Programmer's Guide to the EGA, VGA, and Super VGA Cards

Third Edition

Programmer's Guide to the EGA, VGA, and Super VGA Cards

Third Edition

Richard F. Ferraro

Addison-Wesley Publishing Company, Inc.

Reading, Massachusetts • Menlo Park, California • New York • Don Mills, Ontario
Wokingham, England • Amsterdam • Bonn • Sydney • Singapore • Tokyo
Madrid • San Juan • Paris • Seoul • Milan • Mexico City • Taipei

Library of Congress Cataloging-in-Publication Data

Ferraro, Richard F.
  Programmer's guide to the EGA, VGA, and Super VGA cards : including XGA cards / Richard F. Ferraro. -- 3rd ed.
    p. cm.
  Includes index.
  ISBN 0-201-62490-7
1. IBM Personal Computer--Programming. 2. IBM Personal System/2 (Computer system)--Programming. 3. Expansion boards (Microcomputers) I. Title.
QA76.8.I2594F48 1994
006.6'765--dc20   93-35645
CIP

Sponsoring Editor: Philip Sutherland
Project Managers: Eleanor McCarthy and Claire Horne
Production Coordinator: Lora L. Ryan
Cover design: Trish LaPointe
Text design: Kenneth J. Wilson (Wilson Graphics & Design)
Set in 10 point New Century Schoolbook by Context Publishing Services

1 2 3 4 5 6 7 8 9 - BAH - 9897969594
First printing, August 1994

Dedication

For my parents Jennie and Joseph, my wife Paula, my children Ricco and Georgia, my brothers Frank and Raymond, and my lifelong friends Rocco, Mario, Bo, John, and Trudy.

For those readers who believe the world is worth protecting—and do something about it.

For the dolphins I have known.

Contents

Chapter 13
The Super VGA 603

Preface

The Video Graphics Array (VGA) has clearly established itself as the color graphics card of choice for the PC family of computers. Millions of Enhanced Graphics Array (EGA) and VGA cards are in use worldwide. VGA controllers have penetrated every PC platform, from laptops through Pentium. Between 20 and 30 million VGA and Super VGA chips are sold each year. Software applictions have expanded from the early illustration and graphics packages. Now applications include workstation resolution CAD, desktop publishing, image processing, animation, and multimedia presentation systems.

When I wrote the first edition of this book, I wanted to find out which software packages used the VGA. Now, I doubt whether any software can be found that does not communicate through the VGA. The important question is, "How much of the VGA is utilized?"

The VGA standard has produced a fertile graphics environment for the PC programmer. Although it still reigns supreme in the PC graphics arena, the VGA has grown beyond its original scope. Nearly all VGA cards exceed the VGA standard in some significant way. I call these *Super VGAs*. While no standard exists for these Super VGA cards, advances have been made in the creation of a Super VGA standard by the Video Electronics Standards Association (VESA).

Few software applications fully use the advanced features of the Super VGAs. Most software developers have been largely on their own. Many software developers cannot resist programming the super cards in the standard VGA modes. This is unfortunate, since the Super VGA advances have become so pronounced that programmers can no longer afford to ignore their powerful new graphics features.

The motivation for a third edition of *Programmer's Guide to the EGA and VGA Cards* is simple. I want to help programmers use the Super VGAs to the fullest extent possible.

This edition provides a comprehensive discussion of the complete VGA standards. Intended as reference material, the book elaborates on the PC graphics environment and includes information on the MDA, CGA, Hercules, EGA, VGA, 8514/A, XGA, and the TIGA standards. This book is a programmer's guide intended to teach the reader how to program the various chips and features. This book is not a review of the Super VGAs. Nowhere in this book do I attempt to compare the relative performance of these chips.

Although the Super VGA chips have several features in common, they differ significantly in how they operate. Chapter 13 describes the Super VGA features, Chapter 14 provides insight into the graphics accelerators found on many of the newer generation Super VGA chips. Chapter 15 describes the theory behind the common features in the Super VGAs and illustrates some of the code examples that will follow.

As previously mentioned, each Super VGA is controlled differently. Chapters 16 through 28 provide an in-depth look at the Super VGA chips that make up 99 percent of all VGA cards on the market. It is not possible within the confines of this book to discuss the Super VGA cards that use these chips.

I have attempted to keep this book up-to-date. However, new chips are always invading the market. The Super VGA Toolbox (see coupon on last page) is always kept up-to-date.

The Super VGA chips discussed in this book and fully supported in Super VGA Toolbox include the following:

Manufacturer	*Chip Names*
ATI	18800,28800 rev1–6, 38800 Mach8 and 68800 Mach32
Avance	Ultra+
Chips & Technology	82c451, 82c452, 82c343, 82c455, 82c456
Cirrus	54xx, 62xx, 64xx
Genoa	5000, GVGA
Headland/Video7	VEGA, V7VGA
Integrated Info Tech (IIT)	AGX-014, AGX-015
NCR	77c22e+
Oak	037, 067, 077, 087, 107
S3	911, 924, 928, 801, 805
Trident	8800, 8900, 8900CL, 8900CxR, 9000, 9420
Tseng Labs	ET3000, ET4000, ET4000-W32
Western Digital	PVGA1a, 90c00, 90c10, 90c11, 90c30, 90c31, 90c33
Weitek	P9000

Discussions focus on how to control, query, optimize, and write to and read from these cards. Armed with these tools, programmers can use the higher resolutions and improved capabilities of the Super VGA cards.

The book provides optimized program examples. The examples use many of the advanced features of these powerful cards. The features included are control of the Super VGAs' many display modes; determination of the state of the VGA and graphics environment; control of alphanumerics; manipulation of character fonts; read- and write-to display memory; draw points, lines, and circles; read- and write-to color tables; and control of the start address to allow panning and scrolling through the 1 Mbyte of display memory.

Richard F. Ferraro   Seattle, Washington

Comprehensive Software Now Available

There are three software options available to the user who wants to get code up and running. This software may be purchased directly from the author. The special order coupon provided in the back of this book makes ordering by phone or mail quick and simple.

COMPANION DISK

The *Programmer's Guide Companion Disk* includes all of the source code listings from this book.

SUPER VGA TOOLBOX

The *Super VGA Toolbox* is a comprehensive graphics toolbox that supports virtually every Super VGA card. New chips available after the third edition was written are added to the toolbox. This keeps the toolbox up-to-date.

The *Super VGA Toolbox* provides some 400 optimized functions that control and manipulate all Super VGA chips. Each function is well-documented and naming conventions are intuitive. A clearly written 100-page manual makes using the toolbox effortless. All source code is included and the functions may be used royalty-free. The toolbox is designed so that programmers can readily add additional functions. Software updates will be made available to handle the new Super VGA chips as they are introduced.

The software is written in C and assembly language. It is compatible with Microsoft and Borland compilers. Due to the ANSI standards used, the code is readily portable to other compilers. The code can run in DOS or protected mode applications. It is compatible with other coding libraries.

Once linked into your executable module, the software will automatically detect the type of Super VGA chip present, eliminating the need for special versions or configurations. In addition, the code is written such that each routine is mode- and color-independent. For example, you would set a mode by indicating the horizontal, vertical, and color resolutions; there is no need to be concerned with nonstandard mode numbers. Similarly, the drawing routines are mode-independent. This allows you to change the mode, say, from 640-by-480 16-color to 1024-by-768 65K color without changing your graphics code.

The code is optimized for speed and size. There is no cumbersome overhead necessary to use the functions in your application. Because the functions are not cross-coupled, only the functions called for will be used. Once the software detects the Super VGA environment, an assembly language call table is used for rapid graphics. No decisions are made in the majority of graphics operations unless a bank is swapped. A complete demonstration program is provide to illustrate how to use the toolbox functions.

The *Super VGA Toolbox* consists of the following functions.

Chip Identification	Able to identify and automatically adjust for all Super VGA Chips supported.
Alphanumerics	Variable fonts, infinite positioning, transparencies, special printf and scanf, output characters, output strings.
Drawing	Points, lines, clipping, circles, arcs, polylines, filled polygons.
BitBlts	Clearing, reading and writing of rectangular image areas, high-speed scrolling.
Modes	Complete access to all popular display modes supported by each chip, special 256-color 420-by-400 mode for standard VGAs.
VESA	Complete VESA support is provided.
Colors	4-bit color, 8-bit color, 15-bit color, 16-bit color and 24-bit color all supported; color manipulation, palette control, display colors, make 256 gray scale.
Special Effects	Panning, zooming, fading, scrolling, smooth scrolling.

THE GRAPHICS ACCELERATOR TOOLBOX

The *Graphics Accelerator Toolbox* is a comprehensive set of functions that control the graphics accelerators present on many Super VGAs. These graphics accelerators are also called Windows accelerators, graphics coprocessors, graphics engines, or 8514 engines. The functions can be used alone or in conjunction with the *Super VGA Toolbox*. The functions conform to the popular *Applications Interface* (AI) standard as fully described in Chapter 16 of this book.

The complexity of these accelerators far exceeds the scope of this book. Each accelerator is complicated and filled with various idiosyncrasies. Rather than trying to understand the accelerators, most programmers should either use the provided functions or combine the source code from these functions into larger modules. An understanding of the accelerators is best obtained by reading the source code. Each accelerator contains 20 to 50 registers. Many fields are non-intuitive and some have to be loaded before others. Some features require redundant data to be loaded into different fields of separate registers. Some registers don't perform as specified.

Fortunately, this toolbox provides ready-to-use functions that fully exercise these graphics accelerators. When these functions are added to the *Super VGA Toolbox*, the toolbox automatically uses the graphics accelerator when present. You can be up-and-running in no time at all with the *Graphics Accelerator Toolbox*.

The *Graphics Accelerator Toolbox* consists of the following functions.

Chip Identification	Able to identify and automatically adjust for all graphics accelerators supported.
Chip Setup	Mode setting, open and close adapter, color palette manipulation.
Chip Control	Set chip registers for various graphics functions.
Alphanumerics	Utilize BitBlt color expansion for rapid display of fonts.
Drawing	Lines, clipping, circles, arcs, polylines, filled polygons where supported.
BitBlts	Clearing, reading, and writing of rectangular image areas, high-speed scrolling.
Colors	4-bit color, 8-bit color, 15-bit color, 16-bit color, and 24-bit color all supported.

Acknowledgments

The challenge of writing this Third Edition could not have been met without the support and assistance of many good people. Special thanks are due to:

Paula Lowe for her patience, love and editing. She kept me on track and running during all phases of writing.

Phil Sutherland, Claire Horne, and the excellent staff at Addison-Wesley for their cheerful understanding and steadfast assistance in seeing this book through its third edition.

Each Super VGA chip manufacturer, and several board manufacturers, who have played a large role in educating me, providing endless cards, technical manuals, phone support and code examples. This book is about their genius and creativity, and it would not have been possible without their excellent support. Those of us who use and enjoy color desktop computers all owe these manufacturers thanks. Their achievements are absolutely amazing.

The hundred thousand readers around the world who have taken the time to read my book. And, especially, to the people who took the time to write me and provide me with, *ahem*, illumination into the errors of my ways. The accuracy of the Third Edition is largely due to their support.

The VESA committee for their excellent technical documentation and, more importantly, for their noble efforts to bring order to the maelstrom.

My expresso machine (I do live in Seattle, you know). The Dolphins of Sanctuary Bay (I am writing the book in the Bahamas).

And lastly, to IBM, for inventing the VGA—for not inventing a standard that replaced it.

Chapter 1

Introduction to the Programmer's Guide

1.1 ABOUT COMPUTER GRAPHICS CARDS

For all of you who want to program graphics on your personal computers, the tools and means to use them are now available. No matter what your computer graphics applications, powerful graphics cards now enable you to generate sharp, effective graphic presentations on the video monitor.

An effective graphics system integrates graphics cards with a variety of graphics software, graphics peripherals, computer memory, and the DOS operating system. Graphics cards are used in personal computers to display data via images created by dots, lines, curves, arbitrary shapes, and alphanumeric characters on the video monitor. Monochrome cards, specifically the Hercules card, display data in black-and-white; the color graphics cards display the data in a variety of colors. The art of programming these graphics cards is known as computer graphics.

This book helps you harness the power of the most popular color graphics cards for your own applications. These include the Enhanced Graphics Adapter (EGA), the Video Graphics Array (VGA), the XGA, 8514, and the Super VGA cards. The EGA/VGA standard provides a consistent foundation upon which to build your programs. Because of these standards, the programs you create today can enjoy long useful lifetimes on the millions of computers equipped with either the EGA or VGA cards. Furthermore, cards introduced in the future are bound to conform to the EGA/VGA and Super VGA standards. The time spent learning to program these cards today will benefit you for years to come. When new cards are introduced, you can focus on learning the improvements that expand upon the EGA/VGA standards.

The EGA and VGA computer graphics standards were developed by IBM for its Personal Computer (PC) and Personal System/2 (PS/2) computer families respectively. Although the Color Graphics Adapter (CGA) was introduced earlier, the CGA exhibited poor resolution and limited colors. The EGA standard and adapter board, developed in 1984, solved these problems. Since then, it has become the third most popular color graphics standard for the PC. Manufacturers have produced several variations of the EGA, and nearly every software application has taken advantage of this powerful standard.

The VGA was introduced by IBM in 1987. It is built into the motherboard of models 50, 60, and 80 of the PS/2. This standard maintains downward compatibility to the EGA while adding some important new features. The most significant of these are the readability of the adapter registers, increased resolution, and a 256-color mode. The Super VGAs have been manufactured by several companies since 1987.

A second adapter released with the PS/2 family is the Multicolor Graphics Array (MCGA). The MCGA is incorporated into Model 30 of the PS/2 and is downwardly compatible to the Color Graphics Adapter (CGA) at the register and display memory level as well as at the BIOS level. This adapter has not been as popular at the EGA or VGA.

The IBM corporation was quick to announce several new standards following the successful introduction of the VGA. Although this was done in best intentions, it was a mistake because IBM had underestimated the combined power of the software and hardware industry.

The marketplace (that is, computer users) began to realize that it was the software that they used that was most important; the hardware was merely a platform for running the software and there was no reason to buy new hardware unless the software ran better on it. After spending a tremendous amount of money rewriting code to conform to the VGA standard, the software industry was finally starting to make money. They would change to another standard only if the marketplace demanded the change. In large part, the software industry influenced the marketplace.

Second, a new industry sprung up designing VGA chips. The catalyst for this industry was the ability to economically design and produce high-density gate arrays. The size of the market was estimated to be millions per month. Several small and large companies began to produce these chips in high quantities. Some built and sold the cards that supported these chips. Others simply sold the chips to card manufacturers. Due to the quantities sold and the effective design and manufacturing tools, the VGA cards became inexpensive.

Two large companies, IBM and Texas Instruments, introduced new graphics products that they believed would outperform and consequently replace the VGA. These were the 8514 by IBM and the 34010/20 by Texas Instruments. Both were powerful graphics processors, but this power imposed a cost penalty. The demand for high-cost graphics cards wasn't that great and these two giants duked it out. Neither saw the Super VGA manufacturers in the shadows improving their products.

Each year the gate arrays became bigger and cheaper. The design tools improved and the expertise of these companies multiplied. Consequently, these companies introduced the Super VGA chips with a cost point only marginally more expensive than the VGAs. The Super VGA cards flooded the market, and their performance rivaled the more expensive IBM and Texas Instrument products. Neither the 8514 or the 34010/20 standards took hold. Severely limiting the success of these products was the fact that both required a VGA to run DOS! Thus, the user was forced into buying a VGA anyway.

An important difference existed between the 8514 and the 34010/20 versus the Super VGAs. The 8514 and the 34010/20 incorporated graphics coprocessors, while the Super VGAs relied on the system processor (80286, 80386). Due to the availability of low-cost high-powered computers, the advantages of graphics coprocessors were not significant. Even more relevant was the fact that software manufacturers were hesitant to program these processors. Consequently, the Super VGAs controlled the graphics marketplace.

It is not that graphics coprocessors aren't a good idea. In fact, today they are essential to graphics performance in systems incorporating the fast 80386, 80486, and Pentium processors. In these systems, a new bottleneck exists. This is the bus between the computer processor and the graphics system. If the bus is the bottleneck, reducing the amount of data carried across the bus would improve performance. This is exactly what a graphics coprocessor accomplishes.

The traditional ISA bus was insufficient. It grew from 8-bit to 16-bit but it was still too slow. Meeting the need, new buses were introduced, including the Micro channel (MCA), extended ISA bus (EISA), the VESA (VL) bus, and the PCI bus. These new graphics buses improved performance while reducing the need for graphics coprocessors. Even though coprocessors could still improve performance, they were expensive to program and software companies were hesitant. That is, until Windows 3 hit the streets.

Once again, the software industry became the driving force for hardware. In order to control the graphics card in Windows, a software driver is necessary. Microsoft released a set of specifications for these software drivers. These included basic primitives like BITBLTS, line draws, pattern fills, solid fills, and so on. Consequently, the Super VGA chip manufacturers could see real benefits in producing chips that performed these functions well. The Windows 3 marketplace was enormous. Rewards for their efforts were virtually guaranteed. Consequently, graphics coprocessors incorporated nearly all of the newest generation of Super VGA chips.

IBM tried one more time with the XGA standard, which combined the VGA with the graphics coprocessors engine found in the 8514 onto the same chip. It seemed like a good idea but they faced an uphill battle and had to compete against the entire Super VGA industry. However, the smarts put into the 8514 were not unnoticed by the Super VGA manufacturers. Consequently, some manufacturers produced XGA-compatible chips; others incorporated aspects of the 8514 into the graphics coprocessors portion of the Super VGAs. The XGA became an eXotic VGA. Exotic is great for perfume but lousy for computers. Although the XGA concept was sound, it merely was folded into the VGA momentum.

A very important concept emerged with the 8514 and the XGA—a graphics applications interface, which was a specification that sat between the applications programmer and the graphics engines. This is important since the graphics engines are extremely complicated to program. In addition, advances in hardware would require only a new AI driver rather than changes in the applications code. A great deal of effort has gone into these AI interfaces. Certainly, Windows 3 is the most popular. Others include the 8514 interface, the VESA interface, and interfaces specific to Super VGA manufacturers.

1.2 ABOUT THE NEED FOR THIS BOOK

Information detailing the operation of the EGA or VGA cards has been available only through a collection of technical manuals. Using these manuals is a frustrating process of "cut and paste" with the information being nearly impossible to decipher even for experienced graphics programmers. In addition, none of the references explained how a programmer would use the cards to perform computer graphics or rated one technique as better suited to a task than another. Graphics programming books presented a selection of graphics routines without providing essential details for programming.

As the capabilities, power, and flexibility of graphics systems increase, programming graphics becomes a more demanding, complex job. It is essential to know the capabilities of the graphics system, whether a programmer is using a preexisting graphics library or programming the graphic cards directly. To fully utilize the graphics system, the programmer must have a detailed understanding of computer graphics algorithms, the graphics system, and how the graphics system integrates into the computer environment. Armed with an understanding of the graphics cards and a knowledge of computer graphics, the programmer can create a wide variety of graphics effects on the video monitor.

The VGA standard has been surpassed in performance by cards called "Super VGA." However, many programmers have chosen to ignore the advanced capabilities of these cards.

1.3 ABOUT THIS BOOK

This book provides a thorough, comprehensive guide for anyone who wants to program the Enhanced Graphics Adapter (EGA), the Video Graphics Array (VGA), or the Super VGAs. The goal of this book is to help each reader acquire the knowledge and skills necessary to program successfully with these graphics cards. Each chapter is a building block organized in a learning sequence, and the chapters are also designed to stand alone. This blend of tutorial and reference manual gives the reader plenty of room for moving around, stopping, studying, and moving on.

The philosophy behind this book is that understanding optimizes programming. The features of the VGA are both numerous and hidden within the range of control registers and BIOS calls. There is more than one way to accomplish a task on the VGA. The programmer who is aware of the options within these adapters will be able to make the best choice.

It is difficult to recognize the significance and utility of several of the features on the VGA. Without an understanding of these features' underlying graphics functions, programmers may find many of these features obscure and therefore may not use them. This book unlocks the secrets of these features by providing a tutorial on relevant graphics devices, applications software, and principles.

Since the introduction of these graphics standards, several manufacturers have introduced VGA compatible cards. Many of these cards have enhanced features that extend the capabilities of the EGA and VGA. These Super VGA cards are discussed in detail in Chapters 18–30.

1.4 COMPANION DISK, TOOLBOX, AND ACCELERATOR TOOLBOXES

Software examples are provided throughout the book. This software covers several of the basic graphics functions one would want to perform on the VGAs and Super VGAs. Certainly, the reader might type in these examples, in whole or in part. Many users will desire these code examples in electronic media. This is standard for most computer software books. Still others will require an integrated, up-to-date toolbox of routines that control the VGAs, Super VGAs, and the graphics accelerator portions of the Super VGAs. For these users, two software toolboxes are available from the author.

The major advantages of the toolboxes are as follows:

- Access to ready-to-use code. You can be up and running within 24 hours of placing your order.

- Access to useful graphics functions whose complexity extend beyond the scope of the book.

- Upgrades that support Super VGA cards that were released after the publish date of the book.

- Telephone support from the author.

It was my goal to provide you with an understanding of the basic features of the Super VGAs in this third edition of my book. Due to the complexity and number of different Super VGA cards, I had to draw the line on what I would discuss and what issues were beyond the scope of the book. This is especially true for the graphics accelerators. Many of the manuals that I have received are 300 to 400 pages long, and these manuals discuss just one chip! Beyond these manuals come the details and idiosyncrasies of programming the accelerators. Every manufacturer that I spoke with—and my publisher and I agree—said that it would be impossible to discuss these accelerators in a book. In fact, even with a complete set of manuals from the manufacturer, and after visits to each and every one, I still have problems programming the accelerators. We believe that the programmer should work from known source code functions. If necessary, the programmer can modify the code once the function is understood.

The companion software available from the author is discussed in the *Comprehensive Software Now Available* section. An order form is on the last page of the book.

1.5 TERMS AND STYLES USED IN THIS BOOK

The VGA and Super VGA are really an enhancement of the EGA, although there are some features on the EGA and VGA that differ. To minimize redundancy, the following terms are used: "VGA" is employed, and sentences are written with singular verbs, when information applies to either or both adapters. "EGA" is utilized when information relates only to the EGA.

Numbers are presented in either a decimal or a hexadecimal format. The decimal numbers are presented as the default case, and the hexadecimal numbers are followed by a "hex" qualifier. For example, "10" means the number 10, and "10 hex" means the number 16.

The VGA registers are described in Chapter 10. Each field is referenced both in the register illustration and in the descriptions. This referencing indicates which adapters are affected by each field. The register illustrations include a code name expressing which bits are used for each field. This code name is preceded by a small square if it applies to the EGA. It is followed by a small square if it applies to the VGA.

Some fields have different meanings depending on the adapter. Two codes are present in these fields separated by a slash. The first name refers to the EGA, and the code after the slash refers to the VGA. Codes that are neither preceded nor followed by a square apply to both the EGA and the VGA. A typical register is illustrated in Figure 1.1.

In Chapter 12, all program examples assume the Microsoft C and assembly language conventions. The "large-model" compiler is used throughout the code,

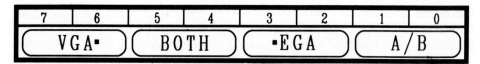

FIGURE 1.1 Typical Register Illustration

although the code can be readily changed to use the "medium-model" compiler option.

1.6   ABOUT THE CHAPTERS IN GENERAL

Chapters 2 through 5 equip the programmer with a thorough understanding of the features of the EGA/VGA and the relationships these adapters have to other display adapters, the PC computer, graphics devices, and graphics software. A tutorial supplies a background in C and assembly language for novice programmers. The graphics algorithms used in the program examples are introduced in the computer graphics tutorial.

Chapters 6 through 11 specify the functions of the EGA/VGA cards. These chapters offer clear, comprehensive information on the display modes, display memory, graphics processor, downloadable fonts, color processing, control registers, and BIOS calls.

This information is translated into programming examples in Chapter 12. Seventy program examples are included to illustrate the power and versatility of the EGA/VGA cards.

Chapter 15 provides a detailed look at the function specifications for the IBM Applications Interface. This powerful interface is used in the Graphics Accelerator Toolkit available from the author and is supported by the XGA, 8514, and many Super VGAs.

Chapter 16 provides an in-depth look at the XGA cards. Included are the relevant register definitions and descriptions of the graphics accelerator. The XGA is treated as if it were another SuperVGA, which in fact it is.

Chapters 13–30 provide detailed descriptions of the Super VGA chips. The scope and depth of this information allows the programmer to identify which chip is present; control, configure and fine-tune the chip; invoke the advanced display modes; access up to one megabyte of display memory; and control the start address and cursor.

Due to the complexity and number of Super VGA cards available, a great deal of important information could not be included in this book. The reader is encouraged to purchase one of the software toolkits available from the author for further information regarding the Super VGAs.

1.7   ABOUT THE CHAPTERS IN DETAIL

Chapter 2 reveals the VGA features so that the programmer is aware of the capacity of these adapters. Issues involving display resolution and color resolution are examined. Features of other graphics adapters are also reviewed.

Chapter 3 describes computer graphics hardware and the impact that this hardware has on the programmer. Relevant computer hardware, graphics adapters, monitors and displays, two monitor systems, and popular computer buses are discussed. Also included is some information on the new "Green PCs" specifications.

Chapter 4 examines the different types of graphics systems including the EGA/VGA, Super VGA, MDA, CGA, MGA, PGA, 8514, XGA, and TIGA. The emphasis of this chapter is to show how the Super VGAs fit in with these other graphics systems.

Chapter 5 explains the principles behind the computer graphics software examples presented in Chapter 12. Coordinate systems and transformations, characters, points, lines, and shapes are described. Special attention is given to the important line drawing, circle drawing, and clipping algorithms.

Chapter 6 furnishes the reader with the necessary tools to program alphanumerics on the EGA/VGA. The alphanumerics processing capabilities of the display adapter are established. Character shapes, sizes, and attributes are described. Each alphanumeric display mode is described and illustrated. The configurations of the display memory for these alphanumeric display modes are presented. Downloadable character sets are also discussed, including the organization of the fonts and techniques for reading, writing, and selecting the fonts.

Chapter 7 furnishes the reader with the necessary tools for programming graphics on the EGA/VGA. Characters, character attributes, and character fonts are described as they apply to the graphics display modes. Each of the graphics display modes is presented. The organization of the display memory for each of these graphics modes in provided. Details of the operation of the internal graphics processor offer the programmer important insights into how to speed up graphics operations. A brief description of video timing provides the programmer with some meaningful definitions.

Chapter 8 illustrates the color processing capabilities of the EGA/VGA. The palette registers and the color registers are described in detail, with special attention paid to techniques for reading and writing data from and to these registers. Techniques for converting data to colors as well as from one color scheme to another are presented.

Chapter 9 focuses on ascertaining the state of the graphics adapters. There are three ways to obtain this information: The registers can read directly, BIOS calls can be invoked, or the BIOS data area in host RAM memory can be interrogated. The register default values for the EGA/VGA are presented in table form. These values are useful to the programmer when trying to understand the operation of the display modes and the interaction of various display registers.

Chapter 10 presents the entire set of registers resident in the EGA/VGA cards. All of the parameters that pertain to the control of these adapters reside on the control registers. Most of the registers are segmented into fields. A single register can control several different graphics functions. Each field of every register is described in detail.

Chapter 11 presents the entire set of BIOS calls on the EGA/VGA cards. The input and output parameters of each call are provided. The effects that each call has on display memory, host registers, EGA/VGA registers, and the BIOS data area are included.

Chapter 12 provides the reader with 70 program examples that exercise the EGA/VGA cards. These examples span the text, font, graphics, and color sections of the adapters. Each program is well-documented and simple to understand. These programs form the basis of a programmer's toolbox.

Chapter 13 describes the many features of the Super VGAs. Chapter 14 provides descriptions and several program examples of features and principles common to all of the Super VGAs.

Chapter 15 provides a detailed look at the IBM Applications (AI) interface. This interface is fully supported with the XGA, 8514, and several of the Super VGAs. It typically comes as a TSR device driver and provides easy access to several popular functions including filling regions, BitBlts, scrolling, state initialization, setting modes, setting patterns, text processing, palette control, and line drawing. This interface is supported in the Graphics Accelerator Toolkit available through the author.

Chapter 16 contains a detailed description of the XGA, which is treated as another Super VGA. Chapters 17 through 30 describe the Super VGAs. In Chapters 16 through 30, the following are provided:

Functional description of chips
How to identify the manufacturer, chip and version number
How to access display memory
How to bank swap
Controlling the start address and cursor
Descriptions of BIOS extensions
Functional description of the graphics accelerators, when one is present
Any special features of concern to the programmer

A software coupon is provided on the last page of this book allowing you to acquire further knowledge of the Super VGAs and to get your software up-and-running quickly.

1.8   PROGRAM EXAMPLES

The program examples found in Chapter 12 and Chapters 14–28 cover a broad variety of graphics topics. These include controlling the EGA/VGA, reading the state of the adapters, performing alphanumerics processing, handling graphics processing, manipulating color, downloading fonts, and using special effects. This collection of routines forms the foundation of a graphics toolbox.

The program examples are written in C and in assembly language. Even the novice programmer should have little trouble understanding the examples.

Several decisions had to be made regarding the routines included in this book. These decisions involved which routines to include, how complicated the routines should be, how specialized each routine should be, and what condition the adapters should be left in at the completion of each routine.

There are several important aspects of the Super VGAs that, because of their complexity, are not discussed in the book. Those readers desiring access to these advanced functions can purchase Toolkits from the author. Included in these toolkits are functioning code, source code, and text descriptions of the registers involved in performing the graphics operations.

The routines selected for this book cover a broad range of graphics topics. These useful routines are valuable in the graphics setting and include string processing; point, line, and circle drawing; clipping; scrolling and panning; windowing; downloading fonts; and manipulating color. The routines illustrate principles taught in the book.

The selected routines are purposefully simple. This book is not the appropriate place to include multipage routines that perform complicated graphics functions. Each routine implements a specific function. The programmer can connect these routines to build more complicated functions. However, the line-drawing routine is a bit complicated because of its optimization. Line drawing is so important in the graphics environment that a very high speed implementation was selected. In addition, this optimization provides the programmer with several tricks that can be used to achieve high-speed graphics.

The degree of specialization for each routine depends on the application. Routines that are too general can complicate the code and slow down the graphics process. Routines that are too specific also cause complications because the programmer must select from a large number of similar routines.

Some of the routines presented in Chapter 12 can handle a wide variety of applications. For example, the window routines can operate in any alphanumeric or graphics display mode. On the other hand, other routines are very specific. The line-drawing routine calls one of five specialized routines to actually draw the line.

Decisions regarding the condition of the adapter at the completion of each routine are critical to effective programming. For example, a particular routine may require several registers to set up. Modification of these registers will likely leave the adapter in an unpredictable state if the registers are not reset to their default values.

It can be very time-consuming to set up these registers at the start of a routine and then reset them at the end of the routine. If a routine is called repetitively, with no other use being made of these registers, a great deal of time is wasted. Therefore, it is advantageous to set up the registers before the routine, call the routine repetitively, and then reset the registers. However, this leaves the adapter in an unpredictable state until the process is completed. The programmer must be aware of this condition and not interrupt the process before the registers are restored to their default values. Herein lies the tradeoff—performance versus programming complexity. Each application dictates the best solution to this problem.

1.9 COMPILERS AND ASSEMBLERS

The routines included in this book are written specifically for the Microsoft C compiler, version 4.0 or later; assembler, version 5.1 or later; and linker, version 3.0 or above. These C routines should be readily transportable to most C compilers. The software toolboxes offered by the author are directly compatible with the Microsoft and Borland compilers. Both standard and protected mode versions are available.

All program examples assume the Microsoft C and assembly language conventions for the large-model compiler. The assembler directives and references to parameters from within the assembly language programs may need to be altered if other compiler models are used.

Chapter 2

The EGA, VGA, and Super VGA Features

2.1 EGA, VGA, AND SUPER VGA FEATURES

The graphics adapters are implemented in Very Large Scale Integrated (VLSI) circuits. The EGA, VGA, and Super VGA integrated circuits are used on several PC-compatible graphics cards. These cards use low-cost, high-speed, high-density memory, and are inexpensive, compact, and easy to maintain. These chips are frequently included in the computer motherboard.

The VGA standard is perhaps the single most important factor contributing to the success of PC graphics. This standard has allowed software houses to develop programs that can reach a wide audience. The VGA boards include their own BIOS. The BIOS is a major factor contributing to compatibility. The routines resident in the BIOS make up for any subtle differences in the hardware implementations. Nearly all of the standard PC software applications are compatible with the VGA.

It is important to recognize that though the VGA standard is well-defined, the standard acts only as a minimum. Nearly all VGA-compatible cards now improve upon the standard with better resolution, wider color selection, more memory, special character fonts, 132-character-wide screen formats, and on-board graphics processors. These additional features have unfortunately not been standardized, although the VESA committee has introduced some standards. Similarly, the popularity of Windows 3 has effectively created a common set of goals. These goals have, in fact, created a standardizing effect.

The abundant and flexible graphics features of the VGA provide the programmer with a powerful graphics tool. The VGA can be configured into one of several alphanumeric or graphics modes and can drive monochrome monitors, low- and high-resolution digital color monitors, and analog monitors.

This chapter includes information about the VGA and Super VGA cards. Standard EGA/VGA card features including display modes, graphics read and write modes, spatial resolutions, color resolutions, and display memory are described. A similar description of the Super VGAs follows.

2.2   STANDARD EGA AND VGA FEATURES

The EGA and VGA standard features provided a powerful platform for graphics software. Although today's Super VGA cards far exceed these standards, an understanding of the basic features is critical to the successful graphics programmer. Even though a Super VGA mode might be in effect, a high percentage of the programming relates to the standard VGA features.

2.2.1   Read and Write Modes

A variety of read and write modes are implemented in the display processor. These modes augment the host processor, allowing many operations to occur within the VGA graphics processor, including display reads and writes of words that are 32 bits wide, as opposed to the standard 8-bit operation. This speeds many graphics applications by a factor of four. Other write modes allow logical operations to be performed with no host processor calculation. One read mode provides a color comparison. This compares a 4-bit color to the color of 8 neighboring pixels, all in one PC read instruction. Once the many hidden and important features of the EGA are understood, new doors open to the graphics programmer.

2.2.2   Display Memory

The programmer can read or write to display memory without having to wait for the horizontal or vertical retrace periods. This speeds up the graphics process significantly compared to that provided by other display adapters.

Memory is organized in a straightforward manner. Once the addressing is understood, the programmer can readily draw lines and shapes directly onto the screen, without relying on the BIOS calls.

The memory is mapped directly into the PC memory address space, allowing the programmer to utilize the PC assembly language *MOV* or *REP MOVS* instructions for rapid data transfers of data between host memory and display memory or between display memory and display memory. However, multiple wait states are common.

The display memory is mapped into the host address space at locations reserved for graphics memory. An EGA configured in a monochrome mode can coexist with a CGA. Similarly, an EGA configured in a color mode can coexist with an MDA.

The display memory is interfaced to the host processor through an 8-bit data bus, regardless of the width of the host data bus.

The display memory consists of up to 256 Kbytes of memory. It can be organized into a variety of resolutions depending on the display mode. It is possible to configure the display memory into several low-resolution pages or one high-resolution page.

The display memory is organized using a packed format or a bit-plane format, depending on the active display mode.

A 32-bit data bus is present in the VGA. The host can initiate a 32-bit host-to-memory data transfer in a single instruction. However, not all 32 bits can be unique. A data transfer that moves data from display memory to display memory can move 32 unique bits of data in a single instruction. This can provide up to a four-to-one increase in speed over the 8-bit data transfers.

2.2.3 Alphanumeric Modes

The display memory is organized so that it is compatible with the MDA and the CGA. This provides complete alphanumeric downward compatibility.

Each character is represented in display memory by two bytes. The ASCII character code describes which character is to be displayed, and the color of the character is determined by the character attributes. Transferring alphanumerics on the screen is very fast, because each character can be represented in the display memory by only two bytes.

In host memory, character and attribute bytes are stored in sequential memory locations. A special addressing mode is available in the EGA/VGA to cause the character and attribute to appear to be in sequential locations within the display memory. This allows the programmer to use the REP MOVS instruction for rapid alphanumeric data transfers.

Characters can be displayed using monochrome or color attributes. Typical attributes are listed in Table 2.1.

Up to eight pages of alphanumeric text can be stored in display memory at a time, depending on the amount of display memory installed.

Several display resolutions are possible in the alphanumeric modes. The default resolutions and characters sizes are listed in Table 2.2.

It is possible to define new character resolutions within the standard display modes by using the 8-by-8 character set. A few examples based on a color display mode are listed in Table 2.3.

Character sets reside in display memory. Up to four character sets may reside simultaneously in the EGA, and eight can reside in the VGA.

TABLE 2.1 Character Attributes

Mode	Attribute
Mono	Normal, Intensified, Reversed, Blinking, Underlined
Color	16 foreground, 16 background colors
Color	16 foreground, 8 background, blinking
Color	8 foreground, 8 background, 512 characters, blinking

TABLE 2.2 Default Alphanumeric Mode Resolutions

Mode	Adapter	Resolution (Characters)	Resolution (Pixels)	Characters (Pixels)
Color	EGA/VGA	40 by 25	320 by 200	8 by 8
Color	EGA/VGA	40 by 25	320 by 350	8 by 14
Color	VGA	40 by 25	360 by 400	9 by 16
Color	EGA/VGA	80 by 25	640 by 200	8 by 8
Color	EGA/VGA	80 by 25	640 by 350	8 by 14
Color	VGA	80 by 25	720 by 400	9 by 16
Mono	EGA/VGA	80 by 25	720 by 350	9 by 14
Mono	VGA	80 by 25	720 by 400	9 by 16

TABLE 2.3 Nonstandard Alphanumeric Mode Resolutions

Mode	Adapter	Resolution (Characters)	Resolution (Pixels)	Characters (Pixels)
Color	EGA/VGA	80 by 25	640 by 200	8 by 8
Color	EGA/VGA	80 by 43	640 by 350	8 by 8
Color	VGA	80 by 50	640 by 400	8 by 8

2.2.4 Graphics Modes

The display memory is organized so that certain modes provide compatibility with the display memory of the CGA. This provides CGA graphics downward compatibility.

The monochrome modes utilize either two bits per pixel or one bit per pixel. When the program is emulating the Hercules, two bits per pixel are used for the various monochrome attributes. Other modes, called two-color modes, can also be thought of as monochrome modes because they can display two colors. The two colors do not need to be black and white.

The color modes utilize two, four, or eight bits per pixel. The "two bits per pixel" mode emulates the CGA, displaying up to four simultaneous colors per image. The four-bits-per-pixel mode allows sixteen simultaneous colors, and the eight-bits-per-pixel mode allows 256 simultaneous colors.

There are several configurations of the display memory, depending on the active display mode. The standard resolutions are listed in Table 2.4.

Character sets reside in host memory space, either in BIOS ROM or in RAM memory.

TABLE 2.4 Standard Graphics Resolutions

Mode	Adapter	Resolution (Pixels)	Number of Colors	Typical Characters (Pixels)
Mono	EGA/VGA	640 by 200	2	8 by 8
Mono	EGA/VGA	640 by 350	4	8 by 14
Mono	VGA	640 by 480	2	8 by 16
Color	VGA	320 by 200	256	8 by 8
Color	EGA/VGA	640 by 200	16	8 by 8
Color	EGA/VGA	640 by 350	16	8 by 8
Color	VGA	640 by 480	16	8 by 16
Color	EGA/VGA	320 by 200	16	8 by 8

2.2.5 Downloadable Character Sets

Each display mode has an assigned default character set. The default character sets reside in the BIOS ROM.

The VGA can utilize user-defined downloadable character sets. Any style of character can be used. The character set can be up to 256 characters long. Each character can be up to nine pixels wide and up to 32 scan lines high.

The EGA BIOS ROM contains three character sets with sizes of 8-by-8, 8-by-14, and 9-by-14 pixels. The 9-by-14 font is supplemental. It contains only the characters that differ in shape from the 8-by-14 character set.

The VGA BIOS ROM contains five character sets with sizes of 8-by-8, 8-by-14, 9-by-14, 8-by-16, and 9-by-16 pixels. The 9-by-14 and 9-by-16 fonts are supplemental. They contain only the characters that differ in shape from the 8-by-14 and 8-by-16 character sets.

Up to four character sets, each 256 characters long, can be resident simultaneously in the EGA display memory. Any two of these can be made active, providing the programmer with a character set that is 512 characters long.

Up to eight character sets, each 256 characters long, can be resident simultaneously in the VGA display memory. Any two of these can be made active, providing the programmer with a character set that is 512 characters long.

2.2.6 Control Registers

Certainly the most complicated aspect of the VGA is understanding the control registers. The registers are divided into five groups, as listed in Table 2.5.

TABLE 2.5 EGA/VGA Register Groups

Number of Registers	Group Name
4	General registers
5	Sequencer registers
28	CRT controller registers
9	Graphics controller registers
22	Attribute controller
5	Color registers

Each register is one byte wide. Several of the registers are subdivided into fields. Often, individual bits within a register control entirely different functions. Some functions require fields that reside in more than one register.

The registers are accessed through the host I/O port address space. The I/O address of a subset of the registers changes depending on the configuration. If the VGA is in a monochrome mode, this subset is mapped into the addresses for the MDA. Similarly, if the VGA is in a color mode, this subset is mapped into the addresses for the CGA.

The register groups, as listed in Table 2.5, are each represented in the host I/O port space by two registers. The VGA registers are indexed by an addressing scheme through an index or address register and a data register.

On the EGA, the great majority of registers are write-only. This restricts the ability of the programmer to interrogate the display adapter. On the VGA, all but one register can be read by the host. The exception is the attribute control flip/flop.

2.2.7 Display Modes

The VGA can be configured in a variety of standardized display formats. These formats control the configuration of the display memory, the resolution of the display, the number of bits per pixel, the default character font, and the starting address of display memory.

All display modes are classified into alphanumeric or graphics modes. The graphics modes are also called *all-points-addressable*. There are important distinctions between these two types of modes.

The programmer can design new modes by manipulating the registers directly. However, this is not advised because of the complexity of the manipulations required to change a mode. A mistake could damage the monitor or the display adapter.

The Set Mode BIOS call changes the display mode simply and effectively.

Alphanumeric display modes are present that emulate the operation of the MDA monochrome system and the CGA color system.

2.2.8 EGA/VGA BIOS

The EGA/VGA BIOS is contained in ROM memory and present in all EGA/VGA implementations. Several alphanumeric and graphics functions can be performed through the BIOS calls.

The BIOS calls are invoked through assembly language calls. In some cases, these can be invoked directly from C routines.

The BIOS calls are organized into several classifications, as listed in Table 2.6.

Perhaps the most important aspect of the EGA/VGA is almost totally ignored. Few BIOS calls are provided to read and write data to the display memory. The calls available are restricted to those for reading and writing a pixel.

2.3 GRAPHICS READ AND WRITE MODES

Four write modes are available to the programmer. These can be used to improve the speed performance of the write operations. In addition, two read modes are available. One reads data directly from display memory, and the second reads the result of a comparison.

2.3.1 Write Mode 0

The programmer can write directly to the display memory through an 8-bit data bus. The byte written by the host can be rotated any number of bits before being written to the display memory. This is useful for lining up bits in the byte with pixel locations.

The byte written by the host can be rotated and masked so that only specified bits in the byte affect the display memory. Up to eight pixels can occupy a single byte. This masking is useful when only a subset of the bits within a byte is to be modified. This operation requires a read/modify/write sequence. A read operation automatically reads all four display planes at the desired address into a 32-bit internal register. This register is used as one of the operands in the read/modify/write operations.

The byte written by the host can perform logical operations on the data that is resident in the display memory at the addressed byte. The logical operations include replacing, ANDing, ORing, and XORing. These operations require a read/modify/write sequence. A read operation automatically reads all four display planes at the desired address into a 32-bit internal register. This register is used as one of the operands in the read/modify/write operations.

Data can be written to multiple display memory bit planes simultaneously by using the Set/Reset and Enable Set/Reset Register. As many as four bit planes can be modified in a single operation. It is possible to write to eight neighboring horizontal pixels in all four bit planes in a single *MOV* instruction. This is effectively a 32-bit write operation, although only four bits are unique.

TABLE 2.6 EGA/VGA BIOS Calls

Control:

Card	Call
EGA/VGA	Mode Set
EGA/VGA	Select Active Display Page
EGA/VGA	Select Alternate Print Screen Routine
VGA	Video Enable/Disable
VGA	Display Switch
VGA	Video Screen On/Off

Return State:

Card	Call
EGA/VGA	Return Current Video State
EGA/VGA	Return Video Information
VGA	Read/Write Display Combination Code
VGA	Return Functionality/State Information
VGA	Save/Restore Video State

Interactive:

Card	Call
EGA/VGA	Set Cursor Type
EGA/VGA	Set Cursor Position
EGA/VGA	Read Cursor Position
EGA	Read Light Pen Position
VGA	Cursor Emulation

Alphanumerics:

Card	Call
EGA/VGA	Scroll Active Page Up
EGA/VGA	Scroll Active Page Down
EGA/VGA	Read Character/Attribute
EGA/VGA	Write Character/Attribute
EGA/VGA	Write Character Only
EGA/VGA	Write Teletypewriter to Active Page
VGA	Select Scan Lines for Alphanumeric Modes
EGA/VGA	Write String

Graphics:

Card	Call
EGA/VGA	Write Dot
EGA/VGA	Read Dot

TABLE 2.6 *(cont.)*

Palette:

Card	Call
EGA/VGA	Set Color Palette
EGA/VGA	Set Individual Palette Register
EGA/VGA	Set Overscan Register
EGA/VGA	Set All Palette Registers and Overscan
EGA/VGA	Toggle Intensity/Blinking Bit
VGA	Read Individual Palette Register
VGA	Read Overscan Register
VGA	Read all Palette Registers and Overscan
VGA	Default Palette Loading During Mode Set

Color Registers:

Card	Call
VGA	Set Individual Color Register
VGA	Set Block of Color Registers
VGA	Select Color Page
VGA	Read Individual Color Registers
VGA	Read Block of Color Registers
VGA	Read Current Color Page Number
VGA	Sum Color Values to Gray Scale
VGA	Default Palette Loading During Mode Set
VGA	Summing to Gray Scales

Character Generator:

Card	Call
EGA/VGA	User Alpha Load with Reset
EGA/VGA	ROM Monochrome Set with Reset
EGA/VGA	ROM 8x8 Character Set Load with Reset
EGA/VGA	Set Block Specifier with Reset
VGA	ROM 8x16 Character Set Load with Reset
EGA/VGA	User Alpha Load
EGA/VGA	ROM Monochrome Set
EGA/VGA	ROM 8x8 Character Set Load
VGA	ROM 8x16 Character Set Load
EGA/VGA	User Graphics Characters INT 1FH (8x8)
EGA/VGA	User Graphics Characters
EGA/VGA	Graphics Mode ROM 8x14 Character Set Load
EGA/VGA	Graphics Mode ROM 8x8 Character Set Load
EGA/VGA	Graphics Mode ROM 8x16 Character Set Load
EGA/VGA	Return Character Generator Information

2.3.2   Write Mode 1

All four display planes can be modified with the 32 bits of data in the EGA/VGA internal 32-bit latch in a single MOV instruction. The 32-bit internal latch is loaded by a host-generated read operation. This mode provides very fast movement of data within the display memory. The display memory often contains storage that is not part of the active display. Data can be moved into and out of the active display region rapidly using this 32-bit write operation.

2.3.3   Write Mode 2

All four display planes can be modified with four bits of data. Each of the four display planes is written to with eight replicated bits. The byte moved from the host to display memory contains four significant bits, bits 0 to 3. Bit 0 is replicated eight times into bit plane 0, and bit 1 is replicated eight times into bit plane 1. The same holds for bits 2 and 3 into bit planes 2 and 3 respectively. This procedure is used in conjunction with the Bit Mask Register to modify selected bits within a byte without having to rotate the byte. It can also be effective for writing a block of eight identical values to the display.

2.3.4   Write Mode 3

This write mode is available on the VGA only and it is a bit complicated. Data is written to the display memory from the Set/Reset Register. Each bit in the Set/Reset Register, bits 0 to 3, is replicated eight times and written to the appropriate bit plane (Bit Planes 0 to 3). These bits are written through a bit mask. The bit mask is a logical AND of the byte written by the host after rotation and the value in the Bit Mask Register. This mode is effective for writing patterns of data to all four display planes when all of the pixels are the same color.

2.3.5   Read Mode 0

Read mode 0 reads a byte of data from the display memory. Only one bit plane can be active at a time. A read operation, while read mode 0 is in effect, will return the data in the active bit plane. If each pixel is represented by one bit in each bit plane, a read operation returns a bit from eight neighboring pixels.

2.3.6   Read Mode 1

Read mode 1 returns the result of a comparison. A 4-bit value can be written into the Color Compare Register. Any or all of the four bit planes can be active in the comparison depending on the value of the Color No Care Register. All active planes are used in a process that compares the value in the addressed pixels of display memory with the value in the Color Compare Register. The byte returned to the host contains the result of eight comparisons, one comparison for each of the eight neighboring horizontal pixels represented in the byte.

2.4   EGA AND VGA RESOLUTION

Two issues that are always important in computer graphics are the amount of spatial resolution and the color resolution. The color resolution includes the total number of possible colors and the number of colors that can be displayed simultaneously.

2.4.1   Spatial Resolution

The resolution of the EGA/VGA in the low-resolution modes is 320 by 200 pixels. In the higher-resolution modes, the EGA/VGA features 640 by 350 pixels, and the VGA provides additional high-resolution modes of 640 by 480 pixels. These resolutions are ideal for a wide variety of color graphics applications, including many scientific and business graphics applications. The spatial resolving power of the human eye at normal screen viewing distances goes far beyond the 640-by-480 resolution of the EGA. In cases involving diagonal lines and curves, the eye can detect jagged lines at resolutions approaching 4,000 by 4,000 on a normal-size monitor. Thus, resolutions 50 times greater than the EGA/VGA's highest resolution could still be considered unsatisfactory. Laser printers can achieve resolutions up to 600 by 600 per inch. To match this resolution, if a normal viewing area of a monitor is 10 inches by 8 inches, the total screen resolution would need to be 6,000 by 4,800. Photosetting equipment can achieve over 1,000 by 1,000 per inch. To match this resolution, a monitor would require a resolution of 10,000 by 8,000.

The question arises: "How much resolution is enough?" The tradeoffs involved in adding resolution are not entirely based on cost. Higher-resolution images involve more processing time and greater storage requirements per image. If cost and processing speed were not issues, the answer clearly would be: "The higher the resolution, the better." As it is, cost and speed are big issues. The cost of high-resolution graphics adapters is easily surpassed by the cost of a compatible high-speed monitor. Each user must select the proper resolution for the application. The resolution of four popular display adapters is illustrated in Figure 2.1.

For business graphics, in which pie charts, bar charts, scatter plots, and simple two- and three-dimensional graphs represent the normal graphics employed, the EGA resolutions are adequate. This may be insufficient, however, if the business graphics are to be projected onto a screen directly from the monitor or if the monitor is to be photographed and put onto a slide. Often special slide-making software and hardware are utilized to create high-resolution slides, and the EGA is used to preview the slides. This is often the case in desktop publishing. The EGA/VGA resolutions are adequate to preview a page in a coarse mode or to view a portion of a page in nearly full resolution. Many frequent desktop publishing users are purchasing WYSIWYG monitors. This acronym stands for "what you see is what you get"; these monitors generally represent a full page.

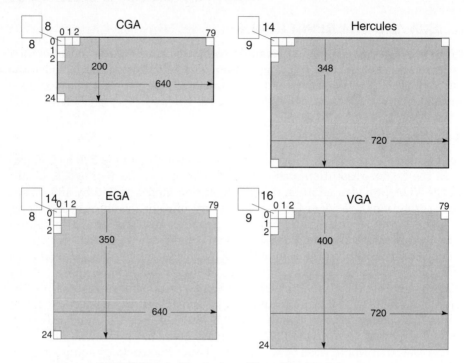

FIGURE 2.1 Resolution of Four Display Adapters

In computer-assisted design (CAD), high-resolution images are required. For some of the three-dimensional modeling packages, resolutions greater than the EGA are almost mandatory. However, the EGA/VGA performs admirably in most CAD applications. Zooming and panning techniques can be used to view the images in high resolutions. The speed at which graphics images can be drawn is significant when using panning and zooming because the image is redrawn frequently. In many packages, the resolution of the image is dictated by the resolution of the output device. Thus, supposing the hardcopy device is 2,400 by 3,150 per image, the image will be drawn to that resolution and a scaled-down version will be drawn on the display. This is often the case with two- and three-dimensional wire drawings; mechanical, electrical, and architectural schematic drawings; and printed circuit layout packages.

The graphic artist using one of the many painting and illustration packages available will usually find the EGA resolution sufficient for illustrations. Like the CAD packages, painting and illustration packages allow the user to zoom and pan to view high-resolution portions of the screen. In fact, portions of the image can be blown up to resolutions of greater than one pixel per dot.

Scientific graphics software is similar to the software mentioned above. Although a higher resolution could represent more information on a single screen, zooming will usually adequately display the results. If the software package is flexible enough, the resolution of the EGA should be sufficient for most scientific applications.

2.4.2   Color Resolution

Several display modes in the EGA/VGA allow the display of sixteen simultaneous colors. These sixteen colors can be selected from a palette of 64 possible colors in the EGA and 256 Kcolors in the VGA. One mode on the VGA allows 256 simultaneous colors from a palette of 256 Kcolors. (The term *Kcolors* is similar to *Kbytes* in that it actually represents a power of two. Thus, 256 Kcolors actually means 262,144 colors, just as 256 Kbytes means 262,144 bytes.)

The number of simultaneous colors is related to the number of bits associated with each pixel in the display memory. The more colors, the more bits. Table 2.7 lists the number of colors according to the number of bits per pixel.

The number of bits per pixel is always a power of two in the EGA/VGA, so that an integer number of pixels will fit into a single byte. The display memory is organized as bytes. In order to utilize memory fully, it is advantageous to pack the pixels evenly into the bytes.

The resolution of the display, in conjunction with the number of bits per pixel determine the total amount of display memory necessary. Table 2.8 lists some common configurations.

The number of bits per pixel dictates the number of simultaneous colors. These bits address a register within the color palette in the EGA or the Color Registers in the VGA. The register accessed by the display memory bits associated with a pixel determines the color output to the monitor. The wider the word in the Palette or Color Register, the more colors that are possible. Each of these registers is segmented into three parts. One part is assigned to represent the intensity of one of the three primary colors: red, green, or blue.

The EGA Palette Registers are six bits wide; therefore, two bits are assigned to each color. This provides a selection of 64 colors. The VGA Color Registers are eighteen bits wide; therefore, six bits are assigned to each color. This provides a selection of 256 Kcolors.

TABLE 2.7   Number of Simultaneous Colors

Bits / Pixel	Number of Colors
1	2
2	4
4	16
8	256
15	32K
16	64K
24	16M

TABLE 2.8 Amount of Display Memory

Resolution		Bytes per Pixel			
X	**Y**	**0.5**	**1**	**2**	**3**
320	200	30000	60000	120000	180000
640	480	153600	307200	614400	921600
800	600	240000	480000	960000	1440000
1024	768	393216	786432	1572864	2359296
1200	1024	614400	1228800	2457600	3686400

A number of techniques can be used to create more than sixteen simultaneous colors. One technique is synchronous loading of the color lookup table. If the color table is modified at some point in the display refresh, a pixel with a value of six at one location of the display would not necessarily have the same color as another pixel with a value of 6 located at a different point of the display. This assumes that the color table was changed somewhere between the refreshing of the first and the second pixels. The easiest place to segment the display would be into horizontal sections. Each section would be separated by horizontal scan lines. The display is updated by counting through the display memory from the top to the bottom. In the 350-line configuration, there are 350 horizontal sync pulses corresponding to displayed lines per frame update. The status of the horizontal refresh can be monitored and the color table can be updated synchronous to the horizontal sync pulse. This would create horizontal windows across the screen, and each window could have its own set of sixteen colors. However, the amount of time available during a horizontal retrace period is typically only a few microseconds.

Another technique that can effectively increase the number of simultaneous colors is *dithering.* Suppose a pattern of blue is interspersed with a random pattern of red dots. This would give the subjective effect of a color somewhere between red and blue. This technique is quite effective over large surfaces but falls apart as the area of color decreases. This technique creates more colors at the expense of resolution.

Many of the questions that exist for resolution also exist for color. The answer once again is application-specific. Having sixteen simultaneous colors is sufficient for most business graphics applications. Bar charts, pie charts, and line graphs of all kinds can usually be drawn effectively in fewer than sixteen colors.

Similarly, CAD and desktop publishing users are usually satisfied with sixteen simultaneous colors. However, these users often desire more than four planes of memory. It is often convenient to overlay drawings on separate planes during the construction of a drawing so that any plane can be modified independently. Most CAD packages maintain independent planes by utilizing host memory or disk storage. This often adds significantly to the processing time.

The output from CAD packages often is directed to color pen plotters; thus, the color on the monitor can be directly represented on the hardcopy. The output from desktop publishing packages, on the other hand, is primarily black and white. Color is often used to differentiate special formatting information. It is also used to differentiate areas of the screen that contain different elements such as messages, text, images, instructions, menus, and overlays.

Surface-shading CAD packages provide effective displays, turning line drawings into realistic representations. In order to achieve shading, subtle changes in color intensity are required. Broadcast standards require digital systems to represent color with 256 intensities per color.

Illustrators may or may not be satisfied with a limited number of colors. The number of colors required is usually directly related to the form the hardcopy output will take.

Scientists often require more than sixteen colors. Being able to represent data with monotonic gray scale or color scale is very important to many scientists.

2.5 THE SUPER VGA FEATURES

The Super VGAs extend the graphics capabilities in a number of directions. These include more memory, additional display modes, increased color resolution, hardware cursors, and hardware-assisted graphics functions. The host interface has also changed on the Super VGAs including linear memory mapping and memory mapping of the I/O registers.

Several advances in the Super VGAs are important to performance yet not really relevant to the programmer. For example, increased caching, queues, and fifos all significantly improve performance. New bus interfaces, VL and PCI for example, significantly improve speed. Similarly, new higher density RAMs in a variety of configurations, along with VRAMs, also improve performance but are, for the most part, transparent to the software.

The new display modes have been standardized by the VESA committee and are typically invoked in a similar fashion as setting the mode on a standard VGA. The increased resolutions are once again handled similarly to the standard VGAs. The hardware cursors are all handled in a similar fashion, however the storage techniques for the hardware cursor patterns vary significantly.

The hardware-assisted graphics functions are nearly identical in function yet each implementation varies in detail. I cannot overemphasize how complicated these hardware-assisted graphics functions are to program. It is best to get a function that works and use it without modification. Such functions are provided in the VGA Coprocessors Toolbox offered by the author.

2.5.1   Read and Write Modes

The most significant new write mode present in the Super VGA is the color expansion write mode. These usually come in two flavors, either opaque or transparent. These are used to convert a monochrome bit map that is one bit per pixel into a color bit map that can be from 4 to 32 bits per pixel. There are several ways of accomplishing this task

The ugly way is to expand every bit in software, convert this bit to a color, and then write the color to the display. Consider a character that is 8-by-16 pixels large occupying 8×16=128 bytes of data. Further suppose that this character is writing into a display that is set up for sixteen bits per pixel. Thus, each character occupies 256 bytes. Writing a character would then require 256 bytes of host transfer in an opaque mode and 512 bytes of host transfer (read/write) for a transparent operation.

If we are in a sixteen-color display mode, a better way is to use the standard VGA write mode 3. This does a color expansion from the one bit per pixel input. In this case, an 8-by-16 character occupies 64 bytes of data. A single host byte transfer corresponds to writing four bytes of data. Thus, eight byte write operations transfer the entire character to display memory—a significant improvement if you can live with sixteen colors. Further, this write mode often requires a read before write for transparent or a double write for opaque, thereby effectively requiring 16-byte memory transfers per character.

A hardware-assisted color expansion present in most new generation Super VGAs is very eloquent. It uses a foreground color, a background color, and a flag that selects either opaque or transparent writes. Suppose that a transparent write is desired of the 8-by-16 character. The host simply sets up the foreground color, the transparent mode, and writes out the sixteen bytes of character pattern. If a 16-bit-per-color display mode is used, only sixteen byte transfers were required, as opposed to the 512 bytes in the first case. Also, the width of the graphics processor might be such that double or quad characters can be written. Thus, sixteen host transfers could result in two or four characters being written simultaneously. This results in a speed improvement of 2048/16 = 128 times faster.

2.5.2   Display Memory

The hardware and software designers see two different things when display memory is discussed. The hardware designer sees DRAM versus VRAM, 1 Mbyte by 1 versus 512 Kbytes by 8 chips, block transfer and refresh cycles, wait-states, bandwidth, refresh rates, and mostly sees dollars and cents. The software designer sees how much memory is present, where the memory is mapped into the host address space, bank swapping, linear addressing, on-screen memory, off-screen memory, and performance. It would seem that the two perspectives have little in common; however, decisions made by one often affect the other.

Most Super VGAs have 1 Mbyte of display memory, while the recent generation are often loaded with either 1, 2, or 4 Mbytes. This memory has to be mapped into the host memory address space. The standard VGA way of doing this is to map the memory into the host address space between A0000 hex and BFFFF hex. To maintain co-compatibility with monochrome cards and to reduce software overhead, the 64 Kbytes between A0000 and AFFFF hex is used in favor of the 128 Kbytes between A0000 and BFFFF hex. A second way of mapping this display memory into the host address space is to use unoccupied regions of host memory. This is called linear mapping.

Bank Swapping

The most common method is bank swapping. In order to map the 1 to 4 Mbytes of memory into this 64 Kbyte space, we need to have some mechanism to bank swap. Since this bank swapping is a feature of the Super VGAs, no standard has been established as to how to accomplish this. Most VGA chips have one or two registers dedicated to bank swapping. There are sixteen 64 Kbyte segments in 1 Mbyte, 32 in 2 Mbytes, and 64 in 4 Mbytes. Therefore, some registers have to be dedicated for the upper addresses. In this example, it would take four bits, five bits, and six bits respectively for bank swapping. These bits would effectively be display memory address bits 16–19, 16–20, and 16–21 respectively.

Dual Banking

A common operation involves moving data from one portion of display memory to another. If the two regions don't share a common 64 Kbyte segment, this operation will be burdened by having to change banks each operation. The assembly language instruction REP MOVS will move data from one place to another at DMA rates. This is very effective. However, the equivalent operation performed one word at a time, interspersed with bank swapping is pathetically slow. For example, consider the following pseudo code that moves a block of 10,000 words from one bank to another.

1. Set source bank

2. Set source inner-bank address

3. Set destination bank

4. Set destination inner-bank address

5. Set word count to 10,000

6. Rep movsw.

The first five steps are done once per 10,000 words. The DMA instruction in step 6 is extremely fast. Now consider the second example where there is only one bank register.

1. Set source inner-bank address

2. Set destination inner-bank address

3. Set word count to 10,000

4. Set source bank

5. Read a word and increment source address

6. Set destination bank

7. Write a word and increment destination address

8. Repeat steps 4–7 10,000 times.

It is clear that steps 4–7 have to be repeated 10,000 times and not at DMA rates. Horrible! Consequently, dual banks are very popular and present throughout the current generation of Super VGA chips.

There are two ways to perform dual bank switching. The first is to have two separate registers, source bank and destination bank, as indicated in the first example. This is very straightforward. One is always dedicated to read operations while the second is dedicated to write operations.

A second approach is to split up the host address space into two chunks and dedicate one bank to one chunk and the second bank to the other. For example, one register is used when addresses between A0000–A7FFF hex are accessed and the second is used when addresses between A8000–AFFFF are accessed. In this case, the bank size would be 32 Kbytes. This would mean that software could write to two separate banks without requiring a bank swap, as well as the read and write operations.

The VESA standard has the capability to handle either single or dual banking systems. Each Super VGA that incorporates dual bank switching will also have a corresponding control bit that will enable either single or dual bank mode. VESA provides an interrupt call to set the bank. Thus, the reader might not need to know how a certain chip actually implements a bank swap. Unfortunately, the interrupt processing takes a considerable amount of time. A faster way to accomplish this task is to get the actual far pointer from the VESA call of the routines that perform the bank swapping and call these routines directly, based on the returned address. This works much better and does provide a consistent interface.

One must be careful, since the VESA implementation might not be in BIOS, and the target computer might not have the VESA TSR driver resident, or the version of the driver might not be current.

Bank Size and Granularity

The bank size is the amount of memory contiguously located in a bank. The Granularity is how much the address changes for each increment in the bank selector. The bank size does not have to be 64 Kbytes, nor does the granularity have to be 64 Kbytes as discussed in the previous examples. In fact these do not have to be the same as each other.

One common way of bank swapping in 1 megabyte cards is to use the one 8-bit port to select the two banks. The lower four bits are used for one bank, while the upper four bits are used for the second bank. In this case, the granularity is 64 Kbytes and the bank size is 64 Kbytes. However, a 2 Mbyte system requires five bits for each, so two 8-bit registers have to be used. Since there are eight bits each, the bank size can stay at 64 Kbytes while the granularity is reduced by a factor of eight to 8 Kbytes. It is reduced by a factor of eight since there are three additional bits in the 8-bit register.

Linear Addressing

Linear addressing gets out of the standard A0000–BFFFF region of host memory and allows the user to map the display memory into one contiguous chunk. Suppose there is 1 Mbyte of display memory and the host has 8 Mbytes of system memory. One could map the Super VGA display memory to occupy the space from 9 Mbytes to 10 Mbytes. Simply write to the display memory as if it were a huge buffer.

Seems too good to be true. Well, it might be. First, the ISA bus can only address up to 32 Mbytes. Therefore, any system with 32 Mbytes and an ISA Super VGA will not be able to use linear mapping. Fortunately, the newer VL and PCI buses do not have this restriction. Second, and perhaps more important, it requires a protected mode environment to access memory above the 1 Mbyte range. As protected mode environments become more popular, this will be less of a problem.

One side note: By default, the Windows 3 specification does not allow for linear display memory addressing. This is due to the version of the DPMI server specified in Windows 3. Some DPMI servers do provide the necessary services to allow for linear display memory mapping but it is not part of the Windows spec. Consequently, software developers are hesitant to jump onto the Windows bandwagon.

One also must ask how much faster linear addressing is anyway. Certainly it is application-dependent, and benchmarks are tough to come by. At the time of this book's writing, the only popular applications that benefit from linear addressing are non-Windows CAD packages such as AutoCAD. This is due to the fact that these applications are already running under a protected mode environment, they don't interface with other concurrently running applications, and it seems that line drawing benefits most from linear addressing.

Refresh Rates versus Memory Bandwidth

A big push is on for the ergonomic display, especially in Europe. Thus we are seeing 70Hz, 72Hz and desires for 80Hz vertical refresh rates. In Europe there is a big push for 100Hz refresh rates. Once again, it seems that if the hardware designers can accomplish it, the users will love it. Right? Maybe not.

In the case of DRAM, the system performance will degrade as the refresh rate increases. It is a simple linear function. The DRAM memory must share its bandwidth between host- and graphics-related accesses and refresh cycles. The higher the refresh rate, the less bandwidth available for graphics. This is **not** the case for VRAM since the VRAM is dual ported and refreshing the display does not subtract from the available bandwidth.

2.5.3   Control Registers

The Super VGA Registers are organized similarly to the Standard VGA Registers. Typically, these are accessed through an index/data register pair. The location of these registers vary across the I/O space of the PC. Sometimes these are tacked onto already existing I/O pairs like 3C3/3C4 hex, 3D6/3D7 by increasing the index values. Other times, new register pairs are selected.

The new generation of Super VGAs that incorporate graphics coprocessors have added a memory mapped I/O feature. Typically, the registers can be accessed through the standard I/O scheme or they can be memory-mapped. The reason for memory mapping is speed. The coprocessors, unlike the standard VGA features, often require several parameters before an operation can begin. By memory mapping the control registers, a control block format exists that is easy and quick to load from software.

A memory location has to be reserved for these memory mapped registers. A typical value is B8000 since this corresponds to the CGA address portion of video memory. The video memory is set up to reside at A0000 in the VGA mode. Consequently, one can find available memory within the VGA allocated memory space for these registers.

2.5.4   Super VGA BIOS

Additional, non-standard BIOS calls, as well as VESA BIOS calls, have been incorporated into many of the Super VGA BIOS ROMS. Unfortunately, only a limited amount of BIOS space has been delegated to the VGA, and it is very hard to cram everything in. Thus, many companies rely on a device driver that must be loaded into system memory.

The BIOS calls are invoked in a similar manner as are the standard VGA BIOS calls. They all suffer from the same speed penalty of using interrupts; however, when complicated functions like mode setting are in place, these are worth their weight in silicon.

2.5.5   Other Hardware on the Super VGA Cards

Two notable improvements, the DAC and the clock generator, have hit the Super VGA cards. The DAC is used to convert the digital data stream into analog voltages compatible with the monitors. The palettes (color registers) are also found in this part. The clock generators provide variable clock rates in a single part, as opposed to requiring multiple crystal oscillators. The older VGAs had four or five metal rectangular cans on the cards, one for each frequency. The newer generation cards have replaced these with an oscillator chip. This represents an obvious cost and space advantage.

The newer high-color and true-color display modes require special DACs. Newer parts also contain separate paths for hardware cursor data and for video overlaying. Thus, the cursor might never actually be written into display memory but rather the digital cursor data is added at the final output stage. The advantage is that the display memory doesn't lose bandwidth to the cursor-related reads and writes. The disadvantage is that if you do a screen dump, the cursor is missing.

There are several versions of both the DACs and the clock generators made by several companies. Any Super VGA chip might be present with any number of these clock generators or DAC chips. The number of permutations becomes difficult to manage. Consequently, pity the person who has to program a display mode without using BIOS. The interface would have to detect which Super VGA Chip, which DAC and which clock generator is present, then understand how to program each for the desired effect. The process is doable but not fun.

One more complication: Even though the Super VGA card can handle a display mode, it may not be advisable for the programmer to use it. There is the monitor to consider. A monitor **can be destroyed** if a display mode is invoked whose resolution is greater that the specified limits of the monitor. Thus, the programmer also has to consider what monitor is present. Most Super VGAs now are bundled with software that lets the user manually input what type of monitor is present. This information is interrogated by BIOS, and the BIOS should stop any unwise mode sets. The programmer will also have to figure this stuff out.

It is beyond the scope of this book to describe these ever-changing complications. That's an author's way of saying I don't want to figure it out myself. If you need this information, call one of the other VGA authors. Tell 'em I sent you.

2.6   SUPER VGA RESOLUTIONS

The Super VGA extends both the spatial and the color resolutions beyond the VGA standard. Workstation graphics is now available to the casual user. The spatial resolutions have been extended to 1280 by 1024. The color resolutions have been extended to 32 bits per pixel. To the software developer, these might seem independent, but they are integrally tied together when considering the amount of display memory required to hold an image and the memory and system bandwidth.

2.6.1 Spatial Resolutions

Spatial resolution is the number of horizontal by vertical pixels of an image. The image resolution might not be the same size as the displayable resolution. The image memory might have a resolution greater than the displayable resolution. The image might be so large that much of it may reside in system memory or on disk. Thus, a scanned 35-mm slide might occupy 4000 by 3000 pixels. The display memory might be able to store only 2048 by 2048 and the monitor might be able to display only 1024 by 768. For the remainder of this section, we will deal with displayable resolutions.

The spatial resolution dictates how fast the monitor will have to be. The monitor size, bandwidth, and dot pitch all need to be considered. The larger the monitor and the finer the dot pitch, the easier to see small detail. The faster the monitor, the more able it is to keep up with higher resolutions.

It should be noted that the resolution of the displayed image is often the same as the resolution of the display. This is not always the case. For example, if the image is 64 by 64 pixels and the display is in a 1024-by-768 graphics mode, then the display resolution is 1024 horizontal pixels. If each pixel is one byte, the display resolution is 1024 bytes. This is called the *display pitch*, and it is a measure of the bytes per scan line. Two adjacent vertical pixels are separated by the display pitch. The opposite case can also occur. In some display modes, on certain cards, the display pitch might be greater than expected.

Consider the following case. A 640-by-480 24-bit color mode would have 640x3=1920 bytes per row. This is a messy number. Many Super VGA manufacturers will actually use a display pitch of 2048. Care must be taken to understand what the actual display pitch is. Unrelated idiosyncrasies of this type are a good reason to buy the Super VGA Toolbox, where all of this nonsense is accounted for transparently.

2.6.2 Color Resolutions

Color resolution is different for palette versus non-palette color modes. The 16-color or 256-color modes are typically palette modes. Each of the sixteen or 256 values are converted into a color at the DAC. The color might be 8-bits for red, green, and blue. Thus, the color resolution would be 24 bits per color, but only sixteen or 256 different colors can be displayed at a time. Color resolution is more straightforward for the non-palette modes where the number of bits dictates the resolution.

The direct color modes are typically 15 bits, 16 bits, or 24 bits per color. Some really nonstandard display modes have direct color for 8-bit modes. This is especially useful in monochrome gray-scale situations. In addition, the early EGA and VGAs used digital monitors where the low color resolutions were directly converted into colors.

Palette Color

The sixteen and 256 color modes utilize a palette. In the case of 256 colors, this palette is called the color register. Palette-based color schemes are great when colors need to be changed rapidly without messing with the actual image data. They are also great when dealing with images that have demanding colors, but not a lot of them. They are a royal pain when trying to display a photographic image.

In the case of 256 colors, the data in display memory ranges from 0–255. Each of these values accesses a color register, number 0–255. The value in the color register is typically an 18-bit value. This value contains six bits of red, green, and blue. Some color registers convert the data to a 24-bit value for eight bits of red, green, and blue. The 24-bit version is far superior, but unfortunately, it wasn't standardized, nor was a method of switching between the two standardized. Thus, it never caught on.

Hi-Color

The 15-bit and 16-bit per color modes are called the Hi-Color modes. The red, green, and blue components share these bits. In the case of the 15-bit color, the blue occupies the lower five bits, the green occupies the next five bits, and the red occupies the next five bits. This leaves bit 15 unused, as shown in Figure 2.2. In some cases, this bit can be used to code the color as either a hi-color or a palette color creating a mixed mode.

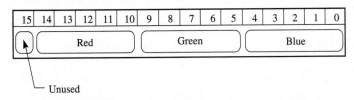

FIGURE 2.2 15-bit-per-Color Word Coding

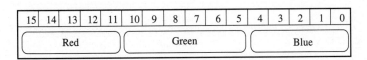

FIGURE 2.3 16-bit-per-Color Word Coding

The 16-bit-per-color mode uses the lower five bits for blue, the next six bits for green, and the highest five bits for red, leaving none left over, as shown in Figure 2.3. The human eye is most sensitive to high frequencies in the green spectrum; thus, the higher green color resolution really pays off.

Hi-color modes are great for images that don't have a lot of fine transition shadings. Since there are only five or six bits per color, we are limited to 32 or 64 shades of each color, which isn't always enough. On the other hand, these modes are very well suited for the graphics coprocessors and only the newer Super VGAs actually accelerate the true-color modes. Due to the limitations of 24 bits per color, the Hi-color modes are often faster. Since most monitors don't really show a true 24 bits of color anyway, the hi-color often work quite well.

True-Color

True-color modes use either 24 or 32 bits per pixel and produce 256 shades of red, green, and blue. Striking photo realism can be achieved in these modes, albeit at the expense of a decrease in speed and an increase in data. As hardware improves, the 32-bit-per-pixel modes will probably dominate the graphics industry. The 24-bit color standard is shown in Figure 2.4

There is not a standard way of coding these colors into three consecutive bytes. Some systems code red, followed by green, followed by blue; others code blue, followed by green, followed by red. Green always seems to be in the middle. The 32-bit color standard is shown in Figure 2.5. Once again, the red and

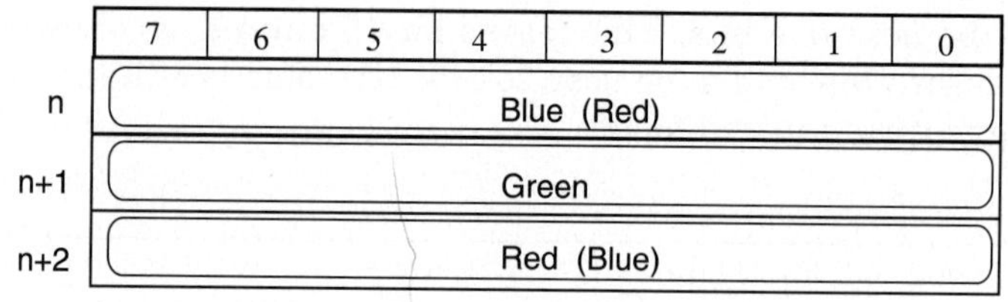

	7	6	5	4	3	2	1	0
n				Blue (Red)				
n+1				Green				
n+2				Red (Blue)				

FIGURE 2.4 24-bit-per-Color Word Coding

	7	6	5	4	3	2	1	0
n				Blue (Red)				
n+1				Green				
n+2				Red (Blue)				
n+3				Overlay				

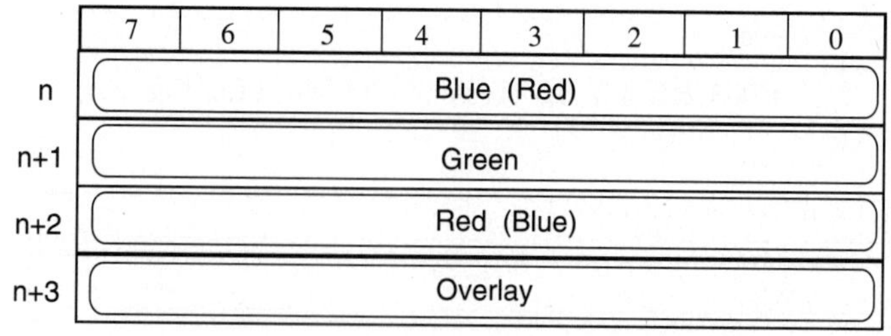

FIGURE 2.5 32-bit-per-Color Word Coding

blue bytes are often swapped depending on the color format adhered to in the graphics card.

2.6.3 Alphanumeric Modes

Due to the popularity of spreadsheets and the availability of high-resolution larger displays, the Super VGAs have accommodated alphanumeric modes with a maximum width of 132 characters and up to 60 character rows high. The standard modes follow, along with the standardized VESA mode numbers as shown in Table 2.9. Each manufacturer that implements these modes also provides its own proprietary display mode numbers. If a VESA driver is not present in BIOS or as a TSR, then the proprietary modes will have to be used.

These modes are accessed identically to the standard VGA alphanumeric modes.

2.6.4 Graphics Modes

The single most important advance in the Super VGAs are the extended resolution display modes. These new modes increase the spatial resolutions as well as the color resolutions. Certainly, the amount of memory and the specific Super VGA chip dictates which new modes are actually present. The VESA graphics modes are provided in Table 2.10.

Programming the 4-bit-per-color and the 8-bit-per-color graphics modes are identical to the 4- and 8-bit-per-color standard VGA modes, with the exception of bank swapping. The 15-bit and 16-bit per color modes are similar to the 8-bit modes, with the exception that two consecutive bytes are used for each pixel. The 24-bit modes are a bit more tricky. It is similar to the 8-bit, 15-bit, and 16-bit per-color modes in that each pixel occupies contiguous memory locations. Unfortunately, in the 24-bit mode, each pixel requires three bytes. Three bytes is not divisible into 65536. Therefore, bank boundaries occur inside a pixel. This is very irritating. The solution, if in a bank-swapping mode, is to check if

TABLE 2.9 VESA Alphanumeric Mode Numbers

VESA Mode Number	Columns	Rows
108 hex	80	60
109 hex	132	25
10A hex	132	43
10B hex	132	50
10C hex	132	60

TABLE 2.10 VESA Graphics Mode Numbers

VESA Mode Number	Columns	Rows	Bits per Color
102 or 6A hex	800	600	4
104 hex	1024	768	4
106 hex	1280	1024	4
100 hex	640	400	8
101 hex	640	480	8
103 hex	800	600	8
104 hex	1024	768	8
106 hex	1280	1024	8
10D hex	320	200	15
110 hex	640	480	15
113 hex	800	600	15
116 hex	1024	768	15
119 hex	1280	1024	15
10E hex	320	200	16
111 hex	640	480	16
114 hex	800	600	16
117 hex	1024	768	16
11A hex	1280	1024	16
10F hex	320	200	24
112 hex	640	480	24
115 hex	800	600	24
118 hex	1024	768	24
11B hex	1280	1024	24

a pixel is going to cross a bank boundary and switch banks inbetween the three bytes output. Like I said, irritating.

The 32-bit modes are similar to the 24-bit modes. Only eight bits are used for each of the red, green, and blue colors. The remaining eight bits might be ignored, used as off-screen memory, or used as an alphanumeric overlay channel. The advantage is that 65536 is divisible by 4, and a single 32-bit write will affect only one pixel. The disadvantage is that 25% more data needs to be stored for the same image.

2.7 RASTER OPS

Microsoft has specified these 256 raster ops. These raster ops are numbered 0–FF hex. Each raster op is therefore an 8-bit value that represents the result of the Boolean operation on predefined pattern bit maps, source bit maps, and destination bit maps. The resultant 256 codes follow. In order to understand this table an example is appropriate.

Consider the OR function. Let's take all possible values of the three inputs and apply the three-way OR operator as shown in Table 2.11. If we read down the OR result table with the top line considered to be bit position 0, we find the result is a hex value of FE hex. Consequently, the OR operation involving all three inputs is numbered FE hex.

If only the OR operator is applied to the Source and Pattern data, the result would be FC hex since the Destination is not considered relevant in the output. This is shown in Table 2.12.

A reverse Polish notation is used to describe each of these values. Using the codes in Table 2.13 as a key, the three-way OR operator would be DPSoo. This is read from inside to the outside as follows: (P OR S) OR D. First take the logical OR function of the Pattern and Source, and then take the logical OR function of the result with the Destination.

Now consider a more complicated example, PSDPSanaxx. Remember that this all occurs as fast as if the destination data were simply replaced with the source. This can be read as:

PSD **(P and S)** naxx	Source AND Pattern
PSD **n(P and S)** axx	NEGATE result
PS **(D a (n(P and S)))** xx	AND with Destination
P **(S x (D a (n(P and S))))** x	XOR with Source
(P x (S x (D a (n(P and S))))	XOR with Pattern

Table 2.14 illustrates the 256 raster ops as defined by Microsoft. Not all of these are relevant, useful, or supported by the variety of Super VGAs.

Not all Super VGAs implement all of the 256 raster codes with a direct operation. Often the common operations, maybe eight to sixteen, are implemented in hardware, and the less common ones are implemented through two or more consecutive combinations of the implemented raster ops.

TABLE 2.11 Three-way Operand OR Raster Op

Pattern	Source	Destination	OR result	Bit #
0	0	0	0	0
0	0	1	1	1
0	1	0	1	2
0	1	1	1	3
1	0	0	1	4
1	0	1	1	5
1	1	0	1	6
1	1	1	1	7

TABLE 2.12 Two-way Operand OR Raster Op

Pattern	Source	Destination	OR result
0	0	0	0
0	0	1	0
0	1	0	1
0	1	1	1
1	0	0	1
1	0	1	1
1	1	0	1
1	1	1	1

TABLE 2.13 Code Letters for Reverse Polish Notation Raster Op Names

P	Pattern
S	Source
D	Destination
o	Logical bitwise OR
a	Logical bitwise AND
n	Negate bitwise (invert)
x	Exclusive-OR bitwise (XOR)

TABLE 2.14 The 256 Raster Ops as Defined by Microsoft

Value	R Polish	Name	Value	R Polish	Name
0	0	Blackness	80	DPSaa	
1	DPSoon		81	SPxDSxon	
2	DPSona		82	DPSxna	
3	PSon		83	SPDSnoaxn	
4	SDPona		84	SDPxna	
5	DPon		85	PDSPnaoaxn	
6	PDSxnon		86	DSPDSoaxx	
7	PDSaon		87	PDSaxn	
8	SDPnaa		88	DSa	SrcAnd
9	PDSxon		89	SDPSnaoxn	
A	DPna		8A	DSPnoa	
B	PSDnaon		8B	DSPSxoxn	
C	SPna		8C	SDPnoa	
D	PDSnaon		8D	SDPSxoxn	
E	PDSonon		8E	SSDxPDxax	
F	Pn		8F	PDSanan	
10	PDSona		90	PDSxna	
11	DSon	NotSrcErase	91	SDPSnoaxn	
12	SDPxnon		92	DOSDOiaxx	
13	SDPaon		93	SPDaxn	
14	DPSxnon		94	PSDPSoaxx	
15	DPSaon		95	DPSaxn	
16	PSDPSanaxx		96	DPSxx	
17	SSPxDSxaxn		97	PSDPSonoxx	
18	SPxPDxa		98	SDPSonoxn	
19	SDPSanaxn		99	SDxn	
1A	PDSPaox		9A	DPSnax	
1B	SDPSxaxn		9B	SDPSoaxn	
1C	PSDPaox		9C	SPDnax	
1D	DSPDxaxn		9D	DSPDSaoxx	
1E	PDSox		9E	DSPDSaoxx	
1F	PDSoan		9F	PDSxan	
20	DPSnaa		A0	DPa	
21	SDPxon		A1	PDSPnaoxn	
22	DSna		A2	DPSn\oa	

(continued)

TABLE 2.14 *(cont.)*

Value	R Polish	Name	Value	R Polish	Name
23	SPDnaon		A3	DPSDxoxn	
24	SPxDSxa		A4	PDSPonoxn	
25	PDSPanaxn		A5	PDxn	
26	SDPSaoxxn		A6	DSPnax	
27	SDPSxnox		A7	PDSPoaxn	
28	DPSxa		A8	DPSoa	
29	PSDPSaoxxn		A9	DPSoxn	
2A	DPSana		AA	D	
2B	SSPxPDxaxn		AB	DPSono	
2C	SPDSoax		AC	SPDSxax	
2D	PSDnox		AD	DPSDaoxn	
2E	PSDPxox		AE	DSPnao	
2F	PSDnoan		AF	DPno	
30	PSna		B0	PDSnoa	
31	SDPnaon		B1	PDSPxoxn	
32	SDPSoox		B2	SSPxDSxox	
33	Sn	NotSrcCopy	B3	SDPanan	
34	S{DSapx		B4	PSDnax	
35	S{DSxmpx		B5	DPSDoaxn	
36	SDPox		B6	DPSDPaoxx	
37	SDPoan		B7	SDPxan	
38	PSDPoax		B8	PSDPxax	
39	SPDnox		B9	DSPDaoxn	
3A	SPDSxox		BA	DPSnao	
3B	SPDnoan		BB	DSno	MergePaint
3C	PSx		BC	SPDSanax	
3D	S{DSpmpx		BD	SDxPDxan	
3E	SPDSnaox		BE	DPSxo	
3F	PSan		BF	DPSano	
40	PSDnaa		C0	PSa	MergeCopy
41	DPSxon		C1	SPDSnaoxn	
42	S|DxPDxa		C2	SPDSonoxn	
43	SPDSanaxn		C3	PSxn	
44	SDna	SrcErase	C4	SPDnoa	
45	DPSnaon		C5	SPDSxoxn	
46	DSPDaox		C6	SDPnax	
47	PSDPsaxn		C7	PSDPoaxn	

TABLE 2.14   *(cont.)*

Value	R Polish	Name	Value	R Polish	Name
48	SDPxa		C8	SDPoa	
49	PDSPDoaxxn		C9	SPDoxn	
4A	DPSDoax		CA	DPSDxax	
4B	PDSnox		CB	SPDSaoxn	
4C	SDPana		CC	S	SrcCopy
4D	SSPxDSxoxn		CD	SDPona	
4E	PDSPxox		CE	SDPnao	
4F	PDSnoan		CF	SPno	
50	PDna		D0	PSDnoa	
51	DSPnaon		D1	PSDPxoxn	
52	DPSDaox		D2	PDSnax	
53	SPDSxaxn		D3	SPDSoaxn	
54	DPSonon		D4	SSPxPDxax	
55	DN	DstInvert	D5	DPSanan	
56	DPSox		D6	PSDPSaoxx	
57	DPSoan		D7	DPSxan	
58	PDSPoax		D8	PDSPxax	
59	DPSnox		D9	SDPSaoxn	
5A	DPx	PatInvert	DA	DPSDanax	
5B	DPSDonox		DB	SPxDSxan	
5C	DPSDxox		DC	SPDnao	
5D	DPSnoan		DD	SDno	
5E	DPSDnaox		DE	SDPxo	
5F	DPan		DF	SDPano	
60	PDSxa		E0	DPSoa	
61	DSPDSaoxxn		E1	PDSoxn	
62	DSPDoax		E2	DSPDxax	
63	SDPnox		E3	PSDPaoxn	
64	SDPSoax		E4	SDPSxax	
65	DSPnox		E5	PDSPaoxn	
66	DSx	SrcInvert	E6	SDPSanax	
67	SDPSonox		E7	SPxPDxan	
68	DSPDSonoxxn		E8	SSPxDSxax	
69	PDSxxn		E9	DSPDSanaxxn	
6A	DPSax		EA	DPSao	
6B	PSDPSoaxxn		EE	DPSxno	
6C	SDPax		EC	SDPao	

(continued)

TABLE 2.14   *(cont.)*

Value	R Polish	Name	Value	R Polish	Name
6D	PDSPDoaxx		ED	SDPxno	
6E	SDPSnoax		EE	DSo	SrcPaint
6F	PDSanan		EF	SDPnoo	
70	PDSana		F0	P	PatCopy
71	SSDxPDxaxn		F1	DPSono	
72	SDPSxox		F2	PDSnao	
73	SDPnoan		F3	PSno	
74	DSPDxox		F4	PSDnao	
75	DSPDxox		F5	PDno	
76	SDPSnaox		F6	PDSxo	
77	DSan		F7	PDSano	
78	PDSax		F8	PDSao	
79	DSPDSoaxxn		F9	PDSxno	
7A	DPSDnoax		FA	DPo	
7B	SDPxnan		FB	DSPnoo	PatPaint
7C	SPDSnoax		FC	PSo	
7D	DPSxnan		FD	PSDnoo	
7E	SPxDSxo		FE	DPSoo	
7F	DPSaan		FF	1	Whiteness

2.8   GRAPHICS ACCELERATORS

No longer is the VGA a simple frame buffer. Now the Super VGAs can be considered to be a powerful graphics system.

2.8.1   What Is a Graphics Accelerator?

There are many flavors of graphics accelerators, but there is really no exact definition of what constitutes a graphics accelerator. Basically, a graphics accelerator performs graphics operations with minimal or no host interaction. Some manufacturers refer to these as coprocessors, graphics engines, accelerators, and Windows accelerators. Many of the newer Super VGAs include graphics accelerators. However, any Super VGA card can claim to be a Windows accelerator because it runs faster than a standard IBM VGA and also runs Windows. In my mind, a graphics accelerator must have silicon dedicated to the performance of most of the following:

   Block Transfers
   Line Drawing

Area Fill
Logical and Arithmetic Mixing
Map Masking
Scissoring
Hardware Cursor

The specific Super VGA implementations vary regarding which functions they support and the extent to which they are supported. For example, the XGA manual by IBM defines a graphics coprocessor as follows:

> "The XGA coprocessor provides autonomous drawing functions for the video system. Autonomous drawing functions means that the coprocessor draws into memory (either video memory or system memory) independently of the system microprocessor, while the system microprocessor is performing some other operation."

This definition is not strictly adhered to in the newest generation of Super VGA accelerators. For example, a true block transfer involving system memory would not require the host. This is not the case due to the bus and software. For the graphics accelerator to take control, it would need to become a bus master. There is no advantage for the graphics system to be a bus master if the host has to be put into a hold mode during the external bus mastering. This is the case on the ISA or VL bus. Therefore, the host has to initiate the DMA transfers through a block move assembly language instruction.

```
rep         movsw
```

Some graphics accelerators do not include certain functions. For example, the line draw and hardware cursor are not supported in all accelerators. In other accelerators, only display memory to display memory block transfers are supported.

All in all, the graphics accelerators perform an important function of limiting the host responsibilities, reducing the amount of data that has to travel across the host-to-graphics system bus, and reducing the host software requirements.

2.8.2 History and Motivations

Shortly after the VGA was introduced, Texas Instruments introduced its 34010 graphics coprocessor. Cards were made for the IBM PCs. They were expensive but filled a niche. Also, they were programmable and similar to microprocessors, with additional graphics-related instructions. Due to their cost and complexity, they really never became mainstream. Several cards are currently available that utilize the 34020 or 34030 graphics accelerators. These cards have been very popular—in fact, nearly mandatory—for true-color applications.

At about the same time, IBM introduced the 8514/A graphics coprocessor. Unlike the VGA, IBM was not willing to disclose the register specification for these parts. Rather, they introduced an Application Interface (AI) that was to be used for interfacing to the chip. Several VGA chip manufacturers quickly set out to reverse-engineer the 8514, and today there are a few 8514 compatible chips available. The 8514 was a micro channel board and, like the micro channel, it never became mainstream.

Both the 340x0 chips and the 8514 had a classic flaw. They also required a VGA in order to run DOS and any DOS applications that didn't support either of these. Most applications did not! In an attempt to correct this problem, IBM introduced the XGA. The XGA incorporated both a VGA and an 8514-type graphics coprocessor. Once again, they relied on the AI interface, although they did publish the register specification.

By the time that Windows 3 was introduced, the hardware manufacturers had a running start with graphics coprocessors. The quick and overpowering popularity of Windows 3 took everyone by surprise. Applications software houses jumped on the bandwagon and the Super VGA manufacturers could get away with shipping a Windows 3 driver, along with some DOS-only drivers like AutoCAD, Lotus, Word Perfect, Word, and so on.

The Windows driver specification had a specific set of tasks. The faster the driver and card could perform these tasks, the faster Windows would run. The race was on. The major way that the Super VGA manufacturers could differentiate their products was by the cost and speed that they would run Windows. Several Super VGA manufacturers introduced the graphics accelerators. These implemented, in whole or in part, several of the most popular graphics functions required by Windows and the popular Windows applications. Consequently, the road was cleared for the profitability of graphics accelerators.

2.8.3 Benchmarks

Benchmarks were designed to test the speed and accuracy of products. They became especially important when rating the speed of graphics cards. They became so important that some manufacturers specially designed their chips or BIOS software to perform well with benchmarks. Others devised ways to detect the benchmark and cheat a bit. The new generation of benchmarks run real-world applications and judge their results. If the graphics system does well on a benchmark that tests an application that is important to you, then, cheating or not, it will likely do a good job for you. The bottom line is that it is difficult to assess what the bottom line is.

2.8.4 Functions of a Graphics Processor

As just mentioned, the specifications for the Super VGA graphics coprocessors were based on the foundation of predecessor coprocessors and on the Windows 3 requirements. Profitability was based on running fast Windows benchmarks. Thus, the motivations for what to include in the graphics coprocessor were based on profit and not on a general purpose graphics engine. Silicon costs money. Each year the amount of transistors achievable in the affordable gate arrays increases. Consequently, as more silicon becomes available, we will see more functions incorporated into the graphics coprocessors. Currently, the following functions are typically integrated into the graphics coprocessors.

Block Transfers	Including host-to-display, display-to-host and display-to-display, with or without color expansion
Line Drawing	Including Bresenham, end-point, short-stroke, patterned, ready-to-fill
Area Fill	Including rectangular fill, patterned fill, polygon fill
Mixing	Controls the way source, mask pattern and destination data are combined including replace, AND, OR, XOR, ADD, and SUBTRACT.
Arithmetic Mixing	Including ADD and SUBTRACT with saturate, with or without a mask
Masking	Allows masking in either through plane or across plane modes.
Scissoring	Allows hardware clipping
Hardware Cursor	Provides a hardware cursor.

Although there are many similarities in how each chip performs these functions, there is really no right or wrong way. Therefore, I will provide generalized cases to discuss the fundamentals of each.

2.8.5 Block Transfers

Block transfers move a block of data from a source location to a destination location. These are often referred to as BitBlts. There are several flavors of block transfers. The source and destination can be in either system memory or display memory as shown next. Since the Super VGA is not a bus master, there is no reason to allow system-to-system transfers.

Case	Source	Destination
1	System memory	Display memory
2	Display memory	System memory
3	Display memory	Display memory

In cases 1 and 2 above, there is no possibility of overlap since the system memory and display memory cannot overlap. In this case, the BitBlt is straightforward and shown in Figure 2.6. Note that the host memory is organ-

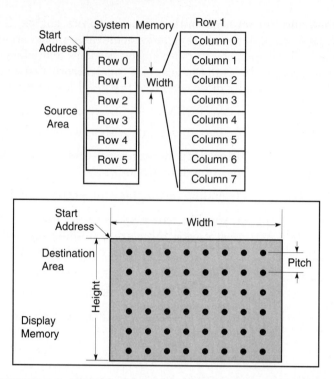

FIGURE 2.6 BitBlt Involving Both System and Display Memory

ized contiguously with the source pitch equal to the width. Thus, a single REP MOVS instruction can be used to move the entire data.

It should be noted that the host has to perform the actual instructions to provide the data to the host in case 1, or to receive the data from the display in case 2. One might ask why the BitBlt is used if the host is doing the work anyway. There is an advantage in doing so because the host does not have to keep track of the display addressing. The display-started address is provided to the coprocessor, and the coprocessor takes care of all of the display-memory addressing. This can yield significant savings since the display memory is often not contiguous, as is the case when the display pitch is not the same as the width. Second—and more important in the future—the Super VGAs will be bus masters. When that happens, case 1 and case 2 will require no host interaction.

The three cases are shown in Figure 2.7. In Figure 2.7a, there is no need to load the destination es:[di] registers and in Figure 2.7b, there is no need to load the source ds:[si] registers. In Figure 2.7c, neither the source nor destination registers need to be loaded. In fact, the host doesn't have to have any interaction with the operation. The coprocessor registers are loaded, and the go command sent. The operation is totally transparent.

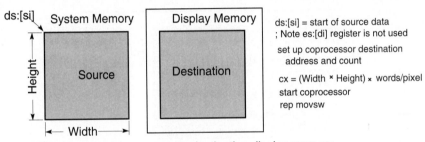

a) BitBlt source system memory to destination display memory

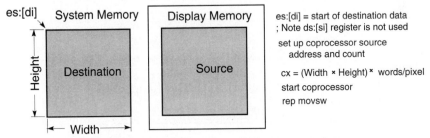

b) BitBlt source destination memory to source display memory

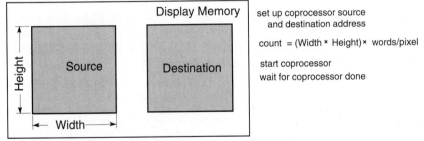

c) BitBlt source display memory to destination display memory

FIGURE 2.7 Controlling the three types of BitBlt. a) From system memory to display. b) From display memory to system. c) From display memory to display memory.

In the case of the display memory to display memory transfer, the coprocessor must be provided with several pieces of information. These are shown in Figure 2.8. Note that there is only one height and one width specification in this example. The proportions are assumed to be the same. There are, however, different source and display pitches.

Different display pitches are necessary in cases 1 and 2, when the data is stored contiguously in the host. It would also be necessary in case 3 when the source and destinations do not share the same display pitch. For example, suppose a 4-by-3 pattern is stored contiguously in 12 bytes and it is desired to

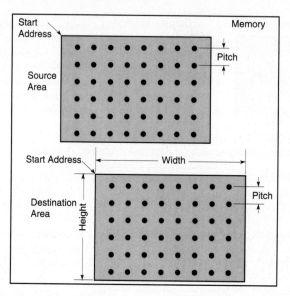

FIGURE 2.8 Display Memory to Display Memory Transfer

display this pattern onto a screen that is 1024 bytes wide. The source pitch would be 4, while the destination pitch would be 1024. Color expansion is discussed later in this section and shown in Figure 2.9. Of course, both the source and destination start addresses have to be specified.

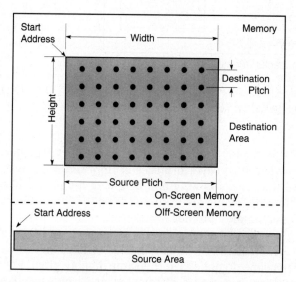

FIGURE 2.9 Display Memory to Display Memory Transfer with Different Source and Destination Pitches

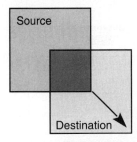

a) Source must start at bottom right, increasing left and up

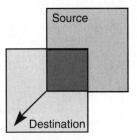

b) Source must start at bottom left, increasing right and up

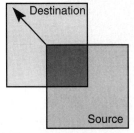

c) Source must start at top left, increasing right and down

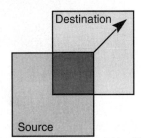

d) Source must start at top right, increasing left and down

FIGURE 2.10 Overlapping Cases When Performing
Display Memory to Display Memory Transfer

Since both source and destination reside in display memory, it is possible for the two to overlap. This requires additional smarts on the part of the graphics accelerator in order to make sure that data isn't destroyed in the source before it is copied. There are four cases where this can occur. These are shown in Figure 2.10. The coprocessor has control registers that tell the coprocessor which corner to start in (upper- or lower-left or lower-right corner) for the source data and which direction to go for incrementing x and y variables (increment to left or right for x and y).

Color Expansion

A popular function in computer graphics is to transfer data that is in a one color format to a second color format during a move operation. A typical example is the display of a character font. Suppose that the font resides in an off-screen region of display memory and you want to store this in as little space as possible (which, of course, is a monochrome format). One could rapidly display a letter from this font into a 24-bit color display mode if the hardware could automatically expand this data during the BitBlt. This is a complicated operation, but the results really pay off when displaying text or other related data. Rudimentary color expansion is provided with the standard VGA write modes 2 and 3.

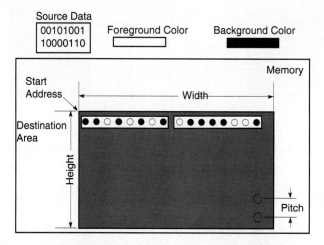

FIGURE 2.11 Typical Color Expansion

Figure 2.11 shows a typical off-screen source of data with an on-screen destination. In this example, two bytes contain the monochrome bit maps for sixteen pixels. Any 0 value in one of these bytes is displayed as a background color and any 1 value is displayed with a foreground color. The background and foreground colors are specified in registers associated with the coprocessor. In this example, the foreground color is white and the background color is black.

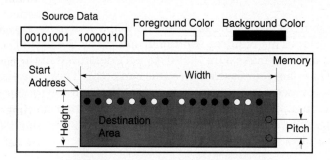

FIGURE 2.12 Opaque Color Expansion

There are two types of popular color expansions, called *opaque* and *transparent*. An opaque transfer is shown in Figure 2.12. Note that the background pixels are displayed with the background color.

The second type is transparent. In this case, the background is assumed to be transparent. Consequently, any 0 in the monochrome source data is ignored. As a result, the character foreground gets written over the screen, and the screen data is untouched when it corresponds to a background 0. This is shown in Figure 2.13.

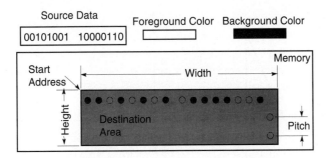

FIGURE 2.13 Transparent Color Expansion

Transparency and Key Colors

More complicated expansions are provided in certain chips allowing for color data to be further color expanded. For example, an 8-bit data source can be BitBlted to a 24-bit true-color screen. A key color is set up that indicates the background pixels. This key color can also have an associated mask value that enables or disables individual bits in the key color. Consequently, a range of key colors can be used. This key color performs the same function as the monochrome 0.

2.8.6 Line Drawing

The most common line drawing algorithm used is the Bresenham algorithm. This involves setting up several registers that control the direction of the line, the axis preference, the starting location, the number of points, and the slope. The line is drawn beginning at the starting location and continuing on until the number of points are output. Typically, a set of registers exist that correspond to the Bresenham parameters. Also common is a second set of registers that drive the Bresenham engine with the line endpoints. This eliminates the need to calculate the Bresenham coefficients from the end points, saving time. Either the Bresenham coefficients or the end points drive the same line drawing engine.

The Bresenham registers that must be initialized by software before the line drawing begins are defined as follows:

CUR_X	Initial x-axis coordinate
CUR_Y	Initial y-axis coordinate
MAJ_AXIS_PCNT	Length of line projected onto major axis (dmajor)
DESTX_DIASTP	2 * dminor – 2 * dmajor
DESTY_AXSTP	2 * dminor
ERROR_TERM	2 * dminor – dmajor

where dminor is the length of the minor axis projection and dmajor is the length of the major axis projection.

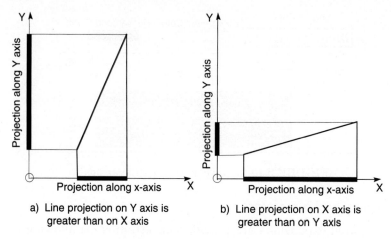

a) Line projection on Y axis is
   greater than on X axis

b) Line projection on X axis is
   greater than on Y axis

FIGURE 2.14 Line Projections

The length of the minor axis projection versus the major axis projection determines the way that the line should be drawn. The longer projection is the major axis also called the *independent axis*. One and only one pixel will be drawn along each pixel of the major axis. Projections are shown in Figure 2.14.

The line draw operation is performed using the following algorithm. Before the line is drawn the image space is decomposed into eight octants, the octant in which the line is drawn is encoded into the INC_Y, YMAJAXIS, and INC_X flags.

```
draw_line()
{
int xstep,ystep,i;
if (INC_Y)     ystep = 1;  else    ystep = -1;
if (INC_X)     ystep = 1;  else    ystep = -1;
for (i=0; i<MAJ_AXIS_PCNT; i++) {
    plot(CUR_X,CUR_Y);     // plot the point to the display
    if(ERROR_TERM>0) {
        CUR_X += xstep;
        CUR_Y += ystep;
        ERROR_TERM += DESTX_DIASTP;
        }
    else {
        // if YMAJAXIS==1 then y axis is the major axis
        if(YMAJAXIS) CUR_Y += ystep;  else CUR_X += xstep;
        ERROR_TERM += DESTY_AXSTP;
        }
    }
}
```

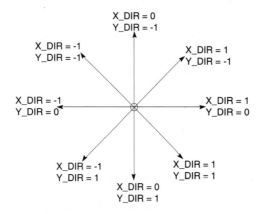

FIGURE 2.15 Short Stroke Directions

Short Stroke

The second common line drawing technique is called the *short stroke*. The short stroke allows lines to be drawn in eight directions corresponding to 45 degree increments, typically up to fifteen points long. These are especially popular and fast when drawing stroke fonts. These lines can be drawn rapidly because it is not necessary to calculate and set the line constants. The implementations usually allow a single 16-bit write operation to completely specify and initiate a short stroke. The short stroke directions are shown in Figure 2.15.

Line Strip

The third (and not so common) line drawing technique employs a different algorithm for drawing lines. This method is called the *line strip*. It provides flexibility in selecting exactly which pixels in a line will be drawn. Line strips are drawn either horizontally or vertically, and are commonly used when the lines are going to be used as the border for a filled polygon. The Bresenham lines can cause problems in this case. A line is drawn in either the horizontal or vertical direction a specified number of points. At the end of the line, the resultant x and y coordinates may be automatically incremented. This allows for rapid repeating of line segments to draw a line. A typical line drawn with this method from 5,3 to 20,8 is shown in Figure 2.16.

2.8.7   Area Fill

It is very important to fill areas. These might be simple fills of a rectangular region with a single color, more complicated fills of a rectangular region with a pattern, and even more complicated fills of irregular polygonal regions. A simple rectangular fill is shown in Figure 2.17. Note that a single fill color is used to fill the entire region. The BitBlt engine is used for this operation.

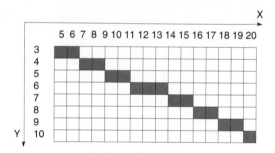

FIGURE 2.16 Line Strip

The more complicated pattern fill is especially important in Windows. A pattern is repeated into a larger region the same way tiles are placed on a floor. This is shown in Figure 2.18. The pattern is typically 32 by 32, but several Super VGAs offer 16 by 16 or even variable size patterns. In some cases, variable offsets are used into the source data allowing the pattern to have a phase offset. For example, consider a pattern with a circle in the middle. A phase offset might start with the circle at the left border. This is important when a pattern is sliding across a window and the start of the pattern is not always aligned with the left border of the window.

The third and most complicated fill is the polygon fill. Important in solid rendering, fast polygon fills are essential for animation and simulated imagery. The polygon fill typically fills a region one line at a time. It assumes that the outside of the region is a solid line comprised of a single color. The algorithm typically starts with an assumed point outside of the region and moves across the scan line alternating between inside and outside the polygon each time a border is reached. Once again, the border is assumed to be the same color. The

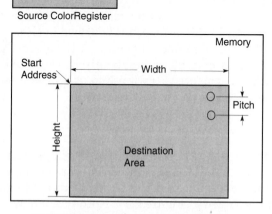

FIGURE 2.17 Rectangular Solid Fill

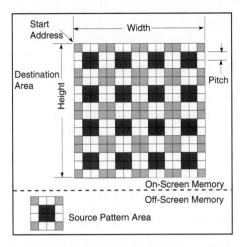

FIGURE 2.18 Rectangular Pattern Fill

border color has to be provided to the filling algorithm. A polygon fill is illustrated in Figure 2.19.

Special line draws are required for effective polygon fills because the typical Bresenham algorithm could complicate a filling algorithm and create errors in the filling. The coprocessors that anticipate a polygon fill or already implement one are equipped with a non-Bresenham algorithm for drawing the outside of a polygon. It is important to remember that there can be no horizontal gaps when scanning horizontally one scan line at a time. Most of us, using one painting package or another, have had a fill operation leak out of an unknown hole.

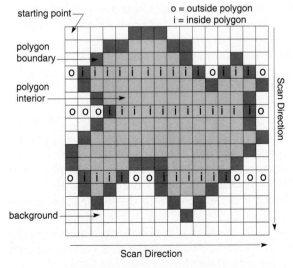

FIGURE 2.19 Polygon Fill

An example of performing an area fill operation follows:

Step 1. Draw the closed outline of the area to be filled. Typically, an area boundary drawing mode is used, as opposed to the standard Bresenham line draw. This closed outline is going to be used as a mask. In order to reduce screen clutter, this could be drawn into an off-screen memory area. The rectangular area where these lines will be drawn should be pre-filled with 0s.

Step 2. If a pattern map is supported, designate this area as the pattern map.

Step 3. Specify the destination where the actual fill operation will occur.

Step 4. Select the foreground mix, source of data, and background mix.

Step 5. Specify the operation to occur with increasing X. This borrows from the BitBlt filling operation.

Step 6. Initiate the area fill.

The algorithm used in this filling operation would be a left-to-right scanning of the pattern, where the first occurrence of the outline would set the pixels to foreground; all subsequent pixels are set to foreground until the next occurrence of a line is encountered. This repeats until the end of the selected region. The background mix should be set to "destination" since the unfilled pixels should remain unmodified.

2.8.8   Logical and Arithmetic Mixing

The simple MOV instruction replaces the destination value with the source value. This is not the only way to alter the destination value. In many cases, it is desirable to replace the destination with some combination of the source and destination. These are commonly refered to as raster ops. In the Standard VGA, it was possible to have four raster ops, corresponding to replace destination with source, AND destination with source, OR destination with source, or XOR destination with source.

The exclusive-or (XOR) operator shown in Table 2.15 is one that is familiar to most graphics programmers, and the nemesis of the original Artificial Intelligence (AI) designers. The most common way of highlighting an area on the screen without destroying the original data is accomplished through the XOR operator. The XOR operation is described in Table 2.15.

Consider the Input B to be the data in the display memory and Input A to be the XOR mask. If the XOR mask is a 0, the display memory value remains unchanged. If the XOR mask is a 1, the display memory value inverts. Thus, the display memory value can be inverted and reinverted to its original value by simply XORing it with the value 1 twice.

TABLE 2.15 The XOR Truth Table

Input A	Input B	Destination
0	0	0
0	1	1
1	0	1
1	1	0

Other operators like AND and OR are also quite useful. The AND operator could be used when a filter type mask is desired. Every value corresponding to a 1 in the AND mask and a 1 in the display memory produces a 1 as an output. If either the AND mask or the display memory is a 0, the resultant display memory value is a 0. Similarly, the OR operator produces a resultant display memory value of 1 if either the display memory or the OR mask is a 1.

There are eight possible outcomes when there are three variables, each capable of 0 or 1 as shown in Table 2.16. In order to account for each, a 3-bit raster op code would be required. Consider the following table.

TABLE 2.16 The Eight Combinations of Three Variables

Source A	Source B	Destination
0	0	0
0	0	1
0	1	0
0	1	1
1	0	0
1	0	1
1	1	0
1	1	1

Arithmetic Operators

Thus far we have discussed only the logical operators. Suppose we wanted to have arithmetic operators to add, subtract, multiply, or divide. These would be excellent for imaging applications containing contrast enhancement, filtering, and brightness control operations.

For example, it would be helpful if we could add a constant to a portion of an image to increase the brightness. Similarly, subtraction would decrease the brightness. It would also be necessary to have clipping with these operators. Suppose 100 was added to 200, producing 300. If 255 was the largest value, the result would be clamped to 255, rather than the 45 remainder. Subtraction would clamp to zero.

A further complication, yet extremely powerful operator would be one that operated in neighborhoods. Consider the destination to be affected not only by a source and pattern mask, but also by immediate neighbors. These would be useful for implementing digital filters such as low-pass, high-pass, or zooming.

Unfortunately, until more silicon becomes available, we will have to wait for these arithmetic operators; thus far, they typically been left out of the Super VGA silicon.

2.8.9 Masking

It is desirable to add a third input along with the source and destination, thereby combining the three inputs into one output. The first input could be the data from the host, the second input could be a mask, and the third input would be the data already present in display memory. This mask is often called the *pattern*. In this case, there are four variables, each with two values. Two raised to the eighth power is 256. Therefore, there are 256 possible combinations requiring an 8-bit raster op code. Each of the 256 outcomes can be achieved, but only a subset actually has much physical significance. The 256 raster ops were described in Section 2.7.

There are two common types of masking—through-plane or across-plane masks. We can consider the memory to be three-dimensional, where the three dimensions are width, height, and bits-per-pixel. Across-plane masking would mask out pixels in the width or height dimension. Through-plane masking would protect individual bits in a single pixel. This is effective in animation when all of the bits are not dedicated to one image. It is also useful when you want to modify only one of the color components associated with a pixel. For example, in a 16-bit per color mode, the mask will enable access to only the lower five bits. Consequently, subsequent operations would affect only the blue-color component.

The simplest form of across-plane masking is the rectangular clipping scissors operation. Any attempt to write to a pixel outside of the scissors region is blocked. This is shown in Figure 2.20.

A more complex across-plane masking operation uses an arbitrary 1-bit-per-pixel mask pattern. This is used in conjunction with the Scissors Registers to mask out individual bits within the rectangular window. This operation could have been accomplished with repetitive writes to the Mask Map Registers, although at a considerable speed penalty. A typical mask is shown in Figure 2.21.

The mask itself is a bit map with one bit per pixel. The location of this bit map is typically in off-screen memory. A mask map is shown in Figure 2.22.

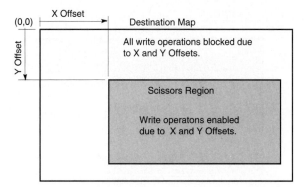

(a) Scissors region defined with respect to the Destination Map

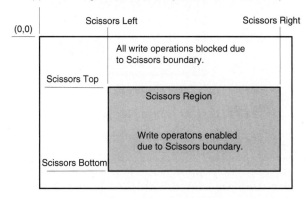

(b) Scissors region defined with respect to the display memory

FIGURE 2.20 Scissors Clipping

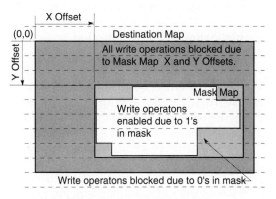

FIGURE 2.21 Mask Map Clipping

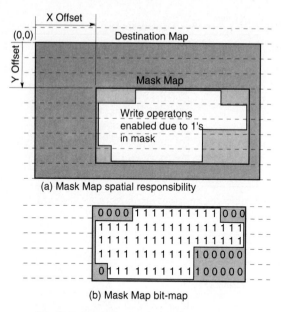

(a) Mask Map spatial responsibility

(b) Mask Map bit-map

FIGURE 2.22 Mask Map Bit Map

2.8.10 Scissoring

Scissoring is a term used for clipping. The two words are synonymous. There are four scissors registers associated with the upper-left and lower-right corners of the clipping rectangle. This was illustrated in Figure 2.20. Any operation that attempts to access data outside of the bounds of the scissors registers would have no effect. It should be noted that even though no data would change outside of the scissors region, the operation would still take time. However, the time would be reduced since the display memory access time would not be relevant.

A faster scissoring algorithm would be one that begins the operation at the edge of the scissors region. For example, consider a line drawn from 0,0 to 100,100. If the scissors region is 25,25 to 75,75, then the line algorithm would step quickly from 0,0 to 24,24 since no memory cycles would occur. It would draw between 25,25 to 75,75, and once again step quickly from 76,76 to 100,100. The faster routine would skip directly to 25,25, draw the line to 75,75 and be done. This, however, requires additional hardware.

2.8.11 Hardware Cursor

The hardware cursor replaces the software mouse pointer commonly used by GUI applications. The hardware cursor eliminates the need for application software to save and restore the screen data as the mouse cursor position changes. In addition, the fast hardware can keep up with the mouse movements providing a smoother moving cursor, as compared with a software cursor.

VESA VCI Standard

The DOS mouse driver is a Terminate-and-Stay Resident (TSR) program that supports the mouse. This program provides support to applications that require mouse-cursor interaction. Consequently, it must talk to the video hardware directly. The VGA BIOS Extension (VBE) written by the VESA committee detailed the Super VGA modes, yet it did not provide any specifications for the video cursor. Today's mouse drivers can acquire the relevant mode information from the VBE to display the cursor but there is not enough information in the VBE to take advantage of hardware cursors.

The VESA Video Cursor Interface (VCI) standard performs the following functions:

- Separates the VGA hardware dependent code from the calling program or driver.

- Takes advantage of hardware cursors when present

- Uses the VBE information to display the cursor

- Adds support for non-VESA modes

- Provides cursor support information to applications.

The applications software passes cursor-related drawing commands to the cursor drawing module. These commands are hardware-independent. The cursor drawing module can be either an overlay program copied to the host mouse driver, a separate TSR program, or a ROM resident code. Communication with this drawing module is accomplished through a table located at a defined offset in the overlay. Any TSR or ROM versions of this module are accessed through an INT 10 hex call.

A table contains VCI module identification, version number, the address of an OEM text-identification string, the address of a string of supported video modes, and several addresses that point to VCI modules. This set of addresses point to a list of 16-bit entries containing video modes for which cursor support is present. Display routines include show/hide cursor, set graphics patterns, and save/restore the cursor module state.

When used with a mouse driver, the VCI interface isn't directly accessible to programs outside the mouse driver. Applications query the mouse driver for information about cursor support through the INT 33 hex call. Two new mouse function calls acquire the Super VGA information. The first returns a pointer to the VCI module table so a calling application can determine if VCI cursor support is available and which VGA modes are supported. The second allows the calling application to get or set cursor information including cursor patterns.

Software support for the VCI interface is available in the Super VGA toolbox offered by the author.

Types of Hardware Cursors

There are three types of hardware cursor. The first actually changes the data in the display memory, saving the underlying image, writing the cursor pattern, and restoring the saved underlying image. This is accomplished in hardware, freeing up the host processor. The second type moves the cursor around in an overlay buffer, never affecting the original data. The cursor simply erases where it was, and draws its pattern at the new location. The display hardware joins these two digital streams before the DAC chip, or at the DAC chip. The third type doesn't actually affect display memory at all. Rather, the hardware cursor is generated in hardware and mixed into the video stream at the DAC chip. The DAC chips then combines these two digital data streams into a single analog data stream sent to the monitor. The cursor pattern never resides in memory.

In order to operate the hardware cursor, the host must set up a set of registers that control where the cursor pattern resides, the cursor size, and the enabling and disabling of the cursor. Typically, the cursor is stored as a monochrome bit pattern with two colors associated with the 1's and 0's. These two cursor colors typically reside as two extra colors in the DAC chip. In addition, some implementations allow each pixel in the cursor pattern to be displayed as a cursor 0 color, cursor 1 color, transparent, or compliment of the image data.

Hardware Cursor Fundamentals.

The cursor shape is defined in off-screen memory. The way that this cursor is stored in memory varies from implementation to implementation. Software developers typically scream when requested to program hardware cursors since each implementation of the pattern is so different. Typically, a cursor pattern is stored with two bits per pixel. A truth table will help. Table 2.17 is the Microsoft Windows specification.

Thus, if the hardware cursor bits are 0, then the resultant pixel will be drawn in Cursor Color 0, as a background color. Similarly, if the bits are 01, the resultant pixel will be drawn in Cursor Color 1, as a foreground color. If the bits are 10, the resultant pixel will **not** be affected by the cursor. If the bits are 11, the resultant pixel will be complemented.

A second way of viewing the cursor pattern still requires two bits per cursor, but considers them as residing in two separate bit planes. The first bit plane is

TABLE 2.17 Hardware Cursor Definitions (Microsoft)

Bit 1	Bit 0	Resultant Displayed Pixel Color
0	0	Cursor Color 0 Background
0	1	Cursor Color 1 Foreground
1	0	Transparent
1	1	Compliment

called the AND plane and the second bit plane is the XOR plane. The hardware cursor is illustrated in Figure 2.23.

The AND plane is used to control which bits in the result will be actually affected by the hardware cursor. If a bit is set to 1 in the AND plane, the resultant pixel will be affected. The way that it is affected is determined by the XOR pixel and the technique employed by the specific Super VGA. If the bit in the AND mask is set to 0, the source image pixels will be zeroed and the resultant pixel value will not be affected by the source pixel. The actual value will be determined by the XOR pixel value. In this case, the XOR value is usually used as a switch bit between one of two colors. This occurs since the XOR implies the use of the underlying source image. It is set to zero due to the zero in the AND mask. Therefore, the XOR mask can't really perform an XOR operation.

The XOR plane dictates which pixels in the input source are inverted and which remain unchanged. Any pixel that remains unchanged creates a back-

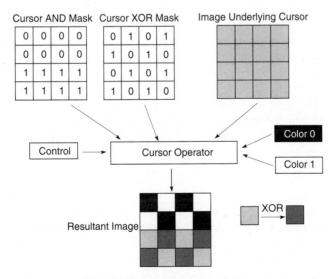

FIGURE 2.23 Hardware Cursor

TABLE 2.18 Four Color Modes Used for Hardware Cursor in One Implementation

Cursor AND	Mask OR	Color Mode 0	Color Mode 1	Color Mode 2	Color Mode 3
0	0	All 0	Color 0	Color 0	Color 0
0	1	All 1	Color 1	Color 1	Color 1
1	0	Transparent	Transparent	Transparent	Transparent
1	1	Inverted	Inverted	XNOR	Color 2

ground transparent result. Any pixel that is inverted produces a noticeable effect on the screen. Using a solid color for the cursor can be problematic if a section of the image happens to be that same color. In this case, the cursor would disappear. This is often rectified by using two complementary colors, one surrounding the cursor pattern, and the second color internal to the pattern. For example, the common Windows cursor is an arrow whose outline is black and interior is white. Therefore, the cursor shows up pretty well under any conditions. Inverting the data can produce weird results when the cursor is floating over a photographic-type image.

Several manufacturers provide distinct color modes that allow a variety of cursor color effects. For example, one Super VGA provides four color modes that produce the results shown in Table 2.18.

Cursor Pattern

The 2-bit cursor pattern is stored in off-screen memory. This is necessary in order for the hardware to directly access the patterns. The way these are stored in memory vary between manufacturers. The two planes can be stored as independent single bit maps; interlaced with one line of AND map and one line of XOR map; as four consecutive lines of AND followed by four lines of XOR; and as packed modes, with four pixels per byte. Similarly, the alignment of the cursor masks are dependent on the implementation. They can require 1 Kbyte alignment; 256 byte alignment; 16-byte alignment; 4-byte alignment; or no alignment.

Cursor Size

Most hardware cursors are 64-by-64 pixels. Often 32-by-32 pixel cursor are available. In some cases, variable sized cursors can be displayed.

Chapter 3

Graphics Hardware and Software

3.1 PC HARDWARE

Graphics has always been an effective tool when used to display information. Trends in data that are obscured when displayed in columns of numbers become obvious when displayed in a graphical format. Since the first computers were used to analyze data, computer graphics has been employed to display the results.

In order to use computer graphics on the PC, the computer hardware, the graphics hardware, and the graphics software must be compatible. This chapter describes these three interrelated elements and emphasizes the impact they have on the programmer. Also provided is a detailed discussion of how the performance of the graphics system is affected by the computer hardware.

3.1.1 Computer Systems

The PC computer may be a PC, PC-XT, PC-AT, PC-386, PC-486, Pentium, or PS/2 model. The computer is typically constructed on a motherboard, though some computers reside on cards that plug into a passive motherboard. The motherboard, also called the *planar* in the PS/2 family of computers, contains the microprocessor, memory, BIOS, interface circuitry, miscellaneous hardware, and card slots. The majority of computers require a video card if video output is desired. Some computers anticipate the need for the video hardware and actually include the video circuitry on the motherboard. No additional video card is necessary in these systems. All circuitry is resident on the motherboard for most laptop and notebook computers.

Graphics chips, including the VGA, have been implemented on the motherboard of several computers. These computers usually can be configured so that an adapter card containing a VGA chip can be used instead of the on-motherboard VGA. This provides additional flexibility to the user who wants to upgrade the VGA; at the same time, it keeps costs down for the user who is satisfied with the on-motherboard VGA. The PS/2 computer family (except Model 30) incorporates the VGA onto the motherboard. In the literature, this is referred to as the *planar VGA*.

There is considerable confusion in the industry regarding the fact that only two distinct cases can be accommodated—the on-motherboard versus adapter card VGAs. The standard, devised by IBM, was designed with their planar VGAs in mind, and was released at the same time as the micro channel. Consequently, no one knows whether the differentiation in the standard is meant to differentiate micro channel versus ISA or on-motherboard versus adapter card.

At that time, IBM thought that a VGA would reside either on the motherboard or on a micro channel bus. Unfortunately, the rest of the world was using the ISA bus. Further complicating the problem was the introduction of additional buses including the EISA, micro channel, VL, and PCI. Currently, no one in the industry understands what the buses are supposed to do. If you are confused, welcome to the gang.

There are two wake-up locations specified for the VGA. One, commonly used for the micro channel but also finding its way into on-motherboard implementations, involves the three ports at 3C3 hex, 94 hex, and 102 hex. An enable bit exists in 3C3 hex. There is also a bit in 94 hex that turns on the port 102 hex. This bit in 102 hex turns on the system enable. Thus, there are two bits, one in port 102 and one in 3C3, that both have to be enabled. In order to get at the bit in 102 hex, you have to first set the bit in 94 hex.

In the ISA bus implementation but now also found on the VL bus is the port at 46E8. There are **two** bits in this register, one corresponding to the enable bit in 3C3 hex and the second corresponding to the bit in 94 hex that enables 102 hex. Many VGAs can be configured to respond to either 46E8 or 3C3 depending on how the chip is integrated into either an adapter card or onto a motherboard. Both registers 3C3 and 46E8 are shown in Figure 3.1.

Video Subsystem Enable Register 3C3

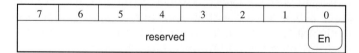

Video Subsystem Enable Register 46E8

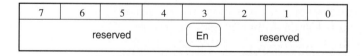

FIGURE 3.1 Wake-up Registers

VL Bus

Unfortunately VESA has provided no guidance regarding the VL bus. The VL bus further complicates the equation since VGAs can reside in three places simultaneously—the VL bus, the ISA bus, and on the motherboard. Having two distinct selection methods is clearly insufficient to select between three devices.

PCI Bus

Fortunately, the PCI bus doesn't add to the mess. The PCI bus contains a set of ID Select Registers that are slot-specific, and the 3C3 or 46E8 registers are not used.

Don't Worry, Be Happy

In most cases, you won't have to worry about any of this since detection and wake-up are typically handled in BIOS during a cold boot operation.

3.1.2 Microprocessors

There are several classes of computers within the PC family. Each class of computer is based on a different microprocessor. The microprocessor plays a large part in whether the computer is well-suited for a graphics application. Typical microprocessors include the 8088, 8086, 80286, 80386, 80486, and Pentium. These integrated circuits can be further subdivided according to their operating speeds. The speed of the processor often plays a major role in the execution time of a graphics algorithm.

Although there are millions of PCs still equipped with 8086 and 80286 processors, the bulk of computing is done on the 80386 and 80486. At the time of the printing of this third edition, the Pentium processor is just being integrated into commercially available systems. The internal speed, external speed, internal data-bus width, external data-bus width, availability of coprocessors, amount, speed, and efficiency of cache memory and bus interface all affect graphics performance.

3.1.3 Coprocessors

Graphics algorithms often require sophisticated and repetitive mathematics. Great improvements in the speed of these algorithms can be achieved with the addition of a math coprocessor. Graphics algorithms often require floating-point calculations. These calculations operate orders of magnitude faster when a coprocessor is present and when the software utilizes it.

Until this time, coprocessors were arithmetic performing fast floating point or fast array operations. The 8087, 80287, and 80387 are three examples. The

80486 and Pentium coprocessors are embedded in the microprocessor chips. Today a wide variety of coprocessors are used including graphics coprocessors, video compression coprocessors, DSP chips, and audio processors.

3.1.4   Computer Buses

There are several buses in today's computer systems. These include the address bus, the data bus, the microprocessor local bus, SCSI, and special purpose buses. The size, speed, and efficiency of these buses determines the effectiveness of the computer's operation. The data bus width varies from eight bits to 64 bits on today's microprocessors. Several microprocessors have different data bus widths internal and external to the part. For example, the 80386-SX or 80486-SX send sixteen bits to the outside world, but use 32 bits internally.

Address Bus

The address bus sends 24 bits to the ISA bus. This means that the ISA bus can address only 16 Mbytes of memory. This has an impact on ISA-based VGAs that are set up for linear addressing. If you have 16 Mbytes or more of memory, there is no space to fit in the linear address mapped VGA. The motherboard, VL, and PCI buses utilize all 32 bits of addressing. Thus, there should be no problem mapping linear addressed VGAs in either of these places. Table 3.1 illustrates address bits and memory address space.

Data Bus

The original ISA bus used an 8-bit data bus. The second generation ISA bus and the micro channel added a second connector providing a 16-bit data bus. The EISA bus provided a 32-bit bus, as did the VL bus and the PCI bus. The wider the data bus, the faster the bus is (assuming the devices on both ends of the bus can keep up).

   The Super VGAs that were designed for a 16-bit bus won't really take advantage of a 32-bit bus. However, the newer chips actually have 32-bit buses and can take advantage of a 32-bit data bus. The next generation chips will incorporate 64-bit buses internally and 32-bit interface buses to the host.

VL Bus

The VL bus, as endorsed by the VESA standard, has become the preferred graphics bus. The newest generation VGA cards that reside on a VL bus report speed improvements of from two to ten times over the ISA-based cards. These cards are designed with appropriate speeds so that they can utilize the high speed VL bus.

   Disk controllers are also being put onto the VL bus, but I experienced problems when trying to run with motherboards, VGAs, and disk controllers all

TABLE 3.1 Address Bits versus Amount of Memory

Bits	Memory
16	64 Kbytes
17	128 Kbytes
18	256 Kbytes
19	512 Kbytes
20	1 Mbyte
21	2 Mbyte
22	4 Mbyte
23	8 Mbyte
24	16 Mbyte
25	32 Mbyte
26	64 Mbyte
27	128 Mbyte
28	256 Mbyte
29	512 Mbyte
30	1 Gigabyte
31	2 Gigabytes
32	4 Gigabytes

residing on the motherboard. This problem originates with the rather loosely interpreted specification regarding loading on the VL bus. It seems that when different manufacturers' motherboards, VGAs, and disk controllers get together, the loading goes out of specification and weird problems occur—the kind of problems that you don't need.

The VL bus is **not** designed to allow bus mastering. VL cards can be bus masters; however, the advantage of this is limited because the host processor must be put into a hold mode during the bus mastering phase.

PCI Bus

Intel has introduced its PCI bus as the bus of the future. This bus is very promising, for it allows bus mastering, which could be an advantage for graphics. The bus mastering PCI bus is really designed for multiple processor systems (that is, network servers). It is important to remember that the speed of the bus and the speed of the Super VGA are relevant only if the software supports them. It is unclear who is actually going to write the bus mastering software. There are definitely motivations for network servers to do so, but the motivations for the wide scope of graphics applications users is questionable in the near future.

There is currently a great deal of controversy surrounding which is better, VL or PCI. Certainly, VL was established first and it is a very simple bus to implement. PCI is more complicated and is currently having problems that limit its speed. Perhaps the future has a place for both buses—VL in the less expensive computers and PCI in the more expensive computers.

3.1.5 Memory

Graphics requires a lot of memory. There is a reason why a picture is worth a thousand words. Typical image sizes and the memory required is shown in Table 3.2.

A scanned image at 600 dpi across an 8- by-10 picture in 24-bit color occupies 86,400,000 bytes. Therefore, the more memory the better. In fact, most graphics applications require a work buffer as well as the image buffer.

TABLE 3.2 Graphics Memory

Width	Height	Bits/Color	Memory (bytes)
640	480	4	153,600
800	600	4	240,000
1024	768	4	393,216
1280	1024	4	655,360
640	480	8	307,200
800	600	8	480,000
1024	768	8	786,432
1280	1024	8	1,310,720
640	480	15–16	614,400
800	600	15–16	960,000
1024	768	15–16	1,572,864
1280	1024	15–16	2,621,440
640	480	24	921,600
800	600	24	1,440,000
1024	768	24	2,359,296
1280	1024	24	3,932,160
640	480	32	1,228,800
800	600	32	1,920,000
1024	768	32	3,145,728
1280	1024	32	5,242,880

Protected Mode

Nonprotected mode DOS applications can access only the lower 1 Mbyte of memory. In order to reach the upper memory without relying on EMS drivers, one needs a protected mode compiler. You cannot talk directly to a memory address when using a protected mode compiler. This is quite common in graphics when sending some data to the display at A0000h. In this case, the segment is A000 hex. In order to use a protected mode compiler, you must request a segment selector from the DPMI server. This value would then be used in lieu of the A000 segment address.

Accessing Memory

Only the lower 24 bits of memory (less than 16 Mbytes) can be accessed on a ISA card. In order to access all 32 bits, you must be on the motherboard, VL, or PCI bus.

Linear Mapped VGAs

The new generation of VGAs allow memory mapping. This maps the 1, 2, or 4 Mbytes of display memory into the computer's address space, outside of the A0000–BFFFF hex address space. There should be neither conventional memory nor other memory-mapped device resident at that location; otherwise memory conflicts will occur.

3.2 GRAPHICS ADAPTERS

Graphics adapters interface the computer to the video monitor. There are several standard graphics adapters used with the PC. The graphics adapters discussed in this book include the Monochrome Display Adapter (MDA), Hercules Graphics Adapter, Color Graphics Adapter (CGA), Enhanced Graphics Adapter (EGA), Video Graphics Array (VGA), Professional Graphics Adapter (PGA), Super VGAs 8514A, XGA, and TIGA-based cards. Both the MDA and the Hercules Adapter are monochrome systems, the CGA is a color system, and the others may be either. A limited downward compatibility exists among these adapters. This limited compatibility is based upon the video BIOS calls, the port addresses, and the data addresses. Downward compatibility implies that software written for the simpler adapters can be executed on the more advanced adapters.

Although these adapters vary in performance, all have certain elements in common. These elements include the host interface, display memory, BIOS, clocks, and the video output circuitry. Display modes resident on the standard MDA, CGA, EGA, and VGA are listed in Table 3.3. Super VGA modes are listed in Table 3.4, located on page 83.

TABLE 3.3 Video Adapters

Adapter Type	Resolution pixels	Number Colors	Display Memory	BIOS
MDA	720 by 348	2/2	4 Kbytes	System
Hercules	720 by 348	2/2	4 Kbytes	System
CGA	320 by 200	4/16	16 Kbytes	System
CGA	640 by 200	2/16	16 Kbytes	System
EGA	640 by 350	16/64	256 Kbytes	Local
VGA	640 by 480	16/256K	256 Kbytes	Local
VGA	320 by 200	256/256K	256 Kbytes	Local

3.2.1 Host Interface

The host can interact with the display adapter in two ways. The first is through the control registers, and the second is through the display memory. The control registers are assigned port addresses in the standard VGAs. These port addresses can be reassigned to memory addresses in several of the Super VGAs. The display memory is mapped into the host memory address space. Both the registers and the display memory can be accessed directly through applications software or indirectly through the BIOS calls.

3.2.2 Display Memory

The display memory can be thought of as a giant shift register that is constantly sending a serial data stream to the monitor. All of the previously mentioned display adapters are raster scan displays. The serial data stream is necessary to refresh the monitor with the data in the display memory. This is illustrated in Figure 3.2.

In reality, a shift register memory is not effective because data need to be accessed by the host in a parallel fashion. The display memory is typically configured as parallel memory. Both the host and the video control logic must compete to gain access to the video memory. The VRAM memory combines both the parallel input and a serial output, both of which can run in parallel.

Bit Planes versus Packed Display Format

There are two ways to segment the display memory. The first technique segments the memory into bit planes. A bit plane contains one bit for each pixel. The number of bit planes must equal the maximum number of bits per pixel, because only one bit exists per plane. The second technique is called *packed display format*. In this mode, there is only one memory plane, and the plane is

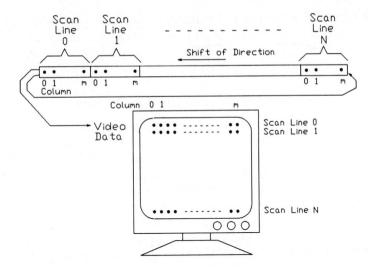

FIGURE 3.2 Shift Register Display Memory

segmented into elements, each being the number of bits in a pixel. Both of these techniques are identical if there is only one bit assigned to every pixel. These two modes are illustrated in Figure 3.3.

The VGA uses the top-left corner of the display as the lowest display memory address. The advantage in using the top-left corner becomes clear when alphanumerics are being displayed. The first character on a page would naturally be in the top-left corner of the page. Similarly, the advantage in using the lower-left corner becomes clear when graphics are being displayed. The origin of a two-dimensional graph is usually in the lower-left corner. The process of

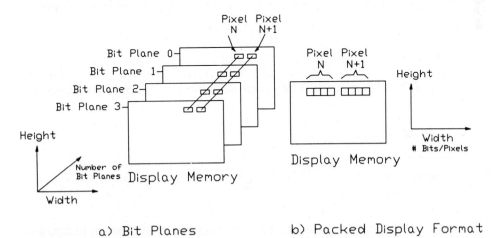

a) Bit Planes   b) Packed Display Format

FIGURE 3.3 Bit-mapped versus Pixel-packed Display Format

drawing a line from a low vertical value to a higher vertical value is normally displayed as a line being drawn in an upward direction. If the lowest address corresponds to the upper-left corner, this line would be drawn in a downward direction.

Mapping Data from Host Memory to Display Memory

Host memory in the PC can be thought of as two-dimensional. One dimension is the number of bits per element, and the second is the number of elements. In the PC, the common element is the byte, which consists of eight bits. Therefore, host memory can be thought of as being two-dimensional, one dimension being very narrow—eight bits—and the second possibly being very long—1 Mbyte. Similarly, we could consider a word to be 32 bits.

Most programmers are accustomed to thinking of host memory as one-dimensional. However, for the examples below, two dimensions work out nicely. In some graphics processors, the basic element is the bit, and the addressing actually accesses single bits. This memory can be construed as being one-dimensional.

The graphics display memory can be thought of as three-dimensional. Later in this book, it is considered to be four-dimensional. The three dimensions are height (called *rows*), width (called *columns*), and depth (called *number of bits per pixel*). The two-dimensional host memory has to be segmented so that it maps into the three-dimensional display memory.

If there is one bit assigned to each pixel, the host two-dimensional memory would be eight pixels per element wide. The length of the memory can be determined from Equation 3.1.

Equation 3.1 Length of Host Memory Buffer

$$\text{Number of elements} = \frac{\text{Number of columns}}{\text{Number of pixels/element}} \times \text{Number of rows}$$

Since an element is equal to a byte, this equation would simplify to Equation 3.2.

Equation 3.2 Byte Length of Host Memory Buffer

$$\text{Number of bytes} = \frac{\text{Number of columns}}{8} \times \text{Number of rows}$$

To speed up the graphics process, the data-transfer rate between host memory and display memory must be maximized. The PC is effective at moving strings of data from one sequential block of memory to another block of memory. In the case of planed or bit-mapped memory, it would be advantageous to keep the data associated with each bit plane in a separate array. A MOVS operation can occur because both the host memory array and the display memory are sequential. Four arrays would be required in the above example, one for each bit plane. In the case of packed display memory, the host array should contain packed bytes, so once again the host memory and the display memory are sequential. The assembly language command that transfers sequential data rapidly is called the REP MOVS. The source address is kept in the DS:SI register, the destination starting address is kept in the ES:DI register, and the number of bytes to move is kept in the CX register. This is illustrated in Figure 3.4a. A similar procedure is followed if the data is to be transferred from display memory to host memory.

In Figure 3.4a, no assumption is made as to the number of bits per pixel, because each bit plane is loaded separately anyway. Each byte contains eight neighboring horizontal pixels. In Figure 3.4b, it is assumed that there are two bits per pixel. This is important because the two bits associated with the same pixel reside in the same byte.

The VGA adapters utilize both techniques. Several display modes are available to the programmer; each segments display memory into a bit-plane format or a packed-display format.

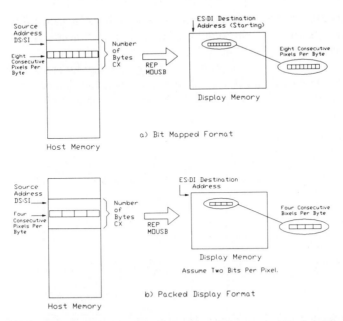

FIGURE 3.4 Transferring Data from Host Memory to Display Memory

advantage and disadvantage

There are advantages and disadvantages to both types of implementations. Bit-plane mapping is advantageous when data is to be modified in a single plane. Eight pixels can be modified through a single byte. In the case of the packed format, this can be difficult. If only one plane is to be modified, the bits associated with the other planes have to be masked out of the write operation. In the VGA, this mapping is done in hardware to eliminate the need for read/modify/write operations. If there are four bits per pixel, three bits would be masked out of the write operation for each pixel. A byte write operation would therefore modify only two bits. In this case, the packed format operates at one-fourth the speed of the bit-mapped format.

The packed format is advantageous when a single pixel is modified. Again, if there are four bits per pixel, two pixels could be modified in a single byte write operation. In the bit-mapped format, four write operations would be necessary to modify the data in each of the display planes. This time, the bit-mapped format operates at one-fourth the speed of the packed format.

Transferring Data from Display Memory to the Monitor

The data in the display memory is output to the monitor through the video hardware section. Each byte in the display memory consists of a number of pixels. If there are eight pixels per byte, a byte in display memory would be translated onto the monitor as eight neighboring horizontal pixels, as shown in Figure 3.5.

Two consecutive bytes in display memory appear as horizontal neighbors on the monitor if the end of the displayed row does not occur between the two bytes. This is illustrated in Figure 3.6.

Vertical neighbors are separated in display memory by the number of bytes per displayed scan row. In Figure 3.7, it is assumed that a scan line is 80 bytes wide. If there are eight pixels per byte, the scan line is 640 pixels wide.

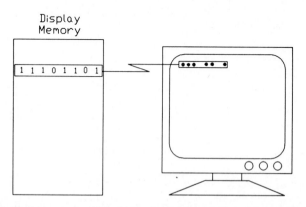

FIGURE 3.5 Mapping a Byte in Display Memory to the Monitor

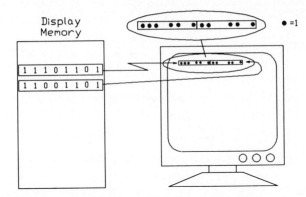

FIGURE 3.6 Horizontal Neighbors in Display Memory

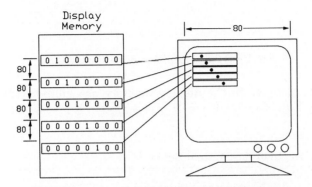

FIGURE 3.7 Vertical Neighbors in Display Memory

The data is output from the display memory to the monitor in a serial fashion. A byte is read out of display memory and parallel loaded into a shift register. The data is subsequently read out of the shift register in a serial bit stream that is output to the electron gun in the monitor. The monitor and the display memory are synchronized so that data read out of the display memory is displayed in the proper positions on the monitor. This data path is illustrated in Figure 3.8.

Virtual and Displayed Images

Data in the display memory is called a *virtual image,* and data on the monitor is called a *viewed image.* A starting address dictates which element in display memory corresponds to the upper-left corner of the monitor. The width of the display is equal to the number of displayed elements per scan line. The width of the virtual image is equal to the number of elements reserved in display memory for a scan line. The virtual image does not have to be the same size as the viewed image.

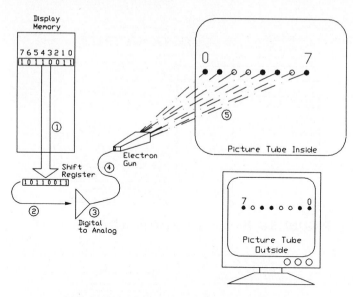

FIGURE 3.8 Parallel to Serial Conversion

The number of bytes in the display memory associated with an image is determined by Equation 3.2 above. It is repeated in Equation 3.3 with the new terminology.

Equation 3.3 Length of Host Virtual Buffer

$$\text{Number of bytes} = \frac{\text{Number of virtual columns}}{8} \times \text{Number of virtual rows}$$

Figure 3.9 illustrates a virtual image. In Figure 3.9a, the number of virtual rows is equal to the display height and the number of virtual columns is equal to the display width. In Figure 3.9b, the number of virtual rows is greater than the display height and the number of virtual columns is greater than the display width.

Window Mapping

The concept of a virtual image can be readily applied to the processing of a window. In the case of a window, the virtual size of the window is usually less than the size of the display. A typical window mapping from host memory to display memory and to the monitor is illustrated in Figure 3.10.

The window can fit compactly and sequentially in host memory with no wasted space, as shown in Figure 3.10a. The window is $J - L + 1$ elements per scan line wide and $M - N + 1$ scan lines high. It is to be displayed beginning at

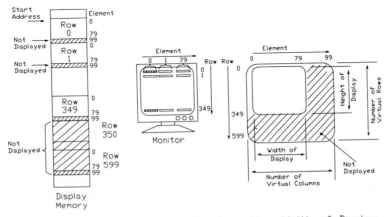

a) Number of Elements in a Row Equals Width of Display

b) Number of Elements in a Row less than Width of Display

FIGURE 3.9 Virtual Image

row N and column J. The window cannot be moved to the display memory with a single MOVSB instruction because it is not in contiguous display memory. This occurs because the width of the window is less than the width of the display. The display memory is illustrated in Figure 3.10b. Only a segment of rows N through M is occupied by the window.

3.2.3 Graphics-related BIOS

Regardless of the memory configuration, most graphics systems have a facility for drawing to a single pixel without requiring in-depth knowledge of the display architecture. BIOS routines are provided on the system board to perform some basic display-related functions. On the VGA, a local BIOS ROM provides enhanced BIOS routines to further assist the programmer. Using the BIOS calls has advantages and disadvantages. They are easy to use, and new graphics boards can provide similar BIOS calls to ensure compatibility. However, in many cases these calls are notoriously slow.

Even the BIOS calls require a certain amount of device-dependent code. Device-independent graphics standards, such as DGIS, VESA, the IBM AI, or

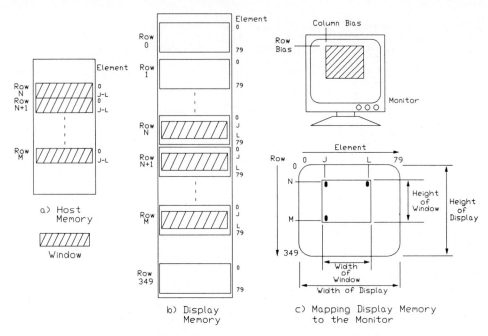

FIGURE 3.10 Window Mapping

TIGA provide a standardized set of routines that the graphics applications can call to control any display adapter.

3.2.4 Video Interface Cable

The video cable contains a number of shielded cables. The number of conductors and the pin numbers on the connectors depend on the graphics adapter and the monitor selected. The signals running inside the cable consist of video information and video control. These signals are listed in Table 3.4.

3.3 MONITORS AND DISPLAYS

The operation of a monitor is simple to understand. A scanning electron beam sweeps across the back face of the monitor. This beam scans across the screen in an orderly fashion. As the beam strikes the back face of the monitor screen, it excites the phosphor coating. The excited phosphor emits light, which is detected by the eye.

The monitor may be a digital or analog monochrome, RGBI or RrGgBb digital color, or an analog RGB color monitor. The resolution and performance of these monitors varies, as does the price. Monochrome monitors—used with the MDA, Hercules, or EGA—are less expensive than color monitors. Because of their simplicity, even inexpensive monochrome monitors are capable of handling high resolutions. A typical monochrome resolution is 720 by 348 pixels.

TABLE 3.4 Video Cable Signals

Adapter	Monitor	Video Signals	Sync Signals
MDA, EGA	Monochrome	Video, Intensity	Horizontal, Vertical
Hercules	Monochrome	Video, Intensity	Horizontal, Vertical
CGA, EGA	RGBI	Red, Green, Blue, Intensity	Horizontal, Vertical
EGA	RrGgBb	Red, Green, Blue, IRed, IGreen, IBlue	Horizontal, Vertical
VGA	Analog RGB	Analog Red, Green, Blue	Horizontal, Vertical
VGA	Analog Monochrome	Analog Green	Horizontal, Vertical

Color monitors vary in performance. RGBI monitors—used with the CGA or EGA—accept digital color inputs, allowing the display of sixteen unique colors. The resolution of these monitors is usually limited to 200 horizontal scan lines. RrGgBb monitors also accept digital color inputs and are used with the EGA. These monitors can display 64 unique colors and handle 350 horizontal scan lines.

Analog monitors must be used with the VGA. Analog RGB monitors can display an unlimited number of colors and typically can handle 480 horizontal scan lines. Analog monochrome monitors can display an unlimited number of shades of gray and, again, typically can handle 480 horizontal scan lines.

Multisync enhanced monitors commonly accept digital or analog color inputs and can display resolutions of 900 by 600 pixels. Advanced monitors, used with high-resolution graphics systems, can display resolutions of 2,000 by 2,000 pixels.

A variety of computer displays has evolved over the years to meet the growing needs of computer processing and computer graphics. Improvements include higher-resolution characters, more characters per line, more lines per screen, x,y addressable cursors, highlighted characters, graphics capabilities, and color.

There are several different types of display monitors, including vector displays, raster scan displays, storage and nonstorage monitors, and flat panel displays. Interfacing the wide variety of displays with the ever-growing number of computers has forced standards to emerge. Monitors are interfaced to the PC through a cable to the graphics hardware.

Storage displays, as in some oscilloscopes, use phosphors with extremely long decay times to store the electron beam's energy. Once the phosphor is excited, it remains excited and therefore does not need to be refreshed. When desired, a large field is energized that erases the entire screen. Selective portions of the screen cannot be erased. Nonstorage scopes use a phosphor with a faster decay time. Shortly after the electron beam leaves an area, that area naturally erases as the phosphor decays. In order for an image to remain on a short decay time phosphor, each area of the monitor's screen has to be refreshed at 50–70 Hz to avoid flicker before the phosphor decays.

3.3.1 Interlaced and Noninterlaced Displays

Displays are either interlaced or noninterlaced. Noninterlaced displays are used exclusively with the EGA/VGA. In an interlaced display, alternate scan lines are updated every frame. In a noninterlaced display, every scan line is updated every frame. This is illustrated in Figure 3.11.

In the interlaced mode, as the frame at *time = t* is displayed, only the even scan lines are updated. The odd scan lines still contain the data from the frame that was displayed at *time = t – 1*. This is illustrated in Figure 3.11a. Similarly, as the frame at *time = t + 1* is displayed, only the odd scan lines are updated. The even scan lines still contain the data from the frame that was displayed at time *t*. This is illustrated in Figure 3.11b. In the noninterlaced mode, all of the scan lines are updated with new data as the frame at *time = t* and is displayed, as shown in Figure 3.11c. Similarly, at *time = t + 1*, all of the scan lines are once again updated, as seen in Figure 3.11d.

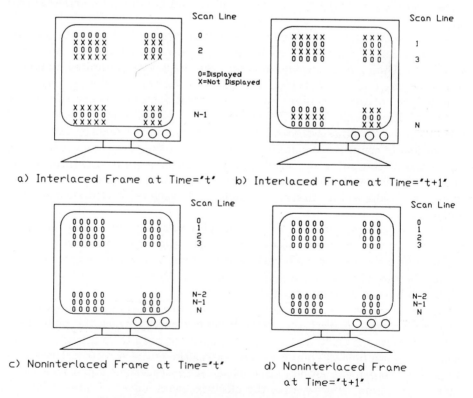

a) Interlaced Frame at Time="t"   b) Interlaced Frame at Time="t+1"

c) Noninterlaced Frame at Time="t"   d) Noninterlaced Frame at Time="t+1"

FIGURE 3.11 Interlaced and Noninterlaced Displays

Interlaced displays are used when the adapter or monitor hardware cannot keep up with the data rates required by the video system. The greater the resolution of the video system, the faster the hardware must be to keep up with the data rates. The interlaced hardware must be only half as fast as the noninterlaced hardware. The disadvantage of the interlaced hardware is that the eye can begin to detect the alternating frequencies on the screen, especially when these interact with the 60-cycle-per-second frequencies present in fluorescent lights.

3.3.2 CRT Monitor Specifications

The CRT monitor manufacturers each have a product line of monitors filling the cost/performance curve. There are several parameters that affect the performance and cost of a monitor. These are listed in Table 3.5. Included are typical specification categories, typical values, and how the values are affected with increasing cost.

3.3.3 Raster Scan Displays

Raster scan displays rely on a memory buffer that contains a full frame of data. An entire picture is stored in this display memory. This memory may be

TABLE 3.5 CRT Specifications

Monitor Parameters	Typical Value	More Expensive
Size	15" diagonal	larger
Dot Ptich	.28	smaller
Flat Surface	subjective	*1
Anti-Glare	subjective	*1
Anti-Static	subjective	*1
High Contrast Surface	subjective	*1
Maximum Resolution	1024 by 768	larger
Horizontal Frequency	27 to 57kHz	wider range
Vertical Frequency	55 to 90 Hz	wider range
PC/Macintosh Compatibility	yes or no	yes
Bandwidth	75MHz	higher
Ergonomic Controls	controls and location of controls	*2
Magnetic Field Emissions	words such as low or reduced	*3
Flicker-Free	subjective	*1

*1 More "pronounced" adjectives and trade-marked terminology.

*2 Swivel base, digital controls, up-front controls.

*3 Currently numbers are not typically quoted.

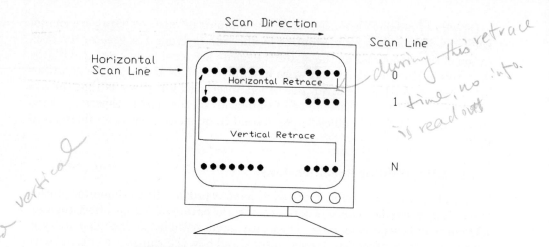

FIGURE 3.12 Raster Scan Display Refresh

(handwritten annotations: "during this retrace time, no info. is read out"; "Horizontal and vertical retrace")

thought of as a giant shift register. The data is read out of the shift register synchronously with the scanning electron beam. Thus, the electron beam is at the top-left corner of the display when the shift register is outputting the first information. This is illustrated in Figure 3.12. As the electron beam scans across one horizontal line, the data that corresponds to the first horizontal line is output from the shift register. At the end of a horizontal line, the electron beam returns to the beginning of the next line. During this retrace time, no information is read out of the shift register. When the electron beam is ready for the second line, data once again is output from the shift register. This process continues until the last scan line is drawn. At this point, a vertical retrace occurs and the electron beam returns to the top-left corner of the screen. This is shown in Figure 3.12.

In reality, a shift register memory is not effective because data needs to be accessed by the host in a parallel fashion. From the host's perspective, the display memory is configured as parallel memory.

Even though the display memory appears to be parallel, eventually it must be converted to a serial data stream in order to interface with the electron beam in the monitor.

3.3.4 Flat Panel Displays

Laptop computers and other portable display systems use flat displays because of size constraints. Liquid crystal displays (LCDs), plasma, and electroluminescent displays are three examples of the flat panel technology. Newer technologies include the newer monochrome panels, the STN,TFT color, the single-scan color, and the dual-scan color panels. Liquid crystals work in low voltage ranges, making them well-suited for portable electronics. Electroluminescent and plasma displays work in the range from 110 to 200 volts. Problems inherent in the liquid crystal technologies include multiplexing difficulties, undesirable response times, and poor electro-optical characteristics, such as charge leakage. Display readability has been improved by twisted crystal techniques and low-power electroluminescent backlighting. Plasma displays are power hungry, but they provide straightforward multiplexing, and high resolutions are readily available. Electroluminescent displays, including ac-thin-film and dc-power displays, are popular in hand-held televisions. LCDs reflect light, whereas gas discharge and electroluminescent displays transmit light. This is a reason that LCDs require less power.

There are several types of flat panel displays. The type of display does not affect the programmer. However, there are several aspects of the flat-panel displays that are of importance to the programmer. These involve the creation of gray scale and color, power management, power sequencing, and simultaneous CRT and LCD operation.

Display Resolutions

The display resolution on flat panels is typically 640 by 480. However, most are required to also drive CRT monitors and thus many support some of the higher resolution modes, for example 1024 by 768 by 16-colors. These modes are used when they drive the CRT. At times, both monitors will be hooked up at the same time. Decisions must be made. Does the VGA drive the 1024 by 768 mode and decimate down to the 640 by 480, or does it drive both at 640 by 480?

Color Displays

Color displays are created from bi-stable elements by dedicating three elements to every pixel. Three horizontal neighbors are used to represent the red, green, and blue primary colors. A filter is placed over each, so that the left-most pixel displays red when on, the center displays green, and the right-most displays blue. This requires a display that has 1320 by 480 pixels to display 440 by 480 pixels.

Gray Scale and Color Shading

Flat panels are inherently on and off devices so how is it that they create gray scale on the monochrome displays or color shading on the color displays? There are two techniques employed for either the gray scale or the color case. The first involves multiplexing the display, and the second involves dithering.

Multiplexing, more properly called frame rate duty cycle, sends a series of pulses at the flat-panel element as opposed to a complete on. The amount of time that the pulse is active determines the effective brightness. The flat-panel element averages the pulses coming at it since it cannot respond as fast as they are switching. The amount of time that the pulse is active determines the effective brightness. About eight distinct levels can be achieved using this technique. When these eight levels are applied to the three colors, red, green, and blue, an effective color screen with 512 colors can be displayed.

The second technique involves dithering. Suppose that four elements are used to display a single pixel. This would be the case when you display a 320-by-200 image on a 640-by-480 display. Since there can be from 0 to 4 elements on, an additional five levels can be achieved.

Power Management

Since most flat panels are on laptops, it is desirable to power down the display when not in use in order to conserve power. There are several states of power down. The "least sleepy" can be awakened immediately. This would be the case when small non-event times occur. The "unconscious" state would require several seconds to awaken. This would be the case when long delays between usage are anticipated. The terminology for power management has not been standard. One manufacturer has six states listed as Normal, Suspend/Resume, Standby, Sleep, Deep Sleep, and Hibernation.

I follow the four-state constituency using Normal, Standby, Suspend, and Shut-down. These are illustrated in Figure 3.13. The four states are described in Table 3.6.

A new and popular feature with laptops is the ability to power down without losing its place. The advantage is that the next time the laptop is started, it immediately goes back to its last state. For example, suppose that on an airplane you are in a word processor. During landing, you close the top without turning off the power switch. The laptop goes into its shut-down mode saving all relevant memory and registers to disk. Later that evening, you open the case and *voilà*—the system restores all relevant memory, powers up the display, and you are back in your word processor. Several sticky areas occur with laptops that can drive both a CRT and LCD at the same time, regarding which mode to pop back into. Certainly on the plane you would be in an LCD mode; at home you might connect to a CRT.

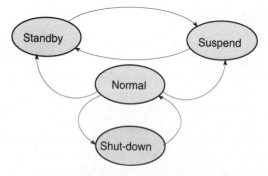

FIGURE 3.13 Power Management

TABLE 3.6 Power Management States

State	Description
Normal Operation	Display is on and fully refreshing
Standby	Turn off display. Application does not know that the display is turned off. When the flat-panel controller detects an event, it turns on the display. An event might be a display access, either through memory or I/O, a keyboard or mouse event, or some other external stimuli.
Suspend	No display. Display memory is refreshed at a slow rate to reserve power. No access to most of the chip, except Resume Register.
Shut-down	Save state of machine, including system memory, display memory, and all control registers. Turn off all power to the graphics subsystem.

Power Sequencing

Power sequencing is the turning on and turning off of the LCD. Watch out! Beware! Don't touch! Don't hack! Leave alone! There are registers associated with power sequencing that can and **will** destroy the flat panel. The panels are made out of CMOS, and CMOS is sensitive. As a result, color flat panels are a bit pricey, so watch out. There are definite sequences that have to be followed to correctly and safely turn on or off the display. The display has power supply and bias and signal voltages that have to be handled carefully. If you ever see color on a monochrome display, turn it off immediately. When experimenting with a flat-panel controller, disconnect the flat panel, use a standard CRT or, better yet, go get a cup of coffee and let the temptation pass.

Simultaneous Display of CRT and LCD

This is often called dual-scan. It is often desirable to have a CRT and LCD displaying data at the same time. This is troublesome for the LCDs that refresh their screen in two halves. This is shown in Figure 3.14. Note that the CRT display refreshes from top down, while the LCD refreshes at the top down to the middle, at the same time as it refreshes the middle to the bottom. Thus, a separate buffer is required. This buffer can be one row or an entire half screen. This buffer may reside in a separate RAM chip or better yet (from a cost perspective), it resides in off-screen memory.

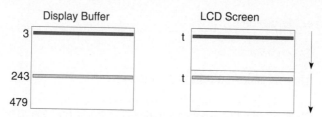

(a) At time t, line 3 is displayed at line 3 of the top LCD panel
     and line 243 is displayed at line 3 of the bottom LCD panel.

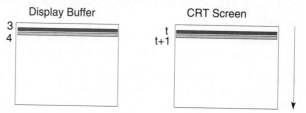

(b) At time t, line 3 is displayed on line 3 of the CRT. At time t+1,
     line 4 is displayed on line 4 of the CRT.

FIGURE 3.14 Dual Scan Display

3.4   THE CO-RESIDENT VGA

Although most computers use one VGA and one monitor, sometimes more than one monitor is desired. For example, there can be more than one VGA resident in a system at a time, the VGA can be co-resident with a more complicated graphics card, the VGA can be co-resident with a monochrome card, video acquisition, NTSC display, or a special purpose multi-VGA card/monitor configuration can be present.

3.4.1   Multiple VGAs

There are a couple of different cases where more than one VGA can be resident in the same system. The first case occurs when two VGAs reside on different buses. It is possible to use both at the same time; most likely, one will be permanently disabled.

In order to use both VGAs, one would have to reside at a wake up of 3C3 hex and the other with a wake up of 46E8 hex. If VGA #1 was at 3C3 hex, and VGA #2 was at 46E8 hex, the procedure would be as follows:

1. Put VGA #2 to sleep.

2. Awaken VGA #1.

3. Control and interact with VGA #1.

4. Put VGA #1 to sleep.

5. Awaken VGA #2.

6. Control and interact with VGA #2.

The second case occurs on the nonstandard multiple VGA cards where a switching mechanism is set up such that one of the co-resident VGAs is enabled at a time. This is definitely nonstandard stuff allowing multiple monitors to display information from separate display memories.

3.4.2 VGA and 8514A/XGA/TIGA/Exotic

Many of the exotic graphics cards require a VGA to be co-resident in order to run DOS and DOS applications that don't talk to the exotic card. The VGA may have its own monitor or a feed-through path might be installed such that both drive a single monitor. This is shown in Figure 3.15.

3.4.3 VGA and NTSC Output

Several VGA cards actually have an NTSC output capable of driving a standard television. As an alternative, there are several add-on NTSC cards or boxes that accept the VGA analog output or digital output from the feature connector. These NTSC cards or boxes then produce the NTSC-compatible signals.

The quality of the NTSC output varies considerably across the different implementations. Care must be taken when selecting the desired system. Typically, high-quality work dictates the need for a TrueVision TARGA^{tm} type board.

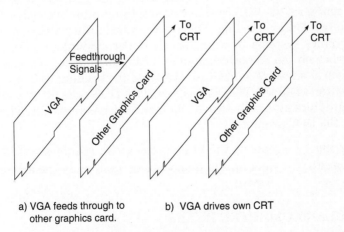

a) VGA feeds through to other graphics card.

b) VGA drives own CRT

Figure 3.15 VGA Feed-through

3.4.4   VGA and NTSC Input

Acquiring NTSC signals is a tricky business. There are systems that can grab one frame at a time, multiple frames at real-time video rates, and systems that can compress the video. Systems range in price from $250 to $1,000,000. Clearly, the quality varies from one system to another and the WYPIWYG applies—"what you pay is what you get."

The VGA was specified with a feature connector. Unfortunately, this specification and implementation is not very good. The connector can sustain transfer rates of images with 800-by-600 resolution. However, in practice, the image quality begins to degrade at resolutions exceeding 640 by 480 due to noise and sync-related problems.

The original specification for the feature connector included the ability to pump in a dot clock to the VGA, as well as the horizontal and vertical sync control signals. This is very advantageous for sync related purposes; however not all cards support this feature. On most NTSC acquisition add-on boards, this feature is not supported, thereby reducing the performance.

There are also a wide range of compatibility problems surrounding which VGA card is used with which video acquisition card, what else is in the system, and what interrupts are available. The clear solution is an integrated VGA card containing the NTSC subsystem. The VGA chip and NTSC acquisition and delivery chips could then be tightly coupled for optimum performance, ease of installation, and reduced cost.

3.4.5   VGA and Monochrome

Many developers use a monochrome card in conjunction with the VGA card. Both can be co-resident; however, if both are on the ISA bus, it is not always possible to configure the VGA card to run in a 16-bit interface mode. This is due to the memory address decoding. There are several utility programs that allow the two graphics systems to work together. For example, CodeView[tm] from Microsoft relies on the monochrome monitor for diagnostic information. There are also several shareware utilities available for sending data to the monochrome monitor when the VGA is enabled. Two DOS calls allow you to switch the active graphics system between the monochrome and VGA. These are invoked from the DOS prompt:

> **> mode co80**   Sets up the VGA as the active graphics system
> **> mode mono**   Sets up the monochrome system as the active graphics
>   system

3.5   POPULAR COMPUTER BUSES

The computer system includes several buses used to transfer data around the system. This section is very brief since these buses typically don't affect the software design. A program designed for a VGA will function on a VGA installed on any of these buses.

There are buses and there are connectors. A bus can reside on the computer motherboard, or it can be brought to a connector. When on the motherboard, there are no mechanical connections to consider and typically the bus can be designed for higher performance. Unfortunately, this limits the expandability of the computer system. In the future we will probably see fewer uses for the adapter cards, and computers will include more features on the motherboards. I believe these features should include graphics, video, image compression, sound, disk controller, additional SCSI, parallel ports, and serial ports.

3.5.1   ISA

The ISA, the first bus on the PC, has a data path eight bits wide. Anticipating slow peripherals, numerous wait states are imposed on each data transfer. Only 22 address bits are brought to the ISA connector providing an address space of 16 Mbytes. Also, the address decoding was limited and produced a minimum address decode space of 128 Kbytes for fast transfers. This causes problems with co-resident VGA and monochrome cards. Ideally, a 64 Kbyte decode space would have been used.

3.5.2   16-bit ISA Extension

A second connector was added to the ISA bus to facilitate 16-bit transfers. The same limitations existed for this bus as for the 8-bit version, with the exception being that 16-bit transfers can occur in a single instruction cycle.

3.5.3   EISA

A consortium of manufacturers came up with an improved bus to extend and replace the ISA bus. This caught on for disk controllers, but was never popular for VGAs.

3.5.4   Micro Channel

Bust city—though it might have been a good idea if it had been released five years earlier. IBM lost its control of the industry and tried to gain it back by requiring manufacturers to license use of the micro channel bus. There are micro channel VGA cards and certainly many micro channel systems in existence. Outside of the 3C3/46E8 hex issue, there is little reason to be concerned about whether a VGA is on a micro channel or on an ISA bus.

3.5.5   VL (VESA Versions)

Finally a fast bus for graphics! The Intel microprocessors have a local bus that was typically used for memory. This bus was extended to drive external devices, typically VGAs and disk controllers. The bus is well-suited for graphics and has become very popular. Many VL buses, especially those that were introduced early, don't conform to the VESA bus. Perhaps they have special proprietary VL bus VGAs. The non-VESA buses are typically **not** compatible with the VESA VL bus.

3.5.6 PCI

The PCI bus is Intel's entry into the bus marketplace. This bus, which has special features for recognizing what devices are present on it, is beginning to find its way into computer systems at the time of writing of this book. At least the PCI bus does not add to the 3C3/46E8 identification problem. It is unclear where the PCI bus will go and how it will compete against the VL bus. The PCI Interface is described in some detail in Sections 25.14 and 28.10.

3.6 THE GREEN PC

A new concern with PCs is power management. The hundreds of millions of PCs out there are requiring a considerable amount of power. The U.S. government is reported to own 5 percent of all PCs. They desire to reduce their electricity bill. In order to do this, the power requirements need to be reduced on the computers. The most power-hungry component of the computer is the monitor. Therefore, it is logical to reduce the power of the monitor. The easiest way to do this is to power down the monitor when not in use.

These techniques have been used before. They are common in lap tops, and screen-saver programs are everywhere. The solution was to integrate some smarts onto the SuperVGAs such that the software could easily power down the monitors when different levels of sleep are required.

3.6.1 Monochrome Monitors

Monochrome monitors typically display data in a bi-stable format, which allows two colors to be displayed. A foreground of white, amber, or green on a black background are common color combinations used in bi-stable displays. Monochrome monitors can also display data in a gray scale format. The gray-scale format requires a modulation of the video signal. As the electron beam is scanned across the phosphor, the amount of energy applied to the phosphor determines the level of brightness. More energy pumped into the phosphor at a given point results in a brighter intensity at that point. Monochrome gray-scale monitors have special analog video inputs that control the gray scale. The enhanced monochrome monitor used with the VGA accepts the analog monochrome signal from the green analog output of the VGA.

The PC monochrome bi-stable monitors have an intensity signal that combines with the video signal to create a tri-stable display. The three intensity states correspond to off, on, and high-intensity on.

Chapter 4

Types of Graphics Systems

4.1 CHIPS, CARDS, AND MOTHERBOARDS

The computer system is indeed a system consisting of hardware and software subsystems. The hardware subsystem consists of a microprocessor, its memory, disk storage, user interface, additional peripherals, and a graphics subsystem. The graphics subsystem consists of a graphics processor chip, graphics memory, BIOS, and video output drivers. The graphics processor chips are based on very large-scale integrated circuits (VLSI). These circuits simplify the production of inexpensive graphics systems. It doesn't matter what graphics system we're talking about. In today's marketplace, VLSI circuitry has to be employed. In this book, these VLSI circuits are called *chips*.

There are several types of graphics chips. Today's popular chips include the Super VGAs, the XGAs, the 8514s, and the 34010,20,30 family of graphics controllers. Several manufacturers make one or more of these graphics controllers, and each manufacturer produces a family of chips. Within each chip family are several chip members, and within each chip member are several version levels. These chips then find their way onto motherboards or adapter cards. Also included are clock generators, DAC chips, and BIOS. There are several manufacturers that make clock chips, DAC chips, and write BIOS software. In the end, the graphics card or graphics system on the motherboard is hooked up to a monitor. As is evident, there are many combinations to deal with. The components of a graphics system are shown in Figure 4.1.

4.1.1 Chip Manufacturers

There are several chip manufacturers producing Super VGA chips. The manufacturers may employ anywhere from several people to several thousand people. Some produce nothing but the Super VGA chips; others produce clock chips or DAC chips to support the Super VGA. Some write their own BIOS software and applications drivers; some produce their own Super VGA cards. The evolu-

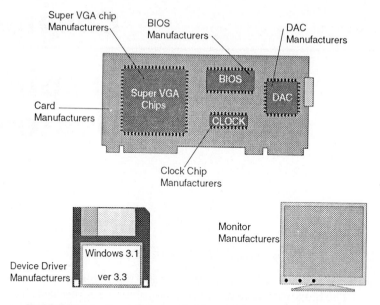

FIGURE 4.1 Components of a Super VGA Graphics System

tion of chip manufacturers is always changing depending on the times and the development tools. Some come and go; others stop producing chips and manufacture cards with other manufacturers' chips on them. Some go public; others stay private. Some are bought out by larger companies; others wish they were. All in all, they produce excellent products.

4.1.2 Chip Families

A typical Super VGA chip manufacturer may make several different families of chips. One might be a low-cost highly integrated basic Super VGA. A second might include high-resolution modes that can access additional memory. A third might include a 16-bit graphics coprocessor. A fourth might include a 32-bit graphics coprocessor. A typical scenario is shown in Figure 4.2. In Figure 4.2a, we see three families of chips. Family 2 has three chip members. Chip 2 in this family has four current revisions. The price performance curve shown in Figure 4.2b shows that Family 3 is more powerful and more expensive than Family 2. When a new family is both more powerful and less expensive, it simply replaces another family.

4.1.3 Family Members

Each family may contain several chip members that may vary only slightly. For example, one chip might only control 1 Mbyte by 1 DRAM memory, while a

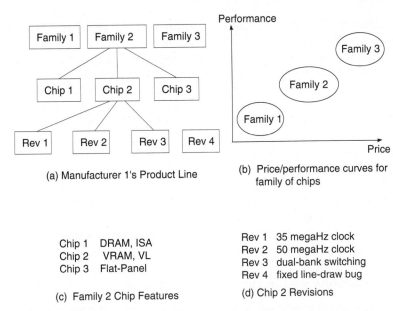

(a) Manufacturer 1's Product Line

(b) Price/performance curves for family of chips

Chip 1   DRAM, ISA
Chip 2   VRAM, VL
Chip 3   Flat-Panel

(c) Family 2 Chip Features

Rev 1   35 megaHz clock
Rev 2   50 megaHz clock
Rev 3   dual-bank switching
Rev 4   fixed line-draw bug

(d) Chip 2 Revisions

FIGURE 4.2 A Typical Super VGA Chip Manufacturer's Product

second might only control 1 Mbyte by 4 DRAMs. In this case, the software developer can ignore the differences. In addition, other chip members might support different buses. As shown in Figure 4.2c, one chip might have an ISA bus interface, while another might have a VL bus interface. Again, this should be invisible to the software developer.

The differences between chip members in a chip family can be very relevant to the software developer. For example, one chip might support flat-panel displays. This chip would have different capabilities and responsibilities than would the CRT controller member in the same family. Similarly, differences might exist in the amount of memory that the chip can address, the resolutions of the display modes, whether true-color is supported, whether dual bank switching is supported, or whether a hardware cursor is present.

4.1.4 Chip Revisions

Within each chip member, there are always chip versions. If at first you don't succeed.... Again, the differences might be invisible or relevant to the software developer. Sample differences are shown in Figure 4.2d. The difference between Rev 1 and Rev 2 in this example has to do with the clock speed. This difference might mean that higher resolution display modes are available on one chip but not on the other. It might mean that there is less jitter, which would be invisible to the software developer. Rev 3 adds dual-bank switching.

Although this could have been called a different chip member, the manufacturer chose to call it a different revision number.

Herein lies the difference between the hardware manufacturer that has a close tie with software and the one that does not. Suppose that a new chip is pin-for-pin compatible with an older chip yet is not completely software-compatible. A hardware-oriented manager would give the same chip member name to each. Conversely, a software-oriented manager would probably give the chips different member names.

Another important revision type is a bug fix. A bug fix might require you to double-load a register in order for the new value to take, or require one register to be loaded before another for no apparent reason, or require a number to be one less than the actual desired number. Nothing is new, but the chip now performs to its original specification. Although software that supported earlier revisions of the chip would have had to compensate for the bug, the new software does not.

4.1.5   Interactions within the Graphics System

A graphics system is composed of both hardware and software. Figure 4.3 is a loose interpretation of the interrelationships between both elements. The software is represented by the operating system and the applications. The tie to the hardware is through the graphics drivers. These drivers might be embedded in the application or loaded as TSR programs. The operating system can interact directly with the device driver and the application can interact directly or through an applications interface (AI). These application interfaces provide a library of graphics routines that are independent of the actual hardware.

The hardware portion consists of the VLSI chip (in this case the Super VGA), the graphics memory and DAC, along with the system microprocessor and its memory. As Figure 4.3 shows, the Super VGA can interact directly with the microprocessor or the system memory, as well as with its own display memory. Similarly, the microprocessor can interact with the Super VGA, the display memory, or its own system memory. Only the DAC actually talks to the display. Note that an additional port is shown into the DAC allowing overlaying.

4.2   THE EGA/VGA STANDARD

The EGA is the basic foundation of today's Super VGAs. Within two years, the EGA was replaced with the VGA. The principal difference was the addition of a 320-by-200 256-color mode and the ability to drive an analog monitor. These differences were enough to spawn an entire industry.

Since the EGAs are long gone, the basic standard is referred to as the VGA. The standard provides a set of registers, BIOS functions, a set of alphanumeric and graphics display modes, access to the color palette and color registers, and a location in host memory space where the display memory resides.

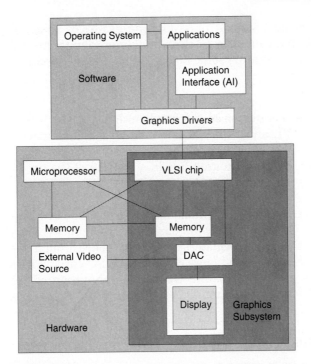

FIGURE 4.3 Interactions within the Graphics System

The features and functions of this VGA standard are described in detail in Chapters 6 through 11. Chapter 6 provides insight into the alphanumeric processing capabilities of the VGA. Chapter 7 discusses the graphics processing capabilities of the VGA. Chapter 8 shows how to get at the color palette and color registers. Chapter 9 discusses how to read the state of the VGA. Chapter 10 provides a comprehensive look at the standard VGA registers. Chapter 11 describes each of the VGA BIOS calls. Chapter 12 discusses software examples that drive the standard VGA.

4.3   THE SUPER VGA

Faster than the speeding bullet, more powerful than a locomotive, able to perform graphics operations in a single instruction cycle...it's Super VGA. The mortal VGA has been genetically reengineered into the Super VGA. Also called the SVGA, these cards build on the basics of the VGA. The Super VGA is much faster than the standard VGA—faster refresh rates, faster graphics operations, faster host interface. The Super VGA is more than the standard VGA. Many enhancements have been added, including more display modes, more colors, and more memory. It's also more affordable.

Chapter 2 describes the features of the Super VGAs, and Chapter 13 provides detailed descriptions. Chapter 14 describes the graphics accelerators, and

Chapter 15 provides several programming examples that control the Super VGAs. In addition, Chapters 16 through 28 describe thirteen different manufacturers' products totaling some 30 different Super VGA chips.

4.3.1 Faster

The Super VGA has increased the bandwidth of its host interface by going to the more exotic VL and PCI buses, by adding FIFO memory, QUEUES, and faster chip response. The Super VGAs can perform graphics operations including BitBlts, line draws, and area fills in a fraction of the time required by the standard VGAs. The Super VGAs can refresh screens at 72Hz and are reaching for the desired 80Hz.

The Super VGAs run applications faster due to the hardware-assisted functions. Many now support hardware cursors and graphics coprocessors. In addition, accessing the control registers can now be done through memory mapping, as opposed to the slower and more cumbersome I/O ports. Faster display memory interfaces are also possible with linear mapping of display memory. Alphanumerics are much faster due to the powerful color expansion write modes.

4.3.2 More Powerful

The Super VGAs have more display modes that boast higher spatial resolutions as well as higher color resolutions. Display modes up to 1024-by-768 by 24-bits-per-color are now supported, as opposed to the 320-by-200 by 8-bits-per-color modes of the standard VGA. That is about 36 times as much data in a single image. Considering that the processors are now 36 times as fast and that disks are 36 times as big, we have increased our information content without sacrificing speed.

The Super VGAs also have more memory. Instead of the 256 Kbytes of the VGA, the Super VGAs now can access up to 4 Mbytes of memory. Because the Super VGAs have more features, many graphics tasks can be offloaded from the host processor due to the on-board coprocessors.

4.3.3 More Able

Every year the tools to create the chips become more powerful, the amount of silicon that can be put onto a chip increases, and the density of transistors that can be put onto that silicon increases. Consequently, the Super VGAs are constantly evolving. Every year the chips are able to integrate tasks that previously required additional circuitry. As a result, more people are able to afford these powerful graphics systems.

With the reduction in size and cost comes the ability to add more circuitry. Additional features including NTSC input and output, sound, mouse interfaces, image compression, and color calibration will soon find their way onto the Super VGA cards.

4.4 THE HERCULES MONOCHROME GRAPHICS CARD

The Hercules adapter is based on the Motorola MC6845 Graphics Controller Chip. The Hercules Corporation quickly dominated the field of monochrome graphics and established the Hercules standard. The Hercules board provides a standard 80-character-by-25-row alphanumeric display and a relatively high resolution in the graphics mode of 720 horizontal by 348 vertical pixels. The outputs drive a digital monochrome monitor with sync frequencies of 50Hz vertical and 18.4kHz horizontal.

The Hercules board was the third display format standardized for the PC family of computers, following the Monochrome Display Adapter (MDA) and Color Graphics Adapter (CGA).

The Hercules adapter allows the programmer to position the cursor and subsequent characters anywhere on the screen. A maximum of 80 characters by 25 lines can be displayed. The columns are numbered from 0 on the far-left column to 79 on the far-right column of the screen. The rows are numbered from 0 on the top row to 23 on the bottom row. This requires a display buffer of 4,000 bytes because each character is two bytes. A character is specified by a one-byte character code and a one-byte attribute code. The size of one character is 7-by-9 dots in a font block of 9-by-14 dots. The additional space in the font block is used for intercharacter spacing. A ROM character generator provides 256 simultaneous characters, including the 96 ASCII graphic characters and sixteen wordprocessor symbols. The attribute code specifies the relationship between foreground and background, underline, blink, and intensity level.

4.4.1 Display Memory

The 4,000 bytes of memory addresses of the display buffer begin with B0000 hex. The characters are organized such that the first character is in the upper-left corner of the screen, the second character to its immediate right, and so on. The 81st character is directly under the first character on the second character line because there are 80 characters per row. The 2,000th character is displayed in the lower-right corner of the screen.

In the alphanumeric mode, the text buffer begins at PC memory address B000–B0FFF comprising 4 Kbytes. A single character is represented by two bytes, one for the character code and one for the attribute byte. To obtain the offset of a character code, use the equation $160 \times \text{Row} + 2 \times \text{Column}$. Remember that the columns are numbered from 0 to 79 starting at the left of the screen, while the rows are numbered from 0 to 24 starting at the top of the screen.

The character codes are contained in even addresses, and the attribute codes are contained in odd addresses. The attribute codes produce the character attributes listed in Table 4.1.

Bit 7 is for blinking or background intensity. If the blinker is off (display mode control port bit 5=0), then B=0 for normal background and B=1 for high-intensity background.

TABLE 4.1 Monochrome Character Attributes

Bit 7 6 5 4 3 2 1 0	Attribute Code
Bit B 0 0 0 I 0 0 0	Blank
B 0 0 0 I 0 0 1	Underline
B 0 0 0 I 1 1 1	Normal Display
B 1 1 1 I 0 0 0	Reverse Video

If the blinker is on (display mode control port bit 5=1), then B=0 for no blinking and B=1 for blinking with a normal-intensity background.

Bit 3 is for the intensity of the foreground; I=0 causes a normal foreground, and I=1 causes a high-intensity foreground.

4.4.2 Registers

The Input/Output (I/O) addresses occupy PC I/O port memory addresses from 3B0 to 3BF hex. In addition, a printer port is typically included on the display board. The printer port occupies I/O addresses in the range from 3BC to 3BF hex. The CRT control registers are accessed through an index register and a data register. The index register is located at address 3B4 hex and the data register is accessed at address 3B5 hex. This index/data register pair is common to many controllers that have several registers but cannot occupy several port addresses on the PC because of PC constraints. In addition to these two registers, a graphics control port is located at 3B8 hex and a monitor status register is located at port 3BA hex.

The internal registers include fourteen registers used to control the display. These registers occupy sixteen-byte locations because two of the registers require sixteen-bit words. Ten of these registers are used for display hardware control. These include the following registers: Horizontal Total, Horizontal Displayed, Horizontal Sync Position, Sync Pulse Width, Vertical Total, Vertical Total Adjust, Vertical Displayed, Vertical Sync Position, Interlace Mode and Skew, and Scan Lines per Character Row. These registers are very similar, although not identical, to registers used in the EGA. The two remaining registers consist of the Cursor Top, Cursor Bottom, Upper-Left Corner Memory Address, and Cursor Position Memory Address registers. The programmer can position and define the shape of the cursor using the cursor registers or can define the address of the upper-left corner of the display using these two remaining registers. If the upper-left address is varied, panning and scrolling of the display can be accomplished, although only 96 extra bytes are available for panning.

The Display Control Register enables the controller through bit 0, enables the display screen through bit 3, and enables the uppermost bit of the attribute code to control blinking through bit 5. The Monitor Status Register provides

TABLE 4.2   Monochrome Output Connector

Pin	Signal
1	Video Ground
2	Synchronization Ground
6	Signal Intensity
7	Video Signal
8	Horizontal Sync Signal
9	Vertical Sync Signal

information regarding the horizontal sync time in bit 0 and the presence of a video signal in bit 3.

4.4.3   Video Connector

The video output connector consists of the standard 9-pin connector. The signals carried on these pins are listed in Table 4.2.

This connector is mechanically identical to the connectors used for the CGA and EGA; however, it is not compatible because of the different electrical signals on the pins.

4.5   THE COLOR GRAPHICS ADAPTER

The Color Graphics Adapter (CGA) combines alphanumeric (A/N) modes and all-points-addressable (APA) graphics. The board provides direct video drive outputs capable of driving a color monitor. The monitor runs at either 7mHz, for the low-resolution mode, or 14mHz, for the high-resolution mode. Like the monochrome adapter described above, the CGA is based on the 6845 CRT controller.

The CGA's operation in the alphanumeric modes is similar to the monochrome adapter described above. The resolution is 40 or 80 columns by 25 rows. The 40-column low-resolution mode was designed for a low-resolution monitor or home television set. The size of one character is 7- by-7 dots in a font block of 8-by-8 dots. Because of the color processing, the characters can be displayed in one of sixteen foreground colors and one of eight or sixteen background colors. Characters may also be blinked on a per-character basis.

4.5.1   Display Memory

In the graphics mode, two resolutions, low and high, are available. Terminology that uses the qualifiers *low*, *medium*, and *high* is often confusing. One adapter's high resolution may be another's low resolution. In the CGA low-resolution mode, the memory is configured as 320 pixels horizontally by 200 pixels vertically. Each pixel can be drawn in one of four colors. Note that 320 times 200 is 64,000. Thus, for the entire display to fit into the 16 Kbyte memory restriction, each pixel can occupy only one-quarter of a byte, or two bits. Thus, one pixel can display up to four different colors. In the high-resolution mode of 640 by 200 pixels, only one color per pixel is allowed because each pixel can occupy only one-eighth of a byte or one bit.

Each byte represents four pixels in the low-resolution mode. These four pixels are horizontal neighbors, with the far-left pixel occupying the two leftmost bits in the byte, bits 7 and 6. The next neighboring pixel to the right is in bits 5 and 4, and so on. Note that care must be taken not to disturb the three neighboring pixels when only one pixel's value should be changed. This can be accomplished by ORing in ones and ANDing in zeros.

Each byte represents eight pixels in the high-resolution mode. These eight pixels are horizontal neighbors, with the leftmost pixel occupying the leftmost bit in the byte, bit 7. The next neighboring pixel to the right is in bit 6, and so on. Care must be taken not to disturb the seven neighboring pixels when only one pixel's value should be changed. Again, this can be accomplished by ORing in ones and ANDing in zeros.

The board contains 16 Kbytes of storage. This memory is mapped into the PC memory space beginning at B8000 hex. Because the maximum alphanumeric resolution of a screen is 80 columns by 25 rows by two bytes per character, one screen takes up 4 Kbytes of memory. Thus, a board can store up to four pages at maximum alphanumeric resolution. The border can also be selected to be displayed in one of sixteen colors. The character set contains the standard ASCII character set, foreign language support, Greek and scientific-notation characters, special characters for games and word processing, and characters for block graphics support.

In the high-resolution alphanumeric mode, the PC processor should access the display buffer only during vertical retrace time when the display is disabled. If this practice is not followed, random speckle will occur during the read or write times.

4.5.2   Color Selection

There are traditionally two color palettes available. These palettes act as lookup tables; they decode a value from display memory into a color. These tables are used in the low-resolution graphics mode. One contains green, red, and brown; the other contains cyan, magenta, and white. This allows a pixel that contains only two bits to produce a color that requires four bits.

Color selection occurs in the alphanumeric mode through the attribute byte. The layout of the attribute byte is identical to the monochrome attribute byte, with the foreground and background representing colors. Bits 0–3 represent the foreground color and bits 4–6 represent the background color. The intensity bit (I) is in bit 7 and is used to highlight the foreground colors. The least signifi-

TABLE 4.3 CGA Color Codes

I R G B	Value	Color
0 0 0 0	0	Black
0 0 0 1	1	Blue
0 0 1 0	2	Green
0 0 1 1	3	Cyan
0 1 0 0	4	Red
0 1 0 1	5	Magenta
0 1 1 0	6	Brown
0 1 1 1	7	White
1 0 0 0	8	Grey
1 0 0 1	9	Blue (intensified)
1 0 1 0	10	Green (intensified)
1 0 1 1	11	Cyan (intensified)
1 1 0 0	12	Red (intensified)
1 1 0 1	13	Magenta (intensified)
1 1 1 0	14	Brown (intensified)
1 1 1 1	15	White (intensified)

cant bit in each of the foreground and background colors represents blue (B), the next significant bit represents green (G), and the next significant bit represents red (R). Table 4.3 illustrates the foreground and background colors.

4.5.3 Control Registers

The 6845 registers are identical to the 6845 registers of the Hercules card described above. The index register is located at port address 3D4 hex and the data register is located at port address 3D5 hex.

Additional registers on the board include the Mode Control Register at 3D8 hex, the Color Select Register at 3D9 hex, the Status Register at 3DA, the Clear Light Pen Latch at 3DB hex, and the Preset Light Pen Latch at 3DC hex.

The Color Select Register contains color and control fields. The function of these fields varies depending on the active display mode. The Color Select Register fields are listed in Table 4.4.

Table 4.5 lists the functions controlled in the Mode Control Register.

Table 4.6 lists the functions of the Status Register.

The Clear Lightpen Latch clears the bit 1 of the Status Register, thereby resetting the light pen trigger status. Any output to this register causes the clearing of this bit.

TABLE 4.4 Color Select Register

Bit	40 by 25 A/N	320 by 200 APA	640 by 200 APA
0	Blue border	Blue background	Blue foreground
1	Green border	Green background	Green foreground
2	Red border	Red background	Red foreground
3	Bright border	Bright background	Bright foreground
4	Background colors	Alternate intensified colors	
5	No function	Selects Palette	

TABLE 4.5 Mode Control Register

Bit	Value	Function
0	0	40-by-25 alphanumeric mode
0	1	80-by-25 alphanumeric mode
1	0	Alphanumeric mode
1	1	320-by-200 APA mode
2	0	Color mode
2	1	Black-and-white mode
3	0	Disable video signal
3	1	Enable video signal
4	1	640-by-200 APA mode
5	0	Bit 7 in attribute controls blinking
5	1	Bit 7 in attribute controls background

TABLE 4.6 Status Register

Bit	Value	Function
0	1	Buffer memory may be accessed by the PC
1	1	Light pen trigger has occurred
2	0	Light pen switch is in on position
2	1	Light pen switch is in off position
3	1	Raster is in vertical retrace

4.5.4 Video Connector

The video output connector consists of the standard 9-pin connector. The signals carried on these pins are listed in Table 4.7.

The composite video output connector is a standard RCA type phono jack, and it contains a 1.5 volt peak-to-peak amplitude composite video signal. The connector also has signal ground available.

The RF modulator connector contains the signals listed in Table 4.8.

The light pen interface connector contains the signals listed in Table 4.9. The light pen interface is rarely used in the PC environment because of the popularity of the mouse, joystick, and digitizing pad. The EGA includes the light pen interface, but it is not included on the VGA.

TABLE 4.7 CGA Video Output Connector

Pin	Signal
1	Video Ground
2	Synchronization Ground
3	Red Signal
4	Green Signal
5	Blue Signal
6	Signal Intensity
7	Reserved
8	Horizontal Sync Signal
9	Vertical Sync Signal

TABLE 4.8 CGA RF Modulator Connector

Pin	Signal
1	12 volts
3	Composite Video
4	Logic ground

TABLE 4.9 Light Pen Interface Connector

Pin	Signal
1	Light Pen Input
3	Light Pen Switch
4	Chassis Ground
5	5 volts
6	12 volts

4.6 THE MULTICOLOR GRAPHICS ARRAY

The Multicolor Graphics Array (MCGA) and the VGA are the two primary adapters designed for the PS/2 series of personal computers. The MCGA is similar in function to the CGA, and the VGA is similar to the EGA. The MCGA is downwardly compatible to the CGA at the BIOS, control register, and display memory levels. Like the CGA, the MCGA can coexist with a monochrome adapter.

The control registers on the MCGA are identical to the sixteen lower control registers of the CGA. These sixteen registers control the video timing of the adapter. Although the registers are identical, the values loaded into these registers are different depending on whether a CGA or an MCGA is used. Therefore, programs that access these registers directly and that expect a CGA may disrupt the video performance of the MCGA. This problem can be alleviated by using the protection bit in the Mode Control Register. This protection write protects the first seven CRT controller registers, which include the horizontal and vertical timing registers. This is identical to the protection method used with the VGA. The VGA can lock out these registers to protect the adapter and monitor from programs that expect an EGA.

The MCGA provides enhanced performance features that are similar to the VGA. Included are downloadable character sets and additional display modes. These features are programmed on the MCGA, as on the EGA and VGA, through the BIOS calls. The additional display modes include a 640-by-480 display mode capable of displaying two colors and a 320-by-200 display mode capable of displaying 256 simultaneous colors.

The MCGA is equipped with a set of 256 Color Registers that are identical to the VGA Color Registers. These store six bits of resolution for each of the three primary colors, red, green, and blue. This provides a total of 256 Kcolors.

The MCGA, like the VGA, drives either an analog monochrome or an analog RGB monitor.

4.7 THE PROFESSIONAL GRAPHICS ADAPTER

The Professional Graphics Adapter (PGA) is the next step up from the EGA in resolution, speed, depth, performance, and cost. The PGA operates at a graphics resolution of 640 by 480 with 256 simultaneous colors. The video output is analog RGB, providing a wide range of colors. Perhaps the most notable improvement over the EGA/VGA is the use of an on-board processor. This processor is capable of performing high-level graphics functions without relying on the host PC processor (that is, the 8088, 8086, 80286, or 80386). The IBM implementation uses a 6845 graphics controller with an 8088 on-board processor. This selection has been improved upon by several other manufacturers who are using more sophisticated processors such as the Texas Instrument 34010 VLSI circuit.

The color lookup table provides 256 simultaneous colors, and each location in the table is twelve bits deep. These twelve bits correspond to four bits of red, green, and blue each. Thus, there are 4,096 possible colors. The alphanumeric section is identical to the above-mentioned display adapters in that there are two bytes assigned to each color, one for the character value and one for the attribute byte. It uses an on-board character generator that produces a character matrix sixteen pixels high by eight pixels wide. Unlike the EGA, the PGA supports no downloadable soft character fonts.

Interfacing to the 6845 and to the other I/O ports on the PGA is similar to the Color Graphics Adapter. This includes the Mode-Select Register and the Status Register.

The on-board processor performs a wide variety of two- and three-dimensional graphics operations including windowing, clipping, viewing transformations, and modeling transformations. Primitives—such as drawing lines, arcs, circles, ellipses, filling enclosed areas, and moving to locations—are also implemented. A wide variety of text commands are also available; these allow control of text size and the placement and orientation of text strings.

These high-level graphics commands can be executed in a single command from the PC processor. Command lists consist of a series of high-level graphics commands, which can also be executed by a single host command.

4.8 THE 8514/A DISPLAY ADAPTER

The 8514/A was designed by IBM and was meant to be plugged into the PS/2 Micro Channel Auxiliary Video Extension Bus. The 8514/A provides advanced graphics functions that can be used in parallel with the planar VGA built onto the IBM Motherboards. IBM kept the 8514/A register set proprietary and requested that programmers interface to the device through the AI interface.

During the past years, there have been a few Super VGAs with downward compatibility to the 8514/A. Many of the concepts used in the graphics accelerator portion of the 8514/A were mimicked in the Super VGA graphics coprocessors.

4.8.1 Features

The 8514/A offers a significant improvement in power and performance over the standard EGA and VGAs. The EGA and VGAs were simple frame buffers with some advanced features. The 8514/A included advanced control capabilities that can offload many low-level operations.

The 8514/A could support either 512 Kbytes or 1 Mbyte of display memory. Offscreen display memory could be configured for use with the advanced features.

4.8.2 Graphics Coprocessor

The 8514/A included the first graphics coprocessor in the IBM product line. The advance features embedded in this processor are listed in Table 4.10.

TABLE 4.10 8514/A Advanced Features

High-speed Line Draw

High-speed Polygon Fill

Rectangle Fill

Color and Monochrome BITBLTS to and from the host and from display-to-display

Full-featured 3-source Raster Ops

Short-stroke Vectors

Scissoring

Downloadable Character Sets

4.8.3   Data Streams

The 8514/A provides a wide variety of sources for the input data. The monochrome input data streams are provided in Table 4.11 and the color input data streams are listed in Table 4.12.

4.8.4   The Pixel Transfer ALU

One pixel from both the color and monochrome data streams are combined with the destination pixel in the pixel transfer ALU. This ALU provides sixteen Boolean functions and sixteen arithmetic functions. The ALU will use one of two independent mixing functions, depending on the value in the monochrome data stream.

TABLE 4.11 Monochrome Data Stream

Host Supplied Data

Selected Planes of the BitBlt Source

Two 4-bit Monochrome Pattern Registers

Always 1

TABLE 4.12 Color Data Stream

Host Supplied Data

The BitBlt Source

Color Expansion of Monochrome Data

The two mixing functions are called the foreground and background mixing functions. If the monochrome data is a 1 for the selected pixel, the foreground mixing function will be used. Similarly, if the monochrome data is a 0, the foreground mixing function will be used.

A destination color comparator is employed such that planes within the destination can be protected during write operations.

4.9   THE XGA

The XGA combined a VGA with an 8514-type graphics coprocessor. IBM did not publish the register specifications for the 8514, which hampered industry acceptance of the 8514. Learning from its mistake, IBM published the register specifications for the XGA. The coprocessor was *not* identical to the 8514.

4.9.1   AI Interface

Compatibility was provided to the 8514 through the XGA Adapter Interface (AI), a device driver supplied with the subsystem as programming support for DOS-based applications. The AI interace was a great idea, but, once again, using questionable decision making, IBM decided to distribute the AI interface specification only to those that purchased an IBM XGA. Once again, the foot takes the bullet. I provide a detailed desciption of this AI in Chapter 15.

4.9.2   High Resolution Display Modes

The XGA provided high-resolution display modes, already common to the Super VGAs. These are listed in Table 4.13.

4.9.3   Graphics Coprocessor

The XGA, like the 8514/A before it, included a graphics coprocessor. Additional features include a hardware cursor, a display identification system, and a graphics coprocessor. The hardware cursor is a 64-by-64 PEL image overlaying the picture without disturbing the contents of video memory. The coprocessor features are listed in Table 4.14.

TABLE 4.13   New XGA Display Modes

Function	Resolution	# bits / color
High-res	1024 by 768	8
Hi-color	640 by 480	16
Alphanumeric	132 by 32	Standard alphanumeric

TABLE 4.14 XGA Coprocessor Features

BitBlts	Including system-to-system, system-to-display, display-to-system, and display to display
Line drawing	Draw and step, area boundary drawing, solid and styled Bresenham lines
Area filling	Fills an outlined area
Mask operations	Spatial masking, ROPs to pixels, bit protection, carry propagation control
Scissoring	Rectangular clipping region
X and Y addressing	Understands X and Y spatial coordinates instead of linear addresses
Control registers	Memory-mapped into an 8-Kbyte-block of memory
Color expansion	Monochrome to color expansion
Color comparison	Compare destination with compare value.

4.10   THE TIGA DISPLAY ADAPTER

Texas Instruments introduced the 34010, 34020, and 34030 chips, and these chips have found their way onto many graphics cards over the past seven years. Since these are not standard, they require a co-resident DOS-compatible card, typically a VGA. Many of the cards employing these chips actually included a VGA chip.

4.10.1   Features

These chips have powerful instruction sets specially suited for graphics operations. These include BitBlts, color expansion, line drawing, text processing, short stroke vectors, and a wide variety of color modes. These cards were the first cards capable of processing true-color and capable of extremely fast line draws. Consequently, they found a niche in the imaging and CAD applications.

4.10.2   The Graphics Coprocessor

These chips were programmable, and consequently the host could download a set of commands and data parameters to the chips and go on with its processing until the graphics coprocessor was done. This produced incredible speed advantages when sending data across the ISA bus when compared with an 8086 or 80286 processor. The speed of these chips, however, could not keep up with the 80386, 80486, or Pentium processors with graphics cards on the local bus; consequently, the speed advantages have become minimized.

4.10.3 TIGA

The graphics coprocessor has its own language, and must be programmed with an assembler, a C compiler, a debugging tool, and a lot of skill. In order to simplify this, TI released the TIGA specification. The TIGA spec is a set of function calls that perform graphics operations—in other words, an AI. This AI became very popular and was distributed as a TSR.

4.10.4 TIGA Cards

Cards that used these chips typically consisted of the host interface, DRAM memory for off-screen memory and program storage, BIOS memory for the TIGA interface, VRAM memory for display memory, and a true-color DAC. These cards were typically expensive and have had a hard time competing with the new generation Super VGAs.

4.10.5 Programmable versus Dedicated Processors

The question exists whether a programmable processor is better suited for graphics applications than a dedicated processor. As algorithms improve, the programmable processor can be upgraded while the dedicated processor becomes obsolete. Conversely, the dedicated processor could perform the functions faster and cheaper. As the industry has changed, it appears that the trend is toward dedicated processors. This is due to the state of maturity of the graphics algorithms, the inexpensive graphics cards, and the rapid turnaround of ASIC chips.

Chapter 5

Principles of Computer Graphics

5.1 COORDINATE SYSTEMS

When wire drawings, graphs, or images are being drawn, some sort of coordinate reference system must be used. Data, extracted from the real world, is measured in a variety of coordinate systems. The range on the real-world data may vary between thousandths of an inch and light years. The numbers can be represented in integers or floating-point numbers. These numbering schemes are usually cumbersome to use in a graphics environment. It is necessary to translate this data to a coordinate system that is more conducive to graphics operations.

The data representing the "real world" is referenced as belonging to the *world coordinate system*. Because the data is to be represented graphically, a display coordinate system must be defined. Raster scan graphics systems, such as the EGA and VGA, are pixelated. Pixelated systems can be represented by an integer coordinate system because there are no fractions. The programmer can save a good deal of time and storage space if the data in the world system is converted to a graphics reference system.

The resolution of the *display coordinate system* should be well-suited to the graphics hardware and to the data being displayed. The output of the display coordinate system is sent to a video monitor for display or to a hard-copy device for output. Because of the variety of resolutions available on these devices, each maintains its own coordinate system, called the *device coordinate system*.

The display coordinate system can be further subdivided. A single display may contain several images, referred to as *viewing windows*. The user views the data through these imaginary windows. It is convenient for each of these windows to maintain its own coordinate system, called the *window coordinate systems*.

The data, represented by pixels, may be organized into functional groups of pixels, called *objects*. These objects can have their own coordinate system, called the *object coordinate system*. An object can be positioned anywhere within the window, but the object definition would not change with respect to its own coordinate system.

5.1.1   World Coordinate System

The world coordinate system refers to the coordinates of the real world. This system exists independently of the graphics systems that represent it. World coordinates can be expressed in any measurement system using either integers or real numbers. The units may be seconds, inches, pounds, number of people, light years, or virtually anything that can be measured. Somewhere in the graphing process these world coordinates must be converted to a display coordinate system.

A transformation is required to convert the data in the real-world coordinate system into the integer-pixelated display coordinate system. The transformation involves translation and scaling. Round-off errors usually occur during this process because the display coordinate system rarely has adequate resolution to represent the world coordinate system.

5.1.2   Display Coordinate System

The display coordinate system relates to the actual resolution of the display memory. This system is measured in horizontal and vertical pixels. The total number of horizontal pixels times the total number of vertical pixels determines the number of pixels per image. Each pixel is represented by a magnitude. This magnitude is represented by a number of bits. The number of bits per pixel times the number of pixels determines the number of bits per image. The display coordinate system is not directly related to any hardware.

The display coordinate system can be larger than the display device coordinate system. In the case of the EGA/VGA, there are 256,000 bytes of display data available on the adapter. At four bits per pixel, this leaves 512,000 pixels per image or approximately 700 by 700 pixels. Zooming and panning allow the selective parts of the display coordinate system to be mapped to EGA/VGA active display. Even larger images can be maintained in host memory, with only sections loaded into the EGA/VGA display memory. Disks can also be utilized to store very large images. This hierarchy of image memory is illustrated in Figure 5.1.

5.1.3   Window Coordinate System

It has become popular to segment an image into separate areas, called *windows*. Each window can represent different data or different views of the same data. To allow programmers to work with these windows efficiently, each is referenced to its own coordinate system. Each window is defined by its shape, size, and position within the display. Windows are typically rectangular, so

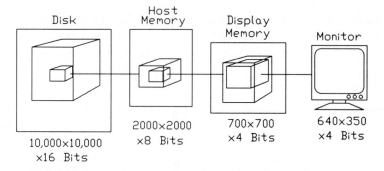

FIGURE 5.1 Hierarchy of the Display Coordinate System

their size can be represented by a height and width. The window is positioned onto the display through some reference point. Generally, the display coordinates of the lower-left corner or the upper-right corner of the window define the placement of the window. Windows may be transparent or opaque depending on how the software defines them. The EGA/VGA has no hardware facility for windows, and all window manipulations must be handled in software. A provision is made for split-screen operation, which may be thought of as two separate windows.

5.1.4 Device Coordinate System — related to hard ware

A typical graphics system may use several device coordinate systems. A device coordinate system relates to the hardware device that will be used to process the data. The EGA/VGA display adapter, when operating in a display mode that features a resolution of 640 by 350 by 4 bits per pixel, has a display device coordinate system that ranges from 0 to 639 on the horizontal axis and from 0 to 349 on the vertical axis. The magnitude of each pixel ranges from 0 to 15.

The input and output of graphics systems also have their own device coordinate systems. A video frame grabber can have a resolution of 512 by 512 pixels at 8 bits per pixel. A dot matrix printer can have a resolution of 638 by 825. An image scanner can have a resolution of 2,550 by 3,300 by 8 bits deep. A laser printer's resolution can exceed 5,100 by 6,600. In the case of an ink jet printer, each dot may be represented by several bits; if a black-and-white printer is used, each dot is one bit. The relationship between the display coordinate system and the device coordinate systems is illustrated in Figure 5.2.

The concept of multiple coordinate systems is extremely important in computer graphics. Suppose the display had a device coordinate system of 640 by 480. If the graphics program operated in the device coordinate system, all of the data would have to be mapped into this resolution. Later, when the time comes to print this image, the image will be restricted to the display device coordinate system. This is true even though the printer has the capability for a higher resolution.

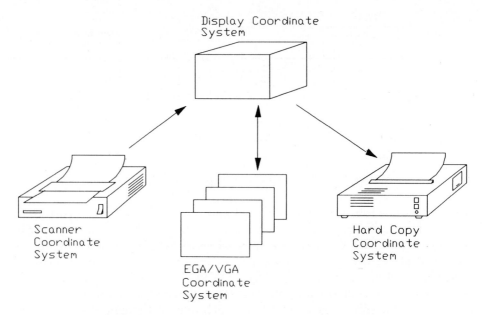

FIGURE 5.2 The Display and Device Coordinate Systems

Suppose the display coordinate system is set to the resolution of the laser printer. Suppose further that the graphics software is vector-driven and that the memory available in the display device adapter is smaller than the maximum resolution of the printer. The display device adapter can display only a portion of the total image at a time. This portion is commonly called a *window*.

5.1.5 Object Coordinate System

In an object-oriented display system, a series of dots, lines, and characters can be associated in such a way that they define an object. Each object maintains its own object coordinate system. If the object is moved or scaled, the entire object coordinate system is affected. These coordinate systems are associated with the display coordinate system or the device coordinate system through a set of reference parameters that are used to position the object in the larger reference system. Each object must have an origin. This origin is related to the origin of the display or device coordinate system by a set of coordinates, typically expressed as polar or rectangular coordinates. Figure 5.3 illustrates the relationship between an object coordinate system and a display coordinate system. The origin of the object coordinate system is referenced to the display coordinate system by the *XC, YC* coordinate pair.

Additional parameters may be necessary in order to map the object coordinate system into the display coordinate system. An object that is rotated by an angle *theta* is illustrated in Figure 5.4. It should be noted that the object did not

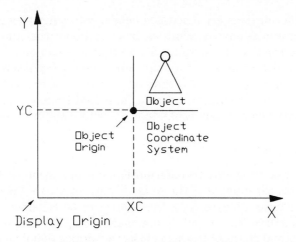

FIGURE 5.3 Object Coordinate Systems

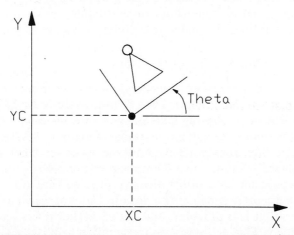

FIGURE 5.4 Object Coordinate System with Rotation

rotate with respect to its own object coordinate system. Rather, the object coordinate system rotated with respect to the display coordinate system.

5.2 COORDINATE TRANSFORMATIONS

Coordinate transformations convert from one coordinate system to another. Common graphics linear transformations include scaling, translation, rotation, and polar-to-rectangular conversion. A single display coordinate system may be composed of several smaller display coordinate systems, or windows. These windows are constantly moved within the larger display space. Within a window there may be several object coordinate systems. Objects can associate and disassociate freely with several coordinate systems in a single operation.

Several transformations are discussed below, with equations given for each. Typically, in a graphics environment, matrix notation rather than equations is used to describe the transformations. These matrices can be combined to perform multiple transformations in a single operation. Graphics processors may include special-purpose hardware that can perform matrix calculations rapidly. The techniques involving two-dimensional and three-dimensional matrix notation are explained in many books that describe computer graphics.

5.2.1 Scaling Data

There are two types of scaling transformation: one operation scales the data; a second scales the coordinates of the data. If data in a two-dimensional space has magnitudes associated with it, the space can be considered to be three-dimensional. The first type of scaling operation changes the magnitudes of the data, and the second changes the size of the two-dimensional space.

Data passes through several stages in the graphics process: from digitization through coordinate transformations to the display system and hard-copy device. The data will likely be scaled in a different way at each of these stages.

5.2.2 Scaling the Magnitude of the Data

Data in the real world that has an associated magnitude must usually be scaled to fit in the limited dynamic range of the display system. An EGA can display a pixel in up to four bits, allowing sixteen simultaneous colors. Thus, the data being displayed is limited to a dynamic range of sixteen. A VGA can display a pixel in up to eight bits, allowing 256 simultaneous colors. This means that the data being displayed is limited to a dynamic range of 256.

The scaling operation is a multiplicative process that may incorporate a translation. The dynamic range of the data in the real world system is determined, shifted so that it is unipolar, and scaled so that it fits into the dynamic range of the display. This is illustrated in Equation 5.1.

Equation 5.1 Scaling the Magnitude of Data

$$\text{Range\_of\_Display} = \text{Display\_Max} - \text{Display\_Min}$$

$$\text{Dynamic\_Range\_of\_Data} = \text{Data\_Max} - \text{Data\_Min}$$

$$\text{Scale\_Factor} = \frac{\text{Range\_of\_Display}}{\text{Dynamic\_Range\_of\_Data}}$$

$$\text{Scaled\_Data}[i] = (\text{Data}[i] - \text{Data\_Min}) \times \text{Scale\_Factor}$$

5.2.3 Scaling the Size of the Data

The transformation from the real-world coordinate system to the display coordinate system involves a coordinate scaling. This scaling is given in Equation 5.2.

Equation 5.2 Determining a Scale Factor

$$X\_Scale = \frac{\text{Integer Range of Display } X \text{ Coordinate}}{\text{Dynamic Range of RealWorld} X \text{ Coordinate}}$$

$$Y\_Scale = \frac{\text{Integer Range of Display } Y \text{ Coordinate}}{\text{Dynamic Range of RealWorld} Y \text{ Coordinate}}$$

The scaling transformation that incorporates these scale factors is listed in Equation 5.3.

Equation 5.3 Scaling Data

$$X \text{ new} = X \times X\_Scale$$

$$Y \text{ new} = Y \times Y\_Scale$$

Below are four examples that describe different scaling transformations.

Example 5.1 Real World Same as Display Space

The real-world coordinate system is measured in integers, the range consisting of 640 horizontal integers by 350 vertical integers. If the display coordinate system is also 640 horizontal by 350 vertical, no transformation is necessary. The transformation is considered one-to-one.

Example 5.2 Real World Measured in Integers

The real-world coordinate system is measured in integers, the range consisting of 1,280 horizontal integers by 700 vertical integers. If the display coordinate system is 640 horizontal by 350 vertical, a two-to-one transformation is necessary. The transformation is considered many-to-one because it is four points in the real-world space map to one point in the display space.

Example 5.3 Real World Smaller than Display Space

The real-world coordinate system is measured in integers, the range consisting of 320 horizontal integers by 175 vertical integers. If the display coordinate system is 640 horizontal by 350 vertical, a one-to-two scaling transformation is necessary. The transformation is considered one-to-many because one point in the real-world space can map to four points in the display space.

Example 5.4 Real World Measured in Reals

The real-world coordinate system is measured in real numbers, the range consisting of 640 horizontal integers by 350 vertical integers, with one significant fractional digit. If the display coordinate system is 640 horizontal by 350 vertical, a ten-to-one scaling transformation is necessary. The transformation is considered many-to-one because ten points in the real-world space map to one point in the display space.

5.2.4 Translation

Translation is used to move one coordinate system with respect to another. The translation can involve no rotations. Translation is an additive process, as shown in Equation 5.4.

Equation 5.4 Translation

X_New = X + X_translation

Y_New = Y + Y_translation

In Equation 5.4, a point, X, Y, is translated by an amount, X_translation and Y_translation. Example 5.5 illustrates a transformation that requires a translation.

Example 5.5 Transformation Requiring Translation

The real-world coordinate system is measured in integers, ranging from 100 to 739 integers along the horizontal axis and 200 to 550 integers along the vertical axis. If the display coordinate system is 640 horizontal by 350 vertical, a translation is required. It would shift the real-world coordinate system so that the value of 100 on the real-world X axis would map to 0 on the display X axis. Similarly, 200 on the real-world Y axis maps to 0 on the display Y axis. No scaling transformation is necessary in conjunction with the translation. The transformation is considered one-to-one because one point in the real-world space maps to one and only one point in the display space.

5.2.5 Rotation

Like translation, rotation moves an object coordinate system within a display or device coordinate system. The object rotates about its object origin by an angle *theta*, as indicated in Figure 5.4 earlier in this chapter.

Rotating an object can be accomplished by Equation 5.5. These equations rotate a point *X, Y* by an angle *theta*. The transcendental functions sine and cosine are used to perform the rotation. Rotations are treated like translations in a polar coordinate system.

Equation 5.5 Rotation

X_new = $X \times$ Cosine(*theta*)

Y_new = $Y \times$ Sine(*theta*)

5.2.6   Combining Transformations

It is possible to combine the linear operators. Scaling and translation equations are listed in Equation 5.6.

Equation 5.6 Scaling and Translation Transformation

X new = (X_Scale $\times X$) – Translation of X

Y new = (X_Scale $\times Y$) – Translation of Y

Example 5.6 illustrates a transformation that requires both a translation and a scaling.

Example 5.6 Transformation Requiring Translation and Rotation

The real-world coordinate system is measured in bipolar integers, ranging from –640 to +639 horizontal integers and from –350 to +349 vertical integers. If the display coordinate system is 640 horizontal by 350 vertical, a two-to-one scaling transformation is necessary in conjunction with a translation. The translation shifts the real-world coordinate system so that the value of –640 on the real-world X axis maps to 0 on the display X axis. Similarly, –350 on the real-world Y axis maps to 0 on the display Y axis. The transformation is considered many-to-one because four points in the real-world space map to one point in the display space. Both a scaling and a translation transformation are required.

5.2.7   Three-dimensional Transformations

A three-dimensional spatial coordinate system has all of the same transformations as discussed in the two-dimensional coordinate system. Often data that is present in a three-dimensional object coordinate system needs to be transformed so that it can be displayed in the two-dimensional display coordinate system. This transformation requires a projection of the three-dimensional space onto the two-dimensional space. A three-dimensional rectangular coordinate system consists of an X axis, a Y axis, and a Z axis. Three-dimensional polar coordinate systems are also popular.

5.3   THE CHARACTER

The shape of a character can be represented by either script or dot matrix techniques. Script techniques represent characters as if they were drawn by a pen. Each character consists of a series of directives that represent line segments. A character is drawn into memory by a series of line segment commands. Script characters are compact and can be drawn rapidly if a fast vector processor is present. Dot matrix techniques consider the character to be a two-dimensional box of pixels. The character is drawn by copying the matrix into the display memory. Dot matrix character shapes tend to be long and contain a great deal of redundant information. Using them is simple and fast because only a copy operation is necessary. No calculations have to be made to determine the shape of the character. A character drawn in each format is shown in Figure 5.5.

5.3.1   Script Characters

Script characters are represented by a sequence of plotting directives. Characters are drawn into a bit-mapped display by translating these plotting directives into foreground and background values. The characters are defined by a

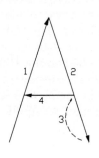
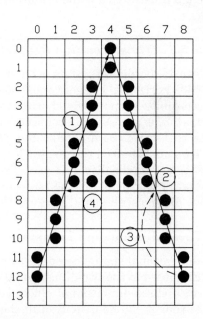

FIGURE 5.5   Script and Dot Matrix Characters

sequence of line segments. A line may be drawn in a color or may be invisible. Drawn lines correspond to moving the pen with it in contact with the paper. Curves would be drawn in a piecewise linear fashion.

Sophisticated script techniques employ shapes other than lines, such as curve segments. Script directives are very efficient when drawing straight lines, especially long straight lines. Also, by controlling the pen width, the character can be drawn in a variety of line widths. Script character sets require minimal storage, because a font can be drawn in any size. All that is required to change the size of a character is a scaling factor.

The display adapters used on the PC utilize dot matrix character sets exclusively in the alphanumerics modes; dot matrix character sets are also used by default in the graphics modes. If script characters are available, the programmer can utilize them in the graphics modes.

5.3.2 Dot Matrix Characters

Dot matrix characters are represented by a rectangle of dots. The width of the character is equal to the width of the box; the height of the character is equal to the height of the box. Intercharacter and interrow space is usually reserved in the character box. In this case, the height and width of the characters must be smaller than the height and width of the character box. When the character matrix is small, 8 by 8, this technique is fast and efficient. A character may be stored with its attribute—color, for example—coded into it. It can also be stored with the attribute separate from it. The latter practice is far more popular and efficient.

The character matrix consists of a matrix of dots. If the character shape is separate from the character attribute, the dots are either "on" or "off." Each row consists of a set of horizontal dots, and each column consists of a set of vertical dots. Typically, the horizontal dots are represented by a byte in memory, each bit representing one of the dots. The vertical dimension of the matrix is represented by an array of these bytes. Character box sizes for the fonts available on the EGA/VGA are illustrated in Figure 5.6.

One character size can be used to draw characters of varying sizes. However, the characters take on a "pixelated" look. A large character can be derived from a small character by representing each dot in the small matrix by a block of dots in the large matrix. A character enlarged by this technique is compared to a character defined by a larger matrix size in Figure 5.7.

5.3.3 Character Sets

Character sets typically consist of 256 characters and symbols. Each set defines a particular font size and type. Typical font types include Gothic, Prestige, Pica, Times, Roman, Elite, and Mathematical, although there are countless others.

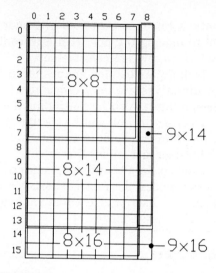

FIGURE 5.6 Dot Matrix Character Storage

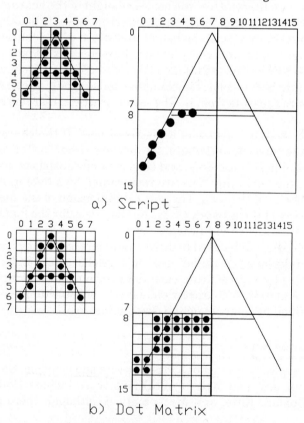

FIGURE 5.7 Enlarging a Character

Font size is measured in points. A small font has a small point size—for example, 8 points—and a large font has a large point size—for example, 20 points. It is difficult for the eye to distinguish between two fonts that are one point apart in size.

5.3.4 ASCII Standard

The ASCII standard ensures that each of the common characters are assigned a unique code that is the same regardless of the keyboard, computer, or monitor. The common characters include uppercase and lowercase characters of the alphabet, numbers, symbols, and a series of nonprintable characters, also referenced by control codes. The ASCII standard is probably the most important standard used in computers.

Typical nonprintable characters include carriage return, tab, backspace, form feed, null, and bell. The nonprintable characters can be accessed from the keyboard by holding the control key down while pressing a character key. For example, the bell code is 07 hex, and the G key is 47 hex. Holding down the control key and the G key simultaneously issues a Control-G. The code for a Control-G is 07 hex, which corresponds to the bell. Only some of the control codes have fixed meanings. The most common of these are found in the lower 32 characters.

The ASCII characters may be represented by a 7- or 8-bit code. The 7-bit code allows 128 unique characters, and the 8-bit code allows 256 characters. The 7-bit code is useful when data is being transmitted over a serial line, providing a 12.5 percent data reduction over the 8-bit code. When data is sent to a serial printer or across a modem, it might be helpful to use 7-bit codes. If the data is processed on a parallel bus, there is little reason to use a 7-bit bus because the bus is a multiple of eight bits wide. In the PC, an 8-bit code is used to represent the alphanumeric characters. The true ASCII standard refers only to the lower 128 character codes.

A second standard is called the *Extended ASCII standard*. These extended characters refer to key codes produced when multiple keys are held down. The Control, Shift, and Alt keys are considered the extended ASCII keys. The cold bootstrap can be initiated by holding down the Control and Alt keys (to create an extended ASCII character set) in conjunction with the Del key. The two Shift keys, one on either side of the keyboard, actually have different codes, and holding both down simultaneously produces a unique code. These character codes are in the range of 128–256.

A standard was also developed to define the shapes of the characters that reside in character code positions 128–256. It is called the IBM Graphics Character Set, and it provides a standardized set of graphics symbols. These characters include specialized symbols, foreign accented characters, Greek characters, and line-drawing symbols. The special symbols are useful when common foreign characters are required or when mathematical symbols must be displayed. The line-drawing symbols are useful when primitive graphics must be drawn on a graphics system that is in an alphanumeric display mode.

5.3.5 Alphanumeric and Graphics Display Modes

The display adapters operate in alphanumeric modes for text processing and graphics modes for graphics processing. This optimizes the performance of the adapter to suit the needs of the software. The alphanumeric modes are faster but less flexible than the graphics modes. Only one of these display modes can be active at a time because it is not possible to display characters in an alphanumeric mode at the same time as graphics are being displayed in the graphics mode. The software must pick one mode or the other.

The smallest element in the alphanumeric modes is a character position. The size of the character determines the number of characters that can fit on a screen. The smallest element in the graphics modes is the pixel. The resolution of the screen is dictated by the active display mode. The techniques used to display data in the alphanumeric modes are different from the techniques used in the graphics modes. In the alphanumeric modes, a code representing a character is loaded into display memory. This code is typically sixteen bits wide, representing the character shape and the character attribute. In the graphics modes, a series of dots is drawn into the display memory, forming the character shape. These dots, representing the actual shape of the character, can require as many as 512 bits if the sixteen-color mode of the VGA is active, using an 8-by-16 character that occupies all four display planes.

Each adapter includes resident character sets. These character sets are used to produce the character patterns displayed on the screen. Each set includes 256 character shapes, consisting of alphabetical, numeric, and special graphics characters. All of the characters in an individual character set have the same size. Some adapters are equipped with multiple character sets, allowing different font sizes. The smaller characters are used to display more characters on the screen, but the larger characters are more legible.

It is possible to draw primitive graphics in an alphanumeric mode. The graphics characters, contained in ASCII codes 128–255, contain line shapes. These allow the programmer to display continuous lines and boxes on the screen. Each graphics character must conform to the character size dictated by the selected character set. Thus, only limited graphics effects can be achieved. Although the graphics potential is limited, it allows the display to stay in an alphanumeric mode.

It is possible to display alphanumeric characters in a graphics mode. The same character sets used in the alphanumeric modes can be used in the graphics modes. The character shapes associated with each character are accessed from the active character set by their ASCII code. Using this technique, the programmer is limited to the character size and shape as loaded in the character set. In contrast, the programmer can draw alphanumeric characters on the screen without using the character sets. One way is to download user-specified character sets. This provides a great deal of flexibility, although the character size is still restricted by limitations in the display adapters. The programmer can draw the characters pixel by pixel, as if they were graphics elements. Any size or shape character can be drawn.

5.3.6   Drawing Characters in an Alphanumeric Mode

The alphanumeric modes represent characters in display memory by a character code and an attribute byte for that character. The actual pixel patterns of each character are not stored in display memory in the alphanumeric modes. Only the code and the attribute byte need to be written into display memory in order to display a character. Similarly, reading from an address in display memory returns the character code and attribute byte. Because only two bytes are stored per character, alphanumeric data transfers are fast. The BIOS routines are typically sufficient for most alphanumeric data transfers.

5.3.7   Drawing Characters in a Graphics Mode

Unlike the alphanumeric modes, the graphics modes store information in the display memory, pixel by pixel. In order to display a character, a program must write every dot in the character box to display memory. The character shape and the attribute are joined when the character is written to display memory. If the foreground attribute of a character is red, the color red is written to each pixel in display memory that corresponds to the character foreground.

The character box consists of a number of horizontal scan lines, each the width of the character. The character width typically includes the horizontal and vertical intercharacter space. A display memory address must be provided to determine where the character will be drawn. Because the display is two-dimensional, the address is most easily defined in two dimensions, row and column. The pixel row and column number can correspond to any point of the character.

Assuming that the starting address refers to the upper-left corner of the pixel, the top scan line of the character is written to this starting address. Each vertical pixel is separated by a value equivalent to the width of the virtual image. If the virtual image is 80 bytes wide, 80 must be added to the starting address to determine the address of the second scan row. This process continues for each scan line, until the last scan line is written to the display.

5.4   THE POINT

A point is the most primitive structure in the graphics environment in a bit-mapped graphics system. All graphics structures are based on groups of points. A character, line, circle, or image can all be defined as a collection of points. A point may be represented in the graphics display system by one or more pixels.

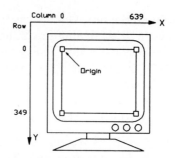

FIGURE 5.8 Screen Coordinate System

In the discussion that follows, it is assumed that a point is represented by one pixel. A pixel may be composed of one or more bits of information. A bit is the most primitive structure in the computer system, and a byte is the smallest addressable structure in the computer. In the EGA, a pixel is represented by one, two, or four bits of information. In the VGA, a pixel is represented by one, two, four, or eight bits of information.

The location of a point, as displayed on the monitor, is best described by a two-dimensional address. It can be described by a horizontal and vertical coordinate pair. The origin of the screen coordinate system, as viewed on the monitor, typically resides at the upper-left or lower-left corner of the monitor. All of the graphics adapters described in this book use the upper-left corner as the origin, as indicated in Figure 5.8.

From a programmer's perspective, this screen coordinate system is the easiest system to use. The screen and the printed page provide an obvious two-dimensional space. If the coordinate values of the pixel are specified and the limits of the horizontal and vertical axes are known, the position of the pixel on the screen can be visualized readily.

From the perspective of the display memory, the location of a pixel is more complex. The display memory is organized in either a bit-plane or a packed display format. The display memory is mapped into the host memory address space, organized into bytes. Each byte consists of eight bits, and these eight bits represent from one to eight pixels. Each display mode in the EGA and VGA organizes the data differently. To further complicate matters, a single display mode can allocate different numbers of bits to a pixel. The programmer must know the condition of the current display mode in order to understand where in display memory a pixel resides.

The graphics modes for the EGA and VGA are listed in Table 5.1. A description of the organization of the display memory for each mode is included. Modes 4 and 5 utilize bit planes 0 and 1. The organization is termed *packed* because a single pixel resides in either bit plane 0 or bit plane 1. Alternate bytes, each byte containing four pixels, are loaded into bit plane 0 or bit plane 1 in an odd/even (O/E) fashion.

TABLE 5.1 Display Memory Organization

Mode (Hex)	Adapter	Format	Number of Colors	Pixels / Byte	Bit Planes
4,5	EGA/VGA	Packed	4	4	0,1 O/E
6	EGA/VGA	Packed	2	8	0,1 O/E
F	EGA/VGA	Bit mapped	2	8	0,2
11	VGA	Packed	2	8	0
D	EGA/VGA	Bit mapped	16	8	0,1,2,3
E	EGA/VGA	Bit mapped	16	8	0,1,2,3
10	EGA/VGA	Bit mapped	16	8	0,1,2,3
12	VGA	Bit mapped	16	8	0,1,2,3
13	VGA	Packed	256	1	0,1,2,3 chained

[handwritten annotations: "odd/even fashion" next to 0,1 O/E; "4" next to the 8 for mode 6; "bit plane"]

Mode F hex uses bit planes 0 and 2, organized in a bit-mapped format. The video bit is stored in bit plane 0, and the intensity bit is stored in bit plane 1.

Modes D, E, 10, and 12 hex use all four bit planes, in a bit-mapped format. A pixel can be represented by any or all of these bit planes. For example, a pixel can be represented by one bit in bit planes 0, 1, 2, or 3. Similarly, the pixel can be represented by two bits in bit planes 0 and 1, 0 and 2, 0 and 3, 1 and 2, 1 and 3, or 2 and 3. A pixel can also be represented by three bits in bit planes 0, 1, or 2, bit planes 1, 2, or 3, or bit planes 0, 2, or 3.

Mode 13 hex uses all four bit planes. The bit planes are organized in a packed format because all eight bits associated with a single pixel reside in a single plane. The four planes are chained so that sequential bytes in host memory are loaded into alternating bit planes.

5.4.1 Bit Addressing

In all but mode 13 hex, more than one pixel is stored per byte. Thus, the smallest addressable structure in the computer, the byte, cannot resolve down to the lowest graphical structure, the pixel. It is not possible to address an individual pixel. Attempting to read a single pixel in modes 4, 5, or 6 will access four pixels from display memory. This occurs because a byte is read in a single instruction. The position of the desired pixel within the byte depends on the horizontal address of the pixel. Because there are four pixels per byte, a modulo 4 division will provide the pixel number within a byte. Figure 5.9 illustrates the pixel numbers within a typical byte.

The modulo 4 division is accomplished in C by the statement "address % 4", where address is an integer. The "%" symbol indicates modulo division. The address can be the horizontal coordinate of the pixel (0-639) or it can be the

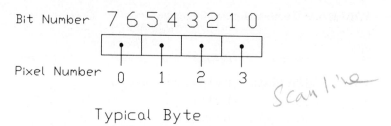

Scan line

Typical Byte

FIGURE 5.9 Pixel Numbers for Modes 4, 5, 6

address relative to the start of display memory. In all of the standard display modes, the number of horizontal pixels per scan line is a multiple of four—either 320 or 640. Therefore, the modulo 4 division will provide the pixel position within a byte regardless of the vertical coordinate.

Suppose the pixel position within a byte is desired for a pixel located at $x=1$, $y=1$ in a mode in which there are 640 pixels per horizontal scan line. The horizontal address of the pixel is 1, and the address with respect to the start of the image is 641. Both 1 and 641 provide a pixel location of 1, as shown in Equation 5.7.

Equation 5.7 Determining Pixel Position

$$\text{pixel position} = \text{address} \ \% \ 4$$

$$\text{pixel position} = 1 = 1 \ \% \ 4$$

$$\text{pixel position} = 1 = 641 \ \% \ 4$$

In modes D, E, F, 10, 11, and 12 hex, there are eight pixels per byte. The pixel location within a byte is determined by using a modulo 8 division. The technique used to determine the pixel position is similar to the technique described for modes 4, 5, and 6. Figure 5.10 illustrates the pixel numbers within a typical byte.

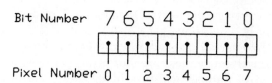

Typical Byte

FIGURE 5.10 Pixel Numbers for Modes D, E, F, 10, 11, 12 hex

In mode 13 hex, one pixel occupies an entire byte. This is the simplest display mode to use when interacting with display memory. The pixel position is always 0 because the pixel occupies the entire byte.

5.4.2 Determining the Display Address

It is possible to determine the display memory address of a pixel given the horizontal coordinates of the pixel, the number of bits per pixel, and the virtual width of the image. The display address and the position of a pixel can be determined using the calculations in Equation 5.8.

Equation 5.8 Determining a Display Address

$$\text{Display address} = \text{Starting address} + \text{Vertical component} + \text{Horizontal component}$$

$$\text{Vertical component} = \left(\text{Virtual width} \middle/ \text{Pixels per byte} \right) \times \text{Vertical coordinate}$$

$$\text{Horizontal component} = \text{Horizontal Coordinate} \middle/ \text{Pixelsperbyte}$$

$$\text{Pixel Location} = \text{Horizontal Coordinate} \% \text{Pixelsperbyte}$$

The display memory consists of 64 Kbytes per plane on most EGA and VGA adapters. The address begins at 0000 hex and extends to FFFF hex. The active display region begins at the *starting address*. The starting address may begin anywhere in this 64 Kbyte region. For the display modes with more than one page, the starting address is typically 0000 hex. Panning and scrolling can affect the position of the starting address. For the display modes in which more than one page is possible, the starting address can be determined from Equation 5.9.

Equation 5.9 Determining the Starting Address

$$\text{Starting address} = \text{Page number} \times \text{Bytes perpage}$$

$$\text{Bytes per page} = \text{Vertical extent} \times \left(\text{Horizontal extent} \middle/ \text{Pixelsperbyte} \right)$$

The page numbers range from 0 to 7 depending on the mode, and the vertical and horizontal extents refer to the number of pixels in the virtual image.

5.4.3 Interacting with Pixels

Once the address and pixel location are determined, the pixel can be accessed in display memory. Reading a pixel really corresponds to reading a number of pixels, either 1, 4, or 8. In the bit-mapped cases, additional bits associated with the pixel might reside in other bit planes. In these cases, additional reads are necessary.

Writing to a pixel is more complex. Although the address and bit position are handled identically, writing to a pixel may mean writing to 1, 4, or 8 pixels. Additional masking is necessary to ensure that only the desired pixel is modified. In the case of four pixels per byte, three of the pixels have to be masked out. In the case of eight pixels per byte, seven of the pixels have to be masked out. When the display is in a bit-mapped mode, additional bits of a pixel may reside in more than one bit plane, and additional write operations may be required.

5.4.4 Reading a Pixel

In the following discussion, it is assumed that the display is in Read Mode 0. Read Mode 0 is the default read-mode.

If the display memory is in a packed or bit-mapped format with one bit plane active, all of the bits associated with a single pixel are in a single plane. In order to read a pixel, the display address that accesses a byte containing the pixel must be determined. The display address is used to read a byte from the appropriate bit plane in display memory. This byte contains the desired pixel. Unfortunately, it also contains undesired pixels.

Once read, the byte from display memory resides in a variable in host memory. The pixel position can then be used to find the starting bit position of the desired pixel, within the variable. In order to obtain the value of the pixel, it is necessary to shift the bits associated with the pixel into the low-order bit positions of the byte. The bits in the variable that correspond to other pixels must be zeroed to provide the value of the desired pixel. Table 5.2 lists the number of bit positions to shift the variable and the value that should be used to zero out the unwanted bit positions. This value can be ANDed with the variable after shifting. A positive value in the "Number of Bits to Shift" column indicates a left shift; a negative value indicates a right shift.

In the modes that use a bit-packed format and have multiple bit planes active, the read operation becomes more complicated. The modes that are bit-packed have eight pixels per byte. In these modes, a pixel may be located in one, two, three, or four display planes. Each of the display planes that contains a bit for the pixel must be read before the value of the pixel can be determined.

bit plane?

TABLE 5.2 Reading a Pixel from Display Memory

Pixels/ Byte	Pixel Position	Pixel in Bits	Number of Bits to Shift	ANDing Mask (hex)
4	0	6,7	−6	03
4	1	4,5	−4	03
4	2	2,3	−2	03
4	3	0,1	0	03
8	0	7	−7	01
8	1	6	−6	01
8	2	5	−5	01
8	3	4	−4	01
8	4	3	−3	01
8	5	2	−2	01
8	6	1	−1	01
8	7	0	0	01

Mode F has data in bit planes 0 and 2, and all of the other modes may have data in all four bit planes.

5.4.5 Mode 6

In mode 6, data resides in both bit planes 0 and 1. The data in bit plane 0 refers to the *video* bit, and the data in bit plane 1 refers to the *intensify* bit. To determine the value of the pixel, the byte that contains the pixel in both display planes is read in a similar fashion to that described above. The display memory address is ascertained, and the byte is read from this address.

All of the display planes reside at the same address and are differentiated by the Read Map Select Register, which chooses one of the bit planes during a read operation. In this example, the Read Map Select Register is loaded with a 0 and the byte containing the desired pixel is read from display memory into a variable in host memory called *Video*. The value in the Read Map Select Register is then changed to 2, and the byte at the same address in display memory is read into a second variable, called *Intensified*.

In order to determine a single value for the variable, these two variables must be joined. Although four values are possible for a pixel with two bits, in this case the values do not correspond to 0, 1, 2, and 3. Rather, the binary code with the two bits in bit positions 0 and 2 corresponds to values of 0, 1, 4 and 5. The *Video* variable must be shifted into bit position 0, and the *Intensify* variable has to be shifted into bit position 2. The number of bit positions to shift

TABLE 5.3 Shifting the Video and Intensified Bits

	Pixel Position							
Variable	0	1	2	3	4	5	6	7
Video	−7	−6	−5	−4	−3	−2	−1	0
Intensified	−5	−4	−3	−2	−1	0	1	2

TABLE 5.4 Zeroing Unwanted Bits

Variable	Mask (Hex)	Comments
Video	01	Only bit 0 is significant
Intensified	04	Only bit 2 is significant

each variable is listed in Table 5.3. A positive shift value indicates a left shift, and a negative shift value indicates a right shift.

The undesired bits corresponding to the other seven pixels in these variables must be zeroed. The mask value is determined from Table 5.4 depending on the pixel position.

Once shifted and masked, the four variables are joined through an ORing operation, as indicated in Equation 5.10. The "|" operator is the symbol used for the logical OR operation in the C language. The variables are denoted *newVideo* and *newIntensified* because they represent the variables *Video* and *Intensified* after the shift and logical AND operation.

Equation 5.10 ORing the Attributes

Pixel value = newVideo | newIntensified

5.4.6   Multiple Bit Planes

In the modes that use a bit-packed format and that have multiple bit planes active, the read operation becomes more complicated. All of the display modes that are bit packed represent eight pixels in each byte. Each pixel may be represented by one, two, three, or four bits. These bits are located in one, two, three, or four display planes. Each of the display planes that contain a bit must be read before the value of the pixel can be ascertained. Mode F hex uses a format of two bits per pixel. It stores the two bits per pixel in bit planes 0 and 2; all of the other modes may have data in all four bit planes.

5.4.7 Modes F, 10, 11, and 12 hex

The bits associated with a pixel in modes F, 10, 11, and 12 hex can be located in any of the four bit planes. The value of the pixel depends on the convention being used. In the case of a pixel occupying a bit in all four bit planes, the value of the pixel ranges from 0 to 15. In the case of a pixel occupying one bit plane, the value of the pixel is either 0 or 1. There is no set convention to determine the value of the pixel in any other cases. The case presented in mode 6 in Section 5.4.5 illustrates this ambiguity. In mode 6, the values correspond to 0, 1, 4, and 5. It is up to the programmer to determine the convention when pixels occupy two or three bit planes.

An example is presented for determining the value of a pixel when the pixel occupies all four bit planes. The same technique can be applied when determining the value of a pixel occupying less than four bit planes. The programmer needs to ascertain the mask values and the number of bits to shift the variables.

Once the address of the byte in display memory that contains the desired pixel is determined, the four bytes from each display plane can be read into four variables called "p0", "p1", "p2", and "p3". These four variables correspond to the values read from bit planes 0, 1, 2, and 3, respectively. Each of the four variables must be shifted the proper amount before being joined into a single variable. Table 5.5 lists the amount of bits to shift the four variables. A positive value indicates a left shift, and a negative value indicates a right shift.

The undesired bits corresponding to the other seven pixels in these variables must be zeroed. The mask value is determined from Table 5.6 depending on the pixel position.

Once shifted and masked, the four variables are joined through an ORing operation, as indicated in Equation 5.11. The "|" operator is the symbol used for the logical OR operation in the C language. The variables are denoted "newP0", "newP1", "newP2", and "newP3" because they represent the four variables "P0", "P1", "P2", and "P3" after the shift and AND operation.

TABLE 5.5 Shifting the Variables from Four Bit Planes

Pixel Position	0	1	2	3	4	5	6	7
Data Bit Position	7	6	5	4	3	2	1	0
P0	−7	−6	−5	−4	−3	−2	−1	0
P1	−6	−5	−4	−3	−2	−1	0	1
P2	−5	−4	−3	−2	−1	0	1	2
P3	−4	−3	−2	−1	0	1	2	3

TABLE 5.6 Zeroing Unwanted Bits

Variable	Mask (Hex)	Comments
P0	01	Only bit 0 is significant
P1	02	Only bit 1 is significant
P2	04	Only bit 2 is significant
P3	08	Only bit 3 is significant

Equation 5.11 ORing the Four Variables

Pixel value = newP0 | newP1 | newP2 | newP3

5.4.8 Writing a Pixel — *read / modify / write*

Writing to a pixel in display memory requires a read/modify/write operation. In the following discussion, it is assumed that the EGA/VGA is in write mode 0, the default write mode. In all modes except mode 13 hex, there is more than one pixel per byte of display memory. However, the byte is the smallest structure that the host memory can access. Writing to one pixel without affecting the other pixels in the byte of display memory requires a masking operation. This ensures that only the desired pixel is modified.

The address of the byte that contains the desired pixel is used to read the byte from display memory. This value is loaded into a variable, "read_val", in the host memory. A mask, called the "read mask" in Table 5.7, zeros out the bits corresponding to the desired pixel. The value of the mask is determined by the number of pixels per byte and the pixel location within the byte. After the zeroing, the bit locations corresponding to the pixel value are 0 and therefore are ready for new data.

The value that is to be loaded into the desired pixel is resident in a variable, "write_val", in host memory. This value occupies the least significant bits of the variable. A mask value, called "write_mask" in Table 5.7, is used to zero all other bits in the variable. This prevents these bits from interfering with the subsequent operations. If the value in this variable does not exceed the maximum value that the pixel can obtain, the zeroing is unnecessary. Once zeroed, the variable "write_val" is shifted to the left so that the pixel value is placed in the bits corresponding to the pixel position. This resultant variable, "write_val", is ORed with the variable "read_val", which inserts the new pixel value into the byte read from display memory. The result is then written back to display memory at the same address that was used for the original read operation. This completes the read/modify/write operation. Table 5.7 contains the necessary constants for this operation. Positive values in the "Number of Bits to Shift" column indicate a left shift, and negative values indicate a right shift.

TABLE 5.7 Reading a Pixel from Display Memory

Pixels/ Byte	Pixel Position	Pixel in Bits	Number of Bits to Shift	Read Mask	Write Mask
4	0	6,7	6	3F	03
4	1	4,5	4	CF	03
4	2	2,3	2	F3	03
4	3	0,1	0	FC	03
8	0	7	7	7F	01
8	1	6	6	BF	01
8	2	5	5	DF	01
8	3	4	4	EF	01
8	4	3	3	F7	01
8	5	2	2	FB	01
8	6	1	1	FD	01
8	7	0	0	FE	01

[handwritten: write mask reg.]   *[handwritten: shift-the data from the host]*

5.4.9 Using the Bit Mask and the Data Rotate Register

This time-consuming operation was anticipated by the designers of the EGA/VGA standard. Internal hardware is built into the EGA/VGA to perform the shifting and masking of the data automatically. A Bit Mask Register is provided in the EGA/VGA to act as a write mask register. A Data Rotate Register is provided in the EGA/VGA to shift the data from the host. These two registers are used for the modify portion of the read/modify/write operation.

The Bit Mask Register is used to protect any bits within a byte of display memory from being modified. A byte of display memory can contain bits associated with more than one pixel. If one pixel needs to be modified, any bits associated with the other pixels have to be protected. Any bit positions within the Bit Mask Register that are reset to 0 are protect bits. A byte written from host memory will affect only those bits in display memory that correspond to a 1 in the Bit Mask Register. This provides the masking necessary for the modify operation. The mask values to load into the Bit Mask Register are determined by the pixel location bits and are listed in Table 5.7.

The Data Rotate Register shifts the byte written from host memory before it is written into display memory. The value that is to be written into a pixel must reside in the bit position associated with that pixel. If it resides in some other location, it must be shifted so that it resides in the proper pixel location. The value loaded into the Data Rotate Register corresponds to the number of pixels to left-shift the host byte. This register is called a *rotate register* because values greater than 8 but less than 16 are considered right shifts. The rotate values to

TABLE 5.8 Bit Mask and Data Rotate Register

Pixels/Byte	Pixel Position	Pixel in Bits	Data Rotate	Bit Mask (Hex)
4	0	6,7	6	C0
4	1	4,5	4	30
4	2	2,3	2	0C
4	3	0,1	0	03
8	0	7	7	80
8	1	6	6	40
8	2	5	5	20
8	3	4	4	10
8	4	3	3	08
8	5	2	2	04
8	6	1	1	02
8	7	0	0	01

load into the Data Rotate Register are also determined by the pixel location register and are listed in Table 5.8.

5.4.10 Multiple Bit Planes

In the modes that use a bit-packed format and have multiple bit planes active, the write operation becomes more complicated. All of these bit-packed modes represent one bit from eight pixels in each byte. A pixel may be represented by one, two, three, or four bits. These bits are located in one, two, three, or four display planes. Each of the display planes that contain a bit must be read before the value of the pixel can be determined. Mode F has data in bit planes 0 and 2; all of the other modes may have data in all four bit planes.

It is possible to write to a pixel in one of the bit planes using the techniques described above. The same techniques can be used. These techniques involving the Bit Mask and Rotate Registers are simply replicated, one for each of the desired bit planes.

It is necessary to understand the hardware in order to understand how to write to the display planes. Internal to the EGA/VGA adapter is a 32-bit-wide data bus. This data bus is segmented into four sections, each section being eight bits wide. Each of the four sections interfaces to one of the four bit planes. The host interfaces to the adapter through an 8-bit data bus. This 8-bit host bus is expanded to the 32-bit data bus. The eight bits from the host bus interface to each of the four EGA/VGA internal data buses, as shown in Figure 5.11.

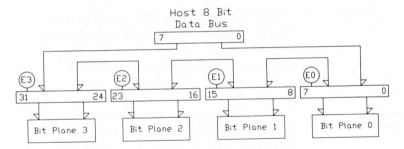

FIGURE 5.11 Host 8-bit to EGA/VGA 32-bit Data Bus

5.4.11 Using the Map Mask Register

Each of the four latches comprising the 32-bit internal latch are enabled separately through signals E0, E1, E2, and E3. If signal E0 is active, the 8-bit data written from the host will affect bit plane 0. Likewise, if signal E1 is active, the 8-bit data written from the host will affect bit plane 1. It is possible for both E0 and E1 to be active. If this is the case, both bit plane 0 and bit plane 1 will be affected. Each will be modified with identical data. In fact, all four bit planes, or any combination of the four bit planes, can be written to simultaneously. This constitutes a 32-bit write operation in a single instruction. The limitation is that the identical eight bits from the host are written to any of the enabled planes. The Map Mask Register determines which bit planes will be affected.

5.4.12 Writing to One Pixel in Multiple Planes

It is possible to write to one pixel in multiple display planes in a single host operation. This can be a big time-saver for the programmer who has to modify a single pixel. Hardware is provided in the EGA/VGA that can access one pixel location in each of the four bit planes. Two techniques can be used to accomplish this. The first utilizes the Set/Reset and Enable Set/Reset Registers. The second utilizes write mode 2.

5.4.13 Set/Reset and Enable Set/Reset Registers

The Set/Reset Register is used to interact with a single pixel in all four bit planes. A 4-bit value is written into the Set/Reset Register. Each bit in this 4-bit value accesses one of the display planes. Bit 0 accesses bit plane 0, bit 1 accesses bit plane 1, and so on. The byte in display memory that contains the desired pixel is accessed by the address used in a host move operation. The individual pixel is enabled through the Bit Mask Register.

It is also possible to write to a pixel that does not occupy all four bit planes. Any number of bit planes can be accessed in a single operation by enabling only the desired bit planes. This is accomplished through the Enable Set/Reset

Register. A 4-bit value is loaded into this register. Each bit within this 4-bit value enables one of the display planes. The enabled display plane is modified with the value in the corresponding bit position of the Set/Reset Register. Any bit in the Enable Set/Reset Register that contains a 1 causes the corresponding bit plane to be modified by the value in the Set/Reset Register. Any bit position in the Enable Set/Reset Register that contains a 0 causes the corresponding bit plane to be modified by the data being output from the host.

The technique employed to write a value to a pixel from one to four bit planes using the Set/Reset and Enable Set/Reset Register is complicated. The appropriate values are loaded into the Set/Reset and Enable Set/Reset Registers. A move operation sends an 8-bit data value to the display adapter. The value in the Map Mask Register determines which bit planes are active. Any bit planes enabled by the Map Mask Register and the Enable Set/Reset Register are modified by the value in the Set/Reset Register. Any bit planes enabled by the Map Mask Register but not enabled by the Enable Set/Reset Register are modified by the value sent by the host in the move operation.

5.4.14 Writing to Multiple Pixels in Multiple Planes

The data in one to eight pixels in each of the four display planes can be modified in a single operation. The Set/Reset Register and the Enable Set/Reset Register are used in an identical fashion, as was described previously. The byte in display memory that contains the desired pixel is accessed by the address referenced in the MOV instruction. When a single pixel is being modified, the Bit Mask Register enables just that one pixel. Additional pixels can be modified if their corresponding bit positions are enabled in the Bit Mask Register.

This technique effectively performs a 32-bit data transfer in a single host instruction. Each bit plane can be modified with different data, permitting up to eight pixels per bit plane to be altered. However, using the Set/Reset and the Enable Set/Reset Registers, all of the bits in a single bit plane can be modified only with the same data. This occurs because the Set/Reset Register contains only four bits, one bit destined for each display plane. Any pixels enabled by the Bit Mask Register will be modified by the same value, either a 0 or a 1, as loaded in the corresponding bit position of the Set/Reset Register.

5.4.15 Writing to All Planes Using Write Mode 2

Any combination of the four bit planes can be modified in a single host instruction by using write mode 2. Write mode 2 is made active by loading a 2 into the WM field of the Mode Register. The host move operation sends a 4-bit word to the display adapter. With write mode 2 active, each of these four bits is associated with one of the four bit planes. Bit 0 in the value sent by the host is associated with bit plane 0. Bits 1, 2, and 3 are associated with Bit Planes 1, 2, and 3, respectively. Each bit is replicated eight times and written to its respective display plane. Up to eight pixels in each bit plane can be modified with this replicated bit. The eight bits are accessed in display memory by the address used in the host move operation. The pixels that are affected depend on the value in the Bit Mask Register. This effectively produces a 32-bit write operation in a single host operation. However, the eight pixels in each plane can be modified only with an identical value, either 0 or 1.

5.5   THE LINE

A single image on the EGA/VGA can consist of thousands of lines. In an interactive graphics session, images can be redrawn hundreds of times. This results in an enormous number of lines being drawn. A line on the EGA/VGA can be composed of more than 600 dots. The line can be drawn by repeatedly calling a point-drawing routine. However, this puts a tremendous constraint on the point-drawing routine. Because it is called repeatedly, the point-drawing routine must be designed as efficiently as possible. Because the line-drawing routine is called repeatedly, it must also be designed as efficiently as possible.

There are several line-drawing algorithms available to the graphics programmer. Three important algorithms are discussed in the following sections. These include the solution of the linear equation, the incremental algorithm, and the Bresenham's line algorithm. The special cases of horizontal and vertical lines are also discussed. Bresenham's line algorithm is far superior to the other techniques when run in a PC environment.

5.5.1   Defining a Line

There are two popular ways to define a line. The first technique defines a line by its endpoints. This defines the line within a rectangular coordinate system. The second technique defines a line by one endpoint, a slope, and a length. This defines the line in a polar coordinate system. Both of these are illustrated in Figure 5.12.

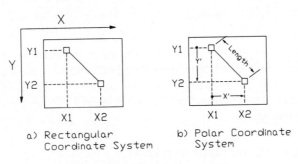

a) Rectangular
Coordinate System

b) Polar Coordinate
System

FIGURE 5.12 Defining a Line

In 5.12a, the endpoints are defined as the two coordinate pairs $(X1,Y1)$ and $(X2,Y2)$. In 5.12b, the one endpoint is defined as $(X1,Y1)$, the length is defined as LENGTH, and the slope is defined as (Y'/X'). The slope is a measure of the change along the vertical axis, Y', divided by the change along the horizontal axis, X'.

5.5.2   Determining the Length of a Line

The length of a line in one dimension can be determined by taking the absolute value of the difference between the endpoints. A line typically is drawn from one endpoint to another. If the position of the drawing device at the end of the line drawing is important, it is necessary to draw the line specifically from one coordinate to another. This is the case with pen plotters.

The length of a line in two dimensions can be determined by taking the length of the projection of that line onto each of two perpendicular axes. These values are squared and added. The square root of the result yields the length of the line. This equation is attributed to Pythagoras and is included in Equation 5.12.

Equation 5.12 Pythagorean Theorem

$$\text{Length} = (\, X^2 + Y^2 \,)^{1/2}$$

The lengths of the projections X and Y are often useful in themselves, and Equation 5.12 does not need to be solved. The lengths of the projections of the line along the X and Y axis are called X and Y. These lengths are described in Equation 5.13.

Equation 5.13 Lengths of Projections

$$X = \text{ABS}\,(\, X2 - X1 \,)$$
$$Y = \text{ABS}\,(\, Y2 - Y1 \,)$$

The programmer must take care when determining the length of a line in a discrete environment. A line that connects two adjacent pixels, say $X=1$ and $X=2$, occupies two pixels yet is only one pixel unit long. This is often a cause of confusion and inaccuracies. If a line having a length of one unit is drawn, two pixels will be involved.

5.5.3   Determining the Slope of a Line

The slope of a line is a measure of the line's direction. The slope of a line is a constant—that is, the slope of a line at one point on the line is equal to the slope of the line everywhere on the line. The slope can be determined by dividing the length of the projection of the line on one axis by the length of the projection of the line on the other axis. The slope of a line can be represented by the change of Y over the change of X or by the change of X divided by the change of Y, as shown in Equation 5.14.

Equation 5.14 Slope of a Line

$$\text{Slope\_Y} = \frac{dy}{dx} = \frac{\text{length of } Y}{\text{length of } X}$$

$$\text{Slope\_X} = \frac{dx}{dy} = \frac{\text{length of } X}{\text{length of } Y}$$

These two slopes are not independent and are related by a reciprocal relationship, as shown in Equation 5.15.

Equation 5.15 Reciprocal Relationship of Slopes

$$\text{SlopeX} = 1 / \text{SlopeY}$$

The angle of a slope is measured counterclockwise from the horizontal axis, as indicated in Figure 5.13a. A horizontal line has a slope of either 0 degrees or 180 degrees. A vertical line has a slope of 90 degrees or –90 degrees.

The slope can also be measured in terms of lengths by Equation 5.13. The slope of a line measured with Y as the independent variable is expressed in Equation 5.14. It should be noted that the vertical orientation is reversed in the EGA/VGA device coordinate system.

The slope corresponding to a horizontal line is 0 in this case because the length of the projection along the vertical axis is 0. The slope corresponding to

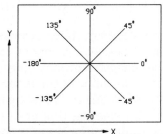
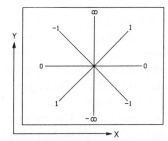

a) Measuring the Slope of a Line in Angles   b) Measuring the Slope of a Line in Lengths

FIGURE 5.13 Measuring the Slope of a Line

a 45-degree line is 1 because both projection lengths are equal. The slope of a vertical line is infinity because the length of the projection along the Y axis is 0, and a scalar divided by 0 yields infinity, in this instance.

5.5.4 The Linear Equation

A line can be drawn by solving either of the linear equations in Equations 5.16 and 5.17.

Equation 5.16 Linear Equation: X Independent Variable

$$Y = (\text{Slope\_Y} \times X) + By$$

Equation 5.17 Linear Equation: Y Independent Variable

$$X = (\text{Slope\_X} \times Y) + Bx$$

In these equations, Y is the vertical coordinate, X is the horizontal coordinate, By is the *y-intercept*, and Bx is the *x-intercept*. Equation 5.16 expresses a line with Y being the dependent variable and X being the independent variable. Equation 5.17 expresses a line with X being the dependent variable and Y being the independent variable.

The slope is defined in Equations 5.14. It is a measure of the amount of change that the dependent variable will incur due to an incremental change in the independent variable. The proper determination of which variable, X or Y, is independent is critical to effective line drawing.

5.5.5 Determining an Independent Variable

When drawing a line, care must be exercised when selecting whether the horizontal or the vertical axis, X or Y, should be the independent axis. In a continuous system, it makes no difference whether Equation 5.16 or 5.17 is selected. However, in a pixelated, discrete system, selecting the proper independent variable affects the quality of the line.

A line is typically drawn from one endpoint to the other. A line-drawing algorithm determines which axis is best thought of as being independent. It starts at the one endpoint with the coordinate of the independent axis plugged into Equation 5.16 or 5.17. This equation determines the value of the independent variable, and a point is drawn at the pixel located at this coordinate pair. The algorithm increments the independent variable, repeating this process until the second endpoint of the line is reached. The resulting line has only one point for each of the incremental values of the independent variable. It may have no

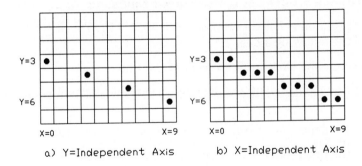

FIGURE 5.14 A Line Using Two Different Independent Axes

point, one point, or many points for any value of the independent variable. This is illustrated in Figure 5.14.

In Figure 5.14, it is evident that the line in *b* is more filled in and looks continuous, while the line in *a* appears to be a dotted line. This occurs because in *b* the independent axis is *X*, and in *a* the independent axis is *Y*.

The criterion used to determine which axis to select as the independent axis involves the slope. If the slope is between −45 degrees and +45 degrees, *X* should be selected as the independent variable. If the slope is less than -45 degrees and greater then −135 degrees or greater than +45 degrees and less than 135 degrees, the *Y* axis should be selected. Measuring the slope in terms of lengths, this means that if the slope is between −1 and +1, select the *X* axis as the independent variable. Otherwise, the *Y* axis should be selected. In other words, if the change in *Y* is less than the change in *X*, select the *X* axis as the independent variable. The selection criterion is illustrated in Figure 5.15.

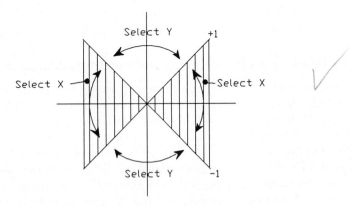

FIGURE 5.15 Selecting an Independent Axis

5.5.6   Drawing a Line Using the Linear Equation

The linear equation is listed in Equations 5.16 or 5.17. This algorithm is implemented by the following steps.

1. Determine the slope and intercept of the line.

2. Select the independent and dependent variable depending on the value of the slope.

3. Set the independent variable to the lesser of the two endpoints.

4. Solve the linear equation for the dependent variable.

5. Draw a point at the pixel selected by the two variables.

6. Increment the independent variable.

7. If the independent variable is not equal to the value at the second endpoint, repeat steps 4–7.

The linear equation requires a multiplication and an addition for every point. The multiplication must be a floating-point multiplication because the slope is a real number. It is possible to estimate the floating-point multiplication with a fractional integer multiplication. Errors can occur unless the precision of the fractional part is high. The floating-point multiplication is time-consuming and slows down the line drawing. The addition requires a rounding operation, which can also be time-consuming. A coprocessor designed to perform rapid floating-point calculations does improve the performance, but these operations are still slow.

Because the display is pixelated, the result of this floating-point multiplication and integer addition must be converted to an integer so that a pixel can be selected. A round-off error will occur. Nevertheless, because the calculation is performed for every point drawn, the errors are usually insignificant. Only when these round-off errors accumulate do significant errors become apparent.

5.5.7   Drawing a Line Using an Incremental Algorithm

A second algorithm that is popular for drawing a line is the incremental technique. This algorithm bases itself on the linear equations in Equations 5.16 and 5.17, but the technique for solving the equation is different.

A slope can be thought of as an incremental change. If the slope is normalized, it represents the change incurred in the dependent variable based on an incremental change in the independent variable. In this case, the increment amount is equal to 1. For example, if a slope of lengthY/lengthX is equal to 5.0, it can be said that for every step of 1.0 in X, a change of 5.0 occurs in Y. Thus, as the algorithm progresses, the value of the independent variable, in this case

X, is incremented and the value in the dependent variable, in this case Y, is increased by 5.0.

This algorithm is implemented by the following steps.

1. The slope is calculated.

2. A decision is made based on the slope regarding which axis should be the independent variable.

3. An incremental slope is determined based on the change in the dependent variable based on a change of 1 in the independent variable.

4. Two floating-point or fractional integer accumulators are set up. These are loaded with the coordinate pair of one of the endpoints.

5. A point is drawn at the coordinate pair indicated by the rounded-off values of the two accumulators.

6. The independent variable is incremented, and the incremental slope is added to the dependent variable.

7. If the independent variable is not equal to the value at the second endpoint, repeat steps 5–7.

This algorithm requires no multiplications, either integer or floating-point, inside the line-drawing loop. The slope must be considered as either a floating-point or fractional integer. Thus, either floating-point or fractional integer additions are required. The horizontal and vertical accumulators that keep track of the X and Y coordinates must be stored as floating-point or fractional integer variables to ensure that the round-off errors do not accumulate. This technique is usually faster than the previous technique because it requires two floating-point or fractional integer additions per point instead of the one floating-point multiplication and one integer addition of the previous technique. This algorithm also requires a single round-off operation per point.

5.5.8   The Bresenham Line Algorithm

The Bresenham algorithm for drawing a line requires no multiplications and no floating-point or fractional integer variables. Because no real variables are necessary, the line-drawing algorithm exhibits no round-off errors. However, the transformation from the real-world coordinate system to the display coordinate system can still produce round-off errors.

The algebra related to the development of this algorithm is described in *Fundamentals of Interactive Computer Graphics*, by J. D. Foley and A. Van Dam (Addison-Wesley, 1982). The derivation of the algorithm is complicated and will not be repeated here. The operation of the algorithm is straightforward.

This algorithm is called a heuristic algorithm because it utilizes the natural constraints of the pixelated graphics system. Utilizing the discrete display space helps to speed the line-drawing processing. The two previous algorithms made calculations in a real number system and then rounded off to obtain the integer pixel values. The incremental algorithm, described in Section 5.5.7, could use an integer accumulator, thereby eliminating the floating-point operations. However, round-off errors accumulate over the length of the line, causing serious problems, especially with long lines. Bresenham's algorithm uses an integer accumulator but bases the accumulation upon a decision. The decision acts as an intelligent rounding-off process. This eliminates accumulation errors.

As the incremental algorithm calculates the coordinate of the dependent variable, a round-off process selects between two pixels. Because the algorithm is solving the equation with X as the independent variable, the two pixels are immediate vertical neighbors. The following discussion assumes that the X axis represents the independent variable. As in the incremental algorithm described previously, the first point is drawn using the coordinates of one of the endpoints of the line. The X coordinate is incremented by 1. The Y coordinate may or may not be incremented, depending on the result of a decision. To eliminate accumulation errors, a decision is made based on the error measured at every point. This limits both the error incurred at each individual point and the total accumulated error to half of one pixel. This is equivalent to the errors associated with round-off.

The decision is based on a running accumulator called D. The initial value of D is obtained from Equation 5.18.

Equation 5.18 Determination of the Decision Value

$$D = (2 \times dY) - dX$$

In this equation, dY and dX are the incremental horizontal and vertical slopes. At each step, X is incremented by 1, and Y will either be incremented by 1 or not be incremented at all. This decision will be based on the current value of the D decision variable. At each step, D is updated by a value depending on the previous value of D. If the previous value of D is less than 0, Equation 5.19 is used to modify the decision variable.

Equation 5.19 Updating the Decision Variable If $D < 0$

$$D = D + (2 \times dY)$$

If the previous value of D is greater than or equal to 0, Equation 5.20 is used to modify the decision variable.

Equation 5.20   Updating the Decision Variable If D >= 0

$$D = D + 2 \times (dY - dX)$$

Each step through the algorithm loop draws one point. Because the X axis is assumed to be the independent variable, this point is drawn one pixel to the right of the previous pixel. It resides at the same Y value or is above the previous Y value by 1. This inner loop requires one integer comparison and two integer additions per pixel. Over many lines, a stochastic analysis of the decisions would determine that less than two additions are occurring per point because decisions are sometimes made not to increment Y. The calculation of D requires a multiplication by 2, which can be accomplished by a shift left.

Although there are multiplications in this algorithm, they are all powers of 2 multiplications, which enables them to be implemented by shift instructions.

5.5.9   Aliasing

All of the line-drawing algorithms exhibit errors attributable to round-off. These round-off errors are apparent on the display as jagged edges and are associated with undersampling. The terms *aliasing* and *anti-aliasing* are used to describe these jagged edges. These terms originate in sampling theory having to do with the digitization process. The digitization process involves the sampling of continuous signals.

A continuous signal is digitized at a sample rate of some number of samples per second. If the signal being sampled has frequencies present that are greater than half of the sample rate, aliasing occurs. This situation constitutes a one-dimensional example of aliasing. The same principle holds for the two-dimensional case. A continuous line has to be digitized in order to be displayed in a pixelated display format.

Representing a line, or any shape for that matter, on a discrete grid of points will likely result in aliasing. If the resolution of the display is high enough, the human eye might not be able to detect the aliasing errors. The EGA/VGA resolution of 640 by 350 is far too small to eliminate the visual perception of aliasing at normal viewing distances.

5.5.10   Anti-aliasing

It is possible to use a technique called *anti-aliasing*, which has the effect of removing these jagged edges. Short of adding more resolution, there is no way to truly remove the effects of aliasing. However, if the display adapter can display sufficient gray scale, the effects of aliasing can be diminished. This technique draws a line in different intensities, even though the line is meant to be drawn in one intensity.

Suppose a dot falls halfway between two pixels. The dot would be drawn in one or the other pixel at full intensity without anti-aliasing. With anti-aliasing, the dot is drawn in both pixels at half intensity. The resulting energy is the same and the result is quite impressive. This technique can be successful at enhancing the appearance of a display that is unappealing because of jagged lines. This enhancement occurs at the expense of blurring and additional processing time. It is usually faster to utilize a higher-resolution display than it is to perform anti-aliasing on a lower-resolution display.

5.5.11 Drawing Horizontal Lines

A special routine to draw horizontal lines can speed up the process of drawing lines. The Y coordinate of the line remains constant, and the line ranges between the X coordinates of the two endpoints. A pixel is drawn at each pixel position between these two endpoints on a single scan line of the display. A pixel is addressed in display memory by a byte address and a pixel location address. In a bit-mapped display, each byte contains up to eight bits from different pixels. A general point-drawing routine would access any of the bits within this byte independently, requiring a move operation per bit. A horizontal line-drawing routine can take advantage of the nature of the bit-map display. All bits within a byte that are included in the horizontal line can be updated in a single move operation.

5.5.12 Drawing Vertical Lines

A special routine to draw vertical lines can likewise speed up the process of drawing lines. The X coordinate of the line remains constant, and the line ranges between the Y coordinates of the two endpoints. A pixel is drawn on each scan line of the display, in one column between the endpoint scan lines. A pixel is addressed in display memory by a byte address and a pixel location address. The pixel location address refers to the bit position within the byte that contains the data relevant to the desired pixel. As the vertical line is drawn, this value will not change. Vertical neighboring pixels are separated in display memory by a number of bytes equal to the width of the virtual image. As each pixel is drawn, a new byte address is calculated. If the line is drawn from the smallest Y coordinate to the largest, the byte address is incremented by the virtual width. Vertical lines can be drawn rapidly, because only one addition is required per point.

5.5.13 Clipping

Keeping data within a window requires a technique called *clipping*. Clipping determines which lines should be drawn into a window, which should not be drawn, and which portions of a line should be drawn when the line is located partially within a window. Other data structures—for example, polygons—must also be calculated to determine which parts fit into a given window. In the case of bit-mapped graphics, all that is necessary to fit a portion of data into a window is to select the starting address and the height and width of the data and to move it into the window. This is much simpler than the situation in which data is being generated in a vector format.

The calculations involved in clipping lines can be difficult and time-consuming. One technique compares each point of the line to the endpoints of the window before it is drawn into the display. This is simple, although it requires four comparisons per point for every point on the line. If the line is much larger than the window, this technique can be extremely time-consuming. A better solution would be to determine where the line intersects the window and to calculate and draw only those points contained within the window.

The brute-force method to determine these intersection points involves calculating the intersection of the line and the edges of the window. If the endpoints of the line fall within the window, they should be used as the endpoints of the line. If the line crosses the window, the intersection points should be used as the line endpoint. Only those points inside the window should be calculated and drawn. This involves an inordinate amount of calculation because both endpoints of every line must be checked. When the window is large and most lines fall completely within it, or when the window is small and both endpoints fall outside of it, this clipping procedure can be very inefficient.

A technique designed by Cohen-Sutherland uses an effective means of determining which lines fall entirely within the window and which fall entirely outside of the window. These lines can be drawn or not drawn without requiring the lengthy intersection calculations. Because the window is assumed to have horizontal and vertical edges, the equation for the line in question can be solved for the intersection point of the line and the horizontal or vertical border of the window. This calculation is far simpler than the calculation of the intersection of the actual window edge and the line in question.

In the Cohen-Sutherland technique, the line is continually subdivided until the remaining line may be trivially accepted or rejected. The standard linear equations $x=x+(1/m)y$ and $y=y+mx$ are used to calculate the intersection point of the line and the lines extended from the borders of the window. The slope of the line, m, is determined by dividing the vertical length of the line by the horizontal length of the line. The line is then translated upward, downward, to the left, or to the right in order to position the endpoint of the line at the intersection point of the extended border. Note that the intersection of the line and the extended border is not the same as the intersection of the line with the actual window edge. For example, the line may intersect with the extended left edge of the window above or below the actual window. Thus, additional decisions are necessary to determine if the new line can be trivially accepted or rejected. A description of this technique can be found in *Fundamentals of Interactive Computer Graphics*, J. D. Foley and A. Van Dam (Addison-Wesley, 1982).

5.6   THE CIRCLE

Several techniques are available for drawing circles. Unlike lines, which have a constant slope, circles have slopes that are constantly changing, ranging from minus infinity through 0 to positive infinity. The constant slope of lines allows the programmer the luxury of deciding which coordinate is best suited to be the independent variable. This is not the case with circles.

A circle is defined by the sum-of-squares equation listed in Equation 5.21.

Equation 5.21   Equation of a Circle

$$\text{Radius}^2 = X^2 + Y^2$$

If the X coordinate is selected as the independent variable, Equation 5.22 can be used to solve this equation. It should be noted that for every value of X there are two values for Y, representing the positive and negative solution to the square root.

Equation 5.22   Solving the Circle Equation for X

$$Y = +/- (\text{Radius}^2 - X^2)^{1/2}$$

5.6.1   Utilizing Symmetry

Symmetry can be utilized to improve the speed of a circle-drawing program because a circle is highly symmetric. Because it is symmetric about the X axis, only angles of 0 to 180 degrees need to be drawn. This symmetry is accounted for in the positive and negative solutions of Equation 5.22. Because the circle is symmetric about the Y axis, only angles of 0 to 90 degrees need to be handled independently. Similarly, the circle is symmetric about the 45-degree axis, requiring only 0 to 45 degrees to be handled. Thus, a circle can be completely drawn by replicating the arc from 0 to 45 degrees eight times. This can save a considerable amount of time. Symmetry about a circle is illustrated in Figure 5.16.

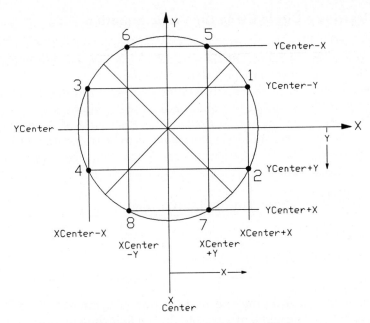

FIGURE 5.16 Symmetry about a Circle

The equations that are used to determine the eight symmetric points given the calculated values of X and Y and the center coordinates X_Center,Y_Center are listed in Equation 5.23.

Equation 5.23 Utilizing the Symmetry of a Circle

X1 = X_Center + X	Y1 = Y_Center + Y	original point
X2 = X_Center + X	Y2 = Y_Center − Y	X reflection
X3 = X_Center − X	Y3 = Y_Center + Y	Y reflection
X4 = X_Center − X	Y4 = Y_Center − Y	X/Y reflection
X5 = X_Center + Y	Y5 = Y_Center + X	45 reflection
X6 = X_Center − Y	Y6 = Y_Center + X	45,X reflection
X7 = X_Center + Y	Y7 = Y_Center − X	45,Y reflection
X8 = X_Center − Y	Y8 = Y_Center − X	45,X,Y reflection

5.6.2 Drawing a Circle Using the Circle Equation

Drawing a circle using Equation 5.22 uses techniques similar to the techniques used to draw a line. A coordinate is selected as the independent variable, and the equation is solved with respect to this variable.

The parameters of a circle usually include the center coordinates of the circle and the radius. The solution to Equation 5.22 will yield bipolar results if the center of the coordinate system is the same as the center of the circle. This is usually not the case, and the circle equation has to be translated to the desired center of the circle. The translation process is accomplished using the calculations in Equations 5.24.

Equation 5.24 Translating a Circle to a Center Point

$$X\_Circle = X + X\_Center$$

$$Y\_Circle = Y + Y\_Center$$

The circle is drawn utilizing the high degree of symmetry. The X axis is assumed to be the independent variable. In the following algorithm, it ranges from the X projection at 0 degrees to the X projection at 45 degrees. The X projections are determined from Equation 5.25.

Equation 5.25 Determining the X Limits

$$XStart = Radius \times Cos(theta) \text{ where } theta = 0 \text{ degrees}$$

$$XStart = Radius \times Cos(0) = Radius$$

$$XEnd = Radius \times Cos(theta) \text{ where } theta = 45 \text{ degrees}$$

$$XEnd = Radius \times Cos(45) = Radius \times .7071$$

Using the circle equation to draw a circle involves the following steps.

1. Determine the X_Start and X_End limits according to Equation 5.25.

2. Solve Equation 5.22 for the positive solution for Y, given X.

3. Translate the X index and the solution for Y to take advantage of the eight-way symmetry. This translation is indicated in Equations 5.23.

4. Draw the eight pixels as indicated in Step 4.

5. Increment the X variable.

6. Repeat steps 2 through 6 until the X value is greater than the value of X_End as determined in Step 1.

This method yields a poor image at locations on the circle where the slope is greater than 1, especially where the slope approaches infinity. The slope approaches infinity at 0 degrees and at 180 degrees. This solution requires two multiplications, an addition, and worst of all, a square root. The multiplications could require floating-point multiplications because the value can exceed the dynamic range of an integer. There are several techniques for performing a square root, none of which is fast.

5.6.3 Drawing a Circle Using Parametric Equations

A second technique for drawing a circle utilizes the parametric equations for a circle. These equations are listed in Equation 5.26.

Equation 5.26 Parametric Equation for a Circle

$$X = \text{Radius} \times \text{Cos}(\textit{theta})$$

$$Y = \text{Radius} \times \text{Sin}(\textit{theta})$$

Theta is an angle that varies from 0 to 360 degrees. In these equations, *theta* is the independent variable. Drawing a circle is accomplished by incrementing *theta* by a constant value. The pixels drawn at the *X,Y* coordinate pair are subsequently drawn so that they are equally distributed around the circle. The smaller the incremental value, the greater the density of dots along the circle. The smaller the radius of the circle, the fewer dots are required. The circumference of a circle is $2 \times \pi \times \text{radius}$. If the radius is 100 pixels, the circumference is 628 pixels. Therefore, at least 628 pixels should be drawn so that the circle appears to be a solid line. If the angular resolution of .5 degrees is selected, 720 pixels will be drawn. This might not be enough for many applications.

When working with these parametric equations, it is important to remember that the center of the circle must be considered as the origin. To draw a circle away from the origin, the center of the circle must be translated to the desired location before drawing occurs.

Another speed enhancer is to create sine and cosine tables and thereby reduce the *sin* and *cosine* calculations to table lookups. These tables can be lengthy, but they are often worth the sizable time savings.

A circle can be drawn using the parametric equations following these steps.

1. Set the *theta* value to 0.

2. Solve Equation 5.26 for *X* and *Y*, given *theta*.

3. Translate the solution *X* and *Y* to take advantage of the eight-way symmetry. This translation is indicated in Equation 5.23.

4. Draw the eight pixels, as indicated in Step 3.

5. Increment the *theta* variable by the desired amount.

6. Repeat Steps 2 through 6 until the *theta* value is greater than 45 degrees.

5.6.4 Bresenham's Circle Equation

A third technique was discovered by Bresenham, and it is similar to his line equation in that it requires no floating-point variables or multiplications. Like the line algorithm, this technique is also based on a decision variable. The decision is based on the value of a decision variable, D, where D is initialized according to Equation 5.27.

Equation 5.27 Initialization of the Decision Variable

$$D = 3 - (2 \times \text{Radius})$$

Either X or Y can be considered as the independent variable because of the symmetry of the circle. Suppose that X is the independent variable. X is initialized to 0 and incremented in each iteration of the algorithm. The X variable ranges from 0 to a value less than Y. Y is initialized to a value equal to the radius. Each iteration through the algorithm draws one pixel. The sign of D determines whether Y should be decremented. It also dictates the adjustment that is to be made on the decision variable, D. The adjustment is indicated in Equation 5.28.

Equation 5.28 Adjustment to the Index Variable

$$D = D + (4 \times X) + 6 \qquad \text{if } D < 0$$
$$D = D + 4 \times (X - Y) + 10 \quad \text{if } D >= 0$$

Because the X variable ranges from 0 to Y, only one-eighth of the circle is calculated. The symmetry is used to draw the remaining points. It should be noted that $X = Y$ at an angle of 45 degrees.

Although there are multiplications in this algorithm, they are all powers-of-two multiplications, which enables them to be implemented by shift instructions.

5.7 THE IMAGE

Images are different than line drawings, just as a photograph of a person is different from a stick figure. Line drawings are referred to as wire drawings because they appear to be objects made from wires. Wire-model drawings are frequently done in two or three dimensions. Images are different from line drawings in that surfaces and shadings are used to give the appearance of realism. Images may or may not represent real-world objects.

The resolution restrictions that affect wire drawings also affect images. Images impose an additional constraint upon graphics systems that involve realistic gray scale or color scale. In order to obtain a lifelike representation of the color shadings of human skin, 24 bits of color may be required. These 24 bits are in contrast to the six bits of color available on the EGA and the eighteen bits of color available on the VGA. Pseudocolor effects can be achieved using dithering techniques. A dithering technique does not rely on solid colors alone to represent shadings. One color can be scattered into a second color to produce a perceived third color. The patterns selected for the scattering are random. The programmer must be willing to sacrifice spatial resolution for the improved color. Black-and-white dithering techniques are common when images are portrayed on printers.

5.7.1 Writing Images

Images in a two-dimensional coordinate space are most commonly represented within a rectangular window. The images typically occupy more than one display plane, providing for gray scale or color scale. The image can be written into display memory a plane at a time or a pixel at a time.

5.7.2 Writing an Image a Bit Plane at a Time

Reading or writing an image a plane at a time is fast because eight neighboring horizontal pixels can be written in a single byte move operation. Neighboring horizontal bytes in display memory occupy sequential location. Therefore, a block move instruction can be used to move one horizontal line at a time. This further speeds up the process. If the image being written is as wide as the virtual image, a single block move instruction can write an entire plane of the image. If four bit planes are active, four block moves are required.

A limitation to reading or writing an image a plane at a time arises when the data is not organized in a bit-mapped format. An image that possesses gray or color scale is often stored one pixel intensity at a time. A C array, for example, stores a two-dimensional array as a series of magnitudes, one magnitude per pixel. This format is called a packed display format. In order to translate the packed display format into a bit plane format, it is necessary to split the elements in the magnitude array into the desired number of bit plane arrays. This is accomplished by a series of shift operations, and it can be time-consuming.

5.7.3 Writing an Image a Pixel at a Time

A display that is organized in a packed display format is designed to be read or written to a pixel at a time. The EGA/VGA has a couple of packed display formats, but the majority are bit plane formats. It is possible to write packed data to the bit plane display a pixel at a time using the Set/Reset and Enable Set/ Reset Registers.

This operation is not as fast as the plane-at-a-time technique because only one pixel can be written at a time. If the image occupies all four display planes, four bits can be modified in a single operation. Both the OUT instruction and the move instructions are necessary to achieve this result, so it operates much slower. In addition, no block move instructions can be utilized because the Set/Reset function is implemented in a register, requiring the OUT instructions.

It is not possible to read the data from the display memory a pixel at a time in the EGA/VGA. The display memory is restricted to a bit plane organization during read operations. Although the Read Point BIOS call reads a byte at a time, it is actually reading each bit plane separately and accumulating the full resolution of the pixel in sequential accesses to each bit plane.

5.7.4 Image Data Compression

Bit-mapped images are large, and even the largest of disks can get overburdened. In addition, it takes a considerable amount of time to read and write this amount of data. Data-compression techniques are used to alleviate some of the storage and speed restrictions inherent in image manipulation. Effective data-compression techniques are highly desirable and most PC-based imaging software packages incorporate some compression technique. The problem is that no image compression standard was incorporated before all of the software houses selected their algorithms. Thus, communication between different packages is limited. There are several techniques used to perform image data compression. The run-length encoding technique is described below.

5.7.5 Run-length Encoding

Run-length encoding is a one-dimensional data-compression technique that is popular in PC-based graphics packages. Run-length encoding takes advantage of the fact that neighboring horizontal pixels often have the same value. Line drawings stored in a raster bit-mapped format usually have a large amount of space between the lines. This space is usually some consistent background color. Horizontal or nearly horizontal lines would also contain several horizontal neighbors with the same intensity. The compression technique selected the horizontal orientation because display memory is usually oriented horizontally.

Run-length encoding stores sequences of repeated values. The number of repetitions of a particular value is stored along with the pixel value that is repeated. If a run consists of 100 pixels, all with an intensity of 10, instead of storing 100 consecutive values of 10, it is possible to store only two values. These values are the run count, which is 100, and the pixel value, which is 10.

A data reduction of 50 is achieved. Because display memory is often organized so that one horizontal row directly follows a second horizontal row, two-dimensional blocks of similar value can also take advantage of this compression.

If pixels in a horizontal line are all different, the data-compression technique can work to a disadvantage. Suppose 100 horizontal pixels have no two adjacent pixels with the same value. The run-length encoding technique would have to store 200 values for these 100 pixels. A compression factor of .5 would occur. It is possible and popular to use hybrid procedures that incorporate both techniques. If the algorithm is given some intelligence, it can search ahead and determine whether a run-length encoding scheme or a direct scheme is more efficient. Based on its decision, the next portion of the data is stored in one of the formats. A data structure is then necessary to ensure that the resulting encoded data can be decoded when the image is redrawn. This structure incorporates some delimiter that indicates whether run-length encoded data or raw data follows. These data structures can be quite complicated, but they are deterministic and can be decoded exactly. This form of data compression does not degrade the image, because the reproduction is an exact duplicate of the original.

5.7.6 Image Processing

Image processing performs mathematical operations on two-dimensional images. Some popular operations include statistical analysis, filtering, edge detection, coordinate transformation, spectral analysis, contrast enhancement, and pattern recognition. Image-processing techniques operate on an entire image or on a window within the image. Many of these techniques are beginning to find their way into computer graphics applications. A primary requirement for many of these image-processing algorithms is a display buffer with a depth of at least eight bits per pixel. A fuzzy border exists between the fields of computer graphics and image processing. Computer graphics primarily involves the synthesis of images; image processing is concerned with the analysis of images. Often these fields overlap.

Statistical analysis algorithms include determining the number of pixels in a window, the intensity histogram, the mean intensity, the median intensity, the standard deviation, and the center of gravity within the window. All of these techniques involve counting and summing the intensities in a given window.

The number of pixels within a window is calculated by subtracting the lower coordinate in the horizontal and vertical directions from the respective higher value coordinate and adding 1. The addition of 1 is very important. Recall that if a window begins at pixel 2 and ends at pixel 3, the window is two pixels wide. These two numbers represent the height and width of the rectangle, and they would be multiplied together to determine the number of pixels per window. If the window were not oriented in the horizontal and vertical directions, more sophisticated techniques would have to be employed.

The intensity histogram is a measure of the magnitude distribution within a window. It is determined by building an array of numbers, the length of which is equal to the number of possible intensities. Each pixel within the window is read and the corresponding counter is incremented. Array element 0 is incremented every time a pixel of 0 intensity is encountered. All other elements within the histogram array are similarly handled. When all pixels have been counted, the resulting array contains the intensity histogram.

The mean intensity of a window provides a measure of the average intensity within the window. The average intensity is obtained by accumulating the intensities of each pixel in the window and dividing the result by the total number of pixels in the window.

The standard deviation of a window is determined by summing the absolute values of the difference between each pixel intensity and the mean. This resultant value is divided by the total number of pixels in the window. It provides a measure of the spread of intensities within the window. A window of constant intensity would provide a standard deviation of 0.

5.8 COLOR THEORY

The computer graphics programmer uses color theory to help select colors to represent data. In the EGA, there are 64 possible colors, and in the VGA, there are 256 Kcolors. Selecting a color or color combination is made easier with even a cursory knowledge of color theory.

Gray scale or color scale is a monotonic progression of color based on intensity or brightness. A low value in the data would be represented by a low-intensity shade of gray. A high value in the data would be represented by a high-intensity shade of gray. Color can also be used to represent monotonic data. The shades of red could be used as effectively as the shades of gray. Color shading can also be used effectively to represent biphasic relationships. Monochrome gray scale can differentiate accurately between lower and higher intensities. However, gray scale cannot effectively display data that ranges from +10 through 0 to −10. In this case, the blue monotonic scale can be assigned to the negative numbers. The value 0 would be represented by no blue, −1 would be the minimum intensity blue, and up to −10 would be the maximum intensity blue. Red can similarly be assigned to the positive values—the value 0 being represented by no red, +1 as minimum red, and up to +10 as the maximum intensity red.

5.8.1 Describing Color

Colors are measured in a variety of ways. Artists have chosen the terms *tints*, *shade*, and *tones* to describe color. Other commonly used terms include *hue*, *saturation* or *chroma*, and *brightness* or *value*. Users of color select terminology that best suits their needs.

Artists are accustomed to pure saturated pigments. When they add black to the pigment to decrease its brightness, they use the term *shade*. In order to change the saturation of the color, they add white to the pigment. The resultant color is termed *tint*, and it relates to the pastel quality of the color. The color can also be modified by adding both white and black. This modifies the *tone* of the color. The addition of black and/or white to a pigment does not affect the *hue* of the color. Either a different pigment must be selected or pigments must be added to one another to affect the hue.

5.8.2   Color Models

Several models are used to represent color. All of these models utilize a three-dimensional space. It is interesting to note that the human eye has three different types of color receptors on the retina. Perhaps four-dimensional models would be required if a fourth color receptor was present. Colors defined by one model can be transformed into other color coordinate systems. Each model is defined to describe colors effectively for specific applications. It would be clumsy to attempt to describe colors with a model that is unsuited for the application in question. As new applications of color arise, new models will be defined to suit the needs of the application.

5.8.3   The CIE Chromaticity Scale

The CIE chromaticity scale decomposes a color into three primary colors termed X, Y, and Z. This scale is used as a reference when colors are compared qualitatively. The CIE chromaticity diagram is used to determine the dominant wavelengths of a color or the complement of a color. The color is decomposed into dominant wavelengths that, when added together in the proper proportions, produce the color. The three CIE primary colors are not visible, but they can be combined to form any color that the eye can perceive.

5.8.4   The RGB Color Model

The RGB color model is based on a three-dimensional Cartesian coordinate system. Color monitors and most color graphics systems utilize the RGB color model. A color cube represents these three dimensions in Figure 5.17.

Red is represented on one axis, blue is on a second and green is on a third. The origin of the color cube is red=0, green=0, and blue=0, which corresponds to black. Moving away from the origin along the cube diagonal produces gray scale, because equal parts of red, green, and blue are represented. The end of the diagonal is at red=maximum, blue=maximum, and green=maximum, which corresponds to white. Any color represented in an RGB format is represented by a dot somewhere within this color cube. The projections of the dot onto the three axes of the cube produce the intensity of each of the three colors.

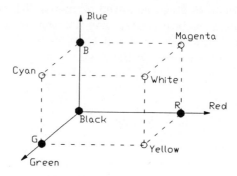

FIGURE 5.17 The Color Cube

5.8.5 The CMY Color Model

The three subtractive primary colors of cyan, magenta, and yellow are used in the CMY color model. These three colors are the complements of red, green and blue. When these three colors are subtracted from white light, red, green, and blue colors are produced. For example, cyan absorbs green and blue and therefore reflects red. This color model is useful when color devices that deposit colored pigments onto paper are used.

5.8.6 The YIQ Color Model

The YIQ model is used in color television. It is based on three coordinates that are especially well suited for coding color signals for display on a monochrome monitor. The YIQ model maximizes the amount of perceived information transmitted in a given frequency band. This was useful in the early days of television. Now that broadcast and receiving electronics have improved, it is easier to handle the higher frequencies. The encoding scheme used in the United States is called the NTSC standard. It is possible to convert from the YIQ model to and from the RGB model. As a result, RGB-to-NTSC converters are possible. This allows computer-based RGB signals that are operating in the proper frequency band to be converted to NTSC signals compatible with standard color televisions and videotape recorders.

5.8.7 The HSV and HLS Color Models

Although the models previously described are effective at implementing color processing equipment, they are awkward when trying to describe the colors in human terms. Two models that are better suited for description are called the HSV and the HLS models. The HSV model stands for hue, saturation, and value, and the HLS model utilizes hue, lightness, and saturation. Conversion techniques are available to convert the HSV or HLS models into the commonly used RGB model. These models are easier to describe. These models can be used during operator interaction and the selected values can then be converted to the RGB mode for the display hardware.

5.8.8 Color Dithering

When a limited color system is involved, it is difficult or impossible to represent accurately colors and color shadings found in the real world. The EGA can display only sixteen simultaneous colors. If the programmer desires more colors, other techniques must be employed. One such technique is called *color dithering*. In contrast, the VGA can provide a mode that displays 256 simultaneous colors. Color dithering may not be necessary or desirable in this mode.

Color dithering works in a similar fashion to black-and-white dithering. It trades off resolution for an increase in the number of perceived colors. A small box of pixels is selected to become the primitive pixel. The size of the box determines the total number of possible colors that can be represented in the pixel. A 2-by-2 pixel box would decrease the overall resolution of the display by a factor of four, but it would greatly increase the number of perceived colors. If the graphics system incorporates four display planes, sixteen simultaneous colors can be displayed. If four pixels are used per pixel box, the number of perceived colors is increased to 64 possible colors per pixel box.

In the high-resolution modes—640 by 350 or 640 by 480—this decrease in resolution may be acceptable. In the low-resolution modes—320 by 200—this decrease in resolution typically will be unacceptable. In a black-and-white system, hard-copy on a laser printer often employs dithering techniques. The high resolution of the laser can produce effective shadings using these techniques. The dot size is small enough that the dithering patterns cannot be detected. If a color high-resolution plotter is used, color dithering can also be effective.

Chapter 6

Alphanumeric Processing

6.1 EGA/VGA CHARACTER PROCESSING

Word processors, spreadsheets, database programs, desktop utilities, the DOS operating system, and user-written applications software are the most common and demanding text-related software products. In order to execute these programs rapidly, the EGA/VGA is designed for high-speed text manipulation. This speed is essential in all text-processing applications, because no one wants to wait while the screen is refreshed. The EGA/VGA provides the programmer with a flexible environment to achieve a wide variety of alphanumeric effects.

Alphanumerics may be displayed in a variety of colors or with various monochrome attributes. In the monochrome modes, characters may be represented in low or high intensity, in reversed intensity, with underlines, or blinking. In the color alphanumeric modes, one of sixteen colors can be selected for the foreground and another for the background of each character. The character code selects a character shape from fonts of 512 characters. In addition, characters may be commanded to blink or be underlined.

6.1.1 Local Character Sets

The EGA/VGA contains character sets in the BIOS ROMS. A character set, once loaded and operational, consists of 256 characters. Two of these character sets may be active at a time, providing a combined character set that is 512 characters long. Because these fonts are downloadable, the programmer may load additional fonts. These fonts are termed *user fonts*.

The EGA is equipped with three character sets. Two of these, one having 8-by-8 characters and the other 8-by-14 characters, are complete 256-character fonts. The third is a 9-by-14 supplemental character set. Up to four character fonts, each 256 characters long, may be loaded into the EGA.

The VGA is equipped with five character sets. Three of these—one having 8-by-8 characters, another 8-by-14, and the third 8-by-16—are complete

256-character fonts. Two are supplemental character sets, one having 9-by-14 characters and the other 9-by-16. Up to eight character fonts, each 256 characters long, may be loaded into the VGA.

6.1.2 Special Alphanumeric Features

Complex alphanumeric screens can be generated utilizing the split screen, panning, and scrolling features. Selected windows within the screen can be programmed to scroll while others remain stationary. Tasteful and effective use of color in conjunction with these complex alphanumeric operations can produce user-friendly screens that are simple to understand and contain a great deal of information.

In order to process text with minimum delay, it is necessary to move large amounts of text rapidly about the screen. To facilitate this, the EGA/VGA incorporates alphanumeric display modes in addition to the graphics modes. Only characters that fit into the active character box size can be displayed during these alphanumeric modes. Although it is not possible to draw dots or lines in the alphanumeric modes, the IBM extended character set does provide a means of drawing horizontal lines, vertical lines, and symbolic characters. These can be used in the alphanumeric modes to perform primitive graphics. In addition, the programmer may select from several user fonts that contain graphic character patterns.

6.1.3 Processing Characters Quickly

Characters can be processed quickly in the alphanumeric modes because they are represented on the screen by a character code and an attribute code, both of which are one byte. As a result, a single character can be represented in 2 bytes. Suppose that a sixteen-color alphanumeric mode is active and the screen resolution is 25 lines of text by 80 characters per line. The 25-by-80 character resolution totals 2,000 characters per screen or 4,000 bytes per screen. Each character is represented by an 8-by-14 character box. If the characters are represented graphically, each character will be represented by 14 bytes per plane, because of the 8-by-14 character box. There are four bit planes. Thus, 14 times 4 produces 56 bytes per character. The total number of bytes needed to represent a full screen would be 56 bytes per character times 2,000 characters per screen, which totals 112,000 bytes per screen. The alphanumeric mode provides a 28-to-1 data-reduction advantage over the same data when represented in a graphics mode. Thus, although the alphanumeric modes are limited in their functionality, they allow rapid character manipulation.

6.1.4 Flexibility of the Alphanumeric Modes

The limited functionality of the alphanumeric modes is compensated for by the variety of features available within these modes. Resolution, character size,

refers to operation of the adapter

TABLE 6.1 Alphanumeric Display Modes

Mode (Hex)	Adapter	# Chars (X/Y)	Char Box	# of Pages	Resolution in Pixels
0 ,1	EGA/VGA	40/25	8 by 8	8	320 by 200
0*,1*	EGA/VGA	40/25	8 by 14	8	320 by 350
0+,1+	VGA	40/25	9 by 16	8	320 by 400
2 ,3	EGA/VGA	80/25	8 by 8	8	640 by 200
2*,3*	EGA/VGA	80/25	8 by 14	4/8	640 by 350
2+,3+	VGA	80/25	9 by 16	4/8	640 by 400
7	EGA/VGA	80/25	9 by 14	8	720 by 350
7+	VGA	80/25	9 by 16	8	720 by 400

refers to operation of the VGA adapter

character color, special character attributes, large character sets, and down-loadable character fonts provide a wide variety of excellent alphanumeric capabilities. These programming features give the programmer the flexibility to configure these boards to accommodate a wide variety of applications.

The EGA/VGA can be programmed to operate in a number of different display resolutions. The display memory is organized so that a tradeoff exists between the resolution of an individual page and the total number of available pages. The screen resolution multiplied by the number of bits per pixel and by the number of available pages must fit within the amount of memory resident in the display memory. Therefore, the greater the screen resolution, the fewer the number of possible pages. Table 6.1 lists the standard EGA alphanumeric display modes and their associated alphanumeric resolutions, display formats, total number of pages, and pixel resolution.

The asterisk in the column entitled "Mode" refers to the operation of the adapter. It applies to the EGA when the EGA is configured with a high-resolution EGA monitor or a multisync monitor. It applies to the VGA when the VGA is programmed to operate in a 350-scan-line mode. This is accomplished by programming the Vertical Size (VS) field of the Miscellaneous Output Register. No such field exists for the EGA. In these cases, the vertical resolution of the display is 350 scan lines.

The plus in the column entitled "Mode" refers to the operation of the VGA adapter. It applies to the VGA when the VGA is programmed to operate in a 400-scan-line mode. This is accomplished by programming the VS field of the Miscellaneous Output Register. No such mode exists for the EGA. In these cases, the vertical resolution of the display is 400 scan lines.

Although these are the standard modes, other display modes are possible. Several manufacturers of EGA boards have programmed 640-by-480 and 800-by-600 display resolutions. Manufacturers will certainly program new display resolutions for the VGA as well. In addition, the programmer can set up specialized display modes. However, because of compatibility issues and the complexity of designing nonstandard display resolutions, programming display mode resolutions is not recommended. See the register definitions in Chapter 10 for details relating to specialized modes.

6.2   CHARACTER SHAPE

An alphanumeric character consists of a pattern contained within a rectangular box of dots. The larger the region, the more dots there are per character, resulting in greater character resolution. Given a fixed screen resolution, the price paid for added character resolution is fewer characters per screen. If both greater character resolution and more characters per screen are desired, additional display memory must be allocated and higher-speed display electronics, along with a higher-bandwidth monitor, must be provided.

6.2.1   Character Box Size

Each character font has a specified character box size. This size dictates the amount of memory necessary to store one character. In order to conserve space, the character shape is stored independently from the character attribute. This means that the character shape can be represented with one bit per pixel, even if the display is in a mode that uses four bits per pixel. Not until the last step before display is the attribute information added to the shape to produce the actual dot pattern output to the monitor.

6.2.2   Representing Characters in Memory

A character is represented in memory by a group of bytes. The EGA/VGA boards allow character widths of eight or nine pixels, and advanced EGA implementations allow characters up to sixteen pixels. A character is represented by a group of horizontal scan lines. A horizontal scan line of a character is represented as a sequence of bytes. Each bit in each byte represents a dot within the character box. The height of the box is represented by consecutive bytes in host or display memory. The first byte corresponds to the top scan line of the character, and the last byte corresponds to the bottom scan line. The most significant bit in each of these bytes represents the far-left pixel of the character. Likewise, the least significant bit represents the far-right pixel. The standard notation for the bits in a byte is represented in Figure 6.1.

This notation allows a one-to-one correspondence between the far-left bit in the byte and the far-left pixel of the character when it is displayed on the screen. This convention is consistent within the many implementations of the EGA. However, it is by no means an industry standard. Many other graphics controllers consider bit 7, the most significant bit, to be the far-right pixel when the character is displayed on the screen.

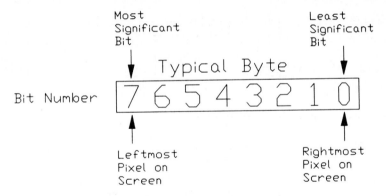

FIGURE 6.1 Bit and Pixel Relationship

6.2.3 Character Tiling

These character boxes are laid onto the screen in a tiled fashion. No space exists between the character boxes, nor is there any overlap between character boxes when they are drawn onto the screen. This is illustrated in Figure 6.2.

Both horizontal and vertical intercharacter space must, therefore, be provided in each character. Normally the intercharacter space is placed at the bottom and right of the character. Figure 6.3 illustrates the typical intercharacter spacing.

6.2.4 Downward-extending Characters

Some characters extend beneath the base of the characters—for example, the lowercase *y*. There are three ways of handling these downward-extending characters. The first two ways are used in small character fonts. The downward-

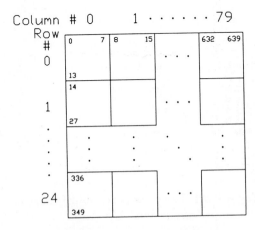

FIGURE 6.2 Character Tiling

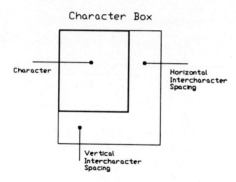

FIGURE 6.3 Intercharacter Spacing

extending portion of the *y* can extend into the intercharacter spacing at the bottom of the character box, or the baseline of the downward-extending character can be pushed up. In large character fonts, the downward extension of the characters can be accommodated by pushing the baseline of all of the characters higher. This provides improved legibility because the lower-extending characters will not touch any tall characters positioned on the line directly above them. These three techniques are illustrated in Figure 6.4.

6.2.5   Character Layout Limitations

Advanced printsetting type functions are possible utilizing the EGA/VGA. Although the alphanumeric modes have no provisions for proportional fonts or kerning, the graphics mode allows software to produce any of these advanced

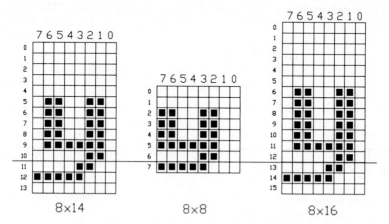

FIGURE 6.4 Downward-extending Characters

printsetting type functions as long as the characters are drawn on a dot-by-dot basis.

Proportional fonts are desirable because they allow characters to have different widths. Thus the character *m* would have a wider character box than would the character *i*. Kerning actually takes into account neighboring pixels to determine the width of characters. For example, the letters *db* appear closer together than the characters *bd*, although the spacing is actually the same. Additional space could be placed between the *d* and *b* in *db* to maintain a uniform appearance. Kerning is effective when lines are justified. Because the EGA can have only one character box size per font but cannot have overlapping characters, neither of these techniques is applicable in the alphanumeric modes. Sophisticated desktop publishing programs utilize kerning techniques in the graphics modes to display alphanumerics on the screen. Again, the tradeoff is speed.

Within the character box, any bit set to 1 will be displayed in the foreground color. Likewise, any bit reset to 0 will be displayed in the background color. The characters are handled differently than in the graphics modes. In the graphics modes, the background or 0 bits are considered transparent, and the characters have no background color other than what was on the screen before the character was drawn.

6.2.6 The 8-by-8 Character Font

The 8-by-8 character font is the smallest of the three local fonts. The character size is typically 7-by-7 pixels within this box. The character is normally left-justified into the character box, leaving the bottom row and right column blank. Special graphics characters and lowercase characters with descenders can extend into these regions. Typically, character boxes are taller than they are wide. Because the 8-by-8 character box is square, additional space exists in the horizontal direction. This permits the characters to be drawn with fatter vertical lines. In most cases, for every pixel that is on, the pixel to the immediate left is turned on. This provides a broader-looking character and fills the extra width available in the character box. For this reason, this character set is often referred to as the *double-dot* character set.

The 8-by-8 character font is typically lacking in character clarity because of its small character box. However, it does allow 25 lines to be displayed on a 200-scan-line monitor or in a 200-scan-line mode. When more than 200 scan lines are available, more than the standard 25 lines may be displayed. At 350 scan lines, it is possible to display 43 character lines using the character font that is 8 scan lines high. The 400-scan-line implementations can display 50 lines, and the 480-line implementations can display 60 lines. A character from the 8-by-8 character font is portrayed in Figure 6.5.

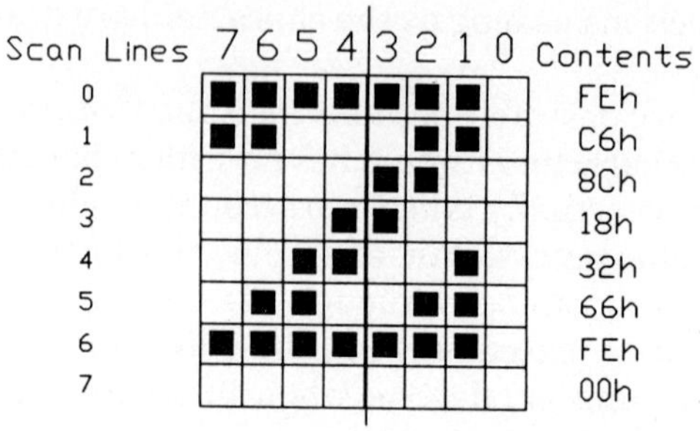

Scan Lines 7 6 5 4 3 2 1 0 Contents

Scan Line	Contents
0	FEh
1	C6h
2	8Ch
3	18h
4	32h
5	66h
6	FEh
7	00h

FIGURE 6.5 Typical 8-by-8 Character

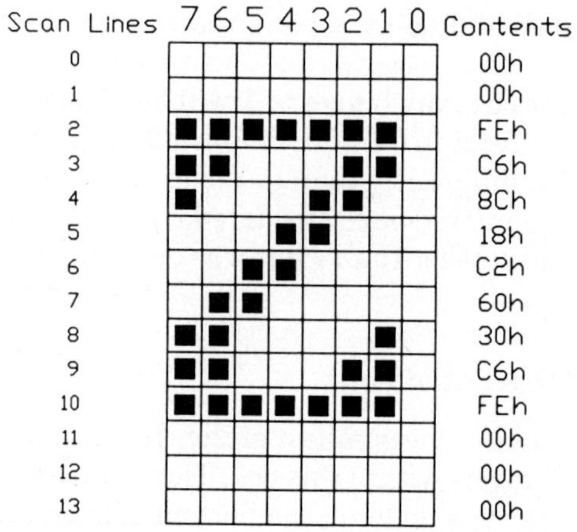

Scan Lines 7 6 5 4 3 2 1 0 Contents

Scan Line	Contents
0	00h
1	00h
2	FEh
3	C6h
4	8Ch
5	18h
6	C2h
7	60h
8	30h
9	C6h
10	FEh
11	00h
12	00h
13	00h

FIGURE 6.6 Typical 8-by-14 Character

6.2.7 The 8-by-14 Character Font

The 8-by-14 character font is similar to the 8-by-8 character font. The characters in this font fill a 7-by-9 area, left-justified in the box. The top two and bottom three scan lines of the character box typically are blank, with the exception of graphics characters and lowercase characters with descenders. The far-right column is typically blank, providing intercharacter spacing.

This font is most often used when the adapter is in a 350-scan-line mode and resolution of 25 character lines per screen is desired. As was true for the 8-by-8 double-dot font, most horizontally neighboring pixels are turned on. A typical 8-by-14 character is represented in Figure 6.6.

6.2.8 The 9-by-14 Character Font

The 9-by-14 character font is the largest of the local fonts. It is actually represented within the BIOS character sets as a supplemental character set. It is called *supplemental* because not all of the 256 characters are provided. This is done to save space because only eight of the nine columns are unique for the majority of the characters. Most characters can be adequately represented within the 8-by-14 character box. In the monochrome alphanumeric display mode 7, there are 720 dots per horizontal scan line. If 80 characters per line are to be displayed, each character may be nine dots wide.

The characters that look good in the 8-by-14 character set are displayed in the 9-by-14 format with the same dot patterns. The 9-by-14 format characters that could benefit from being wider contain dot patterns that are different from the 8-by-14 patterns. These characters are represented within the BIOS supplemental table with one byte per scan line. The ninth bit of the 9-by-14 format is always assumed to be a horizontal intercharacter space and is not represented in the character set. The character shape occupies an 8-by-9 character box, completely filling the width of the character box. The top two and bottom three scan lines of the character box are usually blank, like those of the 8-by-14 box. Typical characters that are included in the supplement are quotation marks (”), the plus sign (+), the minus sign (–), $M, T, V, W, X, Y, Z, m, v,$ and w. Each character within the supplemental font is preceded by its ASCII code. An ASCII code of 00 indicates the end of the supplemental character set. When the 9-by-14 set is loaded, the 8-by-14 character set is first loaded into display memory. All of the character patterns contained within the supplemental character set are then written over the respective 8-by-14 characters. This results in the 9-by-14 character set.

The ninth column can be set either to the background color or to the same value as the eighth dot of the character code being displayed. This is controlled by the B/I field of the Mode Control Register. Setting the ninth dot to the background color is done for characters as indicated above. In the line graphics mode, ASCII characters between 128 and 255 are often used as pseudographics characters. Primitive lines may be drawn using these characters. In order for horizontal lines to be connected, the technique of assuming that the ninth pixel is background will not work. It would cause discontinuities. For these characters, the hardware will copy whatever is in the eighth dot position into the ninth dot position. If the eighth dot position is a 1, signifying a foreground pixel, the ninth dot will subsequently be displayed as a foreground pixel, thereby allowing continuous horizontal lines.

A typical character from the 9-by-14 character font is portrayed in Figure 6.7.

6.2.9 The 8-by-16 Character Font

In the VGA, an 8-by-16 character font is available. This font is used when the VGA is in a 400-scan-line mode, providing 25 character rows per screen. The character patterns are similar to those in the 8-by-14 font, with the exception of an additional two vertical scan lines. A typical 8-by-16 character is shown in Figure 6.8.

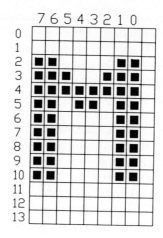

FIGURE 6.7 Typical 9-by-14 Character

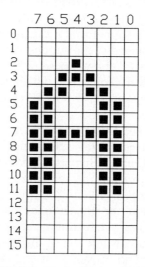

FIGURE 6.8 Typical 8-by-16 Character

6.2.10 The 9-by-16 Character Font

In the VGA, a 9-by-16 character font is available. Like the 8-by-16 character font, this font is used when the VGA is in a 400-scan-line mode, providing 25 character rows per screen. In the VGA, this font is used in display mode 7, which has 720 horizontal pixels per scan line. The 9-dot-wide character provides 80 characters per row. This font is a supplemental font because only a subset of the ASCII character set is provided. The techniques employed to

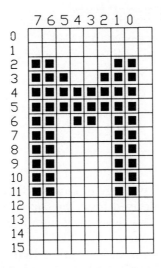

FIGURE 6.9 Typical 9-by-16 Character

display this font are identical to the techniques used for the 9-by-14 font, with the exception of two additional vertical scan lines. A typical 9-by-16 character is shown in Figure 6.9.

6.3 CHARACTER ATTRIBUTES

The alphanumeric modes include modes 0, 1, 2, 3, and 7. Modes 0, 1, 2, and 3 are 16-color modes. Mode 7 is a monochrome mode.

In the alphanumeric modes, the attributes of each character are stored independently from the character shape. The character shapes are stored in the character sets resident in the BIOS or in a user-defined buffer. Once made resident, the character shapes from the character fonts are loaded into display memory. When the characters are displayed on the screen in alphanumeric modes, the character is represented by a one-byte ASCII character code followed by a byte-wide attribute. The attributes define the appearance of the character. The EGA/VGA is alerted to the display type by the Display Type (DT) field in the Mode Control Register. This field dictates whether the character attributes should be considered to be color display attributes or monochrome display attributes.

6.3.1 Monochrome Mode

The only alphanumeric monochrome mode is mode 7. It emulates the MDA or Hercules alphanumeric modes when a monochrome monitor is attached to the graphics system. In this mode, two bits are dedicated to each pixel. Thus, each

TABLE 6.2 Mode 7: Monochrome Attributes

Background (Bits 6–4)	Foreground (Bits 2–0)	Resulting Attribute
0	0	Black
0	1	Underline
0	7	Normal Video (white on black)
7	0	Reverse Video (black on white)
7	7	White

character can be displayed with one of four attributes. The attributes associated with a character are derived from the three least significant bits of the foreground color and from the three least significant bits of the background color in the attribute byte.

If mode 7 is enabled when a monitor other than a monochrome monitor is installed, the EGA typically will not operate correctly with the monitor. The VGA is capable of driving the enhanced color monitor in mode 7.

The functions of the attribute byte, given that a monochrome monitor is attached, are listed in Table 6.2. The foreground field occupies bits 2–0, and the background field occupies bits 4–6.

These fields operate in conjunction with the two special attribute fields that control the intensity and blinking. Bit 3 contains the intensify field and bit 7 contains the blinking field. Some typical display attributes that combine the special fields with the foreground and background fields are listed in Table 6.3.

It should be noted that the underline function is normally disabled when any mode other than mode 7 is active. At Mode Set, the underline feature is disabled for all modes other than mode 7. The programmer must write the proper underline location into the Underline Location Register after a Mode Set. The

TABLE 6.3 Mode 7: Examples of Monochrome Attributes

Blink (Bit 7)	Backgrnd (Bits 6–4)	Intens (Bit 3)	Foregrnd (Bits 2–0)	Code (Hex)	Attribute
0	0	0	7	07	Normal
0	0	1	7	0F	Intense
0	0	0	1	01	Underline
0	0	1	1	09	Intense Underline
0	7	0	0	70	Reversed
1	7	0	0	F0	Blinking Reversed

TABLE 6.4 Mode 7: Palette Registers

Register # (Hex)	Register Value (Hex)	Register # (Hex)	Register Value (Hex)
0	00	8	10
1	08	9	18
2	08	A	18
3	08	B	18
4	08	C	18
5	08	D	18
6	08	E	18
7	08	F	18

Underline Location Register determines the scan line in the character box where this underlining occurs.

The monochrome monitor uses bit 3 for the video field and bit 4 for the intensify field. Thus, an 8 hex causes bit 3, the video bit, to be activated; a 10 hex causes bit 4, the intensified bit, to be activated. An 18 hex results in both being activated. Table 6.4 lists the default values present in the Palette Registers in mode 7.

Note that an attribute value of 0 maps to an output color of 00 hex. Any attribute value between 1 and 7 maps to an output color of 08 hex. An attribute value of 8 maps to an output color of 10 hex. Any attribute value between 9 and F hex maps to an output color of 18 hex.

6.3.2 Sixteen-color Mode

In the sixteen-color mode, the character has a variety of different attributes. One option allows the attribute byte to select from one of sixteen colors for the foreground and one of sixteen colors for the background of each character. A second option allows the attribute byte to select from one of sixteen colors for the foreground and one of eight colors for the background. In addition, the character may be programmed to blink. A third option allows the attribute byte to select from one of eight foreground colors, and the character may be represented by one of 512 character patterns. These 512 character patterns come from the chaining of two of the 256-long character sets. The background may be one of sixteen background colors or one of eight background colors; in addition, the option of blinking is available. These attribute options are illustrated in Figure 6.10.

The default colors loaded into the sixteen Palette Registers associated with the colors called out by the attribute byte are listed in Table 6.5.

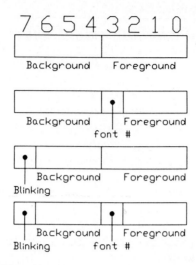

FIGURE 6.10 Attribute Byte in the 16-color Mode

TABLE 6.5 Default Colors for a 16-color Palette

Palette Register (Hex)	Color
0	Black
1	Blue
2	Green
3	Cyan
4	Red
5	Magenta
6	Brown
7	White
8	Gray
9	Light blue
A	Light green
B	Light cyan
C	Light red
D	Light magenta
E	Light brown (yellow)
F	Bright white

6.4 DISPLAY MEMORY

The EGA/VGA display memory is organized into four bit planes, each up to 64 Kbytes long. These bit planes contain from one to eight pages, depending on the size of each display page and the total amount of display memory available. When the EGA/VGA is in an alphanumeric mode, the display memory is used to store the character codes, the character attribute bytes, and the character fonts. The display memory is accessed indirectly by the hardware to obtain the actual character dot patterns for output to the monitor. This is quite different from the operation of the display in a graphics mode. In a graphics mode, the data in the bit planes is a bit-by-bit representation of the character dot patterns.

The four bit planes are accessed at the same address. The address referring to one byte in the host memory address space refers to four bytes in the display memory. Each of these four bytes resides at the same host address, and one byte is associated with each of the four bit planes. From the perspective of the host, the display memory can be thought of as a 32-bit-wide memory. In fact, a 32-bit data bus does exist inside the EGA/VGA and is used to access display memory.

6.4.1 Display Memory in Host Memory Address Space

The Memory Map (MM) field of the Miscellaneous Register dictates the host starting address of the display memory. The possible memory addresses and the associated Memory Map field values are listed in Table 6.6.

Invoking the Set Mode BIOS call (AH = 0) loads the Memory Map field with a starting address, as indicated in Table 6.7.

6.4.2 Bit Plane Utilization

In the alphanumeric modes, codes that represent the character and the character attribute are stored in memory. A single byte is dedicated to each character code, allowing 256 characters to be accessed. A single byte is also dedicated to the attribute of the character.

TABLE 6.6 Display Memory in Host Memory Address Space

Memory Map Field (MM Value)	Beginning Address (Hex)	Amount of Display Memory
0	A0000 – BFFFF	128 Kbytes
1	A0000 – AFFFF	64 Kbytes
2	B0000 – B7FFF	32 Kbytes
3	B8000 – BFFFF	32 Kbytes

TABLE 6.7 Alphanumeric Display Mode Starting Addresses

Mode (Hex)	MM Field	Alpha Format	Address (Hex)
0	3	40 by 25	B8000
1	3	40 by 25	B8000
2	3	80 by 25	B8000
3	3	80 by 25	B8000
7	2	80 by 25	B0000

Bit plane 0 is used to store the character code, and bit plane 1 is used to store the character attribute. The character and attribute pair is stored in host memory, with the character code preceding the character attribute. When the program needs to write to or read from the display memory, the character code should be written to an even address and the attribute should be written to an odd address. Data written to even addresses will be directed to bit plane 0; data written to odd addresses will be directed to bit plane 1.

Display plane 2 is used to store the character font bit patterns. The EGA display memory is segmented into four blocks, each separated by 16 Kbytes. The upper 8 Kbytes of each of these blocks are used to store the bit patterns, and the remaining 8 Kbytes of each block are unused. The VGA is segmented into eight blocks, each separated by 8 Kbytes. The dot patterns of one 256-character set can fit in each of these blocks. Thus, the EGA can hold four resident fonts, and the VGA can hold eight resident fonts.

6.4.3 Display Memory Address Compatibility

In order to maintain compatibility with older displays, it is desirable to begin the alphanumeric memory at the host address of B8000 hex for the Monochrome Display Adapter (MDA) or the Color Graphics Adapter (CGA). In order for the EGA to operate properly with software that produces text output, the default active page 0 of alphanumeric display memory must reside at B0000 hex. When the Monochrome Display Adapter (MDA) or the Hercules Graphics Standard is being emulated, the display memory begins at B0000 hex.

The host memory environment provides 128 Kbytes of address space for display adapters. The 64 Kbytes between host addresses A0000 and AFFFF are dedicated to the EGA, and the 32 Kbytes between host addresses B8000 hex and BFFFF hex are reserved for the MDA and CGA. A fully populated EGA contains 256 Kbytes of display memory organized into four bit planes, each being 64 Kbytes long. The memory will completely fill the space and must be physically strapped to begin at A0000 hex and end at BFFFF hex. This means that the first page of text does not correspond to the lowest address in the EGA display memory. Page 0 of text resides at B8000. Therefore, the first of text resides halfway through the display memory.

6.4.4 Fonts in Display Memory

The smallest character box used on the EGA/VGA is 8 pixels wide by 8 scan lines high. The maximum horizontal resolution of the EGA/VGA in a color mode is 640 pixels. Thus, 80 characters could exist on one horizontal line. The maximum resolution on the standard EGA is 350 scan lines. For the VGA, it is 480 scan lines. This means that 43 character lines can be displayed on one screen using the EGA, and 60 lines can be displayed on one screen using the VGA.

For the EGA, at 80 characters per line by 43 lines, a single screen can display 3,440 characters. At two bytes per character, this translates to 6,880 bytes per page. The specification calls for the EGA to support eight memory resident pages of text. Thus, 55,040 bytes must be reserved for the alphanumerics buffer. For the VGA, at 80 characters per line by 60 lines, a single screen can display 4,800 characters. At two bytes per character, this translates to 9,960 bytes per page. Multiplied by eight display pages, this is equivalent to 76,800 bytes for the alphanumeric buffer.

There are 32,768 bytes available between B8000 hex and the end of the buffer at BFFFF hex. It is therefore necessary to utilize two of the bit planes to store the character and attribute pairs. Using this technique, it is possible to store all eight bit planes of the EGA and seven full display pages of the VGA. One plane is used to store the ASCII character code, and the second plane is used to store the attribute byte associated with the character code. This requires 27,520 bytes for the EGA and 38,400 bytes for the VGA. The memory between A0000 hex and B7FFF hex in these two bit planes is not utilized in these modes.

In order to utilize downloadable character fonts, random access memory (RAM) is allocated to store the actual bit patterns of the characters. The EGA display memory, bit planes 2 and sometimes 3, holds the bit patterns. Host memory could have been used for this purpose, but accessing the bit patterns from host memory is time-consuming. The host memory is used to hold the bit patterns when the EGA/VGA is in a graphics mode because bit planes 2 and 3 are not available. In the EGA/VGA, internal hardware is provided to allow rapid accessing of the character code and the character attribute byte. Once accessed, the character code is quickly converted to an address that points into bit plane 2 and sometimes bit plane 3. The character bit pattern is retrieved from these bit planes and output to the monitor via the output logic. All of this occurs in hardware. If the bit patterns reside in host memory, however, this has to be done with software.

For the EGA, an 8-bit data bus exists between the host and the EGA. This is slow compared to the EGA 32-bit internal data bus. For the planar VGA, a 16-bit path exists between the host and the VGA. A planar VGA is a VGA that is physically located on the backplane of the host, as is true of the IBM System/2 computers. Even this 16-bit data path is slow compared to the internal 32-bit data path. A VGA adapter plugged into a host backplane conforms to the

8-bit bus standard and again is limited by the 8-bit wide bus. Thus, planar VGA implementations are faster than VGA adapters.

6.4.5 Odd/Even Operation

A term that comes up repeatedly in the EGA/VGA documentation is *odd/even*. The Odd/Even (O/E) field of the Mode Register controls whether the odd/even or a sequential addressing mode is active. In a sequential mode, the least significant bit of the host address bus drives the least significant bit of the display memory address bus. In odd/even addressing, the least significant bit of the host address bus is not connected to the least significant bit of the display memory address bus. Rather, it is connected to a multiplexer that selects between odd or even planes. The least significant bit of the memory address bus is obtained from a higher-order host address bus bit, such as bit 14 or bit 16. All other bits of the host memory address bus map directly to the display memory bus. This address bus mapping is illustrated in Table 6.8.

TABLE 6.8 Odd/Even Address Bus Mapping

EGA/VGA Address	Host Memory Address
MA17	A17
MA16	A16
MA15	A15
MA14	A14
MA13	A13
MA12	A12
MA11	A11
MA10	A10
MA09	A09
MA08	A08
MA07	A07
MA06	A06
MA05	A05
MA04	A04
MA03	A03
MA02	A02
MA01	A01
MA00*	A14/A16
MA00†	A00

*word mode

†byte mode

The word mode or byte mode is selected by the Word/Byte (W/B) field in the Mode Control Register. Host address bit A14 or A16 is selected for use as EGA/VGA address bit MA00 by the Address Wrap (AW) field in the Mode Control Register.

This address-switching causes the EGA/VGA display memory to become segmented. A write of two consecutive bytes from host memory is mapped to the same address in the display memory space, but the two bytes are written to different bit planes. Data written to even host addresses is mapped to even bit planes—that is, bit planes 0 or 2. Data written to odd host addresses is mapped to odd bit planes—that is, bit planes 1 or 3.

In the textual convention established in the PC family of computers, the character code is stored first, followed immediately by the attribute byte. This character/attribute pair, when written to display memory, places all character codes into bit plane 0 and all attribute bytes into bit plane 1. Both reside at the same physical address. Thus, a single address in the display memory accesses both the character code and the character attribute. Strings composed of character/attribute pairs can be copied directly to the display memory using an assembly language move string word, MOVSW. No further software manipulations are necessary because the data is placed directly into the proper bit planes through address swapping. This is especially useful in view of the processing time necessary to load the character into plane 0 and the attribute into plane 1 using a brute-force method. The Map Mask Register would need to be loaded with a 1 to access plane 0 when writing the character code. The Map Mask Register would then need to be changed to a 2 in order for the attribute byte to be written into plane 1.

Two consecutive character codes in the host would occupy consecutive even addresses in the display memory. This occurs because the high-order host address line, bit A14 or bit A16, is used in place of host address bit 0. Thus, a high-order address bit is used to select either even or odd memory locations for the character/attribute pairs. If either A14 or A16 is low, all character/attribute pairs will be consecutive even memory locations. Likewise, if either A14 or A16 is high, the character/attribute pairs will be written to consecutive odd locations.

6.4.6 Reading Fonts in Odd/Even Modes

The odd/even addressing mode complicates the task of reading directly from display memory when the display is in an alphanumeric mode. It is still possible to read the character font bit patterns directly from display memory when the display is in an alphanumeric mode, although BIOS provides a call that will read the pattern. The technique to accomplish this is complicated because of the addressing protocol used in the alphanumeric modes, but it is useful to understand it because it helps clarify the operation of the odd/even modes.

TABLE 6.9 Font Size: Alphanumeric Modes

Mode (Hex)	Adapter	Columns / Rows	Address Page 0	Font Size
0 ,1	EGA/VGA	40/25	B8000	8 by 8
0*,1*	EGA/VGA	40/25	B8000	8 by 14
0+,1+	VGA	40/25	B8000	9 by 16
2 ,3	EGA/VGA	80/25	B8000	8 by 8
2*,3*	EGA/VGA	80/25	B8000	8 by 14
2+,3+	VGA	80/25	B8000	9 by 16
7	EGA/VGA	80/25	B0000	9 by 14
7+	VGA	80/25	B0000	9 by 16

The alphanumeric display modes include modes 0, 1, 2, 3, and 7. The features of each of these modes are listed in Table 6.9.

The alphanumeric modes 0, 1, 2, and 3 all emulate the CGA color standard, and the alphanumeric mode 7 emulates the MDA monochrome standard. In all cases, the display memory is organized so that the character codes reside in bit plane 0, the character attributes reside in bit plane 1, and the character font bit patterns reside in bit plane 2.

Each character code occupies one byte, and each character attribute occupies another byte. In host memory, these bytes are ordered so that the character code is followed in the next higher memory byte address by its associated attribute byte. A typical string of three character/attribute pairs is shown in Table 6.10.

Note that this string of three characters occupies six bytes in host memory. To achieve fast data transfers, the move string instructions can be used to move the character/attribute string from host memory to display memory. This sequential transfer involves some address shuffling so that the character and attribute codes end up in the proper display bit planes.

TABLE 6.10 Typical Character String

Byte Location	Value
0	Character code for the first character
1	Attribute code for the first character
2	Character code for the second character
3	Attribute code for the second character
4	Character code for the third character
5	Attribute code for the third character

The hardware that causes the odd/even shuffling during write operations also affects read operations. The odd/even addressing affects bit planes 0 and 1 as well as bit planes 2 and 3. Suppose that a string move operation is used to move a character font bit pattern consisting of eight sequential bytes into display memory bit plane 2. Because of the odd/even hardware, half of these bytes will end up in bit plane 2 and half in bit plane 3. Likewise, if a read operation from display memory bit plane 2 is attempted using a move string operation, half of the data will be read from bit plane 2 and half from bit plane 3. This is obviously undesirable.

To achieve correct results, it is necessary to employ alternative methods to load or read the bit patterns. One technique that works correctly places zero bytes between each of the character font bit pattern bytes. Loading an 8-byte-long font subsequently requires sixteen bytes to be transferred to the display memory. When this technique is used, the character bit patterns are directed to bit plane 2, and the zero bytes are directed to bit plane 3.

In order for the bit pattern contained in bit plane 2 to be read, it is necessary to change the display mode from an alphanumeric mode to a graphics mode. The graphics mode does not utilize the odd/even automatic addressing shuffle. Once the system is in a graphics mode, it is possible to read bit plane 2 directly. However, the host addresses in which the fonts reside in the alphanumeric modes are different from the addresses in which the font resides in the graphics modes. In the alphanumeric modes, page 0 resides at host memory address B8000 hex; in graphics mode 10 hex, page 0 resides at address A0000.

6.4.7 Writing Directly to Memory

In order to write characters and or character attributes directly to memory, the programmer must keep track of the display configuration parameters. The alphanumeric display is normally considered to be composed of a grid of characters, each with a two-dimensional row and column address. It is necessary for the programmer to be able to calculate the physical display memory address from the row and column values. To do this, a number of other display parameters must be known. Typical parameters include the number of columns per character line, the number of character lines per page, the beginning address of each page, and the position of the cursor.

6.4.8 Determining a Physical Memory Address

The EGA/VGA display memory is mapped into a contiguous block of memory in the host address space. The lowest address of the display memory is called the *display memory base address*. The display memory is organized into display pages. The lowest address of each display page, referenced to the beginning of display memory, is called the *page offset*. A character occupies a byte location within this memory space. The address of the character, referenced to the

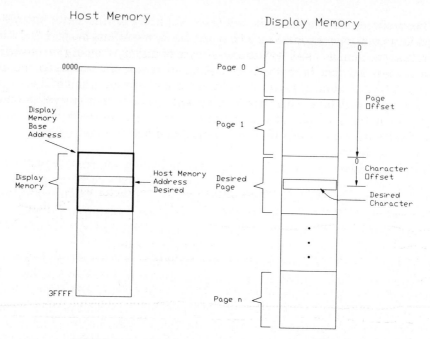

FIGURE 6.11 Calculating a Host Memory Address

display page, is called the *character offset*. These parameters are illustrated in Figure 6.11.

Equation 6.1 may be used to calculate the address of a character.

Equation 6.1 Determining the Host Address of a Character

$$\begin{array}{c} \text{Host memory} \\ \text{address} \end{array} = \begin{array}{c} \text{Display memory} \\ \text{base address} \end{array} + \begin{array}{c} \text{Page} \\ \text{offset} \end{array} + \begin{array}{c} \text{Character} \\ \text{offset} \end{array}$$

Each parameter in Equation 6.1 is described below.

Display Memory Base Address

The display memory base address is the address of the first byte of display memory mapped into the host address space. For a 256-Kbyte graphics system, this must be A0000. This value is determined by the Memory Map (MM) field in the Miscellaneous Register.

Page Offset

The page offset is the address of the first byte of the desired display page with respect to the top of the display memory. The page offset is the distance from the beginning of display memory to the lowest address of the desired display page. It is a relative offset referenced to the top of display memory. A "relative" addressing scheme is used, so the lowest byte of display memory is considered to be address 0. In the EGA/VGA, for a given display mode, each page must be the same length. However, the display pages are not contiguous. This means that for a given display mode, the first byte of one page does not follow immediately after the last byte of the previous page. Therefore, it is necessary to keep track of the base address of each display page.

what is lot contiguous.

Character Offset

The character offset is the address of the desired character with respect to the top of the selected display page. The character offset is usually determined from a row and column value. The screen is typically perceived to be a two-dimensional grid of rows and columns, as shown in Figure 6.12.

In addition to the row and column, the number of characters per row is necessary. The display memory is organized so that the first byte in a display page corresponds to the character in the upper-left corner of the monitor screen. The second byte represents the nearest right neighbor, and following bytes continue from right to left until the end of the scan row on the display monitor. The far right pixel displayed on the monitor is determined by the active display mode. Typical values are 320 or 640 pixels. These are loaded in the Horizontal Display End Register. The following byte may represent the next horizontal character or it may represent the far left character in the next row down the page. Which ever one it represents is determined by the value in the Offset Register. The Offset Register dictates the number of characters per line. This value may be thought of as the number of bytes separating two vertical neighboring pixels.

Vertical neighboring characters are thus separated by the number of characters in a row. Because there is one byte per character, this distance also corresponds to the number of bytes between vertically neighboring characters. The

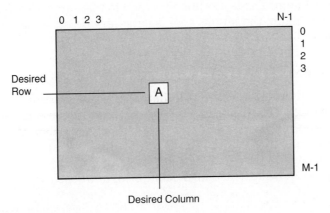

FIGURE 6.12 Two-dimensional Character Screen

term *pitch* is often used to represent the number of bytes between successive vertical neighboring pixels. The address of the character with respect to the beginning of the page in which the character resides can be determined from the desired row number, column number, and number of characters per row, as shown in Equation 6.2.

Equation 6.2 Determining the Display Address of a Character

$$
\begin{array}{l}
\text{Character} \\
\text{address}
\end{array}
=
\left(
\begin{array}{l}
\text{Row} \\
\text{number}
\end{array}
\times
\begin{array}{l}
\text{\#Characters} \\
\text{per row}
\end{array}
\right)
+
\begin{array}{l}
\text{Column} \\
\text{number}
\end{array}
$$

Row Number

As seen in Figure 6.12, the row-numbering scheme begins with row number 0 as the top row. It is followed immediately by row number 1, row number 2, and so on, until the last row. The last row is equal to the number of rows per page minus one. The "minus one" is necessary because the first row is numbered 0. Thus, the fourth row of the display is actually row number 3.

Number of Characters Per Row

The number of characters per row determines how many characters are displayed on the monitor screen in a single character row. This value is found in the Horizontal Display End Register.

Column Number

The column-numbering scheme is similar to the row-numbering scheme. It begins with column number 0 as the far left column. The next column to the right is column number 1. The column number increments from left to right until the last column. The last column is equal to the number of characters per line minus one. Again, the "minus one" is necessary because the first column is numbered 0.

6.4.9 Writing Characters and Attributes

Once the host address of the desired character is determined, either a single byte representing the character code or two bytes representing the character code and the attribute byte can be written directly to memory.

A horizontal string of characters can be written to the display. An array could be moved to display memory using a move string command, such as the assembly language MOVSW instruction. The lower byte in each word would be the character code, and the upper byte would be the attribute byte. The array would consist of alternating bytes of character codes and attribute bytes.

The host-PC protocol employed when copying a 16-bit word across an 8-bit bus is to copy the least significant byte first, followed by the most significant byte. The lower byte, which corresponds to the character code, is written to bit plane 0; the upper byte, the attribute byte, is written to bit plane 1. This occurs automatically through the odd/even hardware address shuffling.

It should be noted that the BIOS routines wait for a horizontal retrace period before modifying the display memory. This eliminates flicker in the alphanumeric modes. Usually one word can be written per horizontal retrace period. At 350 horizontal retrace periods per page and 60 pages per second, this means that 21,000 bytes, or 15,500 character/attribute pairs, can be written per second. A typical page consists of 80 columns by 25 rows, or 2,000 characters per page. Thus, nearly eight pages can be written per second. This seems to be more than adequate for most applications.

If no modification of the attribute byte is desired, a MOVS block move instruction cannot be used because the attribute bytes interleave the character codes. Software would have to write the character codes to even display memory addresses and increment the display address variable by 2 after each character code is written. This would skip over the attribute bytes and, therefore, would write only to bit plane 0, not to bit plane 1. Thus, it would modify only the characters. Likewise, the attributes can be changed without modifying the characters by writing the attribute bytes to odd display memory addresses. The attribute bytes are written to bit plane 1. A string of attributes can be written by writing the first attribute byte to the desired odd host address. After each write operation, the address is incremented by 2, skipping over the character attributes.

A vertical string of characters cannot be written using a single MOVS instruction because vertically neighboring characters do not occupy contiguous spaces in the display memory. It would be necessary to provide software that adds a constant to the address pointer as each character code and attribute byte pair is written to the display memory. This constant would be equal to the value in the Offset Register.

Writing character strings in other orientations is possible by simply adding the proper value to the display address variable after each character/attribute pair is output. Adding the value in the Offset Register plus 1 after every character causes the string to be written at a 45-degree angle in the downward direction. Subtracting the same offset produces a string written at a 45-degree angle in an upward direction.

Reading the character/attribute pair from display memory is done in a fashion similar to writing the pair. Again, the odd/even feature of the hardware automatically accesses the character byte from page 0 and the attribute byte from page 1.

TABLE 6.11 Character-manipulation BIOS Calls

BIOS	Code	Function
AH	AL	
05	—	Select active display page
08	—	Read attribute/character at current cursor position
09	—	Write attribute/character at current cursor position
0A	—	Write character only at current cursor position
0E	—	Write TTY character
13	0	Write character string, do not affect cursor position
13	1	Write character string, position cursor at end of string when done
13	2	Write character/attribute pair string, do not affect cursor position
13	3	Write character/attribute pair string, position cursor at end of string when done

6.4.10 Reading and Writing Characters via BIOS

Another method for reading and writing characters, much simpler than that presented in the previous section, is to rely on the BIOS calls. There is a bit of overhead that must be accepted when using the alphanumeric BIOS calls. However, the simplicity of using BIOS may overcome the speed penalty. In reality, the BIOS calls are simply following the same algorithms described above. The overhead involved when using BIOS includes time spent on the interrupt response, ascertaining which BIOS routine to process, determining the current status of the display, and saving registers.

The BIOS routines dedicated to character manipulation are listed in Table 6.11, along with the BIOS codes used to call them. All of these calls are invoked through the interrupt INT 10 hex. Once the interrupt is invoked, the AH and sometimes the AL registers are used to distinguish which BIOS call to invoke.

6.5 ALPHANUMERIC DISPLAY MODES

In the alphanumeric modes, the EGA/VGA bit planes are used to store the character codes, the character attributes, and the character font bit patterns. There are four CGA-compatible display modes available in the EGA/VGA. The CGA can be configured in either a 40- or 80-column alphanumeric mode. Display modes 0 and 1 provide 40 columns, and display modes 2 and 3 provide an 80-column format. The difference between modes 0 and 1 and between modes 2 and 3 has to do with the generation of a composite color signal on the CGA

TABLE 6.12 Color Graphics Alphanumeric Modes

Display Mode (Hex)	Resolution in Characters	Number of Colors	Starting Address	Number of Pages
0,1	40 by 25	16	B8000	8
2,3	80 by 25	16	B8000	4/8

board. There is no distinction between these two modes at the direct drive color outputs on the EGA/VGA board.

The configuration sense switches on the EGA board alert the EGA as to the type of monitor in use. The VGA is software-configured via a batch file. In the CGA emulation modes, a standard PC-compatible color monitor is assumed to be connected to the EGA/VGA. These monitors are often called RGBI monitors because the red, green, and blue colors are each represented by one line. An intensity control bit can make the resultant color brighter. An RGBI monitor is capable of displaying sixteen possible colors because there are four digital color control lines driving the color monitor.

In modes 0 through 3, if an enhanced color monitor is installed on the EGA/VGA board, a total of 16 out of 64 colors is possible. There are 64 possible colors because there are six digital color control lines driving the color monitor. Enhanced color monitors are sometimes called RrGgBb monitors because there are two lines dedicated to each color.

Both modes begin at host address B8000 hex. The color graphic alphanumeric modes are listed in Table 6.12.

There are several similarities found in these display modes. Details for each mode are described completely within each section.

6.5.1 Modes 0 and 1 (EGA/VGA)

Modes 0 and 1 are 40-column alphanumeric modes, compatible with the Color Graphics Adapter (CGA). As far as the EGA/VGA is concerned, there is no functional difference between modes 0 and 1.

In the EGA, these modes use 320 pixels per horizontal scan line. The EGA can operate with a resolution of 200 or 350 scan lines, as determined by the type of monitor connected to the EGA. The VGA uses 320 pixels per horizontal scan line in the modes with 200 and 350 scan lines and 360 pixels per horizontal scan line in the 400-scan-line mode. The VGA can operate with resolutions of 200, 350, or 400 scan lines, as determined by the setting of the number of scan lines in the BIOS call Select Scan Lines for Alphanumeric Mode.

The default character size for the EGA is an 8-by-8 character box in the 200-scan-line mode and an 8-by-14 character box for the 350-scan-line mode. The

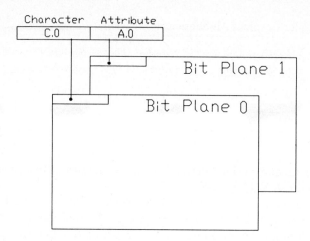

FIGURE 6.13   Modes 0,1: Mapping Character/Attributes into Display Memory

default character size for the VGA is an 8-by-8 character box in the 200-scan-line mode, an 8-by-14 character box in the 350-scan-line mode, and an 8-by-16 character box in the 400-scan-line mode.

These modes allow a display resolution of 40 characters per row by 25 rows per screen, totaling $40 \times 25 = 1,000$ characters. Each character is represented by two bytes, one byte for the character code and one for the attribute byte. This is equivalent to 2,000 bytes per page. The character code is loaded into bit plane 0, and the attribute byte is loaded into bit plane 1, as shown in Figure 6.13.

When display memory is read from or written to, the transfer of data to the two display bit planes occurs automatically because of special hardware in the EGA/VGA. This addressing mode is called *odd/even* because data read from or written to even locations affects bit plane 0, and data read from or written to odd locations affects bit plane 1.

In Figure 6.14, a byte array in host memory called a *string* is copied to display memory. The array consists of alternating character codes and attribute bytes. In the array, the "C" refers to the character code, the "A" refers to the attribute byte, and the number following the "C" or "A" is the index number—that is, 0, 1, 2, . . . 79. The data in the string buffer is written to display memory bit planes 0 and 1, as indicated in Figure 6.14.

Although 2,000 bytes of memory are required per display page, only 1,000 bytes are required in each of the two bit planes because the character codes and attributes are loaded into separate bit planes. Because of the odd/even memory mapping in effect, only even addresses are accessible in bit plane 0, and only odd addresses are accessible in bit plane 1. A display page, therefore, requires 2,000 bytes and occupies 2,048 bytes of host memory address space. Up to eight display pages can be resident in display memory simultaneously. The mapping of display pages into memory is illustrated in Figure 6.15.

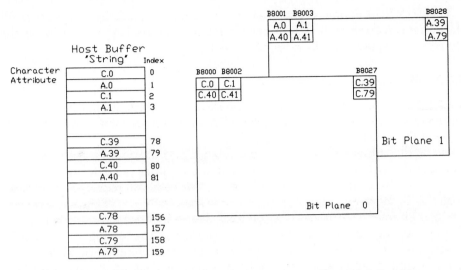

FIGURE 6.14 Modes 0,1: Moving Data from a Host Array to Display Memory

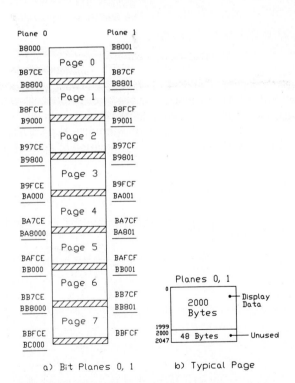

a) Bit Planes 0, 1   b) Typical Page

FIGURE 6.15 Modes 0,1: Display Memory Map

The EGA/VGA divides certain horizontal clocking signals by 2 in order to fill the entire screen with the 40 characters. Each character is twice as wide as the characters displayed in the 80-column modes.

6.5.2   Modes 2 and 3 (EGA/VGA)

Modes 2 and 3 are 80-column alphanumeric modes, compatible with the Color Graphics Adapter (CGA). As far as the EGA/VGA is concerned, there is no functional difference between modes 2 and 3.

In the EGA, these modes use 640 pixels per horizontal scan line. The EGA can operate with a resolution of 200 or 350 scan lines, as determined by the type of monitor connected to the EGA. The VGA uses 640 pixels per horizontal scan line in the modes that use 200 and 350 scan lines and 720 pixels per horizontal scan line in the 400-scan-line mode. The VGA can operate with a resolution of 200, 350, or 400 scan lines, as determined by the setting of the number of scan lines in the BIOS call Select Scan Lines for Alphanumeric Mode.

The default character size for the EGA is an 8-by-8 character box in the 200-scan-line mode and an 8-by-14 character box for the 350-scan-line mode. The default character size for the VGA is an 8-by-8 character box in the 200-scan-line mode, an 8-by-14 character box in the 350-scan-line mode, and a 9-by-16 character box in the 400-scan-line mode.

These modes allow a display resolution of 80 characters per row by 25 rows per screen, totaling $80 \times 25 = 2,000$ characters. Each character is represented by two bytes, one byte for the character code and one for the attribute byte. This is equivalent to 4,000 bytes per page. The character code is loaded into bit plane 0, and the attribute byte is loaded into bit plane 1, as shown in Figure 6.16.

When reading from or writing to display memory, the transfer of data to the two display bit planes occurs automatically because of special hardware in the

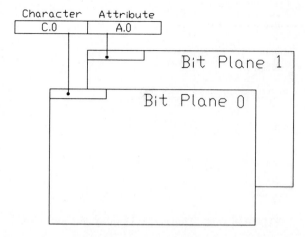

FIGURE 6.16   Modes 2,3: Mapping Character/Attributes into Display Memory

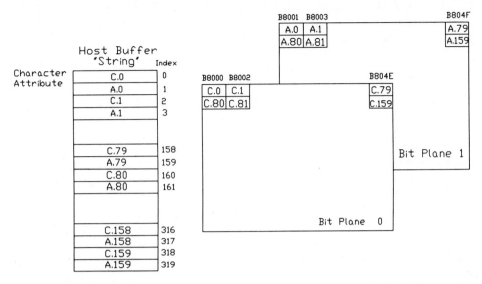

FIGURE 6.17 Modes 2,3: Moving Data from a Host Array to Display Memory

EGA/VGA. This addressing mode is called odd/even because data read from or written to even locations affects bit plane 0, and data read from or written to odd locations affects bit plane 1.

In Figure 6.17, a byte array in host memory called string is copied to display memory. The array consists of alternating character codes and attribute bytes. In the array, the "C" refers to the character code, the "A" refers to the attribute byte, and the "X" is the index number—that is, 0, 1, 2, . . . 79. The data in the string buffer is written to display memory bit planes 0 and 1, as indicated in Figure 6.17.

Although 4,000 bytes of memory are required per display page, only 2,000 bytes are required in each of the two bit planes because the character codes and attributes are loaded into separate bit planes. Because odd/even memory mapping is in effect, only even addresses are accessible in bit plane 0, and only odd addresses are accessible in bit plane 1. A display page, therefore, requires 4,000 bytes and occupies 4,096 bytes of host memory address space. Up to eight display pages can be resident in display memory simultaneously. The mapping of display pages into memory is illustrated in Figure 6.18.

6.5.3 Mode 7 (EGA/VGA)

Mode 7 is an 80-column alphanumeric mode compatible with the Monochrome Display Adapter (MDA).

Mode 7 is the only mode that has the underline feature enabled at a Mode Set. All other modes disable this feature at a Mode Set. Underlining is enabled for a particular character when the attribute byte of a character is a 1 or a 9 for

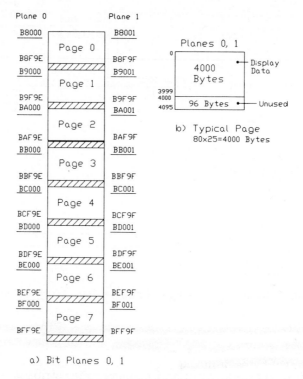

a) Bit Planes 0, 1

FIGURE 6.18 Modes 2,3: Display Memory Map

the foreground color and a 0 for a background color. The Underline Location Register must be programmed after a Mode Set occurs if underlining is desired.

In the EGA/VGA, this mode uses 720 pixels per horizontal scan line. The EGA can operate with a resolution of 350 scan lines. The VGA can operate with a resolution of 350 or 400 scan lines, as determined by the setting of the number of scan lines in the BIOS call Select Scan Lines for Alphanumeric Mode.

The default character size for the EGA is a 9-by-14 character box. The default character size for the VGA is a 9-by-14 character box in the 350-scan-line mode and a 9-by-16 character box in the 400-scan-line mode.

This mode allows a display resolution of 80 characters per row by 25 rows per screen, totaling $80 \times 25 = 2,000$ characters. Each character is represented by two bytes, one byte for the character code and one for the attribute byte. This is equivalent to 4,000 bytes per page. The character code is loaded into bit plane 0, and the attribute byte is loaded into bit plane 1, as shown in Figure 6.19.

When display memory is being read from or written to, the transfer of data to the two display bit planes occurs automatically because of special hardware in the EGA/VGA. This addressing mode is called *odd/even* because data read from or written to even locations affects bit plane 0, and data read from or written to odd locations affects bit plane 1.

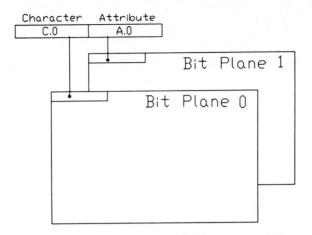

FIGURE 6.19 Mode 7: Mapping Character/Attributes into Display Memory

In Figure 6.20, a byte array in host memory called *string* is copied to display memory. The array consists of alternating character codes and attribute bytes. In the array, the "C" refers to the character code, the "A" refers to the attribute byte, and the "X" is the index number—that is, 0, 1, 2 . . . 79. The data in the string buffer is written to display memory bit planes 0 and 1, as indicated in Figure 6.20.

Although 4,000 bytes of memory are required per display page, only 2,000 bytes are required in each of the two bit planes because the character codes and

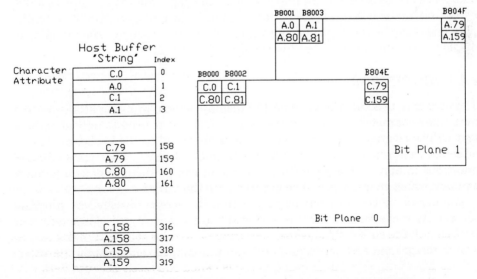

FIGURE 6.20 Mode 7: Moving Data from a Host Array to Display Memory

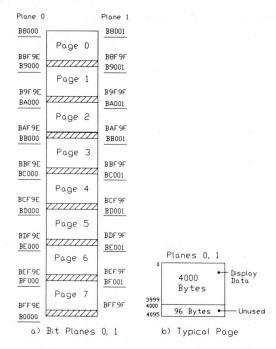

FIGURE 6.21 Mode 7: Display Memory Map

attributes are loaded into separate bit planes. Because odd/even memory mapping is in effect, only even addresses are accessible in bit plane 0, and only odd addresses are accessible in bit plane 1. A display page, therefore, requires 4,000 bytes and occupies 4,096 bytes of host memory address space. Up to eight display pages can be resident in display memory simultaneously. The mapping of display pages into memory is illustrated in Figure 6.21.

6.6 THE CURSOR

The cursor is used as a pointer on the display screen, bringing attention to a particular character position on the screen. Often it is used to indicate where text will be positioned on the screen as keys are typed on the keyboard. This is often the case when word processors are used or when users are responding to questions in application programs. The cursor can be thought of as a window through which characters will be entered onto the screen.

The cursor moves nondestructively across the screen, directed by program control. As it overwrites characters already on the screen, the characters that lay beneath the cursor change their attribute. In a color system, the characters switch foreground and background colors. In a monochrome system, the char-

TABLE 6.13 Cursor-related BIOS Calls

BIOS Code AH (Hex)	Function
01	Set Cursor Type
02	Set Cursor Position
03	Read Cursor Position
12 BL=34	Cursor Emulation (VGA only)

acter foreground and background video and reversed video attributes are switched. As the cursor leaves a character position, the original character is restored.

The cursor blinks at a rate of 1/16th of the vertical frame rate. Because the vertical scan rate is 60 frames per second, the blink rate is nearly four on/off pairs, blinking at a rate of nearly two blinks per second.

6.6.1 Cursor-related BIOS Calls

There are several BIOS routines that interact with the cursor. The BIOS codes and their functions are listed in Table 6.13. All of the cursor BIOS calls are invoked through interrupt INT 10 hex. The AH register is used to distinguish which call is invoked.

6.6.2 Cursor Shape

The cursor shape is determined by the Cursor Start and the Cursor End Register. The cursor shape is always a rectangle that fills the scan lines of the character box beginning at the scan line number loaded in the Cursor Start Register and ending with the scan line loaded in the Cursor End Register. The BIOS call Set Cursor Type, AH = 01, loads these two registers. The cursor shape is illustrated in Figure 6.22.

6.6.3 Enabling and Disabling the Cursor

In the VGA, the cursor may be turned off by setting the value in Cursor On/Off (COO) field of the Cursor Start Register. If the cursor start value is larger than the cursor end value, no cursor will be displayed. In the EGA, if the cursor start value is larger than the value in the cursor end value, two rectangles will be drawn within the character box. The first box will begin at the cursor start value and end at the bottom scan line of the cursor box. The second box will reside above the first box and will begin with the top scan line of the character box and end at the cursor end value.

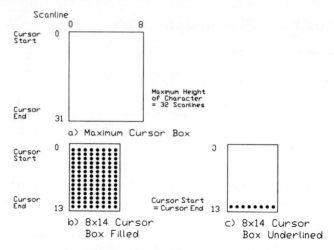

FIGURE 6.22 Cursor Shape

It is possible to enable a cursor emulation mode in the VGA. This mode is enabled or disabled by a call to the Cursor Emulation BIOS call. If this mode is enabled, the type of cursor and the starting and ending values of the cursor may be adjusted depending on the values input to Set Cursor Type BIOS call, AH = 01. Various conditions are checked. If the conditions are met, specific cursor shapes will be drawn. This provides the programmer with a convenient way to draw underline cursors, full-block cursors, and half-block cursors.

An underline cursor is produced by setting the end value to be less than or equal to the start value plus 2. An overbar cursor is produced by setting the start value to be less than the end value, both of which are less than or equal to 3. A full-block cursor is produced by setting the start value to be less than or equal to 2 or the end value less than the start value. A half-block cursor is produced by setting the start value to be less than 2. Note that these cursor shapes were formed without the programmer's needing to be concerned with the current character box size.

6.7 DOWNLOADABLE CHARACTER SETS

The EGA/VGA is capable of utilizing downloadable character fonts. Two complete fonts and one supplemental font are supplied in the EGA BIOS ROM. Three complete fonts and one supplemental font are supplied in the VGA BIOS ROM. Additional fonts may be supplied by the user. Each character font consists of 256 characters. Each character is represented by a rectangular box filled with a grid of dots. Each dot in the box represents a pixel in the display memory and is represented by a bit in the character font.

The way that the character fonts are handled depends on whether the EGA/VGA is in an alphanumeric mode or a graphics mode.

6.7.1 Character Size

The character widths currently supported by the EGA/VGA are eight pixels per character row in the color modes and nine pixels per character row in the monochrome mode. Although the characters are nine pixels wide in the monochrome mode, the character sets store a horizontal line of a character as eight pixels per character. A byte in the character set represents eight consecutive neighboring horizontal pixels. Consecutive bytes within a character represent vertical neighboring scan lines.

The character heights available in the character sets resident in BIOS range from 8 scan lines to 14 scan lines per character in the EGA and 8-to-16 scan lines per character in the VGA. The maximum height of a character to be accessed in the alphanumeric modes is 32 scan lines high. A typical character from character sets of each size is presented in Figure 6.23.

6.7.2 Fonts Resident in Display Memory

When a character is referenced by an ASCII code, its bit pattern is found in the active resident display font. In the alphanumeric modes, four character sets may be resident in the EGA display memory and eight character sets may be resident in the VGA display memory. Each resident display font is 256 characters long. Two of these 256-long character sets may be active at a time, allowing any character to access any of 512 characters.

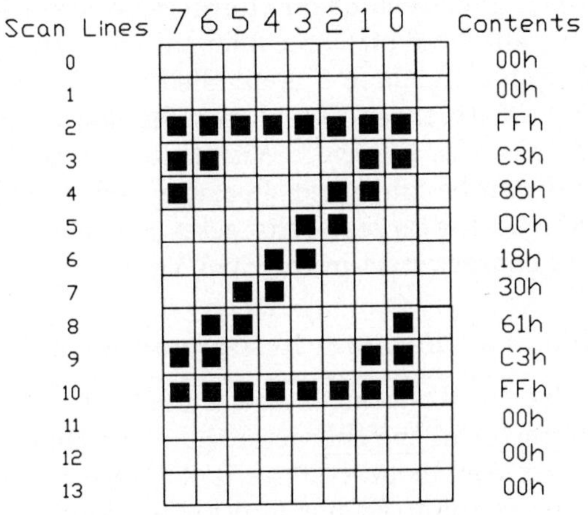

Scan Lines	7 6 5 4 3 2 1 0	Contents
0		00h
1		00h
2		FFh
3		C3h
4		86h
5		0Ch
6		18h
7		30h
8		61h
9		C3h
10		FFh
11		00h
12		00h
13		00h

FIGURE 6.23 A Typical Character

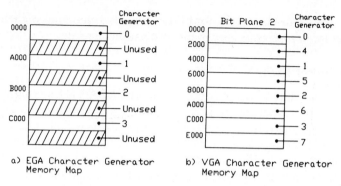

FIGURE 6.24 Resident Fonts in Bit Plane 2

6.7.3 Fonts in the Alphanumeric Modes

In the alphanumeric modes, the EGA display memory planes store the character codes, character attributes, and character font bit patterns. The bit patterns corresponding to the character codes reside in bit plane 0; the character attributes reside in bit plane 1; and the character bit patterns reside in bit plane 2. Up to four character sets can be resident in the EGA bit plane 2. Up to eight character sets can be resident in the VGA bit plane 2. One or two of these character sets can be active, allowing a character set of either 256 or 512 characters.

In the EGA, bit plane 2 is subdivided into four blocks, each 16 Kbytes long. The 8 Kbytes of storage at the beginning of each of these blocks is reserved for the four resident fonts. In the VGA, bit plane 2 is subdivided into eight blocks, each 8 Kbytes long. Figure 6.24 illustrates the EGA/VGA resident fonts in bit plane 2.

In order to obtain higher-resolution character fonts, nonstandard EGA implementations have allocated bit plane 3 for the character font bit patterns. In these implementations, bit plane 3 is handled in a fashion similar to that used with bit plane 2. With these two planes chained together, a character width of sixteen pixels can be achieved. With this increased character width, larger character fonts can be employed. Because each character has storage allocated for 32 scan lines, the largest a character can be is 16 by 32, four times the size of the 8-by-14 character set in the EGA/VGA.

6.7.4 The Location of a Character in Alphanumeric Modes

Regardless of the active font's character size, a single-sized block of memory is reserved for each character in the character set. Each character has 32 bytes reserved for it. Because each character set is 256 characters long, a total of 8,192 bytes of storage is required per font. This number—8,192 bytes—is referred to in computer terminology as *8 Kbytes*. Thus, 8 Kbytes literally means

8,192 bytes, not 8,000 bytes. These 32 bytes of storage refer to the maximum number of scan lines per character that can be displayed in an alphanumeric mode. It is computationally advantageous for this number to be a power of 2 because it facilitates rapid addressing. The character codes that are used to access these character bit patterns within the font follow the ASCII standard and vary from 00 hex to FF hex. In order to determine where the character shape exists in memory, it is necessary to multiply the character code number by the number of bytes per character and add in the base of the character font, as shown in Equation 6.3.

Equation 6.3 Determining the Address of a Character

$$\text{Character shape address} = \text{Character base address} + \left(\text{Font Character Code} \times \text{\# of bytes per Character} \right)$$

It is possible to substitute a logical shift operation for the multiplication operation if the number of bytes per character is a power of 2. Because there are 32 bytes per character, the address of the character bit pattern can be determined by shifting the ASCII character code by 5 positions to the left. This left shift is equivalent to a multiplication by 32. Because the fonts do not overlap, it is possible to substitute a logical OR operation for the addition. Using these simplifications, the address of the character can be determined as shown in Equation 6.4.

Equation 6.4 Fast Determination of the Address of a Character

$$\text{Character shape address} = \text{Font base address} \mid [\,(\,\text{Character code} << 5\,)$$

The logical OR operation is denoted with the "|" symbol and the logical shift right operation is denoted with the "<<" symbol, which is consistent with the notation used in the C language. The resulting 16-bit address points to the desired character bit pattern. It can be split up into three fields, as shown in Figure 6.25. This figure illustrates the logical operations from Equation 6.4.

6.7.5 Fonts in the Graphics Modes

In the graphics modes, pointers are provided to point to the active character set. This character set resides in host memory and can be one of either the ROM-based or the user-defined character sets. Only one 256-character-long character set may be active at a time.

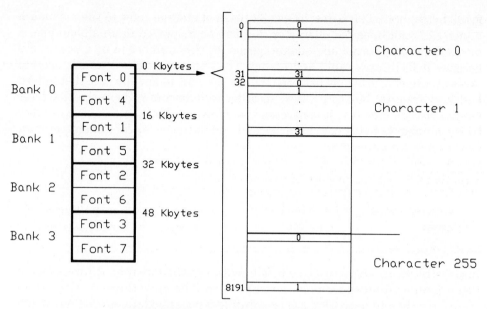

FIGURE 6.25 Character Font Addressing

6.7.6 The Location of a Character in the Graphics Modes

The location of a character in host memory is determined by locating the address of the starting location of the character set and adding the offset that points to the desired character, as shown in Equation 6.5.

Equation 6.5 Determining the Location of a Character

$$\text{Address of character} = \text{Pointer to character set} + \text{Offset to character}$$

The pointer to the character set is located in the interrupt vector locations of interrupt INT 43 hex or interrupt INT 1F hex. These interrupts are located in host memory offset from address 0000:0000 hex by the interrupt number times 4. This occurs because each interrupt vector is four bytes long in order to store the long pointer. The long pointer must load both the segment and offset registers with 16-bit values. The vector at interrupt INT 1F hex contains the pointer to the upper 128 characters of the 256-character-long character set when the EGA/VGA is in display mode 4, 5, or 6.

The offset value that points to the desired character is determined by multiplying the number of bytes in each character by the ASCII character code, as shown in Equation 6.6.

Equation 6.6 Determining the Offset to a Character (Not Modes 4, 5, or 6)

Offset = ASCII code × Number of bytes per character

If the display is in mode 4, 5, or 6, the bias is determined by multiplying the number of bytes in each character by the ASCII character code minus 128, as shown in Equation 6.7.

Equation 6.7 Determining the Offset to a Character (Modes 4, 5, and 6)

Offset = (ASCII code − 128) × Number of bytes per character

6.7.7 Font-related BIOS Calls

Several BIOS calls are associated with the character fonts. These calls are listed in Table 6.14.

The programmer may load a user-defined or ROM-based character set in one of two ways. The first way, invoked by BIOS calls AL = 00 hex to AL = 04 hex, automatically issues a Set Mode without clearing the display memory. The

TABLE 6.14 BIOS-related Character Font Calls. AH = 11 Hex. Load Character Generator BIOS Routines

AL (Hex)	Title	Display Mode	Adapter
00	Load User Character Set	Alpha	EGA/VGA
01	Load ROM 8-by-14 Monochrome Set	Alpha	EGA/VGA
02	Load ROM 8-by-8 Color Set	Alpha	EGA/VGA
03	Set Block Specifier	Alpha	EGA/VGA
04	Load ROM 8-by-16 Character Set	Alpha	VGA
10	Load User Character Set	Alpha	EGA/VGA
11	Load ROM 8-by-14 Monochrome Set	Alpha	EGA/VGA
12	Load ROM 8-by-8 Color Set	Alpha	EGA/VGA
14	Load ROM 8-by-16 Character Set	Alpha	VGA
20	Load User 8-by-8 Color Set	Alpha	EGA/VGA
21	Load User Set	Graphics	EGA/VGA
22	Load ROM 8-by-14 Set	Graphics	EGA/VGA
23	Load Rom 8-by-8 Color Set	Graphics	EGA/VGA
24	Load Rom 8-by-16 Color Set	Graphics	VGA
30	Return Font Information	—	EGA/VGA

Maximum Scan Line = Bytes per character − 1

Cursor Start = Bytes per character − 2

Cursor End = 0

Vertical Display End = [(row + 1) × bytes per character] − 1

FIGURE 6.26 EGA Register Modifications

Maximum Scan Line = Bytes per character − 1

Cursor Start = Bytes per character − 2

Cursor End = 0

For 400-scan-line modes:

Vertical Display End = [(rows + 1) × bytes/character] − 1

For 200-scan-line modes:

Vertical Display End = [(rows + 1) × bytes/character*2] − 1

ROWS = [(Number of Scan Lines) / bytes/character] − 1

CRT_LEN = (ROWS + 1) * CRT_COLS × 2

FIGURE 6.27 VGA Register Modifications

second way, invoked by BIOS calls AL = 10 to AL = 14, requires the programmer to issue a Set Mode immediately before invoking one of these BIOS calls. In addition, display page 0 must be active. Once the BIOS call has been invoked, several of the character-related parameters and display registers will be modified to adjust to the new character set. The display registers affected in the EGA are listed in Figure 6.26.

The display parameters and display registers affected in the VGA are listed in Figure 6.27.

Active Character Sets

The Set Block Specifier BIOS call, AH=11 hex AL=03 hex, allows the programmer to select two active character sets from the resident character sets. If two of the character sets are active, a character can select from 256 possible characters.

Resident Character Sets

The font-related BIOS calls provide a means of loading character sets into the resident slots available in bit plane 2 of display memory. In the EGA, up to four 256-long character sets may be resident at a time. In the VGA, up to eight 256-long character sets may be resident at a time.

TABLE 6.15 Alphanumeric Default Character Sets at Mode Set

Mode (Hex)	Character Box Size	EGA Monitor	VGA # of Scan Lines
0 ,1	8 by 8	RGBI	200
0*,1*	8 by 14	RrGgBb	350
0+,1+	9 by 16	—	400
2 ,3	8 by 8	RGBI	200
2*,3*	8 by 14	RrGgBb	350
2+,3+	9 by 16	—	400
7	9 by 14	Mono/RrGgBb	350
7+	9 by 16	—	400

6.7.8 Character Sets in the Alphanumeric Modes

All of the alphanumeric modes load a default character set into display memory bit plane 2 at a Mode Set. The default character set chosen depends on the display mode selected and on the system configuration. Table 6.15 lists the default character sets selected during a Mode Set.

6.7.9 EGA Alphanumeric Default Character Sets

In the EGA, the configuration is determined by the type of monitor attached to the adapter. If an RGBI monitor is attached, the EGA is forced into a 200-scan-line mode and an 8-by-8 character set is employed. If an enhanced RrGgBb monitor is attached, the EGA goes into a 350-scan-line mode and an 8-by-14 character set is employed. In the monochrome mode, mode 7, either a monochrome monitor or the enhanced color monitor allows for 350 scan lines. The 9-by-14 character set is employed.

6.7.10 VGA Alphanumeric Default Character Sets

In the VGA, the configuration is determined by the number of scan lines selected. The number of scan lines is adjusted by the BIOS call Select Scan Line for Alphanumeric Modes, AH = 12 hex, BL = 30 hex. It can be set to 200, 350, or 400 scan lines. In the color alphanumeric modes, selecting 200 scan lines forces the VGA to use the 8-by-8 character set. Selecting 350 scan lines allows the VGA to use an 8-by-14 character set while selecting 400 scan lines allows use of the 8-by-16 character set. In these color modes, only the enhanced color monitor may be used. In the monochrome mode, mode 7, either the enhanced monochrome or the enhanced color monitor may be used. If 350 scan lines are selected, the 9-by-14 character set is used. If 400 scan lines are selected, the 9-by-16 character set is used. The 200-scan-line mode cannot be used while the VGA is in mode 7.

TABLE 6.16 Character Set Pointers for the BIOS Call Return Font Information

BH	Adapter	Pointer
0	EGA/VGA	User-defined graphics, 8-by-8 ASCII (128–255)
1	EGA/VGA	User-defined graphics
2	EGA/VGA	ROM 8 by 14
3	EGA/VGA	ROM 8-by-8 ASCII (0–127)
4	EGA/VGA	ROM 8-by-8 ASCII (128–255)
5	EGA/VGA	ROM alpha supplement 9 by 14
6	VGA	ROM 8 by 16
7	VGA	ROM alpha supplement 9 by 16

6.7.11   Loading Character Sets Into Display Memory

There are several character fonts resident in the BIOS ROM. These fonts may be accessed by the BIOS call Return Font Information. The pointer to the top of each of these character fonts is returned to the calling program by invoking this BIOS Call. Recall that the supplemental fonts are not complete fonts but rather a collection of character bit patterns. The various font pointers are presented in Table 6.16.

6.7.12   Character Sets in the Graphics Modes

The graphics modes do not load a character set into display memory—rather, these modes depend on a pointer that points to a character set bit pattern. The bit patterns reside in host memory address space, either in RAM or in BIOS ROM. In the graphics modes, the programmer provides the BIOS with a pointer to the desired character set bit patterns. Default pointers are used for the different modes depending on the resolution of the selected mode. The default pointers select a specific-sized character set as indicated in Table 6.17.

A variety of character sets is available, including the 8-by-8 and 8-by-14 characters for the EGA/VGA and the 8-by-16 characters for the VGA. In addition, the user may provide pointers to user-defined character sets. A BIOS call, AL = 30 hex, is provided to return information to the calling program regarding the value of the pointers that reference the above-mentioned character sets. Table 6.16 lists the character set pointers.

The character set provided to the EGA/VGA when a graphics mode is active is pointed to by a pointer located in the Interrupt 43 hex vector. In all graphics modes, with the exception of modes 4, 5, and 6, this pointer points to the entire 256-character-long character set.

In the graphics modes 4, 5, and 6, the EGA/VGA is maintaining the CGA standard. In this standard, the pointer in the INT 43 hex vector points to the

TABLE 6.17 Alphanumeric Default Character Sets at Mode Set

Mode (Hex)	Character Box Size	Adapter Applicable	EGA Monitor	VGA Monitor
4,5	8 by 8	EGA, VGA	RGBI,RrGgBb	Color
6	8 by 8	EGA, VGA	RGBI,RrGgBb	Mono/color
D,E	8 by 8	EGA, VGA	RGBI,RrGgBb	Color
F	8 by 14	EGA, VGA	Mono,RrGgBb	Mono/color
10	8 by 14	EGA, VGA	RrGgBb	Color
11	8 by 16	VGA	—	Mono/color
12	8 by 16	VGA	—	Color
13	8 by 8	VGA	—	Color

first 128 characters in the character set, ASCII 0 through 127. A second pointer is required to access the upper 128 characters of the character set. This pointer resides in the INT 1F hex vector. In these display modes, modes 4, 5, and 6, only the 8-by-8 character set is utilized.

6.7.13 Default Character Sets in the Graphics Modes

The pointer to the default character set is loaded into the proper interrupt vector location, as determined by the active display mode. In the EGA, a pointer to either the 8-by-8 character set or the 8-by-14 character set is selected depending on the display mode. In the VGA, a pointer to the 8-by-8, the 8-by-14, or the 8-by-16 character set is selected depending on the display mode. These character sets are presented in Table 6.18.

TABLE 6.18 Graphics Mode Default Character Sets at Mode Set

Mode (Hex)	Character Box Size	Adapter Applicable	EGA Monitor	VGA Monitor
0,1	8 by 8	EGA, VGA	RGBI,RrGgBb	Color
0,1	8 by 14	EGA, VGA	RrGgBb	Color
0,1	9 by 16	VGA	—	Color
2,3	8 by 8	EGA/VGA	RGBI,RrGgBb	Color
2,3	8 by 14	EGA/VGA	RrGgBb	Color
2,3	9 by 16	VGA	—	Color
7	9 by 14	EGA/VGA	Mono	Mono/Color
7	9 by 16	VGA	—	Mono/Color

Chapter 7

Graphics Processing

7.1 CHARACTERS

When the EGA/VGA is in a graphics mode, the display memory bit planes contain bit patterns that correspond directly to the dot patterns viewed on the screen. This is distinctly different from the configuration during an alphanumeric mode in which each bit plane has a specific function. The actual dot patterns displayed on the monitor are derived from the codes stored in the bit planes. In the graphics modes, these displayed dot patterns are output directly from the bit planes into the color lookup table and out to the monitor.

A character can be written to the display memory when the EGA/VGA is in a graphics mode by writing directly to the display or by going through the BIOS routines. Certainly, going to the display memory through the BIOS routines is the simpler, albeit slower, path. When writing single characters or character strings, the BIOS calls may be fast enough for many applications. However, applications that require rapid full-screen updates or scrolling windows of text may find the BIOS calls to be too slow.

7.1.1 Character Sets

The character-generation section of the EGA/VGA is based on *downloadable* character fonts. To be called downloadable, the adapter must have the capability of accepting user-defined character fonts as well as its own. In the alphanumeric modes, bit plane 2, and in some cases bit plane 3, is reserved to hold the character font dot patterns. Thus, the fonts are downloaded to the display memory. Because the bit patterns reside within the display memory, special hardware within the EGA/VGA accesses the patterns in a rapid fashion.

Any font of the proper size may be loaded into the display memory and used as the active character set. These fonts may originate from an external source or may be one of the resident character fonts contained within the BIOS ROM. The display memory of the EGA is capable of storing four character sets simultaneously, and the VGA is capable of storing eight. Each character set is 256 characters long. The programmer may select either one or two of the 256 character fonts to be active at a time. The attribute byte associated with each character dictates which of the two fonts to use for that particular character.

7.1.2   Storing Characters in Display Memory

The display memory cannot be used to store the character fonts when the EGA is in a graphics mode because bit planes 2 and 3 are not available. All four bit planes are occupied in storing the bit-mapped graphics data. The programmer may write the characters directly into display memory or may use the character-related BIOS routines while the EGA/VGA is in one of the graphics modes.

The programmer has complete flexibility when writing characters directly to the display memory while the EGA/VGA is in a graphics mode. The characters may be any size, shape, color, or combination of colors. Suppose that the EGA/VGA is in display mode 10 hex and all four bit planes are active. A pixel is represented by one bit in each of the four bit planes. A character is constructed by loading the character's bit patterns into each bit plane. The Set/Reset Register may be used to write the character to the display memory. The Set/Reset Register writes one pixel to all bit planes simultaneously. Thus, an 8-by-14 character box can be written to the display memory in 14 ö 8 = 112 byte move operations. If a full 80-by-25 screen is updated using this technique, nearly 224,000 bytes will be written to the display memory. Add in the necessary addressing operations associated with this data move operation and a full-screen write could take several seconds.

7.1.3   Writing Characters Quickly

If a few assumptions are made regarding the nature and orientation of the characters, the number of operations required to write characters to the display can be drastically reduced. The first assumption is that, in most cases, characters will be oriented horizontally, with each character displayed in one color. In addition, only the character foreground will be displayed, leaving the background transparent. A further assumption would be that the characters all fall on byte boundaries. Based on these assumptions, an 8-by-14 character can be written to the display memory in 14 byte operations. This reduces a full-screen write to 28,000 byte operations, providing an improvement of 8 to 1 over the previously described method.

The technique used to write characters takes advantage of these assumptions. It updates an entire character scan line in one byte move operation. All four bit planes are written to simultaneously. Because the character is 8 pixels wide, an entire character scan line can be contained in one byte. The byte that represents the bit pattern of one scan line is written into the Bit Mask Register. Each bit of the Bit Mask Register corresponds to one of the eight horizontal neighboring pixels of the display. Any bit set to a 1 in this register allows the corresponding pixel in the display memory to be modified. Likewise, any pixel reset to 0 protects the corresponding pixel in the display memory from being modified. The character foreground pixels are represented with a 1, and background pixels are represented with a 0. Thus, foreground pixels will overwritethe corresponding locations in the display memory, and background pixels will have no effect on the display memory.

The character color is loaded into the Set/Reset Register. All planes are configured to respond to this Register by loading an 0F hex into the Enable Set/Reset Register. Ultimately, only those planes selected in the Map Mask Register will actually be affected, regardless of the setting in the Enable Set/Reset Register. The bit positions within each of the three Registers will correspond to a bit plane. All bit planes enabled by the Map Mask Register and set in the Enable Set/Reset Register will be updated by the subsequent write operation. A 0 in a bit position of the Set/Reset Register will cause the selected pixel in the corresponding bit plane to be overwritten with a 0. A 1 in a bit position will cause the pixel in the corresponding bit plane to be overwritten with a 1.

The Map Mask Register and the Enable Set/Reset Register are loaded to select the desired bit planes. The foreground color of the character is loaded into the Set/Reset Register. The first scan line from the character bit pattern is fetched and loaded into the Bit Mask Register. A byte, 00 hex, is written to the display memory using a MOV instruction to the desired position of the first scan line. All planes selected will be updated with the corresponding bit value in the Set/Reset Register. Because a Write Mode 0 is in effect, eight consecutive horizontal pixels will be written to the display. The Bit Mask Register assigns one bit per pixel. All pixels set to a 1 in the Bit Mask Register will cause the corresponding pixels to be loaded with the value from the Set/Reset Register. The single MOV instruction causes up to eight pixels in up to four bit planes to be updated with the value in the Set/Reset Register. The process is repeated for each character scan line by adjusting the address used in the MOV instruction so that it addresses the next scan line of the selected character. A new value that corresponds to the bit pattern of the second scan line of the character is written into the Bit Mask Register. Again, a 0 byte is written to display memory via a MOV instruction, updating the second scan line. This process repeats for all scan lines in the character.

If more sophisticated text output is desired, it is likely that the characters will not always fall on an even byte boundary. A single scan line in a character may take two byte write operations, requiring the Bit Mask Register and the address to be modified twice for each scan line output. A host buffer can be used to build up the character in a rectangular grid. Each bit can be written independently. Once constructed, the resultant two-dimensional matrix is output to the display one byte at a time. If a character string needs to be written to the display, a host buffer can be used to store an entire character line of data. Eight pixels at a time would still be written to the display. However, these eight pixels do not necessarily correspond to one character. The move string instructions MOVSB or MOVSW could be used to move the host buffer rapidly to the display.

Thus far, it has been assumed that the character strings are oriented horizontally. Writing characters that are not oriented in a horizontal direction is more difficult. Vertically oriented characters can be written by transposing the rows and columns of a character in a host buffer and then writing the host buffer to the display as if the characters were horizontal. A transposed 8-by-14 character box can be thought of as a 14-by-8 character box. Because 14 dots are written horizontally, two byte operations are necessary to output each character scan line for all eight scan lines. Other than this transposition, the character output process is identical to the horizontal character strings.

Angular orientations can be produced by first rotating the character bit patterns within a host memory array and then writing one horizontal line at a time. The maximum number of bytes for an 8-by-14 character would be two bytes per scan line for fourteen scan lines. By rotating the characters within a host buffer, strings can be output one byte at a time, and each byte may contain data from more than one character.

7.1.4   Graphics Text Processing through BIOS

The programmer may utilize the BIOS character routines to read and write characters to the display when the EGA/VGA is in a graphics mode. Because the downloadable character fonts are not located in display memory, the location of the desired font must be provided to the BIOS routine. This is done by one of the BIOS calls, as invoked by AH = 11, which is the Load Character Generator BIOS call. The parameter passed to the interrupt routine in the AL register determines the type of font loaded, as indicated in Table 7.1.

The BIOS software must be told where the character set resides so that it can find the character bit patterns when drawing characters. These pointers may refer to user-defined downloadable character fonts located in host memory or to one of the character fonts located in the BIOS ROM. The character fonts are limited to 256 active characters at a time, because the attribute byte cannot contain the font selection bit as is done in the alphanumeric modes.

TABLE 7.1   Load Character Generator BIOS Routines

AH=11 Hex AL (Hex)	Title	Display Mode
21	Load User Set	Graphics
22	Load ROM 8-by-14 Set	Graphics
23	Load ROM 8-by-8 Color Set	Graphics

7.1.5 Finding a Character Set

When a character is accessed through a BIOS call, the character code and attribute byte are sent to the BIOS routine. The display memory address where the character will be placed is determined by the current cursor position of the selected page. Depending on the display mode, the pointer to the character font located at either the interrupt 43 hex or the 1F hex vector will be selected to point to the character bit pattern. If the current display mode is less than 7, a CGA emulation mode is in effect and the 8-by-8 character font is selected. If the character code is less than 80 hex, the vector at interrupt 43 hex is selected as the pointer to the base of the character bit patterns. Otherwise, the vector at interrupt 1F hex is selected.

7.1.6 Locating a Bit Pattern within a Character Set

To determine the location of the selected character bit pattern, the character code is multiplied by 8 and added to the font base pointer found in the interrupt vector. If the current display mode is greater than 7, the vector at interrupt 43 hex is selected as the pointer to the base of the character bit patterns. To determine a character position, the number of bytes per character, as stored in host memory at 485 hex, is multiplied by the character code. This is necessary because a user-specified character size may be selected in these modes.

7.1.7 Writing the Bit Pattern to Display Memory

Once the bit pattern for the selected character is located within the character set, the pattern is written directly to the display memory at the current cursor position. The color of the character is determined by the attribute byte associated with the character. The foreground color ranges from 0 to 15 in bit positions 0 to 3 of the attribute byte. Bit 7 of the attribute byte is a flag that determines the type of write operation. If bit 7 is reset to 0, the write operation is straightforward. All pixels in the display memory corresponding to foreground pixels in the character are overwritten with the value indicated by the foreground color. If bit 7 of the attribute byte is set to a 1, the operation becomes an XOR logical operation. The new character data is XORed with the current data in the corresponding display memory location before the result is written to the display memory. The BIOS routine actually loads the Function Select (FS) field of the Data Rotate Register with a 3 to indicate that the XOR operation should take place.

With the XOR function enabled, the character will be written to the display memory without modifications if the area of the display memory selected contains all 0s. This occurs because any value XORed with a 0 remains unmodified. If the area of the display memory selected contains the same bit pattern as the new data being written, the character will be erased. This occurs because any value XORed with itself results in 0. The most common use of this XOR function is to draw and erase a character with minimal overhead. The programmer must simply output the character to the blank display, thereby writing the character to the display. Without modifying anything, the character can be rewritten to the display, causing the character to be erased.

If the area of the display memory to be modified contains all 1s, the resulting character color will be inverted. This occurs because any value XORed with 1 results in an inversion. This is a simple way to highlight a character on the screen. A character bit pattern of FF hex, all 1s, can be written to the display using the XOR feature. Any characters existing in the desired display memory locations will have their colors inverted. Color inversion means that all bits will be inverted. Thus, a character with color 5 (0101 binary) will be modified to color A hex (1010 binary). This process can be reversed by rewriting the same FF hex pattern to the character position with the XOR function enabled. The result in the above example is to redraw the character in its original color of 5.

If the data in the display memory is not all 0s, all 1s, or identical to the new data, the resultant character pattern written to the display will depend on the data present. If other data is present in the display area, the result will appear to be the original character overwritten with the new character. The result will be three colors, corresponding to the original character foreground color, the XOR of the original and the new character's foreground color, and the new character's foreground color.

7.2 GRAPHICS ATTRIBUTES

The character attributes are handled differently in graphics modes than in alphanumeric modes. In the graphics modes, the actual bit patterns for the character are stored in display memory. Each pixel is 1, 2, or 4 bits wide. The values loaded into the bits associated with each pixel are determined by the attribute byte. The attribute byte is interrogated as to the desired color or monochrome attribute for the character. The foreground portion of this attribute code is loaded into the pixels that correspond to the foreground of the character. Any background attribute value is ignored because the character is drawn in a transparent mode. All pixels associated with the background pixels of a character are ignored.

7.2.1 Two-color Mode

The two-color graphics mode in the EGA/VGA is invoked in mode 6. In addition, the VGA mode 11 uses the two-color mode. The foreground color of all characters is displayed in white. This white is obtained by setting all bits in each of the three colors to on. In the Palette Registers, this corresponds to a 17 hex. In the default Palette Register, all Palette Registers with the exception of Register 0 are loaded with a 17 hex. Any character attribute value other than 0 will result in the character being displayed in maximum intensity white. The 0 corresponds to the background color of the character.

7.2.2 Monochrome Mode

The monochrome mode emulates the EGA/VGA graphics on a monochrome display. This is associated with display mode F hex. Two bits are dedicated to each pixel in this mode. Thus, each character can be displayed with one of four attributes. The attributes associated with a character are derived from the two least significant bits of the foreground color in the attribute byte. The background color is ignored.

The two bits associated with each pixel are stored in bit planes 0 and 2. Bit planes 1 and 3 are disabled; thus, they do not contribute to the Palette Register address. This can be seen in the value of the Plane Select Register, index 12 hex, in the EGA or VGA Default Register Values Tables, found in Chapter 9, Tables 9.5 and 9.6, respectively. The value is 05, which corresponds to a 1 in bit positions 0 and 2 and a 0 in bit positions 1 and 3.

The standard monochrome attributes are listed in Table 7.2.

The possible attribute values, the associated Palette Register number, the default Palette Register value, and the resulting character attribute are listed in Table 7.3.

TABLE 7.2 Monochrome Attributes

Character Attribute	Attribute
0,8	Black
1,9	Video
2,A	Black
3,B	Video
4,C	Blinking
5,D	Intensified Video
6,E	Blinking
7,F	Intensified Video

TABLE 7.3 Two-color Attributes

Attribute Value	Palette Number	Palette Value (Hex)	Resulting Color
0	0	00	Black
1	1	08	Video
4	4	18	Blinking
5	5	18	Intensified Video

TABLE 7.4 Four-color Attributes

Attribute	Palette Value (Hex)	Color Select 1	Color Select 2
0	00	Black	Black
1	13	Light cyan	Green
2	15	Light magenta	Red
3	17	Intensified white	Brown

Note that the monochrome adapter uses bit 3 for the video and bit 4 for intensified. Thus, an 8 hex causes bit 3, the video bit, to be activated; a 10 hex causes bit 4, the intensified bit, to be activated. An 18 hex results in both being activated.

7.2.3 Four-color Mode

The four-color graphics modes in the EGA/VGA are invoked in modes 4 and 7. These modes emulate the CGA graphics standard. The color of each character is determined by the two least significant bits of the foreground portion of the attribute byte. Each pixel is represented by two bits. These two bits allow the pixel to access Palette Registers 0 through 3. These Palette Registers are loaded with values that allow the character to be displayed in one of the two standard CGA color selections. The attribute values, the associated default Palette Register values, and the associated colors are listed in Table 7.4.

7.2.4 Sixteen-color Mode

The sixteen-color graphics modes are modes D, E, and 10 hex for the EGA and VGA. In addition, mode 12 hex is available in the VGA. These modes assign four bits to each pixel. The four bits per pixel are loaded with the foreground attribute color of each character. Only the foreground pixel of each character is affected. The foreground attribute values, the associated Palette register value, and resultant colors are listed in Table 7.5.

7.2.5 256-color Mode

The 256-color mode is available through mode 13 hex of the VGA only. Eight pixels are reserved for each pixel. The attribute byte associated with each character contains four bits of foreground color. These four bits correspond to one of sixteen foreground colors. These sixteen values map to the sixteen palette registers. In the VGA, the outputs of the Palette Registers address the Color Registers. The actual color codes reside in the Color Registers.

TABLE 7.5 Sixteen-color Attributes

Attribute Value (Hex)	Palette Value (Hex)	Default Color
0	00	Black
1	01	Blue
2	02	Green
3	03	Cyan
4	04	Red
5	05	Magenta
6	06	Brown
7	07	White
8	38	Dark gray
9	39	Light blue
A	3A	Light green
B	3B	Light cyan
C	3C	Light red
D	3D	Light magenta
E	3E	Yellow
F	3F	Intensified white

This is the only mode in the VGA that requires that the Palette Registers not be changed. If a color needs to be changed, the associated Color Register, not the Palette Register, should be modified. According to the Default Palette Register Values, found in Chapter 9, in Table 9.6, the sixteen Palette Registers are loaded with incrementing values from 0 to 15.

The sixteen Color Registers selected by Palette Registers 0 through 15 are determined by the Color Select Register. The first sixteen Color Registers contain the EGA-compatible colors, as listed in Table 7.5. The second set of sixteen registers contains gray scales. The remaining Color Registers contain combinations of colors based on the hue-saturation-intensity model.

7.3 DISPLAY MEMORY

The EGA/VGA display memory is constructed from dynamic read/write memory. It is segmented into four bit planes. These bit planes operate in a wide variety of ways depending on the display mode. In the literature, the four bit planes are also referred to as *bit maps*. Each bit plane may be from 16 Kbytes to 64 Kbytes long. Typical EGA/VGA implementations include four 64-Kbyte bit planes for a total of 256 Kbytes of memory. The organization of the display memory as four bit planes is shown in Figure 7.1.

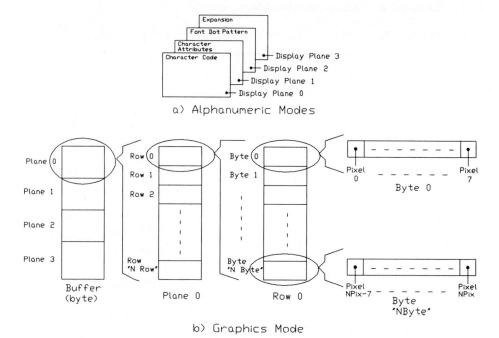

a) Alphanumeric Modes

b) Graphics Mode

FIGURE 7.1 Display Memory Bit Planes

7.3.1 Display Memory in Host Memory Address Space

The display memory is mapped into the host memory address space. It can occupy a maximum area of 128 Kbytes from A0000 hex to BFFFF hex in the host memory space per plane. The starting address is adjustable depending on the setting of the Memory Map (MM) field in the Miscellaneous Register. The possible values of this field, along with the corresponding starting addresses, are listed in Table 7.6.

Note that the fully populated EGA/VGA cannot coexist with any other graphics board because a host memory and host port addressing conflict will occur. A half-populated EGA/VGA, which most such cards are, can coexist with an

TABLE 7.6 Memory Map Field

MM Field	Starting Address	Amount of Memory	Compatibility Emulation
0	A0000–BFFFF	128 Kbytes	Can't coexist
1	A0000–AFFFF	64 Kbytes	Can coexist
2	B0000–BFFFF	64 Kbytes	Hercules/MDA
3	B8000–BFFFF	16 Kbytes	CGA

MDA, Hercules, or CGA board. If the EGA is configured in a color mode, however, only a monochrome or Hercules board may act as the other adapter. If the EGA/VGA is configured as a monochrome board, only a color adapter can coexist with it. The EGA/VGA memory can be mapped to look like a Hercules board when MM = 2; it can look like a CGA board when MM = 3.

A VGA adapter board can coexist with another VGA planar video. The planar video is contained on the host motherboard. Either can be selected as the active video device by invoking the Display Switch BIOS call, AH = 12 hex, BL = 35 hex.

7.3.2   Display Pages

The resolution of a single page and the total amount of display memory determine the number of display pages available in each display mode. Assuming 64 Kbytes per plane and a host starting address of A0000 hex, the starting addresses of the display pages are listed in Table 7.7. This table refers to the EGA/VGA graphics modes.

The VGA has three graphics modes that are not available on the EGA. Two of these modes, mode 11 hex and mode 12 hex, utilize a 640-by-480 resolution. One mode, mode 13 hex, uses a 320-by-200 resolution with eight bits dedicated to every pixel. These VGA-specific graphics modes are listed in Table 7.8.

TABLE 7.7   Display Pages: EGA/VGA Graphics Modes

Page	Mode 4,5 Hex	Mode D Hex	Mode E Hex	Mode 10 Hex
0	B8000	A0000	A0000	A0000
1	—	A2000	A4000	A8000
2	—	A4000	A8000	—
3	—	A6000	AC000	—
4	—	A8000	—	—
5	—	AA000	—	—
6	—	AC000	—	—
7	—	AE000	—	—

TABLE 7.8   Display Pages: VGA Graphics Modes

Page	Mode 11 Hex	Mode 12 Hex	Mode 13 Hex
0	A0000	A0000	A0000

TABLE 7.9   Display Pages: EGA/VGA Alphanumeric Modes

Page	Modes 0,1 Hex	Modes 2,3 Hex	Mode 7 Hex
0	B8000	B8000	B8000
1	B8400	B8800	B8800
2	B8800	B9000	B9000
3	B8C00	B9800	B9800
4	B9000	BA000	BA000
5	B9400	BA800	BA800
6	B9800	BB000	BB000
7	B9C00	BB800	BB800

Assuming 64 Kbytes per plane and a host starting address of B8000 hex, the starting addresses of the display pages when the EGA/VGA is in an alphanumeric mode are listed in Table 7.9.

7.3.3   Display Memory Organization

There are two basic types of display modes called the alphanumeric modes and the graphics modes. The functioning of the display memory is different depending on which of these modes is in effect. When in an alphanumeric mode, the display memory is used to hold character codes, attribute bytes, and character font bit patterns. Once decoded, the data in the display memory is converted to bit patterns that are sent to the monitor. When a graphics mode is in effect, the display memory is used to hold a bit-per-bit representation of the data being displayed on the monitor. The addressing is handled so that the bit stream coming from the display memory is output directly to be displayed on the monitor.

7.4   GRAPHICS DISPLAY MODES

The EGA/VGA graphics modes use each of the four bit planes to store the bit-mapped data to be displayed. The color of a pixel when viewed on the monitor is represented by one or more bits in one or more of the bit planes. The exact number of bits in different planes depends on the display modes. Table 7.10 lists the number of bits per plane and the number of planes that affect the color of a pixel.

7.4.1   Number of Colors versus Display Planes

The color determined from Table 7.10 may be modified depending on whether a particular bit plane is enabled or disabled. This is controlled through the Color Plane Enable Register. Table 7.11 illustrates the increasing color resolution available by enabling bit planes.

TABLE 7.10 Graphics Mode Pixels, Bits, and Bit Planes

Mode (Hex)	# of Colors	# Bits per Plane	Bit Planes Affected	Notes
4,5	4	2	0 or 1	1
6	2	1	0	2
D	16	1	0,1,2 and 3	3
E	16	1	0,1,2 and 3	3
F	4	1	0 and 2	4
10	16	1	0,1,2 and 3	3
11	2	1	0	2
12	16	1	0,1,2 and 3	3
13	256	8	0,1,2 or 3	5

Notes:

1. In modes 6 and 11 hex, each pixel consists of one bit in bit plane 0.

2. In modes 4 and 5, alternate bytes of data, each containing four pixels, are stored in bit plane 0 and bit plane 1. Bit plane 0 contributes the low-order bit, and bit plane 1 contributes the high-order bit of the 2-bit pixel.

3. In modes D, E, 10, and 12 hex, each pixel corresponds to one bit in each of the four bit planes. Bit plane 0 contributes the low-order bit, followed by bit plane 1 and bit plane 2. Bit plane 3 contributes the high-order bit of the 4-bit pixel.

4. In mode F hex, bit plane 0 contributes the low-order bit and bit plane 2 contributes the high-order bit of the 2-bit pixel.

5. In mode 13 hex, all four bit planes are chained together and each pixel consists of eight bits. The plane in which a pixel resides depends on the position of the pixel on the display. Each plane holds one-quarter of the pixels.

TABLE 7.11 Number of Colors versus Planes Enabled

# of Display Planes Enabled	# of Colors
1	2
2	4
3	8
4	16

7.4.2 CGA Emulation

The EGA/VGA can emulate the alphanumeric or graphics modes available in the CGA. This emulation includes the BIOS calls and the addressing of the display memory. Programs that command the CGA directly through the registers may not operate properly on the EGA/VGA. Some EGA/VGA implementations feature true CGA emulation. In the CGA modes, the EGA/VGA display memory is mapped into the host memory address space beginning at B8000 hex. The base address of the I/O ports is set at 3D4 hex.

7.4.3 CGA Graphics Modes

In the CGA emulation modes, the EGA display memory is organized in a packed display format. The 320-by-200 modes, 4 and 5, simulate the CGA low-resolution mode, and the 640-by-200 mode 6 simulates the CGA medium-resolution mode. In the low-resolution mode, each byte contains four neighboring horizontal pixels. In the medium-resolution mode, each byte contains eight neighboring horizontal pixels. Notice that both display modes store an entire horizontal line in 80 bytes.

The CGA does not store display memory contiguously when operating in a graphics mode. Consecutive scan lines are separated by half of the display. Even-numbered scan lines are displayed at the scan line positions 0 to 99, and odd scan lines are displayed at the scan line positions 100 to 199.

Suppose that an image is stored in display memory in a contiguous byte array. The display format requires 80 bytes per horizontal line, with 200 horizontal lines per page. The array contains $80 \times 200 = 1,600$ bytes. The far-left byte of row *n+1* immediately follows the far-right byte of row *n*. Each byte in the array is numbered continuously from 0 to 1,599. Figure 7.2 illustrates the way in which this contiguous display array is mapped onto the display. There

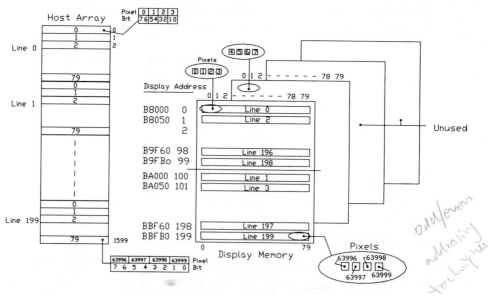

FIGURE 7.2 CGA Addressing Scheme

TABLE 7.12 CGA Graphics Emulation Modes

Display Mode (Hex)	Resolution Pixels	Number of Colors	Starting Address	Number of Pages
4,5	320 by 200	4	B8000	1
6	640 by 200	2	B8000	1
D	320 by 200	16	A0000	4/8
E	640 by 200	16	A0000	2/4

are 80 characters per scan line and 200 scan lines per display. The Offset Register is set to 80, indicating that the virtual width of the image is 80 bytes.

The CGA graphics emulation modes are listed in Table 7.12. Modes 4, 5, and 6 actually emulate the memory configuration of the CGA, and modes D and E operate differently but also have 200 scan lines per screen.

7.4.4 Modes 4 and 5 (EGA/VGA)

Modes 4 and 5 are graphics modes that use display memory bit planes 0 and 1 to store the graphics information. As far as the EGA/VGA is concerned, there is no functional difference between modes 4 and 5. These modes use a display resolution of 320 horizontal pixels per scan line and 200 scan lines. The default character set invoked in these modes is the 8-by-8 character set.

Odd/even addressing techniques force even-numbered bytes to reside in bit plane 0 and odd-numbered bytes to reside in bit plane 1. There are four possible colors for each pixel, requiring two bits per pixel. The EGA/VGA display memory is organized in a packed display form as opposed to a bit-mapped format.

Each pixel is stored in two consecutive bits of a single byte in display memory. Each byte in display memory contains four neighboring horizontal pixels, as indicated in Figure 7.3. Pixel 0 is located to the immediate left of pixel 1, and so on. Only one page is available in either mode 4 or mode 5.

These modes allow a display resolution of 320 pixels per horizontal row by 200 rows per screen. This is equivalent to 64,000 pixels per page. There are four pixels per byte, totaling 16,000 bytes per page. Because two bit planes, bit planes 0 and 1, are used to store the data, only 8,000 bytes are required per page. Alternating bytes of data from the host memory are loaded into bit planes 0 and 1, as shown in Figure 7.4. Each byte of data contains four pixels; thus, one byte containing pixels 0 through 3 resides in bit plane 0; the following byte, containing pixels 4 through 7, resides in bit plane 1.

When display memory is read from or written to, the transfer of data to the two display bit planes occurs automatically because of special hardware in the EGA/VGA. This addressing mode is called odd/even, because data read from or

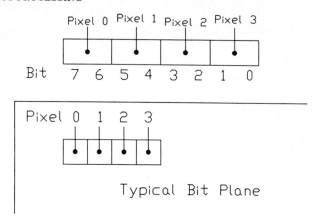

FIGURE 7.3 Mode 4,5: Pixel Packing

written to even locations affects bit plane 0, and data read from or written to odd locations affects bit plane 1.

In Figure 7.5, a byte array in host memory called *data* is copied to display memory. The array consists of alternating character codes and attribute bytes. In the array, the "D" refers to the data byte and the "X" is the index number—that is, 0, 1, 2, . . 79. The data in the data buffer is written to display memory bit planes 0 and 1, as indicated in Figure 7.5.

It should be noted that the memory in the bit plane is segmented into two halves. The upper half contains even scan rows, and the lower half contains odd scan rows. This is added to the fact that alternating bytes are contained in different bit planes. Figure 7.5 shows how four consecutive bytes of host memory, "D158", "D159", "D160", and "D161", are spread through display memory.

Although 16,000 bytes of memory are required per display page, only 8,000 bytes are required in each of the two bit planes because the alternating bytes are loaded into separate bit planes. Because odd/even memory mapping is in effect, only even addresses are accessible in bit plane 0, and only odd addresses

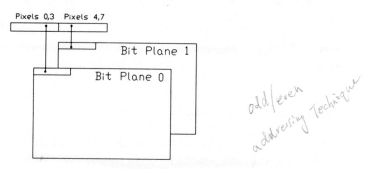

FIGURE 7.4 Modes 4,5: Mapping Data into Display Memory

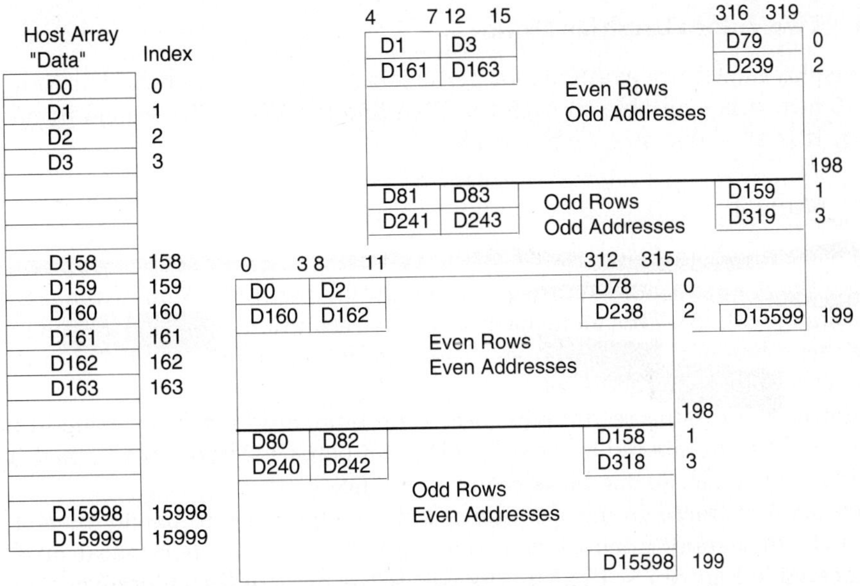

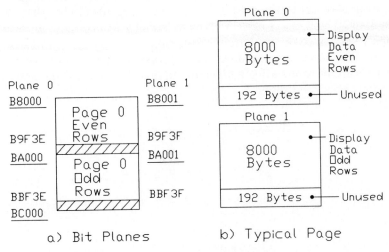

FIGURE 7.5 Modes 4,5: Moving Data from a Host Array to Display Memory

are accessible in bit plane 1. A display page therefore requires 16,000 bytes and occupies 16,384 bytes of display memory address space. Up to two display pages can be resident in display memory simultaneously. The mapping of display pages into memory is illustrated in Figure 7.6.

FIGURE 7.6 Modes 4,5: Display Memory Map

7.4.5   Two-color Graphics Modes

Two display modes are available for performing two-color graphics. The first is mode 6 hex. It is available on both the EGA and the VGA. The second is mode 11 hex. It is available on only the VGA.

7.4.6   Mode 6

Mode 6 is a graphics display mode and uses display memory bit planes 0 and 1 to store the graphics information. It is compatible with the Monochrome Display Adapter (MDA). This mode uses a display resolution of 640 horizontal pixels per scan line and 200 scan lines. The default character set invoked in this mode is the 8-by-8 character set.

Odd/even addressing techniques force even-numbered bytes to reside in bit plane 0 and odd-numbered bytes to reside in bit plane 1. There are two possible colors for each pixel, so one bit is required per pixel.

Each pixel is stored in one bit position of a single byte in display memory. Each byte in display memory contains eight neighboring horizontal pixels, as indicated in Figure 7.7. Pixel 0 is located to the immediate left of pixel 1, and so on.

This mode allows a display resolution of 640 pixels per horizontal row by 200 rows per screen. This is equivalent to 128,000 pixels per page. Because there are eight pixels per byte, this totals 16,000 bytes per page. Because two bit planes, bit planes 0 and 1, are used to store the data, only 8,000 bytes are required per page. Alternating bytes of data from the host memory are loaded into bit planes 0 and 1, as shown in Figure 7.8. Each byte of data contains eight pixels; thus, one byte, containing pixels 0 through 7, resides in bit plane 0, and the following byte, containing pixels 8 through 15, resides in bit plane 1.

When display memory is read from or written to, the transfer of data to the two display bit planes occurs automatically because of special hardware in the EGA/VGA. This addressing mode is called odd/even because data read from or written to even locations affects bit plane 0, and data read from or written to odd locations affects bit plane 1.

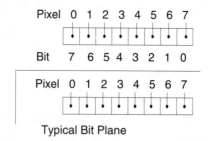

Typical Bit Plane

FIGURE 7.7   Mode 6: Pixel Packing

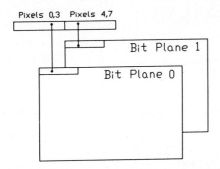

FIGURE 7.8 Mode 6: Mapping Data into Display Memory

In Figure 7.9, a byte array in host memory called *data* is copied to display memory. The array consists of alternating character codes and attribute bytes. In the array, the "D" refers to the data byte and the "X" is the index number—that is, 0, 1, 2, . . . 79. The data in the data buffer is written to display memory bit planes 0 and 1, as indicated in Figure 7.9.

It should be noted that the memory in the bit plane is segmented into two halves. The upper half contains even scan rows and the lower half contains odd scan rows. This is added to the fact that alternating bytes are contained in different bit planes. Figure 7.9 shows how four consecutive bytes of host-memory, "D158", "D159", "D160", and "D161," are spread through display memory.

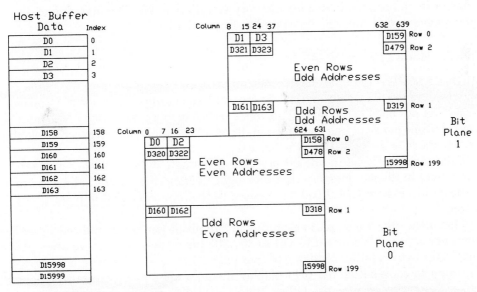

FIGURE 7.9 Mode 6: Moving Data from a Host Array to Display Memory

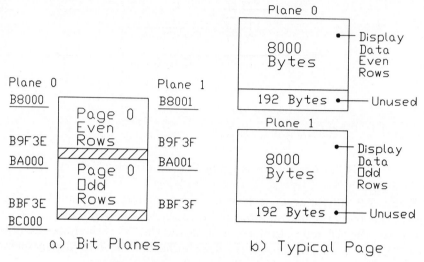

FIGURE 7.10 Mode 6: Display Memory Map

Although 16,000 bytes of memory are required per display page, only 8,000 bytes are required in each of the two bit planes because the alternating bytes are loaded into separate bit planes. Because odd/even memory mapping is in effect, only even addresses are accessible in bit plane 0, and only odd addresses are accessible in bit plane 1. A display page therefore requires 16,000 bytes and occupies 16,384 bytes of display memory address space. Up to two display pages can be resident in display memory simultaneously. The mapping of display pages into memory is illustrated in Figure 7.10.

7.4.7 Mode 11 Hex (VGA)

Mode 11 hex is a graphics display mode that uses display memory bit plane 0 to store the graphics information. There are two possible colors for each pixel, so one bit per pixel is required. This mode uses a display resolution of 640 horizontal pixels per scan line and 480 scan lines. The default character set invoked in this mode is the 8-by-16 character set.

Each pixel is stored in one bit position of a single byte in display memory. Each byte in display memory contains eight neighboring horizontal pixels, as indicated in Figure 7.11. Pixel 0 is located to the immediate left of pixel 1, and so on.

This mode allows a display resolution of 640 pixels per horizontal row by 480 rows per screen. This is equivalent to 307,200 pixels per page. There are eight pixels per byte, totaling 38,400 bytes per page. Consecutive bytes in host memory map to consecutive bytes in display memory. The exception is when the offset value loaded into the Offset Register is different from the number of bytes per line. The memory mapping is illustrated in Figure 7.12.

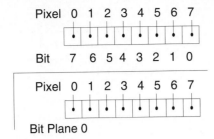

FIGURE 7.11 Mode 11 Hex: Pixel Packing

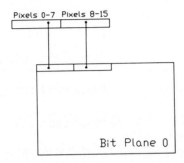

FIGURE 7.12 Mode 11 Hex: Mapping Data into Display Memory

In the following example, a data array in host memory called data is written to display memory. The host array is defined as a *char* array, so every element in the array is a byte wide. The elements in the data array each represent eight pixels. An element is named "D.X". The "D" refers to data and the "X" is the index number—that is, 0, 1, 2 . . . 159. If the data in the data buffer is written to display memory, it is loaded into bit plane 0, as indicated in Figure 7.13.

A single page requires 38,400 bytes of memory. Only one display page can be resident in display memory. However, display memory bit planes 1, 2, and 3 are unoccupied. The mapping of a display page into memory is illustrated in Figure 7.14.

7.4.8 Hercules/MDA Emulation

The EGA/VGA can emulate the Hercules or MDA standards to a certain degree, depending on the EGA implementation. The standard EGA can emulate the alphanumeric mode of the Hercules/MDA, and advanced boards can boast total compatibility. The monochrome graphics systems rely on a high-resolution display screen capable of displaying 720 by 350 pixels. The VGA allows a resolution of 720 by 400 pixels. A corresponding high-resolution character font size of 9-by-14 is used, producing the standard alphanumeric display format of 80 columns by 25 rows for the 350-scan-line mode. A 9-by-16

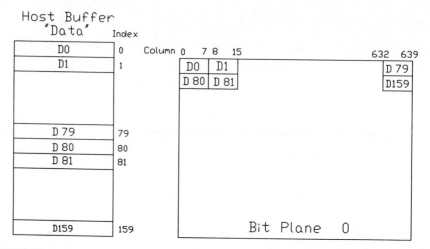

FIGURE 7.13 Mode 11 Hex: Moving Data from a Host Array to Display Memory

font is used to produce the same 80-by-25 character resolution when a 400-scan-line mode is active in the VGA.

The monochrome graphics half mode utilizes 32 Kbytes beginning at address B0000 hex; the full mode occupies 64 Kbytes, also beginning at B0000 hex. The Hercules operates with separate contiguous memory banks in a manner similar to that used by the CGA. However, the CGA splits the display into two banks, whereas the Hercules splits the display into four banks. Therefore, each scan line is separated from its nearest neighbors by one-quarter of the display.

When the EGA is emulating the Hercules, its memory is organized so that two of the four bit planes are used for display memory. Each byte in the display memory represents eight horizontal neighboring pixels. Each pixel is represented by one bit in bit plane 0 and one bit in bit plane 1. Each pixel may be displayed in one of two colors. Two display pages are available, called display

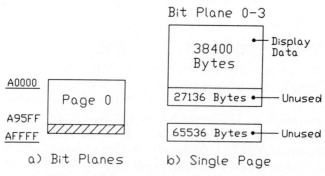

FIGURE 7.14 Mode 11 Hex: Display Memory Map

TABLE 7.13 Monochrome Graphics Emulation Modes

Display Mode (Hex)	Resolution	Number of Colors	Starting Address
F	640;ti350	3	A0000

TABLE 7.14 Monochrome Graphics Attributes

Plane 2	Plane 0	Pixel Color	Attribute Value
0	0	Black	0
0	1	Video	1
1	0	Blinking	4
1	1	Intensify	5

page 0 and display page 1. One of these is selected as the active display page in the Page Select field of the Hercules Mode Control Register.

There is only one monochrome graphics mode in the standard EGA/VGA implementation. It can be used as an enhanced Hercules/MDA graphics display mode. This mode can operate with either a monochrome monitor or an enhanced color monitor. The monochrome graphics display mode is listed in Table 7.13.

Note that the graphics mode F hex is not mapped at the same address as the Hercules graphics memory. In addition, this mode allows a 350-line resolution. Two bit planes, plane 0 and plane 2, are used to contain all of the display data. One bit from plane 0 and one from plane 2 are used together to represent the color. Table 7.14 illustrates the different monochrome attributes possible by representing a pixel in two planes.

If only 16 Kbytes are available per bit plane, two consecutive bit planes can be chained together to form a 32-Kbyte plane. Because four bit planes are available, plane 1 is chained to plane 0, and plane 3 is chained to plane 2. In this way, two 32-Kbyte bit planes are formed. This chaining is controlled in the Chain Odd/Even (COE) field of the Miscellaneous Register.

7.4.9 Mode F Hex (EGA/VGA)

Mode F hex is a four-color graphics display mode. On the EGA, it is designed to drive monochrome monitors that are capable of displaying black, video (white), blinking video, and intensified video. On the VGA, it is designed to drive the enhanced monochrome display monitor. This mode uses a display resolution of 640 horizontal pixels per scan line and 350 scan lines. The default character set invoked in this mode is the 8-by-14 character set.

Mode F hex assumes that a monochrome monitor is attached to the EGA. Any other monitor will not necessarily display the data correctly if mode F is active. The VGA can drive the enhanced color monitor or the enhanced monochrome monitor when mode F is active.

Mode F hex uses display memory bit plane 0 and bit plane 2 to store the graphics information. There are four possible colors for each pixel, so two bits per pixel are required.

Two bit planes are used to store the data. The attributes associated with this mode contain a video bit field and an intensity bit field. The video bit fields are stored in bit plane 0, and the intensity bit fields are stored in bit plane 2.

In EGA implementations of less than 64 Kbytes per plane, bit planes 0 and 1 are chained together, as are bit planes 2 and 3, in order to provide sufficient memory for an entire page.

Each pixel is stored in one bit position of a single byte in two bit planes of display memory. Each byte in display memory contains eight neighboring horizontal pixels, as indicated in Figure 7.15. Pixel 0 is located to the immediate left of pixel 1, and so on.

This mode allows a display resolution of 640 pixels per horizontal row by 350 rows per screen. This is equivalent to 224,000 pixels per page. There are eight pixels per byte, totaling 28,000 bytes per page. The two bit attributes associated with each pixel are mapped into separate bit planes. The video fields asso-

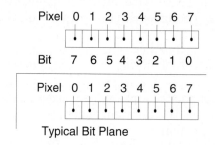

FIGURE 7.15 Mode F Hex: Pixel Packing

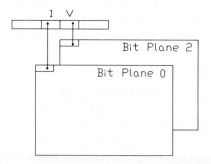

FIGURE 7.16 Mode F Hex: Mapping Data into Display Memory

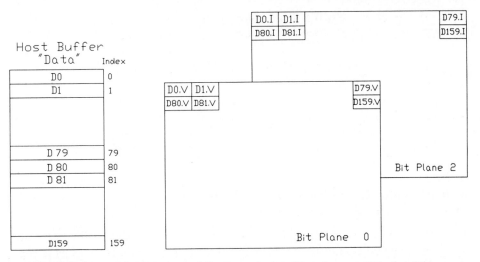

FIGURE 7.17 Mode F Hex: Moving Data from a Host Array to Display Memory

ciated with each pixel are stored in bit plane 0, and the intensity fields associated with each pixel are stored in bit plane 2. The memory mapping is illustrated in Figure 7.16.

In the following example, a byte array in host memory called data is written to display memory. The elements in the data array each represent four pixels. An element is named "D.X". The "D" refers to data and "X" is the index number—that is, 0, 1, 2 . . . 159. The video portion of the data in the data buffer is written to display memory bit plane 0, and the intensity portion of the data is written into bit plane 0. This is illustrated in Figure 7.17.

A single page requires 28,000 bytes of memory. Only one display page can be resident in display memory simultaneously. However, in EGA and VGA systems with 64 Kbytes per bit plane, display memory bit planes 1 and 3 are unoccupied. The mapping of the display page into memory is illustrated in Figure 7.18.

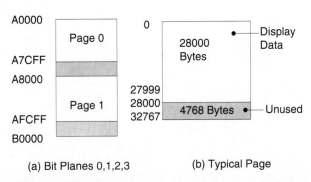

(a) Bit Planes 0,1,2,3   (b) Typical Page

FIGURE 7.18 Mode F Hex: Display Memory Map

TABLE 7.15 Mapping Bit
Position to Bit Planes

Bit Position	Bit Plane
0	0
1	1
2	2
3	3

7.4.10   16-color Graphics Modes D, E, 10, and 12 Hex (D, E, 10 EGA/VGA; 12 VGA)

Modes D, E, 10, and 12 hex are graphics display modes that utilize all four display memory bit planes to store the graphics information. Each pixel is represented by four bits, one bit per bit plane. Each byte in display memory represents one bit of eight neighboring horizontal pixels. Because there are four bits per pixel, each pixel can be represented in one of sixteen colors. The mapping of bit position to bit plane is shown in Table 7.15.

Each pixel is stored in one bit position of up to four bytes in display memory. This is illustrated in Figure 7.19.

Each byte in the four bit planes contains eight neighboring horizontal pixels, as indicated in Figure 7.20. Pixel 0 is located to the immediate left of pixel 1, and so on.

In the following example, a byte array in host memory called data is written to display memory. The elements in the data array each represent four pixels. An element is named "D.X". The "D" refers to data and "X" is the index number—that is, 0, 1, 2 . . . 159. The video portion of the data in the data buffer corresponding to bit plane 0 is written to display memory bit plane 0. This is illustrated in Figure 7.21.

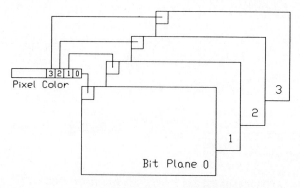

FIGURE 7.19 Modes D, E, 10, and 12 Hex: Mapping Data into Display Memory

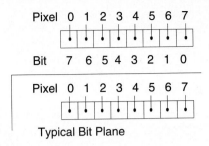

FIGURE 7.20 Modes D, E, 10, and 12 Hex: Pixel Packing

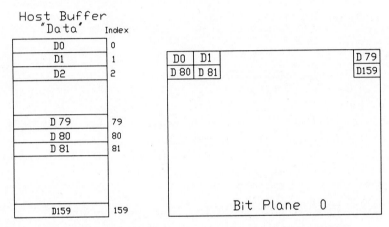

FIGURE 7.21 Modes D, E, 10, and 12 Hex: Moving Data
from a Host Array to Display Memory

7.4.11 Mode D Hex (EGA/VGA)

This mode uses a display resolution of 320 horizontal pixels per scan line and 200 scan lines. This is equivalent to 64,000 pixels per page. There are eight pixels per byte, totaling 8,000 bytes per bit plane per page. Eight pages can reside in display memory simultaneously. The default character set invoked in this mode is the 8-by-8 character set. This allows 40 horizontal characters by 25 character rows. The mapping of display pages into memory is illustrated in Figure 7.22.

7.4.12 Mode E Hex (EGA/VGA)

Mode E hex uses a display resolution of 640 horizontal pixels per scan line and 200 scan lines. This is equivalent to 128,000 pixels per page. There are eight pixels per byte, totaling 16,000 bytes per bit plane per page. Four pages can reside in display memory simultaneously. The default character set invoked in this mode is the 8-by-8 character set. This allows 80 horizontal characters by 25

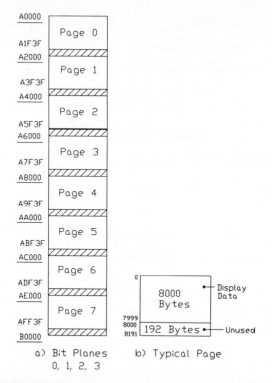

FIGURE 7.22 Mode D Hex: Display Memory Map

character rows. The mapping of display pages into memory is illustrated in Figure 7.23.

7.4.13 Mode 10 Hex (EGA/VGA)

Mode 10 hex uses a display resolution of 640 horizontal pixels per scan line and 350 scan lines. This is equivalent to 224,000 pixels per page. There are eight pixels per byte, totaling 28,000 bytes per bit plane per page. Two pages can reside in display memory simultaneously. The default character set invoked in this mode is the 8-by-14 character set. This allows 80 horizontal characters by 25 character rows. The mapping of display pages into memory is illustrated in Figure 7.24.

7.4.14 Mode 12 Hex (VGA Only)

Mode 12 hex uses a display resolution of 640 horizontal pixels per scan line and 480 scan lines. This is equivalent to 307,200 pixels per page. There are eight

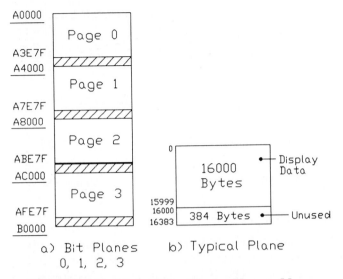

FIGURE 7.23 Mode E Hex: Display Memory Map

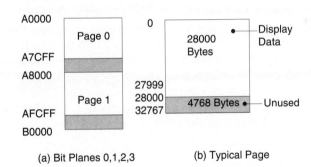

FIGURE 7.24 Mode 10 Hex: Display Memory Map

pixels per byte, totaling 38,400 bytes per bit plane per page. Only one page can reside in display memory. The default character set invoked in this mode is the 8-by-16 character set. This allows 80 horizontal characters by 25 character rows. The mapping of display pages into memory is illustrated in Figure 7.25.

7.4.15 256-color Mode (VGA Only)

Only one mode is currently available that allows 256 simultaneous colors. This mode is available only on the VGA, and it is numbered mode 13 hex. The 256 Color Registers are accessed directly by the data in display memory. Each pixel is represented by eight bits, providing the 256 simultaneous colors.

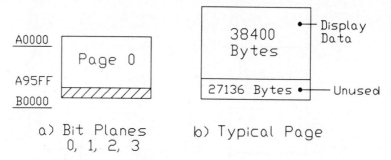

a) Bit Planes
0, 1, 2, 3   b) Typical Page

FIGURE 7.25 Mode 12 Hex: Display Memory Map

7.4.16 Mode 13 Hex (VGA Only)

There are 256 possible colors for each pixel, so eight bits per pixel are required. Each pixel is stored in one byte of display memory. This byte can reside in any one of the four bit planes. The default character set invoked in this mode is the 8-by-8 character set. This allows 40 horizontal characters by 25 character rows.

This mode allows a display resolution of 320 pixels per horizontal row by 200 rows per screen. This is equivalent to 64,000 pixels per page. Because there is one pixel per byte, there are 64,000 bytes per page. Four bit planes are used to store the data, so only 16,000 bytes are required per page. Consecutive bytes of data from the host memory are loaded into bit planes 0, 1, 2, and 3 as shown in Figure 7.26. Each byte of data contains one pixel. The first byte, containing pixel 0, resides in bit plane 0, the second in bit plane 1, the third in bit plane 2, and the fourth in bit plane 3. A fifth byte would reside following pixel 0 in bit plane 0.

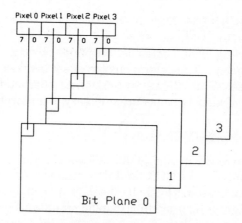

FIGURE 7.26 Mode 13 Hex: Mapping Data into Display Memory

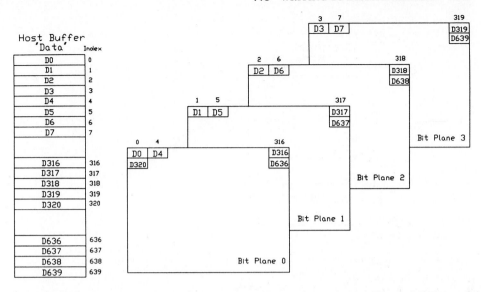

FIGURE 7.27   Mode 13 Hex: Moving Data from a Host Array to Display Memory

When display memory is read from or written to, the transfer of data from the host array to the four display bit planes in display memory occurs automatically because of special hardware in the VGA.

In the following example, a byte array in host memory called data is written to display memory. The elements in the data array each represent four pixels. An element is named "D.X". The "D" refers to data and "X" is the index number—that is, 0, 1, 2 . . . 159. The video portion of the data in the data buffer is written to display memory bit plane 0, 1, 2, and 3. This is illustrated in Figure 7.27.

A total of 16,000 bytes of memory is required per bit plane. Three out of four bytes in each bit plane are unused and cannot be accessed by the host in this display mode. Thus, the 16,000 bytes actually occupy 64,000 bytes of all four bit planes. At the end of each bit plane is an unused buffer of 1,535 bytes. Similarly, three out of four bytes are not available to the host. Only one display page can be resident in display memory. The mapping of this display page into memory is illustrated in Figure 7.28. Enhanced VGAs use this memory.

7.5   WRITING TO DISPLAY MEMORY

There are two general ways to write to display memory. The first, by far the simplest and slowest, is to use the BIOS call entitled Write Pixel. The second involves writing directly to the display memory.

The display memory can be thought of as a four-dimensional space. The two standard dimensions are height, or row, and width, or column. The third dimension is depth and relates to the intensity or color of the pixel. This depth

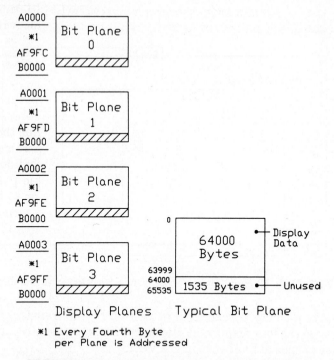

FIGURE 7.28 Mode 13 Hex: Display Memory Map

value might be located in any or all of the four bit planes, depending on the display mode and the number of planes enabled. The fourth dimension spans across the number of pages. Figure 7.29 illustrates this generalized four-dimensional space.

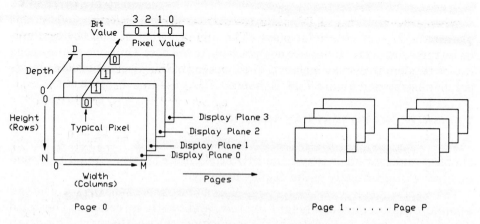

FIGURE 7.29 Four-dimensional Display Memory

In Figure 7.29, the height ranges from 0 to n rows; the width ranges from 0 to m columns; the depth ranges from 0 to 15; and the page number ranges from 0 to 7 pages.

7.5.1 Writing to Display Memory: BIOS

The Write Dot BIOS call, AH = 0C hex, modifies the value in one pixel location. Depending on the current display mode, this pixel may be represented by a one-bit, two-bit, or four-bit value. The programmer must provide the row number, column number, pixel value, and page number. These parameters correspond to the generalized four-dimensional graphic representation of display memory. A special feature is provided within the pixel value parameter. It causes the pixel value to be written directly into memory or to be logically XORed with the current value in that pixel location of display memory.

Although this BIOS call is simple to use and general enough to handle all display modes, it is extremely slow when a series of dots must be drawn.

7.5.2 Writing to Display Memory: Direct

The descriptions in the sections below involve writing directly to the display memory. To avoid repeating each description for each display format, the most commonly used display format was chosen. These descriptions are targeted for the display mode 10 hex, although they may be readily applied to the other graphics display modes.

7.5.3 Graphics Data Structures

Some general information about graphics data structures is appropriate before the details of writing to display memory are addressed. A pixel is the most primitive graphics element, and a bit is the most primitive computer element. A pixel may be represented by up to four bits in a 16-color system like the EGA.

When a computer has an 8-bit bus, the byte is the most primitive addressable element. A byte consists of eight bits. The smallest element that the computer can write to in a single instruction cycle is a byte.

The display memory is bit mapped and stores the image data in four separate bit planes. Each bit plane is organized into bytes, and each begins at the same host address. This provides an effective 32-bit display word, as illustrated in Figure 7.30.

This 32-bit bus is used in several display operations and may be accessed in a single instruction cycle. Note that at a single host address, one byte from each of the four bit planes contributes to form the 32-bit word. This 32-bit bus is the largest structure that the EGA can manipulate.

The EGA contains a byte-wide interface to the host. The VGA contains a 16-bit-wide bus interface to the host if the VGA is planar. In the Series/2

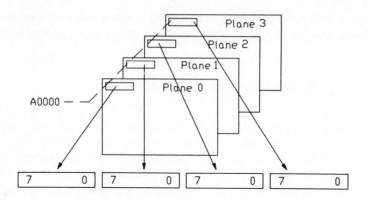

FIGURE 7.30 32-Bit Internal Display Bus

computers, the VGA is planar if it resides on the host backplane. The VGA contains an 8-bit-wide bus interface to the host if the VGA is an adapter plugged into a computer. This byte-wide bus is multiplexed by the dispatcher onto any or all of the four 8-bit bit plane buses. The Map Mask Register controls which of the planes the data will be written to. If all four planes are selected, the same eight bits will be written to each of the four bit planes. The byte-to-32-bit interface is illustrated in Figure 7.31.

7.5.4 Writing to a Pixel

Three write modes are available in the EGA/VGA. These are set in the Write Mode (WM) field of the Mode Register. The selected write mode dictates the nature of the write operation. Write modes 0, 2, and 3 are used when data is being transferred from the host to the EGA/VGA. Write mode 1 is used when data is being moved from one location in display memory to a second location. Write mode 2 is a convenient tool for writing to one or all bit planes of an individual pixel.

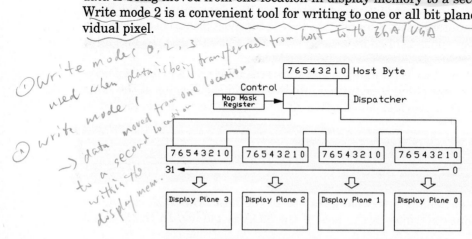

FIGURE 7.31 Host Byte to the 32-Bit Bus Display

Two values must be determined in order to locate a pixel within the display memory. The first value corresponds to the byte address of display memory that contains the pixel. This value is determined by the row and column coordinates of the desired pixel.

The following example illustrates this process. Suppose that the display format is 640 horizontal dots by 350 vertical dots. Let the pixel location be at row number 85 and column number 243, resident on display page 0. The display memory address for display page 0 begins at A0000 hex. Each row of the display contains 80 bytes of information. Thus, row 85 corresponds to byte number 6,960 which is 1B30 hex. This is determined by multiplying 80 by 87. The address of the beginning of row 85 is A0000+1A90 hex, or A1A90 hex. Each byte in display memory corresponds to eight pixels. Therefore, the byte that contains the pixel at column 243 is obtained by dividing the column number by 8. This gives the whole part of 30 with a remainder of 3. The whole part of 30, or 1E hex, is the offset from the start of the row to the byte that contains column 243. The address A1AAE is the address of the desired byte in display memory.

The second value that must be determined in order to find the desired pixel is the bit number within the byte A1AAE hex that corresponds to column 243. This is obtained from the remainder of 3. The byte at A1AAE corresponds to pixels 240 to 247. These pixels correspond to the remainders of 0 to 7 when using modulo 8 arithmetic. A remainder of 0 indicates that the far-left pixel in the eight neighboring horizontal pixels is selected. This far-left pixel is equivalent to the most significant bit of the byte. In this example, the remainder of 3 indicates the fourth pixel from the left in byte A1AAE. In order to enable only this pixel, the Bit Mask Register is used. It must be set to 10 hex to enable this pixel alone. The bit mask value of 10 hex is the second value required to access the pixel. Table 7.16 illustrates the values used to determine the bit mask value.

7.5.5 Write Mode 0 (EGA/VGA)

Write mode 0 is the most commonly used write mode when data is written from the host to the EGA. There are many options within write mode 0, depending on the setting of several of the EGA registers. The most general operation

TABLE 7.16 Pixels in Display Memory at Byte A000:1AAE

Bit	7	6	5	4	3	2	1	0
Column	240	241	242	243	244	245	246	247
Remainder	0	1	2	3	4	5	6	7
Mask (hex)	80	40	20	10	08	04	02	01

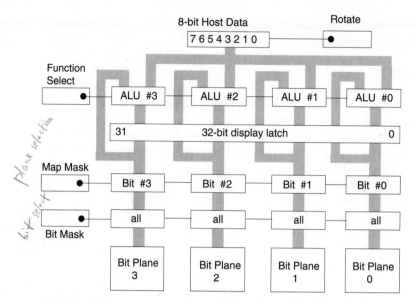

FIGURE 7.32 Write Mode 0: Host-to-Display-Memory Write Path

involves taking a byte from the host and writing it directly to one or more of the display memory planes. The data will pass through several hardware sections on its way from the host to the display memory. The path from the host to the display memory is illustrated in Figure 7.32.

7.5.6 Data Rotator

The first section through which the data passes is the barrel rotator. The barrel rotator is capable of shifting the input data from zero to seven bits to the right. Bits shifted out of the byte from the right are rotated back into the byte from the left. The number of bits that the input byte are rotated depends on the rotate count in the RC field of the Data Rotate Register. Figure 7.33 illustrates the operation of the barrel rotator, showing it shifting the input byte three bits.

7.5.7 Function Select

Once through the rotator, the data passes into the Arithmetic Logic Unit (ALU). Four 8-bit ALU sections are used to modify the data. Four logical operations may occur in the ALU as dictated by the Function Control (FC) field of the Data Rotate Register. These functions are listed in Table 7.17.

Functions 1, 2, and 3 logically combine the input byte with data stored in the 32-bit processor latch. The 32-bit processor latch is loaded by performing a read operation from the display memory. Eight bits are loaded from each of the four

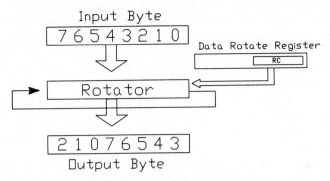

FIGURE 7.33 Barrel Rotator

TABLE 7.17 Function Control Field

FC Field	Logical Function
0	Data unmodified
1	Data ANDed with latched data
2	Data ORed with latched data
3	Data XORed with latched data

bit planes. An assembly language MOV instruction can be used to read data from the display memory. The source field of this instruction should point to a byte location in display memory. Once this instruction has been executed, 32 bits of data from the four addressed bytes in the four bit planes will be accessed and loaded into the 32-bit processor latch. Each read operation updates this 32-bit register. The data in the latch remains unchanged until the next read operation.

A read-modify-write operation is normally used to logically modify data. For example, the equation $A = A \& B$ would be read "the value A is equal to the logical ANDing of A and B." To perform this operation, the value A would be read. This value is modified by logically ANDing it with B. The result is written in place of the original A value in display memory.

In assembly language, this operation could be accomplished without the display arithmetic logic unit by the following commands. Assume that the register pair DS:SI points to the selected byte in display memory and that the data to be used in the AND operation is in the AL register.

```
MOV   BL,DS:SI    ;move the display byte into the BL register
AND   AL,BL       ;AL = AL & BL
MOV   DS:SI,AL    ;restore the display byte with the result
```

It should be noted that only one bit plane at a time can be accessed by a read operation. Thus, these instructions affect eight pixels in one and only one bit plane. If all four bit planes need to be modified, these instructions would be repeated four times, enabling a different bit plane before each iteration. The plane read is determined by the value in the Read Map Select Register.

This procedure can also be accomplished totally within the confines of the EGA/VGA as follows. A byte in display memory is read into the internal 32-bit EGA/VGA register. This value is ANDed with the data byte being transferred from the host. The result is written back to the display memory in place of the original data.

This technique is implemented in assembly language using the display ALU by first setting the Function Select (FS) field of the Data Rotate Register to the value 1. Again, assuming that the register pair DS:SI points to the desired location in display memory, the same operation can be performed as follows.

```
MOV   BL,DS:SI     ;move the data into the 32-bit register
MOV   DS:SI,AL     ;move the data back into the bit planes
```

The first instruction causes a read to occur. This loads the EGA/VGA 32-bit internal register with the four bytes from the addressed location in the display memory. The data is read into the BL register. However, the BL register in this example is actually a dummy register, since the value loaded into it will not be used. This is called a *dummy read* because it is unimportant whether the data gets to the host. The entire operation will occur within the EGA. The second instruction causes each of the four fields in the 32-bit register to be ANDed with the byte value in the AL register. The result is then written to all planes that are enabled in the Map Mask register. Remember that the AND operation occurs because of the FS field being previously set to 1.

It is important to realize that many instructions were saved using the second technique. The speed advantage was realized because of the internal EGA/VGA 32-bit register. This allows all four bit planes to be accessed in one instruction cycle.

In the previous example, both instructions accessed the same display data causing the $A = A \ \& \ B$ operation to be properly performed. If the address is changed between these instructions, the operation $C = A \ \& \ B$ will be performed. In this case, the result is not written over the original data because the data in the 32-bit latch remains there until another read operation from display memory occurs. At that time, it is overwritten with the new data. Thus, it is important not to change the address referencing the display memory in between the read and the write operations.

7.5.8   Plane Selection

The Map Mask Register was discussed above. It selects which bit planes will be affected in the write operation. Any plane selected will be modified according to the Function Select field. The logical operation selected by the Function Select field has two operands. The first operand is an 8-bit value provided to the ALU by the MOV instruction. This value will be replicated from one to four times, depending on the number of planes selected, in order to create the 32-bit word. The second operand is a 32-bit value having been loaded into the 32-bit display register.

Suppose that it is desired to XOR the value 55 hex with the byte values in each of the four bit planes at a desired address in the display memory. This byte is denoted in Equation 7.1 by "Byte(Bit Plane n)". All four display memory planes are enabled by loading a 0F hex into the Map Mask Register. An XOR operation is selected by loading a 03 into the Function Select field of the Data Rotate Register. Equation 7.1 illustrates this 32-bit XOR operation.

Equation 7.1 Using the XOR Function

Byte(bit plane 0) = 55 hex .XOR. byte(bit plane 0)

Byte(bit plane 1) = 55 hex .XOR. byte(bit plane 1)

Byte(bit plane 2) = 55 hex .XOR. byte(bit plane 2)

Byte(bit plane 3) = 55 hex .XOR. byte(bit plane 3)

Note that the second operand in each equation is unique, depending on the value in the display memory. Only one unique first operand, equal to 55 in this example, is possible for all four display planes.

The Color Plane Enable (CPE) field of the Color Plane Enable Register is a four-bit field. Each bit is associated with a bit plane, and any bit set to 1 causes the corresponding bit plane to be enabled. Table 7.18 lists the functions of the four bits within this register.

7.5.9 Bit Selection

Only selected bit positions within the four bit planes will be affected during a write operation. There are two levels of selection, the first being the bit plane selection and the second being the bit selection. The 32-bit data is organized as

TABLE 7.18 Color Plane Enable Field

CPE Field	Display Plane Enabled
Bit 0 = 1	Select display plane 0
Bit 1 = 1	Select display plane 1
Bit 2 = 1	Select display plane 2
Bit 3 = 1	Select display plane 3

four parallel 8-bit buses, one bus to each of the bit planes. The Map Mask Register is used to determine which bit planes should be affected. The Bit Mask Register is used to determine which bits within all of the selected planes should be affected.

It is often desirable to enable only selected bits within the byte to be written to display memory. To accomplish this, it is necessary to mask certain bits from the write operation. A pixel is represented by a single bit in one or more of the bit planes. A byte is the smallest data structure that the host processor can update in a single instruction. Because a byte contains eight bits, masking is necessary if fewer than eight pixels are to be modified in a single instruction. The Set/Reset Register can also be used when writing to a single pixel. The Bit Mask Register is used to mask bits from the write operation.

Each bit in the Bit Mask Register corresponds to one of eight neighboring horizontal pixels. Any bit set to 1 enables that particular bit to be modified; likewise, any bit reset to 0 protects that bit. The most significant bit in the Bit Mask Register corresponds to the far-left pixel on the display. All four bitplanes are affected by the same bit plane mask, replicated from one to four times.

7.5.10 Set/Reset Function

The write mode 0 operation described above assumed that all four bits in the Enable Set/Reset Register were disabled. In effect, this disabled the Set/Reset function, and the selected bit planes were modified according to the data byte sent through the host MOV instruction. If one or more of the bits in the Enable Set/Reset Register were enabled, the write operation would take into account the value in the Set/Reset Register.

A single pixel often needs to be modified in all four bit planes. Using the direct approach, as illustrated above, four bytes would have to be sent to the display memory, one for each bit plane. Between each of these byte MOV operations, the Map Mask Register would be modified to select each of the four bit planes independently. The Bit Mask Register would mask out all bits other than the bit in the position associated with the desired pixel location. This requires a good many instructions and therefore a lot of processor time. A useful alternative is the Set/Reset function, which can modify a single pixel in all four bit planes with unique data. The direct approach could enable all four bit planes and thereby load all four bits of a pixel. However, each bit plane would be written with identical data—that is, a 1 or a 0.

Suppose a pixel is to be loaded with the value A hex. The value A hex is equivalent to a 1010 binary. Table 7.19 illustrates which bits will be loaded into the four bit planes to achieve this color.

In order to load a pixel with the value A hex, using the Set/Reset approach, the value A hex would be written into the Set/Reset Register and the value F hex would be written into the Enable Set/Reset Register. The A hex corre-

TABLE 7.19 Set/Reset Field

Bit Plane	Bit Value
0	0
1	1
2	0
3	1

sponds to the desired color, and the value F hex causes all four bit planes to be selected for the Set/Reset function. Once these steps are taken, any write operation to display memory will invoke the Set/Reset function.

A pixel is loaded with the color A hex by writing a dummy value to the desired memory address. Both the address of the byte in display memory that contains the desired pixel and the pixel location within the byte must be determined. Using the same coordinates from the previous example, row 85 and column 243, the host address of A1AAE hex and the Bit Plane Mask value of 10 hex are used to access the desired pixel. Thus, a 10 hex is loaded into the Bit Mask Register. A MOV operation to address A1AAE hex causes the value A hex to be written to the desired pixel. A dummy write operation is used because all four planes will be updated from the Set/Reset Register rather than the host data path. The data coming from the host is ignored. The write instruction itself, regardless of the data, will cause the display update.

The operations that were described to occur on the host data will also modify the Set/Reset data. The Function Select field allows the Set/Reset data to be logically combined with the data resident in the display memory. The Map Mask Register controls which bit planes will be affected, and the Bit Mask Register determines which pixels within a given byte will be affected.

Figure 7.34 illustrates the Set/Reset data path. In this example the Enable Set/Reset Register is set to F hex, thereby selecting the data in the Set/Reset Register for all four data selectors. The value in each of the bit positions is replicated eight times before it is MASKed with the value in the Bit Mask Register. Note that each of the four bytes is MASKed with the identical byte loaded in the Bit Mask Register. Only the bit position enabled in the Bit Mask Register is modified in the bit planes. This bit position corresponds to the desired pixel. All four bit planes are enabled because the Map Mask Register is set to F hex. The write operation occurs directly because the Function Select Field of the Data Rotate Register is set to 0. As a result, no logical operations occur within the ALU.

It is possible to enable all planes in the Enable Set/Reset Register, yet not select desired planes in the Map Mask Register. The Map Mask Register takes precedence. No data will be modified in a bit plane that is not selected.

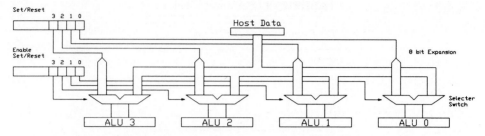

FIGURE 7.34 Set/Reset Example Data Flow

It is also possible to enable only selected planes in the Enable Set/Reset Register even though those bit planes are selected in the Map Mask Register. The effect is that all planes enabled in the Enable Set/Reset Register will be modified according to the corresponding value in the Set/Reset Register. The other planes will be modified depending on the data sent by the host. It therefore is possible to perform two independent operations in a single instruction cycle.

Suppose the Set/Reset Register contains an A hex and the Enable Set/Reset Register contains a 3 hex. The 3 in the Enable Set/Reset Register enables bit planes 0 and 1 for the Set/Reset Function. The corresponding bits in the Set/Reset register are 0 and 1 respectively. Further, suppose that the value of 40 hex is in the Bit Mask Register, thereby selecting one pixel. The Function Select field is assumed to be 0, thereby allowing a straight write operation. The following instruction would move the byte value BB hex to a byte in display memory addressed by DS:SI. Because the Bit Mask Register is a 40 hex, bit 6 of the host word will be copied to both display planes 2 and 3.

```
MOV   AL,0BBh         ;Load the AL register with BB hex
MOV   DS:SI,AL        ;Write BB hex to display memory
```

The effects on the pixel in display memory are shown in Table 7.20.

Programmers may find unique applications for this combined technique.

TABLE 7.20 Effects of the Set/Reset Function

Bit Plane	Pixel Value	Reason
0	0	Bit 0 of Set/Reset = 0
1	1	Bit 1 of Set/Reset = 1
2	0	Bit 6 of host byte = 1
3	0	Bit 6 of host byte = 1

7.5.11 Write Mode 1 (EGA/VGA)

It is possible to move 32 bits of data from one display memory location to another in a single instruction cycle using write mode 1. This can greatly enhance the performance of the EGA by speeding up move operations. Combined with the MOV string instructions, large amounts of display memory can be moved rapidly. In the MOV string operation, both the source and destination fields must address display memory because this 32-bit move operation cannot be extended into the host memory, which is usually restricted to an 8-bit bus. The Data Rotator, the Set/Reset function, the ALU, and the bit mask are completely ignored in this write mode.

The internal bus of the EGA/VGA is 32 bits wide. This bus is written to during a processor read operation. The four bit planes contribute a byte of data each to the 32-bit latch when the processor reads a byte of information from display memory. The read operation occurs when a MOV instruction is executed with the source field addressing display memory. When write mode 1 is enabled, the data written to display memory in a MOV instruction comes from the display 32-bit latch; it is not presented by the host in the MOV instruction. All planes that are selected in the Map Mask Register will be updated with the data in the corresponding byte of the 32-bit display latch.

This powerful feature is a prime reason for having a display memory that is larger than the active display region. Images can be stored in nondisplayed regions of the display memory and then rapidly moved into the display region, 32 bits at a time. Using the MOV string operation, a contiguous block of data can be moved from one area of display memory to another. The host CX Register contains the number of bytes to move. The DS:SI Register pair points to the source data, and the ES:DI Register pair points to the destination data. Again, both must address display memory. This operation is illustrated in Figure 7.35.

The Move String Byte (MOVSB) instruction first reads a byte of data as addressed by the source address field. The source address points to a byte in each of the display memory planes. These four bytes are written into the 32-bit display latch. The next function of the MOVSB instruction is to write the byte into memory as addressed by the destination address field. Again the data byte itself is ignored, and the 32-bit data in the display latch is loaded into the four bit planes. The CX count register is decremented and the process repeats until the count is zero, thereby moving a continuous block of data. The Move String Word (MOVSW) instruction could have been used. It operates identically to the Move String Byte (MOVSB) instruction except that a word is moved. Because the EGA has a byte interface to the host, this results in a slight speed improvement by reducing the instruction cycle time within the host. Because the internal display bus is 32 bits wide, it is not possible for the MOVSW instruction to result in sixteen bits from each of the four bit planes being moved simultaneously.

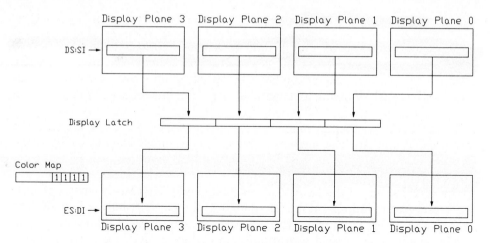

FIGURE 7.35 Write Mode 1

A severe limitation of the write mode 1 feature is that each of the bytes in each bit plane represents eight pixels. Ideally, the 32-bit MOV instruction should shift the data before it is rewritten to the display memory. This would allow pixel alignment to occur. Without this ability, the source and destination blocks of data in the display memory are constrained to be byte-aligned data. This coarse movement results from the fact that each byte actually corresponds to eight pixels. It is only possible to move a group of pixels beginning at a pixel address that is a multiple of eight to a pixel address that is also a multiple of eight. The display can be considered as having a set of grid lines drawn every eighth pixel. The minimum block size that can be moved is eight pixels, corresponding to the eight bits in a byte. The block size to be moved must be a multiple of eight, and the source and destination blocks must begin on the grid lines.

For example, suppose it is desirable to move a section of the image that begins at pixel 111 to a section that ends at pixel 317. The closest a programmer can come to pixel 111 is either 104 or 112. To include pixel 111 in the MOV operation, it is necessary to begin the move at pixel 104. The destination of the move must also be aligned to a multiple of eight. The nearest grid lines are 312 or 320. To include pixel 317, the best approximation to this move operation would be from pixel 104 to pixel 320.

7.5.12 Write Mode 2 (EGA/VGA)

The operation of write mode 2 is similar to the Set/Reset function in write mode 0. The purpose of this mode is to update a single pixel, represented in up to four bit planes. This mode, rather than the Set/Reset mode, would be selected when a group of pixels is to be updated. The group of bytes representing these pixels would be in a format where each byte would contain the four bits of the intensity to be loaded into each pixel. If 100 pixels are to be loaded, the host byte array would be 100 bytes long, and each byte would contain a four-bit value for each pixel. A MOVS string operation could copy this data quickly from the host array into the contiguous block of pixels. The data rotator and the Set/Reset function are ignored in this write mode.

The four-bit value to be loaded into the pixel is written to display memory via a MOV instruction in a similar fashion as the direct approach in write mode 0. For a single pixel to be modified, the Bit Mask Register must be loaded with the proper code byte to enable only that selected pixel. (Multiple pixels can be selected for the write operation by setting more than one bit in the Bit Mask Register.) Each bit in the four-bit value being moved to display memory is replicated eight times before it gets to the ALU. This is similar to the replication of the bits from the Set/Reset Register. This replication ensures that the data will be in the proper bit position for each of the four bit planes, regardless of which bit or bits are enabled in the Bit Mask Register. Figure 7.36 illustrates the functioning of write mode 2.

The destination field of the MOV instruction is contained in the DS:SI host register pair. The data to be moved in this example is B hex. The following instructions perform this operation, assuming that write mode 2 is in effect.

```
MOV   AL,0Bh         ;Move B hex into the AL register
MOV   DS:SI,AL       ;Move the B hex into all four bit planes
```

Note that up to eight pixels can be loaded with identical data if more than one bit in the Bit Mask Register is enabled.

7.5.13   Write Mode 3 (VGA Only)

Write mode 3 is relevant to the VGA only. Each plane is written to with eight identical bits. The bit value (1 or 0) selected for each of the four display planes (3–0) are derived from the corresponding bit positions in the SR field of the Set/Reset Register. Recall that the SR field has four bits, bits 3–0. The data written from the host is rotated according to the value in the Data Rotate Reg-

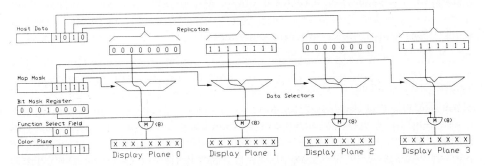

FIGURE 7.36 Write Mode 2

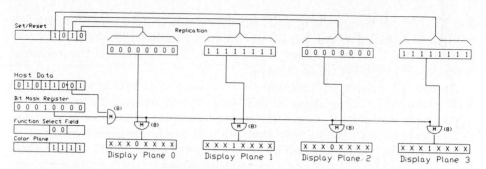

FIGURE 7.37 Write Mode 3

ister. It is then ANDed with the Bit Mask Register to form an 8-bit value that acts as the Bit Mask for the write operation. The eight identical bits derived from the Set/Reset Register are masked with this resultant value before being written to the display memory. Figure 7.37 illustrates the operation of write mode 3.

7.6   READING FROM DISPLAY MEMORY

As is the case when writing to display memory, programmers may select to read from display memory using BIOS calls or by reading directly from the display memory.

7.6.1   Reading Display Memory: BIOS

The Read Dot BIOS call, AH=0D hex, reads the value in one pixel location. Depending on the current display mode, this pixel may be represented by a one-bit, two-bit, or four-bit value. The programmer must provide the desired page number and the row and column coordinates. These coordinates correspond to the generalized four-dimensional graphic representation. Although this BIOS call is simple to use and general enough to handle all display modes, it is extremely slow when a series of dots must be read.

7.6.2   Reading Display Memory: Direct

Two means can be used to read data from the display memory to the host. The first is a direct transfer from display memory to host, and the second reads the result of a comparison. These two read modes are selected through the Read Mode (RM) field of the Mode Register.

Only eight bits of information can be read back from the display memory at a time. The display memory is organized into four bit planes. A pixel may be represented by one or more bits in one or more of the bit planes. A read operation, invoked through a MOV instruction, reads from one of these four bit planes. The Read Map Select Register is used to select which of the bit planes will be selected. Only one bit plane may be read from the display memory to the host in a single instruction cycle. It is referred to as read mode 0.

A second type of read operation involves reading the result of a comparison. This is useful when color comparisons are being made. A great deal of time can be saved when it is necessary to determine if a pixel or group of pixels are a certain value. This comparison allows a maximum of eight pixels, each spanning up to four bit planes, to be compared to a selected color. The byte result of these comparisons is returned to the host as a byte value. Pixels that match the desired color cause a 1 to be returned in their corresponding bits of the returned byte. Pixels that do not match cause a 0 to be returned in their corresponding bit position.

7.6.3   Read Mode 0

Read mode 0 allows the programmer to read the contents of the display memory. Because each of the four bit planes is accessed at the same location in host address space, only one of the bit planes can be accessed in a read instruction. A read operation can be initiated from the host via a MOV instruction with the source field addressing display memory. This instruction causes all four bit planes to be loaded simultaneously into the 32-bit EGA/VGA internal register. Although all four bit planes are read in the instruction, only one byte can be directed to the host via a MOV instruction. The Read Map Select Register is used to select which of the four bit planes will be read. The Read Map Select field contains a two-bit binary encoded value that determines which plane should be selected. Table 7.21 lists the possible options. Note that only one plane can be selected at a time. This contrasts with the Map Mask Register, in which any combination of planes can be enabled at one time during write operations.

A block diagram of read mode 0 is illustrated in Figure 7.38.

In this example, the MOV instruction addresses the desired byte in all four planes through the DS:SI register pair. The Read Map Register is loaded with

TABLE 7.21   Read Map Register

Read Map Field	Display Plane Selected
0	0
1	1
2	2
3	3

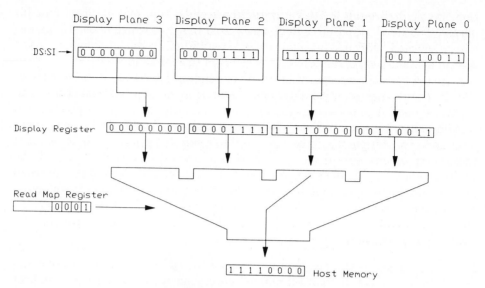

FIGURE 7.38 Read Mode 0

a 1, which selects bit plane 0. The byte value in bit plane 0 at DS:SI is transferred to the AL Register by the following instruction.

```
MOV  AL,DS:[SI]          ;read a byte from display memory to AL
```

Note that a block of display memory can be transferred readily to the host memory using the string instructions.

If the EGA/VGA has the odd/even addressing fields enabled, reading data from the bit planes may not produce the desired result. The odd/even addressing automatically directs bytes of data from the host that correspond to even addresses to even bit planes. Similarly, bytes of data that correspond to odd addresses are directed to odd bit planes. This is used in the alphanumeric modes so that the character codes are placed into bit plane 0 and the attribute bytes are placed in bit plane 1. Reading data in read mode 0 while the odd/even addressing mode is active will cause every other byte to be read from alternate planes, regardless of the setting of the Read Map Register. Thus, it is impossible to read ten bytes of contiguous data from bit plane 0 with the odd/even mode in effect. Every other byte—that is, the odd addresses—of bit plane 0 will be ignored. These will be replaced with data corresponding to the even addresses from bit plane 1. To read these ten contiguous bytes of memory, the display mode needs to be changed so that odd/even addressing is disabled.

The odd/even addressing mode is complicated to control and it is perhaps best changed by getting out of the alphanumeric modes without a screen erase. The odd/even related fields are listed in Table 7.22.

TABLE 7.22 Odd/Even Related Fields

Field	Register Name
O/E Odd/Even	Memory Mode
O/E Odd/Even Page	Misc. Output
O/E Odd/Even	Mode Register
COE Chain Odd to Even	Miscellaneous

Read mode 0 ignores the value in the Read Map Select Register when the VGA is in display mode 13 hex. In this mode, all four planes are chained together and a pixel is represented by one byte.

7.6.4 Read Mode 1

Read mode 1 returns the result of a comparison to the host via a MOV instruction. A block of comparisons can be invoked by using the REP MOV instructions. The Color Compare Register holds a four-bit value corresponding to the four-bit value of a pixel. Each bit in the Color Compare Register represents the bit value in each of the four bit planes. The relationship between the bits in the Color Compare Register and the bit planes is illustrated in Figure 7.39.

In Figure 7.39, if the Color Compare Register is loaded with the value 6, and the pixel addressed in display memory also has a value of 6, the result of the comparison will be true.

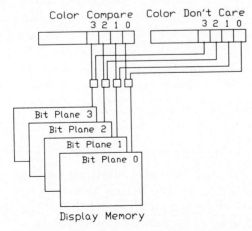

FIGURE 7.39 Color Compare Register Bits

A positive comparison will result in a 1 being loaded into the corresponding bit position of the byte returned to the host. Likewise, a negative comparison will result in a 0 being loaded into the corresponding bit position of the byte returned to the host. The results of eight comparisons, each up to four bits wide, can be returned to the host in a single instruction.

It is not necessary to use all of the four bits in the Color Compare Register when comparing the pixel values in display memory. Bit planes can be selected as being significant in the comparison or deselected as insignificant, depending on the corresponding values set in the Color Don't Care Register. Similar to the bit positions in the Color Compare Register, those in the Color Don't Care Register correspond to the bit planes. Thus, the value in bit position 0 dictates whether bit plane 0 should be considered in the comparison. Any bit set to a 1 in the Color Don't Care Register causes the corresponding bit in the Color Compare Register and the pixel value in the corresponding bit plane not to be used in the comparison. Likewise, any bit reset to a 0 in the Color Don't Care Register causes the corresponding bit plane to be used in the comparison. By selecting only desired planes, programmers can have comparisons performed on images that have pixels that are less than four bits deep. In addition, it is possible to compare classifications of pixels.

For example, a comparison can be made to determine all pixels whose most significant bit is a 1. To accomplish this, the Color Compare Register must be loaded with an 8, indicating that the comparison should look for a pixel whose value in bit plane 3 is a 1. In fact, this register could be loaded with any value whose most significant bit is a 1 because the other three bits will be ignored anyway. The Color Don't Care Register would be loaded with 7, indicating that only bit 3, the most significant bit, should be considered as being significant.

In the following example, a byte of display memory is accessed through a MOV instruction. The 8-bit result of the comparison will be loaded into the AL register. The DS:SI register pair points to the desired display memory address. Assuming that the Read Mode (RM) field of the Mode Register is set to 0, the following instruction would return the result of the comparison into the AL register.

```
MOV   AL,DS:[SI]        ;load the comparison result into AL
```

Each byte addressed in the four display memory planes contains eight pixels of information. All four planes are considered significant because a 0 is loaded into the Color Don't Care Register. The result of the comparison shows that there are three pixels in the group of eight pixels that compare true to the Color Compare value of A hex. This example is illustrated in Figure 7.40.

The Color Don't Care Register can be used to select which planes are significant. Table 7.23 illustrates some possible outcomes of the above example had the Color Don't Care Register contained different values.

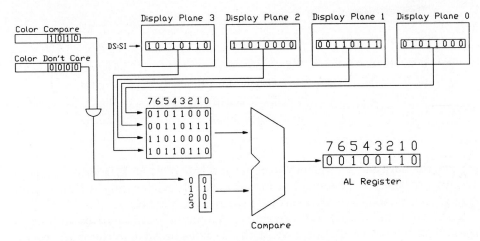

FIGURE 7.40 Read Mode 1 Example

TABLE 7.23 Color Don't Care Values

Color Don't Care Binary	Result of Comparison	Compare x = Either	Significant Planes
0111	10110110	1xxx	3
0011	10010000	10xx	3,2
1011	00101111	x0xx	2
1000	00100111	x010	2,1,0
0000	00100110	1010	3,2,1,0

7.7 DISPLAY MEMORY TIMING

The EGA/VGA controls the video bus sent to the monitor. This bus consists of the horizontal sync pulse, the vertical sync pulse, and the video signals. The video signals vary depending on the type of monitor being used. These signals are listed in Table 7.24 according to monitor type.

7.7.1 Sync Pulses

The horizontal and vertical sync pulses dictate the scan rate of the display. The horizontal sync pulse occurs once every horizontal line. The vertical sync pulse occurs once every screen refresh period. The monitor must be capable of operating at the frequencies being generated by the EGA or the VGA. In a low-resolution color mode with 320-by-200 or 640-by-200 resolution, most monitors expect the horizontal sync pulses to occur at a rate of 17.75 kHz with a vertical sync rate of 60 Hz. A high-resolution EGA monitor or a monochrome monitor

TABLE 7.24 Monitor Types

Monitor Type	Video Signals	Type
Monochrome	Video, Intensity	Digital
RGBI Color	Red, Green, Blue, Intensity	Digital
RrGgBb Color	Red (2), Green (2), Blue (2)	Digital
RGB Color	Red, Green, Blue	Analog

expects the horizontal frequency to occur at a rate of 21.85 kHz with a vertical sync rate of 60 Hz. A VGA monitor must be capable of operating at a horizontal sync rate of 31.46 kHz with a vertical sync rate of 70.08 Hz.

It should be noted that at these rates a maximum of 262 horizontal lines is possible in the low-resolution case, with 364 lines possible in the EGA resolution. Because the monitor must allow time for the vertical refresh period, the maximum number of lines is limited to 200 and 350 for the EGA and 480 for the VGA. The autosync monitors, called *multisync,* are capable of operating over a wide range of frequencies, allowing even higher resolutions than are currently output.

7.7.2 Horizontal Refresh Timing

The horizontal sync pulse synchronizes the monitor to the EGA/VGA. The EGA/VGA sends data on the video lines to the monitor. The serial data stream that feeds the monitor begins at the left of the screen and scans across to the right of the screen. At the end of a line, a horizontal sync pulse indicates the end of the line. Upon receiving this pulse, the monitor will send the electron beam back to the left border of the screen and begin scanning to the right again. The rate at which the monitor scans the electron beam across the phosphor is generated inside the monitor. This is one reason why the EGA/VGA and the monitor must be compatible. If the EGA/VGA is sending data too slowly, the monitor scanning will reach the right side of the screen and then wait for the next horizontal sync pulse. This results in the left portion of the data being displayed on the monitor. This section of data would appear to be stretched across the screen. Likewise, if the data is being output too quickly, the data will be squeezed on the right side of the screen. If the sync pulses are sent out too quickly, the monitor scanning will never refresh the right portion of the screen.

The horizontal timing pulses are illustrated in Figure 7.41.

The top part of Figure 7.41 represents the monitor screen. On the left of the screen is the border region, also called the *front porch*. It is followed by the displayed video data portion of the screen. The data representing one horizontal scan line is displayed in this portion of the display. This is followed by a right border, also called the *back porch*.

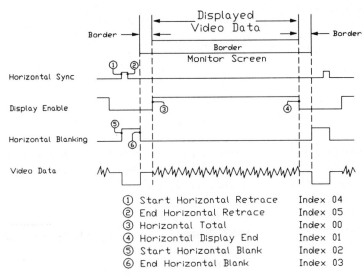

① Start Horizontal Retrace   Index 04
② End Horizontal Retrace   Index 05
③ Horizontal Total   Index 00
④ Horizontal Display End   Index 01
⑤ Start Horizontal Blank   Index 02
⑥ End Horizontal Blank   Index 03

FIGURE 7.41 Horizontal Timing

The EGA/VGA contains an internal character counter. It is reset to 0 when its value is equal to the value loaded into the Horizontal Total Register. The character counter increments by 1 for each character scan line output. In the EGA/VGA, the number of pixels per scan line in a character is typically eight or nine. Horizontal events are driven when the character counter equals one of the values set in the relevant horizontal registers. The basic horizontal events are horizontal sync, display enable, and horizontal blanking.

The horizontal sync pulse is the master timing pulse in the horizontal timing cycle. It is an active high pulse that begins when the character counter equals the value in the Start Horizontal Retrace Register. It ends when the low-order five bits of the character counter equal the value in the End Horizontal Retrace Register. The horizontal sync pulse signals the monitor to begin the retrace period.

The horizontal display enable signifies when the video data input from the display memory is being output to the display. The Horizontal Total Register dictates how many characters are present on a scan line. When the character counter reaches this value, the end of the scan line is issued and the character counter is reset. It is important to realize that the start of the horizontal timing period does not begin at the same time as when the display electron beam is at the left side of the screen. Intuitively, this would seem logical. However, displays are set up so that the start of the horizontal timing period coincides with the start of the display enable period. This positions the refresh period and left border after the right border.

Figure 7.42 illustrates the timing as it appears from the character counter. The numbers are the actual values used in the IBM EGA when the display is in

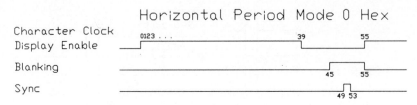

FIGURE 7.42 Horizontal Timing Mode 0

a 40-character-per-line alphanumeric mode called display mode 0. Note that the active display region, which is indicated by the Display Enable signal being high, displays 40 characters numbered 0 to 39. The entire horizontal timing period consists of 55 characters, 40 displayed and 15 undisplayed.

Figure 7.43 shows the numbers used by the IBM during the 640-dots-per-line graphics mode called display mode 10 hex. *display 80 characters.*

Note that the horizontal sync period takes up the entire horizontal blanking period. This is necessary when enhanced EGA multisync-type monitors are being driven.

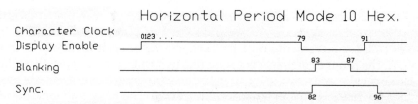

FIGURE 7.43 Horizontal Timing Mode 10 hex

7.7.3 Vertical Refresh Timing

The EGA/VGA controls the vertical refresh rate of the display system. The monitor must be properly synchronized with the EGA for the system to maintain proper vertical sync. The vertical timings are similar to the horizontal timings, including a vertical sync pulse, vertical display enable, and vertical blanking. Figure 7.44 illustrates the vertical timing signals.

The left portion of this figure represents the monitor screen. On the top of the screen is the top border region, also called the front porch. It is followed by the displayed video data portion of the screen. The data representing each horizontal scan line is displayed in this portion of the display. This is followed by a bottom border, also called the back porch.

Internal to the EGA/VGA is a horizontal scan line counter. When its value is equal to the value loaded into the Vertical Total Register it is reset to 0. The scan-line counter increments by one for each scan-line output. Vertical events are driven when the scan-line counter equals one of the values set in the rele-

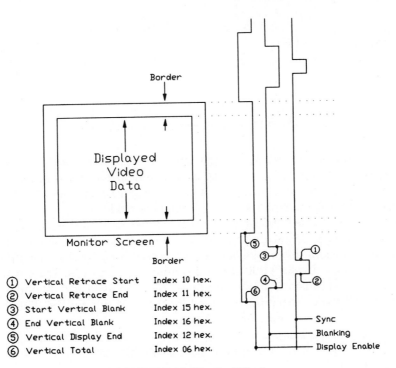

FIGURE 7.44 Vertical Timing

vant vertical registers. The basic vertical events are vertical sync, display enable, and vertical blanking. Each of these is represented in several of the EGA/VGA registers. It should be noted that the scan-line counter will get larger than 256, which is the largest value that can be stored in a byte register. An additional register called the Overflow Register is necessary to hold the ninth bit of the relevant vertical registers.

The vertical sync pulse is the master timing pulse in the vertical timing cycle. It is an active high pulse that begins when the scan-line counter equals the value in the Start Vertical Retrace Register. It ends when the low-order five bits of the scan-line counter equal the value in the End Vertical Retrace Register. The vertical sync pulse signals the monitor to begin a new screen, sending the electron beam back to the top-left corner of the display.

The vertical display enable signifies when the horizontal lines of video data input from the display memory are being output to the display. The Vertical Total Register dictates how many scan lines are present on a display screen. When the scan-line counter reaches this value, the end of the scan line is issued and the scan-line counter is reset. It is important to realize that the start of the vertical timing period does not begin at the same time as when the display electron beam is at the top of the screen. Intuitively, it would seem logical.

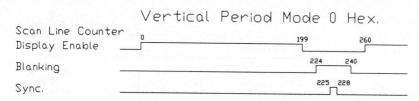

FIGURE 7.45 Vertical Timing Mode 0

However, displays are set up so that the start of the vertical timing period coincides with the start of the display enable period. This positions the refresh period and top border after the bottom border. Figure 7.45 draws the timing as it appears from the character counter for display mode 0.

The numbers in this figure are the actual values used in the IBM EGA when the display is in a 200-scan-line alphanumeric mode called display mode 0. Note that the active display region, which is indicated by the Display Enable signal being high, displays 200 scan lines numbered 0 to 199. The entire vertical timing period consists of 260 scan lines, 200 displayed and 60 undisplayed.

Figure 7.46 shows the numbers used by the IBM during the 350-scan-line graphics mode called display mode 10 hex.

Note that the vertical sync period takes up the entire vertical blanking period. This is necessary when enhanced EGA/VGA multisync-type monitors are being driven.

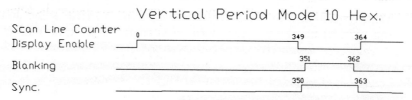

FIGURE 7.46 Vertical Timing Mode 10 hex

Chapter 8

Color Palette and Color Registers

8.1   COLOR PALETTE

A color palette is a lookup table that is used to convert the data associated with a pixel in the display memory into a color. A color palette provides a graphics adapter with a great deal of power and flexibility. In the VGA, the color palette is enhanced by the Color Registers.

A color palette allows the programmer to change the colors rapidly. For example, an image on the EGA/VGA can occupy 256 Kbytes of display memory. In a 16-color mode, only sixteen colors can be displayed simultaneously. All 256 Kbytes of data in the display memory must be modified to change the colors on the display if a color palette is not present. With a color palette, only sixteen bytes would have to be changed.

Another advantage of using a color palette is that the total number of possible colors can be greater than the number of colors that can be displayed simultaneously. In the 16-color modes, sixteen colors can be displayed simultaneously. However, because of the Palette Registers in the EGA, these sixteen colors can be selected from 64 possible colors. Each color in the Palette Registers is represented by six bits. In the VGA, this expansion is even more significant. In the 256-color mode, 256 simultaneous colors can be displayed. Each color is represented by eighteen bits within the Color Registers, providing a selection from 256 Kcolors.

8.1.1   Palette Registers

The color palette consists of 16 Palette Registers. The data in the bit planes consists of from one to eight bits of information per pixel. The data corresponding to each pixel addresses one of the Palette Registers. In the EGA, the selected Palette Register produces a color that is output to the monitor. This path is illustrated in Figure 8.1.

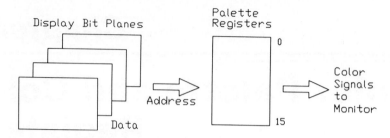

FIGURE 8.1 EGA Conversion of Data to Colors

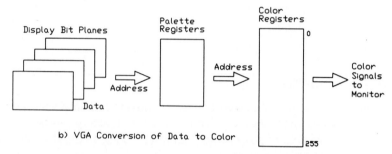

FIGURE 8.2 VGA Conversion of Data to Colors

In the VGA, the selected Palette Register produces another address, not a color code. This address is used to access one of the Color Registers that contain the color codes. There are 256 Color Registers on the VGA. This process is illustrated in Figure 8.2.

In the alphanumeric modes, each character is represented by two values. One is for the foreground pixels of a character, and a second is for the background pixels. Each of these foreground and background values accesses a Palette Register. These values are stored in the character attribute.

In the graphics modes, each pixel is represented by one to eight bits in the display bit plane memory. The location of these bits, which represent a single pixel, depends on the active display mode. Figure 8.3 illustrates the palette addressing schemes used in the various display modes.

8.1.2 Codes Contained in the Palette Registers

Each of the Palette Registers contains six bits of information. In all of the display modes, with the exception of mode 13 hex in the VGA, these six bits define a color. In mode 13 hex, these six bits define a sequential address that accesses a Color Register. The color code contained in the Palette Register must conform to the monitor connected to the video system. For the EGA, a monochrome, RGBI color, or RrGgBb enhanced color monitor may be used. The color coding used in the EGA Palette Registers is illustrated in Figure 8.4.

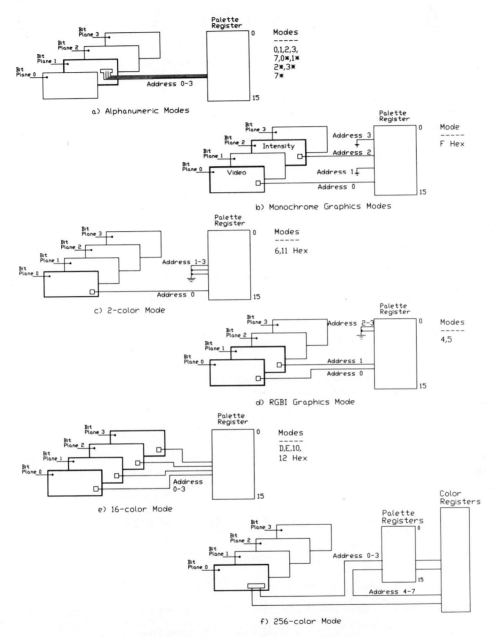

FIGURE 8.3 Palette Register Addressing

8.1.3 EGA Palette Register Outputs

In the EGA, the colors output to the monitor are contained in the Palette Registers according to the color codes in Figures 8.4a–c. Figure 8.5 illustrates the variety of output color codes presented to the monitors. The output format is

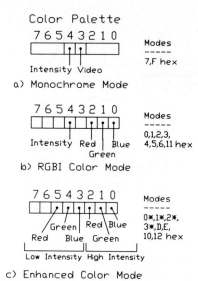

FIGURE 8.4 EGA Palette Register Color Codes

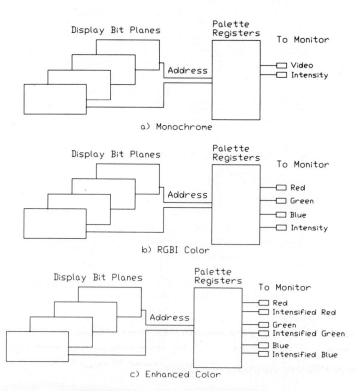

FIGURE 8.5 EGA Palette Outputs

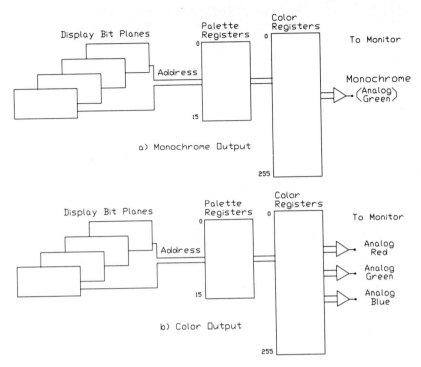

FIGURE 8.6 VGA Palette Outputs

determined by the configuration sense switch settings, which in turn depend on the monitor type.

8.1.4 VGA Palette Register Outputs

For the VGA, either an enhanced monochrome or enhanced color monitor may be used. The VGA automatically determines the monitor installed. The output format used in the VGA Palette Registers is illustrated in Figure 8.6.

In the VGA, the colors output to the monitor are contained in the Color Registers. These registers are accessed by the value in the Palette Registers, as illustrated in Figure 8.7.

8.1.5 Accessing the Palette Registers

The Palette Registers are contained in a dual-ported memory. The display memory requires access to the Palette Registers in order to refresh the display. The host requires access to the Palette Registers during read or write operations. The process of accessing the dual-ported Palette Registers is illustrated in Figure 8.8.

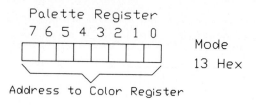

256-color Mode

FIGURE 8.7 VGA Conversion of Data to Colors

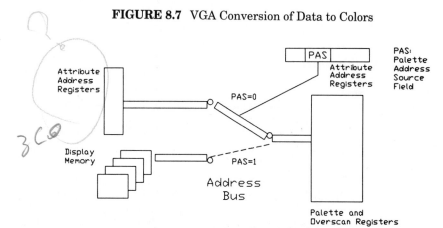

FIGURE 8.8 Accessing the Palette Registers

This dual-ported memory is accessed through a host port register at host I/O address 3C0. This port has two different functions. One is to index the Palette Registers. In this mode, it is called the Attribute Address Register. A second is to act as a portal to the Palette Registers. In this mode, it may be thought of as a data register, similar to the data registers of the other EGA/VGA register groups.

An internal hardware flip-flop is used that multiplexes this port to load either this Attribute Address Register or one of the Attribute Registers. When the flip-flop is in the clear state, data output from the host to port 3C0 hex is directed to this Attribute Address Register. When the flip-flop is in the set state, data written to this port is directed to whichever Attribute Register index is loaded into the ADR field of this register.

The flip-flop is controlled indirectly by the host. When a host assembly language input port instruction, IN, is issued to the Input Status #1 Register, the flip-flop is cleared. This register resides at port address 3BA hex for monochrome implementations or port addresses 3DA hex for color implementations. Once the flip-flop is cleared, the path is set so that outputs to this 3C0 hex port load an index that points to one of the Attribute Registers. This is equivalent to loading any of the other Address Registers. The next assembly language output port instruction written to this 3C0 hex port (OUT) will load the indexed Attribute Register. After the output occurs, the flip-flop automatically changes state. The following output will be directed once again to the Attribute Address Register.

In addition to the address field, the Attribute Address Register contains a Palette Address Source (PAS) field. This field is used to control the operation of the dual-ported palette RAM. If the host is to have control of the palette registers during a load operation, it must reset the PA field to 0. In order for the display memory to access this palette RAM, the PAS field must be set to a 1.

8.2 CONVERTING DATA TO COLORS

The variety of display modes available on the EGA/VGA provides a number of different possible color schemes. These include 2-color modes, 4-color modes, and 16-color modes. In addition, the VGA provides for a 256-color mode. The color modes and the bit planes affected are listed in Table 8.1.

8.2.1 Monochrome Modes

In the monochrome modes, the Palette Registers contain two fields, each one bit wide. These two bits are output to the monochrome monitor. The monochrome monitor requires two control signals that determine the intensity of the video signal. Together, these bits can produce four monochrome attributes. The possible monochrome intensities are shown in Table 8.2. The monochrome intensities are video (V) and intensify (I).

TABLE 8.1 Palette Utilization

Display Mode (Hex)	Number of Colors	Palette Registers Affected
0,1	16	0–15
2,3	16	0–15
4,5	4	0,1,2,3
6	2	0,1
7	4	0,1,4,5
D	16	0–15
E	16	0–15
F	4	0,1,4,5
10	16	0–15
11	2	0,1
12	16	0–15
13	256	0–15

TABLE 8.2 Monochrome Intensity Values

Video	Intensify	Saturation
0	0	0% saturation = Black
0	1	50% saturation = Normal intensity
1	1	100% saturation = High intensity
1	0	Blinking normal intensity

8.2.2 Monochrome Alphanumeric Mode

In the monochrome alphanumeric mode, mode 7, the code that determines the monochrome attribute for each character is contained in the attribute byte of the character. The attribute bytes are located in bit plane 2. The attribute byte may access any of the sixteen Palette Registers. However, the values in the Palette Registers reflect the fact that only four codes are possible. The convention used is compatible with the monochrome adapter boards. The 2-bit code resides in bits 3 and 4. Bits 7–5 and bits 2–0 are not relevant. Any attribute in display memory that has the video bit on—bit 3=1, for example—produces an output that has the video bit on. Likewise, any attribute in display memory that has the intensity bit on—bit 4=1, for example—produces an output that has the intensity bit on. This occurs because the Palette Registers are loaded with the values indicated in Table 8.3.

8.2.3 Monochrome Graphics Mode

In the monochrome graphics mode, mode F hex, a 2-bit-wide code is assigned to every pixel. This 2-bit-wide field also represents the video and intensity bits of the monochrome attributes. Four of these 2-bit-wide attributes are loaded into display memory, packed into a byte format. This is illustrated in Figure 8.9.

Each byte contains the attributes associated with four neighboring pixels. If all of the pixels are located on a line, attribute n is associated with the far left pixel. When display mode F hex is active, special hardware intercepts the data written to the display memory and loads all of the video attribute bits into bit plane 0 and all of the intensity attribute bits into bit plane 2. This is illustrated in Figure 8.3b earlier in this chapter.

TABLE 8.3 Mode 7 Palette Default Values

Register	0	1	2	3	4	5	6	7	8	9	A	B	C	D	E	F
Value	0	8	8	8	8	8	8	8	10	18	18	18	18	18	18	18

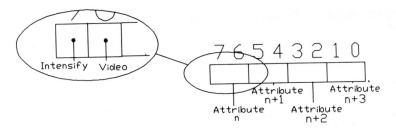

FIGURE 8.9 Monochrome Graphics Attribute Byte Packing

TABLE 8.4 Mode F Hex Palette Default Values

Register	0	1	2	3	4	5	6	7	8	9	A	B	C	D	E	F
Value	0	8	—	—	18	18	—	—	—	—	—	—	—	—	—	—

The sixteen Palette Registers are addressed by two active bits, bit 0 and bit 2. Bits 1 and 3 are reset to 0, resulting in only four of the sixteen Palette Registers being relevant. The four Palette Registers accessed are registers 0, 1, 4, and 5, as shown in Table 8.4.

8.2.4 RGBI Color Mode —digital

In the CGA-emulation modes, the Palette Registers contain the RGBI codes. This code is represented with four bits, which together can produce up to sixteen different colors. The three color bits—R=red, G=green, and B=blue—define eight colors, black included. The fourth bit, S=secondary, dims the preceding eight possible colors.

The EGA is capable of driving an RGBI monitor directly in the 200-scan-line modes. Thus, the 4-bit color code is output from the EGA adapter. The VGA cannot drive an RGBI monitor. However, the Palette Registers and the Color Registers are loaded with appropriate colors to provide compatibility. The bit positions in the palette registers contain the red, green, blue, and intensity fields, as listed in Figure 8.4b earlier in this chapter.

8.2.5 RGBI Alphanumeric Modes digital

In the RGBI alphanumeric modes—modes 0, 1, 2, and 3—the code that determines the color attribute for each character is contained in the attribute byte of the character. The attribute bytes are located in bit plane 2. The attribute byte may access any of the sixteen Palette Registers. Each character can reference one Palette Register for the foreground color and one Palette Register for the background color.

TABLE 8.5 Modes 0, 1, 2, and 3 Palette Default Values

Register	0	1	2	3	4	5	6	7	8	9	A	B	C	D	E	F
Value	0	1	2	3	4	5	6	7	8	9	A	B	C	D	E	F

TABLE 8.6 Modes 0*, 1*, 2*, 3* Palette Default Values

Register	0	1	2	3	4	5	6	7	8	9	A	B	C	D	E	F
Value	0	1	2	3	4	5	14	7	38	39	3A	3B	3C	3D	3E	3F

*Enhanced graphics mode

In the EGA, either an RGBI monitor or an enhanced RrGgBb monitor is attached. If the RGBI monitor is attached, the lower four bits of the Palette output are output as the RGBI signals to the monitor. The Palette Registers represent a one-to-one mapping scheme, so that an attribute is output directly to the monitor. This is seen in the default values of the Palette Registers. All of the values in the Palette Registers are equal to the addresses of the Palette Register. The default values used for the RGBI modes are listed in Table 8.5.

If the RrGgBb monitor is attached, all six bits of the output of the Palette are output as the RrGgBb signals to the monitor. The Palette Registers simulate the color mapping used on the RGBI systems. The default values used for the RrGgBb modes are listed in Table 8.6. Because bit 4 is the intensity bit, all attributes that have the intensity bit set to 1 address Palette Registers number 8 through F hex. The values in these registers are all greater than or equal to 38 hex, which is 111xxx binary. Because bits 3, 4, and 5 are set to 1, the secondary R, G, and B bits are activated, producing less bright colors.

Palette Register 6 is loaded with a 14 hex instead of the expected 6 hex, and its intensified brother, Palette Register E hex, is loaded with a 3E hex as expected. Both of these values represent a brown or yellow, which is a combination of red and green. The 14 hex loaded into Palette Register 6 uses a secondary green with a primary red. A value of 6 in the Palette Register 6 would produce primary green and primary red.

8.2.6 RGBI Graphics Modes

In the RGBI graphics modes, modes 4 and 5, each pixel is represented by two color attribute bits. These four bits allow each pixel to be displayed in one of four colors. These graphics modes are compatible with the Color Graphics Adapter (CGA).

In the CGA adapter, these two attribute bits produce four colors, although the RGBI monitor is capable of displaying sixteen colors. Two default palettes are present in the CGA. The programmer can select one of these two palettes to

TABLE 8.7 CGA-compatible Color Selection

ATR 1	ATR 0	Set 1	Set 0	EGA Palette Register
0	0	Background	Background	0
0	1	Cyan	Green	1
1	0	Magenta	Red	2
1	1	White	Brown	3

convert the 2-bit attribute to an RGBI color. Table 8.7 lists the colors for each of the default palettes.

In the EGA/VGA, the two default colors can be loaded into the sixteen Palette Registers through the Set Color Palette BIOS call, AH=0B hex. In the EGA/VGA, Palette Registers 0 through 3 are accessed by the two attribute bits. These four registers can be loaded with any colors desired.

The two attribute bits associated with each pixel are named ATR1 and ATR0. The bit ATR1 is the most significant bit, and ATR0 is the least significant bit. The process used to convert a host address to a Palette Register address is not straightforward. The attribute bit ATR1 eventually becomes the color palette address bit 1. The attribute bit ATR0 becomes the color palette address bit 0.

In modes 4 and 5, the two attribute bits are located as neighbors in the same byte of data. This precludes simply loading one attribute bit in each of bit planes 0 and 1. Hardware controlled by the odd/even flags automatically directs even bytes of information to bit plane 0 and odd bytes of information to bit plane 1. Data input to the EGA/VGA when the EGA/VGA is in modes 4 or 5 is separated into bit planes 0 and 1, depending on the even or odd address of the data. The data present in these two planes is automatically unwrapped by more hardware, so that ATR1 and ATR0 address bits 1 and 0 of the color palette.

Four pixels are packed into each byte of the host byte buffer. Four consecutive bytes of display memory contain sixteen pixels in host memory. When these four bytes are written to the display memory, the bytes located at the even host addresses are loaded into bit plane 0, and the odd host addresses are loaded into bit plane 1. The two attribute bits associated with each pixel are unwrapped and presented to the Palette Registers as address bits 0 and 1.

8.2.7 Two-color Modes

In the 2-color graphics modes, modes 6 and 11 hex, each pixel is represented by one bit. Both of these modes are graphics modes, and there are no associated 2-color alphanumeric modes. Mode 6 is meant to be compatible with the CGA graphics mode, and mode 11 hex is specially designed for the VGA to provide 2-color graphics.

TABLE 8.8 Mode 6 Hex Palette Default Values

Register	0	1	2	3	4	5	6	7	8	9	A	B	C	D	E	F
Value	0	17	17	17	17	17	17	17	17	17	17	17	17	17	17	17

TABLE 8.9 Mode 11 Hex Palette Default Values

Register	0	1	2	3	4	5	6	7	8	9	A	B	C	D	E	F
Value	0	37	37	37	37	37	37	37	37	37	37	37	37	37	37	37

8.2.8 CGA Two-color Emulation

In mode 6 of the EGA/VGA, the one bit per pixel selects one of two palette locations. The default values loaded into the Palette Registers are listed in Table 8.8.

Eight consecutive pixels are packed into each byte of display memory. The processing is identical to the RGBI graphics modes 4 and 5 except that there are only two colors instead of four colors. As is true in the RGBI display modes, bit planes 0 and 1 in mode 6 are used to store even and odd bytes of the data. When the color palette is addressed, the single attribute bit for each pixel is presented to the Palette Registers as address bit 0.

8.2.9 VGA Two-color Emulation

In mode 11 of the VGA, the one bit per pixel selects one of two palette locations. The default values loaded into the Palette Registers are listed in Table 8.9.

Eight consecutive pixels are packed into each byte of display memory. The memory mapping is straightforward, using only bit plane 0 to store the data. When the color palette is addressed, the single attribute bit for each pixel is presented to the Palette Registers as address bit 0.

8.2.10 Enhanced Color Modes

In the enhanced color modes—modes D, E, 10, and 12 hex—a pixel is represented by four bits in display memory. These four bits reside in bit planes 0 through 3. One bit is assigned to each of the four bit planes. These four bits are combined to make the 4-bit address to the Palette Registers. Any of these four bits can be disabled by using the Color Plane Enable Register. Any plane that is disabled causes the associated address bit to the Palette Registers to be reset to 0. Thus, if all four bit planes are disabled, all four address bits will be reset to 0, causing the color in Palette Register 0 to be displayed.

8.2.11 Enhanced Color: EGA

The EGA requires an enhanced color monitor that has six control lines to determine the color. Two lines are assigned for each of the red, green, and blue colors, which allows the monitor to display up to 64 different colors.

Each 2-bit field in the Palette Registers corresponds to an intensity value of the three primary colors—red, green, and blue. The sum of these six bits determines the color displayed. Because each primary color is represented by two bits, each color can have four intensities. The possible values of a typical color are listed in Table 8.10.

The six bits are organized within the Palette Registers as shown in Figure 8.4c. The default values for the Palette Registers in these modes are identical to those for the RGBI color modes. The default values are repeated in Table 8.11.

8.2.12 Enhanced Color: VGA

The VGA requires an analog RGB monitor. There are three lines, one each of red, green, and blue, permitting the monitor to display an infinite number of colors. The VGA is restricted to six bits per color, which limits the possible number of colors to 256 Kcolors.

8.2.13 256-color Mode

The VGA provides mode 13 hex, which allows 256 colors. Every pixel is represented by eight bits of data. The eight bits when loaded into display memory are spread through the four bit planes. The eight bits are split into two 4-bit fields. The first field, corresponding to the lower four bits (bits 0–3), addresses the Palette Registers. The four low-order outputs of the Palette Registers are used as the four low-order address bits, bits 0–3, for the Color Registers. The

TABLE 8.10 Color Intensities

Intensified Color Bit	Color Bit	Percentage of Saturation
0	0	0 % saturation
0	1	33 % saturation
1	0	66 % saturation
1	1	100 % saturation

TABLE 8.11 Modes D, E, 10, and 12 Hex Palette Default Values

Register	0	1	2	3	4	5	6	7	8	9	A	B	C	D	E	F
Value	0	1	2	3	4	5	14	7	38	39	3A	3B	3C	3D	3E	3F

TABLE 8.12 Mode 13 Hex Palette Default Values

Register	0	1	2	3	4	5	6	7	8	9	A	B	C	D	E	F
Value	0	1	2	3	4	5	6	7	8	9	A	B	C	D	E	F

second field, corresponding to bits 4–7 from the display memory, are presented to the Color Registers as address bits 4–7.

The Palette Registers are restricted to provide a one-to-one transfer of address to data. The default values of the Palette Registers are listed in Table 8.12; they should not be modified by the programmer.

8.3 COLOR REGISTERS

The VGA is equipped with 256 Color Registers. A pixel or character in display memory consists of from one to eight bits of data. This data is used to address the sixteen Palette Registers. The output of these Palette Registers is used in conjunction with the data in display memory to address the Color Registers. The Color Registers contain the color codes that are output to the digital-to-analog converters (DAC). The outputs of the DAC are sent to the monitor. Each of the Color Registers consists of a red, green, and blue component. Each of these color components is six bits wide.

8.3.1 Color Register Addressing

The Color Registers are addressed according to Figure 8.10.

Each of the sixteen Palette Registers contains six bits of data. In the EGA and in the VGA, with mode 13 hex excluded, these six bits are used as a color code. In mode 13 hex, these six bits are used as an address. They provide the low-order six bits of an 8-bit address that is presented to the Color Registers. Because there are 256 Color Registers, eight address bits are required.

The Palette Registers are present in the VGA to provide compatibility with the EGA. There is no need to have two layers of color conversion registers—that is, both the Palette Registers and the Color Registers. The Color Registers would be sufficient in themselves.

Suppose that Palette Register 5 contains a value of 3. The value 3 is a binary 000011, which translates to the color cyan, because both high-intensity blue and high-intensity green are active. Color Register 3 would be addressed if this value 3 is used as an address to present to the Color Registers. If Color Register 3 contains a value that activates a high-intensity green and a high-intensity blue, the resultant color will still be cyan. Thus, Palette Register 5 may be thought of either as containing a color 3 or as an address 3.

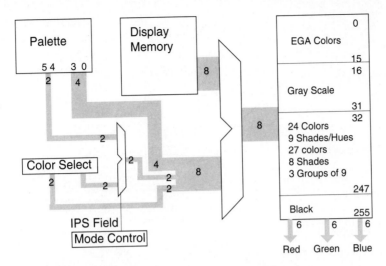

FIGURE 8.10 Color Register Addressing

If the Palette Registers are thought of as an address for the Color Registers, a transparency should exist. An address presented to the Palette Registers should produce a value on the output of the Palette Registers that is identical to the address. The display bit planes provide the four low-order address bits to the Palette Registers. To provide transparency, the Palette Registers should provide four bits of output. These four bits access sixteen of the Color Registers. Because there are 256 Color Registers, they may be segmented into sixteen banks, each bank containing sixteen registers. One bank is active at a time. The Palette Registers provide the address to an individual register in a bank.

If the Palette Registers are thought of as a color, six bits of output are provided. These six bits are used as the low-order six bits of the address provided to the Color Registers; they also access 64 of the Color Registers. Because there are 256 Color Registers, these may be segmented into four banks, each bank containing 64 registers. One bank is active at a time. The Palette Registers provide the address to an individual register in a bank.

8.3.2 Four Banks of 64 Color Registers

The Color Select Register provides two address bits, named bits C7 and C6. Combined with the six output bits from the Palette Registers, an 8-bit Color Register address is formed. In this configuration, the C7 and C6 fields of the Color Select Register act as a bank select. A bank, in this case, consists of 64 Color Registers. In the 16-color modes, sixteen Color Registers must be reserved to hold the sixteen colors. Each Palette Register contains a 6-bit color code. Because the output of the Palette Registers address the Color Registers,

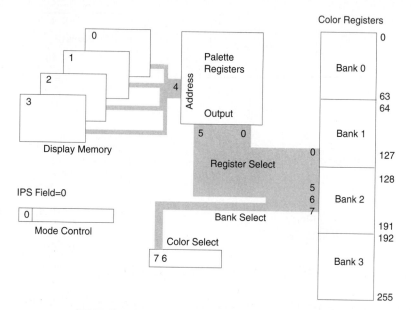

FIGURE 8.11 Four Banks of 64-color Registers

these six bits can be used to select one of 64 Color Registers within a bank. The two high-order address bits, C7 and C6, are provided from the Color Select Register and act as a bank select. Rapid selections of other banks of Color Registers can be made by simply changing the value in the C7 and C6 fields.

This bank select mode is enabled by the Palette Size Select (IPS) field of the Mode Control Register. If this field is set to 1, the address bits C7 and C6 are used as the upper two bits of the address presented to the Color Registers. The six bits output from the Palette Registers are used as the six low-order address bits presented to the Color Registers. Thus, one of four banks can be selected. This color selection mode is illustrated in Figure 8.11.

8.3.3 Sixteen Banks of 16 Color Registers

In addition to fields C7 and C6, the Color Select Register provides two other address fields called C5 and C4. When these fields are combined with the four low-order output bits from the Palette Register, an 8-bit Color Register address is formed. In this configuration, the C7, C6, C5, and C4 fields of the Color Select Register act to select a bank. The four low-order output bits from the Palette Registers select a Color Register within a bank.

This bank-select mode is enabled by the Palette Size Select (IPS) field of the Mode Control Register. If this field is reset to 0, the address bits C5 and C4 are used in conjunction with C7 and C6 to form the four upper-order address bits presented to the Color Registers. Thus, one of sixteen banks can be selected. This color-selection mode is illustrated in Figure 8.12.

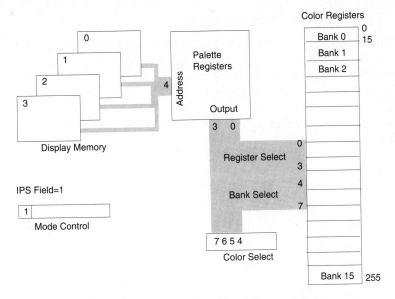

FIGURE 8.12 Sixteen Banks of 16-color Registers

8.3.4 Color Register Organization

Each of 256 Color Registers is composed of three parts, corresponding to the red, green, and blue components. Each of these components is six bits wide, providing each of these three primary colors with 64 possible intensities or levels of saturation. When combined, the three primary colors provide the programmer with the opportunity to select any color from a possible selection of 256 Kcolors. The notation "256 Kcolors" actually translates into 262,144 possible colors.

The Color Registers may be set up to provide any combination of colors that appeals to the programmer. At initialization, the registers are set up as shown in Table 8.13.

TABLE 8.13 Initial State of the Color Registers

Registers	Color Scheme
0–15	Identical to the 16 EGA colors initially loaded into the EGA Palette Registers
16–31	16 evenly spaced shades of gray.
32–247	24 color groups, each consisting of nine shades of a color. Three intensity levels and three saturation levels are provided for each shade.
248–255	Preloaded with 0, for black

8.3.5 Color Register Default Values

The Color Registers may be loaded with the initial values at a mode set by enabling the preload function. Likewise, the Color Registers may remain un-modified during a mode set if the preload function is disabled. The preload function is controlled by invoking the BIOS call named Default Palette Loading During Mode Set, AH = 12 hex, BL = 31 hex. A listing of the initial state of the Color Registers is given in Table 8.14. In this table, R = red, G = green, and B = blue.

TABLE 8.14 Initial Values in the Color Registers

Index	*Colors (R = Red, G = Green, B = Blue) (Values in Decimal)*											
	R	G	B	R	G	B	R	G	B	R	G	B
0	0	0	0	0	0	42	0	42	0	0	42	42
4	42	0	0	42	0	42	42	21	0	42	42	42
8	21	21	21	21	21	63	21	63	21	21	63	63
12	63	21	21	63	21	63	63	63	21	63	63	63
16	0	0	0	5	5	5	8	8	8	11	11	11
20	14	14	14	17	17	17	20	20	20	24	24	24
24	28	28	28	32	32	32	36	36	36	40	40	40
28	45	45	45	50	50	50	56	56	56	63	63	63
32	0	0	63	16	0	63	31	0	63	47	0	63
36	63	0	63	63	0	47	63	0	31	63	0	16
40	63	0	0	63	16	0	63	31	0	63	47	0
44	63	63	0	47	63	0	31	63	0	16	63	0
48	0	63	0	0	63	16	0	63	31	0	63	47
52	0	63	63	0	47	63	0	31	63	0	16	63
56	31	31	63	39	31	63	47	31	63	55	31	63
60	63	31	63	63	31	55	63	31	47	63	31	39
64	63	31	31	63	39	31	63	47	31	63	55	31
68	63	63	31	55	63	31	47	63	31	39	63	31
72	31	63	31	31	63	39	31	63	47	31	63	55
76	31	63	63	31	55	63	31	47	63	31	39	63
80	45	45	63	49	45	63	54	45	63	58	45	63
84	63	45	63	63	45	58	63	45	54	63	45	49
88	63	45	45	63	49	45	63	54	45	63	58	45
92	63	63	45	58	63	45	54	63	45	49	63	45
96	45	63	45	45	63	49	45	63	54	45	63	58
100	45	63	63	45	58	63	45	54	63	45	49	63
104	0	0	28	7	0	28	14	0	28	21	0	28
108	28	0	28	28	0	21	28	0	14	28	0	7

(continued)

TABLE 8.14 *(cont.)*

Index	Colors (R = Red, G = Green, B = Blue) (Values in Decimal)											
	R	G	B	R	G	B	R	G	B	R	G	B
112	28	0	0	28	7	0	28	14	0	28	21	0
116	28	28	0	21	28	0	14	28	0	7	28	0
120	0	28	0	0	28	7	0	28	14	0	28	21
124	0	28	28	0	21	28	0	14	28	0	7	28
128	14	14	28	17	14	28	21	14	28	24	14	28
132	28	14	28	28	14	24	28	14	21	28	14	17
136	28	14	14	28	17	14	28	21	14	28	24	14
140	28	28	14	24	28	14	21	28	14	17	28	14
144	14	28	14	14	28	17	14	28	21	14	28	24
148	14	28	28	14	24	28	14	21	28	14	17	28
152	20	20	28	22	20	28	24	20	28	26	20	28
156	28	20	28	28	20	26	28	20	24	28	20	22
160	28	20	20	28	22	20	28	24	20	28	26	20
164	28	28	20	26	28	20	24	28	20	22	28	20
168	20	28	20	20	28	22	20	28	24	20	28	26
172	20	28	28	20	26	28	20	24	28	20	22	28
176	0	0	16	4	0	16	8	0	16	12	0	16
180	16	0	16	16	0	12	16	0	8	16	0	4
184	16	0	0	16	4	0	16	8	0	16	12	0
188	16	16	0	12	16	0	8	16	0	4	16	0
192	0	16	0	0	16	4	0	16	8	0	16	12
196	0	16	16	0	12	16	0	8	16	0	4	16
200	8	8	16	10	8	16	12	8	16	14	8	16
204	16	8	16	16	8	14	16	8	12	16	8	10
208	16	8	8	16	10	8	16	12	8	16	14	8
212	16	16	8	14	16	8	12	16	8	10	16	8
216	8	16	8	8	16	10	8	16	12	8	16	14
220	8	16	16	8	14	16	8	12	16	8	10	16
224	11	11	16	12	11	16	13	11	16	15	11	16
228	16	11	16	16	11	15	16	11	13	16	11	12
232	16	11	11	16	12	11	16	13	11	16	15	11
236	16	16	11	15	16	11	13	16	11	12	16	11
240	11	16	11	11	16	12	11	16	13	11	16	15
244	11	16	16	11	15	16	11	13	16	11	12	16
248	0	0	0	0	0	0	0	0	0	0	0	0
252	0	0	0	0	0	0	0	0	0	0	0	0

Note: All Color Register values are in decimal.

8.3.6   Accessing the Color Registers

The Color Registers can be written to or read from by using the BIOS calls or by programming the Color Registers directly. The same arguments that apply to programming the control registers directly or through BIOS also apply to the programming of the Color Registers. Speed versus portability are the two key issues.

8.3.7   Modifying the Color Registers through BIOS

Several BIOS calls are available that relate to the Color Registers. All of these calls are found on the VGA only because there are no Color Registers on the EGA. Programmers may set or read a single Color Register or a group of Color Registers, or they may select or read the color page or bank. The Color Registers can be loaded during a mode set by enabling the Palette Loading function. Likewise, the Color Registers can remain unmodified during a mode set by disabling this function. These calls are invoked with interrupt INT 10 hex, with AH=10 hex or AH=12 hex. A listing of the Color Register BIOS-related calls is found in Table 8.15.

8.3.8   Modifying the Color Registers Directly

Four registers in the VGA are dedicated to the Video digital-to-analog converters. These registers are listed in Table 8.16.

Data is read from or written to the Color Registers through the PEL Address and PEL Data Registers. This register pair operates in a similar fashion to that used by the other EGA/VGA address and data register pairs. An index is set up in the address register that points to one of the internal Color Registers. This

TABLE 8.15   Color Register BIOS-related Calls

AH (Hex)	AL (Hex)	Function of Call
10	10	Set individual Color Register
10	12	Set block of Color Registers
10	13	Select color page or paging mode
10	15	Read individual Color Register
10	17	Read block of Color Registers
10	1A	Read current color page number
12	BL = 31	Default palette loading during mode set

TABLE 8.16 Video Digital-to-Analog Converter Registers

Address	Read/Write	Function
3C8 hex	Read/write	PEL address during write
3C7 hex	Write only	PEL address during read
3C7 hex	Read only	DAC state
3C9 hex	Read/write	PEL Data Register
3C6 hex	Read/write	PEL mask

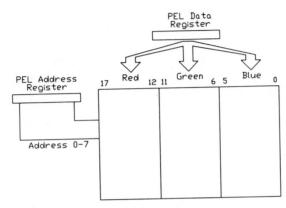

FIGURE 8.13 Direct Addressing of the Color Registers

register is then accessed through the data register. Special hardware features included in the PEL Address and Data Registers can be used to speed up the read and write operations. This addressing is illustrated in Figure 8.13.

PEL Address Register

The PEL Address Register is eight bits wide and addresses one of the 256 Color Registers. The PEL Address Register has two addresses in the host port I/O space. Writing to port address 3C8 hex provides an address to the Color Register and alerts the hardware that the host desires to write to the Color Registers. Similarly, writing to port address 3C7 hex provides an address to the Color Register and alerts the hardware that the host desires to read to the Color Registers.

The PEL Address Register autoincrements after three consecutive read or write operations to the PEL Data Register. This is provided so that consecutive Color Registers can be accessed without requiring the programmer to update the PEL Address Register.

PEL Data Register

The PEL Data Register contains a 6-bit field that is used by the host to read data from or write it to the Color Registers. After the address to the Color Registers is set up in either of the ports associated with the PEL Address Register, the Color Register hardware is ready to accept three simultaneous read or write operations. The first read or write operation accesses the red field of the color register, the second accesses the green field, and the third accesses the blue field. It is important that a series of three read or write operations occurs before the index in the PEL Address Register is modified.

Due to hardware limitations, a slight delay is necessary between successive read or write operations performed to the PEL Data Register. The minimum period between successive accesses is 240 nanoseconds.

When the Color Registers are modified, "snow" may appear on the monitor. To eliminate this "snow," the programmer must ensure that the display is not in an active refresh period. This can be accomplished in two ways. The programmer can modify the Color Registers only when the display is in a retrace period rather than an active display period, or the programmer can turn the refreshing off by using the Screen Off field in the Clocking Mode Register.

DAC State Register

The condition of the host interface section of the Color Registers can be monitored through the DAC State Register. This condition is important because the hardware expects three consecutive read or write operations after data is written to the PEL Address Register. Data corruption within the Color Registers can occur if a second write to the PEL Address Register occurs before the sequence of three read or write operations to the PEL Data Register has completed.

The status bits are located in bits 0 and 1 of the DAC State Register. The values returned during a read to this register reflect the state of the Color Register hardware. These states are listed in Table 8.17.

After the PEL Address Register is written to at one of its two addresses, the mode does not change until another write operation occurs to the alternate PEL Address Register port address. The mode stays in effect since sequential read or write operations are anticipated by the controller. The autoincrementing feature automatically updates index address.

TABLE 8.17 DAC State Register

Bits 0,1	Meaning
00 binary	DAC is currently in a read mode
11 binary	DAC is currently in a write mode

PEL Mask Register

The PEL Mask Register is initialized to FF hex by the BIOS initialization procedure. This register should not be modified by the programmer.

8.3.9 Color Conversion

A variety of color-coding techniques is available with the EGA/VGA. These include using the 2-bit color codes on the EGA and the 6-bit color codes on the VGA. Color coding includes monochrome gray scales, RGBI color, RrGgBb color, and analog color. It is often necessary to convert from one color scheme to another.

Gray Scale

Gray shades are composed of equal amounts of red, green, and blue. White is the maximum gray scale value, and black is the minimum value. Thus, the number of gray scales is directly related to the number of bits reserved for each of the three primary colors.

The EGA allocates two bits per color. These two bits can produce four independent gray scales. The four levels of gray scale can be achieved using the color fields within the Palette Registers, as shown in Table 8.18.

The VGA allocates six bits per color that provides 64 possible gray scales. These 64 levels of gray scale are achieved using the six-bit color fields within the Color Registers, as shown in Table 8.19.

Converting RrGgBb, RGBI, and Monochrome

Thus far, three color schemes have been discussed. These include the monochrome intensities, the RGBI color outputs, and the enhanced color output, RrGbBb. It is sometimes necessary to convert the enhanced color outputs to the RGBI outputs or vice versa. Table 8.20 provides a conversion reference for the RrGbBb, RGBI, and monochrome formats.

TABLE 8.18 EGA: Gray Scale Using the Color Registers

Intensified Color Bits			Color Bits			
SR	SG	SB	R	G	B	Gray Scale
0	0	0	0	0	0	0 % saturation
0	0	0	1	1	1	33 % saturation
1	1	1	0	0	0	66 % saturation
1	1	1	1	1	1	100 % saturation

TABLE 8.19 VGA: Gray Scale Using the Color Registers

Color Register Value			
Red	*Green*	*Blue*	*Gray Scale*
0	0	0	0 % saturation
1	1	1	1.6 % saturation
2	2	2	3.2 % saturation
.	.	.	.
.	.	.	.
.	.	.	.
63	63	63	100 % saturation

Summing Colors to Gray Scale

In the VGA, the colors loaded into the Color Registers can be converted into gray scales. A formula is used to convert the intensity found in each of the three primary color components—red, green, and blue—into a gray scale value. The formula is listed in Equation 8.1.

Equation 8.1 Determining Gray Scale

$$\text{Gray Scale} = (.30 \times \text{red}) + (.59 \times \text{green}) + (.11 \times \text{blue})$$

Because the sum of the multipliers, .30 + .59 + .11, totals 1.00, gray scale values are preserved. In other words, a gray scale input to the equation produces a gray scale of the same intensity as an output.

The summing to gray scale function can be invoked automatically during a mode set if the summing feature is enabled. All 256 Color Registers will be summed to form the gray scales. If this summing feature is disabled, the Color Registers will not be summed to a gray scale during a mode set. The programmer can cause a summing operation on any number of Color Registers to occur at command by using the BIOS routines. The BIOS calls that relate to the summing operation are listed in Table 8.21.

8.3.10   Selective Color Planes

The four bit planes address the color palette. However, not all of the planes will necessarily affect the address of a particular pixel. A logical AND operation occurs with the 4-bit value in the Color Plane Enable Register and the four address bits coming from the four bit planes. This logical function is illustrated in Figure 8.14.

TABLE 8.20 Converting RGBI and Monochrome

			RrGgBb						RGBI			Monochrome	
r	g	b	R	G	B	Code	I	R	G	B		I	V
							Red						
0	0	0	1	0	0	4	0	1	0	0		0	1
1	0	0	0	0	0	32	0	1	0	0		0	1
1	0	0	1	0	0	36	1	1	0	0		0	1
1	0	0	1	1	1	39	1	1	0	0		0	1
1	1	1	1	0	0	60	1	1	0	0		0	1
							Blue						
0	0	0	0	0	1	1	0	0	0	1		0	1
0	0	1	0	0	0	8	0	0	0	1		0	1
0	0	1	0	0	1	9	1	0	0	1		0	1
0	0	1	1	1	1	15	1	0	0	1		0	1
1	1	1	0	0	1	57	1	0	0	1		0	1
							Green						
0	0	0	0	1	0	2	0	0	1	0		0	1
0	1	0	0	0	0	16	0	0	1	0		0	1
0	1	0	0	1	0	18	1	0	1	0		0	1
0	1	0	1	1	1	23	1	0	1	0		0	1
1	1	1	0	1	0	58	1	0	1	0		0	1
							Violet						
0	0	0	1	0	1	5	0	1	0	1		0	1
1	0	1	0	0	0	40	0	1	0	1		0	1
0	0	1	1	0	0	12	0	1	0	1		0	1
1	0	0	0	0	1	33	0	1	0	1		0	1
0	0	1	1	0	1	13	1	1	0	1		0	1
1	0	0	1	0	1	37	1	1	0	1		0	1
1	0	1	0	0	1	41	1	1	0	1		0	1
1	0	1	1	0	0	44	1	1	0	1		0	1
1	0	1	1	1	1	47	1	1	0	1		0	1
1	0	1	0	0	1	41	1	1	0	1		0	1
1	1	1	1	0	1	61	1	1	0	1		0	1
1	0	1	1	0	1	45	1	1	0	1		0	1
							Cyan						
0	0	0	0	1	1	3	0	0	1	1		0	1
0	1	1	0	0	0	24	0	0	1	1		0	1
0	1	0	0	0	1	17	0	0	1	1		0	1
0	0	1	0	1	0	10	0	0	1	1		0	1
0	0	1	0	1	1	11	1	0	1	1		0	1

(continued)

TABLE 8.20   *(cont.)*

		RrGgBb						RGBI			Monochrome	
r	g	b	R	G	B	Code	I	R	G	B	I	V
0	1	0	1	1	1	19	1	0	1	1	0	1
0	1	1	0	0	1	25	1	0	1	1	0	1
0	1	1	0	1	0	26	1	0	1	1	0	1
0	1	1	1	1	1	31	1	0	1	1	0	1
1	1	1	0	1	1	59	1	0	1	1	0	1
0	1	1	0	1	1	27	1	0	1	1	0	1
						Yellow						
0	0	0	1	1	0	6	0	1	1	0	0	1
1	1	0	0	0	0	48	0	1	1	0	0	1
0	1	0	1	0	0	20	0	1	1	0	0	1
0	1	0	1	1	0	22	1	1	1	0	0	1
1	0	0	0	1	0	34	0	1	1	0	0	1
1	0	0	1	1	0	38	1	1	1	0	0	1
1	1	0	0	1	0	50	1	1	1	0	0	1
1	1	0	1	0	0	52	1	1	1	0	0	1
1	1	0	1	1	0	54	1	1	1	0	0	1
1	1	0	1	1	1	55	1	1	1	0	0	1
1	1	1	1	1	0	62	1	1	1	0	0	1
						Gray						
0	0	0	0	0	0	0	0	0	0	0	0	0
0	0	0	1	1	1	7	0	1	1	1	0	1
1	1	1	0	0	0	56	0	1	1	1	0	1
0	0	1	1	1	0	14	0	1	1	1	0	1
0	1	0	1	0	1	21	0	1	1	1	0	1
1	0	0	0	1	1	35	0	1	1	1	0	1
1	1	0	0	0	1	49	0	1	1	1	0	1
1	0	1	0	1	0	42	0	1	1	1	0	1
0	1	1	1	0	1	29	1	1	1	1	1	1
0	1	1	1	1	0	30	1	1	1	1	1	1
1	0	1	0	1	1	43	1	1	1	1	1	1
1	0	1	1	1	0	46	1	1	1	1	1	1
1	1	0	0	1	1	51	1	1	1	1	1	1
1	1	0	1	0	1	53	1	1	1	1	1	1
1	1	1	1	1	1	63	1	1	1	1	1	1
						Blinking						
—	—	—	—	—	—	—	1	0	0	0	1	0

TABLE 8.21 Summing to Gray Scale: Related BIOS Calls

AH (Hex)	Subcall (Hex)	Function of Call
10	AL = 1B	Sum color values immediately to gray scale
12	BL = 33	Enable/Disable summing to gray scale at mode set

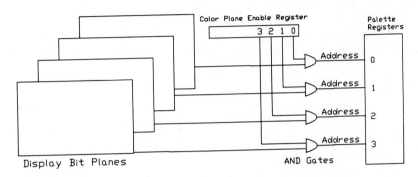

FIGURE 8.14 Selective Addressing of the Palette Registers

Any color palette address bit that equals 0 as a result of the AND operation (because a 0 existed in the corresponding bit field in the Color Plane Enable Register) is set to 0. For example, suppose the color palette address bits have a value of 7 (0111 binary) and the Color Plane Enable Register has a value of 3 (0011) binary. The AND operation would result in a 3 (0011 binary). Thus, Palette Register number 3 would be accessed.

Chapter 9

Reading the State of the EGA and VGA

9.1 READING THE STATE OF THE ADAPTER

Programs must often read the state of the adapter to determine which graphics adapters are present in the computer system. Further, it is important to know which of these are active and what monitors are present. Once the adapter and monitor are known, it is frequently necessary to determine the mode and display parameters under which the adapter is currently operating.

The adapters present in the system can be ascertained by searching the host I/O ports for any active devices or by searching through BIOS ROM memory for adapter identifiers. Once the adapters are found, the attached monitor type can be determined from the state of the adapter. The display system configuration information can be obtained from tables that reside in the host memory. This information includes the starting address and the amount of display memory, the resolution of the display memory, the base port address of the control registers, the location of character fonts, and the state of the configuration switches. Information regarding the dynamic condition of the display can be determined by interrogating the display registers or from the BIOS tables stored in host memory. Typical parameters include the active display mode, the active display page, the cursor position, the number of rows and columns on the display, and the dimensions of the characters.

9.2 READING THE DISPLAY REGISTERS

The control registers resident on the EGA/VGA contain the most primitive information regarding the state of the graphics system. The EGA registers, for the most part, cannot be read. All of the VGA registers can be read. Both the EGA and the VGA maintain a table in BIOS that contains the default register values loaded into the registers during a Mode Set BIOS call.

TABLE 9.1 EGA Readable Registers

Register Name	Register Group	Index
Input Status # 0	Miscellaneous	—
Input Status # 1	Miscellaneous	—
Start Address High	CRTC	0C hex
Start Address Low	CRTC	0D hex
Cursor Location High	CRTC	0E hex
Cursor Location Low	CRTC	0F hex
Light pen High	CRTC	10 hex
Light pen Low	CRTC	11 hex

9.2.1 Reading EGA Registers

The EGA adapter is limited in its ability to allow the programmer to read the state of its registers. The great majority of registers in the EGA are write-only. This is a severe limitation because memory resident programs have no way of determining the state of the EGA. This means that if a memory resident program desires to change the state of the EGA, it cannot restore the state back to the original condition. The readable EGA registers are listed in Table 9.1. Some EGA cards allow reading of the registers. The owner's manual should be consulted as to the readability of the EGA registers.

9.2.2 EGA Video Parameter Table

The default state of the EGA registers can be read from the Video Parameter Table in BIOS memory. The location of this table is pointed to by the Video Parameter Table Pointer, a double-word pointer that resides in the first location of the Table of Save Area Pointers. The Table of Save Area Pointers is pointed to by a second pointer. This pointer is called the Pointer to Table of Save Area Pointers. It resides in host memory at location 0000:04A8. Thus, it takes two pointers to arrive at the actual address of the Video Parameter Table.

The Video Parameter Table consists of a group of subtables, each 64 bytes long. Each subtable contains default values for the supported active modes. The number of modes present for the display adapter depends on the implementation. The standard EGA implementation contains nineteen of these 64 subtables; one subtable for each of the display modes 0, 1, 2, 3, 4, 5, 6, 7, D, E, F, 10, F*, 10*, 0*, 1*, 2*, 3*. (The asterisk refers to the enhanced graphics modes.)

The form of these subtables is listed in Table 9.2. The page length for each of these tables is listed in Table 9.3.

TABLE 9.2 Form of the Video Parameter Table

Byte #	Description
0	Number of columns per page
1	Number of rows per page
2	Number of pixels per character
3,4	Page length
5–8	Sequencer Registers
9	Miscellaneous Register
10–34	CRTC Registers
35–54	Attribute Registers
55–63	Graphics Controller Registers

TABLE 9.3 Page Length According to Parameter Table

Mode (Hex)	Page Length (Decimal)
0	2,048
1	2,048
2	4,096
3	4,096
4	16,386
5	16,386
6	16,386
7	4,096
D	8,196
E	16,386
F	32,768
10	32,768
F*	32,768
10*	32,768
0*	2,048
1*	2,048
2*	4,096
3*	4,096

TABLE 9.4 Video Parameter Table

	Mode																	
	00	01	02	03	04	05	06	07	0D	0E	0F	10	0F*	10*	00*	01*	02*	03*
Col/Row	28	28	50	50	28	28	50	50	28	50	50	50	50	50	28	28	50	50
Row/Screen	18	18	18	18	18	18	18	18	18	18	18	18	18	18	18	18	18	18
Pel/Char	8	8	8	8	8	8	8	E	8	8	E	E	E	E	E	E	E	E
Col/Row	0	0	0	0	0	0	0	0	0	0	0	0	0	0	0	0	0	0

9.2.3 Initial Values of the EGA Registers

The values contained in this Video Parameter Table for the standard EGA implementation are listed in Table 9.4.

Also contained in the Video Parameter Table are the initial settings for all of the control registers. The initial settings are listed in Table 9.5.

9.2.4 Reading VGA Registers

The VGA, in contrast to the EGA, has given the programmer access to all of the registers. This important feature allows the programmer to read the status of any of the control registers. The Input Status #0 and Input Status #1 Registers are the only read-only registers on the VGA. All other registers are read/write. The typical default values of the VGA registers are listed in Table 9.6. All register values are listed in hex.

9.3 READING BIOS TABLES FROM MEMORY

The BIOS routines keep track of important video parameters in host RAM memory.

9.3.1 Reading Interrupt Vectors

The video-related interrupt parameters are stored in lower host memory, as indicated in Table 9.7.

In Table 9.7, note that the memory location is equivalent to four times the interrupt vector—that is, $4 \times 05 = 20 = 14$ hex. Multiplying by 4 is necessary because there are four bytes in each of the vector locations. There are four bytes because each location must contain a long pointer.

TABLE 9.5 Control Register Initial Values: EGA

Miscellaneous Register

								Mode									
0	1	2	3	4	5	6	7	D	E	F	10	0F*	10*	00*	01*	02*	03*
23	23	23	23	23	23	23	A6	23	23	A2	A7	A2	A7	A7	A7	A7	A7

Sequencer Registers

Index	0	1	2	3	4	5	6	7	D	E	F	10	0F*	10*	00*	01*	02*	03*
									Mode									
0	B	B	1	1	B	B	1	0	B	1	5	5	1	1	B	B	1	1
1	3	3	3	3	3	3	1	3	F	F	F	F	F	F	3	3	3	3
2	0	0	0	0	0	0	0	0	0	0	0	0	0	0	0	0	0	0
3	3	3	3	3	2	2	6	3	6	6	0	0	6	6	3	3	3	3
4	23	23	23	23	23	23	23	A6	23	23	A2	A7	A2	A7	A7	A7	A7	A7

CRTC Registers

Index	0	1	2	3	4	5	6	7	D	E	F	10	0F*	10*	00*	01*	02*	03*
									Mode									
0	37	37	70	70	37	37	70	60	37	70	60	5B	60	5B	2D	2D	5B	5B
1	27	27	4F	4F	27	27	4F	4F	27	4F	4F	4F	4F	4F	27	27	4F	4F
2	2D	2D	5C	5C	2D	2D	59	56	2D	59	56	53	56	53	2B	2B	53	53
3	37	37	2F	2F	37	37	2D	3A	37	2D	1A	17	3A	37	2D	2D	37	37
4	31	31	5F	5F	30	30	5E	51	30	5E	50	50	50	52	28	28	51	51
5	15	15	7	7	14	14	6	60	14	6	E0	BA	60	0	6D	6D	5B	5B
6	4	4	4	4	4	4	4	70	4	4	70	6C	70	6C	6C	6C	6C	6C
7	11	11	11	11	11	11	11	1F	11	11	1F	1F	1F	1F	1F	1F	1F	1F
8	0	0	0	0	0	0	0	0	0	0	0	0	0	0	0	0	0	0
9	7	7	7	7	1	1	1	D	0	0	0	0	0	0	D	D	D	D
A	6	6	6	6	0	0	0	B	0	0	0	0	0	0	6	6	6	6
B	7	7	7	7	0	0	0	C	0	0	0	0	0	0	7	7	7	7
C	0	0	0	0	0	0	0	0	0	0	0	0	0	0	0	0	0	0
D	0	0	0	0	0	0	0	0	0	0	0	0	0	0	0	0	0	0
E	0	0	0	0	0	0	0	0	0	0	0	0	0	0	0	0	0	0
F	0	0	0	0	0	0	0	0	0	0	0	0	0	0	0	0	0	0
10	E1	E1	E1	E1	E1	E1	E0	5E	E1	E0	5E	5E	5E	5E	5E	5E	5E	5E
11	24	24	24	24	24	24	23	2E	24	23	2E	2B	2E	2B	2B	2B	2B	2B
12	C7	C7	C7	C7	C7	C7	C7	5D	C7	C7	5D	5D	5D	5D	5D	5D	5D	5D
13	14	14	28	28	14	14	28	28	14	28	14	14	28	28	14	14	28	28
14	8	8	8	8	0	0	0	D	0	0	D	F	D	F	F	F	F	F
15	E0	E0	E0	E0	E0	E0	DF	5E	E0	DF	5E	5F	5E	5F	5E	5E	5E	5E
16	F0	F0	F0	F0	F0	F0	EF	6E	F0	EF	6E	A	6E	A	A	A	A	A
17	A3	A3	A3	A3	A2	A2	C2	A3	E3	E3	8B	8B	E3	E3	A3	A3	A3	A3

(continued)

TABLE 9.5 (cont.)

CRTC Registers

Index	0	1	2	3	4	5	6	7	D	E	F	10	0F*	10*	00*	01*	02*	03*
18	FF	FF	FF	FF	FF	FF	FF	FF	FF	FF	FF	FF	FF	FF	FF	FF	FF	FF
19	0	0	0	0	0	0	0	0	0	0	0	0	0	0	0	0	0	0

Graphics Controller Registers

Index	0	1	2	3	4	5	6	7	D	E	F	10	0F*	10*	00*	01*	02*	03*
0	0	0	0	0	0	0	0	0	0	0	0	0	0	0	0	0	0	0
1	0	0	0	0	0	0	0	0	0	0	0	0	0	0	0	0	0	0
2	0	0	0	0	0	0	0	0	0	0	0	0	0	0	0	0	0	0
3	0	0	0	0	0	0	0	0	0	0	0	0	0	0	0	0	0	0
4	0	0	0	0	0	0	0	0	0	0	0	0	0	0	0	0	0	0
5	10	10	10	10	30	30	0	10	0	0	10	10	0	0	10	10	10	10
6	E	E	E	E	F	F	D	A	5	5	7	7	5	5	E	E	E	E
7	0	0	0	0	0	0	0	0	F	F	F	F	F	F	0	0	0	0
8	FF	FF	FF	FF	FF	FF	FF	FF	FF	FF	FF	FF	FF	FF	FF	FF	FF	FF

Attribute Controller Registers

Index	0	1	2	3	4	5	6	7	D	E	F	10	0F*	10*	00*	01*	02*	03*
0	0	0	0	0	0	0	0	0	0	0	0	0	0	0	0	0	0	0
1	1	1	1	1	13	13	17	8	1	1	8	1	8	1	1	1	1	1
2	2	2	2	2	15	14	17	8	2	2	0	0	0	2	2	2	2	2
3	3	3	3	3	17	17	17	8	3	3	0	0	0	3	3	3	3	3
4	4	4	4	4	2	2	17	8	4	4	18	4	18	4	4	4	4	4
5	5	5	5	5	4	4	17	8	5	5	18	7	18	5	5	5	5	5
6	6	6	6	6	6	6	17	8	6	6	0	0	0	14	14	14	14	14
7	7	7	7	7	7	7	17	8	7	7	0	0	0	7	7	7	7	7
8	10	10	10	10	10	10	17	10	10	10	0	0	0	38	38	38	38	38
9	11	11	11	11	11	11	17	18	11	11	8	1	8	39	39	39	39	39
A	12	12	12	12	12	12	17	18	12	12	0	0	0	3A	3A	3A	3A	3A
B	13	13	13	13	13	13	17	18	13	13	0	0	0	3B	3B	3B	3B	3B
C	14	14	14	14	14	14	17	18	14	14	0	4	0	3C	3C	3C	3C	3C
D	15	15	15	15	15	15	17	18	15	15	18	7	18	3D	3D	3D	3D	3D
E	16	16	16	16	16	16	17	18	16	16	0	0	0	3E	3E	3E	3E	3E
F	17	17	17	17	17	17	17	18	17	17	0	0	0	3F	3F	3F	3F	3F
10	8	8	8	8	1	1	1	E	1	1	B	1	B	1	8	8	8	8
11	0	0	0	0	0	0	0	0	0	0	0	0	0	0	0	0	0	0
12	F	F	F	F	3	3	1	F	F	F	5	5	5	F	F	F	F	F
13	0	0	0	0	0	0	0	8	0	0	0	0	0	0	0	0	0	0

TABLE 9.6 Control Register Initial Values: VGA

General Registers
Mode

Index	00	01	02	03	04	05	06	07	0D	0E	0F	10	11	12	13
0	63	63	63	63	63	63	63	A6	63	63	A2	A3	E3	E3	63
1	00	00	00	00	00	00	00	00	00	00	00	00	00	00	00
2	70	70	70	70	70	70	70	70	70	70	70	70	70	70	70
3	04	04	05	05	04	04	05	FF	04	04	FF	04	04	04	04

Sequence Registers
Mode

Index	00	01	02	03	04	05	06	07	0D	0E	0F	10	11	12	13
0	03	03	03	03	03	03	03	03	03	03	03	03	03	03	03
1	09	09	01	01	09	09	01	00	09	01	01	01	01	01	01
2	03	03	03	03	03	03	01	03	0F	0F	0F	0F	0F	0F	0F
3	00	00	00	00	00	00	00	00	00	00	00	00	00	00	00
4	02	02	02	02	02	02	06	02	06	06	06	06	06	06	0E

CRTC Registers
Mode

Index	00	01	02	03	04	05	06	07	0D	0E	0F	10	11	12	13
0	2D	2D	5F	5F	2D	2D	5F	FF	2D	5F	FF	5F	5F	5F	5F
1	27	27	4F	4F	27	27	4F	FF	27	4F	FF	4F	4F	4F	4F
2	28	28	50	50	28	28	50	FF	28	50	FF	50	50	50	50
3	90	90	82	82	90	90	82	FF	90	82	FF	82	82	82	82
4	2B	2B	55	55	2B	2B	54	FF	2B	54	FF	54	54	54	24
5	A0	A0	81	81	80	80	80	FF	80	80	FF	80	80	80	80
6	BF	BF	BF	BF	BF	BF	BF	FF	BF	BF	FF	BF	0B	0B	BF
7	1F	1F	1F	1F	1F	1F	1F	FF	1F	1F	FF	1F	3E	3E	1F
8	00	00	00	00	00	00	00	FF	00	00	FF	00	00	00	00
9	C7	C7	C7	C7	C1	C1	C1	FF	C0	C0	FF	40	40	40	41
A	06	06	06	06	00	00	00	FF	00	00	FF	00	00	00	00
B	07	07	07	07	00	00	00	FF	00	00	FF	00	00	00	00
C	00	00	00	00	00	00	00	FF	00	00	FF	00	00	00	00
D	00	00	00	00	00	00	00	FF	00	00	FF	00	00	00	00
E	00	00	00	00	00	00	00	FF	00	00	FF	00	00	00	00
F	31	31	59	59	31	31	59	FF	31	59	FF	59	59	59	31
10	9C	9C	9C	9C	9C	9C	9C	FF	9C	9C	FF	83	EA	EA	9C
11	8E	8E	8E	8E	8E	8E	8E	FF	8E	8E	FF	85	8C	8C	8E
12	8F	8F	8F	8F	8F	8F	8F	FF	8F	8F	FF	5D	DF	DF	8F
13	14	14	28	28	14	14	28	FF	14	28	FF	28	28	28	28
14	1F	1F	1F	1F	00	00	00	FF	00	00	FF	0F	00	00	40

(continued)

TABLE 9.6 *(cont.)*

CRTC Registers

	Mode														
Index	*00*	*01*	*02*	*03*	*04*	*05*	*06*	*07*	*0D*	*0E*	*0F*	*10*	*11*	*12*	*13*
15	96	96	96	96	96	96	96	FF	96	96	FF	63	E7	E7	96
16	B9	B9	B9	B9	B9	B9	B9	FF	B9	B9	FF	BA	04	04	B9
17	A3	A3	A3	A3	A2	A2	C2	FF	E3	E3	FF	E3	C3	E3	A3
18	FF	FF	FF	FF	FF	FF	FF	FF	FF	FF	FF	FF	FF	FF	FF

Graphics Controller Registers

	Mode														
Index	*00*	*01*	*02*	*03*	*04*	*05*	*06*	*07*	*0D*	*0E*	*0F*	*10*	*11*	*12*	*13*
0	00	00	00	00	00	00	00	00	00	00	00	00	00	00	00
1	00	00	00	00	00	00	00	00	00	00	00	00	00	00	00
2	00	00	00	00	00	00	00	00	00	00	00	00	00	00	00
3	00	00	00	00	00	00	00	00	00	00	00	00	00	00	00
4	00	00	00	00	00	00	00	00	00	00	00	00	00	00	00
5	10	10	10	10	30	30	00	10	10	00	00	10	00	00	40
6	0E	0E	0E	0E	0F	0F	0D	0A	05	05	05	05	05	05	05
7	00	00	00	00	00	00	00	00	00	0F	05	00	05	0F	0F
8	FF	FF	FF	FF	FF	FF	FF	FF	FF	FF	FF	FF	FF	FF	FF

Attribute Controller Registers

	Mode														
Index	*00*	*01*	*02*	*03*	*04*	*05*	*06*	*07*	*0D*	*0E*	*0F*	*10*	*11*	*12*	*13*
0	00	00	00	00	00	00	00	00	00	00	00	00	00	00	00
1	01	01	01	01	13	13	17	08	01	01	08	01	3F	01	01
2	02	02	02	02	15	15	17	08	02	02	00	02	3F	02	02
3	03	03	03	03	17	17	17	08	03	03	00	03	3F	03	03
4	04	04	04	04	02	02	17	08	04	04	18	04	3F	04	04
5	05	05	05	05	04	04	17	08	05	05	18	05	3F	05	05
6	06	06	06	06	06	06	17	08	06	06	00	14	3F	14	06
7	07	07	07	07	07	07	17	08	07	07	00	07	3F	07	07
8	10	10	10	10	10	10	17	10	10	10	00	38	3F	38	08
9	11	11	11	11	11	11	17	18	11	11	08	39	3F	39	09
A	12	12	12	12	12	12	17	18	12	12	00	3A	3F	3A	0A
B	13	13	13	13	13	13	17	18	13	13	00	3B	3F	3B	0B
C	14	14	14	14	14	14	17	18	14	14	00	3C	3F	3C	0C
D	15	15	15	15	15	15	17	18	15	15	18	3D	3F	3D	0D
E	16	16	16	16	16	16	17	18	16	16	00	3E	3F	3E	0E

TABLE 9.6 *(cont.)*

Attribute Controller Registers

Mode

Index	00	01	02	03	04	05	06	07	0D	0E	0F	10	11	12	13
F	17	17	17	17	17	17	17	18	17	17	00	3F	3F	3F	0F
10	08	08	08	08	01	01	01	0E	01	01	0B	01	01	01	41
11	00	00	00	00	00	00	00	00	00	00	00	00	00	00	00
12	0F	0F	0F	0F	03	03	01	0F	0F	0F	05	0F	0F	0F	0F
13	00	00	00	00	00	00	00	00	00	00	00	00	00	00	00
14	00	00	00	00	00	00	00	00	00	00	00	00	00	00	00

TABLE 9.7 Interrupt Vectors

Memory Location (Hex)	*Function*
0000:0014	Interrupt INT 05 hex vector
0000:0028	Interrupt INT 0A hex vector
0000:0040	Interrupt INT 10 hex vector
0000:007C	Interrupt INT 1F hex vector
0000:0108	Interrupt INT 42 hex vector
0000:010C	Interrupt INT 43 hex vector

9.3.2 BIOS Storage in Host Memory

In addition to the vector locations, the BIOS routines store information in host memory. Memory locations range from 0000:0410 to 0000:04A8. Location 0000:0100 is reserved for print-screen status. Table 9.8 lists the relevant video memory storage locations.

These variables are critical to the programmer, especially in the EGA, because the majority of the EGA registers are write-only. Not being able to read the EGA registers forces the programmer to use these storage locations. Fortunately, all registers in the VGA are read/write, allowing the programmer to read the state of each register directly. Often, the variables stored in memory are the results of calculations based on the values in the EGA/VGA registers, and reading these locations is more convenient than calculating the value. The meaning of these memory variables is discussed in the following sections.

TABLE 9.8 EGA: Host Memory Locations Reserved for Video

Memory Location (Hex)	Function
0000:0449	Active video mode
0000:044A	Number of character columns
0000:044C	Length of current display page
0000:044E	Start of current page in display memory
0000:0450	Cursor save area
0000:0450	Page 0: row / column
0000:0452	Page 1: row / column
0000:0454	Page 2: row / column
0000:0456	Page 3: row / column
0000:0458	Page 4: row / column
0000:045A	Page 5: row / column
0000:045C	Page 6: row / column
0000:045E	Page 7: row / column
0000:0460	Cursor mode: start / end
0000:0462	Current display page
0000:0463	Base host address of port I/O
0000:0465	Current mode
0000:0466	Current color
0000:0484	Number of character rows on screen − 1
0000:0485	Bytes per character
0000:0487	Miscellaneous information
0000:0488	Configuration bits
0000:04A8	Pointer to Table of Save Area Pointers
0000:0100	Print-screen status

9.4 READING THE STATE OF THE EGA AND VGA ADAPTERS

Perhaps the greatest difference between the EGA and the VGA is the VGA's ability to provide information to the host program. This section describes how to access information to ascertain the state of the EGA and VGA.

9.4.1 Reading the EGA State

Unlike the VGA, the EGA has no provision in the BIOS calls for returning the adapter state information. This information can be obtained from the memory locations reserved for the video system as listed in Table 9.8. The relevant values for each of the described display modes of the EGA are listed in Table 9.9.

TABLE 9.9 EGA State Information

Active display mode = 0 hex

Number of character columns = 40
Length of display buffer = 800 hex
Start of active buffer = 0 hex
Cursor starting line = 7, ending line = 6

CRTC port address = 3D4 hex
Number of character rows per screen = 25
Character height = 14 rows

Active display mode = 1 hex

Number of character columns = 40
Length of display buffer = 800 hex
Start of active buffer = 0 hex
Cursor starting line = 7, ending line = 6

CRTC port address = 3D4 hex
Number of character rows per screen = 25
Character height = 14 rows

Active display mode = 2 hex

Number of character columns = 80
Length of display buffer = 1000 hex
Start of active buffer = 0 hex
Cursor starting line = 7, ending line = 6

CRTC port address = 3D4 hex
Number of character rows per screen = 25
Character height = 14 rows

Active display mode = 3 hex

Number of character columns = 80
Length of display buffer = 1000 hex
Start of active buffer = 0 hex
Cursor starting line = 7, ending line = 6

CRTC port address = 3D4 hex
Number of character rows per screen = 25
Character height = 14 rows

Active display mode = 4 hex

Number of character columns = 40
Length of display buffer = 4000 hex
Start of active buffer = 0 hex
Cursor starting line = 0, ending line = 0

CRTC port address = 3D4 hex
Number of character rows per screen = 25
Character height = 8 rows

Active display mode = 5 hex

Number of character columns = 40
Length of display buffer = 4000 hex
Start of active buffer = 0 hex
Cursor starting line = 0, ending line = 0

CRTC port address = 3D4 hex
Number of character rows per screen = 25
Character height = 8 rows

Active display mode = 6 hex

Number of character columns = 80
Length of display buffer = 4000 hex
Start of active buffer = 0 hex
Cursor starting line = 0, ending line = 0

CRTC port address = 3D4 hex
Number of character rows per screen = 25
Character height = 8 rows

Active display mode = 7 hex

Number of character columns = 80
Length of display buffer = 1000 hex
Start of active buffer = 0 hex
Cursor starting line = 12, ending line = 11

CRTC port address = 3D4 hex
Number of character rows per screen = 25
Character height = 14 rows

(continued)

TABLE 9.9 *(cont.)*

Active display mode = D hex

Number of character columns = 40	CRTC port address = 3D4 hex
Length of display buffer = 2000 hex	Number of character rows per screen = 25
Start of active buffer = 0 hex	Character height = 8 rows
Cursor starting line = 0, ending line = 0	

Active display mode = E hex

Number of character columns = 80	CRTC port address = 3D4 hex
Length of display buffer = 4000 hex	Number of character rows per screen = 25
Start of active buffer = 0 hex	Character height = 8 rows
Cursor starting line = 0, ending line = 0	

Active display mode = F hex

Number of character columns = 80	CRTC port address = 3D4 hex
Length of display buffer = 8000 hex	Number of character rows per screen = 25
Start of active buffer = 0 hex	Character height = 14 rows
Cursor starting line = 0, ending line = 0	

Active display mode = 10 hex

Number of character columns = 80	CRTC port address = 3D4 hex
Length of display buffer = 8000 hex	Number of character rows per screen = 25
Start of active buffer = 0 hex	Character height = 14 rows
Cursor starting line = 0, ending line = 0	

Note that this table does not contain elements that are relevant to the dynamic condition of these display modes. For example, the cursor position tables are not included in Table 9.9.

9.4.2   Reading the VGA State

The VGA BIOS provides a useful BIOS call that returns the current information regarding the state of the VGA. The BIOS call AH=1B hex invokes the Return Functionality/State Information. The programmer provides this BIOS call with a pointer to an array. The BIOS routine fills this array with the functionality and state information. The information returned to the calling program closely resembles the state table illustrated in Table 9.9. The values returned by this BIOS call and their associated offsets from the top of the array are listed in Table 9.10.

TABLE 9.10 Functionality/State Information

Offset (Hex)	Notes	Length	Function
00	1	Word	Static Functionality Info. Table Offset
02	1	Word	Static Functionality Info. Table Segment
04		Byte	Active display mode
05		Word	Number of character columns per screen
07		Word	Length of current display page
09		Word	Start address of current display page
0B		Word	Cursor position table
0B		Word	Page 0: row / column
0D		Word	Page 1: row / column
0F		Word	Page 2: row / column
11		Word	Page 3: row / column
13		Word	Page 4: row / column
15		Word	Page 5: row / column
17		Word	Page 6: row / column
19		Word	Page 7: row / column
1B		Word	Cursor mode: start / end
1D		Byte	Current display page
1E		Word	Base host address of Port I/O
20		Byte	Current mode
21		Byte	Current color palette
22	2	Byte	Number of character rows on screen
23		Word	Bytes per character
25	3	Byte	Display combination code (DCC) (active)
26	3	Byte	Display combination code (DCC) (alternate)
27		Word	Number of colors supported in current mode
29		Byte	Number of pages supported in current mode
2A	4	Byte	Number of scan lines in current mode
2B	5	Byte	Primary active character block
2C	5	Byte	Secondary active character block
2D	6	Byte	Miscellaneous state information
2E–30			Reserved
31	7	Byte	Display memory installed
32	8	Byte	Save pointer state information
33–3F			Reserved

Notes:

1. The Static Information Table is pointed to by the Offset and Segment address located in offsets 00 and 02. (See the Static Information Table.)

(continued)

TABLE 9.10   *(cont.)*

2. The number of character rows on the screen is one greater than the similar value in the EGA. However, in the EGA, the value at host address 0000:0084 is one less than the number of columns.

3. The Display Combination Code signifies which type of monitor is installed in the active and alternate display adapter. (See the Display Combination Code.)

4. The number of scan lines in the current mode ranges from 200 to 480 scan lines depending on the active display mode. The code in this byte represents the number of scan lines, as indicated in Table 9.11.

5. The values in the primary and secondary active character block locations range from 0 to 259. These numbers represent block 0 to block 255, respectively.

6. The Miscellaneous state information is different from the Miscellaneous information byte of the EGA residing at host address 0000:0487. Each bit in the Miscellaneous state information byte has a special meaning. The function of each of these bits is listed in Table 9.12.

7. The amount of display memory installed can range from 64 Kbyte to 256 Kbytes. It is conceivable to load 512 Kbytes on the display adapter, because the PC memory map allows 512 Kbytes of storage between A000:0000 and BFFF:FFFF hex. Table 9.13 lists the possible display memory configurations.

8. Each bit in the save pointer state information byte contains a flag representing the active or inactive state of a variety of features in the VGA. Any bit set to 1 indicates that the respective state is active. Likewise, any bit reset to a 0 indicates an inactive state. The meaning of each bit is listed in Table 9.14.

TABLE 9.11   Number of Scan Lines in Alphanumeric Mode

Code	Number of Scan Lines
0	200
1	350
2	400
3	480

9.4.3   Functionality/State Information

Invoking the BIOS call to read the functionality/state information using a VGA planar system results in the information listed in Tables 9.11 through 9.15. Note that several parameters called out in the functionality/state specification from Table 9.15 are not included in this table. These parameters were eliminated from the Table 9.15 because they referred to non–mode-related functions. For example, cursor shape and cursor position are independent of the active display mode.

TABLE 9.12 Miscellaneous State Information Byte

Bit Number	Function
0	Monitor state =0 All modes on all monitors are inactive =1 All modes on all monitors are active
1	Color Register summing mode =0 Summing Mode inactive =1 Summing Mode active
2	Monochrome display =0 Monochrome display not attached =1 Monochrome display attached
3	Default palette loading during Mode Set =0 Palette, Color Registers not affected =1 Palette, Color Registers loaded
4	Cursor Emulation =0 Cursor emulation inactive =1 Cursor emulation active
5	Function of bit 3 of attribute byte =0 Use as part of background color =1 Use to signify blinking or non-blinking
6,7	Reserved

TABLE 9.13 Amount of Display Memory

Code	Amount of Display Memory
0	64 Kbytes
1	128 Kbytes
2	256 Kbytes
3	384 Kbytes
4–255	Reserved

TABLE 9.14 Save Pointer State Information Byte

Bit Number	Function (1 = Active)
0	512-character set
1	Dynamic save area
2	Alpha font override
3	Graphics font override
4	Palette override
5	Display combination code extension
6,7	Reserved

TABLE 9.15 Typical Functionality/State Information

Display mode = 0 hex

Number of character columns = 40
Length of display buffer = 800 hex
CRTC address = 3D4 hex
CRT_MODE_SET = 2C hex,
CRT_PALETTE = 30 hex
Number of character rows per screen = 25

Character height = 16
Number of colors = 16
Number of display pages supported = 8
Miscellaneous state information = 31 hex

Display mode = 1 hex

Number of character columns = 40
Length of display buffer = 800 hex
CRTC address = 3D4 hex
CRT_MODE_SET = 28 hex,
CRT_PALETTE = 30 hex
Number of character rows per screen = 25

Character height = 16
Number of colors = 16
Number of display pages supported = 8
Miscellaneous state information = 31 hex

Display mode = 2 hex

Number of character columns = 80
Length of display buffer = 1000 hex
CRTC address = 3D4 hex
CRT_MODE_SET = 2D hex,
CRT_PALETTE = 30 hex
Number of character rows per screen = 25

Character height = 16
Number of colors = 16
Number of display pages supported = 8
Miscellaneous state information = 31 hex

Display mode = 3 hex

Number of character columns = 80
Length of display buffer = 1000 hex
CRTC address = 3D4 hex
CRT_MODE_SET = 29 hex,
CRT_PALETTE = 30 hex
Number of character rows per screen = 25

Character height = 16
Number of colors = 16
Number of display pages supported = 8
Miscellaneous state information = 31 hex

Display mode = 4 hex

Number of character columns = 40
Length of display buffer = 4000 hex
CRTC address = 3D4 hex
CRT_MODE_SET = 2A hex,
CRT_PALETTE = 30 hex
Number of character rows per screen = 25

Character height = 8
Number of colors = 4
Number of display pages supported = 1
Miscellaneous state information = 11 hex

Display mode = 5 hex

Number of character columns = 40
Length of display buffer = 4000 hex
CRTC address = 3D4 hex
CRT_MODE_SET = 2E hex,
CRT_PALETTE = 30 hex
Number of character rows per screen = 25

Character height = 8
Number of colors = 4
Number of display pages supported = 1
Miscellaneous state information = 11 hex

TABLE 9.15 *(cont.)*

Display mode = 6 hex

Number of character columns = 80
Length of display buffer = 4000 hex
CRTC address = 3D4 hex
CRT_MODE_SET = 1E hex,
CRT_PALETTE = 3F hex
Number of character rows per screen = 25

Character height = 8
Number of colors = 2
Number of display pages supported = 1
Miscellaneous state information = 11 hex

Display mode = 7 hex

Number of character columns = 80
Length of display buffer = 1000 hex
CRTC address = 3B4 hex
CRT_MODE_SET = 29 hex,
CRT_PALETTE = 30 hex
Number of character rows per screen = 25

Character height = 16
Number of colors = 0
Number of display pages supported = 8
Miscellaneous state information = 31 hex

Display mode = D hex

Number of character columns = 40
Length of display buffer = 2000 hex
CRTC address = 3D4 hex
CRT_MODE_SET = 29 hex,
CRT_PALETTE = 30 hex
Number of character rows per screen = 25

Character height = 8
Number of colors = 16
Number of display pages supported = 8
Miscellaneous state information = 11 hex

Display mode = E hex

Number of character columns = 80
Length of display buffer = 4000 hex
CRTC address = 3D4 hex
CRT_MODE_SET = 29 hex,
CRT_PALETTE = 30 hex
Number of character rows per screen = 25

Character height = 8
Number of colors = 16
Number of display pages supported = 4
Miscellaneous state information = 11 hex

Display mode = F hex

Number of character columns = 80
Length of display buffer = 8000 hex
CRTC address = 3B4 hex
CRT_MODE_SET = 29 hex,
CRT_PALETTE = 30 hex
Number of character rows per screen = 25

Character height = 14
Number of colors = 0
Number of display pages supported = 2
Miscellaneous state information = 31 hex

Display mode = 10 hex

Number of character columns = 80
Length of display buffer = 8000 hex
CRTC address = 3D4 hex
CRT_MODE_SET = 29 hex,
CRT_PALETTE = 30 hex
Number of character rows per screen = 25

Character height = 14
Number of colors = 16
Number of display pages supported = 2
Miscellaneous state information = 11 hex

(continued)

TABLE 9.15 *(cont.)*

Display mode = 11 hex

Number of character columns = 80
Length of display buffer = A000 hex
CRTC address = 3D4 hex
CRT_MODE_SET = 29 hex,
CRT_PALETTE = 30 hex
Number of character rows per screen = 30

Character height = 16
Number of colors = 2
Number of display pages supported = 1
Miscellaneous state information = 11 hex

Display mode = 12 hex

Number of character columns = 80
Length of display buffer = A000 hex
CRTC address = 3D4 hex
CRT_MODE_SET = 29 hex,
CRT_PALETTE = 30 hex
Number of character rows per screen = 30

Character height = 16
Number of colors = 16
Number of display pages supported = 1
Miscellaneous state information = 11 hex

Display mode = 13 hex

Number of character columns = 40
Length of display buffer = 2000 hex
CRTC address = 3D4 hex
CRT_MODE_SET = 29 hex,
CRT_PALETTE = 30 hex
Number of character rows per screen = 25

Character height = 8
Number of colors = 0
Number of display pages supported = 1
Miscellaneous state information = 11 hex

9.4.4 VGA Static Information Table

The static information table consists of a group of static parameters that describe the condition of the VGA. This table is called *static* because the values do not change during the operation of the VGA. Rather, this table lists the configuration of the VGA, which is similar to the information provided by sense switches. The values stored in the Static Information Table and their associated offsets from the start of the table are listed in Table 9.16.

9.4.5 Typical Static Function Block

A typical static function block is listed in Table 9.17. From the Functionality/State Information, it was determined that this block resides in BIOS ROM beginning at address E000:305F hex.

TABLE 9.16 Static Information Table

Offset (Hex)	Notes	Length	Function
00	1	Byte	Video modes (BIOS call AH = 00)
01	1	Byte	Video modes (BIOS call AH = 00)
02	1	Byte	Video modes (BIOS call AH = 00)
03–06			Reserved
07	2	Byte	Scan lines of text available (BIOS call AH = 12 BL = 30 hex)
08		Byte	Character blocks available: alpha modes (BIOS call AH = 11)
09		Byte	Max. # of character blocks: alpha modes (BIOS call AH = 11)
0A	3	Byte	Miscellaneous functions (BIOS calls are bit-dependent)
0B	3	Byte	Miscellaneous functions (BIOS calls are bit-dependent)
0C–0D			Reserved
0E	4	Byte	Save pointer functions

Notes:

1. The availability of the video modes is contained in three contiguous bytes of the static function table. The three bytes contain a total of eighteen bits. Each bit is associated with a display mode. A bit position within one of these three bytes that is set to a 1 indicates that the respective mode is supported on this video system. The display modes and their associated bits are listed in Table 9.18.

2. In the VGA, it is possible to configure the alphanumeric display modes with 200, 350, or 400 lines as indicated in Table 9.19.

3. There are two bytes dedicated to miscellaneous functions of the VGA. In these two bytes, any bit set to a 1 indicates that the associated function is enabled. Likewise, any bit reset to a 0 indicates that the function is disabled. The meaning of each bit in the two bytes is listed in Table 9.20.

9.4.6 VGA Display Combination Code

The display combination code (DCC) contains information relevant to the type of display adapters installed in the computer and the monitors connected to the active and inactive display adapters. Because there can be two VGA systems

TABLE 9.17 Static Function Information Block

Video modes 0–7 = FF hex (1 = enabled)
Video modes 8–F = E0 hex (1 = enabled)
Video modes 10–13 = 0F hex (1 = enabled)
Scan lines available in text modes = 07 hex
Character blocks available in text modes = 2
Maximum # of active character blocks: alpha modes = 8
Miscellaneous functions = FF hex (1 = enabled)
Miscellaneous functions = 0E hex (1 = enabled)
Save Pointer functions = 0 hex (1 = enabled)

TABLE 9.18 Display Modes Available (BIOS Call AH = 00 Hex)

Byte	Bit	Display Mode (Hex) (1 = Supported 0 = Not supported)
00	0	Mode 0
00	1	Mode 1
00	2	Mode 2
00	3	Mode 3
00	4	Mode 4
00	5	Mode 5
00	6	Mode 6
00	7	Mode 7
01	0	Mode 8
01	1	Mode 9
01	2	Mode A
01	3	Mode B
01	4	Mode C
01	5	Mode D
01	6	Mode E
01	7	Mode F
02	0	Mode 10
02	1	Mode 11
02	2	Mode 12
02	3	Mode 13
02	4–7	Reserved

TABLE 9.19 Scan Lines Available in Alphanumeric Modes (BIOS Call AH = 12 Hex)

Bit	Number of Scan Lines
0	200
1	350
2	400
3–7	Reserved

TABLE 9.20 Miscellaneous Functions

Byte	Bit	Function (1 = Active)
00	0	All modes on all monitors
00	1	Color Registers summing (BIOS call AH = 10 AL = 1B hex) (BIOS call AH = 12 BL = 33 hex)
00	2	Character font loading (BIOS call AH = 11 hex)
00	3	Default palette loading on mode set (BIOS call AH = 12 BL = 31 hex)
00	4	Cursor emulation (BIOS call AH = 01, AH = 12 BL = 34 hex)
00	5	EGA palette (BIOS call AH = 10 hex)
	6	DAC color palette (BIOS call AH = 10 hex)
00	7	DAC color paging (BIOS call AH = 10 hex)
01	0	Light pen (BIOS call AH = 04 hex)
01	1	Save/restore (BIOS call AH = 1C hex)
01	2	Background intensity/blinking control (BIOS call AH = 11 hex)
01	3	Display combination code (DCC) (BIOS call AH = 1A hex)
01	4–7	Reserved

TABLE 9.21   Display Combination Code (BIOS Call AH = 1A Hex)

Code	Type of Adapter	Type of Monitor
0	None	None
1	Monochrome	Monochrome
2	Color Graphics Adapter	
7	PS/2 Display Adapter	Monochrome
8	PS/2 Display Adapter	Color

installed in the same computer, one planar and one adapter, it is possible to have any combination of monitors on either system. Both the active and the inactive display systems have their own DCC. The inactive display system is also called the *alternate display system*. The DCC codes and their meanings are listed in Table 9.21.

9.4.7   VGA: Saving and Restoring

A BIOS call is provided in the VGA that allows the video state to be saved or restored. This BIOS call, AH=1C hex, allows the programmer to load the video system with data provided in a buffer. The buffer can contain the video hardware state, the video data areas, or the video palette state and color registers. This buffer can contain any combination of these groups of parameters. Upon invoking a save operation, a buffer provided by the programmer is loaded automatically by BIOS with the desired groups of parameters. Upon invoking a restore operation, the programmer provides the loaded buffer to BIOS and BIOS loads the groups of parameters into the VGA.

9.5   TESTING FOR HARDWARE

For software to operate in an environment that may contain different graphics adapters and monitors, it first must determine which hardware is present. Certain standardized techniques and some not-so-standard techniques are defined to assist the programmer in this task. The Micro Channel requires that the cards contain a registered ID number. In this case, it is necessary only to read the ID numbers on the bus to determine what hardware is present. This is not the case, however, for the EGA/VGA.

9.5.1   Testing for Adapters

Tests are often necessary to determine if an MDA, CGA, EGA, PGA, MEGA, or VGA is present. In addition, a system might have one adapter configured as a monochrome adapter and a second adapter configured as a color adapter. The System/2 computer family allows two VGA display systems to be resident in the same computer. In addition, both can be configured with color monitors. In the System/2, only one of these VGA systems, either the planar or the adapter, can be active at a time.

The EGA may be tested in a number of ways. One way to differentiate the MDA, CGA, and EGA is to read the system configuration word at host memory address 0040:0010. A primary display field is contained in bits 4 and 5 of the byte at this location. Table 9.22 lists the options for this field.

Another way to check for the EGA is to determine if the copyright information is present in the EGA BIOS ROM. The BIOS ROM starts at location A000:0000. The first two bytes contain the traditional BIOS identifiers 55 hex followed by AA. The copyright information begins at C000:0009. Although it is not a recommended method, an IBM identifier can be found at memory location C000:001E, as shown in Table 9.23.

Several software products use this flag to determine if an EGA is present. Compatible EGA adapters will usually contain these bytes in the proper memory locations.

If it is determined that an EGA monitor does not exist, it is possible to search for other adapters by writing to the appropriate Cursor Position Register for the other adapters. The monochrome and color adapters both rely on the 6845 graphics controller chip. A group of CRT Controller Registers are contained in this chip, one of which is the Cursor Location Register. This register is a read/write register because it is necessary to command the cursor to move to a desired location as well as reading the current location.

The monochrome adapter maps the CRTC Registers at host port address 3B4 hex, and the color adapter maps the register at 3D4 hex. This register must be

TABLE 9.22 Primary Display Field

Bit 5	Bit 4	Primary Display
0	0	EGA
0	1	CGA 40-column mode
1	0	CGA 80-column mode
1	1	MDA

TABLE 9.23 IBM Logo

Address	Character	Code (Hex)
C000:001E	I	49
C000:001F	B	42
C000:0020	M	4D

loaded with a 0F hex in order to access the Cursor Location Register. The Cursor Position Register is then accessed, through host port 3B5 for monochrome adapters or host port 3D5 for color adapters. The programmer can read this register, saving the value for later, write a new value into this register, and then read it again. The register exists if the second read operation returns the same value as was written into the register. If the register exists, the adapter must be present. If the test is positive, the original data read from the cursor position can be returned to the Cursor Position Register.

9.5.2   Testing for Monitors

If the EGA is present, a test can be performed to determine whether a monochrome or monitor is attached to the adapter. A Miscellaneous Information Byte is located at memory address 0000:487. A monitor type field is kept in bit 1 of this byte. Table 9.24 lists the meaning of this field.

If an EGA is present with a monochrome monitor, it is possible that a second display adapter exists with a color monitor—for example, the CGA. Likewise, if the EGA is using a color monitor, a second display adapter may exist with a monochrome monitor—for example, the MDA or the Hercules.

9.5.3   Reading System Parameters

The EGA/VGA registers are accessed through the host input/output ports. If the system is configured as a monochrome system, certain ports will be configured at port addresses beginning with a 3Bx. Likewise, if the system is configured as a color system, certain ports will be configured at port addresses beginning with a 3Dx. The x refers to the least significant hexadecimal digit of the port address. Examples of these registers are the CRTC Address and Data Registers, the Feature Control Register, and the Input Status #1 Register. The other registers reside at host port addresses beginning with a 3Cx. It is possible to determine whether the ports can be accessed through ports 3Bx or 3Dx by the value in host memory address 0000:0463, called the Base Address of Active Video Interface Board. The value in this location will be loaded with a 3B4 or a 3D4, indicating the base port address.

It is possible to determine all relevant information regarding the EGA/VGA display memory. The base of the EGA display memory is at host address A000:0000. The amount of EGA display memory available can be obtained by a

TABLE 9.24   Monitor Field

Bit 1	Monitor Type
0	Color
1	Monochrome

TABLE 9.25 Amount of Display Memory

BL Register	Amount of Memory	Memory per Plane
0	64 Kbytes	16 Kbytes
1	128 Kbytes	32 Kbytes
2	192 Kbytes	48 Kbytes
3	256 Kbytes	64 Kbytes

BIOS call. The Alternate Select BIOS call entitled Return Video Information can provide information regarding the amount of display memory installed on the board. Table 9.25 lists the possible memory configurations and the associated codes returned in the BL register. Most EGA implementations and all VGA implementations are configured with 256 Kbytes of display memory.

The EGA/VGA segments the display memory into display pages. The number of display pages available depends on the amount of display memory and the current display mode. The base address of the active display page relative to the host address of the EGA display memory can be determined from 0000:044E. This word contains the offset to the top of the current display page. The length of the display page is loaded into host address 0000:044C.

The horizontal and vertical resolution of a page can be measured in units of characters or pixels. The number of character rows minus 1 is loaded into host address 0000:0484, and the number of character columns is loaded into host address 0000:044A.

The number of vertical pixels can be determined by multiplying the number of rows per character by the number of character rows per screen. The number of rows per character is loaded in host memory address 0000:0485, commonly called the number of bytes per character. This terminology is slightly confusing. The characters are stored in the character font bit patterns using a format that relies on one byte per character row. When displayed, however, a character does not necessarily represent eight horizontal pixels. Character sets whose characters are nine pixels wide are available.

The number of horizontal pixels can be determined by multiplying the number of character rows (as determined above) by 8. The 9-bit-wide characters do not have to be considered when a pixel coordinate system is used. The only time a pixel coordinate system would be used is when the EGA/VGA is in a graphics mode, and no graphics modes use nine-bit-wide character sets.

9.5.4 Reading the Cursor Status

Information regarding the cursor is kept in host memory and can be accessed through the Read Cursor Position BIOS call, AH = 03. The EGA display memory can be segmented into a maximum of eight display pages. The BIOS call returns the cursor position of any desired page.

A table of cursor row and column positions is kept in host memory beginning at host address 0000:0450. This table consists of eight row and column coordinate pairs, one for each possible display page. The row values are in the even byte addresses, and the column values are in the odd byte addresses. The values in each of the row and column positions refer to the character position instead of the pixel position. The shape of the cursor can be read from host memory address 0000:0460. The lower byte of this word contains the start scan line, and the upper byte contains the end scan line of the cursor block.

9.5.5 Video Parameters

The current video mode number is contained in host memory address 0000:0449. The active video page number is contained in host memory address 0000:0462. Miscellaneous information is available in a byte at host address 0000:0487. Each bit in this byte refers to a specific function. These functions are listed in Table 9.26.

TABLE 9.26 Miscellaneous State Information

Bit Number	Information
0	Cursor emulation 0 = Direct cursor setting 1 = Emulate 8-by-8 cursor
1	Display monitor 0 = Color 1 = Monochrome
2	Display buffer access 0 = CPU can access memory at any time 1 = CPU must wait for display inactive
3	EGA status 0 = EGA active 1 = EGA inactive
4	(Reserved)
6,5	Amount of display memory 0 = 64 Kbytes 1 = 128 Kbytes 2 = 192 Kbytes 3 = 256 Kbytes
7	Status of display memory after mode set 0 = Display memory cleared 1 = Display memory preserved

TABLE 9.27 Sense Switch Field of Video Configuration

Field (Hex)	Primary Display	Secondary Display
0	MDA Mono 80c	EGA RGBI 40c
1	MDA Mono 80c	EGA RGBI 80c
2	MDA Mono 80c	EGA RrGgBb 200p
3	MDA Mono 80c	EGA RrGgBb 350p
4	CGA RGBI 40c	EGA Mono 720p
5	CGA RGBI 80c	EGA Mono 720p
6	EGA RGBI 40c	MDA Mono 80c
7	EGA RGBI 80c	MDA Mono 80c
8	EGA RrGgBb 200p	MDA Mono 80c
9	EGA RrGgBb 350p	MDA Mono 80c
A	EGA Mono 720p	CGA RGBI 40c
B	EGA Mono 720p	CGA RGBI 80c

Legend:

MDA	= Monochrome Display Adapter
CGA	= Color Graphics Adapter
EGA	= Enhanced Graphics Adapter
Mono	= Monochrome monitor
RGBI	= 16-color monitor
RrGgBb	= Enhanced Color Monitor
#p	= Number of horizontal pixels per line
#c	= Number of horizontal characters per line

The video configuration can be determined by reading host memory address 0000:0488, called the configuration bits byte. The low-order four bits correspond to the sense switches on the EGA, and the high-order four bits correspond to the feature bits. The sense switches tell the EGA which monitor is attached and if the EGA is coexisting with any other display adapter. The meanings of these four bits of this memory byte are listed in Table 9.27.

The EGA has a feature connector with two parallel inputs and two parallel outputs. The inputs to the feature connector are labeled FEAT 0 and FEAT 1. These inputs may be read in the Input Status #0 Register. The outputs are controlled through the Feature Control Register. The organization of these bits is listed in Table 9.28.

The EGA stores a list of double-word (long) pointers beginning at host memory address 0000:04A8. This table is called the Video Parameter Table Pointer. It consists of four pointers to other tables also resident in host memory. The four pointers address each of these other pointers. The Video Parameter Table Pointer is illustrated in Table 9.29.

TABLE 9.28 Feature Control Field of Video Configuration

Bit Number	Information
4	Input value of FEAT 0 with FC1 ON
5	Input value of FEAT 1 with FC1 ON
6	Input value of FEAT 0 with FC1 OFF
7	Input value of FEAT 1 with FC1 OFF

TABLE 9.29 Video Table Pointer

Memory Address	Pointer
0000:04A8	Video Parameter Table
0000:04AC	Dynamic Save Area (optional)
0000:04B0	Alpha Aux Char Generator (optional)
0000:04B4	Text Aux Char Generator (optional)

The Video Parameter Table consists of 1,472 bytes of data organized as 23 blocks of information, each 64 bytes long. Each block is associated with a display mode and contains the values that are to be loaded into the EGA/VGA registers during a Set Mode command. This table is typically located in the EGA BIOS ROM. Table 9.30 lists the modes and the offset from the long pointer in 0000:04A8 at which the register values can be found.

TABLE 9.30 Video Parameter Table

Offset	Mode	Offset	Mode	Offset	Mode
000	0	040	1	080	2
0C0	3	100	4	140	5
180	6	1C0	7	200	8
240	9	280	A	2C0	B
300	C	340	D	380	E
3C0	F	400	10	440	F*
480	10*	4C0	0*	500	1*
540	2*	580	3*		

TABLE 9.31 Block Structure of Video Parameter Table

Offset	# Bytes	Contents
0	1	# columns
1	1	# rows
2	1	Pixels/character
3–4	2	Page length
5–8	4	Sequencer Registers
9	1	Miscellaneous Register
10–34	25	CRTC Registers
35–54	20	Attribute Registers
55–63	9	Graphics Controller Registers

Each block of 64 bytes contains the values that will be loaded into the EGA registers. The meanings of the bytes within these blocks are listed in Table 9.31.

Chapter 10

The EGA/VGA Registers

10.1 THE EGA/VGA REGISTERS

All graphics functions of the EGA/VGA are controlled through a set of registers. The EGA/VGA standard dictates the placement and function of each of these registers. These registers are mapped into the host port address space and are accessed via assembly language IN and OUT instructions. Each of these registers is one byte wide and is segmented into one to eight independent fields. Graphics functions are controlled from these fields. A single function may require a field that spans more than one register. An example of this is seen in the Start Address Registers.

To specify the starting address of the display, it is necessary to load the Start Address Registers with a value that points to an individual byte within the display memory. Because there are 64 Kbytes possible, a 16-bit value is required to fully specify the start address. Thus, two registers, each a byte wide, are required. These are named the Start Address High and Start Address Low Registers.

In most cases, the EGA and VGA registers are identical. The VGA has added several features not available on the EGA, and many fields within the registers are specified for the VGA only. Some of the existing fields apply only to the EGA. Moreover, there are four fields that have one function for the EGA and a different function for the VGA.

10.1.1 Register Groups

The registers are grouped into five basic sets consisting of the General or External Registers, the Sequencer Registers, the CRTC Registers, the Graphics Registers, and the Attribute Registers. Note that certain registers exist at one of two host port addresses. These registers exist at host port address 3Bx hex if the VGA/EGA adapter is in a monochrome emulation mode and at host port address 3Dx hex if the adapter is in a color emulation mode. These registers

TABLE 10.1   Register Port Addresses

Register Groups	I/O Port Addresses (Hex)
General or External	3BA or 3DA, 3CA, 3C2, and 3CC
Sequencer	3C4, 3C5
CRTC	3B4, 3B5 or 3D4, 3D5
Graphics	3CE, 3CF
Attribute	3CO, 3C1

are mapped in this manner to ensure downward compatibility. In addition, because the monochrome and color adapters are mapped into different I/O port addresses, a monochrome and color adapter can coexist in the same system. Table 10.1 illustrates the I/O port addresses used by these registers.

In many applications, it is advisable to use the BIOS routines to modify the registers in the EGA/VGA. All basic graphics functions can be programmed using the BIOS calls. However, several important features within the EGA/VGA can improve processing speed, and these are not implemented within the BIOS calls. In order to use these features, it is necessary for the programmer to access the registers directly. In addition, many of the graphics features that are programmed within the BIOS calls require a prohibitively long time to execute due to the BIOS overhead. In these cases, it is necessary to program the EGA/VGA by writing to the registers and display memory directly. It is possible to achieve a significant improvement in execution time by optimizing the data path to and from the host and the EGA/VGA.

Future graphics adapters may be compatible at the BIOS level, and direct programming of the registers may then cause erroneous results. However, the processing speed advantages of direct programming often outweigh the disadvantages of lost portability.

The EGA and VGA are compatible at the BIOS level. The VGA has additional features that can be accessed through the VGA BIOS calls but not through the EGA BIOS calls. All of the EGA BIOS calls are implemented in the VGA. The VGA is therefore downwardly compatible to the EGA. Code written for the EGA will run directly on the VGA if the code always uses the BIOS calls. Code that controls the EGA registers directly will not necessarily execute correctly on the VGA.

There are several cases in which the programmer should use the BIOS calls. Graphics functions that are performed once per session—for example, setting a mode or a color table—can be accomplished through the BIOS calls with little or no impact on processing time. Other functions may be called often throughout a program, yet the inherent BIOS delays may not be objectionable. Manipulating the cursor or writing a text string are two examples of situations in which BIOS calls can greatly simplify the programmer's task without causing significant delays. The programmer is well advised to use the BIOS calls for these operations.

10.1.2 Accessing the Registers

The General Registers, also called the External Registers, and the Color Select Register in the Attribute Register group are accessed directly. Each of these registers has a unique host port I/O port address. Reading or writing data to these registers is accomplished by using the assembly language IN and OUT instructions. All of the other registers are accessed indirectly.

The indirect addressing technique uses two I/O host port locations to access a group of registers within the EGA/VGA. The two host port locations are called the index or address register and the data register. Each register within the group is assigned a unique index value. Registers within a group have index values that start at 0 and increment, ending with the last register in the group. The address register is used to point to one of the actual EGA/VGA registers within the group. If it is desired to write to a register, this register is loaded with the index value of the desired register. Once this is loaded, a byte is written from the host to the data register. The byte of data is automatically written to the selected register. This is illustrated in Figure 10.1.

In Figure 10.1, the index value, 03, is output to the address register. The data byte, AB hex, is then output to the data register. Because the address register contains an 03, register 03 is selected. The data byte, AB hex, is automatically written to this register.

The registers are read in a similar manner. Again, the address register is loaded with the desired register index, and a data byte is read from the data register. The majority of registers within the standard EGA cannot be read. In contrast, all registers within the VGA can be read.

Reading and writing to the Attribute Registers is more complicated. Instead of the address and data register occupying two host port I/O addresses, they occupy the same port address. An internal flip-flop in the EGA/VGA is used to select either the Attribute Index Register or the Attribute Data Register. Both of these registers reside at I/O port address 3CO hex. The flip-flop is initialized to point to the index register by executing an I/O read instruction to either port 3BA or port 3DA hex. The actual address depends on whether the EGA is emulating a

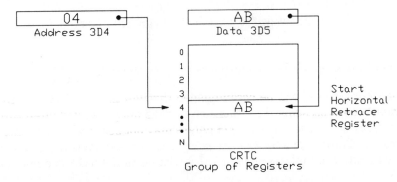

FIGURE 10.1 Accessing the EGA/VGA Registers

monochrome or a color adapter. After an output port instruction, OUT, is issued to the Attribute Index Register, the flip-flop toggles and points to the Attribute Data Register. Subsequent outputs to the Attribute Register at 3C0 hex cause the flip-flop to toggle repeatedly between the index and the data registers.

A problem exists because of this obscure addressing format. The state of the flip-flop cannot be interrogated or saved. Should a context switch occur, the state of this register is lost. If interrupts are a possible source of context changes, then interrupts should be disabled while the Attribute Registers are being accessed.

In the VGA, the lower seven registers in the CRTC Registers have a protect bit associated with them. It is located in the PR field of the Vertical Retrace End Register. If this field is set to a 1, CRTC registers 0 through 7 cannot be modified. The exception to this is the Line Compare (LC) field of the Overflow Register. This function protects the critical horizontal and vertical timing generator registers contained in these locations from modification. Programs that expect the EGA may attempt to load these registers with values that are appropriate for the EGA but not for the VGA. The Vertical Retrace Start Register, at index 10 hex, and the Vertical Retrace End Register, at index 11 hex, can be accessed only when the Compatible Read (CR) field of the End Horizontal Blanking Register is set to a 1.

10.1.3   The Register Diagrams

Each of the EGA/VGA register groups, registers, and fields is described in the following section. Each register is preceded by an illustration of the register. The fields within each register are indicated by an oval in the register. The placement of the oval dictates which bits within the register are dedicated to this field. Each oval contains a code of up to three letters that is used to identify the field. The functions of these fields are described in the text.

A field that applies only to the EGA is designated by a small square to the immediate left of the code. A field that applies only to the VGA is designated by a small square to the immediate right of the code. If a field has no squares, it applies to either the EGA or the VGA. A field with two codes separated by a square indicates that there are two separate meanings for the field, one for the EGA and one for the VGA.

10.2   THE GENERAL OR EXTERNAL REGISTERS

There are four General or External Registers in the EGA/VGA. These registers have their own port addresses. Because of these port assignments, the programmer accesses these registers directly, with no need of an index and data register pair. These registers are referred to as the External Registers in the EGA documentation and as the General Registers in the VGA documentation.

TABLE 10.2 General or External Registers

Register Name	Write (Hex) (EGA / VGA)	Read (Hex) (EGA)	Read (Hex) (VGA)
Misc. Output	3C2		3CC
Feature Control	3DA/3BA		3CA
Input Status #0		3C2	3C2
Input Status #1		3DA/3BA	3DA/3BA

Both implementations consist of the same four registers, although the fields within these registers vary. The General or External Registers are listed in Table 10.2.

Note that there are two addresses listed that allow writing to the Feature Control Register and the Input Status #1 Register. These two addresses are in the form 3Dx/3Bx. The first address, 3Bx, is applicable when the adapter is configured in a monochrome mode. The second address, 3Dx, is applicable when the adapter is configured in a color mode.

10.2.1 Miscellaneous Output Register

```
EGA    Write Port 3C2 hex
VGA    Write Port 3C2 hex
       Read Port 3CC hex
```

VSP Vertical Sync Polarity   EGA, VGA **Bit 7**

Determines the polarity of the vertical sync pulse. Hardware manufacturers can use this field to control the pulse shape of the vertical sync pulse. On the VGA, this field is also used to control the vertical size of the monitor. The monitors that are supported by the VGA are autosynchronizing. These monitors must be capable of achieving vertical synchronization. To do so, they detect the polarity of the horizontal and vertical sync signals. The polarity of these sync pulses alerts the monitor as to how many vertical lines should be displayed. This is illustrated in Table 10.3.

=0 Select a positive vertical retrace sync pulse.

=1 Select a negative vertical retrace sync pulse.

TABLE 10.3 Vertical Size and Sync Polarity

Bit 7	Bit 6	Vertical Size	Active Lines
0(+)	0(+)	Reserved	Reserved
0(+)	1(−)	400 lines	414 lines
1(−)	0(+)	350 lines	362 lines
1(−)	1(−)	480 lines	496 lines

HSP Horizontal Sync Polarity   EGA, VG **Bit 6**

Determines the polarity of the horizontal sync pulse. Hardware manufacturers can use this field to control the pulse shape of the horizontal sync pulse. On the VGA, this field is also used to control the vertical size of the monitor. The monitors that are supported by the VGA are autosynchronizing. They must be capable of achieving vertical synchronization. To do so, they detect the polarity of the horizontal and vertical sync signals. The polarity of these sync pulses alerts the monitor as to how many vertical lines should be displayed. This is illustrated in Table 10.3 above.

=0 Select a positive horizontal retrace sync pulse.

=1 Select a negative horizontal retrace sync pulse.

PB Page Bit for Odd/Even   EGA, VGA **Bit 5**

Selects the 64K page of memory when the system is in one of the odd or even modes. The display modes that utilize the odd/even modes are modes 0, 1, 2, 3 and 7.

=0 Select the low 64K page of memory.

=1 Select the high 64K page of memory.

DVD Disable the Video Drivers   EGA **Bit 4**

The video drivers on the EGA normally control the video direct drive video outputs. It is possible to utilize the direct drive video inputs from the feature connector. In order to use these feature connector inputs as the direct drive outputs, the internal video drivers must be taken off the bus. This field enables or disables the internal video drivers.

=0 Enable the internal video drivers.

=1 Disable the internal video drivers.

TABLE 10.4 Clock Source

Bit 3	Bit 2	EGA Clock Source	VGA Clock Source
0	0	14-mHz clock	25-mHz
0	1	16-mHz clock	28-mHz clock
1	0	external clock	Reserved

CS Clock Select   EGA, VGA **Bits 3,2**

The frequency of the clock used to drive the EGA hardware determines the overall speed of the graphics process. The horizontal frequency of the video output controls the number of dots that may be displayed on a line and the number of lines that can be displayed on the screen. The mode of the display, color or monochrome, also determines the number of dots and lines possible.

The monitor type that is being utilized controls which clock frequencies may be used. For a standard color monitor, a 14-mHz clock signal is required to produce the desired horizontal frequency. For an EGA monitor, a 16-mHz clock signal may be utilized. If a multisync monitor is used, even higher clock frequencies may be implemented. Again, the higher the clock frequency, the greater the display resolution.

Anticipating the need for higher frequencies, the feature connector provides an input pin. A clock may be provided on this pin when higher horizontal resolutions are desired. For example, a 132-column display utilizing an 8-dot-wide character would require a higher frequency clock than 16mHz. This CS field determines the clock rate and, in the case of CS=2, the source of the clock. Table 10.4 illustrates the different clocks possible.

ER Enable RAM   EGA, VGA **Bit 1**

Enable Access of CPU to video memory. All display modes allow CPU access to the display memory.

=0 Disable access of the video memory from the CPU.

=1 Enable access of the video memory from the CPU.

IOA Input/Output Address   EGA, VGA **Bit 0**

The EGA may emulate either the monochrome or the color display adapters. This emulation exists only at the BIOS level on standard EGAs and may exist at the register level on specially equipped EGA boards. For monochrome emulation, the CRTC addresses are set to 3Bx. The Input Status #1 Register is set at 3B2, and the Feature Control Register is set at 3BA. For color adapters, the CRTC registers are set to 3Dx. The Input Status #1 Register is set to 3D2, and the Feature Control Register is set at 3DA.

=0 Monochrome emulation. Address based at 3Bx.

=1 Color emulation. Address based at 3Dx.

10.2.2 Feature Control Register

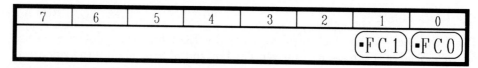

7	6	5	4	3	2	1	0
						•FC 1	•FC 0

EGA	Write Port 3BA hex Monochrome, 3DA hex Color
VGA	Write Port 3BA hex Monochrome, 3DA hex Color
	Read Port 3CA hex

The feature connector on the EGA provides two output pins called FC0 and FC1. The host processor can use these pins to convey information to the external devices in the same way that a parallel output port is programmed. Setting this bit to 1 causes the corresponding bit on the feature connector to go to a logical high state; setting it to a 0 causes the pin to go to a low state.

VSS Vertical sync select   VGA **Bit 3**

Controls the signal output to the vertical sync line that controls the monitor.

=0 Normal vertical sync output to the monitor.

=1 Vertical sync output to the monitor is the logical OR of the vertical sync and the vertical display enable.

FC1 Feature control bit 1   EGA **Bit 1**

Feature control bit 1 is on pin 20 of the feature connector.

=0 The logical state of FC1 is set to 0 (logical low).

=1 The logical state of FC1 is set to 1 (logical high).

FC0 Feature control bit 0   EGA **Bit 0**

Feature control bit 0 is on pin 21 of the feature connector.

=0 The logical state of FC0 is set to 0 (logical low).

=1 The logical state of FC0 is set to 1 (logical high).

10.2.3 Input Status #0 Register

7	6	5	4	3	2	1	0
•VRI	•FS1	•FS0	SS				

EGA   Read Port 3C2 hex
VGA   Read Port 3C2 hex

VRI Vertical Retrace Interrupt   EGA **Bit 7**

Reports the status of the Vertical Interrupt.

=0 Vertical retrace is occurring.

=1 Vertical retrace is not occurring. Video is being displayed.

FS1 Feature Status 1   EGA **Bit 6**

Reports the status of the feature 1 (FEAT1) on pin 17 of the feature connector.

=0 Feat1 = 0 (logical low level).

=1 Feat1 = 1 (logical high level).

FS0 Feature Status 0   EGA **Bit 5**

Reports the status of the feature 0 (FEAT0) on pin 19 of the feature connector.

=0 Feat0 = 0 (logical low level).

=1 Feat0 = 1 (logical high level).

SS Switch Sense   EGA, VGA **Bit 4**

Reports the status from one of the four sense switches as determined by the CS field of the Misc. Output Register.

=0 Selected sense switch = 0 (off).

=1 Selected sense switch = 1 (on).

10.2.4 Input Status #1 Register

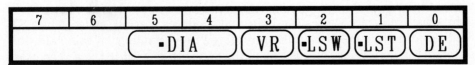

7	6	5	4	3	2	1	0
		•DIA		VR	•LSW	•LST	DE

EGA Read Port 3BA hex monochrome, 3DA hex color.
VGA Read Port 3BA hex monochrome, 3DA hex color.

TABLE 10.5 DIA Field

DIA Field		Input Status #1 Register	
Bit 5	Bit 4	Bit 5	Bit 4
0	0	Red	Blue
0	1	I Blue	Green
1	0	I Red	I Green

DIA Diagnostic   EGA **Bits 5,4**

Reports the status of two of the six color outputs. The values set into the VSM field of the Color Plane Enable Register determine which colors are input to these two diagnostic pins according to Table 10.5.

VR Vertical Retrace   EGA, VGA **Bit 3**

Reports the status of the display regarding whether the display is in a display mode or a vertical retrace mode. The occurrence of a 1 in this bit, indicating a vertical retrace, can generate a level-2 interrupt depending on the status of the Disable Vertical Interrupt (DVI) field of the Vertical Retrace End Register. This is used when software synchronization with the display is desired.

=0 Display is in the display mode.
=1 Display is in the vertical retrace mode.

LSW Light Pen Switch   EGA **Bit 2**

Monitors the status of the light pen switch. Light pens are all equipped with a switch that allows the operator another degree of control. The switch may be on the side of the light pen. More often, it is found on the tip of the pen. By pushing the pen against the screen, the user activates the pen switch.

=0 Light pen switch is pushed in (closed).
=1 Light pen switch is not pushed (open).

LST Light Pen Strobe   EGA **Bit 1**

Monitors the status of the light pen strobe. When the electron beam scans across the area of the screen where the light pen is pointing, the light pen's light sensitive device senses the light and produces a strobe pulse. The LST field monitors this pulse. By taking repeated rapid readings of this field, the software can determine the position of the pen with respect to the screen coordinates. When this field is active (LST = 1), the Light Pen Position Low and

TABLE 10.6 Retrace Period

VR	DE	Display Status
0	0	Display mode
1	1	Vertical retrace time
0	1	Horizontal retrace time

Light Pen Position High registers may be read to determine the position of the light pen.

=0 Light pen has not been triggered.

=1 Light pen is triggered (electron beam is at the light pen position).

DE Display Enable NOT   EGA, VGA **Bit 0**

Monitors the status of the display. Alerts the software that the display is in a horizontal or vertical retrace mode or in a display mode. Some older display adapters required that data in display memory be modified only during a retrace period. During a retrace period, no active display refreshing occurred. On these older displays, noise would occur on the screen if the display was modified during refreshing. This is not the case with the EGA/VGA. When DE is used in conjunction with the VR field of this register, it is possible to determine if the display is in a horizontal or vertical retrace period; see Table 10.6.

The horizontal retrace time can be used to synchronize the software with the horizontal scanning. This allows the programmer to update the color palette in a way that produces more than sixteen simultaneous colors on the display.

=0 The display is in the display mode.

=1 The display is not in the display mode. Either the horizontal or vertical retrace period is active.

10.3 THE SEQUENCER REGISTERS

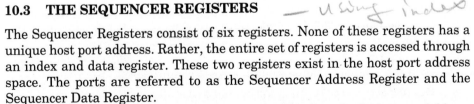

The Sequencer Registers consist of six registers. None of these registers has a unique host port address. Rather, the entire set of registers is accessed through an index and data register. These two registers exist in the host port address space. The ports are referred to as the Sequencer Address Register and the Sequencer Data Register.

The program accesses these registers by first loading the Sequencer Address Register with an index value ranging from 0 to 4. Next, it selects one of the five Sequencer Data Registers as the current active register. Reading or writing to this Sequencer Data Registers will repeatedly access the register selected by the index value until the Sequencer Address Register is modified. The

TABLE 10.7 Sequencer Registers

Register Name	Index	Write (Hex) (EGA/VGA)	Read Hex (VGA)
Address	—	3C4	3C4
Reset	0	3C5	3C5
Clocking Mode	1	3C5	3C5
Map Mask	2	3C5	3C5
Character Map Select	3	3C5	3C5
Memory Mode	4	3C5	3C5

Sequencer Address Register resides at port 3C4 hex, and the Sequencer Data Register resides at port 3C5 hex. All of the Sequencer Registers are write-only in the standard EGA and read/write in the VGA. The Sequencer Registers are listed in Table 10.7.

10.3.1 Reset Register

7	6	5	4	3	2	1	0
						SR	AR·SR

Index 00 hex

The Reset register provides two ways to reset the processor. Either reset—SR or AR—will cause the sequencer to reset, thereby stopping the functioning of the EGA. Both resets must be off (logical 1) in order for the EGA to operate. Both cause a clear-and-halt condition to occur. All outputs are placed in a high-impedance state during a reset condition.

SR Synchronous Reset   EGA, VGA **Bit 1**

Control the state of the sequencer by producing a synchronous reset. A synchronous reset preserves memory contents. It must be used before changing the Clocking Mode Register in order to preserve memory contents.

=0 Generate and hold the system in a reset condition.

=1 Release the reset if bit 0 is in the inactive state.

SR Synchronous Reset (No Asynchronous Reset on VGA)   VGA **Bit 0**

Control the state of the sequencer by producing a synchronous reset. A synchronous reset preserves memory contents and must be used before changing the Clocking Mode Register to avoid loss of memory contents.

=0 Generate and hold the system in a reset condition.

=1 Release the reset if bit 1 is in the inactive state.

AR Asynchronous Reset   EGA **Bit 0**

Control the state of the sequencer by producing an asynchronous reset. An asynchronous reset may cause a loss of display memory contents.

=0 Generate and hold the system in a reset condition.

=1 Release the reset if bit 1 is in the inactive state.

10.3.2 Clocking Mode Register

7	6	5	4	3	2	1	0
		SO •	S4 •	DC	SL	• BW	8/9

Index 01 hex
Determine the clock timing.

SO Screen Off   VGA **Bit 5**

Turns the screen off along with the picture-generating logic. Because there is no time spent refreshing the screen, the video processor has direct control of the video memory, which facilitates rapid memory access.

=0 Screen is turned on.

=1 Screen is turned off.

S4 Shift Four   VGA **Bit 4**

Controls how often the video serializers should be loaded.

=0 Load the serializers every character clock cycle.

=1 Load the serializers every fourth character clock cycle.

DC Dot Clock   EGA, VGA **Bit 3**

The dot clock is the basic graphics clock of the system. It is generated from the master clock input, the source of which is determined by the CS field of the Misc. Output Register. If the Dot Clock is generated every input clock, high-resolution outputs are possible. It also divides the master clock by 2 before generating the Dot Clock. This has the effect of slowing down the system, thereby stretching out the other timing signals. The divide-by-2 mode is used when a horizontal resolution of 320 for the EGA or a horizontal resolution of 320 or 360 for the VGA is selected. Display modes 0, 1, 4, 5, and D utilize this feature.

=0 Set the Dot Clock to the same frequency as the Master Clock.

=1 Divide the Master Clock by 2 to derive the Dot Clock.

SL Shift Load   EGA, VGA **Bit 2**

The EGA provides the two standard horizontal resolutions of 640 or 320 dots per line. The display memory is organized in parallel words. The display output, however, requires a serial output stream. Hardware associated with the EGA converts this parallel data in a device called a video serializer. The high-resolution mode with 640 dots per line requires that the video serializers be loaded every character clock. The lower resolution mode of 320 dots per line allows the video serializers to be loaded every other character clock.

The VGA operates in a similar fashion to the EGA, except that this bit is significant only if the Shift Four (S4) field is set to a 0 to cause the serializers to be loaded every character clock. Combined, these two fields allow the serializers to be loaded every cycle, every other cycle, or every fourth cycle of the character clock.

=0 Load the video serializers every character clock. Use with 640 (EGA) or 720 (VGA) horizontal resolutions.

=1 Load the video serializers every other character clock. Use with 320 (EGA) or 360 (VGA) horizontal resolutions.

BW Bandwidth   EGA **Bit 1**

The video memory may be thought of as a triple-ported memory. This means that there are three devices attempting to access the memory. The CPU is one device. Its purpose is to load new data into the display memory or to read data out of the display memory. A second source desiring control of the display memory is the dynamic memory refresh timing. Because the EGA/VGA display memory is typically constructed from dynamic memory, the dynamic memory must be refreshed periodically or data will be lost. The addressing required to perform the dynamic memory refreshing must also share the memory bus. The third device is an output device. The video serializers must be loaded in order to refresh the display. The CRT display expects constant updating as the electron beam scans across its face. The serial data driving the electron beam must be read from the display memory.

The type of dynamic memory dictates how often the dynamic memory refreshing must take place on the memory bus. For every scan line, a certain amount of data must be read out into the video serializers. The amount of data is determined by the number of pixels being output per line. Therefore, the more data read out during this predetermined time, the more time the video serializers require the memory bus. This means that the CPU must wait for these two higher-priority devices before it can gain control of the memory bus.

The high-resolution modes require that the CRTC controller have four out of five memory cycles to fulfill the needs of the screen refresh. In lower-resolution modes, the CRTC can get by with two out of five memory cycles. Thus, in the high-resolution modes, the CPU must wait for one out of five memory cycles before it can read or write to memory. This slows down system throughput. However, it does allow for inexpensive dynamic memory to be used as display memory.

An equivalent field for the VGA is located in the BW field of the Horizontal Retrace End Register.

=0   The CRTC will control the memory bus on four out of five memory cycles.
     Used in all high-resolution modes.

=1   The CRTC will control the memory bus on two out of five memory cycles.
     Used in all lower resolution modes.

8/9   8/9 Dot Clocks   EGA, VGA   **Bit 0**

The size of the character box determines the resolution of the resulting characters. The monochrome display mode 7 utilizes a 9-dot character. All other modes utilize an 8-dot character. Because 80 characters are desired, a total of 80×9, or 720, horizontal dots are necessary for mode 7. In all other modes with 80 dots per line, 80×8, or 640, dots per line are required. At times in the monochrome mode, the character font is nine dots wide. Thus, two bytes are required to represent a single line of a character. It is also possible to represent the 9-dot character with an 8-dot matrix. Although this decreases the resolution of the character, it halves the amount of memory required to represent a single line, reducing it to 1 byte. In the case of graphics characters, character codes C0 hex to DF hex, it is desired that horizontal lines connect. Thus, it is necessary to extend the eight dots to nine dots. This is done by copying the dot representing the eighth dot, found in bit 7, into the position of the ninth dot. The effect is that horizontal lines are extended. A line in one character position will touch a character in the adjacent horizontal positions.

The EGA uses the 9-dots-per-character clock in mode 7, while the VGA uses the 9-dots-per-character clock in modes 0+, 1+, 2+, 3+, 7, and 7+.

=0   Character clocks eight dots wide are generated. Used in all modes by
     mode 7, in which there are 320 or 640 horizontal dots.

=1   Character clocks nine dots wide are generated. Used in the monochrome
     mode 7, in which there are 720 horizontal dots.

10.3.3 Map Mask Register

7	6	5	4	3	2	1	0
				EM3	EM2	EM1	EM0

Index 02 hex

The display memory is organized as nonstandard read/write memory with respect to the host processor. Each byte of memory represents from one to eight consecutive horizontal pixels. The display memory is viewed as being serial memory to the output drivers due to the video serializer. The CRTC controller views this memory through a 32-bit port. A 32-bit register sits between the CRTC graphics controller and the display memory.

The EGA/VGA consists of four display planes. Because each plane is organized as bytes, $4 \times 8 = 32$ bits. Each plane is mapped into the same host memory address space. When the host outputs a byte to display memory at a specific memory address, this byte may be written to any combination of the display memory planes. The Write Plane Mask Register determines which planes are written to. Any combination is allowed because the 32-bit-wide display memory path permits all four planes to be updated simultaneously. Because there are four display memory planes, one bit in this register is assigned to each plane; thus, four control bits are required. Each control bit corresponds to one memory plane. If the bit is disabled, the plane cannot be written to, and the plane is masked out of the system. Thus, this register is called the Plane Mask Register or the Map Mask Register.

On read operations, the 32-bit buffer register is also used. On a single read, all four memory planes can be read simultaneously. However, unlike the write operation, in which one byte is written to four bytes, the read operation can transfer only one byte to the host at a time. The Read Map Select Register determines which plane is read back to the host.

There are write modes that allow the EGA to take advantage of this 32-bit memory path. For example, it is possible to copy EGA memory from one location to another 32 bits at a time. This is one reason for having display memory in excess of the display requirements. Patterns may be stored in the excess region and then copied at high speed to the portion of display memory being displayed. The write mode that selects this function is determined by the WM field of the Mode Register.

Another type of masking is possible. A byte references one to eight consecutive horizontal pixels, and it may be desired to modify only one pixel. This can be accomplished by masking out all pixels other than the desired pixel. This is done in the BM field of the Bit Mask Register.

The four memory planes are combined to produce a color for an individual pixel. The data bit from memory plane 0 is placed into the resulting 4-bit word in bit position 0. It may be thought of as the least significant bit of the resulting color nibble. The data bit from memory plane 1 is placed into bit position 1, and so on, until memory plane 3 places a bit into bit position 3. Memory plane 3 may be thought of as the most significant memory plane.

EM3 Mask Memory Plane 3   EGA, VGA **Bit 3**

=0 Disable memory plane 3 on CPU write operations.
=1 Enable memory plane 3 on CPU write operations.

EM2 Mask Memory Plane 2   EGA, VGA **Bit 2**

=0 Disable memory plane 2 on CPU write operations.
=1 Enable memory plane 2 on CPU write operations.

EM1 Mask Memory Plane 1   EGA, VGA **Bit 1**

=0 Disable memory plane 1 on CPU write operations.
=1 Enable memory plane 1 on CPU write operations.

EM0 Mask Memory Plane 0   EGA, VGA **Bit 0**

=0 Disable memory plane 0 on CPU write operations.
=1 Enable memory plane 0 on CPU write operations.

10.3.4 Character Map Select Register

7	6	5	4	3	2	1	0
		SAH■	SBH■	SA		SB	

Index 03 hex

The EGA allows downloadable character fonts. These fonts are used when the display is in one of the alphanumeric modes. When an alphanumeric mode is in effect, display plane 0 is used for the character data, plane 1 is used for the character attribute, and plane 2 is used for the character fonts. In some cases, plane 3 is also used for character fonts that are wider than 8 dots per character line. Up to four fonts may be loaded simultaneously in plane 2 or planes 2 and 3. Each plane is 64 Kbytes long.

In the text modes, each character is represented by a character ASCII code and an attribute. The attribute determines the color of the character on a color system; on a monochrome system, the attribute sets any special features of the character—underline, blinking, or high intensity, for example. Bit 3 of the attribute is reserved for one of two purposes. In one configuration, it selects one of sixteen colors as the foreground color of the character. In the second mode, it selects which of two character sets to use for the character. In this second mode, character sets of 512 characters may be used. This is possible because the ASCII character code is capable of selecting one of 256 characters. This additional attribute bit permits the character to be from one of two character sets.

In the EGA, the display planes are split into four banks, each being 16 Kbytes long. One font may be loaded into the first 8 Kbytes of each bank. In the VGA, the display planes are split into eight banks, each being 8 Kbytes long.

Suppose that a character is eight bits per line wide and 32 lines long, each character requiring 32 bytes of memory. A 256-character set would then require 8 Kbytes of storage. If the character is wider than eight dots per line, the upper byte of storage will be analogously stored into the first 8 Kbytes of each of the four banks of display plane 3. Restricting each character to 32 lines allows the characters to be aligned on 32-byte boundaries. Accessing a character is then a simple task of shifting the ASCII code five bits to the left.

Whether the system responds to bit 3 of the attribute byte as an intensity or as a character-set selector is determined by whether the two fields SB and SA are different. If these have the same value, the system assumes that bit 3 should be used to select the intensified colors. If they have different values, the system assumes that bit 3 should be used to select the character set. Although four fonts may be loaded simultaneously, only two can be active at a time.

The character maps for the EGA are illustrated in Table 10.8.

The character maps for the VGA are illustrated in Table 10.9. It should be noted that bits 4 and 5 contain the third bit for each of the two character map fields.

SAH Select Character Generator A (High Order)   VGA **Bit 5**

Selects which of eight possible character sets to select when the attribute byte has bit 3 = 1. Combines with SA field.

SBH Select Character Generator B (High Order)   VGA **Bit 4**

Selects which of eight possible character sets to select when the attribute byte has bit 3 = 0. Combines with SB field.

TABLE 10.8 EGA Character Mapping

Bit 1	Bit 2	Map	Table Location
0	0	0	First 8K of bank 0 at 0–7 K
0	1	1	First 8K of bank 1 at 16–23 K
1	0	2	First 8K of bank 2 at 32–39 K
1	1	3	First 8K of bank 3 at 48–55 K

TABLE 10.9 VGA Character Mapping

Bits 5,4	Bits 3,1	Bits 2,0	Character Map	Address Offset to First Character
0	0	0	0	0 K
0	0	1	1	16 K
0	1	0	2	32 K
0	1	1	3	48 K
1	0	0	4	8 K
1	0	1	5	24 K
1	1	0	6	40 K
1	1	1	7	56 K

SA Select Character Generator A   EGA, VGA **Bits 3,2**

Selects which of the eight possible character sets to select when the attribute byte has bit 3 = 1. Combines with SAH field for VGA.

SB Select Character Generator B   EGA, VGA **Bits 1,0**

Selects which of the eight possible character sets to select when the attribute byte has bit 3 = 0. Combines with SBH field for VGA.

10.3.5 Memory Mode Register

7	6	5	4	3	2	1	0
				C4 •	O/E	EM	•A/G

Index 04 hex

This register contains several fields that control the way in which the display memory functions.

C4 Chain Four   VGA **Bit 3**

Controls the manner in which the display memory bit planes are accessed. In a write mode, the display bit plane is normally selected by the EM0–EM3 enable memory mask fields of the Map Mask Register. Any combination of the four display planes may be accessed simultaneously. In mode 13 hex, the four display memory bit planes are chained together, and only one can be selected at a time. In this mode, the two low-order address bits are used to select which of the four display bit planes are enabled. Thus, four sequential bytes written to the display memory are stored so that one byte occupies an identical addressed location in each of the four display planes.

In a read mode, only one display memory bit plane can be active at a time. The active bit plane is normally selected by the Read Map Select (RMS) field of the Read Map Select Register. In mode 13 hex, the operation is identical to the write operation above, with the Read Map Select Register being ignored and the display plane being selected by the low-order A1 and A0 address bits.

=0 The display planes are selected via the Map Mask and the Read Map Select Registers.

=1 The display planes are selected by the low-order A1 and A0 address bits; the four display planes are assumed to be chained.

O/E Odd/Even   EGA, VGA **Bit 2**

Determines whether the processor addresses a display memory plane sequentially, or whether odd addresses access display planes 1 and 3 and even addresses access display planes 0 and 2. The odd/even mode is enabled when memory addressing compatibility is desired between the EGA/VGA and the Color Graphics Adapter.

Note that the value of this bit should be the complement of the value in the OE field of the Mode Register.

=0 Enables the odd/even addressing mode.

=1 Directs the system to use a sequential addressing mode.

EM Extended Memory   EGA,VGA **Bit 1**

Alerts the graphics processors to the fact that extended memory is present. All EGA/VGA implementations with greater than 64 Kbytes should have this field enabled.

=0 No extended memory present. Display memory is less than 64 Kbytes.

=1 Extended memory is present. Display memory is greater than 64 Kbytes.

A/G Alpha/Graphics Mode   EGA **Bit 0**

Dictates whether the system is in an alphanumeric mode or a graphics mode. In an alphanumeric mode, characters are addressed by code and the memory planes are used to display the code, the attribute, and the character generators. In a graphics mode, the memory is used directly to display graphics data. A character would be represented by a two-dimensional series of dots.

In the EGA, three fields in the control registers redundantly control this function. The second and third fields are in the G/A field of the Mode Control Register and the G/A field of the Miscellaneous Register. Note that these values should be the complement of the A/G field in the appropriate register.

In the VGA, the alphanumeric and graphics modes are selected from the G/A fields in the Mode Control Register and the G/A field in the Miscellaneous Register.

=0   Select a graphics mode.

=1   Select an alphanumerics mode.

10.4   THE CRT CONTROLLER REGISTERS

The CRT Controller Registers, commonly called the CRTC Registers, consist of 26 registers in the EGA and 24 registers in the VGA. None of these registers has a unique host port address. Instead, an address and data register pair exists in the host port address space. The programmer accesses these registers by first loading the CRTC Address Register with an index value. This index value ranges from 0 to 24 decimal. However, the hexadecimal numbering convention of 0 to 18 hex is more commonly used.

In the EGA, the 26 registers map into 24 indexes because four registers share two identical indexes. Two of these are read-only registers dedicated to the light pen interface. Two other registers, at identical indexes (indexes 10 and 11 hex) are write-only registers. Thus, there is no addressing conflict.

In the VGA, there are no light pen registers, and all of the CRTC Registers are read/write. The CRTC Address Register selects one of the CRTC Data Registers as the current active register. Reading or writing to this CRTC Data Register will repeatedly access the register selected by the index value, until the CRTC Address Register is modified.

The CRTC Address Register resides at port 3B4 hex for monochrome systems and port 3D4 hex for color systems. The CRTC Data Register resides at port 3B5 hex for the monochrome systems and port 3D5 hex for the color systems. The CRTC Registers are listed in Table 10.10.

10.4.1   Horizontal Total Register

7	6	5	4	3	2	1	0
			H T				

Index 00 hex

The Horizontal Total Register determines the horizontal scan time. It includes the borders, active display time, and horizontal retrace time. Internal to the CRT controller is a horizontal character counter. In the alphanumeric modes, this counter is initialized at the beginning of each scan line with a value of 0 and incremented after each character is output to the screen. In the graphics modes, the counter is incremented after either eight or nine pixels are output

TABLE 10.10 CRT Controller Registers

Register Name	Index (Hex)	Write (Hex) (EGA/VGA)	Read (Hex) (EGA)	Read (Hex) (VGA)
Address	—	3D4/3B4	—	3D4/3B4
Horizontal Total	0	3D5/3B5	—	3D5/3B5
Horizontal Display End	1	3D5/3B5	—	3D5/3B5
Start Horizontal Blank	2	3D5/3B5	—	3D5/3B5
End Horizontal Blank	3	3D5/3B5	—	3D5/3B5
Start Horizontal Retrace	4	3D5/3B5	—	3D5/3B5
End Horizontal Retrace	5	3D5/3B5	—	3D5/3B5
Vertical Total	6	3D5/3B5	—	3D5/3B5
Overflow	7	—	—	3D5/3B5
Preset Row Scan	8	3D5/3B5	—	3D5/3B5
Max Scan Line	9	3D5/3B5	—	3D5/3B5
Cursor Start	A	3D5/3B5	—	3D5/3B5
Cursor End	B	—	—	3D5/3B5
Start Address High	C	3D5/3B5	3D5/3B5	3D5/3B5
Start Address Low	D	3D5/3B5	3D5/3B5	3D5/3B5
Cursor Location High	E	3D5/3B5	3D5/3B5	3D5/3B5
Cursor Location Low	F	3D5/3B5	3D5/3B5	3D5/3B5
Vertical Retrace Start	10	3D5/3B5	—	3D5/3B5
Light Pen High (EGA only)	10	—	3D5/3B5	—
Vertical Retrace Low	11	3D5/3B5	—	3D5/3B5
Light Pen Low (EGA only)	11	—	3D5/3B5	—
Vertical Display End	12	3D5/3B5	—	3D5/3B5
Offset	13	3D5/3B5	—	3D5/3B5
Underline Location	14	3D5/3B5	—	3D5/3B5
Start Vertical Blank	15	3D5/3B5	—	3D5/3B5
End Vertical Blank	16	3D5/3B5	—	3D5/3B5
Mode Control	17	3D5/3B5	—	3D5/3B5
Line Compare	18	3D5/3B5	—	3D5/3B5

to the screen. These eight or nine pixels correspond to the width of the character in pixels as specified in the 8/9 field of the Clocking Mode Register.

The horizontal character counter counts from 0 to a maximum value indicated in the Horizontal Total Register. When the character counter reaches this value, it is reset to 0. This character counter overflow is the basis of all of the display timing. Because the horizontal counter increments on a character basis, a single byte is sufficient to store the number of characters per line. At the maximum value of 255 with eight pixels per character, the display can handle about 2,000 pixels per horizontal scan line.

In the EGA, the value loaded into this register is actually the total character count minus 2. Thus, if 90 characters are desired per line, the value 88 should be loaded into this register. In the VGA, the value loaded into this register is actually the total character count minus 5. If 90 characters are desired per line, a value of 85 should be loaded into this register.

HT Horizontal Total   EGA,VGA **Bits 7–0**

EGA HT = The horizontal total – 2
VGA HT = The horizontal total – 5

10.4.2 Horizontal Display End Register

7	6	5	4	3	2	1	0
H D E								

Index 01 hex

This register determines the number of displayed characters or character positions on a horizontal line. The internal horizontal character counter counts from 0 to the value indicated in the Horizontal Total register. However, not all of the characters on a horizontal line are to be displayed. The horizontal scan time consists of the border or porch, displayed data, and horizontal refresh times. Both the borders and the displayed data must fit into the horizontal display period.

At the end of each horizontal line, the CRT electron beam moves from the right extent of the current line to the left extent of the next lower line. The electron beam always scans from left to right on the screen in a top to bottom format. The time taken for the electron beam to get ready for the next line is called the horizontal retrace time. During this retrace time, no data should be written to the display. A display enable signal is generated to control when the display is enabled. Blanking occurs during the time that the display enable signal is inactive. The period of time surrounds the active display area on the screen and is called the border or porch. The overscan color is displayed during this border period and is controlled by the Overscan Register.

HDE Horizontal Display Enable   EGA,VGA **Bits 7–0**

The total number of displayed characters or character positions on a horizontal scan line.

EGA HDE = The number of displayed characters – 1.

VGA HDE = The number of displayed characters.

10.4.3 Start Horizontal Blanking Register

7	6	5	4	3	2	1	0
			S H B				

Index 02 hex

The horizontal blanking signal is generated when the horizontal character counter equals the value in the Start Horizontal Blanking Register. It ends when the value equals the value of the End Horizontal Blanking Register. The horizontal blanking signal is generated to stop the display of data during the CRT refresh time. Most blanking signals sent to the monitor are the composite of both the horizontal and vertical blanking times. The vertical blanking time is dictated by the Start Vertical Blanking and the End Vertical Blanking Registers. The blanking signal may be sent on its own line or combined into a composite signal that also includes either monochrome or color video data and sync information.

SHB Start Horizontal Blanking   EGA,VGA **Bits 7–0**

The value of the character counter at the time the horizontal blanking period should begin.

SHB = Start of Horizontal Blanking

10.4.4 End Horizontal Blanking Register

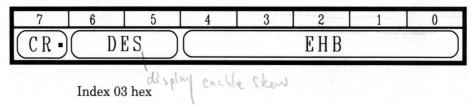

7	6	5	4	3	2	1	0
CR ·	D E S			E H B			

Index 03 hex

The end of the horizontal blanking period is determined by the value in this register. The character counter is an 8-bit counter. The start of the horizontal blanking period is determined by comparing the character counter and the value in the Start Horizontal Blanking Register. Both of these are 8-bit values.

The width of the horizontal blanking period consists of the number of character positions that should be output during this period. The value in the End Horizontal Blanking (EHB) field of this register is used to determine the width of the blanking period.

In the EGA, the EHB field of this register is only five bits wide. These five bits represent the lower five bits of the character count that will cause the end of horizontal blanking. Thus, it represents a mod 32 counter. Because the three most significant bits of the character counter are not used, there will be eight times as many End Horizontal Blanking signals as there are Start Horizontal Blanking Signals. The only End Blanking pulse that is relevant is the pulse that occurs after the start of the blanking period. It is important to note that the value in this field does not represent the width of the blanking pulse. The width is determined by subtracting the beginning of the blanking signal from the end of the blanking signal, taking special care with the upper three bits. Note that the maximum length for the blanking signal is 31 character positions. The lower five bits of the value in the Start Horizontal Blanking Register should never equal the value in the End Horizontal Blanking field. The manner in which the width of the blanking period is determined is identical to the technique used to determine the width of the retrace period. The End Horizontal Retrace (EHR) field of the End Horizontal Retrace Register is also used for this purpose.

In the VGA, the functioning of this register is identical to its functioning in the EGA, with the exception that a sixth bit is added for the EHB field of the End Horizontal Retrace Register. Thus, a mod 64 counter is operating, allowing a blanking width of 63 character positions.

The Display Enable Skew Control field is used to compensate for hardware delays caused by accessing the attribute and character codes, accessing the character generator font, and reading the Pixel Panning Register. Certain modes require a one-character skew, and others use no character skew.

In the VGA, an additional field called the Compatible Read Field is used to enable access to the Vertical Retrace Start and the Vertical Retrace End Registers.

CR Compatible Read   VGA **Bit 7**

Enables or disables access to the Vertical Retrace Start and the Vertical Retrace End Registers.

=0 Disable access to these registers.

=1 Enable access to these registers.

DES Display Enable Skew   VGA, EGA **Bits 6,5**

The number of character clocks to skew the position of the horizontal timing to achieve proper synchronization. The 2-bit binary value in this register represents the number of character clocks used to delay the timing.

EHB End Horizontal Blanking   VGA, EGA **Bits 4–0**

This field is used to determine the end of the horizontal blanking period as discussed above. In the VGA, a sixth bit is found in the EHB field of the End Horizontal Retrace Period.

10.4.5 Start Horizontal Retrace Register

7	6	5	4	3	2	1	0
			S H R				

Index 04 hex

The horizontal sync pulse is the master horizontal synchronization reference used in the graphics system. The pulse begins when the character counter equals the value set in this register. Increasing this value causes the displayed area of the screen to be shifted horizontally to the right on the monitor.

The polarity of the horizontal sync pulse is set in the HSP field of the Miscellaneous Output Register.

SHR Start Horizontal Retrace   EGA, VGA **Bits 7–0**

The value used to determine the start of the horizontal retrace period.

10.4.6 End Horizontal Retrace Register

7	6	5	4	3	2	1	0
SOM·EHB	HRD			EHR			

Index 05 hex

The value in this register determines where the end of the horizontal retrace period occurs. The width of the retrace period is determined in a manner similar to the technique used to determine the width of the blanking period. Unlike the EHB field, this field is a 5-bit value for both the EGA and the VGA. These five bits represents the lower five bits of the 8-bit character counter. When the lower five bits of the character counter equal the five bits in the End Horizontal Retrace field, the retrace time will end. See the End Horizontal Blanking Register for details.

SOM Start Odd/Even Memory Address   EGA **Bit 7**

Determines whether an odd or even memory address should be used as the first memory address after a horizontal refresh. This value is normally set to zero indicating that an even address should be used. This field is used during horizontal pixel panning operations.

=0 Start at an even memory address. ✓

=1 Start at an odd memory address. ✓

EHB End Horizontal Blanking   VGA **Bit 7**

The sixth bit of the EHB field found in the End Horizontal Blanking Register.

HRD Horizontal Retrace Delay   EGA,VGA **Bits 6–5**

The skew of the horizontal retrace signal used to synchronize the display adapter with the monitor. The high-resolution advanced EGA modes require retrace delays. The binary number in this 2-bit field determines the number of character clocks to skew the system.

EHR End Horizontal Retrace   EGA,VGA **Bits 4–0**

The 5-bit value used to determine the end of the horizontal retrace period as described above.

10.4.7 Vertical Total Register

7	6	5	4	3	2	1	0
			V T				

Index 06 hex

This register determines the number of scan lines on the monitor, including both displayed and nondisplayed lines. It determines the frequency at which the vertical sync pulses will be generated. This is called the *vertical frequency*. Only the eight least significant bits of the vertical total are contained in this register. In the EGA, the ninth bit is found in the VT0 field of the Overflow Register. In the VGA, the ninth and tenth bits are found in the VT0 and VT1 fields of the Overflow Register respectively.

The vertical timing dictated by this register is similar to the horizontal timing dictated in the Horizontal Total Register. A line counter is used to count the horizontal scan lines. When the line counter equals the vertical total, a vertical retrace period begins.

VT Vertical Total   EGA,VGA **Bits 7–0**

The low-order eight bits of the value that determines the total number of vertical scan lines, including the vertical retrace period. The EGA has a ninth bit in the VT0 field of the Overflow Register. The VGA has a ninth and tenth bit in the VT1 field of the Overflow Register.

EGA VT = vertical retrace + # of horizontal scan lines.

VGA VT = vertical retrace + # of horizontal scan lines − 2.

10.4.8 Overflow Register

7	6	5	4	3	2	1	0
VRS▪	VDE▪	CL▪VT1	LC	VBS	VRS	VDE	VT

Index 07 hex

Certain registers associated with the vertical counter require field sizes larger than eight bits. Several of the registers require nine bits of accuracy because the vertical counter is greater than 256. In the VGA, the vertical total period requires a 10-bit value. The high-order bit fields of several of these registers are included in this register.

VRS Vertical Retrace Start Bit 9   VGA **Bit 7**

The ninth bit of the vertical retrace start value. The low-order eight bits are found in the Vertical Retrace Start Register.

VDE Vertical Display Enable End Bit 9   VGA **Bit 6**

The ninth bit of the vertical display enable value. The low-order eight bits are found in the Vertical Display Enable End Register.

CL Cursor Location Bit 8   EGA **Bit 5**

The ninth bit of the cursor location value. The low-order eight bits are found in the Cursor Location Register.

VT1 Vertical Total Bit 9   VGA **Bit 5**

The tenth bit of the vertical total value. The low-order eight bits are found in the Vertical Total Register. The ninth bit is found in the VT field of this register.

LC Line Compare Bit 8   EGA, VGA **Bit 4**

The ninth bit of the line compare value. The low-order eight bits are found in the Line Compare Register.

VBS   Start Vertical Blanking Bit 8   EGA, VGA   **Bit 3**

The ninth bit of the start vertical blanking value. The low-order eight bits are found in the Start Vertical Blanking Register.

VRS   Vertical Retrace Start Bit 8   EGA, VGA   **Bit 2**

The ninth bit of the start vertical retrace start value. The low-order eight bits are found in the Vertical Retrace Start Register.

VDE   Vertical Display Enable End Bit 8   EGA, VGA   **Bit 1**

The ninth bit of the start vertical display end value. The low-order eight bits are found in the Vertical Display End Register.

VT   Vertical Total Bit 8   EGA, VGA   **Bit 0**

The ninth bit of the start vertical total value. The low-order eight bits are found in the Vertical Total Register. For the VGA, the tenth bit is found in the VT1 field of this register.

10.4.9   Preset Row Scan Register

7	6	5	4	3	2	1	0
	BP■			PRS			

Index 08 hex

This register is used during scrolling operations in the EGA and the VGA. In the VGA, the BP field in this register is dedicated to panning operations. During scrolling, the first row of characters may not be full height. This occurs when the display is being panned and only a fraction of the top row of characters is visible. This register determines which scan line within the top row of characters should be displayed as the top scan line of that character row. This preset value is in effect only immediately after the vertical retrace period. The top row of data displayed on the monitor occurs immediately after the vertical retrace period.

The EGA/VGA is controlled as if the display consisted entirely of characters, even if the adapter is in a graphics mode. Each character is composed of a character box that consists of a matrix of dots equal to the number of rows in the character times the number of columns in the character. The rows in the character, also called scan lines, are numbered from the top down, beginning at zero and ending at the maximum row scan. The maximum row scan is equal to the number of scan lines in the character box and is contained in the Maximum Scan Line Register.

character — scan lines.

Scrolling is the effect achieved when the data on the screen appears to move up or down. The terminology in scrolling is reversed from the terminology used when viewing the screen as if through a window. When text is moved upward it is said that the text is "scrolled up." In a windows notation, one would view the window as moving downward through the text. This downward motion of the window would give the appearance of the displayed data moving upward.

There are two types of scrolling, a *character row scroll* (or *rough scroll*) and a *smooth scroll*. A character row scroll is used to scroll one complete row of characters at a time. For example, if the display were scrolling upward, the top row of characters on the display would disappear and the second row would become the top row. A new row of characters would appear at the bottom of the display. This would be a rough scroll because the entire group of scan lines representing a character was moved at one time.

A smooth scroll would scroll one scan line at a time. If a character consists of fourteen scan lines, it would take fourteen single-line scrolls before a new character row would appear. In this case, the characters in the first row would not be full height. The Preset Row Scan Register determines which scan line in the top row of characters to output to the display as the top scan line of the top row of characters. Again, this is in effect only for the first row following a vertical retrace, which is the top row of the display. The maximum character matrix height is 32 rows. Therefore, this preset row scan can range from row 0 to row 31. Smooth scrolling is illustrated in Figure 10.2.

In the VGA, an additional field, BP, is present that enhances the control of the panning operation. It allows up to three characters to be panned, which

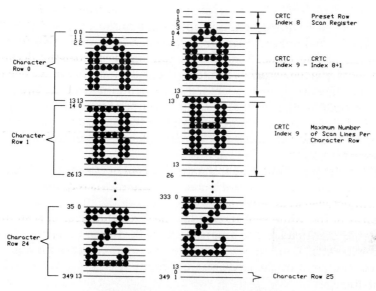

FIGURE 10.2 Smooth Scrolling

corresponds to 24 pixels in an 8-pixel-per-character mode or 27 pixels in a 9-pixel-per-character mode.

BP Byte Panning   VGA **Bits 6–5**

This field controls the number of bytes to pan during a panning operation. The Horizontal Panning Register determines the number of pixels to pan, and this field determines the number of bytes to pan. Together, these fields allow up to three characters to be panned.

PRS Preset Row Scan   EGA,VGA **Bits 4–0**

The starting row of a character box displayed on the top row of characters on a screen. Normally, the value in this register is 0, which displays the entire vertical extent of the top row of characters.

10.4.10 Maximum Scan Line Register

7	6	5	4	3	2	1	0
2T4•	LC•	VBS•			MSL		

Index 09 hex

The size of the rectangular character box is variable. The number of scan lines in a character ranges from 0 to 31 pixels. This register contains the maximum number of scan lines per character rows minus 1. This "minus 1" occurs because the topmost row of a character is row 0 rather than row 1.

The adapter can have only one maximum scan line count in effect at a time. If characters with different character heights are desired, the Maximum Scan Line Register should be set to the maximum character height. Because two character fonts may be active at a given time, it is possible to have one character set taller than the other. Each character in the shorter of the two character sets will be padded with zeros. When the smaller character set is selected, the character will be written to the screen with the additional rows of padded zeros as background. In the alphanumeric modes, the character background is displayed according to the background color. In the graphics modes, the background of the character is transparent and does not overwrite what is currently displayed. Therefore, the unused portion of the character, considered background, will not overwrite any data.

Regardless of the value selected for the maximum number of scan lines per character, the downloadable character fonts will be stored in display memory with each character consisting of 32 rows. If the character set contains eight rows per character, the character would occupy the first eight of the 32 available positions. The remaining 24 positions would be unused. These 32 rows are reserved for each character in order to achieve fast addressing of the character fonts. Because each character is 32 bytes apart in display memory, a shift operation is all that is required to determine the position of the character pattern. To determine the character position from the ASCII code, the code value is simply shifted five bits to the left. This is equivalent to a multiplication by 32.

In the VGA, the upper three bits of this register are used to allow 200 lines to be displayed as 400 lines and as additional overflow fields for the Line Compare and Start Vertical Blanking Registers.

2T4 200-to-400-line Conversion   VGA **Bit 7**

Allows a 200-line mode to be displayed on 400 display scan lines. This permits the 200-line display modes to fill the entire screen. Each line is duplicated twice by dividing the clock to the row scan counter by 2.

  =0 Normal operation.

  =1 Display 200 lines on the full display.

LC Line Compare Bit 9   VGA **Bit 6**

The tenth bit of the Line Compare value. The lower eight bits are in the Line Compare Register, and the ninth bit is in the LC field of the Overflow Register.

VBS Start Vertical Blanking Bit 9   VGA **Bit 5**

The tenth bit of the start vertical blanking value. The lower eight bits are in the Start Vertical Blanking Register, and the ninth bit is in the VBS field of the overflow register.

MSL Maximum Scan Line   EGA, VGA **Bits 4–0**

The number of scan lines in a character row minus 1.

10.4.11 Cursor Start Register

7	6	5	4	3	2	1	0
		(C 0 0■)		(	C S		)

Index 0A hex

The hardware cursor is represented as a block of pixels occupying a character position. Like any character, the cursor is composed of a number of scan lines. In conjunction with the Cursor End Register, this register allows the height of the cursor to be variable. This register determines the first scan line within the character box that should be filled in. The scan lines within a character box are numbered from the top down. The count begins at 0, with the exception of the top scan line (see Preset Row Scan Register), and ends at the maximum character height defined in the Maximum Scan Line Register. A cursor that fills the entire character box should begin at scan line 0.

The cursor may be enabled or disabled by the COO field for the VGA.

COO Cursor On/OFF   VGA **Bit 5**

Allows the cursor to be turned on or off.

=0 Turn the cursor off.

=1 Turn the cursor on.

CS Cursor Start   EGA,VGA **Bits 4–0**

The number of the scan line within a character box that will be the first scan line displayed for the cursor. Because the maximum character size is 32 scan lines, this value may range from 0 to 31.

10.4.12 Cursor End Register

7	6	5	4	3	2	1	0
	C S K				C E		

Index 0B hex

The hardware cursor is represented as a block of pixels occupying a character position. Like any character, the cursor is composed of a number of scan lines. In conjunction with the Cursor Start Register, this register allows the height of the cursor to be variable. This register determines the last scan line within the character box that should be displayed as part of the cursor. The scan lines within a character box are numbered from the top down. The count begins at 0, with the exception of the top scan line (see Preset Row Scan Register), and ends at the maximum character height defined in the Maximum Scan Line Register. A cursor that fills the entire character box should end at the scan line equal to the maximum scan lines per character.

Because of the internal timing of the EGA, it is necessary in the high-resolution modes to skew the timing of the signals to achieve proper synchronization. The Cursor Skew field of this register is similar to the DES field in the End Horizontal Blanking Register and the HRD delay field in the End Horizontal Retrace Register.

CSK Cursor Skew   EGA, VGA **Bits 6–5**

The number of characters to delay the cursor data in order to achieve proper synchronization. The binary amount in this field is equal to the number of characters to skew.

CE Cursor End   EGA, VGA **Bits 4–0**

The bottom scan line to display per character row for the cursor.

10.4.13 Start Address High Register

7	6	5	4	3	2	1	0
			S A H				

Index 0C hex

The upper-left corner of the display represents the origin of the display. The data to be displayed at this location is resident in the display buffer. The address of this data is determined by the 16-bit value found in the Start Address Registers. The maximum display buffer size is 64 Kbytes. Thus, a 16-bit address is required to address any given byte. Because the CRTC registers are eight bits each, it takes two registers to fully specify the start address. The Start Address High Register represents the upper eight bits of the 16-bit address, and the Start Address Low Register represents the lower eight bits of the 16-bit address.

The screen may be considered to be a window through which data can be viewed. The size of the window is not necessarily the same as the size of the data. The maximum window size for a display would be the maximum resolution of the EGA/VGA. The display memory may be, and in fact often is, larger than this maximum resolution. If the starting address is modified, the window will move through the data, giving the effect of horizontal panning or vertical scrolling.

The display memory is 64 Kbytes per plane. Each plane begins with relative address 0. In the graphics modes, modifying the value in the starting address by one will change the position of the data to be displayed on the screen by one byte. In the EGA modes, this translates to eight horizontal pixels because there are eight pixels per byte, one pixel per bit. Thus, increasing the address by one will have the effect of shifting the display to the left by eight pixels. Assuming that the dimensions of the display are not modified, the data corresponding to the left eight columns on the screen will no longer be displayed. New data will be displayed in the right eight pixels of the screen.

Likewise, decreasing the starting address by one will cause the displayed data to shift eight pixels to the right. If the starting address is increased by the number of horizontal pixels per row, the display will appear to scroll one row downward. The number of pixels in a horizontal row is determined by the number of character positions per row loaded in the Horizontal Display Enable End Register and the number of pixels per character loaded in the 8/9 field of the

Clocking Mode Register. If there are 80 characters per row, corresponding to 640 pixels, increasing the starting address by 80 would cause the display to scroll one row upward. The previous top row of the display would no longer be displayed, and a new row would scroll into the bottom of the screen. Remember that this row represents one scan line, not one character row.

SAH Start Address High   EGA, VGA **Bits 7–0**

The high-order eight bits of the starting address that will determine the first data to be displayed after a vertical refresh. The low-order eight bits of the starting address are found in the Start Address Low Register.

10.4.14 Start Address Low Register

7	6	5	4	3	2	1	0
			S A L				

Index 0D hex

The upper-left corner of the display represents the origin of the display. The data to be displayed at this location is resident in the display buffer. The address of this data is determined by the 16-bit value found in the Start Address Registers. The display buffer is 64 Kbytes long. Thus, a 16-bit address is required to address any given byte. Because the CRTC registers are eight bits each, it takes two registers to fully specify the start address. The Start Address Low Register represents the lower eight bits of the 16-bit address, and the Start Address High Register represents the higher eight bits of the 16-bit address. See the Start Address High Register for details.

SAL Start Address Low   EGA, VGA **Bits 7–0**

The low-order eight bits of the starting address that will determine the first data to be displayed after a vertical refresh. The high-order eight bits of the starting address are found in the Start Address High Register.

10.4.15 Cursor Location High Register

7	6	5	4	3	2	1	0
			C L H				

Index 0E hex

The cursor position is determined by the 16-bit address that points to a byte in display memory. This register represents the upper eight bits of the 16-bit address. The lower eight bits of the 16-bit address are found in the Cursor Location Low Register. See the Start Address High Register for addressing details. It is necessary to specify the cursor address in this way because the cursor will nondestructively overwrite data on the screen. The EGA keeps track of which data is being overwritten by the cursor so that the original data occupying that location on the screen may be restored when the cursor moves. This allows the cursor to move about the screen without destroying data. The nondestructive activity of the cursor is transparent to the programmer. Note that the cursor location may point to a non-displayed location on the screen. In this case, the cursor would not be displayed.

CLH Cursor Location High   EGA, VGA **Bits 7–0**

The eight high-order bits of the 16-bit address that determines where the cursor will be located.

10.4.16   Cursor Location Low Register

7	6	5	4	3	2	1	0
			C L L				

        Index 0F hex

The cursor position is determined by the 16-bit address that points to a byte in display memory. This register represents the lower eight bits of the 16-bit address. The upper eight bits of the 16-bit address are found in the Cursor Location High Register. See the Cursor Location High Register and the Start Address High Register for addressing details.

CLL Cursor Location Low   EGA, VGA **Bits 7–0**

The eight low-order bits of the 16-bit address that determines where the cursor will be located.

10.4.17   Vertical Retrace Start Register

7	6	5	4	3	2	1	0
			V R S				

        Index 10 hex

In the VGA, this register may be accessed only if the Compatible Read (CR) field of the End Horizontal Blanking Register is set to a 1.

The vertical sync pulse is output when the scan line counter is equal to the value loaded into this register. The status of the display can be monitored through the VRI field of the Input Status #0 Register and through the DE or VR field of the Input Status #1 Register. These fields are used to indicate whether the system is in a vertical retrace, a horizontal retrace, or a display condition. As is true during the horizontal retrace, no information is drawn onto the screen during the vertical retrace.

The vertical retrace period is significantly longer than the horizontal retrace because of the longer distance that the electron beam needs to travel to get back to the top-left corner of the monitor. Also, more time can be taken because the vertical retrace occurs only 50–60 times per second. This time can be utilized for internal display adapter housekeeping.

The sync pulse is a master timing pulse used internally for the display and externally to synchronize the monitor. Because the vertical counters are a minimum of nine bits, this register can hold only the low-order eight bits. The ninth bit is located in the VT field of the Overflow Register for the EGA. The ninth and tenth bits are located in the VT and VT1 fields of the Overflow Register for the VGA.

In the EGA, the occurrence of a vertical retrace period can generate an interrupt if the vertical retrace interrupt is enabled. It is enabled by resetting the DVI field of the Vertical Retrace End Register. The polarity of the vertical retrace period is set in the VSP field of the Miscellaneous Output Register.

VRS Vertical Retrace Start   EGA, VGA **Bits 7–0**

The low-order eight bits of the value that determines when a vertical retrace pulse begins. The scan line counter is compared to this register at each horizontal retrace time. When the scan-line counter equals this value, the vertical retrace period begins.

10.4.18   Vertical Retrace End Register

7	6	5	4	3	2	1	0
PR	BW	DVI	CVI	EVR			

Index 11 hex

In the VGA, this register may be accessed only if the Compatible Read (CR) field of the End Horizontal Blanking Register is set to a 1.

The vertical sync pulse becomes inactive when the low-order five bits of the scan line counter, also called the horizontal scan count, is equal to this value.

The vertical sync pulse begins when the scan count is equal to the value in the Vertical Retrace Start Register. The operation of this function is identical to the operation of the Horizontal Retrace End Register. Like that register, this register represents only the five low-order bits of the end value. After the vertical retrace begins, the five low-order bits of the scan line counter will be compared to this register. When they are equal, the retrace pulse will become inactive. See the Horizontal Retrace End Register for more details on this mod 32 counter.

In the EGA, the status of the display can be monitored through the VRI field of the Input Status #0 Register and through the DE or VR field of the Input Status #1 Register. These fields are used to indicate whether the system is in a vertical retrace, a horizontal retrace, or a display condition. The occurrence of a vertical retrace signal can generate an interrupt if the interrupt is enabled. It is enabled by resetting the DVI field in this register. Note: The vertical interrupt is disabled if this field is equal to a 1. Thus, it is termed the Disable Vertical Interrupt field.

Further, in the EGA, when the vertical interrupt is enabled and a vertical retrace period occurs, an interrupt level 2 on a PC or level 9 on an AT is generated on the host processor. The CVI field of this register clears this vertical interrupt. Again, the notation is confusing because of the polarity of this field. A 0 in this field will cause the interrupt to be cleared. It is important for the interrupt service routine to reset the interrupt. The first thing that an interrupt service routine should do is to disable any further undesired interrupts from occurring. This ensures that the interrupt service routine is not interrupted by undesired sources.

Disabling interrupts is particularly important in time-sensitive applications. Suppose that it is necessary to modify some parameter in the graphics system during the vertical retrace period, and the modification is to occur within the interrupt service routine. If non–time-sensitive interrupts such as keyboard or disk are serviced during this time, the vertical retrace period could well be over before control is returned to the vertical interrupt service routine. This could be avoided by disabling the disk and keyboard interrupts, along with any other undesirable interrupts.

At the end of the interrupt service routine, the interrupts are reenabled. Because the EGA is generating the interrupt, as soon as the interrupts are reenabled, the vertical interrupt will regenerate itself because the interrupt is still active. This occurs regardless of the fact that the interrupt was handled. The vertical interrupt signal does not go away when the vertical retrace period ends. It is necessary for the software to clear the interrupt. Thus, the second thing that the interrupt service routine should do is to clear the vertical interrupt by resetting a 0 into the CVI field of this register. This is done to ensure that a vertical interrupt is not missed.

If an event is to be synchronized with the vertical retrace period, it is not necessary to perform any function within the vertical retrace period itself, as long as the occurrence of the vertical retrace period is noted. Further, if a different time-sensitive interrupt occurs during the time that a vertical retrace period occurs, and if this time-sensitive interrupt service routine disables the level-2 interrupts and finishes after the vertical retrace period, the vertical retrace interrupt will still be pending. This would not be the case if the interrupt had been removed automatically at the end of the vertical retrace period.

In the VGA, bits 6 and 7 are used to protect the CRTC registers at indexes 0 through 7. The exception is the line compare field (LC) in the Overflow Register. The bandwidth of the system is also controlled for the VGA by allowing three or five dynamic RAM (DRAM) refresh cycles per horizontal line. A similar field is found in the BW field of the Clocking Mode Register for the EGA.

PR Protect Registers 0–7   VGA **Bit 7**

Protects CRTC registers at indexes 0 to 7 from being modified. The lower eight registers in the CRTC contain sensitive horizontal and vertical timing settings. Software expecting the EGA may program these registers unwittingly.

  =0 No protection is active.

  =1 Writing from the host to CRTC registers 0–7 is disabled.

BW Bandwidth   VGA **Bit 6**

Selects three or five DRAM refresh cycles per horizontal line.

  =0 Select three DRAM cycles.

  =1 Select five DRAM cycles.

DVI Disable Vertical Interrupts   EGA **Bits 5**

Controls the ability of the EGA to generate a level-2 interrupt on the occurrence of a vertical interrupt.

  =0 Enable vertical interrupts.

  =1 Disable vertical interrupts.

CVI Clear Vertical Interrupts   EGA **Bit 4**

Removes a vertical interrupt when reset to 0. Note that setting this field to a 1 has no effect because it cannot generate an interrupt.

  =0 Clear the vertical interrupt.

  =1 No effect.

EVR Vertical Retrace End   EGA, VGA **Bits 3–0**

The low-order five bits of the value that will cause the vertical retrace period to end. The horizontal scan line count is compared to the Vertical Retrace Start Register. When the values are equal, a vertical retrace period is started. After this time, the low-order five bits of the scan line count are compared to the five bits in the **EVR** field. When they are equal, the vertical retrace period ends.

10.4.19 Light Pen High Register

7	6	5	4	3	2	1	0
			·LPH				

Index 10 hex (EGA only)

The light pen interface generates a trigger pulse when the electron beam crosses in front of the light pen. When this trigger occurs, the display memory address of the current data being refreshed corresponds to the position of the light pen. This 16-bit value is automatically written into the two light pen registers. This register contains the high-order eight bits of the 16-bit display memory address that corresponds to the current position of the light pen. The low-order eight bits are automatically written into the Light Pen Low Register.

It is important to note that if the electron beam is not drawing any data onto the screen at the location of the light pen, no trigger will be generated. The electron beam must be exciting the screen phosphor before the light pen can detect the presence of light.

LPH Light Pen High   EGA **Bits 7–0**

The high-order eight bits of the current position of the light pen as generated by the light pen trigger.

10.4.20 Light Pen Low Register

7	6	5	4	3	2	1	0
			·LPL				

Index 11 hex (EGA only)

This register contains the low-order eight bits of the 16-bit display memory address that corresponds to the current position of the light pen. The high-order eight bits are automatically written into the Light Pen High Register. See the Light Pen High Register for details.

LPL Light Pen Low   EGA **Bits 7–0**

The low-order eight bits of the current position of the light pen as generated by the light pen trigger.

10.4.21 Vertical Display End Register

7	6	5	4	3	2	1	0
			V D E				

Index 13 hex

This register determines the number of the last horizontal scan line occurring on the bottom of the screen. The scan-line counter increments until the value in the Vertical Display Enable End Register is reached. Because this value is greater than 256, only the low-order eight bits of the enable end value can be stored in this register. The ninth bit is stored in the VDE field of the Overflow Register for the EGA. The ninth and tenth bits are stored in the VDE field of the Overflow Register for the VGA. The vertical blanking usually occurs before the value in the Vertical Display Enable End Register occurs. The horizontal lines that occur between these two values are considered to be the border area. The color of the border is determined by the value in the Overscan Register.

VDE Vertical Display End Enable   EGA, VGA **Bits 7–0**

The low-order eight bits of the value in the Vertical Display Enable End Register. This determines the last horizontal line to be displayed on the bottom of the monitor, including the overscan region.

10.4.22 Offset Register

7	6	5	4	3	2	1	0
			O F F				

Index 13 hex

This register specifies the width of the display. The EGA/VGA may be addressed in a byte mode or a word mode as specified in the CBT field of the Mode Control Register. This offset value corresponds to the difference between the addresses of two vertically neighboring pixels. This is often called *display pitch* in other graphic processors. The address of the next display row is computed by the current byte start address + (value in the Offset Register $\times$ K), where K = 2 for byte addressing and K = 4 for word addressing.

OFF Offset   EGA, VGA **Bits 7–0**

The difference in byte or words between vertically adjacent scan lines.

10.4.23   Underline Location Register

7	6	5	4	3	2	1	0
	DW ■	CB4 ■			UL		

Index 14 hex

The EGA/VGA allows each character to be underlined as determined in each character's underline field. Each character is composed of up to 32 scan lines in the vertical dimension, as dictated in the Maximum Scan Line Register. The horizontal line used for the underlining will occur on one of these scan lines. The number of the scan line minus 1 is loaded into this register. The "minus 1" occurs because the scan lines are counted beginning with scan line number zero. Thus, the fourth scan line of the character is actually scan line number three.

The VGA uses bits 5 and 6 to enable double-word addressing and, when double-word addressing is enabled, to divide the character clock input to the memory address counter by 4. This is utilized when the four display modes are chained in mode 13 hex.

DW   Double Word Mode   VGA   **Bit 6**

Allows normal addressing or double-word addressing.

   =0   Normal word addressing.
   =1   Double word addressing.

CB4   Count by Four   VGA   **Bit 5**

If the double-word addressing is enabled in the DW field of this register, this field controls the clock to the memory address counter. It is possible to divide this clock by 4, which would be done when the four display planes are chained in Mode 13 hex.

   =0   Normal clocking.
   =1   Divide the character clock to the memory address counter by 4.

UL   Underline Location   EGA, VGA   **Bits 4–0**

The value in this field minus 1 determines the horizontal scan line within a character box on which the underline will occur.

10.4.24 Start Vertical Blank Register

7	6	5	4	3	2	1	0
			VBS				

Index 15 hex

The vertical blanking period begins when the horizontal scan line counter equals the start vertical blanking value. The vertical blanking period is used to turn off the data stream being output to the display during the vertical retrace period. The display enable period is normally concluded, as indicated by the value in the Vertical Display End Register, before the blanking begins. This allows a border region, the color of which is determined by the value in the Overscan Register. Because the horizontal scan line counter is greater than eight bits, only the low-order eight bits are contained in this register. The ninth bit is contained in the VBS field of the Overflow Register for the EGA. For the VGA, the ninth bit is contained in the VBS field of the Overflow Register and the tenth bit is located in the VBS field of the Maximum Scan Line Register.

VBS Vertical Blank Start   EGA, VGA **Bits 7–0**

The low-order eight bits of the value that is compared to the horizontal scan line counter. When these two values are equal, the vertical blanking period begins.

10.4.25 End Vertical Blank Register

7	6	5	4	3	2	1	0
	VBE•			VBE			

Index 16 hex

This register determines the end of the vertical blanking period. It is similar in operation to the End Horizontal Blanking, End Horizontal Retrace, and End Vertical Retrace Registers. In the EGA, the 5-bit value in this register is compared to the low-order five bits of the horizontal scan line counter. The comparison causes the vertical blanking period to end after a vertical blanking period begins. It begins when the scan-line counter and the value in the Start Vertical Blanking Register are equal. Because only the low five bits are used, the comparison is based on mod 32 arithmetic. This limits the vertical blanking period to 32 character positions. In the VGA, this field is seven bits long, facilitating a mode 128 arithmetic.

VBE End Vertical Blanking   EGA **Bits 4–0**

The value that determines when the vertical blanking interval should end. This value is compared to the low-order five bits of the horizontal scan line counter.

VBE End Vertical Blanking   VGA **Bits 6–0**

The value that determines when the vertical blanking interval should end. This value is compared to the low-order seven bits of the horizontal scan line counter.

10.4.26   Mode Control Register

7	6	5	4	3	2	1	0
HR	W/B	AW	•OC	CBT	HRS	SRS	CMS

Index 17 hex

A multifunction register that assists in the control of the display. This register can generally be left alone by the programmer. When the mode of the display is changed, the BIOS commands will automatically adjust the value in this register to match the mode.

HR Hardware Reset   EGA, VGA **Bit 7**

Enables or disables the ability of the display to generate hardware horizontal and vertical retrace signals, display enable signals, and blanking signals.

=0   Places all horizontal and vertical control timings into a hold state, thereby forcing a reset condition.

=1   Enables the occurrence of the horizontal and vertical control signals.

W/B Word/Byte Mode   EGA, VGA **Bit 6**

Controls the way the internal addresses generated in the EGA are output to the display memory address bus. Word mode is used in CGA emulation.

=0   The word mode is selected, causing the addresses' bits to be shifted left one position before being output to the display memory. A more significant address bit is output on the least significant memory address line. This bit is either bit 13 or bit 15 depending on the value in the AW field in this register.

=1   The byte mode is selected, causing the addresses to be output to the display memory without being shifted.

AW Address Wrap   EGA, VGA **Bit 5**

Determines whether bit 13 or bit 15 should be output on the least significant
address line to the display memory when the system is in a word mode, as
indicated in the W/B field in this register. This field is used during CGA emulation. Shifting the address bits one position has the effect of halving memory.
The CGA maps the even memory addresses in the first block of memory and the
odd memory addresses in the second block of memory. This contrasts with
using address bit 1 as a switch, as is done in the SRS field, which quarters the
memory for Hercules emulation.

  If bit 0 is substituted for memory address bit 13, consecutive scan lines are
separated by 8 Kbytes. If bit 0 is substituted for memory address bit 15, successive scan lines are separated by 32 Kbytes.

=0 Select address bit 13 to be sent to the least significant address bit to the
    display memory. This should be used when 64 Kbytes of memory is
    installed on the EGA/VGA board.

=1 Select address bit 15 to be sent to the least significant address bit to the
    display memory. This should be used when greater than 64 Kbytes of
    memory is installed on the EGA board.

OC Output Control   EGA **Bit 4**

Enables or disables the output drivers. Note that this bit is used for alternative
memory addressing by EGA/VGA chip manufacturers. Only the IBM EGA
standard usage for this register is discussed here. Consult the manufacturers'
specifications for the use of this bit on other EGA boards.

=0 Enable the EGA output drivers.

=1 Disable the EGA output drivers.

CBT Count by Two   EGA, VGA **Bit 3**

Determines whether the EGA/VGA memory address counter is clocked every
character clock or every other character clock. This creates either a byte or a
word refresh address for the display buffer. It determines the actual address
difference in conjunction with the Offset Register.

=0 The memory address counter is clocked with the character clock input.

=1 The memory address counter is clocked with every other character clock
    input.

HRS Horizontal Retrace Select   EGA, VGA **Bit 2**

Controls the vertical resolution capability of the display. Normally, the vertical
resolution of the display is limited to 512 horizontal lines because of the 9-bit
scan-line counter in the EGA. In the VGA, it is limited to 1,024 horizontal lines

because of the 10-bit scan-line counter in the VGA. If the scan-line counter is clocked with the horizontal retrace divided by 2, it will be clocked twice as often. This increases the possible vertical resolution to 1,024 horizontal scan lines in the EGA and 2,048 horizontal scan lines in the VGA.

=0 Clock the scan-line counter with every horizontal retrace.

=1 Clock the scan-line counter with every horizontal retrace divided by 2, allowing up to 1,024 addressable scan lines for the EGA and 2,048 horizontal scan lines for the VGA.

SRS Select Row Scan Counter   EGA, VGA Bit 1

This field allows the EGA/VGA to be compatible at the memory addressing level with a graphics system that uses a four-bank memory. The graphics system that most frequently uses such a four-bank memory is the Hercules monochrome adapter. The memory address bit 14 is multiplexed. The occurrence of the display enable period is indicated by the DE field of the Input Status #1 Register and is controlled by the Horizontal Display End Register and the Vertical Display End Register. During the display enable period, the memory address line corresponding to bit 14 is replaced with bit 1. This makes successive scan lines 16 Kbytes apart. This is similar to the multiplexing of bit 0 onto memory address bit 13 or bit 15 for CGA compatibility. In this mode, successive scan lines are 32 Kbytes apart. This function is controlled by the AW field of this register.

=0 Row scan counter bit 1 is placed on the memory address bus bit 14 during active display time. Bit 1, placed on memory address bit 14, has the effect of quartering the memory.

=1 Memory addresses are output sequentially.

CMS Compatibility Mode Support   EGA, VGA Bit 0

This field allows the EGA/VGA to address memory in a similar fashion to that used by the CGA. During the active display time, row scan address bit 0 is substituted for memory address bit 13. The CGA is controlled by the 6845 controller chip and uses the row scan address to increase the 6845 address potential. The 6845 normally can address only 128 lines. To achieve the desired 200-line resolution, the 6845 is programmed for a 100-scan-line resolution with two row scan addresses per character row. This chip places successive scan lines of the display memory in two separate odd and even memory banks. The CGA has 16 Kbytes of memory, and successive scan lines are placed 8 Kbytes apart. Row scan address bit 0 is used as the most significant address bit on the CGA to split up the memory into these two 8 Kbyte blocks. Bit 13 corresponds to the 8 Kbyte boundary, and row scan address bit 0 corresponds to odd and even scan lines. This causes the EGA/VGA to address memory in a similar fashion to that used by the CGA.

=0 Substitutes row scan address bit 0 for memory address bit 13, causing the memory of the EGA/VGA during the graphics modes to be compatible with the CGA's 6845 controller chip.

=1 Performs no substitution, causing the EGA to access memory sequentially.

10.4.27 Line Compare Register

7	6	5	4	3	2	1	0
			LC				

Index 18 hex

This register allows split-screen display. The low-order eight bits of a value are compared to the horizontal scan line counter. The ninth bit is located in the LC field of the Overflow Register for the EGA. In the VGA, the ninth bit is located in the LC field in the Maximum Scan Register and the tenth bit is located in the LC field in the Maximum Scan Register. When the scan line counter equals the value in this register, the line counter is cleared, causing the display to begin refreshing the top section of the display again. This causes the display to be split. The bottom portion of the display represents the difference between the value in the Line Compare Register and the value in the Vertical Display End Register. Split-screen operation is illustrated in Figure 10.3.

The starting address loaded into the Start Address High and Start Address Low Registers determines the location of the data that will be displayed in the upper-right corner of the display. The length of each display is determined by

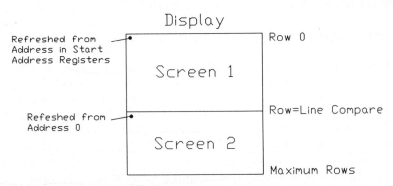

FIGURE 10.3 Split-screen Operation

the Horizontal Display End and Vertical Display End Registers. In normal operation, the Line Compare Register is loaded with a maximum value of 511 for the EGA and 1,023 for the VGA. This causes data to fill the entire screen. The line counter is not reset because it will never reach the maximum values in the Line Compare Register. The horizontal line counter, also called the vertical counter, will be reset only when the Vertical Display End value is reached at the bottom of the screen.

Now suppose that the Line Compare Register and its associated ninth bit are loaded with the value 175. In a 350-line display, this corresponds to a line half-way down the screen. When the vertical counter reaches 175, the memory address counter will be reset, causing the screen refreshing to begin at memory location 0. There will be no observable change to the top half of the screen if no other parameters have changed. The reason is that the starting address still dictates where the data begins for the top half of the display. The bottom half of the screen now reflects the data beginning at memory address 0, the beginning of the display planes. Thus, two screens are displayed on the monitor. The top half begins at the address in the Start Address High and Start Address Low Registers; the bottom half begins at memory location 0. If the Start Address registers are set to 0, a single screen will result.

This register is often used to provide split-screen operation that allows one portion of the screen to be scrolled independently of the other. If the Start Address registers are loaded with a new value, the top half of the screen will reflect the change, and the bottom half will remain unchanged. See the Start Address High and Start Address Low Registers for addressing details.

LC Line Compare   EGA, VGA **Bits 7–0**

When the line counter is equal to the 9-bit line-compare value, the refresh address will be cleared, causing the horizontal display lines beneath the line compare value to be refreshed from display memory address 0. The effect is a dual-screen operation. This register contains the low-order eight bits of the line-compare value. This is illustrated in Figure 10.3.

10.5 THE GRAPHICS CONTROLLER REGISTERS

The Graphics Controller Registers consist of nine registers. None of these registers has a unique host port address. Instead, an address and data register pair exists in the host port address space. The programmer accesses these registers by first loading the Graphics Address Register with an index value ranging from 0 to 8. The Graphics Address Register selects one of the Graphics Data Registers as the current active register. Reading or writing to this Graphics Data Register will repeatedly access the register selected by the index value, until the Graphics Address Register is modified. The Graphics Address Register resides at port 3CE hex, and the Graphics Data Register resides at port 3CF hex.

TABLE 10.11 Graphics Controller Registers

Register Name	Index (Hex)	Write (Hex) (EGA/VGA)	Read (Hex) (VGA)
Graphics 1 Position	—	3CC (EGA only)	—
Graphics 2 Position	—	3CA (EGA only)	—
Graphics Address	—	3CE	3CE
Set/Reset	0	3CF	3CF
Enable Set/Reset	1	3CF	3CF
Color Compare	2	3CF	3CF
Data Rotate	3	3CF	3CF
Read Map Select	4	3CF	3CF
Mode	5	3CF	3CF
Miscellaneous	6	3CF	3CF
Color Don't Care	7	3CF	3CF
Bit Mask	8	3CF	3CF

In addition to these indexed registers, the EGA contains two registers that have their own host port addresses. These registers are called the Graphics 1 Position and the Graphics 2 Position Registers. They reside at host port addresses 3CC and 3CA hex, respectively. The Graphics Controller Registers are listed in Table 10.11.

10.5.1 Graphics #1 Position Register (EGA only)

7	6	5	4	3	2	1	0
						▪G P 1	

Write Port 3CC hex (EGA)

The EGA was originally implemented by IBM using two Graphics Controller Chips. It was necessary to program each to respond to a different set of two consecutive bits of the 8-bit host data bus. In the IBM EGA implementation, a 0 must be loaded into this register. In the VGA, there is no analogous register.

GP1 Graphics Position #1   EGA **Bits 2–1**

A zero should be loaded into this location to map host data bus bits 0 and 1 to display planes 0 and 1 respectively.

10.5.2 Graphics #2 Position Register (EGA only)

7	6	5	4	3	2	1	0
						•G P 2	

Write Port 3CA hex (EGA)

The EGA was originally implemented by IBM using two Graphics Controller Chips. This register is used to program the Graphics #2 chip. See the Graphics #1 Position Register for details.

GP2 Graphics Position #2   EGA **Bits 1–0**

A 1 should be loaded into this location to map host data bus bits 2 and 3 to display planes 2 and 3, respectively.

10.5.3 Set/Reset Register

7	6	5	4	3	2	1	0
				S / R			

Index 00 hex

In normal display operation, the Set/Reset function is disabled through the Enable Set/Reset Register. Assuming a write mode of 0, as loaded in the MW field of the Write Mode Register, writing to display memory occurs in a horizontal block of up to eight consecutive pixels in one, two, three, or four planes. The data that is written into the display planes comes from the host processor data bus. The byte-wide data bus, bits 7–0, is sent to the EGA/VGA. It is interpreted as being eight neighboring horizontal pixels, where bit 7 corresponds to the far left pixel and bit 0 corresponds to the far right pixel. Depending on the value in the Bit Plane Mask Register, any or all of these bits might be written to the display memory. If more than one plane is enabled via the Map Mask Register, an identical pattern is written to each plane. This mode of writing to a display is termed *Bit Plane Mode* in the graphics world because unique data is written to consecutive locations in a single plane. Although multiple planes may be selected, these will be written with the same data as is written to a single plane.

It is sometimes desirable to write unique data to all display planes in a single operation. This mode of writing to a display is called *raster mode* because a multiplane pixel is written to in a single operation. The value in the Bit Plane Mask Register determines the number of horizontal neighboring pixels that will be affected in the byte addressed by the host processor. If more than one bit is enabled in the Bit Plane Mask Register, more than one pixel will be written to in a single operation. These multiple pixels will be loaded with the same data as presented in the Set/Reset Register.

In summary, the "Bit Plane Mode" writes unique information to horizontally neighboring pixels and copies this pattern to between 1 and 4 display planes. In the raster mode, unique information is written to between 1 and 4 display planes and copied to horizontally neighboring pixels.

The Set/Reset Register is loaded with the pattern that will be written to the display planes. There is a one-to-one correspondence between the bit positions in the Set/Reset register and the display plane numbers. Thus, bit 0 in the Set/Reset Register corresponds to memory plane 0, bit 1 corresponds to memory plane 1, and so on. Not all display planes need to be affected in a set/reset operation. The Enable Set/Reset Resister determines which planes should be affected in such an operation.

The bit locations in the Enable Set/Reset Register correspond to the bit locations in the Set/Reset register and the memory display plane numbers. Any bit that is set to 1 in the Enable Set/Reset Register causes the data in the corresponding display bit plane to be modified by the corresponding bit in the Set/Reset Register. If a bit is reset to 0 in the Enable Set/Reset Register, the corresponding display bit plane remains unmodified. Originally, all bits in the Enable Set/Reset Register were reset to 0, which had the effect of disabling the set/reset function. In this case, the data presented by the host processor was used to modify the data in the selected display planes as normal for write mode 0. The display planes that were modified in this case were those that were enabled in the Map Mask Register. Again, the bit positions (3–0) in the Set/Reset Register, Enable Set/Reset Register, and the Map Mask Register correspond to the display bit plane number (3–0).

It is also possible, and sometimes desirable, to combine the normal writing mode with the Set/Reset mode. In either mode, writing to the display memory requires data to be moved into the display memory address space. The specific address determines where the data will be written to with respect to the display. This data move is accomplished through an assembly language MOV instruction, either directly through assembly language or indirectly through a C command. This move command will move a byte of data to the desired location. A word move will simply write two consecutive bytes, similar to two consecutive byte move instructions.

Assume that all planes are enabled through the Map Mask Register. If the set/reset function is enabled in all four display planes, the data being referred to in the MOV instruction will be totally ignored. This occurs because all planes will be written to with the value in the Set/Reset Register. However, any planes that are not enabled in the Enable Set/Reset Register will ignore the data in the Set/Reset Register and will respond to the data in the MOV instruction in a normal manner. This is usually not desired unless the programmer is doing some very tricky programming. To get around the problem, the display planes that should not be modified must be disabled in the Map Mask Register before the set/reset function.

S/R Set/Reset   EGA, VGA **Bits 3–0**

The bit positions of this field correspond to the respective display planes and to the bit positions in the Enable Set/Reset Register. The display planes that correspond to the bits enabled in the Enable Set/Reset Register will be modified by the corresponding bits in this Set/Reset Register. This allows up to four display planes to be modified with unique data in a single operation. See the Enable Set/Reset Register.

10.5.4   Enable Set/Reset Register

7	6	5	4	3	2	1	0
				E S R			

Index 01 hex

Any bits set in this register will enable the set/reset write mode. This mode allows up to four display planes to be written with unique data in a single operation. See the Set/Reset Register for details.

ESR Enable Set Reset   EGA, VGA **Bits 3–0**

The bit numbers in this field correspond to the respective display planes and to the bit positions in the Set/Reset Register. The display planes corresponding to the bits enabled in this field will be modified by the corresponding bits in this Set/Reset Register. This allows up to four display planes to be modified with unique data in a single operation.

10.5.5   Color Compare Register

7	6	5	4	3	2	1	0
				C C			

Index 02 hex

It is possible to read the result from a comparison of the data in the display planes with the value loaded into the Color Compare Register. The EGA has two read modes controlled by the RM field of the Mode Register. The more common read mode #0 causes data to be read from eight consecutive horizontal pixels from one of the four display memory planes. This data move is accomplished using an assembly language MOV instruction.

The memory plane selected is dictated by the binary value in the Read Map Select Register. The selected pixels are determined by the address referenced in the MOV instruction. In one byte move instruction, eight consecutive pixels will be read from one display plane. Word MOV instructions act similarly to two consecutive byte MOV instruction.

The second read mode (read mode #1), as loaded in the RM field of the Mode Register, is used when the result of a comparison is desired. A common computer graphics application is to fill a closed polygon or arbitrary shape. To fill the shape, it is necessary to know where the boundary of the shape is located. If the boundary is in a single color, it is necessary to determine which pixels correspond to that color. This can be done by reading the data using the read mode #0. Four consecutive reads are necessary, one from each display plane. Next, the data from the four reads must be reorganized into a word that represents the data from all four planes at one pixel's location. This must be compared to the boundary color. A positive comparison indicates that the specified pixel is the same color as the boundary color and is therefore part of the boundary. As is evident, a good deal of processing is necessary.

The internal hardware of the EGA/VGA uses a 32-bit data bus, and the host processor uses an 8-bit data bus. The 32-bit bus is composed of eight bits from each display plane. A read operation actually loads all 32 bits simultaneously. A write also uses all 32 of these bits. All of the write modes utilize this 32-bit bus to speed writing operations. Read mode #1 also utilizes this 32-bit bus for compare operations. The EGA/VGA hardware also includes an internal 32-bit comparator. If read mode #1 is active, the 32-bit data read from the four display memory planes is compared on a pixel-by-pixel basis with the value in the Color Compare Register. Any or all planes may take part in the comparison, depending on the corresponding bits in the Color Don't Care Register. Each pixel is composed of up to four bits that correspond to the four display planes. The bit positions in the Color Compare Register and in the Color Don't Care Register correspond to the display bit plane numbers. Any bits in the Color Don't Care Register that are reset to 0 will cause the corresponding bit planes in the display memory to be compared to the data in the corresponding bit positions in the Color Compare Register. Any bits set to 1 in the Color Don't Care Register will not be considered in the comparison.

Suppose that the Color Don't Care Register contained a C hex, which is a 1100 binary. This value would indicate that display planes 0 and 1 should be compared to bit positions 0 and 1 in the Color Compare Register. Note that the 1 in bit positions 2 and 3 causes those corresponding bits in the Color Compare register not to be compared with the corresponding display planes. Also suppose that the Color Compare Register was loaded with the value A hex, which is 1010 binary. If the pixel addressed in the MOV instruction contained a color value of E hex, which is 1110 binary, a positive comparison would occur. This occurs because bits 0 and 1 are identical to bits 0 and 1 of the Color Compare Register, regardless of the values of bits 2 and 3.

Further, consider that the eight neighboring horizontal pixels as addressed by the MOV instruction have hex color values 0, 1, 2, 3, 4, 5, 6, and 7, from left to right. Using the same E hex in the Color Compare Register and C hex in the Color Don't Care Register would result in a comparison being read by the MOV instruction of 22 hex, which is 00100010. This occurs because only the pixel positions corresponding to colors 2 and 6 test positive. Both colors 2 and 6 have a 1 in bit position 1 and a 0 in bit position 0.

The read instruction, as commanded by the MOV byte instruction, reads eight bits of information. The information read is the result of comparing the value in this Color Compare Register with the eight horizontal neighboring pixels addressed in the MOV instruction. All pixels that have the same color as the value in the Color Compare Register test positive and cause a 1 to be loaded into the corresponding bit position in the resultant byte of the MOV instruction. All pixels that are not the same color cause a 0 to be loaded into the corresponding bit position.

The speed benefit is obvious. A single MOV instruction utilizing read mode #1 performs the comparison of eight neighboring horizontal pixels.

CC Color Compare   EGA, VGA **Bits 3–0**

The value in this register represents a 4-bit color. This color value will be compared to eight neighboring horizontal pixels when read mode #1 is selected. The result of this comparison will be returned to the host processor through a MOV instruction. Not all four display planes need to take an active part in the comparison. The Color Don't Care Register determines which planes should be considered in the comparison. This read mode is contrasted to read mode #0, in which the MOV instruction would return the actual data located in the eight pixels of the selected display plane.

10.5.6 Data Rotate Register

7	6	5	4	3	2	1	0
			FS		RC		

Index 03 hex

This register consists of two independent fields, both of which affect the data being written from the host processor to the display memory. The Rotate Count field consists of the binary value used as the number of bits to shift the data input from the host before writing the data to the display planes. This field is set to 0 by default, which causes the data not to be rotated. The binary number in the Rotate Count field determines the number of bits to rotate the byte to the right. The term *rotate* is used because the least significant bit in the byte, bit 0, will be shifted right out of the byte. It will then be rotated back into the byte from the most significant bit, bit 7. This rotate operation occurs before any other operations are performed on the data on its way from the host to the display memory.

Other functions that affect the data are the set/reset function controlled by the Set/Reset and Enable Set/Reset Registers, the write mode selected in the Mode Register, the logical read before write operations controlled by the Function Select field of this register, and the bit mask controlled in the Bit Mask Register. Again, the data rotate operation occurs before any of these other operations.

The rotate field is important because the display memory is organized into independent bit planes. Each byte of display memory consists of eight horizontal neighboring pixels. To write data to a desired bit, it is often necessary to shift the data to properly align the data with the bit position. For example, suppose a 1 needs to be written into horizontal pixel number 101 in the first row of the display. Pixel 101 will be found in the twelfth byte from the starting display address as loaded in the Start Address High and Start Address Low Registers. If the starting address is 0, pixel 101 will be located in byte number 11, which is the twelfth byte. The most significant bit of this byte, bit 7, corresponds to the far-left pixel associated with that byte. This would be pixel number 96. Because pixel number 101 is five pixels to the left of pixel 96, the bit position that corresponds to pixel 101 would be five bits to the right of bit 7. This, of course, is bit 2.

The data byte to be written to pixel 101 is a 01 hex. Therefore, to write a 1 into this bit 2 location, it is necessary to shift into bit position 2 the 1 in bit 0 of the byte to be written. This can be done by rotating the data 7 positions to the right, creating 02 hex. This byte can then be written to the byte number 11, causing pixel 101 to be set to a 1. This operation also has the effect of writing a 0 to pixels 96 through 100 and a 0 in pixel 102 and 103. The Bit Plane Mask Register could be used to mask off all bit positions other than bit 2. This could be accomplished by loading the Bit Plane Mask Register with a 02 hex. This masking operation occurs after the rotation.

The EGA/VGA maintains a 32-bit internal data bus. Certain write modes, as loaded in the WM field of the Mode Register, take advantage of this wide bus to speed up operations. In write mode #2, a full 32 bits of data can be moved in a single instruction cycle from one location in display memory to another location in display memory. It would have been quite useful if the data rotater was placed in this path so that data could be shifted during the move operation. However, this is not the case, and the only place the rotater can be used is in the path from the host processor to the display memory.

The Function Select field modifies the data written by the host with data already in the display memory, before the data is written to the display memory. This operation occurs as the last step before the data is actually written to the display memory. The default setting for this field is 0, which causes the data to be unmodified by the data already present in the display memory. The logical functions possible all require read-before-write operations. The EGA/VGA uses the 32-bit internal latch to temporarily hold the data being read from all four display planes. This latch is then used to logically modify the new data before it is loaded into the display memory. The logical functions of AND, OR, or XOR can be performed on the new data with the data in the 32-bit internal latch. This latch must be preloaded with the correct display data if the logical operation is to perform correctly. This is usually accomplished by a read-before-write operation. Two consecutive move operations would be required, the first to read the data into some dummy register and the second to write the new data to the display.

The data that is read from the display memory can be loaded into a dummy register or memory location because it does not need to be used. The logical operation selected in this field occurs internal to the EGA/VGA. If data is read from the display memory at address A and is to be written into the display memory at address B, the logical operation will involve the data at address A being logically combined with the host data and then stored into the display at address B. This occurs because the read operation at address A loads the 32-bit internal latch with the data located at address A.

The AND operation may be used to reset individual pixels within a bit plane without modifying the neighboring pixels contained within the same byte. Any bits that correspond to a 0 in the host byte to be written will cause the associated bits in the display memory to be reset to 0 after the read-before-write operation. Any bits that are 1s in the host byte will cause the associated bits in the display memory to remain unchanged.

The OR operation may be used to set individual pixels within a bit plane without modifying the neighboring pixels contained within the same byte. Any bits that correspond to 1s in the host byte to be written will cause the associated bits in the display memory to be set to 1 after the read-before-write operation. Any bits that are 0 in the host byte will cause the associated bits in the display memory to remain unchanged.

The XOR operation may be used to invert individual pixels within a bit plane without modifying the neighboring pixels contained within the same byte. Any bits that correspond to 1s in the host byte to be written will cause the associated bits in the display memory to be inverted after the read-before-write operation. Any bits that are 0s in the host byte will cause the associated bits in the display memory to remain unchanged. Inversion means that bits in the display memory that are 1s will be changed to 0s; bits that are 0s in display memory will be changed to 1s.

TABLE 10.12 Function Select Field

Bit 5	Bit 4	Logical Function
0	0	Data is written unmodified
0	1	Data is ANDed with the latched data
1	0	Data is ORed with the latched data
1	1	Data is XORed with the latched data

FS Function Select   EGA, VGA **Bits 5–4**

Data written from the host to the display memory may be logically modified with data already present in the display memory. The logical function selected is determined by the value in this field. The logical functions are listed in Table 10.12.

DR Data Rotate   EGA, VGA **Bits 3–0**

Data written from the host to the display memory will be rotated to the right the number of bits indicated in this field. This rotation will occur before any other logical operations happen to this data on its way to the display memory.

10.5.7 Read Map Select Register

7	6	5	4	3	2	1	0
						R M S	

Index 04 hex

The value in this register determines which of the bit planes should be accessed during a read operation when the EGA/VGA is in READ MODE #0. The EGA/VGA has an internal bus that is 32 bits wide. A 32-bit register is used to latch eight bits of data from each of the four display planes during a read operation. This 32-bit bus must be narrowed to an 8-bit bus when transferring this data to the PC in a typical read operation.

When a bit plane is selected, eight bits from that plane are sent to the host through a multiplexor. When the EGA/VGA is in read mode #0, as set in the RM field of the Mode Register, the data located in the display memory will be sent to the host during a read operation. These eight bits correspond to the single bit values of eight horizontal neighboring pixels in that bit plane. Only one bit plane can be enabled at a time.

This register has no effect when the EGA/VGA is in the Read Mode #1 corresponding to the color compare mode.

RMS Read Map Select   EGA/VGA **Bits 1–0**

Selects which plane to read in Read Mode 0.

10.5.8   Mode Register

7	6	5	4	3	2	1	0
	SR ▪		O/E	RM	▪ TC	WM	

Index 05 hex

The Mode Register contains four fields used to control the EGA/VGA read and write modes. Differences exist in this register between the EGA and the VGA. The EGA has a Test Condition (TC) field in this register that is not present in the VGA. The VGA has a Shift Register Control Field (SR) and an additional bit reserved to allow special shift-register handling for mode 13 hex.

SR Shift Register   VGA **Bit 6–5**

This field controls the output shift registers in order to format the data for straight EGA/VGA addressing, CGA compatibility, or VGA mode 13 hex addressing. The parallel data stored in the display memory must be serialized and placed onto the four bit planes. Data is accessed from display memory 32 bits at a time. The order in which the data is taken from the parallel display memory and placed onto the four serial bit plane outputs determines how the data is supplied.

In the EGA/VGA mode, the data is serialized so that the display memory in bit plane 0 is output on the serial output bit that corresponds to bit plane 0. Likewise, the display memory in bit plane 1 is output on the serial output bit that corresponds to bit plane 1. Bit planes 2 and 3 operate similarly. This is the normal direct addressing EGA/VGA mode of operation. The eight bits from display memory plane 0 are serialized and output so that the far right pixel in the horizontal group of pixels is shifted out first.

In the CGA emulation mode, the data is serialized so that the even bits in the four display bit planes are output on the even bit plane serial outputs, plane 0 and plane 2, and the odd bits are output on the odd bit plane serial outputs, plane 1 and plane 3. Bit plane 0 is output on both the plane 0 and plane 1 serial outputs. Bit plane 1 is also output on both the plane 0 and plane 1 serial outputs. Bit plane 2 is output on both the plane 2 and plane 3 serial outputs, and bit plane 3 is also output on bit plane 2 and bit plane 3. The resultant output to the monitor will be composed of a pixel from bit planes 0 and 1 followed by a pixel from bit planes 2 and 3. At any time, the four serial plane outputs represent two consecutive horizontally neighboring pixels. The 2-bit binary code in these two bits determines the color to use. This emulates the CGA 4-color mode.

In the VGA emulation mode for mode 13 hex, the shift registers are loaded with the four most significant bits of each plane, followed by the four least significant bits of the same plane. Display plane 0 is followed by display plane 1, plane 2, and plane 3. Each plane stores a byte that represents a single pixel. At an identical host address, the four display planes contain four neighboring pixels. All eight bits from each plane are shifted out in order.

=0 Output the data in a straightforward serial fashion with each display plane output on its associated serial output. This is the standard EGA/VGA format.

=1 Output the data in a CGA-compatible 320-by-200, 4-color graphics mode. This is used in display modes 4 and 5.

=2 Output the data eight bits at a time from the four bit planes. This is the format for the VGA mode 13 hex.

SR Shift Register   EGA **Bit 5**

This field controls the output shift registers to format the data for straight EGA addressing or for CGA compatibility. See the SR field above for details.

=0 Output the data in a straightforward serial fashion with each display plane output on its associated serial output. This is the standard EGA format.

=1 Output the data in a CGA compatible 320-by-200, 4-color graphics mode. This is used in display modes 4 and 5.

O/E Odd/Even   EGA, VGA **Bit 4**

Used to select between the EGA/VGA mode or the CGA-compatible mode of operation. This bit should always be the complement of the O/E field in the Memory Mode Register because that field requires the value to be 0 to select the CGA-compatible mode.

=0 Normal operating EGA/VGA mode.

=1 Controls the EGA/VGA so that even host addresses access even display planes, planes 0 and 2, and odd host address access odd display planes, planes 1 and 3.

RM Read Mode   EGA, VGA **Bit 3**

This bit selects which read mode is active in the EGA/VGA. In the default read mode #0, the host processor reads data from the display memory through an assembly language MOV instruction. This instruction addresses eight consecutive horizontal neighboring pixels. The EGA/VGA has an internal 32-bit register that latches eight bits from each of the four display planes. These 32 bits are then multiplexed down to eight bits so that the data can be put onto the 8-bit host bus. Only one plane can be accessed at a time; the plane selected is determined by the Read Map Select Register. Consult this register for further details regarding reading data in the read mode #0.

In read mode #1, the host processor does not read the data from the display memory. Rather, it reads the result of a comparison. The comparison is made between the data in the display memory addressed by the assembly language MOV instruction and the value set in the Color Compare Register. Only those bits enabled in the Color Don't Care Register are used in the comparison. The Read Map Select Register has no effect when the EGA/VGA is in this mode. The resulting eight bits read by the MOV instruction represent eight comparisons. A 1 in a bit position indicates that the comparison is true; a 0 indicates that the comparison is false. See the Color Compare Register for details on read mode #1.

=0 Select read mode #0. Data read from the EGA/VGA represents eight neighboring horizontal pixels in one display plane, as specified in the Read Map Select Register.

=1 Select read mode #1. Data read from the EGA/VGA represents the result of a comparison made between the eight neighboring horizontal pixels from any or all display planes with the value in the Color Compare Register. The display planes selected for the comparison are determined in the Color Don't Care Register.

TC Test Condition   EGA **Bit 2**

This field was specified in the original IBM EGA to cause all EGA outputs to be placed in a high impedance state for testing purposes. Most implementations require that this bit always be set to a 0.

=0 Normal operation.

=1 Forces all EGA outputs to a high-impedance state for testing.

WM Write Mode   EGA, VGA **Bits 1–0**

The EGA/VGA features three write modes that control the manner in which data is written to the display memory.

=0 The default mode, write mode #0, provides several ways to get data from the host to the display memory. One technique allows eight consecutive neighboring horizontal pixels to be written to one or all selected display planes. The Bit Plane Mask Register determines which planes should be written to. The EGA maintains a 32-bit internal data bus. If all four planes are selected, the eight bits presented by the 8-bit host interface bus are copied into all four planes. This mode allows a unique pattern of eight bits to be written to one or all display planes. It does not allow eight pixels of unique data to be written simultaneously to more than one plane. Data written to more than one plane at a time must be identical.

On the way to the display, the data is passed through a pipeline of operations that occur transparently to the host. The first operation is a rotation of the data. The number of bits that the data is rotated to the right is dictated in the Rotate Register. The second operation either selects the data coming from the host and loads it onto the 32-bit bus or selects data from the Set/Reset Register.

The internal 32-bit bus will write to eight neighboring horizontal pixels in all four planes simultaneously. The Enable Set/Reset register determines which of the four planes are loaded with the eight bits from the host and which are written with the value in the Set/Reset register. Any plane not selected in the Enable Set/Reset Register will be loaded with the eight bits from the host. However, only those planes enabled in the Bit Plane Mask Register will actually be affected. Any plane that is selected by the Enable Set/Reset Register will be loaded with the corresponding bits in the Set/Reset Register. The Set/Reset function allows all four display planes to be written with unique data in a single operation. However, only one pixel may be written to with unique data. Eight neighboring pixels will be written to simultaneously with identical data in each pixel.

Once the 32-bit bus is primed, the pipeline passes through a 32-bit arithmetic unit. One input to the arithmetic logic unit is the 32-bit data just described. The second input is the 32-bit internal data latch that contains the last 32 bits of data that were loaded into it. Data is loaded into this read register when a read operation occurs from display memory.

When an assembly language MOV statement addresses display memory, eight consecutive horizontal pixels are read from all four planes into the 32-bit register. In normal operation, a read-before-write operation will occur through back-to-back MOV instructions. The first move instruction will refer to an address in the display memory address space as its source address. It can read this data into any dummy register because it will not be used. This operation is utilized only to load the 32-bit internal latch.

The second MOV instruction uses this same address as the destination field. The source for this instruction is the byte that is to be written to the display memory. If the Set/Reset mode is selected for all four bit planes, via the Enable Set/Reset Register, the source field of this MOV instruction may also be dummy data because it will not be used.

Once the 32-bit read register is primed, the arithmetic unit will perform an "AND," "OR," or "XOR" instruction depending on the Function Select field of the Data Rotate Register. The result of this arithmetic operation will be written to the display memory. However, only those bits selected in the Bit Mask Register will be affected by this arithmetic operation. All bits not selected in the Bit Mask Register will be unmodified.

Refer to the Data Rotate, Bit Plane Mask, Set/Reset, Enable Set/Reset, and Bit Mask Registers for more details on the writing operations related to write mode #0.

=1 Write mode #1. This mode allows eight unique neighboring horizontal pixels in all four bit planes to be moved from one display memory location to another display memory location. The EGA maintains a 32-bit data bus. When this bus is interfaced to the host 8-bit bus, it is restricted to eight unique bits. However, when the bus is used internally, 32 bits may be transferred at a time. This feature provides fast data-transfer operations when the data source and destination is display memory.

An assembly language move-string-of-bytes instruction, MOVSB, or move-string-of-words operation, MOVSW, is best suited for this write mode. The source address is set up in the host DS:SI registers to point to the address in display memory that corresponds to the source data. Likewise, the host ES:DI registers are set to point to the address in display memory that corresponds to the destination. The host CX register is set to the number of words or bytes to transfer, and the MOVSW or MOVSB instruction is executed. Data will be transferred 32 bits at a time.

=2 Write mode #2 writes to eight neighboring horizontal pixels in all four display planes simultaneously. The horizontal pixels are written to with eight identical values in a given plane. Bit plane 0 is written with eight bits of 0 or 1, as determined by the value in bit position 0 of the data byte sent to the EGA from the host. Likewise, planes 1, 2, and 3 are written with eight identical 0 or 1 values corresponding to the value in bit positions 1, 2, and 3 respectively in the data byte sent to the EGA from the host. The result is eight identical neighboring horizontal pixels. In this way, blocks of eight pixels can be written to quickly. However, this is not the purpose of this write mode.

This write mode is most effective when used in conjunction with the Bit Mask Register. If an individual pixel is to be written to, that pixel can be enabled in the Bit Mask Register. When write mode #2 is selected, the four bits of data can reside in the lower four bits of data being sent from the host to the display memory. A MOV instruction can be used for this purpose. Because this pixel's data will be replicated eight times because of the write mode, it is not necessary to shift the data. If more than one pixel is to be written to with the same value, a time savings can be achieved. The pixels do not need to be neighbors because any pattern of up to eight pixels can be enabled through the Bit Mask Register.

=3 Write mode #3 is relevant to the VGA only. Each plane is written to with eight identical bits. The bit value (1 or 0) selected for each of the four display planes (3–0) is derived from the corresponding bit positions in the SR field of the Set/Reset Register. Recall that the Set/Reset Field has four bits, bits 3–0. The data written from the host is rotated according to the value in the Data Rotate Register. It is then ANDed with the Bit Mask Register to form an 8-bit value that acts as the Bit Mask for the write operation. The eight identical bits derived from the Set/Reset Register are masked with this resultant value before being written to the display memory.

10.5.9 Miscellaneous Register

7	6	5	4	3	2	1	0
				M M		C O E	G/A

Index 06 hex

The Miscellaneous Register contains four fields used to control the EGA/VGA display mode, monochrome graphics emulation, and memory mapping.

MM Memory Map   EGA, VGA **Bit 3–2**

The display memory is mapped into the host processor's memory address space. The starting location and the length of the display memory are set in this field, as indicated in Table 10.13.

Memory mode 0 represents a full EGA/VGA. No other display adapter can be resident in the system. Memory mode 1 is also for the EGA/VGA, although other display adapters may reside in the system. Memory mode 2 is for Hercules emulation, and memory mode 3 is for CGA emulation. Some implementations of VGA cards allow up to 1 mbyte of memory.

COE Chain Odd-Even   EGA, VGA **Bit 1**

The host address bit 0 is replaced with a higher-order address bit, causing even host addresses to access planes 0 and 2 and odd CPU addresses to access planes

TABLE 10.13 Display Memory Starting Address

MM	Bit 3	Bit 2	Memory Location	Memory Length
0	0	0	A0000–BFFFF hex	128 K
1	0	1	A0000–AFFFF hex	64 K
2	1	0	B0000–B7FFF hex	32 K
3	1	1	B8000–BFFFF hex	32 K

1 and 3. This mode is useful for Monochrome Graphics Adapter emulation. It allows a 128-Kbyte display buffer with two bits per pixel.

=0 Standard EGA/VGA addressing.

=1 Replace host address bit 0 with a higher-order address bit so that even host addresses access even planes and odd addresses access odd planes. Used for MDA emulation.

G/A Graphics/Alphanumerics Mode   EGA, VGA **Bit 0**

Selects whether the system should be operating in a graphics or an alphanumeric mode. In the EGA, this field should be the complement of the A/G field in the Memory Mode Register.

=0 Select the alphanumeric mode of operation.

=1 Select the graphics mode of operation.

10.5.10   Color Don't Care Register

7	6	5	4	3	2	1	0
				C D C			

Index 07 hex

If the EGA/VGA is in read mode #1, as dictated by the RM field of the Mode Register, host reads from display memory will produce a bit pattern that represents the comparison of eight consecutive horizontal neighboring pixels with selected bits of a color loaded into the Color Compare Register. The bits included in the compare are determined by the bits that are reset in this register. Only bits that are reset to 0 in this register will be considered in the comparison between the display memory and the Color Compare Register. The read instruction is initiated via a MOV instruction.

The source field of this instruction is the desired starting address for the eight consecutive horizontal pixels in the display memory that are to be compared. The destination field is the place where the resultant bits from the eight comparisons should be loaded in the host. A 1 in a bit position corresponds to a positive comparison; a 0 corresponds to the associated bits not comparing. See the Read Mode (RM) field in the Mode Register and the Color Compare Register for more details.

Each of the four bits in this field operate independently, and each adheres to Table 10.14.

=0 Do not consider the corresponding bit in the Color Compare register and the data from the corresponding bit plane in the comparison.

TABLE 10.14 Color Don't Care Fields

Bit #	Bit Plane Affected
0	0
1	1
2	2
3	3

=1 Consider the corresponding bit in the Color Compare register and the data from the corresponding bit plane in the comparison.

10.5.11 Bit Mask Register

7	6	5	4	3	2	1	0
				BM			

Index 08 hex

The display memory is organized into bit four planes. Each pixel is represented by one bit in each bit plane. A byte of data in a bit plane in display memory corresponds to a single bit in eight horizontal neighboring pixels. The low-order bit of the byte represents the far-right pixel in the group, and the high-order bit in the byte represents the far-left pixel in the group. To write to a pixel or group of pixels within an eight-pixel group without disturbing the contents of the other pixels in the group, it is necessary to mask out the undesired pixels.

The undesired pixels can be masked from the write operation by setting the corresponding bits in this register to a 0. The low-order bit of this register corresponds to the far-right pixel, and the high-order bit corresponds to the far-left pixel. If all bits in this register are set to 0, writing data will have no effect in display memory because all bits will be masked out. Bit masking occurs as the last step before data is written to display memory.

In write mode 3, the value in the Bit Mask Register is ANDed with the host data byte before it is used as the bit mask. See the Memory Mode Register for details of Write Mode #3.

Each of the eight bits in this field operates independently, and each adheres to the following rule.

=0 All bits reset to 0 mask the corresponding bits in the display memory; thus, these pixels cannot be modified during a host write operation.

=1 All bits set to 1 allow the corresponding bits in the display memory to be modified by a write operation.

TABLE 10.15   Attribute Controller Registers

Register Name	Index (Hex)	Write (Hex) (EGA / VGA)	Read (Hex) (VGA)
Address	—	3C0	3C1
Palette	0–F	3C0	3C1
Mode Control	10	3C0	3C1
Overscan Color	11	3C0	3C1
Color Plane Enable	12	3C0	3C1
Horizontal Pixel Panning	13	3C0	3C1
Color Plane Enable (VGA only)	14	3C0	3C1

10.6   THE ATTRIBUTE CONTROLLER REGISTERS

The Attribute Controller Registers consist of 20 registers for the EGA and 21 registers for the VGA. None of these registers has a unique host port address. One register exists in the host port address space at 3C0 hex. This register represents both the Attribute Controller Address Register and the Attribute Controller Data Register. The programmer accesses the Attribute Controller Data Registers by alternately loading index values and data values into this 3C0 hex port address. The index values range from 0 to 13 hex for the EGA and 0 to 14 hex for the VGA. An additional register called the Color Enable Register is available on the VGA. The Attribute Address Register selects one of the Attribute Data Registers as the current active register. See the Attribute Address Register below for details. The Attribute Controller Registers are listed in Table 10.15.

10.6.1   Attribute Address Register

7	6	5	4	3	2	1	0
		P A S		A D R			

Write Port 3C0 hex (EGA)
Write Port 3C0 hex (VGA)
Read Port 3C1 hex (VGA)

This register selects the attribute controller registers that will be selected during a write operation for the EGA/VGA or a read operation for the VGA. This address register is different from the other EGA/VGA address registers. Unlike all other address/data port pairs, the attribute controller has only one port dedicated to it. This port resides at host location 3C0 hex. An internal hardware flip-flop is used to multiplex this port to load either this Address Attribute Register or one of the Attribute Registers. When the flip-flop is in the clear state, it causes data output from the host to port 3C0 hex to be directed to this Address Attribute Register. When the flip-flop is in the set state, data written to this port is directed to whichever Attribute Register index is loaded into the AA field of this register.

The Attribute Registers consist of the sixteen Palette Registers, the Mode Control Register, the Overscan Color Register, the Color Plane Enable Register, and the Horizontal Pixel Panning Register. The VGA also includes the Color Select Register.

The flip-flop is controlled indirectly by the host. When a host assembly language input port instruction, IN, is issued to the Input Status #1 Register, the flip-flop is cleared. This register resides at port address 3BA hex for monochrome implementations and 3DA hex for color implementations. Once cleared, the path is set so that outputs to this 3C0 hex port load an index that points to one of the Attribute Registers into the Address Register itself. This is equivalent to loading any of the other Address Registers. The next assembly language output port (OUT) instruction written to this 3C0 hex port will load the indexed Attribute Register. After the output occurs, the flip-flop automatically changes state. The following output will be directed once again to the Attribute Address Register.

In addition to the address field the Attribute Address Register contains a Palette Address Source (PAS) field. This field is used to control the operation of the dual-ported palette RAM. If the host is to have control of the palette registers during a load operation, it must reset the PA field to 0. In order for the display memory to access this palette RAM, the PAS field must be set to a 1.

PAS   Palette Address Source   EGA, VGA **Bit 5**

Determines whether the palette dual-ported RAM should be accessed by the host or by the EGA display memory.

=0   Allows the host to access the palette RAM. Disables the display memory from gaining access to the palette.

=1   Allows the display memory to access the palette RAM. Disables the host from gaining access to the palette.

ADR   Attribute Address   EGA, VGA **Bits 4–0**

Points to one of the Attribute Address Registers, as shown in Table 10.16.

TABLE 10.16 Attribute Address Registers

AA Field	Register
00–0F hex	Palette Registers 0–15
10 hex	Mode Control Register
11 hex	Overscan Color Register
12 hex	Color Plane Enable Register
13 hex	Horizontal Pixel Panning Register

10.6.2 Palette Registers

Secondary Red

7	6	5	4	3	2	1	0
		SR	SG	SB	R	G	B

from color select Reg.

Index 00–0F hex

The color palette is a random access memory (RAM) that is used to indirectly map the data contained in the individual pixel locations of the display memory into colors. The palette consists of a RAM memory that is sixteen locations long. It is addressed by the value in each pixel location of the display memory. From the host's perspective, the functioning of the palette in the EGA and VGA is identical. However, the manner in which a color is produced by the EGA or VGA is drastically different. The EGA Palette Registers contain the color codes. The output of the EGA palette drives the monitor directly. The VGA palette contains addresses. The output of the VGA palette addresses a second set of registers called the Color Registers. The actual color codes are stored in the Color Registers. This double level of registers serves no purpose other than providing compatibility between the VGA and EGA. One of the greatest advantages of the VGA is the extended set of Color Registers.

The concept of a palette greatly enhances a graphics system. A pixel in display memory is not associated with any color. Rather, the pixel simply contains a binary code. This binary value is used to address a particular location within the palette. Changing the value of the pixel merely changes the address presented to the color palette. The color codes reside inside the palette. The width of each location in the palette RAM determines the number of colors possible. The number of registers within the palette RAM determines the number of simultaneous colors that can be displayed.

A second advantage of the palette RAM is that colors may be modified without altering the actual data within the color table. For example, suppose several pixels have the value 1 and several others have the value 2. It might be desirable to map both the value 1 and value 2 pixels into the same color, say color 3. If no palette were available, a program would have to read all of the display memory, determine which pixels had values 1 or 2, and change them all to color 3. This process would be irreversible; there would be no way to get back to the original colors because it would not be possible to distinguish which of the color 3 values originally came from the value 1 colors and which came from the value 2 colors. By contrast, with the palette it is necessary only to change the values in palette locations 1 and 2 to the value 3. Reversing the process simply requires changing palette location 1 back to a 1 and changing location 2 back to a 2.

The number of bits per pixel determines the number of simultaneous colors that may be displayed. The four display planes of the EGA, or the EGA-compatible modes of the VGA, allow sixteen simultaneous colors to be displayed. In the VGA advanced mode 13 hex, eight bits are assigned per pixel, allowing 256 simultaneous colors. The Color Registers are eighteen bits wide with six bits assigned to each color. Thus, there are 32 possible levels of saturation for each color, or 256K possible colors. In this mode, the VGA palette acts as an index into the Color Registers and should not be modified.

In the EGA, an individual palette RAM location consists of a field dedicated to each of the three colors, red, green, and blue. Two bits are used for each color, totaling six bits per palette RAM location. As a result, the width of the palette is six bits. These red, green, and blue 2-bit color codes produce the color code sent to the monitor. In the EGA, the two bits representing each color are sent to the monitor as six digital signals. This format is called *direct drive* or *digital RGB*. The term *RGB* stands for *red, green, and blue*.

In the VGA, each register in the palette consists of a six-bit field that addresses one of the first 64 Color Registers. The color codes are stored in these Color Registers. The output of the Color Registers drive three digital-to-analog (D/A) converters. These three analog signals are output to the monitor. This format is called *analog RGB*.

In the EGA and in the EGA-compatible modes of the VGA, the data in the Palette Registers determines the amount of red, green, and blue in the resultant color. Because there are two bits per color, there are four possible levels of saturation for each color. The coding is *R* for red and *SR* for secondary red. Likewise, *G* and *B* are for green and blue, and *SG* and *SB* are for secondary green and secondary blue. The 2-bit code determines the intensity or saturation of the color, as listed in Table 10.17.

The colors may be combined to produce different hues or shades of colors. For example, if all six fields are set to 1, the resultant color would be highest-intensity white. If the secondary red (R) and the secondary green (G) are both set, the resultant color will be secondary yellow.

SR Secondary Red   EGA, VGA **Bit 5**

  0 = No secondary red present.

  1 = Secondary red present.

TABLE 10.17 Sixteen-color Intensity Saturation

(SR, SG, SB)	(R, G, B)	Color Saturation	
0	0	No intensity	0%
0	1	Lowest intensity	33%
1	0	Medium intensity	66%
1	1	Highest intensity	100%

SG Secondary Green   EGA, VGA **Bit 4**

  0 = No secondary green present.
  1 = Secondary green present.

SB Secondary Blue   EGA, VGA **Bit 3**

  0 = No secondary blue present.
  1 = Secondary blue present.

R Red   EGA, VGA **Bit 2**

  0 = No red present.
  1 = Red present.

G Green   EGA, VGA **Bit 1**

  0 = No green present.
  1 = Green present.

B Blue   EGA, VGA **Bit 0**

  0 = No blue present.
  1 = Blue present.

10.6.3 Mode Control Register

7	6	5	4	3	2	1	0
IPS▪	PCS▪	PPC▪		B/I	ELG	DT	G/A

Index 10 hex

This register contains four fields that control the EGA/VGA mode with respect to the attributes. It also contains three fields that control the VGA.

IPS Internal Palette Size   VGA **Bit 7**

The VGA Palette Registers each contain a field that is six bits wide. The output of the Palette Registers address the 256 Color Registers. The VGA contains four display planes that allow sixteen simultaneous colors to be displayed.

It is possible to segment the Color Registers into sixteen groups of registers, each group consisting of sixteen registers. It is also possible to segment the Color Registers into four groups of registers, each group consisting of 64 registers. The first segmentation uses all six bits from the Palette Registers as the six low-order bits addressing the Color Registers. The upper-order two bits are provided through the C67 field of the Color Select Register. Thus, it is possible to select from four possible EGA-type palettes by simply changing the value in the C67 field. The second segmentation uses the four low-order bits in the Palette Registers as the four low-order address bits. It uses the C45 and C67 fields of the Color Select Register to obtain the four high-order address bits. In this way, the Color Registers can be used to rapidly select one of sixteen possible color selections, each selection consisting of the sixteen simultaneously displayed colors.

=0 The Palette Register's bits 4 and 5 provide the address bits 4 and 5 to the Color Registers.

=1 The C45 field of the Color Register provides the address bits 4 and 5 to the Color Registers.

PCS Pixel Clock Select   VGA **Bit 6**

Controls the clocking of the PELs to allow eight bits of data to select a color in mode 13 hex. This field is used in conjunction with the Shift Register (SR) field of the Mode Register. When the SR field is set to 2, data is loaded into the Shift Registers in two operations, providing eight bits of data from each display plane. This value of 2 is operative only during mode 13 hex. During this mode, the PCS field is set to 1.

=0 The pixel data is changed at each cycle of the dot clock.

=1 The pixel data is changed every second cycle of the dot clock.

PPC Pixel Panning Compatibility   VGA **Bit 5**

This field allows a section of the screen to be panned independently from the second section during a split-screen mode of operation.

=0 Prevents a line compare from affecting the output of the Pixel Panning Register.

=1 Allows a line compare to affect the output of the Horizontal Pixel Panning Register and the Byte Panning (BP) field of the Preset Row Scan Register.

B/I Enable Blink or Intensity   EGA, VGA **Bit 3**

This field controls whether the most significant bit of the character attribute byte, bit 7, is used to select background colors or to enable blinking. If it is used to enable blinking, whenever bit 7 of the character attribute byte is a 1, the character will blink. If bit 7 is a 0, the character will not blink. In this mode of operation, the background color is limited to one of eight possible colors. This occurs because the background color field of the character attribute byte is limited to three bits. These three bits address Color Palette Registers 0–7.

The blinking rate is determined from the vertical refresh period. In the standard implementations of the EGA, the vertical sync rate is divided by 32 to determine the blink rate. Because the vertical sync rate is normally on the order of 60 cycles per second, the resultant blink rate is about two blinks per second. Other implementations of the EGA may control the blinking in a different manner.

In monochrome modes, blinking causes the character to switch between on and off. In color modes, the most significant bit feeding the color palette is toggled. This causes the character color to switch between the lower and upper halves of the color palette. For example, a character with foreground color 3 and background color E hex would alternately change to foreground color D hex and background color 6 during the blinking cycle. In the graphics modes, the most significant bit addressing the color palette is switched, similarly altering the color codes.

The cursor blinks at its own rate. The standard implementations blink the cursor at twice the rate at which the character blinks. The vertical sync pulse is divided by 16 to derive this blink rate.

If this field is used to select a background intensity, bit 7 of the character attribute byte is used in conjunction with bits 4–6 to select a background color, and no blinking feature is available. The four most significant bits of the attribute byte are thus dedicated to the background color and are used to select one of sixteen background colors in palette locations 0–15.

=0 Use bit 7 of the character attribute code to select a background color. Do not allow blinking.

=1 Use bit 7 of the character attribute code to enable or disable blinking. This is the default mode of operation.

ELG Enable Line Graphics Character Codes   EGA, VGA **Bit 2**

The line graphics character codes in the Monochrome Display Adapter are C0 hex to DF hex. These character codes represent graphics characters that include lines, corners, and some shapes. These were used to perform rudimentary graphics without relying on a graphics display adapter or forcing a display adapter to go into a graphics mode. When character fonts that are nine characters wide are used, as is common in the Monochrome Display Adapter, the ninth horizontal dot of the character in the graphics set should mimic the eighth dot of the same line. This extends the lines through the intercharacter spacing and connects horizontal lines from one character to the next.

When character sets are used that do not have special characters associated with line graphics in character codes C0 hex to DF hex, this field should be set to 0.

=0 Set the ninth dot of the character to the background color, regardless of the character code.

=1 Set the ninth dot of the character to the same value as the eighth dot of the character for all graphics line characters.

DT Display type   EGA, VGA **Bit 1**

Dictates whether the display attributes should be displayed as color display attributes or as IBM Monochrome Display Adapter attributes.

=0 Select color display attributes.

=1 Select IBM Monochrome Display Adapter attributes.

G/A Graphics/Alphanumeric   EGA, VGA **Bit 0**

Selects whether the display is in an alphanumeric or graphics mode. In the EGA, this field should be the inverse of the A/G field in the Memory Mode Register and the same value as the G/A field in the Miscellaneous Register. In the VGA, this field should be the same value as the G/A field in the Miscellaneous Register.

=0 Select alphanumeric mode.

=1 Select graphics mode.

10.6.4 Overscan Color Register

7	6	5	4	3	2	1	0
		SR	SG	SB	R	G	B

Index 11 hex

The border region or porch of the display surrounds the active display region. It exists on the top and bottom of the active display region. Its vertical size is determined by the distance between the vertical display enable period and the vertical blanking, as dictated by the Vertical Display End Register and the Start and End Vertical Blanking Registers. Its horizontal extent exists between the horizontal display enable period and the horizontal blanking, as dictated by the Horizontal Display End Register and the Start and End Horizontal Blanking Registers.

The border region occurs before the blanking begins in both the horizontal and vertical dimensions. Thus, a color needs to be selected for display during this period. Normally this color is 0, which is black. *Note:* Most EGA/VGA implementations do not operate satisfactorily when a color other than black is selected for the border region.

The color coding in this Overscan Register is identical to the color coding used in the Color Palette Registers. See the Color Palette Registers for details.

SR Secondary Red   EGA, VGA   **Bit 5**

0 = No secondary red present.
1 = Secondary red present.

SG Secondary Green   EGA, VGA   **Bit 4**

0 = No secondary green present.
1 = Secondary green present.

SB Secondary Blue   EGA, VGA   **Bit 3**

0 = No secondary blue present.
1 = Secondary blue present.

R Red   EGA, VGA   **Bit 2**

0 = No red present.
1 = Red present.

G Green   EGA, VGA   **Bit 1**

0 = No green present.
1 = Green present.

B Blue   EGA, VGA   **Bit 0**

0 = No blue present.
1 = Blue present.

10.6.5 Color Plane Enable Register

7	6	5	4	3	2	1	0
		▪V S M			C P	E	

Index 12 hex

This register controls which plane will be enabled during the display process. Normally all planes are enabled, providing four address lines to the sixteen palette registers. If a plane is deselected, the corresponding data that addresses the palette registers is set to 0. Deselected planes can still be written to or read from in a normal fashion. This Color Plane Enable field affects only the output path between the display memory and the color palette. The effect of deselecting a plane is that the display will not contain any data located in that plane. Selecting color planes is illustrated in Figure 10.4.

If only plane 0 is selected, a 0 will address palette location 0 and a 1 will address palette location 1. If only plane 1 is selected, a 0 will address palette location 0 and a 1 will address palette location 2.

Table 10.18 illustrates this single-plane palette addressing. Note that a pixel in the selected plane that is a 0 always addresses palette location 0, regardless of the plane in which pixel is located. This occurs because all other planes are forced to 0.

The ability to select or deselect display planes is by no means limited to single planes. It is possible that at a given pixel location, neither plane will be on, either plane will be on, or both planes will be on. Table 10.19 illustrates the two plane possibilities using planes 1 and 2.

Table 10.20 illustrates the three plane possibilities using plane 1, 2, and 3.

This Color Plane Enable Register can also be used to display animation. One plane can be selected while the other planes are being manipulated. If the selected

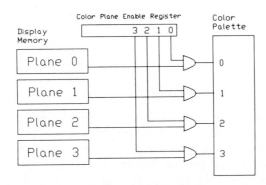

Figure 10.4 Selecting Colors

TABLE 10.18 One-plane Palette Addressing

	Palette Location	
Single Plane Selected	Pixel=0	Pixel=1
0	0	1
1	0	2
2	0	4
3	0	8

TABLE 10.19 Two-plane Palette Addressing

Plane 2	Plane 1	Palette Location
0	0	0
0	1	2
1	0	4
1	1	6

TABLE 10.20 Three-plane Palette Addressing

Plane 3	Plane 2	Plane 1	Palette Location
0	0	0	0
0	0	1	2
0	1	0	4
0	1	1	6
1	0	0	8
1	0	1	10
1	1	0	12
1	1	1	14

display planes are changed periodically, motion effects can be achieved. Consider a case in which each display plane is enabled for a tenth of a second. The selecting sequence is planes 0, 1, 2, 3, 0, 1, 2, 3, ... enabled. In a motion picture, each frame on the film is shot in sequence. A figure moving across the screen moves a little bit in each successive frame. The frames on the film are numbered sequentially and never repeat. These frames could be mapped into a mod 4 picture plane counter to simulate the playback of this film.

Plane 0 would represent the image taken at t=0.0 second, plane 1 would represent the image taken at t=0.1 second, plane 2 at t = 0.2 second, plane 3 at t = 0.4 second, and plane 0 at t = 0.5 second. If the playback rate is slow enough to handle the time necessary to get the image being represented onto the next display plane, animation can be achieved. Again, this animation is not limited to one plane at a time.

In the EGA, this register also contains a Video Status MUX field. This selects two of the RGB direct-drive six-color outputs to be available on the DIA field of the Input Status #1 Register. This is used for diagnostic purposes.

VSM Video Status MUX   EGA **Bits 5–4**

Selects two of the six RGB outputs to be loaded into the DIA field of the Input Status #1 Register. See Input Status #1 Register for details on which colors get selected depending on this 2-bit field.

CPE Color Planes Enable   EGA, VGA **Bits 3–0**

The display planes may be selected or deselected depending on the values in this field. Any combination of display planes can be selected simultaneously.

bit 0 = 0 Do not select display plane 0.
bit 0 = 1 Select display plane 0.
bit 1 = 0 Do not select display plane 1.
bit 1 = 1 Select display plane 1.
bit 2 = 0 Do not select display plane 2.
bit 2 = 1 Select display plane 2.
bit 3 = 0 Do not select display plane 3.
bit 3 = 1 Select display plane 3.

10.6.6 Horizontal Pixel Panning Register

7	6	5	4	3	2	1	0
				H P P			

Index 12 hex

The display memory is organized into four bit planes. Each plane is organized as consecutive bytes with respect to the host processor and the graphics processor, and as individual pixels with respect to the output video refresh circuitry. Each byte of each of the four display planes has up to eight horizontally neighboring pixels. The first byte of information displayed on the screen in the upper left corner is determined by the value in the Start Address High and Start Address Low Registers. In an alphanumeric mode, the starting address value corresponds to a character; in a graphics mode, this corresponds to eight neighboring horizontal pixels.

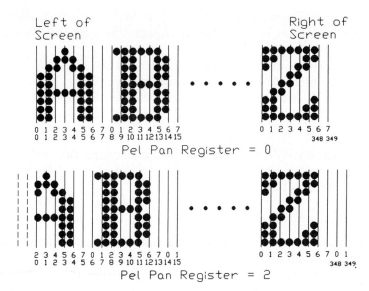

Figure 10.5 Smooth Panning

Panning is the term used when the display slides horizontally across the display. Using "windows" terminology, this would be stated as "moving the window horizontally across the data." It is possible to pan the display in an alphanumeric mode one character at a time by incrementing or decrementing the starting address.

If smooth panning is desired, this character-by-character panning will not suffice. It is therefore necessary to pan horizontally on a pixel-by-pixel basis. Smooth panning is illustrated in Figure 10.5.

In the standard font sizes, the character box is eight pixels wide. However, in larger character fonts or in the monochrome mode, the character box is greater than eight pixels wide. The standard EGA/VGA implementations allow a maximum character width of nine characters when in the monochrome alphanumeric mode. The standard selected for shifting the image is determined by the pixel size and is illustrated in Table 10.21.

This table is read as follows: If an 8-dot/character alphanumeric mode is selected and the HPP field is 0, the first dot shifted out will be the bit 0 in the word. This corresponds to the less significant bit and to the far right pixel displayed.

Likewise, if the 9-dot/character alphanumeric mode is selected and the HPP field is 4, the first dot to be shifted out will be the dot corresponding to the bit 3. Note that in the nine-dot/character mode, bit 8, which is the copy of bit 7, is actually displayed on the right side of the character and bit 7 is displayed on the left side. This does not affect the display because neighboring character boxes touch anyway. The left side of one pixel touches the right side of the next

TABLE 10.21 Horizontal Pixel Panning

	Value in the HPP Field
Dots / Character	*0,1,2,3,4,5,6,7,8,9,A,B,C,D,E,F*
6	2,3,4,5,6,7
8	0,1,2,3,4,5,6,7
9	8,0,1,2,3,4,5,6,7
12	B,A,9,8,0,1,2,3,4,5,6,7
16	F,E,D,C,B,A,9,8,0,1,2,3,4,5,6,7

pixel. In this table, the sequence from left to right of the bit positions corresponds to the shifting sequence. Because the CRT is refreshing from left to right, the first pixel out the shifter should be the far right pixel in the word. The far right pixel corresponds to the least significant bit.

In a graphics mode, incrementing or decrementing the starting address would shift the display eight pixels to the left or right. To achieve a smooth pan, the panning must also occur on a pixel-by-pixel basis. Graphics modes always assume an 8-dot/character size.

HPP Horizontal Pixel Pan   EGA, VGA **Bits 3–0**

The number of pixels to shift the video data horizontally to the left. This affects the starting far left pixel and the ending far right pixel on the screen. It is used in conjunction with the starting address for smooth panning applications.

10.6.7 Color Select Register

7	6	5	4	3	2	1	0
				C67∙		C45∙	

Index 14 hex

This register contains two fields which, combined with the output bits from the palette register, determine the 8-bit address used to select one of the 256 Color Registers. It is possible to segment the Color Registers into sixteen groups with each group consisting of sixteen registers. This is useful because in all but mode 13 hex, the maximum number of simultaneous colors that can be displayed is sixteen. Thus, it is possible to rapidly select from sixteen different color palettes by simply modifying the C45 and C67 fields of this register.

A second technique segments the Color Registers into four groups with each group consisting of 64 registers. This is useful because the EGA palette is 64 colors long. Thus, it is possible to rapidly select from four different EGA palettes by modifying the C67 field of this register. See the Mode Control Register for details.

C67 Color Register Address Bits 6 and 7 VGA **Bits 3–2**

Address bits 6 and 7 combine with the six output bits from the color palette to form the eight address bits to the Color Registers.

C45 Color Register Address Bits 4 and 5 VGA **Bits 1–0**

Address bits 4 and 5 combine with the two address bits from the C67 field above and the four low-order output bits from the color palette to form the eight address bits to the Color Registers. This field is used only if the IPS field of the Mode Control Register is set to 1.

10.7 COLOR REGISTERS

10.7.1 PEL Address Write Mode Register

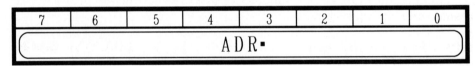

7	6	5	4	3	2	1	0

ADR ▪

VGA Write Port 3C8 hex
      Read Port 3C8 hex

ADR Address During Write Mode VGA **Bits 7–0**

This register contains the 8-bit address used to access one of the 256 Color Registers during a write operation. This register is similar to the address registers associated with the other register groups in that it occupies a location in the host I/O port address space and that it indexes one of the internal registers. It differs from the others in that it signifies that a write operation is to occur. A write operation consists of three byte outputs to the PEL Data Register. These three outputs load the red, green, and blue components of the indexed Color Register. The PEL Data Register can be thought of as an 18-bit-wide register that loads six bits during each output operation.

At the conclusion of the third output to the PEL Data Register, the address in this PEL Address Write Register automatically increments. This feature allows the programmer to output up to 768 consecutive bytes to the PEL Data Register without having to modify the PEL Address Write Register after its initial setting.

The PEL Address Write Register is a read/write register that allows the programmer to interrogate its current value. The operation of the PEL Address

Register Write Register is identical to that of the PEL Address Read Register except that the latter is used for read operations and the former is a write-only register.

10.7.2 PEL Address Read Mode Register

7	6	5	4	3	2	1	0
			ADR ▪				

VGA   Write Port 3C7 hex

ADR Address During Read Mode   **VGA Bits 7–0**

This register contains the 8-bit address used to access one of the 256 Color Registers during a read operation. This register is identical in function to the PEL Address Write Mode Register. It differs from this register in that it signifies that a read operation is to occur. A read operation consists of three byte inputs from the PEL Data Register. These three inputs read the red, green, and blue components of the indexed Color Register. The PEL Data Register can be thought of as an 18-bit-wide register. Six of these bits are loading into the PEL Data Register before each input operation. The first load occurs when the PEL Address Read Register is loaded.

At the conclusion of the third input from the PEL Data Register, the address in this PEL Address Read Register automatically increments. This feature allows the programmer to input up to 768 consecutive bytes from the PEL Data Register without having to modify the PEL Address Read Register after its initial setting.

10.7.3 PEL Data Register

7	6	5	4	3	2	1	0
			DATA ▪				

VGA   Write Port 3C9 hex
       Read Port 3C9 hex

DATA Data Value   **VGA Bits 7–0**

This register is an 18-bit-wide register used to interface the host and the 256 Color Registers. This data register is similar to the other data registers except that it is eighteen bits wide. Each Color Register contains three primary colors, each color represented by six bits. The host data bus is eight bits wide, and therefore only one of these components can be accessed at a time. The data written to and read from this register interacts with the Color Register that is indexed by the PEL Address Write or PEL Address Read Register. When the PEL Address Write Register is loaded with an index, internal hardware automatically selects the red component of the PEL Data Register. An output to this register loads this component with the six low-order bits. The hardware automatically changes to point to the green component of this register. Again an output loads this component with the six low-order bits. Similarly, the blue portion is loaded next. Once all three outputs have occurred, the PEL Address Write Register is autoincremented and the next output to the PEL Data Register will load the red portion once again. Because the address is incremented, the next higher Color Register will be affected. The function is identical in the read operations, with the PEL Address Read Register being affected.

10.7.4   DAC State Register

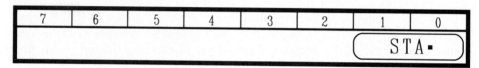

VGA   Read Port 3C7 hex

STA DAC State Value   VGA **Bits 1–0**

These two bits reflect whether a read or a write operation is in effect.

  =0 A read operation is in effect. The PEL Address Read Register was accessed last.

  =3 A write operation is in effect. The PEL Address Write Register was accessed last.

10.7.5   PEL Mask Register

VGA   Write Port 3C6 hex
VGA   Read Port 3C6 hex

MASK Mask Value   VGA **Bits 7–0**

This register is a read/write register; however, it is not to be modified by the programmer. It is initialized to FF hex by the BIOS Mode Set call.

Chapter 11

The EGA/VGA BIOS

11.1 EGA/VGA BIOS DESCRIPTIONS

The EGA/VGA Basic Input Output System (BIOS) resides in the host memory space beginning at address C0000 hex and extending to C4000 hex. This BIOS contains an initialization section invoked during bootstrap operations, code to control the EGA/VGA, and several character generators. The EGA BIOS source listings are provided in the IBM documentation. However, the BIOS source listings of the VGA are not provided. Because of the lack of source listings for the VGA, the EGA BIOS descriptions in this book are more comprehensive than are the VGA descriptions.

During the bootstrap operation, the host system BIOS scans the ROM space, looking for a ROM header that indicates that an EGA is present. If it finds this header, it performs a FAR CALL to address C0003 hex. This is the location of the start of the EGA BIOS initialization code. The first three bytes of ROM, beginning at address C0000 hex, contain a signature. At the starting address of C0003 hex resides a JMP SHORT instruction to the beginning of the EGA BIOS code. The jump is necessary because more signature information is present in the next several bytes, including the IBM copyright information and the BIOS creation date.

Once the short jump is taken, the code initializes the video vectors within the PC interrupt locations in the lower PC memory space. Next, it determines the configuration of the card and performs a hardware diagnostic. At the conclusion of the diagnostics, a tone will be issued indicating that the bootstrap operation was completed successfully. If this operation was not successful, a series of tones will signify the nature of the problem. At completion, a FAR RET instruction returns control to the host system's BIOS ROM.

The second section of the BIOS is dedicated to routines that provide all of the processing necessary to respond to the interrupt 10 hex calls. In this book, these interrupt calls are commonly referred to as the INT 10h calls. All INT

10h calls are directed to the BIOS through the interrupt vector located in the four bytes of memory beginning at 00040 hex in the interrupt vector table.

This interrupt was set up during initialization. Once the interrupt has been invoked, all registers are saved, and the AH register is interrogated to see which software handler to call. The AH register must contain a value from 0 to 13hex for the EGA and from 0 to 1C hex for the VGA. This value determines which BIOS subroutine is invoked. If the value of the AH register is greater than 13 hex for the EGA or 1C hex for the VGA, another interrupt is invoked. This interrupt is number 42 hex. This gives the programmer the added facility of extending the EGA BIOS into a different BIOS or into host RAM memory.

If the value in the AH register is within the range of the EGA/VGA, it is used to determine which subroutine to invoke. In some cases, the AH register defines a group of similar functions, and the value in the AL register is used to determine which subroutine within the group should be invoked.

The host processor general-purpose registers—for example, BX, CX, and DX, are most often used to hold additional input parameters. At other times, these registers are used to hold output parameters passed back to the routine that invoked the BIOS. The SI or DI and DS or ES register pairs are sometimes used as input or output parameters. They traditionally hold pointers to some data buffer.

The third section of the BIOS is filled with the character tables. An 8-by-8 character table and an 8-by-14 dot table are available on the EGA. An 8-by-8 character table, an 8-by-14 character table, and an 8-by-16 character table are available on the VGA. The address within host memory at which these tables reside is made available to the programmer through a BIOS call.

11.2 DISPLAY MODES

11.2.1 AH = 00 Hex: Set Video Mode (EGA/VGA)

The EGA/VGA board has a standard set of display modes that control the resolution, type of display, and number of pages, along with several other features. These modes require a number of registers to be modified to achieve the desired result. It is advisable to use the interrupt 10 hex feature of the EGA/VGA BIOS when changing modes. This ensures that all of the features, some of which are redundant within several registers, are properly handled. However, it is possible to alter these registers individually to achieve similar modes or to create new modes. Caution is advised because modifying these registers incorrectly can, in some reported cases, damage the monitor and/or the EGA/VGA adapter board.

The current video mode is stored in host memory in the video buffer used by the BIOS interrupt routines. The mode is stored in location 449 hex. The selected display mode determines the number of characters in a scan row and is equivalent to the number of columns. The number of characters is loaded into memory location 44A hex. The mode also dictates the total length, in bytes, of the active display page. The total length is loaded into memory location 44C hex.

The key value sent to this interrupt routine in AL and the corresponding display mode that will become active are contained in Table 11.1 for the EGA and Table 11.2 for the VGA. Also included are the resolution of the screen in columns and rows, the character box size, the total number of possible colors, the number of possible pages available in this mode, the display format, and the resolution of the display page.

The "Pages" column in Table 11.1 contains entries with more than one number—for example, "1, 2, 4". This indicates the number of pages available when the EGA is equipped with 64 Kbytes, 128 Kbytes, or 256 Kbytes of display memory, respectively.

The code "bw" stands for black-and-white or synonymously monochrome. The codes "16-color," "4-color," and "2-color" stand for the 16-, 4-, and 2-color modes

TABLE 11.1 EGA Display Modes

AL (Hex)	Mode (Hex)	Resolution (# Cols. by # Rows)	Box Size	# Colors	# Pages	Display Format	Resolution in Pixels
00	0	40 by 25	8 by 8	16-color bw	8	Alpha	320 by 200
	0*	40 by 25	8 by 14	16-color bw	8	Alpha	320 by 350
01	1	40 by 25	8 by 8	16-color	8	Alpha	320 by 200
	1*	40 by 25	8 by 14	16-color	8	Alpha	320 by 350
02	2	80 by 25	8 by 8	16-color bw	8	Alpha	640 by 200
	2*	80 by 25	8 by 14	16-color bw	4,8	Alpha	640 by 350
03	3	80 by 25	8 by 8	16-color	8	Alpha	640 by 200
	3*	80 by 25	8 by 14	16-color	4,8	Alpha	640 by 350
04	4	40 by 25	8 by 8	4-color	1	Graph	320 by 200
05	5	40 by 25	8 by 8	4-color bw	1	Graph	320 by 200
06	6	80 by 25	8 by 8	2-color bw	1	Graph	640 by 200
07	7	80 by 25	9 by 14	bw	8	Alpha	720 by 350
0D	D	40 by 25	8 by 8	16-color	2,4,8	Graph	320 by 200
0E	E	80 by 25	8 by 8	16-color	1,2,4	Graph	640 by 200
0F	F	80 by 25	8 by 14	bw	1,2	Graph	640 by 350
10	10	80 by 25	8 by 14	16/64-color	1,2	Graph	640 by 350

TABLE 11.2 VGA Display Modes

AL (Hex)	Mode (Hex)	Resolution (# Cols by # Rows)	Box Size	Display Format	# Pages	Display Mode	Resolution in Pixels
00	0	40 by 25	8 by 8	16/256K bw	8	Alpha	320 by 200
	0*	40 by 25	8 by 14	16/256K bw	8	Alpha	320 by 350
	0+	40 by 25	9 by 16	16/256K bw	8	Alpha	360 by 400
01	1	40 by 25	8 by 8	16/256K	8	Alpha	320 by 200
	1*	40 by 25	8 by 14	16/256K	8	Alpha	320 by 350
	1+	40 by 25	9 by 16	16/256K	8	Alpha	360 by 400
02	2	80 by 25	8 by 8	16/256K bw	8	Alpha	640 by 200
	2*	80 by 25	8 by 14	16/256K bw	8	Alpha	640 by 350
	2+	80 by 25	9 by 16	16/256K bw	8	Alpha	720 by 400
03	3	80 by 25	8 by 8	16/256K	8	Alpha	720 by 200
	3*	80 by 25	8 by 14	16/256K	8	Alpha	640 by 350
	3+	80 by 25	9 by 16	16/256K	8	Alpha	720 by 400
04	4	40 by 25	8 by 8	4/256K	1	Graph	320 by 200
05	5	40 by 25	8 by 8	4/256K bw	1	Graph	320 by 200
06	6	80 by 25	8 by 8	2/256K bw	1	Graph	640 by 200
07	7	80 by 25	9 by 14	bw	8	Alpha	720 by 350
07	7+	80 by 25	9 by 16	bw	8	Alpha	720 by 400
0D	D	40 by 25	8 by 8	16/256K	8	Graph	320 by 200
0E	E	80 by 25	8 by 8	16/256K	4	Graph	640 by 200
0F	F	80 by 25	8 by 14	bw	2	Graph	640 by 350
10	10	80 by 25	8 by 14	16/256K	2	Graph	640 by 350
11	11	80 by 30	8 by 16	2/256K	1	Graph	640 by 480
12	12	80 by 30	8 by 16	16/256K	1	Graph	640 by 480
13	13	40 by 25	8 by 8	256/256K	1	Graph	320 by 200

normally associated with the Color Graphics Adapter (CGA). The code "16/64-colors" represents sixteen simultaneously displayable colors out of the possible palette of 64 colors. This condition occurs when the monitor connected to the EGA is equipped with six color inputs—IR, IG, IB, R, G, and B.

The asterisk in the "Display Mode" column indicates that an Enhanced Color Monitor is installed. The Enhanced Color Monitor must be capable of display-ing 350 scan lines at a 21.85-kHz horizontal scan rate and a 60-Hz vertical scan rate. Modes 0, 1, 2, and 3 are automatically converted to modes 0*, 1*, 2*, or 3* when the EGA is configured for a high-resolution monitor. These advanced modes are invoked automatically through the settings of the sense switches on the EGA board.

The VGA has only one memory configuration. As a result, there is only one entry per mode for the number of possible pages. The asterisk used in the "Display Mode" column indicates that the VGA is in a text mode with 350 vertical lines. The plus sign indicates that the VGA is in a text mode with 400 vertical lines. The number of vertical lines is controlled through the Vertical Size (VS) field of the Misc. Output Register.

Character Size

The alphanumeric modes, indicated by "Alpha" in Tables 11.1 and 11.2, use display memory plane 2 and, in some implementations, plane 3 for the character generator. Because these memory planes are random access memory (RAM), downloadable character fonts may be employed. The graphics modes, indicated by "Graph" in Tables 11.1 and 11.2, use the character generator programmed into the Read Only Memory (ROM). This generator typically shares the same ROM as the EGA BIOS. Three character patterns are resident in most EGA implementations.

Erasure During Mode Change

It is possible to erase the display memory at the time of a mode change. The AL register is used to select the mode when the AH=0 (Set Mode) command is invoked. If the most significant bit of AL is set to 1, the display memory is not erased after a mode change. If the most significant bit of AL is reset to 0, the display memory is erased after a mode change. Thus, if mode 3 with a screen erasure is desired, the value in the AL register should be a 3 (Hex 3). If mode 3 with no screen erasure is desired, the value in the AL register should be set to a 131 (hex 83). When changing from an alphanumeric mode to a graphics mode, it is usually advisable to erase the display memory because the character ASCII codes, attributes, and the current character fonts are loaded into the four planes of display memory.

Display Mode Emulation

Display modes 0 through 6 emulate the Color Graphics Adapter (CGA). Mode 7 emulates the IBM Monochrome MDA or the Hercules Monochrome graphics standard. The modes with asterisks—0*, 1*, 2*, 3*, and 10*—are modes that are supported when a high-resolution monitor is being used. The only difference between modes 0 and 1 and modes 2 and 3 is the presence of a color burst signal, such as that used in a composite video.

The RCA video connectors on the back of most EGA boards were originally intended for composite video input and output. Most EGA implementations do not include any composite video output. As a result, these modes are identical. Mode 7, the monochrome alphanumeric mode, is the only mode that utilizes the 9-by-14-dot character cell.

Input Parameters:

AL = The desired mode number. Note that setting bit 7 to 1 in the mode value contained in AL causes the screen not to be erased during a mode change. Resetting bit 7 to 0 causes the screen to be erased during a mode change.

Output Parameters:

None.

EGA Registers Affected:

Several of the fields in many of the EGA registers are affected.

Host Memory Affected:

449 hex = Current video mode.
44A hex = Number of columns on screen.
44C hex = Length of active screen buffer.
44E hex = Start of current page.
450 = Cursor positions.
460 = Cursor mode.
462 = Current display page.
463 = Base host address of port.
465 = Current mode.
466 = Current color.
484 = Number of character rows.

11.3   CURSOR CONTROL

The shape of the cursor can be controlled by the programmer. A full character box or an underline is used as the common cursor shape. The row and column position of the cursor can be set or read by the programmer.

11.3.1   AH = 01 Hex: Set Cursor Type (EGA/VGA)

Set the shape of the cursor by setting the starting and ending scan lines of the cursor. The maximum character box height is 32 scan lines. The top of the character box is referred to as scan line 0. The bottom scan line is referred to as scan line 31. The cursor may be enabled or disabled in the alphanumeric modes through the Cursor On/Off (COO) field of the Cursor Start Register in the VGA. In the graphics modes the cursor is not displayed, although BIOS does keep track of its position.

It is possible to set the ending line of the cursor to be less than the starting scan line. In the EGA, this will cause the cursor box to start at the selected ending scan line, extend to the bottom of the character box, wrap around to the top of the character box, and end at the starting scan line. The effect is two disjoined boxes. In the VGA, setting the ending line of the cursor to be less than the beginning line causes no cursor to be displayed.

Certain memory locations within the host RAM are used to store graphics parameters. Location 460 hex in the host memory space contains the Cursor Mode Area. This area consists of two bytes of information corresponding to the current starting and ending scan lines of the cursor. This function loads these locations with the starting and ending cursor scan lines.

Input Parameters:
   CH = The starting scan line for the cursor.
   CL = The ending scan line for the cursor.

Output Parameters:
   None.

EGA Registers Affected:
   Cursor Start, Cursor End.

Host Memory Affected:
   460 hex = Cursor ending scan line number.
   461 hex = Cursor starting scan line number.

11.3.2   AH = 02 Hex: Set Cursor Position (EGA/VGA)

The cursor may be located at any character position in the display memory. Certain display modes have multiple display pages. The number of pages available for each mode depends on the amount of display memory installed. The number of pages per mode is listed in Tables 11.1 and 11.2 above.

The cursor position is a 16-bit word that corresponds to a character position. The display memory begins with character position 0 at the top left of the display and increments from left to right and then from the top down. The display mode determines the number of horizontal and vertical characters per page. Thus, an address in display memory can be translated to a page number, a horizontal row value, and a vertical column value. The cursor resides at one character position on one page only. If the cursor is on a display page other than the display page that is currently active, the cursor will not be visible.

This BIOS function uses the desired page, row, and column numbers rather than the character address. These input parameters, used in conjunction with the current display mode, determine the 16-bit cursor location. Remember that the cursor is not displayed in the graphics modes.

Certain memory locations within the host RAM are used to store graphics parameters. Location 450 hex contains the Cursor Save Area. This area consists of sixteen bytes of information segmented into eight sections, two bytes per section. Each section corresponds to one of the display pages. Eight sections are provided because the maximum number of display pages for any mode is eight. Each section consists of two bytes, one for the row position and one for the column position. This function loads the appropriate locations within the table.

Input Parameters:
BH = The page number where the cursor will reside.
DH = The row number to position the cursor.
DL = The column number to position the cursor.

Output Parameters:
None.

EGA Registers Affected:
Cursor Location High, Cursor Location Low.

Host Memory Affected:
450 hex + pagenumber × 2 = Cursor position column number.
451 hex + pagenumber × 2 = Cursor position row number.

11.3.3   AH = 03 Hex: Read Cursor Position (EGA/VGA)

This function provides information to the calling routine regarding the position and the cursor type. The functioning of the cursor position is described in the Set Cursor Position BIOS call (AH = 02). Reading the cursor position reverses the process used to write the cursor to a selected position. It converts the 16-bit cursor location into row and column numbers. It is necessary to provide the desired page number as an input parameter because each display page maintains its own cursor. The location of the cursor within each display page is stored in the Cursor Save Area of host RAM. The page number is necessary because the BIOS routine will check for the cursor position in the Cursor Save Area rather than deriving it from the Cursor Location Registers. The Cursor Location Registers store the location of the cursor associated with the current display page.

The Cursor Save Area resides in host RAM at location 450 hex. This area consists of sixteen bytes of information segmented into eight sections, two bytes per section. Each section corresponds to one of the display pages. Eight sections are provided because the maximum number of display pages for any mode is eight. Each section consists of two bytes, one for the row position and one for the column position. This function reads the appropriate locations within the table to determine the current cursor position.

Input Parameters:
None.

Output Parameters:
DH, HL = Row, column of cursor.
CH, CL = Cursor type.

EGA Registers Affected:
None.

Host Memory Affected:
None.

11.4 LIGHT PEN POSITION

11.4.1 AH = 04 Hex: Read Light Pen Position (EGA)

The light pen is not the most popular of operator interactive devices for the PC, although as windows environments become more popular the light pen may see a resurgence in popularity. This function is available for the EGA only because the VGA has no light pen facilities. The function reports the status and position of the light pen to the calling program. The light pen position will be considered valid if the light pen has been triggered. The light pen triggers when the electron beam of the CRT excites the phosphor of the screen immediately in front of the light pen. When this occurs, the light pen trigger strobe (LST) field of the Input #1 Status Register is set.

It may be desirable to clear this field, indicating that the light pen strobe has not occurred. This BIOS routine clears this field upon completion. Clearing the light pen latch is accomplished in some implementations in the following manner. In an EGA mode, an I/O output instruction, OUT, must be executed to address 3DB hex to clear the light pen trigger field. In a CGA mode, this may be accomplished by reading or writing to this port through an IN or OUT instruction. In the Hercules modes, an I/O output to port 3BB hex is necessary.

The location of the light pen during the last trigger is returned as pixel locations.

Input Parameters:
None.

Output Parameters:
AH = 0 Light pen trigger has not occurred. No valid data.
AH = 1 Light pen trigger has occurred. The data is valid.
BX = Vertical pixel column in which light pen was located during the last trigger.
CX = Horizontal pixel raster line in which light pen was located during the last trigger. This occurs in modes 4,5, and 6.
DH = Horizontal character row in which light pen was located during the last trigger.

DL = Vertical character column in which light pen was located during the last trigger.

EGA Registers Affected:
The Light Pen Strobe (LST) field of the Input Status #1 Register is cleared, indicating that the data is no longer valid.

Host Memory Affected:
None.

11.5   DISPLAY PAGE SELECTION

11.5.1   AH = 05 Hex: Select Active Display Page (EGA/VGA)

Depending on the current display mode and the amount of display memory, the EGA/VGA may be configured to have from one to eight pages of full-screen graphics. Only one page may be selected at a time for display. This page is called the *active page*. A list of the number of display pages available for the display modes is found in Table 11.1 for the EGA and Table 11.2 for the VGA. The default active display page is page number 0.

The display memory contains more memory than is required for a single display page. In some cases, it is segmented into multiple display pages. The selected active display page dictates where the data to be displayed resides within the display memory. The EGA/VGA determines where to start refreshing the display by the values in the Start Address Registers. This BIOS routine will load the Start Address Registers with a value derived from the current video parameters and the new active display page requested.

The host memory video storage area contains a byte storage location for the active display page at 462 hex. The actual address of the starting location, as loaded in the EGA/VGA Start Address Register pair, is loaded into the two-byte location beginning at 44E hex.

In the alphanumeric modes, it is advantageous to store data on multiple pages. To view different pages, simply select a new active display page. A great deal of time can be saved this way because the BIOS call to change the active display page requires far less time than saving the current display page and rewriting another page in its place. This is especially useful for the diagnostic stages of programming. Variables, flags, and arrays can be easily stored on multiple pages, allowing a great deal of information to be readily available.

In the graphics modes, multiple graphs may be stored on separate pages to speed display operation or for pseudo-animation. It is possible to load one display page while another is being displayed. Alternate display and loading can achieve basic animation effects.

Input Parameters:
   AL = The page number for the new active display page.

Output Parameters:
   None.

EGA Registers Affected:
   Start Address High, Start Address Low.

Host Memory Affected:
   44E hex = Start of active display page.
   462 hex = Active display page number.

11.6 SCROLL SCREEN

A rectangular region of any size on the screen can be scrolled upward or downward any desired number of lines.

11.6.1 AH = 06 Hex: Scroll Active Page Up (EGA/VGA)

In a windows environment, it is often desirable to scroll selected areas of the screen without disturbing the rest of the screen. The BIOS interrupt allows a window to be defined on the screen by its upper-left and lower-right corners. Each of these corners is defined by its corresponding row and column value. These values represent the character positions at the corner locations.

   Scrolling means the moving up or down of information on the screen. In addition to defining the position and size of the window, it is also necessary to define the number of scan lines that will be scrolled. If the number of scan lines requested is 0, the entire window will be blanked, providing a rapid means of clearing a portion of the display.

   Character scrolling one line upward brings one new row of characters into the window at the bottom and scrolls one row of characters out of the window at the top. Similarly, scrolling two lines upward brings in two new lines at the bottom of the screen and scrolls the top two lines off the top of the window. This scroll routine does not bring in new text information at the bottom of the screen. Rather, it outputs blank lines with a new attribute for the new character lines being scrolled into the window. It is the programmer's responsibility to follow this scroll routine with a character string output to the selected line positions that have been scrolled onto the bottom of the screen.

It should be noted that this scrolling operation is totally unrelated to the hardware scrolling available through the Start Address Registers.

Input Parameters:

AL = The number of scan lines to scroll. Note that if zero lines are requested, the entire window will be blanked.

BH = The attribute to be used on the new blank lines entering the window from the bottom.

CH = The upper-left character row number of the window.

CL = The upper-left character column number of the window.

DH = The lower-right character row number of the window.

DL = The lower-right character column number of the window.

Output Parameters:

None.

EGA Registers Affected:

None.

Host Memory Affected:

None.

Display Memory Affected:

The character codes of the display memory contained within the described window. The attribute codes of the display memory contained at the bottom of the window. The number of lines to scroll, as input in AL, dictates how many lines will have their attribute bytes changed. The character codes reside in display memory plane 0, and the attributes reside in display memory plane 1.

11.6.2   AH = 07 Hex: Scroll Active Page Down (EGA/VGA)

This BIOS interrupt routine is similar in function to Scroll Active Page Up routine mentioned above. This routine scrolls the display window downward. New blank lines are input from the top of the window, and the data at the bottom of the window is lost. See the Scroll Active Page Up call above.

If the number of scan lines requested is 0, the entire window will be blanked. This provides a rapid means of clearing a portion of the display.

Input Parameters:

AL = The number of scan lines to scroll. Note that if zero lines are requested, the entire window will be blanked.

BH = The attribute to be used on the new blank lines entering the window from the top.

CH = The upper-left character row number of the window.

CL = The upper-left character column number of the window.

DH = The lower-right character row number of the window.
DL = The lower-right character column number of the window.

Output Parameters:
None.

EGA Registers Affected:
None.

Host Memory Affected:
None.

Display Memory Affected:
The character codes of the display memory contained within the described window. The attribute codes of the display memory contained at the top of the window. The number of lines to scroll, as input in AL, dictates how many lines will have their attribute bytes changed. The character codes reside in display memory plane 0, and the attributes reside in display memory plane 1.

11.7 READ/WRITE CHARACTERS

Three calls allow the programmer to read an attribute and character byte, write an attribute and character byte, or write a character only. These calls can be included into program loops that read or write strings of characters.

11.7.1 AH=08 Hex: Read Attribute/Character Pair (EGA/VGA)

This function returns the character code and attribute byte of the character located at the current cursor position. No attribute code is returned when the display is in one of the graphics modes. The page number input to this routine determines which display page will be used for the read operation. The cursor position is determined by the Cursor Save Area contained in the display information area buffer of host memory. See Set Cursor Position in section 11.3.2 for a description of this area.

Character Storage

In the alphanumeric display modes, the character codes are stored in display page 0, and the character attributes are stored in display page 1. The current display mode, in conjunction with the desired page, determines the actual physical memory address corresponding to the cursor position. It is then a simple matter to read the character code from plane 0 and the attribute byte from plane 1.

In the graphics display modes, the problem is far more complicated. As in the alphanumeric modes, the current display mode and the desired page are used to determine the actual physical memory address corresponding to the cursor position. The next step involves determining which character is in the character box pointed to by the cursor position.

This BIOS function must determine which characters, if any, are written into a selected memory location corresponding to the cursor position. The cursor points to a rectangular area on the screen that contains a character box. The size of this area is dictated by the number of bytes per character. The character box contains a group of pixels. This routine must determine whether these pixels correspond exactly to one of the character pixel patterns in the active display font.

In the graphics mode, the characters are compared to a block of 128 characters in the character-generator section of the EGA BIOS ROM. It is often desirable to read a character code from the full 256 characters in the character generator. However, only the lower 128 characters of the character set can be accessed using this function. To access the upper 128 characters of the character set, the program must reset the interrupt 1F hex vector, located at 7C hex in host memory. This value must be set to point to the second set of character dot patterns associated with characters 128–256 of the selected character font.

The number of bytes per character is located in the display information area of host memory. This area, located in the host memory space, contains a byte at 485 hex that holds the current number of bytes per character.

To determine which character, if any, is present in this character box, it is necessary to compare the pixels in the character box with all of the possible character patterns in ROM. The Color Compare and Color No Care Registers and read mode #1 are used to speed up this function. If no character is found, a 0 code is returned in the character read position. Reading the character code at this position would return the "space" code of 20 hex, as expected.

Reading a Space

It is not possible to read a "space" in the graphics modes. Because a "space" character is all background, nothing will be present in that character position of the display memory. As a result, reading a character position corresponding to a "space" or a "tab" will return a 0 character code, indicating that no character was found.

Input Parameters:
BH = The page number.

Output Parameters:
AL = Character read. The character code of the character occupying the space in display memory corresponding to the current cursor position on the selected page.

AH = Character attribute. The attribute code of the character occupying the memory space at the current cursor position on the selected page.

EGA Registers Affected:
None.

Host Memory Affected:
None.

11.7.2   AH = 09 Hex: Write Attribute/Character Pair (EGA/VGA)

This function writes the character code and attribute byte to display memory at the current cursor position. The page number, an input parameter, determines which display page will be used for the write operation. The character count, also an input parameter, determines the number of times to replicate this character. In the alphanumeric modes, this number is limited to the number of characters left until the end of the current display page is reached. In the graphics modes, this number is limited to the number of remaining character positions to the right of the cursor position until the end of the line. The cursor position is determined by the Cursor Save Area contained in the display information area buffer of host memory. See Set Cursor Position in section 11.3.2 for a description of this area.

Character Patterns

In the alphanumeric display modes, the character codes are written to display page 0, and the character attributes are written to display page 1. The current display mode, in conjunction with the desired page, determines the actual physical memory address corresponding to the cursor position.

In the graphics display modes, the character pattern is written to the display memory. As in the alphanumeric modes, the current display mode and the desired page are used to determine the actual physical memory address corresponding to the cursor position. In the graphics display modes, the characters are written into the display memory as a sequence of foreground dots. Writing a character to the display involves copying the character pattern that corresponds to the character code from the character generator into the display memory. This character generator is located in the EGA/VGA BIOS ROM. The size of the active font determines the size of the character box that contains the dot pattern of the selected character.

When a particular character is written onto the display, the character pattern corresponding to this character code is copied to the display memory at the selected position. The color of the character is determined by the attribute byte associated with the character to be written. The foreground color determines the color of the character, and thus, which display planes should be updated. If the foreground color is 0F hex, all planes will be requested for update. Likewise, if the foreground color is 1 hex, only plane 0 will be requested. It may not be possible to write into all planes requested. Only those planes enabled by the Map Mask Register may be modified.

In the graphics mode, the characters are formed from a block of 128 characters in the character-generator section of the BIOS ROM. It is often desirable to utilize the full 256 characters in the character generator. However, only the lower 128 characters of the character set can be accessed in this function. To access the upper 128 characters of the character set, the program must reset the interrupt 1F hex vector, located at 7C hex in host memory. This value must be set to point to the second set of character dot patterns associated with characters 128–256.

In the graphics modes, the most significant bit of the attribute byte, bit 7, determines the write mode. If this bit is 0, the dots in the foreground of the character overwrite the dots in the display memory. If this bit is a 1, the dots in the foreground of the character are logically XORed with the dots in the display memory. This XORing has the effect of erasing the character if it is already present in that location and writing the character if it is not present.

Writing a "Space" Character

Writing a "space" character to the display while the display is in an alphanumeric mode causes a 20 hex code to be written into display memory. The space character consists of a character box composed entirely of background dots. The attribute byte associated with this space character determines the color of the background dots. This background color fills the character box of the screen corresponding to the space position on the screen.

Writing a space character to the display while the display is in a graphics mode has no effect on the display. Nothing happens when a space is written because the graphics modes utilize a character transparency function. This function ignores all of the background pixels and writes only the foreground pixels associated with the selected character. The effect is that any data behind the background area of the character box will show through the character box.

Input Parameters:

BH = The page number.

AL = Character to write.   The character code of the character to be written to the display memory at the current cursor position on the selected page.

BL = Character attribute.   The attribute code of the character to be written to the display memory at the current cursor position on the selected page. Only the foreground pixels are written to the screen in the graphics modes. Note that bit 7 affects the way in which these foreground pixels modify the screen:

Bit 7=0   Overwrite whatever pixels are in the selected character box in display memory with the foreground pixels of the character.

Bit 7=1   Logically XOR the pixels in the selected character box in display memory with the foreground pixels of the character.

CX = Replication count.   The number of times to repeat this character/attribute pair.

Output Parameters:
None.

EGA Registers Affected:
None.

Display Memory Affected:
The display memory corresponding to the current cursor position. In the alphanumeric mode, planes 0 and 1 will be modified to contain the new character code and attribute byte, respectively. In the graphics modes, the display memory corresponding to the character box at the selected cursor position will be modified.

11.7.3 AH=0A Hex. Write Character Only (EGA/VGA)

This function writes a character to the display memory beginning at the current cursor position. The attribute byte of the character positions is not affected. The page number, an input parameter, determines which display page will be used for the write operation. The character count, also an input parameter, determines the number of times to replicate this character. In the alphanumeric modes, this number is limited to the number of characters left until the end of the current display page is reached. In the graphics modes, this number is limited to the number of remaining character positions to the right of the cursor position until the end of the line. The cursor position is determined by the Cursor Save Area contained in the display information area buffer of host memory.

See Set Cursor Position in section 11.3.2 for a description of this area. See the Write Character/Attribute call for details on writing characters in both the alphanumeric and graphics modes.

Input Parameters:
BH = The page number.
AL = Character to write. The character code of the character to be written to the display memory at the current cursor position on the selected page.
BL = Character attribute. In the alphanumeric modes, this field is ignored. In the graphics modes, bit 7 of this register affects the way in which the character foreground pixels modify the screen:
Bit 7=0 Overwrite whatever pixels are in the selected character box in display memory with the foreground pixels of the character.
Bit 7=1 Logically XOR the pixels in the selected character box in display memory with the foreground pixels of the character.
CX = Replication count. The number of times to repeat this character/attribute pair.

Output Parameters:
None.

EGA Registers Affected:
None.

Display Memory Affected:
The display memory corresponding to the current cursor position. In the alphanumeric mode, plane 0 will be modified to contain the new character code. In the graphics modes, the display memory corresponding to the character box at the selected cursor position will be modified.

11.8   COLOR PALETTE

There is one function that is used to set the color palette. This function should be used only when in an EGA mode.

11.8.1   AH = 0B Hex: Set Color Palette (EGA/VGA)

This function sets the color palette when the system is operating in modes 4 or 5, which are the 320-by-200 CGA display modes. This function is used to provide color compatibility with the CGA. In some nonstandard EGA implementations, mode 6, which corresponds to the 640-by-200 graphics mode, is also controlled by this function. Information relating to the graphics modes is provided in Table 11.3.

In the 4-color mode, there are two bits that correspond to each pixel's color. These two bits are horizontal neighbors. Because these two bits can access only four locations in the palette, only four colors are possible. In the standard IBM implementation, one of two color schemes is loaded into the palette. Each of these palettes represents four colors. In some nonstandard implementations,

TABLE 11.3   Graphics Modes

Mode (Hex)	Adapter	Rows	Columns	Page	Color
4,5	EGA/VGA	0–199	0–319	0	0–3
6	EGA/VGA	0–199	0–639	0	0–1
D	EGA/VGA	0–199	0–319	0–7	0–15
E	EGA/VGA	0–199	0–639	0–3	0–15
F–10	EGA/VGA	0–349	0–639	0,1	0–15
11	VGA	0–479	0–639	1	0–1
12	VGA	0–479	0–639	1	0–15
13	VGA	0–199	0–319	1	0–255

the programmer may actually select which colors will be loaded into these palette registers.

In modes 4 or 5 (4-color modes), the palette color ID operates as follows: If the color ID = 0, the color value will select the background and intensity. The values from 0 to 15 select normal background colors, and the values 16–31 select the high-intensity background colors.

If the color ID = 1, the color value will select the four colors to be loaded into the first four positions of the color palette. The four colors that can be selected are as follows:

Color Value = 0 *Select Palette #0*	*Color Value = 1* *Select Palette #1*
0 = black	0 = black
1 = green	1 = cyan
2 = red	2 = magenta
3 = brown	3 = white

Note that in certain implementations of this BIOS function, variations exist regarding how the color palette compatibility is set. Some implementations of this BIOS function allows the programmer to select the colors to be loaded into the palette. This function may also control the color selection of mode 6. In mode 6 (2-color mode), each pixel is represented by one pixel. In some cases a CGA Color Select Register at port address 3D9 hex is present. This register allows additional control to achieve CGA color compatibility.

Input Parameters:
 BH = Color ID.   Selects the function of the Color Value.
 BL = Color Value.   Controlled by the Color ID field above; provides the color for the background or the current palette number.

Output Parameters:
 None.

EGA Registers Affected:
 Color Palette Registers.

Host Memory Affected:
 466 hex current color.

11.9   READ/WRITE PIXEL

Certainly the weakest aspect of the BIOS is the reading and writing of data while the display is in the graphics modes. There are only two routines, AH = 0C hex and AH = 0D hex. These read from or write to a pixel. These routines are notoriously slow when used in any graphics operations.

11.9.1   AH = 0C Hex: Write Pixel (EGA/VGA)

This function is a slow but sure way to write a pixel to the display memory when the EGA/VGA is in a graphics mode. The programmer provides the color, page number, row number, and column number. The possible values of these parameters are listed below.

Note that this function does not affect the cursor position. The position of the pixel to be modified is obtained by converting the mode and page number to a display memory address. The pixel written to is not necessarily on the current page, so it is possible that the write operation will have no effect on the displayed page. The active page does not change according to the page parameter sent to this function.

Input Parameters:

AL = Color value. Value to load into display memory at the desired position.

BH = Display page. The display page that contains the pixel that should be written to by this function.

CX = Column number. The horizontal pixel coordinate of the pixel. Note that this number represents a pixel number, not a character number. The columns count from 0, on the left of the screen, to a maximum value dictated by the display mode, on the right side of the screen.

DX = Row number. The vertical pixel coordinate of the pixel. Note that this number represents a pixel number, not a character number. The rows count from 0, on the top of the screen, to a maximum row number dictated by the display mode, on the left side of the screen.

Output Parameters:

None.

EGA Registers Affected:

None.

Display Memory Affected:

The bit or bits corresponding to the display mode, the horizontal and vertical coordinate input parameters, the selected page, and the value of the Map Mask Register. The Map Mask Register determines which planes are enabled for write operations.

11.9.2   AH = 0D Hex: Read Pixel (EGA/VGA)

This function is a slow but sure way to read the value in a pixel location in display memory when the EGA/VGA is in a graphics mode. The programmer provides the page number, row number, and column number as input parameters. The function returns the color of the pixel to the calling program as addressed by the input parameters. See the Write Pixel function in section 11.9.1 for more details.

The pixel read is not necessarily on the current page. The active page does not change according to the page number parameter sent to this function. Thus, if display page 0 is active, it is possible to read a pixel from display page 1.

Input Parameters:

BH = Display page. The display page that contains the pixel that should be written to by this function.

CX = Column number. The horizontal pixel coordinate of the pixel. Note that this number represents a pixel number, not a character number. The columns count from 0, on the left of the screen, to a maximum value dictated by the display mode, on the right side of the screen.

DX = Row number. The vertical pixel coordinate of the pixel. Note that this number represents a pixel number, not a character number. The rows count from 0, on the top of the screen, to a maximum row number dictated by the display mode, on the left side of the screen.

Output Parameters:

AL = Color value. Value to load into display memory at the desired position.

EGA Registers Affected:

None.

Display Memory Affected:

None.

11.9.3   AH = 0E Hex: Write TTY Character (EGA/VGA)

This function writes a character to the display memory. In addition to the regular characters that can be displayed, this function understands several carriage-control functions. It causes the display to operate in a similar manner to a TTY-type terminal. This write function operates on the carriage return, line feed, backspace, and bell key.

The TTY character is written to the display memory at the cursor position on the active page. After the character is written, the cursor is advanced one position. When the end of the current horizontal line is reached, an effective carriage return and line feed are issued, thereby moving the cursor to column 0 of the next line. When a line feed is issued and the cursor is already on the bottom line, the entire screen is scrolled. The attribute of the new line being scrolled in from the bottom is the same as the attribute of the far-left character in the bottom line of the display.

TABLE 11.4 Cursor-control Keystrikes

Symbol	Name	Action
CR	Carriage Return	Moves the cursor to column 0 of the next character line.
LF	Line Feed	Moves the cursor down one character row. If the current character row is on the bottom of the screen, the entire screen is scrolled upward. The attribute of the new line is assigned to be the attribute of the previous last line's far left character. It is assumed that each line has only one attribute in these scrolling operations.
BS	Backspace	The cursor is moved to the left one character position. No action occurs if the cursor is at the far left column, column 0, of the line.
BELL	Bell	Causes the bell to ring.

The attribute bytes associated with the characters when the display is in an alphanumeric mode remain unmodified, with the exception of a screen scroll previously discussed. In the graphics modes, it is necessary to specify the foreground color of the character.

Table 11.4 illustrates the operation of these cursor-control keystrikes.

The Write String BIOS call, AH = 13 hex, utilizes this Write TTY BIOS call when writing strings of characters to the display. Thus, character-control codes contained within the strings are treated as indicated in Table 11.4.

Input Parameters:

AL = Character code to write to the display at the current cursor position on the current page. The attribute byte of this character is not modified. This code may also be one of the four codes mentioned above.

BL = Foreground color for the graphics modes. If the display is in one of the graphics modes, this parameter contains the color that will be used to draw the character. Because there is no background color for characters in the graphics modes, this is the only color that needs to be specified.

Output Parameters:

None.

Display Memory Affected:

If the character is a printable character, display memory is modified. The location of the modified display memory depends on the current cursor position, the active display page, and the display mode.

TABLE 11.5 Video State Memory Locations

Host Memory	Function
449 hex	Display mode
44A hex	Number of character columns
462 hex	Active display page

TABLE 11.6 Number of Character Columns

Mode (Hex)	# of Columns
0,1,4,5,D,13	40
2,3,5,6,7,E,F,10,11,12	80

11.9.4   AH = 0F Hex: Read Current Video State (EGA/VGA)

This function reads the current state of the EGA/VGA, including the display mode, the number of character columns on the screen, and the current active display page. All of these values are located in the information buffer in host memory, as shown in Table 11.5.

Input Parameters:
  None.

Output Parameters:
  AH = Number of character columns on the screen. Table 11.6 illustrates the number of character columns possible for the different display modes.
  AL = Current display mode. The low-order 7-bit value in this register ranges from 0 to 10 hex in the standard EGA implementations. Bit 7 in the display mode corresponds to whether the display was cleared during the last mode change. If it was cleared, this bit will be a 0; if it was not cleared, this bit will be a 1. See the Set Mode Function for details on the display modes.
  BH = Active display page. Table 11.7 illustrates the possible page values for the different display modes.

11.10   PALETTE REGISTERS

The sixteen Palette Registers can be written to on the EGA. They can be written to and read from on the VGA. Individual registers or all sixteen registers can be accessed by the BIOS routines. Other functions within the Attribute Register Group, including the Intensity/Blinking Bit and the Overscan Register, are controlled in these BIOS calls.

TABLE 11.7 Possible Number of Pages

Mode (Hex)	Page Numbers
4–6	0
D	0–7
E	0–3
F–10	0–7
11	1
12	1
13	1

11.10.1 AH = 10, AL = 0: Set Individual Palette Registers (EGA/VGA)

This function loads an individual Palette Register with a specified color. A better title for this BIOS function would be "Set Individual Attribute Registers," and the description would be "this function loads an individual Attribute Register with a specified value." The Palette Registers are only a subgroup of the Attribute Registers that can be programmed with this BIOS call. The Palette Registers are the first sixteen of twenty Attribute Registers for the EGA and the first sixteen out of 21 Attribute Registers for the VGA.

The colors loaded into the Palette Register determine the color output to the monitor. The EGA provides for 64 possible colors by allocating two bits per three primary colors—red, green, and blue. The coding of these six bits, according to the monitor type, is illustrated in Table 11.8.

The Color Palette consists of sixteen registers that are used to map the values representing the intensity of each pixel into a color. The address of each palette register corresponds to the number of unique states available in the display memory. Table 11.9 illustrates the Color Palette addresses used according to the different display modes.

TABLE 11.8 Palette Color Codes

Bit #	Color EGA Monitor	Color RGBI Monitor	Monochrome Monitor
5	Secondary red	—	—
4	Secondary green	Intensity	Intensity
3	Secondary blue	—	Video
2	Red	Red	—
1	Green	Green	—
0	Blue	Blue	—

TABLE 11.9 Color Palette Utilization

Mode (Hex)	Color	Palette Addresses Used
0,1,2,3,D,E,10	16-color	0–15
4,5	4-color	0–3
6	2-color	0–1
7,F	Monochrome	0–1
11	2-color	0–1
12	16-color	0–15
13	256-color	0–15, VGA Color Registers

16-color Mode

In the 16-color mode, the color palette is accessed by one bit from each of the four memory planes. Bit plane 0 represents bit 0 of the 4-bit address, bit plane 1 represents bit 1, bit plane 2 represents bit 2, and bit plane 3 represents bit 3. This 4-bit address accesses a given location in the palette during the screen refreshing. Only those memory planes that are selected in the Enable Color Plane Register control the address feeding the palette. The bit planes that are deselected cause a 0 in that bit position of the 4-bit address. Suppose that bit plane 1 and 2 are disabled. This would mean that the only Palette Registers that could be accessed would be 0, 1, 8, and 9, as shown in Table 11.10.

256-color Mode

The 256-color mode is specific to the VGA and is associated with display mode 13 hex. The colors output to the monitor are derived from the 256 Color Registers on the VGA rather than the sixteen Palette Registers used in all other display modes. In this mode, the sixteen Color Palette Registers act as the low-order four bits of the address to the Color Registers. In this mode 13 hex, the sixteen Palette Registers should not be modified. If it is desired to modify a color, the color code should be changed within the desired Color Register.

TABLE 11.10 Examples of Palette Addressing

Bit Plane 3	Bit Plane 0	Palette Address
0	0	0
0	1	1
1	0	8
1	1	9

Nonpalette Attribute Registers

There are 20 registers in the EGA and 21 registers in the VGA that belong to the Attribute Registers. The first sixteen are dedicated to the palette registers. The Attribute Registers are tricky to program because a single port address is used both to index the Attribute Registers and as the data port for them. It is sometimes more convenient to use this BIOS call rather than to program the registers directly.

Register 10 hex is the Attributes Mode Control Register. This register controls several functions related to the output configuration of the EGA. See the Attributes Mode Control Register in section 10.6.3 for further details.

Register 11 hex is called the Overscan Register. This register controls the color of the border region surrounding the graphics display area. The 6-bit color coding of this register is identical to the color coding of the lower sixteen palette registers that was described above. See the Overscan Register in section 10.6.4 for further details.

Register 12 hex is the Color Plane Enable Register. This register controls the selecting and deselecting of display planes. Only selected display planes can be written to or can affect the output colors addressed by the lower sixteen palette registers. See the Color Plane Enable Register in section 10.6.5 for further details.

Register 13 hex is the Horizontal Pel Panning Register. This register is used when it is desired to smooth-pan the display area to the left or to the right. Rough panning moves the screen a character position at a time while smooth panning moves the screen one pixel location at a time. See the Horizontal Pel Panning Register in section 10.6.6 for further details.

Register 14 hex is the Color Select Register. It is available only on the VGA. It selects either the upper two address bits or the upper four address bits, which select one of the 256 Color Registers.

Input Parameters:

BH = Coded color value to be loaded into the palette.

BL = Attribute Register address of the register to be loaded. The most commonly used registers in this group are the sixteen Color Palette registers.

Output Parameters:

None.

EGA Registers Affected:

The selected Attribute Register.

11.10.2   AH = 10, AL = 1: Set Overscan Register (EGA/VGA)

This function loads the Overscan Registers with a color code. This color code will be displayed in the border region of the display. The border region is the region surrounding the graphics display area. It is bounded by the active display area and the horizontal and vertical blanking timing. The Overscan Register is actually Attribute Register 10 hex and can be also programmed by the Set Individual Palette Register above.

The EGA has great difficulty displaying colors other than black in the 350-line modes. This difficulty, related to timing, causes undesirable effects. The border region does operate properly in the 200-scan-line modes. To achieve a reasonable display, the Overscan Register should be set to 0 for the color black.

The VGA does not support overscan borders in the 40-column display modes. In other display modes, with the exception of mode 13 hex, all borders are restricted to one character wide.

The color codes in the Overscan Register use the same coding as that described in the Set Individual Palette Register BIOS call.

Input Parameters:
BH = Color code for the border region.

Output Parameters:
None.

EGA Registers Affected:
Overscan Register.

11.10.3   AH = 10, AL = 2: Set All Palette Registers and Overscan Register (EGA/VGA)

This function loads all of the 16-color Palette Registers and the Overscan Register with the values in a 17-byte array. The values in the array are coded color values that are described in the Set Individual Palette Register BIOS call.

Input Parameters:
ES:DX Pointer to the 17-byte array containing the color codes for the sixteen Palette Registers and for the Overscan Register. The ES Register is the segment register, and the DX register is the offset register. The actual 20-bit address is obtained by shifting the segment register by four bits to the left and ORing in the value in the offset register.

Output Parameters:
None.

EGA Registers Affected:
Sixteen Palette Registers, Overscan Register.

11.10.4 AH = 10 Hex, AL = 3 Hex: Toggle Blink/Intensity Bit (EGA/VGA)

This function loads the Blink/Intensity field, B/I, of the Mode Control Register. This field defines whether bit 7 of the character attribute bytes controls blinking or background intensity.

It was desirable to maintain a one-byte character attribute. It was also desirable to allow the character to have one of sixteen foreground colors, to have one of sixteen background colors, and to be able to blink. This required nine bits of coded information, four for the foreground, four for the background and one for the blinking. A compromise was struck: the blinking field and the fourth bit of the background intensity bit share the same bit-7 position of the character attribute byte.

In order to select which function this bit 7 is controlling, a single bit in the Mode Control Register called the B/I field was created. This B/I field controls the blinking/intensity function for the entire display.

If the B/I field is set to 1, blinking is enabled, but only one of eight unique colors can be selected for the background intensity of the character. A character will blink if its associated attribute byte bit 7=1. The character will not blink if its associated attribute byte bit 7=0. Likewise, if the B/I field is reset to 0, blinking is disabled, but the background color can be represented by one of sixteen colors. Table 11.11 illustrates the possibilities.

Input Parameters:
   BL = Value to load into the B/I field of the Mode Control Register, controlling the blinking/intensity function of bit 7 in the character attribute bit.
   0 = Enable background intensities.
   1 = Enable blinking.

Output Parameters:
   None.

EGA Registers Affected:
   B/I field of the Mode Control Register.

TABLE 11.11 Blinking/Background Intensity

B/I Field Mode Control	Bit 7 Attribute	Blinking	Background Intensity
0	0	No blink,	16 background colors
0	1	No blink,	16 background colors
1	0	No blink,	8 background colors
1	1	Blink,	8 background colors

11.10.5   AH = 10 Hex, AL = 07 Hex: Read Individual Palette Register (VGA)

The Palette Registers may be read in the VGA. This very important feature allows programs to save the palette registers before modifying them. The original palette can then be restored after a program exits. This is useful when memory resident programs are competing for the display resource but have no way of communicating with one another regarding the state of the EGA.

The selected palette register color code is returned to the calling program.

Input Parameters:
BL = Palette Register to read.

Output Parameters:
BH = Color code read from the selected Palette Register.

EGA Registers Affected:
None.

11.10.6   AH = 10 Hex, AL = 08 Hex: Read Overscan Register (VGA)

The color code in the Overscan Register can be read with the value returned to the calling program.

Input Parameters:
None.

Output Parameters:
BH = Color code read from the Overscan Register

EGA Registers Affected:
None.

11.10.7   AH = 10 Hex, AL = 09 Hex: Read All Palette Registers and Overscan Register (VGA)

The color codes of the sixteen Palette Registers and the Overscan Register can be read with the 17 byte values returned into a buffer pointed to by the output parameter register pair ES:DX.

Input Parameters:
ES = Segment Address pointing to the array that will contain the Palette and Overscan Register color codes.
DX = Offset Address pointing to the array that will contain the Palette and Overscan Register color codes.

Output Parameters:
  None.

EGA Registers Affected:
  None.

Host Memory Affected:
  The 17-character array in host memory pointed to by the ES:DX register pair.

11.11 COLOR REGISTERS

The 256 Color Registers are available in the VGA but not the EGA. The BIOS routines can read from or write to individual registers or groups of them. The 256 Color Registers can be segmented into pages, and the active page can also be controlled. The colors present in these registers can be summed to produce gray scale values through one of these calls.

11.11.1 AH = 10 Hex, AL = 10 Hex: Set Individual Color Register (VGA)

This function allows the programmer to set one of the Color Registers. The VGA is equipped with 256 Color Registers that contain the actual color codes output to the monitor. Each contains three 6-bit fields: one for the red intensity, one for the blue intensity, and one for the green intensity. Because each field is six bits wide, it is possible to display 64 levels of intensity for each of the three primary colors. Because all three 6-bit fields are combined to produce the resultant color code, an 18-bit field is used to create the color. These eighteen bits allow 256 K possible colors.

In the VGA display mode 13 hex, it is possible to exhibit all 256 of these Color Registers simultaneously. In all other modes, only a subset of 2, 4, or 16 registers may be used simultaneously. By using the Color Select Register, it is feasible to rapidly select from groups of sixteen or 64 Color Registers without having to modify the Color Registers.

Input Parameters:
  BX = Color Register number to set.
  CH = Intensity of the green color, ranging from 0–63.
  CL = Intensity of the blue color, ranging from 0–63.
  DH = Intensity of the red color, ranging from 0–63.

Output Parameters:
  None.

EGA Registers Affected:
  None.

11.11.2   AH = 10 Hex, AL = 12 Hex: Set Block of Color Registers (VGA)

This function permits the programmer to set a block of the Color Registers. The VGA is equipped with 256 Color Registers that contain the actual color codes output to the monitor. See the Set Individual Color Register for details.

The selected number of Color Registers are loaded from a buffer in host memory as addressed by the ES:DX register pair. Any number of registers, up to the maximum of 256, can be written, starting at an arbitrary register number. Thus, it is possible to write to two consecutive Color Registers beginning at Color Register number 100.

The format of the data buffer consists of a sequence of three bytes per Color Register. The sequence is red, green, blue. This arrangement is followed by the next sequence, which corresponds to the next sequential Color Register. The buffer should be three times the number of Color Registers to be written. In the above example, the buffer would appear as indicated in Table 11.12.

Input Parameters:
   BX = Number of first Color Register to set.
   CX = Number of Color Registers to set.
   ES:DX = Segment/Offset Address of host array containing the color codes. The buffer should be three times the length of the number of Color Registers to set as indicated in the CX parameter.

Output Parameters:
   None.

EGA Registers Affected:
   Selected Color Registers.

11.11.3   AH = 10 Hex, AL = 13 Hex: Select Color Page (VGA)

There are 256 Color Registers, but only in mode 13 hex can all 256 be simultaneously displayed. There are two ways to segment the Color Registers. The

TABLE 11.12 Example of an Array of Colors

Byte Index	Color Value
0	Red intensity for Color Register 100
1	Green intensity for Color Register 100
2	Blue intensity for Color Register 100
3	Red intensity for Color Register 101
4	Green intensity for Color Register 101
5	Blue intensity for Color Register 101

TABLE 11.13 Selecting the Color Page

Input BL	Parameters (BH Function)	BH Possible Values
0	Select paging mode	0=4 pages of 64 Color Registers
		1=16 pages of 16 Color Registers
1	Select color page	0–3 if paging mode=0
		0–15 if paging mode=1

first way segments the 256 registers into sixteen blocks with sixteen registers per block. This is useful when the VGA is in a 16-color mode. It allows the programmer to rapidly select from sixteen possible palettes without having to reload any of the Color Registers. The second segmentation creates four blocks with 64 colors per block. This is useful when the programmer desires to modify the 64 possible colors accessed by the Palette Registers in the 16-color modes.

This BIOS call allows the programmer to select one of two functions. The first, selected with the input parameter BL = 0, allows the programmer to select the paging mode. The second, selected with BL=1, permits the programmer to change the active color page depending on the active color paging mode. The possible values for this call are illustrated in Table 11.13.

This BIOS call allows the programmer to select the page according to the current paging mode. The Internal Palette Size Select (IPS) field of the Mode Control Register is loaded depending on the input parameter to this BIOS call. This field is used in conjunction with the Color Select Register to determine the addressing technique used to select the Color Registers. See the IPS field of the Mode Control Register and the Color Select Register for details.

Input Parameters:
    BH = Paging mode or active color page.
        If BL = 0, Paging mode is selected.
            BH = 0   Select four pages of 64 Color Registers.
            BH = 1   Select sixteen pages of 16 Color Registers.
        If BL = 1, Select page is selected.
            BH = 0–3 if in 4-page mode.
            BH = 0–15 if in 16-page mode.
    BL = Select function of this BIOS call
            BL = 0 Select Paging Mode
            BL = 1 Select Active Color Page Mode

Output Parameters:
    None.

EGA Registers Affected:
    Mode Control Register, Color Select Register

11.11.4   AH = 10 Hex, AL = 15 Hex: Read Individual Color Register (VGA)

This function allows the programmer to read one of the Color Registers. The VGA is equipped with 256 Color Registers that contain the actual color codes output to the monitor. See the Set Individual Palette Register in section 11.10.1 for details.

Input Parameters:
BX = Color Register number to read.

Output Parameters:
CH = Intensity of the green color, ranging from 0–63.
CL = Intensity of the blue color, ranging from 0–63.
DH = Intensity of the red color, ranging from 0–63.

EGA Registers Affected:
None.

11.11.5   AH = 10 Hex, AL = 17 Hex: Read Block of Color Register (VGA)

This function allows the programmer to read a block of the Color Registers. The VGA is equipped with 256 Color Registers that contain the actual color codes output to the monitor. See the Set Block of Color Registers in section 10.7 for details.

The selected number of Color Registers are loaded into a buffer in host memory that is addressed by the ES:DX register pair. Any number of registers, up to the maximum of 256, can be read, starting at an arbitrary register number.

The format of the data buffer consists of a sequence of three bytes per Color Register. The sequence is red, green, blue. This arrangement would be followed by the next sequence, which corresponds to the next sequential Color Register. The buffer should be three times the number of Color Registers to be written.

Input Parameters:
BX = Number of first Color Register to set.
CX = Number of Color Registers to set.

Output Parameters:
ES:DX = Segment/Offset Address of host array containing the color codes. The buffer should be three times the length of the number of Color Registers to set as indicated in the CX parameter.

Host Memory Affected:
The host memory that is addressed by the ES:DX register pair. Three times the number of bytes as input in the CX registers will be affected. The resultant

array in no way reflects which registers are associated with the color sequences.

11.11.6   AH = 10 Hex, AL = 1A Hex: Read Current Color Page Number (VGA)

The 256 Color Registers may be configured either as sixteen groups with sixteen registers per group or as four groups with 64 registers per group. This is determined by the Internal Palette Size Select (IPS) field of the Mode Control Register and may be loaded through the Select Color Page BIOS CALL, AH=10 hex, AL=13 hex. Both the current paging mode and the active color page are returned to the calling routine. See the Select Color Page BIOS call in section 11.11.3 for details.

Input Parameters:
   None.

Output Parameters:
   BH = Current active color page.
   BL = Active paging mode.

EGA Registers Affected:
   None.

11.11.7   AH = 10 Hex, AL = 1B Hex: Sum Color Values to Gray Scale (VGA)

This call converts the color values in the Color Registers into gray scale values. A weighted average is used to convert the intensity values of the three primary colors—red, green, and blue—into a gray scale according to Equation 11.1. Any number of consecutive Color Registers can be converted using this call. The programmer provides the starting Color Register number and the number of Color Registers to convert.

Equation 11.1 Determining Gray Scale

Gray Scale = $(.30 \times \text{Red}) + (.59 \times \text{Green}) + (.11 \times \text{Blue})$

In creating the gray scale, 30 percent of the red intensity is added to 59 percent of the green intensity and added to 11 percent of the blue intensity. Because the resultant intensity is equal to 100 percent of the intensity of the three colors, the intensity of a gray scale will result in a gray scale of the same value. For example, assume that the three color values are 40, 40, and 40 for red, green, and blue respectively. This produces a gray scale of intensity 40. The resultant gray scale would be $(.30 \times 40) + (.59 \times 40) + (.11 \times 40) = 1.0 \times 40 = 40$.

This call is similar to the Summing to Gray Scales BIOS call, AH = 12 hex, BL = 33 hex. It differs in that the summing operation occurs automatically when this call is invoked. The Summing to Gray Scales call does not actually alter any Color Registers until subsequent mode sets occur and operations take place that access the Color Registers. If implemented in C, this operation would be similar to Listing 11.1. This example assumes that the three primary colors of each Color Register have been read from the Color Registers and loaded into the red, green, and blue arrays. The values start_reg and number_regs contain the starting Color Register number and the number of Color Registers to convert.

LISTING 11.1 Summing Selected Registers to Gray Scale

```
unsigned char Red[256], Blue[256], Green[256], Gray;
int i,start_reg,number_regs;
for (i=start_reg; i<=number_regs; i++)
 { Gray = (.30 * Red[i])+(.59 * Green[i])+(.11 * Blue[i]);
   Red[i] = Gray; Green[i] = Gray; Blue[i] = Gray;
 }
```

This BIOS call reads a set of the Color Registers, calculates the above equation, and rewrites the result into the red, green, and blue portions of the selected Color Registers. Any number of Color Registers, up to the maximum of 256, can be selected, beginning at any Color Register index.

Input Parameters:
   BX = First Color Register to be converted to gray scale.
   CX = Number of Color Registers to be converted.

Output Parameters:
   None.

EGA Registers Affected:
   The selected Color Registers.

11.12 CHARACTER GENERATION

Several BIOS routines allow the programmer to download ROM-based or user-based character sets into the display memory. Two sets of calls are provided for use during the alphanumeric modes. One set forces a mode set reset, and the second set automatically adjusts certain display parameters. In the graphics modes, the pointers to ROM-based or user-based character sets are loaded. Up to eight fonts can be resident in display memory. A BIOS call is provided that selects two of these fonts to be active. The active character font information can be returned to the programmer through one of these BIOS calls.

11.12.1 AH = 11, AL = 0: User ALPHA Load (with Reset) (EGA/VGA)

This function loads a character set into one of the font areas reserved in the display memory. The character set may consist of any number of bytes per character, up to the 32-byte limit. The programmer provides this routine with a long pointer that points to the character set that is to be loaded. All or any portion of a character set may be loaded into the display memory font area. This call can be used only when the EGA/VGA is in an alphanumeric mode.

Fonts in Display Memory

There are four areas reserved for the display fonts in the EGA and eight areas on the VGA. Before the character set is loaded, a Set Mode is automatically executed. See the Set Mode BIOS call in section 11.2.1 for details. This Set Mode operation is executed without clearing the display. Thus, character codes and attributes located in display memory will not be erased. This feature of not erasing the display memory also allows the programmer to load partial fonts without erasing the original character fonts previously loaded in the display memory. The character fonts are located in bit plane 2 and, in some implementations, bit plane 3 of the display memory.

The memory plane, or planes, dedicated to holding the character sets, are each segmented into four blocks of 16 Kbytes each for the EGA and eight blocks of 8 Kbytes each for the VGA. In the EGA, the first 8 Kbytes of each of these four buffers are dedicated to a character font. Four fonts, each 256 characters long, may be loaded in memory simultaneously. In the VGA, all 8 Kbytes of each of the eight buffers are dedicated to the character fonts. In both the EGA and the VGA, only two of these four fonts may be active at a time, allowing a maximum of 512 different characters on the screen at one time.

In some implementations, character sets with character boxes wider than eight bits are allowed. These characters may be up to sixteen pixels wide. The left eight bits of each scan line are stored in bit plane 2, and the right eight bits of the scan lines are stored in bit plane 3.

Character Generator

The character generator consists of the dot patterns that represent each character in the character set. The character dot patterns are stored in character boxes, each of which is 32 bytes long. Bits set to 1 in the character font will be displayed in the foreground color, and bits reset to 0 will be displayed in the background color. The display memory consists of four display planes called bit planes, each being 32 Kbytes long. In the alphanumeric modes, bit plane 2 is used to hold the character generator. This limits the characters to an 8-bit-wide character box.

In the EGA, the single exception to this rule is the 9-by-14 monochrome character set. This 9-bit-wide character box is actually represented by eight bits in the character generator. The ninth bit is derived from a copy of the eighth bit. For most characters, the 8-by-14 font is used to represent the 9-by-14 font. The difference, once displayed, is the additional column of background values in the 9-by-14 format.

Certain characters, however, require alternate font patterns to better utilize the 9-by-14 format. A supplemental character set is provided. The wider-bodied characters are represented in this new format and leave no blank column on the right side of the character. That is, the character foreground values extend to the far-right limit of the character box. Once the character has been drawn, the ninth column of background colors will be drawn on the right of the character. Each character in this 9-by-14 supplement is represented in the BIOS character-generator bit patterns by fifteen bytes of information. The first byte of each character is the ASCII code of the character that follows. These ASCII codes are necessary because all characters are not represented in the supplement. As a result, a simple indexed addressing scheme cannot be used. The characters in the supplement include upper case *M*, *T*, *V*, *W*, *X*, *Y*, and *Z*. The lower case characters include *m*, *v*, and *w*. Symbolic characters such as quotation marks, plus sign, and minus sign are included, along with six nonalphanumeric characters. The supplement is terminated with a 0 byte in the ASCII code location.

In the VGA, the characters sets are similar, with the exception of an additional 8-by-16 character set and a 9-by-16 alphanumeric supplement. These two fonts work in an identical fashion to that used by the 8-by-14 font and the 9-by-14 supplement in the EGA.

Input Parameters:

BH = The number of bytes per character. The maximum length of a character is 32 bytes. The character generator reserves 32 scan lines for each character, and each character will be stored in the 32 bytes regardless of the number of bytes per character. This facilitates rapid addressing. Because the number of bytes per character is specified, the BIOS routine knows how many bytes from the input user table to copy into each of the 32-byte character slots in the display memory.

BL = Block to Load. This dictates which of the four blocks of display memory dedicated to the character sets should be loaded.

CX = The number of characters to load. The number of characters is specified to let the BIOS routine know how many blocks of bytes associated with each character should be loaded into the display memory. The total number of bytes in the user array is equal to the number of bytes per character times the number of characters to load.

DX = The character offset into the selected block of memory. This value determines where in the display memory font area the incoming user character array should be loaded. The character patterns in the user character array are organized sequentially, with one character following the previous character. It is not necessary for the first character in the array to be the first character in the character set. This offset is specified to let the BIOS routine know where the user array should be loaded in the selected 8-Kbyte block in display memory.

ES:BP = The pointer to the user downloadable font contained in a sequential byte buffer. The ES register should contain the segment address of the array, and the BP register should contain the offset address of the array.

Output Parameters:
None.

Display Memory Affected:
Plane 2 of display memory beginning at the character offset times 32 and extending for the number of characters times 32. The "times 32" is needed because each character in the display buffer occupies 32 bytes, regardless of how many bytes it actually uses.

11.12.2 AH = 11, AL = 1: ROM Monochrome Set (with Reset) (EGA/VGA)

This subroutine loads the ROM-resident monochrome 9-by-14 character set into the selected 8-Kbyte block of memory in the display memory. It must be used only when the display is in an alphanumeric mode. Although the character width is nine bits, the character box size is eight bits wide. This function operates similarly to the Load User Character Set with Reset function above. Unlike that function, which loads a user-defined array into display memory, this function copies the 9-by-14 monochrome character set from ROM into the display memory. The entire character set is loaded into display memory.

The 9-by-14 monochrome character set consists of the 8-by-14 character set with supplemental 9-by-14 characters. Using this font size allows higher-resolution characters to be used when the display is operating in mode 7, which has a resolution of 720 dots per scan line. See the Load User Character Set with Reset BIOS call in section 11.12.1 for details.

Input Parameters:
BL = The number of the block in display memory to load the 9-by-14 character font. This value may range from 0 to 3 in the EGA and from 0 to 7 in the VGA. It references the desired 8-Kbyte block of memory where this monochrome font should be loaded.

Output Parameters:
None.

Display Memory Affected:
The entire 8-Kbyte block of memory in display memory bit plane 2, and possibly bit plane 3, as specified in the Block Number parameter.

11.12.3 AH = 11, AL = 2: ROM 8-by-8 (with Reset) (EGA/VGA)

This function loads the ROM-resident 8-by-8 character set into the selected 8-Kbyte block of the display memory. This function operates similarly to the Load ROM Monochrome Character Set with Reset BIOS call. Unlike that function, which loads the 9-by-14 character set into display memory, this function copies the 8-by-8 character set into display memory. The entire character set is loaded.

This 8-by-8 font allows 43 lines of text to be displayed on a single screen when one of the 350-scan-line modes is active. It allows 60 lines of text to be displayed when the 480-line mode is active. All 8-bit-wide fonts allow 80 characters per line in the standard 640-pixel horizontal formats. See the Load ROM Monochrome Character Set and the Load User Character Set with Reset BIOS calls in section 11.12.1 for details.

Input Parameters:
  BL = The number of the block in display memory to load the 8-by-8 character font. This value may range from 0 to 3 for the EGA and 0 to 7 for the VGA. It references the desired 8-Kbyte blocks of display memory where the 8-by-8 font should be loaded.

Output Parameters:
  None.

Display Memory Affected:
  The entire 8-Kbyte block in display memory bit plane 2, and possibly bit plane 3, as specified in the Block Number parameter.

11.12.4 AH = 11, AL = 3: Set Block Specifier (EGA/VGA)

This subroutine selects which of the character sets resident in the display memory should be used to determine the character dot pattern for a given character. In the EGA, four simultaneous character sets may be resident in display memory. In the VGA, eight simultaneous character sets may be resident in display memory. It is possible to have two of these resident character fonts loaded into display memory (active) at a time. Each character set is 256 characters long. When they are chained together, 512 unique characters can be displayed simultaneously.

Bit 3 of the character attribute byte is used either to select one of sixteen foreground colors for the associated character or to choose from one of two resident character sets. Because each character set has 256 characters, an 8-bit-wide character code is required, thus utilizing the 8-bit character code. This leaves eight bits in the character attribute byte to determine the character color, to determine the blinking status, and to select from one of the two character sets. All eight bits of the attribute byte can be dedicated to selecting the character color because it is possible to select one of sixteen foreground colors and one of sixteen background colors. In order to select blinking or not blinking and to select from one of the two character sets, it is necessary to double up on the function of two of the bits within the attribute byte. Bit 7 was selected to have the dual function of either being part of the background color code or being a switch for the blinking feature. Bit 3 was selected to have the dual function of either being part of the foreground color or being a switch for selecting one of the two character fonts.

When it is part of the foreground color, bit 3 is defined as the high-order bit of the 4-bit foreground color field. If a 512-character set is desired, only eight unique foreground colors will be allowed, and the fourth bit, bit 3, will be dedicated to selecting one of the two active character sets. A switch in the attribute byte determines whether sixteen foreground colors and one 256-character set or eight foreground colors and two 256-character sets is used. Bit 3 of the attribute byte is used to select which of the two 256 character sets is selected if the values in the SA and SB fields are different.

The Character Map Select Register consists of two fields called the Character Generator Select A (SA) and the Character Generator Select B (SB) fields. Each of these fields may select one of the four or eight character fonts resident in display memory. If the values in both the SA and SB fields are identical, only one character set is active, and the system automatically considers bit 3 of the attribute byte to be part of the character foreground color code. Only one 256-character set is allowed. If the SA and SB fields are different, bit 3 is automatically assumed to be a switch that selects one of the two 256-character sets for its associated character code. Only one of eight foreground colors is possible per character.

In both the EGA and the VGA, it is recommended that the BIOS call at Int 10 hex, Set Palette Registers, be called before this Block Specifier call is invoked. The Set Individual Palette Register subfunction at AL = 00 hex should be used with the palette register number 12 hex selected by setting the BL Register to 12 hex. This register, number 12 hex, is not actually a palette register. It is the Color Plane Enable Register. If its value is set to 07 hex by setting the BH register to 07 hex, the value in the fourth bit, bit 3, of the character attribute byte is ignored when the color is generated. This is important because if bit 3 is being used to select one of the two character fonts, two character attribute bytes could have different values in bit 3, although both desire to be displayed in the same color.

Input Parameters:

BL = The value to load into the Character Map Select Register. This value contains the A and B fields. The format of this byte input parameter is identical to the bit fields of the Character Map Select Register. The map select fields in the Character Map Select Register on the EGA are shown in Figure 11.1.

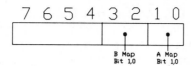

FIGURE 11.1 EGA Character Map Select Fields

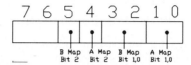

FIGURE 11.2 VGA Character Map Select Fields

In Figure 11.1, each of the fields SA and SB consists of two bits that allow the selection of one of four simultaneously loaded character sets.

The map select fields in the Character Map Select Register on the VGA are shown in Figure 11.2.

In Figure 11.2, each of the A and B select fields consists of three bits that allow the selection of one of eight simultaneously loaded character sets.

Output Parameters:
None.

EGA Registers Affected:
The Character Map Select Register.

11.12.5   AH = 11, AL = 04: ROM 8-by-16 Character Set (with Reset) (VGA)

This function loads the ROM-resident 8-by-16 character set into the selected 8-Kbyte block of the display memory. This function operates similarly to the Load ROM 8×8 Character Set with Reset BIOS call. Unlike that function, which loads the 8-by-8 character set into display memory, this function copies the 8-by-16 character set into display memory. The entire character set is loaded.

This 8-by-16 font allows 30 lines of text to be displayed on a single screen when one of the 480-scan-line modes is active. All 8-bit-wide fonts allow 80 characters per line in the standard 640-pixel horizontal formats. See the Load User Character Set with Reset BIOS calls in section 11.12.1 for details.

Input Parameters:
BL = The number of the block in display memory to load the 8-by-8 character font. This value may range from 0 to 7 for the VGA. It references the desired 8-Kbyte blocks of display memory where the 8-by-16 font should be loaded.

Output Parameters:
None.

Display Memory Affected:
The entire 8-Kbyte block in display memory bit plane 2, and possibly bit plane 3, as specified in the Block Number parameter.

11.12.6   AH = 11, AL = 10: User Alpha Load (EGA/VGA)

This function loads a character set into one of the four or eight blocks of display memory reserved for the resident character sets. This function is nearly identical to the Load User Character Set AH = 11, AL = 0 function. The difference is that this function will recalculate several of the CRT Controller Registers (CRTC Registers) in the EGA/VGA. Recalculating these registers modifies the operational mode. It is modified according to the parameters input to this BIOS call. It should be noted that erratic results may occur if the recalculations are not close to the original values of the modified registers.

A second difference is that no Set Mode is automatically executed before the character set is downloaded. It is highly recommended to execute the Set Mode BIOS call immediately before invoking this function. In addition, the active display page must be 0 before this function is invoked. See the Load User Character Set with Reset function in section 11.12.1 for details on downloading user character sets. Also see the Set Mode function in section 11.2.1 for details on resetting the display mode.

Input Parameters:
BH = The number of bytes per character. The maximum length of a character is 32 bytes. Specifying the number of bytes per character lets the BIOS routine know how many bytes from the user table to copy into each of the 32-byte character slots in the display memory.

BL = Block to Load. This dictates which of the four or eight blocks of display memory dedicated to the character sets should be loaded.

CX = The number of characters to load. Specifying the number of characters lets the BIOS routine know how many blocks of bytes associated with each character to load into the display memory. The total number of bytes in the user array is equal to the number of bytes per character times the number of characters to load.

DX = The character offset into the selected block of memory. This value determines where to load the incoming user character array in the display memory font area. The character patterns in the user character array are organized sequentially, with one character following the previous character. It is not necessary for the first character in the array to be the first character in the character set. Specifying this offset lets the BIOS routine know where in the selected 8-Kbyte block in display memory the user array should be loaded.

ES:BP = The pointer to the user downloadable font contained in a sequential byte buffer. The ES register should contain the segment address of the array and the BP register should contain the offset address of the array.

Output Parameters:
None.

Display Memory Affected:
Plane 2 of display memory beginning at the character offset times 32 and extending for the number of characters times 32. The "times 32" is needed because each character in the display buffer occupies 32 bytes regardless of how many bytes per character are specified in the user array.

EGA Registers Affected:
Maximum Scan Line Register. The number of scan lines per character. Set equal to the bytes per character input parameter minus 1.

Cursor Start Register. Defines at which scan line in the character box to begin drawing the rectangular cursor block. In the EGA, this is set to the number of bytes per character parameter minus 1. This is the bottom line of the character box. In conjunction with the Cursor End Register (see below), this defines a cursor that fills the entire character box.

In the VGA, this is set to the number of bytes per character parameter minus 2. This is the next-to-the-bottom line of the character box. In conjunction with the Cursor End Register below, this defines a cursor that fills the bottom two lines of the character box.

Cursor End Register. Defines at which scan line in the character box to end drawing the rectangular cursor block. In the EGA, this is set to 0, which is the top line of the character box. In the VGA, it is set to the number of bytes per character parameter minus 1.

Vertical Display End Register. Determines the number of scan lines to include in the display portion of the screen. In the EGA/VGA, this is set according to the calculations in Equation 11.2 if the display is in a 350- or 480-scan-line display mode and according to the calculations in Equation 11.3 if the display is in a 200-scan-line display mode.

Equation 11.2 350- or 480-line Vertical Displacement

Vertical Displacement   =   (the number of rows + 1)
                          × (the number of bytes per character) − 1.

Equation 11.3 200-line Vertical Displacement

Vertical Displacement = (the number of rows + 1)
                          $\times$ (the number of bytes per character $\times$ 2) – 1.

Overflow Register. The Vertical Display End (VDE) field of this register is adjusted. In the EGA, this field is bit 8 of the 9-bit Vertical Display End value. Bits 0–7 are contained in the Vertical Display End Register. In the VGA, this field is bits 8 and 9 of the 10-bit Vertical Display End value. Bits 0–7 are contained in the Vertical Display End Register.

In the VGA, two parameters are also affected by this BIOS call. The first is the number of character rows on the screen. It is modified according to Equation 11.4. In this equation, the number of scan lines is 200, 350, or 400. The 480-scan-line mode is applicable only in the graphics modes 11 hex and 12 hex. Thus, it is not relevant to this alphanumeric mode BIOS call.

Equation 11.4 Number of Rows on a Screen

Rows = (Number of Character rows / Character Height) – 1

The number of rows are calculated from Equation 11.4. The CRT length value, called CRTLEN, is modified according to Equation 11.5.

Equation 11.5 CRT Length Parameter

CRT_LEN = (Rows+1) $\times$ (CRT_COLS $\times$ 2)

11.12.7   AH = 11 Hex, AL = 11 Hex: ROM Monochrome Set (EGA/VGA)

This function loads the ROM-resident monochrome 9-by-14 character set into the selected 8-KByte block of the display memory. It operates similarly to the Load ROM Monochrome Character Set with Reset BIOS call, number 01 hex, with the exception that the Set Mode function is not automatically invoked when this function is called. In addition, the active display page must be 0 before this function is invoked. Display parameters and registers will be modified according to the new font being loaded. See the Load ROM Monochrome Character Set with Reset BIOS call, number 01 hex, and the User Alpha Load BIOS call, number 10 hex, for details.

Input Parameters:
   BL = The number of the block in display memory to load the 9-by-14 character font. This value may range from 0 to 3 in the EGA and 0 to 7 in the VGA. It references one of 8-Kbyte blocks of memory reserved for the character fonts.

Output Parameters:
   None.

Display Memory Affected:
   The entire 8-Kbyte block of memory in display memory bit plane 2, and possibly bit plane 3, as specified in the Block Number parameter.

11.12.8   AH = 11 Hex, AL = 12 Hex: ROM 8-by-8 Set (EGA/VGA)

This call loads the ROM-resident 8-by-8 character set into the selected 8-Kbyte block of display memory. This call operates similarly to the Load ROM 8-by-8 Character Set with Reset BIOS call, 02 hex. Unlike that function, it does not automatically issue a Set Mode command. In addition, the active display page must be 0, and certain display parameters and registers will be modified. See the Load ROM Monochrome Character Set with Reset BIOS call, number 02 hex, in section 11.12.2, and the User Alpha Load BIOS call, number 10 hex, in section 11.12.6, for details.

Input Parameters:
   BL = The number of the block in display memory to load the 8-by-8 character font. This value may range from 0 to 3 for the EGA and 0 to 7 for the VGA. It references one of 8-Kbyte blocks of memory reserved for the character fonts.

Output Parameters:
   None.

Display Memory Affected:
   The entire 8-Kbyte block of memory in display memory bit plane 2, and possibly bit plane 3, as specified in the Block Number parameter.

11.12.9   AH = 11 Hex, AL = 14 Hex: ROM 8-by-16 Set (VGA Only)

This call loads the ROM-resident 8-by-16 character set into the selected 8-Kbyte block of display memory. This call operates similarly to the Load ROM 8-by-16 Character Set with Reset function, 04 hex. Unlike that function, it does not automatically issue a Set Mode command. In addition, the active display page must be 0, and certain display parameters and registers will be modified. See the Load ROM 8-by-16 Character Set with Reset BIOS call, number 04 hex, in section 11.2.5, and the User Alpha Load BIOS call, number 10 hex, in section 11.2.6, for details.

Input Parameters:
   BL = The number of the block in display memory to load the 8-by-16 character font. This value may range from 0 to 3 for the EGA and 0 to 7 for the VGA. It references one of the 8-Kbyte blocks of memory reserved for the character fonts.

Output Parameters:
None.

Display Memory Affected:
The entire 8-Kbyte block of memory in display memory bit plane 2, and possibly bit plane 3, as specified in the Block Number parameter.

11.12.10 AH = 11 Hex, AL = 20 Hex: User Graphics Characters INT 1FH 8 by 8 (EGA/VGA)

This call loads a pointer to an 8-by-8 user-defined character set. This pointer is loaded into the host memory as a vector to the second half of the 8-by-8 character font. This second half refers to characters with ASCII codes from 128 to 256. Only display modes 4, 5, and 6 utilize this pointer. The pointer can be read by invoking the Return Font BIOS call 30 hex with input parameter BH=01 hex. See the Return Font call in section 11.12.15 for details.

In the graphics modes, it is necessary for the character set to reside in host memory because the display memory is dedicated to pixel graphics, and there is no room for character sets. Therefore, in order to allow downloadable character sets, the host memory must be used to store the character bit patterns. Either host RAM or BIOS memory space may be referenced by this pointer.

The character set pointer is a long pointer requiring a segment:offset register pair. In the special case of the 8-by-8 font, the character set pointer refers to the second 128 characters of the character set. The video interrupt 1F hex must be invoked to load the pointer to the second 128 characters, characters 128–255, of the character set. The Set Mode function should be invoked immediately preceding this function. See the Set Mode function in section 11.2.1 for details.

In the EGA, a Parameter Table is maintained in host memory that provides a list of seven long pointers to other tables. Four of these tables are currently implemented, and three are reserved for future use. This Parameter Table is described in Table 11.14.

TABLE 11.14 Parameter Table

Offset (Hex)	Pointer Function (Long Pointer)
0	Video Parameter Table
4	Dynamic Save Area
8	Text Mode Auxiliary Character Generator Table
C	Graphics Mode Auxiliary Character Generator Table
10	Reserved
14	Reserved
18	Reserved

TABLE 11.15 Text Mode Auxiliary Character-Generator Table

Offset (hex)	Type	Function
0	Byte	Bytes per character
1	Byte	Block to load
2	Word	Count to store
4	Word	Character offset
6	Long	Font table pointer
A	Byte	Number of displayed rows. 0 = Maximum.
B	Byte	First mode value
C	Byte	Second mode value
.	.	.
.	.	.

TABLE 11.16 Graphics Mode Auxiliary Character-Generator Table

Offset (Hex)	Type	Function
0	Byte	Number of displayable rows. 0 = maximum.
1	Word	Bytes per character
3	Long	Font table pointer
7	Byte	First mode value
8	Byte	Second mode value
.	.	.
.	.	.

The Text Mode Auxiliary Character Generator Table and the Graphics Mode Auxiliary Character Generator Table apply to these character-set functions. The Text Mode Auxiliary Character Generator Table is described in Table 11.15.

This list is terminated when the mode value is equal to FF hex.

The Graphics Mode Auxiliary Character Generator Table is described in Table 11.16.

This list is terminated when the mode value is equal to FF hex.

Input Parameters:

ES:BP = The pointer to the user downloadable font contained in a sequential byte buffer. The ES register should contain the segment address of the array, and the BP register should contain the offset address of the array.

Output Parameters:

None.

Host Memory Affected:
The Graphics Mode Auxiliary Character Generator Table.

11.12.11 AH = 11 Hex, AL = 21 Hex: User Graphics Characters (EGA/VGA)

This call loads a pointer to a variable-sized user-defined character set. This pointer is loaded into the host memory through the Int 43 hex vector. This call is used in the graphics modes to point to the graphics characters. It is meant to be called immediately after a Set Mode command is issued. See the Load User Graphics Characters BIOS call 20 hex in section 11.12.10 for details.

This pointer can be read by invoking the Return Font BIOS call 30 hex with input parameter BH=01 hex. See the Return Font call in section 11.12.15 for details.

Input Parameters:
BL = Rows specifier. Defines how many character rows are to be on the screen. The standard number is 14, 25, or 43. In the EGA, the programmer may select any number by specifying a count of 0. The DL field then determines the number of rows. The possible row specifiers are listed in Table 11.17.

CX = The number of bytes per character. This dictates the height of the character box.

DL = In the EGA only, the number of character rows on the display if the rows specifier parameter is 0.

ES:BP = The pointer to the user downloadable font contained in a sequential byte buffer. The ES register should contain the segment address of the array, and the BP register should contain the offset address of the array.

Output Parameters:
None.

Host Memory Affected:
The Graphics Mode Auxiliary Character Generator Table.

TABLE 11.17 User Row Specifier

Rows Specifier	Number of Rows
0 (EGA Only)	User-defined in the DL Register
1	14 rows
2	25 rows
3	43 rows

11.12.12   AH = 11 Hex, AL = 22 Hex: Graphics Mode ROM 8-by-14 Character Set (EGA/VGA)

This call loads the long pointer to the 8-by-14 character set located in the EGA/VGA BIOS ROM. A description of the host memory parameter tables is discussed in Load User 8-by-8 Character Set Pointer BIOS call 20 hex. This pointer can be read back by invoking the Return Font BIOS call 30 hex with input parameter BH=02 hex. See the Return Font call in section 11.12.15 for details.

Input Parameters:

BL = Rows specifier. Defines how many character rows are to be on the screen. The standard number is 14, 25, or 43. In the EGA, the programmer may select any number by specifying a count of 0. The DL field then determines the number of rows. The possible values for the row specifier are listed in Table 11.18.

In the VGA, the programmer is restricted to one of the three predetermined number of rows. Thus, the programmer must select 14, 25, or 43 rows on the screen.

DL = In the EGA, the number of character rows on the display if the rows specifier parameter is 0.

Output Parameters:

None.

Host Memory Affected:

The Graphics Mode Auxiliary Character Generator Table.

11.12.13   AH = 11 Hex, AL = 23 Hex: Graphics Mode ROM 8-by-8 Set (Double Dot) (EGA/VGA)

This call loads the long pointer to the lower half of the 8-by-8 character set located in the EGA/VGA BIOS ROM. A description of the host memory parameter tables is given in Load User 8-by-8 Character Set Pointer BIOS call number

TABLE 11.18   8-by-14 Row Specifier

Rows Specifier	Number of Rows
0 (EGA Only)	User-defined in the DL register
1	14 rows
2	25 rows
3	43 rows

TABLE 11.19   8-by-8 Row Specifier

Rows Specifier	Number of Rows
0 (EGA Only)	User-defined in the DL register
1	14 rows
2	25 rows
3	43 rows

12 hex. This pointer can be read by invoking the Return Font BIOS call 30 hex with input parameter BH = 03 hex. See the Return Font call in section 11.12.15 for details.

Input Parameters:

BL = Rows specifier. Defines how many character rows are to be on the screen. The standard number is 14, 25, or 43. In the EGA, the programmer may select any number by specifying a count of 0. The DL field then determines the number of rows. The possible values for the row specifier are listed in Table 11.19.

In the VGA, the programmer is restricted to one of the three predetermined number of rows. Thus, the programmer must select 14, 25, or 43 rows on the screen.

DL = In the EGA, the number of character rows on the display if the rows specifier parameter is 0.

Output Parameters:

None.

Host Memory Affected:

The Graphics Mode Auxiliary Character Generator Table.

11.12.14   AH = 11 Hex, AL = 24 Hex: Graphics Mode ROM 8-by-16 Set (VGA)

This call loads the long pointer to the 8-by-16 character set located in the EGA BIOS ROM. A description of the host memory parameter tables is given in Load User 8-by-8 Character Set Pointer BIOS call number 12 hex. This pointer can be read by invoking the Return Font BIOS call 30 hex with input parameter BH = 08 hex. See the Return Font call in section 11.12.15 for details.

Input Parameters:

BL = Rows specifier. Defines how many character rows are to be on the screen. The standard number is 14, 25, or 43. The possible values for the row specifier are listed in Table 11.20.

TABLE 11.20 8-by-16 Row Specifier

Rows Specifier	Number of Rows
0	User-defined in the DL register
1	14 rows
2	25 rows
3	43 rows

In the VGA, the programmer is restricted to one of the three predetermined number of rows. Thus, the programmer must select 14, 25, or 43 rows on the screen.

DL = In the EGA, the number of character rows on the display if the rows specifier parameter is 0.

Output Parameters:
None.

Host Memory Affected:
The Graphics Mode Auxiliary Character Generator Table.

11.12.15 AH = 11 Hex, AL = 30 Hex: Return Character Generator Information (EGA/VGA)

This call returns information related to the current character font to the calling program. The information returned includes the bytes per character, the number of character rows on the screen, and the pointer to one of the character sets. The programmer may select which of six pointers for the EGA or eight pointers for the VGA should be returned. These pointers indicate the starting location in host memory space of the respective character sets. The pointers returned to the calling program are listed in Table 11.21.

In addition to interrupt 10 hex, there are two video BIOS interrupts that affect the operation of the EGA/VGA font selection. These interrupts, 1F hex and 43 hex, specify the location of user-defined character sets resident in host memory. It is necessary to use host memory to store the downloadable character sets when in a graphics mode. This is necessary because all of the four display memory bit planes are reserved for graphics data. Unlike in the alphanumeric modes, in the graphics modes, bit planes 2 and 3 are not available to hold the character fonts.

The interrupt 1F hex pointer refers to the upper 128 characters of the 8-by-8 character set used in the graphics display modes 4, 5, or 6. The interrupt 43 hex pointer refers to the 8-by-14 character set or the lower 128 characters of the 8-by-8 character set.

TABLE 11.21 Return Character Generator Information

Pointer Specifier	Adapter	Character Set Pointer Selected
0	EGA,VGA	Interrupt 1F hex (user 8-by-8 upper)
1	EGA,VGA	Interrupt 43 hex (user 8-by-8 lower, 8-by-14)
2	EGA,VGA	ROM 8-by-14
3	EGA,VGA	ROM 8-by-8 lower 128 characters
4	EGA,VGA	ROM 8-by-8 upper 128 characters
5	EGA,VGA	ROM 9-by-14 supplement
6	VGA	ROM 8-by-16
7	VGA	ROM 9-by-16 supplement

There are three fonts loaded into the EGA ROM BIOS and five in the VGA ROM BIOS. The 8-by-8 font is special because it is split up into two character sets, one representing the lower 128 characters and the second representing the upper 128 characters. Initially, the 8-by-8 character font was split into two halves, each having 128 characters. It was believed that room could be saved by separating the graphics characters from the alphanumeric characters. In retrospect, this seems to have been a poor decision.

Input Parameters:
BH = Pointer specifier. See Table 11.21.

Output Parameters:
CX = The number of bytes per character in the selected character set.

DL = In the EGA, the number of character rows on the screen; in the VGA, the number of character rows on the screen minus 1.

ES = The segment pointer to the beginning of the selected character font. The entire address is specified in the ES:BP register pair.

BP = The offset pointer to the beginning of the selected character font. The entire address is specified in the ES:BP register pair.

11.13   ALTERNATE SELECT

The alternate select functions perform a variety of seemingly unrelated tasks. These tasks range from returning video information to selecting the number of scan lines in an alphanumeric mode.

11.13.1   AH = 12 Hex, AL = 0 Hex, BL = 10 Hex: Return Video Information (EGA/VGA)

This function returns information related to the current display mode and the configuration of the EGA/VGA. Information returned includes whether a color or monochrome mode is active, the amount of memory on the adapter, the status of the feature bits on the adapter feature connector, and the video configuration code. The video configuration code is determined from the four sense switches on the EGA and from the configuration set by the adapter POST on the VGA. There are no sense switches on the VGA.

Input Parameters:
  None.

Output Parameters:
  BH = Video Controller Mode.
  0 = Color. This indicates that several EGA/VGA registers are mapped into the host port space at 3Dx hex. The value of x depends on the selected register.
  1 = Monochrome. This indicates that several EGA/VGA registers are mapped into the host port space at 3Bx hex. The value of x depends on the selected register.
  BL = Memory Size. The 2-bit code returned indicates the size of the display memory as follows:
  0 = 64 Kbytes
  1 = 128 Kbytes
  2 = 192 Kbytes
  3 = 256 Kbytes

  CH = Feature control bits. At power up, the feature bits FEAT0 and FEAT1, located on pin 19 and 17 respectively, are read and the values of these pins are recorded. This BIOS call returns the status of these bits as they appeared during power up. Subsequent changes made to these bits can be determined only by reading the DIA field of the Input Status #1 Register. See the Input Status #1 Register in section 10.2.4 for details. This is valid on the EGA only.
  CL = Video configuration code. There are typically four sense switches located on the rear panel of EGA that dictate the desired configuration. Some EGA implementations utilize six sense switches, the additional two being used for compatibility modes. The value returned as the configuration code indicates which display adapter is configured as the primary and secondary display adapter and which monitor is connected to it. Typical display adapters include the MDA, CGA, EGA, and VGA. Typical monitors include the monochrome, color RGBI, and enhanced color RrGgBb. Which adapters and monitors correspond to which configuration code varies with the particular manufacturer's version of the EGA/VGA adapter board.

11.13.2 AH = 12 Hex, AL = 0 Hex, BL = 20 Hex: Select Alternate Print Screen Routine (EGA/VGA)

This call allows a user-defined print-screen routine to be invoked instead of the print-screen handler normally invoked through the BIOS call. The normally used handler resides in host system BIOS and is called by the ROM interrupt 05 hex. This alternate print handler may be utilized to output the screen image to specific devices or to print all of the data on the screen if the EGA/VGA is in a nonstandard display mode that uses 43 rows per page or 132 columns per line.

When this Select Alternate Print Screen Routine function is invoked, the vector loaded into the EGA BIOS 05 hex interrupt is used to direct control to the proper print handler. It is the responsibility of the programmer to supply the print handler. In addition, the programmer must load the interrupt vector corresponding to interrupt 05 hex in location 14 hex of host memory.

The print-screen status is located in the EGA information buffer in host memory at address 500 hex. If the printer is offline or not ready, a timeout will occur and control will return to the calling program.

Input Parameters:
   None.

Output Parameters:
   None.

Host Memory Affected:
   500 hex = Print Screen Status. The codes in the status byte are described in the Table 11.22.

11.13.3   AH = 12 Hex, BL=30 Hex: Select Scan Lines for Alphanumeric Modes (VGA)

This call selects the number of scan lines and the default character set to use for an upcoming alphanumeric mode. The change takes effect at the next occurrence of a mode set. It is possible to configure the VGA to have either 200, 350, or 400 scan lines per screen in the alphanumeric modes. In addition, a 480-scan-line mode is possible in the graphics modes 11 hex and 12 hex. This feature provides some flexibility in the display modes.

TABLE 11.22   Print Screen Status Code

Value (Hex)	Meaning
0	Idle
1	Printing
FF	Error occurred during printing

Input Parameters:
AL = The number of scan lines per page.
=0 200 scan lines per page. (Can't be used in mode 7.)
=1 350 scan lines per page.
=2 400 scan lines per page.

Output Parameters:
AL = Indicates that the call was valid or invalid.
=12 hex   Call was valid.
=any other value.   Call was invalid.

Registers Affected:
The Vertical Size (VS) field of the VGA Miscellaneous Output Register.

11.13.4   AH = 12 Hex, BL=31 Hex: Default Palette Loading During Mode Set (VGA)

This call selects whether the Palette Registers, Overscan Registers, and Color Registers will be loaded with default values during following mode sets. If this feature is disabled, these registers will remain untouched. Together with the clearing or not clearing of the display memory during a mode set, these calls provide the programmer with a certain amount of flexibility during mode sets.

Input Parameters:
AL = Select or deselect the loading of the Palette Registers, Overscan Register, and Color Registers
=0 Enable register loading during a mode set.
=1 Do not load registers during a mode set.

Output Parameters:
AL = Indicates that the call was valid or invalid.
=12 hex   Call was valid
=any other value.   Call was invalid.

Registers Affected:
Palette Registers, Overscan Registers, Color Registers, if enabled.

11.13.5   AH = 12 Hex, BL = 32 Hex: Video Enable/Disable (VGA)

This call selects whether the video should be enabled or disabled. The video input ports and the host address decoding are enabled or disabled as determined by this call. This is useful if more than one device is residing in the system with the same host port addresses or host memory addresses. It allows the VGA to be effectively pulled out of the system to avoid bus conflicts. This is especially important on systems where the VGA is part of the backplane.

Disabling the video can improve the data transfer speed when data is sent from the host to the VGA. The video refresh logic is not competing for the memory bus. When the video is enabled, both the host and the video refresh logic must compete for the display memory bus. Data transfer throughput increases of 3 to 1 were observed when loading the buffer with the video disabled as opposed to loading the buffer with the video screen enabled. A similar but less pronounced speed advantage is observed when the video screen is turned off. This can be accomplished by invoking the Video Screen On/Off BIOS call AH = 12 hex, BL = 36 hex.

Input Parameters:
AL = Enable or disable the VGA video port and memory addressing.
=0 Enable the video.
=1 Disable the video.

Output Parameters:
AL = Indicates that the call was valid or invalid.
=12 hex   Call was valid
=any other value. Call was invalid.

Registers Affected:

11.13.6 AH = 12 Hex, BL = 33 Hex: Summing to Gray Scales (VGA)

This call selects whether the colors in the Color Registers will be summed to convert the values in the Color Registers from colors to gray scales. The summing operation occurs during Mode Set and during calls that affect the Color Registers. All 256 Color Registers will be summed if this summing feature is enabled.

This call, like the Sum Color Values, performs a function similar to that performed by Gray Scale BIOS call AH=10 hex, AL = 1B hex. However, in this call no actual summing operation takes place. The composite color output from the Color Registers to the monitor is derived from the values of the three primary colors—red, green, and blue. These three primary color values are stored in each of the 256 Color Registers. Each primary color value ranges from 0 to 63. The higher the value is for each color, the brighter the color. The composite color observed on the monitor is derived by adding together the three values of red, green, and blue. When the values in each of the three primary colors are equal, the resultant color is a gray scale. The amount of intensity in each of the three colors determines the brightness value of the gray scale. This is similar to viewing a color video on a monochrome monitor.

A weighted sum is used to produce the gray scale value. The equation used is listed in Equation 11.6.

Equation 11.6 Summing to Gray Scale

$$Gray = (.30 \times Red) + (.59 \times Green) + (.11 \times Blue)$$

In this equation, the three primary colors refer to the values in the red, green, and blue components of each Color Register. The "gray scale" result of this equation is then loaded into the red, green, and blue components of the same Color Register. If the original color is a gray scale, the resultant color will also be a gray scale of the same intensity because the three multipliers sum to 1.0. When enabled, this operation modifies all 256 Color Registers.

The summing operation occurs during Mode Set and during operations that access the Color Registers. If implemented in C, this operation would be similar to Listing 11.2. The code in Listing 11.2 assumes that the three primary colors of each Color Register have been read from the Color Registers and loaded into the red, green and blue arrays.

LISTING 11.2 Summing to All Registers to Gray Scale

```
unsigned char Red[256], Blue[256], Green[256], Gray;
int i;
for (i=0; i<256; i++)
{ Gray = (.30 * Red[i])+(.59 * Green[i])+(.11 * Blue[i]);
 Red[i] = Gray;
 Green[i] = Gray;
 Blue[i] = Gray;
}
```

Input Parameters:
AL = Enable or disable the Color Registers summing.
=0 Enable the summing.
=1 Disable the summing.

Output Parameters:
AL = Indicates that the call was valid or invalid.
=12 hex   Call was valid
=any other value.   Call was invalid.

Registers Affected:
If enabled, all 256 Color Registers.

11.13.7 AH = 12 Hex, BL = 34 Hex: Cursor Emulation (VGA)

This call selects whether the cursor will be drawn according to the current character definition. The cursor shape is initialized to be a horizontal line two scan lines wide at the bottom of the character box. If the emulation mode is active, the cursor will be drawn according to the current character height. Calls made to Set Cursor Type, the BIOS call at AH=01 hex, will cause software to be invoked automatically. This software will determine the type of cursor and whether any modifications are needed because of the new cursor height.

If there is no cursor or an overbar cursor, no modifications are made. If there is an underline cursor, a full-block cursor or a half-block cursor, adjustments are made. These states are determined by the Start and End parameters passed to the Set Cursor Type call. The values are listed in Table 11.23.

If the program detects that adjustments are active and the start or end of the cursor are out of bounds, adjustments are made until neither the Start Cursor nor End Cursor occur out of bounds. The adjustments made if the Start or End Cursor are out of bounds are listed in Table 11.24.

TABLE 11.23 Cursor Type During Cursor Emulation

Cursor Type	Parameters Set	Adjustable Cursor Type
Bit 5=1	None	No
Start End<=3	Overbar	No
Start+2>= End	Underline	Yes
Start <= 2 or End < Start	Full Block	Yes
Start > 2 Half	Half Block	Yes

TABLE 11.24 Start and End Cursor Adjustments

Cursor Type	Start and End Cursor Adjustments.
Full Block	Modify End to the last line in the character box.
Half Block	Modify Start to be equal to the scan line half way in the character height. Modify End to the bottom scan line of the box.
Height > 16	An underline cursor is positioned on the last line in the character box.

Input Parameters:
AL = Enable or disable the cursor emulation mode.
=0 Enable the cursor emulation.
=1 Disable the cursor emulation.

Output Parameters:
AL = Indicates that the call was valid or invalid.
=12 hex   Call was valid
=any other value.   Call was invalid.

11.13.8 AH = 12 Hex, BL = 35 Hex: Display Switch (VGA)

This call allows the programmer to select between the Personal System/2 Display Adapter and the video adapter that resides on the system motherboard. The system motherboard is also referred to as the *planar. The addresses in the host I/O space of the input/output ports, the addresses in host memory address space of the display memory, and the BIOS routines may be configured to cause bus conflicts. If this is the case, it is necessary to disable one of the video systems before enabling the other.*

At power-up, the power-on self-test (POST) determines if there are multiple display adapters resident. If there is an addressing conflict between the planar video and the adapter video, the POST initializes the adapter video and disables the planar video. If there is no addressing conflict, the POST initializes both video systems.

If the adapter video and the planar video are in conflict, only one can be active at a time. This BIOS call is used to select which video should be active and which should be inactive. In order for the BIOS routine to be able to make a system active or inactive, it must have access to a 128-byte buffer to save the current display state. It is necessary for the BIOS to store the current display state of each of the video systems in two such buffers. The programmer must call this BIOS routine twice to initialize both buffers. This is accomplished by invoking this BIOS call with the AL input parameter set to a 0 for the adapter video and a 1 for the planar video. The programmer must provide the routine with a long pointer to a 128-byte buffer for both of these calls.

Subsequent switching of the active video can be accomplished by switching the active video off and switching the inactive video on. These functions are invoked by setting the AL input parameter to 2 and 3 respectively.

Input Parameters:
AL = Desired function of call.
=0 Switch off the adapter video. This also saves the system status in the buffer pointed to by the ES:DX register pair. The adapter video is enabled at the power-on self-test (POST). This call is useful when the display adapter is

being changed for the first time after POST. It would be called first to disable the adapter video and to save the display state. It would then be followed by a call to this routine to switch on the planar video using the AL = 1 option.

=1 Switch on the planar video. This also saves the system status in the buffer pointed to by the ES:DX register pair. Because the planar video is disabled at POST, this call will be useful when changing the display adapter for the first time after POST.

=2 Switch off the active video. Assuming that either the planar video or the adapter video is active, a call to this routine switches whichever video is active to an inactive state. This would precede a call to this routine to switch on the inactive video using the AL= 4 option.

=3 Switch on the inactive video. The inactive video will be made active. No buffers are initialized as they are in options AL = 0 and AL = 1.

Output Parameters:
AL = Indicates that the call was valid or invalid.
=12 hex   Call was valid
=any other value.   Call was invalid.

11.13.9   AH = 12 Hex, BL = 36 Hex: Video Screen On/Off (VGA)

This call selects whether the video outputs to the display monitor should be enabled or disabled. This provides a convenient way for turning off the display which can improve the data-transfer speed from the host to the VGA by eliminating the video refresh logic's demand for the memory bus. When the video screen is turned on, both the host and the video refresh logic must compete for the display memory bus. Data transfer throughput increases of 2 to 1 are observed when the buffer is loaded with the video screen off as opposed to with the video screen on. A similar but even more pronounced speed advantage is observed when the entire video system is disabled. This can be accomplished by invoking the Video Enable/Disable BIOS call AH = 12 hex, BL = 32 hex.

Turning off the video screen is also beneficial to the monitor when the monitor is not in use. It protects the phosphor from being burned out at specific locations but does not require turning on and off the power to the monitor.

Several software products incorporate this video screen on/off feature into a memory resident program that senses when a specified amount of time has passed without a keyboard keystroke. The program concludes from the inactivity at the keyboard that the user is not at the monitor; it therefore turns off the screen. Any keystrike will turn it on again.

Input Parameters:
AL = Enable or disable the VGA video port and memory addressing.
=0 Turn on the video.
=1 Turn off the video.

Output Parameters:
   AL = Indicates that the call was valid or invalid.
   =12 hex   Call was valid
   =any other value.   Call was invalid.

Registers Affected:
   The Screen Off (SO) field of the Clocking Mode Register.

11.14 WRITING A STRING OF CHARACTERS

11.14.1   AH = 13 Hex: Write String of Characters (EGA/VGA)

This call writes a string of one or more characters to the specified page of the display. This function uses the Write TTY function to write the data to the display. The Write TTY feature handles carriage returns (0D hex), line feeds (0A hex), backspace (08 hex) and bell (07 hex) characters as control characters rather than printable characters. The "line feed" control code causes the screen to be scrolled when it is encountered at the bottom of the active display page.

There are four variations of the Write TTY function; the appropriate variation is selected by the Format Code parameter in the AL register. Two of the four options consider the input character string to consist entirely of character codes. The string is written to the display with a common attribute byte. This value of this attribute byte is also input to the BIOS call. The other two options consider the input character string to consist of alternating character codes and attribute bytes. This allows each individual character to have its own unique attribute.

The Write TTY function normally moves the cursor one position to the right for every character that is output, somewhat as a typewriter does. Two of these options leave the cursor position unmodified. The other two options leave the cursor positioned at the end of the string just written to the display.

This function exhibits a few peculiarities. Although the function can write to pages other than the active page, the active page will scroll. When the host processor is an Intel 80286 microprocessor, as is the case in AT computers, the page parameter in BH is ignored, and the data is always written to the active page.

When the input character string consists of alternating character and attribute bytes, it is assumed that each character code is followed by an attribute byte. Together, each of these pairs determines the character dot pattern, colors, and blinking. The special carriage-movement characters are not printable on the screen and therefore require no attribute byte. These characters are loaded into the input character string with no attribute byte, causing strings of consecutive character codes to occur in the input parameter array with no separating attribute bytes.

TABLE 11.25 Write String Options

Format Code	Function	Cursor Motion
0	Character,character	None
1	Character,character	Moves to end of string
2	Character,attribute	None
3	Character,attribute	Moves to end of string

Input Parameters:

AL = Option code. The code selects which of the four types of write string operations is desired. The possible options and their associated functions are listed in Table 11.25.

BH = Page number. Directs the output to the selected page. The number of possible pages depends on the display mode and the amount of memory resident on the adapter.

BL = Attribute byte if the Format Code in AL is a 0 or 1. This attribute byte is associated with all of the printable characters in the string that are output to the display.

CX = Length of the string. In this function, as in the Write TTY function, the length is limited by the screen size in the alphanumeric modes and by the end of the current line if one of the display graphics modes is used.

DH = Cursor row position to begin writing the character string.

DL = Cursor column position to begin writing the character string.

ES = Pointer to the segment of the input string. The entire long pointer is input in the ES:BP register pair.

BP = Pointer to the offset of the input string. The entire long pointer is input in the ES:BP register pair.

Host Memory Affected:

450 Cursor position.

11.15   RETURN CONDITION OF THE VGA

Three BIOS calls are provided to return information regarding the state of the VGA. These include reading and writing the display combination code, returning the functionality/state information, and saving and restoring the video state.

11.15.1   AH = 1B Hex: Read/Write Display Combination Code (VGA)

This call reads or writes the Display Combination Code (DCC) into low memory. This call is meant to be used as a system function and typically is not invoked by the applications programmer. This call is invoked by the Power-on Self-test (POST) to initialize the BIOS. It reads or writes to the active video system and to the inactive video system.

The Display Combination Codes are listed in Table 11.26. The monitor information is not supported when the VGA is in a dual-screen configuration.

Input Parameters:
AL = Selects whether the call performs a read or write of the DCC.
=0 Read the Display Combination Code (DCC).
=1 Write the Display Combination Code (DCC).
BH = Inactive video system Display Combination Code (DCC).
BL = Active video system Display Combination Code (DCC).

Output Parameters:
AL = Indicates that the call was valid or invalid.
=1A hex   Call was valid
=any other value.   Call was invalid.
BH = Inactive video system Display Combination Code (DCC).
BL = Active video system (DCC).

Registers Affected:
None.

Host Memory Affected:
Low memory storage location for the Display Combination Code (DCC).

TABLE 11.26   Display Combination Codes (DCC)

Code	Description	Monitor
0	Monochrome Display Adapter (MDA)	No monitor
1	Monochrome Display Adapter (MDA)	Monochrome
2	Color Graphics Adapter (CGA)	Color
7	Personal System/2 Display Adapter	Monochrome
8	Personal System/2 Display Adapter	Color

11.15.2   AH = 1B Hex: Return Functionality/State Information (VGA)

This call reads the functionality/state table and returns the table to the calling routine. The table is loaded into a buffer that is pointed to by a long pointer passed to the call.

Input Parameters:

BX = Implementation type. Currently, this value must be 0.

ES = Pointer to the offset of the functionality/state table. The entire long pointer is input in the ES:DI register pair.

DI = Pointer to the segment of the functionality/state table. The entire long pointer is input in the ES:DI register pair.

Output Parameters:

AL = Indicates that the call was valid or invalid.
=1B hex   Call was valid
=any other value.   Call was invalid.

Host Memory Affected:

The array as pointed to by the ES:DI long pointer.

11.15.3   AH = 1C Hex: Save/Restore Video State (VGA)

This call either reads the active video state and returns the information from the video system to a host buffer or writes the active video state to the video system from the host buffer. The buffer is pointed to by the long pointer passed to this call in the ES:BX register pair. This call is not supported in dual-screen configurations when the active adapter is an alternate adapter—that is, the Monochrome Display Adapter or the Color Display Adapter.

This call has three options that allow the programmer to store any or all combinations of the video hardware state, the video data areas, and the video palette state and the Color Registers.

Input Parameters:

AL = Call option indicating desired function.

=0 Return the size of the save or restore buffer depending on the value passed in the selection field in the CX register.

=1 Save the video state by reading the desired values in the selection field in the CX registers and sending this data back to the host memory buffer. The host memory buffer is pointed to by the long pointer in the ES:BX register pair.

=2 Restore the video state by writing the desired values, as indicated in the selection field in the CX registers from the host buffer, and loading this data into the video system. The host memory buffer is pointed to by the long pointer in the ES:BX register pair.

CX = Selection of areas of the video system to save or restore. Any or all of these areas can be saved by setting the associated bits 0 through 2 in CX register. Setting the bit to 1 causes the associated video area to be saved or restored. For example, if bits 0 and 1 are set, both the video hardware state and the video data areas will be saved or restored.

Bit 0 = Video hardware state.

Bit 1 = Video data areas.

Bit 2 = Video DAC state and Color Registers.

ES = Pointer to the offset of the save/restore buffer. The entire long pointer is input in the ES:BX register pair.

BX = Pointer to the segment of the save/restore buffer. The entire long pointer is input in the ES:BX register pair.

Output Parameters:

AL = Indicates that the call was valid or invalid.

=1C hex   Call was valid

=any other value.   Call was invalid.

BX = The size block count of the save or restore buffer when the "return size" selection is invoked, which happens when the AL = 0 option is used.

Chapter 12

Programming Examples

12.1 LIST OF STANDARD VGA FUNCTIONS

This chapter covers several functions written in both C and assembly language that interact with the Standard EGA/VGA. Many of these functions write directly to the EGA/VGA; others rely on BIOS. Wherever possible, non-BIOS functions are used for time-sensitive operations. Many of these functions are relevant to the Super VGAs. Others require specially tailored functions for the Super VGA. For example, the *RdColors* function reads the color registers. The color registers have not changed from the Standard VGA to the Super VGAs. This is not the case for memory-related functions like *WrWin_256*. The Standard VGA assumes a single bank of 64 Kbytes. This is not the case for the Super VGAs. Consequently, bank swapping is necessary in the Super VGA version of *WrWin_256*. Any of these functions can be used when either a Standard VGA or Super VGA is being used in display modes 1–13 hex since these are the Standard VGA modes.

Tables 12.1 through 12.11 provide brief descriptions of each function present in Chapter 12. Table 12.12 provides the function prototypes for each function.

TABLE 12.1 Control and Request Status

Listing	Name	Function	Page
12.1	OnVideo	Turn on the video output drivers	491
12.1	OffVideo	Turn off the video output drivers	491
12.2	SetMode	Set the active display mode	491
12.2	SetPage	Set the active display page	491

(continued)

TABLE 12.1   (cont.)

TABLE 12.2   Alphanumerics

TABLE 12.2 *(cont.)*

Listing	Name	Function	Page
12.14	WrCursor	Position the cursor (BIOS)	510
12.14	RdCursor	Read the cursor (BIOS)	511
12.14	DefCurs	Define the cursor position	511
12.14	Wr_Cursor	Position cursor	512
12.14	Rd_Cursor	Read the cursor	512
12.15	ScrollUp	Scroll a rectangular region up	513
12.15	ScrollDw	Scroll a rectangular region down	514

TABLE 12.3 Drawing Functions Regarding a Point

Listing	Name	Function	Page
12.16	Wr_Point	Write a point using BIOS	515
12.16	Wr_Point_16	Write a point in 16-color mode without setup	516
12.16	Wr_Pixel_16	Write a point in 16-color mode	517
12.16	Wr_Pixel_256	Write a point in 256-color mode	518
12.17	Rd_Point	Read a point using BIOS	519
12.17	Rd_Pixel_16	Read a point in 16-color mode	519
12.17	Rd_Pixel_256	Read a point in 256-color mode	521

TABLE 12.4 Drawing Functions Regarding a Line

Listing	Name	Function	Page
12.18	Wr_HLine_16	Draw a horizontal line in 16-color mode	523
12.18	Hsub1	Horizontal subroutine for 1 byte in 16-color mode	524
12.18	Hsub2	Horizontal subroutine for 2 bytes in 16-color mode	525
12.18	Hsub3	Horizontal subroutine for more bytes in 16-color mode	526
12.18	Wr_HLine_256	Draw a horizontal line in 256-color mode	527
12.18	Clr_Part	Clear part of the display used in 256-color mode above	527

(continued)

TABLE 12.4 *(cont.)*

Listing	Name	Function	Page
12.19	Wr_VLine_16	Draw a vertical line in 16-color mode	529
12.19	Wr_VLine_256	Draw a vertical line in 256-color mode	531
12.20	Wr_Line_16	Draw a vertical line in 16-color mode	534
12.20	Wr_Line_256	Draw a vertical line in 256-color mode	536

TABLE 12.5 Drawing Functions Regarding a Circle

Listing	Name	Function	Page
12.21	Wr_Circle_16	Draw a circle in 16-color mode	539
12.21	Wr_Circle_256	Draw a circle in 256-color mode	541
12.21	Circ_Pnt_16	Circle subroutine for 16-color circle	541
12.21	Circ_Pnt_256	Circle subroutine for 256-color circle	542

TABLE 12.6 Drawing Functions Regarding a Rectangular Window

Listing	Name	Function	Page
12.22	Wr_Win_16	Write a window in 16-color mode	544
12.22	Wr_Win_256	Write a window in 256-color mode	544
12.22	MapMask	Set the Map Mask Register for 16-color mode	545
12.22	Wr_Graph_Win	Write a graphics window subroutine	545
12.22	Wr_Part	Write to part or all of a 64 Kbyte bank of memory	546
12.23	Wr_Alpha_Win	Write an alphanumeric window	547
12.24	Rd_Win_16	Read a window in 16-color mode	547
12.24	Rd_Win_256	Read a window in 256-color mode	548

TABLE 12.6 *(cont.)*

Listing	Name	Function	Page
12.24	ReadMap	Set the Read Map Register for 16-color mode	549
12.24	Rd_Graph_Win	Read a graphics window subroutine	549
12.24	Rd_Part	Read from part or all of a 64 Kbyte bank of memory	550
12.25	Rd_Alpha_Win	Read an alphanumeric window	551

TABLE 12.7 Utility Drawing Functions Table Caption

Listing	Name	Function	Page
12.26	DeMux	Demultiplex eight planar pixels into packed	552
12.26	Mux	Demultiplex eight packed pixels into planar	553
12.27	Clipper	Clip a line coordinate	555
12.27	OutCode	Clipping subroutine	556
12.27	Reject	Clipping subroutine for trivial reject	556
12.27	Accept	Clipping subroutine for trivial accept	557

TABLE 12.8 Drawing Functions Regarding Clearing

Listing	Name	Function	Page
12.28	Clr_Alpha_Lines	Clear one or more alphanumeric lines	558
12.29	Clr_Win_16	Clear a rectangular window in 16-color mode	560
12.29	Clr_Win_256	Clear a rectangular window in 256-color mode	561
12.29	Clr_Graph_Win	Clear a graphics window subroutine	561
12.30	Clr_Alpha_Win	Clear an alphanumeric window subroutine	562

TABLE 12.9 Font-Related Functions

Listing	Name	Function	Page
12.31	Wrfont	Write a font to display memory	563
12.32	UserSet	Load a pointer to a user-defined font	564
12.32	Rom8x8	Load a pointer to an 8-by-8 lower 128 long font	565
12.32	Rom8x14	Load a pointer to an 8-by-14 256 long font	565
12.32	Rom8x16	Load a pointer to an 8-by-16 256 long font	566
12.33	Guser8x8	Load a user-defined 8-by-8 128 long font	567
12.33	GuserSet	Load a user-defined 8-by-8 128 font graphics mode	567
12.33	Grom8x8	Load an 8-by-8 Rom-based 128 long font	568
12.33	Grom8x14	Load an 8-by-14 Rom-based 256 long font	568
12.33	Grom8x16	Load an 8-by-16 Rom-based 256 long font	569
12.34	FontInfo	Return font pointer and other info	569
12.35	RdBlock	Read the A and B font block numbers	571
12.35	WrBlock	Write the A and B font block numbers	572
12.35	BlockVal	Set the value for the A and B block subroutine	572
12.36	MaxScan	Set the maximum scan lines per display	573
12.37	F25row	Set up for a 25-row display	574
12.37	F43row	Set up for a 25-row display	575
12.37	F50row	Set up for a 25-row display	576
12.38	SetLines	Set either 200, 350, or 400 scan lines per display	578
12.39	Get_Font_Pattern	Read a selected font into a buffer	579
12.39	RdFont	Read a font subroutine	579
12.40	Make_Italic	Create an italic font	580

TABLE 12.10 Graphics Mode Font-Related Functions

Listing	Name	Function	Page
12.41	Wr_StringG	Write a string in graphics mode	581
12.41	Wr_CharG_16	Write a string in a 16-color graphics mode	582
12.41	Wr_CharG_256	Write a string in a 256-color graphics mode	582
12.41	Write_Points	Write points internal subroutine for above	586
12.41	PutGString	Write a character string in graphics mode	586
12.41	Put_GChar	Write a character in graphics mode with setup	587
12.41	Put_G_Char	Write a character in graphics mode without setup	587
12.41	GraphChr	Draw a graphics character	588
12.41	Setup_for_Write_Mode	Setup for write mode 1, 2, or 3	589
12.41	Restore_to_Write_Mode_0	Restore to write mode 0	589

TABLE 12.11 Palette and Color Register Functions

Listing	Name	Function	Page
12.42	EnCol	Encode a red, green, blue color to a palette format	590
12.42	DecCol	Decode a palette format to red, green, blue color	591
12.42	EnCols	Encode several red, green, blue to palette formats	591
12.42	DecCols	Decode several palette formats to red, green, blue	592
12.43	WrPal	Write a palette register	592
12.43	WrPals	Write several palette registers	593
12.43	RdPal	Read a palette register	593
12.43	RdPals	Read all 17 palette registers (Note Overscan=17)	594
12.44	RdColor	Read a color register through BIOS	594
12.44	RdColors	Read 17 color registers through BIOS	594
12.44	ColorsRd	Read color registers directly	594

(continued)

TABLE 12.11 *(cont.)*

Listing	Name	Function	Page
12.45	WrColor	Write a color register through BIOS	597
12.45	WrColors	Write 17 color registers through BIOS	597
12.45	ColorsWr	Write color registers directly	598
12.46	SumGray	Sum up colors to gray scale values	599
12.47	DefaultP	Return the system to the default palette	599
12.48	Fade	Fade in or out using the color registers	600

The function prototype for each of these functions is provided in Table 12.12. These prototypes would normally be included in the prototype include file when linking to these functions. The functions included in Table 12.12 are described in Tables 12.1 through 12.12 and provided in Listings 12.1 through 12.48. The ASSEM directive is left blank for Microsoft C6 and set to *extern "C"* for Microsoft C7 as follows:

```
#ifdef Microsoftc7
  #define ASSEM extern "C"
#endif

#ifdef Microsoftc6
  #define ASSEM
#endif

#ifdef Borland
  #define ASSEM
#endif
```

Other defines relevant to this software define SHORT and BYTE as follows:

```
#define SHORT      unsigned int
#define BYTE       unsigned char
```

In addition, the assembly language directives and data definitions must be present at the start of the assembly language file. Note that the data definitions would have to be declared as *externs* if more than one file contains the assembly language. The data definitions utilize variables that point to absolute memory locations. If assembled directly, the code is correct for unprotected environments. Later, protected mode code will be provided that will modify these variables. Thus, the assembly language functions do not have to change based on whether protected mode or unprotected mode programs are desired.

TABLE 12.12 Function Prototypes for the Standard VGA Functions

Listing	Function	Prototype
12.1	OnVideo	ASSEM void OnVideo();
12.1	OffVideo	ASSEM void OffVideo();
12.2	SetMode	ASSEM void SetMode(BYTE mode);
12.2	SetPage	ASSEM void SetPage(BYTE page);
12.2	Wr_Start	ASSEM void Wr_Start(SHORT value);
12.2	Rd_Start	ASSEM SHORTtart(void);
12.2	SetRes	void SetRes(BYTE value);
12.2	ESetRes	void ESetRes(BYTE value);
12.2	BitMask	void BitMask(BYTE value);
12.3	Get_Screen_Size	void Get_Screen_Size(int *columns, int *rows, int *char_columns, int *char_rows);
12.4	Get_Screen_Height	ASSEM int Get_Screen_Width(void);
12.4	Get_Screen_Width	ASSEM int Get_Screen_Height(void);
12.5	Get_Char_Width	int Get_Char_Width(void);
12.5	Get_Char_Height	ASSEM int Get_Char_Height(void);
12.6	Is_It_Graphics	int Is_It_Graphics(void);
12.6	Get_Bytes_per_Row	int Get_Bytes_per_Row(void);
12.6	Get_Number_of_Colors	int Get_Number_of_Colors(void);
12.7	Get_Rows_per_Screen	ASSEM int Get_Rows_per_Screen(void);
12.7	Get_Columns_per_Screen	ASSEM int Get_Columns_per_Screen(void);
12.8	VidState	ASSEM int Vidstate(BYTE *buf,int state,BYTE operation);
12.9	RdChar	ASSEM SHORT RdChar(BYTE page,int row,int column);
12.9	WrChar	ASSEM void Wrchar(BYTE page,SHORT charatr,int row,int column);
12.10	RdChars	ASSEM void RdChars(BYTE page,SHORT *charatr_string,int numchar, BYTE row, BYTE column,BYTE rowInc,BYTE colInc);
12.10	WrChars	ASSEM void WrChars(BYTE page,char *string,BYTE forg,BYTE back, BYTE row,BYTE column,BYTE rowInc,BYTE colInc);
12.11	WrStrC	ASSEM void WrStrC(char *string,BYTE attr,BYTE cursor);
12.12	WrStrA	ASSEM void WrStrA(SHORT *charatr,BYTE cursor);
12.13	WrString	ASSEM void WrString(BYTE page,char *string,BYTE grattr);

(continued)

TABLE 12.12 *(cont.)*

Listing	Function	Prototype
12.13	RepChar	ASSEM void RepChar(BYTE page,char character,int numchar,BYTE grattr);
12.14	WrCursor	ASSEM void WrCursor(BYTE page,BYTE row,BYTE column);
12.14	RdCursor	ASSEM void RdCursor(BYTE page,int *row, int *column);
12.14	DefCurs	ASSEM void DefCurs(BYTE start, BYTE end);
12.14	Wr_Cursor	ASSEM void Wr_Cursor(SHORT position);
12.14	Rd_Cursor	ASSEM SHORT Rd_Cursor(void);
12.15	ScrollUp	ASSEM void ScrollUp(int num, int ulRow, int ulCol, int blRow, int blCol, int _for, int back);
12.15	ScrollDw	ASSEM void ScrollDw(int num, int ulRow, int ulCol, int blRow, int blCol, int _for, int back);
12.16	Wr_Point	ASSEM void Wr_Point(BYTE page,int x_addr, int y_addr, BYTE color);
12.16	Wr_Point_16	ASSEM void Wr_Point_16(int x, int y, int bytes_per_row);
12.16	Wr_Pixel_16	ASSEM void Wr_Pixel_16(int x, int y, BYTE color, int bytes_per_row);
12.16	Wr_Pixel_256	ASSEM void Wr_Pixel_256(int x, int y, BYTE color, int bytes_per_row);
12.17	Rd_Point	ASSEM BYTE Rd_Point(int page, int x, int y);
12.17	Rd_Pixel_16	ASSEM BYTE Rd_Pixel_16(int x, int y, int bytes_per_row);
12.17	Rd_Pixel_256	ASSEM BYTE Rd_Pixel_256(int x, int y, int bytes_per_row);
12.18	Wr_HLine_16	ASSEM void Wr_HLine_16(int x1,int x2,int y,BYTE color,int bytes_per_row);
12.18	Wr_HLine_256	ASSEM void WrHLine_256(int x1,int x2,int y,BYTE color,int bytes_per_row);
12.18	Hsub1	ASSEM void Hsub1(SHORT address,BYTE mask);
12.18	Hsub2	ASSEM void HSub2(SHORT address,BYTE mask1,BYTE mask2);
12.18	Hsub3	ASSEM void HSub3(SHORT address,BYTE mask1,BYTE mask2,int nbytes);
12.18	Clr_Part	ASSEM void Clr_Part(BYTE color,int npix,int start);

TABLE 12.12 *(cont.)*

Listing	Function	Prototype
12.19	Wr_VLine_16	ASSEM void WrVLine_16(int x,int y,int npix,BYTE color,int bytes_per_row);
12.19	Wr_VLine_256	ASSEM void WrVLine_256(int x,int y,int npix,BYTE color,int bytes_per_row);
12.20	Wr_Line_16	void Wr_Line_16(int x1,int y1,int x2,int y2,BYTE color,int bytes_per_row);
12.20	Wr_Line_256	void Wr_Line_256(int x1,int y1,int x2,int y2,BYTE color,int bytes_per_row);
12.21	Wr_Circle_16	void Wr_Circle_16(int xc, int yc, int radius, BYTE color, int bytes_per_row);
12.21	Wr_Circle_256	void Wr_Circle_256(int xc, int yc, int radius, BYTE color, int bytes_per_row);
12.21	Circ_Pnt_16	void Circ_Pnt_16(int x,int y,int xc,int yc,int bytes_per_row);
12.21	Circ_Pnt_256	void Circ_Pnt_256(int x,int y,int xc,int yc,BYTE color,int bytes_per_row);
12.22	Wr_Win_16	void Wr_Win_16(int x1, int y1, int x2, int y2, BYTE *buf, int bytes_per_row);
12.22	Wr_Win_256	void Wr_Win_256(int x1, int y1, int x2, int y2, BYTE *buf, int bytes_per_row);
12.22	MapMask	void MapMask(BYTE plane);
12.22	Wr_Graph_Win	ASSEM void Wr_Graph_Win(int x, int y, BYTE *buffer, int nbyte, int nrow, int bytes_per_row);
12.22	Wr_Part	ASSEM void Wr_Part(BYTE *buf, int npix, int start);
12.23	Wr_Alpha_Win	void Wr_Alpha_Win(int page, char *buf, int col1, int row1, int col2, int row2);
12.24	Rd_Win_16	void Rd_Win_16(int x1, int y1, int x2, int y2, BYTE *buf, int bytes_per_row);
12.24	Rd_Win_256	void Rd_Win_256(int x1, int y1, int x2, int y2, BYTE *buf, int bytes_per_row);
12.24	ReadMap	void ReadMap(BYTE map);
12.24	Rd_Graph_Win	ASSEM void Rd_Graph_Win(int x, int y, BYTE *buffer, int nbyte, int nrow, int bytes_per_row);
12.24	Rd_Part	ASSEM void Wr_Part(BYTE *buf, int npix, int start);
12.25	Rd_Alpha_Win	void Rd_Alpha_Win(int page, char *buf, int col1, int row1, int col2, int row2);

(continued)

TABLE 12.12 *(cont.)*

Listing	Function	Prototype
12.26	DeMux	DeMux(BYTE *inbuf, BYTE *outbuf);
12.26	Mux	Mux(BYTE *inbuf, BYTE *outbuf);
12.27	Clipper	Clipper(int *x1, int *y1, int *x2, int *y2, int xmin, int xmax, int ymin, int ymax);
12.27	OutCode	int OutCode(int x,int y,int xmin,int xmax,int ymin,int ymax);
12.27	Reject	int Reject(int code1,int code2);
12.27	Accept	int Accept(int code1,int code2);
12.28	Clr_Alpha_Lines	void Clr_Alpha_Lines(BYTE page, BYTE row, BYTE numrow, BYTE attribute);
12.29	Clr_Win_16	void Clr_Win_16(int x1, int y1, int x2, int y2, BYTE color, int bytes_per_row);
12.29	Clr_Win_256	void Clr_Win_256(int x1, int y1, int x2, int y2, BYTE color, int bytes_per_row);
12.29	Clr_Graph_Win	ASSEM void Clr_Graph_Win(int x, int y, BYTE color, int nbyte, int nrow, int bytes_per_row);
12.30	Clr_Alpha_Win	ASSEM void Clr_Alpha_Win(BYTE color,BYTE column1,BYTE row1, BYTE column2,BYTE row2);
12.31	Wrfont	ASSEM void WrFont(BYTE *input, int blknum, int numline);
12.32	UserSet	ASSEM void UserSet(int segment, int offset, int numchar, int bpc, int block, int modeset);
12.32	Rom8x8	ASSEM void Rom8x8(int block, int modeset);
12.32	Rom8x14	ASSEM void Rom8x14(int block, int modeset);
12.32	Rom8x16	ASSEM void Rom8x16(int block, int modeset);
12.33	Guser8x8	ASSEM void GUser8x8(int segment, int offset);
12.33	GuserSet	ASSEM void GUserSet(int segment, int offset, int numrow, int bpc);
12.33	Grom8x8	ASSEM void GRom8x8(int segment, int offset, int numrow);
12.33	Grom8x14	ASSEM void GRom8x14(int segment, int offset, int numrow);

TABLE 12.12 *(cont.)*

Listing	Function	Prototype
12.33	Grom8x16	ASSEM void GRom8x16(int segment, int offset, int numrow);
12.34	FontInfo	ASSEM void FontInfo(SHORT *buf, int choice);
12.35	RdBlock	ASSEM void RdBlock(int *buf);
12.35	WrBlock	ASSEM void WrBlock(int a, int b);
12.35	BlockVal	ASSEM void BlockVal(int block);
12.36	MaxScan	void MaxScan(BYTE value);
12.37	F25row	ASSEM void F25row(int block);
12.37	F43row	ASSEM void F43row(int block);
12.37	F50row	ASSEM void F50row(int block);
12.38	SetLines	ASSEM void SetLines(int numlines);
12.39	Get_Font_Pattern	void Get_Font_Pattern(BYTE *fontbuf);
12.39	RdFont	ASSEM void RdFont(SHORT inseg,SHORT inoffset, BYTE *output, int nchar, int bpc);
12.40	Make_Italic	void Make_Italic(BYTE *buf, int font_height, int nchar);
12.41	Wr_StringG	void Wr_StringG(char *string,int foreground,int background,int x,int y, int is_transparent,BYTE *fontbuf,int font_height,int font_width)
12.41	Wr_CharG_16	void Wr_CharG_16(char char_code,int foreground,int background,int x1,int y1, int is_transparent,BYTE *fontbuf,int font_height,int font_width)
12.41	Wr_CharG_256	void Wr_CharG_256(char char_code,int foreground,int background,int x1,int y1, int is_transparent,BYTE *fontbuf,int font_height,int font_width)
12.41	Write_Points	void Write_Points(BYTE rc,int x,int y,int bytes_per_row);
12.41	PutGString	void PutGString(SHORT x, SHORT y, BYTE *fontbuf, char *charbuf, BYTE color, int bytes_per_row);
12.41	Put_GChar	void Put_GChar(SHORT x, SHORT y, BYTE *charbuf,BYTE color, int bytes_per_row);

(continued)

TABLE 12.12 *(cont.)*

Listing	Function	Prototype
12.41	Put_G_Char	void Put_G_Char(SHORT x, SHORT y, BYTE *charbuf, BYTE color, int bytes_per_row);
12.41	GraphChr	ASSEM void GraphChr(BYTE *charbuf, SHORT address, int offset, int bpc, BYTE color);
12.41	Setup_for_Write_Mode	ASSEM void Setup_for_Write_Mode(BYTE mode);
12.41	Restore_to_Write_Mode_0	ASSEM void Restore_to_Write_Mode_0(void);
12.42	EnCol	BYTE EnCol(BYTE red, BYTE green, BYTE blue);
12.42	DecCol	void DecCol(BYTE color, BYTE *buf);
12.42	EnCols	void EnCols(BYTE *buf, BYTE *r, BYTE *g, BYTE *b);
12.42	DecCols	void DecCols(BYTE *inbuf, BYTE *red, BYTE *green, BYTE *blue);
12.43	WrPal	ASSEM void WrPal(int regnum, BYTE value);
12.43	WrPals	ASSEM void WrPals(BYTE *colorbuf);
12.43	RdPal	ASSEM BYTE RdPal(int palnum);
12.43	RdPals	ASSEM void RdPals(BYTE *palbuf);
12.44	RdColor	ASSEM void RdColor(BYTE *buf, int regnum);
12.44	RdColors	ASSEM void RdColors(BYTE *buf, int first, int numreg);
12.44	ColorsRd	ASSEM void ColorsRd(BYTE *buf);
12.45	WrColor	ASSEM void WrColor(BYTE *buf, int regnum);
12.45	WrColors	ASSEM void WrColors(BYTE *buf, int first, int numreg);
12.45	ColorsWr	ASSEM void ColorsWr(BYTE *buf);
12.46	SumGray	ASSEM void SumGray(int first, int numreg);
12.47	DefaultP	ASSEM void DefaultP(int choice);
12.48	Fade	void Fade(BYTE *color_reg_buf, int direction);

```
.LARGE   ; set up for large model
.286     ; allow for 286 instructions

; Local macros
TRUE      equ      1
FALSE     equ      0

; create a local data segment containing the segment pointers.
; These contain the segment addresses of absolute memory
; locations commonly used in graphics.  These variables can be
; overwritten in the case of protected mode programs.
.DATA    ; local data segment

PUBLIC    Seg0040, SegA000, SegB000, SegB800, SegC000, SegF000,
SelInc

Seg0040  dw  00040H    ;BIOS data area
SegA000  dw  0A000H    ;EGA/VGA display segment
SegB000  dw  0B000H    ;Monochrome display segment
SegB800  dw  0B800H    ;CGA display segment
SegC000  dw  0C000H    ;Video ROM BIOS segment
SegF000  dw  0F000H    ;ROM BIOS segment
SelInc   dw  01000H    ;Selector increment
PMInit   dw  FALSE     ;Protected Mode initialized flag

.CODE    ; put source into code segment
```

The end of each assembly language function should contain the end directive:

```
end
```

The C source code requires the following includes:

```
#include <stdio.h>
#include <conio.h>
#include <stdlib.h>
#include <string.h>
#include <stdarg.h>
#include <dos.h>

#include "proto12.h"
```

12.2   INTRODUCTION

The C and assembly language routines presented in this chapter illustrate the operation of the EGA/VGA and constitute the basis of a programmer's toolbox. The examples selected are in an understandable yet flexible format. More than

100 routines are included. These routines by no means form a complete toolbox; space would not allow one. Programmers can obtain a disk containing the source code to this toolbox for all of the routines presented in this chapter. Purchasing instructions are provided on the last page of this book.

The routines provide control of the EGA/VGA, read and write alphanumerics, points, lines, and images. Routines utilize the downloadable character fonts and the palette, color, and general registers. The List of Standard VGA Functions in section 12.1 enumerates the routines that are meant to be called by the programmer. Several other routines included in this chapter are invoked by these routines. These lower-order routines are also well documented and may be used by the programmer.

The Microsoft C compiler Version 7 convention is assumed throughout this book. However, the C code is highly portable and should operate on any C compiler with little modification. The assembly language routines also assume the Microsoft C Version 6 interface conventions. Using other compilers may require the names of these routines and the code segment names to be modified.

12.3 NAMING CONVENTIONS

Trying to maintain order in naming routines is difficult if not impossible. Because of the file name limitations in DOS, the subroutine names in these examples are limited to eight characters. Most compilers can handle more than eight characters. However, files can become confused when DOS truncates the letters in the name to eight characters.

The display is considered as an external device on the system. Data is written from the host to the display. As a result, names of routines that involve transferring data from the host to the display usually begin with Wr. Similarly, names of routines that read data from the display to the host usually begin with Rd.

The names of routines that process along a horizontal direction contain an H; those that have a vertical orientation will contain a V. Rows are called row, and columns are called col. This can present a problem because colors can also be abbreviated as col.

Routines that process alphanumerics contain an A; those that process graphics contain a G in a conspicuous location. An example of the former is RdAWin, which stands for **R**ead an **A**lphanumerics **Win**dow.

One source of common confusion is the mixing of rows and columns with X and Y addresses. Rows are measured along the vertical dimension, from top to bottom, and are thus associated with the Y dimension. Columns are measured along the horizontal dimension, from left to right, and are associated with the X dimension. Because the vertical dimension counts from top to bottom, the Y value increments as it goes down. This means that a 1 pixel beneath a second will have a greater Y value.

12.4 CONTROLLING AND READING THE STATUS OF THE DISPLAY

The state of the EGA/VGA adapters is best controlled through the BIOS calls. The most fundamental element of control is to turn off and turn on the video drivers. This tends to save the screen during periods of non-use as well as speeding up data transfers. The routine OnVideo turns on the video, and Off-Video turns off the video. Both appear in Listing 12.1.

LISTING 12.1 Turning the Video Screen On and Off

```
; Enable the video screen

; Calling protocol
;     OnVideo();

OnVideo proc FAR C PUBLIC
        mov     bl,36h     ;turn on the video
        mov     ax,1200h
        int     10h
        ret
OnVideo endp

; Disable the video screen
; Calling protocol
;     OffVideo();

OffVideoproc FAR C PUBLIC
        mov     bl,36h     ;turn off the video
        mov     ax,1201h
        int     10h
        ret
OffVideoendp
```

The display mode and active display page can be set using the SetMode and SetPage routines in Listing 12.2. The BIOS calls are used in these routines because of the complexity involved in trying to perform the functions directly.

LISTING 12.2 Setting the Active Display Mode and Page

```
; Set the display mode
; Input parameters
;    mode    desired display mode (byte)

; Calling protocol
;     SetMode(mode);
```

(continued)

```
SetMode proc FAR C PUBLIC mode:byte
        mov    ah,00h      ;get current video state
        mov    al,mode     ;get desired mode
        int    10h         ;interrupt 10
        ret
SetMode endp

; Select a new active page
; Input parameters:
;  page      desired page (byte)

; Calling protocol:
;    SetPage(npage);

SetPage proc   FAR C PUBLIC npage:byte
        mov    al,npage    ;get active page
        mov    ah,05       ;select page
        int    10h         ;call bios
        ret
SetPage endp


; Write the starting address from the CRTC registers.  This
; determines where the top left corner begins grabbing pixels
; from display memory.

; Input Parameters:
;        value  new starting address

; Calling Protocol:
;    Wr_Start(value);

Wr_Start proc FAR C PUBLIC  value:word

;       wait for the vertical interrupt so no snow
        mov    dx,3dah
s2o:    in     al,dx
        test   al,8
        jz     s2o         ;wait for vertical interupt

s1o:    in     al,dx       ;wait for NOT vertical interupt
        test   al,8
        jnz    s1o

        mov    dx,3d4h
        mov    ax,value     ;get start address low and high
        mov    bl,al        ;save low
```

```
        mov     al,0ch      ;address high
        out     dx,ax       ;output high
        inc     al
        mov     ah,bl       ;get low
        out     dx,ax       ;output low
        ret
Wr_Start endp

;  Read the starting address from the CRTC registers.  This
;  determines where the top left corner begins grabbing pixels
;  from display memory.

; Output Parameters:
;       start  starting address

; Calling Protocol:
; start = Rd_Start();

Rd_Start proc FAR C PUBLIC
        mov     dx,3d4h
        mov     al,0ch      ;address high
        out     dx,al       ;output high index
        inc     dx
        in      al,dx       ;get high
        mov     ah,al       ;save high

        dec     dx
        mov     al,0dh      ;address low
        out     dx,al       ;output low index
        in      al,dx       ;get low
        ret
Rd_Start endp


/* Load the Set/Reset Register

Input Parameters:
  value value to load into the register

Calling Protocol:
SetRes(value); */

void SetRes(BYTE value)
{ outp(0x3ce,0);  outp(0x3cf,value); }


/* Load the Enable Set/Reset Register
```

(continued)

```
Input Parameters:
 value  value to load into the register

Calling Protocol:
  ESetRes(value); */

void  ESetRes(BYTE value)
{ outp(0x3ce,1);  outp(0x3cf,value); }



/* Load the Bit Mask Register

Input Parameters:
 value  value to load into the register

Calling Protocol:
BitMask(value); */

void  BitMask(BYTE value)
{ outp(0x3ce,8); outp(0x3cf,value); }
```

The EGA/VGA operational parameters can be determined by reading the control registers in the VGA, invoking the return parameter BIOS calls in the EGA/VGA, or reading the section of host RAM memory dedicated for the BIOS storage. The routines that follow utilize the BIOS calls.

It is far easier to determine the condition of the VGA than it is to determine the condition of the EGA. The VGA provides a much richer combination of routines for use in determining its state. All of the control registers on the VGA can be read; few of the EGA registers can be read.

Even though the registers can be read on the VGA, not all parameters are easily determined by the registers alone. The active display mode and active display page are two examples. These functions are not associated with a single register, but rather are determined by the combination of several of the registers.

Certain display parameters can be returned by calling the routine in Listing 12.3. It should be noted that this BIOS call requires the BP register. Certain display parameters can be returned by the functions in Listing 12.3 through 12.7. These are listed in Table 12.13.

LISTING 12.3 Get the Display Status

```
/*  Get the screen size from the hardware

Output Parameters:
        columns        # of active columns on the screen
        rows           # of active rows on the screen
```

TABLE 12.13 Functions that Return Information about the VGA

Listing	Function name	Function returns the
12.3	Get_Screen_Size	Screen resolution
12.4	Get_Screen_Height	# of screen rows in pixels
12.4	Get_Screen_Width	# of screen columns in pixels
12.5	Get_Char_Width	# of pixel rows per character
12.5	Get_Char_Height	# of pixel columns per character
12.6	Is_It_Graphics	Alphanumeric or graphics status
12.6	Get_Number_of_Colors	Number of colors
12.6	Get_Bytes_per_Row	Bytes in a row
12.7	Get_Rows_Per_Screen	# of character rows per screen
12.7	Get_Columns_Per_Screen	# of character columns per screen

```
          char_columns  # of active character columns on the screen
          char_rows     # of active character rows on the screen

Calling Protocol:
  Get_Screen_Size(&columns,&rows,&char_columns,&char_rows);    */

void    Get_Screen_Size(int *columns, int *rows, int *char_columns,
int *char_rows)
{
int     screen_width,
screen_height,columns_per_screen,rows_per_screen;

          screen_height = Get_Screen_Height();
          screen_width = Get_Screen_Width();
          columns_per_screen = Get_Columns_per_Screen();
          rows_per_screen = Get_Rows_per_Screen();

          *rows = screen_height;
          *columns = screen_width;
          *char_columns= columns_per_screen;
          *char_rows = rows_per_screen;
}
```

LISTING 12.4 Get Screen Height

```
/* Get Screen Height in pixels

Output Parameters:
          screen_height    screen height in pixels
```

(continued)

```
Calling Protocol:
 screen_height = Get_Screen_Height() */

int Get_Screen_Height()

{ int height,overflow,crtc_port,rows_per_screen,char_height;

// determine whether monochrome or color
if(inp(0x3cc) & 1) crtc_port = 0x3d4; else crtc_port = 0x3b4;

        outp(crtc_port, 0x12);  // Vertical Display Enable End
        height = inp(crtc_port+1) + 1;
        outp(crtc_port, 7);     // Vertical Overflow
        overflow = inp(crtc_port+1);
        if((overflow & 0x02)!=0)   height += 256;
        if((overflow & 0x40)!=0)   height += 512;
        rows_per_screen = Get_Rows_per_Screen();
        char_height = Get_Char_Height();
        if((rows_per_screen*char_height)>height) height *= 2;

//      check for 320x200 special case
        if((Get_Screen_Width()==320) & (height==400)) height=200;

        return(height);
}

/* Get Screen Width in pixels

Output Parameters:
        screen_width  screen width in pixels

Calling Protocol:
 screen_width = Get_Screen_Width() */

int  Get_Screen_Width()

{ int width,columns_per_screen,char_width;

        columns_per_screen = Get_Columns_per_Screen();
        char_width = Get_Char_Width();
        width = columns_per_screen * char_width;

 return(width);
}
```

LISTING 12.5 Is an 8 or 9 Pixel Font Active?

```
/*  Determine if an 8 or 9 pixel font  is active

Output Parameters:
        char_width        8 = 8 pixels wide    9 = 9 pixels wide

Calling Protocol:
 char_width = Get_Char_Width() */

int Get_Char_Width()

{ int gmode,char_width;

        outp(0x3ce, 6);
        gmode = inp(0x3cf) & 1; // 1 for graphics mode
        outp(0x3c4, 1);
        if(inp(0x3c5) & 1)  char_width = 8;
        else   char_width = 9;
        return(char_width);
}

; Return the number of pixel rows per character
; Output Parameters
;       char_height   character height in pixels
; Calling Protocol:
;       char_height = Get_Char_Height()

Get_Char_Height proc FAR C PUBLIC USES DS SI
;       set up ds segment pointers point to VGA BIOS segment
;       at 0000h
        get_bios_segment ds    ;load ds with BIOS segment

;       set up source pointer for character height
        mov   si,0485h      ;location of identification
        mov   ax,ds:[si]    ;return the character height
        ret
Get_Char_Height     endp
```

LISTING 12.6 Is a Graphics Mode Active?

```
/* Determine if a graphics mode is active

Output Parameters:
        graphics        1=graphics mode 0=alphanumerics mode
```

(continued)

```
Calling Protocol:
 graphics = Is_It_Graphics() */

int Is_It_Graphics()

{ int gmode;

        outp(0x3ce, 6);
        gmode = inp(0x3cf) & 1;    /* 1 for graphics mode */
        return(gmode);
}

/*   Determine if a 16 or 256 color mode is active

Output Parameters:
        number_of_colors    16 = 16 colors  256 = 256 colors

Calling Protocol:
 number_of_colors = Get_Number_of_Colors() */

int Get_Number_of_Colors()

{ BYTE ncol;

        outp(0x3c4, 4);         // miscellaneous register
        ncol = inp(0x3c5) & 0x08;     // bit 4
        if (ncol==0) return(16);      // bit 4=0 for 16-color
        else return(256);       // bit 4=1 for 256-color
}

/* Determine number of bytes per row

Output Parameters:
        bytes_per_row    number of bytes per display row

Calling Protocol:
 bytes_per_row = Get_Bytes_per_Row();    */

int Get_Bytes_per_Row()

{ int ncol,screen_width;

 screen_width = Get_Screen_Width();   // Get screen width
 ncol = Get_Number_of_Colors();       // Get number of colors
        if (ncol==16) return(screen_width/8);   //  16-color
        else return(screen_width);    //  256-color
}
```

LISTING 12.7 Get Number of Rows per Screen

```
; Get the number of pixel Rows per screen
Calling Protocol:
;  rows_per_screen = Get_Rows_per_Screen()

Get_Rows_per_Screen proc FAR C PUBLIC USES DS SI
;       set up ds segment pointers to BIOS
        mov     ds,Seg0040

;       set up source pointer for character height
        mov     si,0084h        ;location of rows per screen
        mov     al,ds:[si]      ;get rows per screen
        xor     ah,ah
        inc     ax              ;add one for actual number
        ret
Get_Rows_per_Screen     endp

; Return the number of pixel columns per screen
; Output Parameters
;        columns_per_screen      number of columns per screen
; Calling Protocol:
;        columns_per_screen = Get_Columns_per_Screen()

Get_Columns_per_Screen proc FAR C PUBLIC USES DS SI
;       set up ds segment pointers to BIOS
        mov     ds,Seg0040

;       set up source pointer for character height
        mov     si,004Ah    ;location of columns per screen
        mov     ax,ds:[si] ;return the number of columns per screen
        ret
Get_Columns_per_Screen     endp
```

12.5 DETERMINING THE STATE OF THE VGA ADAPTER

The VGA adapter provides a BIOS call named Save/Restore Video State, which accesses control parameters. This function allows the programmer to read the video state into a buffer, modify the state, and then return the state to normal by writing the state back to the adapter. Any combination of the video hardware, video data areas, or video color palette and color registers can be saved or restored, as shown in Table 12.14. Any combination of the bits in the CX register can be used in the same call to provide a concatenation of the different areas. When more than one area is selected, the order in which the data is read from or written to the table is determined by the precedence of Table 12.14.

TABLE 12.14 Areas of the Video Adapter to Save or Restore

Code (CX)	Area of Adapter
bit 0	Video hardware state
bit 1	Video data areas
bit 2	Video Color Palette and Color Registers

The first element in the table, the video hardware state, will always appear first if it is included. It will be followed by video data area, if it is present, followed by the color palette and color registers, if it is present.

The VidState routine in Listing 12.8 can be used either to save or to restore these video areas.

LISTING 12.8 Saving and Restoring the Video State

```
; Save or restore the video state
; Input parameters
;  buf      "C" buffer which contains the video state data
;              during an AL=2, restore video state, request.
;  state    desired data to save or restore
;              bit 0 = video hardware
;              bit 1 = video data areas
;              bit 2 = dac state and color registers
; operation desired operation
;              0 = return size of buffer
;              1 = save video state
;              2 = restore video state

; Output parameters
;  buf      "C" buffer which will contain the video state data
;              during an AL=1, save video state, request.
;  size     The size of the buffer*64 in bytes, only returned
;              during a AL=0 selection requesting a return size

; Calling protocol
;  size = Vidstate(buf,state,operation);

Vidstate    proc FAR C PUBLIC USES ES, buf:FAR PTR, state,
operation:byte
            les    bx,buf      ;get buffer pointer
            mov    cx,state    ;get state to save
            mov    ah,1Ch      ;1C=save/restore
```

```
        mov     al,operation  ;desired operation
        int     10h           ;save data

        mov     ax,bx         ;return buffer size block count
        ret
Vidstateendp
```

12.6 ALPHANUMERICS

Alphanumeric processing involves reading and writing characters to the display. There are several ways in which the programmer can read or write single characters or character strings. The orientation of the character strings is typically horizontal; however, routines are presented that allow any orientation using variable intercharacter spacing.

Because the EGA/VGA allows color alphanumerics, each character is represented by a character code and attribute byte. The organization of the display memory is illustrated in Figure 12.1.

It is useful to write a string with one attribute for the entire string. At other times, it is useful to write a string with an attribute associated with each character. In addition, a string of characters can be written without modifying the attribute bytes.

12.6.1 Reading and Writing Characters

The most basic alphanumeric functions are reading and writing characters. The RdChar and WrChar routines in Listing 12.9 read and write a character to

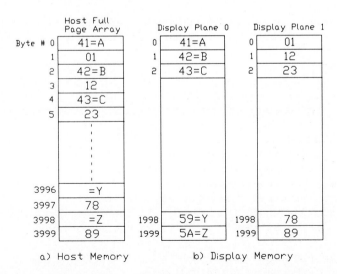

FIGURE 12.1 Alphanumeric Display Memory

the display memory. The character is input or output through an integer whose lower byte contains the character code and whose upper byte contains the attribute byte.

LISTING 12.9 Reading and Writing a Character

```
; Read a character and its attribute.

; Input parameters
;  page     desired display page
;  row      desired row
;  column   desired column

; Output parameters
;  charatr  returned character and attribute.
;           The character code is returned in the lower byte.
;           The attribute byte is returned in the upper byte.

; Calling protocol:
;  charatr = RdChar(page,row,column);

RdChar proc FAR C PUBLIC npage:byte,row:byte,column:byte
        mov    bh,npage   ;get active page
        mov    dh,row     ;get row
        mov    dl,column  ;get column
        mov    ah,2       ;move Cursor to desired position
        int    10h

        mov    ah,8       ;read character and attribute into ax
        int    10h        ;return with character/ attribute in ax
        ret
RdChar endp


; Output a character and its attribute to the display

; Input parameters
;  page     desired display page
;  row      desired row
;  column   desired column
;  charatr  returned character and attribute.
;           The character code is in the lower byte.
;           The attribute byte is in the upper byte.

; Calling protocol:
;  Wrchar(page,charatr,row,column);
```

```
WrChar proc FAR C PUBLIC npage:byte,charatr,row:byte,column:byte
        mov     bh,npage        ;get desired page
        mov     dh,row          ;get row to start string
        mov     dl,column       ;get column to start string
        mov     ah,2            ;move Cursor to desired position
        int     10h

        mov     ax,charatr      ;get char in al, attribute in ah
        mov     bl,ah           ;attribute is in bl
        mov     cx,01           ;one character
        mov     ah,09           ;write character/attribute
        int     10h             ;display character/attribute
        ret
WrChar endp
```

12.6.2 Character Strings

Writing a string of characters in any orientation is accomplished by the WrChars routine in Listing 12.10. The string of characters input to the routine is in a byte array containing only the character codes. Thus, the standard C string manipulation routines can be utilized. The string will be written in one color that is determined by the foreground and background colors also input to the routine. The first character is read at position row, column. The location of each subsequent character is determined by adding the row and column increment values.

LISTING 12.10 Writing a Character String in Any Orientation

```
; Read a string of characters and attributes from the display

; Input parameters:
;   page      desired display page
;   string    byte "C" array to place the characters and
;             attribute pairs.  Even bytes as character and odd
;             bytes as attributes.
;   numchar   number of characters to read from the display
;   row       desired row
;   column    desired column
;   rowInc    # of vertical spaces to place between characters
;   colInc    # of horizontal spaces to place between characters

; Calling protocol:
;   RdChars(page,string,numchar,row,column,rowInc,colInc);

RdChars proc FAR C PUBLIC  USES ES DI, npage:byte, string:FAR PTR,
```

(continued)

```
            nchar, row:byte, column:byte, rowInc:byte, colInc:byte
            les    di,string      ;get pointer
            mov    cx,nchar       ;get number of characters
            mov    bh,npage       ;get active page
            mov    dh,row         ;get row
            mov    dl,column      ;get column

re1:        mov    ah,02          ;request set cursor
            int    10h            ;call bios
            mov    ah,8           ;read character and attribute into ax
            int    10h
            stosw                 ;return char and attribute
            add    dh,rowInc      ;add row increment
            add    dl,colInc      ;add column increment
            loop   re1            ;repeat til done

            ret
RdChars endp


; Write a string of characters in a given color on the display

; Input parameters:
;    page       desired display page
;    string     host "C" byte array of the character codes
;    for        desired foreground color of the string
;    back       desired background color of the string
;    row        desired row
;    column     desired column
;    rowinc     # of vertical spaces to place between characters
;    colinc     # of horizontal spaces to place between characters

; Calling protocol:
;    WrChars(page,string,for,back,row,column,rowInc,colInc);

WrChars proc FAR C PUBLIC USES DS SI, npage:byte, string:FAR PTR,
            fore:byte, back:byte, row:byte, column:byte, rowinc:byte,
            colinc:byte
            mov    dh,row         ;get row
            mov    dl,column      ;get column
            mov    ah,02          ;set cursor position
            mov    bh,npage       ;desired page
            int    10h            ;set cursor row=dh

            lds    si,string      ;get address of string
            mov    bl,fore        ;get foreground color
            and    bl,0fh
            mov    al,back        ;get background color
            mov    cx,04          ;put for and back into
```

```
          shl    al,cl           ;attribute
          and    al,0f0h
          or     bl,al           ;attribute is in bl

dloop:    mov    ah,09
          mov    al,[si]         ;get character
          cmp    al,00           ;last character in string ?
          jz     ddone           ;exit if done

          inc    si              ;next char in string
          mov    bh,npage        ;page #
          mov    cx,01           ;one character
          int    10h             ;display
          add    dh,rowinc       ;add row increment
          add    dl,colinc       ;add column increment
          mov    ah,02           ;set cursor position
          mov    bh,npage        ;get page
          int    10h             ;set cursor row=dh col=dl
          jmp    dloop           ;display another if not

ddone:    ret

WrChars endp
```

Reading a string of characters in any orientation is accomplished by the RdChars routine in Listing 12.10. The string of characters output from this routine is sent to a C byte array. Because every character on the display is represented by a character and attribute byte, the array contains alternating character codes and attribute bytes. The first character is read at position row, column. The location of each subsequent character is determined by adding the row and column increment values.

Horizontal strings can be written to the character using either the WrStrC routine in Listing 12.11 or the WrStrA routine in Listing 12.12. The WrStrC routine writes a character string in one color; the WrStrA routine writes an attribute with each character.

A character string and an attribute byte are passed as parameters to the WrStrC routine. The character string contains only the character codes, which makes it directly compatible with the C string-handling routines. The end of the character string is terminated by a null character, which is equivalent to a 0 and which may be invoked in C by using the "\0" notation within the string. The attribute byte is written into the display memory associated with each character. Note that the BP register must be saved because the BIOS call will modify it. The string is written beginning at the current cursor position.

The cursor position is moved at the end of the BIOS call to the position immediately following the last character output. If the last character represents the end of a line, the cursor is placed on the far-left position of the following line. If the string fills the last line, the cursor is positioned down one line, forcing a scroll up one line. If this presents undesirable results, the BIOS call AH = 13 hex, AL = 01 hex can be changed to AH = 13 hex, AL = 00.

LISTING 12.11 Writing a String of Character/Attribute Pairs

```
; Write a string to the display at the current cursor position
; and page. The cursor is moved to the end of the string at
; completion.  Maximum string limit is set to 500.

; Input parameters:
;  string   Host byte string of character codes terminated with
;              a null=0 code.
;  attr     Attribute for string of characters
;  cursor   Determines whether the cursor will be moved or not
;              at the end of the string output.
;              0 = don't move cursor   1 = move cursor

; calling protocol
;  WrStrC(string,attr,cursor);

WrStrC proc FAR C PUBLIC USES ES DS DI SI, string:FAR
PTR,attr:byte,cursor:byte
;         determine # of characters in the string
          xor    cx,cx      ;determine # of chars in string
          lds    si,string  ;point to character array

a1:       lodsb             ;get character and increment si
          cmp    al,0       ;end of string
          jz     a2         ;exit if end
          inc    cx
          cmp    cx,500     ;character limit
          jb     a1         ;exit if more than limit

a2:       cmp    cx,0
          jz     a3         ;exit it no characters

;         set up parameters
          mov    ah,attr    ;get attribute in bl
          mov    al,cursor  ;get cursor control in al

          les    di,string  ;get pointer to string
          push   bp
          push   cx
          push   ax

          mov    bp,di
```

```
        mov     ah,0fh          ;get status
        int     10h             ;al=mode, ah=# char, bh=page

        mov     ah,03           ;get cursor position
        int     10h             ;dh,dl=position

        pop     ax
        mov     bl,ah
        mov     ah,13h          ;output string, move cursor
        pop     cx
        int     10h             ;cx - number of characters

        pop     bp              ;restore base point register
a3:     ret
WrStrC endp
```

A character string consisting of alternating character codes and attribute bytes
is passed to the WrStrCA routine. The string is terminated by a *null* character
in the character position at the end of the string. A null character is equivalent
to a 0 and may be invoked in C by using the "\0" notation within the string.

LISTING 12.12 Writing a String with a Single Attribute

```
; Write a string to the display at the current cursor position
; and page. The cursor is moved to the end of the string at
; completion. Maximum string limit is set to 500.

; Input parameters:
;   charatr  Host "C" array consisting of a string of character
;            attribute pairs. The string is terminated by a
;            null = 0 in the character position.
;   cursor   Determines whether the cursor will be moved or not
;            at the end of the string output.
;            0 = don't move cursor   1 = move cursor

; calling protocol
;   WrStrA(charatr,cursor);

WrStrA proc FAR C PUBLIC USES DS SI, charatr:FAR PTR,cursor:byte
        push    bp              ;save base pointer

;       determine # of characters in the string
        xor     cx,cx           ;determine # of chars in string
        lds     si,charatr      ;point to character array
        push    ds
        push    si
```

(continued)

```
b1:     lodsw                       ;get character and increment si
        cmp     al,0                ;end of string
        jz      b2                  ;exit if end
        inc     cx
        cmp     cx,500              ;character limit
        jb      b1                  ;exit if more than limit

b2:     cmp     cx,0
        jz      b3                  ;exit it no characters

        push    cx
        mov     ah,0fh              ;get status
        int     10h                 ;al=mode, ah=# char, bh=page
        mov     ah,03               ;get cursor position
        int     10h                 ;dh,dl=position cx type

        mov     al,cursor           ;get cursor control
        pop     cx
        pop     bp
        pop     es
        add     al,2                      ;make code be 2=no move or 3=move
        mov     ah,13h                    ;output string, move cursor
        int     10h

        pop     bp                  ;restore base pointer
b3:     ret
WrStrA endp
```

Two additional horizontal character string routines, WrString and RepChar, are provided in Listing 12.13. These routines write a character, repeated character, or string of characters but do not modify the character attribute bytes already in the display memory. For example, a character or string written at row 10 will be displayed in whatever attribute was previously assigned to the characters in row 10.

In the graphics mode, the attribute of a character must be supplied for each character drawn. An attribute is provided to these routines for the graphics modes. In the alphanumeric modes, the attribute is ignored.

In WrString, a character string is written to the display. The character string contains only the character codes, which makes it directly compatible with the C string-handling routines. The character string is terminated by a null character at the end of the character string. A null character is equivalent to a 0 and may be invoked in C by using the "\0" notation within the string. This routine utilizes the Write TTY BIOS call. Cursor-control characters present in the character string affect the positioning of the cursor, as shown in Table 12.15.

The RepChar routine writes a character a number of times into the display memory at the current cursor position. This routine is useful for initializing areas of the screen with a character pattern.

TABLE 12.15 Cursor-control Characters

Character	Action
CR	Move the cursor to column 0 of the current row
LF	Move the cursor down one row. If the cursor is on the bottom row, scroll the screen up one row. The attribute of the new bottom row is the same as the attribute present in column 0 of the previous bottom row.
BS	Move the cursor one position to the left
BEL	Ring the bell

LISTING 12.13 Writing a String of Characters Only

```
; Output a character string.  In the alphanumerics modes, no
; attributes are modified.
; In the graphics modes, the  character string is written with
; the "grattr" attribute.

; Input parameters:
;   page    desired display page
;   string  character string containing character codes,
;           terminated in a "null" character
;   grattr  -graphics mode only-  character attribute

; Calling protocol:
;   WrString(page,string,grattr);

WrString proc FAR C PUBLIC  USES DS SI,  npage:byte, string:FAR
PTR, grattr:byte
        mov    al,npage   ;get desired page select the active page
        mov    ah,05      ;select page
        int    10h

        lds    si,string    ;point to character array
        mov    bl,grattr    ;graphics mode attribute

runloop:lodsb               ;get the character into AL
        cmp    al,0         ;end of string AL=null?
        jz     done         ;exit if end
        mov    ah,0Eh       ;tty write character only
        int    10h
        jmp    runloop      ;repeat til done
done:   ret
WrString endp
```

(continued)

```
; Output a single character a multiple number of times. In the
; alphanumerics modes, no attributes are modified. In the
; graphics modes, the character string is written with the
; "grattr" attribute.

; Input parameters:
;   page      desired display page
;   char      character to repeat
;   nchar     number of times to write the character
;   grattr    -graphics mode only-  character attribute

; Calling protocol:
;   RepChar(page,char,numchar,grattr);

RepChar proc FAR C PUBLIC      npage:byte, tchar:byte, nchar,
grattr:byte
          mov      cx,nchar         ;get repeat count
          mov      bh,npage         ;get desired page
          mov      al,tchar         ;get character
          mov      bl,grattr        ;graphics mode attribute
          mov      ah,0Ah           ;write character only
          int      10h
          ret
RepChar endp
```

12.7   CURSOR CONTROL

The programmer can position the cursor, read the position of the cursor, or define the cursor shape using the functions in Listing 12.14. Note that the WrCursor and RdCursor functions use BIOS calls while the Wr_Cursor and Rd_Cursor functions do not. The function DefCurs provides a means for setting the bottom and top lines of the cursor shape.

LISTING 12.14 Cursor Control

```
; Set the position of the cursor Uses BIOS

; Input parameters:
;   page      = page number for cursor
;   row       = row number to position cursor
;   column    = column number to position cursor

; Calling protocol:
;   WrCursor(page,row,column);

WrCursor proc   FAR C PUBLIC npage:byte, row:byte, column:byte
          mov      ah,02           ;request set cursor
          mov      bh,npage        ;page number
```

```
              mov     dh,row           ;row
              mov     dl,column        ;column
              int     10h              ;call BIOS to position cursor
              ret
WrCursor endp

; Read the cursor position.  Uses BIOS
; Input parameters:
;  page      current page to read cursor from

; Output parameters:
;  row        The row is returned in the low-order byte.
;  column     The column is returned in the high-order byte

; Calling protocol:
;   RdCursor(page,&row,&column);

RdCursor proc FAR C PUBLIC USES ES DI, npage:byte, row:FAR PTR,
column:FAR PTR

              mov     ah,03            ;read cursor position
              mov     bh,npage         ;page number
              int     10h              ;row in dh, col in dl

              les     di,row           ;point to row
              xor     ah,ah
              mov     al,dh            ;return row
              stosw
              les     di,column        ;point to row
              mov     al,dl            ;return column
              stosw
              ret

RdCursor endp

; Define the shape of the cursor.

; Input parameters:
;  start    starting scan line for the cursor
;  end      ending scan line for the cursor

; Calling protocol:
;   DefCurs(start,end);

DefCurs proc FAR C PUBLIC      start:byte,last:byte
              mov     ch,start         ;get Cursor start
              mov     cl,last          ;get Cursor end
              and     cx,1f1fh         ;assure bits (7-5) of low and high=0
```

(continued)

```
        mov     ah,01           ;read character and attribute into ax
        int     10h             ;define the cursor
        ret
DefCurs endp

; Load a new cursor position

; Input Parameters:
;       position  new starting address

; Calling Protocol:
;   Wr_Cursor(position);

Wr_Cursor proc FAR C PUBLIC position:word
        mov     dx,3d4h
        mov     ax,position     ;get cursor position low and high
        mov     bl,al           ;save low
        mov     al,0eh          ;address high
        out     dx,ax           ;output high
        inc     al
        mov     ah,bl           ;get low
        out     dx,ax           ;output low
        ret
Wr_Cursor endp

; Read the Cursor position

; Output Parameters:
;       position  starting address

; Calling Protocol:
; position = Rd_Cursor();

Rd_Cursor proc FAR C PUBLIC

        mov     dx,3d4h
        mov     al,0eh    ;address high
        out     dx,al     ;output high index
        inc     dx
        in      al,dx     ;get high
        mov     ah,al     ;save high

        dec     dx
        mov     al,0fh    ;address low
        out     dx,al     ;output low index
        in      al,dx     ;get low
        ret

Rd_Cursor endp
```

12.8   SCROLLING

Two scrolling routines are provided to scroll a window on the active display page. The ScrollUp and ScrollDw routines in Listing 12.15 scroll a portion of the display up or down. The upper-left and lower-right corner row and column coordinates are passed to the routine, along with the number of lines to scroll. For example, a window that consists of 20 character rows can be scrolled one row up, causing all 20 rows to shift up one character row. In this example, the top row would scroll out of the window, and the bottom row would be filled with an attribute byte. The attribute byte consists of a foreground and background color that are also input as parameters.

LISTING 12.15   Scrolling Alphanumerics

```
; Scroll an Alphanumerics window upward

; Input parameters:
;   num                number of lines to scroll the window upward
;   ulRow,ulCol        upper left row, column coordinate of window
;   blRow,blCol        bottom left row, column coordinate of window
;   fore               foreground color to be scrolled in
;   back               background color to be scrolled in

; Calling protocol:
; ScrollUp(num,ulRow,ulCol,blRow,blCol,for,back);

ScrollUpproc    FAR C
PUBLIC    num:byte,ulRow:byte,ulCol:byte,blRow:byte,blCol:byte,
          fore:byte,back:byte
          mov    bh,fore        ;get foreground color
          and    bh,0fh
          mov    al,back        ;get background color
          mov    cx,04          ;put for and back into
          shl    al,cl          ;attribute
          and    al,0f0h
          or     bh,al          ;attribute is in bh
          mov    ah,06          ;request scroll screen up
          mov    al,num         ;get number of lines to scroll
          mov    ch,ulRow       ;get upper left corner row
          mov    cl,ulcol       ;get upper left corner column
          mov    dh,blRow       ;get lower left corner row
          mov    dl,blCol       ;get lower left corner column
          int    10h            ;call bios
          ret
ScrollUpendp
```

(continued)

```
; Scroll an Alphanumerics window downward

; Input parameters:
;   num             number of lines to scroll the window downward
;   ulRow,ulCol     upper left row, column coordinate of window
;   blRow,blCol     bottom left row, column coordinate of window
;   fore            foreground color to be scrolled in
;   back            background color to be scrolled in

; Calling protocol:
;   ScrollDw(num,ulRow,ulCol,blRow,blCol,for,back);

ScrollDwproc    FAR C
PUBLIC   num:byte,ulRow:byte,ulCol:byte,blRow:byte,blCol:byte,
         fore:byte,back:byte
         mov    bh,fore      ;get foreground color
         and    bh,0fh
         mov    al,back      ;get background color
         mov    cx,04        ;put for and back into
         shl    al,cl        ;attribute
         and    al,0f0h
         or     bh,al        ;attribute is in bh
         mov    ah,07        ;request scroll screen down
         mov    al,num       ;get number of lines to scroll
         mov    ch,ulRow     ;get upper left corner row
         mov    cl,ulCol     ;get upper left corner column
         mov    dh,blRow     ;get lower left corner row
         mov    dl,blCol     ;get lower left corner column
         int    10h          ;call bios
         ret
ScrollDw    endp
```

12.9   DRAWING A POINT

A single point may occupy from one to four planes of memory. The BIOS call Draw Point utilizes the Set/Reset Register to access the point. Typically, points are drawn in combination with other points. In these cases, it may be appropriate to modify the point-drawing algorithm, bypassing the BIOS call to achieve faster throughputs.

This is the case in the line-drawing routine presented in Section 12.10. Care must be taken to ensure that the state of the display adapter is handled properly. For example, eliminating redundant loading or reloading of a register may achieve a time savings. However, doing so may leave the display adapter in an undesirable condition if these registers are not properly reset.

The functions in Listing 12.16 write a pixel to the screen. The simplest and slowest is Wr_Point since it is based on the BIOS call. The Wr_Point_16 and Wr_Point_256 are specifically tailored for the 16-color or 256-color modes. Note that you should provide the number of bytes per row to these functions. This provides flexibility when the virtual image is not the same as the screen width. The Wr_Point_16 function assumes that the Set/Reset and Enable Set/Reset register has been set up with the desired color before this routine is called. In addition, it is important to reset the Bit Mask Register to FF hex and the Enable Set/Reset Register to 0 after this function is called. This allows the function to be called repetitively without calling unnecessary setup and clean-up operations each time. An alternative function, Wr_Pixel_16 performs this setup and clean-up.

The functions in Listing 12.17 read a pixel from the screen. Similar to the functions of Listing 12.16, the simplest and slowest is Rd_Point since it is based on the BIOS call. The Rd_Point_16 and Rd_Point_256 are specifically tailored for the sixteen-color or 256-color modes. Note that you should provide the number of bytes per row to these functions. This provides flexibility when the virtual image is not the same as the screen width.

LISTING 12.16 Writing a Point

```
; Write a point into display memory using BIOS

; Input parameters
;   page       display page to receive point
;   x,y        horizontal and vertical coordinates of point
;   color      color to draw point

; Calling protocol
;   Wr_Point(page,x,y,color);

Wr_Point proc FAR C PUBLIC page:byte,x_addr,y_addr,color:byte
        mov     bh,page       ;get page number
        mov     cx,x_addr     ;get x address column
        mov     dx,y_addr     ;get y address row
        mov     al,color      ;get color
        mov     ah,0Ch        ;write dot
        int     10h           ;draw the point
        ret
Wr_Point endp


; Draw a point into display memory  16 color  modes.

;   NOTE:  ASSUMES that Set Reset and Enable Set Reset Register
;   are preset with color.

; Input parameters
;    x_addr           horizontal coordinate of point
```

(continued)

```
;   y_addr        vertical coordinate of point
;   color         color to draw point
;   bytes_per_row display bytes_per_row = # of pixels per line

; Calling protocol
;   Wr_Point_16(x,y,bytes_per_row);

Wr_Point_16 proc FAR C PUBLIC USES ES
DI,x_addr,y_addr,bytes_per_row

; set up the Bit Mask Register
        mov     ax,3ceh     ;point to address port
        mov     dx,ax
        mov     ax,8
        out     dx,al       ;address bit plane mask
        inc     dx          ;DX points to data port

;       load the Bit Mask Register
        mov     cx,x_addr   ;get x address
        push    cx          ;save the address
        and     cx,0007h    ;only want bit position
        mov     al,80h      ;bit mask
        shr     al,cl       ;put bit mask into proper position
        out     dx,al       ;output bit plane mask

; get the x index and divide by 8 for 16-color
        pop     ax          ; get the x address
        shr     ax,1        ; divide by 8
        shr     ax,1
        shr     ax,1
        push    ax          ;save byte address for later

; determine the address = ( y * bytes_per_row ) + x
        mov     ax,bytes_per_row ; get bytes_per_row in ax
        mov     bx,y_addr      ; get y in bx
        mul     bx           ; y*bytes_per_row in dx:ax
        pop     cx           ; get the x byte address
        add     ax,cx        ; (y*bytes_per_row)+x lower 16 bits in ax
        mov     di,ax        ; load as display offset for es:di

; send the data to the display memory through set reset.  Set
; up display segment in es
        mov     es,SegA000
        mov     bl,es:[di]    ;dummy read from display memory
        mov     es:[di],bl    ;store color in memory through Set/Reset
        ret
Wr_Point_16 endp
```

```
;   Drawing a Point in one of the 16-color modes

; Input parameters:
;   x,y              x,y coordinate of point
;   color            color of the line
;   bytes_per_row    offset of display

; Calling protocol */
;       Wr_Pixel_16(int x, int y, BYTE color, int bytes_per_row)

Wr_Pixel_16 proc FAR C PUBLIC USES ES DS DI SI,
x_adr,y_adr,color:byte,bytes_per_row

;       set up the display segment pointer in es (always in 64K)
        mov     es,SegA000

;       enable the set reset function and load the color
        mov     dx,3ceh    ;point to address port
        mov     ax,0f01h   ;enable set reset index 1 to 0f
        out     dx,ax

;       set up set/reset register
        mov     al,0       ;set reset index 0 to color
        mov     ah,color
        out     dx,ax

;       set up the Bit Mask Register
        mov     al,8
        out     dx,al      ;address bit plane mask
        inc     dx         ;DX points to data port

;       load the Bit Mask Register
        mov     cx,x_adr   ;get x address
        and     cx,0007h   ;only want bit position
        mov     al,80h     ;bit mask
        shr     al,cl      ;put bit mask into proper position
        out     dx,al      ;output bit plane mask

; get the x index and divide by 8 for 16-color
        mov     ax,x_adr   ; get the x address
        shr     ax,1       ; divide by 8
        shr     ax,1
        shr     ax,1
        push    ax         ;save byte address for later

; determine the address = ( y * bytes_per_row ) + x
        mov     ax,bytes_per_row ; get bytes_per_row in ax
        mov     bx,y_adr   ;get y in bx
```

(continued)

```
        mul    bx              ;y*bytes_per_row in dx:ax
        pop    cx              ;get the x byte address
        add    ax,cx           ;(y*bytes_per_row)+x lower 16 bits in ax
        mov    di,ax           ;load as display offset for es:di

; send the data to the display memory through set reset
        mov    bl,es:[di]      ;dummy read from display memory
        mov    es:[di],bl      ;store color in memory through Set/Reset

; reset for normal vga operaton
        mov    dx,3ceh         ;point to address port
        mov    ax,0ff08h       ;bit mask index to ff
        out    dx,ax

;       restore enable set/reset register
        mov    ax,0001h        ;enable set reset index 1 to 0
        out    dx,ax
        ret
Wr_Pixel_16 endp


; Write a point into display memory in a 256-color mode

; Input parameters
;  x,y       horizontal and vertical coordinates of point
;  color     color to draw point
;  offset    display offset = # of pixels per line

; Calling protocol
;  Wr_Pixel_256(x,y,color,offset);

Wr_Pixel_256 proc FAR C PUBLIC USES ES
DI,x_addr,y_addr,color:byte,bytes_per_row
; determine the (long) address = ( y * offset ) + x.  segment
; is in dx and the offset is in ax
        mov    ax,bytes_per_row ;get offset
        mov    bx,y_addr        ;get y
        mul    bx               ;y * offset
        add    ax,x_addr        ;(y * offset) + x (lower 16 bits)
        adc    dx,0             ;(y * offset) + x (upper n bits)
        and    dx,0fh           ;only keep lower 4 bits of segment

; load the segment register
        push   ax               ;save the offset for later
        mov    al,dl            ;get the segment value
        mov    dx,3cdh          ;point to segment register
        out    dx,al            ;load the segment register

; send the data to the display memory in es
```

```
        mov     es,SegA000
        pop     di                    ;get display offset value
        mov     al,color              ;get color
        mov     es:[di],al            ;store color in display memory
        ret
Wr_Pixel_256 endp
```

LISTING 12.17 Reading a Point

```
; Read a point from the display memory (BIOS)

; Input parameters:
;  page display page to receive point
;  x,y  horizontal and vertical coordinates of point to read

; Output parameter:
;  colorcolor of point read

; Calling protocol
;  color = Rd_Point(page,x,y);

Rd_Point proc FAR C PUBLIC npage:byte,x_addr,y_addr
        mov     bh,npage        ;get page number
        mov     cx,x_addr       ;get x address column
        mov     dx,y_addr       ;get y address row
        mov     ah,0Dh          ;read dot
        int     10h             ;read the pixel
        xor     ah,ah           ;return color in ax
        ret
Rd_Point endp

; Read a point from display memory16 color modes.

; Input parameters
;  x        horizontal coordinate of point
;  y        vertical coordinate of point
;  bytes_per_row display bytes_per_row = # of pixels per line

; Output Parameters:
;  color    color to draw point

; Calling protocol
;  color = Rd_Pixel_16(x,y,bytes_per_row);

Rd_Pixel_16 proc FAR C PUBLIC USES DS
SI,x_addr,y_addr,bytes_per_row
        mov     ax,x_addr       ;get the x address
```

(continued)

```
        push    ax              ;save the x address
        shr     ax,1            ;divide by 8
        shr     ax,1
        shr     ax,1
        push    ax              ;save byte address for later

; determine the address = ( y * bytes_per_row ) + x
        mov     ax,bytes_per_row ; get bytes_per_row in ax
        mov     bx,y_addr       ;get y in bx
        mul     bx              ;y*bytes_per_row in dx:ax
        pop     cx              ;get the x byte address
        add     ax,cx           ; (y*bytes_per_row)+x lower 16 bits in ax
        mov     si,ax           ;load as display offset for ds:di

;       read the data from the display memory  in ds once for
;       each plane
        mov     ds,SegA000

;       set up the Read Plane Register
        mov     dx,3ceh    ;point to address port
        mov     ax,4
        out     dx,al      ;address read map mask
        inc     dx         ;DX points read map register data port

;       determine the number of bits to shift
        pop     ax         ;get x address
        and     ax,0007h   ;only want bit position
        mov     cl,07      ;bit mask
        sub     cl,al      ;7-remainder = # bits to right shift plane 0
        mov     bl,cl      ;save shift amount

;       read plane 0
        mov     al,0       ;read from plane 0
        out     dx,al
        mov     al,ds:[si];read from display memory
        shr     al,cl
        and     al,01h     ;only want bit 0
        mov     ah,al      ;save in ah

;       read plane 1
        mov     al,1       ;read from plane 1
        out     dx,al
        mov     al,ds:[si];read from display memory
        mov     cl,bl      ;get shift count
        shr     al,cl
        and     al,01h     ;only want bit 0
        shl     al,1
        or      ah,al      ;save in ah
```

```
;       read plane 2
        mov     al,2            ;read from plane 2
        out     dx,al
        mov     al,ds:[si]      ;read from display memory
        mov     cl,bl
        shr     al,cl
        and     al,01h          ;only want bit 0
        shl     al,1
        shl     al,1
        or      ah,al           ;save in ah

;       read plane 3
        mov     al,3            ;read from plane 3
        out     dx,al
        mov     al,ds:[si]      ;read from display memory
        mov     cl,bl
        shr     al,cl
        and     al,01h          ;only want bit 1
        shl     al,1
        shl     al,1
        shl     al,1
        or      ah,al           ;save in ah

        mov     al,ah
        xor     ah,ah           ;send back in ax
        ret
Rd_Pixel_16 endp



; Read a point into display memory in a 256-color mode

; Input parameters
;  x,y       horizontal and vertical coordinates of point
;  offset    display offset = # of pixels per line

; Output parameters
;  color     color of selected point

; Calling protocol
;  color = Rd_Pixel_256(x,y,offset);

Rd_Pixel_256 proc FAR C PUBLIC USES
DS,x_addr,y_addr,bytes_per_row

; determine the (long) address = ( y * offset ) + x
; where the segment is in dx and the offset is in ax
        mov     ax,bytes_per_row ;get offset
        mov     bx,y_addr       ;get y
```

(continued)

```
        mul     bx              ; y * offset
        add     ax,x_addr       ; (y * offset) + x (lower 16 bits)
        adc     dx,0            ; (y * offset) + x (upper n bits)
        and     dx,07h          ; only keep lower 3 bits of segment

; load the segment register
        push    ax              ; save the offset for later
        mov     al,dl           ; get the segment value
        shl     al,1
        shl     al,1
        shl     al,1
        shl     al,1            ; bits 3-0 into read bank bits 7-4
        mov     dx,3cdh         ; point to segment register
        out     dx,ax           ; load the segment register

; send the data to the display memory in ds
        mov     ds,A000
        pop     si              ; get display offset value
        mov     al,ds:[si]      ; send color to "C"
        xor     ah,ah

        ret
Rd_Pixel_256 endp
```

12.10   DRAWING A LINE

Probably the most important algorithm in computer graphics is the line-drawing algorithm. The algorithm included in this book is highly optimized for the EGA/VGA. This routine, called Line, is split up into three separate line-drawing algorithms. Two of these are special cases of line-drawing concerned with drawing horizontal and vertical lines. The third routine uses Bresenham's line algorithm and is used for all other lines. All three of these routines are specially written for optimal operation on the EGA/VGA.

The line algorithm is invoked by calling either the routine Line or the routine Line13. The Line routine operates in all display modes that use sixteen colors. These modes utilize all four display modes to store a single pixel value. Eight pixels are represented in each byte of all four display planes. The Line13 routine is written specifically for the display mode 13 hex. This mode allows 256 simultaneous colors, with each byte containing the 8-bit color code for each pixel.

The Line and Line13 routine rely on special-purpose line-drawing routines to handle the horizontal and vertical lines. These horizontal and vertical line routines may be called directly if a horizontal or vertical line is required.

12.10.1 Horizontal Lines

The EGA/VGA configured in display modes D, E, F, or 10 hex, or the VGA configured in modes 11 or 12 hex, stores bits from eight neighboring horizontal
pixels in a single byte of display memory. The smallest element that can be
written to display memory is a single byte. Using a point-drawing routine to
draw every point in the line would be wasteful because up to eight pixels can be
handled in a single byte operation.

The algorithm used to draw horizontal lines calls upon one of three subroutines to actually draw the line. The routine Wr_HLine_16 in Listing 12.18 is
called to draw horizontal lines. Also in Listing 12.18 are the three assembly
routines that actually write to the display.

LISTING 12.18 Drawing Horizontal Lines

```
/*    Draw a horizontal line in a 16_color mode

Input parameters:
x1          = x-coordinate 1
x2          = x-coordinate 2
y           = y-coordinate
color       = desired color of line

Calling Protocol:
Wr_HLine_16(page,x1,x2,y,color);        */

void Wr_HLine_16(int x1,int x2,int y,BYTE color,int
bytes_per_row);
{ int i,x,x1byte,x2byte,nbyte,address,dx,offset;
  char mask1,mask2;

ESetRes(15);    SetRes(color);

// reverse x-coordinates
if (x1>x2) { x=x1; x1=x2; x2=x; }

x1byte=x1>>3; x2byte=x2>>3;
dx=x2byte-x1byte; nbyte=x2byte-x1byte-1;
address = (y*bytes_per_row) + x1byte;

switch (x1%8) {
    case 0: mask1=0xff; break;    case 1: mask1=0x7f; break;
    case 2: mask1=0x3f; break;    case 3: mask1=0x1f; break;
    case 4: mask1=0x0f; break;    case 5: mask1=0x07; break;
    case 6: mask1=0x03; break;    case 7: mask1=0x01; break;
    }
```

(continued)

```
switch (x2%8) {
   case 0: mask2=0x80; break;   case 1: mask2=0xc0; break;
   case 2: mask2=0xe0; break;   case 3: mask2=0xf0; break;
   case 4: mask2=0xf8; break;   case 5: mask2=0xfc; break;
   case 6: mask2=0xfe; break;   case 7: mask2=0xff; break;
    }

 if(dx == 0) Hsub1(address,mask1&mask2);
 if(dx == 1) HSub2(address,mask1,mask2);
 if(dx>1)    HSub3(address,mask1,mask2,nbyte);

BitMask(255);  ESetRes(0);  MapMask(15);
 }



; Output a horizontal line containing one byte
; Input assumptions:
;  Enable Set/Reset Register set to desired planes
;  Set/Reset Register set to color

; Output assumptions:
;  Enable Set/Reset Register reset to 0
;  Bit Mask Register reset to 0xff

; Input parameters:
;  address = display memory offset address
;  mask    = mask of single byte containing the line

; Calling protocol:
;  Hsub1(addr,mask);

Hsub1  proc far USES DS SI, address, nmask:byte
        mov    ds,SegA000
        mov    si,address   ;get address

; load the Bit Mask Register
        mov    ax,3ceh       ;point to mask address
        mov    dx,ax
        mov    al,8          ;8 for mask
        out    dx,al
        inc    dx            ;point to mask register
        mov    al,nmask      ;get mask
        out    dx,al         ;load mask

        mov    al,ds:[si]    ;dummy read before write
        mov    ds:[si],al    ;output color
```

```
            ret
Hsub1   endp


; Output a horizontal line contained within two bytes
; Input assumptions:
;   Enable Set/Reset Register set to desired planes
;   Set/Reset Register set to color

; Output assumptions:
;   Enable Set/Reset Register reset to 0
;   Bit Mask Register reset to 0xff

; Input parameters:
;   address  = display memory offset address
;   mask1    = first (left-most) mask for line
;   mask2    = second (right-most) mask for line

; Calling protocol:
;   HSub2(address,mask1,mask2);
HSub2   proc far USES DS SI, address,mask1:byte,mask2:byte
            mov     ds,SegA000
            mov     si,address     ;get address

; load the Bit Mask Register
            mov     ax,3ceh        ;point to mask address
            mov     dx,ax
            mov     al,8           ;8 for mask
            out     dx,al
            inc     dx             ;point to mask register

; output first byte
            mov     al,mask1       ;get mask1
            out     dx,al          ;load Bit Mask with mask1

            mov     al,ds:[si]     ;dummy read
            mov     ds:[si],al     ;output color

; output second byte
            mov     al,mask2       ;get mask2
            out     dx,al          ;load Bit Mask with mask2

            inc     si             ;increment address
            mov     al,ds:[si]     ;dummy read
            mov     ds:[si],al     ;output color
            ret
HSub2   endp
```

(continued)

```
; Output a horizontal line containing more than two bytes

; Input assumptions:
;   Enable Set/Reset Register set to desired planes
;   Set/Reset Register set to color

; Output assumptions:
;   Enable Set/Reset Register reset to 0
;   Bit Mask Register reset to 0xff

; Input parameters:
;   address = display memory offset address
;   mask1   = first (left-most) mask for line
;   mask2   = second (right-most) mask for line
;   nbytes  = number of bytes inbetween end bytes

; Calling protocol:
;   HSub3(address,mask1,mask2,nbyte);

HSub3   proc far USES DS SI, address,mask1:byte,mask2:byte,nbytes
        mov     dsSegA000
        mov     si,address      ;get address

; load the Bit Mask Register
        mov     ax,3ceh         ;point to mask address
        mov     dx,ax
        mov     al,8            ;8 for mask
        out     dx,al
        inc     dx              ;point to mask register

; load the first byte
        mov     al,mask1        ;get mask1
        out     dx,al           ;load Bit Mask with mask1

        mov     al,ds:[si]      ;dummy read
        mov     ds:[si],al      ;output color

; load the middle bytes
        mov     al,0ffh
        out     dx,al           ;load mask with FFh = all on

        mov     cx,nbytes       ;get repeat count
o31:    inc     si              ;increment address
        mov     al,ds:[si]      ;dummy read
        mov     ds:[si],al      ;output color to a middle byte
        loop    o31
```

```
; load the end byte
        mov     al,mask2                ;get mask2
        out     dx,al                   ;load Bit Mask with mask2

        inc     si                      ;increment address
        mov     al,ds:[si]              ;dummy read
        mov     ds:[si],al              ;output color
        ret
HSub3   endp
```

```
/* Drawing a Horizontal Line in one of the 256-color modes

  Input parameters:
   x1,x2              endpoints of x coordinates of line
   y                  y coordinate of horizontal line
   color              color of the line
   bytes_per_row      offset of display

Calling protocol */
void WrHLine_256(int x1,int x2,int y,BYTE color,int
bytes_per_row)

{ SHORT offset;  int length;

 length = 1+x2-x1;
 // determine the starting offset of  the line
offset = ((SHORT)y*bytes_per_row) + x1;

Clr_Part(color,length,offset);

}

; Clear a portion of a segment beginning at a start address
; Input parameters
;   color   color to set segment
;   npix    number of pixels
;   start   offset of window to start at

; Calling protocol
;   Clr_Part(color,npix,start);

Clr_Part proc FAR C PUBLIC USES ES DI, color:byte, npix, start
        mov     es,SegA000
        mov     di,start        ;starting address of segment
        mov     cx,npix         ;desired number of bytes
```

(continued)

```
        mov     al,color       ;get color
        rep     stosb          ;fill memory
        ret
Clr_Part endp
```

The first subroutine, named Hsub1, draws a horizontal line if the entire line is located in one byte. The second, named Hsub2, draws a horizontal line if the line fits in two bytes, and the third, Hsub3, draws a horizontal line when more than two bytes are contained. Dhline determines a bit mask for the single byte in Hsub1 and two masks, one for each end, for Hsub2 and Hsub3.

All of the bytes contained in the center of the line have a mask of FF hex because all bits represent pixels contained in the line. These mask values contain a 1 in the bit positions of pixels contained in the line and a 0 in the other bit positions. These masks are loaded into the Bit Mask Register. The Set/Reset Register and Enable Set/Reset Register are utilized in Write Mode 0 to actually draw the points. The Bit Mask Register and the Enable Set/Reset Register are reset by DhLine at completion of the line. Figure 12.2 illustrates these three cases.

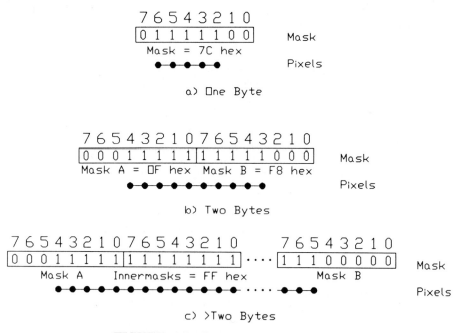

FIGURE 12.2 Drawing a Horizontal Line

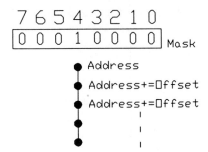

FIGURE 12.3 Drawing a Vertical Line

12.10.2 Vertical Lines

The address of a pixel in these specific display modes is determined by the byte address of display memory and the pixel location within this addressed byte. Drawing vertical lines involves setting up a mask that determines which pixel in the accessed bytes is affected. This mask does not have to change during the drawing of the line because the line is vertical. The address of each point in the line is determined by adding or subtracting an offset value from the display address. This offset value represents the distance in bytes between two neighboring vertical pixels. Figure 12.3 illustrates the drawing of a vertical line. Vertical line-drawing functions are provided in Listing 12.19.

LISTING 12.19 Drawing a Vertical Line

```
;    Drawing a vertical line in a 16-color modes

; Input parameters:
;    x              x coordinates of line
;    y              y coordinate of horizontal line
;    npix           number of pixels
;    color          buffer containing data
;    bytes_per_row  offset of display

; Calling protocol
void  Wr_VLine_16(int x,int y,int npix,BYTE color,int
bytes_per_row)

Wr_VLine_16 proc FAR C PUBLIC USES ES
DI,x_addr,y_addr,npix,color:byte,bytes_per_row

;        set up the display segment pointer (always in 64K)
         mov    es,SegA000
```

(continued)

```
;       enable the set reset function and load the color
        mov     dx,3ceh        ;point to address port
        mov     ax,0f01h       ;enable set reset index 1 to 0f
        out     dx,ax

;       set up set/reset register
        mov     al,0           ;set reset index 0 to color
        mov     ah,color
        out     dx,ax

;       set up the Bit Mask Register
        mov     al,8
        out     dx,al          ;address bit plane mask
        inc     dx             ;DX points to data port

;       load the Bit Mask Register
        mov     cx,x_addr      ;get x address
        and     cx,0007h       ;only want bit position
        mov     al,80h         ;bit mask
        shr     al,cl          ;put bit mask into proper position
        out     dx,al          ;output bit plane mask

; get the x index and divide by 8 for 16-color
        mov     ax,x_addr      ; get the x address
        shr     ax,1           ; divide by 8
        shr     ax,1
        shr     ax,1
        push    ax             ;save byte address for later

; determine the address = ( y * bytes_per_row ) + x
        mov     ax,bytes_per_row    ; get bytes_per_row in ax
        mov     bx,y_addr           ; get y in bx
        mul     bx             ; y*bytes_per_row in dx:ax
        pop     cx             ; get the x byte address
        add     ax,cx          ; (y*bytes_per_row)+x lower 16 bits in ax
        mov     di,ax          ; load as display offset for es:di

        mov     cx,npix   ; set up the line count
        mov     dx,bytes_per_row    ;get bytes_per_row into dx
wrv_l16:
        mov     al,es:[di]     ; dummy read from display memory
        mov     es:[di],al     ; store color in display memory
        add     di,dx          ;add bytes_per_row to address next row
        loop    wrv_l16

; reset for normal vga operaton
        mov     dx,3ceh        ;point to address port
```

```
        mov     ax,0ff08h       ;bit mask index to ff
        out     dx,ax


;       restore enable set/reset register
        mov     ax,0001h        ;enable set reset index 1 to 0
        out     dx,ax
        ret
Wr_VLine_16 endp


; Write a vertical line in a 256-color mode

; Input parameters
;  x              x coordinates of line
;  y              y coordinate of horizontal line
;  npix           number of pixels
;  color          buffer containing data
;  bytes_per_row  offset of display

; Calling protocol
; void  Wr_VLine_256(int x,int y,int npix,BYTE color,int
bytes_per_row)

Wr_VLine_256 proc FAR C PUBLIC USES ES
DI,x_addr,y_addr,npix,color:byte,bytes_per_row
; determine the (long) address = ( y * offset ) + x.  segment
; is in dx and the offset is in ax
        mov     ax,bytes_per_row ;get offset
        push    ax                      ;save bytes per row for later
        mov     bx,y_addr       ;get y
        mul     bx              ;y * offset
        add     ax,x_addr       ;(y * offset) + x (lower 16 bits)
        mov     di,ax           ;load into di

; send the data to the display memory
        mov     es,SegA000

        mov     cx,npix         ;set up the line count
        mov     al,color        ;get color
        pop     dx              ;get bytes_per_row into dx
wrv_1256:
        mov     es:[di],al      ;store color in display memory
        add     di,dx           ;add bytes_per_row to address next row
        loop    wrv_1256
        ret
Wr_VLine_256 endp
```

12.10.3   Bresenham's Algorithm

Bresenham's line algorithm is based on the fact that a line is composed of a series of connected pixels. An independent axis is selected, and a single pixel is drawn at each point on the independent axis between the two end points. Thus, the one coordinate of the point is determined by incrementing that variable. Because the points are connected, the dependent variable can either maintain the same value or change it by one. A decision variable is used to determine whether or not the dependent variable should change.

The independent variable is selected depending on the slope of the line. The line's slope is determined by dividing the number of pixels included in one direction by the number of pixels included in the other. The axis that has the greater number of pixels is elected as the independent axis. This process is illustrated in Figure 12.4.

In Figure 12.4, a line is drawn from coordinates $X = 20$, $Y = 10$ to the point $X = 32$, $Y = 18$. The difference is determined by Equation 12.1. Because the XDIF is larger, the X axis is selected as the independent variable.

Equation 12.1   Determining the Independent Axis

$$XDIF = ABS\ (X2 - X1) = ABS\ (32 - 20) = 12$$

$$YDIF = ABS\ (Y2 - Y1) = ABS\ (18 - 10) = 8$$

The line is drawn by incrementing the X variable from 20 to 32. At each point, a decision is made regarding the incrementing of the Y variable. The decision variable is modified at each point by one of two constants. The constants are determined by the slope of the line. These constants assume that the independent axis increments positively. This constrains the direction of the

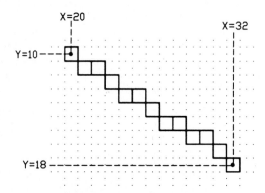

FIGURE 12.4   Drawing a Line

lines to positive motion along the independent variable. The dependent variable can move in a positive or negative direction. The difference of the independent variable, as calculated in Equation 12.1, must be positive. In other words, $X2$ or $Y2$ must be greater than $X1$ or $Y1$ respectively. It is a simple matter to reverse the coordinates, $X2 = X1$, $X1 = X2$, $Y1 = Y2$, and $Y2 = Y1$, if the line moves in the wrong direction.

Implementing the algorithm for the EGA/VGA requires heuristic knowledge of the operation of the EGA/VGA. At each coordinate, along the independent axis, a point is drawn. The BIOS Draw Point call could be invoked to draw each point. This provides portability but imposes a heavy penalty because of the unnecessary operations that occur. An optimum implementation is presented that minimizes the unnecessary operations.

Drawing a line on the EGA/VGA is accomplished using different techniques depending on which of the X or Y axes is the independent axis. The exception is display mode 13 hex on the VGA. This mode assigns one byte for every pixel, creating a symmetry between the horizontal and vertical axes. In all other modes, multiple pixels are represented in a single byte. A group of pixels—two, four, or eight—is accessed by a single address. An individual pixel within this byte is accessed by a bit position. When data is written to the display memory, a mask locates the pixel within the addressed byte. Moving to the left or right on the display involves shifting a pattern within the mask, and moving up or down involves adding an offset to the address. A single pixel can be accessed by representing the pixel with a 1 in one bit of the mask.

Moving one pixel to the left involves shifting this mask byte one bit to the left. Similarly, moving one pixel to the right involves shifting the mask one bit to the right. If an overflow occurs when shifting to the left, the address is decremented and the mask is reset to 01 hex. If an overflow occurs when shifting to the right, the address is incremented and the mask is reset to 80 hex. This is illustrated in Table 12.4 for the display modes D, E, F, 10, 11, and 12 hex. Shifting to the right is represented by reading from the top of the table downward, and shifting to the left is represented by reading from the bottom of the table upward.

In contrast, the Y axis is incremented by adding a constant value to the display address. The constant is equal to the number of bytes that separate two adjacent vertical bytes in the virtual image. This value is stored in the Offset Register, which cannot be read in the EGA. This value can be obtained by interrogating the system status through the BIOS call.

Because the mask value represents which pixel within the addressed byte is active, the mask value does not change when the Y axis is modified. In Table 12.16, the Y byte address is observed to change from 10 to 18. If the offset is 80, this corresponds to addresses 800 to 1,440. The row number is multiplied by the offset to produce the Y address. The display memory address, which accesses a single byte in display memory, is obtained by adding the X address to the Y address. Moving in the positive Y direction is accomplished by adding

TABLE 12.16   Changing the X Address

X Coordinate	X Address	Bit Mask (Hex)	Y Address × Offset
20	2	08	10
21	2	04	11
22	2	02	11
23	2	01	12
24	3	80	13
25	3	40	13
26	3	20	14
27	2	10	15
28	3	08	15
29	3	04	16
30	3	02	17
31	3	01	17
32	4	80	18

to the display address a constant value that is equal to the display offset. Similarly, moving in the negative Y direction is accomplished by subtracting the offset from the display address.

Because of speed-related issues, line drawing is more complicated to implement than one would at first suspect. There are horizontal and vertical lines as well as lines of arbitrary slope. Each type of line needs to be implemented with an optimized routine. Two line-draw routines are provided in Listing 12.20, one for 16-color and one for 256-color modes. These may call upon the horizontal line drawing functions in Listing 12.18 or the vertical line drawing functions in Listing 12.19.

LISTING 12.20   Drawing a Line

```
/*   Draw a Line in one of the 16-color modes

   Input parameters:
     x1,y1              first endpoint x,y coordinates of line
     x2,y2              second endpoint x,y coordinates of line
     color              color of the line
     bytes_per_row      offset of display

Calling Protocol */
void    Wr_Line_16(int x1,int y1,int x2,int y2,BYTE color,
        int bytes_per_row)
{
    int dx,dy,incr1,incr2,d,x,y,xend,yend,yinc,xinc;
```

```
    // draw a vertical line if so directed
 if(x1 == x2) {
      if(y1 > y2) {  yend = y1;     y1 = y2;     y2 = yend;   }
      Wr_VLine_16(x1,y1,y2,color,bytes_per_row);
      }
  else {  // draw a non-vertical line

   // draw a horizontal line if so directed
 if(y1 == y2) {
      if(x1 > x2) {  xend = x1;     x1 = x2;     x2 = xend;   }
      Wr_HLine_16(x1,x2,y1,color,bytes_per_row);
      }
  else {   // draw a non-horizontal line

    // enable the set/reset function and load the color
    ESetRes(15);  SetRes(color);

    // determine whether the line should be drawn along the x
or y axis
    dy = abs(y2-y1);       dx = abs(x2-x1);
    if(dx>=dy) {   // slope < 1 so draw along x axis
     // determine which direction to draw line along x axis
     if(x1>x2) {
        x = x2;  y = y2; xend = x1;
        if(dy==0) yinc=0;
          else { if(y2>y1) yinc = -1; else yinc =  1; }
        }
      else {
        x = x1;  y = y1; xend = x2;
        if(dy==0) { yinc=0; }
          else        { if(y2>y1) yinc =  1; else yinc = -1; }
        }

     // draw first point
     incr1 = 2*dy;  d = incr1-dx;  incr2 = 2*(dy-dx);
     Wr_Point_16(x,y,bytes_per_row);

    // draw rest of points
     while (x<xend) {
        x ++;
        if (d<0) { d += incr1; }
          else     { y += yinc;  d += incr2; }
        Wr_Point_16(x,y,bytes_per_row);
          }
   } // end of draw along x axis

 else {  // draw along y axis
```

(continued)

```c
                // determine which direction to draw line along y axis
                 if(y1>y2) {
                     x = x2;  y = y2; yend = y1;
                     if(dx==0) xinc=0;
                     else  { if(x2>x1) xinc = -1;  else xinc =  1; }
                     }
                 else {
                     x = x1;  y = y1; yend = y2;
                     if(dx==0) { xinc=0; }
                      else {  if(x2>x1) xinc =  1;  else       xinc = -1; }
                     }

                 incr1 = 2*dx;   d = incr1-dy; incr2 = 2*(dx-dy);
                 Wr_Point_16(x,y,bytes_per_row);

                 while (y<yend) {
                     y ++;
                     if (d<0) d += incr1;
                      else {  x += xinc;  d += incr2;    }
                     Wr_Point_16(x,y,bytes_per_row);
                     }  // end of draw til end of y
          }   // end of line draw
        BitMask(255); ESetRes(0);  // reset the EGA/VGA registers
} }   // end of not horizontal or vertical line
}


/*      Drawing a Line in one of the 256-color modes

 Input parameters:
  x1,y1             first endpoint x,y coordinates of line
  x2,y2             second endpoint x,y coordinates of line
  color             color of the line
  bytes_per_row     offset of display

Calling protocol */
void      Wr_Line_256(int x1,int y1,int x2,int y2,BYTE color,
          int bytes_per_row)

{ int dx,dy,incr1,incr2,d,x,y,xend,yend,yinc,xinc;

   // draw a vertical line if so directed
  if(x1 == x2) {
        if(y1 > y2) {  yend = y1;     y1 = y2;     y2 = yend;   }
        Wr_VLine_256(x1,y1,y2,color,bytes_per_row);
        }
    else {  // draw a non-vertical line
```

```
// draw a horizontal line if so directed
if(y2==y1) {
      if(x1 > x2) {  xend = x1;    x1 = x2;    x2 = xend;  }
      Wr_HLine_256(x1,x2,y1,color,bytes_per_row);
       }
   else {
     dx = abs(x2-x1);  dy = abs(y2-y1);
     // determine whether the line should be drawn along
     // the x or y axis
     if(dx>=dy) {  // slope < 1 so draw along x axis
      if(x1>x2) {
         x = x2;  y = y2; xend = x1;
         if(dy==0) {yinc=0; }
           else {if(y2>y1) yinc = -1;  else yinc = 1; }
         }
        else   {
           x = x1;  y = y1; xend = x2;
           if(dy==0) yinc=0;
             else {if(y2>y1) yinc = 1;  else yinc = -1; }
             }

  // draw first point
  incr1 = 2*dy;   d = incr1-dx; incr2 = 2*(dy-dx);
  Wr_Pixel_256(x,y,color,bytes_per_row);

     // draw rest of points
     while (x<xend) {
       x ++;
       if (d<0) { d += incr1; }
         else { y +=yinc; d = d + incr2;  }
       Wr_Pixel_256(x,y,color,bytes_per_row);
       }
     }  // end of draw along x axis

   else {  // draw along y axis
      // determine which direction to draw line along y axis
      if(y1>y2) {
        x = x2;  y = y2; yend = y1;
        if(dx==0) { xinc=0; }
         else { if(x2>x1) xinc = -1;  else xinc = 1;}
         }
        else {
          x = x1;  y = y1; yend = y2;
          if(dx==0) { xinc=0; }
          else { if(x2>x1) xinc =  1;  else xinc = -1;}
          }
```

(continued)

```
incr1 = 2*dx;   d = incr1-dy; incr2 = 2*(dx-dy);
Wr_Pixel_256(x,y,color,bytes_per_row);

while (y<yend) {
   y ++;
   if (d<0) { d += incr1; }
    else { x +=xinc; d = d + incr2;  }
   Wr_Pixel_256(x,y,color,bytes_per_row);
   }  // end of draw til end of y
}  // end of line draw
} }  // end of not horizontal or vertical line
}
```

Figure 12.5 illustrates the eight quadrants that segment the 360 degrees surrounding a point. A line is drawn into one of these quadrants, depending on the slope of the line.

12.11 DRAWING A CIRCLE

A circle exhibits an eight-quadrant symmetry, as shown in Figure 12.6. Thus, the points on the circumference of a circle need only be calculated from 0 to 45 degrees.

Bresenham's circle algorithm is implemented in the routine called Circle, presented in Listing 12.21. This routine operates in a similar fashion to that used by the line-drawing routine. Because the circle is symmetric about the X

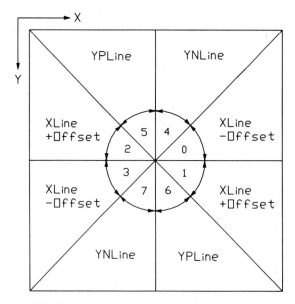

FIGURE 12.5 Selecting a Line-drawing Routine

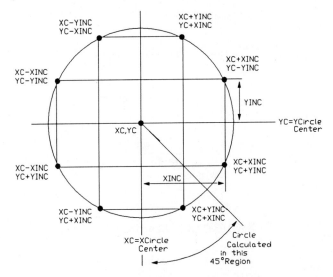

FIGURE 12.6 Eight-point Symmetry

and Y axis, either the X or Y axis may be chosen as the independent variable. The initial condition sets the first point according to Equation 12.2.

Equation 12.2 Initial Conditions for the Circle

$X = X$ center

$Y = Y$ center + radius

This positions the point at the 270-degree point. The 45-degree span that will be calculated travels from this 270-degree point to the 315-degree point. In this routine, the X axis is selected as the independent variable, and it increments for each point. A decision variable is used to determine whether the Y axis should be decremented for every point. Remember that decrementing the address corresponds to an upward motion along the Y axis on the EGA/VGA. The process of drawing a circle is illustrated in Figure 12.7.

LISTING 12.21 Drawing a Circle

```
/*   Draw a 16-color Circle

Input parameters:
  xc      horizontal center coordinate
  yc      vertical center coordinate
```

(continued)

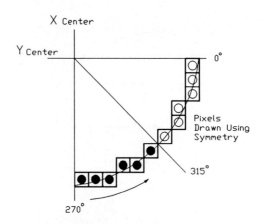

FIGURE 12.7 Drawing a Circle

```
radius              radius of circle
color               color of circle
bytes_per_row       = display offset

Calling protocol:
Wr_Circle_16( xc,  yc,  radius,  color,  bytes_per_row);    */

void    Wr_Circle_16(int xc, int yc, int radius, BYTE color,
        int bytes_per_row)
{ int x=0,y,d;
// enable the set reset function and load the color
ESetRes(15); SetRes(color); //  load registers

  y = radius; // initialize y to radius
 // with x=0 and y=radius,  first point is at 270 degrees
  d = 3 - (2*radius);  // initialize the decision variable

  while (x<y)
  { Circ_Pnt_16(x,y,xc,yc,bytes_per_row); // draw a point in
all four quadrants
        if(d<0) // don't decrement y
           d += 4*x + 6; // update the decision variable
        else
        { d += 4*(x-y) + 10; // update the decision variable
          y --; }  // decrement y
        x++; // increment the x variable
  } // end of while (x<y)
  if(x==y) Circ_Pnt_16(x,y,xc,yc,bytes_per_row);
  // draw a point in four quadrants
BitMask(255); ESetRes(0);  // reset the EGA/VGA registers
}
```

```
/*  Draw a 256-color Circle

Input parameters:
 xc                 horizontal center coordinate
 yc                 vertical center coordinate
 radius             radius of circle
 color              color of circle
 bytes_per_row      = display offset

Calling protocol:
Wr_Circle_256( xc,  yc,  radius, color,  bytes_per_row) */

void    Wr_Circle_256(int xc, int yc, int radius, BYTE color,
        int bytes_per_row)
{ int x=0,y,d;

  y = radius; // initialize y to radius
 // with x=0 and y=radius,  first point is at 270 degrees
  d = 3 - (2*radius);  // initialize the decision variable

  while (x<y)
  // draw a point in all four quadrants
  { Circ_Pnt_256(x,y,xc,yc,color,bytes_per_row);
       if(d<0) // don't decrement y
          d += 4*x + 6; // update the decision variable
       else
       { d += 4*(x-y) + 10; // update the decision variable
          y --; }  // decrement y
       x++; // increment the x variable
  } // end of while (x<y)
 if(x==y) Circ_Pnt_256(x,y,xc,yc,color,bytes_per_row);
 // draw a point in four quadrants
}


/*  Determining the sixteen-color Eight-point Symmetry

Input parameters:
 x,y        = coordinate of point to replicate eight times
 xc,yc  = center of circle
 bytes_per_row = display offset

Calling protocol:
Circ_Pnt_16( x, y, xc, yc, bytes_per_row);   */

void Circ_Pnt_16(int x,int y,int xc,int yc,int bytes_per_row)
{ int   xxcp,xxcm,xycp,xycm,yxcp,yxcm,yycp,yycm;
```

(continued)

```
   // draw points using eight-point symmetry
xxcp = xc+x; xxcm = xc-x; xycp = xc+y; xycm = xc-y;
yxcp = yc+x; yxcm = yc-x; yycp = yc+y; yycm = yc-y;
Wr_Point_16(xxcp,yycp,bytes_per_row);
Wr_Point_16(xxcp,yycm,bytes_per_row);
Wr_Point_16(xxcm,yycp,bytes_per_row);
Wr_Point_16(xxcm,yycm,bytes_per_row);
Wr_Point_16(xycp,yxcp,bytes_per_row);
Wr_Point_16(xycp,yxcm,bytes_per_row);
Wr_Point_16(xycm,yxcp,bytes_per_row);
Wr_Point_16(xycm,yxcm,bytes_per_row);
}

/*  Determining the 256-color (internal) Eight-point Symmetry

Input parameters:
 x,y            = coordinate of point to replicate eight times
 xc,yc          = center of circle
 bytes_per_row = display offset

Calling protocol:
Circ_Pnt_256(x,y,xc,yc, color,bytes_per_row) */

void    Circ_Pnt_256(int x,int y,int xc,int yc,BYTE color,
        int bytes_per_row)
{
    int  xxcp,xxcm,xycp,xycm,yxcp,yxcm,yycp,yycm;

 // draw points using eight point symmetry
xxcp = xc+x; xxcm = xc-x; xycp = xc+y; xycm = xc-y;
yxcp = yc+x; yxcm = yc-x; yycp = yc+y; yycm = yc-y;
Wr_Pixel_256(xxcp,yycp,color,bytes_per_row);
Wr_Pixel_256(xxcp,yycm,color,bytes_per_row);
Wr_Pixel_256(xxcm,yycp,color,bytes_per_row);
Wr_Pixel_256(xxcm,yycm,color,bytes_per_row);
Wr_Pixel_256(xycp,yxcp,color,bytes_per_row);
Wr_Pixel_256(xycp,yxcm,color,bytes_per_row);
Wr_Pixel_256(xycm,yxcp,color,bytes_per_row);
Wr_Pixel_256(xycm,yxcm,color,bytes_per_row);
}
```

Each *X* and *Y* coordinate pair is drawn in eight places on the display by calling the functions CircPnt_16 or CircPnt_256. This routine calculates the eight symmetric points that are shown in Figure 12.6 and writes the eight points to the screen using the DrawPnt routine.

12.12 DRAWING AN IMAGE

An image, also called a *window*, consists of a rectangular area filled with pixels of any value. The windows are written to the screen in horizontal lines. Each pixel may have its own color. This is different from the line-drawing routine, in which the entire horizontal line was drawn in a single color.

The window may be associated with an alphanumeric or graphics display mode. In the alphanumeric display modes, its dimensions are measured in character positions along both the horizontal and vertical axes. In the graphics display modes, its dimensions are measured in pixels along the horizontal axis and in scan lines along the vertical axis.

The data that resides inside the window fills a two-dimensional space in the display memory. Lines are not necessarily contiguous because the width of the window does not necessarily correspond to the width of the virtual display. The width of the virtual display is stored in the Offset Register, as illustrated in Figure 12.8.

The buffer may be declared as a one-dimensional or a two-dimensional C array. The format used for the data in the window routines is identical to the C data convention. The elements of each row are stored sequentially, each row loaded contiguously in the C array.

12.12.1 Writing to a Window

The routine WrWin in Listing 12.22 writes a data buffer to the display memory at a specified location. The calculations that determine the position of the window in the display memory vary depending on the active display mode. The position and size of the window are determined by the horizontal and vertical dimensions passed to the routine. The parameters passed to this routine represent the horizontal and vertical coordinates of the upper-left and lower-right corners of the window.

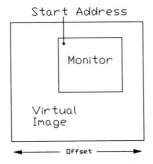

FIGURE 12.8 The Monitor Window within a Virtual Image

LISTING 12.22 Writing a Window to Display Memory

```c
/*  Write to a Rectangular Window in a 16-color mode
/*  ..NOTE.. x1,x2 must be byte aligned

 Input Parameters:
 x1,y1              starting coordinates of window
 x2,y2              ending coordinates of window
 buf               buffer containing the data
 bytes_per_row     number of bytes per horizontal display line

Calling protocol:
Wr_Win_16( x1,  y1,   x2,  y2,  buf,  bytes_per_row); */

void    Wr_Win_16(int x1, int y1, int x2, int y2, BYTE *buf,
          int bytes_per_row)
{ BYTE *buf_pnt;  int numbyte,nrow,byteperwin;
 x1=x1>>3;    x2=x2>>3;    // account for 16-color mode
 numbyte = (x2 - x1) + 1;    // number of bytes per row
 nrow  = (y2 - y1) + 1;      // number of rows
 buf_pnt = &buf[0];          // pointer buf_pnt points to buf
 byteperwin = numbyte * nrow;

 MapMask(1);
 Wr_Graph_Win(x1,y1,buf_pnt,numbyte,nrow,bytes_per_row);

 buf_pnt += byteperwin;  // plane 1 after plane 0 in buf
 MapMask(2);
 Wr_Graph_Win(x1,y1,buf_pnt,numbyte,nrow,bytes_per_row);

 buf_pnt += byteperwin;  // plane 2 after plane 1 in buf
 MapMask(4);
 Wr_Graph_Win(x1,y1,buf_pnt,numbyte,nrow,bytes_per_row);

 buf_pnt += byteperwin;  // plane 3 after plane 2 in buf
 MapMask(8);
 Wr_Graph_Win(x1,y1,buf_pnt,numbyte,nrow,bytes_per_row);
 MapMask(0x0f);
}

/*   Write a Rectangular Window in a 256-color mode

Input Parameters:
 x1,y1              starting coordinates of window
 x2,y2              ending coordinates of window
 buf               buffer containing the data
 bytes_per_row     number of bytes per horizontal display line
```

```
Calling protocol:
Wr_Win_256( x1, int y1,   x2,   y2,   *buf,   bytes_per_row);
*/

void    Wr_Win_256(int x1, int y1, int x2, int y2, BYTE *buf,
        int bytes_per_row)
{ int numbyte,nrow;
 numbyte = (x2 - x1) + 1;   // number of bytes per row
 nrow  = (y2 - y1) + 1;     // number of rows
 Wr_Graph_Win(x1,y1,buf,numbyte,nrow,bytes_per_row);
}


/*   Load the Map Mask Register

Input Parameters:
 plane  value to load into the register

Calling Protocol: */
void MapMask(BYTE plane)

{ outp(0x3c4,2); outp(0x3c5,plane); }



;    Writing an Image to Display Memory

; Function:
; Write a plane of data to the display memory

; Input Parameters
;  x              byte address (8-pixels if in 16-color mode)
;  y              coordinates of starting point
;  buf            host "C" buffer containing the data
;  nbyte          number of bytes per row
;  nrow           number of rows per window
;  bytes_per_row  bytes per virtual row

; Calling protocol
;  Wr_Graph_Win(x,y,buf,nbyte,nrow,bytes_per_row);

Wr_Graph_Win proc FAR C PUBLIC USES ES DS DI SI,
x_addr,y_addr,buf:FAR PTR,nbyte,nrow,bytes_per_row
;        determine segment:offset address
        mov    es,SegA000
        mov    ax,bytes_per_row ; get pitch in ax
        mov    bx,y_addr      ; get y in bx
        mul    bx             ; y*pitch in dx:ax
```

(continued)

```
        add     ax,x_addr    ; add x_coordinate
        mov     di,ax        ; put offset to display memory in di

; load the segment:offset address of the "C" buffer in DS:SI
        lds     si,buf     ;get segment and offset of buffer

; set up constants for the data moving
        mov     dx,nrow      ;get the number of rows per window
        mov     bx,bytes_per_row    ;get window bytes per row
        sub     bx,nbyte   ;(virtual - window )bytes per row
        mov     ax,nbyte   ;get bytes per window

; move one row per loop
loopwrg1:
        mov     cx,ax        ;number of bytes per row
        rep     movsb        ;move the data
        add     di,bx        ;add offset for display address
        dec     dx           ;decrement the row counter
        jg      loopwrg1     ;repeat for all rows
        ret
Wr_Graph_Win endp

; Write to a portion of a display segment beginning at a start
; address from a "C" array beginning at a specified  byte

; Input parameters
;   buf       host "C" buffer containing data
;   npix      number of pixels
;   start     offset of window to start at

; Calling protocol
;   Wr_Part(buf,npix,start);

Wr_Part proc FAR C PUBLIC USES DS ES SI DI, arg1:FAR
PTR,arg2,arg3
        lds     si,arg1    ;get pointer to top of array
        mov     cx,arg2    ;desired number of bytes
        mov     es,SegA000
        mov     di,arg3    ;starting address of display
        rep     movsb        ;write to memory
        ret
Wr_Part endp
```

In the alphanumeric modes, the routine WrAWin in Listing 12.23 is called to output the data to the screen. In this case, the buffer is assumed to be composed of character and attribute pairs for each character. This routine relies on the

WrChar routine in Listing 12.9 to perform the character output a horizontal line at a time.

LISTING 12.23 Writing an Alphanumeric Window

```
/*  Writing an Alphanumeric Window

Input parameters:
 page             desired display page
 buf              buffer which contains char/attribute pairs
 row1,col1        character coordinates of upper-left corner
 row2,col2        character coordinates of lower-right corner

Calling protocol:
Wr_Alpha_Win( page, buf, col1, row1, col2, row2);    */

void    Wr_Alpha_Win(int page, char *buf, int col1, int row1,
          int col2, int row2)
{SHORT charatr;
 int row,column,i=0;

 for (row=row1; row<=row2; row++)
   for (column=col1; column<=col2; column++)
       { charatr =  buf[i] + (buf[i+1]<<8);
         WrChar(page,charatr,row,column); i+=2;
       }
}
```

12.12.2 Reading from a Window

Reading a window from display memory is accomplished in a similar fashion to writing the window to display memory. The descriptions associated with the write routines apply to the read routines. The parameters are identical, with the exception of the plane parameter. Unlike the write operation, the read operation can read only one bit plane at a time. The desired bit plane is selected in the plane parameter as a binary number. Thus, if the parameter 1 is sent to the MapMask routine, bit plane 0 will be selected. However, if the parameter 1 is sent to the ReadMap routine, bit plane 1 is selected. Because this routine is also meant to be used with the larger-resolution display modes, it is limited to reading from either page 0 or page 1.

The functions RdWin_16 and RdWin_256 in Listing 12.24 read a window from the display memory and return the data to a C buffer. The format of this buffer is identical to the format of the buffer passed to the WrWin_16 and WrWin_256 functions.

LISTING 12.24 Reading an Image from Display Memory

```
/*   Read a Window in a 16-color mode

Input Parameters:
 x1,y1              starting coordinates of window
 x2,y2              ending coordinates of window
 buf                buffer which will contain the data
 bytes_per_row      number of bytes per horizontal display line

Calling protocol:
Rd_Win_16( x1,   y1,   x2,   y2,  buf,  bytes_per_row); */

void     Rd_Win_16(int x1, int y1, int x2, int y2, BYTE *buf,
         int bytes_per_row)
{ BYTE *buf_pnt;   int numbyte,nrow,byteperwin;
 x1=x1>>3;    x2=x2>>3;    // account for 16-color mode
 numbyte = (x2 - x1) + 1;    // number of bytes per row
 nrow  = (y2 - y1) + 1;       // number of rows
 byteperwin = numbyte * nrow;
 buf_pnt = &buf[0];        // pointer buf_pnt points to buf

 ReadMap(0);       // plane 0  begins buf
 Rd_Graph_Win(x1,y1,buf_pnt,numbyte,nrow,bytes_per_row);

 buf_pnt += byteperwin;      // plane 1 after plane 0 in buf
 ReadMap(1);
 Rd_Graph_Win(x1,y1,buf_pnt,numbyte,nrow,bytes_per_row);

 buf_pnt += byteperwin;      // plane 2 after plane 1 in buf
 ReadMap(2);
 Rd_Graph_Win(x1,y1,buf_pnt,numbyte,nrow,bytes_per_row);

 buf_pnt += byteperwin;   // plane 3 after plane 2 in buf
 ReadMap(3);
 Rd_Graph_Win(x1,y1,buf_pnt,numbyte,nrow,bytes_per_row);
 ReadMap(0);
}

/*      Read the data to a window in 256-color mode

Input Parameters:
 x1,y1              starting coordinates of window
 x2,y2              ending coordinates of window
 buf                buffer containing the data
 bytes_per_row      number of bytes per horizontal display line
```

```
Calling protocol:
Rd_Win_256( x1,   y1,   x2,   y2,   buf,   bytes_per_row); */

void     Rd_Win_256(int x1, int y1, int x2, int y2, BYTE *buf,
         int bytes_per_row)
{ int numbyte,nrow;
 numbyte = (x2 - x1) + 1;    // number of bytes per row
 nrow  = (y2 - y1) + 1;       // number of rows
 Rd_Graph_Win(x1,y1,buf,numbyte,nrow,bytes_per_row);
}


/*   Load the Read Map Select Register

Input Parameters:
 mapcode     value to load into the register

Calling Protocol:
 ReadMap(mapcode); */

void  ReadMap(BYTE mapcode)
{ outp(0x3ce,4);  outp(0x3cf,mapcode); }

;    Reading an Image to Display Memory

; Input Parameters
;   x               byte address (8-pixels if in 16-color mode)
;   y               coordinates of starting point
;   buf             host "C" buffer containing the data
;   nbyte           number of bytes per row
;   nrow            number of rows per window
;   bytes_per_row   bytes per virtual row

; Calling protocol
;   Rd_Graph_Win(x,y,buffer,nbyte,nrow,bytes_per_row);

Rd_Graph_Win proc FAR C PUBLIC USES ES DS DI SI,
x_addr,y_addr,buf:FAR PTR,nbyte,brow,bytes_per_row

;         determine segment:offset address in DS:SI
          mov   ds,SegA000
          mov   ax,bytes_per_row    ; get pitch in ax
          mov   bx,y_addr           ; get y in bx
          mul   bx                  ; y*pitch in dx:ax
          add   ax,x_addr           ; add x_coordinate
          mov   si,ax               ; put offset to display memory in si
```

(continued)

```
; load the segment:offset address of the "C" buffer in ES:DI
        les    di,buf         ;get segment and offset of buffer

; set up constants for the data moving
        mov    dx,brow         ;get the number of rows per window
        mov    bx,bytes_per_row    ;get window bytes per row
        sub    bx,nbyte       ;(virtual - window )bytes per row
        mov    ax,nbyte       ;get bytes per window

; move one row per loop
loopwrg2:
        mov    cx,ax      ;number of bytes per row
        rep    movsb      ;move the data
        add    si,bx      ;add offset for display address
        dec    dx         ;decrement the row counter
        jg     loopwrg2   ;repeat for all rows
        ret

Rd_Graph_Win endp

; Read from a portion of a display segment beginning at a start
; address to a "C" array beginning at a specified byte

; Input parameters
; npix      number of pixels
; start     offset of window to start at

; Output parameters
; buf       host "C" buffer to receive data

; Calling protocol
; Rd_Part(buf,npix,start);

Rd_Part proc FAR C PUBLIC USES ES DS DI SI, buf:FAR
PTR,npix,start
        les    di,buf      ;get pointer to top of array
        mov    cx,npix     ;desired number of bytes
        mov    ds,SegA000
        mov    si,start    ;starting address of display
        rep    movsb       ;write to memory
        ret
Rd_Part endp
```

In the alphanumeric modes, the window is read by calling the RdAWin routine
in Listing 12.25.

LISTING 12.25 Reading a Window in the Alphanumeric Modes

```
/*    Reading a Window in the Alphanumeric Modes

Input parameters:
 page        desired display page
 buf         buffer to contain char/attribute pairs
 row1,col1   character coordinates of upper-left corner
 row2,col2   character coordinates of lower-right corner

Calling protocol:
  Rd_Alpha_Win(  page,  buf,   col1,   row1,   col2,   row2); */

void    Rd_Alpha_Win(int page, char *buf, int col1, int row1,
          int col2, int row2)
{SHORT charatr,row,column,i=0;

  for (row=row1; row<=row2; row++)
    for (column=col1; column<=col2; column++)
        { charatr = RdChar(page,row,column);
          buf[i] = charatr & 0xff; i++;
          buf[i] = (charatr>>8) & 0xff; i++;
        }
}
```

12.13   DATA DECODING

In the 16-color modes, each pixel is represented by a four-bit value. Multiple pixels can be stored in a byte array, with each byte containing a four-bit intensity. This data format is called pixel-packed because each pixel is represented within a single byte. Eight bytes of data, each byte consisting of four relevant bits, total 32 bits of data to represent eight pixels. The data resident in the display bit planes is stored in a bit-mapped format because a single pixel can be located in up to four display planes. Reading four bytes, one from each of the display bit planes, produces 32 bits that represent eight pixels. Two routines are presented to convert data from the bit-mapped into the pixel-packed format and vice-versa.

The routine Demux in Listing 12.26 converts four bytes in bit-mapped format into an array of eight bytes in which each byte contains a single pixel intensity. The most significant bit in each of the four bytes, bit 7, represents a bit from the far left pixel in the eight neighboring horizontal pixels. The value determined from the four bit 7s is returned in the output buffer element 0. The value determined from the four bit 6s is returned in the output buffer element 1. Similarly, the value from the four bit 0s is returned in the output buffer element 7. Upon completion, the 8-byte array contains eight pixel elements reading from left to right across the screen.

LISTING 12.26 Demultiplexing Four Bytes into Eight Pixels

```
;   Demultiplexing Four Bytes into Eight Pixels Demultiplex four
;   byte which contain eight pixels in a bit mapped format, into
;   eight color values.

;   Input parameters:
;   inbuf[] input buffer containing four bytes

;   Output parameters:
;   outbuf[] output buffer containing eight bytes

;   Calling protocol
;   DeMux(inbuf,outbuf);

DeMux proc FAR C PUBLIC USES DS DI, inbuf:FAR PTR,outbuf:FAR PTR

           les     di,outbuf ;point to the output buffer
           mov     cx,8        ;zero that buffer
           xor     al,al       ;zero al
           rep     stosb       ;zero all eight values

           lds     si,inbuf  ;point to the input buffer DS:SI
           mov     dx,04
           mov     bl,01       ;set up mask

loop_de:les     di,outbuf ;point to the output buffer ES:DI
           lodsb               ;get the input, inc DS:SI
           mov     cx,0        ;eight pixels in a byte

loop4:   rcl     al,1        ;get bit into carry
           jnc     zero4       ;jump if bit is 0

           or      es:[di],bl    ;or in a 1 into the output buffer
zero4:   inc     di              ;increment the output array ES:DI
           loop    loop4           ;finish plane 0

           shl     bl,1        ; shift the mask
           dec     dx
           jne     loop_de     ; repeat til done with four bytes

           ret
DeMux endp


;   Multiplexing Eight pixels into Four Bytes.  Multiplex four
;   bytes in a Bit Mapped format into eight color values.
```

```
; Input parameters:
;   inbuf[]  buffer containing eight pixel values

; Output parameters:
;   outbuf[] output buffer containing four bytes

; Calling protocol
;   Mux(inbuf,outbuf)

Mux proc FAR C PUBLIC USES ES DI, inbuf:FAR PTR,outbuf:FAR PTR

; zero the four output bytes
        les     di,outbuf       ;point to output
        xor     al,al           ;zero al
        mov     cx,04           ;do for all four output bytes
rep     stosb

        lds     si,inbuf        ;point to the input buffer
        mov     dx,08           ;do for all eight bytes
        mov     bl,80h          ;process bit 0

l8mux:  les     di,outbuf       ;point to the output buffer
        lodsb                   ;get the input, inc DS:SI
        mov     cx,8            ;eight pixels in a byte
loop8:  rcl     al,1            ;get bit into carry
        jnc     zero8           ;jump if bit is 0

        or      es:[di],bl      ;or in a 1 into the output buffer
zero8:  inc     di              ;increment the output array ES:DI
        loop    loop8           ;finish plane 0

        shr     bl,1            ;shift left mask
        dec     dx
        jne     l8mux           ;repeat til done

        ret
Mux endp
```

The routine Mux converts an 8-byte array, each element of which contains a pixel value, into four bytes, each byte containing a bit-mapped format. The first byte in the output array, element 0, represents bit plane 0, element 1 represents bit plane 1, etc. The most significant bit in the output bytes, bit 7, represents a bit in the far-left pixel in the eight neighboring horizontal pixels. The value loaded into the four bit 7s is determined from the input buffer element 0. The value loaded into the four bit 6s is determined from the input buffer element 1. Similarly, the value loaded into the four bit 0s is determined from the output buffer element 7. Upon completion, the 4-byte array contains the data representing each of the four bit planes.

The DeMux and Mux routines each call a subroutine to perform the shifting operation; these subroutines are called Fill8 and Fill4, respectively.

12.14   CLIPPING

The Cohen-Sutherland algorithm is implemented for clipping a line. It is based upon the divide-and-conquer technique of continually segmenting a line until the entire line can be either accepted or rejected. A set of endpoints is provided to the routine, and a reject flag or a new set of endpoints is returned from this routine. The reject flag indicates that none of the line is contained within the specified window. The new set of endpoints indicate the portion of the line that does fit into the window. These endpoints may then be used to draw the line, improving performance because only the points actually contained in the window are calculated.

The Clipper routine in Listing 12.27 performs this clipping operation. The coordinates of the endpoints of the line are passed to the routine in an X and Y array. The upper-left and lower-right coordinates of the window are also passed to the routine. If the line is rejected, the return variable is set to 1. If it is accepted, the return variable is reset to 0, and the new coordinates are returned in the X and Y arrays.

The clipping operation is illustrated in Figure 12.9. Lines a and b are rejected by the reject routine without segmentation because both set of endpoints violate a single border line. Line c is rejected after calculation because both endpoints violate two border lines. Line d is accepted after calculation because a portion of the line resides in the window. The original endpoints of both lines c and d are in the same quadrants; thus, segmentation is required before a decision can be made. Line e is accepted without calculation because both endpoints reside in the window.

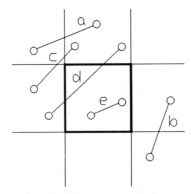

FIGURE 12.9 Clipping a Line

LISTING 12.27 Clipping a Line

```
/*   Clipping a Line. Clip a line so that it fits into a
/*   rectangular window

Input Parameters:
   x[]          = x-coordinates of endpoints of line x[0],x[1]
   y[]          = y-coordinates of endpoints of line y[0],y[1]
   xmin,ymin    = coordinates of lower left corner of rectangular
   xmax,ymax    = coordinates of upper right corner of rectangular

Output Parameters:
   x[]          = clipped x-coordinates x[0],x[1] of line
   y[]          = clipped y-coordinates y[0],y[1] of line
   function returns a 1 if line is trivially rejected

Calling protocol:
reject = Clipper(x,y,xmin,xmax,ymin,ymax)   */

int Clipper(int *x1, int *y1,int *x2, int *y2, int xmin,
        int ymin, int xmax, int ymax)

{  int code1,code2,rejected,accepted,done=0,t1,t2,t3,dummy;

do  {
   // determine the OutCode of point 1
   code1=OutCode(*x1,*y1,xmin,xmax,ymin,ymax);
   // determine the OutCode of point 2
   code2=OutCode(*x2,*y2,xmin,xmax,ymin,ymax);

   if((rejected=Reject(code1,code2))!=0) return(1);
    else {
     if((accepted=Accept(code1,code2))!=0) return(0);
         else {
         if(code1==0)
         { t1=*x1; t2=*y1; t3=code1;
             *x1=*x2; *y1=*y2; code1=code2;
             *x2=t1; *y2=t2; code2=t3; }

         if((code1 & 0x01)!=0) {
     *x1+=(*x2-*x1)*(float)(ymax-*y1)/(*y2-*y1);
     *y1=ymax; }

         else if((code1 & 0x02)!=0) {
     *x1+=(*x2-*x1)*(float)(ymin-*y1)/(*y2-*y1);
     *y1=ymin; }
```

(continued)

```
        else if((code1 & 0x04)!=0) {
 *y1+=(*y2-*y1)*(float)(xmax-*x1)/(*x2-*x1);
 *x1=xmax; }

        else if((code1 & 0x08)!=0) {
 *y1+=(*y2-*y1)*(float)(xmin-*x1)/(*x2-*x1);
 *x1=xmin;
 }}} // end of elses
} while (1==1);
}
```

```
/* Outcode clipping Subroutines. Determine the outcode of a
/* point at x,y with respect to a window which is limited by
 /* xmin,ymin and xmax,ymax

Input parameters:
 x,y         point to determine outcode
 xmin,ymin  coordinates of lower left corner of rectangular
 xmax,ymax  coordinates of upper right corner of rectangular

Output parameter:
 Function Returns a binary four bit code as follows:
        bit 0  = point is to top of window
        bit 1  = point is to bottom of window
        bit 2  = point is to right of window
        bit 3  = point is to left of window

Calling protocol
code = OutCode(x,y,xmin,xmax,ymin,ymax)   */

int OutCode(int x,int y,int xmin,int xmax,int ymin,int ymax)
{ int code; code=0;
if(y>ymax) code |= 0x01;     // beneath window
 else if(y<ymin) code |= 0x02; // above  window
if(x>xmax) code |= 0x04;     // to right of window
 else if(x<xmin) code |= 0x08;  // to left of window
return(code);
}
```

```
/*  Reject clipping sub-function. Determine if a code can be
/*  rejected trivially

Input parameters:
 code1      out code of point 1
 code2      out code of point 2
```

```
Output parameter:
 Function Returns a 0 if cannot reject and a 1 if reject

Calling protocol:
 rejected = Reject(code1,code2) */

int Reject(int code1,int code2)
{ if ((code1&code2)==0) return(0); // cannot reject
       else return(1);         // reject the line
}


/*  Accept  clipping sub-function.  Determine if a code can be
    accepted trivially

Input parameters:
 code1       out code of point 1
 code2       out code of point 2

Calling protocol:
 accepted = Accept(code1,code2) */

int Accept(int code1,int code2)
{ if ((code1|code2)==0) return(1);    // accept the line
       else return(0);                // cannot accept
}
```

The Clipper routine calls upon three subroutines. The first, named OutCode, is used to determine the quadrant where a point exists with respect to the window. The OutCode values depend on the quadrant and are shown in Figure 12.10.

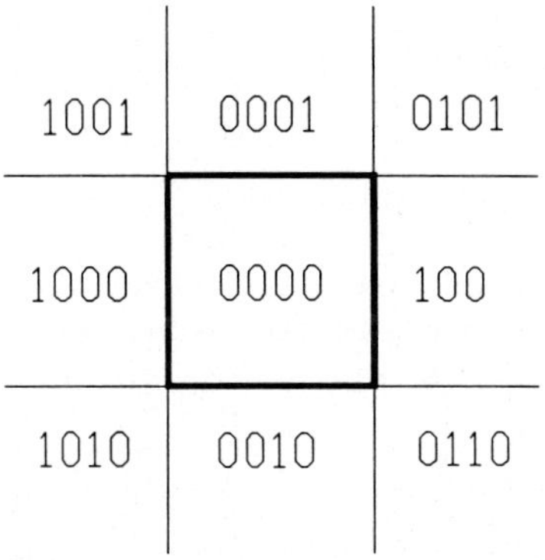

1001	0001	0101
1000	0000	100
1010	0010	0110

FIGURE 12.10 Definition of the OutCodes

The other routines, Accept and Reject, are used to determine if a point can be trivially accepted or rejected.

12.15   CLEARING DISPLAY MEMORY

Clearing the display memory is actually a special case of setting the display memory to a constant value. Routines are provided to clear a character line, a group of character lines, a rectangular window, or an entire page. The techniques employed to clear alphanumerics are different from those employed to clear graphics. Clearing alphanumerics is accomplished by setting character codes to a "space" and by setting the attributes to a desired value. Clearing graphics is accomplished by setting all pixels to a desired value.

12.15.1   Clearing a Character Row

A character row consists of a set of characters in a horizontal line. The length of a character row is determined by the virtual window defined in the Offset Register. The height of a character row is determined by the number of scan lines in the active character font, as set in the Maximum Scan Line Register.

A character row or multiple character rows can be cleared by using the Clr_Alpha_Lines routine in Listing 12.28. This routine is useful when displaying text on the screen. The selected lines are cleared, and the cursor is positioned to the far left character position of the top line cleared. The lines can be cleared on any display page, not necessarily the active display page. The desired page number is passed to the routine; however, this page does not become the active display page. The line number and the number of lines to clear are also passed to the routine as parameters.

LISTING 12.28   Clearing a Line or Multiple Lines

```
;   Clear  Lines.  Although this can be used in the graphics
;   modes, it is slow and should be used only in the
;   alphanumerics modes

; Input parameters:
;   page        desired display page
;   row         starting row to clear
;   numrow      number of rows to clear
;   attribute   Color to clear to. Typically set to 7 for white
;               foreground and black background

; Calling protocol:
;   Clr_Alpha_Lines(page,row,numrow,attribute);

Clr_Alpha_Lines proc  FAR C
PUBLIC   npage:byte,row:byte,numrow:Byte,attribute:byte
```

```
;         determine state,   page=bh   ah=number of columns
          mov     ah,0fh
          int     10h
          push    bx      ;save page in bh
          dec     ah      ;number of columns -1
          push    ax      ;save number of columns in ah

;         select new page
          mov     al,npage  ;get page into al
          mov     ah,05     ;select active display page
          int     10h       ;select active page

          mov     ah,07     ;request scroll screen down
          mov     bh,attribute ;attribute
          mov     al,numrow    ;get number of rows to clear
          xor     cl,cl     ;starting column number = 0
          mov     ch,row    ;get starting row number
          pop     dx        ;get number of columns in dh
          mov     dl,dh     ;ending column in dl
          mov     dh,al     ;get number of rows
          add     dh,ch     ;end row = start row + # of rows
          dec     dh        ;minus 1
          int     10h       ;call bios for scroll

;         reset to original page
          pop     ax
          mov     al,ah     ;get page number in al
          mov     ah,05     ;select active display page
          int     10h       ;select active page
          ret

Clr_Alpha_Lines endp
```

The Clr_Alpha_Lines function operates in any of the alphanumeric or graphics modes. In the alphanumeric modes, an attribute of 07 hex is written to the cleared region of the display. This translates into a 0 background color, typically black, and a 7 foreground color, typically white. In the graphics modes, an attribute of 00 hex is written to the cleared region. The foreground color is 0, typically black, and there is no background color written to the display in the alphanumeric modes. Not writing a background color produces a transparent effect.

This routine utilizes the scroll-up command. The starting row and column coordinates and the number of rows are passed to the routine as parameters. The number of characters per line is automatically determined and is used as the number of columns to scroll. Because the scroll operation operates only on the active display page, it is necessary to change the active display page before executing the scroll operation. The original active display page is reactivated at the conclusion of this routine.

Functions that clear a graphics window in either the 16- or 256-color modes are shown in Listing 12.29. These function similarly to the write window functions in Listing 12.22 except that a solid color is used instead of a buffer.

LISTING 12.29 Clearing a Window

```
/*    Clear a Window in a 16-color mode

Input Parameters:
 x1,y1              starting coordinates of window
 x2,y2              ending coordinates of window
 color              color to clear window with
 bytes_per_row      number of bytes per horizontal display line

Calling protocol:
Clr_Win_16(  x1, y1, x2, y2, color, bytes_per_row); */

void    Clr_Win_16(int x1, int y1, int x2, int y2, BYTE color,
        int bytes_per_row)
{ int numbyte,nrow; BYTE bmask;
 x1=x1>>3;   x2=x2>>3;   // account for 16-color mode
 numbyte = (x2 - x1) + 1;   // number of bytes per row
 nrow  = (y2 - y1) + 1;     // number of rows

  if ((color&1)!=0) bmask = 0xff; else bmask = 0;
 MapMask(1);
 Clr_Graph_Win(x1,y1,bmask,numbyte,nrow,bytes_per_row);

  if ((color&2)!=0) bmask = 0xff; else bmask = 0;
 MapMask(2);
 Clr_Graph_Win(x1,y1,bmask,numbyte,nrow,bytes_per_row);

  if ((color&4)!=0) bmask = 0xff; else bmask = 0;
 MapMask(4);
 Clr_Graph_Win(x1,y1,bmask,numbyte,nrow,bytes_per_row);

  if ((color&8)!=0) bmask = 0xff; else bmask = 0;
 MapMask(8);
 Clr_Graph_Win(x1,y1,bmask,numbyte,nrow,bytes_per_row);
 MapMask(0x0f);
 }


/*    Clear  a window in 256-color mode
```

```
Input Parameters:
 x1,y1                 starting coordinates of window
 x2,y2                 ending coordinates of window
 color                 color
 bytes_per_row     number of bytes per horizontal display line

Calling protocol:
Clr_Win_256(  x1,   y1,   x2,   y2,   color,  bytes_per_row); */

void    Clr_Win_256(int x1, int y1, int x2, int y2, BYTE color,
        int bytes_per_row)
{ int numbyte,nrow;
 numbyte = (x2 - x1) + 1;        // number of bytes per row
 nrow  = (y2 - y1) + 1;          // number of rows
 Clr_Graph_Win(x1,y1,color,numbyte,nrow,bytes_per_row);
}


;   Clearing a Graphics Window

; Input Parameters
;  x              byte address (8-pixels if in 16-color mode)
;  y              coordinates of starting point
;  color          bit to fill into window
;  nbyte          number of bytes per row
;  nrow           number of rows
;  bytes_per_row  bytes per virtual row

; Calling protocol
;  Clr_Graph_Win(x,y,color,nbyte,nrow,bytes_per_row);

Clr_Graph_Win proc FAR C PUBLIC USES ES DI,
x_addr,y_addr,color:byte,nbyte,nrow,color,bytes_per_row

;        determine segment:offset address
        mov    es,SegA000
        mov    ax,bytes_per_row     ; get pitch in ax
        mov    bx,y_addr       ; get y in bx
        mul    bx              ; y*pitch in dx:ax
        add    ax,x_addr       ; add x_coordinate
        mov    di,ax           ; put offset to display memory in di


; set up constants for the data moving
        mov    dx,nrow             ;get the number of rows per window
        mov    bx,bytes_per_row    ;get virtual bytes per row
        sub    bx,nbyte            ;(virtual - window )bytes per row
```

(continued)

```
        mov     cx,nbyte            ;get bytes per window per row
        mov     al,color            ;get color

; move one row per loop
runloop:push    cx          ;save number of bytes per line
        rep     stosb       ;load with constant
        pop     cx          ;restore number of bytes per line
        add     di,bx       ;add byte increment
        dec     dx          ;decrement the row counter
        jg      runloop     ;repeat for all rows
        ret

Clr_Graph_Win endp
```

The Clr_Alpha_Win function, shown in Listing 12.30, clears a window in the alphanumeric modes. This routine performs the scrolling operation on the desired window.

LISTING 12.30 Clearing an Alphanumeric Window

```
;   Clear an Alphanumeric Window   Clear the display at the
current page by scrolling in blanks

; Input parameters:
;   attribute       attribute to scroll into window
;   row1,col1       top-left corner of window
;   row2,col2       bottom-right corner of window

; Calling protocol
;   Clr_Alpha_Win(color,column1,row1,column2,row2);

Clr_Alpha_Win proc FAR C PUBLIC
color:byte,column1:byte,row1:byte,column2:byte,row2:byte
        mov     bh,color        ;attribute to scroll in
        mov     ch,row1         ;get top-left row
        mov     cl,column1      ;get top-left column
        mov     al,row2         ;get bottom-right row
        mov     dl,column2      ;get bottom-right column
        mov     dh,al         ;get bottom-right row
        sub     al,ch         ;bottom row -  top row in AL
        inc     al            ;number of rows +1
        mov     ah,06h        ;request scroll screen
        int     10h           ;call bios
        ret
Clr_Alpha_Win   endp
```

12.16   DOWNLOADING CHARACTER FONTS

In the alphanumeric modes, four character fonts can reside in the EGA simultaneously, and eight can reside in the VGA. These fonts reside in bit plane 2, which is segmented into four or eight blocks. Fonts, either user-defined or ROM-resident, are loaded into these blocks.

12.16.1   Writing a Font in the Alphanumeric Modes

User-defined character sets are loaded into display memory by using the routine WrFont in Listing 12.31. The font bit patterns are passed to this routine in a byte array along with the number of scan lines per character. Each block in display memory can contain 256 characters, each character occupying up to 32 bytes. This routine can download any number of characters, beginning at any character position within the block. For example, three characters can be loaded into ASCII positions 65 through 67, thus overwriting *A*, *B*, and *C*. The BIOS call Load User Text Set at AH = 11 and AL = 10 is used. This does not force a mode set.

LISTING 12.31   Writing a Character Set to Display Memory

```
;   Writing a Character Set to Display Memory

; Function:
; Write a font into one of the font blocks in display memory

; Input parameters:
;   input        array containing character bit patterns
;   blknum       block number
;                (0-3) for EGA    (0-7) for VGA
;   numline      number of scan lines per character

; Calling protocol:
;   WrFont(input,blknum,numline);

WrFont proc FAR C PUBLIC USES ES, input:FAR
PTR,blknum:byte,numline:byte
        push    bp              ;save the base point register
        mov     bl,blknum       ;get block number
        and     bl,07           ;limit to 0-7  block number

        les     ax,input        ;point to "C" buffer es:ax
        mov     bh,numline      ;# bytes per character
        mov     bp,ax           ;load offset to "C" buffer es:bp
        mov     cx,100h         ;do for 256 characters
```

(continued)

```
        xor    dx,dx            ;begin at 0
        mov    ax,1110h         ;load font
        int    10h
        pop    bp               ;restore the base point register
        ret
WrFont endp
```

The programmer may select to download a character set into the display memory by using one of the BIOS calls. The selected font is loaded into one of the blocks of bit plane 2 reserved for the character sets. The programmer may download a user-defined character set or a ROM-resident character set. The routines UserSet, Rom8×8, Rom8×14, and Rom8×16 in Listing 12.32 perform this function. A parameter passed to these routines dictates whether a mode set will occur during the loading process.

LISTING 12.32 Loading ROM-Resident Character Sets

```
    ;    Loading ROM Resident Character Sets   Load a pointer to a
    ;    user-defined alphanumeric character set

    ; Input parameters:
    ;   segment     segment address of font
    ;   offset      offset address of font
    ;   numchar     number of characters to load
    ;   bpc         bytes per character
    ;   block       desired block
    ;               0-3   EGA   0-7   VGA
    ;   modeset     Mode set flag   0=No Mode Set  1-Mode Set

    ; Calling protocol:
    ;   UserSet(segment,offset,numchar,bpc,block,modeset);

UserSet proc FAR C PUBLIC USES ES,
segval,offval,numchar,bpc:byte,block:byte,modeset:byte
        push   bp               ;save the base point register
        mov    es,segval        ;get segment address
        mov    cx,numchar       ;get number of characters
        mov    bh,bpc           ;get bytes per character
        mov    bl,block         ;get block number
        mov    dl,modeset       ;get mode flag

        mov    al,00h           ;assume no mode set
        cmp    dl,1             ;test for mode set
        je     u0
        mov    al,10h           ;no mode set
```

```
u0:       mov     ah,11h          ;load font pointer
          mov     bp,offval       ;get offset address
          int     10h

          pop     bp              ;restore the base point register
          ret
UserSet endp

;     Load a pointer to an 8x8 (lower 128) graphics character set

; Input parameters:
;  block     block number to load font into.
;            0-3  EGA  0-7  VGA
;  modeset Mode set flag   0=No Mode Set 1=Mode Set

; Calling protocol:
;  Rom8x8(block,modeset);

Rom8x8 proc FAR C PUBLIC block:byte,modeset:byte
          mov     bl,block        ;get block number
          mov     dl,modeset      ;get mode set parameter
          mov     al,02h          ;assume no mode set
          cmp     dl,1            ;test for mode set
          je      u2
          mov     al,12h          ;no mode set

u2:       mov     ah,11h          ;load font pointer 8x8
          int     10h
          ret
Rom8x8 endp


;     Load a pointer to an 8x14 graphics character set

; Input parameters:
;  block     block number to load font into.
;            0-3  EGA  0-7  VGA
;  modeset Mode set flag   0=No Mode Set 1=Mode Set

; Calling protocol:
;  Rom8x14(block,modeset);
Rom8x14 proc FAR C PUBLIC block:byte,modeset:byte
          mov     bl,block        ;get block number
          mov     dl,modeset      ;get mode set parameter
          mov     al,01h          ;assume no mode set
          cmp     dl,1            ;test for mode set
```

(continued)

```
        je     u1
        mov    al,11h          ;no mode set

u1:     mov    ah,11h          ;load font pointer 8x8
        int    10h
        ret
Rom8x14 endp



;  Load a pointer to an 8x16 graphics character set -VGA ONLY-

; Input parameters:
;  block    block number to load font into.
;                0-3  EGA   0-7   VGA
;  modeset  Mode set flag   0=No Mode Set  1=Mode Set

; Calling protocol:
;  Rom8x16(block,modeset);

Rom8x16 proc FAR C PUBLIC block:byte,modeset:byte
        mov    bl,block         ;get block number
        mov    dl,modeset       ;get mode set parameter
        mov    al,04h           ;assume no mode set
        cmp    dl,1             ;test for mode set
        je     u4
        mov    al,14h           ;no mode set

u4:     mov    ah,11h           ;load font pointer 8x8
        int    10h
        ret
Rom8x16 endp
```

12.16.2   Writing a Font in the Graphics Modes

In the graphics modes, it is not necessary—or possible—to load the character sets into bit plane 2 because bit plane 2 is used for graphics information. Two pointers are provided through interrupt vector 1F hex and interrupt vector 43 hex. Only one character set can be active at a time. The 8-by-8 character set is actually split into two character sets, each 128 characters long. This is done to provide downward compatibility to the 7-bit ASCII code; it has no other real purpose. This pointer references either a user-defined font in RAM memory or a preprogrammed ROM-resident font. BIOS must be told the number of character rows that are present on a single image. This value is necessary so that BIOS can determine the location of a character row in display memory.

The BIOS character string routines operate in the graphics modes as well as the alphanumeric modes. In the graphics modes, the BIOS string-related routines are asked to write characters on the display at specified row and column positions. The BIOS routines are passed the ASCII character code, the row and column, and the foreground color of the character. In order to draw the character, the BIOS routine must know where to begin drawing the character and how many characters to draw. In the graphics modes, all characters are eight bits wide.

In the graphics modes, pointers to either user-defined character sets or ROM-based character sets can be passed to BIOS by using the GUser8×8, GUserSet, GRom8×8, GRom8×14, and GROM8×16 routines in Listing 12.33.

LISTING 12.33 Loading Graphics Modes Character Sets

```
;  Load a Graphics Modes Character Sets    Load a pointer to a
;  user defined 8x8 (upper 128) graphics character set for
;  interrupt INT 1F hex.

; Input parameters:
;  segment       segment address of font
;  offset        offset address of font

; Calling protocol:
;  GUser8x8(segment,offset);

Guser8x8 proc FAR C PUBLIC USES ES, segval,offval
        push    bp              ;save the base point register
        mov     es,segval       ;get segment address
        mov     bp,offval       ;get offset address
        mov     ax,1120h        ;load font pointer 8x8
        int     10h
        pop     bp              ;restore the base point register
        ret
Guser8x8 endp


; Load a pointer to a user defined graphics character set
; Function:
; Load a pointer to a user defined graphics character set

; Input parameters:
;  segment       segment address of font
;  offset        offset address of font
;  numrow        number of scan lines on the display
;                1=14 scan lines  2=25 scan lines  3=43 scan lines
;  bpc           bytes per character

; Calling protocol:
;  GUserSet(segment,offset,numrow,bpc);
```

(continued)

```
GuserSet proc FAR C PUBLIC USES ES,
segval,offval,numrow:byte,bpc
        push    bp              ;save the base point register
        mov     es,segval       ;get segment address
        mov     bp,offval       ;get offset address
        mov     bl,numrow       ;get number of scan lines per display
        mov     cx,bpc          ;get bytes per character
        mov     ax,1121h        ;load font pointer
        int     10h
        pop     bp              ;restore the base point register
        ret
GuserSet endp



;    Load a pointer to an 8x8 (lower 128) graphics character set
; Function:
; Load a pointer to an 8x8 (lower 128) graphics character set

; Input parameters:
;  segment       segment address of font
;  offset        offset address of font
;  numrow        number of scan lines on the display
;                1=14 scan lines  2=25 scan lines  3=43 scan lines

; Calling protocol:
;   GRom8x8(segment,offset,numrow);

Grom8x8 proc FAR C PUBLIC USES ES, segval,offval,numrow
        push    bp              ;save the base point register
        mov     es,segval       ;get segment address
        mov     bp,offval       ;get offset address
        mov     cx,numrow       ;number of scan lines on display
        mov     ax,1123h        ;load font pointer 8x8
        int     10h
        pop     bp              ;restore the base point register
        ret
Grom8x8 endp

;    Load a pointer to an 8x14 graphics set

; Input parameters:
;  segment          segment address of font
;  offset           offset address of font
;  numrow           number of scan lines on the display
;                1=14 scan lines  2=25 scan lines  3=43 scan lines

; Calling protocol:
;   GRom8x14(segment,offval,numrow);
```

```
Grom8x14 proc FAR C PUBLIC USES ES, segval,offval,numrow
        push    bp              ;save the base point register
        mov     es,segval       ;get segment address
        mov     bp,offval       ;get offset address
        mov     cx,numrow       ;number of scan lines on display
        mov     ax,1122h        ;load font pointer 8x14
        int     10h
        pop     bp              ;restore the base point register
        ret
Grom8x14 endp


; Listing 3.4.3.8 Load a pointer to an 8x16 graphics
; set  -VGA ONLY-

; Input parameters
;  segment      segment address of font
;  offset       offset address of font
;  numrow       number of scan lines on the display
;               1=14 scan lines 2=25 scan lines 3=43 scan lines

; Calling protocol:
;  GRom8x16(segment,offset,numrow);
Grom8x16 proc FAR C PUBLIC USES ES, segval,offval,numrow
        push    bp              ;save the base point register
        mov     es,segval       ;get segment address
        mov     bp,offval       ;get offset address
        mov     cx,numrow       ;number of scan lines on display
        mov     ax,1124h        ;load font pointer 8x16
        int     10h
        pop     bp              ;restore the base point register
        ret
Grom8x16 endp
```

12.16.3   Reading the Font Information

The location of the characters sets can be determined by calling the routine
FontInfo in Listing 12.34.

LISTING 12.34 Return Font Information

```
;  Return Font Information

; Input parameters:
;  choice       particular information desired (0-9)

; Output parameters:
;  buf  integer return information buffer
```

(continued)

```
;              [0]  pointer segment      [1]   pointer offset
;              [2]  bytes per character  [3]   number of rows

; Calling protocol:
;   FontInfo(buf,choice);

     FontInfo proc FAR C PUBLIC USES DS SI , buf:FAR PTR,choice:byte
             push    bp                  ;save the base pointer
             lds     si,buf              ;point to buffer
             mov     ah,11h              ;font
             mov     al,30h              ;return character generator info
             mov     bh,choice           ;get selection
             int     10h

             mov     ax,es
             mov     ds:[si],ax     ;return segment
             inc     si
             inc     si
             mov     ax,bp
             mov     ds:[si],ax     ;return offset
             inc     si
             inc     si
             mov     ds:[si],cx     ;return bytes per character
             inc     si
             inc     si
             xor     dh,dh
             inc     dx                  ;number of char rows = dl+1
             mov     ds:[si],dx     ;return rows per screen
             pop     bp                  ;restore the base pointer
             ret
     FontInfo endp
```

The FontInfo routine is passed a font number, 0–7, that specifies which of the pointers should be returned. Table 12.17 lists the possibilities for this routine.

A long pointer is returned to the calling program to point to the top of the current font buffer. The ROM-resident fonts are usually located in the EGA/VGA BIOS ROM, which is located in host memory space C000:xxxx. In addition to the font pointer, information regarding the current number of character rows on the screen and the number of scan lines per character is also returned to the calling routine.

It should be noted that these parameters refer to the active character set, not the character set referenced in this subroutine call. For example, if an 8-by-14 character set is active, and information is requested regarding an 8-by-8 character set, the number of bytes per character returned from this subroutine will be 12, reflecting the active mode.

TABLE 12.17 Return Font Information

Font #	Font Size	Adapter	Mode
0	Int 1F hex	EGA/VGA	Graphics
1	Int 43 hex	EGA/VGA	Graphics
2	8-by-14	EGA/VGA	Alphanumeric
3	8-by-8 (Lower)	EGA/VGA	Alphanumeric
4	8-by-8 (Upper)	EGA/VGA	Alphanumeric
5	9-by-14	EGA/VGA	Alphanumeric
6	8-by-16	VGA	Alphanumeric
7	9-by-16	VGA	Alphanumeric

12.16.4 Selecting a Character Set

Once the fonts are downloaded in the alphanumeric modes, the programmer can select which font or fonts are active. Up to two fonts, each 256 characters long, can be active at a time, providing a 512-character resident set. The ASCII code for each character is eight bits wide, which allows a single character to be selected from the 256 characters in one set. An additional bit, bit 3, is provided in the character attribute byte that can select from among eight of these sets of characters.

These two resident sets are called *A* and *B*. The Character Map Select Register is provided to associate each of the *A* and *B* active fonts with one of the four or eight resident fonts. The default condition is *A* = 0 and *B* = 0 which results in all characters referencing the 256 characters in block 0. Block 0 is the only resident block of memory loaded with a character set at a mode set initialization command.

The active character sets, *A* and *B*, are modified by calling the WrBlock routine. The VGA can interrogate this register by using the RdBlock routine. Both are listed in Listing 12.35.

LISTING 12.35 Read and Write the Character Set Block

```
/* Listing 12.35  Read  the Character Set Block Returns A
   font # in buf[0] and B font # in buf[1] -VGA ONLY-

Input parameters:
buf[]   buffer which contains the A font and B font block numbers
        buf[0] = A font number   buf[1] = B font number
```

(continued)

```
Calling protocol:
  RdBlock(buf); */

void    RdBlock(int *buf)
{ int block,a,b;
outp(0x3c4,3); block = inp(0x3c5);
b = (block >>2) & 0x03;
a = block & 0x03;
if((block & 0x20)!=0) b += 4;
if((block & 0x10)!=0) a += 4;
buf[0] = a; buf[1] = b;
}

/*   Write the block specifier  from  "a" and "b" block #'s

Input parameters:
 a       block number for font a
 b       block number for font b

Calling Protocol
  WrBlock( a,   b); */

void    WrBlock(int a, int b)
{ int block;

block = (a&3)|((b&3)<<2);
if((a & 0x4)!=0) block += 0x10;
if((b & 0x4)!=0) block += 0x20;
BlockVal(block);
}

; Invoking the Set Block BIOS Call.   Set the value for the A
; and B active blocks

; Input parameters
; block    desired block code containing A and B block numbers

; Calling parameters
; BlockVal(block);

BlockVal proc FAR C PUBLIC block:byte
        mov    bl,block      ;get desired mode
        mov    ax,1103h      ;set blocks
        int    10h           ;interupt 10
        ret
BlockVal endp
```

The WrBlock routine calls an assembly language routine named BlockVal to actually invoke the BIOS call.

If both the *A* and *B* block pointers are loaded with the value 1, both active sets refer to the character set resident in block 1. Loading an 8-by-8 character set into block 1 while an 8-by-14 character set is in block 0 will result in an 8-by-8 character being displayed when block 1 is active and an 8-by-14 character set being displayed when block 0 is active. However, the Max Scan Line Register must be set each time the block is changed; otherwise, the wrong number of scan lines per character will be displayed. Because there is only one Max Scan Line Register, two character sets that have a different number of scan lines per character cannot be used simultaneously. The Max Screen Line Register can be loaded through the MaxLine routine in Listing 12.36.

LISTING 12.36 Loading the Max Scan Line Register

```
/* Listing 12.36  Load the Max Scan Line Register

Input Parameters:
 value   value to load into the register-1

Calling Protocol:
MaxScan(value);   */

void  MaxScan(BYTE value)
{
 outp(0x3D4,9);  outp(0x3D5,value-1);
}
```

Three routines are provided to handle all of the necessary parameters to set the screen to a format that has 25, 43, or 50 lines per screen. The cursor shape and the underline locations are related to the number of scan lines per character. The routine F25row sets up an 8-by-14 character set, and the routines F43row and F50row set up an 8-by-8 character set in display formats that have 43 and 50 character rows. The cursor shape and the underline location must be modified to be compatible with these display formats. Note that this routine sets and resets the Cursor Emulation bit of the Miscellaneous byte stored in the BIOS storage area of host memory at location 0040:0087. All are shown in Listing 12.37.

LISTING 12.37 Setting Up the Number of Rows per Display

```
;  Setting up a 25 Row Display

; Input parameters:
;   block        block number to load font
;                0-3 for EGA   0-7 for VGA

; Calling protocol:
;   F25row(block);

F25row proc FAR C PUBLIC USES DS SI, block:byte
; determine the active page
        mov     ah,0fh
        int     10h         ;bh=page
        mov     bl,bh       ;get page in lower
        push    bx          ;save the current page in upper

; make page 0 active
        mov     ax,0500h    ;set active page to 0
        int     10h

; load the 8x14 character set
        mov     ax,1111h       ;set to 8x14 character set
        mov     bl,block       ;into desired block
        int     10h

; set to 1 bit 0 of the Miscellaneous Information byte in
; host memory to enable the cursor emulation.
        mov     ds,Seg0040
        mov     si,0087h
        or      byte ptr ds:[si],01

; set the cursor position to a three line underline
        mov     cx,0B0Dh    ;set cursor to begin at 11
        mov     ah,01       ;and end at 13
        int     10h

; reset to 0 bit 0 of the Miscellaneous Information byte in
; host memory to disable the cursor emulation.
        mov     dsSeg0040
        mov     si,0087h
        and     byte ptr ds:[si],0FEh

; adjust the underline location
        mov     dx,03d4h
        mov     al,14h
        out     dx,al
```

```
        inc     dx
        mov     al,0Dh
        out     dx,al

; reset the active page to its previous value
        pop     ax          ;get original page
        mov     ah,05h      ;set original active page
        int     10h
        ret
F25row endp


;   Setting up a 43 Row Display

; Input parameters
;   block         block number to load font
;                 0-3 for EGA   0-7 for VGA

; Calling protocol:
; F43row(block);

F43row proc FAR C PUBLIC USES DS SI, block:byte
; determine the active page
        mov     ah,0fh
        int     10h             ;bh=page
        mov     bl,bh           ;get page in lower
        push    bx              ;save the current page in upper

; make page 0 active
        mov     ax,0500h        ;set active page to 0
        int     10h

; load the 8x8 character set
        mov     ax,1112h        ;set to 8x8 character set
        mov     bl,block        ;into desired block
        int     10h

; set to 1 bit 0 of the Miscellaneous Information byte in
; host memory to enable the cursor emulation.
        mov     ds,Seg0040
        mov     si,0087h
        or      byte ptr ds:[si],01

; set the cursor position to a block
        mov     cx,0600h        ;begin at 6 end at 0
        mov     ah,01
        int     10h             ;set the cursor
```

(continued)

```
; reset to 0 bit 0 of the Miscellaneous Information byte in
; host memory to disable the cursor emulation.
        mov    ds,Seg0040
        mov    si,0087h
        and    byte ptr ds:[si],0FEh

; adjust the underline location
        mov    dx,03d4h        ;adjust underline location
        mov    al,14h
        out    dx,al
        inc    dx
        mov    al,07h          ;set underline to line 7
        out    dx,al

; reset the active page to its previous value
        pop    ax              ;get original page
        mov    ah,05h          ;get old active page
        int    10h
        ret
F43row endp



;   Setting up a 50 Row Display

; Input parameters:
;   block       block number to load font
;               0-3 for EGA  0-7 for VGA

; Calling protocol:
; F50row(block);

F50row proc FAR C PUBLIC USES DS SI, block:byte
; determine the active page
        mov    ah,0fh
        int    10h             ;bh=page
        mov    bl,bh           ;get page in lower
        push   bx              ;save the current page in upper

; make page 0 active
        mov    ax,0500h        ;set active page to 0
        int    10h

; select 50 lines
        mov    ax,1202h        ;select 400 scan lines
        mov    bl,30h
        int    10h
```

```
; perform a mode set without changing display mode
        mov    ah,0fh         ;determine the current mode
        int    10h            ;mode returned in al
        mov    ah,00h         ;set mode
        int    10h

; load the 8x8 character set
        mov    ax,1112h       ;set to 8x8 character set
        mov    bl,block       ;get block number
        int    10h

; set to 1 bit 0 of the Miscellaneous Information byte in
; host memory to enable the cursor emulation.
        mov    ds,Seg0040
        mov    si,0087h
        or     byte ptr ds:[si],01

; set the cursor position to a block
        mov    cx,0600h       ;begin at 6 end at 0
        mov    ah,01
        int    10h            ;set the cursor

; reset to 0 bit 0 of the Miscellaneous Information byte in
; host memory to disable the cursor emulation.
        mov    ds,Seg0040
        mov    si,0087h
        and    byte ptr ds:[si],0FEh

; adjust the underline location
        mov    dx,03d4h   ;adjust underline location
        mov    al,14h
        out    dx,al
        inc    dx
        mov    al,07h     ;set underline to line 7
        out    dx,al

; reset the active page to its previous value
        pop    ax             ;get original page
        mov    ah,05h         ;get old active page
        int    10h
        ret
F50row endp
```

In the VGA, it is possible to set the number of scan lines per display to 200, 350, or 400. The number of scan lines per page divided by the number of scan lines per character yields the number of character rows per screen. The routine called SetLines, presented in Listing 12.38, performs this function.

LISTING 12.38 Setting the Number of Scan Lines per Page

```
; Setting the Number of Scan Lines per Page -VGA only -

; Input parameters: numlinesnumber of lines per screen
;        0 = 200 scan lines  (not available in mode 7)
;        1 = 350 scan lines  2 = 400 scan lines

; Calling protocol:
;  SetLines(numlines);

SetLines    proc FAR C PUBLIC numlines:byte
            mov    al,numlines    ;get number of scan lines
            mov    ah,12h         ;set number of scan lines
            mov    bl,30h         ;part of definition
            int    10h
            ret
SetLines    endp
```

12.16.5   Reading a Character Font

It is possible to read a font bit pattern into a C buffer by calling the RdFont routine in Listing 12.39. This routine performs a move string (REP MOVSB) operation that transfers a specified number of characters from one memory location to another. In this case, the source of the move is the character font and the destination is the C buffer. The pointer to the character font bit patterns to read, the number of characters, and the number of bytes per character are also provided to this routine. The character set bit patterns are returned to the C buffer. The pointer to desired bit patterns can be provided by the FontInfo routine.

LISTING 12.39 Reading a Font

```
/* Read a character font into fontbuf.  It must be a 16 byte
   per character font.

Input Parameters:
        which_font      which font to get an address to.  Can be
                        the following:
;                       2 = 8x14             3=8x8 (lower 128)
;                       4=8x8 (upper 128)    6=8x16
 Output Parameters:
        fontbuf         font buffer.  should be the following
                        2 = 256*14=3584 3=128*8=1024 bytes
                        4=128*8=1024    6=256*16=4096  bytes
        returned        0 = no font returned     1=ok
```

```
Calling Protocol:
  ok_font = Get_Font_Pattern(which_font,fontbuf);    */

int  Get_Font_Pattern(int which_font,BYTE *fontbuf)
{ SHORT point[4];
  FontInfo(point,which_font);  // get pointer to selected font

  switch(which_font) {
      case 2:  RdFont(point[0],point[1],fontbuf,256,14); break;
      case 3:  RdFont(point[0],point[1],fontbuf,128,8); break;
      case 4:  RdFont(point[0],point[1],fontbuf,128,8); break;
      case 6:  RdFont(point[0],point[1],fontbuf,256,16);  break;
      default:  return(0);
      }
return(1);
}


;  Read a font from one memory location to another

; Input parameters:
;  insegment        array segment address to read from
;  inoffset         array offset address to read from
;  buf              output array to write to
;  nchar            number of characters to read
;  bpc              bytes per character

; Calling protocol:
;  RdFont(insegment,inoffset,buf,nchar,bpc);

RdFont proc FAR C PUBLIC USES ES DS SI DI,
insegment,inoffset,buf:FAR PTR,nchar,bpc
        mov     ax,nchar         ;do for "nchar" characters
        mul     word PTR bpc     ;# character * bytes/character
        mov     cx,ax            ;into counter for number of bytes
        mov     ds,insegment     ;point to source segment
        mov     si,inoffset      ;point to source offset
        les     di,buf           ;point to destination
        rep     movsb
        ret
RdFont endp
```

12.16.6 Modifying a Character Set

The character set bit patterns, once entered into the C buffer, can be modified and written back to the display. One popular technique involves shifting the bit patterns in a character set so that an italic effect is achieved. The Ital14 routine in Listing 12.40 illustrates a typical shift operation for a fourteen-byte-long character set. The modified bit patterns can be written back to the display memory by using the "WrFont" routine.

LISTING 12.40 Creating an Italic Character Set

```
/* Create an Italics character set out of a character set by
   shifting the bit patterns to create an italics effect

Input parameters:
 buf[]      buffer containing the bit patterns
 nchar      number of characters in the buffer

Calling Protocol:
  Make_Italic(buf, font_height, nchar);    */

void    Make_Italic(BYTE *buf, int font_height, int nchar)
{ int i,j;

switch(font_height) {

case 8:
  for (i=0; i<nchar; i++) {
    j = i*8;
    buf[j]=buf[j]>>2;        buf[j+1]=buf[j+1]>>2;
    buf[j+2]=buf[j+2]>>1;    buf[j+3]=buf[j+3]>>1;
    buf[j+6]=buf[j+6]<<1;    buf[j+7]=buf[j+7]<<1;
    }
  break;

case 14:
  for (i=0; i<nchar; i++) {
    j = i*14;
    buf[j]=buf[j]>>3;          buf[j+1]=buf[j+1]>>3;
    buf[j+2]=buf[j+2]>>2;      buf[j+3]=buf[j+3]>>2;
    buf[j+4]=buf[j+4]>>1;      buf[j+5]=buf[j+5]>>1;
    buf[j+8]=buf[j+8]<<1;      buf[j+9]=buf[j+9]<<1;
    buf[j+10]=buf[j+10]<<2;   buf[j+11]=buf[j+11]<<2;
    buf[j+12]=buf[j+12]<<3;   buf[j+13]=buf[j+13]<<3;
    }
  break;

case 16:
  for (i=0; i<nchar; i++) {
    j = i*16;
    buf[j]=buf[j]>>3;        buf[j+1]=buf[j+1]>>3;
    buf[j+2]=buf[j+2]>>2;    buf[j+3]=buf[j+3]>>2;
    buf[j+4]=buf[j+4]>>1;    buf[j+5]=buf[j+5]>>1;
```

```
          buf[j+8]=buf[j+8]<<1;    buf[j+9]=buf[j+9]<<1;
          buf[j+10]=buf[j+10]<<2;  buf[j+11]=buf[j+11]<<2;
          buf[j+12]=buf[j+12]<<3;  buf[j+13]=buf[j+13]<<3;
          buf[j+14]=buf[j+15]<<4;  buf[j+15]=buf[j+15]<<4;
          }
      break;
      }
}
```

12.16.7 Writing Characters without BIOS

In the graphics modes, it is possible to write a bit pattern directly to memory without going through BIOS. This provides the programmer with additional flexibility. The routine called GraphChr, presented in Listing 12.41, provides a means of writing a character to a specified address in display memory. It utilizes write mode 3 to achieve a high data-transfer rate. A character bit pattern of a specified number of scan lines is written to a specified address in display memory. The character color is also passed to this routine. The offset parameter refers to the number of bytes per scan line in the virtual display. Note that the display can be set up before a text output by calling Setup_for_Write_Mode_3. After the text output, it can be restored to normal operation by calling Restore_to_Write_Mode_0.

LISTING 12.41 Writing a Character Directly to the Display

```
/* Draw a string on the screen  where the characters are
   drawn using graphics calls on a per-pixel basis.

Input Parameters:
        string    ASCII character string NULL terminated
        x1,y1     position of first character

Calling Protocol:
Wr_StringG(string,foreground,background,x,y,
        is_transparent,fontbuf,font_height,font_width);   */

void    Wr_StringG(char *string,int foreground,int background,
        int x,int y, int is_transparent,BYTE *fontbuf,
        int font_height,int font_width)
{ int i,length;
length = strlen(string);

for (i=0; i<length; i++) {
   if(Get_Number_of_Colors()==16)
```

(continued)

```
       Wr_CharG_16(string[i],foreground,background,x,y,is_transparent,
                  fontbuf,font_height,font_width);
          else

       Wr_CharG_256(string[i],foreground,background,x,y,is_transparent,
                  fontbuf,font_height,font_width);
         x += font_width;
         }
       }


/* Draw a character on the screen 256-color mode where the
   characters are drawn using graphics calls on a per-pixel basis.

   Input Parameters:
      char_code                 ASCII character code
      foreground,background     character colors
      x1,y1                     position of character
      is_transparent            display code  0=opaque  1=transparent
      fontbuf                   character buffer containing the font
                                bit patterns
      font_height               character height in scan lines
      font_width                character width in pixels

   Calling Protocol:
   Wr_CharG_256(char char_code,foreground,background,x1,y1,
          is_transparent,BYTE *fontbuf,font_height,font_width); */

   void Wr_CharG_256(char char_code,int foreground,int
   background,int x1,int y1,
          int is_transparent,BYTE *fontbuf,int font_height,
          int font_width)
   {
     int i,index,bytes_per_row,buf_ptr=0,x1_pos,x2_pos,font_byte,
       char_base;
     BYTE pattern[512];

   font_byte = font_width/8;  // width of font in font buffer
   char_base = char_code*font_height*font_byte;
   bytes_per_row=Get_Bytes_per_Row();

   switch(font_width) {
     case 8:
        x1_pos = x1; x2_pos = x1_pos + 7;
        // fill the pattern buffer with the background character
     switch(is_transparent) {
        case 0:
   for (i=0; i<128; i++) pattern[i] = background;  break;
```

```
      case 1:
Rd_Win_256(x1_pos,y1,x2_pos,y1+font_height-1,pattern,
bytes_per_row);  break;
      }

 // extract the code of letter, draw it into the buffer pattern
 for (i=0; i<font_height; i++)  {
   index = (i*font_byte)+char_base;
   buf_ptr = 8 * i;
   if(fontbuf[index] & 0x80) pattern[buf_ptr]   = foreground;
   if(fontbuf[index] & 0x40) pattern[buf_ptr+1] = foreground;
   if(fontbuf[index] & 0x20) pattern[buf_ptr+2] = foreground;
   if(fontbuf[index] & 0x10) pattern[buf_ptr+3] = foreground;
   if(fontbuf[index] & 0x08) pattern[buf_ptr+4] = foreground;
   if(fontbuf[index] & 0x04) pattern[buf_ptr+5] = foreground;
   if(fontbuf[index] & 0x02) pattern[buf_ptr+6] = foreground;
   if(fontbuf[index] & 0x01) pattern[buf_ptr+7] = foreground;
   }

 // draw the character buffer into display memory
 Wr_Win_256(x1_pos,y1,x2_pos,y1+font_height-1,pattern,
 bytes_per_row);
break;

case 16:
   x1_pos = x1; x2_pos = x1_pos + 15;

   // fill the pattern buffer with the background character
   switch(is_transparent) {
     case 0:
for (i=0; i<512; i++)  pattern[i] = background;  break;
     case 1:
Rd_Win_256(x1_pos,y1,x2_pos,y1+font_height-1,pattern,
bytes_per_row);  break;
     }

  // extract the code of letter, draw it into the buffer pattern
 for (i=0; i<font_height; i++)  {
   index = (i*font_byte)+char_base;
   buf_ptr = i * font_width;
   if(fontbuf[index] & 0x80) pattern[buf_ptr]   = foreground;
   if(fontbuf[index] & 0x40) pattern[buf_ptr+1] = foreground;
   if(fontbuf[index] & 0x20) pattern[buf_ptr+2] = foreground;
   if(fontbuf[index] & 0x10) pattern[buf_ptr+3] = foreground;
   if(fontbuf[index] & 0x08) pattern[buf_ptr+4] = foreground;
   if(fontbuf[index] & 0x04) pattern[buf_ptr+5] = foreground;
   if(fontbuf[index] & 0x02) pattern[buf_ptr+6] = foreground;
   if(fontbuf[index] & 0x01) pattern[buf_ptr+7] = foreground;
```

(continued)

```
   if(fontbuf[index+1] & 0x80) pattern[buf_ptr+8]  = foreground;
   if(fontbuf[index+1] & 0x40) pattern[buf_ptr+9]  = foreground;
   if(fontbuf[index+1] & 0x20) pattern[buf_ptr+10] = foreground;
   if(fontbuf[index+1] & 0x10) pattern[buf_ptr+11] = foreground;
   if(fontbuf[index+1] & 0x08) pattern[buf_ptr+12] = foreground;
   if(fontbuf[index+1] & 0x04) pattern[buf_ptr+13] = foreground;
   if(fontbuf[index+1] & 0x02) pattern[buf_ptr+14] = foreground;
   if(fontbuf[index+1] & 0x01) pattern[buf_ptr+15] = foreground;
   }

// draw the character buffer into display memory/
Wr_Win_256(x1_pos,y1,x2_pos,y1+font_height-1,pattern,
bytes_per_row);
break;
 }
}


/*  Draw a character on the screen 16-color mode  where the
    characters are drawn using graphics calls on a per-pixel
    basis.

Input Parameters:
    char_code                ASCII character code
    foreground,background    character colors
    x1,y1                    position of character
    is_transparent           display code  0=opaque  1=transparent
    fontbuf                  character buffer containing the font
                             bit patterns
    font_height              character height in scan lines
    font_width               character width in pixels

Calling Protocol:
    Wr_CharG_16(char char_code,foreground,background,x1,y1,
        is_transparent,BYTE *fontbuf,font_height,font_width);  */

void Wr_CharG_16(char char_code,int foreground,int
background,int x1,int y1,
        int is_transparent,BYTE *fontbuf,int font_height,
        int font_width)
{
int i,index,y_pos,x2,x3,char_base,font_byte,bytes_per_row;

font_byte = font_width/8;

x2 = x1 + 8;   x3 = x2 + 8;
char_base = char_code*font_height*font_byte;
bytes_per_row=Get_Bytes_per_Row();
```

```
// if not transparent set background pixels to the
   background color
if(is_transparent==0)
  Clr_Win_16(x1,y1,x1+font_width-1,y1+font_height-1,background,
  bytes_per_row);

ESetRes(15); SetRes((BYTE)foreground); //change to foreground color

// draw the foreground pixels
switch(font_byte) {
  case 1:
     for (i=0; i<font_height; i++)  {
        y_pos = y1 + i;
        index = (i*font_byte)+char_base;
        Write_Points(fontbuf[index],x1,y_pos,bytes_per_row);
        }
  break;

  case 2:
     for (i=0; i<font_height; i++)  {
        y_pos = y1 + i;
        index = (i*font_byte)+char_base;
  // left
        Write_Points(fontbuf[index]  ,x1,y_pos,bytes_per_row);
  // right
        Write_Points(fontbuf[index+1],x2,y_pos,bytes_per_row);
        }
  break;

  case 3:
     for (i=0; i<font_height; i++)  {
        y_pos = y1 + i;
        index = (i*font_byte)+char_base;
 // left
      Write_Points(fontbuf[index]  ,x1,y_pos,bytes_per_row);
 // center
      Write_Points(fontbuf[index+1],x2,y_pos,bytes_per_row);
 //right
      Write_Points(fontbuf[index+2],x3,y_pos,bytes_per_row);
        }
  break;
  }
BitMask(255); ESetRes(0);  /* reset the EGA/VGA registers */
}

/* Internal function for 16_color write character
```

(continued)

```
Input Parameters:
    rc        character bit pattern byte
    x,y       coordinates of leftmost pixel

Calling Protocol: */
Write_Points(rc,x,y,bytes_per_row)

void Write_Points(BYTE rc,int x,int y,int bytes_per_row)
{
   if((rc & 0x80))Wr_Point_16(x  ,y,bytes_per_row);
   if((rc & 0x40))Wr_Point_16(x+1,y,bytes_per_row);
   if((rc & 0x20))Wr_Point_16(x+2,y,bytes_per_row);
   if((rc & 0x10))Wr_Point_16(x+3,y,bytes_per_row);
   if((rc & 0x08))Wr_Point_16(x+4,y,bytes_per_row);
   if((rc & 0x04))Wr_Point_16(x+5,y,bytes_per_row);
   if((rc & 0x02))Wr_Point_16(x+6,y,bytes_per_row);
   if((rc & 0x01))Wr_Point_16(x+7,y,bytes_per_row);
}


/*   Write a graphics-based string assuming font is loaded in
     fontbuf.  It must be a 16 byte per character font.

  Input Parameters:
         x,y                starting pixels for character
                            (note x is byte aligned)
         fontbuf            font
         charbuf            ascii null terminated string
         bytes_per_row      display bytes per row
         color              foreground color

Calling Protocol:
  PutGString(x,   y,   fontbuf,   charbuf,   color,
  bytes_per_row);   */

void     PutGString(SHORT x, SHORT y,  BYTE *fontbuf,
         char *charbuf, BYTE color, int bytes_per_row)
 { SHORT i=0,ascii; BYTE value,*pat,old_value;

Setup_for_Write_Mode(2);

while(charbuf[i]!=(char)NULL) {
   ascii = charbuf[i++];
   pat = &fontbuf[16*ascii];// point to current buffer
   Put_G_Char(x,y,pat,color,bytes_per_row);
   x += 8;
   }
Restore_to_Write_Mode_0();
 }
```

```
/* Write a graphics based character assuming font data for
   character is loaded in charbuf.  It must be a 16 byte per
   character font.  This handles the VGA registers.

   Input Parameters:
         x,y                 starting pixels for character
                             (note x is byte aligned)
         charbuf             ascii null terminated string
         bytes_per_row       display bytes per row
         color               foreground color

  Calling Protocol:
   Put_GChar(  x,    y,  charbuf, color,  bytes_per_row);  */

void     Put_GChar(SHORT x, SHORT y, BYTE *charbuf,
            BYTE color, int bytes_per_row)
{
 SHORT address; BYTE value;
address = (x/8) + (y * bytes_per_row);

Setup_for_Write_Mode(2);
GraphChr(charbuf,address,bytes_per_row,16,color);
Restore_to_Write_Mode_0();
}

/* Write a graphics based character assuming font data for
   character is loaded in charbuf. It must be a 16 byte per
   character font.  This does NOT handle the VGA registers.

   Input Parameters:
         x,y                 starting pixels for character
                             (note x is byte aligned)
         charbuf             ascii null terminated string
         bytes_per_row       display bytes per row
         color               foreground color

  Calling Protocol:
   Put_G_Char(  x,    y,  charbuf, color,  bytes_per_row);  */

void     Put_G_Char(SHORT x, SHORT y, BYTE *charbuf,
            BYTE color, int bytes_per_row)
{
    SHORT address;
    address = (x/8) + (y * bytes_per_row);
    GraphChr(charbuf,address,bytes_per_row,16,color);
}
```

(continued)

```
;  Write a Character Directly to the Display.

; Input assumptions:
;        The display is in a graphics mode
;        Write mode 3 is in effect
;    This is accomplished by calling Setup_for_Write_Mode_2();

; Output assumptions:
;        Write Mode reset to 0
;        Bit mask is retored to ff
;    This is accomplished by calling Restore_to_Write_Mode_0();

; Input parameters
;  charbuf[]    array containing bit pattern
;  address      display address to load character
;  offset       display offset (bytes/row)
;  bpc          bytes per character (# of rows)
;  color        foreground color of character

; calling protocol
; GraphChr(charbuf,address,offset,bpc,color);

GraphChr proc FAR C PUBLIC USES DS SI DI, charbuf:FAR
PTR,address,offval,bpc,color:byte

; point to the Bit Plane Mask
        mov     dx,3ceh        ;point to address port
        mov     al,8
        out     dx,al          ;load bit plane mask index
        inc     dx             ;dx points to data port

        lds     si,charbuf     ;character bit pattern in DS:SI
        mov     es,SegA000
        mov     di,address     ;display memory address in DI
        mov     bx,offval      ;display offset (#bytes per row) in BX
        mov     cx,bpc         ;# of rows in character in CX
        mov     ah,color       ;get color

runloop:lodsb                  ;get bit pattern byte al=ds:[si++]
        out     dx,al          ;load Bit Plane Mask Register
        mov     al,es:[di]     ;dummy read
        mov     es:[di],ah     ;write color
        add     di,bx          ;add offset to DI destination
        loop    runloop        ;repeat for bpc characters
        ret
GraphChr endp
```

```
;   Setup for write mode.  Can be used for 0-3 although
;   typically it is used for 1,2 or 3, since going back to Write
;   Mode 0 usually involves other register restoring.

; Calling Protocol:
;           Setup_for_Write_Mode(choice)

Setup_for_Write_Mode proc FAR C PUBLIC, choice:byte
;           setup for write mode without disturbing the other bits
            mov     dx,3ceh
            mov     al,05           ;index 5 for mode register
            out     dx,al

            inc     dx
            in      al,dx           ;get value
            and     al,0fch         ;zero bits 0-1
            mov     ah,choice       ;set for write mode
            and     ah,03
            or      al,ah
            out     dx,al
            ret
Setup_for_Write_Mode   endp


;   Restore to write mode 0

; Calling Protocol:
;           Restore_to_Write_Mode_0();

Restore_to_Write_Mode_0 proc FAR C PUBLIC
;           restore for write mode 0 without disturbing other bits
            mov     dx,3ceh
            mov     al,05       ;index 5 for mode register
            out     dx,al

            inc     dx
            in      al,dx       ;get value
            and     al,0fch     ;zero bits 0-1
            out     dx,al

;           restore the bit mask register to ff
            mov     dx,3ceh
            mov     al,8        ;bit mask index
            mov     ah,0ffh     ;all on
            out     dx,ax
            ret
Restore_to_Write_Mode_0 endp
```

12.17   COLOR PALETTE

A color, when displayed on the video monitor, is composed of red, green, and blue components. In the Palette Registers, two bits are assigned to each of these three primary colors. Each primary color ranges in intensity from 0 to 3. Because the final color value is composed from a 6-bit word, there can be 64 possible colors. The six bits are located in the lower six bits in each of the sixteen Palette Registers. Each Palette Register is one byte wide.

12.17.1   Encoding and Decoding Colors

It is common for the programmer to consider each of these primary color intensities as independent values. The EnCol routine encodes a color from the three intensities of red, green, and blue to a single coded value. The coding of this value is compatible with the Palette Registers. The DeCol routine decodes a single color byte, coded in the Palette Register format, into the three primary intensities. Because there are sixteen Palette Registers, two additional routines—EnCols and DeCols—are provided to encode or decode a buffer of sixteen colors. These four routines are listed in Listing 12.42.

LISTING 12.42   Encoding and Decoding Colors

```
/*   Encoding and Decoding Colors using the palette encoding
     scheme from the RGB inputs.

Input parameters:
 red        red (0-3)
 grccn      green (0-3)
 blue       blue (0-3)

Output parameters:
 code    The encoded color is returned as the character function
         return parameter.

Calling protocol:
 code = EnCol(red,green,blue);   */

BYTE    EnCol(BYTE red, BYTE green, BYTE blue)
{ BYTE g0,b0,r0,g1,b1,r1,color;
  green&=3; blue&=3; red&=3;     // limit inputs to 0-3
  g0=(green&2);      g1=(green&1)<<4;    // position green
  r0=(red&2)<<1;     r1=(red&1)<<5;      // position red
  b0=(blue&2)>>1;    b1=(blue&1)<<3;     // position blue
  color=g0+g1+r0+r1+b0+b1;    // resultant coded color
  return(color);
}
```

```
/*  Decode an array of Color coded in the palette encoding
    scheme, into the three primary colors "red", "green" and
    "blue".

Input parameters:
 color   coded color containing red, green, and blue

Output parameters:
 buf     output buffer where buf[0]=red, buf[1]=green, buf[2]=blue

Calling protocol:
DecCol( color,  buf); */

void    DecCol(BYTE color, BYTE *buf)
{ buf[0] = ((color&0x20)>>5)+((color&4)>>1); // red
  buf[1] = ((color&0x10)>>4)+ (color&2);      // green
  buf[2] = ((color&0x08)>>3)+((color&1)<<1); // blue
}


/* Encode an array of Colors using the palette encoding scheme,
   from the RGB inputs.

Input parameters:
 red        buffer of 16 red (0-3) values
 green      buffer of 16 green (0-3) values
 blue       buffer of 16 blue (0-3) values

Output parameters:
   buf      Encoded color buffer containing 16 coded colors.

Calling protocol:
EnCols( buf,  r,  g, b); */

void    EnCols(BYTE *buf, BYTE *r, BYTE *g, BYTE *b)
{ int i;
  for (i=0; i<16; i++) buf[i] = EnCol(r[i],g[i],b[i]);
}


/* Decode an array of Colors from "inbuf", using the palette
   encoding scheme into three primary color byte arrays "red",
   "green" and "blue".

Input parameters:
 inbuf[]    buffer containing 16 encoded color values

Output parameters:
 red[]      buffer containing 16 red intensities
```

(continued)

```
green[]    buffer containing 16 green intensities
blue[]     buffer containing 16 blue intensities

Calling protocol:
DecCols( inbuf,  red,  green,  blue); */

void    DecCols(BYTE *inbuf, BYTE *red, BYTE *green, BYTE *blue)
{ int i; BYTE colbuf[3];

  for (i=0; i<16; i++) {
      DecCol(inbuf[i],colbuf);
      red[i]   = colbuf[0];
      green[i] = colbuf[1];
      blue[i]  = colbuf[2];
      }
}
```

12.17.2   Writing to the Palette Registers

An individual Palette Register can be loaded with the routine WrPal; the entire
group of 16-color registers can be loaded with the routine WrPals. Both of these
routines are listed in Listing 12.43.

LISTING 12.43 Loading the Palette Registers

```
;  Load a Palette Register.  Set an individual palette register

; Input parameters
;  regnum   desired palette register
;  color    color to load into the palette register

; Calling protocol
;  WrPal(regnum,value);
WrPal  proc FAR C PUBLIC regnum:byte, value:byte
        mov    bl,regnum     ;load palette register
        mov    bh,value      ;load palette value
        mov    ax,1000h      ;load palette register
        int    10h
        ret
WrPal  endp

;  Load all color palette registers

; Input parameters
;  colorbuf host "C" byte array containing the 16 color registers

; Calling protocol
;  WrPals(palbuf);
```

```
WrPals proc FAR C PUBLIC USES DS SI, palbuf:FAR PTR
        lds     si,palbuf  ;load address of byte buffer
        mov     cx,16      ;do for 16 registers
        xor     bl,bl      ;start at 0 register

wr1:    mov     bh,[si]    ;get color byte
        mov     ax,1000h   ;load palette register
        int     10h        ;load a value
        inc     si         ;point to next value
        inc     bl         ;point to next register
        loop    wr1


        ret
WrPals endp



; Read the Palette Registers    (VGA Only)

; Input parameters
; palnum       number of the desired palette register

; Return parameters
; color     color value read from the selected Palette Register

; Calling protocol
;  color = RdPal(palnum);

RdPal  proc FAR C PUBLIC palbuf:byte
        mov     bl,palbuf      ;get palette number
        mov     ax,1007h       ;read a Palette Register
        int     10h            ;save data

        xor     ah,ah
        mov     al,bh          ;return palette value
        ret
RdPal   endp

;  Read all Palette Registers  (VGA Only)

; Input parameters
; palnum   number of desired palette register

; Return parameters
; palbuf   A 17 byte "C" buffer which will contain the values
;          in the 16 Palette Registers and the Overscan Register.

; Calling protocol
;  RdPals(palbuf);
```

(continued)

```
RdPals proc FAR C PUBLIC USES ES, palbuf:FAR PTR
        les    dx,palbuf      ;point to "C" buffer
        mov    ax,1009h       ;read Palette Registers
        int    10h            ;save data
        ret
RdPals endp
```

12.17.3   Reading from the Palette Registers

It is not possible to read the Palette Registers in the EGA, but it is possible to read them in the VGA. The RdPal and RdPals routines in Listing 12.43 read one or all of the Palette Registers. It should be noted that the RdPals routine actually returns seventeen bytes, the last byte being the overscan color code. This can be a source of errors if the C array is only sixteen bytes long.

12.18   COLOR REGISTERS

The VGA is equipped with 256 color registers. These color registers are similar in function to the palette registers. Each contains a red, green, and blue component. Each is eighteen bits long, requiring three host read or write cycles.

12.18.1   Reading from the Color Registers

The operator can read from or write to one or more of these color registers. The routines RdColor and RdColors in Listing 12.44 read the red, green, and blue components from one or more of the color registers. The function ColorsRd does not use BIOS and operates during the vertical retrace.

LISTING 12.44   Reading or Writing to the Color Registers

```
;   Read the Color Registers through BIOS

;  Input parameters:
;  regnum   number of the Color Register to read.

;  Output parameters:
;   buf "C" byte buffer which will contain the selected Color
;  Register.  The Color Register is represented by three bytes.

;  calling protocol
;   RdColor(buf,regnum);

RdColor proc FAR C PUBLIC USES ES DI, buf:FAR PTR,regnum
        les    di,buf     ;get buffer pointer
        mov    bx,regnum  ;register number
        mov    ax,1015h   ;read a color registers
        int    10h
```

```
        mov     al,dh       ;return red
        stosb
        mov     al,ch       ;return green
        stosb
        mov     al,cl       ;return blue
        stosb
        ret
RdColor endp


;  Read several of  the Color Registers through BIOS

; Input parameters:
; first   number of the first Color Register to read.
; numreg  number of registers to read.

; Output parameters:
; buf[]  "C" byte buffer which will contain the selected
;        Color Registers.
;        Each value representing a Color Register occupies
;        three bytes in this array. The order is red, followed
;        by green, followed by blue. The first byte in the array
;        is the red component of the first element selected.
;        The length of the buffer is 3 * the # of registers.

; calling protocol
;  RdColors(buf,first,numreg);

RdColorsproc FAR C PUBLIC USES ES DS, buf:FAR PTR, first, numreg
        les     dx,buf          ;get buffer pointer
        mov     bx,first        ;starting register
        mov     cx,numreg       ;number of registers to read
        mov     ax,1017h        ;read block of color registers
        int     10h
        ret
RdColorsendp


;  Read all 256 Color Registers directly.  Waits for vertical
;  retrace to avoid undesirable flicker.  Does NOT use BIOS

; Input parameters:
;  buf "C" byte buffer which contains the selected Color
;        Register.  The Color Register buffer is represented by
;        three bytes as follows: buf[k+0] = red, buf[k+1] = green,
;        buf[k+2] = blue;
```

(continued)

```
; calling protocol
;   ColorsRd(buf);

ColorsRdproc FAR C PUBLIC USES ES DI, buf:FAR PTR
        les     di,buf      ;get buffer pointer
        mov     cx,256*3    ;read all registers
        mov     bx,3c7h     ;get ready for address read mode register

;       wait for a vertical retrace
        mov     dx,3dah
; wait for the vertical active display period
11a:    in      al,dx
        test    al,08h
        jnz     11a

; wait for the vertical retrace period
12a:    in      al,dx
        test    al,08h
        jz      12a

        mov     dx,bx       ;point to the address write mode register
        xor     al,al       ;start with first register number
        out     dx,al       ;output index to write mode register
        inc     dx          ;point to the data register 3c9h
        inc     dx          ;point to the data register 3c9h

        rep     insb
        ret
ColorsRdendp
```

12.18.2   Writing to the Color Registers

Writing to the color registers is similar to reading from the color registers. The routines WrColor and WrColors in Listing 12.45 write the red, green, and blue components to one or more of the Color Registers. The function ColorsWr does not use BIOS and operates during the vertical retrace.

LISTING 12.45 Writing to the Color Registers

```
;   Write to a Color Register

; Input parameters:
;   first   number of the first Color Register to load.
;   numreg  number of the register to load.

; Output parameters:
;   buf[]   "C" byte buffer which contains the selected Color
```

```
;            Register.  The Color Register is represented by three
             bytes. The first is red, followed by green,followed
;            by blue.

; calling protocol
;  WrColor(buf,regnum);

WrColor proc FAR C PUBLIC USES DS SI, buf:FAR PTR,regnum
        lds    si,buf          ;get buffer pointer
        lodsb
        mov    dh,al           ;load red
        lodsb
        mov    ch,al           ;load green
        lodsb
        mov    cl,al           ;load blue

        mov    bx,regnum       ;register number
        mov    ax,1010h        ;write a color register
        int    10h
        ret
WrColor endp


;   Write to a number of Color Registers

; Input parameters:
;  first    number of the first Color Register to write.
;  numreg   number of registers to write.

; Output parameters:
;   buf "C" byte buffer which contains the selected Color
;       Registers. Each value representing a Color Register
;       occupies three bytes in this array. The order is red,
;       followed by green, followed by blue.  The first byte in
;       the array is the red component of the first element
;       selected.  The length of the buffer is three times the
;       number of registers selected.

; Calling protocol:
;  WrColors(buf,first,numreg);

WrColorsproc FAR C PUBLIC USES ES, buf:FAR PTR,first, numreg
        les    dx,buf          ;get buffer pointer
        mov    bx,first        ;starting register
        mov    cx,numreg       ;number of registers to read
        mov    ax,1012h        ;read block of color registers
```

(continued)

```
            int     10h
            ret
WrColors        endp

; Write all 256 Color Registers directly without bios

; Input parameters:
;   buf "C" byte buffer which contains the selected Color
;       Register.  The Color Register buffer is represented by
;       three bytes as follows:
;           buf[k+0] = red,  buf[k+1] = green,  buf[k+2] = blue;

; calling protocol
;   ColorsWr(buf);

ColorsWrproc FAR C PUBLIC USES DS SI, arg1:FAR PTR
            lds     si,arg1     ;get buffer pointer
            mov     cx,256*3    ;read all registers
            mov     bx,3c8h     ;get ready for address write mode
                                ; register

;           wait for a vertical retrace
            mov     dx,3dah
11b:        in      al,dx       ; wait for the vertical active display
            test    al,08h      ; period
            jnz     11b

12b:        in      al,dx       ; wait for the vertical retrace period
            tcst    al,08h
            jz      12b

            mov     dx,bx       ;point to the address write mode register
            xor     al,al       ;start with first register number
            out     dx,al       ;output index to write mode register
            inc     dx          ;point to the data register 3c9h

            rep     outsb
            ret

ColorsWrendp
```

12.18.3 Summing to Gray Scale

The values in the color registers can be summed to produce a gray scale. The routine SumGray in Listing 12.46 sums the values in any number of the Color Registers.

LISTING 12.46 Summing Colors to Gray Scale

```
;  Summing Colors to Gray Scale   Sum a block of color registers
;  to gray scale

;  Input parameters:
;  first    number of the first Color Register to sum.
;  numreg   number of registers to sum.

;  calling protocol
;  SumGray(first,numreg);

SumGray proc FAR C PUBLIC, first, numreg
        mov    bx,first       ;starting register
        mov    cx,numreg      ;number of registers to write
        mov    ax,101Bh       ;set block of color registers
        int    10h
        ret
SumGray endp
```

12.18.4   Default Loading of the Palette and Color Registers

The palette registers and the color registers can be loaded with default values at a mode set. The DefaultP routine in Listing 12.47 enables or disables this function.

LISTING 12.47 Default Palette and Color Register Loading

```
;  Default Palette and Color Register Loading   Enables or
;  disables the loading of the
;  Palette and Color Rgisters during a Mode Set.

;  Input parameters:
;  choice   Enable or disable default color loading
;           0 = Enable default color loading
;           1 = Disable default color loading

;  Calling protocol
;  DefaultP(choice);

DefaultP   proc FAR C PUBLIC choice:byte
           mov    al,choice      ;get choice
           mov    bl,31h         ;select default palette load
           mov    ah,12h
           int    10h
           ret
DefaultP   endp
```

12.18.5 Producing a Fade Effect

The 256-color registers can be used to produce a fade effect. The display must be in 256-color mode for this effect to work. The technique is simple. An image can be faded-in by starting with all black values. At a prescribed time interval, each of the red, green, and blue color registers is incremented. The result of each increment produces a slightly brighter image. When any red, green, or blue component of a color reaches the final state, that component stops incrementing. Therefore, when all have reached their final state, the true brightness of the image is displayed.

Similarly, to fade-out an image, the color registers begin with the true brightness of the image. At a prescribed time interval, each of the red, green, and blue color registers is decremented. The result of each decrement produces a slightly darker image. When any red, green, or blue component of a color reaches zero, that component stops decrementing. Therefore, when all have reached their final state, the resultant image is displayed as black.

The function in Listing 12.48 illustrates this process. Note that the ColorsWr and ColorsRd functions are invoked. These wait for the vertical refresh cycle before loading the color registers with new values. These functions do not use BIOS due to speed. It is necessary to change the color registers during refresh so that no image data is displayed on the screen. This reduces the visible noise. This is not required unless repetitive changes to the color registers are required. Otherwise, the effect is negligible.

LISTING 12.48 Producing a Fade Effect

```
/* Fade whatever image is on the screen in or out using the
   color registers.

   NOTE:  Image must be in a palette color mode using the VGA
   color regs.

Input Parameters:
   color_reg    768 byte color register buffer containing colors
   direction    fade in or out.  1=in  other=out

Calling Protocol:
   void Fade(color_reg_buf, direction)  */

void Fade(BYTE *color_reg_buf, int direction)
{
int i, j,k;
BYTE buf[768];
```

```
if (direction==1) {         // fade from black to colors
   // start out as black (all zeros)
   for (k=0; k<768; k++) buf[k] = 0;
   for (j=0; j<64; j++)   { // increase to color_reg_buf levels
      for (i=0; i<768; i++) if (j >=(63-color_reg_buf[i]))
buf[i]++;
      ColorsWr(buf);
      }
   }
else  {          // fade to black
   for (k=0; k<768; k++) buf[k] = color_reg_buf[k];   //start
with colors

   for (j=0; j<64; j++) {    // decrease all levels evenly to zero
      for (i=0; i<768; i++) if (buf[i] >=1) buf[i]--;
      ColorsWr(buf);
      }
   }
}
```

Chapter 13

The Super VGA

13.1 THE SUPER VGA CARD

The VGA graphics controller reigns as the most popular color graphics system for the IBM PC family of computers. A staggering number of VGAs and related software are in use. Although new graphics controllers are knocking at the door, the momentum gained by the VGA has kept it firmly in place as the graphics adapter of choice.

Nearly all VGA cards manufactured today exceed the VGA standard (as described in Chapters 1–12) in some significant way. These new and improved VGAs have been labeled *Super VGAs*, *Extended VGAs*, or *Advanced VGAs*. For the remainder of this book I will refer to these cards as *Super VGAs*.

With no *super* standards to go by, VGA chip designers have developed their own specific implementations. As a result, each super card implementation is different. Whatever the superlative title, a programmer must have an understanding of the techniques used to program these cards.

13.1.1 Super VGA Terminology

Several different manufacturers produce VGA cards. Each of these VGA cards is based upon a VGA controller chip. The performance of the card depends on the particular VGA controller chip and the supporting implementation. Although each chip set is different, most of these cards are based on one of several VGA chips sets from seven major manufacturers. This solves some problems for the programmer. Cards using the same chip can be programmed identically.

To help the programmer even further, the performance features of each of these cards are very similar. Display resolutions, for the most part, are the same for each card (that is, 640 by 480, 800 by 600, 1024 by 768). Other features are also similar. For example, memory is mapped (memory squeezing) into the PC address space through paging registers for each implementation.

The Video Electronics Standards Association (VESA) has made an after-the-fact attempt to create a set of standards for the Super VGAs. These standards are beginning to trickle down.

In summary, the Super VGA cards surpass the VGA standard by doing more, doing it faster, in less space, and for less money. A summary of the improvements is found in Table 13.1.

13.1.2 Super VGA Feature Enhancements

The Super VGA now boasts resolutions and processing speeds that can adequately perform many graphics tasks. The most important advance is unquestionably the higher spatial resolutions. To support these display resolutions, VGA controllers can now directly access 1 through 4 Mbytes of display memory. The higher resolutions in the 16-color modes have made CAD and desktop

TABLE 13.1 Super VGA Features

Description	Super VGA	Standard VGA
More functionality	1024-by-768 16-color 1024-by-768 256-color 8, 16, 24 bit-per-color DACs 4 Mbytes memory Hardware cursor Larger and smaller fonts Interrupt capability Downward compatibility Graphics accelerators	640-by-480 16-color 320-by-200 256-color 6-bit per color DACs 256 Kbytes memory Software cursor
Faster	16-bit ISA, VL, PCI bus Interface queue Dual paging Video RAM Shadow RAM BIOS Linear address space Graphics accelerators	8-bit ISA bus
Smaller	Single VLSI ASIC chip Higher level of integration 4 megabit memory chips Programmable clock chip Surface mount technology	Chip sets Lots of support chips 64 Kbyte or 256 Kbyte memory chips Multiple crystal oscillators
Cheaper	Large production runs Shorter design cycles Cheaper memory Fewer parts	

publishing much more effective. The higher resolutions in the 8-, 16-, and 24-bit color modes have brought a whole new collection of imaging applications to the VGA arena.

The penalty for increased resolution is additional memory. For example, a 1024-by-768 24-bit graphics image requires 2.4 Mbytes. Two problems occur when using this much memory. The first problem arises because the size of the image—in fact the size of most sub-windows—is larger than 64 Kbytes. Sixteen-bit addressing no longer suffices, and 32-bit addressing arithmetic must be employed. The second problem is that there is only one 64 Kbyte chunk of memory available at A0000 hex for the VGA display memory in the PC/DOS environment. Thus, display memory has to be overlayed.

Additional color acuity is available through new color DACs featuring 8-, 15-, 16-, and 24-bits per color, as opposed to the 6-bit per color DACs, on the standard VGAs.

Programmers will appreciate several other features. Hardware cursors are ideal for mouse interaction due to their high speed responsiveness. These cursors also allow for a variety of effects due to their programmability. The ability to generate and handle vertical retrace interrupts has also been included. Improved character handling permits larger character fonts (up to 32 by 32) to be used in the alphanumeric modes and smaller character fonts to be used in 143-character/line applications. Anti-aliasing techniques are used to improve the readability of the smaller fonts.

13.1.3 Super VGA Speed Enhancements

The Super VGAs can move pixels and text around on the screen considerably faster than the first generation VGAs. A much larger memory makes this possible. To achieve the same effective processing rate on a 1024-by-768 24-bit image as opposed to a 320-by-200 8-bit image, the electronics system must be over 36 times faster. Speed enhancements are present in the host to VGA interface, the display memory to VGA controller interface, and the graphics operations themselves. The 16-bit bus interface greatly reduces the wait-states imposed with 8-bit systems. It allows twice the data to be transferred per operation. Caches are present in several of the Super VGAs to speed data transfers. The new high-speed buses of preference for the Super VGAs are the VL (VESA) local bus and the PCI bus. In order to take full advantage of these high-speed computer buses, the Super VGAs had to really soup-up their host-interface. The speed benefits are extraordinary.

The real bottleneck in graphics operations is the multi-ported display memory. The host, the VGA controller, the video refresh circuitry and the dynamic memory refresh cycles, all vie for time on the precious display memory bus. Faster display memory and video RAM memory help reduce the delays. Many of the new generation Super VGAs incorporate graphics accelerators. These accelerators also compete for the display memory resource. An exorbitant amount of the display memory's limited bandwidth can be spent on the CRT refresh cycles. The only way out of this is through the use of Video Ram (VRAM) memory since this memory is truly two-ported and CRT refresh does not reduce effective bandwidth.

Graphics operations are also enhanced when the VGA BIOS is executed from RAM memory (shadow RAM)—as opposed to the EPROMs—because the RAM has inherently faster access times. Most computers incorporate special Shadow masking of the BIOS areas. Special dedicated memory on the computer motherboards is used for this purpose.

With the 286, 386, 486, and Pentium processors, and operating systems such as OS/2, Windows, and DOS extensions, the potential exists to improve the speed performance of the VGA by getting the VGA out of the A0000 segment and into upper memory. The additional space eliminates the cumbersome overlapped memory schemes and the display memory can be accessed using a linear address scheme. In addition, the 32-bit addressing instructions in the 386, 486, and Pentiums can be utilized in conjunction with this linear addressing.

13.1.4 Super VGA Cost Reductions

Without a doubt, a major factor contributing to the VGA's success is cost. Not only have the Super VGAs improved performance, but they have done so without an increase in cost. The costs associated with a graphics system include the graphics adapter card, the display memory, the monitor, and the software that runs on it. With increased production runs, the production cost per card decreases as do the amortized design and nonrecurring engineering costs. Programmers can rely on the VGA for high-performance, low-cost graphics.

The same principle applies to the display monitors. The display memory cost is dictated by density, size, speed, and the principle of supply and demand. Because VGAs utilize the same memory chips already used in computer memory, graphics users can ride the coattails of the computer industry and benefit from the low costs and competitive environment for this memory. The VGA was based upon this principle. Last, but by no means least, is the reduced cost of software.

13.2 COMPONENTS OF THE SUPER VGA

The VGA card is really a graphics system unto itself. The components of a standard VGA and Super VGA are shown in Figure 13.1. Both systems rely on a clock oscillator, a VGA chip, display memory, video output, and a host interface. Each component in the Super VGA, Figure 13.1b, contains improvements and refinements over the same component in the standard VGA, Figure 13.1a. Some implementations place the VGA chip on the host computer motherboard, but the components remain the same.

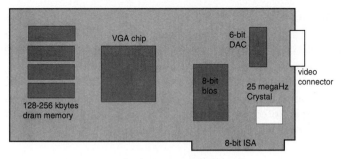

(a) Standard VGA Adapter

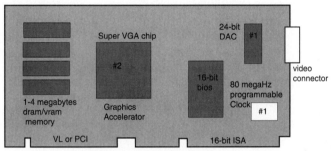

#1 NOTE: Clock and DAC may be incorporated onto Super VGA chip.
#2 NOTE: Some accelerators are on a second chip.

(b) Super VGA Adapter

FIGURE 13.1 Two VGA Implementations

13.2.1 Clock Oscillators

The *clock oscillator* is the heart of the VGA, generating the principle clock. The speed of the clock generated dictates the performance of the graphics card. In synchronous VGA implementations, the higher the speed of the clock, the more operations the system can perform in a unit of time. This translates directly into the amount of data per unit time that can be moved around the system. As the clock ticks faster, the resolutions can get larger. The resolution includes both spatial and color resolution. The eventual data rate is based upon the number of bits per second that can be thrown at the monitor. In asynchronous VGA implementations, separate clock oscillators are used, one for the CPU interface and one for the CRTC.

Suppose that a spatial resolution of 1024 by 768 pixels with eight bits per pixel is desired. This translates to 786,432 bytes per screen. Further, suppose that the system is to be noninterlaced with refreshes 60 times a second. The data rate has to be 47,185,920 bytes per second.

Typical oscillator frequencies are shown in Table 13.2. In order to achieve each designated frequency, a unique oscillator set to each frequency must be present on the card. A highly compacted surface mount card with four crystal oscillators is a rare sight. Since the oscillator's activities interfere with radio transmissions, it is doubtful if designers, aware of the stringent rules for Federal Communications Commission (FCC) approval regarding radio transmission, readily comply to construct such a product. New advances in electronic circuitry incorporate these multiple frequencies into a single device.

TABLE 13.2   Clock Frequencies for Display Modes

# Colors	Character Resolution	Pixel Resolution	Mode	VGA Clock	EGA Clock
16	40x25	360x400	0,1	28 MHz	14 MHz
16	80x25	640x200	0*,1*	25 MHz	16 MHz
16	80x25	640x350	0+,1+	25 MHz	14 MHz
16	80x25	720x400	2,3	28 MHz	16 MHz
16	40x25	320x200	2*,3*	25 MHz	14 MHz
16	80x25	720x400	2+,3+	28 MHz	14 MHz
4	40x25	320x200	4,5	25 MHz	14 MHz
2	80x25	640x200	6	25 MHz	14 MHz
2	80x25	720x350	7	28 MHz	16 MHz
2	80x25	720x400	7+	28 MHz	–
16	40x25	320x200	D	25 MHz	14 MHz
16	80x25	640x200	E	25 MHz	14 MHz
2	80x25	640x350	F	25 MHz	14 MHz
16	80x25	640x350	10	25 MHz	16 MHz
2	80x25	640x480	11	25 MHz	–
16	80x25	640x480	12	25 MHz	–
256	40x25	320x200	13	25 MHz	–
16	132x25	1056x400	*	40 MHz	–
16	100x37	800x600	6A (VESA)	50 MHz	–
16	120x45	960x720	*	50 MHz	–
16	128x48	1024x768	*	65 MHz	–
256	80x25	640x400	*	50 MHz	–

* non-standard mode

– not an EGA mode

13.2.2 VGA ASIC Chip

The VGA controller is a dedicated *graphics controller chip*, and it is programmable to a certain degree. However complicated, it is not classified as a graphics coprocessor because it lacks the general programmable capabilities of a coprocessor. The programmer can select specific graphics operations (that is, write mode, read mode, bit mask), but cannot combine these into a program through which the VGA controller can sequence.

Application Specific Integrated Circuits

The VGA controllers are implemented in *Application Specific Integrated Circuits* (ASICs). An EPROM is probably the most simple of the ASICs. An EPROM is application specific, and it is certainly an integrated circuit. A Programmable Array Logic (PALs) is another example of a simple application-specific, integrated ciruit. EPROMs and PALs are not typically called ASICs. Instead, they are usually referred to as programmable logic. Confusing? Perhaps, but let it suffice that EPROMs and PALs are not complicated enough to be called ASICs. Both rely on a program, or some sort of fuse, to mold the design of a circuit.

Next in the chain of complexity is the programmable gate array. Gate arrays can be thought of as generalized PALS, or circuit boards on a chip. The non-reprogammable gate arrays use fuses to form links among the logic elements, and the reprogrammable gate arrays use RAM elements. Certainly there are advantages to both, but the non-reprogrammable gate arrays are typically faster and yield higher densities. Programmable gate arrays are getting complex enough to be classified as ASICs. Although the densities and performance of the programmables are increasing, they still lag far behind the features of the non-programmable gate arrays.

Integrated circuit designers have a broad range of platforms to work from when actually designing silicon. Designers use three technologies when producing VGA chips. The lowest level of silicon design uses a full custom method. The second level uses standard cells. The designer can design the chip from the base up, using predefined elements, called standard cells. These elements include memory, gates, counters, FIFOs, shift registers, and adders. Standard cell designs yield all sorts of circuits, including the powerful microprocessors. Standard cell design is expensive and entails large non-recurring engineering fees, ranging from \$100,000 to several million dollars.

The next level down is the gate array. The gate array already has the lowest levels of silicon laid down on the chip, and the designer is constrained to work with this configuration. Different gate arrays have different basic architectures. Again, the designer has a selection of gates to design with including most of the standard cell elements, with the exception of random access memory elements. Gate arrays can be typically designed with non-recurring engineering costs of between $30,000 and $100,000, depending on their complexity.

Designing memory elements into a gate array is costly in terms of space and used gates. Typically a designer selects either standard-cell or gate-array technology, based upon whether the application requires memory. If an application requires memory, the designer can use a gate array and interface it to a standard SRAM. Now, however, pin-out becomes a problem because the ASICs have limitations on the number of pins a package can support. The VGA chips typically come in 144 and 160 pin packages.

The VGA ASIC

The VGA, standard or super, has a set of functions that it must perform. These include memory management, pixel processing, host interface and CRT control, and sequence and attribute control. The *VGA ASIC* determines the performance features and details of each VGA implementation. In most cases, compatibility with the IBM VGA has been strictly observed.

The Super VGA ASICs shown in Figure 13.2 have gone far beyond this standard and are really considered in a class by themselves. Six manufacturers of Super VGAs are presented in this book, and most have more than one Super VGA chip. Each chip is different and must be dealt with separately.

Memory Management

The *memory management* portion of the VGA is a complex mechanism. It must provide memory control timing and sequence control, including dynamic memory refresh control, memory address control, and memory data. The memory

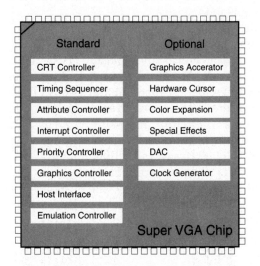

FIGURE 13.2 The VGA ASIC Chips

address bus is formed by two 8-bit buses that interface to memory; the data bus is 32 bits wide, accommodating the four 8-bit planes. The memory and data bus architecture was designed to fit well into the standard memory sizes. Suppose memory chips are configured with 1 Mbyte locations by one bit per location, as shown in Figure 13.3a. In this case, the chip would require 20 bits of address and one bit of data.

Another configuration would be 256 Kbytes locations by four bits per location as shown in Figure 13.3b. This configuration would require eighteen bits of address and four bits of data.

If the VGA is configured in a 16-color mode, each pixel is represented by four bits, and these bits could be located in each of the four RAM chips. Thus, it would be simple to gate in data into one bit-plane (one RAM) while leaving the other bits (other three RAMs) untouched. This would take four chips. There would be enough memory with these four chips to store a 1024-by-1024 pixel image (1 Mbyte of four bit words). With the second configuration, the four-bit planes could reside in one chip. This would mean that a single chip could be used to store an image that is 640-by-400 pixels. Of course, it would take four chips to store the 1024-by-1024 image. However, it is no longer an easy task to store data in one bit without disrupting the other three bits since the memory chip accesses all four bits at a time. Thus, a read-modify-write operation would be required, using two memory accesses per operation. If a 256-color mode is in effect, each pixel is eight bits. There is little need to write into a single-bit position within the byte.

If a 16-bit-wide display memory data bus is desired, sixteen 1-bit memory chips would be required, as shown in Figure 13.4a. Better suited to this 16-bit memory, only four 4-bit per memory chips would be required, as shown in Figure 13.4b.

Host Interface

As listed in Chapter 10, all of the standard registers are implemented within the VGA gate array. In addition, the Super VGA registers are also implemented in the gate arrays. These registers form the *host interface* between the host and the VGA. All host-modified functions that the VGA performs are controlled through these registers. The VGA must decode the addresses from the host address bus and the I/O bus to determine whether the VGA is being accessed. The range of memory and port addresses are fixed, based upon the VGA standard.

The Super VGAs extend the port addresses to accommodate the new registers. An especially interesting feature of some of the Super VGAs is their ability to remap the memory and I/O addresses to other places. Remapping the memory allows the VGA to reside in upper memory, out of the A0000 hex segment. This feature will be used by non-DOS-operating systems that can access this upper memory.

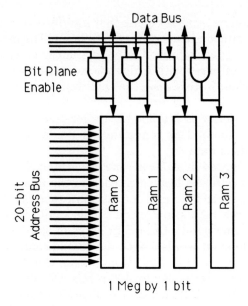

a) Using four 1 Meg x 1bit RAM
for a 1024x1024 16–color display buffer

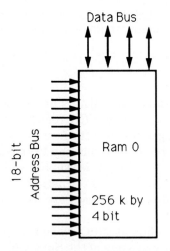

b) Using a single 256k x 4bit
RAM for a 640x400 16–color display buffer

FIGURE 13.3 Small System Implementation of VGA Display Mode

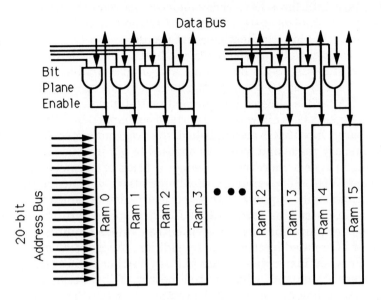

a) Implementing a 16-bit data bus using 1-bit
1Meg memory chips

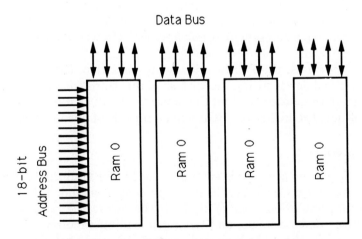

b) Implementing a 16-bit data bus using 4-bit
1Meg memory chips

FIGURE 13.4 Large System Implementation of VGA Display Memory

Some VGA host interfaces have cache memory between the host and VGA. This allows data or control instructions to be queued up and can reduce the wait-states interjected into the host's system timing.

Super VGAs can typically interface with the host through the 16-bit, AT bus, or through the standard 8-bit bus. Some are programmable, regardless of whether they have 8- or 16-bit bus interfaces. Others automatically sense whether the VGA card is plugged into an 8-bit or 16-bit slot.

Many of the Super VGAs allow the I/O ports to be mapped into the host memory address space. Once this is accomplished, the programmer can access these ports using memory reads and writes as opposed to I/O instructions. This can produce dramatic speed improvements when a block of parameters must be sent to the Super VGA. For example, a BitBlt operation, when using the graphics accelerator, typically requires that seventeen registers be loaded before a line-draw operation can be initiated. If I/O is mapped into the standard index/data register pairs, loading these seventeen values requires a considerable amount of I/O related instructions. In addition, I/O instructions cause the 80386/80486/Pentium instruction caches to flush, further causing delays.

Due to increased demand, which is the mother of invention, new system buses have been designed to speed up the computer system. These include the VL local bus (VESA) and the PCI bus. The local bus borrows its terminology from the CPU local bus, typically used for memory. An extension of this bus and a standardization by the VESA committee has created an excellent bus for video adapters. Most new Super VGA cards have a VL VESA bus version. The VL bus is not meant to be bus mastered (technically, it can be a bus master, but the CPU would have to be put into a hold mode negating the benefit). The VL bus is very fast and excellent video performance can be achieved. There are no programming changes necessary to drive a Super VGA when it's on either a VL or an ISA bus.

The second new bus, the PCI bus, is an Intel creation, the specification of which is being tied down during the writing of this third edition. The PCI bus will have ID requirements such that the Super VGA will be required to identify itself. In addition, the PCI Super VGA will be capable of bus mastering.

Timing Sequencer

The *Timing Sequencer* provides basic timing control for both the CRT Controller and the Attribute Controller. The timing control includes the following: horizontal count resolution (eight or nine dots/character), the various dot clocks and their divide down cousins, and the video loading circuitry, which determines whether data should be loaded at every 8-, 16-, or 32-dot clock. The Timing Sequencer is controlled through the Timing Sequencer registers discussed in Chapter 10.4.

CRT Controller

The *CRT controller* (CRTC) provides an 18-bit linear address, vertical and horizontal sync signals, and cursor addresses to control the raster-scan CRT displays. Internal to the VGA, the addresses and timing are stored in two-dimensions, horizontal and vertical, while externally the memory is sequential. This control is derived from the CRTC registers in Chapter 10.4.

Attribute Controller

The internal *Attribute Controller* provides high-speed video shifting and processing for the alphanumeric and graphics modes. The attribute controller handles 8- or 9-bit font data widths in the alphanumeric modes and must reformat pixel data into one, two, or eight bits of adjacent data for the graphics modes. Some Super VGAs can reformat the pixel data into sixteen bits of adjacent data per pixel. In either mode, this data is translated through an internal lookup table called the palette and sent out to the color lookup table. The Attribute Registers are described in Chapter 10.6; the Color Registers are described in Chapter 10.7. The standard VGA Attribute Registers support *Plane* (16-color mode) or Byte (256-color mode). Some VGAs support *Word* (65,536-color mode) pixel structures.

Graphics Display Controller

The *graphics controller*, described in Chapter 10.5, helps the host CPU in graphics-related operations. These include rotate, bit masking, and z-plane operations with four boolean operations in response to a single CPU write. In a sense, this controller may be thought of as a primitive graphics coprocessor. Placing bitmap operations in the gate array high-speed hardware improves the graphics performance of the VGA significantly over a dumb frame buffer. This processing is restricted to Plane operations and cannot be used in byte or word operations. This limits the effectiveness of using the 16-bit host interface.

13.2.3 Display Memory

Display memory causes bottleneck in the system because there is competition for this memory. To a large extent, the speed of the display memory dictates the performance of the system. When the EGA was first introduced, systems utilized 256 Kbit DRAM chips. The highest EGA mode was 640 by 350 with 16-color mode using a total of 128 Kbytes, thereby requiring four memory chips. The 1024-by-768 256-color resolution of the Super VGA requires 786,432 bytes as well as eight 1 Mbit chips or two 4 Mbit chips.

Three types of memory chips would fit the bill for video memory. These are dynamic RAM (DRAM), video-RAM (VRAM), and Static Ram (SRAM). Both the DRAM and the VRAM require memory refresh; the SRAM does not. Typically, SRAM is not used due to the lower density and higher cost penalties paid for this memory.

In the standard VGA, 256 Kbytes of memory is needed in the display buffer to support both 4-bit per pixel and 8-bit per pixel. In the newer Super VGAs, 15-, 16-, and 24-bit-per-pixel configurations are provided.

Dynamic Memory

Dynamic memory is by far the most popular memory used in VGA systems. Dynamic memory requirements are outlined in Table 13.3. There are three tyrants competing for this memory resource. The first is the VGA chip itself. It must read the memory, write the memory, and perform the ever-present memory refresh necessary for dynamic memory. The second is the host computer. It must read and write into the memory. The third, and most persistent, is the video circuitry which must read the memory and use the contents to refresh the CRT tube. The host computer can turn off the port to the video circuitry, thereby cutting it off from the display memory. Consequently, the video screen goes blank.

Video Memory

Some VGAs have gone the extra half-mile to support video memory, VRAM. In and of itself, VRAM is dual-ported. It anticipates the requirements of the video circuitry and provides a special serial port just for that purpose. It knows that the video circuitry never wants to write to this memory. The video frame grabber is an exception. VRAM also knows that the video circuitry desires a sequential output from this memory.

TABLE 13.3 Dynamic Memory Requirements

# Colors	Pixel Resolution	# 256K x 4 Dram Memory Chips	# 1 Mbyte x 4 Dram Memory Chips	Memory Speed
16	640x480	2	1	100 nsec
256	640x480	4	1	100 nsec
16	800x600	2	1	80 nsec
256	800x600	8	2	100 nsec
16	1024x768 *1	4	2	100 nsec
256	1024x768 *1	8	2	100 nsec
16	1024x768	4	2	80 nsec
256	1024x768	8	2	80 nsec

*1 interlaced

The density of VRAMs track the density of DRAMs closely, since the memory elements are the same in each case. The problem centers on cost and availability. Typically, the cost of the VRAM is twice that of the DRAM.

Static RAM

SRAMs are beautiful. As long as power is present, they remember what they are doing, and no refreshing is necessary. They are also exceedingly fast. The only problem is that their densities are lower, their power requirements greater, and their cost even higher. Typically, the cost of the SRAM is five times that of the DRAM, and advances usually lag behind DRAM by one generation.

13.2.4 Video Output Circuitry

The *Video Output Refresh Circuitry* must feed a near-constant stream of data to the CRT. Typically 80 percent of the memory accesses must be dedicated to the Video Refresh Circuitry. The host is prevented from accessing memory during memory refreshing. If, in the worst case, 80 percent of the memory accesses are for video refresh, only one out of five host memory accesses will get through. The host is told that the VGA is not ready if it attempts to read too quickly. This "not ready" signal comes to the host in the form of wait-states. Be aware that the speed of the graphics system is principally dependent on the wait-states generated by the host interface and the inability of the host to access display memory.

The interface to the CRT monitor is through the video output circuitry. The immediate buffer between the video memory and the CRT is the color palette chip. The width of the palette dictates the number of colors per pixel, and the length of the palette dictates the number of simultaneous colors that can be displayed. Super VGAs can easily interface to palettes that can display eight bits per color totaling 24 bits per pixel. This is compared to six bits per color for the standard VGA. Note this is not what is termed 24-bit color, since the length of the palette is still restricted to 256 registers (that is, 256 simultaneous colors). 24-bit true color means 24 bits per color with sixteen million simultaneous colors.

The new generation of color palette chips allow more colors and feed through modes that provide access to 16-bit and 24-bit true-color images. These chips are significantly better for imaging applications. A 16-bit color per pixel allows 64 Kbytes color possibilities per pixel. Typically, this is split between 32 shades of red and blue and 64 shades of green. Others split these sixteen bits into 64 shades of red and green and sixteen shades of blue. Blue is always given the least resolution because human vision is less sensitive to the blue spectrum of color but highly sensitive to green and red spectrums.

True color has 24 bits per pixel images. It allows 16.8 million colors to be displayed. The resultant colors really are staggering. The difference between the green of a dollar bill and the green of grass are subtle, yet significant.

13.2.5 Host Interface

The *host interface* affects the performance of any graphics system. It has a profound effect on graphics systems that have no coprocessor. The host interface also has an impact on the VGA. Every command, every byte, every pixel must pass through the hands of the host interface. Like any middleman, the interface keeps a little for itself.

Graphics systems with coprocessors can get by with sending a single command through the interface. This sets in motion thousands of operations within the graphics system. A little tax paid here and there may appear to be scant. The VGA, however, must send everything through the interface, and the penalties are striking. The design generalities and idiosyncrasies of the IBM PC environment compound the problem.

The IBM "true blue" VGA was first introduced on the system board of the PS/2 family of computers. The interface relied on the MCA, the microchannel bus. The non-IBM, but standard VGAs, were designed to interface to the host processor through the PC/AT bus. Severe penalties are paid when one ventures through the PC/AT bus in the form of wait-states. Wait-states occur when some external device wants the host to slow down. The device might have slow memory or be a slow I/O device unable to keep up with the host. The inserted and sometimes unnecessary wait-states can bring the graphics system to its knees. One would expect the IBM VGA to have an advantage and to operate faster than the adapter card VGA versions. In a sense it does because bus wait-states are not interjected. However, unfortunately, the IBM VGA is so slow that the increased performance due to fewer wait-states has been eaten by the graphics processor and memory.

The Super VGAs rely on the 16-bit AT bus, as opposed to the 8-bit PC bus of the original VGA adapters. (Most of the first VGAs relied on the 8-bit PC bus to interface to the host processor.) The latter creates an unnecessary slowdown since the AT automatically inserts six additional cycles of wait-states when accessing an 8-bit device. The PC was designed as a 4.77 MHz bus. The AT assumes that it has to slow down to this bus rate for an 8-bit card. The AT inserts only two additional cycles of wait-states when accessing a 16-bit device. In addition, a 16-bit transfer also transfers twice as much data as an 8-bit transfer. Thus, theoretically, the 16-bit VGAs should outperform the 8-bit VGAs by two to six times. Unfortunately, this is not the case, since the VGA is inherently an 8-bit device. A bottleneck occurs further down the line, which forces the interjection of additional wait-states.

The VGA is based on an 8-bit architecture. Designers have done a great deal of creative "souping up" to help the chips take advantage of the 16-bit transfers.

Especially suited to the 16-bit transfer is the alphanumeric mode, where a character is represented by an 8-bit ASCII code and an 8-bit attribute totaling 16 bits. Other operations vary, depending upon speed advantages when using the 16-bit interface, and are highly chip-implementation specific.

The BIOS routines associated with interrupt 10 hex are usually located in EPROMs on the VGA adapter card. Utilizing 16-bit word wide, EPROMs can help speed things up since, once again, 16-bit transfers are occurring out of the inherently slow EPROMs. Most Super VGAs include two EPROMs to ensure 16-bit transfers.

Another popular technique employs shadow RAM. Shadow RAM is popular in the 80386 systems where the data resident in the VGA EPROMs is copied to RAM, and the BIOS operates from this location. Yet another technique uses RAM-resident BIOS device drivers that reside in host memory. The device drivers get loaded as terminate and stay resident programs. They redirect the video interrupt 10 hex from the VGA EPROM to the RAM location to which they are loaded.

13.2.6   16-bit Memory Transfers

Designing a 16-bit interface for memory transfers is not trivial on the AT bus. The PC bus was designed by IBM. Once it was carved in stone there was no turning back. There is a problem with the latched and unlatched address bus on the AT. These two address buses are passed to the adapters through the AT connectors. When 16-bit memory accesses are desired, a tri-stated line called MEM16 must be pulled low by the adapter, indicating to the host processor that a 16-bit transfer is desired. The host has to do some fancy footwork to determine whether it should output two 8-bit bytes on data lines 0–7 or one 16-bit word on data lines 0–15. In order to have enough time, the AT bus requires that the MEM16 line be asserted shortly after the address lines settle. The address lines are used by the adapter to determine whether it should respond at all to the bus address. Thus, it has to be decoded by the adapter.

Consider the following example. The VGA display memory resides at address A0000–B0000 hex in the PC memory address space. The host wants to read a word from the VGA at address A1000. It exerts the address A1000 on the bus and waits for a bit. During this time, all devices on the memory bus have to look at the address, A1000, to determine if they should respond. In this case, the VGA address decoder would detect that A1000 resides between A0000 and Affff and so gears itself up. It still does not know if the host wants to read or write. Since this VGA is a 16-bit device, it wants to exert MEM16 to alert the host to this fact. As soon as it decodes the A0000 hex, it sends out the low signal on the MEM16 line. The host in turn identifies the MEM16 line and sends its memory read pulse. Then it waits for a bit before it reads the 16-bit data on the data bus bits 0–15. During this second wait, this VGA has to use the read pulse to enable the output of its memory (previously addressed at a1000) and send the 16-bit signal onto the data bus bits 0–15.

The problem is that decoding the address takes time for the VGA, and it has to send out the MEM16 line quickly. The address cannot be decoded until the address lines settle. On the PC, there are two sets of address lines on the PC being latched and unlatched. The unlatched lines settle before MEM16 has to be asserted, while the latched lines settle after MEM16 has to be asserted. We can rule out using the latched address lines. The problem is that no complete set of unlatched address lines is available, the lowest being address bit 17. As a result, the address decoding circuitry cannot detect memory locations that are smaller than 128 Kbytes. Therefore, the VGA can only detect that a memory access is required somewhere between A0000 and Bffff before it can decide whether to respond with a MEM16 signal. Unfortunately, in dual monitor systems, a Hercules card may well be residing at B0000 with unpredictable results. I have yet to see a 16-bit Hercules implementation.

The MEM16 line is another reason why 16-bit VGAs will operate in an 8-bit mode but will not operate in a 16-bit mode in AT systems with bus speeds greater than 8 MHz. The increased speed of the bus and the subsequent decreased time for the MEM16 line to be asserted exceeds the decoding rate of the VGA.

13.2.7   System Throughput

The pipeline existing between the host and the VGA is primarily limited by the serial connection of the host interface and the display memory bottlenecks. In such instances, the system performance is dictated by the worse of the two. For example, if the host can only pass data across the bus at a 1.5 Mbyte/second rate and the display memory can only allow data into display memory at a 1.5 Mbyte/second rate, the system throughput will be around 1.5 Mbyte/second. If the host bus passes 10 Mbyte/second while the display memory still operates at 1.5 Mbyte/second, then the throughput rate will still be approximately 1.5 Mbyte/second.

13.2.8   Graphics Displays

The output of the video circuitry must drive some type of display. These include monochrome, color, digital, analog, fixed frequency, multi-syncing, and monochrome or color flat panel displays. Table 13.4 lists some common monitor types.

Monitors and Emulation

The Super VGAs share the ability to perform some type of downward compatibility. It is necessary to ensure that the proper monitor is installed. Otherwise, damage can occur to the monitor. Some Super VGAs check to see the monitor

TABLE 13.4 Common Display Types

Display	Characteristics	Graphics Card Compatibility
Monochrome	Black and white	Hercules/MDA
Color <= 200 lines	Digital 16-color	CGA
Fixed freq. <= 350 lines	Digital 64-color	EGA
Fixed freq. <= 480 lines	Analog color	VGA
Enhanced monochrome	Analog monochrome	VGA
Multi-syncing interlaced	Analog color	8514/A, Super VGA
Multi-syncing	Analog color	Super VGA
Mono flat panel	4 shades of gray	Laptops CGA, EGA, VGA
Color flat panel	64 colors	Laptops EGA, VGA

type and report the findings. Others leave it to the user to ensure that the proper monitor is in place.

Fixed Frequency Monitors

The MDA, Hercules, CGA, EGA, VGA, and 8514/A are *fixed frequency monitors.* They provide a standardized set of display resolutions. The simpler cards provide fewer resolutions from which to choose. For example, the CGA or Hercules has only one resolution and, consequently, only requires the monitor to synchronize one known set of horizontal and vertical frequencies. As the number of required frequencies has increased and the industry has lost its apparent fear of non-standard frequencies, the fixed frequency monitors have given way to multi-syncing monitors.

Multi-syncing Monitors

With the EGA, the number of possibilities increased and the concept of multi-syncing monitors became popular. The *multi-syncing monitors* have lower and upper bounds on the synchronization frequencies. This has raised some problems regarding downward compatibility. It is not cost-effective to design a monitor to sync to both high and low frequencies. Consequently, high performance monitors cannot necessarily display low-resolution images that conform to the timing specifications of the low-performance monitors.

Interlaced and Non-interlaced Monitors

Interlaced monitors are cheaper to build than non-interlaced monitors in the same range of performance. The issue came up when IBM decided to formalize the interlaced 1024-by-768 graphics mode of the 8514/A. It is agreed by virtually all that the interlacing has an annoying flicker. The 8514/A clones do not follow suit. These have predominantly incorporated non-interlaced 1024-by-768 modes. Unfortunately, for these clones to be compatible they should also be capable of supporting an interlaced 1024-by-768 mode. Most of the later generation Super VGA chips do support the interlaced display modes in addition to the non-interlaced display modes.

NTSC compatibility

Interlacing also plays a part in the display of images on televisions and VCRs that adhere to the NTSC standard. Several new cards are now available that convert the VGA modes to the NTSC standard and allow the output of the VGA to be displayed on a television or recorded on a VCR. However, the designers work under great restrictions in order to reduce the costs of production. I have yet to see a system to recommend. More expensive graphics systems, designed specifically for broadcast-quality video, do a great job. For instance, the TARGA or VISTA cards produce beautiful video. On the other hand, these same cards cannot come close to competing with the VGA as far as high-resolution display modes are concerned.

Flat Panels

Flat-panel displays can be either monochrome or color. The monochrome systems are based upon liquid LCD or gas discharge technologies. These can be made to display gray scale by time-modulating the signal. For example, suppose the frame rate is divided into four cycles. A pixel can be set to On in none, one, two, three, or four of these time cycles producing five possible shades of gray. Dithering is another technique used. However, using it means decreased resolution.

Color displays are based on the active matrix Thin Film Transistor (TFT) or the Super Twist (STN) Technologies. Currently, 64 colors can be produced on these color flat panels.

A typical panel consists of 640 by 240 pixels. Mounting one panel on top of the other provides a 640-by-480 display resolution. The number of horizontal and vertical pixels filling a screen is fixed. Thus, there can be no compensation in timing to affect screen size or position. For example, a 640-by-350 display cannot be continuously stretched to fill a 640-by-480 pixel flat panel. Special techniques called *vertical compensation* must be used to fill the screen.

One vertical-compensation technique involves offsetting the display so that the 350 lines are at least centered. Another repeats lines or inserts blank lines evenly spaced through the display. It is possible to stretch the display through interpolation. However, the calculation requirements on the processor to perform interpolation rule out this technique.

Clever color compression techniques must be employed to reduce the amount of colors inherent in the VGA to a number that can be displayed on the flat panel. In addition, contrast enhancement techniques must be used when mapping color to gray scale. Colors can have the same monochromic value, meaning they would look very different on a color monitor but identical on the monochrome flat panel. Some VGAs have algorithms implemented in hardware to perform the color compression and contrast enhancement.

13.3 SUPER VGA BIOS

The Standard VGA BIOS is described in Chapter 11. Some of the Super VGAs have added additional calls to the video BIOS. These additional calls allow the user to set up extended graphics modes, access extended registers, save and restore the state of the VGA extended registers, set up emulation modes, return VGA information, and set power on video conditions. The VESA standards group has recommended that a new set of BIOS calls be mandatory as listed in Table 13.5. More discussion of the VESA BIOS recommendations will follow in the next section.

The VGA BIOS is resident in one or two EPROMs located on the VGA adapter card. If only one EPROM is present, an 8-bit BIOS interface is used. If two are present, a 16-bit BIOS interface is present. The BIOS memory is mapped into PC memory space at c0000 to c5fff and at c6800–c7fff hex. providing 30 Kbytes of code space for the BIOS memory. When this occurs, the video BIOS is located on the motherboard. In this case, the VGA controller typically has to be alerted so that it can map out the aforementioned address space. In addition, many computers have the facility to copy the video BIOS into shadow RAM. When this function is enabled, execution of BIOS calls occurs from RAM memory as opposed to the slower ROM memory. This shadow RAM is non-DOS memory specifically dedicated for this purpose.

A potential problem involving a clash between the VGA BIOS and the 8514/A BIOS was headed off at the pass by the VESA committee. The base address of

TABLE 13.5 VESA BIOS Recommendations

Function	Function Number	Section
Return Super VGA Information	0	13.5.3
Return Super VGA Mode Information	1	13.5.4
Set Super VGA Video Mode	2	13.5.5
Return Current Video Mode	3	13.5.6
Save/Restore Super VGA State	4	13.5.7
CPU Video Memory Window Control	5	13.5.8

the ROM for the 8514/A depends on the ROM size, the type of host interface, and the base address field of the 8514/A Extension Register 2. The ROM size might be 8 Kbytes or 32 Kbytes. The Host interface might be a PC/AT or a microchannel. If the 8514/A is in a microchannel, its ROM exists at C6800 to C7FFF. The VESA committee recommends that this base address be used when the 8514/A is installed in a microchannel system while the default address of C8000 to C9FFF be used in the PC/AT systems.

13.4 THE SUPER VGA STANDARDS

The Super VGA cards have improved upon the VGA standard, but unfortunately, they have done so in a non-standard way. Each implementation is similar to the others; all try and accomplish basically the same things. Yet each is slightly different from the others and none stands out as the clear champion with the slickest solution.

All of the Super VGAs take advantage of the VGA standard and remain downwardly compatible. However, they all suffer from this compatibility since many of the additions must be patched in. This process is often awkward and slow.

Some Super VGAs actually have two modes. The first conforms to the VGA standard. The second does not conform, but it is better suited to fast programming. Luckily, the paths taken by the VGA manufacturers have not diverged very much. It is not that difficult to modify the code that drives one Super VGA while allowing it to operate on any other. Chapter 14 and 15 contain details on just how to do this.

VESA is a consortium of electronic manufacturers spearheaded by NEC. They have attempted to standardize some display modes and BIOS calls for the Super VGAs. The VESA standards will be discussed in detail in Section 13.5 of this chapter.

13.4.1 Standardizing the Super VGA

Every programmer should be familiar with the five major areas in the Super VGAs. These five are terminology, identifying the VGA card and its capabilities, accessing the extended registers, accessing the display modes, and accessing the display memory.

13.4.2 Standardizing Terminology

The Super VGA terminology is shrouded in problems. The first problem relates to labeling a VGA that functions beyond the standard VGA. Some call them *extended*, others *advanced,* and others *super*. I have selected the terminology super.

The second problem has to do with defining the terms *page, plane, bank* and *window*. There is general agreement regarding the use of plane. Display mem-

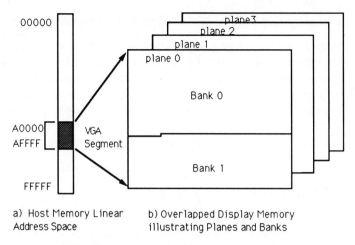

a) Host Memory Linear Address Space

b) Overlapped Display Memory illustrating Planes and Banks

FIGURE 13.5 VGA Memory Technology

ory is overlayed into four display planes, each 8 bits wide. This creates an effective data bus, which is 32 bits wide. This *planar* memory configuration was ideal for the 16-color modes.

In the standard VGA, the terminology page is used to indicate when more than one display screen fits into display memory. For example, in the alphanumeric display mode 3, the resolution is 80 by 25 characters and totals 2,000 characters. Each character occupies one byte in each of the four display planes. Since each plane is 64 Kbytes long, it is possible to fit 32 display pages in the 256 Kbyte VGA display memory. Thus, like a book, the VGA has multiple pages. Within each page it has multiple planes. This is illustrated in Figure 13.5.

From here the terminology goes out to pasture. As more memory was added to the VGA, it had to be further overlayed to fit into the 64 Kbyte segment. Terms for the resultant sub-page, sub-plane units eluded the terminology departments at the VGA manufacturers. Some called them pages while others called them banks. As described in Section 13.5, VESA has named these windows. VESA may have selected a neutral term to avoid siding with any one of the manufacturers. I prefer and use banks throughout this book since pages was already taken and windows means too many things. Besides, Apple, Microsoft or Xerox do not take kindly to the use of the word windows without a trademark.

13.4.3 Identifying the VGA and Card Capabilities

Some Super VGA cards have well-defined functions for determining the chip type and capabilities of the card. Others do not. In some cases, it is necessary to poke around with registers and memory locations. Writing patterns and reading them back can help determine what is and is not present. Techniques for identifying the VGA and its capabilities are presented in Chapter 14.

13.4.4   Accessing the Super VGA Extended Registers

All Super VGAs have extended registers in addition to the Standard VGA registers. Where these registers reside and how the programmer accesses them varies from one implementation to another. Some are grouped within the standard VGA register groups. Others are in an address space by themselves. The extended registers are often locked and access to them can require special programming. Complete listings of several manufacturers' extended registers are described in Chapter 14, Appendix A, and in the chapters that discuss the Super VGA.

13.4.5   Using the Super VGA Display Modes

The implementations of the Super VGAs support several Extended display modes, each with its own spatial and color resolutions. Not every card supports every display mode. Several cards do not extend beyond 640 by 480 for the 256-color modes. Common display modes, and some not so common ones, are listed in Table 13.6 and Table 13.7. In certain implementations, the display modes are accessed through the standard AH=0 Set Mode BIOS call described in Section 11.2.1. Some of the display modes are accessed through a separate BIOS call. The actual mode numbers for each of these resolutions vary according to the particular implementation. The more common screen resolutions are displayed in Figure 13.6.

13.4.6   Accessing the Super VGA Display Memory

All Super VGAs support at least 512 Kbytes of memory. This means that the 512 Kbytes must be overlayed in some fashion, or in several ways, to fit within the 64-Kbyte segment in host memory address space at A0000 hex. To access this memory, paging or bankswitching techniques are employed.

Each implementation has defined its own locations for these Bank Switching Registers. Some have placed them in more than one location. Some have one Bank Switch Register, while others have separate registers for read and write. Some have two general registers; unfortunately, others have split up the single feature into several locations.

In the 4-bit-per-color modes, these 512 Kbytes are overlayed into four display planes, each being 128 Kbytes. The 128 Kbytes is further overlayed into the 64-Kbyte segment A0000 hex in the PC memory address space. The 1024 by 768 pixel resolution in the 16-color display mode is the only currently implemented 16-color mode that requires more than 256 Kbytes of total display memory. This translates into a single 64-Kbyte segment per display plane.

TABLE 13.6 Commonly Used Super VGA Display Modes

Resolution	Bits / Color	Memory	# of 64 Kbyte Banks
800 by 600	4	256 Kbytes	4
1024 by 768	4	512 Kbytes	8
1280 by 1024	4	1 Mbyte	16
640 by 400	8	256 Kbytes	4
640 by 480	8	512 Kbytes	8
800 by 600	8	512 Kbytes	8
1024 by 768	8	1 Mbyte	16
1280 by 1024	8	1 Mbyte	16
320 by 200	15	256 Kbytes	4
640 by 480	15	1 Mbyte	16
800 by 600	15	1 Mbyte	16
1024 by 768	15	1 Mbyte	16
1280 by 1024	15	2 Mbytes	32
320 by 200	16	256 Kbytes	4
640 by 480	16	1 Mbyte	16
800 by 600	16	1 Mbyte	16
1024 by 768	16	1 Mbyte	16
1280 by 1024	16	2 Mbytes	32
320 by 200	24	256 Kbytes	4
640 by 480	24	1 Mbyte	16
800 by 600	24	2 Mbytes	32
1024 by 768	24	4 Mbytes	64
1280 by 1024	24	4 Mbytes	64
320 by 200	32	256 Kbytes	4
640 by 480	32	2 Mbytes	32
800 by 600	32	2 Mbytes	32
1024 by 768	32	4 Mbytes	64
1280 by 1024	32	8 Mbytes	128

In the 8-bit-per-color modes, the overlaying is more severe. The four display planes are chained together, called *chain 4*, and extend in a linear address space within a 64-Kbyte segment. In a 640-by-400 display mode, 256,000 bytes

TABLE 13.7 Commonly Used Super VGA Alphanumerics Display Modes

Resolution	# of Colors	Display Memory	# of Banks
132 by 25	2, 4, or 16	256 Kbytes	1
132 by 28	2, 4, or 16	256 Kbytes	1
132 by 44	2, 4, or 16	256 Kbytes	1
132 by 50	2, 4, or 16	256 Kbytes	1
80 by 60	16	256 Kbytes	1
100 by 40	16	256 Kbytes	1
100 by 60	16	256 Kbytes	1

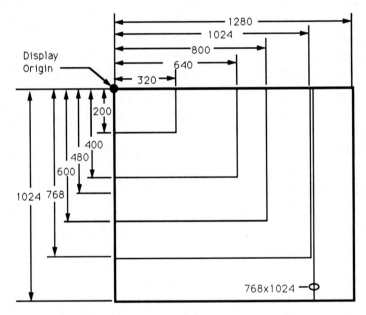

FIGURE 13.6 Super VGA Spatial Resolutions

are required. This fits within 256 Kbytes of total display memory. However, it must be overlayed into four banks to fit within the 64-Kbyte host address space at A0000 hex.

In the 15-, 16-, 24-, and 32-bit-per-color modes, the overlaying requires even more bank switching. Many Super VGAs had to add additional bits to their bank control registers to accommodate these modes. For example, it was common for a single byte control register to contain both the read and write bank controls, each being four bits. Now, modes can require 32, 64, and even 128 banks requiring up to eight bits per bank.

13.4.7 Other Super VGA Features

Not all features are shared by the Super VGA cards. The exclusive features are downward compatibility, hardware cursors, large character fonts in alphanumeric modes, anti-aliased character sets also for the alphanumeric modes, interrupt counters, sliding registers, and bit masking.

Downward compatibility means that the VGA can emulate either the MDA, Hercules, CGA, or EGA. One Super VGA even emulates the 8514/A standard. The techniques and levels of emulation vary according to each implementation. Typically, a set of registers is specifically present for emulation use. In some cases, BIOS calls are present to set up the emulation. Sophisticated duplication of CRT Controller timing registers is provided so that emulation modes do not have to overwrite the normal values for these registers when in a VGA mode.

Hardware cursors are very important in graphical interface environments and are included in two of the Super VGA implementations discussed in this book. A cursor pattern is software-generated and is stored in high display memory. This pattern will be displayed at a specified position. A mouse or another pointing device typically dictates the position to load the cursor. The position of the cursor can also be interrogated.

The cursor can be thought of as containing a foreground and a background. For example, the cursor is surrounded by a rectangular region. If the cursor shape is an arrow, then the arrow could be considered foreground. The space in the rectangular box, not covered by the arrow itself, could be considered the background. The application can specify a color for the foreground and background of the cursor.

It is also possible to program how the cursor affects the pixels that it overlays. For example, the cursor can overwrite or be drawn in an opaque or transparent color. It can also be quickly enabled or disabled, caused to blink at varying rates, or zoom in dimension.

The "hot-spot" of the cursor is also programmable. This allows any point within the cursor pattern to be programmed as the coordinates to return when the cursor position is queried. A hardware cursor and its relevant terminology are illustrated in Figure 13.7.

Large-character fonts are also available on several of the Super VGAs. Character sizes up to 32 pixels by 32 scan lines can be programmed to operate in the alphanumeric modes. Of course, any character size can be programmed in the graphics modes, but the alphanumeric modes will operate much quicker when text is the only output desired. It is certainly possible to load non-character symbols within these large character boxes. This permits the eloquent use of icons within the alphanumeric modes.

Small-character sets are also advantageous, especially when high-resolution screens are desired. The problem is readability. One solution is called *anti-aliased* character fonts, available on at least one Super VGA. Aliasing is a term borrowed from signal processing. It has to do with violating the constraints set

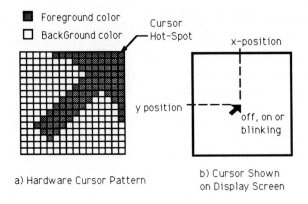

a) Hardware Cursor Pattern   b) Cursor Shown
                                       on Display Screen

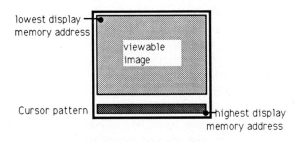

c) Location of Cursor Pattern
in Display Memory

FIGURE 13.7 Hardware Cursor

up when sampling continuous signals into a digital format. In imaging, it may
be thought of as an undesirable effect associated with *pixelation*. A character
that suffers from not having enough pixels can be enhanced by adding gray
scale to the character. This is illustrated in Figure 13.8.

The most notable new feature in the Super VGAs is the graphics accelerator.
The graphics accelerators have evolved the VGA from a dumb frame buffer into
a powerful graphics system. The details of the graphics accelerators are provided in Chapter 14.

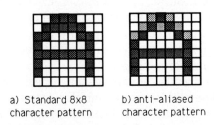

a) Standard 8x8   b) anti-aliased
character pattern   character pattern

FIGURE 13.8 Anti-aliased Character Pattern

13.5 VIDEO ELECTRONICS STANDARDS ASSOCIATION (VESA)

The consortium of graphics card and video monitor manufacturers (VESA) has made an attempt to standardize the Super VGAs. Unfortunately, this attempt comes after most of the damage has already been done. VESA has recommended that an 800-by-600 16-color graphics mode be standardized; I hope that 1024-by-768 16-color and 640-by-480, 800-by-600 and 1024-by-768 256-color mode standards will follow. In addition, VESA has recommended several new video BIOS calls.

13.5.1 VESA Display Mode 6a hex

The standard defines a common BIOS interface to the VGA 800-by-600 16-color mode. This interface is an extension to the standard VGA interface.

The mode is invoked by the Set Mode video BIOS function as normal, using the mode number 6a hex to indicate the 800-by-600 16-color mode. The BIOS data area changes are listed in Table 13.8.

13.5.2 VESA Video BIOS Extensions

The two goals of the VESA BIOS Extension are to return information about the video environment to the application and to assist the application in initializing and programming the hardware. A software application has no standardized mechanism for determining the presence of a particular video card. To make this determination, the application must read specific I/O registers within the VGA and the extended VGA register space. A set of routines for determining the video card is provided in Chapters 14 and 15. Without a close-up knowledge of the particular VGA chip used on the interrogated card and the surrounding features of the card, the application cannot take advantage of the card's special features.

The VESA BIOS Extension provides functions to return information about the video environment. These functions return system level information and video mode specific details. These functions are listed in Table 13.9 and are further described in Table 13.10.

TABLE 13.8 Video BIOS Data Area Changes with Mode 6a hex

Name	Address	Size	Description	New Value
CRT Mode	40:0049	Byte	Current BIOS video mode	Not Specified
CRT Cols	40:004a	Word	Number of video columns	64hex = 100
CRT Len	40:004c	Word	Size of video buffer	F000h=61,440
Rows	40:0084	Byte	# of character rows-1	Not Specified
Points	40:0085	Word	# of bytes per character	Not Specified

TABLE 13.9 VESA BIOS Extensions

Function	Name	Description
00	Return Super VGA Information	Return general system information about the general capabilities of the Super VGA environment. A 256-byte buffer is return to the caller.
01	Return Super VGA Mode Information	Return information about a specific Super VGA video mode. A 256-byte buffer is return to the caller.
02	Set Super VGA Video Mode	Initialize a Super VGA video mode in a similar way that the standard Set Mode BIOS call operates.
03	Return Current Video Mode	Return the current video mode number in a similar way that the standard Read Current Video State BIOS call operates.
04	Save/Restore Video State	Save or restore the Super VGA video state, including all registers, DAC registers, and BIOS Data Area.
05	CPU Video Memory Control	Provide access to the video memory through bank switching.

Details of each of these functions follow in the following four sections. The status word returned by the following BIOS calls is described in Table 13.10. This code applies to all of the VESA Extended BIOS function calls.

TABLE 13.10 Return Status Information

Register	Value	Description
AL	== 4F hex	Function is supported
AL	!= 4F hex	Function is NOT supported
AH	== 00 hex	Function call was executed successfully
AH	!= 00 hex	Function call was NOT executed successfully

13.5.3 BIOS Return Super VGA Information

The AH = 4f hex, Al=00h function 00h provide information regarding the general capabilites of the Super VGA environment. The function fills an information block structure at the address specified by the caller. The information block size is 256 bytes.

Output Parameters:

ES:DI = segment:offset far pointer to calling routine buffer where the information block should be loaded.

AX = Status as indicated in Table 13.10

The VGA block information is described in Table 13.11.

The *VESASignature* field contains the character string *VESA* if this is a valid VESA structure. (Note: The string is not terminated with a Null character to indicate the end of a string.)

The *VESAVersion* field is the VESA standard to which the Super VGA BIOS conforms. The higher byte specifies the major version number, and the lower byte specifies the minor version number. The intial VESA version number is 1.0. VESA versions are upwardly compatible.

The *OEMStringPtr* field is a far pointer to a Null terminated OEM-defined string. The string may be used to identify the video chip, video board, memory configuration and others. The only restriction for the format of the string is the NULL termination.

The *Capabilities* field describes the general features supported in the video environment. The long integer contains 32 bits, and none has been defined.

TABLE 13.11 The VGA Information Block Structure

Name	Size	Value	Description
VESASignature	4 bytes	'VESA'	4-byte signature indicating this is a valid VESA structure.
VESAVersion	word	?	Current VESA BIOS version number
OEMStringPtr	long	?	Far pointer to OEM string identifying the VGA implementation
Capabilities	4 bytes	?	Capability of the video environment indicating the supported features.
VideoModePtr	long	?	Far pointer to supported VGA mode list.

TABLE 13.12   VESA Mode Number Format

Bit Position	Description	Value
Bit 15	Reserved	set to 0
Bit 14–9	Reserved by VESA for future expansion	set to 0
Bit 8	VESA mode	0 = Not a VESA mode 1 = VESA mode
Bit 7–0	Mode number	0–ff hex

The *VideoModePtr* field is a far pointer to a list of supported Super VGA mode numbers. These mode numbers may be VESA standard modes or manufacture specific mode numbers. Each mode number is one 16-bit word long. (Note: The list is terminated with a–1 value FFFF hex. This list might be a static list located in ROM or a dynamic list loaded in RAM. The mode numbers as defined by VESA are described in Table 13.11.)

The standard mode numbers are seven bits wide and the standard VGA modes range from 0 to 13 hex. The extended modes, as defined by the manufacturers, range from 14 hex to 7f hex. Values greater than 7f hex = 127 cannot be used since bit 7 indicates to the BIOS mode Set command, whether the display memory to be used in the desired mode will be cleared or not.

The VESA mode numbers are 15 bits wide, as shown in Table 13.12. Note that the VESA mode numbers range from 100 hex to 1FF hex. There can only be 256 possible VESA modes since bit 8 is a flag that indicates whether the mode is a VESA-defined mode.

The one mode that VESA has defined, mode 6A hex, is an 800-by-600 16-color mode. The official VESA mode number for this mode is 102 hex. Additional modes defined by VESA are listed in Table 13.13.

13.5.4   BIOS Return Super VGA Mode Information

The AH = 4f hex, Al=01h function 00h provides information to the calling program about a specific Super VGA video mode. The function fills an information block structure at the address specified by the caller. The information block size is a maximum of 256 bytes. Both a VESA-defined mode and a non-VESA-defined mode can be queried for using this BIOS mode. Note that some implementations may not support the non-VESA-defined modes.

Input Parameters:
   CX = super VESA or non-VESA VGA video mode of which information is desired

TABLE 13.13   VESA-Defined Modes

VESA Mode Number	Columns	Rows	Bits per Color
102 or 6A hex	800	600	4
104 hex	1024	768	4
106 hex	1280	1024	4
100 hex	640	400	8
101 hex	640	480	8
103 hex	800	600	8
104 hex	1024	768	8
106 hex	1280	1024	8
10D hex	320	200	15
110 hex	640	480	15
113 hex	800	600	15
116 hex	1024	768	15
119 hex	1280	1024	15
10E hex	320	200	16
111 hex	640	480	16
114 hex	800	600	16
117 hex	1024	768	16
11A hex	1280	1024	16
10F hex	320	200	24
112 hex	640	480	24
115 hex	800	600	24
118 hex	1024	768	24
11B hex	1280	1024	24
??? hex	320	200	32
??? hex	640	480	32
??? hex	800	600	32
??? hex	1024	768	32
??? hex	1280	1024	32

Output Parameters:
   ES:DI = segment:offset far pointer to calling routine buffer where the information block should be loaded.
   AX = Status as indicated in Table 13.10

TABLE 13.14 Mandatory Information Structure Describing a Video Mode

Name	Size	Description
ModeAttributes	word	Mode attributes describing important characteristics of the video mode
WinAAttributes	byte	Describe characteristics of the CPU windowing scheme for window A
WinBAttributes	byte	Describe characteristics of the CPU windowing scheme for window B
WinGranularity	word	Defines the smallest boundary, in Kbytes, on which the window can be placed in video memory.
WinSize	word	Specifies the size of the window in Kbytes
WinASegment	word	Segment address of where the window A is located in host address space
WinBSegment	word	Segment address of where the window B is located in host address space
WinFuncPtr	long	Far Pointer to the function that actually performs the windowing
BytesPerScanLine	word	Number of bytes that each logical scanline consists of. A logical scan line can be equal or greater than the displayed scanline

The mandatory mode information block is described in Table 13.14. The optional Mode Information Block is described in Table 13.15. The optional mode information block will be present if bit 1 of the ModeAttributes bit is set to 1.

The mode attribute field, *ModeAttributes*, describes certain important characteristics of the video memory, as indicated in Table 13.15. The window attributes fields, *WinAAttributes* and *WinBAttributes* describe characteristics of the windowing scheme, as described in Table 13.16.

Examples of optional information that can be found in the mode information block are included in Table 13.17.

The memory model field, *MemoryModel*, describes the memory organization, as indicated in Table 13.18.

The number of banks field, *NumberOfBanks*, contains the number of banks in which the scan lines are grouped. For example, the CGA and Hercules have distinct banks of memory that are not sequentially mapped to the screen. CGA graphics modes have two banks, and the Hercules graphics modes have four

TABLE 13.15 Mode Attribute Bit Fields

Bit	Function
0	Specifies whether this mode can be initialled in the current video configuration. This bit can block access to a video mode if there is some environmental condition precluding its usage; that is, the monitor attached to the VGA is not sufficient to handle the blocked mode's resolution.
1	Specifies whether the extended mode information is available. Video modes defined by VESA will have certain known characteristics. This extended information is an optional provision in the information block as described in Table 13.14. It is optional due to the space constraints for ROM-based implementations of the VESA BIOS extensions. Since the VESA-defined modes are standardized, this optional information is already known and need not be included.
2	Indicates whether the BIOS has support for output functions. Some typical output functions include TTY output, scrolling, and pixel. VESA recommends that the BIOS support all output functions.
3	Indicates whether the mode is a monochrome or color mode. Monochrome modes, as indicated by a 0 in bit 3 of Table 13.12, maps the CRTC register pairs to addresses 3B4/3B5 hex. Color modes, as indicated by a 1 in bit 3 of Table 13.12, maps the CRTC register pairs to addresses 3D4/3D5. 0= monochrome mode 1 = color mode
4	Indicates whether the mode is a text mode or a graphics mode. Text modes utilize bit planes 0 and 1 for character and attribute codes respectively. They utilize bit planes 2 and 3 for the character font bit patterns. 0 = text mode 1 = graphics mode

banks. If the scan line number is divided by the number of banks, the remainder is the bank that contains the scan line. The resultant quotient is the scan line number within the bank.

Consider the following example. Suppose a CGA mode with two banks is in effect. To locate scan line 131, divide 131 by two. This yields a quotient of 65 and a remainder of 1. Thus, the scan line is in bank 1 and is located in scan line 65 within that bank.

TABLE 13.16 Window Attribute Bit Fields

Bit	Function
0	Whether the window A or B is supported.
	0 = Window A or B is not supported
	1 = Window A or B is supported
1	Whether the window A or B is readable
	0 = Window A or B is not readable
	1 = Window A or B is readable
2	Whether the window A or B is writeable
	0 = Window A or B is not writeable
	1 = Window A or B is writeable
3–15	Reserved for future expansion.

TABLE 13.17 Optional Information in the Mode Information Block

Name	Size	Description
XResolution	word	Horizontal resolution in pixels
YResolution	word	Vertical resolution in pixels
XCharSize	byte	Character cell width
YCharSize	byte	Character cell height
NumbeofPlanes	byte	Number of memory planes
BitsPerPixel	byte	Number of bits per pixel
NumberofBanks	byte	Number of banks. The bank size is indicated in the BankSize field.
MemoryModel	byte	Memory model type. See Table 13.18.
BankSize	byte	Size of each memory bank in Kbytes. Modes that do not use scan line banks would set this field to 0.

The bank size field, *BankSize*, specifies the size of each bank as previously described in units of Kbytes. The CGA-compatible modes and the Hercules compatible modes each have 8192 bytes per bank. Thus, the value of this field would be set to 8. Modes that do not have scanline banks would set this field to 0.

13.5.5 BIOS Set Super VGA Video Mode

The AH = 4f hex, Al=02h function 02 initializes a super video mode. The BX register contains the Super VGA mode to set. The format of the VESA mode numbers is described in Table 13.13. If the mode cannot be set, the BIOS

TABLE 13.18 Memory Model Types

Code	Memory Type
00 hex	Text mode
01 hex	CGA mode
02 hex	Hercules graphics mode
03 hex	4-plane planar mode
04 hex	Packed pixel mode
05 hex	Non-chain 4, 256-color mode
06–0F hex	Reserved for future use by VESA
10–FF hex	To be defined by the card or chip manufacturer

should leave the video environment unchanged. An error code is returned as described in Table 13.10.

Input Parameters:
BX   Video Mode
        Bit 0–14 = video mode as per Table 13.13
        Bit 15 is a flag indicating whether the display memory that will be affected by this mode should be cleared.
            Bit 15=1   Clear video memory
            Bit 15=0   Do not clear video memory

Output Parameters:
AX   Status as described in Table 13.10

13.5.6   AH = 4f Hex, Al=03h: Return Current VGA Video Mode

Function 03 returns the current video mode. The BX Register contains the desired VGA mode to return. The format of the VESA mode numbers is described in Table 13.10. This function is similar to the Read Current Video State BIOS call, AH=0F hex, described in Chapter 11.9.4. The main difference is that the video mode is returned in the AL Register as a byte, and this function returns the mode as a word in the BX Register. A second difference is that the clear option is not indicated in the mode number. The BIOS Set Mode, Function 00 hex described in Chapter 11.2.1, and the VESA Set Super VGA Video Mode, Function 02 hex just described in Section 13.5.5, allow the user to optionally clear the memory. In the AH=OF BIOS call, the state of the display memory clearing is returned in bit 7. This is not the case in this VESA Function 03 hex call. The Memory-Clear bit will not be returned in the BX Register since the purpose of this call is to return the mode number. If the clear state is desired, the application should inquire through bit 7 of the mode value in the

BIOS state area of host memory at byte location 40:0087. It can also be determined by calling the BIOS Read Current Video Mode function 0F.

Output Parameters:
BX   Video Mode
        Bit 0–14 = video mode as per Table 13.10
AX   Status as described in Table 13.10

13.5.7   BIOS Save/Restore Super VGA Video State

The AH = 4f hex, Al=04h function 04 hex provides a means to save and restore the Super VGA video state. The functions are a superset of the three subfunctions of the standard VGA BIOS call Function 1C hex described in Section 11.15.3. There are three subfunctions within this BIOS call. These determine the actual operation of this call and are selected through the DL Register. The three subfunctions allow the return of the size of the save/restore state buffer. This saves the Super VGA video state and restores the Super VGA video state described in Table 13.19.

There are four possible states that can be saved. These include the video hardware state, the video BIOS data state, the video DAC state, and the Super VGA state. The first three are identical to the three states stored in the standard BIOS Save/Restore Video State function AH=1C hex call described in

TABLE 13.19   Save/Restore Super VGA Video States Subfunctions

Subfunction	Description
00 hex	Return the size of the buffer to be loaded with data if a save state is called or read from if a restore state is called. The size indicates the number of 64-byte blocks needed to hold the data. For example, if the size, as returned in the BX register, is 15, the buffer should be 15*64=960 bytes long.
01 hex	Save the Super VGA video state. The state of the VGA will be read as indicated in the requested states field described in Table 13.17. When the states are combined, the data relevant to these states will be loaded into the buffer in a specific order. This same order will be used for the analogous Restore State function.
02 hex	Restore the Super VGA video state. The state of the VGA will be written as indicated in the requested states field described in Table 13.17. When the states are combined, the data relevant to these states will be read from the buffer in a specific order. This same order would have been used by the analogous Save State function.

TABLE 13.20 Save/Restore Function Requested States

Blt	Requested State
0	Save/restore the video hardware state
1	Save/restore the video BIOS data state
2	Save/restore the video DAC state
3	Save/restore the Super VGA state

Section 11.15.3. The fourth handles the Super VGA states. These are described in Table 13.20. The first three states should be the same from one VGA adapter to another. The fourth state should not be assumed to be compatible across different VGA adapters.

The four possible requested states can be combined to form sixteen possible combinations. For example, a request state code of A hex = 1010 binary would indicate that the data in the save/restore buffer would contain the Super VGA state and the video hardware state.

Subfunction DL=00

Subfunction DL=00 returns the size of the buffer in 64-byte blocks necessary for a save state or expected for a restore state BIOS call. The size is determined by the requested states.

Input Parameters:
DL=0   Return the buffer size of the save/restore buffer
CX   Requested states as indicated in Table 13.19

Output Parameters:
AX   Status as indicated in Table 13.10
BX   Number of 64-byte blocks that are required for the size of the buffer in order to store/restore the requested states.

Subfunction DL=01

Subfunction DL=01 saves the Super VGA state. The requested states, as indicated in the CX Register, will determine the areas of the VGA to be saved and the order in which they will be loaded into the buffer. It is possible to determine the size of each area and the order in which each is saved in the buffer by experimentation. The size, in 64-byte blocks, of each state can be determined by calling subfunction 1 four times with one state requested for each call. The order within the buffer can be determined by searching through the data for matching patterns. This really should not be necessary as long as the same states are requested for complimentary save and restore calls.

Input Parameters:

DL=1   Save the Super VGA state

CX   Requested states as indicated in Table 13.17

ES:BX   Segment:Offset address of buffer that will contain the data as saved from the Super VGA. The size and ordering of this buffer conforms to the requested states.

Output Parameters:

AX   Status as indicated in Table 13.10

Subfunction DL=02

Subfunction DL=2 restores the Super VGA state. The requested states, as indicated in the CX Register, will determine the areas of the VGA to be restored and the order in which they will be loaded into the buffer. It is possible to determine the size of each area and the order in which each is saved in the buffer by experimentation. The size, in 64-byte blocks of each state, can be determined by calling subfunction 1 four times with one state requested for each call. The order within the buffer can be determined by searching through the data for matching patterns. This should not be necessary as long as the same states are requested for complimentary save and restore calls.

Input Parameters:

DL=2   Restore the Super VGA state

CX   Requested states as indicated in Table 13.17

ES:BX   Segment:Offset address of buffer that is expected to contain the data which will be restored into the Super VGA. The size and ordering of this buffer conforms to the requested states.

Output Parameters:

AX   Status as indicated in Table 13.10

13.5.8   BIOS CPU Video Memory Window Control

The AH = 4f hex, Al=05h function 04 hex provides a means to set or get the position of a specified window in the video memory. This function allows direct access to the hardware paging registers. To use this function, the application can obtain the size, location, and granularity of the desired window through the Return Super VGA mode information, VESA BIOS function 01 hex described in

Section 13.5.4. This function has two subfunctions for selecting the video memory window or the returning of the window position.

Two windows are possible—windows A and B. These are described and defined in Table 13.11. The two windows exist because several of the Super VGAs use two-paging schemes. The ability to use two pages is important because speed is usually an issue.

When moving memory from one location to another it is necessary to maintain two sets of pointers, one for the source data and another for the destination data. In the host, this is accomplished by the DS:SI source address register pair and ES:DI for the destination address register pair. These segment:offset registers describe the 18-bit address necessary to completely describe the address. In the VGA, when mapped into the PC address space A0000–AFFFF space, this is a bit more complex. Paging or Bank Registers are necessary to hold the upper address because the display memory is no longer contiguous. Maintaining two Page Registers allows data to be transferred without constantly fiddling with the page (bank) registers.

An example is when the MOVSx instruction is used. If dual paging is engaged, the DS and ES Registers are set to the display memory segment address A000. The DI and SI offset Registers point to the offset of the data within each segment. The Page (bank) Registers are set to their respective banks. At this point all necessary pointers are initialized, and a REP MOVSx instruction can be executed. Up to 64 Kbytes can be transferred without ever touching a Page (bank) Register.

The two Page (bank) Registers correspond to the windows A and B pointers described below. If only one Page Register is used, only one window should be utilized. Otherwise, both windows A and B should point to identical locations.

Both windows A and B functions can be directly accessed through a far call from the application. The address of the BIOS function may be obtained from the VESA BIOS function 01 as described in Section 13.5.4. A field in the ModeInfoBlock, described in Table 13.11, contains the far pointer address to this function. The location of this function may change when the VGA is in different video modes. Therefore, the location of this function should be interrogated after each mode set. Note that even this direct function call might be too time consuming. It may be desirable to directly access the Super VGA registers responsible for the bank setting. Techniques vary for each VGA implementation. Several techniques are described in Chapter 15.

In the far call version, the AX and DX registers are not preserved. The application must load the input parameters in the BX and DX registers for the set window command. However, it is not necessary to load the AX Register when using the far call version of this function. When using the direct, register-setting techniques described in Chapter 15, each function must be scrutinized to determine the specific registers involved.

Subfunction BH=00

Subfunction BH=00 selects a Super VGA window memory window. There are two possible windows, either A or B. The window number, window A or B, is input to this subfunction. The window position in video memory, according to the window granularity units, is returned.

In the following example, the window granularity is 4 Kbytes and 64 windows would describe the full 1 Mbyte space. This is the case when a 256-color mode is engaged, and the 4 Kbyte segment corresponds to 4 Kbytes in each of the four planes totaling 16 Kbytes. Thus, 16 Kbytes * 64 = 1 Mbyte. When the window points to 512 Kbytes, it is equivalent to half way into memory, which corresponds to a window location of 32.

Input Parameters:

BH=00   Select Super VGA video memory window

BL   Window number

           0 = Window A

           1 = WindowB

DX   Window position in video memory. This value is according to window granularity.

Output Parameters:

AX   Status as indicated in Table 13.10

Subfunction BH=01

Subfunction BH=01 return the Super VGA window memory window number. Windows A and B are the only two possible windows. The window number for one of these two is input to this subfunction, and the window position in video memory, according to the window granularity units, is returned. This function returns the current window number of the selected window.

Input Parameters:

BH=00   Return Super VGA video memory window

BL   Window number

           0 = Window A

           1 = Window B

Output Parameters:

AX   Status as indicated in Table 13.10

DX   Window position in video memory. This value is according to window granularity.

13.6 IDENTIFYING THE GRAPHICS ENVIRONMENT

Each implementation of the VGA has its own specific potential and programming specifics. However, there are many similarities. Section 13.6 presents the theory and background of some of the similarities. Chapter 14 provides application specific details. Chapter 15 contains program examples that implement these basic features.

The discussions in this section provide details about the following: definitions, techniques and problems associated with identifying the VGA, controlling the VGA, saving and restoring the state of the VGA, memory addressing techniques, writing to display memory, and selecting a start address.

The first three items, identifying the VGA, controlling the VGA, and saving and restoring the state of the VGA, will become much simpler when the VGA adapter manufacturers and the BIOS programmers implement the VESA standards associated with identifying which VGA chip is present, the capabilities of the adapter surrounding the chip, and a BIOS call to save and restore the Extended registers. Section 13.6.1, 13.6.2 and 13.6.3 help describe these functions. The corresponding VESA definitions are found in Sections 13.5.

The last three items, memory addressing techniques, writing to display memory, and selecting a starting address, will describe in detail how memory is actually organized. The reader may select to use these techniques and the program examples provided in Chapter 15 instead of the VESA standard BIOS call, which handles changing banks (pages, windows). The principle reason for this choice is speed. Although the Al=05h BIOS call named *CPU Video Memory Window Control* described in Section13.5.8 has an associated direct function call, this may still be too slow for several applications.

Any program that intends to use the advanced features of the Super VGAs will have to determine the graphics environment installed on the host computer. This can be a simple or a complex task. In general, the pertinent questions that must be answered about the graphics environment are which other cards beside the VGA are present, which VGA chip is present, and the potentials of the VGA card itself. Several of these important issues are listed in Table 13.21.

13.6.1 The Graphics Environment

Most computer systems contain one graphics card, although some contain none or multiple cards. It is assumed that at least one VGA is present. Other graphics cards can coexist with the VGA card. There are monochrome graphics cards, MDA and Hercules, less powerful color graphics cards, CGA, EGA, other VGA graphics cards, and cards including 8514/A, TIGA, or special purpose cards.

If a monochrome card coexists with the VGA, the VGA must be configured in a color mode. By configuring the VGA into a color mode, the CRTC registers will be located at 3D4/3D5. Other registers in the Super VGA register sets may

TABLE 13.21 Assessing the Graphics Environment

Question	Possibilities
Other graphics cards?	Yes, No
Which graphics cards?	CGA, MDA, VGA, multiple VGAs, Super VGA, XGA, 8514/A, TIGA, other
VESA supported?	No, Yes
VESA version implemented?	Integer
Manufacturer of VAG chip?	ATI, Chips and Tech, Genoa, Paradise, Trident, Tseng, Video 7
Chip identification number?	Integer
Chip version?	Integer
Location?	Motherboard or Adapter Card
Host interface?	8 bit, 16 bit or 32 bit
Amount of display memory?	256 Kbytes, 512 Kbytes, 1 Mbyte, 2 Mbytes, 4 Mbytes
16-color display modes accommodated?	800x600, 1024X768, 1280x1024, etc. interlaced or noninterlaced
256-color display modes accommodated?	640x400, 640x480, 800x600, 1024x768, etc.
Emulation modes available?	No, CGA, MDA, Hercules, EGA, 8514/A
Color DAC?	6-bit, 8-bit, 16-bit, 24-bit per color
Type of Monitor?	Monochrome, Standard Frequency, Multi-syncing

be affected by this setting. The monochrome memory will reside at B0000–B7FFF hex while the VGA memory will reside between A0000–AFFFF hex. There are exceptions to this location, as certain VGA cards will allow their memory, when configured in a color mode, to be mapped into A0000–BFFFF hex. Details are discussed in Chapter 14.

There seem to be no 16-bit monochrome cards. This can cause a problem if 16-bit memory accesses are desired to and from the VGA. Since the VGA has no way of enabling 16-bit address to addresses A0000–AFFFF without including B0000–BFFFF, 16-bit accesses will be forced upon the poor and unsuspecting monochrome card. This can cause bus conflicts and/or unpredictable results. I find that using a monochrome monitor in conjunction with a VGA card is essential when debugging graphics applications. This is especially true when using a debugger, like Microsoft's *CodeView*, which has the facility to handle two simultaneous graphics systems.

Some VGA manufacturers claim that no other graphics card can coexist with their VGA. In these cases, I recommend using the monochrome card with their VGA anyway. This restriction was created by IBM designers who designed the AT bus with such a major limitation as 128 Kbyte accesses limited to 16-bit transfers.

If a color graphics card, CGA, coexists with the VGA in question, that VGA must be set up in a monochrome mode. The CRTC registers will be mapped to 3B4/3B5, and the memory will reside at B0000–B7FFF hex. Once again, unpredictable results will occur if the VGA is configured in a 16-bit memory access mode.

The EGA, being so similar to the VGA, cannot coexist with the VGA unless the VGA card can be disabled. This situation is similar to having multiple VGAs in the same system. The IBM PS/2 VGA was designed on the motherboard and had the capability of being disabled. Several of the Super VGAs share this capability, allowing multiple VGA systems to operate in parallel. One can immediately see the importance of this feature once multi-user operating systems, such as UNIX, hit the PC platforms with graphical interfaces such as X-Windows.

There are three ways of approaching multiple monitors. The first is to utilize a high-speed data link such as ethernet going to an ethernet-compatible user station. This link is standard in the workstation environment. Currently, monitors supporting X-Windows are available. They eliminate the need for multiple processors on the network. It would be possible to interface a microprocessor, ethernet adapter, some memory and a VGA chip to a monitor and keyboard and have a remote VGA workstation. This would be especially well suited to applications requiring remote stations.

A second possibility is to have multiple VGAs with only one active at a time on the host bus. In this case, all but one VGA would be "asleep" with respect to the host. Each could have the same port and memory addresses and a single control register with a ID code. Most VGAs have the ability to be asleep. Of course, all monitors would have to be within video monitor cable distance from the VGA cards. Some cards are equipped with multiple VGAs on a single card.

A third and preferable condition is for the VGAs to map into different memory and I/O space when distances are not an issue. With the 80386 address space, there is enough elbow room for about a thousand or so VGAs. In some cases, the Super VGAs can remap memory and I/O address space to accommodate multiple VGA implementations. Typically, this re-mapping would be used in conjunction with a restructuring of the VGA address space to remove overlapping memory. The advantages of the linear address space with the 80386's 32 bit instructions are significant.

The 8514/A adapter is compatible with the VGA and requires a VGA to operate. In 1987, IBM introduced the VGA and the 8514/A at the same time. The hooks for the 8514/A are designed into the IBM standard video BIOS on the

VGA. Similar to the TIGA graphics adapters described in the following paragraph, the 8514/A requires a standard DOS adapter. This is certainly a drawback. 8514/A cards have either a feedthrough capability for a VGA or an on-board VGA. Transfer of control from one display mode that runs on the VGA to one that runs on the 8514/A is easily and eloquently accomplished through the BIOS on the VGA. This is one advantage that the 8514/A has over the TIGA-based cards.

The TIGA graphics adapters, based on the Texas Instruments TI34010 and TI34020 coprocessors, coexist with the VGA. Currently, the PC has to have a standard adapter in order to boot up. This might be an MDA, Hercules, CGA, EGA, VGA, or 8514/A. Several of the TIGA cards have an onboard VGA, or a feedthrough path for the VGA. Having a separate VGA card means a separate monitor. Having a feedthrough path allows the user to utilize the same monitor. Of course, the monitor has to have syncing capabilities to handle both the VGA and the TIGA adapter.

There is no simple technique to inquire as to which cards are available on the system. In the case of an MDA or Hercules card, the VGA is set up in a color mode, and its display memory is typically mapped at A0000–AFFFF or from B8000–BFFFF. The CRTC registers is mapped at 3D4/3D5. The Hercules or MDA display memory is located at B0000–B0FFF, and its control registers are located between 3B0–3BF. It is possible to read a value in this memory space, replace it with another value, and read it again and see if the value changed. If this can be performed, a Hercules or MDA is present. The original value should then be replaced. Another technique is to read/modify/rewrite one of the Control Registers in a similar fashion as was done to the memory.

If a CGA is present, the VGA will be set up as a monochrome system with its display memory at B0000–B7FFF and the CRTC Registers located at 3B4/3B5. The CGA display memory resides at B8000–B8FFF, and its Control Registers reside at 3D4/3D5. Similar techniques to those used in the preceding paragraph could be used to determine whether a CGA card is present.

If multiple VGAs are present, the specific VGA card documentation must be consulted to determine how the VGA discriminates between the multiple VGAs.

13.6.2 Is VESA Supported?

Luckily, VESA has a well-defined BIOS call that identifies whether VESA is present and if so, which version. This is outlined in Table 13.10.

13.6.3 Determining Which VGA Is Present

Each Super VGA has a fingerprint that can be traced by looking for certain clues. A message may be hiding in BIOS; a particular register that is not present in the other Super VGA implementations may be present.

TABLE 13.22 Super VGA Chips Detailed in This Book

Manufacturer	Chip Numbers
ATI	18800,28800, 38800 (Mach8) and 68800 (Mach32)
Avance	Ultra+
Chips & Technology	82c451, 82c452, 82c343, 82c455, 82c456
Cirrus	54xx, 62xx, 64xx
Genoa	5000, GVGA
Headland/Video7	VEGA, V7VGA,
Integrated Info Tech (IIT)	AGX-014, AGX-015
NCR	77c22e+
Oak	037, 067, 077, 087, 107
S3	911, 924, 928, 801,805
Trident	8800, 8900, 8900CL, 8900CxR, 9000, 9200, 9420
Tseng Labs	ET3000, ET4000, ET4000-W32
Western Digital	PVGA1a, 90c00, 90c10, 90c11, 90c30, 90c31, 90c33
Weitek	P9000

Chapters 14 through 19 provide detailed descriptions for identifying six of the popular VGA chips. The chips selected include ATI, Chips and Technologies, Paradise, Trident, Tseng Labs, and the Video7 VGA Chips. In certain cases, these manufacturers have more than one VGA chip and it is necessary to distinguish which particular chip is present. The chips described in this book are listed in Table 13.22.

13.6.4 Determining the VGA Host Interface

It is necessary to identify the type of host interface in order to interface to these chips. In some cases, registers will be located in different locations depending on whether the VGA is on the motherboard or on an adapter. The speed advantages inherent with the motherboard-located VGAs is significant, and the future will certainly see a growing popularity of VGA implementations on the motherboard.

A second reason to determine the type of host interface deals with the 8- and 16-bit interfaces. All Super VGA chips can handle the 16-bit host interface. The three aspects of this interface include the BIOS, the I/O ports, and the display memory. All 16-bit cards can be configured to operate in either the 8-bit or 16-bit mode. Some have auto sensing; others have switch settings or jumpers. Still others have programmable registers that control the interface; a few more have a combination of the above.

It is not always true that "more is better." Quite often "more" means more trouble. In cases when the width of the interface uses automatic sensing through switch settings or through jumpers, the programmer is relinquished of responsibility. However, a programmable interface is another story and defies solution.

Here is the problem. The PC bus interface can either transfer memory or I/O. Both are presented with a 16-bit enable control line called MEM16 and IO16 respectively. The I/O ports are the easiest to interface. Typically they interface to hardware registers that are fast and simple. The host has considerable time to set up a 16-bit I/O transfer, and the adapter can decode all of the slow address lines. Thus, every port address can be decoded individually to determine if that particular port address is an 8- or 16-bit port. Usually the speed of the host bus will not affect the operation of the 16-bit ports.

The memory transfers are more complicated. These encompass both the BIOS instruction execution transfers and the display memory data transfers. The host does not have much time to set up the 8- or 16-bit transfer, and consequently, the adapter cannot decode all of the address lines. Chunks of address space in 128 Kbyte increments have to be decoded as one entity. The problem is that there are no 128 Kbyte segments dedicated just to the VGA. The host memory address space utilization is generally mapped in Table 13.23.

As for BIOS transfers, Table 13.23 shows that the Video BIOS area shares the 128 Kbyte space with the Hard Disk BIOS and host BIOS. Typically, the host BIOS and the disk BIOS are not a source of problems. The Host BIOS is not a problem since it is typically sixteen bits wide and does not depend on the MEM16 line since it is not on an adapter card. The disk BIOS is typically not a problem because most disk controllers used in 16-bit bus systems utilize the 16-bit interface.

The MEM16 and IO16 line are open-collector lines. This means that more than one source can pull the line down at a time without any hardware con-

TABLE 13.23 16-bit Memory Address Decoding Map

Host Address Range	Typical Usage
00000–1FFFF	Interrupt Vectors, ROM BIOS Communications Area, DOS Communications Area
20000–3FFFF	DOS
40000–5FFFF	Device drivers, Resident command.com
60000–7FFFF	RAM, random buffers, control blocks
80000–9FFFF	RAM
A0000–BFFFF	Video Display Memory for Monochrome and Color
C0000–DFFFF	Video BIOS, Hard Disk BIOS and host BIOS
E0000–FFFFF	Host BIOS

flicts. Thus, it is likely that both the Super VGA and the hard disk controller are always both pulling down MEM16.

A problem does exist in the non-defined memory area between the Video BIOS, which starts at C000 hex, and the Hard Disk BIOS, which starts at C8000. Industrious third-party manufacturers have squeezed their BIOS codes into this area. If their 8-bit or 16-bit card cannot support an 8-bit BIOS, their card will not function properly.

Consider the following example. Suppose the VGA in question is just sitting idle while a third-party scanner card is being accessed. Further suppose the scanner sends an interrupt, and the host interrupt vector sends the program counter to location C6000, location of the scanner BIOS. The scanner BIOS is only eight bits wide and does not even interface to the connector that contains the MEM16 signal. It is innocent. It is just in the wrong place at the wrong time. The address C6000 gets exerted onto the bus and before the scanner can respond, the superfast decoding logic on the Super VGA determines that the address did reside within C0000 and DFFFF. It exerts MEM16 and then remains off the bus since it has no business with C6000. Unfortunately, the damage is already done! The host has sensed the MEM16 line and reads in an instruction from the scanner, which it is expecting to be sixteen bits wide. Nobody is responding to C6000 and so the upper eight bits of the bus are in a tri-stated condition. The instruction makes no sense to the host and trouble results.

So, what is a programmer to do? Perhaps an interactive operator setup procedure is necessary before engaging the 16-bit interface. More typically, an application will simply kick-in the 16-bit interface and let the buyer sort it out.

13.6.5 Determining Which Modes are Supported

A Super VGA BIOS can have defined several high resolution modes and will respond to commands to install these modes. However, the VGA card may not be equipped with enough memory or the monitor attached to the VGA may not be sufficient to handle all of the display modes.

Let us consider the issue of having enough memory. The Super VGAs are equipped with either 256 Kbytes, 512 Kbytes, or 1 Mbyte. Soon versions will appear with 4 Mbytes. Each Super VGA has its own display modes, but not all defined modes will run on a given implementation. This is due to variations in the amount of display memory present, as well as the type of adapter and monitor. It is a simple issue to perform a start-up test to determine the amount of memory residing on the card. One performs read/modify writes through the various banks until the memory runs out.

The monitor is more difficult to detect. The VESA standard includes a table indicating valid display modes. This table can be interrogated to determine whether a mode can be used. In some Super VGAs, a register contains information regarding the monitor type. These cards perform automatic monitor sensing and set up themselves at power on. Warnings are provided to ensure that a different monitor is not attached while power is on. These user-friendly cards do not allow display modes inappropriate for the monitor type. The programmer can attempt to set a mode and look for an error in the return parameter.

13.6.6 Determining the Emulation Modes

The techniques used for setting up downward compatibility vary from one Super VGA card to another. It is necessary to consult the documentation of individual cards to set up their emulation modes. Some cards provide BIOS calls; others provide set-up programs. Still others provide registers that can be programmed for proper emulation. In any case, the appropriate monitor has to be installed for these emulation modes to function well.

13.6.7 Determining the Resolution of the Color DAC

VGAs operate in either a 1-, 2-, 4-, 8-, 15-, 16-, 24-, or 32-bit per color mode. In any of these modes, the two, four, sixteen, or 256 colors can be either 18-bit or 24-bit color. Unfortunately, there is no standard way to set up the final color resolution. The DAC chips are compatible pin for pin. For a few extra dollars, one can have 24-bit color. Note that this is not "true color," which is also called 24-bit color. There can only be 256 different colors.

It is not the responsibility of the VGA chip to keep track of the type of DAC chip present. The cards that do support the 8-bit-per-color DACS have external decoding, and their documentation should be consulted for details on selecting or determining the DAC color resolution.

In some DACs, there are special conditions such as mixed mode or gray scale. In mixed mode, the image data can be combinations of both hi-color 15-bit per color and palette color. The high-order bit, bit 15, is used to switch each pixel between the straight hi-color or palette color. For example, if bit 15=1, then the DAC is switched such that the lower eight bits are used as a palette DAC lookup. If bit 15=0, the lower fifteen bits are used for the 5-bits per red, green, and blue hi-color. The DACs that are capable of true gray scale require eight bits per output such that there can be 256 distinct shades of gray.

13.7 CONTROLLING THE SUPER VGA

Techniques used to control the Super VGAs range in complexity from turning the VGA on to setting up complex emulation states. Fortunately, the manufacturers have helped programmers by coding many control features in the BIOS. Hardware engineers have implemented the features in hardware.

Some of the control aspects are performed immediately at power up while others occur inside a tight and frequently-used loop. Thus, the speed at which these control functions must be executed varies. The word control is, of course, very broad. Almost anything can be lumped into the category of control.

TABLE 13.24 Controlling the Super VGA

Feature	Technique
Enabling and disabling the VGA	Register, Switch, Autosense
Configuring up the host interface	Register
Accessing the VGA registers	Register, BIOS
Setting display modes	BIOS
Controlling emulation	BIOS, Register
Locking out or protecting registers	Register
Controlling vertical interrupts	Register
Saving and restoring the VGA state	BIOS, Register

Table 13.24 includes those features of the Super VGAs categorized as control features.

13.7.1 Enabling and Disabling the VGA

There are several on/off switches for the VGA. The many techniques for taking firm control of the standard VGA are listed in Table 13.25. Each item is discussed in the following paragraphs. References are made to the appropriate sections in Chapters 1–12 when features are part of the VGA standard.

TABLE 13.25 Resetting and Enabling the Standard VGAs

Function	Purpose	Technique
Asynchronous reset	Reset sequencer	Reset Register Bit 0=0
Synchronous reset	Reset sequencer	Reset Register Bit 1=0
Turn off the screen	Fast memory access	Clocking Mode Register Bit 5=1
Turn on the screen	Display image	Clocking Mode Register Bit 5=0
Enable RAM	Enable host access to RAM	Miscellaneous Output Register Bit 1=1
Disable RAM	Disable host access to RAM	Miscellaneous Output Register Bit 1=0
Disable display	Blank the screen	Attribute Address Register Bit 5=0
Enable display	Normal operation	Attribute Address Register Bit 5=1

As discussed in Section 10.3.2, the standard VGA allows the screen to be turned off by setting bit 5 of the Clocking Mode Register. When turned off, the programmer can achieve maximum bandwidth transfers to the display memory since the host will not be wait-stated due to display refresh cycles. The display monitor is still provided with horizontal and vertical sync pulses and a blanking color. In most implementations, this blanking color is black, while in some this color can be programmed.

To adjust the Clocking Mode Register without destroying memory contents, the sequencer must first be reset through a synchronous reset, using the Reset Register. As discussed in Section 10.3.1, this is accomplished by writing a 0 to bit 1 followed by writing a 1 to bit 1. This causes a synchronous reset pulse to be issued. A similar pulse written to Bit 0 causes an asynchronous reset. This, in turn, causes data loss in the display memory. Recall that the display memory is constructed of dynamic RAM memory.

The display memory can be cut off from the host through the Miscellaneous Output Register. As presented in Section 10.2.1, this is one way in which to allow multiple VGAs to reside in the same host system with their respective memories mapped to the same host memory addresses. Only one VGA would have its memory enabled at a time. The rest would be put "to sleep."

The display can be enabled or disabled through the Attribute Address Register. As indicated in Section 10.6.1, the palette and other attribute registers are dual-ported. Either the host or the display video circuitry has access to them. One can inadvertently cut the video drivers off, thereby blanking the screen, by keeping Bit 5 of this reset after indexing the attribute registers.

Mismanaging the registers in any number of ways can cause the display to go blank. In addition, all of display memory could be loaded with black color, or all of the Color Registers could be set to black. If the programmer desires to blank the screen, one of these techniques can be used.

Some of the Super VGAs have additional facilities to enable and disable the card. In addition, the card can be awoken or put to sleep. These cases are shown in Table 13.26. Detailed descriptions can be found in Chapters 15–21.

13.7.2   Configuring the Host Interface

The Super VGAs have the ability to handle 16-bit transfers. The three types of controlled transfer include the display memory accesses, the ROM accesses, and the I/O port accesses. The Super VGAs cards can be inserted into 8- or 16-bit card slots. The user can often select 8- or 16-bit I/O accesses, 8- or 16-bit display memory addresses, or 8- or 16-bit BIOS accesses by setting switches or by placing or removing jumpers. Some cards are auto-configurable. These automatically adapt to an 8- or 16-bit card. In addition, the user can select to enable or disable on-card BIOS. Typical cases are listed in Table 13.27. Detailed descriptions for each Super VGA manufacturer are found in Chapters 15–21.

TABLE 13.26 Controlling the Super VGAs

Feature	Typical Implementation Technique
Enable or disable VGA	Register
Put VGA asleep or awake	Register
Enter/exit setup mode	Register

TABLE 13.27 Configuring the Host Interface

Feature	Typical Implementation Technique
Select 8- or 16-bit I/O	Register, switch, autosense
Select 8- or 16-bit memory	Register, switch, autosense
Select 8- or 16-bit BIOS	Register, switch, autosense
Enable on-card BIOS	Register, switch
Select Slow/Fast address decode	Register, switch
Fast write	Register
Fast scroll	Register

Most of the Super VGAs have a facility for fine-tuning the speed of the host to VGA interface. Typical features are fast decoding, fast writing, and fast scrolling. Some host systems do not allow fast decoding. The features of fast writing and scrolling release the host as soon as the instruction is completed; they do not generate host wait-states.

13.7.3 Accessing the VGA Registers

As we know by now, the VGA is composed of the standard VGA registers, emulation registers, and extended or super registers. A programmer must know how to access these registers while preventing other applications from accessing them. Table 13.28 lists some issues related to accessing registers.

The VGA is assumed to be awake. Otherwise, no registers will be accessible as discussed in the preceding paragraphs. The BIOS Mode Set command accesses nearly all of the registers as does the Save/Restore State BIOS call. Both of these are described in the remaining sections of this chapter.

In certain implementations, an extended BIOS call is provided to access the extended registers. One chip manufacturer provides a disclaimer as to where the enable key is for the extended registers. The manufacturer may want to move it around in the future; an indirect memory location in BIOS for this address has been provided.

TABLE 13.28 Accessing the Super VGA Registers

Feature	Typical Implementation Technique
Enter set-up mode	Register at 46E8 for PC/AT or 3C3 for microchannel
Enable extended registers	Register
Lcok registers	Register
Accessing extended registers	Register, BIOS

Chapter 10 described how to access the standard VGA registers. Accessing the extended or Super VGA registers is typically accomplished through additional port addresses in the same range of port addresses as the standard VGA registers. Usually there is a technique for enabling and disabling access to these registers. In addition, several of the Super VGAs have a setup mode that acts as a key to the extended registers. This setup facility was designed and specified by IBM because its VGA is designed onto the motherboard and the use of multiple VGAs in a single system was anticipated. The setup concept is well-suited to putting VGAs to sleep. Some manufacturers have followed suit and implemented a 46E8 register.

The extended register addresses vary according to whether the implementation is on a microchannel or an AT bus. The Setup Control Register was placed at 46E8 hex in the I/O space for the PC/AT and at 3C3 hex for the microchannel. The value 46E8 was selected based on the result of an extensive search through computer history that concluded that no one has ever used the port address 46E8 willingly.

There are several cases where it is desirable to lock out applications from getting to registers. Of course, this lock-out facility is not meant to keep out the user—just the applications that were designed before all of this sophistication. Consider this example. Due to downward compatibility, an old game program might be running on a Super VGA that is operating in a CGA emulation mode. The application will probably want to write to the CGA registers. However, the emulation is not exact. It is therefore advisable to keep the old application out of certain registers. Locking the registers creates the illusion in old applications that they are in control, despite reality.

The first example of a lock-out is in the standard VGA mode set. I stumbled around trying to restore registers after a mode set. The display was not correct unless the mode remained unchanged. After considerable effort combined with some guidance, I found that the CRTC registers 0-7 are locked automatically after a mode set. These registers must be unlocked through the Vertical Sync End Register bit 7 as discussed in Section 10.4.18 of this book.

The reason for this write protection is to enable EGA applications to function on a VGA. Some EGA applications write directly to the EGA CRT controller.

Such applications will fail on a VGA since the EGA and VGA monitors require different timing signals.

A second reason to lock registers is to protect the hardware and software from inadvertently messing them up. By locking the registers, it is less likely that a program will mistakenly unlock the registers. There are several levels of locking, and several groups of registers can be locked or unlocked. This provides a great deal of flexibility for the programmer who is dealing with emulation or older applications.

13.7.4 Setting the Display Mode

Typically, the display modes are set through a BIOS call. There are over 50 registers that must be set up to perform a correct mode set. In addition, a BIOS data area in host memory must be considered. The values loaded into the VGA registers, both standard and extended for a mode set depend on the particular implementation and are not standard across different VGA cards. This is true, even if the same VGA chip is used. It is best to leave mode sets up to the BIOS. There is nothing mystical about a mode set. An effective mode set can be achieved by copying and restoring the proper registers and BIOS data area. However, many have tried and failed.

Most of the Super VGAs utilize the Mode Set BIOS call AH=0, as described in Section 11.2.1. In certain instances, a special BIOS call is necessary to activate the non-standard VGA display modes. Some routines return a parameter that indicates if the mode set was successful. Others simply ignore the command if the mode number is invalid. A parametric mode set BIOS call is also available, which allows the programmer to enter the desired horizontal and vertical resolutions and the number of colors. If a predefined mode equivalent to these parameters is available, the corresponding mode will be set. This would be a useful way to initialize a particular mode when the VGA chip manufacturer is unknown. Unfortunately, not all video chips support this function, and it needs to be universally accepted to be useful. The VESA standard does take care of this problem for you through a BIOS call.

The majority of modes are standard. Sixteen-color modes are stored in a planar fashion, and 256-color modes are stored in a packed fashion. The four-color modes of the CGA have been left behind. In some cases, two-color modes have made it to the big time of higher resolutions. There are exceptions to these rules.

In one case, a four-color 1024-by-768 mode is provided, and the same manufacturer provides a 1024-by-768 16-color mode, where the pixels are stored in a packed fashion. The packed technique is advantageous when a natural separation into display planes is not evident. For example, suppose the source of image data is a photograph, and the image is represented in sixteen colors. The smallest logical element into which the pixel can be decomposed is the four bit element representing each of the sixteen colors. In contrast, suppose the source of the image was a CAD package, and the image represents four overlayed line drawings. Each of these line drawings is represented in one plane and is therefore bimodal (0 or 1). The smallest logical element in this instance is a single bit, where a pixel would be represented as a combination of four such bits. In a planar mode, it would be possible to draw one plane at a time (one bit per pixel), without spending time transferring data relevant to the other planes. In a packed mode, it would be necessary to transfer all information relevant to the pixel (four bits per pixel), even if just one plane needed to be drawn.

In this sixteen-color display mode, two consecutive pixels are stored in a single byte. This creates problems when the transfer is not byte-aligned. For example, suppose there was a horizontal row of 100 pixels stored in a 50-byte array with bytes 0 and 1 stored together, 2 and 3 stored together, and so on. In this case, pixel 0 would be in the upper four bits and pixel 1 would be in the lower four bits of the byte. Further, suppose it was desired to move the data to the display beginning at pixel 201. Now pixel 201 is in the lower four bits of byte 100 relevant to that display row. Thus, there is a shifting of four bits required to align the input data to the destination. This is very time-consuming. Those familiar with the planar modes are familiar with this problem. A solution is presented in Chapter 16 on Chips and Technologies.

13.7.5   Controlling Emulation

A common feature among the Super VGAs is the ability to emulate the MDA, Hercules, CGA, and EGA. Some treat the EGA as a special case of the VGA. As is shown in Chapter 10, nearly all fields of the EGA are contained in the VGA. However, there are a few minor exceptions. A new ability is to emulate the 8514/A. I am not convinced that this will prove to be important because any application having an 8514/A driver also has a VGA driver. The VGA driver will be faster than the 8514/A emulation.

The emulation modes are controlled by directly accessing the registers. In some cases, it is wise to also lock register groups after the emulation is set up. BIOS calls to set up emulation are also provided for some of the Super VGAs.

13.7.6   Controlling Vertical Interrupts

Certain VGAs have the facility for generating interrupts when a vertical retrace period is encountered. Typically, the application interrupt service routine will count down from this 30 frame per second (approximately) rate and perform some function. Animation would be one example. One Super VGA has the facility to generate vertical interrupts after a prescribed number of vertical retrace periods. This is very useful since it limits unnecessary processing time for countdown to occur from the 30-frame-per-second rate. Vertical interrupts are handled through the standard VGA registers. These include the Input Status Register, described in Section 10.2.3, and the Vertical Retrace End Register, described in Section 10.4.18.

If no interrupt-generation facility is provided, the vertical retrace period can be determined by reading bit 3 of the Input Status One Register, described in Section 10.2.4.

13.7.7 Saving and Restoring the VGA State

Last but not least in the control category is the tricky issue of saving and restoring the VGA state. The standard VGA has three areas considered unique by the BIOS Save and Restore State function described in Section 11.15.3. These are the video hardware registers, the video data areas, and the video DAC state and color registers. The Super VGAs do not have any standardized areas reserved in the BIOS data area of host RAM to store information, nor do they have any additional DAC registers. All that is necessary to save or restore the super state is to save or restore the super registers.

The Save and Restore Video State BIOS call has a peculiar characteristic. The Save function actually alters the original contents of the registers or data areas involved. To maintain the original state after a Save BIOS call, the programmer should immediately perform a Restore BIOS call using this same function.

The information in the hardware-state area is described in Table 13.29 and totals 70 bytes.

TABLE 13.29 Hardware State Save Area

Offset into Save Buffer (hex)	Registers
0	Sequencer Index
1	CRT Controller Index
2	Graphics Controller Index
3	Attribute Controller Index
4	Feature Control Register
5–8	Sequencer Registers Index 1–5
9	Sequencer Registers Index 0
A–22	CRT Controller Registers 0–8 hex
23–32	Palette Registers 0–F hex
33–36	Attribute Registers 10–3 hex
37–3F	Graphics Controller Registers 0–8
40	CRTC Base Address low
41	CRTC Base Address high
42	Plane 0 latch
43	Plane 1 latch
44	Plane 2 latch
45	Plane 3 latch

TABLE 13.30 DAC Storage Area

Offset	Value
0	Read/write mode DAC
1	Pixel address
2	Pixel mask
3–302 hex	256 pairs of 3-color registers totalling 768 bytes
303 hex	Color Select Register

TABLE 13.31 Bytes Required to Save the Standard State

DAC Area Requested	Bios Data Requested	Hardware Requested	# of Bytes Required	# Returned from BIOS Call
No	No	Yes	70	128
No	Yes	No	96	128
No	Yes	Yes	166	192
Yes	No	No	772	832
Yes	No	Yes	842	896
Yes	Yes	No	868	896
Yes	Yes	Yes	938	960

The video data definition area resides in the host memory address space 400 hex–500 hex. This is typically referred to as *locations in segment 40 hex*. The Save state command reads the consecutive memory locations beginning at segment 40 hex : offset 49 hex and ending with segment 40 hex : offset A9 hex. This totals 96 bytes. This information is described in Table 9.8.

The DAC storage area contains the values of the DAC registers and the DAC color registers themselves. This is described in Table 13.30. The DAC storage area requires 772 bytes.

The possible combinations of storage and the number of types required for each are listed in Table 13.31. Also presented in this table is the number of bytes requested by the BIOS call. Remember that the BIOS call returns the number of 64-byte data chunks. Thus, the BIOS total is equal to the closest multiple of 64 greater or equal to the actual number of bytes.

13.8 MEMORY ADDRESSING TECHNIQUES

In order to use the Super VGAs, the programmer must first understand how display memory is accessed. In the unprotected DOS environment, 128 Kbytes are reserved for display memory in the space A0000–BFFFF hex. The VGA has to share this area with the MDA or CGA. Typically, a 64 Kbyte block of memory is used in the space A0000–AFFFF hex for the graphics modes of the Super VGA.

In the protected DOS environment, there is unlimited space above the 1 Mbyte DOS area to use for display memory. No convention has been laid out for what should go into this memory. Many computer systems are equipped with between 1 and 32 Mbytes of memory. Soon, I am sure, hundreds of megabytes will not be uncommon.

In order to use the A0000–AFFFF DOS memory area, it is necessary to bank switch the 1 to 4 Mbytes of memory on the SuperVGAs such that all 1 to 4 Mbytes can be accessed from DOS. Bank swapping is described in Sections 13.8.1 and 13.8.2. In order to use upper memory, the Super VGA has to be capable of linear addressing. Linear addressing is described in Section 13.11.

13.8.1   Single Paging Systems

Figure 13.9 illustrates a paging technique. In this figure, and in subsequent figures, the amount of VGA memory can vary from 1 to 4 Mbytes. The principles remain the same. It just takes more banks for more memory.

A bank start address determines where the bank resides within the VGA 1 Mbyte address space. The length of the bank and the bank start address completely describe the bank as far as the host address generation is concerned. In this figure, a bank is 64 Kbytes long and maps directly into the host address space between A0000–AFFFF hex. To read or write into this bank from the host, one simply sets the ES Segment Register to A0000 and the DI Offset

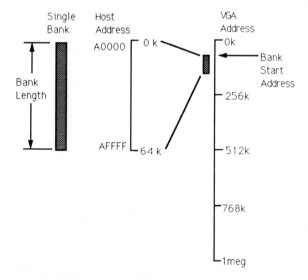

FIGURE 13.9 Single-Bank (Paging) System

Register to the desired location within the bank. To access memory outside of the current bank, the programmer changes the Bank Start Address so that the desired memory locations fall within the newly located bank.

This technique is a bit cumbersome copying memory from one location to another. Suppose the source of the data resided between 768 Kbytes and 832 Kbytes and the destination of the data resided between 0 Kbytes and 64 Kbytes. The program would have to set the Bank Start Address to the source area, read a value, change the Bank Start Address to the destination area, and write the value. This cycle would repeat for every value copied. The value might be a byte, a 16-bit word, or a 32-bit word depending on the write mode.

In the preceding example, we are accessing 1 Mbyte of memory requiring 20 address bits. Assuming that the bank length is 64 Kbytes, sixteen of these address bits are used to span a segment, called intra-segment. This leaves the high four address bits to describe the bank number.

There are several techniques that one can employ to read/write to this memory. One technique would be to restrict each data transfer to 64 Kbytes. Thus, the total transfer would be accomplished by segmenting it into several chunks of transfers, one leaving off where the previous ended and none crossing a bank boundary. The Bank Start Address would be loaded before each transfer. This technique is especially well-suited for BITBLTs since it allows the use of the move string DMA instructions.

A second technique uses 32-bit arithmetic for the address generation and checks for overflows. When an overflow occurs, the Bank Start Address is incremented. This technique is well-suited for writing lines that are not horizontal. This type of structure cannot take advantage of the DMA string instructions anyway as there is no pre-calculation.

Constrained to one Bank Start Address Register, a programmer would design this register so that it resides in a place that is both fast and easy to access. Unfortunately, this is not always the case. In one early implementation, the four bits were split up into four different registers, so that the number of instructions per pixel became quite ridiculous.

13.8.2   Dual-Paging Systems

Dual-Paging systems alleviate the problem of moving data from one display location to another by keeping two Bank Start Addresses as shown in Figure 13.10. The process would be to set up the one Bank Start Address to the start of the source segment and the second to the start of the destination segment. With both the ES and DS registers set to A0000, the SI and DI registers pointing to their respective source and destination offsets, and the CX Register containing the number of words to transfer, it is then possible to transfer data through the repeat move string DMA instruction.

Like the single paging system, the value moved during each cycle of the DMA instruction could be a byte, 16-bit word, or 32-bit word. The only limiting

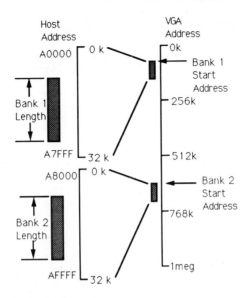

FIGURE 13.10 Dual-Bank (Paging System)

element here would be the wait-states issued by the display memory. If the display can withstand being disabled (see Section 13.7.1), wait-states can be minimized. If the VGA is mounted on the motherboard and the display memory is fast enough, zero-wait-state data transfers can be accomplished. Since 32 bits can be moved at a time, this translates into respectable data transfers. Unfortunately, there are a lot of "ifs" between zero-wait-states and the reliability of today's implementations.

13.8.3 Banks, Planes, and Pages

There are several ways to organize memory within the VGA, depending on the display mode. Some common techniques used in the Super VGA's advanced modes are given in Table 13.32. The first mode has four colors per pixel and is unique. Its organization is reminiscent of the CGA modes using odd and even banks. It is included here for completeness. Note, however, that it will not be discussed further. All remaining modes implemented in the Super VGAs fit into the planar or packed format. The second mode, which uses sixteen colors in a packed mode, is also unique with the sixteen colors represented in a packed format. Thus, two pixels adjoin in a single byte instead of the one pixel per byte in the 256-color modes. Other than this, it fits into the packed memory organization category.

The Macintosh uses a similar organization for its 16-color mode. The rest of this section will discuss only the third and fourth modes. These assume that a 16-color mode is planar and a 256-color mode is packed.

TABLE 13.32 Super VGA Advanced Display Modes

# of Colors	Bits per plane	Planes per pixel	Bytes per bank	Plane Organization	Terminology
4	2	1	256 Kbytes	Sequential	Unique
16	4	1	64 Kbytes	Sequential	Packed
16	1	4	256 Kbytes	Overlapped	Planar
256	8	1	64 Kbytes	Sequential	Packed

13.8.4   16-color Mode Planar Memory Organization

As a review, planar memory means that a pixel is represented by bits of information spread out across a set of planes. When this occurs, sixteen colors are possible, requiring four bits. The four display planes have the pixel represented by one bit per plane. Display memory is organized as bytes. There are eight pixels per byte. The memory planes are overlayed in the host memory address space so that each plane occupies exactly the same host addresses. These can be accessed independently by virtue of the read and write plane select registers.

The Map Mask Register, described in Section 10.3.3, controls the plane selection during write operations. The four bit field allows any combination of the four planes to be written to at the same time. The Read Map Select Register, described in Section 10.5.7, on the other hand allows the selection of one of the four planes with a two bit-field. This prevents bus conflicts on read operations, no conflict occurs on write operations. The planar organization is illustrated in Figure 13.11.

There can be greater than 64 Kbytes of memory on the Super VGAs. As a result, additional memory segmentation is necessary. This is where the banks come in. In Figure 13.12, a 1-Mbyte system is shown. Note that each plane, 0–3, is drawn so that it is overlayed to span the address range from A0000–AFFFF hex. The four memory banks, 0–3, are shown across the figure. Each consists of a set of four planes. Important to note from this figure is that each bank actually consists of 256 Kbytes of memory. This is an important fact and distinguishes the planar from the packed memory organizations.

Suppose a programmer wants to write to a byte at the location 400 hex, in plane 0 of bank 3. In host memory space this is accomplished by enabling plane 0, accessing bank 3, setting the ES segment register to A0000 hex, setting the DI register to 400 hex, and writing the byte through the ES:[DI] registers. The question is how one accesses bank 3.

Each Super VGA is different but similar. As was mentioned in the previous section, each bank has a Bank Length and a Bank Start Address. Suppose the bank is 64 Kbytes long and the Start Address can increment in chunks of 64 Kbytes. This incremental value is referred to as the granularity. Although each

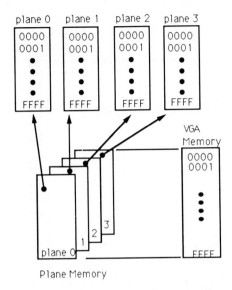

FIGURE 13.11 Planar Memory Organization in 16-color Mode

bank is 256 Kbytes long with respect to the VGA memory, these banks are only 64 Kbytes long with respect to the host. Thus, this location would be located in the fourth bank, bank 3. The Bank Start Address would be loaded with a three. Programmers should again note that this is a very important point and feature-specific to the planar VGA display modes.

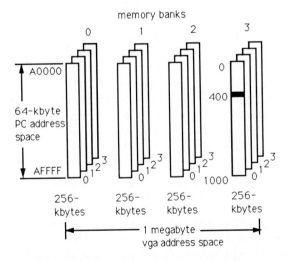

FIGURE 13.12 Planar Memory Banks

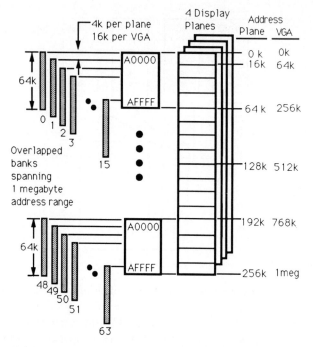

FIGURE 13.13 Overlapped Banks in a Planar Display Mode

The granularity just mentioned is "pretty granular" at 64 Kbytes. Most VGA implementations set the granularity to 4 Kbytes while keeping the Bank Length at 64 Kbytes. This causes the banks to overlap by 60 Kbytes. Figure 13.13 illustrates this case. The right-most column is the 1-Mbyte address space with respect to the VGA. The second column from the right is the 256-Kbyte memory space with respect to a single plane. The third column from the right shows that there are four display planes, which accounts for the scale factor of four. Each bank is 64 Kbytes long; each overlaps its neighbor by 60 Kbytes, stepping 4 Kbytes at a time. It takes sixteen overlapped banks to span one 64-Kbyte plane segment, which translates into one 256-VGA-Kbyte segment. Sixty-four banks are required to span the entire 256-Kbyte plane memory space. This translates into the entire 1 Mbyte VGA memory space.

13.8.5 Common 16-Color Planar Display Modes

This section contains maps of the display memory for all common Super VGA modes. The basic organization of the 16-color planar modes is shown in Figure 13.14. This figure illustrates a display mode utilizing two banks of memory across the four display planes as shown in Figure 13.14a. Note that the boundary between bank 0 and bank 1 does not occur at the start of a scan line but rather somewhere in the middle. This is the case when the number of bytes per

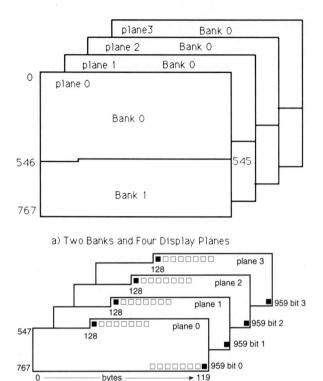

a) Two Banks and Four Display Planes

(b) Bank 1 Exploded View

FIGURE 13.14 Typical 16-color Planar Memory Map

scan line is not an integer divisor of 64 Kbytes, which is 65536 bytes in actuality. Described later in this section is a technique that ensures that all 16-color planar modes that can be displayed in two banks can be made to have bank transitions at the beginning of a scan row. This can simplify code considerably.

Figure 13.14b shows an exploded view of Bank 1. Note that bank boundary occurs at pixel 128, which translates to byte 16, of scan line 546. Pixel 128 is actually located in bit position 7 in all four planes of the byte at this location. When writing to this pixel, the byte that contains this pixel would be written to the first byte in bank 1. The last pixel in the displayed portion of bank 1 is labeled pixel 959, indicating that there are 960 pixels per scan line. This pixel is actually in bit position 0 of all four planes of the 120th byte in the 767th scan line. This would be byte 26,623 in bank 1.

The number 26,623 is derived as follows: The image has a resolution of 960 pixels (120 bytes) by 768 scan lines. It requires two banks of memory, the first occupying 545+ scan lines. If 65536 is divided by 120, the result is 546, with a remainder of 16. Thus, there are 546 complete scan lines (0–545) plus one scan line that contains 16 bytes (128 pixels). The second bank must contain the

TABLE 13.33 16-color Planar Display Memory Maps

Figure Number	Resolution Pixels	Memory Required	# of Pages with 1 Mbyte	# of Banks
13.15	320 by 200	32,000	2	1
13.16	640 by 480	153,600	6	1
13.17	800 by 600	240,000	4	1
13.18	960 by 720	345,600	3	2
13.19	1024 by 768	393,216	2	2
13.20	1280 by 1024	655,360	1	3

remaining 104 bytes of scan line 546 and 221 full scan lines to reach the scan line total of 768. The 120th byte of scan line 767 would be

(221*120) + 104 = 26,624 bytes,

which is byte number 26,623 in bank 1.

There is a set of common VGA 16-color resolutions ranging from 320 by 200 to 1024 by 768 and proposed 1280 by 1024. A pictorial map of each of these display modes follow. These maps are useful when writing code or trying to understand the code presented in Chapter 15. These maps are presented in Figures 13.15–13.20 as itemized in Table 13.33.

In Figure 13.15, a 320-by-200 pixel display mode is presented. This mode requires 320/8 = 40 bytes per scan line per plane. A single bank can contain 65536/40 =1,638 scan lines. There are four display planes. Thus, 40*4=160

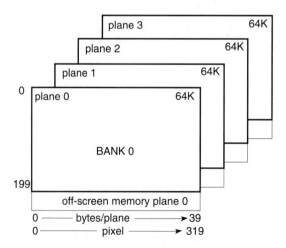

FIGURE 13.15 320-by-200 16-color Mode

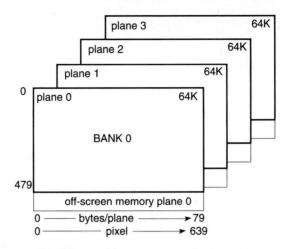

FIGURE 13.16 640-by-480 16-color Mode

bytes per scan line is the total for all display planes. A single image would occupy 32,000 bytes of display memory, 8000 bytes per plane. This image is considered a page. Of course, the effective or virtual resolution of the image could be much larger than 320 by 200, and the user could pan or scroll to see other 320x200 windows.

Figures 13.16 and 13.17 are similar, in that an image fits in a single bank. No bank switching is necessary if the virtual image size fits within this single bank as well. Image manipulation is much quicker if the arithmetic and graphics instructions do not have to worry about bank switching.

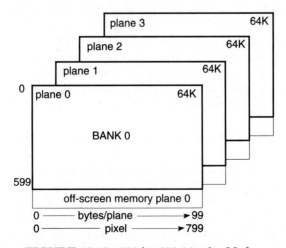

FIGURE 13.17 800-by-600 16-color Mode

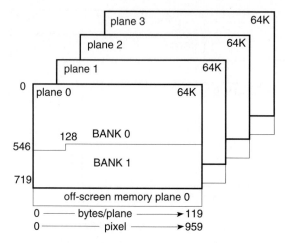

FIGURE 13.18 960-by-720 16-color Mode

Figure 13.18 is a 960-by-720 display mode. This display mode is possible because monitors that cannot keep up with a full 1024-by-768 non-interlaced can sometimes keep up with a 960-by-720 mode. Note that the image in this mode does span two banks and that the bank transition does not occur at the start of a scan line.

Figure 13.19 and Figure 13.20 illustrate the high-resolution 16-color modes. The 1280-by-1024 mode requires three banks of memory.

Aligning Banks to the Start of Scan Lines

If the display mode, be it 16-color planar or 256-color packed, can fit in two banks, the boundary of the two banks can be forced to align to the start of a scan line by adjusting the start address. The start address is a 16-bit address. This address dictates which byte contains the first pixel that will be displayed. The Start Address Low and High Registers are described in Section 10.4.13 and 10.4.14 respectively. The start address is typically set to 0, but can be modified to create a panning or scrolling effect. In this case, it is desirable to align the bank boundary.

If there are only two banks, there are two boundaries. One is at the start of the first bank; the second is at the transition between the first and second bank. It is always assumed that the start of the first bank is aligned to the beginning of a scan line since it starts at the start of scan line 0. If the number of bytes per scan line does not divide evenly into 65,536, the transition boundary will not align to the start of a scan line. If the start address is set equal to the number of bytes that occur as the remainder in the divide of 65,536 / (# of bytes per scan line), the fractional part is accounted for and the number of bytes per scan line will divide equally into (65,536 − remainder). First encountered through ATI, I have found no penalty in doing this neat little trick.

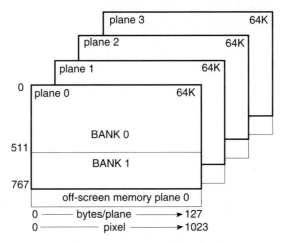

FIGURE 13.19 1024-by-768 16-color Mode

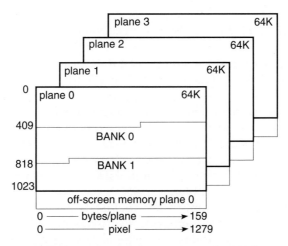

FIGURE 13.20 1280-by-1024 16-color Mode

13.8.6 Common 256-Color Packed Display Modes

The 256-color modes are stored in memory as one byte per pixel, contained in a single plane. This is called *packed* since a pixel is packed into a single byte. In the 16-color packed mode, two pixels are packed into a byte, as opposed to being spread across the various planes. The memory is still organized as planes. However, the addressing is completely different from the 16-color planar modes described in Section 13.8.5. Figure 13.21 illustrates the packed memory organization in a packed display mode. Note that the four display planes are organized so that sequential addressing jumps from plane 0, to 1, to 2, to 3 and back

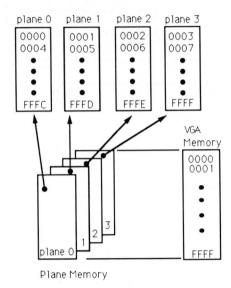

FIGURE 13.21 Packed Memory Organization in 256-color Modes

to plane 0 again. As a result, eight consecutive pixels are actually loaded so that pixels 0 and 4 are in plane 0, pixels 1 and 5 are in plane 1, pixels 2 and 6 are in plane 2, and pixels 3 and 7 are in plane 3.

Fortunately, the memory address controller takes care of all this. The programmer does not even need to consider which plane memory would be going into. In the above example, it would only be necessary to write out eight bytes to consecutive display memory locations. The only time that a programmer must consider the display planes is when data is read or written in a packed mode and written or read in a planar mode.

It is interesting and important to note that a 64-Kbyte segment in host memory address space actually encompasses 16 Kbytes in each display plane. The Super VGAs support resolutions that extend beyond a single 64-Kbyte segment. Thus, as with the 16-bit planar examples, paging is necessary. The requirement for paging is far more stringent with respect to the packed display modes for two reasons. First, the packed mode considered uses eight bits per pixel in the 256-color modes as opposed to four bits per pixel in the 16-color modes. Thus, twice the memory must be stored for the same spatial resolution image. Secondly, the display planes are not overlapped with respect to the host memory address space. This causes a 64-Kbyte segment in host memory address space to access 64 Kbytes of memory in the VGA memory address space. This is four times less than the planar alternative where 256 Kbytes of VGA memory address space is spanned by the single 64-Kbyte segment in host memory address space. Consequently, many more banks are required in the 256-color modes.

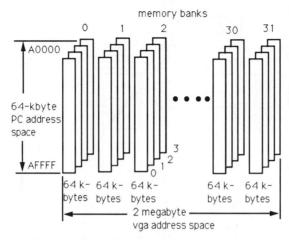

FIGURE 13.22 256-color Overlapped Memory

The packed memory banks organization is illustrated in Figure 13.22. This figure is similar to and should be compared to Figure 13.12. In Figure 13.22, the planes are numbered 0 to 3 and are shown as being overlapped. The single 64-Kbyte segment A0000–AFFFF hex is shown to span all four display planes as opposed to the single display plane in Figure 13.12. A bank of four display planes is shown to contain 64 Kbytes as opposed to the 256 Kbytes in the planar example of Figure 13.12. One last difference is that there are 32 memory banks in the packed mode as opposed to the four memory banks in the planar example. This factor of 8 is derived from the 2 times as much data factor in the 8 versus 4 bits per pixel ratio multiplied by the 4 display planes.

Once again, similar to the 16-color planar mode, there is a need to reduce the granularity of a bank. The question is how much. If a 4-Kbyte granularity is selected, it would require 256 banks to span the 1-Mbyte host address space. Due to the planar organization of memory (even in the packed modes) of the Super VGAs, the decision was made to have a packed granularity of 16 Kbytes. Thus, the total number of banks is 64, analogous to the planar case. The catch is that the terminology is such that the granularity can still be considered to be 4 Kbytes if one is operating in the plane address space. Programmers should be careful with the terminology and the corresponding VGA implementation. It is important to understand both the difference and the sameness of the 4-Kbyte planar granularity and the 16-Kbyte VGA granularity. This is illustrated in Figure 13.23. This figure should be compared to Figure 13.13, which portrays the analogous 16-color planar situation.

A typical 256-color packed memory map is pictorially represented in Figure 13.22. The relationship of the four display planes and the five banks necessary to represent a single image are shown in this figure. Note that the bank boundaries do not align to the start of scan lines. This figure should be

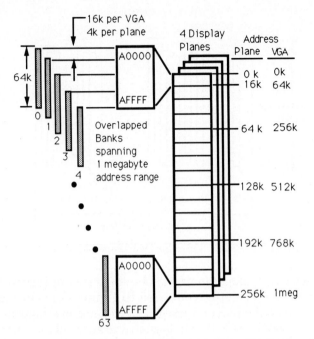

Note: Address increments by one in VGA address space and
it increments by four in the plane address space

FIGURE 13.23 Overlapped Banks in a Packed Mode

compared to Figure 13.14, which portrays the analogous planar representation. The text associated with Figure 13.14 also applies to the location of a pixel within a bank.

In this packed case, the right-most four pixels in the last scan line of an image are labeled byte *n* through *n+3*. A scan line containing 640 pixels translates into 640 bytes per scan line. Since 640 does not divide evenly into 65,536, the bank boundaries will not be aligned to the start of a scan line. Since there are more than two planes in this relatively low-resolution image, there is no chance of forcing the alignment by using the start address technique discussed in Section 13.8.5. A typical 256-color memory map is shown in Figure 13.24.

There are a set of common VGA 16-color resolutions ranging from 320 by 200 to 1024 by 768 and proposed 1280 by 1024. A pictorial map of each of these display modes follow. These maps are useful when writing code or trying to understand the code presented in Chapters 15–21. The maps are presented in Figures 13.15–13.20 as itemized in Table 13.34.

In Figure 13.25, a 320-by-200 pixel display mode is presented. This mode requires 320 bytes per scan line per plane. A single bank can contain

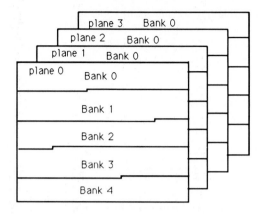

a) Five Banks and Four Display Planes

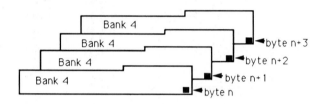

b) Bank 4 Exploded View

FIGURE 13.24 Typical 256-color Packed Memory Map

65536/320 = 204 scan lines. This image is considered a page. Of course, the effective or virtual resolution of the image could be much larger than 320-by-200, and the user could pan or scroll to see other 320- by-200 windows.

TABLE 13.34 256-color Packed Display Memory Maps

Figure number	Resolution pixels	Bytes required	# of pages with 1 Mbyte	# of banks
13.24	320 by 200	64,000	16	1
13.25	640 by 400	256,000	4	4
13.26	640 by 480	307,200	3	5
13.27	800 by 600	480,000	2	7
13.28	1024 by 768	786,432	1	12
13.29	1280 by 1024	1,310,720	0 (*1)	20

Note: *1 1280-by-1024 mode requires 2 Mbyte implementation

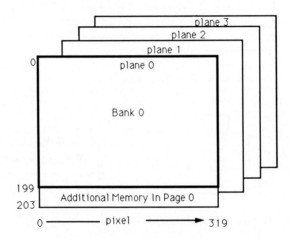

FIGURE 13.25 320-by-200 256-color Mode

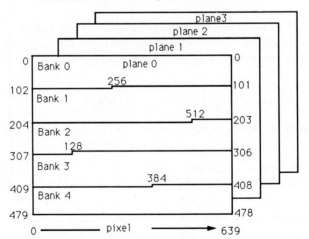

FIGURE 13.26 640-by-400 or 640-by-480 256-color Mode

800 pitch in a 256-color mode

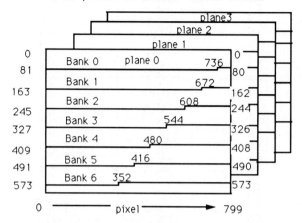

FIGURE 13.27 800-by-600 256-color Mode

In Figures 13.26–13.29, 256-color display modes typically are displayed. Note that the only display mode used, an even divisor into 65,536, is the 1024 pitch of Figure 13.28. The 1280-by-1024 mode displayed in Figure 13.29 would require a VGA with more than 1 Mbyte as shown in Table 13.34.

1024 pitch in a 256-color mode

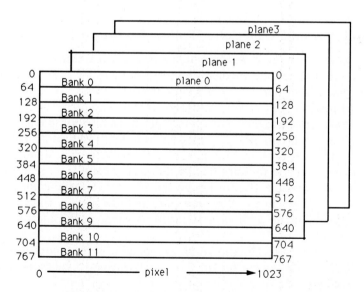

FIGURE 13.28 1024-by-768 256-color Mode

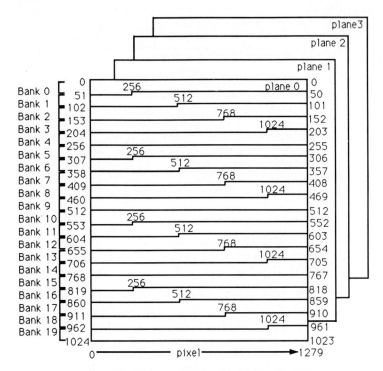

FIGURE 13.29 1280-by-1024 256-color Mode

13.8.7 Hi-Color and True-Color Display Modes

An exciting advancement in several of the Super VGA chips is the ability to display hi-color or true-color modes. The term "true color" implies either 24 or 32 bits per pixel. In either case, eight bits are dedicated to each of red, green, and blue and produce 16.8 million different colors. The term "hi-color" implies fifteen or sixteen bits per pixel. The 15-bits-per-pixel hi-color mode has five bits for red, five bits for green, and five bits for blue and produce 32,768 different colors. The 16-bits per pixel hi-color mode has five bits for red, six bits for green, and five bits for blue and produce 65,536 different colors.

It is important to realize that although the 15- and 16-bit hi-color modes produce more colors than do the 8-bit-per-color palette modes, there is actually more color accuity in the 8-bit palette modes because each palette entry uses six bits per color.

The data format for the 15- and 16-bit-per-pixel hi-color modes are shown in Figure 13.30. The data format for the 24- and 32-bit-per-pixel true-color modes are shown in Figure 13.31.

The organization of these 15-, 16-, and 24-bit-per-color memory modes is displayed in Figures 13.32 and 13.33. These display modes are very similar to the

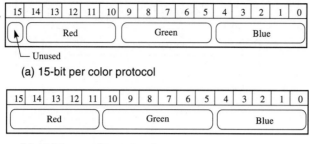

(a) 15-bit per color protocol

(b) 16-bit per color protocol

FIGURE 13.30 Hi-color Display Mode Color Format

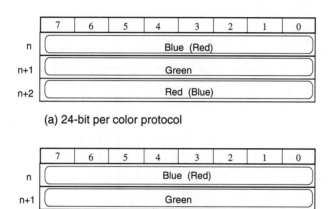

(a) 24-bit per color protocol

(a) 32-bit per color protocol

FIGURE 13.31 True-Color Display Mode Color Format

256-color memory configurations with an exception occurring when a single pixel is represented by more than one byte.

In Figure 13.32 two pixels are represented in a 16-bit display mode. This could also apply to a 15-bit display mode with the exception that bit 15 would be unused. In Figure 13.32a, the 16-bit pixels are shown in a memory configuration such that there are four bit planes. This could be thought of as a chain-4 mode. In this case, each byte of the two pixels is stored in its own plane. Figure 13.32b shows that the four bytes of the two pixels are stored contiguously in memory in Intel order (lower before upper). Figure 13.32c shows 16-bit pixels in a memory configuration such that there are sixteen bit planes. This could be

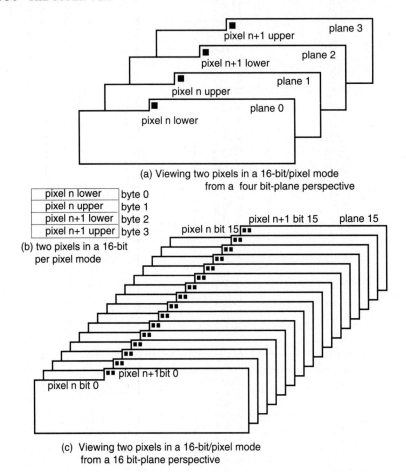

(a) Viewing two pixels in a 16-bit/pixel mode
from a four bit-plane perspective

pixel n lower	byte 0
pixel n upper	byte 1
pixel n+1 lower	byte 2
pixel n+1 upper	byte 3

(b) two pixels in a 16-bit
per pixel mode

(c) Viewing two pixels in a 16-bit/pixel mode
from a 16 bit-plane perspective

FIGURE 13.32 Display memory in a 16-bit-per-pixel mode.
(a) From a 4-bit plane perspective. (b) Four bytes of two pixels stored
contiguously. (c) From a 16-bit plane perspective

thought of as a chain-16 mode. In this case, each bit of each color component of
each pixel is stored in its own plane.

Similarly, in Figure 13.33 two pixels are represented in a 24-bit display
mode. In Figure 13.33a, the 24-bit pixels are shown in a memory configuration
such that there are eight bit planes. This could be thought of as a chain-8 mode.
In this case, each bit of all three color components of the two pixels is stored in
its own plane. In other words, bit 0 is in the same bit plane for each of the red,
green, and blue components of the pixel. Figure 13.32b shows that the six bytes
of the two pixels are stored contiguously in memory in Intel order (lower before
upper). Figure 13.33c shows 24-bit pixels in a memory configuration such that
there are 24 bit planes. This could be thought of as a chain-24 mode. In this
case, each bit of each color component of each pixel is stored in its own plane.

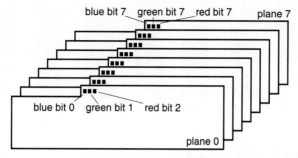

(a) Viewing two pixels in a 24-bit/pixel mode
from a eight bit-plane perspective

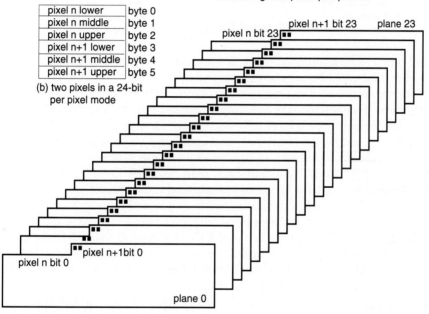

pixel n lower	byte 0
pixel n middle	byte 1
pixel n upper	byte 2
pixel n+1 lower	byte 3
pixel n+1 middle	byte 4
pixel n+1 upper	byte 5

(b) two pixels in a 24-bit
per pixel mode

(c) Viewing two pixels in a 24-bit/pixel mode
from a 24 bit-plane perspective

FIGURE 13.33 Display memory in a 24-bit-per-pixel mode.
(a) From an 8-bit plane perspective. (b) Six bytes of two pixels stored
contiguously. (c) From a 24-bit plane perspective

The number of bit planes is important because of hardware. As everyone knows, the display memory is made of memory chips. The configuration of the chips varies in both the amount of memory per chip and in the number of data bits per chip. For example, 4 Mbyte RAM might be organized as 1 bit by 4 Mbytes, 4 bits by 1 Mbyte, 8 bits by 512 Kbytes, 16 bits by 256 Kbytes, and so on. The organization affects performance.

For example, suppose that each chip has a separate chip enable. It would then be possible to mask out the data write going to the RAM chips by a single

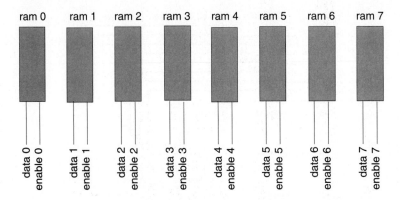

FIGURE 13.34 Bit Masking Ram Chips

control line and no additional chips. If the chip was 1 bit by 4 Mbytes, then each bit in the pixel could be selectively enabled or disabled. This could be very useful since there are no time-consuming read/modify/write software operations taking place. The desired bits are simply masked out. Alternatively, the 8-bits-by-512-Kbytes chip would have only one enable for eight bits while the 16-bits-by-256-Kbytes chip would have only one enable for sixteen bits.

A typical situation is shown in Figure 13.34 where there are eight chips each with one bit per pixel. Note that each chip gets one data line and one chip select. Thus, each of these bits could be masked independently.

The 16-bit or 24-bit data in display memory gets fed directly to the DAC producing the red, green, and blue analog outputs as seen in Figure 13.35.

It should be noted that there is a real difficulty related to bank crossing when dealing with 24-bit-per-pixel true-color modes. Since there are three bytes per pixel, there will be 21,845 pixels per 65,536 byte bank. However, 21,845 times 3 yields only 65,535 bytes. Therefore, the 21,846th pixel, numbered 21,845, will straddle a bank crossing such that the first byte, blue, will be in bank 0, while

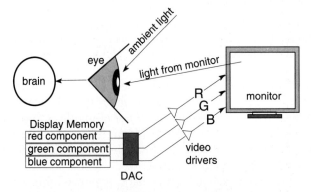

FIGURE 13.35 True-Color DAC Outputs

the second and third bytes, green and red, will fall into the bank 1. The next bank crossing will have the 43,690th pixel such that the blue and green components will be in bank 1, while the red component will be in bank 2. The software overhead necessary to maintain this intra-pixel bank crossing can slow down graphics algorithms.

13.9 WORKING WITH COLOR

Several factors affect color. Some are measurable, some are subjective, some are simple to understand, some are quite complex, some are understood, and others remain elusive. Books are written on the topic of color theory. This section will discuss color from the perspective of the Super VGAs.

13.9.1 Factors That Influence Color

Figure 13.36 illustrates some of the factors that influence color. The eye, which responds to light and nothing more, contains three narrow band filters that can respond to three different frequencies of light. These frequencies correspond to what we call red, green, and blue. The electrical signals are data compressed as they are sent from the eye to the cerebral cortex. Once in the cortex, they are further reduced and interpreted. The eye is a receptor, part of our physiology. The brain is a thinker and responder, influenced by our perception. Therefore, even given exactly the same conditions, one cannot say that the color that one person "sees" is identical to the color that another person "sees."

The light that strikes the eye's receptors comes from two sources—the phosphor illumination on the monitor and ambient light. Both affect our perception of color. The monitor is certainly a prime factor in the color that we see. Color balance, linearity, convergence, stability, and accuracy all affect the color seen on the surface of the tube or flat panel. The monitor is driven by red, green, and blue analog signals provided from video drivers on the output stage of the DAC. The video drivers and the digital-to-analog converters all affect color. The DAC

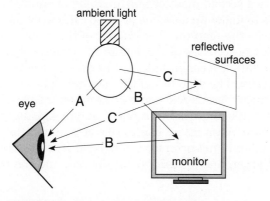

FIGURE 13.36 Factors That Influence Color

is driven by the red, green, and blue components of the color associated with each pixel in display memory. The number of bits available for each color component affect the color.

Ambient light is broken down into three additive sources, labeled A, B and C, as shown in Figure 13.36. First, the ambient light directly strikes the eye, as shown in A. Next, it reflects off of the monitor face and then strikes the eye, as shown in B. Finally, it reflects off other surfaces in the room and then strikes the eye, as shown in C.

13.9.2 Displaying Color

The VGA and now the Super VGA bring color to desktop computing. Color-coded information is stored in the display memory, converted to video signals in the DAC, and displayed on a monitor. The information is stored in the display memory in a red, green, and blue format. This is not the only way to store color, and several other color formats could be used besides red, green, and blue. However, all Super VGAs currently store the information as RGB.

The color data is stored in display memory. Display memory is made of either DRAM or VRAM memory. VRAM memory has a second port dedicated to refreshing the CRT. As a result, Super VGAs using VRAM memory are faster (and more expensive) than their DRAM counterparts.

The digital data stored in display memory is converted to analog data in the color or video DAC. The DAC may be part of the Super VGA chip or it may be a separate part. At the time of the VGA, the DAC was relatively simple and, consequently, the DAC standard was simple. It could not anticipate how complex the DACs would become. Therefore, the new DACs present on most Super VGAs have additional features that extend beyond the VGA standard. The quality and configuration of the DAC determines how well the digital data is actually converted to analog data. It also determines how well the monitor is driven. For example, the gain of the DAC determines how "hard" the monitor is driven. One DAC's settings might be well suited for one monitor driving it to its maximum, but would overdrive a second monitor. Fortunately, monitors have contrast and brightness controls to make up for some of these calibration issues.

DAC output drives the monitor. The quality of the monitor determines how the colors look, and the accuracy of the monitor determines how closely changes in the analog color data are converted into changes on the face of the monitor. This is called *linearity*. The stability of the monitor determines how a specific color looks five minutes versus five hours after monitor turn on, in a room that is 50 degrees versus 100 degrees Fahrenheit, and on the day the monitor was purchased versus two years later. The purity of the monitor determines how pure the red, green, and blue primary colors look. If the colors are not pure, a certain amount of green may be present in the red, and the colors will not be fully saturated.

13.9.3 Direct versus Palette Color

This data might be an index into a Palette Register or an actual color value. There are two things to consider when displaying color—how many different colors and how many shades of each color. Using direct color, these two are implicitly the same; using palette color, these two are typically different.

When a palette is used, its length determines the number of simultaneous colors that can be displayed. The depth of the palette determines the color resolution. For example, the palette might be 256 entries long with each entry being eighteen bits. There would therefore be 2^{18} or 256 Kbytes colors possible. However, only 256 different colors could be displayed at a time. When direct color is used, the number of bits per pixel dictates both the color resolution and the number of simultaneous colors that can be displayed.

13.9.4 Hi-color versus True-color modes

The two most popular types of direct color are hi-color (fifteen or sixteen bits per color) and true-color (24 or 32 bits per color). Although there is no absolute way of determining when to use hi-color or true-color, Table 13.35 provides some insight.

Comparing color accuracy is impacted by linearity. There are 32 shades per color in hi-color. The eye can definitely detect more that 32 shades, especially in certain color regions where the eye is more sensitive. Therefore, when displaying photographic images on the screen, one will see distinct lines within what should be a smooth transition. If you don't want to see these lines, you will need to go to the true-color modes. One good approach is to leave the file in a 24-bit color format on disk, but display it in a hi-color mode. This allows you to keep the data in its raw high-resolution form while taking advantage of the faster hi-color Super VGA processing. However, these speed advantages might be diminished due to the 24-bit to 16-bit conversions.

TABLE 13.35 Selecting Hi-Color versus True-Color

Characteristics of Hi-Color	*Characteristics of True-Color*
Easy to manage data	Difficult to maintain data
Fast due to less data	Slow due to more data
Slow due to awkward format	Fast due to byte per color
Smaller files	Larger files
Supported by current accelerators	Not supported by many accelerators
Difficult time with shading	Can accurately represent photographic images

13.9.5   16-color Modes

The 16-color modes use the first sixteen entries in the color registers to produce colors. The standard default color registers values are shown in Table 13.36. The VESA standardized display modes are shown in Table 13.37.

13.9.6   256-color Modes

The 256-color modes are popular in the Super VGA due both to the compact byte-per-pixel notation and the flooding of Super VGAs on the market when only 8-bit-per-color modes were available. These modes utilize all 256 locations

TABLE 13.36   16-color Default Color Register Values

Color Register	Red	Green	Blue	Color	Usage
0	0	0	0	Black	Background, off, border
1	0	0	42	Mid Blue	
2	0	42	0	Mid Green	
3	0	42	42	Mid Cyan	
4	42	0	0	Mid Red	
5	42	0	42	Mid Magenta	
6	42	21	0	Mid Yellow	
7	42	42	42	Dim White	Text foreground color
8	21	21	21	Gray	
9	21	21	63	Blue	
10	21	63	21	Green	
11	21	63	63	Cyan	
12	63	21	21	Red	
13	63	21	63	Magenta	
14	63	63	21	Yellow	
15	63	63	63	White	
16					

TABLE 13.37   16-color VESA Display Modes

VESA Mode Number	Columns	Rows
12 hex (standard)	640	480
102 or 6A hex	800	600
104 hex	1024	768
106 hex	1280	1024

TABLE 13.38   256-color VESA Display Modes

VESA Mode Number	Columns	Rows	Bits per Color
13 hex (standard)	320	200	8
100 hex	640	400	8
101 hex	640	480	8
103 hex	800	600	8
104 hex	1024	768	8
106 hex	1280	1024	8

of the color registers. The default values for these registers are provided in Table 13.38. The standardized 256-color display modes are described in Table 8.13. The actual values are shown in Table 8.14.

13.9.7   Hi-color Modes

The two hi-color modes are very similar except that green has 64 possible shades in the 16-bits-per-color mode but has 32 possible shades in the 15-bits-per-color mode. Each pixel is stored in two consecutive byte locations in display memory. This can be described as a single word location in display memory. The color format within this pixel is provided once again in Figure 13.37.

The hi-color modes are efficient in memory due to the even word alignment of each pixel. Unfortunately, the color coding of red, green, and blue are not so effective and a great deal of time can be wasted getting data into and out of these particular bit locations. The VESA standardized hi-color modes are shown in Table 13.39.

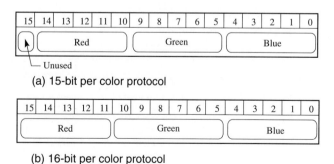

(a) 15-bit per color protocol

(b) 16-bit per color protocol

FIGURE 13.37   Hi-Color Display Mode Color Format

TABLE 13.39 Hi-color VESA Display Modes

VESA Mode Number	Columns	Rows	Bits per Color
10D hex	320	200	15
110 hex	640	480	15
113 hex	800	600	15
116 hex	1024	768	15
119 hex	1280	1024	15
10E hex	320	200	16
111 hex	640	480	16
114 hex	800	600	16
117 hex	1024	768	16
11A hex	1280	1024	16

13.9.8   True-Color

The two true-color modes are 24 bits per pixel and 32 bits per pixel. These modes each store eight bits of red, green, and blue data providing 256 shades of each for a total of 2^{24} = 16.8 million possible colors. The data format is shown in Figure 13.38.

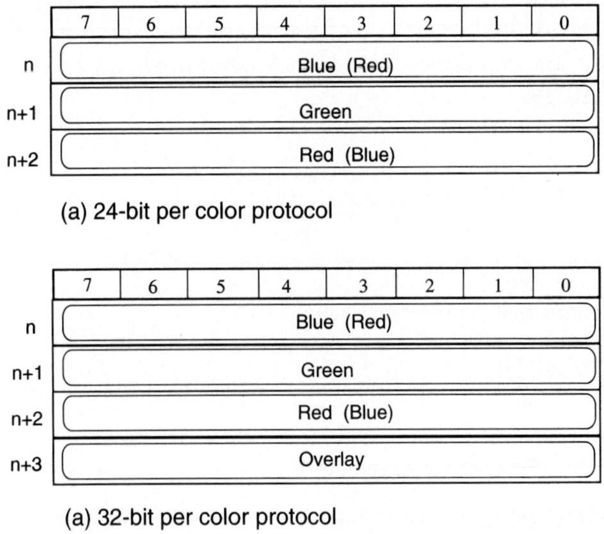

	7	6	5	4	3	2	1	0
n				Blue (Red)				
n+1				Green				
n+2				Red (Blue)				

(a) 24-bit per color protocol

	7	6	5	4	3	2	1	0
n				Blue (Red)				
n+1				Green				
n+2				Red (Blue)				
n+3				Overlay				

(a) 32-bit per color protocol

FIGURE 13.38 True-Color Display Mode Color Format

It should be noted that not all Super VGAs use this format of blue, followed by green, followed by red. Some use red, followed by green, followed by blue. This definitely adds to the confusion, and chips that utilize this format are described in their individual chapters.

The 24-bit color mode is problematic since it requires three bytes per pixel, forcing an odd 3-byte alignment. Since a typical display bank is 65,536 bytes, a single pixel can straddle a 65,536 bank boundary. This is illustrated in Figure 13.39. The VESA standardized hi-color modes are shown in Table 13.40.

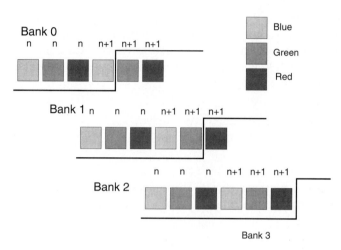

FIGURE 13.39 A Pixel Crossing a Bank Boundary in a 24-bit Color Mode

TABLE 13.40 True-color VESA Display Modes

VESA Mode Number	Columns	Rows	Bits per Color
10F hex	320	200	24
112 hex	640	480	24
115 hex	800	600	24
118 hex	1024	768	24
11B hex	1280	1024	24
??? hex	320	200	32
??? hex	640	480	32
??? hex	800	600	32
??? hex	1024	768	32
??? hex	1280	1024	32

13.10 BITBLTS

If the display memory is the most important part of the Super VGA, then certainly the BitBlt is the most important operation required of the Super VGA. A BitBlt moves a rectangular block of data from one location to another location. These transfers can be from host-to-display, display-to-display, or display-to-host memory.

13.10.1 Software BitBlt

A BitBlt can be performed in software. Suppose that the data is organized as a two-dimensional source and destination arrays. The source and destination is being moved from [x1,y1] to [x2,y2]. Code to move data from one location to another follows. The following examples assume that the source array does not overlap the destination array.

```
for (row=y1; row<=y2; row++) {
    for (column=x1; column<=x2; column++) {
        destination[row][column] = source[row][column]
        }
    }
```

Data is typically not stored in two-dimensional arrays. If the data was in a one-dimensional array, the code would be as follows:

```
height = (1+y2-y1);
width = (1+x2-x1);
number_of_pixels = height *width;
for (i=0; i<number_of_pixels; i++) {
  destination[i] - source[i];
  }
```

This is an oversimplification since it implies that the data is contiguously stored in both the source and destination using the same coordinate system. Suppose you want to move a block from one location of the source to a different location in the destination, say, starting at [first_row, first_column]. Further suppose that you want to move a section of the source to a section of the destination. This is illustrated in Figure 13.40.

Note that the start of the second line to move does not immediately follow the end of the first line. The code sample gets a bit more complicated, taking into account the data that is being skipped in the source and destination. Suppose that the source has a certain number of pixels per row called the *source_pitch* and the destination has *destination_pitch* pixels per row.

```
// notice there is only one height and one width since the
transfer is one-to-one
height = (1+source_y2-source_y1);
```

```
    width = (1+source_x2-source_x1);
// transfer the data
for (row=0; row<height; row++) {
  source_row = source_x1 + row;
  destination_row = destination_y1 + row;
  for (column=0; column<width; column++) {
    source_column = source_x1 + column;
    destination_column = destination_y1 + column;
    source_address = (source_row * source_pitch) + source_column;
    destination_address = (destination_row * destination_pitch)
      + destination_column;
    destination[destination_address] = source[source_address]
  }
}
```

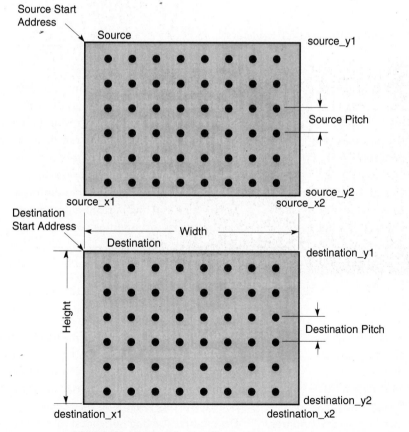

FIGURE 13.40 Moving Non-contiguous Data

13.10.2 Hardware BitBlts

In order to perform the same operation in hardware, the following parameters have to be passed to the graphics coprocessor. The exact implementation, register names, locations of registers, and locations of fields within registers and control fields vary from implementation to implementation. One typical example of the BilBlt Registers is shown in Table 13.41.

The coordinates are provided in terms of a two-dimensional coordinate system as indicated by the X1,Y1 coordinates. In many instances, a one-dimensional coordinate system is used, where the one dimension refers to a memory address. In this case, the typical registers are shown in Table 13.42. The start address for the source and destination follow the software example as follows:

```
source_address = (source_Y1 * source_pitch) + source_X1;
destination_address = (destination_Y1 * destination_pitch) +
    destination_X1;
```

TABLE 13.41 Typical BLT Registers

Register	Function
BLT Width Register	Width of transfer for both source and destination
BLT Height Register	Height of transfer for both source and destination
BLT Source Pitch	Number of pixels per display row in source
BLT Destination Pitch	Number of pixels per display row in destination
BLT Source X1	Source starting horizontal coordinate
BLT Source Y1	Source starting horizontal coordinate
BLT Destination X1	Destination starting horizontal coordinate
BLT Destination Y1	Destination starting horizontal coordinate
BLT Control Register	Control register containing go command

TABLE 13.42 Typical BLT Registers

Register	Function
BLT Width Register	Width of transfer for both source and destination
BLT Height Register	Height of transfer for both source and destination
BLT Source Pitch	Number of pixels per display row in source
BLT Destination Pitch	Number of pixels per display row in destination
BLT Source Start Address	Source starting horizontal coordinate
BLT Destination Start Address	Destination starting horizontal coordinate
BLT Control Register	Control register containing various fields

TABLE 13.43 Source and Destination

Source	Destination
Host memory	Host memory
Host memory	Display memory
Display memory	Display memory
Display memory	Host memory

13.10.3 Sources and Destinations

In the most general case, it is possible to transfer data from a source to a destination in four ways as shown in Table 13.43. Transfers from host memory to host memory are uncommon using the hardware BitBlt since the Super VGAs are not typically bus masters. Perhaps with the PCI bus, the Super VGAs will become bus masters allowing the BitBlt hardware accelerator to be useful when moving data from a source two-dimensional array in host memory to a destination two-dimensional array in host memory.

13.10.4 Direction of Transfers

If the source array and destination array overlap, then the direction of the transfer becomes critical. Otherwise, portions of the data in the source array can be destroyed before being written to the destination. For example, suppose that the source and destination arrays overlap as shown in Figure 13.41. If the data is moved in the standard left-to-right and top-to-bottom direction, then before the pixel S at Sx1,Sy1 can be written from the source to the destination D at Dx1,Dy1, it will be overwritten with the data from pixel 0 at Sx0,Sy0.

In order for this transfer to occur properly, the source starting address would have to be at pixel E at Ex1,Ex2 and the direction would have to proceed from right-to-left and from bottom-to-top. Figure 13.42 illustrates the four possibilities of overlapped data. Since there are four cases, two bits in the BLT Control Register are required to specify the direction of the transfer.

13.10.5 Solid and Pattern Fills

A common graphics operation involves filling a rectangular region on the screen with either a solid color or a pattern. This is actually a simplification of the full two-dimensional BitBlt since the source data is either a constant or a pattern. A solid fill would simply write a constant color into the destination rectangle. This color could come from either the Foreground or Background Color Registers. A field is required to enable solid fill. In some Super VGAs there is no implicit function for the solid fill; rather, the pattern fill is required.

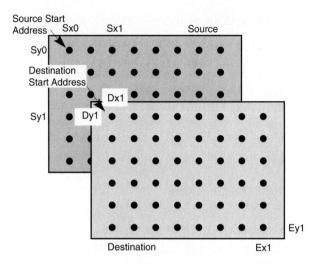

FIGURE 13.41 Overlapping Source and Destination

The pattern fill repeats a source pattern, typically 8 by 8 pixels, into an output. For example, suppose that a scroll bar is to be filled with a dithered pattern as shown in the off-screen memory portion of Figure 13.43. The pattern fill would be enabled, the BitBlt source would point to the off-screen memory

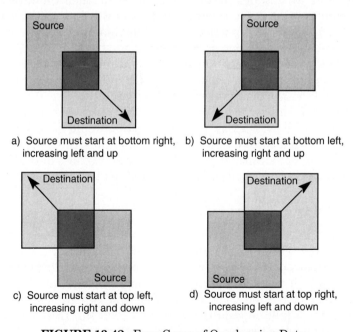

a) Source must start at bottom right, increasing left and up

b) Source must start at bottom left, increasing right and up

c) Source must start at top left, increasing right and down

d) Source must start at top right, increasing left and down

FIGURE 13.42 Four Cases of Overlapping Data

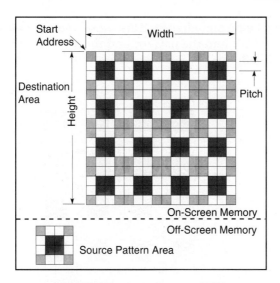

FIGURE 13.43 Pattern Fill

location of the source pattern, and the BitBlt would automatically repeat, in a tiled fashion, the 8-by-8 source into the destination. If all of the 8-by-8 pixels were set to a constant, then a solid fill would occur. Note that color expansion can often be used in conjunction with the pattern fill. Thus, the pattern would consist of a background and foreground color. Registers associated with the pattern fill require only an additional control flag that enables the pattern fill.

13.10.6 Aligning Patterns

In some cases, it is necessary to draw a pattern such that the start of the pattern doesn't correspond to the upper-left corner of the pattern. For example, suppose that a 128-by-128 destination rectangle contains a tiling of 16-by-16 patterns, where each pattern is an 8-by-8 rectangle. Now further suppose that a section of this 128-by-128 rectangle is removed and then later has to be filled in. If the section removed is aligned to the 8-by-8 original rectangles, then no problem occurs as shown in Figure 13.44a. If it is not aligned, then repeating the pattern would cause a crease in the resultant pattern in Figure 13.44b.

One could rewrite the pattern shifted the appropriate amount corresponding to the new pattern as seen in Figure 13.44b. Another technique is to draw each 8-by-8 pattern four times. Thereafter, it would be simple to shift the pattern by simply adjusting the source address to point at the correct upper-left corner of the pattern. This is shown in Figure 13.45.

Some VGAs allow the pattern to have an offset such that the pattern doesn't have to start at the upper-left corner. This is important when the pattern is to be overlaid into a background that contains a similar pattern, without having the pattern end up being non-aligned. This would require two additional registers, one for the x-offset into the pattern and the second is the y-offset. This is shown in Figure 13.46.

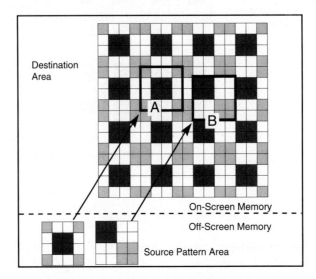

FIGURE 13.44 Offset Problems when Replicating Patterns

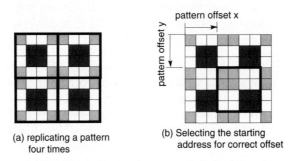

(a) replicating a pattern four times

(b) Selecting the starting address for correct offset

FIGURE 13.45 Repeating a Pattern

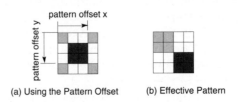

(a) Using the Pattern Offset

(b) Effective Pattern

FIGURE 13.46 Offset Pattern Parameters

TABLE 13.44   Solid and Pattern Fill Registers

Register	Function
Control	Contains enable solid fill, enable pattern fill
Pattern X Offset	Contains x offset into pattern
Pattern Y Offset	Contains y offset into pattern

13.10.7   Solid and Pattern Fill Registers.

The solid and pattern fills rely mostly on already-existing registers. Added would be the enable pattern replication flag in a Control Register and the X and Y Offset Registers if offsetting of patterns is allowed. These are shown in Table 13.44.

13.11   COLOR EXPANSION

A common task encountered in color graphics is the expansion of monochrome data, one bit per pixel, into color data, either four, eight, fifteen, sixteen, 24, or 32 bits per pixel. This is called *color expansion*. Color expansion is not necessarily limited to monochrome-to-color transfers. One could expand a 4-bit-per-color pixel to a 32-bit-per-color pixel, but this is not common. The standard VGA provided a primitive color expansion technique using write modes 2 and 3. Code examples using these modes are provided in Chapter 12. This color expansion was limited to expansion of a monochrome byte containing eight pixels into eight consecutive pixels in a 4-bit-per-color output. Further, the transfer was transparent (that is, only the foreground pixels were written).

Many Super VGAs incorporate a fully flexible color expansion mode capable of expanding into many color formats in either opaque or transparent modes. In addition, many of the graphics processors can process up to 64 pixels in a single instruction cycle. The Super VGAs implement this color expansion capability differently. Some implement it in the Super VGA portion of the chip. Others implement it in the graphics accelerator. Still others implement it in both. Color expansion can go from host memory to display memory or from display memory to display memory.

13.11.1   Transparent or Opaque Background

Many graphics objects can be described as containing a foreground and background. These might be as simple as a character or as complicated as an animation sprite moving across a background image. When drawing objects onto the screen, a decision needs to be made regarding what to do with the background.

An "opaque" draw occurs when the pixels corresponding to the background of the object are drawn over the existing data on the screen. A "transparent" draw occurs when the pixels corresponding to the background of the object are **not** drawn over the existing data on the screen. There are actually several types of transparency-related operations. These are discussed in detail in Section 13.12.

13.11.2 Expanding Monochrome Data

The most common form of monochrome expansion involves character fonts. Characters are seldom drawn such that there are more than two colors, called the foreground and background. The binary representation of the font is stored in memory. The character font could reside in either host memory or display memory. If the character font is in host memory, then a color-expanded BitBlt would occur from system memory to display memory. If the character font is in display memory, then a color-expanded BitBlt would occur from display memory to display memory. Typically, the display memory to display memory transfers are quicker dependent on the host-display bus. Also, if a graphics accelerator is used, the host is free to perform other tasks while the display-to-display transfer is taking place. There is no reason to store this data in its true color expanded form when color expansion is present since there is no time penalty to expand the data.

An example of expanding a "word" is shown in Figure 13.47. The width of the graphics processor determines how much data can be moved at a time. Two

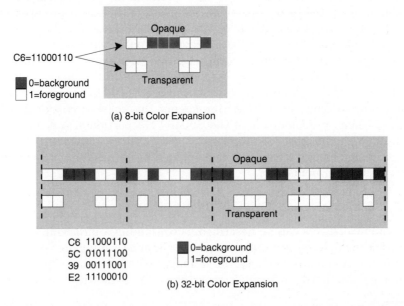

FIGURE 13.47 Color Expansion. (a) 8-bit color expansion (b) 32-bit color expansion

examples are provided, one in Figure 13.47a where an 8-bit transfer occurs and a second in Figure 13.47b, showing that a 32-bit transfer can occur in a single "word" cycle. In the first case, the "word" is eight bits wide, and in the second it is 32 bits wide. It is likely that the 8-bit data would be used to create text on the screen since a common character width is eight bits wide. In some cases, wider fonts might be used, thereby requiring more than eight bits to be transferred at a time.

A second common application of color expansion are sprites. A sprite might be a cursor that once again is stored in binary form and color expanded when it is actually copied to display memory. In this case, the width of the sprite would determine the optimum "word" size.

13.11.3 Expansion of a Two-Dimensional Block of Monochrome Data

In the previous section, we saw how to expand a one-dimensional array. In most graphics applications, we are dealing with two-dimensional arrays. For example, the character pattern would be 8 by 14 pixels or a cursor might be 32 by 32 pixels. It is desirable to color expand the entire two-dimensional array in a single instruction. This is accomplished using the BitBlt discussed in Section 13.10. A typical block color expansion is shown in Figure 13.48, in which an entire character is transferred in a single operation.

In order to perform a color expansion BitBlt into display memory, the programmer would set up the BitBlt such that the source pointed to the binary data, whether in host or display memory, and the destination to the desired location in display memory. The destination pitch is set up in the same way as a non-color expanded BitBlt. The source pitch is a bit different. We need to look at the input memory format to understand how this source pitch works.

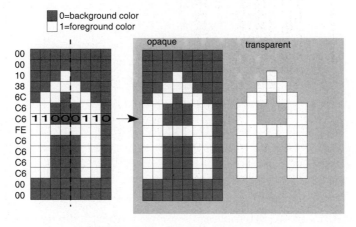

FIGURE 13.48 Block Color Expansion

13.11.4   Source Pitch

The source data can reside in host memory or in display memory. If it resides in host memory, the memory format is considered to be one dimensional. There is, in reality, only one memory address pointer. Therefore, the font data is stored contiguously with one character immediately following the previous character. In this case, the source pitch would be considered to be the width of the destination. This is shown in Figure 13.49.

Since we are expanding a binary two-dimensional array, the width of the input data, be it eight, sixteen, or 32 bits, is equivalent to the width of the output. Since the input data is stored in a one-dimensional array, there is no true meaning to pitch. However, the BitBlt system needs to know how many bytes to read before skipping to the next line as described in Section 13.10. In the case of a character box that is one byte wide (eight bits), we would write the byte, then bump the address by the pitch of the source data to find the next scan lines worth of data. Since the next scan lines worth of data is the next byte, the BitBlt would want to add 8 to the address. Thus the pitch is 8. This is the width of the BitBlt since the character is eight pixels wide. However, there is an ambiguity here and different Super VGAs handle it differently. Should the pitch of the source be 8 for the eight pixels or 1 for the one byte containing the input? Each Super VGA must be dealt with independently regarding the actual implementation.

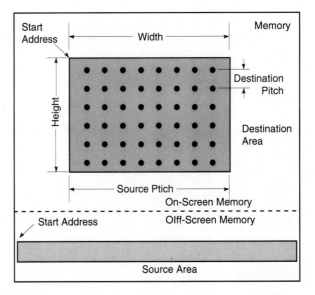

FIGURE 13.49 Determining the Source Pitch with Binary Data

When the source data is contained in the off-screen memory, as shown in Figure 13.44, the source pitch would not necessarily be the same for each object contained there. For example, there may be both color and binary data in off-screen memory. The source pitch would be determined by the object. Therefore, the off-screen memory has no inherent pitch. It is simply memory.

13.11.5 Color-Expanded BitBlt Registers

In order to accomplish the two-dimensional block color expansion, we need to add a few items to the BitBlt register list. These are shown in Table 13.45. In order to provide the proper control, two flags are necessary. These are an enable flag that turns on the color expansion and a transparent/opaque flag.

13.12 TRANSPARENCY

Many graphics objects can be described as containing a foreground and background. These might be as simple as a character or as complicated as an animation sprite moving across a background image. When drawing objects onto the screen, one needs to decide what to do with the background. An *opaque* draw occurs when the pixels corresponding to the background of the object are drawn over the existing data on the screen. A *transparent* draw occurs when the pixels corresponding to the background of the object are **not** drawn over the existing data on the screen.

There are two types of transparent operations. The more common type of transparency operation, as discussed in the previous paragraph, involves the input data. The input data contains the key. If a pixel in the input data is a background, it keys the transparency/opaque operation. In the case of color expansion, this pixel is always 0 since the input data is binary. In a non-color expansion mode, this pixel might be any value.

Suppose you want to draw a sprite onto a screen and that sprite contains both foreground and background information. Further suppose that the sprite contains the image of a person standing in front of a blue background. The foreground would be the portion of the image corresponding to the person and the background would be everything that wasn't the foreground.

TABLE 13.45 Color Expansion Registers

Register	Function
Register	*Function*
Background Color	Contains background color
Foreground Color	Contains foreground color
Control	Contains transparent/opaque background flag and expansion enable flag

13.12.1   Background Key Color

In the previous example, no simple binary input data can determine the foreground versus the background. One simple way is to create a background key value. This would be the value that would be compared to the input data. Any match would force the pixel that matched to be the background. Any NOT match would force the pixel that didn't match to be the foreground. In the previous example, suppose the background was a constant Red=0, Green=0, Blue=127. In this case, the background key value would be Red=0, Green=0, Blue=140. See any problems here? I see at least two. The first is that the background key color cannot be contained in the foreground image. If the person in the image is wearing a blue a shirt with a blue circle in the middle of it whose value happens to be Red=0, Green=0, Blue=140, the circle will be viewed as background. Consequently, there will be a hole in the middle of the person. The second problem arises if the blue circle has shading within it. Say the blue varies from 130 to 150. In this example, only pixels that have blue set to 140 would be considered as background.

13.12.2   Background Key Color Mask

The problem occurring when the background contains a range of colors can be partially fixed by the use of a background Mask Register. The background Mask Register is used to compare the bits in the background key color with the bits in the source image. Any bit in the Mask Register that is set to 1 forces the same bits in the source image and in the background key color to be compared. All bits in the source data and the background key color corresponding to 1s in the background mask must compare for the resultant pixel to be considered as a background. All other pixels are no-cares.

For example, suppose that the background key color Mask Register is set to Red=0, Green=0, Blue=224. Now red and green are all no-cares. Blue is set to 224, which corresponds to C0 hex. That means that only bits 7, 6, and 5 will be compared. Therefore, we need to look at the background key color and see what bits 7, 6, and 5 are set to. In this example, let's set them to 1, 0, 0 respectively. The value could then be 80 hex or 128. Now, any pixels in the source image that have bits 7=1, 6=0, and 5=0 will cause a background match. These pixels correspond to values within the range of 128 through 159. This would cover all of the pixels ranging from 130 to 150 in the input circle. Certainly, not all situations can be handled with this method.

13.12.3   Background Masking

A more powerful method enabling foreground and background differentiation is masking. Masking provides a flag for each pixel, which determines implicitly whether the pixel is a foreground or background. Masking is available in the Standard VGA through the Bit Mask Register. This masks out only the eight pixels in a single byte when using a 16-color mode. This approach is very limited.

The Super VGAs have extended this 8-bit mask to fit the entire word with perhaps sixteen, 32 or even 64 bits. Some Super VGAs incorporate a two-dimensional mask. This powerful function allows desired bits to be masked in or out and is very similar to the Hardware Cursors mask patterns. Masking is discussed in Section 13.13.

13.12.4 Background Related Registers

We have included two new registers: the Background Key Color Register and the Background Key Color Mask Register as shown in Table 13.46. Although not all Super VGAs use this technique, it is fairly common.

13.13 MASKING

Display memory can be thought of as a three-dimensional space where the horizontal and vertical dimensions are as expected with the third dimension being the depth of each pixel. This is illustrated in Figure 13.50. In Figure 13.50a the three dimensions are shown as horizontal, vertical and pixel depth. In Figure 13.50b, the popular pixel depths are shown.

TABLE 13.46 Background Key Registers

Register	Function
Background Key Color	Contains background key color
Background Key Color Mask	Contains background key color mask
Control	Enable Color Masking flag

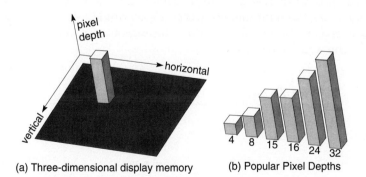

(a) Three-dimensional display memory   (b) Popular Pixel Depths

FIGURE 13.50 Three-dimensional Display Memory

There are three types of masking. The first type is a horizontal-line–based mask. It operates on a certain number of pixels, usually up to 64 bits, per horizontally contiguous pixels. The second type is a two-dimensional mask that operates across both the horizontal and vertical dimensions at the same time. The third type operates across the pixel height. The first two are called *across-plane masks,* and the third is called a *through-plane mask.*

13.13.1 Across-Plane Masks

The most common masks are the across-plane masks. These include the horizontal mask, typically called a bit mask and a two-dimensional mask. Since these masks affect only one plane at a time, they are referred to as across-plane masks. The first type is common in the standard VGA and resides in the Bit Mask Register. Each pixel in the mask is either a 0 or a 1. If 0, the data is masked out; if 1, the data is allowed through. Table 13.47 illustrates an AND operation as applied to a bit mask.

The standard VGA Bit Mask Register was only eight bits and worked only with 4-bit-per-color modes. In the Super VGAs, these masks can be to 64 bits long, accommodating a maximum 64-bit data bus width. A bit mask is shown in Figure 13.51. A register the size of the mask is required to store the mask data. Typically, the mask is always enabled and should be pre-loaded to all 1s.

Two-dimensional masks are more exotic. Their most common application is in hardware cursors, which are discussed in Section 13.14. The theory is the same as for the one-dimensional case. Any mask value that is a 1 allows the source data into the destination. Any mask value that is a 0 masks the destination data from any change. Since the mask can be an arbitrary size, it is not possible to store the mask in registers, and off-screen memory is typically used. In Figure 13.52, the data consists of the typical cursor arrow with white on the outside getting darker towards the inside. The black pixels in the data mask are don't cares. The mask contains either 0s or 1s where 0s are represented in black and 1s are represented in white. This is analogous to a filter where the black would block the light and the white (clear) would allow the light through. Only those pixels associated with the white=clear=1 pixels in the mask are affected by the write operation.

TABLE 13.47 AND Logical Operation

Data	Mask	Output
0	0	No change
1	0	No change
0	1	0 input allowed through
1	1	1 input allowed through

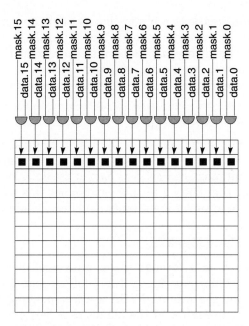

FIGURE 13.51 One-dimensional Bit Mask

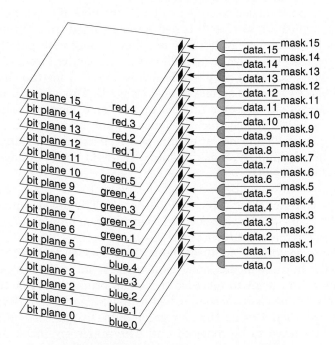

FIGURE 13.52 Two-Dimensional Bit Mask

The two-dimensional mask is a binary image. This image has to be stored somewhere, typically in display memory, and typically in off-screen display memory. The display hardware has to be made aware of the horizontal and vertical size of the mask as well as its starting location. In addition, a control field in a register is required to enable the across-plane masking.

13.13.2 Alpha-Channel Masks

The simplest two-dimensional mask is the alpha-channel mask. The alpha channel is present in 32-bit-per-pixel display modes. If the hardware is present, the two-dimensional bit mask can exist as part of the data itself resident in the alpha channel. Recall that the 32 bit per pixel mode has 24 bits of color and eight bits left over. The left-over eight bits are called the alpha channel.

13.13.3 Through-Plane Masking

The second type of masking is through-plane masking. The standard VGA had four bit planes, each containing one of the four bits per pixel. A Map Mask Register was provided in the standard VGA to allow masking of the planes. The register allowed any combination of the planes to be written into. A 4-bit field was required for the mask, one bit for each plane. Since the mask affected all planes, it was called through-plane masking.

When 8-bit-per-pixel modes became available, the idea of masking was kind of lost, even though there were still benefits to be gained from through-plane masking. This is not immediately obvious when dealing with palette modes. But consider the case where you would like two independent images to reside in display memory. It would be possible to use bits 0–3 for the first image, Image A, and bits 4–7 for the second image, Image B. This would produce two completely independent 16-color images in the same memory. The palette would repeat the pattern such that the images were independent. Any write operation to Image A should not affect Image B. Therefore, masking bits 4–7 could protect them. Similarly, masking bits 0–3 would protect Image A when writes occurred to Image B.

Another application would be to dedicate bit plane 7 to a binary mask, similar to the alpha channel mask discussed previously. The image data would be restricted to 7 bits, 0–127. The mask could then reside in bit plane 7. Of course, the hardware would have to support this feature.

Through-plane masking is more relevant when working in the 15-, 16-, 24- and 32-bit modes. In these modes, one is able to mask out individual colors. For example, suppose you want to increase the green brightness in a 16 bit-per-color mode. This can be easily accomplished by masking off the bits associated with blue and red, then writing the new green data. In this case bits 0–4 and bits 10–15 would have to be masked out. The mask would be 07E0 hex.

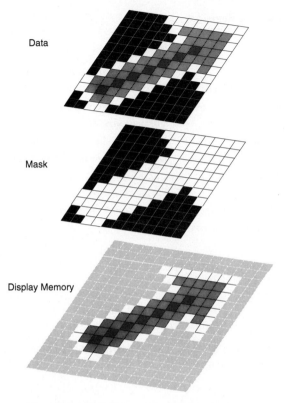

FIGURE 13.53 Through-Plane Masking

Through-plane masking is shown in Figure 13.53. Typically, through-plane masking is always enabled and all bits are preset to 1.

13.13.4 Registers Associated with Masking

For the across-plane masks, it is necessary to provide a Bit Mask Register, a pointer to the two-dimensional mask, a horizontal and vertical Size Mask Register, and a control to enable the two-dimensional masking. Most Super VGAs that support two-dimensional masking have implicit sizes for the masks, typically 32-by-32 or 64-by-64 masks. The size registers are included for completeness in Table 13.48.

13.14 RASTER OPERATIONS (RASTER OPS) / MIXES

Raster operations are arithmetic or logical operations that occur on the image data. Since there are several arithmetic and logical operations that one performs on graphics data, they are quite handy. The most common raster

TABLE 13.48 Masking Registers

Register	Description
Across-plane Bit Mask	Must be as large as the display data bus
Two-dimensional Mask Address	Address to upper-left corner of binary mask
Mask X-dimension	Horizontal size of mask
Mask Y-dimension	Vertical size of mask
Through-plane Bit Mask	Must be as large as the maximum bits-per-pixel
Control	Enable 2-D across plane mask

operation is *replace destination with source*. Common software instructions that perform this operation are

```
mov  ax,bx       ; replace the value of ax with the value in bx
mov  es:[di],ax  ; replace the memory location pointed to by
es:[di] with the value in ax
destination = source; // replace the value of the variable
                     // "destination" with the value in the
                     // variable "source"
```

Often our operation of replacing the destination with a source follows some other logical or arithmetic operation, as shown in the following examples:

```
add  ax,20       ; replace the value of ax with the sum of the old
                 ; value in ax and the constant 20
xor  ax,bx       ; replace the value of ax with the XOR of the old
                 ; value in ax and the value in bx
destination += source;  // replace the value of "destination"
                        // with the sum of the old "destination"
                        // and "source"
```

These operations are also common in graphics memory. The problem is that many of these operations require read-modify-write operations, and this can be extremely time-consuming when going across the display-host interface. A much better idea is to incorporate the arithmetic/logic unit in the graphics processor, as shown in Figure 13.54. The programmer sets up the logical operation desired, then provides the source and destination information. The read-modify-write operations occur in the graphics processor. In the following code, the destination would be replaced by the XOR of the current value in the destination with the value provided by the host in the ax register. The difference is even more exaggerated when an arithmetic raster op is used like *add with saturate*.

```
mov  cx,10000    ; do all 10000 operations at DMA rates
rep  stosw       ; perform the logical XOR of the old value in
                 ; display memory with the value in ax
```

TABLE 13.49 Raster Operations

Function Select	Operation
0	Replace destination with source
1	Destination = source AND latched data
2	Destination = source OR latched data
3	Destination = source XOR latched data

This is far superior to the following:

```
mov     cx,10000    ; do 10,000 operations at a snail's pace
loop1:  lodsw       ; read the value from display memory
xor     ax,value    ; perform the logical XOR of ax and value
stosw               ; write the value into display memory
loop    loop1       ; repeat tile done
```

The standard VGA had raster operations, which are found in the Function Select Field (FS) of the Data Rotate Register. The four operations are shown in Table 13.49. A further limitation was that the source of the second operand had to be the latched data held in the 32-bit VGA read-back latch. The purpose of this latch was to allow read/modify/write operations. You first had to read the selected display memory location, thus latching it in the read-back latch. Next you would write the new data to the selected display memory location. The latched data and the new data were then logically combined as per the Function Select field to form the new destination value. This was better than nothing but still cumbersome because it required the read-before-write operation.

13.14.1 Data Flow

During a graphics operation, source data is combined with destination data, under the control of pattern data, and the result is written back to the destination. The mask data, discussed in Section 13.13, can also be included in the operation to selectively inhibit updating of the destination data. The data flow is specific to Super VGA. I will discuss the XGA in this section. Most Super VGAs have a technique similar to the XGA, although there is a tremendous amount of variation depending on the implementation. The XGA data flow is shown in Figure 13.54.

13.14.2 Source Data

The foreground and background sources can be either the source bit map or from the foreground and background Color Registers. The bit map data might come from the host or display memory. The display memory might be from on-screen memory during a pan or from off-screen during a screen re-draw.

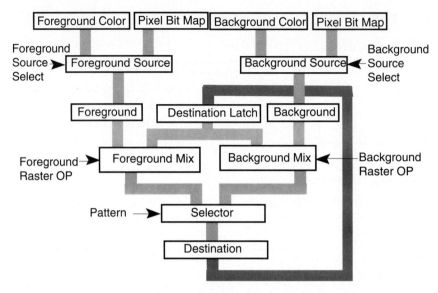

FIGURE 13.54 Data Flow Diagram

Whether the source of data is from the foreground or background mix is determined by the pattern bit map.

13.14.3 Pattern Bit map

The pattern bit map is described in the mask section in Section 13.13. Each pixel in the Pattern Register determines whether the foreground or background mix data is written into the destination. In the example describing the XGA, a color expansion would occur by sending the font pattern of a character into the pattern stream as opposed to the data stream as described for the Super VGAs in earlier sections.

NOTE: If this seems overly confusing, that's because it actually **is** overly confusing! Every manufacturer interprets how to accomplish the data flow differently. The end results are usually very similar, but how they get there is often different. In large part, this is why I cannot completely describe the details of each Super VGA graphics accelerator in this book.

Pattern data can be supplied by a bit map or it can be set to a constant. The constant is always 1, indicating that the foreground source should be used throughout the entire operation. The pattern data can be generated from the coprocessor using a source color compare operations. The pattern data is generated on the fly. As the source data comes in, it is checked for 0. For any value of 0, the comparitor generates a 0 pattern bit. This 0 pattern bit then forces use of the background color and background mix. Any non-zero value in the source data generates a 1 pattern bit indicating foreground. This allows multi-colored text, as is used in anti-aliased text. More complicated color comparison is discussed in Section 13.14.5.

13.14.4 Foreground and Background Mix

The foreground and background are each put into their own Arithmetic Logic Unit (ALU), called the *foreground mix* and *background mix*. The foreground source is combined with the destination using the foreground mix and the background source is combined with the destination using the background mix. The terminology gets a bit out of hand here since we use the terms "raster op" and "mix" interchangeably. The mix or raster op is the operation that occurs in the ALU.

In Chapter 2.7, the complete 256 raster op table is provided. This follows the Microsoft conventions. Table 13.50 provides the XGA Mix tables. Remember that the foreground mix is separate from the background mix.

One might ask, "What is all of the NOT Source OR NOT Destination stuff anyway ?" I think it will be useful to spend some time looking at each of these functions. In Figure 13.55, a logic diagram is provided for each of the fifteen

TABLE 13.50 Foreground and Background Mix (Raster Ops) for the XGA

Code	Function
00	Zeros
01	Source AND Destination
02	Source AND NOT Destination
03	Source
04	NOT Source AND Destination
05	Destination
06	Source XOR Destination
07	Source OR Destination
08	NOT Source AND NOT Destination
09	Source XOR NOT Destination
0A	NOT Destination
0B	Source OR NOT Destination
0C	NOT Source
0D	NOT Source OR Destination
0E	NOT Source OR NOT Destination
0F	Ones
10	Maximum
11	Minimum
12	Add with Saturate
13	Subtract (Destination-Source) with Saturate
14	Subtract (Source-Destination) with Saturate
15	Average

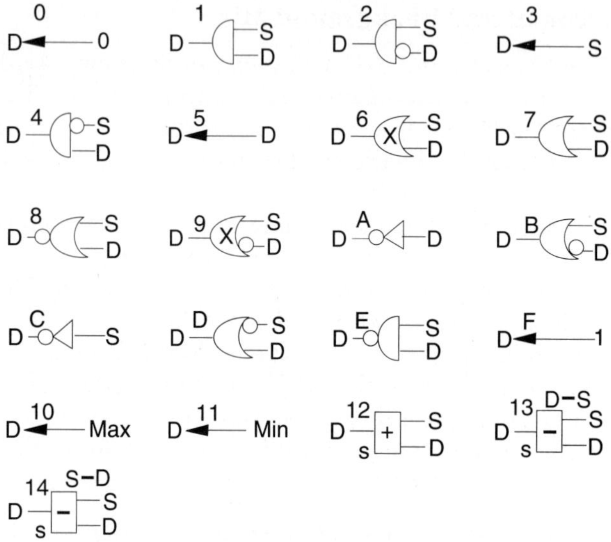

FIGURE 13.55 Logic Diagrams

logical operations in Table 13.40. There are basically three types of logical operations. These include setting the destination to a constant, setting the destination to either the source or destination, and using an AND operation, an OR operation, or an XOR operation. The NOT operation is an inversion. What does it mean to invert a color?

Color Inversion

The inverse of black is white. Easy one. The inverse of red is cyan. Not so simple. The inverse of Red=125, Green=73, Blue=201 is Red=130, Green=182, Blue=54 using 24-bit color. Really obscure. Now let's get really obnoxious. Suppose the color present in palette index of 14 is Red=20, Green=20, Blue=20 and that the color present in palette index of 241 is Red=21, Green=20, Blue=20. Since the inverse of 14 is 241, the inverse color of Red=20, Green=20, Blue=20 is Red=21, Green=20, Blue=20. Certainly there is no physical reason why this is the case. Let's look at each case.

The inverse of black is certainly white due to the binary relationship between 0 and 1. For all other colors, the inverse operation can be thought of as a compliment operation. Using basic color theory, the compliments to Red, Green, and Blue are Cyan, Magenta, and Yellow respectively. This is described in Table 13.51.

The operation used to form a compliment is to invert the value. This inversion can be thought of as subtraction. For example, there are five bits per color in a 15-bit-per-color mode . Thus, there are 32 possible shades. The inverse of color X

TABLE 13.51   Color Compliments

Color			Compliment		
Red	Green	Blue	Red	Green	Blue
255	0	0	0	255	255
0	255	0	255	0	255
0	0	255	255	255	0
125	73	201	130	182	54

would be $Y = 1 + (32 - X)$. There are eight bits per color in a 24-bit per color mode. Using the same logic, the inverse of color X would be $Y = 1 + (255 - X)$.

It should be noted that color negative film is the inverse of color positive film...kind of. There is actually a much more complicated operation that is required to invert the color.

AND Operations

The logical AND operation is an *intersection* operation. Consider an example in which two objects have 1 as a foreground and 0 as a background. The result is 1 any place where the two objects intersect. This AND operation is commonly used in masking. Consider two transparencies, called A and B, each consisting of a clear circle on a black background. Put A on top of B and both on to a light table. As you slide one across the other, the light that gets through both transparencies represents the intersection and consequently the AND operation. In this case destination = A AND B.

Using the AND operation with inverted inputs simply allows you to reverse the color of the inputs and still maintain the AND function. For example, consider transparency A to be a black circle with a clear background. This is clearly the inverse of transparency A in the previous example. One might well desire the same result as above. Instead of inverting A before the AND operation, we could simply use the inverted input NOT A. In this case: destination = NOT A AND B.

Inverting the output of the AND operation is called a NAND operation. This says simply perform the AND, and then invert the output. Suppose that the desired result is 0 anywhere A and B intersect and 1 everywhere else. No problem; simply use destination = NOT (A AND B). There is no entry for NOT (A AND B) in Figure 13.55. However, there is an exact alternative in the OR operators, number E, called NOT Source OR NOT Destination. This is not intuitive unless one looks at the truth tables. They are indeed identical. This says that the output is a 1 if either of the inputs is a 0. This is an OR operation since it uses the "either" keyword. It is also an AND operation since one could equivalently say that the output is a 0 if both of the inputs are a 1.

OR Operations

The logical OR operation is a *union* operation. Consider an example in which the same two objects have 1 as a foreground and a 0 as a background. Any place that either of the objects has a 1 produces a result of 1. This OR operation is commonly used when filtering two objects. We have to choose a subtractive analogy as opposed to the additive analogy in the AND section. Suppose that our two objects each have a black circle on top of a clear background and both are sliding across each other atop our light table. The light will be blocked anywhere that a circle exists, regardless of whether the circles touch each other. Our analogy has to change. Suppose the desired result is blackness. Therefore, blackness gets assigned 1 in both the input A and B space and the output space. Now the logic works. The destination = A OR B; that is, the destination is black anywhere that either of the circles exists.

Using the OR operation with inverted inputs is analogous to the AND operations. It is still the OR operation without having to invert one of the inputs.

Inverting the output of the OR operation is called a NOR operation. Once again, simply perform the OR and then invert the output. Suppose you want a white result wherever either A or B is black. Thus destination = NOT (A OR B). Once again this does not show up in Figure 13.55 and we have to use the exact alternative in the AND operations, number 8, destination = NOT Source AND NOT Destination. This says that the output is a 1 if both of the inputs are a 0. This is an AND operation since it uses the "both" keyword. It is also an OR operation since one could equivalently say that the output is a 0 if either of the inputs is a 1.

XOR Operations

The XOR operator allows selective inversion. If one operator is a 1, the other operator is inverted. This is very useful when you want to non-destructively change data. Since two inversions result in a non-inversion, one could XOR a destination with a 1 to change the color, then XOR it again with a 1 to restore the original value. The difference between an XOR and a NOT function is that the XOR allows a choice between inversion and leave-alone. Suppose that one source is considered as a mask, A, and a second, B, is considered the data. If a value in the mask is a 1, the destination will be NOT B. If the mask is a 0, the destination will be B. If the destination is B, then we have our most common use of the XOR operator.

The XOR operator and the AND operator are used in conjunction to produce a hardware cursor. The AND operator is used as a mask and the XOR operator is used to change the destination. When the cursor overlays a region of the display, there is no need to save the underlying data. It is only necessary to NOT the destination when the cursor passes over, and then NOT it again when the cursor leaves.

Arithmetic Operations

The arithmetic operations of maximum, minimum, add, and subtract are self-evident. The "saturate" protects the data during addition and subtraction. Suppose maximum saturation of a color is 255, as is the case in 24-bit color. If we add 100 to the value of 200, we would (typically) like the result to be 255 and not 300 = 25 after truncation. Similarly, if the minimum saturation is 0, subtracting 200 from the value of 100 should (typically) produce 0, and not –100 = 155.

13.14.5 Color Comparison

The value that the destination pixels are compared with is stored in the Destination Color Compare Value Register. The way in which the data is compared is stored in the Destination Color Compare Condition Register. The possible conditions are provided in Table 13.52. The result of the color comparison determines whether the destination should be masked. If the result is true, the destination is masked. If the result is false, the destination is updated.

13.14.6 Raster Op/Mix Registers

The registers required to implement the Raster Op/Mix functions vary greatly depending on the implementation. The XGA implementation is shown in Table 13.53. Super VGA implementations are similar. Several of these entries are bit fields combined within other registers to save space. The address to the source and destination are the same as the BitBlt addresses.

The foreground and background source control select the actual source of data into the foreground and background ALUs. The choices are shown in Table 13.54.

TABLE 13.52 Color Comparison Condition Codes

Condition Code	Condition
0	Always True (Disable update)
1	Destination Data > Color Compare Value
2	Destination Data = Color Compare Value
3	Destination Data < Color Compare Value
4	Always False (Enable update)
5	Destination Data > = Color Compare Value
6	Destination Data != Color Compare Value
7	Destination Data <= Color Compare Value

TABLE 13.53 Raster Op/Mix Registers

Register	Function
Background Source	Selects the source for the background data (see Table 13.54)
Foreground Source	Selects the source for the foreground data (see Table 13.54)
Source Bit Map	Address pointing to source. Note 1.
Destination Bit Map	Address pointing to destination. Note 1.
Pattern Bit Map	Address pointing to pattern. Note 1.
Foreground Mix	Raster Op used for foreground
Background Mix	Raster Op used for background

Note 1. In the XGA, there is an indirect address scheme such that the Source, Destination, and pattern bit map addresses actually point to one of three actual address registers called PEL Map A, PEL Map B, PEL MAP C. See Chapter 18 for details.

TABLE 13.54 Foreground and Background Source Control

Value	Source
0	Fixed value. Foreground or Background Color Register provides value.
1	Reserved.
2	Source Bit Memory. May be host or display memory.
3	Reserved.

13.15   HARDWARE CURSOR

Hardware cursors reduce the software overhead required to maintain a graphics cursor. The hardware is completely responsible for updating the display with respect to the cursor. Either the mouse driver or direct control of the cursor position determines where the cursor should be positioned. The hardware cursor is very easy to understand yet very difficult to implement since each and every SuperVGA seems to do it differently. See Section 2.8.10. for an additional discussion of the hardware cursor .

13.15.1   Cursor Technique

The technique employed for a hardware cursor either mixes the cursor pattern at the input to the DAC or actually overwrites display memory with the cursor pattern. Three examples are shown in Figure 13.56.

When writing directly into display memory, the color of the cursor determines how the operation proceeds. If solid cursor controllable cursor colors are desired, the original data in the display memory has to be saved before the cursor is drawn and then restored when the cursor is moved. If the cursor color

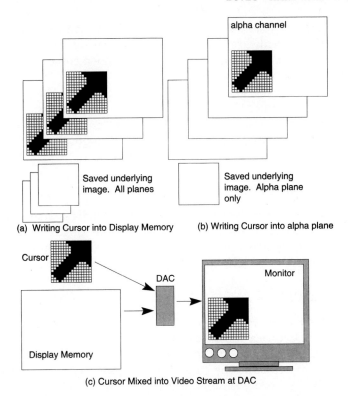

FIGURE 13.56 Methods of Creating a Hardware Cursor. (a) Writing into display memory. (b) Writing into an overlay plane. (c) Writing directly into the DAC.

is to be an XOR of the original data, no display data must be saved. If an alpha channel is used, then the same relationships exist, except this time only the alpha channel needs to be saved or XORed. If the data is written to the DAC directly, display memory is never modified and no saving or XORing is necessary. If this is the case, don't expect to find the cursor when doing a screen grab. If you need to show the cursor, you will have to read the cursor location and the cursor pattern and draw it into display memory yourself.

The hardware cursor pattern is stored in off-screen memory. If enabled, it is drawn in the selected colors to the display memory at the specified cursor location.

13.15.2 Cursor Colors

The cursor can be displayed in a number of ways. One color scheme uses a combination of two solid colors. Only two colors can be used since the cursor is a binary pattern. The advantage is that you always know what color the cursor will be. The disadvantages are that the cursor can disappear if the colors of the underlying image are too close to the cursor. The second disadvantage is a speed penalty if the hardware cursor is actually writing into display memory since it forces a save/restore operation. A well-designed cursor would have two very different colors to ensure visibility.

A second technique uses an XOR function for the cursor colors such that the underlying data determines the color of the cursor. Color inversion is used. The advantage is that the cursor is always visible and no save/restore operations are required. The disadvantage is that the cursor can get pretty weird looking when displayed over regions of rapidly changing colors.

13.15.3   Cursor Location

The cursor is located onto the screen based on an address that points to the upper-left corner of the cursor pattern. This address might be a one-dimensional display memory address or a two-dimensional horizontal and vertical address pair. The address is shown in Figure 13.57.

13.15.4   Cursor Offsets

The cursor pattern is stored in off-screen memory. A one-dimensional address pointer is required to direct the hardware to its location in off-screen memory. This is called the *Cursor_Offset* as shown in Figure 13.57 and Figure 13.58.

It is not necessary to start the cursor at the upper-left corner. Some hardware cursors are equipped with an offset that allow the start of the cursor to shift across the pattern. This offset is typically specified as a two-dimensional offset, called the *Horz_Cursor_Offset* and the *Vert_Cursor_Offset*. These are

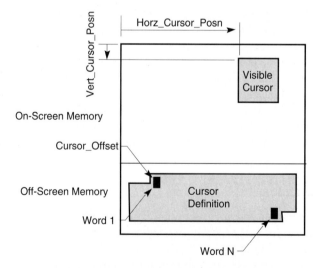

FIGURE 13.57 Hardware Cursor Location

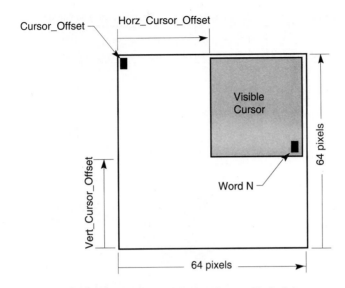

FIGURE 13.58 Hardware Cursor Definition

shown in Figure 13.57. There are two uses for this offset. The first is when a 32-by-32-sized cursor is desired. The offset points into the 64-by-64 cursor pattern, thereby accessing the desired portion of the pattern. The second reason for offsets is when the cursor is partially hidden behind another object. In order to achieve the three-dimensional effect, it is necessary to slide the visible portion of the cursor. This is shown in Figure 13.59. The offset into the cursor pattern should not be confused with the *Cursor_Offset* address that tells the hardware where the start of the cursor pattern resides.

13.15.5 Cursor Patterns

The cursor pattern is a two-bit-per-pixel pattern. There are, unfortunately, a variety of protocols used to store the cursor. Some common techniques are shown in Figure 13.60. The two bits per pixel can be used in a variety of ways; usage typically depends on other control bits that affect their usage. For

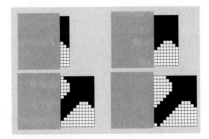

FIGURE 13.59 Displaying a Portion of the Cursor

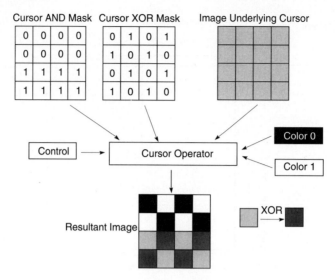

FIGURE 13.60 Hardware Cursor Patterns

example, these two bits can have four different functions if a two-bit control field is provided that determines their function. An example is provided in Table 2.29.

The hardware cursor pattern contains two masks. These are the AND mask and the XOR mask. The AND mask and XOR mask operate on the principles discussed in Section 13.14. The behavior of the hardware cursor based on the AND and XOR masks varies among the different Super VGA implementations. A typical usage is shown in Table 13.55. In this example, the hardware cursor can be displayed as either a two-color cursor or as an XOR cursor. The XOR cursor bases its colors on the inverted colors from the destination display memory. The AND mask selects which of these two color schemes are used. If the AND mask pixel is a 0, the corresponding pixel in display memory is set to a solid color. The color, either Color 0 or Color 1, is selected by the value in the corresponding XOR mask pixel. If the Cursor mask pixel is a 1, the

TABLE 13.55 Typical Color Mode Used for Hardware Cursor

Cursor Mask		Function
AND	*XOR*	
0	0	Color 0
0	1	Color 1
1	0	Transparent
1	1	Inverted

corresponding destination display memory pixel will either remain untouched or be inverted depending on the value in the XOR mask.

The AND mask determines which pixels in the destination display memory should be modified based on the data in the hardware cursor XOR mask. The XOR mask is used to modify those pixels in the destination display memory that are selected by the corresponding pixels in the AND mask. An example is provided in Figure 13.60. In this example, the top half of the AND mask is 0 and the bottom half is 1. Therefore, the top half of the resultant pixel contains solid colors. Since the top half of the XOR mask alternates between 0 and 1, the resultant image alternates between Color 0 and Color 1. The bottom half of the resultant image is based on the pixel values that resided in the image underlying the cursor. In this example, the XOR mask alternates between 0 and 1. Therefore, the resultant image corresponding to the bottom half of the cursor pattern alternates between untouched and inverted versions of the original data.

13.15.6 Hardware Cursor Registers

The registers dedicated to the hardware cursor are shown in Table 13.56. Of course, implementation differences exist among the different Super VGAs.

13.16 LINE DRAWING

Line drawing is especially useful in CAD, graphics data display, three-dimensional rendering, and illustration software applications. Several Super VGAs have incorporated line drawing into their graphics accelerators. There are several types of lines, each having a special use. Since the most common lines are horizontal or vertical, high-speed horizontal and vertical line drawing routines are important. Since the algorithm used to draw these lines is faster than the arbitrary sloped line, it is wise to determine if a desired line is horizontal or

TABLE 13.56 Hardware Cursor Registers

Register	Function
Cursor_Offset	Address of start of off-screen cursor pattern
Horz_Cursor_Posn	Horizontal position of cursor on screen
Vert_Cursor_Posn	Vertical position of cursor on screen
Cursor_Color_0	Cursor Color #0
Cursor_Color_1	Cursor Color #1
Horz_Cursor_Offset	Horizontal offset to start of visible cursor within pattern
Vert_Cursor_Offset	Vertical offset to start of visible cursor within pattern
Control	Cursor Enable, Cursor Color Code

vertical before the line is drawn. Lines of arbitrary slope are drawn using the Bresenham algorithm. Lines of 45 degrees are also special cases common in the short stroke vectors. The short stroke vector is a line of limited length that can be drawn along the eight 45 degree increments. These fast lines are ideal for vector font drawing. In addition, alternate line drawing routines are used when the lines represent the boundary of a shape that is destined to be filled. When several lines are joined at their endpoints, they are called *polylines*. It is essential that no gaps occur along the polyline outline of a to-be-filled shape. These gaps might cause the filling algorithm to "spill out" or incorrectly be identified as a boundary crossing. These lines are typically called line fill, polyline, or trapezoid lines.

13.16.1 Bresenham Algorithm Revisited

The most common line drawing algorithm used is the Bresenham algorithm. This involves setting up several registers that control the direction of the line, the axis preference, the starting location, the number of points, and the slope. The line is drawn beginning at the starting location and continues until the number of points are output. The Bresenham engine requires a set of parameters. These might be provided through registers that directly mimic the Bresenham parameters. Alternatively, a second set of registers could contain the lines endpoints. This eliminates the need to calculate the Bresenham coefficients from the end points. Since the majority of lines are drawn based on endpoints, not calculating the Bresenham coefficients could save time. Both the Bresenham coefficients and the end points drive the same line-drawing engine.

13.16.2 Line Endpoint Parameters

The most common way to specify a line is through the line's endpoints. A line-drawing routine would calculate the slope and draw the line using one of the following equations:

```
dx = 1+X_END-X_START; // projection of line along x axis
dy = 1+Y_END-Y_START; // projection of line along y axis

if (dy > dx) {  // draw the line with one point per every y
                // since y projection is major axis
   slope = (float) dx / dy;
   for (i=0; i<dy; i++ ) {
      y = Y_START + i;
      x = (slope * i) + X_START;
      draw_point(x,y);
      }
   }
```

```
else {   // draw the line with one point per every x since x
         // projection is major axis
  slope = (float) dy / dx;
  for (i=0; i<dx; i++ )  {
     x = X_START + i;
     y = (slope * i) + Y_START;
    draw_point(x,y);
    }
  }
```

All that this algorithm requires is the lines' endpoints. In order to draw a line by endpoint specification, the following line specification registers would be required as shown in Table 13.57.

13.16.3 Bresenham Parameters

The Bresenham line draw algorithm eliminates the need for floating point slopes and multiplies. It requires a different set of parameters based on the Bresenham algorithm. The calculation of the Bresenham parameters is trivial given the endpoints as specified in 13.16.2. Some hardware line-draw implementations allow the line to be specified through use of the endpoints. The hardware would internally port the endpoint parameters to the Bresenham parameters using the same line-drawing algorithm regardless of which parameter method is selected.

The Bresenham parameters that must be initialized by software before the line drawing begins are defined in Table 13.58. In this table, the two parameters dminor and dmajor are the major and minor axis projections and are defined by

```
// if y axis projection is greater than the x axis projection
if (dy>dx)  { dmajor = dy;  minor = dx; }
  // if x axis projection is greater than the y axis projection
  else { dmajor = dy;  dminor = dx; }
```

TABLE 13.57 End Point Parameter Line Draw Registers

Register	Function
X_START	starting x coordinate
X_END	ending x coordinate
Y_START	starting y coordinate
Y_END	ending y coordinate
Control	control required to start line draw

TABLE 13.58   End-Point Parameter Line Draw Registers

Register	Function
CUR_X	Initial x-axis coordinate
CUR_Y	Initial y-axis coordinate
MAJ_AXIS_PCNT	Length of line projected onto major axis (dmajor)
DESTX_DIASTP	2 * dminor – 2 * dmajor
DESTY_AXSTP	2 * dminor
ERROR_TERM	2 * dminor – dmajor

13.16.4   Line Projections

The lengths of the major and minor axis projections determine the manner in which the line should be drawn. The longer of these two projections is the *major axis,* also called the *independent axis.* One and only one pixel will be drawn along each pixel of the major axis. Line projections are shown in Figure 2.14. If the line's endpoints are specified, the projections along the x and y axis are as follows:

```
dx = 1 + (x2-x1); // projection along x axis
dy = 1 + (y2-y1); // projection along y axis
```

Different lines are drawn depending on which axis is the major or minor axis. If the wrong axis is specified, the line will be drawn sparsely. For example, if a line's x projection is 2 and y projection is 100, 100 points will be drawn if y is the major axis. If x is the major axis, only 2 points will be drawn. In the case of a 45 degree line, there is no difference.

13.16.5   Direction

In many line-drawing implementations it is necessary to specify the direction of the line. When specifying the line direction, positive in the x direction means moving to the right. Positive in the y direction means moving downward.

The Bresenham and short stroke vectors decomposed the image space into eight quadrants with the starting point of the line at the center . The direction of the horizontal and vertical lines and the major and minor axis can be determined by the quadrant that contains the endpoint of the line as shown in Figure 13.61.

13.16.6   Bresenham Line Drawing Algorithm

The Bresenham line-drawing algorithm follows a straightforward and very clever algorithm that determines where each pixel should be drawn based on an error term. The algorithm therefore minimizes the error in a line. Before the

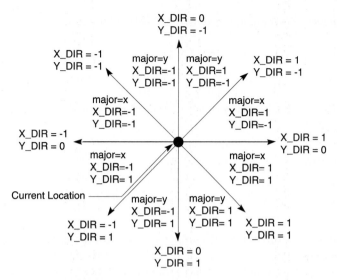

FIGURE 13.61 Line Drawing Quadrants

line is drawn, the image space is decomposed into eight octants, as shown in Figure 13.61, and the octant in which the line is drawn is encoded into the INC_Y, YMAJAXIS, and INC_X flags.

```
draw_line()
{
int xstep,ystep,i;
if (INC_Y)     ystep = 1;  else    ystep = -1;
if (INC_X)     ystep = 1;  else    ystep = -1;
for (i=0; i<MAJ_AXIS_PCNT; i++) {
        plot(CUR_X,CUR_Y);  // plot the point to the display
        if(ERROR_TERM>0) {
            CUR_X += xstep;
            CUR_Y += ystep;
            ERROR_TERM += DESTX_DIASTP;
            }
        else {
            // if YMAJAXIS==1 then y axis is the major axis
            if(YMAJAXIS) CUR_Y += ystep;  else CUR_X += xstep;
            ERROR_TERM += DESTY_AXSTP;
            }
        }
}
```

13.16.7   Bresenham Line Drawing Registers

The Bresenham registers that must be initialized by software before the line drawing begins are defined in Table 13.59. Oftentimes the control field used to

TABLE 13.59 Bresenham Parameter Line Draw Registers

Register	Function
CUR_X	Initial x-axis coordinate
CUR_Y	Initial y-axis coordinate
MAJ_AXIS_PCNT	Length of line projected onto major axis (dmajor)
DESTX_DIASTP	2 * dminor – 2 * dmajor
DESTY_AXSTP	2 * dminor
ERROR_TERM	2 * dminor – dmajor
Control	control required to start line draw

start the line draw is appended onto one of the parameter registers. This register would then always be the last register loaded, initiating the line draw at the same time. This reduces the host instructions required to generate a line.

13.16.8 Short Stroke Lines

The second line-drawing technique is called the *short stroke*. The short stroke allows lines to be drawn in eight directions corresponding to 45-degree increments, typically up to fifteen points long. These are especially popular and fast when drawing stroke fonts. These lines can be drawn rapidly because it is not necessary to calculate and set the line constants. The implementations usually allow a single 16-bit write operation to completely specify and initiate a short stroke. The short stroke directions are shown in Figure 13.62.

13.16.9 Short Stroke Line Registers

Short stroke vectors are simple to specify. These only need three parameters, all of which can fit into a single byte. This allows the host to generate a short stroke line in a single byte transfer. Some coprocessor implementations allow several of these short stroke parameters to fill a word, either 16-bit or 32-bit, allowing up to four short stroke lines to be generated in a single host instruction cycle.

The three parameters include the direction, length, and operation. There are eight possible directions, as shown in Figure 13.62, requiring three bits. The length of the line is limited to sixteen pixels requiring four bits. The length is the number of pixels along the major axis. The operation is either move or draw, requiring one bit. A typical register is shown in Figure 13.63 along with a 16-bit word implementation.

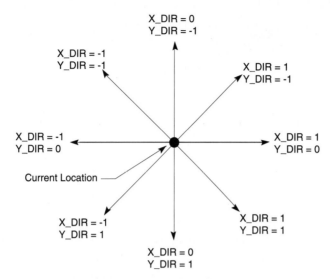

FIGURE 13.62 Line Drawing Directions

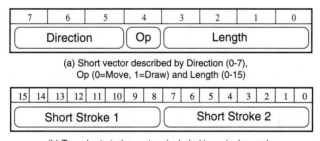

FIGURE 13.63 Short Stroke Line Register. (a) Specification of a short stroke line. (b) Two short stroke lines in a single register.

13.16.10 Line Strips

A third line-drawing technique is called the *line strip*. It provides flexibility in selecting exactly which pixels in a line will be drawn. Line strips are drawn either horizontally or vertically. These are commonly used when the lines are going to be used as the border for a filled polygon since exact control can be achieved. A line is drawn in either the horizontal or vertical direction a specified number of points. At the end of the line, the resultant X and Y coordinates may be automatically incremented or decremented. Thus, lines of arbitrary slope can be rapidly drawn. A typical line drawn with this method from 5,3 to 20,8 is shown in Figure 13.64.

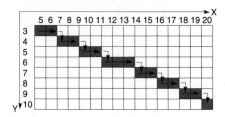

FIGURE 13.64 Line Strip

There is another shortcut that one can use to rapidly draw lines. This uses the alternate length register as a line counter. If horizontal lines are being drawn, the vertical length register is used as a line counter. Similarly, if vertical lines are being drawn, the horizontal length register is used as a line counter. In this case only four lines need to be drawn. Setting up for the line strips requires the following:

```
X_INC=+,  Y_INC=+,  X_ORIGIN = 5,  Y_ORIGIN=3,MAJOR = X Axis,
Enable Line Strip
```

Drawing independent lines requires the following line outputs. Note that the "go" command is automatically generated with the output to the X_LENGTH field.

```
Y_LENGTH=1    X_LENGTH = 2
Y_LENGTH=1    X_LENGTH = 2
Y_LENGTH=1    X_LENGTH = 2
Y_LENGTH=1    X_LENGTH = 3
Y_LENGTH=1    X_LENGTH = 2
Y_LENGTH=1    X_LENGTH = 2
Y_LENGTH=1    X_LENGTH = 2
Y_LENGTH=1    X_LENGTH = 1
```

Alternatively, we could use the Y_LENGTH field as a line counter as follows:

```
Y_LENGTH=3    X_LENGTH = 2
Y_LENGTH=1    X_LENGTH = 3
Y_LENGTH=3    X_LENGTH = 2
Y_LENGTH=1    X_LENGTH = 1
```

The line strip method must be disabled after the line strip operations are completed or future writes to the X_LENGTH field will generate a line strip due to the implicit Go.

13.16.11   Line Strip Registers

In order to draw a line strip, it is necessary to specify the length of the line, either horizontal or vertical, and whether the alternative axis should be incremented at the end of the line. The starting point of the line strip is also required. A control field is needed to start the line draw and to put the coprocessor into a line strip mode. In order to facilitate rapid line drawing, the origin is updated at the end of a line strip operation such that this new origin is ready for the next line strip. This new origin will be the end point of the previous line strip plus or minus 1 in both the horizontal or vertical direction. The only register operation required would then be the horizontal or vertical length.

If we are drawing horizontal lines, the LENGTH_Y filed is used as a repeat count. Since the usage of line strips typically involves repeated application of the line strip, often a repeated sequence is desired. For example, in Figure 13.64 we saw repeated horizontal lines each two pixels wide being drawn. Instead of commanding each line separately, the vertical length register can be used as a line counter. It is common for the line strip to be drawn whenever either the vertical or horizontal length registers are written into. Thus, only one host instruction is required to generate a line strip. The registers required to specify a line strip are shown in Table 13.60. It should be noted that the actual number indicated in a length field is oftentimes one less than the desired amount. For example, a length of 1 would actually generate a length 2. This allows a length of 0 to generate a length of 1. Therefore, an 8-bit field can actually generate lines that are 256 long as opposed to 255.

13.16.12 Line Color and Patterned Lines

Thus far, we have looked only at the coordinates and control of a line and not the color or pattern that will be used for the line draw. Lines can be drawn in either a solid color or in a pattern. This requires the foreground Color Register when drawing a solid line. When a patterned line is required, an additional

TABLE 13.60 Line Strip Registers

Register	Function
DEST_X	Initial x-axis coordinate
DEST_Y	Initial y-axis coordinate
LENGTH_X	Length of horizontal line strip (see Note 1)
LENGTH_Y	Length of vertical line strip (see Note 2)
DIR_X	Flag to increment or decrement X after line strip
DIR_Y	Flag to increment or decrement Y after line strip
MAJOR	Draw either horizontal or vertical
CONTROL	Enable line strip mode, start line strip (see Note 3)

Note 1. The LENGTH_X field is a line counter when drawing vertical line segments.

Note 2. The LENGTH_Y field is a line counter when drawing horizontal line segments.

Note 3. Start line strip often automatically generated with write to LENGTH_X or LENGTH_Y.

Pattern/Texture Register

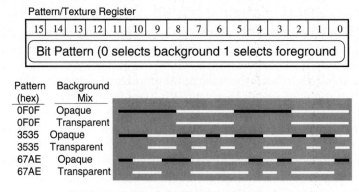

FIGURE 13.65 Patterned or Textured Lines

Pattern Register is required, along with the background Color Register. Patterned lines are also called textured lines by some manufacturers. The Pattern Register is typically a 16-bit register that determines whether a foreground or background color/mix should be used. Remember that the foreground and background colors are fed through ALUs before being written to display memory. Therefore, we already have the capability for mixing the line color or colors into the display memory. One example would be the patterned line. Suppose the patterned line is a simple alternating on/off dotted line and that you want to have the foreground portion shown in the foreground color and the background transparent. This can be accomplished by setting the foreground mix to replace destination with source and the background mix to select the destination data. Some examples of textured lines are shown in Figure 13.65.

13.16.13 Trapezoidal Fill

A trapezoidal fill is really a streamlined way of performing line strips. It incorporates the same basic algorithm as a line strip except the lines are drawn only in a horizontal direction and there is no repeat count. An example is shown in Figure 13.66. In this example, fifteen lines are drawn beginning at DEST_X=15, DEST_Y=100. The Y axis automatically increments at the end of each line. The LENGTH_X has to be loaded for each line as does the DEST_X. The DEST_X issues the go command so it should follow the associated load to LENGTH_X.

13.16.14 Polygon Fill

The polygon fill assumes that the outside of the region is a solid line comprised of a single color. This color is also assumed to be distinct from other colors not associated with the background. For example, consider the simple case of a square with an outline color of Red=255, Green=0, Blue=0 on a black background. The fill algorithm would interpret every pixel in the selected region

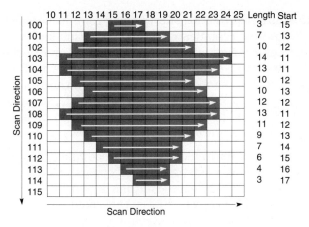

FIGURE 13.66 Trapezoidal fill

that is Red=255, Green=0, Blue=0 to be part of the object outline. Problems will likely occur if any pixels other than the square outline in the selected region are also Red=255, Green=0, Blue=0.

The algorithms used to fill polygons vary among the implementations that support this feature. The algorithm typically requires a starting point inside of the region of interest yet outside of the object to be filled. The algorithm scans horizontally across the selected region one scan line at a time. Each time a border color is encountered, the state of inside or outside of the object switches. The border color, starting point, and region of interest have to be provided to the filling algorithm. A polygon fill is illustrated in Figure 13.67.

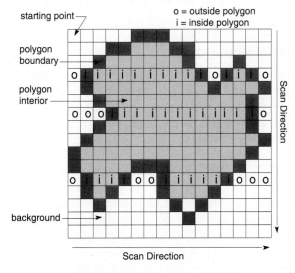

FIGURE 13.67 Polygon Fill

Special line draws are required for effective polygon fills because the typical Bresenham algorithm could complicate a filling algorithm and create errors in the filling. The coprocessors that anticipate a polygon fill or already implement one are equipped with a non-Bresenham algorithm for drawing the outside of a polygon. It is important to remember that there can be no horizontal gaps when scanning horizontally one scan line at a time. Most of us, using one painting package or another, have had a fill operation leak out of an unknown hole.

An example of performing an area fill operation follows.

Step 1. Draw the closed outline of the area to be filled. Typically, an area boundary drawing mode is used, as opposed to the standard Bresenham line draw. This closed outline is going to be used as a mask. In order to reduce screen clutter, this could be drawn into an off-screen memory area. The rectangular area where these lines will be drawn should be pre-filled with 0s.

Step 2. Designate this area as the pattern map, if a pattern map is supported.

Step 3. Specify the destination where the actual fill operation will occur.

Step 4. Select the foreground mix, source of data, and background mix.

Step 5. Specify the operation to occur with increasing X. This borrows from the BitBlt filling operation.

Step 6. Initiate the area fill.

The algorithm used in this filling operation would be a left-to-right scanning of the pattern, where the first occurrence of the outline would set the pixels to foreground. All subsequent pixels are set to foreground until the next occurrence of a line is encountered. This repeats until the end of the selected region. The background mix should be set to "destination" since the unfilled pixels should remain unmodified.

13.16.15 Scissoring/Clipping

Scissoring is a term used for clipping. There are four scissors registers associated with the upper-left and lower-right corners of the clipping rectangle. This was illustrated in Figure 2.20 and is shown in Figure 13.68. Any operation that attempts to access data outside of the bounds of the scissors registers would not have any effect. It should be noted that even though no data would change outside of the scissors region, the operation would still take time. The time would be reduced, though, since the display memory access time would not be relevant.

A faster scissoring algorithm would be one that begins the operation at the edge of the scissors region. For example, consider a line drawn from 90,220 to 960,650. If the scissors region is 256,256 to 768,768, the line algorithm would

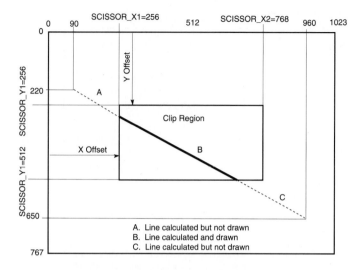

FIGURE 13.68 Scissoring/Clipping Lines

step quickly from 90,220 to 256,280 (the entry point of intersection with the clip rectangle), since no memory cycles would occur. It would draw between 256,280 to 650,512, the exit point of intersection with the clip region. Once again, it would step quickly from 650,512 to 960,650. A faster technique would begin drawing the line at 256,280 and finish the line at 650,512. This, however, requires additional hardware that may not be present.

There are four registers that have to be loaded in order to specify the rectangular clip region. The dimensional system may be with respect to the display memory or with respect to the destination coordinates depending on the implementation. When drawing lines, the display memory coordinate system is typically used. Both examples are shown in Figure 13.69.

There are four registers required to specify the clipping region. These are shown in Table 13.61. These specify the upper-left and lower-right corner of the clip region. It is usually assumed that any pixel drawn on the boundary of the clip region will be DRAWN.

13.16.16 Scissoring/Clipping a Polygon

A special case exists when clipping a polygon. Since the clipping hardware has to understand how to close an area, the simple clipping algorithm used on a line-by-line basis cannot be used when dealing with polygons. For example, suppose a polygon vertex exists out of the clipping region. A properly drawn polygon would clip the line proceeding out of the clipping region at the point of intersection. It would then trace the line and draw the portion of the line that extends out of the clipping region as a projection onto the clipping boundary. It

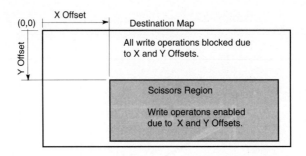

(a) Scissors region defined with respect to the Destination Map

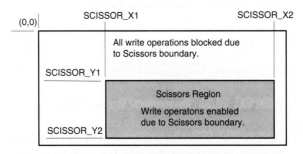

(b) Scissors region defined with respect to the display memory

FIGURE 13.69 Clipping Coordinate System (a) Defined with respect to the destination map. (b) Defined with respect to the display memory.

TABLE 13.61 Registers Required for Scissoring/Clipping

Register	Function
SCISSORS_X1	Left edge of clip region
SCISSORS_Y1	Top edge of clip region
SCISSORS_X2	Right edge of clip region
SCISSORS_Y2	Bottom edge of clip region

would continue doing this until the polygon returns into the clipping region. This is shown in Figure 13.70.

13.17 LINEAR ADDRESSING

Most programmers are sick to death of bank swapping. With the gigabytes of host memory address space, it is time that the (32-bit) 4 megabytes of Super VGA display memory fit into a contiguous address space. Until recently, the

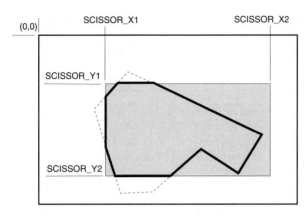

FIGURE 13.70 Scissoring/Clipping Polygons

VGA display memory resided in the A0000–BFFFF display region. Most implementations provided a 64 Kbyte region of memory in the A0000–AFFFF region. A standard VGA had 256 Kbytes organized as four planes all overlapping the 64 Kbyte address space. The Super VGAs are equipped with from 1 to 4 Mbytes. The memory is organized as sixteen banks of 64 Kbytes each overlaid in the 64 Kbyte address space. A memory map of the standard VGA and Super VGA with 1 Mbyte memory map is shown in Figure 13.71.

Figure 13.72 attempts to illustrate exactly how much memory is in the 32-bit address space with respect to the 64 Kbytes of DOS VGA allocated memory

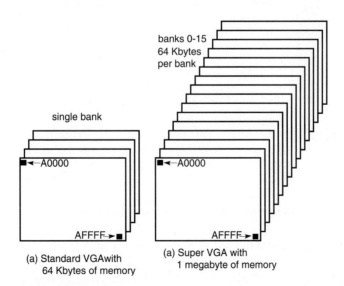

FIGURE 13.71 Display Memory Configuration. (a) Standard Super VGA with 256 Kbytes of memory. (b) Super VGA with 1 Mbyte of memory

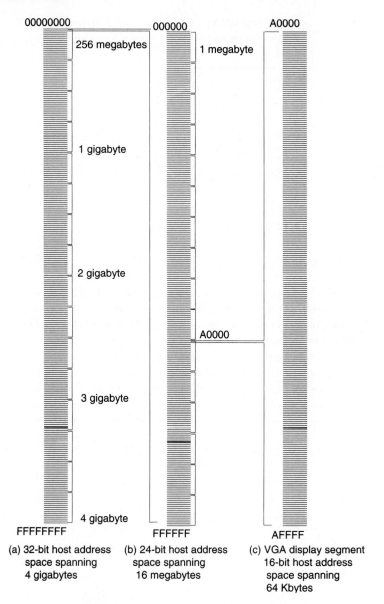

FIGURE 13.72 Linear Address Space

space. Figure 13.72a shows the entire 4 gigabyte space. Each large grid denotes 256 Mbytes, and each small grid space is equivalent to 16 Mbytes. Figure 13.72b expands the first 16 Mbytes such that each large grid is 1 Mbyte and each small grid is 64 Kbytes. Figure 13.72c further expands this 64-Kbyte range, where each small grid is 256 bytes. Let's suppose that there are 40 million PCs in existence with an average of 1 Mbyte per unit. That's a total of 40 million Mbytes, or 40,000 gigabytes of memory, or 10,000 fully loaded PCs.

Linear addressing allows the Super VGA display memory to be mapped out of the standard A0000–BFFFF region of host memory and allows the user to map the display memory into one contiguous chunk. Suppose there is 1 Mbyte of display memory and the host has 8 Mbytes of system memory. One could map the Super VGA display memory to occupy the host memory address space from 9 Mbytes to 10 Mbytes. One could simply write to the display memory as if it were a huge buffer. Looking at Figure 13.72, a Super VGA equipped with 1 Mbyte of display memory would be mapped somewhere into the 4-gigabyte address space. This 1 Mbyte would correspond to the larger grid marks in Figure 13.72b. You should not map Super VGA memory into an address space that is already occupied by host memory. Therefore, if your system has 4 gigabytes of memory you are out of luck (and probably out of power and money as well).

13.17.1 Setting up the Linear Addressing

In order for the Super VGA to accept linear addressing, a 32-bit address and an aperture size have to be provided. The address lets the Super VGA know where the display memory resides. The aperture size tells the Super VGA how much memory to map into this space. This is shown in Figure 13.73.

One could configure a Super VGA into a linear addressing mode such that it responded to the standard, non-linear addressing software. This would be done by setting the 32-bit address to 000A0000 hex. The aperture size would be set to 64 Kbytes. Everything would work as expected. Bank swapping would be

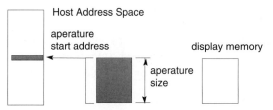

(a) Linear address aperature same size as display memory

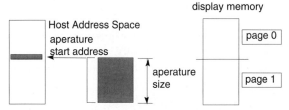

(b) Linear address aperature smaller than display memory

FIGURE 13.73 Linear Address Parameters

necessary as is the case in the non-linear addressing scenario. In one system, the chip is always set up for linear addressing initialized with the above mentioned settings. On other chips this will not work because there are separate banking registers.

13.17.2 Linear Addressing Registers

Each Super VGA that supports linear addressing does it differently. Some allow a wide variety of aperture sizes. Others restrict it to 1 or 4 Mbytes. Some pick an address space where it has to go; others allow you to select a space based on a particular granularity (say 256 Mbyte boundaries).

Consider the general case that allows you to position the Super VGA anywhere in host memory. A 32-bit register would be required to point to the start of the space that the Super VGA will occupy. A second register (or field) would be required to select how large a space the Super VGA will occupy. This can be rephrased as we must have a register that points to the start of the aperture and one that dictates the size of the aperture. If the size of the aperture is smaller than the amount of display memory, it is necessary to also have aperture paging. In addition, a control bit is probably resident that enables the linear addressing. These are shown in Table 13.62.

13.17.3 Linear Addressing on the ISA Bus

The ISA bus provides 24 bits of address bus. The ISA bus can address only up to 16 Mbytes. Therefore, any computer system with 16 Mbytes and an ISA Super VGA will not be able to use linear mapping.

13.17.4 VL and PCI

Fortunately, all 32 bits of address bus are available on the VL or PCI bus. Therefore, the Super VGA can be mapped anywhere in the 4 gigabyte, 32-bit address space when installed on a VL or PCI bus.

TABLE 13.62 Linear Addressing Registers

Register	Function
APERATURE_START	Up to 32 bits of start address of the aperture
APERATURE_SIZE	Size of the aperture
APERATURE_PAGE	Page number when aperture size < amount of display memory
Control	Enable flag for linear addressing

13.17.5 Protected Mode Programming

It is necessary to use a DOS extender to access memory above the lower 1 Mbyte limit imposed by DOS. Soon a true 32-bit DOS will arrive making the DOS extenders unnecessary. The DOS extenders run in protected mode and therefore a protected mode environment is required. This book supports the PharLap 286 extender.

13.17.6 Windows Device Drivers

The Windows 3 specification does not, by default, allow for linear display memory addressing. This is due to the version of the DPMI server specified in Windows 3. Some DPMI servers do provide the necessary services to allow for linear display memory mapping, but it is not part of the Windows spec. Consequently, software developers are hesitant to program the linear addressing feature of the Super VGAs in their Windows display drivers.

13.18 MAPPING I/O REGISTERS INTO HOST MEMORY ADDRESS SPACE

The VGA is controlled through sets of index/data register pairs and a few other registers, which are mapped into the host I/O space. This technique allows 256 registers to be resident at a single I/O word address. The host I/O space has lots of room anyway, especially when a single-word address can contain 256 registers. This abundant I/O space seems ideal for peripheral devices. Unfortunately, there are drawbacks.

The primary fault with I/O instructions is their speed. Using I/O instructions is slow. They flush the host processor cache and cause wait states. This isn't much of a problem if a few I/O instructions are sprinkled here and there in your code. However, if several control registers have to be accessed for a single operation, the overhead for accessing these ports can be unacceptable. This is the case in the Super VGAs coprocessors where up to ten registers need to be loaded for a single operation.

The I/O addressing of the standard VGA worked out just fine. IBM created standards, and everyone else followed. The speed wasn't so much of an issue since the VGA wasn't that fast anyway. Times have changed. With the faster host processors, faster buses, faster Super VGAs, and with the new graphics accelerators, the I/O addressing was no longer sufficient. In order to speed up their products, Super VGA manufacturers began mapping the control registers into memory address space. Figure 13.74 illustrates the difference between memory mapping and I/O mapping.

13.18.1 Memory Mapping Super VGA Control Registers

Even on those Super VGA implementations that support memory-mapped I/O, not all control registers are involved. Typically, only the graphics coprocessor

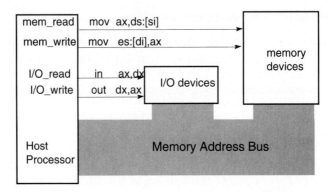

FIGURE 13.74 I/O Mapping versus Memory Mapping

registers were mapped into memory space. The default configuration uses the I/O mapping for these registers. A control field somewhere in the I/O space is used to switch the Super VGA into a memory-mapped I/O configuration. Figure 13.75 illustrates how the selected control registers are mapped into the host memory address space.

The registers associated with the control register memory mapping are simpler than the display memory mapping. The reason is that there are only a small number of I/O registers to map, typically under 100. Therefore, there is no reason to be concerned with aperture size or page swapping. The only register necessary is the address register that points to the top of the control register aperture. A control field is required to enable or disable this mapping. These are shown in Table 13.63.

13.18.2 Choosing a Memory Address for the Control Registers

There is no reason to worry about where the control registers should be mapped. The VGA has memory address space in the B0000–BFFFF range. Remember that when the VGA is in a VGA mode, it maps its display memory into the A0000–AFFFF space. This leaves the MDA space at B0000 or the CGA

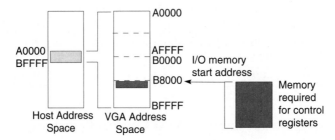

FIGURE 13.75 Mapping I/O into Host Address Space

TABLE 13.63 I/O Memory Mapping Registers

Register	Function
IO_MEMORY_START	Up to 32-bits of start address of the control registers aperture
Control	Enable flag for linear addressing

space at B8000 available. If you have a co-resident MDA, select the B8000 address. If you have a co-resident CGA, select the B0000 address.

13.18.3 Multiple Instances

The ability to reposition the I/O addresses into host-memory address can also be an effective means to setting up systems with multiple display cards. All of the I/O address would have to be mapped to host memory. Linear mapping of display memory, as discussed in Section 13.17, would also be required. In this case, the entire VGA system would be mapped to host memory. Unfortunately, because the sleep-awake thing wasn't worked out well, it could be a real challenge to software configure these multiple cards such that each would reside at a different location. The PCI bus should solve these problems due to its more rigorous identification system. Multiple, configurable, memory-mapped Super VGAs could then become popular.

13.19 OFF-SCREEN MEMORY

Off-screen display memory is the display memory on the Super VGA that is not dedicated to the display of data for the current display mode. For example, a 1024-by-768, 8 bit-per-pixel display mode would occupy 786,432 bytes. Since a 1-Mbyte Super VGA has 1,048,576 bytes, this leaves 262,144 bytes of display memory available for general use.

13.19.1 Virtual Images

One common use of this memory is the virtual display. Suppose an image is 1024 by 1024. The entire image could be loaded into display memory, occupying every byte. Even though the user might be able to display only 1024 by 768 pixels at a time, the rest of the image could be instantaneously accessed through panning by changing the CRTC start address. In this example, the image was taller than the display mode.

A second application of virtual displays occurs when the image is wider than the display mode. Suppose the image is 2048 by 500 pixels. It is possible to load this entire image into display memory and set the display pitch to 2048. Only

1024 horizontal pixels can be displayed at a time, but, once again, the image can be instantaneously panned.

Both of these examples utilize the off-screen memory for image storage and would consequently reduce the amount of storage available for other uses.

13.19.2 Font Storage

A second use of off-screen memory is the storage of fonts. The alphanumeric modes used in the standard and Super VGAs utilize display plane 2 and plane 3 for storage of font patterns. As you will recall, plane 0 and plane 1 are used for the ASCII character code and the character attribute.

In graphics modes, the off-screen memory is often used to store the font patterns. This is especially efficient if color expansion is available. Refer to Section 13.11 for a detailed description of color expansion. Let it suffice to say that the binary font pattern is stored in off-screen memory. When the application desires to draw a character, the display driver software figures out the address of the ASCII character and performs a color expansion BitBlt into the desired location in on-screen display memory. Even the primitive color expansion capabilities of the VGA could be used in the event that the color expansion BitBlt is not available. The address of the off-screen memory ASCII character bit pattern would be as follows:

Address = display_memory_base_address + offset_address_to_top_of_font + (bytes_per_character * ASCII code);

The font patterns are stored in off-screen display memory contiguously. They are **not** stored in the same display format as the on-screen display mode.

13.19.3 Cache Storage

For lack of a better term, cache storage is space in off-screen memory dedicated to storing and retrieving image data that is accessed receptively. Like the host cache memory, it is a valuable resource and must be treated carefully. The reason for storing image data in these areas is the throughput. The display memory could well have a 32 to 64 bit bus, and display-to-display memory transfers can be very fast. This is especially true when hardware BitBlts are available and the host processor is freed for other tasks while the BitBlt is taking place.

If the image data is similar in format and not well-suited to color expansion, it **is** stored in off-screen memory using the same memory organization as the on-screen memory. For example, if a 16-by-16 icon is stored off-screen, it would **not** be stored contiguously in the off-screen memory. Suppose the 1024-by-768, 8-bit-per-color mode is active. Let's say we store the 16-by-16 icon at column 0 on scan line 768. This is the first available off-screen memory. The first 16 bytes of off-screen memory would contain the top row of the icon. The next (1024–16) bytes would not be occupied. The second line of the icon would begin at the 0th column on the 769th scan line and so on. Other areas of off-screen memory might contain other icons stored non-contiguously or contiguously stored font patterns or combinations of the two.

13.19.4 Hardware Cursors

Hardware cursors store their cursor patterns in off-screen memory. The hardware cursor generator has its own type of color expansion where the hardware cursor data is stored in a 2-bit-per-pixel format. The hardware cursor is stored contiguously and, like a font pattern, does not use the display format of the on-screen memory.

Every Super VGA imposes its own rules regarding the alignment of the hardware cursor pattern in off-screen memory. Each has to be consulted regarding where the starting address of the cursor can reside.

In many applications, the cursor rapidly changes pattern when highlighting different portions of the screen. This helps differentiate the use of the cursor. This also means that multiple hardware cursor patterns are stored in display memory. Changing the pattern address pointer is all that is necessary to change the pattern.

13.19.5 Simultaneous CRT and Flat-Panel Display

In order to refresh a dual-panel flat-panel display and a CRT at the same time, a buffer memory is required. Many flat panel VGA controllers use off-screen memory to hold this buffer. In these instances, do not use this memory dedicated to refreshing the screen.

13.19.6 Animation and Real-Time Video

One way to achieve 15 or 30 frames a second playback on the Super VGAs is to allocate several image frames within the display memory. Each image frame would contain one frame of the animation or video data. The playback software would display a frame for a 30th of a second, then change the CRTC start address to point to the next frame. This next frame would be on for the next 30th of a second time period. The host could modify the image data in any display memory frame that was not currently being displayed, thereby eliminating the nasty screen artifacts that can occur when data is modified while being displayed. The number of frames corresponds to the speed of the host processor, the size of the frame, the animation or video frame rate, and the sound synchronization requirements. For example, if there are six frames, you have to be able to rewrite a worse case complete frame in less than 5/30ths of a second. In the long run, you have to be much faster than this, averaging one frame per 30th of a second or else you will fall behind. However, the time required to write frames varies greatly depending on disk accesses, the complexity of the frame, and, most significantly, the usage of the frame in the image compression scheme.

13.19.7   Task Switching

In multitasking environments, entire screens may be saved in off-screen memory facilitating rapid swapping of screens. This, of course, is an expensive way to save time, but in some instances it is necessary.

13.19.8   Multiple Views

In CAD or imaging packages, you might want to rapidly switch rapidly between a zoomed view of an image and the original image. These different views can be stored in off-screen memory and rapidly switched or copied into view upon request.

13.19.9   Mixed Memory

In the future, we may well see display memory that uses VRAM for the anticipated on-screen memory and DRAM for the off-screen memory. The display system could increase its performance by using additional off-screen memory without requiring the expensive VRAM memory in areas that aren't required to refresh the screen.

13.19.10   Off-Screen Memory Management

As more and more tasks require off-screen memory, the challenge of managing this memory becomes more complex. Consider the case where off-screen memory has non-contiguous icons stored with contiguous fonts, multiple contiguous hardware cursor patterns, and a smattering of frequently used image data. The off-screen memory manager would have to take a lot into consideration, following standard memory management procedures regarding fragmentation, garbage collection, and swapping algorithms.

Chapter 14

Graphics Coprocessors

Graphics coprocessors are also called graphics accelerators, windows accelerators and graphics engines. When I refer to one of these in this book, I am referring to the dedicated silicon found on or co-existing with the Super VGA used to accelerate BitBlts, line draws, color expansions, hardware cursors, and area and polygon fills. These may or may not work independently or in conjunction with the host processor. The terms coprocessors, accelerators, or engines are used interchangeably.

These accelerators are powerful—and ugly. (Perhaps the politically correct term for ugly is "programmingly challenging.") This chapter will attempt to highlight their power and capabilities as well as their drawbacks. In Chapter 13, I discussed the theory of operation of these coprocessors and provided a generic set of registers describing how each operation can be controlled. These generic registers descriptions apply to every graphics accelerator. Of course, there are differences among the various Super VGA cards and graphics accelerator chips, and you won't be able to program any without further chip-specific details. However, the fundamentals of Chapter 13 are essential to all of the graphics accelerators.

In this chapter I will further describe the accelerators. I will use several as examples and try to discuss some of the pitfalls you will encounter when you attempt to program these devices. Armed with the feature descriptions of Chapter 13 and the functional descriptions of this chapter, you will be ready to digest the programming examples available in the Graphics Accelerator Toolbox.

14.1 GETTING MORE INFORMATION

I wish I could cover all of the information regarding the graphics coprocessors in this book. However, this is impossible due to space constraints, complexity issues, and the rapidly changing products. An alternative and better solution is the Graphics Accelerator Toolbox, which is available for all of the popular graphics coprocessors. The Toolbox contains detailed information regarding what each instruction is doing. The code is tested and kept up-to-date. The Graphics Accelerator Toolbox is the only sane approach to working with the code. Purchase the necessary Toolboxes, try them out, incorporate the functions into your code, and modify them as you dare and desire.

14.2 GRAPHICS COPROCESSORS

As you recall, a graphics coprocessor performs an operation after it is given a GO command. An exception occurs with host memory operations. BitBlts from or to host memory require the host to initiate the read or writes. This is necessary because the Super VGA is typically not a bus master. Thus, the minimum register fields include a function register and function parameter registers, a GO command field, and a done status field.

The function register specifies the operation to be performed by the coprocessor. The function might be in a single field of a register or distributed among several registers. For example, the BitBlt might have a 2-bit field in one place indicating the source and destination and additional function fields used for transparency and color expansion. In addition, each function might require several parameters. The BitBlt would require source address, destination address, width, height, and display pitch. The function registers are described in Section 14.5.

The GO command field starts the process. As shown in several examples in Chapter 13, this field is often hidden in the write pulse to a given register, thus eliminating an unnecessary write cycle. For example, the GO command for a short-stroke line draw is provided whenever the short-stroke register is written to. Therefore, if you load the direction field and length, then move or draw fields in a single host write operation, the line is automatically drawn. Controlling the coprocessors is described in Section 14.6.

The "done" field in a status register may have several components. The simplest consists of a done bit. The host software would start the operation and then poll the done bit until the coprocessor was done before interacting with the coprocessor. A more complicated done would involve an interrupt. There are several sources for interrupts associated with the graphics coprocessors. Still more complicated are the instruction FIFOs and queues where the number of available registers in the queue also has to be considered. The coprocessor status, interrupts, queues, and FIFOs are discussed in Section 14.7.

14.3 TYPES OF COPROCESSORS

There are several types of coprocessors. Some reside inside the Super VGA chip; others are found on separate chips that are tightly coupled to the Super VGA chips. Some resemble or emulate the 8514/A or the XGA coprocessors. Some can work in parallel with the Super VGA portion of the chips; others

TABLE 14.1   Trivial Differences Among the Coprocessors

Identical registers with different names

Identical function parameters distributed differently among registers and fields in registers

8-bit register repeated twice in a 16-bit register or four times in a 32-bit register

Cursor patterns using different formats

Off-screen memory boundary limitations

One-dimensional versus two-dimensional address specifications

Different codes for identical ALU functions

---

require the VGA to be disabled in order to function properly. In certain cases, the system can hang if the Super VGA attempts to access display memory while the coprocessor is active and vice versa.

It is not difficult to understand the theory behind the coprocessor functions. What can be confusing, however, is trying to describe how to use more than one, if not all, of them. This chapter provides a number of tables and figures that attempt to describe the principles behind the coprocessor operations. The fundamentals are very similar among the different coprocessors, although the implementations are different. Differences can be trivial or significant. Common trivial differences are provided in Table 14.1. Significant differences are provided in Table 14.2.

I am faced with a difficult decision regarding how to describe the several popular coprocessors available today. I will attempt to describe the union of all coprocessors, because this will help you deal with the specifics of a single coprocessor. For example, one coprocessor might use a one-dimensional start address and another might use a two-dimensional start address. Since I describe both coprocessors, programmers of either should be able to figure out

TABLE 14.2   Significant Differences Among the Coprocessors

New functions not supported in other coprocessors

Similar functions that operate differently

Different registers that actually create a go command

Binary versus color patterns

Different ALU functions

Different line-drawing algorithms

Different levels of coprocessor support

Different color modes supported in coprocessor

what is going on and not get confused because the other coprocessor's registers are present. In fact, there are coprocessors that have both one- and two-dimensional start addresses. One implementation where both are present allows you to select either. A second implementation where both are present requires you to load both. An address is an address regardless of the implementation details. If you understand the principle, you will be able to figure out how to use any given coprocessor once you are provided with the details.

Figure 14.1 illustrates a data flow block diagram. This is a very powerful architecture and not all Super VGAs currently support this amount of flexibility. This architecture is very similar to the 8514/A. I am providing this powerful architecture since almost all of the coprocessors present in the 8514/A, VGA, or Super VGAs can be described with this figure. Several sources of data can be used to modify a pixel in the destination. The destination in this figure is assumed to be display memory. This is the first point of divergence. Some coprocessors allow the host memory to be a destination. This is important when reading display data back to the host. However, this operation is typically straightforward, and the data is simply copied to the host and the complexities of the mixes and ALU are used. The color comparison feature is used when the host is the destination. For example, the host might desire to read a binary

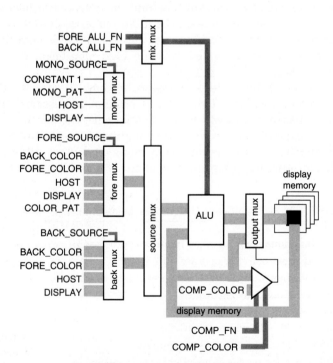

FIGURE 14.1 Data Flow Diagram

representation of the data in the display memory where the 0 or 1 is based on a comparison.

A few definitions are in order. A multiplexor, or mux, is a switch that selects one output from many inputs. A control is necessary to select which input is used as the output. The input is never modified in any way in a mux. The control is a binary value that has enough bits to select from all inputs. For example, a 5-input mux would require a 3-bit control field. An ALU is a processor that combines a set of inputs (operands) in some fashion (operation) to produce an output. These operations are sometimes called mixes, sometimes called functions, sometimes called raster ops. The operands in this case are the source data and the display memory destination data. For example, output of ALU = source + destination. Three operand raster operations provide 256 different RasterOps. The first two were source and destination, as we see here, but the third used a pattern (for example, output of ALU = (source AND destination) OR pattern). This can be implemented using the architecture of Figure 14.1 by using a two-pass operation. The first pass would select the host source (HOST) as the foreground source. The ALU operation would be AND. The output would be written to display memory. The second pass would select the pattern (COLOR_PAT) as the foreground source and the ALU operation would be OR. Similarly, more complex operations might require additional operations. The color compare logic selectively compares bits of the two inputs. In this case, the one source is always the destination and the second is a compare key color (COMP_COLOR). Only selective bits are used in the operation as determined by the comparison function (DEST_COMP_FN).

The source data used to modify the destination (in this case display memory) can come from the host, from off-screen display memory, or be some function of the destination data (invert, for example). The source data is organized into three distinct categories: foreground, background, or monochrome. This model is chosen based on its effectiveness at describing common graphics functions. For example, a character has a background and foreground. An object is either behind or in front of another object. A window is hidden by another window. A person sits in a field of grass. The foreground and background sources are color sources. In several cases, a monochrome source of data is desired. For example, a character font or a cursor pattern are monochrome data sources. In our foreground/background model, we often need to rapidly change from pixel to pixel. The monochrome data is used as the selector that determines whether a particular pixel is a foreground or background pixel. This is seen in Figure 14.1 by the monochrome multiplexor output driving the source mux and mix mux.

14.4 COPROCESSOR FUNCTIONS

As one would suspect, the functionality of the coprocessors varies from part to part. However, there is an amazing consistency based on the Microsoft Windows 3 display driver specification. The coprocessor hardware manufacturers

TABLE 14.3 Coprocessor Functions

Function	Qualifiers
Compatibility	8514/A, XGA
Color Modes Supported	4-bit, 8-bit, hi-color, true-color
Memory Bus Size	16-bit, 32-bit, 32-bit multiplexed, 64-bit
Simultaneous Operation	With or without VGA
Interrupts	Operation, ready, full
Host Interface	Input cache, FIFO
BitBlt	Host-to-host, host-to-display, display-to-host, display-to-display
Color Expansion	Opaque, transparent
Color Expansion Source	Host or display
Mixing	Foreground, background
Masking	Pattern mask
Hardware Cursor	Color patterns, variable size, wrap-around offset
Line Draw	Solid, pattern
Short Stroke	Solid, pattern
Line Segment	Solid, pattern
Clipping	Line, BitBlt
Rectangle Fill	Solid, pattern
Polygon Fill	Solid, pattern
Raster Ops	Logical, arithmetic

are not going to spend time and money developing features on the chips that people won't use. People won't use features if programmers don't support them, and programmers won't support features if people don't buy their products. This is a vicious cycle. Fortunately, enough people buy Windows that Windows device driver programmers support features that make Windows run faster (or at least Windows benchmarks). Consequently, a consistent set of coprocessor functions shows up in the various coprocessor implementations. Several important functions are shown in Table 14.3. Corresponding to each function in this table are qualifiers that provide important details about the functions.

14.5 PROGRAMMING THE COPROCESSORS

Once more I must provide this warning: "Programming the coprocessors is not a trivial task." In most cases, you can accomplish it without devoting a major portion of your career to it.

14.5.1 Foreground, Background, Patterns, and Masks

As Figure 14.1 shows, there are several foreground and background sources provided to the foreground and background multiplexes. The desired foreground and background source is selected by the foreground (FORE_SOURCE) and background source control (BACK_SOURCE) respectively. The sources of data include the background constant color (BACK_COLOR), foreground constant color (FORE_COLOR), image data from the host, image data from display memory and a color pattern (COL_PAT). The color pattern is a 32-pixel color pattern register block used for repeating a pattern. This is often used for patterned fills. The one-dimensional source is considered NOT destination-aligned. Destination aligned means that there is not a one-to-one correspondence with the pattern and the destination. A single 32-pixel color pattern source is shown in Figure 14.2.

The foreground and background sources are listed in Table 14.4. When the host data is selected, the data is usually provided through a host interface register or FIFO. When the display data is selected, the data is provided from a read-back latch.

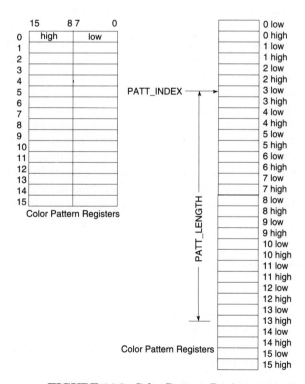

FIGURE 14.2 Color Pattern Registers

TABLE 14.4 Foreground and Background Sources

Index	Description	Register Name
0	Background color	BACK_COLOR
1	Foreground color	FORE_COLOR
2	Host data	HOST_REGISTER
3	Display data	DISPLAY_REGISTER
4	Pattern data	COL_PAT

In the 8514/A, the source can be selected from the two registers, FORE_COLOR or BACK_COLOR, the pattern data, COL_PAT, or the host or display data. The selection is made based on the value in the foreground mux (FORE_SOURCE) and background mux (BACK_SOURCE) control lines and as shown in Table 14.5. The 8514/A provides a considerable amount of flexibility. Many Super VGAs don't include all of the features but are likely to include many in the future.

In the 8514/A, the sources of data are described as being either the host data or the display data. The destination is always assumed to be the display memory. This is **not** the case in most Super VGAs. In the Super VGAs the destination and source can be either display memory or host. (The exception is host-to-host transfers, in which the source and destination addresses are provided and no pointer is given as to the pointer referring to host or display.) If the address is a host address, the transfer will use host memory. Similarly, if the address is a display memory address, the result will use display memory.

Operations involving the source and destination are often influenced by the pattern and mask bit maps. Some or all of these addresses of these bit maps must be provided to the coprocessor and are described in Table 14.6. Once again, in some cases the start address might be a long pointer or it might be an X and Y two-dimensional coordinate. Both are equivalent. In some cases, both are required.

TABLE 14.5 Selecting the Source Registers

Register	Description
BACK_SOURCE	Selects the source for the background data from the choices in Table 14.2
FORE_SOURCE	Selects the source for the foreground data from the choices in Table 14.2

TABLE 14.6 Bit Map Sources of Data

Address	Description
SOURCE_START	Address pointing to source bit map
SOURCE_X	X-address of source data viewed from 2-dimensional perspective
SOURCE_Y	Y-address of source data viewed from 2-dimensional perspective
DEST_START	Address pointing to destination bit map
DEST_X	X-address of destination data viewed from 2-dimensional perspective
DEST_Y	Y-address of destination data viewed from 2-dimensional perspective
PATTERN_START	Address pointing to binary or color pattern bit map
MASK_START	Address pointing to binary mask bit map

Don't get lost in the details here. Each chip, be it Super VGA, 8514/A, or XGA, performs the same functions, but differently. Whether the source is display memory, host memory, a linear address, or a two-dimensional address really doesn't matter much when it comes to understanding the theory—they're just different ways of accomplishing the same goals. The details become critical only when it is time to actually program a chip. At that time, each chip has to be specifically handled. Only the registers and techniques specific to that chip will be included—that's where the Graphics Coprocessor Toolbox becomes essential. Several of the BitBlt registers are illustrated in Figure 14.3.

14.5.2 Monochrome Source

Four monochrome sources of data are provided as inputs to the monochrome multiplexor listed in Table 14.7. The output of the monochrome multiplexor controls the source multiplexor. The monochrome data is selected by the monochrome source control (MONO_SOURCE). If the monochrome control value is a 1, the output of the foreground multiplexor is selected as the source for that pixel. Alternatively, if the monochrome control value is a 0, the output of the background multiplexor is selected as the source for that pixel. The four sources of data are the constant 1 (always foreground), a monochrome pattern register (MONO_PAT), a binary bit pattern in host, or a monochrome bit pattern in display memory. The monochrome binary pattern may either be a 32-pixel (32-bit) or an 8-by-8 (64-bit) pattern register used for repeating a pattern.

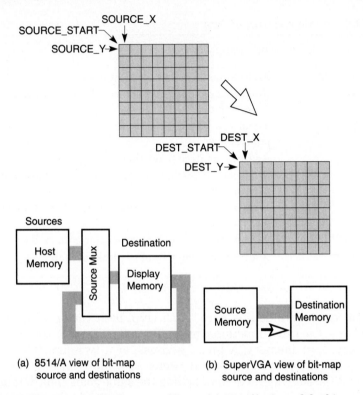

(a) 8514/A view of bit-map
source and destinations

(b) SuperVGA view of bit-map
source and destinations

FIGURE 14.3 BitBlt Sources of Data. (a) 8514/A view of the bit map
(b) Super VGA view of the bit map

This is often used for patterned lines allowing the pattern-based selection of foreground or background colors for the lines.

A single 32-pixel monochrome pattern source is shown in Figure 14.4a. A two-dimensional 8-by-8 monochrome pattern is shown in Figure 14.4b. The one-dimensional source is considered NOT destination-aligned; the 8-by-8 pattern is destination-aligned. In the two-dimensional case, it is easy to see the correspondence. The [row 1:column 1] value in the pattern will affect the [row1:column1] pixel in the destination.

TABLE 14.7 Monochrome Sources

Index	Description	Register Name
0	Bit pattern used is always 1	1
1	Monochrome pattern	MONO_PAT
2	Host data	
3	Display data	

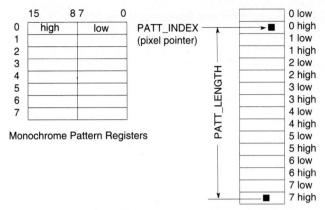

(a) One-dimensional 32-pixel Monochrome Pattern Registers

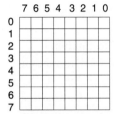

(b) Two-dimensional 8 by 8 pixel Monochrome Pattern Registers

FIGURE 14.4 Monochrome Patterns. (a) One-dimensional 32-pixel Monochrome Pattern Registers. (b) Two-dimensional 8-by-8 pixel Monochrome Pattern Registers.

14.5.3 ALU

The arithmetic logic unit, ALU, is provided the output of the source multiplexor and the display memory data. The function performed in the ALU is determined by either the foreground function (FORE_MIX) or the background function (BACK_MIX). These are shown in Table 14.8.

TABLE 14.8 Controlling the Raster Op/Mix ALU

ALU Function	Description
FORE_MIX	Raster Op used for foreground; controls code in Table 14.4 if foreground is selected in the mix mux
BACK_MIX	Raster Op used for background; controls code in Table 14.4 if background is selected in the mix mux

TABLE 14.9 Foreground and Background Mix (Raster Ops) for the XGA

Code	Function
00	Zeros
01	Source AND Destination
02	Source AND NOT Destination
03	Source
04	NOT Source AND Destination
05	Destination
06	Source XOR Destination
07	Source OR Destination
08	NOT Source AND NOT Destination
09	Source XOR NOT Destination
0A	NOT Destination
0B	Source OR NOT Destination
0C	NOT Source
0D	NOT Source OR Destination
0E	NOT Source OR NOT Destination
0F	Ones
10	Maximum of Source – Destination
11	Minimum of Source – Destination
12	Add Source + Destination with Saturate
13	Subtract (Destination – Source) with Saturate
14	Subtract (Source – Destination) with Saturate
15	Average

Similar to the source multiplexor, the foreground or background ALU function is selected by the output of the monochrome multiplexor. Consequently, if the monochrome pattern indicates that the foreground should be used, then the foreground ALU operation is also used. The ALU performs either a foreground mix operation or a background mix operation depending on the monochrome pattern being 1 or 0 respectively. These mix operations are also commonly called raster ops. The codes are listed in Table 14.9.

14.5.4 Output Multiplexor

The output multiplexor is provided two inputs—either the output of the ALU or the output data. The output multiplexor is controlled by the output of a color compare logic. This facilitates color transparency based on the value of the output pixel. For example, the data in the image in display memory would control whether portions of that image data were changed. This allows for data to be written behind sections of image data. Typical transparency uses the values in the input data stream to determine which values in the output will change. This is just the opposite. The color compare logic is provided the data from the display memory along with a color constant (COMP_COLOR). These values are compared in some fashion. The result of the comparison selects if the output of the ALU modifies the output pixel or if the pixel is left unmodified. The function performed by the color compare logic is provided by the destination compare function (DEST_COMP_FN). The color compare functions are listed in Table 14.10.

This comparison may be based on a key. The key selects which bits in the color (COLOR_CMP) and destination color are used in the comparison. All other bits are ignored. This key color (COMP_MASK) may be a special register or it may be part of a read mask (READ_MASK) depending on the implementation. The read mask is a register that has one bit assigned per plane. A 16-bit color would be organized as sixteen planes. The read mask would then have sixteen bits, one bit per plane. The Background Key Registers are shown in Table 14.11.

TABLE 14.10 Color Compare Functions

Code	Function
0	Destination overwritten (Always false)
1	Destination untouched (Always true)
2	Destination Color >= COLOR_CMP
3	Destination Color < COLOR_CMP
4	Destination Color != COLOR_CMP
5	Destination Color = COLOR_CMP
6	Destination Color <= COLOR_CMP
7	Destination Color > COLOR_CMP

TABLE 14.11 Background Key Registers

COMP_COLOR	Contains color for comparison
COMP_MASK	Contains mask for compare
READ_MASK	Contains mask for compare

14.6   PROGRAMMING COPROCESSOR EXAMPLES

The most common functions performed by the coprocessors include BitBlts, drawing line, filling rectangles or polygons, and hardware cursors. There are several variations of these functions including the use of patterns or solid colors, color expansion, masking, and patterns.

14.6.1   BitBlts

A BitBlt requires a source, a destination, spatial information relating to display pitch, rectangle width and height, whether color expansion is desired, masking, and raster operation. These are shown in Figure 14.5.

A typical BitBlt is flow charted in Figure 14.6. The first two blocks set up the source and destination address. These might be a one-dimensional memory address or the horizontal and vertical two-dimensional addresses. The width (WIDTH) and height (HEIGHT) of the source rectangle must be provided. In non-color expansion modes, the width and height of the source are identical to the width and height of the destination. It is necessary to set up for color expansion if the source data is in a binary format. When color expansion is engaged, the width and height refer to the destination since the source data is always contiguous.

Display pitch is the number of bytes or pixels per horizontal row. In some implementations, it is necessary to provide the coprocessor with the display pitch. In other cases, the display pitch is not provided and the coprocessor determines the pitch from other Super VGA registers. At times, only one display pitch is provided and it refers to all of the on-screen display memory. In

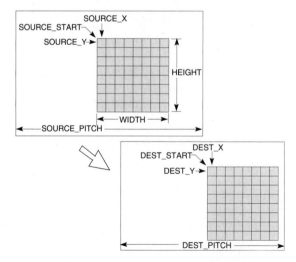

FIGURE 14.5   BitBlt Register Definitions

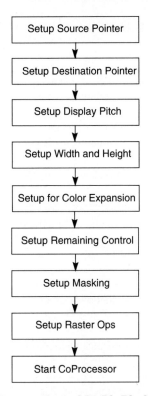

FIGURE 14.6 Typical BitBlt Block Diagram

other cases, it is necessary to provide both the source pitch (SOURCE_PITCH) and the destination pitch (DEST_PITCH). Table 14.12 summarizes the BitBlt related parameters.

The source, destination, and mask addresses were provided in Table 14.4. In some implementations, a mask bit mask is used to selectively mask pixels in the destination from being updated. The address to the mask bit map (MASK_START) must be provided to the coprocessor. The raster operation must also be provided. Common raster operations are listed in Table 14.7.

14.6.2 Solid and Pattern Area Fills

Special purpose BitBlts include the rectangular solid or pattern area fills, which fill the destination rectangle with either a solid color or a pattern. If the solid color is selected, the foreground color or background color registers are typically selected as the source of data. A solid fill is shown in Figure 14.7. Note that the solid color is provided in a register and that no additional source pointers or parameters are required. The rest is identical to a BitBlt with the destination address, width, height, display pitch, masking, and raster op features all required. See the description in Section 14.4.2 for details.

TABLE 14.12 BitBlt Related Parameters

Field	Function
WIDTH	Width of transfer for both source and destination when in non-color expansion; width of destination when in color expansion
HEIGHT	Height of transfer for both source and destination when in non-color expansion; width of destination when in color expansion
DISPLAY_PITCH	Number of pixels (or bytes) per display row in all on-screen memory
SOURCE_PITCH	Number of pixels (or bytes) per display row in source
DEST_PITCH	Number of pixels (or bytes) per display row in destination

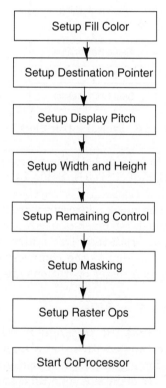

FIGURE 14.7 Solid Fill Block Diagram

The area or pattern fill BitBlt is in between the solid fill and the general BitBlt. A pattern is provided instead of a constant color. The details of the pattern vary widely from implementation to implementation. For some coprocessors, the pattern is in a set of registers. In others it is an actual bit map provided by the host or resident in display memory. This bit map is typically smaller than the destination and the destination is filled by repeating the pattern in a tiled format. Often this pattern is 8-by-8 pixels large. A pattern fill block diagram is shown in Figure 14.8. Note that the pattern pointer and pattern itself must be set up. The pattern bit map either resides in host memory or in display memory. The pointer to the pattern must be provided to the coprocessor. If the pattern resides in display memory, it must be copied into display memory, perhaps using the BitBlt operation. The pattern might be a binary pattern, a 2-bit per color pattern (as is the case in the hardware cursor), or a color pattern conforming to the current display mode. If a binary pattern is used, then color expansion must be employed during the pattern fill operation.

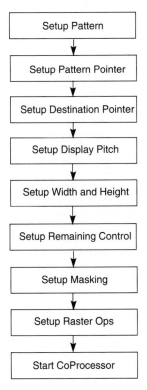

FIGURE 14.8 Pattern Fill Block Diagram

14.6.3 Bresenham Line Drawing

There are several ways to draw a line. The basic flow is shown in Figure 14.9. The line end points, color or pattern, clipping, masking, and raster ops must be defined. The masking and raster operations are identical to the BitBlts. The line color is described in 14.6.7. Clipping is described in Section 14.6.4.

The most common line-drawing algorithm is the Bresenham technique. Bresenham lines may be specified as a set of two endpoints or as a starting point, slope, and length. In the first case, the X and Y coordinates of the starting point (X_START,Y_START) and the ending point (X_END,Y_END) must be specified. These are shown in Table 14.13. In this case, the endpoints are converted to the Bresenham initial conditions inside the coprocessor.

In many cases, these endpoint registers are not provided. Only the actual Bresenham initial condition registers are available. If the line is defined as endpoints, the software must convert these endpoints to the Bresenham coordinates before setting up the coprocessor registers. The Bresenham registers and the necessary conversion formulas are listed in Table 14.14.

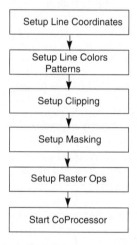

FIGURE 14.9 Drawing a Line Block Diagram

TABLE 14.13 End Point Parameter Line Draw Registers

Field	Function
X_START	starting x coordinate
X_END	ending x coordinate
Y_START	starting y coordinate
Y_END	ending y coordinate

TABLE 14.14 Bresenham Parameter Line Draw Registers

Field	Function
CUR_X	Initial x-axis coordinate
CUR_Y	Initial y-axis coordinate
MAJ_AXIS_PCNT	Length of line projected onto major axis (dmajor)
DESTX_DIASTP	2 * dminor − 2 * dmajor
DESTY_AXSTP	2 * dminor
ERROR_TERM	2 * dminor − dmajor

Once all of the line parameters are initialized, either through Table 14.200 or 14.201, the line draw is started. The operation is typically started through a control register.

14.6.4 Scissors/Clipping

We are all familiar with clipping. I have yet to determine why the term "scissors" was used as opposed to "clipping." The analogy is clear anyway. The clipping region is defined by a rectangle, and the rectangle is defined by four registers as shown in Table 14.15.

Typically, the actual border of this clipping rectangle is considered to be part of the allowed region; consequently, any point that falls inside the following will be drawn. This is not always the case and care must be taken regarding specific boundary conditions.

SCISSORS_X1 <= X <= SCISSORS_X2
SCISSORS_Y1 <= Y <= SCISSORS_Y2

14.6.5 Short Strokes

A short-stroke vector is a rapid way to draw sequences of several short lines as shown in Figure 14.10. For example, a vector font requires several lines to be drawn. Imagine the way an X-Y plotter works. The pen either moves (pen up)

TABLE 14.15 Registers Required for Scissoring/Clipping

Field	Function
SCISSORS_X1	Left edge of clip region
SCISSORS_Y1	Top edge of clip region
SCISSORS_X2	Right edge of clip region
SCISSORS_Y2	Bottom edge of clip region

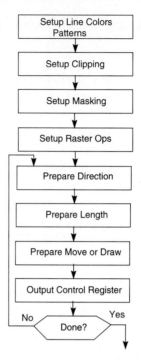

FIGURE 14.10 Short-Stroke Vectors Block Diagram

or draws (pen down) from a source to a destination location. The data to be drawn is typically in a list of bytes already in short-stroke format. In order to draw the sequence of lines, the byte list is output to the graphics coprocessor. The clipping, masking, and raster ops are identical to the Bresenham line.

In order to facilitate quick line drawing, each line segment must be less than sixteen pixels long and be aligned to a 45-degree angle. A starting point is specified (CUR_X,CUR_Y). At the end of the short-stroke line, the starting point is automatically updated to reflect the destination of that line. Three factors enable a single-byte write to generate a line stroke: automatic updating, the fact that all parameters fit in one byte, and a draw command that is automatically generated when the register is written to. The XGA and 8514/A allow two consecutive line segments in a 16-bit write. Some coprocessors allow a 32-bit write to generate four lines by concatenating four bytes into a 32-bit register. The only short-stroke register is shown in Table 14.16.

14.6.6 Line Strips

Line strips allow drawing lines with exact control; the pixels are actually part of the lines, which can be horizontal or vertical. A starting coordinate (CUR_X,CUR_Y) is provided along with a horizontal and vertical length and increment direction. The line strip registers are shown in Table 14.17.

TABLE 14.16 Short-Stroke Registers

Field	Function
SHORT_STROKE	Short-stroke register containing the necessary length, direction, and move or draw command for one to four lines

TABLE 14.17 Line Strip Registers

Field	Function
CUR_X	Initial x-axis coordinate
CUR_Y	Initial y-axis coordinate
LENGTH_X	Length of horizontal line strip
LENGTH_Y	Length of vertical line strip
DIR_X	Flag to increment or decrement X after line strip
DIR_Y	Flag to increment or decrement Y after line strip
MAJOR	Draw either horizontal or vertical

14.6.7   Line Colors

A line may be drawn in either a solid color (FORE_COLOR) or in an alternating sequence of two colors (FORE_COLOR, BACK_COLOR). The sequence of foreground and background colors is determined by a pattern register, which is typically sixteen bits long. Any bit that is a 1 in the register creates a foreground color in the next pixel on the line. Similarly, any bit that is a 0 in the register creates a background color in the next pixel of the line. The pattern repeats for the length of the line. The line pattern is in a Motorola format; that is, the first bit to be used is bit 15. The sequence is 15, 14, 13, 12, 11, 10, 9, 8, 7, 6, 5, 4, 3, 2, 1, 0, 15, 14, ... until the line is completed. If a transparent mode is selected, the pixels corresponding to 0's in the pattern are not be updated. The colors for the lines may be derived from the foreground and background mix as described in 14.5.1 and Figures 14.1, 14.2, and 14.3. A special line-specific color register and pattern register may be provided as listed in Table 14.18.

14.6.8   Polygon Fills

The polygon fill operation requires a closed polygon, which must have a continuous border. Typically, a special line draw operation is used to draw the border. This requires that one and only one pixel is drawn per scan line. There is typically only a polygon fill type field in a control register associated with polygon fill operations. All other relevant variables are parts of other functions as described later.

TABLE 14.18   Line Color Registers

Field	Function
LINE_COLOR	Line color
PATTERN	Pattern register

The color of this border must be consistent with the type of polygon fill. The simplest form of polygon fill operation requires the border to be the same color. In many implementations, the color of the border can vary according to the color comparison circuitry. Two examples are provided.

In the first example, the color compare function uses a color comparison value (BACK_KEY_COLOR) and a color mask (BACK_KEY_MASK) as discussed in Section 14.5.4. The polygon border can be traced as long as the comparison between the (color or colors) in the border compare with the BACK_KEY_COLOR masked by the BACK_KEY_MASK. The result of the comparison is a monochrome bit map. A 1 indicates that the comparison was true for the masked comparison.

In the second example, a plane mask is used. In the 8514/A, a RD_MASK is compared with the polygon border color. Only certain planes of the data are used in the comparison. The compared planes are based on bits selected as "enabled" in the RD_MASK. All other planes are not used in the comparison. The result of the comparison is a monochrome bit map. A 1 indicates that the comparison was true for all enabled bit planes.

An outer rectangular boundary must be declared for the polygon fill. The technique for filling a polygon requires a horizontal scan across the width of the outer rectangular boundary. The starting point, which is the upper-left corner of the boundary rectangle, must be on the outside of the polygon. The 8514/A uses the Rectangle Fill operation to perform the polygon fill. The normal rectangle fill fills the entire rectangular region with a solid color. The polygon fill fills only the region inside the boundary color with a solid color. The 8514/A has two modes for filling polygons called Mode A and Mode B. Essentially, Mode A fills the polygon with the fill color but does not include the right edge of the border. Mode B includes the right edge of the border in the fill operation. The constant color used in the fill is consistent with other update operations using the appropriate bit plane masks, pattern masks, and so on.

14.6.9   Hardware Cursor

Setting up the hardware cursor is pretty straightforward as shown in Figure 14.11. The cursor bit map has to be organized in the format specified by the particular Super VGA used. This pattern must be loaded into memory, typically off-screen display memory. A pointer must be alerted to the location of

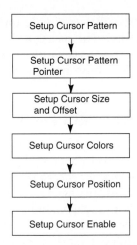

FIGURE 14.11 Hardware Cursor Block Diagram

this cursor pattern (CURS_OFFSET). There are two cursor sizes commonly used—32 by 32 and 64 by 64. Some implementations allow sizable cursors up to 64 by 64 (HORZ_CURS_SIZE, VERT_CURS_SIZE). Still others allow the starting address of the cursor pattern to be non-zero (HORZ_CURS_OFFSET, VERT_CURS_OFFSET). In the simplest implementation, the cursor is always assumed to be 64 by 64 and only the CURS_OFFSET pointer to where the pattern resides needs to be loaded.

The cursor color scheme also varies. Some allow a simple AND-XOR operation that either uses a foreground (Curs_Color_0) and background (Curs_Color_1) color or an invert or leave-alone color scheme as selected in the

TABLE 14.19 Hardware Cursor Registers

Field	Function
CURS_OFFSET	Address of start of off-screen cursor pattern
HORZ_CURS_SIZE	Cursor Size in X direction
VERT_CURS_SIZE	Cursor Size in Y direction
HORZ_CURS_OFFSET	Horizontal offset to start of visible cursor within pattern
VERT_CURS_OFFSET	Vertical offset to start of visible cursor within pattern
HORZ_CURS_POSN	Horizontal position of cursor on screen
VERT_CURS_POSN	Vertical position of cursor on screen
CURS_COLOR_0	Cursor Color #0
CURS_COLOR_1	Cursor Color #1
CURS_ENABLE	Enable Cursor
CURS_COLOR	Cursor color scheme

control field (CURS_COLOR). The cursor is enabled or disabled through the control field CURS_ENABLE. The position that the cursor is displayed at on the screen is determined through the (HORZ_CURS_POSN, VERT_CURS_POSN) registers. These hardware cursor related registers are listed in Table 14.19.

14.7 CONTROLLING THE COPROCESSORS

Once the coprocessor parameters are loaded, the coprocessor can be engaged. The simplest form of engagement is by setting the start field (GO). The GO field is not the only way to start the coprocessor. At times, writing to specific parameter registers will automatically send a GO command to the coprocessor. This saves a step. In turn, it is the responsibility of the software to make sure that all other parameters are loaded before the register in question is written. Since the coprocessor works independently from the host, the host has to find out when the coprocessor is done. This can be most easily accomplished by polling a done flag (DONE_FLAG). This is shown in the flow chart of Figure 14.12.

In this example, the host must set up the operation and then load the parameters into the coprocessor registers. The host always waits for the coprocessor to be done. Note that repetitive calls to the coprocessor can be accomplished by the load parameters, start coprocessor, and wait for coprocessor sequence. This is obviously not the most efficient means to communicate with a coprocessor. This simple technique is shown in Figure 14.13. The host sends control information and receives status information from the coprocessor engine through the coprocessor registers. Similarly, the coprocessor takes its commands from the coprocessor registers and provides status information back into them.

It would be nice to keep the host processor busy while the coprocessor is working on the graphics. This is shown in Figure 14.14. In this example, the host is setting up the operation while the coprocessor is working. The only real

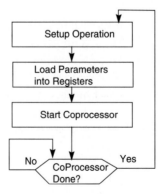

FIGURE 14.12 Simple Coprocessor Control Block Diagram

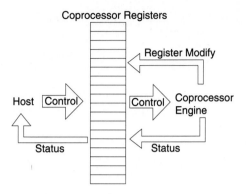

FIGURE 14.13 Host-Coprocessor Communication

gain here is in the time saved in setting up the operation, which comes at the expense of more complicated software.

It would also be nice if the host could actually load the parameters into the coprocessor while the coprocessor is working. This can be accomplished in two ways. The first is through a second set of registers in the coprocessor, commonly called a *queue*. Once the coprocessor is given the GO command, it loads its own private registers from the host-coprocessor registers. This allows the host to immediately modify the coprocessor registers. This is shown in Figure 14.15, in which the host controls the coprocessor through a queue while receiving status information from the coprocessor registers themselves. The coprocessor reads the queue into its registers before processing, thereby freeing up the queue for the host.

A second technique employs a FIFO. In this case, the host loads the FIFO and the coprocessor reads out the registers from the FIFO. The status registers

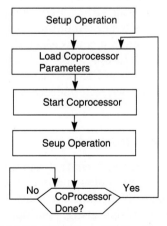

FIGURE 14.14 Working with the Coprocessor

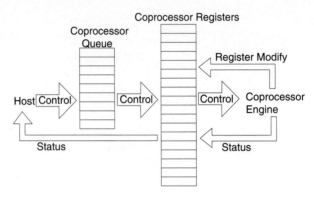

FIGURE 14.15 Communicating with a Coprocessor Queue

do not use the FIFO as seen in Figure 14.16. In Figure 14.16a, the FIFO is similar to the queue in the previous figure. First of all, the FIFO has limited length. The host communicates to the FIFO through only one port. Therefore an address has to be present for each data value or the ordering of the values for each command has to be location-specific. In the first case, the FIFO would be wide enough to hold the index to the coprocessor register and the coprocessor register data. If the data is 32 bits wide and there are 60 registers, the FIFO would have to be 38 bits wide. This is the more popular approach. In the second case, no address is required but the ordering is critical. For example, suppose the line draw command required the X1, Y1, X2, Y2 parameters followed by the line draw code. The host would simply load these registers, in order, into the FIFO. In Figure 14.16b, three commands are loaded into the FIFO. These commands are five, three, and seven words long; this leaves three available FIFO slots. If the next command is three words long, it can also be loaded into the FIFO. Otherwise, you have to wait until more space frees up in the FIFO. This would occur when the coprocessor either loads the parameters for command 1 or it finishes command 1. This is implementation-specific.

The steps required to command a coprocessor through a FIFO are shown in Figure 14.17. The host sets up the operation and before loading the coprocessor, determines if there is space in the FIFO. If there is, the host loads the FIFO and starts the coprocessor. Subsequent operations repeat this sequence.

14.7.1 Control and Status Registers

The simplest coprocessor has a single control register as shown in Figure 14.18. This register contains two control fields and two status fields. The control fields include start (GO) and reset. Note that the start field is alternatively a suspend field. If the coprocessor is operating, loading a 1 into the S field causes a

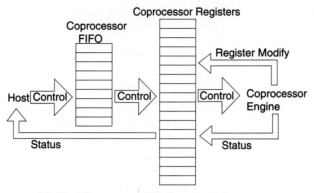

(a) Host-Coprocessor Fifo Communications

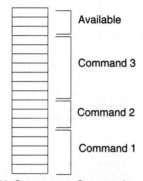

(b) Fifo filled with Coprocessor Commands

FIGURE 14.16 Host-Coprocessor FIFO (a) Host-Coprocessor FIFO Data Flow
(b) Commands in a FIFO

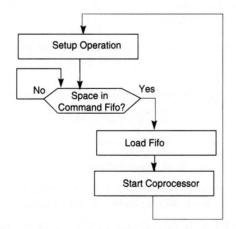

FIGURE 14.17 Communicating with a Coprocessor FIFO

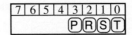

7	6	5	4	3	2	1	0
				P	R	S	T

P Progress Status
R Reset
S Start/Suspend
T Status

FIGURE 14.18 Simple Control Register

suspend. The status fields include the status field (STATUS) and the Progress Status field.

A more typical control register is shown in Figure 14.19. This is the XGA Control Register scheme. Remember that by my definition, a control register actually starts an operation whereas a parameter register doesn't initiate anything. The XGA has two control registers. In Figure 14.19a, the actual XGA Control Register is shown. In Figure 14.19b, the XGA Direction Step Register is shown. This register also initiates a draw operation. As can be seen in Figure 14.19a, there are several fields in the control register, so several parameters can be loaded at the same time as the coprocessor is commanded to GO.

Both registers are 32 bits wide. The GO command is implicitly issued when the software writes into Byte 3. If a 32-bit-wide bus interface is present, this

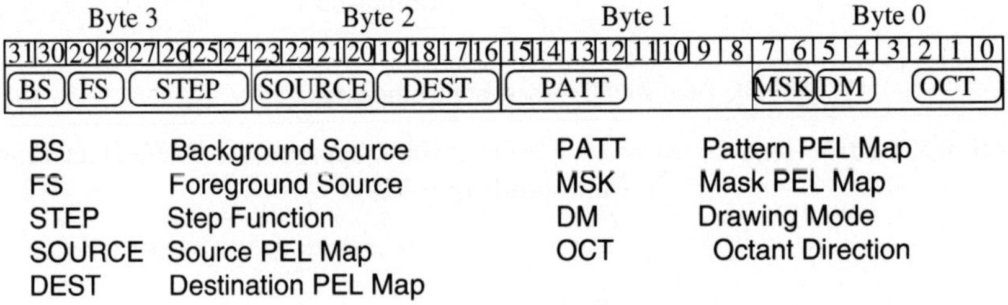

Byte 3	Byte 2	Byte 1	Byte 0
31 30 29 28 27 26 25 24	23 22 21 20 19 18 17 16	15 14 13 12 11 10 9 8	7 6 5 4 3 2 1 0
BS FS STEP	SOURCE DEST	PATT	MSK DM OCT

BS   Background Source
FS   Foreground Source
STEP   Step Function
SOURCE   Source PEL Map
DEST   Destination PEL Map

PATT   Pattern PEL Map
MSK   Mask PEL Map
DM   Drawing Mode
OCT   Octant Direction

(a) XGA Control Register. Writes into Byte 3 cause execution to begin

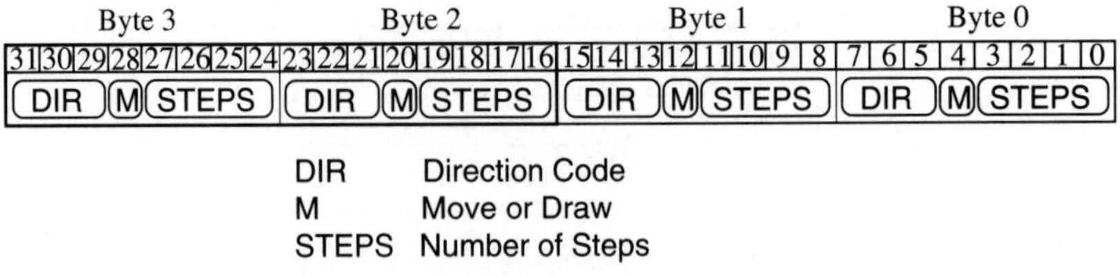

Byte 3	Byte 2	Byte 1	Byte 0
31 30 29 28 27 26 25 24	23 22 21 20 19 18 17 16	15 14 13 12 11 10 9 8	7 6 5 4 3 2 1 0
DIR M STEPS	DIR M STEPS	DIR M STEPS	DIR M STEPS

DIR   Direction Code
M   Move or Draw
STEPS   Number of Steps

(b) XGA Direction Step Registers allowing up to 4 draw and step operations with a single write. Writes into Byte 3 cause execution to begin

FIGURE 14.19 XGA Control Registers. (a) XGA Control Register (b) XGA Direction Step Register

occurs during the single 32-bit-wide write. If a 16-bit wide bus is present, this occurs during the high-order word write. Since Intel ordering (low then high) is assumed, this is handled automatically with the 32-bit write (broken into two 16-bit writes). If a 16-bit-wide write software instruction is used, then the lower sixteen bits of the control register should be written first, followed by a 16-bit-wide write to the upper sixteen bits.

A 16-bit wide control and status register for a coprocessor that employs a FIFO is shown in Figure 14.20. The Control Register contains several fields, similar to Figure 14.19. Similarly, the Status Register also contains several status fields. In the status register is a FIFO field, which indicates the number of FIFO slots that are available. Suppose that the FIFO is 128 words long. This FIFO field would then tell how many slots are available (0 to 127). Also in the Status Register is an A field. The A field indicates when all FIFO slots are empty. This is useful since the software can assume that any operation will fit into the FIFO without further decision making. It also indicates that the coprocessor has read all of the FIFO information. A coprocessor busy flag, B, is also provided in the Status Register, indicating the coprocessor status. An R field indicates when Read Data is available. If the coprocessor has status information for the host to read, it sets this field.

Thus far we have seen two typical control registers—the more general Control Register and the Direction and Step Register. The Direction and Step Register has been standardized by IBM in the 8514/A. Since it accomplishes its

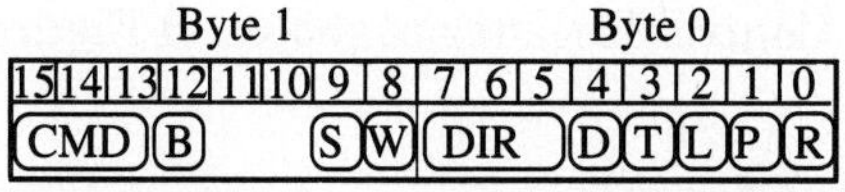

C MD	Command	DIR	Drawing Direction
B	Byte Swap	T	Direction Type
S	Bus Size	L	Last Pixel Drawn
W	Wait on CPU	P	Pixel Mode
		R	Read or Write

(a) Drawing Command Register

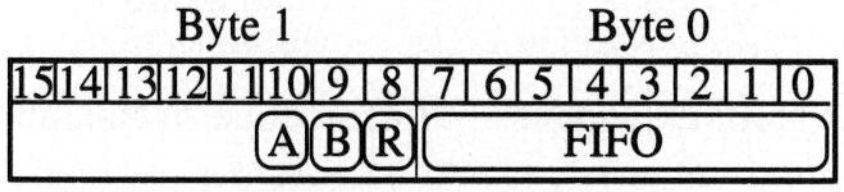

A	All Fifo Slots Empty
B	Coprocessor Busy
R	Read Data Available
FIFO	# of Slots in Fifo Available

(a) Coprocessor Status Register

FIGURE 14.20 Control and Status Registers.
(a) Control Register (b) Status Register

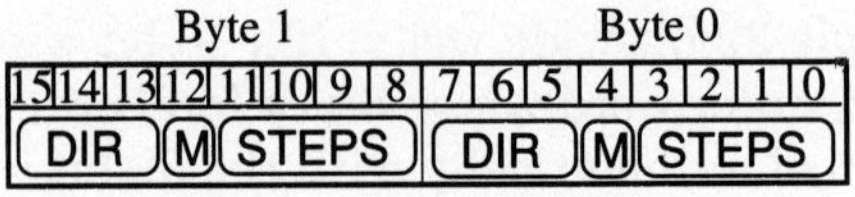

Byte 1   Byte 0

```
15 14 13 12 11 10 9 8  7 6 5 4 3 2 1 0
( DIR )(M)(STEPS)  ( DIR )(M)(STEPS)
```

DIR   Direction Code
M   Move or Draw
STEPS   Number of Steps

FIGURE 14.21   IBM Standard Direction and Step Register

task perfectly, no one has modified it. This register is shown in Figure 14.21.
All four essential components are present, including the direction, length, draw
or move flag, and GO command. As seen earlier, several implementations have
concatenated these 8-bit wide register into 16 or 32-bit registers allowing more
than one line segment to be queued up at a time.

The 8514/A has a Control Register shown in Figure 14.22a. In this register
are several control fields and the implicit GO field. The Status Register shown
in Figure 14.22b includes a coprocessor busy field, a data ready from host field,
and a set of eight fields that indicate which FIFO positions are occupied. This
is NOT a binary value indicating the number of available slots (which would
have made more sense); rather, each bit represents one FIFO position.

A third control register is the Line Strip Register found in some Super VGA
coprocessors. This register contains the parameters and controls necessary to
generate a line strip. Rapid writing to this register can create arbitrary lines
suitable for filling algorithms. A write to this register generates a GO command. The Line Strip Control Register is shown in Figure 14.23.

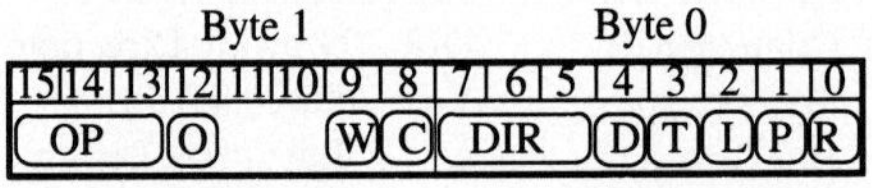

Byte 1   Byte 0

```
15 14 13 12 11 10 9 8  7 6 5 4 3 2 1 0
( OP )(O)      (W)(C)( DIR )(D)(T)(L)(P)(R)
```

OP   Operation Code   D   Draw or Move
O   Byte ordering   T   Direction Type
W   Data Width   L   Last Pixel Drawn
C   CPU Wait   P   Pixel Mode
DIR   Direction of Line   R   Read/Write

(a) 8514/A Control Register. Writes cause execution to begin.

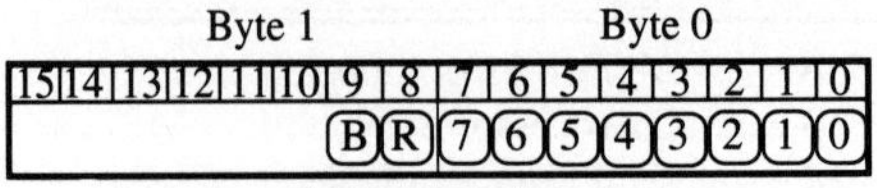

Byte 1   Byte 0

```
15 14 13 12 11 10 9 8  7 6 5 4 3 2 1 0
                (B)(R)(7)(6)(5)(4)(3)(2)(1)(0)
```

B   Coprocessor Busy
R   Data is Ready from Host
7-0   Fifo Position (7-0) occupied

(b) 8514/A Status Register.

FIGURE 14.22   8514/A Control and Status Register

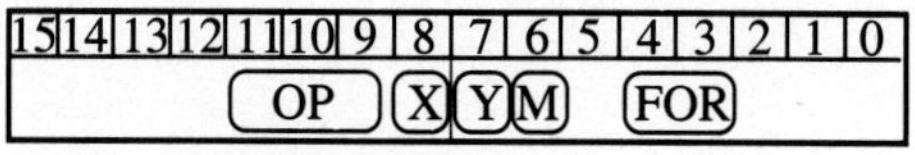

OP   Drawing Operation
X   X direction
Y   Y direction
M   Major axis
FOR Source Format

FIGURE 14.23 Line Strip Control Register

14.7.2 Registers

The registers associated with controlling the coprocessor are shown in Table 14.20.

TABLE 14.20 Control Registers

Register	Description
GO	Go field that starts a coprocessor operation
STATUS	Fields that report the condition of the coprocessor
COMMAND	Provide additional controls and parameters for the GO command
STEP	Line step registers that draw short-stroke vectors

Chapter 15

Super VGA Code Basics

15.1 INTRODUCTION

The programmer faces a true challenge when trying to create a fast and eloquent program that accommodates multiple display modes, pages, planes, and banks. In addition, the programmer must make this program operate under a variety of VGA chips, each with its own operational specifics.

Two basic functions encountered repeatedly are the bitblt and the single-pixel operations. The bitblts are common in imaging applications when manipulating a rectangular region. The single-pixel operations are most commonly encountered when objects are based on non-horizontal or vertical lines. Several techniques are available for each of these two cases. Some of them are presented in this section. Details and program examples for particular implementations on different Super VGAs can be found in Chapters 16–30.

It is the philosophy of this book that similar functions must be written in order to optimize performance. These similar routines need to handle planar or packed display modes. They must be further segmented into two cases according to whether or not bank boundaries are involved. These cases are then repeated for each Super VGA implementation. This encompasses a number of functions. However, it eliminates the need for decisions at the time-critical, low-level functions.

15.1.1 Determining Where the Super VGA Ports Are Mapped

In most cases, the Super VGA cards have their standard VGA ports mapped into the same locations. Their extended ports are spread through the immediate vicinity of the standard VGA port addresses. The ports at 3B4/3D4 hex and 3B5/3D5 hex are the exceptions. In monochrome configurations, the 3Bx hex mapping is used. In color configurations, the 3Dx configuration is used. The macro provided in Listing 15.1 determines whether these ports are located at 3Bx or 3Dx hex.

LISTING 15.1 Determine if the VGA is in a Monochrome or Color Mode

```
; Output Parameters:
;       dx      either 3D0 or 3B0
; Calling Protocol:
;       mono_or_color

mono_or_color   macro
        local   mono,go_on
        push    ax

        mov     dx,3cch     ;point to miscellaneous register
        in      al,dx       ;get byte
        test    al,1        ;test bit 0
        jz      mono        ;is zero so monochrome

;       is color
        mov     dx,3d0h     ;color port at 3dx
        jmp     go_on

;       is monochrome
mono:   mov     dx,3b0h     ;color port at 3dx
go_on:  pop     ax
        endm
```

In some Super VGA configurations, the attribute registers can be mapped differently from the VGA standard. The 3C0/3C1 hex register pair can be configured to act as an index/data pair as opposed to the standard VGA configuration. The state of the Attribute Index or internal attribute flip-flop can be read in certain Super VGAs.

Because of port mapping conflicts, it is also possible to map the VGAs into the 2xx hex address space instead of the 3xx hex port address space.

15.2 TRANSFERRING DATA WITHIN A SINGLE BANK

A block transfer typically involves a rectangular region consisting of a number of rows and columns. The most simple special case of this block transfer occurs when the number of rows is equal to one. In this case, the transfer involves all or part of a single row. Since the row is organized contiguously in display memory, a DMA Repeat Move String instruction can be used.

15.2.1 Determining the Starting Address

The starting address can be thought of as either a linear address or an x, y coordinate pair. The linear address, assumed to be a long integer (32 bits), is determined from the x, y coordinate pair by Equation 15.1.

Equation 15.1 Determining Linear Address

Linear_Address = x + (y * bytes_per_row)

The bank number, assuming the bank granularity is 64 Kbytes, can be determined by the Equation 15.2.

Equation 15.2 Determining a Bank Address

Bank Number = (Linear_Address & 0x00FF) >> 16;

Thus, the whole part of a mod 65536 operation produces the bank address. The bank address is equivalent to the high-order sixteen bits of the long integer. Typically, a maximum of one megabyte of display memory is provided on the Super VGAs. This translates into a 4-bit bank number (bits 20–17).

The fractional part of this arithmetic produces the intra-segment offset address of the pixel. The fractional part is equivalent to the low-order sixteen bits of the long integer. This is termed the pixel offset and can be calculated from Equation 15.3.

Equation 15.3 Determining a Pixel Offset Address

Pixel Offset = Linear_Address & 0x0000FFFFF;

This equation can be coded concisely in assembly language by the code examples in Listings 15.2 and 15.3. The starting, left-most x-coordinate is used in Listing 15.2; the ending, right-most x-coordinate is used in Listing 15.3. This assembly language code determines the (long) linear address from the equation (y * bytes_per_row) + x. This can be used to determine the bank and offset values of the start and end of the single scanline block to be transferred. The long arithmetic places the 64-Kbyte bank number in DX Register and the lower 16-bit intra-bank offset in the AX Register.

LISTING 15.2 Calculation of an Offset and a Bank Address of the Starting Point

---

```
;Input Parameters:
;       bytes_per_row     = bytes per row
;       x_start_coord     = starting x coord (left-most)
;       y_coord           = y coord
;Output Parameters:
;       dx     = Start_Bank_Number (64-kbyte granularity)
;       ax     = Start_Offset address
```

(continued)

```
; Calling Protocol
;         Start_Address    bytes_per_row, x_start_coord, y_coord

Start_Address  macro bytes_per_row, x_start_coord, y_coord
        mov    ax,bytes_per_row    ; get pitch in ax
        mov    bx,y_coord          ; get y in bx
        mul    bx                  ; y*pitch in dx:ax
        add    ax,x_start_coord    ; add x_coord
endm
```

LISTING 15.3 Calculation of an Offset and a Bank Address of the Ending Point

```
; Input Parameters:
;         bytes_per_row    = bytes per row
;         x_end_coord      = ending x coord (right-most)
;         y_coord          = y coord
; Output Parameters:
;         dx      = Start_Bank_Number (64-kbyte granularity)
;         ax      = Start_Offset address
; Calling Protocol:
;         End_Address    bytes_per_row, x_start_coord, y_coord

End_Address    macro bytes_per_row, x_end_coord, y_coord
        mov    ax,bytes_per_row    ; get pitch in ax
        mov    bx,y_coord          ; get y in bx
        mul    bx                  ; y*pitch in dx:ax
        add    ax,x_end_coord      ; add x_coord
endm
```

The *Bank_Off* function determines the starting bank number and offset address within the bank that corresponds to a given x, y and the number of bytes per row. This function can be called from a C program and is provided in Listing 15.4.

LISTING 15.4 Determine the Segment and Offset. (a) 4-bit Color Mode (b) 8-bit Color Mode (c) Hi-color mode (d) True-color mode

```
; (a) Function: Determine the segment and offset of a point in
; memory (4-bit color)

; Input parameters
;  x,y           horizontal and vertical coordinates of point
;  pitch         display pitch = # of pixels in a row
; Output parameters
;   *offset      pointer to offset of point within segment
;   *segment     pointer to segment which contains point
```

```
; Calling protocol
;   Seg_Off_16(x,y,pitch,&offset,&segment);

Seg_Off_16 proc FAR USES ES DI,  arg1,arg2,arg3,arg4:FAR
PTR,arg5:FAR PTR
; (long) address = ( y * offset ) + x; segment in dx, offset in ax
        mov    ax,arg3    ; get bytes per row
        mov    bx,arg2    ; get y
        mul    bx         ; y * bytes per row
        mov    cx,arg1    ; get x
        shr    cx,1       ; divide x by 8 for 16 color addressing
        shr    cx,1
        shr    cx,1
        add    ax,cx      ; (y * bytes per row) + x (lower 16 bits)
        adc    dx,0       ; (y * bytes per row) + x (upper n bits)

        les    di,arg4       ;get point to return offset
        mov    es:[di],ax    ;send back ax=offset
        les    di,arg5       ;get pointer to return segment
        mov    es:[di],dx    ;send back ax=segment
        ret
Seg_Off_16 endp

; (b) Function: Determine the segment and offset of a point in
; memory (8-bit color)

; Input parameters
;   x,y           horizontal and vertical coordinates of point
;   pitch         display pitch = # of pixels in a row
; Output parameters
;   *offset       pointer to offset of point within segment
;   *segment      pointer to segment which contains point
; Calling protocol
;   Seg_Off_256(x,y,pitch,&offset,&segment);

Seg_Off_256 proc FAR USES ES DI,  arg1,arg2,arg3,arg4:FAR
PTR,arg5:FAR PTR
; (long) address = ( y * offset ) + x; segment in dx, offset in ax
        mov    ax,arg3    ; get offset
        mov    bx,arg2    ; get y
        mul    bx         ; y * offset
        add    ax,arg1    ; (y * offset) + x (lower 16 bits)
        adc    dx,0       ; (y * offset) + x (upper n bits)

        les    di,arg4       ;get point to return offset
        mov    es:[di],ax    ;send back ax=offset
        les    di,arg5       ;get pointer to return segment
```

(continued)

```
            mov     es:[di],dx     ;send back ax=segment
            ret
    Seg_Off_256 endp


    ; (c) Function: Determine the segment and offset of a point in
    ; memory (Hi-color)

    ; Input parameters
    ;  x,y         horizontal and vertical coordinates of point
    ;  pitch       display pitch = # of pixels in a row
    ; Output parameters
    ;   *offset    pointer to offset of point within segment
    ;   *segment   pointer to segment which contains point
    ; Calling protocol
    ;  Seg_Off_Hi(x,y,pitch,&offset,&segment);

    Seg_Off_Hi proc FAR  USES ES DI,  arg1,arg2,arg3,arg4:FAR
    PTR,arg5:FAR PTR
    ; (long) address = ( y * offset ) + x; segment in dx, offset in ax
            mov     ax,arg3    ; get offset
            mov     bx,arg2    ; get y
            mul     bx         ; y * offset
            mov     bx,arg1    ; (y * offset) + 2*x (lower 16 bits)
            shl     bx,1
            add     ax,bx
            adc     dx,0       ; (y * offset) + x (upper n bits)

            les     di,arg4       ;get point to return offset
            mov     es:[di],ax    ;scnd back ax-offset
            les     di,arg5       ;get pointer to return segment
            mov     es:[di],dx    ;send back ax=segment
            ret
    Seg_Off_Hi endp


    ; (d) Function: Determine the segment and offset of a point in
    ; memory (True-color)

    ; Input parameters
    ;  x,y         horizontal and vertical coordinates of point
    ;  pitch       display pitch = # of pixels in a row
    ; Output parameters
    ;   *offset    pointer to offset of point within segment
    ;   *segment   pointer to segment which contains point
    ; Calling protocol
    ;  Seg_Off_True(x,y,pitch,&offset,&segment);

    Seg_Off_True proc FAR  USES ES DI,  arg1,arg2,arg3,arg4:FAR
    PTR,arg5:FAR PTR
```

```
; (long) address = ( y * offset ) + x; segment in dx, offset in ax
        mov     ax,arg3         ; get offset
        mov     bx,arg2         ; get y
        mul     bx              ; y * offset
        mov     bx,arg1         ; (y * offset) + 3*x (lower 16 bits)
        shl     bx,1
        add     bx,arg1
        add     ax,bx
        adc     dx,0            ; (y * offset) + x (upper n bits)

        les     di,arg4         ;get point to return offset
        mov     es:[di],ax      ;send back ax=offset
        les     di,arg5         ;get pointer to return segment
        mov     es:[di],dx      ;send back ax=segment
        ret
Seg_Off_True endp
```

15.2.2 Writing to a Single Bank

In the simplest case of transfers contained within a single bank, data can be written to display memory without concern for long arithmetic or bank crossing. The *Wr_Part* function loads a block of data into display memory and is provided in Listing 15.5.

In some cases, the Super VGAs will be configured as 128-Kbyte segments ranging from A0000–BFFFF hex in host address space. It is necessary to pass the display segment address, A0000h or B0000h, to the write function in these cases. In the majority of cases, the display memory is configured as 64 Kbytes between A0000–AFFFF. In these cases, it is not necessary to pass the segment address since A0000 will always suffice. Note that the variable SegA000 is used instead of a constant A000h. This provides the ability to change the segment address when in protected mode.

LISTING 15.5 Writing to a Portion of Display memory. (a) Write Bytes to a Single Bank of Display Memory (b) Write to a Portion of a Display Segment (Hi-color) (d) Write to a Portion of a Display Segment Point (True-color)

```
; Function:  Write to a portion of a display segment beginning at
; a start address from a "C" array beginning at a specified  byte
; Input parameters
;  buf      host "C" buffer containing data
;  npix     number of pixels
;  start    offset of window to start at
; Calling protocol
;  Wr_Part(buf,npix,start);

Wr_Part proc FAR USES DS ES SI DI, buf:FAR PTR,npix,start
```

(continued)

```
            mov     es,SegA000
            lds     si,buf          ;get pointer to top of array
            mov     cx,npix         ;desired number of bytes
            mov     di,start        ;starting address of display
            rep     movsb           ;write to memory
            ret
Wr_Part endp
```

```
; (b) Function:  Write to a portion of a segment beginning at a
; specified point (hi-color)

; Input parameters
;  buf      host "C" buffer containing data
;  npix     number of pixels
;  start    offset of window to start at
; Calling protocol
;  Wr_Part_Hi(buf,npix,start);

Wr_Part_Hi proc FAR  USES DS ES SI DI, buf:FAR PTR,npix,start
            mov     es,SegA000      ;point to base of display
            lds     si,buf          ;get pointer to top of array
            mov     cx,npix         ;desired number of bytes
            mov     di,start        ;starting address of display
            rep     movsw           ;write to memory
            ret
Wr_Part_Hi endp
```

```
; (c) Function:  Write to a portion of a segment beginning at a
; specified point (true-color)

; Input parameters
;  buf      host "C" buffer containing data
;  npix     number of pixels
;  start    offset of window to start at
; Calling protocol
;  Wr_Part_True(buf,npix,start);

Wr_Part_True proc FAR  USES DS ES SI DI, arg1:FAR PTR,arg2,arg3
            mov     es,SegA000      ;point to base of display
            lds     si,arg1         ;get pointer to top of array
            mov     cx,arg2         ;desired number of bytes
            mov     di,arg3         ;starting address of display
            rep     movsb           ;write to memory
            ret
Wr_Part_True endp
```

15.2.3 Reading from a Single Bank

Nearly identical to the write function, data can be read from a single plane using the Rd_Part function, which reads a block of data from display memory, assuming a 64-Kbyte memory map, and is provided in Listing 15.6.

LISTING 15.6 Reading from a Portion of Display Memory (a) Read Bytes from a Single Bank of Display Memory (b) Read from a Portion of a Display Segment (Hi-color) (c) Read from a Portion of a Display Segment (True-color)

```
; Function: Read from a portion of a display segment beginning at
; a start address to a "C" array beginning at a specified byte
; Input parameters
; npix      number of pixels
; start     offset of window to start at
; Output parameters
; buf       host "C" buffer to receive data
; Calling protocol
; Rd_Part(buf,npix,start);

Rd_Part proc FAR USES ES DS DI SI, arg1:FAR PTR,arg2,arg3
        les    di,arg1        ;get pointer to top of array
        mov    cx,arg2        ;desired number of bytes
        mov    ds,SegA000
        mov    si,arg3        ;starting address of display
        rep    movsb          ;write to memory
        ret
Rd_Part endp

; (b) Function  Read from a portion of a segment beginning at a
; specified point (hi-color)

; Input parameters
; npix      number of pixels
; start     offset of window to start at
; Output parameters
; buf       host "C" buffer to receive data
; Calling protocol
; Rd_Part_Hi(buf,npix,start);

Rd_Part_Hi proc FAR  USES ES DS DI SI, arg1:FAR PTR,arg2,arg3
        les    di,arg1        ;get pointer to top of array
        mov    cx,arg2        ;desired number of bytes
        mov    ds,SegA000     ;point to base of display
        mov    si,arg3        ;starting address of display
        rep    movsw          ;write to memory
        ret
```

(continued)

```
Rd_Part_Hi endp


; (c) Function:  Read from a portion of a segment beginning at
; a specified point (true-color)

; Input parameters
;  npix     number of pixels
;  start    offset of window to start at
; Output parameters
;  buf      host "C" buffer to receive data
; Calling protocol
;  Rd_Part_True(buf,npix,start);

Rd_Part_True proc FAR  USES ES DS DI SI, arg1:FAR PTR,arg2,arg3
        les   di,arg1   ;get pointer to top of array
        mov   cx,arg2   ;desired number of bytes
        mov   ds,SegA000      ;point to base of display
        mov   si,arg3   ;starting address of display
        rep   movsb     ;write to memory
        ret
Rd_Part_True endp
```

15.2.4 Clearing a Single Bank

The Read and Write functions require a buffer since every pixel can be different. When clearing a window, only one color is necessary. The Clr_Part function loads a single color into a display memory window, assuming a 64-Kbyte memory map, and is provided in Listing 15.7.

LISTING 15.7 Clearing a Portion of Display Memory to a Specified Value (a) Clear Bytes to a Single Bank of Display Memory (b) Clear to a Portion of a Display Segment (Hi-color) (c) Clear to a Portion of a Display Segment (True-color)

```
; Function: Clear a portion of a display segment beginning
; at a start address to a specified value
; Input parameters
;  color    color to set segment
;  npix     number of pixels
;  start    offset of window to start at
; Calling protocol
;  Clr_Part(color,npix,start);

Clr_Part proc FAR USES ES DI, color:byte, npix, start
        mov   es,SegA000
        mov   di,start    ;starting address of segment
        mov   cx,npix     ;desired number of bytes
        mov   al,color    ;get color
```

```
        rep stosb        ;fill memory
        ret
Clr_Part endp


; (b) Function:  Clear a portion of a segment beginning at a
; specified point (hi-color)

; Input parameters
;  color    color to set segment
;  npix     number of pixels
;  start    offset of window to start at
; Calling protocol
;  Clr_Part_Hi(color,npix,start);

Clr_Part_Hi proc FAR  USES ES DI, arg1,arg2,arg3
        mov     es,SegA000    ;point to base of display
        mov     di,arg3       ;starting address of segment
        mov     cx,arg2       ;desired number of pixels
        mov     ax,arg1       ;get color
        rep     stosw         ;fill memory
        ret
Clr_Part_Hi endp


; (c) Function:  Clear a portion of a segment beginning at a
; specified point (true-color)

; Input parameters
;  color    color to set segment
;  npix     number of pixels
;  start    offset of window to start at
; Output Parameters:
;        returns   0=output all bytes 1=output only 1 byte
;                        2=output only 2 bytes

; Calling protocol
;  Clr_Part_True(color,npix,start);

Clr_Part_True proc FAR  USES DS SI ES DI, arg1:FAR PTR,arg2,arg3
        mov     es,SegA000    ;point to base of display
        mov     di,arg3       ;starting address of segment
        mov     cx,arg2       ;desired number of pixels (loop count)

cpt1:   lds     si,arg1       ;point to start of buffer
        movsb                 ;fill memory with a pixel blue
        dec     cx
        jz      cpt_end1
```

(continued)

```
        movsb           ;fill memory with a pixel red
        dec     cx
        jz      cpt_end2

        movsb           ;fill memory with a pixel green
        dec     cx
        jnz     cpt1

        xor     ax,ax
        ret
cpt_end1: mov ax,01
        ret
cpt_end2: mov ax,02
        ret
Clr_Part_True endp
```

15.2.5 Writing to Four Display Planes

The function provided in Listing 15.8 writes data from an array into all four planes of display memory. The number of bytes involved in the transfer to each display plane is input to the function in the *num_bytes* variable. The data resides in a character buffer pointed to by *buf_ptr*. The data in the buffer is 4 * *num_bytes* bytes long since the buffer contains distinct data for all four display planes. The data is organized so that the num_bytes relevant to plane 0 are first, followed by *num_bytes* of data for plane 1, plane 2 and plane 3.

Four calls to the *Wr_Part* function follow the enabling of the appropriate write plane. Since all four display planes can be enabled at once, only one plane is enabled at a time through the codes, 01, 02, 04, and 08. After each output, the buffer pointer, *buf_ptr*, is incremented by the number of bytes output, *num_bytes*.

LISTING 15.8 Write to Part of a Display in a 16-color Mode

```
/* Function:  Write a horizontal line in a 16-bit mode.  The
lines worth of data consists of 4 * dx bytes.  The line is
embedded within the "buf" array and must be extracted.  The data
is organized a line at a time in a single plane.  Thus, each
byte contains one bit of eight pixels.
It consists of  "dx" bytes of plane 0 followed by "dx" bytes of
plane 1,2, and 3.
Input Parameters:
        dx        number of bytes in the line
        off_addr  offset address into current bank of
                  display memory
        buf_ptr   buffer pointer pointing to a byte buffer
                  containing the data
```

```
Calling Protocol:   */

void    Wr_Part_16(BYTE *buf_ptr, SHORT dx, SHORT off_addr)
{
 MapMask(1);    // write to bit plane 0
Wr_Part(buf_ptr,dx,off_addr);   buf_ptr += dx;
 MapMask(2);    // write to bit plane 1
Wr_Part(buf_ptr,dx,off_addr);   buf_ptr += dx;
 MapMask(4);    // write to bit plane 2
Wr_Part(buf_ptr,dx,off_addr);   buf_ptr += dx;
 MapMask(8);    // write to bit plane 3
Wr_Part(buf_ptr,dx,off_addr);
 MapMask(0x0f);    // write to bit plane 0-3
 }
```

15.2.6   Reading from Four Display Planes

Reading from all four display planes is accomplished through the code in Listing 15.9. This code is very similar to the write function in Section 15.2.4. The main difference is the coding to the Read Map Register. Only one display plane can be read from at a time; consequently, the codes are *01, 02, 03,* and *04.*

15.2.7   Clearing Four Display Planes

Clearing all four display planes is similar to writing to the display planes, except that a single color is used for the transfer. As a result, there is no input buffer or buffer pointer. Code that clears all four display planes is presented in Listing 15.10. Since all four display planes can be written to simultaneously, only one call to *Wr_Part* is necessary. All four display planes are enabled by the code *0x0F*.

LISTING 15.9 Read from Part of a Display in a 16-color Mode

```
/* Function:  Read a horizontal line in a 16-bit mode.  The
line's worth of data consists of 4 * dx bytes.  The line is
embedded within the "buf" array and must be extracted.  The data
is organized a line at a time in a single plane.  Thus, each
byte contains one bit of eight pixels.
It consists of  "dx" bytes of plane 0 followed by "dx" bytes of
plane 1,2, and 3.
Input Parameters:
          dx        number of bytes in the line
          off_addr  offset address into current bank of
                    display memory
          buf_ptr   buffer pointer pointing to a byte buffer
                    containing the data
```

(continued)

```
Calling Protocol:  */

void    Rd_Part_16(BYTE *buf_ptr, SHORT dx, SHORT off_addr)
{
 ReadMap(0);   // Read from plane 0
Rd_Part(buf_ptr,dx,off_addr); buf_ptr += dx;
 ReadMap(1);   // Read from plane 1
Rd_Part(buf_ptr,dx,off_addr); buf_ptr += dx;
 ReadMap(2);   // Read from plane 2
Rd_Part(buf_ptr,dx,off_addr); buf_ptr += dx;
 ReadMap(3);   // Read from plane 3
Rd_Part(buf_ptr,dx,off_addr);
 ReadMap(0);   // Read from plane 0
}
```

LISTING 15.10 Clear Part of a Display in a 16-color Mode

```
/* Function:   Clear part of a display in a 16-color mode
Input Parameters:
        color     color to use to clear memory
        num_byte  number of bytes to clear
        address   starting address in buffer to clear
Calling Protocol: */

void Clr_Part_16(BYTE color,SHORT num_byte,SHORT address)
{
    BYTE bmask,check;
    for(check=1 ; check<16 ; check <<= 1) {
      if(color&check)  bmask = 0xff;
      else     bmask = 0;
      MapMask(check);
      Clr_Part(bmask,num_byte,address);
      }
    MapMask(0x0f);        // reset mask
}
```

15.3   TRANSFERRING DATA TO TWO BANKS

If the banks associated with the first and last points in a window are not equal, special care must be taken to ensure that the upper-order bank addresses and lower-order bank offset addresses are handled properly. The special case when only two banks are crossed is considered in this section.

In the case of a rectangular window, the transfer of data that crosses a single bank boundary can be split into two transfers. The first transfer starts at the beginning of the window and ends with the last pixel contained in the window that falls in the first bank. The second transfer starts with the first pixel in the window that falls into the second bank and ends with the last pixel contained in the window.

The most simple example occurs when the width of the window is equal to the virtual width of the display. The number of pixels in the first bank can be derived by determining the distance from the starting pixel to the last pixel in the bank. The number of pixels in the second bank is equal to the offset of the last pixel in the window. Two DMA transfers can be initiated to accomplish the entire transfer. Note that the start offset of the first DMA transfer will be the offset address of the first pixel. The offset of the second bank is 0 (it begins at the bank boundary by default). The number of pixels in the first bank and the starting offset address of the first bank can be calculated by the Equations 15.4 and 15.5, respectively.

Equation 15.4   Calculating the Number of Pixels in the First Bank

$$\text{Pixels\_in\_First\_Bank} = 65536 - \text{Start\_Offset}$$

Equation 15.5   Calculating the Starting Offset Address in the First Bank

$$\text{Start\_Offset\_First\_Bank} = \text{Start\_Offset}$$

The number of pixels in the second bank and the starting offset address of the second bank can be calculated by the Equations 15.6 and 15.7, respectively.

Equation 15.6   Calculating the Number of Pixels in the Second Bank

$$\text{Pixels\_in\_Second\_Bank} = \text{Enbytes\_per\_rowset}$$

Equation 15.7   Calculating the Starting Offset Address in the Second Bank

$$\text{Start\_Offset\_Second\_Bank} = 0$$

15.4   TRANSFERRING DATA TO MULTIPLE BANKS

Transferring data to multiple banks using the simplification where the width of the rectangular window to be transferred is equal to the virtual width of the display is handled in a similar fashion. Additional DMA instructions are issued, one for each intermediate bank. The start address of all intermediate banks is 0, and the number of bytes to transfer is 65536.

When the width of the window is less than the virtual width of the display, separate DMA instructions are issued, one for each horizontal line in the window.

15.4.1   Techniques

There is a technique for moving blocks of data across bank boundaries. It involves pretesting where the bank transitions will occur before any data is moved. This can be accomplished by comparing the start and end points of the window against the bank transition points.

15.4.2   Single-Row Transfers

The simplest case occurs when the rectangular window is only one scan-line high. There are four special circumstances considered in this section, as illustrated in Figure 15.1.

The first, shown in Figure 15.1a, occurs when the transfer does not happen at a bank transition row. This is the most elementary of the four cases. The bank start address and the intra-bank offset address are determined, and the number of pixels in the single line are transferred to the display memory. Since the line is not on a bank transition row, no bank crossing is possible.

The remaining three circumstances, shown in Figure 15.1b–d, occur when the block transfer is on a bank transition line. Figure 15.1b illustrates what happens when the actual transfer crosses the boundary. Figure 15.1c–d show the cases when the actual transition is not crossed. In this case, the entire transfer occurs to the left or right of the point of transition and is functionally

Single Row DMA Transfers

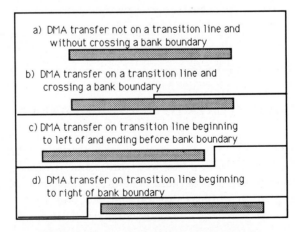

FIGURE 15.1 Single Row DMA Transfers

equivalent to the case where the line does not occur on a bank transition line. Determining whether the scan row is on a bank transition line may seem cumbersome for a single-line transfer. However, this technique is very useful when generalizing to non-single, scan-line transfers.

15.4.3 Multiple-Row Transfers

Next, we consider the case when the window is more than one line high. Like the single-row case, the first example of this occurs when the width of the scan line is the same as the virtual width of the display. This is the simplest case since the first (left-most) pixel of scan line n+1 immediately follows the last (right-most) pixel of scan line n. This case is illustrated in Figure 15.2. Note that the virtual image size, as loaded into the Offset Register, is not necessarily the number of bytes per displayed scan line. The virtual width of the display is based on the number of pixels per byte and whether the addressing mode is byte, word, or double word. The Offset Register is described in Section 10.4.22.

The starting and ending bank numbers involved in the transfer are determined by left-top and bottom-right coordinates of the window. The bank starting address and the number of pixels to transfer are determined as shown in Equations 15.8 and 15.9, respectively.

Equation 15.8 Calculating the Number of Pixels in the First Bank

Pixels_in_First_Bank = 65536 - Start_Offset

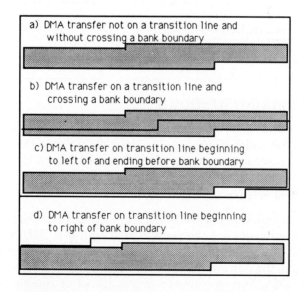

a) DMA transfer not on a transition line and without crossing a bank boundary

b) DMA transfer on a transition line and crossing a bank boundary

c) DMA transfer on transition line beginning to left of and ending before bank boundary

d) DMA transfer on transition line beginning to right of bank boundary

FIGURE 15.2 Multiple Full-Row DMA Transfers

Equation 15.9 Calculating the Starting Offset Address in the First Bank

Start_Offset_First_Bank = Start_Offset

If the transfer spans more than two banks, all intermediate banks are full, 64-Kbyte transfers. These fill the entire bank as shown in Equations 15.10 and 15.11, respectively.

Equation 15.10 Calculating the Number of Pixels in the Middle Banks

Pixels_in_Middle_Banks = 65536

Equation 15.11 Calculating the Starting Offset Address in the Middle Banks

Start_Offset_Middle_Bank = 0

The number of pixels and the starting offset address for the last bank can be determined by Equations 15.12 and 15.13, respectively.

Equation 15.12 Calculating the Number of Pixels in the Last Bank

Pixels_in_Last_Bank = Enbytes_per_rowset

Equation 15.13 Calculating the Starting Offset Address in the Last Bank

Start_Offset_Second_Bank = 0

15.5   TRANSFERRING WINDOWS

The last case considered here occurs when the transfer height is not limited to a single row and the width is not equal to the virtual display width. There are, once again, three cases to be considered as shown in Figure 15.3.

15.5.1   Transfers Within a Single Bank

The first case, illustrated in Figure 15.3a, transfers data to one block. The start and ending bank numbers are the same. The length of a DMA transfer is limited to the width of the window since the right-most pixel of one scan line is NOT contiguous to the left-most pixel of the following scan line.

The routine *DMA_Transfer* moves *length* bytes of image data into the selected bank beginning at a *start_offset* as determined by Equation 15.14. The

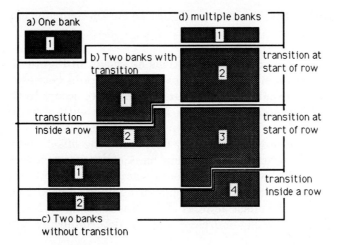

FIGURE 15.3 Transfering Rectangular Blocks

start_offset variable can be an unsigned single precision integer since overflow is guaranteed not to occur within a single bank.

Equation 15.14 Calculating a Starting Offset Address

Start_Offset = (y * bytes_per_row) + x;

15.5.2 Transfers Crossing Multiple Banks

The second and third cases, shown in Figure 15.3b–c, are special cases of the fourth case shown in Figure 15.3d. The transfer either crosses two bank boundaries or more than two bank boundaries respectively. If it crosses two bank boundaries, the transfer operation could be accomplished through two DMA loops, one for each bank. If it crosses more than two boundaries, the first and last transfer are identical to the first and second transfer in the two bank cases of Figure 15.3b–c. Each has to account for the possibility of encountering a bank transition at either the bottom line (of the top window) or the top line (of the bottom window). The intermediate transfers have to account for the possibility of encountering a bank transition at both the top and bottom lines. Section 15.6 provides a discussion of the more general cases.

15.6 TRANSFERRING DATA ACROSS GENERALIZED BANK TRANSITIONS

The following code that writes, reads, or clears a window makes no assumptions regarding where bank transitions occur. The bank transitions can occur in between rows, to the left of the window, to the right of the window or somewhere within the window. In Figure 15.3c, the transfer crosses a bank boundary that is within the block, that is, x_start <= x_bank_transfer <= x_end.

There are four types of bank transitions as shown in Figure 15.4. The first type of transition, illustrated in Figure 15.4a, occurs in between rows and is row-aligned. The second, illustrated in Figure 15.4b, occurs to the left of the window. The third, shown in Figure 15.4c, occurs within the window. The fourth, shown in Figure 15.4d, occurs to the right of the window. These have to be differentiated in order to correctly determine the offset address within a given bank. In this figure, there are four bank crossings each with a left-most pixel marked *X1*. The bank transition occurs at the x-coordinate *xt* in each case. Each case represents two vertically neighboring lines, labeled 1 and 2.

In the first case, the offset address of the line 2 begins at X1. In the second case, the beginning of offset address of line 2 is determined by Equation 15.15.

Equation 15.15 Offset Address When Transition Is to Left of Window

---

offset_address = X1 − xt

In the third case, there would be two offset addresses associated with line 2. The first represents the portion of the line still in the top-most bank. The second represents the portion of the line in the bottom-most bank. The first

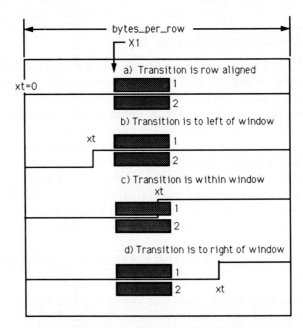

FIGURE 15.4 Crossing Bank Transitions

portion's offset would be bytes_per_row bytes beyond line 1; the second portion's offset would be zero.

In the fourth case, the offset of line 2 would be determined by the Equation 15.16.

Equation 15.16 Offset Address When Transition Is to Right of Window

offset_address = x1 + (bytes_per_row − xt)

15.7 HANDLING A WINDOW IN THE PACKED COLOR MODES

Packed color modes store the data associated with each pixel sequentially. This is simplest to understand in the 8-bit-per-color mode, in which each pixel is represented by a single byte. Pixel 1000 would be found at byte 1000. In the hi-color modes, each pixel is represented by two bytes. Therefore, pixel number 1000 would be found at byte location 2000–2001. In the true-color modes, each pixel is represented by three bytes. This is called 24-bit color where each byte represents the red, green, and blue content. Thus, pixel number 1000 would be found at byte number 3000–3002. A second form of the true-color modes exists when each pixel is represented by four bytes. This is called 32-bit color. The fourth byte, besides the red, green, and blue may be unused, used for masking, or used as an alphanumeric overlay. In this case, pixel 1000 would be found at byte number 4000–4003.

With the 24-bit color modes, there is a complication that occurs at the bank borders. This complication occurs since the 65,536-byte-long bank is not evenly divisible by three. Consequently, there is a remainder involved, which means that a pixel at the end of a bank will cross a bank boundary. This non-pixel aligned bank boundary requires very messy code and is a principal reason for going to either a linear memory map or to a 32-bit-per-pixel mode. Obviously, a 32-bit-per-pixel mode has pixel-aligned banks since 65,536 is evenly divisible by 4. The 24-bit-per-pixel mode bank crossing is shown in Figure 15.5.

15.7.1 Writing a Window in a Packed Color Mode

Writing a window with generalized bank transitions is very similar to the aligned bank transition case described in Section 15.6.1. An additional step is required since a bank transition can occur in the middle of a line. The implementation presented in Listing 15.20 bases its operation on a line-by-line basis within a do...while loop, similar to the aligned case. Within the loop a test is made before each line is output. This test determines if the line to be output will cross a bank boundary. Separate code is executed according to whether it will or will not.

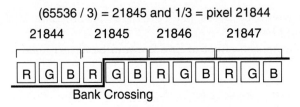

FIGURE 15.5 Non-pixel aligned bank crossings
in the 24-bit per pixel color modes

If the line to be drawn will cross the bank boundary, two lines must be drawn. The first line extends to the end of the bank from the current offset. The second line extends to the end of the line from the start of the next bank. The display and buffer pointers, display_ptr and buf_ptr, accurately reflect the buffer locations. The length of the two line segments, length_1 and length_2, are calculated based on the example in Figure 15.4 and Equations 15.15 and 15.16. The first line segment is drawn and the source buffer pointer, buf_ptr, incremented.

At this point it is necessary to change banks. The bank number, bank_num, is incremented and output to the Write Bank Register. Since the transition occurred within a bank, the first pixel drawn in the second line segment corresponds to the first pixel in the next bank. The display buffer offset pointer, display_ptr, is thus set to 0. The second line segment is drawn and the display buffer pointer, display_ptr, adjusted.

The second case occurs when a transition will not happen during the drawing of the next line. The line is drawn and the buffer pointer, buf_ptr, is incremented. The number of bytes per row, bytes_per_row, is added to the long integer display offset variable, display_offset. If the resultant number exceeds 65,536, a transition occurs before the next line is drawn. If this is the case, the bank must be switched, and the offset of the first pixel of the next line must be determined. The bank counter is incremented and output to the Write Bank Register.

Calculation of the offset to the first pixel in the next line is dependent on where the bank transition occurs. This is described in Figure 15.4 and Equations 15.15 through 15.16. To reduce calculation, a table is constructed that contains the x-axis bank transition points. These points vary depending on the number of bytes per row of the display. Three examples are given for 640, 800, and 1024 bytes per row. Note that the bank transitions in the 1024-byte case always occur at x=0. This is due to the fact that the banks are aligned. The code presented in Section 15.6 is better suited to the task.

The x-axis transition of the new bank, found in *sx[bank_num]*, is compared to the left-most pixel of the window, x1. The appropriate display pointer offset is determined according to whether the bank transition occurs to the left or to the right of the window. It is already known that the bank transition will occur outside of the last drawn line. This ensures that if the bank transition occurs to the right of x1, that it will actually occur to the right of x2.

The display pointer is adjusted, the row counter is incremented, and the do...while loop continues until the last row is drawn.

LISTING 15.11 Write Image Data to a Packed Color Mode Window in Display Memory (a) In a 256-color Mode (b) In a 256-color Row-aligned Mode (c) In a Hi-color Mode (d) In a True-color Mode

```
/* (a) Function:  Write data to a window in display memory in a
   256-color mode

Input Parameters:
 x1,y1       top-left corner coordinates
 x2,y2       bottom-right corner coordinates
 buf         byte containing color
 bytes_per_row bytes per display row

Calling Protocol:  */
void    WrWin_256(int x1, int y1, int x2, int y2, BYTE *buf,
        int bytes_per_row)
{
SHORT b_bank,b_offset,display_ptr;
int dx,length_1,length_2,bank_num,row,sx[12];
long end_of_line,display_offset;   BYTE *buf_ptr;

if(bytes_per_row==1024)  WrWin_1024(x1,y1,x2,y2,buf);
else {
  if(bytes_per_row==640) {
   sx[0]=0; sx[1]=256; sx[2]=512; sx[3]=128; sx[4]=384; sx[5]=0;
   }
  if(bytes_per_row==800) {
    sx[0]=0; sx[1]=736; sx[2]=672; sx[3]=608; sx[4]=544;
    sx[5]=480; sx[6]=416; sx[7]=352;
    }

// determine the offsets and banks of the starting and ending
   points
 Seg_Off_256(x1,y1,bytes_per_row,&b_offset,&b_bank);
 dx = (x2-x1)+1;  // determine the width of the window

// initialize the bank and pointers
 row = y1;      // start with starting row number
 // load the intra-window offset address
 display_offset = b_offset;
 display_ptr = (SHORT)display_offset;
 buf_ptr = &buf[0];  // point to top of buffer
```

(continued)

```
        bank_num=b_bank;
        Load_Write_Bank_256((BYTE)bank_num);  // setup first bank

    do {
      // does this line cross a bank
      end_of_line = (long)display_ptr + (x2-x1);
      if(end_of_line>=65536L)    {
          // must draw line as two line segments. Draw first segment
          // length of second line segment
          length_2 = (SHORT)(1 + end_of_line - 65536L);
          length_1 = dx - length_2;  // length of first line segment
          Wr_Part(buf_ptr,length_1,display_ptr);  // write the line
          buf_ptr += length_1;    // increment buffer pointer

          // change banks
          bank_num ++;    // increment to next bank
          Load_Write_Bank_256((BYTE)bank_num);  // setup first bank
          display_ptr = 0; // setup display offset

          // draw second line segment
          Wr_Part(buf_ptr,length_2,display_ptr);  // write the line
          buf_ptr += length_2;    // increment buffer pointer
          display_ptr = bytes_per_row - length_1; // inc display offset
          }
      else  {
          Wr_Part(buf_ptr,dx,display_ptr);      // draw a single line
          buf_ptr += dx; // increment buffer pointer

          // check to see if this was the last line in the bank
          display_offset = (long)display_ptr + bytes_per_row;
          if(display_offset>=65536L)    {
          // change banks
          bank_num ++;    // increment to next bank
          Load_Write_Bank_256((BYTE)bank_num);  // setup first bank
          if(sx[bank_num]<=x1)        display_ptr = x1-sx[bank_num];
          else        display_ptr = x1+(bytes_per_row-sx[bank_num]);
          }
      else
          display_ptr += bytes_per_row;
          }
     row ++;                  // increment row counter
    } while (row<=y2);
    Load_Write_Bank_256(0);  // restore the bank to bank 0
     }
    }

    /* (b) Function:  Write data to a window in display memory.
       (256-color row aligned)
```

```
Input Parameters:
 x1,y1      top-left corner coordinates
 x2,y2      bottom-right corner coordinates
 buf        "C" byte buffer containing colors

Calling Protocol:    */
void     WrWin_1024(int x1, int y1, int x2, int y2, BYTE *buf)
{ SHORT b_offset,display_ptr,b_bank;
  int dx,bank_num,row,bytes_per_row;
  BYTE *buf_ptr;    long display_offset;

 bytes_per_row=1024;  // determine the starting bank and offset
 Seg_Off_256(x1,y1,bytes_per_row,&b_offset,&b_bank);

 dx = (x2-x1)+1;  // determine the width of the window
 display_offset = b_offset;
 buf_ptr = &buf[0];  // point to top of buffer
 bank_num=b_bank;
 Load_Write_Bank_256((BYTE)bank_num);  // increment bank
 row = y1;              // start with starting row number

do {
 display_ptr = (SHORT)display_offset;
 Wr_Part(buf_ptr,dx,display_ptr);
 buf_ptr += dx;        // increment source buffer pointer
 display_offset += bytes_per_row;  // inc display offset
 if(display_offset>=65536L)  {
    bank_num++;
    Load_Write_Bank_256((BYTE)bank_num);  // increment bank
    display_offset = x1;
    }
 row ++;            // increment row counter
} while (row<=y2);// repeat til last row

 Load_Write_Bank_256(0);  // restore the bank to bank 0
}


/* (c) Function:  Write data to a window in display memory in a
   Hi-color mode

Input Parameters:
 x1,y1         top-left corner coordinates
 x2,y2         bottom-right corner coordinates
 buf           byte containing color
 bytes_per_row bytes per display row
```

(continued)

```
Calling Protocol:  */
void    WrWin_Hi(int x1, int y1, int x2, int y2, int *buf,
        int bytes_per_row)
{
SHORT b_bank,b_offset,display_ptr;
int dx,length_1,length_2,bank_num,row,i,*buf_ptr;
long end_of_line,display_offset;

// determine the offsets and banks of the starting and ending
   points
 Seg_Off_Hi(x1,y1,bytes_per_row,&b_offset,&b_bank);
 dx = (x2-x1)+1;  // determine the width of the window

// initialize the bank and pointers
 row = y1;              // start with starting row number
 // load the intra-window offset address
 display_offset = b_offset;
 display_ptr = (SHORT)display_offset;
 buf_ptr = &buf[0];  // point to top of buffer
 bank_num=b_bank;
 Load_Write_Bank_256((BYTE)bank_num);  // setup first bank

 do  {
  // does this line cross a bank
  end_of_line = (long)display_ptr + (2*(x2-x1));
  if(end_of_line>=65536L)  {
// must draw line as two line segments.  Draw first segment
length_2 = (SHORT)(1 + (end_of_line - 65536L)/2);
length_1 = dx - length 2;  // length of first line segment

Wr_Part_Hi(buf_ptr,length_1,display_ptr);  // write the line

buf_ptr += length_1;  // increment buffer pointer

// change banks
bank_num ++;    // increment to next bank
Load_Write_Bank_256((BYTE)bank_num);  // setup first bank
display_ptr = 0;  // setup display offset

// draw second line segment
Wr_Part_Hi(buf_ptr,length_2,display_ptr);  // write the line
buf_ptr += length_2;  // increment buffer pointer
display_ptr = 2*(Pixels_per_Row - length_1); // inc display
offset
      }
  else   {
     // draw a single line
     Wr_Part_Hi(buf_ptr,dx,display_ptr);
     buf_ptr += dx;// increment buffer pointer
```

```
    // check to see if this was the last line in the bank
    display_offset = (long)display_ptr + bytes_per_row;
    if(display_offset>=65536L) {
      bank_num ++;   // increment to next bank
      Load_Write_Bank_256((BYTE)bank_num);  // setup first bank
     display_ptr = display_offset - 65536L;
      }
    else {
     display_ptr += bytes_per_row;
      }
    }
 row ++;                 // increment row counter
 } while (row<=y2);
 Load_Write_Bank_256(0);  // restore the bank to bank 0
}


/* (d) Function:  Write data to a window in display memory in a
   True-color mode

Input Parameters:
 x1,y1         top-left corner coordinates
 x2,y2         bottom-right corner coordinates
 buf           byte containing color
 bytes_per_row bytes per display row

Calling Protocol:  */
void    WrWin_True(int x1, int y1, int x2, int y2, BYTE *buf,
        int bytes_per_row)
{
SHORT b_bank,b_offset,display_ptr;
int length_1,length_2,bank_num,row,i,bytes_in_this_line;
long end_of_line,display_offset; BYTE *buf_ptr;

// determine the offsets and banks of the starting and ending
   points
 Seg_Off_True(x1,y1,bytes_per_row,&b_offset,&b_bank);

// initialize the bank and pointers
 row = y1;             // start with starting row number
 // load the intra-window offset address
 display_offset = b_offset;
 display_ptr = (SHORT)display_offset;
 buf_ptr = &buf[0];  // point to top of buffer

 bank_num=b_bank;
 Load_Write_Bank_256((BYTE)bank_num);  // setup first bank
```

(continued)

```
bytes_in_this_line = 3*(1+x2-x1);
do  {
 // does this line cross a bank
 end_of_line = (long)display_ptr + bytes_in_this_line;
 if(end_of_line>=65536L)  {
// must draw line as two line segments.  Draw first segment
length_1 = 65536L - display_ptr;
length_2 = bytes_in_this_line - length_1;

Wr_Part_True(buf_ptr,length_1,display_ptr);  // write the line

buf_ptr += length_1;  // increment buffer pointer

// change banks
bank_num ++;    // increment to next bank
Load_Write_Bank_256((BYTE)bank_num);  // setup first bank
display_ptr = 0;  // setup display offset

// draw second line segment
Wr_Part_True(buf_ptr,length_2,display_ptr);  // write the line
buf_ptr += length_2; // increment buffer pointer
display_ptr = bytes_per_row - length_1;   // inc display offset
     }
 else   {
    // draw a single line
    Wr_Part_True(buf_ptr,bytes_in_this_line,display_ptr);
    buf_ptr += bytes_in_this_line; // increment buffer pointer

     // check to see if this was the last line in the bank
    display_offset = (long)display_ptr + bytes_per_row;
    if(display_offset>=65536L)  {
      bank_num ++;    // increment to next bank
      Load_Write_Bank_256((BYTE)bank_num);  // setup first bank
      display_ptr = display_offset - 65536L;
      }
     else {
      display_ptr += bytes_per_row;
      }
    }
 row ++;      // increment row counter
} while (row<=y2);
Load_Write_Bank_256(0);  // restore the bank to bank 0
}
```

15.7.2 Reading a Window in a Packed Color Mode

A similar routine, presented in Listing 15.12, reads the data from the display and places it into the *buf* buffer. There is only one difference between the read routine and the write function. This is the call to Rd_Part as opposed to Wr_Part and the setting of the read bank as opposed to the write bank.

LISTING 15.12 Read Image Data from a Packed Color Window in Display Memory (a) In a 256-color Mode (b) In a 256-color Row-aligned Mode (c) In a Hi-color Mode (d) In a True-color Mode

```
/* (a) Function:  Read data from display (256-color).

Input Parameters:
 x1,y1          top-left corner coordinates
 x2,y2          bottom-right corner coordinates
 buf            byte containing color
 bytes_per_row bytes per display row
Calling Protocol:  */
void    RdWin_256(int x1, int y1, int x2, int y2, BYTE *buf,
        int bytes_per_row)
{ SHORT b_bank,b_offset,display_ptr;
  int dx,length_1,length_2,bank_num,row,sx[12];
  long end_of_line,display_offset;  BYTE *buf_ptr;

if(bytes_per_row==1024)  RdWin_1024(x1,y1,x2,y2,buf);
else  {
  if(bytes_per_row==640) {
    sx[0]=0;   sx[1]=256; sx[2]=512; sx[3]=128; sx[4]=384;
sx[5]=0;
    }
  if(bytes_per_row==800) {
    sx[0]=0;   sx[1]=736; sx[2]=672; sx[3]=608; sx[4]=544;
sx[5]=480;
    sx[6]=416; sx[7]=352;
    }

// determine the offsets and banks of the starting and ending
   points
 Seg_Off_256(x1,y1,bytes_per_row,&b_offset,&b_bank);
 dx = (x2-x1)+1;  // determine the width of the window

// initialize the bank and pointers
 row = y1;               // start with starting row number
 // load the intra-window offset address
 display_offset = b_offset;
 display_ptr = (SHORT)display_offset;
 buf_ptr = &buf[0];  // point to top of buffer
 bank_num=b_bank;
 Load_Read_Bank_256((BYTE)bank_num);  // setup first bank
```

(continued)

```
do {
 // does this line cross a bank
 end_of_line = (long)display_ptr + (x2-x1);
 if(end_of_line>=65536L)    {
      // must draw line as two line segments. Draw first segment
      // length of second line segment
      length_2 = (SHORT)(1+end_of_line - 65536L);
      length_1 = dx - length_2; // length of first line segment
      Rd_Part(buf_ptr,length_1,display_ptr); // Read the line
      buf_ptr += length_1;   // increment buffer pointer

      // change banks
      bank_num ++;    // increment to next bank
      Load_Read_Bank_256((BYTE)bank_num);  // setup first bank
      display_ptr = 0;    // setup display offset

      // draw second line segment
      Rd_Part(buf_ptr,length_2,display_ptr);   // Read the line
      buf_ptr += length_2;   // increment buffer pointer
      // inc display offset
      display_ptr = bytes_per_row - length_1;
      }
 else    {
      // draw a single line
      Rd_Part(buf_ptr,dx,display_ptr);
      buf_ptr += dx;  // increment buffer pointer

      // check to see if this was the last line in the bank
      display_offset = (long)display ptr + bytes_per_row;
      if(display_offset>=65536L) {
        bank_num ++;    // increment to next bank
        Load_Read_Bank_256((BYTE)bank_num); // setup first bank

        if(sx[bank_num]<=x1)  display_ptr = x1-sx[bank_num];
        else display_ptr = x1+(bytes_per_row-sx[bank_num]);
        }
   else
     display_ptr += bytes_per_row;
      }
 row ++;              // increment row counter
} while (row<=y2);
Load_Read_Bank_256(0);  // restore the bank to bank 0
 }
}
```

```
/* (b) Function:  Read data from display (256-color row-aligned)

Input Parameters:
 x1,y1       top-left corner coordinates
 x2,y2       bottom-right corner coordinates
 buf         "C" byte buffer containing colors

Calling Protocol:  */
void     RdWin_1024(int x1, int y1, int x2, int y2, BYTE *buf)
{ SHORT b_bank,b_offset,display_ptr;
  int dx,bank_num,row,bytes_per_row;
  BYTE *buf_ptr;    long display_offset;

 bytes_per_row=1024;  // determine the starting bank and offset
 Seg_Off_256(x1,y1,bytes_per_row,&b_offset,&b_bank);

 dx = (x2-x1)+1;  // determine the width of the window
 display_offset = b_offset;
 buf_ptr = &buf[0];  // point to top of buffer
 bank_num=b_bank;
 Load_Read_Bank_256((BYTE)bank_num);   // increment bank
 row = y1;              // start with starting row number

do {
 display_ptr = (SHORT)display_offset;
 Rd_Part(buf_ptr,dx,display_ptr);
 buf_ptr += dx;        // increment source buffer pointer
 display_offset += bytes_per_row;  // inc display offset
 if(display_offset>=65536L)  {
    bank_num++;
    Load_Read_Bank_256((BYTE)bank_num);  // increment bank
    display_offset = x1;
    }
 row ++;             // increment row counter
} while (row<=y2);// repeat til last row
 Load_Read_Bank_256(0);  // restore the bank to bank 0
}


/* (c) Function:  Read data to a window from display memory in
   a Hi-color mode

Input Parameters:
 x1,y1         top-left corner coordinates
 x2,y2         bottom-right corner coordinates
 bytes_per_row bytes per display row
```

(continued)

```
Output Parameters:
 buf            byte containing color
Calling Protocol:  */
void    RdWin_Hi(int x1, int y1, int x2, int y2, int *buf,
        int bytes_per_row)
{
SHORT b_bank,b_offset,display_ptr;
int dx,length_1,length_2,bank_num,row,*buf_ptr;
long end_of_line,display_offset;

// determine the offsets and banks of the starting and ending
   points
 Seg_Off_Hi(x1,y1,bytes_per_row,&b_offset,&b_bank);
 dx = (x2-x1)+1;  // determine the width of the window

// initialize the bank and pointers
 row = y1;  // start with starting row number
 // load the intra-window offset address
 display_offset = b_offset;
 display_ptr = (SHORT)display_offset;
 buf_ptr = &buf[0];  // point to top of buffer
 bank_num=b_bank;
 Load_Read_Bank_256((BYTE)bank_num);  // setup first bank

 do {
  // does this line cross a bank
  end_of_line = (long)display_ptr + (2*(x2-x1));
  if(end_of_line>=65536L)  {
    // must draw line as two line segments.  Draw first segment
    length_2 = (SHORT)(1 + (end_of_line - 65536L)/2);
    length_1 = dx - length_2;  // length of first line segment
    Rd_Part_Hi(buf_ptr,length_1,display_ptr);  // Read the line
    buf_ptr += length_1; // increment buffer pointer

    // change banks
    bank_num ++;   // increment to next bank
    Load_Read_Bank_256((BYTE)bank_num);  // setup first bank
    display_ptr = 0;  // setup display offset

    // draw second line segment
    Rd_Part_Hi(buf_ptr,length_2,display_ptr);  // Read the line
    buf_ptr += length_2; // increment buffer pointer
    // inc display offset
    display_ptr = 2*(Pixels_per_Row - length_1);
     }
  else  {
    // draw a single line
    Rd_Part_Hi(buf_ptr,dx,display_ptr);
```

```
    buf_ptr += dx; // increment buffer pointer

    // check to see if this was the last line in the bank
    display_offset = (long)display_ptr + bytes_per_row;
    if(display_offset>=65536L) {
     bank_num ++;    // increment to next bank
     Load_Read_Bank_256((BYTE)bank_num);  // setup first bank
     display_ptr = display_offset - 65536L;
      }
     else {
      display_ptr += bytes_per_row;
       }
     }
  row ++;                // increment row counter
 } while (row<=y2);
 Load_Read_Bank_256(0);  // restore the bank to bank 0
}

/* (d) Function:  Read data to a window from display memory in
   a True-color mode

Input Parameters:
 x1,y1          top-left corner coordinates
 x2,y2          bottom-right corner coordinates
 bytes_per_row bytes per display row
Output Parameters:
 buf            byte containing color
Calling Protocol:  */
void    RdWin_True(int x1, int y1, int x2, int y2, BYTE *buf,
        int bytes_per_row)
{
SHORT b_bank,b_offset,display_ptr;
int length_1,length_2,bank_num,row,bytes_in_this_line;
long end_of_line,display_offset;   BYTE *buf_ptr;

// determine the offsets and banks of the starting and ending
   points
 Seg_Off_True(x1,y1,bytes_per_row,&b_offset,&b_bank);

// initialize the bank and pointers
 row = y1;  // start with starting row number
 // load the intra-window offset address
 display_offset = b_offset;
 display_ptr = (SHORT)display_offset;
 buf_ptr = &buf[0];  // point to top of buffer

 bank_num=b_bank;
 Load_Read_Bank_256((BYTE)bank_num);  // setup first bank
```

(continued)

```
  bytes_in_this_line = 3*(1+x2-x1);
  do {
   // does this line cross a bank
   end_of_line = (long)display_ptr + bytes_in_this_line;
   if(end_of_line>=65536L) {
// must draw line as two line segments.  Draw first segment
length_1 = 65536L - display_ptr;
length_2 = bytes_in_this_line - length_1;

Rd_Part_True(buf_ptr,length_1,display_ptr);  // Read the line
buf_ptr += length_1; // increment buffer pointer

// change banks
bank_num ++;    // increment to next bank
Load_Read_Bank_256((BYTE)bank_num);  // setup first bank
display_ptr = 0;  // setup display offset

// draw second line segment
Rd_Part_True(buf_ptr,length_2,display_ptr);  // Read the line
buf_ptr += length_2; // increment buffer pointer
display_ptr = bytes_per_row - length_1;  // inc display offset
     }
   else   {
     // draw a single line
     Rd_Part_True(buf_ptr,bytes_in_this_line,display_ptr);
     buf_ptr += bytes_in_this_line; // increment buffer pointer

   // check to see if this was the last line in the bank
   display_offset = (long)display_ptr + bytes_per_row;
    if(display_offset>=65536L) {
     bank_num ++;    // increment to next bank
     Load_Read_Bank_256((BYTE)bank_num);  // setup first bank
     display_ptr = display_offset - 65536L;
      }
     else {
      display_ptr += bytes_per_row;
       }
     }
  row ++;                // increment row counter
 } while (row<=y2);
 Load_Read_Bank_256(0);  // restore the bank to bank 0
}
```

15.7.3 Clearing a Window in a Packed Color Mode

The Clear function, presented in Listing 15.13, is nearly identical to the Write Window function. Since the Clear function sends a single color to every pixel within the window, no buffer or buffer pointer are required. Consequently, there is no addressing problem, and the window can be any size.

LISTING 15.13 Clear Image Data from a Packed Color Window in Display Memory (a) In a 256-color Mode (b) In a 256-color Row-aligned Mode (c) In a Hi-color Mode (d) In a True-color Mode

```
/* (a) Function:  Clear a window in display memory in a 256-
   color mode

Input Parameters:
 x1,y1         top-left corner coordinates
 x2,y2         bottom-right corner coordinates
 color         byte containing color
 bytes_per_row bytes per display row

Calling Protocol:    */
void    ClrWin_256(int x1, int y1, int x2, int y2, int color,
        int bytes_per_row)
{
SHORT b_bank,b_offset,display_ptr;
int   dx,length_1,length_2,bank_num,row,sx[12],bank,enmem;
long end_of_line,display_offset;

if(bytes_per_row==1024)  ClrWin_1024(x1,y1,x2,y2,color);
else {
 if(bytes_per_row==640) {
   sx[0]=0;   sx[1]=256; sx[2]=512; sx[3]=128; sx[4]=384;
sx[5]=0;
   }
 if(bytes_per_row==800) {
   sx[0]=0;   sx[1]=736; sx[2]=672; sx[3]=608; sx[4]=544;
   sx[5]=480; sx[6]=416; sx[7]=352;
   }

// determine the offsets and banks of the starting and ending
   points
 Seg_Off_256(x1,y1,bytes_per_row,&b_offset,&b_bank);
 dx = (x2-x1)+1;  // determine the width of the window

// initialize the bank and pointers
 row = y1;               // start with starting row number
 // load the intra-window offset address
 display_offset = b_offset;
 display_ptr = (SHORT)display_offset;
```

(continued)

```
   bank_num=b_bank;
   Load_Write_Bank_256((BYTE)bank_num);  // setup first bank

 do {
   end_of_line = (long)display_ptr + (x2-x1);     // does this
line cross a bank
   if(end_of_line>=65536L)      {
      // must draw line as two line segments.  Draw first segment
      // length of second line segment
      length_2 = (SHORT)(1+end_of_line - 65536L);
      length_1 = dx - length_2;  // length of first line segment
      // write the line
      Clr_Part((BYTE)(BYTE)color,length_1,display_ptr);

      // change banks
      bank_num ++;    // increment to next bank
      Load_Write_Bank_256((BYTE)bank_num);  // setup first bank
      display_ptr = 0;  // setup display offset

      // draw second line segment
      // write the line
      Clr_Part((BYTE)(BYTE)color,length_2,display_ptr);
      display_ptr = bytes_per_row - length_1; // inc display offset
      }
   else     {
      // draw a single line
      Clr_Part((BYTE)(BYTE)color,dx,display_ptr);

      // check to see if this was the last line in the bank
      display_offset = (long)display_ptr + bytes_per_row;
      if(display_offset>=65536L) {
      bank_num ++;    // increment to next bank
      Load_Write_Bank_256((BYTE)bank_num);  // setup first bank

      if(sx[bank_num]<=x1)      display_ptr = x1-sx[bank_num];
      else     display_ptr = x1+(bytes_per_row-sx[bank_num]);
      }
    else
      display_ptr += bytes_per_row;
  }
  row ++;                // increment row counter
 } while (row<=y2);
 Load_Write_Bank_256(0);  // restore the bank to bank 0
 }
}
```

```
/* (b) Function Clear a window  in a 256-color aligned mode

Input Parameters:
 x1,y1      top-left corner coordinates
 x2,y2      bottom-right corner coordinates
 color      byte value containing color
Calling Protocol:    */
void     ClrWin_1024(int x1, int y1, int x2, int y2, int color)
{ SHORT b_bank,b_offset,display_ptr;
  int dx,bank_num,row,bytes_per_row,enmem,bank;
  long display_offset;

 bytes_per_row=1024;  // determine the starting bank and offset
 Seg_Off_256(x1,y1,bytes_per_row,&b_offset,&b_bank);

 dx = (x2-x1)+1;  // determine the width of the window
 display_offset = b_offset;
 bank_num=b_bank;
 Load_Write_Bank_256((BYTE)bank_num);  // increment bank
 row = y1;               // start with starting row number

do {
 display_ptr = (SHORT)display_offset;
 Clr_Part((BYTE)color,dx,display_ptr);
 display_offset += bytes_per_row;  // inc display offset
 if(display_offset>=65536L) {
    bank_num++;
    Load_Write_Bank_256((BYTE)bank_num);  // increment bank
    display_offset = x1;
     }
 row ++;            // increment row counter
 } while (row<=y2);   // repeat til last row
 Load_Write_Bank_256(0);  // restore the bank to bank 0
}

 /* (c)  Function:  Clear a window in display memory in a
Hi-color mode

Input Parameters:
 x1,y1          top-left corner coordinates
 x2,y2          bottom-right corner coordinates
 color          byte containing color
 bytes_per_row bytes per display row
Calling Protocol:  */
void     ClrWin_Hi(int x1, int y1, int x2, int y2, int color,
        int bytes_per_row)
{
```

(continued)

```
 SHORT b_bank,b_offset,display_ptr;
 int  dx,length_1,length_2,bank_num,row;
 long end_of_line,display_offset;

// determine the offsets and banks of the starting and ending
   points
Seg_Off_Hi(x1,y1,bytes_per_row,&b_offset,&b_bank);
dx = (x2-x1)+1;  // determine the width of the window in pixels

// initialize the bank and pointers
row = y1;             // start with starting row number
// load the intra-window offset address
display_offset = b_offset;
display_ptr = (SHORT)display_offset;
bank_num=b_bank;
Load_Write_Bank_256((BYTE)bank_num);  // setup first bank

do  {
 // does this line cross a bank
 end_of_line = (long)display_ptr + (2*(x2-x1));
 if(end_of_line>=65536L)    {
   // must draw line as two line segments.  Draw first segment
   length_2 = (SHORT)(1+ (end_of_line - 65536L)/2);
   length_1 = dx - length_2;

   Clr_Part_Hi(color,length_1,display_ptr);  // write the line

   bank_num ++;    // increment to next bank
   Load_Write_Bank_256((BYTE)bank_num);  // setup first bank
   display_ptr = 0;  // setup display offset

   // draw second line segment
   Clr_Part_Hi(color,length_2,display_ptr);  // write the line
   // inc display offset
   display_ptr = 2*(Pixels_per_Row - length_1);
    }
else  {
   // draw a single line
   Clr_Part_Hi(color,dx,display_ptr);

   // check to see if this was the last line in the bank
   display_offset = (long)display_ptr + bytes_per_row;

   if(display_offset>=65536L) {
     bank_num ++;    // increment to next bank
     Load_Write_Bank_256((BYTE)bank_num);  // setup first bank
    display_ptr = display_offset - 65536L;
    }
```

```
    else {
      display_ptr += bytes_per_row;
      }
    }
 row ++;                  // increment row counter
} while (row<=y2);
Load_Write_Bank_256(0);  // restore the bank to bank 0
}


/* (d) Function:  Clear a window in display memory in a True-
   color mode

Input Parameters:
 x1,y1          top-left corner coordinates
 x2,y2          bottom-right corner coordinates
 color          byte containing color
 bytes_per_row bytes per display row
Calling Protocol:  */
void    ClrWin_True(int x1, int y1, int x2, int y2, long color,
        int bytes_per_row)
{
SHORT b_bank,b_offset,display_ptr;
int length_1,length_2,bank_num,row,bytes_in_this_line,rval;
long end_of_line,display_offset; BYTE cbuf[3],ct;

cbuf[0] = (BYTE) color;  cbuf[1] = (BYTE)(color>> 8);
cbuf[2] = (BYTE)(color>>16);

// determine the offsets and banks of the starting and ending
   points
 Seg_Off_True(x1,y1,bytes_per_row,&b_offset,&b_bank);

// initialize the bank and pointers
 row = y1;                // start with starting row number
 // load the intra-window offset address
 display_offset = b_offset;
 display_ptr = (SHORT)display_offset;

 bank_num=b_bank;
 Load_Write_Bank_256((BYTE)bank_num);  // setup first bank

 bytes_in_this_line = 3*(1+x2-x1);
 do {
  // does this line cross a bank
  end_of_line = (long)display_ptr + bytes_in_this_line;
  if(end_of_line>=65536L)    {
    // must draw line as two line segments.  Draw first segment
```

(continued)

```
   length_1 = 65536L - display_ptr;
   length_2 = bytes_in_this_line - length_1;
rval = Clr_Part_True(cbuf,length_1,display_ptr); // write line
switch(rval) {
  case 1:
    ct=cbuf[0]; cbuf[0]=cbuf[1]; cbuf[1]=cbuf[2]; cbuf[2]=ct;
  break;
  case 2:
    ct=cbuf[0]; cbuf[0]=cbuf[2]; cbuf[2]=cbuf[1]; cbuf[1]=ct;
  break;
  }
bank_num ++;   // increment to next bank
Load_Write_Bank_256((BYTE)bank_num);  // setup first bank
display_ptr = 0;  // setup display offset

// draw second line segment
rval = Clr_Part_True(cbuf,length_2,display_ptr); // write line
display_ptr = bytes_per_row - length_1;   // inc display offset
switch(rval) {
  case 1:
    ct=cbuf[0]; cbuf[0]=cbuf[1]; cbuf[1]=cbuf[2]; cbuf[2]=ct;
  break;
  case 2:
    ct=cbuf[0]; cbuf[0]=cbuf[2]; cbuf[2]=cbuf[1]; cbuf[1]=ct;
  break;
  }
}
else {
  // draw a single line
  rval = Clr_Part_True(cbuf,bytes_in_this_line,display_ptr);

  // check to see if this was the last line in the bank
  display_offset = (long)display_ptr + bytes_per_row;

  if(display_offset>=65536L) {
    bank_num ++;    // increment to next bank
    Load_Write_Bank_256((BYTE)bank_num);  // setup first bank
    display_ptr = display_offset - 65536L;
    }
   else {
    display_ptr += bytes_per_row;
    }
  }
 row ++;                  // increment row counter
} while (row<=y2);
Load_Write_Bank_256(0);  // restore the bank to bank 0
}
```

15.8   HANDLING A WINDOW IN 16-COLOR MODES

These same Write, Read, and Clear functions could be used in the 16-color modes by dividing the x-coordinates by 8 and using 16-bit versions of the Wr_Part function. However, the most common 16-color display mode that crosses a bank boundary is the 1024-by-768 mode. This mode has only one bank crossing, between lines 511 and 512, so the write, read, and clear functions are much simpler. These are provided in Listings 15.14 through 15.16 respectively.

The buffer used in the Write and Read functions consists of data from all four display planes. It is organized so that the first (top-most) line of the window is at the start of the buffer. The length of each line is a given number of bytes. The data from the first line of all four display planes is loaded contiguously, followed by the data from the next scan line's four display planes.

Imagine that there are N bytes per line. The data that resides in the buffer is described in Table 15.1. It assumes that the first scan line is at row 0. Thus, the length of the buffer is equal to four times the number of pixels in the window.

15.8.1   Writing a Window in 16-color Modes

In the code of Listing 15.14, data is written to display memory in a 16-color mode. It is assumed that a 1024-by-768 display mode is active. The code in Listing 15.14 also assumes that the left-most and right-most edges of the window, x1 and x2, are byte-aligned. Code presented in Chapter 12 can be incorporated to handle non-byte-aligned cases.

The byte addresses of the left and right-most edges of the window are determined by dividing the x1 and x2 coordinates by eight. This accounts for the eight pixels per byte (in one plane). The function has two cases. In the first, the window extends across the bank boundary. In the second, the window is completely contained in one bank.

TABLE 15.1   Data Format in the 16-color Window Buffer

Byte	Row	Plane
0 to (N–1)	0	0
N to (2N–1)	0	1
2N to (3N–1)	0	2
3N to (4N–1)	0	3
4N to (5N–1)	1	0
5N to (6N–1)	1	1
6N to (7N–1)	1	2
7N to (8N–1)	1	3

In the first case, the first write bank, bank 0, is selected. The destination display pointer, display_ptr, is set to the starting location and the buffer pointer, buf_ptr, is initialized to the top of the buffer. The transfer of data is accomplished through two do...while loops. The first outputs data to the first bank, bank 0, and the second outputs data to bank 1. One line is output at a time. The Wr_Part_16 function outputs 4 * dx bytes, dx bytes to each of the four display memory planes. Thus, the display offset pointer is incremented by 4 * dx. The first loop outputs data until line 512 is reached.

At line 512, the bank is switched to bank 1, and a similar do..while loop is executed. The display pointer, display_ptr, is initialized to the left-most byte of the window since it will be starting at the first row in the bank. The single-bank case is identical to the dual bank case with the exception that only one do...while loop is executed, either to bank 0 or bank 1.

LISTING 15.14 Write a Window in 4-bit-per-color Mode in a 1024-by-768 Resolution

```
/* Function: Write a window to display memory from a "C"
   buffer. Byte-aligned.
Input parameters:
 x1,y1          top-left corner coordinates
 x2,y2          bottom-right corner coordinates
 buf            host buffer containing data
 bytes_per_row bytes per display row
Calling protocol:  */

void    WrWin_16(int x1, int y1, int x2, int y2, BYTE *buf,
        int bytes_per_row)
{ int row,dx;  SHORT b_offset,off_addr,b_bank;
  BYTE *buf_ptr;
  buf_ptr = &buf[0];  // point to top of buffer

// there are 8 bits per pixel in the 16-color mode
 Seg_Off_16(x1,y1,bytes_per_row,&b_offset,&b_bank);
 x1 = x1>>3;    x2 = x2>>3;
 dx = (x2-x1)+1; row = y1;

if(Pixels_per_Row==1024)
if((y1<512) && (y2>=512)) {  // does it span both banks

    // write to the first bank
    Load_Write_Bank_16(0);
    off_addr = b_offset;  // starting offset
    do {
        Wr_Part_16(buf_ptr,dx,off_addr);
```

```
        buf_ptr += 4*dx;  off_addr += bytes_per_row;  row ++;
        } while (row<512);

    // write to the second bank
    Load_Write_Bank_16((BYTE)1);
    off_addr = x1;  // starting offset
    do {
        Wr_Part_16(buf_ptr,dx,off_addr);
        buf_ptr += 4*dx;  off_addr += bytes_per_row;  row ++;
        } while (row<=y2);
  }

else {  // contained in one segment
    if(y1<512) {     // contained in bank 1
        Load_Write_Bank_16(0);
        off_addr = b_offset;  // starting offset
         do   {
            Wr_Part_16(buf_ptr,dx,off_addr);
            buf_ptr += 4*dx; off_addr+=bytes_per_row; row++;
             } while (row<=y2);
        }
    else {        // contained in bank 2
        Load_Write_Bank_16((BYTE)1);
        off_addr = b_offset;  // starting offset
          do {
            Wr_Part_16(buf_ptr,dx,off_addr);
            buf_ptr += 4*dx; off_addr+=bytes_per_row; row++;
            } while (row<=y2);
        }
  }

else    {
        off_addr = b_offset;  // starting offset
          do {
            Wr_Part_16(buf_ptr,dx,off_addr);
          off_addr+=bytes_per_row; row++;
          } while (row<=y2);
        }
  }
```

15.8.2   Reading a Window in 16-color Modes

The Read function is presented in Listing 15.15. It is similar to the Write function, with the source and destination pointers reversed. In addition, the Read bank is used instead of the Write bank.

LISTING 15.15 Read a Window in a 4-bit-per-color Mode in a 1024-by-768 Resolution

```
/* Function:    Read a window to display memory from a "C"
   buffer. Byte-aligned
Input parameters:
 x1,y1           top-left corner coordinates
 x2,y2           bottom-right corner coordinates
 buf             host buffer containing data
 bytes_per_row bytes per display row
Calling protocol:   */

void    RdWin_16(int x1, int y1, int x2, int y2, BYTE *buf,
         int bytes_per_row)
{ int row,dx;  SHORT off_addr,b_offset,b_bank;
  BYTE *buf_ptr;
  buf_ptr = &buf[0];   // point to top of buffer

// there are 8 bits per pixel in the 16-color mode
 Seg_Off_16(x1,y1,bytes_per_row,&b_offset,&b_bank);
 x1 = x1>>3;   x2 = x2>>3;
 dx = (x2-x1)+1; row = y1;

if(Pixels_per_Row==1024)
if((y1<512)&&(y2>=512))  {   // does it span both banks
    // read from the first bank
    Load_Read_Bank_16(0);
    off_addr = b_offset;  // starting offset
    do {
         Rd_Part_16(buf_ptr,dx,off_addr);
         buf_ptr += 4*dx;  off_addr += bytes_per_row;  row ++;
         } while (row<512);

    // read from the second bank
    Load_Read_Bank_16((BYTE)1);
    off_addr = x1;  // starting offset
    do {
         Rd_Part_16(buf_ptr,dx,off_addr);
         buf_ptr += 4*dx;  off_addr += bytes_per_row;  row ++;
         } while (row<=y2);
  }

 else  {     // contained in one segment
   if(y1<512) {           // contained in bank 1
        Load_Read_Bank_16(0);
        off_addr = b_offset;  // starting offset
          do  {
```

```
                Rd_Part_16(buf_ptr,dx,off_addr);
                buf_ptr += 4*dx; off_addr+=bytes_per_row; row++;
              } while (row<=y2);
          }
      else  {       // contained in bank 2
          Load_Read_Bank_16((BYTE)1);
          off_addr = b_offset;  // starting offset
            do
            { Rd_Part_16(buf_ptr,dx,off_addr);
              buf_ptr += 4*dx; off_addr+=bytes_per_row; row++;
              } while (row<=y2);
          }
    }
  else  {
        off_addr = b_offset;  // starting offset
         do {
              Rd_Part_16(buf_ptr,dx,off_addr);
              off_addr+=bytes_per_row; row++;
            } while (row<=y2);
        }
  }
```

15.8.3 Clearing a Window in 16-color Modes

The Clear function, presented in Listing 15.16, is nearly identical to the Write function. The difference is that there is no buffer or buffer pointer. Consequently, no restriction regarding window size is imposed on this function. In addition, this function supports non-byte aligned resolutions greater than 1024 by 768.

LISTING 15.16 Clear a Window in a 4-bit-per-color Mode in a 1024-by-768 Resolution

```
/*  Function: Preset a window in display memory to a specific
    color.  Non-byte aligned.
Input parameters:
 x1,y1          top-left corner coordinates
 x2,y2          bottom-right corner coordinates
 color          desired color
 bytes_per_row bytes per display row
Calling protocol:   */

void    ClrWin_16(int x1, int y1, int x2, int y2, int color,
        int bytes_per_row)
{
      int     irow[2];  BYTE      left,right;
```

(continued)

```
    SHORT   i,ib,ib1,ib2,x1bytes,x2bytes,row,rowchk,sbit1,
            ebit1,ebit2, nxbytes,nmidbytes,off_addr;

// there are 8 bits per pixel in the 16-color mode
    x1bytes = x1>>3;     x2bytes = x2>>3;
    nxbytes = x2bytes-x1bytes+1;  // total number of bytes to set

    irow[0] = y2;      irow[1] = 511;
    sbit1=(x1&0x07);     ebit2=(x2&0x07);
    if(nxbytes == 1) {  // no byte boundary? yes...only one byte
to set
        ebit1 = ebit2;
        nmidbytes = 0;  // no middle, or right bytes
        right = FALSE;
    }
    else {                       // at least 2 bytes
        // total number of bytes minus left and right bytes
        nmidbytes = nxbytes-2;
        ebit1   = 7;           // to 8-th bit of left byte
        right=(ebit2 !=7);     // less than 8 bits to set?
        if(!right)   nmidbytes++;     // no one more middle byte
    }

    left=!((sbit1==0) && (ebit1==7)); // less than 8 bits to set?
    if(!left)                         // no...
      nmidbytes++;                    // no one more middle byte

    Seg_Off_16(x1,y1,bytes_per_row,&off_addr,&ib);
    row = y1;

    if(Pixels_per_Row == 1024) {
        ib1 = y1/512;                 // initial bank number
        ib2 = y2/512;                 // final bank number
    }
    else
        ib1 = ib2 = 0;
    for(ib=ib1 ; ib<=ib2 ; ib++)  {   // loop thru banks
        Load_Write_Bank_16((BYTE)ib);  // load current write bank
        // set variable for row check rule
        rowchk   = irow [ib2-ib];
        do {                          // do remainder of fill
            if(left) {
                ESetRes(15); SetRes((BYTE)color); // load registers
                for(i=sbit1 ; i<=ebit1 ; i++)
                    WrPoint_16(x1+i-sbit1,row,bytes_per_row);
                BitMask(255); ESetRes(0); // reset EGA/VGA registers
            }
```

```
            if(nmidbytes > 0)
               Clr_Part_16((BYTE)color,nmidbytes,off_addr+left);
            if(right) {
               ESetRes(15); SetRes((BYTE)color);  // load registers
               for(i=0 ; i<=ebit2 ; i++)
                   WrPoint_16(x2-i,row,bytes_per_row);
               // reset the EGA/VGA registers
               BitMask(255); ESetRes(0);
            }
            off_addr += bytes_per_row;
            row++;
         } while (row<=rowchk);
         off_addr = x1bytes;               // offset for 2nd bank
      }
   MapMask(0x0f);                          // reset mask
}
```

15.8.4   Color Expansion: Writing to or Clearing Display Planes

In the planar display modes, it is possible to write to any combination of planes at a time. It is often useful to write a monochrome image to a single plane. With the proper palette manipulation, this can create a fast color expansion. A function that writes a monochrome image to a display plane is provided in Listing 15.17a. Note that any combination of display planes can be written using the binary 4-bit pattern in the "plane" parameter.

LISTING 15.17 Display or Clear a Monochrome Image into Any Combination of Planes in the 16-color Mode. (a) Write an Image Plane (b) Clear an Image Plane

```
/* (a) Function:  Write a monochrome image into any
   combination of planes in a 16-color mode.
Parameters:
         x, y       starting coordinates
         numbyte    number of bytes per row
         nrow       number of rows
         plane      combination of display planes 0-15

Calling Protocol: */
void Wr_ImagePlane_16(int x,int y,int numbyte,int nrow,BYTE
*buf,int plane)

{ SHORT num_row,last_row; BYTE *buf_ptr;

 buf_ptr = &buf[0];
 MapMask((BYTE)plane);  // draw into plane only.
 last_row = y+nrow-1;
 if(Pixels_per_Row>=1024) {
```

(continued)

```
    if(y>=512) {  // all in bank 1
       Load_Write_Bank_16((BYTE)1);
      Wr_Graph_Win(x,y,buf,numbyte,nrow,Row_Width);
      } // y >= 512
    else { // y < 512 therefore may be more than one bank
          if(last_row<512) {  // all in bank 0
               Load_Write_Bank_16(0);
               Wr_Graph_Win(x,y,buf,numbyte,nrow,Row_Width);
               } // last row < 512
          else {  // starts in bank 0 and ends in bank 1
               num_row = 512 - y;
               Load_Write_Bank_16(0);
               Wr_Graph_Win(x,y,buf_ptr,numbyte,num_row,Row_Width);

               buf_ptr += num_row * numbyte;
               num_row = nrow - num_row;
               Load_Write_Bank_16((BYTE)1);
               Wr_Graph_Win(x,512,buf,numbyte,num_row,Row_Width);
                      } //starts in bank 0 and ends in bank 1
         } // y < 512
   } // maybe more than one bank
  else  Wr_Graph_Win(x,y,buf,numbyte,nrow,Row_Width);

 MapMask(0x0f);  // reset plane mask
}


/* (b) Function:  Clear any combination of planes in the
   16-color mode.

Input Parameters:
         x, y      starting coordinates
         numbyte   number of bytes per row
         nrow      number of rows
         plane     combination of display planes 0-15

Calling Protocol: */
void Clr_ImagePlane_16(int x,int y,int numbyte,int nrow,BYTE
color,int plane)


{ int num_row,last_row;


 MapMask((BYTE)plane);  // draw into plane

 last_row = y+nrow-1;
```

```
    if(Pixels_per_Row>=1024) {  // if more than one bank in image

    if(y>=512) {  // all in bank 1
        Load_Write_Bank_16((BYTE)1);
        Clr_Graph_Win(x,y,color,numbyte,nrow,Row_Width);
        } // end of all in 1

    else { // if not all in 1
            if(last_row<512) {  // all in bank 0
                Load_Write_Bank_16(0);
                Clr_Graph_Win(x,y,color,numbyte,nrow,Row_Width);
                } // end of all in zero

            else {  // starts in bank 0 and ends in bank 1
                    num_row = 512 - y;
                Load_Write_Bank_16(0);
                Clr_Graph_Win(x,y,color,numbyte,num_row,Row_Width);

                num_row = nrow - num_row;
                Load_Write_Bank_16((BYTE)1);
                Clr_Graph_Win(x,512,color,numbyte,num_row,Row_Width);
                } // end of starts in 0 and ends in 1
        } // y < 512
    } // maybe more than one bank
    else  Clr_Graph_Win(x,y,color,numbyte,nrow,Row_Width);

  MapMask(0x0f);  // reset plane mask
  }
```

A second common function is the clear plane function provided in Listing 15.17b. Once again, any combination of display planes can be written to at a time. The clear function can be used to quickly clear regions of the display since each output writes to all four display planes. A 32-bit write on a local bus would therefore cause 32*4=128 bits to be written per instruction cycle output. The write and clear function can be called repetitively creating a scrolling or panning effect.

15.9 DRAWING SINGLE PIXELS

Transferring single pixels is easier than transferring blocks. There are several techniques. One technique determines the bank number and offset of the pixel in question by referencing the x,y coordinate-pair inputs and the offset of the display. It then loads the bank and transfers the pixel. Code that draws a pixel in a planar mode is more complicated than code that draws a pixel in a packed mode. Examples of each follow.

A packed display mode is organized so that each pixel is stored contiguously in one to four bytes. Typical code for drawing a pixel in such a mode is provided in Listing 15.18.

15.9.1 Drawing a Pixel in the Packed Display Modes

LISTING 15.18 Reading and Writing Pixels in a Packed Mode. (a) Draw a Point in 256-color (b) Draw an XOR Point in 256-color (c) Read a Point (Hi-color) (d) Draw a Point (Hi-color) (e) Draw an XOR Point (Hi-color) (f) Read a Point (True-color) (g) Draw a Point (True-color) (h) Draw an XOR Point (True-color)

```
; (a) Function: Draw a point into display memory in extended
  resolution 256 color modes.

; Input parameters
;  arg1:x                  horizontal coordinate of point
;  arg2:y                  vertical coordinate of point
;  arg3:color              color to draw point
;  arg4:bytes_per_row      display bytes_per_row = # of
;                          pixels per line
; Calling protocol
;  WrPixel_256(x,y,color,bytes_per_row);

WrPixel_256 PROC FAR  USES ES DI ,arg1,arg2,arg3:byte,arg4
        get_address_write_256
        call FAR PTR Set_Write_Bank_256   ;load the write bank
        write_pixel_256
        ret
WrPixel_256 endp


; (b) Function: Draw an XOR point into display memory in
  extended resolution 256 color modes.

; Input parameters
;  arg1: x                 horizontal coordinate of point
;  arg2: y                 vertical coordinate of point
;  arg3: color             color to draw point
;  arg4: bytes_per_row     display bytes_per_row = # of
;                          pixels per line
; Calling protocol
;  WrXPixel_256(x,y,color,bytes_per_row);

WrXPixel_256 PROC FAR  USES ES DI ,arg1,arg2,arg3:byte,arg4
        get_address_write_256
        call FAR PTR Set_Write_Bank_256   ;load the write bank
        call FAR PTR Set_Read_Bank_256    ;load the read bank
        write_Xpixel_256
```

```
        ret
WrXPixel_256 endp

; (c) Function:   Read a point (Hi-color)

; Input parameters
;  arg1: x                  horizontal coordinate of point
;  arg2: y                  vertical coordinate of point
;  arg3: bytes_per_row      display bytes_per_row = # of
;                           pixels per line
; Output parameters:
;  color     color to draw point
; Calling protocol
;  color = RdPixel_Hi(x,y,bytes_per_row);

RdPixel_Hi PROC FAR  USES DS SI,arg1,arg2,arg3
        get_address_read_Hi ;determine address
        call  FAR PTR Set_Read_Bank_256   ;load the read bank
        read_pixel_Hi ;read pixel
        ret
RdPixel_Hi endp

; (d) Function:   Draw a point (Hi-color)

; Input parameters
;  arg1: x                  horizontal coordinate of point
;  arg2: y                  vertical coordinate of point
;  arg3: color              color to draw point
;  arg4: bytes_per_row      display bytes_per_row = # of
;                           pixels per line
; Calling protocol
;  WrPixel_Hi(x,y,color,bytes_per_row);

WrPixel_Hi PROC FAR  USES ES DI ,arg1,arg2,arg3,arg4
        get_address_write_Hi
        call FAR PTR Set_Write_Bank_256   ;load the write bank
        write_pixel_Hi
        ret
WrPixel_Hi endp

; (e) Function:   Draw a XOR point (Hi-color)

; Input parameters
;  arg1: x                  horizontal coordinate of point
;  arg2: y                  vertical coordinate of point
;  arg3: color              color to draw point
;  arg4: bytes_per_row      display bytes_per_row = # of
;                           pixels per line
```

(continued)

```
; Calling protocol
;   WrXPixel_Hi(x,y,color,bytes_per_row);

WrXPixel_Hi PROC FAR   USES ES DI ,arg1,arg2,arg3,arg4
        get_address_write_Hi
        call FAR PTR Set_Write_Bank_256   ;load the write bank
        call FAR PTR Set_Read_Bank_256    ;load the read bank
        write_Xpixel_Hi
        ret
WrXPixel_Hi endp


; (f) Function   Read a point (True-color)

; Input parameters
;   arg1: x                 horizontal coordinate of point
;   arg2: y                 vertical coordinate of point
;   arg3: bytes_per_row     display bytes_per_row = # of
;                              pixels per line
;   arg4: buf        buffer to contain 3 bytes
; Output parameters:
;   color    color to draw point
; Calling protocol
;   RdPixel_True(x,y,bytes_per_row,buf);

RdPixel_True PROC FAR   USES ES DI DS SI,arg1,arg2,arg3,arg4:FAR
PTR
        get_address_read_True   ;get address in bl:si
        push   si
        ;load the read bank for 1'st pixel
        call FAR PTR Set_Read_Bank_256
        pop    si
        push   bx              ;save the bank for later (if needed)

;       now check if the true pixel itself crosses a bank
        cmp    si,65535
        je     rdpt1

        cmp    si,65534
        je     rdpt2

        read_pixel_true        ;ok to read all three pixels
        pop bx                 ;fix stack
        ret

rdpt1:                         ;at 65535 so read one byte
        read_pixel1a_True      ;read 1 byte
        pop bx                 ;fix stack
        inc    bx              ;increment bank
```

```
                ;load the read bank for next 2 pixels
                call FAR PTR Set_Read_Bank_256
                read_pixel1b_True   ;read 1 byte
                ret

rdpt2:                      ;at 65535 so read one byte
                read_pixel2a_True   ;read 2 bytes
                pop bx              ;fix stack
                inc   bx            ;increment bank
                ;load the read bank for next 2 pixels
                call FAR PTR Set_Read_Bank_256
                read_pixel2b_True   ;read one byte


                ret
RdPixel_True endp



; (g) Function:  Draw a point (True-color)

; Input parameters
;   arg1: x               horizontal coordinate of point
;   arg2: y               vertical coordinate of point
;   arg3: buf             buffer of 3-byte color to draw point
;   arg4: bytes_per_row   display bytes_per_row = # of
;                         pixels per line
; Calling protocol
;   WrPixel_True(x,y,buf,bytes_per_row);

WrPixel_True PROC FAR  USES ES DI DS SI,arg1,arg2,arg3:FAR
PTR,arg4

                get_address_write_True ;get address.  leave in bl:di
                ;load the write bank for 1st pixel
                call FAR PTR Set_Write_Bank_256
                push   bx            ;save the bank for later (if needed)

;               now check if the true pixel itself crosses a bank
                cmp    di,65535
                je     wrpt1

                cmp    di,65534
                je     wrpt2

                write_pixel_true     ;ok to write all three pixels
                pop bx               ;fix stack
;               mov    ax,0          ;used for diagnostics
                ret
```

(continued)

```
wrpt1:              ;at 65535 so write one byte
          write_pixel1a_True  ;write 1 byte
          pop bx              ;fix stack
          inc   bx            ;increment bank
          ;load the write bank for next 2 pixels
          call FAR PTR Set_Write_Bank_256
          write_pixel1b_True  ;write 1 byte
;         mov   ax,1          ;used for diagnostics
          ret


wrpt2:              ;at 65535 so write one byte
          write_pixel2a_True  ;write 2 bytes
          pop bx              ;fix stack
          inc   bx            ;increment bank
          ;load the write bank for next 2 pixels
          call FAR PTR Set_Write_Bank_256
          write_pixel2b_True  ;write one byte
;         mov   ax,2          ;used for diagnostics
          ret

WrPixel_True endp


; (h) Function:   Draw an XOR point (True-color)

; Input parameters
;  arg1: x                horizontal coordinate of point
;  arg2: y                vertical coordinate of point
;  arg3: buf              buf of 3-btye color to draw point
;  arg4: bytes_pcr_row    display bytes_per_row = # of
                          pixels per line
; Calling protocol
;  WrXPixel_True(x,y,color,bytes_per_row);

WrXPixel_True PROC FAR  USES ES DI DS SI,arg1,arg2,arg3:FAR
PTR,arg4
          get_address_write_256
          call FAR PTR Set_Write_Bank_256   ;load the write bank
          call FAR PTR Set_Read_Bank_256    ;load the read bank
          write_Xpixel_true
          ret
WrXPixel_True endp
```

15.9.2   Drawing a Pixel in 16-color Modes

A planar display mode is organized for each byte to contain multiple pixels and be distributed across all four display planes. The Set/Reset Register and Enable Set/Reset Register can be used to write to all display planes simultaneously. The Bit Mask Register can be used to mask off the bits corresponding to other pixels in the byte.

Two functions are provided that write a pixel in the planar display modes. The first handles the Set/Reset Register and Enable Set/Reset Register; the second does not. In the case of a single-color line drawing routine, the Set/Reset Register and Enable Set/Reset Register can be set once before the line is drawn.

Listing 15.19 provides typical code to draw a pixel using the Set/Reset Register and Enable Set/Reset Register.

LISTING 15.19 Draw a Pixel in the 16-color Modes (a) Draw a Point with Set/Reset (b) Draw a Point in 16-color Modes (Assuming Set/Reset Set) (c) Draw an XOR Point in 16-color Modes (Assuming Set/Reset Set)

```
/* (a) Drawing a Point in one of the 16-color modes

  Input parameters:
    x1,y1              first endpoint x,y coordinates of line
    x2,y2              second endpoint x,y coordinates of line
    color              color of the line
    bytes_per_row      offset of display

Calling protocol */
void    WrPixel_16(int x, int y, int color, int bytes_per_row)
{
// enable the set reset function and load the color
ESetRes(15); SetRes((BYTE)color);  //  load registers
WrPoint_16(x,y,bytes_per_row);
BitMask(255); ESetRes(0);          // reset the EGA/VGA registers
}

; (b) Function: Draw a point into display memory in extended
   resolution 16 color modes.
;  NOTE:  ASSUMES that Set Reset and Enable Set Reset Register
;   are preset with color.

; Input parameters
;  arg1: x                horizontal coordinate of point
;  arg2: y                vertical coordinate of point
;  arg3: bytes_per_row    display bytes_per_row = # of
;                         pixels per line

; Calling protocol
;  WrPoint_16(x,y,bytes_per_row);

WrPoint_16 PROC FAR   USES ES DI,arg1,arg2,arg3
```

(continued)

```
; set up the Bit Mask Register
        load_bit_mask_16     ;load bit mask register
; get the x index and divide by 8 for 16-color
        mov    ax,arg1       ; get the x address
        shr    ax,1          ; divide by 8
        shr    ax,1
        shr    ax,1
        push   ax            ;save byte address for later
; (long) address = ( y * bytes_per_row ) + x:; segment in dx
; and bytes_per_row  in ax
        mov    ax,arg3   ; get bytes_per_row in ax
        mov    bx,arg2   ; get y in bx
        mul    bx        ; y*bytes_per_row in dx:ax
        pop    cx        ; get the x byte address
        add    ax,cx  ; (y*bytes_per_row)+x lower 16 bits in ax
        adc    dx,0   ; (y*bytes_per_row)+x upper n bits in dx
        mov    di,ax  ; load as display offset for es:di

;       determine bank register
        mov    bl,dl  ;put page value into bl for port output
        push   bx     ;save
        call FAR PTR Set_Read_Bank_16 ;load the read bank
        pop bx         ;restore
        call FAR PTR Set_Write_Bank_16    ;load the write bank
        ;send the data to display memory through set reset
        write_pixel_16
        ret
WrPoint_16 endp

;   (d) Function: Draw a point into display memory in extended
;   resolution 16 color modes.
;   NOTE:  ASSUMES that Set Reset and Enable Set Reset Register
;   are preset with color.

; Input parameters
;  arg1: x               horizontal coordinate of point
;  arg2: y               vertical coordinate of point
;  arg3: bytes_per_row   display bytes_per_row = # of
                         pixels per line

; Calling protocol
;  WrXPoint_16(x,y,bytes_per_row);

WrXPoint_16 PROC FAR  USES ES DI,arg1,arg2,arg3
        load_bit_mask_16          ;load bit mask register
; get the x index and divide by 8 for 16-color
        mov    ax,arg1   ; get the x address
        shr    ax,1      ; divide by 8
```

```
        shr     ax,1
        shr     ax,1
        push    ax          ;save byte address for later
; (long) address = ( y * bytes_per_row ) + x:; segment in dx
; and bytes_per_row  in ax
        mov     ax,arg3     ; get bytes_per_row in ax
        mov     bx,arg2     ; get y in bx
        mul     bx          ; y*bytes_per_row in dx:ax
        pop     cx          ; get the x byte address
        add     ax,cx   ; (y*bytes_per_row)+x lower 16 bits in ax
        adc     dx,0    ; (y*bytes_per_row)|x upper n bits in dx
        mov     di,ax   ; load as display offset for es:di

;       determine bank register
        mov     bl,dl   ;put page value into bl for port output
        call FAR PTR Set_Read_Bank_16      ;load the read bank
        mov     bl,dl   ;put page value into bl for port output
        call FAR PTR Set_Write_Bank_16     ;load the write bank
        ;send the data to display memory through set reset
        write_pixel_16
        ret
WrXPoint_16 endp
```

15.10   DRAWING A LINE

Drawing a line is accomplished by using the Bresenham algorithm calling upon the draw pixel functions described in Section 15.9. The lines are drawn in the planar and packed display modes. Standard lines and the special cases of horizontal, vertical, and XOR lines are covered.

15.10.1   Drawing a Line in the Packed Color Modes

The packed color modes include the 8-bit, hi-color, and 24-bit true-color modes. Functions for standard lines are provided in Listing 15.20. Horizontal line drawing routines are provided in Listing 15.21. XOR line drawing routines are provided in Listing 15.22.

LISTING 15.20 (a) Drawing a Line in One of the 8-bit Color Modes (b) Drawing a Line in One of the Hi-color Modes (c) Drawing a Line in One of the True-color Modes

```
// Drawing a Line in one of the 256, hi or true-color modes

  Input parameters:
    x1,y1           first endpoint x,y coordinates of line
    x2,y2           second endpoint x,y coordinates of line
    color           color of the line:  int if 256 or hi-color,
                    long if true-color
```

(continued)

```
    bytes_per_row    offset of display

Calling protocol */

// (a) Function:  Drawing a Line in one of the 256-color modes
void    WrLine_256(int x1,int y1,int x2,int y2,int color,
        int bytes_per_row)
{ int dx,dy,incr1,incr2,d,x,y,xend,yend,yinc,xinc;

if(y2==y1) {
        if(x1 > x2) {    xend = x1;      x1 = x2;    x2 = xend; }
        WrHLine_256(x1,x2,y1,color,bytes_per_row);
        }
  else {
     dx = abs(x2-x1);    dy = abs(y2-y1);

   if(dx>=dy) {   // slope < 1
    if(x1>x2) {
        x = x2;  y = y2; xend = x1;
        if(dy==0) yinc=0;
        else {if(y2>y1) yinc = -1;  else yinc = 1; }
        }
    else {
        x = x1;  y = y1; xend = x2;
        if(dy==0) yinc=0;
         else {if(y2>y1) yinc = 1;  else yinc = -1; }
        }
    incr1 = 2*dy;   d = incr1-dx; incr2 = 2*(dy-dx);
    WrPixel_256(x,y,color,bytes_per_row);
    while (x<xend) {
        x ++;
        if (d<0) d += incr1;
        else { y +=yinc; d = d + incr2;  }
        WrPixel_256(x,y,color,bytes_per_row);
        }
  }
  else  {
   if(y1>y2) {
        x = x2;  y = y2; yend = y1;
        if(dx==0) xinc=0;
        else { if(x2>x1) xinc = -1;  else xinc = 1;}
        }
    else {
        x = x1;  y = y1; yend = y2;
        if(dx==0) xinc=0;
        else { if(x2>x1) xinc =  1;  else xinc = -1;}
        }
   incr1 = 2*dx;   d = incr1-dy; incr2 = 2*(dx-dy);
```

```
    WrPixel_256(x,y,color,bytes_per_row);
    while (y<yend) {
          y ++;
          if (d<0) d += incr1;
          else { x +=xinc; d = d + incr2;  }
          WrPixel_256(x,y,color,bytes_per_row);
          }
     }
  }
}


// (b)   Write a line in a Hi-color mode
void    WrLine_Hi(int x1,int y1,int x2,int y2,int color,
        int bytes_per_row)
{ int dx,dy,incr1,incr2,d,x,y,xend,yend,yinc,xinc;

if(y2==y1) {
      if(x1 > x2) {
        xend = x1; x1 = x2;  x2 = xend;
        }
        WrHLine_Hi(x1,x2,y1,color,bytes_per_row);
        }
else {
dx = abs(x2-x1);  dy = abs(y2-y1);

if(dx>=dy) {   /* slope < 1 */
 if(x1>x2) {
        x = x2;  y = y2; xend = x1;
        if(dy==0) yinc=0;
        else {if(y2>y1) yinc = -1;  else yinc = 1; }
        }
   else {
        x = x1;  y = y1; xend = x2;
        if(dy==0) yinc=0;
         else {if(y2>y1) yinc = 1;  else yinc = -1; }
        }
  incr1 = 2*dy;  d = incr1-dx; incr2 = 2*(dy-dx);
  WrPixel_Hi(x,y,color,bytes_per_row);
  while (x<xend) {
        x ++;
        if (d<0) d += incr1;
        else { y +=yinc; d = d + incr2;  }
        WrPixel_Hi(x,y,color,bytes_per_row);
        }
  }
 else  {
  if(y1>y2) {
```

(continued)

```
            x = x2;  y = y2; yend = y1;
            if(dx==0) xinc=0;
            else { if(x2>x1) xinc = -1;  else xinc = 1;}
            }
      else {
            x = x1;  y = y1; yend = y2;
            if(dx==0) xinc=0;
            else { if(x2>x1) xinc =  1;  else xinc = -1;}
            }
      incr1 = 2*dx;  d = incr1-dy; incr2 = 2*(dx-dy);
      WrPixel_Hi(x,y,color,bytes_per_row);
      while (y<yend) {
            y ++;
            if (d<0) d += incr1;
            else { x +=xinc; d = d + incr2;  }
            WrPixel_Hi(x,y,color,bytes_per_row);
            }
      }
   }
}


// (d)  Write a line in a True-color mode
void    WrLine_True(int x1,int y1,int x2,int y2,long color,
        int bytes_per_row)
{ int dx,dy,incr1,incr2,d,x,y,xend,yend,yinc,xinc;
  BYTE cbuf[3];
 cbuf[0] = (BYTE)color;  cbuf[1] = (BYTE)(color>> 8);
 cbuf[2] = (BYTE)(color>>16);

if(y2==y1) {
      if(x1 > x2) {
        xend = x1; x1 = x2;  x2 = xend;
        }
        WrHLine_True(x1,x2,y1,color,bytes_per_row);
        }
else {
    dx = abs(x2-x1); dy = abs(y2-y1);

  if(dx>=dy) {  /* slope < 1 */
    if(x1>x2) {
        x = x2;  y = y2; xend = x1;
        if(dy==0) yinc=0;
        else {if(y2>y1) yinc = -1;  else yinc = 1; }
        }
    else {
        x = x1;  y = y1; xend = x2;
        if(dy==0) yinc=0;
         else {if(y2>y1) yinc = 1;  else yinc = -1; }
        }
```

```
        incr1 = 2*dy;   d = incr1-dx; incr2 = 2*(dy-dx);
        WrPixel_True(x,y,cbuf,bytes_per_row);
        while (x<xend) {
               x ++;
               if (d<0) d += incr1;
               else { y +=yinc; d = d + incr2;  }
               WrPixel_True(x,y,cbuf,bytes_per_row);
               }
       }
      else  {
       if(y1>y2) {
               x = x2;   y = y2; yend = y1;
               if(dx==0) xinc=0;
               else { if(x2>x1) xinc = -1;  else xinc = 1;}
               }
         else {
               x = x1;   y = y1; yend = y2;
               if(dx==0) xinc=0;
               else { if(x2>x1) xinc =  1;  else xinc = -1;}
               }
       incr1 = 2*dx;   d = incr1-dy; incr2 = 2*(dx-dy);
       WrPixel_True(x,y,cbuf,bytes_per_row);
       while (y<yend) {
               y ++;
               if (d<0) d += incr1;
               else { x +=xinc; d = d + incr2;  }
               WrPixel_True(x,y,cbuf,bytes_per_row);
               }
        }
      }
    }
```

LISTING 15.21 Drawing a Horizontal Line (a) In an 8-bit Color Mode (b) In a
Hi-color Mode (c) In a True-color Mode

```
/* Drawing a Horizontal Line in one of the 256, Hi or True-
   color modes

 Input parameters:
  x1,x2             endpoints of x coordinates of line
  y                 y coordinate of horizontal line
  color             color of the line:  int if 256 or Hi-color,
                    long if True-color
  bytes_per_row     offset of display

Calling protocol */
// (a) Draw a horizontal line in an 8-bit color mode
```

(continued)

```c
void    WrHLine_256(int x1,int x2,int y,int color,
        int bytes_per_row)

{ SHORT b_offset,b_segment,e_offset,e_segment,line_segment;
  int length;

 length = 1+x2-x1;
 // determine the segment of the end of the line
 // end of line
 Seg_Off_256(x2,y,bytes_per_row,&e_offset,&e_segment);
 // start of line
 Seg_Off_256(x1,y,bytes_per_row,&b_offset,&b_segment);
 Load_Write_Bank_256((BYTE)b_segment); // set beginning bank

 // draw line as one line segment
 if(b_segment==e_segment) Clr_Part((BYTE)color,length,b_offset);

 else { // draw line as two line segments
   // draw first portion of line in first bank
   line_segment = 65536L - b_offset;
   Clr_Part((BYTE)color,line_segment,b_offset);
   // draw second portion of line in second bank
   Load_Write_Bank_256(e_segment);
   Clr_Part((BYTE)color,e_offset,0);
   }
}

// (b) Draw a horizontal line in a Hi-color mode
void  WrHLine_Hi(int x1,int x2,int y,int color,int bytes_per_row)

{ SHORT b_offset,e_offset,b_segment,e_segment,line_segment;
  int length;
 length = 1+x2-x1;
 // end of line
 Seg_Off_Hi(x2,y,bytes_per_row,&e_offset,&e_segment);
 // start of line
 Seg_Off_Hi(x1,y,bytes_per_row,&b_offset,&b_segment);
 Load_Write_Bank_256((BYTE)b_segment);  // set beginning bank

 // draw line as one line segment
 if (b_segment==e_segment) Clr_Part_Hi(color,length,b_offset);
   else { // draw line as two line segments
     // draw first portion of line in first bank
     line_segment = 65536L - b_offset;
     Clr_Part_Hi(color,line_segment/2,b_offset);
     // draw second portion of line in second bank
     Load_Write_Bank_256(e_segment);
```

```
      Clr_Part_Hi(color,e_offset/2,0);
      }
}


// (c) Draw a horizontal line in a True-color mode
void    WrHLine_True(int x1,int x2,int y,long color,
        int bytes_per_row)
{
SHORT display_ptr,bank_num;
int length_1,length_2,row,bytes_in_this_line,rval;
long end_of_line;  BYTE cbuf[3],ct;
cbuf[0] = (BYTE)( color; cbuf[1] = (BYTE)(color>> 8); cbuf[2] =
(BYTE)(color>>16);

// determine the offsets and banks of the starting and ending
   points
 Seg_Off_True(x1,y,bytes_per_row,&display_ptr,&bank_num);
 Load_Write_Bank_256((BYTE)bank_num);  // setup first bank

 bytes_in_this_line = 3*(1+x2-x1);

// does this line cross a bank
end_of_line = (long)display_ptr + bytes_in_this_line;
  if(end_of_line>=65536L)    {
    // must draw line as two line segments. Draw first segment
    length_1 = 65536L - display_ptr;
    // write line
    rval = Clr_Part_True(cbuf,length_1,display_ptr);
    switch(rval) {
        case 1:
          ct=cbuf[0]; cbuf[0]=cbuf[1]; cbuf[1]=cbuf[2]; cbuf[2]=ct;
          break;
        case 2:
          ct=cbuf[0]; cbuf[0]=cbuf[2]; cbuf[2]=cbuf[1]; cbuf[1]=ct;
           break;
           }
  Load_Write_Bank_256((BYTE)bank_num+1);  // setup next bank
  // draw second line segment
  length_2 = bytes_in_this_line - length_1;
  Clr_Part_True(cbuf,length_2,0);  // write line beginning at 0
  }
  // draw single line
  else  rval = Clr_Part_True(cbuf,bytes_in_this_line,display_ptr);
 Load_Write_Bank_256(0);  // restore the bank to bank 0
}
```

LISTING 15.22 Drawing an XOR Line. (a) In an 8-bit color mode (b) In a Hi-color Mode (c) In a True-color Mode

```
/* Function Draw an XOR Line

 Input parameters:
  x1,y1             first endpoint x,y coordinates of line
  x2,y2             second endpoint x,y coordinates of line
  color             color of the line
  bytes_per_row     offset of display

Calling protocols */

//  (a)  Drawing an XOR Line in one of the 256-color modes
void    WrXLine_256(int x1,int y1,int x2,int y2,int color,
        int bytes_per_row)
{ int dx,dy,incr1,incr2,d,x,y,xend,yend,yinc,xinc;

dx = abs(x2-x1);   dy = abs(y2-y1);
if(dx>=dy)  {  // slope < 1
   if(x1>x2) {
        x = x2;  y = y2; xend = x1;
        if(dy==0) yinc=0;
        else {if(y2>y1) yinc = -1;  else yinc = 1; }
        }
   else  {
        x = x1;  y = y1; xend = x2;
        if(dy==0) yinc=0;
        else {if(y2>y1) yinc = 1;  else yinc = -1; }
        }
   incr1 = 2*dy;  d = incr1-dx; incr2 = 2*(dy-dx);
   WrXPixel_256(x,y,color,bytes_per_row);
   while (x<xend)  {
        x ++;
        if (d<0) d += incr1;
        else { y +=yinc; d = d + incr2;   }
        WrXPixel_256(x,y,color,bytes_per_row);
        }
 }
 else {
  if(y1>y2)  {
        x = x2;  y = y2; yend = y1;
        if(dx==0) xinc=0;
        else { if(x2>x1) xinc = -1;  else xinc = 1;}
        }
   else  {
        x = x1;   y = y1; yend = y2;
```

```
          if(dx==0) xinc=0;
          else { if(x2>x1) xinc =  1;  else xinc = -1;}
          }
    incr1 = 2*dx;   d = incr1-dy; incr2 = 2*(dx-dy);
    WrXPixel_256(x,y,color,bytes_per_row);
    while (y<yend)   {
          y ++;
          if (d<0) d += incr1;
          else { x +=xinc; d = d + incr2;   }
          WrXPixel_256(x,y,color,bytes_per_row);
          }
     }
}



// (b)   Drawing an XOR Line in one of the Hi-color modes
void     WrXLine_Hi(int x1,int y1,int x2,int y2,int color,
         int bytes_per_row)
{ int dx,dy,incr1,incr2,d,x,y,xend,yend,yinc,xinc;
dx = abs(x2-x1);   dy = abs(y2-y1);

if(dx>=dy)   {   /* slope < 1 */
    if(x1>x2) {
          x = x2;   y = y2; xend = x1;
          if(dy==0) yinc=0;
          else {if(y2>y1) yinc = -1;  else yinc = 1; }
          }
     else  {
          x = x1;   y = y1; xend = x2;
          if(dy==0) yinc=0;
           else {if(y2>y1) yinc = 1;  else yinc = -1; }
          }
    incr1 = 2*dy;   d = incr1-dx; incr2 = 2*(dy-dx);
    WrXPixel_Hi(x,y,color,bytes_per_row);
    while (x<xend)   {
          x ++;
          if (d<0) d += incr1;
          else { y +=yinc; d = d + incr2;   }
          WrXPixel_Hi(x,y,color,bytes_per_row);
          }
     }
  else  {
   if(y1>y2)   {
          x = x2;   y = y2; yend = y1;
          if(dx==0) xinc=0;
          else { if(x2>x1) xinc = -1;   else xinc = 1;}
          }
```

(continued)

```
      else  {
            x = x1;   y = y1; yend = y2;
            if(dx==0) xinc=0;
            else { if(x2>x1) xinc =  1;   else xinc = -1;}
            }
    incr1 = 2*dx;   d = incr1-dy; incr2 = 2*(dx-dy);
    WrXPixel_Hi(x,y,color,bytes_per_row);
    while (y<yend)   {
            y ++;
            if (d<0)  d += incr1;
            else { x +=xinc; d = d + incr2;   }
            WrXPixel_Hi(x,y,color,bytes_per_row);
            }
    }
}


// (c)   Drawing an XOR Line in one of the True-color modes
void    WrXLine_True(int x1,int y1,int x2,int y2,long color,
        int bytes_per_row)

{ int dx,dy,incr1,incr2,d,x,y,xend,yend,yinc,xinc;
BYTE cbuf[3];

cbuf[0] = (BYTE)color; cbuf[1] = (BYTE)(color>> 8); cbuf[2] =
(BYTE)(color>>16);
dx = abs(x2-x1);   dy = abs(y2-y1);

if(dx>=dy) {     /* slope < 1 */
   if(x1>x2) {
        x = x2;  y = y2; xend = x1;
        if(dy==0) yinc=0;
        else {if(y2>y1) yinc = -1;   else yinc = 1; }
        }
   else  {
        x = x1;   y = y1; xend = x2;
        if(dy==0) yinc=0;
         else {if(y2>y1) yinc = 1;   else yinc = -1; }
        }
    incr1 = 2*dy;   d = incr1-dx; incr2 = 2*(dy-dx);
    WrXPixel_True(x,y,cbuf,bytes_per_row);
    while (x<xend) {
        x ++;
        if (d<0) d += incr1;
        else { y +=yinc; d = d + incr2;   }
        WrXPixel_True(x,y,cbuf,bytes_per_row);
        }
    }
```

```
else {
   if(y1>y2) {
        x = x2;  y = y2; yend = y1;
        if(dx==0) xinc=0;
        else { if(x2>x1) xinc = -1;  else xinc = 1;}
        }
   else {
        x = x1;  y = y1; yend = y2;
        if(dx==0) xinc=0;
        else { if(x2>x1) xinc =  1;  else xinc = -1;}
        }
   incr1 = 2*dx;  d = incr1-dy; incr2 = 2*(dx-dy);
   WrXPixel_True(x,y,cbuf,bytes_per_row);
   while (y<yend) {
        y ++;
        if (d<0) d += incr1;
        else { x +=xinc; d = d + incr2;  }
        WrXPixel_True(x,y,cbuf,bytes_per_row);
        }
  }
}
```

15.10.2 Drawing a Line in 16-color Modes

Code that draws a line in a 16-color mode is provided in Listing 15.23. Since a single pixel is spread across four display planes and a single byte contains data for eight pixels, the mapping from pixels to bytes is not as straightforward as the example in Listing 15.20. The functions are used to draw in the single pixel, across all four display banks, without disturbing neighboring pixels. The four display planes are handled by utilization of the Set/Reset Register and Enable Set/Reset Register. These functions assume that the Set/Reset Register and Enable Set/Reset Register are preset. This can be accommodated since the line is drawn in only one color. At the end of this function, the Bit Mask, Set/Reset Register, and Enable Set/Reset Register are reset to their normal operating condition. Standard, horizontal, and XOR lines are provided.

LISTING 15.23 (a) Drawing a Line in One of the 16-color Modes (b) Drawing a Horizontal Line in One of the 16-color Modes (c) Drawing an XOR Line in One of the 16-color Modes

```
/*     (a) Function:  Drawing a Line in one of the 16-color modes

Input parameters:
  x1,y1              first endpoint x,y coordinates of line
  x2,y2              second endpoint x,y coordinates of line
  color              color of the line
```

(continued)

```
    bytes_per_row    offset of display

Calling Protocol */
void    WrLine_16(int x1,int y1,int x2,int y2,int color,
        int bytes_per_row)
{
    int dx,dy,incr1,incr2,d,x,y,xend,yend,yinc,xinc;

    if(y1 == y2) {
        if(x1 > x2) { xend = x1;    x1 = x2;   x2 = xend;  }
        WrHLine_16(x1,x2,y1,color,bytes_per_row);
          }
    else {
            // enable the set reset function and load the color
            dy = abs(y2-y1);
            dx = abs(x2-x1);
            ESetRes(15); SetRes((BYTE)color); //  load registers

            if(dx>=dy) {  // slope < 1
        if(x1>x2) {
            x = x2;  y = y2; xend = x1;
            if(dy==0) yinc=0;
            else { if(y2>y1) yinc = -1; else yinc =  1; } }
        else {
            x = x1;  y = y1; xend = x2;
            if(dy==0) yinc=0;
            else { if(y2>y1) yinc =  1; else yinc = -1; }
        }

        incr1 = 2*dy;  d = incr1-dx; incr2 = 2*(dy-dx);
        WrPoint_16(x,y,bytes_per_row);

        while (x<xend) {
            x ++;
            if (d<0) d += incr1;
            else {
                y += yinc;
                d += incr2;
            }
            WrPoint_16(x,y,bytes_per_row);
        }
          else {
        if(y1>y2){
            x = x2;  y = y2; yend = y1;
            if(dx==0) xinc=0;
            else  {
                if(x2>x1) xinc = -1;
```

```
                else xinc =  1;
          }
      }
      else {
          x = x1;  y = y1; yend = y2;
          if(dx==0) xinc=0;
          else {
              if(x2>x1) xinc =  1;
              else      xinc = -1;
          }
      }

      incr1 = 2*dx;  d = incr1-dy; incr2 = 2*(dx-dy);
      WrPoint_16(x,y,bytes_per_row);

      while (y<yend) {
          y ++;
          if (d<0) d += incr1;
          else {
              x += xinc;
              d += incr2;
          }
          WrPoint_16(x,y,bytes_per_row);
      }
   }
   BitMask(255); ESetRes(0);  // reset the EGA/VGA registers
   }
}

/* (b) Function:  Drawing a Horizontal Line in one of the 16-
   color modes

 Input parameters:
  x1,x2             endpoints of x coordinates of line
  y                 y coordinate of horizontal line
  color             color of the line
  bytes_per_row     offset of display

Calling protocol */

void WrHLine_16(int x1,int x2,int y,int color,int bytes_per_row)
{
        BYTE    left,right;
        SHORT
i,ib,x1bytes,x2bytes,sbit1,ebit1,ebit2,nxbytes,nmidbytes,off_addr;
```

(continued)

```
// there are 8 bits per pixel in the 16-color mode
   x1bytes = x1>>3;     x2bytes = x2>>3;
   nxbytes = x2bytes-x1bytes+1;  // total number of bytes to set

   sbit1=(x1&0x07);
   ebit2=(x2&0x07);
   if(nxbytes == 1)    {          // no byte boundary?
      nmidbytes = 0;              // no middle, or right bytes
      ebit1 = ebit2;
      right = FALSE;
    }
   else   {                       // at least 2 bytes
      // total number of bytes minus left and right bytes
      nmidbytes = nxbytes-2;
      ebit1  = 7;                 // to 8-th bit of left byte
      right=(ebit2 !=7);          // less than 8 bits to set?
      if(!right)     nmidbytes++; // no one more middle byte
   }
   left=!((sbit1==0) && (ebit1==7)); // less than 8 bits to set?
   if(!left)  nmidbytes++;         // one more middle byte
   Seg_Off_16(x1,y,bytes_per_row,&off_addr,&ib);
   if(Pixels_per_Row == 1024)  {
      ib  = y/512;                // initial bank number
      Load_Write_Bank_16((BYTE)ib);  // load current write bank
   }
   else
      Load_Write_Bank_16(0);      // load current write bank
   if(left)    {
      ESetRes(15); SetRes((BYTE)color);  // load registers
      for(i=sbit1 ; i<=ebit1 ; i++)
         WrPoint_16(x1+i-sbit1,y,bytes_per_row);
      BitMask(255); ESetRes(0);  // reset the EGA/VGA registers
   }
   if(nmidbytes > 0)
      Clr_Part_16((BYTE)color,nmidbytes,off_addr+left);
   if(right)    {
      ESetRes(15); SetRes((BYTE)color);  // load registers
      for(i=0 ; i<=ebit2 ; i++) WrPoint_16(x2-i,y,bytes_per_row);
      BitMask(255); ESetRes(0);   // reset the EGA/VGA registers
   }
   MapMask(0x0f);                           // reset mask
}


/* (c) Function:Drawing an XOR Line in one of the 16-color modes

 Input parameters:
  x1,y1            first endpoint x,y coordinates of line
```

```
  x2,y2              second endpoint x,y coordinates of line
  color              color of the line
  bytes_per_row    offset of display

Calling Protocol */
void    WrXLine_16(int x1,int y1,int x2,int y2,int color,
        int bytes_per_row)

{ int dx,dy,incr1,incr2,d,x,y,xend,yend,yinc,xinc;

// enable the set reset function and load the color
ESetRes(15); SetRes((BYTE)color);     // load registers
dx = abs(x2-x1); dy = abs(y2-y1);

if(dx>=dy) {    // slope < 1
   if(x1>x2)   {
        x = x2;   y = y2; xend = x1;
        if(dy==0) yinc=0;
         else {if(y2>y1) yinc = -1;  else yinc = 1; }}
   else   {
        x = x1;   y = y1; xend = x2;
        if(dy==0) yinc=0;
         else {if(y2>y1) yinc = 1;  else yinc = -1; }}

  incr1 = 2*dy;   d = incr1-dx; incr2 = 2*(dy-dx);
        //mask =   WrXPoint_16(x,y,bytes_per_row);

  while (x<xend)   {
        x ++;
        if (d<0) d += incr1;
        else { y +=yinc; d = d + incr2;   }
        WrXPoint_16(x,y,bytes_per_row);
        }
 }
 else {
  if(y1>y2)   {
        x = x2;   y = y2; yend = y1;
        if(dx==0) xinc=0;
         else {if(x2>x1) xinc = -1;  else xinc = 1; }}
   else
        { x = x1;   y = y1; yend = y2;
        if(dx==0) xinc=0;
         else {if(x2>x1) xinc =  1;  else xinc = -1; }}

  incr1 = 2*dx;   d = incr1-dy; incr2 = 2*(dx-dy);
        WrXPoint_16(x,y,bytes_per_row);
```

(continued)

```
  while (y<yend)  {
        y ++;
        if (d<0) d += incr1;
        else { x +=xinc; d = d + incr2;  }
        WrXPoint_16(x,y,bytes_per_row);
        }
 }
 BitMask(255); ESetRes(0);  // reset the EGA/VGA registers
 }
```

15.11   READING AND WRITING VECTORS

In this book, a vector is defined as a line where every pixel has a separate value. For example, suppose we wrote one horizontal line of an image. This would be called a horizontal vector. This is by no means a standard definition, but it serves the purposes of this book. It is often useful to be able to read either a horizontal or vertical vector line. This is often the case when scrolling in a waterfall type display.

Horizontal vectors are the most commonly used. They are very fast due to the sequential and, consequently, DMA-oriented data. Several functions are provided that write horizontal vectors as shown in Listing 15.24. Typically, vectors are used in images and therefore only the packed display formats are provided. Several functions are provided in Listing 15.25 for reading these vectors.

LISTING 15.24 Write a Horizontal Vector. (a) A 256-color Mode (c) A 256-color 1024x768 Mode (c) A Hi-Color Mode (d) A True-Color Mode

---

```
/* Write an image row  in one of four color mode

Input parameters:
 x                 starting left coordinate
 length            length of line
 y                 starting y coordinate
 buf               buffer containing data
 bytes_per_row     display offset

Calling protocol:  */

(a) Write Horizontal Vector in 8-bit color Mode
void    WrVecH_256(int x, int y, int length, BYTE *buf,
        int bytes_per_row)

{ SHORT b_offset,b_segment,e_offset,e_segment,line_segment;
  BYTE *buf_ptr;    buf_ptr = &buf[0];

 // determine the segment of the end of the line
```

```
   Seg_Off_256(x+length,y,bytes_per_row,&e_offset,&e_segment);
   // determine the segment of the start of the line
   Seg_Off_256(x,y,bytes_per_row,&b_offset,&b_segment);

   Load_Write_Bank_256(b_segment);  // set beginning bank

   // draw line as one line segment
   if(b_segment==e_segment)
        Wr_Part(buf_ptr,length,b_offset);
   else {    // draw line as two line segments
        line_segment = 65536L - b_offset;
        Wr_Part(buf_ptr,line_segment,b_offset);

        // draw second portion of line in second bank
        Load_Write_Bank_256(e_segment);
        buf_ptr += line_segment;
        Wr_Part(buf_ptr,e_offset,0);
        }
}

(b)Write Horizontal Vector in 8-bit color mode in 1024x768
void     WrVecH_1024(int x, int y, int length, BYTE *buf)

{ SHORT b_segment,b_offset;

// determine the segment and offset of the line
 Seg_Off_256(x,y,1024,&b_offset,&b_segment);

 Load_Write_Bank_256((BYTE)b_offset);
 Wr_Part(buf,length,b_offset);
}

(c) Write Horizontal Vector in  Hi-Color Mode
void     WrVecH_Hi(int x, int y, int length, int *buf,int
bytes_per_row)
{
SHORT display_ptr,bank_num;
int length_1,length_2,*buf_ptr;
long end_of_line,display_offset;

// determine the offsets and banks of the starting and ending
   points
 Seg_Off_Hi(x,y,bytes_per_row,&display_ptr,&bank_num);

 buf_ptr = &buf[0];  // point to top of buffer
 Load_Write_Bank_256((BYTE)bank_num);  // setup first bank

  // does this line cross a bank
```

(continued)

```
     end_of_line = (long)display_ptr + 2*length;
    if(end_of_line>=65536L)   {
      length_1 = (65536L - display_ptr)/2;
      // write the line
      Wr_Part_Hi(buf_ptr,length_1,display_ptr);
      buf_ptr += length_1;  // increment buffer pointer
      Load_Write_Bank_256((BYTE)bank_num+1);  // setup next bank
      length_2 = length - length_1;
      Wr_Part_Hi(buf_ptr,length_2,0);  // write the line
      }
   else  Wr_Part_Hi(buf_ptr,length,display_ptr);

  Load_Write_Bank_256(0);  // restore the bank to bank 0
 }


(d)   Write Horizontal Vector in True-Color Mode
void    WrVecH_True(int x, int y, int length, BYTE *buf,
        int bytes_per_row)
{
SHORT display_ptr,bank_num;
int length_1,length_2,bytes_in_this_line;
long end_of_line,display_offset;
BYTE *buf_ptr;

// determine the offsets and banks of the starting and ending
   points
 Seg_Off_True(x,y,bytes_per_row,&display_ptr,&bank_num);

 buf_ptr = &buf[0];  // point to top of buffer
 Load_Write_Bank_256((BYTE)bank_num);  // setup first bank
 bytes_in_this_line = 3*length;

  end_of_line = (long)display_ptr + bytes_in_this_line;
  if(end_of_line>=65536L)   {
   // must draw line as two line segments.  Draw first segment
   length_1 = 65536L - display_ptr;
   // write the line
   Wr_Part_True(buf_ptr,length_1,display_ptr);
   buf_ptr += length_1;  // increment buffer pointer
   Load_Write_Bank_256((BYTE)bank_num+1);    // setup next bank
   length_2 = bytes_in_this_line - length_1; // draw second line
segment
   Wr_Part_True(buf_ptr,length_2,0);  // write the line
   }
  else   Wr_Part_True(buf_ptr,bytes_in_this_line,display_ptr);

 Load_Write_Bank_256(0);  // restore the bank to bank 0
 }
```

LISTING 15.25 Read a Horizontal Vector (a) An 8-bit Color Mode (b) A 1024x768 8-bit Color Mode (c) A Hi-color Mode (d) A True-Color Mode

```
/* Function:  Read an image row  in a 256-color mode

Input parameters:
 x                 starting left coordinate
 length            length of line
 y                 starting y coordinate
 buf               buffer which will contain data
 bytes_per_row     display offset

Calling protocol:  */


// (a) Read a horizontal vector to the display  in an 8-bit
//    color mode
void    RdVecH_256(int x, int y, int length, BYTE *buf,
        int bytes_per_row)
{ SHORT b_offset,b_segment,e_offset,e_segment,line_segment;
  BYTE *buf_ptr;
  buf_ptr = &buf[0];

 // determine the segment of the end of the line
 Seg_Off_256(x+length,y,bytes_per_row,&e_offset,&e_segment);
 // determine the segment of the start of the line
 Seg_Off_256(x,y,bytes_per_row,&b_offset,&b_segment);

 // set beginning bank
 Load_Read_Bank_256(b_segment);

 // read line as one line segment
 if(b_segment==e_segment)  Rd_Part(buf_ptr,length,b_offset);

 else   {      // draw line as two line segments
    // draw first portion of line in first bank
    line_segment = 65536L - b_offset;
    Rd_Part(buf_ptr,line_segment,b_offset);
    // draw second portion of line in second bank
    Load_Read_Bank_256(e_segment);
    buf_ptr += line_segment;
    Rd_Part(buf_ptr,e_offset,0);
    }
}

// (b) Read a horizontal vector to the display  hex 1024x768
//    8-bit color mode
```

(continued)

```
void     RdVecH_1024(int x, int y, int length, BYTE *buf)
{ SHORT b_segment,b_offset;

 // determine the segment and offset of the line
 Seg_Off_256(x,y,1024,&b_offset,&b_segment);

 Load_Read_Bank_256((BYTE)b_segment);  // setup first bank
 Rd_Part(buf,length,b_offset);
}


// (c)  Read an image row  in a Hi-color mode
void     RdVecH_Hi(int x, int y, int length, int *buf, int
bytes_per_row)
{
SHORT display_ptr,bank_num;
int length_1,length_2,*buf_ptr;
long end_of_line,display_offset;

// determine the offsets and banks of the starting and ending
   points
 Seg_Off_Hi(x,y,bytes_per_row,&display_ptr,&bank_num);

 buf_ptr = &buf[0];  // point to top of buffer
 Load_Read_Bank_256((BYTE)bank_num);  // setup first bank

  // does this line cross a bank
  end_of_line = (long)display_ptr + 2*length;
  if(end_of_line>=65536L)  {
    // must draw line as two line segments.  Draw first segment
    length_1 = (65536L - display_ptr)/2;
    Rd_Part_Hi(buf_ptr,length_1,display_ptr);  // Read the line
    buf_ptr += length_1;  // increment buffer pointer
    Load_Read_Bank_256((BYTE)bank_num+1);  // setup next bank
    length_2 = length - length_1;  // draw second line segment
    Rd_Part_Hi(buf_ptr,length_2,0);  // Read the line
    }
 else    Rd_Part_Hi(buf_ptr,length,display_ptr);

 Load_Read_Bank_256(0);  // restore the bank to bank 0
}


// (d) Read an image row  in a True-color mode
void     RdVecH_True(int x, int y, int length, BYTE *buf,
        int bytes_per_row)
{
SHORT display_ptr,bank_num;
int length_1,length_2,bytes_in_this_line;
```

```
long end_of_line,display_offset;
BYTE *buf_ptr;

// determine the offsets and banks of the starting and ending
   points
 Seg_Off_True(x,y,bytes_per_row,&display_ptr,&bank_num);

 buf_ptr = &buf[0];  // point to top of buffer
 Load_Read_Bank_256((BYTE)bank_num);  // setup first bank
 bytes_in_this_line = 3*length;

  // does this line cross a bank
  end_of_line = (long)display_ptr + bytes_in_this_line;
  if(end_of_line>=65536L)  {
    // must draw line as two line segments.  Draw first segment
    length_1 = 65536L - display_ptr;
    // Read the line
    Rd_Part_True(buf_ptr,length_1,display_ptr);
    buf_ptr += length_1; // increment buffer pointer
    Load_Read_Bank_256((BYTE)bank_num+1);  // setup next bank
    // draw second line segment
    length_2 = bytes_in_this_line - length_1;
    Rd_Part_True(buf_ptr,length_2,0);  // Read the line
    }
  else  Rd_Part_True(buf_ptr,bytes_in_this_line,display_ptr);

 Load_Read_Bank_256(0);  // restore the bank to bank 0
 }
```

Vertical vectors are commonly used when displaying data that scroll horizontally across the screen. Functions are provided in Listing 15.26 for reading and writing these vertical vectors.

LISTING 15.26 (a) Write a Vertical Vector 256-color or Hi-color Mode (b) Read a Vertical Vector 256-color or Hi-color Mode (c) Drawing a Vertical Line in one of the True-color Modes (d) Reading a Vertical Line in one of the True-color Modes

```
; Function:
; Write a vertical vector 256-color or Hi-color

; Input parameters
;  arg1: x                horizontal coordinate of column
;  arg2: start_y          starting vertical coordinate of column
;  arg3: npix             number of pixels
;  arg4: buf              host "C" buffer containing data
;  arg5: bytes_per_row    display bytes_per_row
```

(continued)

```
; Calling protocol
;   WrVecV_256(x,start_y,npix,buf,bytes_per_row);

WrVecV_256   PROC FAR   USES DS ES SI DI,
arg1,arg2,arg3,arg4:FAR PTR,arg5

; set up the display address segment, number of points and
; pointer to "C" buffer
        mov     es,SegA000
        mov     cx,arg3     ;get desired number of bytes in cx
        lds     si,arg4     ;get pointer to data vector ds:si

; determine the address  = ( y * bytes_per_row ) + x
        mov     ax,arg5     ; get bytes_per_row in ax
        mov     bx,arg2     ; get y in bx
        mul     bx          ; y*bytes_per_row in dx:ax
        add     ax,arg1     ; (y*bytes_per_row)+x lower 16 bits in ax
        mov     di,ax       ; load as display offset for es:di

;       determine page register
        adc     dx,0        ; (y*bytes_per_row)+x upper n bits in dx
        mov     bl,dl
        call FAR PTR Set_Write_Bank_256   ;load the write bank

; main program loop
pixel_loop1:
        lodsb   ;get value from "C" input buffer and inc pointer
        mov     es:[di],al  ;send to display
        add     di,arg5     ;add y increment to di
        jnc     same_page1  ;don't change the current page since
                            ;no carry

; load the new page value into the page register
        inc     dx              ;increment page adress
        mov     bl,dl
        call FAR PTR Set_Write_Bank_256   ;load the write bank

same_page1:
        loop    pixel_loop1  ;repeat for number of points
        ret
WrVecV_256 endp


; (b)  Function:  Read a vertical vector 256-color or Hi-color

; Input parameters
;  arg1: x              horizontal coordinate of column
;  arg2: start_y        starting vertical coordinate of column
```

```
;   arg3: npix              number of pixels
;   arg4: buf               host "C" buffer which will contain data
;   arg5: bytes_per_row     display bytes_per_row

; Calling protocol
;   RdVecV_256(x,start_y,npix,buf,bytes_per_row);

RdVecV_256   PROC FAR   USES DS ES SI DI,
arg1,arg2,arg3,arg4:FAR PTR,arg5

; set up the display address segment, number of points and
; pointer to "C" buffer
        mov     cx,arg3    ;get desired number of bytes in cx
        les     di,arg4    ;get pointer to data vector es:di
        mov     ds,SegA000

; determine the address  = ( y * bytes_per_row ) + x
        mov     ax,arg5    ; get bytes_per_row in ax
        mov     bx,arg2    ; get y in bx
        mul     bx         ; y*bytes_per_row in dx:ax
        add     ax,arg1    ; (y*bytes_per_row)+x lower 16 bits in ax
        mov     si,ax      ; load as display offset for ds:si

;       determine page register
        adc     dx,0       ; (y*bytes_per_row)+x upper n bits in dx
        mov     bl,dl
        call FAR PTR Set_Read_Bank_256    ;load the read bank

; main program loop
pixel_loop2:
        mov     al,ds:[si]   ;get from display
        stosb                ;put value to "C" input buffer and
                             ;inc pointer
        add     si,arg5      ;add y increment to si
        jnc     same_page2   ;don't change the current page since
                             ;no carry

; load the new page value into the page register
        inc     dx           ;increment page adress
        mov     bl,dl
        call FAR PTR Set_Read_Bank_256     ;load the read bank

same_page2:
        loop    pixel_loop2  ;repeat for number of points
        ret
RdVecV_256 endp
```

(continued)

```
/* (c)  Drawing a Vertical Line in one of the True-color modes

 Input parameters:
  x              x coordinates of line
  y              y coordinate of horizontal line
  npix           number of pixels
  buf            buffer containing data
  bytes_per_row  offset of display

Calling protocol */
void  WrVecV_True(int x,int y,int npix,BYTE *buf,int bytes_per_row)
{
BYTE *buf_ptr;  int j;

buf_ptr = &buf[0];
for (j=0; j<npix; j++) {
  WrPixel_True(x,y+j,buf_ptr,bytes_per_row);
  buf_ptr += 3;
  }
}

/* (d)  Reading a Vertical Line in one of the True-color modes

 Input parameters:
  x              x coordinates of line
  y              y coordinate of horizontal line
  npix           number of pixels
  bytes_per_row  offset of display

 Output Parameters:
  buf       buffer containing data

Calling protocol */
void  RdVecV_True(int x,int y,int npix,BYTE *buf,int
bytes_per_row)
{
BYTE *buf_ptr;   int j;

buf_ptr = &buf[0];
for (j=0; j<npix; j++) {
  RdPixel_True(x,y+j,bytes_per_row,buf_ptr);
  buf_ptr += 3;
  }
}
```

15.12 SWITCHING DISPLAY BANKS

Bank swapping is probably the most common task that is different for each Super VGA. The display aperture is mapped into the host memory address space, typically at the 64-Kbyte location beginning at A0000 hex. The software examples that follow assume that the bank swapping mechanism is configured such that each Super VGA's aperture is indeed 64 Kbytes located at A0000 hex.

Several Super VGAs have separate read and write banks. This allows data to be transferred from one bank in display memory to another without constantly changing the banks. The examples that follow load values into the read and write banks assuming either a 4-bit or 8-bit-per-color display mode.

The 4-bit-per-color mode is planar while the 8-bit-per-color mode is packed. There are eight pixels for every byte of data written or read from display memory. Consequently, the bank swapping occurs one-eighth as often as in the 8-bit-per-color modes. Note that all packed display modes can use these packed bank swapping functions.

Examples of bank swapping are provided in Listing 15.27. Note that they rely on a get_vga_key macro, which is found in Listing 15.27. It takes the bank number in the BX register and returns an index pointer into a table based on the specific Super VGA chip resident in the system. This index, returned in the SI register, is used as an offset in a function table. The function table contains addresses of the specific bank swapping functions for each Super VGA.

LISTING 15.27 Loading the Read and Write Banks. (a) Load the Write Bank (256-color) with Parameter (b) Load the Read Bank (256-color) with Parameter (c) Set the Write Bank (256-color) with Value in bl (d) Load the Read Bank (256-color) with value in bl (e) Load the Write Bank (16-color) with the Parameter (f) Load the Read Bank (16-color) with the Parameter (g) Load the Write Bank (16-color) with the Value in bl (h) Load the Read Bank (16-color) with the Value in bl

```
; (a) Function  Load the Write Bank (256-color) with parameter

; Input Parameters:
;     arg1   Write Bank_Number
;            0-15 bank number = desired 64-kbyte bank
; Calling Protocol:
;     Load_Write_Bank_256

Load_Write_Bank_256   PROC FAR  USES SI,  arg1
        mov   bx,arg1   ;get write bank
        get_vga_key
        call  write_bank_256_table [si]
        ret
Load_Write_Bank_256   endp
```

(continued)

```
; (b) Function:  Load the Read Bank  (256-color) with parameter

;  Input Parameters:
;       arg1   Read Bank_Number
;              0-15 bank number = desired 64-kbyte bank
;  Calling Protocol:
;       Load_Read_Bank_256

Load_Read_Bank_256   PROC FAR   USES SI, arg1
        mov    bx,arg1        ;get read bank
        get_vga_key
        call   read_bank_256_table [si]
        ret
Load_Read_Bank_256  endp

; (c) Function:  Set the Write Bank (256-color) with value in bl

;  Input Parameters:
;       bl     Write Bank_Number
;              0-15 bank number = desired 64-kbyte bank
;  Calling Protocol:
;       Set_Write_Bank_256

Set_Write_Bank_256   PROC FAR USES SI DX
        get_vga_key
        call   write_bank_256_table [si]
        ret
Set_Write_Bank_256     endp

; (d) Function  Load the Read Bank (256-color)  with value in bl

;  Input Parameters:
;       bl     Read Bank_Number
;              0-15 bank number = desired 64-kbyte bank
;  Calling Protocol:
;       Set_Read_Bank_256

Set_Read_Bank_256   PROC FAR  USES SI DX
        get_vga_key
        call   read_bank_256_table [si]
        ret
Set_Read_Bank_256  endp

; (e) Function: Load the Write Bank (16-color) with the parameter

;  Input Parameters:
;       arg1   Write Bank_Number
;              0-15 bank number = desired 64-kbyte bank
```

```
;   Calling Protocol:
;        Load_Write_Bank_16

Load_Write_Bank_16    PROC FAR   USES SI,   arg1
        mov     bx,arg1   ;get write bank
        get_vga_key
        call    write_bank_16_table [si]
        ret
Load_Write_Bank_16    endp

; (f) Function: Load the Read Bank (16-color) with the parameter

;   Input Parameters:
;        arg1    Read Bank_Number
;                0-15 bank number = desired 64-kbyte bank
;   Calling Protocol:
;        Load_Read_Bank_16

Load_Read_Bank_16    PROC FAR    USES SI, arg1
        mov     bx,arg1   ;get read bank
        get_vga_key
        call    read_bank_16_table [si]
        ret
Load_Read_Bank_16    endp

; (g) Function: Load the Write Bank (16-color) with the value in bl

;   Input Parameters:
;        bl      Write Bank_Number
;                0-15 bank number = desired 64-kbyte bank
;   Calling Protocol:
;        Set_Write_Bank_16

Set_Write_Bank_16    PROC FAR USES SI DX
        get_vga_key
        call    write_bank_16_table [si]
        ret
Set_Write_Bank_16    endp

; (h) Function: Load the Read Bank (16-color) with the value in bl

;   Input Parameters:
;        bl      Read Bank_Number
;                0-15 bank number = desired 64-kbyte bank
;   Calling Protocol:
;        Set_Read_Bank_16
```

(continued)

```
Set_Read_Bank_16    PROC FAR   USES SI DX
        get_vga_key
        call    read_bank_16_table [si]
        ret
Set_Read_Bank_16   endp
```

For example, suppose that it is desired to write a 4 to a write bank register while in a 256-color mode. One would call the Load_Write_Bank function passing a 4 as an argument. Further suppose that the get_vga_key reported that a Tseng ET4000 chip was present in the system. It might return a 10, indicating that the ET4000 chip's specific bank swapping routine would be found in the tenth location of all of the function tables. In the case of a far code segment, each function entry would be four bytes long, producing the 32-bit address. Thus the SI register would contain a 40. The call write_bank_256_table [SI] assembly language function would call the appropriate bank swapping function.

15.13   COLOR CONVERSIONS

The several color conversion functions that are useful have to do with changing the format of the data. For example, a true color might be 24 bits or 32 bits. This conveniently fits into a long variable. However, it might also be useful to consider each pixel as an array of three or four bytes. Also, the byte ordering of the red, green, and blue content of a true-color word is not consistent among the Super VGAs. Some use a RGB ordering, and others use a BGR ordering (Intel vs. Motorola ordering issues). Several useful color conversion functions are provided in Listing 15.28.

LISTING 15.28 Functions that Manipulate Colors. (a) Should we Reverse the Colors from BGR to RGB Ordering (b) Create an RGB Buffer of Colors from a True-color (c) Create an RGB Buffer of Colors from a True-color (d) Create a True-color (long) from an RGB Buffer (byte*) of Colors (e) Create an RGB Buffer (byte*) of Colors from a Hi-color (int) (f) Create a Hi-color (int) from an RGB Buffer (byte *) of Colors

```
/* (a) Function:  Should we reverse the colors from BGR to RGB
   ordering?  The decision is based on the particular chip or
   card.

Input Parameters:
        buf 3 byte BGR: where buf[0]=blue, buf[1]=green, buf[2]=red

Output Parameters:
        buf 3-byte RGB  buf[0]=red, buf[1]=green, buf[2]=blue
        reversed      1 = was reversed 0 = not reversed
```

```
Calling Protocol:
 reversed = should_reverse_24(buf); */

int should_reverse_24(BYTE *buf)
{ BYTE temp; int ret_val=0;

switch(VGA_id) {
    case 33:
        temp = buf[2];  buf[2] = buf[0];  buf[0] = temp;
        ret_val = 1;
    break;
 }
return(ret_val);
}

/* (b) Function:  Create an RGB buffer of colors from a
true-color

Input Parameters:
        in_color  15 or 16-bit true-color value

Output Parameters:
        buf 3-byte  RGB: where buf[0]=red, buf[1]=green, buf[2]=blue

Calling Protocol: */
 void Make_RGB_from_True(unsigned long color,BYTE *cbuf)
{
    cbuf[0] = (BYTE)( color      & 0x000000ffL);
    cbuf[1] = (BYTE)((color>> 8) & 0x000000ffL);
    cbuf[2] = (BYTE)((color>>16) & 0x000000ffL);
}

/*  (c) Function: Create an RGB buffer of colors from a true-color
Input Parameters:
        buf 3-byte RGB: where buf[0]=red, buf[1]=green, buf[2]=blue

Output Parameters:
        color  long value containing 24-bit or 15 or
                16-bit color value

Calling Protocol:
  long_color =  Make_Color_from_RGB(cbuf); */

  long Make_Color_from_RGB(BYTE *cbuf)
{ long out_color; SHORT short_color;
```

(continued)

```
switch(Pixel_Bits) {
  case c15_bit: case c16_bit:
  out_color = (long)Make_Hi_from_RGB(cbuf);
  break;
  case c24_bit:
  out_color = Make_True_from_RGB(cbuf);
  break;
  }
return(out_color);
}


/* (d) Function: Create a true-color (long) from an RGB buffer
   (byte*) of colors
Input Parameters:
        buf 3-byte RGB: where buf[0]=red, buf[1]=green, buf[2]=blue


Output Parameters:
        true_color     24-bit true-color value red=23-16
                       green=15-8 blue=7-0


Calling Protocol: */
  long Make_True_from_RGB(BYTE *cbuf)
{
 long true_color=0L;
 true_color =    (long) cbuf[0] |          //blue
              ( ((long) cbuf[1])<<8) |     //green
              ( ((long) cbuf[2])<<16) ;    //red
return(true_color);
}


/* (e) Function: Create an RGB buffer (byte*) of colors from a
   hi-color (int)
Input Parameters:
        in_color  15 or 16-bit hi-color value


Output Parameters:
        buf 3-byte RGB: where buf[0]=red, buf[1]=green, buf[2]=blue


Calling Protocol: */
 void Make_RGB_from_Hi(SHORT in_color,BYTE *buf)
{
if(Pixel_Bits==c15_bit) {
 buf[2] = in_color & 0x001f;            //blue
 buf[1] = (in_color & 0x03e0)>>5;       //green
 buf[0] = (in_color & 0x7300)>>10;      //red
 }
else {  //16-bit hi-color
 buf[2] = in_color & 0x001f;            //blue
```

```
  buf[1] = (in_color & 0x07e0)>>5;      //green
  buf[0] = (in_color & 0xf100)>>11;     //red
  }
}


/* (f) Function: Create a hi-color (int) from an RGB buffer
   (byte *) of colors
Input Parameters:
        buf 3-byte RGB: where buf[0]=red, buf[1]=green, buf[2]=blue

Output Parameters:
        hi_color  15 or 16-bit hi-color value

Calling Protocol: */
  SHORT Make_Hi_from_RGB(BYTE *buf)
{
SHORT hi_color;

if(Pixel_Bits==c15_bit)
    hi_color =  buf[2]&0x1f |          //blue
               ((buf[1]&0x1f)<<5) |    //green
               ((buf[0]&0x1f)<<10);    //red
else  //16-bit hi-color
    hi_color =  buf[2]&0x1f |          //blue
               ((buf[1]&0x3f)<<5) |    //green
               ((buf[0]&0x1f)<<11);    //red
return(hi_color);
}
```

A 32-bit data structure is defined below that is useful when describing a color. Note that the ordering of the red, green, and blue could vary.

```
// Color (32-bit)
typedef struct {
unsigned char red,green,blue;   // could be blue,green,red
int index;
} vga_color_t;
```

15.14 GRAPHICS CHARACTER DISPLAY

In alphanumeric modes, one most often uses BIOS (which is typically fast enough) to output characters. BIOS can also be used in graphics modes, although there is a major limitation related to character cell size. For example, an 8-by-16 character font can be displayed only every eighth pixel horizontally and every sixteenth pixel vertically. There is no way to display a character at location (4,4) using BIOS. Therefore, it is often necessary to provide your own character write functions.

15.14.1 A Graphics Character Write Function

Graphics character sets are typically stored in a monochrome bit map. This data has to be written to display memory. A fast way of accomplishing this is to use the VGA's write mode 2. In this write mode, a color value is written to the display memory at each pixel corresponding to a 1 in the data mask. Thus, eight pixels can be written to in every output. The function provided in Listing 15.29 requires that the characters be byte-aligned in display memory. This function is transparent since any value in the font bit pattern that is a 0 does not affect the display data. Consequently, all pixels associated with the background are left untouched.

LISTING 15.29 Load a Graphics Character into Display Memory

```
; Function: Load a graphics character into display memory
;           directly
; Input assumptions:
;   The display is in a graphics mode. Write mode 2 is in effect
; Output assumptions:
;   Write Mode reset to 0.  Bit mask is restored to ff

; Input Parameters
;   charbuf[]    array containing bit pattern
;   address      display address to load character
;   offset       display offset (bytes/row)
;   bpc          bytes per character (# of rows)
;   color        foreground color of character

; calling protocol
; Graph_Chr(charbuf,address,offset,bpc,color);

_Graph_Chr PROC FAR  USES DS SI DI, arg1:FAR
PTR,arg2,arg3,arg4,arg5:byte
          mov     dx,3ceh    ;point to  Bit Plane Mask address port
          mov     al,8
          out     dx,al      ;load bit plane mask index
          inc     dx         ;DX points to data port

          mov     es,SegA000   ;display memory offset in ES
          lds     si,arg1      ;character bit pattern in DS:SI
          mov     di,arg2      ;display memory address in DI
          mov     bx,arg3      ;display offset (#bytes per row) in BX
          mov     cx,arg4      ;# of rows in character in CX
          mov     ah,arg5      ;get color

runloop:          lodsb              ;get bit pattern byte al=ds:[si++]
          out     dx,al              ;load Bit Plane Mask Register
```

```
        mov     al,es:[di]      ;dummy read
        mov     es:[di],ah      ;write color
        add     di,bx           ;add offset to DI destination
        loop    runloop         ;repeat for bpc characters

        ret
_Graph_Chr endp
```

15.14.2   More General Graphics Character Write Functions

The output process slows down when one desires to locate the character in a non-byte aligned location. Several functions are provided in Listing 15.30 that write a character to the display in a 4-bit, 8-bit, 16-bit or 32-bit format. In addition, a function is provided that creates a 16-by-32 font from an 8-by-16 font.

LISTING 15.30   Draw a Character on the Screen (a) Draw a Character on the Screen in 16-color Mode (b) Internal Function for 16-color Write Character (c) Draw a Character on the Screen in 256-color Mode (d) Draw a Character on the Screen in Hi-color Mode (e) Draw a Character on the Screen in True-color Mode (f) Create a 16x32 Font out of the 8x16 Font

```
/*  (a) Function:  Draw a character on the screen in 16-color
mode

Input Parameters:
        char_code       ASCII character code
        fgnd            fgnd color
        bgnd            bgnd color (if opaque)
        x1,y1           position of character
        display_code    display code  0=opaque  1=transparent
        font_buf        character buffer containing the font bit pats
        font_height     character height in scan lines
        font_width      width in bytes of character

Calling Protocol: */
void    Wr_Char_16(char char_code,int fgnd,int bgnd,int x1,int y1,
        int display_code,BYTE *font_buf,int font_height,
        int font_width)
{
 int i,index,y_pos,x2,x3,char_base,font_byte;
font_byte = font_width/8;
x2 = x1 + 8;   x3 = x2 + 8;
char_base = char_code*font_height*font_byte;
```

(continued)

```
if(display_code==0)  // if not transparent set bgnd to the bgnd
color

ClrWin_16(x1,y1,x1+font_width-1,y1+font_height-1,bgnd,Row_Width);


ESetRes(15); SetRes((BYTE)fgnd); // change to fgnd color

switch(font_byte) {    // draw the fgnd pixels
  case 1:  for (i=0; i<font_height; i++)  {
             y_pos = y1 + i;
             index = (i*font_byte)+char_base;
             Write_Points(font_buf[index],x1,y_pos);
             }
  break;
  case 2:  for (i=0; i<font_height; i++)  {
             y_pos = y1 + i;
             index = (i*font_byte)+char_base;
             Write_Points(font_buf[index]  ,x1,y_pos);  // left
             Write_Points(font_buf[index+1],x2,y_pos);  // right
             }
  break;
  case 3:  for (i=0; i<font_height; i++)  {
             y_pos = y1 + i;
             index = (i*font_byte)+char_base;
             Write_Points(font_buf[index]  ,x1,y_pos); // left
             Write_Points(font_buf[index+1],x2,y_pos); // center
             Write_Points(font_buf[index+2],x3,y_pos); //right
             }
  break;
  }
BitMask(255); ESetRes(0);  // reset the EGA/VGA registers
}


/* (b) Internal function for 16_color write character
Input Parameters:
        rc          character bit pat byte
        x,y         coordinates of leftmost pixel

Calling Protocol: */
void Write_Points(BYTE rc,int x,int y)
{
 if((rc & 0x80))  WrPoint_16(x  ,y,Row_Width);
 if((rc & 0x40))  WrPoint_16(x+1,y,Row_Width);
 if((rc & 0x20))  WrPoint_16(x+2,y,Row_Width);
 if((rc & 0x10))  WrPoint_16(x+3,y,Row_Width);
 if((rc & 0x08))  WrPoint_16(x+4,y,Row_Width);
```

```
 if((rc & 0x04))   WrPoint_16(x+5,y,Row_Width);
 if((rc & 0x02))   WrPoint_16(x+6,y,Row_Width);
 if((rc & 0x01))   WrPoint_16(x+7,y,Row_Width);
}


/* (c) Function: Draw a character on the screen in 256-color mode

Input Parameters:
        char_code     ASCII character code
        fgnd          fgnd color
        bgnd          bgnd color (if opaque)
        x1,y1         position of character
        display_code  display code  0=opaque  1=transparent
        font_buf      character buffer containing the font bit pats
        font_height   character height in scan lines
        font_width    character width in pixels

Calling Protocol: */
void    Wr_Char_256(char char_code,int fgnd,int bgnd,int x1,
        int y1,int display_code,BYTE *font_buf,int font_height,
        int font_width)
{
  int i,index,bptr=0,x1_pos,x2_pos,font_byte,char_base;
  BYTE pat[512];

font_byte = font_width/8;  // width of font in font buffer
char_base = char_code*font_height*font_byte;

switch(font_width) {
  case 8:
    x1_pos = x1; x2_pos = x1_pos + 7;

    // fill the pat buffer with the bgnd character
    switch(display_code) {
     case 0:
        for (i=0; i<128; i++)  pat[i] = bgnd;
      break;
      case 1: case 2:
        RdWin_256(x1_pos,y1,x2_pos,y1+font_height-1,pat,Row_Width);
      break;
  }

 // extract the code of letter, draw it into the buffer pat
 for (i=0; i<font_height; i++)  {
   index = (i*font_byte)+char_base;
   bptr = 8 * i;
```

(continued)

```
        if(font_buf[index] & 0x80) pat[bptr]   = fgnd;
        if(font_buf[index] & 0x40) pat[bptr+1] = fgnd;
        if(font_buf[index] & 0x20) pat[bptr+2] = fgnd;
        if(font_buf[index] & 0x10) pat[bptr+3] = fgnd;
        if(font_buf[index] & 0x08) pat[bptr+4] = fgnd;
        if(font_buf[index] & 0x04) pat[bptr+5] = fgnd;
        if(font_buf[index] & 0x02) pat[bptr+6] = fgnd;
        if(font_buf[index] & 0x01) pat[bptr+7] = fgnd;
        }

// draw the character buffer into display memory/
WrWin_256(x1_pos,y1,x2_pos,y1+font_height-1,pat,Row_Width);
  break;

  case 16:
      x1_pos = x1; x2_pos = x1_pos + 15;
      // fill the pat buffer with the bgnd character
      switch(display_code) {
        case 0:
         for (i=0; i<512; i++)  pat[i] = bgnd;
        break;
        case 1: case 2:
         RdWin_256(x1_pos,y1,x2_pos,y1+font_height-1,pat,Row_Width);
        break;
        }

for (i=0; i<font_height; i++)  {   // extract the code of
letter, draw it into the buffer pat
    index = (i*font_byte)+char_base;
    bptr = i * font_width;
    if(font_buf[index] & 0x80) pat[bptr]   = fgnd;
    if(font_buf[index] & 0x40) pat[bptr+1] = fgnd;
    if(font_buf[index] & 0x20) pat[bptr+2] = fgnd;
    if(font_buf[index] & 0x10) pat[bptr+3] = fgnd;
    if(font_buf[index] & 0x08) pat[bptr+4] = fgnd;
    if(font_buf[index] & 0x04) pat[bptr+5] = fgnd;
    if(font_buf[index] & 0x02) pat[bptr+6] = fgnd;
    if(font_buf[index] & 0x01) pat[bptr+7] = fgnd;

    if(font_buf[index+1] & 0x80) pat[bptr+8]  = fgnd;
    if(font_buf[index+1] & 0x40) pat[bptr+9]  = fgnd;
    if(font_buf[index+1] & 0x20) pat[bptr+10] = fgnd;
    if(font_buf[index+1] & 0x10) pat[bptr+11] = fgnd;
    if(font_buf[index+1] & 0x08) pat[bptr+12] = fgnd;
    if(font_buf[index+1] & 0x04) pat[bptr+13] = fgnd;
    if(font_buf[index+1] & 0x02) pat[bptr+14] = fgnd;
    if(font_buf[index+1] & 0x01) pat[bptr+15] = fgnd;
    }
```

```
  // draw the character buffer into display memory
  WrWin_256(x1_pos,y1,x2_pos,y1+font_height-1,pat,Row_Width);
  break;
  }
}


/* (d) Function: Draw a character on the screen in Hi-color mode

Input Parameters:
          char_code    ASCII character code
          fgnd         fgnd color
          bgnd         bgnd color (if opaque)
          x1,y1        position of character
          display_code display code  0=opaque  1=transparent
          font_buf     character buffer containing the font bit pats
          font_height  character height in scan lines
          font_width   character width in pixels

Calling Protocol: */
void    Wr_Char_Hi(char char_code,int fgnd,int bgnd,int x1,int y1,
        int display_code,BYTE *font_buf,int font_height,
        int font_width)
{
  int i,index,bptr=0,x1_pos,x2_pos,font_byte,char_base,pat[512];

 font_byte = font_width/8;   // width of font in font buffer
 char_base = char_code*font_height*font_byte;

switch(font_width) {

  case 8:
    x1_pos = x1; x2_pos = x1_pos + 7;
    // fill the pat buffer with the bgnd character
    switch(display_code) {
        for (i=0; i<128; i++)  pat[i] = bgnd;
      break;
      case 1: case 2:
        RdWin_Hi(x1_pos,y1,x2_pos,y1+font_height-1,pat,Row_Width);
      break;
      }

// extract the code of letter, draw it into the buffer pat
for (i=0; i<font_height; i++)  {
   index = (i*font_byte)+char_base;
   bptr = 8 * i;
   if(font_buf[index] & 0x80) pat[bptr]    = fgnd;
```

(continued)

```
    if(font_buf[index] & 0x40) pat[bptr+1] = fgnd;
    if(font_buf[index] & 0x20) pat[bptr+2] = fgnd;
    if(font_buf[index] & 0x10) pat[bptr+3] = fgnd;
    if(font_buf[index] & 0x08) pat[bptr+4] = fgnd;
    if(font_buf[index] & 0x04) pat[bptr+5] = fgnd;
    if(font_buf[index] & 0x02) pat[bptr+6] = fgnd;
    if(font_buf[index] & 0x01) pat[bptr+7] = fgnd;
    }

    // draw the character buffer into display memory/
    WrWin_Hi(x1_pos,y1,x2_pos,y1+font_height-1,pat,Row_Width);
    break;

  case 16:
    x1_pos = x1; x2_pos = x1_pos + 15;
    // fill the pat buffer with the bgnd character
    switch(display_code) {
       case 0:
         for (i=0; i<512; i++)  pat[i] = bgnd;
       break;
       case 1: case 2:
         RdWin_Hi(x1_pos,y1,x2_pos,y1+font_height-1,pat,Row Width);
       break;
       }

  // extract the code of letter, draw it into the buffer pat
  for (i=0; i<font_height; i++)  {
    index = (i*font_byte)+char_base;
    bptr = i * font_width;
    if(font_buf[index] & 0x80) pat[bptr]     = fgnd;
    if(font_buf[index] & 0x40) pat[bptr+1]  = fgnd;
    if(font_buf[index] & 0x20) pat[bptr+2]  = fgnd;
    if(font_buf[index] & 0x10) pat[bptr+3]  = fgnd;
    if(font_buf[index] & 0x08) pat[bptr+4]  = fgnd;
    if(font_buf[index] & 0x04) pat[bptr+5]  = fgnd;
    if(font_buf[index] & 0x02) pat[bptr+6]  = fgnd;
    if(font_buf[index] & 0x01) pat[bptr+7]  = fgnd;

    if(font_buf[index+1] & 0x80) pat[bptr+8]  = fgnd;
    if(font_buf[index+1] & 0x40) pat[bptr+9]  = fgnd;
    if(font_buf[index+1] & 0x20) pat[bptr+10] = fgnd;
    if(font_buf[index+1] & 0x10) pat[bptr+11] = fgnd;
    if(font_buf[index+1] & 0x08) pat[bptr+12] = fgnd;
    if(font_buf[index+1] & 0x04) pat[bptr+13] = fgnd;
    if(font_buf[index+1] & 0x02) pat[bptr+14] = fgnd;
    if(font_buf[index+1] & 0x01) pat[bptr+15] = fgnd;


    }
```

```
// draw the character buffer into display memory/
WrWin_Hi(x1_pos,y1,x2_pos,y1+font_height-1,pat,Row_Width);

   break;
   }
}


/* (e) Function: Draw a character on the screen in True-color mode

Input Paramters:
           char_code    ASCII character code
           fgnd         fgnd color
           bgnd         bgnd color (if opaque)
           x1,y1        position of character
           display_code display code 0=opaque 1=transparent
           font_buf     character buffer containing the font bit
                        patterns
           font_height  character height in scan lines
           font_width   character width in pixels

Calling Protocol: */
void    Wr_Char_True(char char_code,long fgnd,long bgnd,int x1,
           int y1,int display_code,BYTE *font_buf,int font_height,
           int font_width)
{
    int i,index,bptr=0,x1_pos,x2_pos,font_byte,char_base;
    BYTE pat[512*3],fbuf[3],bbuf[3];

    fbuf[0] = (BYTE) fgnd; fbuf[1] = (BYTE)(fgnd>> 8);
fbuf[2] = (BYTE)(fgnd>>16);
    bbuf[0] = (BYTE) bgnd; bbuf[1] = (BYTE)(bgnd>> 8);
bbuf[2] = (BYTE)(bgnd>>16);

   font_byte = font_width/8;  // width of font in font buffer
   char_base = char_code*font_height*font_byte;

switch(font_width) {
  case 8:
   x1_pos = x1; x2_pos = x1_pos + 7;

   // fill the pat buffer with the bgnd character
   switch(display_code) {
   case 0:
       for (i=0; i<128; i++)  {
         index = 3*i;
         pat[index] = bbuf[0]; pat[index+1] = bbuf[1];
pat[index+2] = bbuf[2];
```

(continued)

```
          }
       break;
       case 1: case 2:

RdWin_True(x1_pos,y1,x2_pos,y1+font_height-1,pat,Row_Width);
       break;
     }

// extract the code of letter, draw it into the buffer pat
for (i=0; i<font_height; i++)  {
     index = (i*font_byte)+char_base;
     bptr = 3 * 8 * i;
     if(font_buf[index] & 0x80) {
        pat[bptr] = fbuf[0]; pat[bptr+1] = fbuf[1];
pat[bptr+2] = fbuf[2];
        }
     if(font_buf[index] & 0x40)  {
        pat[bptr+3] = fbuf[0]; pat[bptr+4] = fbuf[1];
pat[bptr+5] = fbuf[2];
        }
     if(font_buf[index] & 0x20) {
       pat[bptr+6] = fbuf[0]; pat[bptr+7] = fbuf[1];
pat[bptr+8] = fbuf[2];
        }
     if(font_buf[index] & 0x10) {
       pat[bptr+9] = fbuf[0]; pat[bptr+10] = fbuf[1];
pat[bptr+11] = fbuf[2];
        }
     if(font_buf[index] & 0x08) {
       pat[bptr+12] = fbuf[0]; pat[bptr+13] = fbuf[1];
pat[bptr+14] = fbuf[2];
        }
     if(font_buf[index] & 0x04) {
       pat[bptr+15] = fbuf[0]; pat[bptr+16] = fbuf[1];
pat[bptr+17] = fbuf[2];
        }
     if(font_buf[index] & 0x02) {
       pat[bptr+18] = fbuf[0]; pat[bptr+19] = fbuf[1];
pat[bptr+20] = fbuf[2];
        }
     if(font_buf[index] & 0x01) {
     pat[bptr+21] = fbuf[0]; pat[bptr+22] = fbuf[1];
pat[bptr+23] = fbuf[2];
        }
  }
// draw the character buffer into display memory/
WrWin_True(x1_pos,y1,x2_pos,y1+font_height-1,pat,Row_Width);
     break;
```

```
    case 16:
      x1_pos = x1; x2_pos = x1_pos + 15;
      // fill the pat buffer with the bgnd character
      switch(display_code) {
        case 0:
          for (i=0; i<512; i++)  {
            index = 3*i;
            pat[index] = bbuf[0]; pat[index+1] = bbuf[1];
pat[index+2] = bbuf[2];
          }
          break;
        case 1: case 2:

RdWin_True(x1_pos,y1,x2_pos,y1+font_height-1,pat,Row_Width);
        break;
      }


// extract the code of letter, draw it into the buffer pat
for (i=0; i<font_height; i++)  {
    index = (i*font_byte)+char_base;
    bptr = 3 * i * font_width;
    if(font_buf[index] & 0x80) {
      pat[bptr] = fbuf[0]; pat[bptr+1] = fbuf[1];
pat[bptr+2] = fbuf[2];
    }
    if(font_buf[index] & 0x40) {
      pat[bptr+3] = fbuf[0]; pat[bptr+4] = fbuf[1];
pat[bptr+5] = fbuf[2];
    }
    if(font_buf[index] & 0x20) {
     pat[bptr+6] = fbuf[0]; pat[bptr+7] = fbuf[1];
pat[bptr+8] = fbuf[2];
    }
    if(font_buf[index] & 0x10) {
      pat[bptr+9] = fbuf[0]; pat[bptr+10] = fbuf[1];
pat[bptr+11] = fbuf[2];
    }
    if(font_buf[index] & 0x08) {
      pat[bptr+12] = fbuf[0]; pat[bptr+13] = fbuf[1];
pat[bptr+14] = fbuf[2];
    }
    if(font_buf[index] & 0x04) {
      pat[bptr+15] = fbuf[0]; pat[bptr+16] = fbuf[1];
pat[bptr+17] = fbuf[2];
    }
    if(font_buf[index] & 0x02) {
      pat[bptr+18] = fbuf[0]; pat[bptr+19] = fbuf[1];
pat[bptr+20] = fbuf[2];
```

(continued)

```
      }
    if(font_buf[index] & 0x01) {
     pat[bptr+21] = fbuf[0]; pat[bptr+22] = fbuf[1];
pat[bptr+23] = fbuf[2];
      }
    if(font_buf[index+1] & 0x80) {
     pat[bptr+24] = fbuf[0]; pat[bptr+25] = fbuf[1];
pat[bptr+26] = fbuf[2];
      }
    if(font_buf[index+1] & 0x40) {
     pat[bptr+27] = fbuf[0]; pat[bptr+28] = fbuf[1];
pat[bptr+29] = fbuf[2];
      }
    if(font_buf[index+1] & 0x20) {
     pat[bptr+30] = fbuf[0]; pat[bptr+31] = fbuf[1];
pat[bptr+32] = fbuf[2];
      }
    if(font_buf[index+1] & 0x10) {
     pat[bptr+33] = fbuf[0]; pat[bptr+34] = fbuf[1];
pat[bptr+35] = fbuf[2];
      }
    if(font_buf[index+1] & 0x08) {
     pat[bptr+36] = fbuf[0]; pat[bptr+37] = fbuf[1];
pat[bptr+38] = fbuf[2];
      }
    if(font_buf[index+1] & 0x04) {
     pat[bptr+39] = fbuf[0]; pat[bptr+40] = fbuf[1];
pat[bptr+41] = fbuf[2];
      }
    if(font_buf[index+1] & 0x02) {
     pat[bptr+42] = fbuf[0]; pat[bptr+43] = fbuf[1];
pat[bptr+44] = fbuf[2];
      }
    if(font_buf[index+1] & 0x01) {
     pat[bptr+45] = fbuf[0]; pat[bptr+46] = fbuf[1];
pat[bptr+47] = fbuf[2];
      }
     }
// draw the character buffer into display memory/
WrWin_True(x1_pos,y1,x2_pos,y1+font_height-1,pat,Row_Width);
  break;
  }
}

/* (f) Function:  Create a 16x32 font out of the 8x16 font

Calling Protocol:    */
void Make_a_16x32_Font(void)
{
```

```
int i,index=0;
BYTE temp_buf[4096],value_left,value_right,dupc[16];

 dupc[0] =0x00; dupc[1] =0x03; dupc[2] =0x0c; dupc[3] =0x0f;
 dupc[4] =0x30; dupc[5] =0x33; dupc[6] =0x3c; dupc[7] =0x3f;
 dupc[8] =0xc0; dupc[9] =0xc3; dupc[10]=0xcc; dupc[11]=0xcf;
 dupc[12]=0xf0; dupc[13]=0xf3; dupc[14]=0xfc; dupc[15]=0xff;

 Char_Height = 16;   Read_Font(6,temp_buf);
 VGA_Text.font_height = 32;   VGA_Text.font_width = 16;
 VGA_Text.font_byte = VGA_Text.font_width/8;

 for (i=0; i<4096; i++) {
        value_left  = dupc[(temp_buf[i]>>4)&0x0f];
        value_right = dupc[ temp_buf[i]&0x0f];

        VGA_Text.font_buf[index++] = value_left;
        VGA_Text.font_buf[index++] = value_right;
        VGA_Text.font_buf[index++] = value_left;
        VGA_Text.font_buf[index++] = value_right;
        }

 Characters_per_Row = Pixels_per_Row/VGA_Text.font_width;
 CharRows_per_Screen =
PixelRows_per_Screen/VGA_Text.font_height;
 }
```

Two data structures are provided that help describe an alphanumeric text region. The first is a text structure that stores the position of a text window, the font parameters, the font data pattern, foreground and background colors, and transparent and move cursor flags.

```
// Text related structure
typedef struct {
    vga_rect_t query,print;
    int
font_height,font_width,printf_pixels,font_byte,transparent;
    long foreground,background;
    char move_cursor;
    // font can be 256 characters by 16 bytes/character
    BYTE font_buf[4096];
} VGA_Text_t;
```

This calls upon a rectangular positioning data structure that could be defined as follows:

```
// Rectangular structure
typedef struct {
    // rectangle window limits
```

```
   int left,right,top,bottom,width,height;
   // background and foreground colors for window
   long background,foreground;
   int x,y;        // desired position of character
   int transparent;    // transparent flag for window
} vga_rect_t;
```

15.15 VESA RELATED FUNCTIONS

Often, the programmer will want to combine VESA and non-VESA related graphics. Several useful functions are provided in Listing 15.31. These check VESA to see if a particular Super VGA chip set is present, set a VESA mode, and return a VESA mode number.

LISTING 15.31 VESA Related Functions (a) Check for a Known String in VESA (b) Set the VESA Mode (c) Find the VESA Mode Number (d) Function: Check the VESA for a Known ID

```
/* (a) Function: Check the VESA for a given string match

Input Parameters:
  key       NULL terminated character string
Output Parameters:
  return    return found code
             1= match was made   0= no match was made

Calling Protocol: */
int Check_VESA(char *key)
 { int i,k,length,found; char *ptr;

 length = strlen(key);   // find length of match key
 ptr = VGA_Info.OEMStringPtr;

 // find the first occurance of key in VGA_Info.OEMStringPtr
 for (i=0; i<=256-length; i++) {
   if((*ptr)==key[0]) {
     found=CHIP_FOUND;
     ptr++;
     for (k=1; k<length; k++) {
         if((*ptr)!=key[k]) found=CHIP_NOT_FOUND;
         ptr++;
         }

     if(found) return(CHIP_FOUND);
     }
  }
return(CHIP_NOT_FOUND);
}
```

```
/* (b)  Function:  Find the mode given the active VGA and the
   resolution specification and then set the mode

Input Parameters:
        VGA_ID          global vga identification code
        width           number of horizontal characters/pixels
        height          number of vertical characters/pixels
        graphics        1=graphics or 0=alphanumeric mode

Output Parameters:
        mode            display mode  -1 = no supported mode
        Pixel_Bits      global number of bits per colors

Calling Protocol:  */
int Set_VESA_VGA_Mode(int width, int height, int
bits_per_color, int graphics)
{ int mode,ret_val;
   mode = Find_VESA_Mode(width,height,bits_per_color,graphics);

 if(mode!=-1) {
  Pixel_Bits=bits_per_color;  // set Global value
  ret_val=Set_VESA_Mode(mode);
  if(ret_val==0x004f) {
    Build_Mode_Structure(mode);
    Handle_Specifics(mode);  // handle the chip specifics
    }
  else mode=-1; // not set for some reason
  }
 return(mode);
 }

/* (c)  Function:  Find the mode given the active VGA and the
   resolution specification

Input Parameters:
        VGA_ID          global vga identification code
        width           number of horizontal characters/pixels
        height          number of vertical characters/pixels
        graphics        1=graphics or 0=alphanumeric mode

Output Parameters:
        mode            display mode  -1 = no supported mode
        Pixel_Bits      global number of bits per colors

Calling Protocol:  */
int Find_VESA_Mode(int width, int height, int bits_per_color,
int graphics)
{
```

(continued)

```
int mode = -1,*mode_ptr ;

if (graphics == 1) {  // ------------- do graphics modes
--------------------------------
  switch (bits_per_color) {
        case c4_bit: // 4-bit
        switch(width) {
         case 800:  if(height==600)  mode=0x102;  break;
         case 1024: if(height==768)  mode=0x104;  break;
         case 1280: if(height==1024) mode=0x106; break;
         }
        break;
        case c8_bit:  // 8-bit
         switch(width) {
          case 640:  if(height==400)  mode=0x100;
                if(height==480) mode=0x101;  break;
          case 800:  if(height==600)  mode=0x103; break;
          case 1024: if(height==768)  mode=0x105; break;
          case 1280: if(height==1024) mode=0x107; break;
          }
        break;
        case c15_bit:  // 15-bit
         switch(width) {
          case 320:  if(height==200)  mode=0x10D; break;
          case 640:  if(height==480)  mode=0x110; break;
          case 800:  if(height==600)  mode=0x113; break;
          case 1024: if(height==768)  mode=0x116; break;
          case 1280: if(height==1024) mode=0x119; break;
          }
        break;
        case c16_bit:  // 16-bit
         switch(width) {
          case 320:  if(height==200)  mode=0x10E; break;
          case 640:  if(height==480)  mode=0x111; break;
          case 800:  if(height==600)  mode=0x114; break;
          case 1024: if(height==768)  mode=0x117; break;
          case 1280: if(height==1024) mode=0x120; break;
          }
        break;
        case c24_bit:  // 24-bit
         switch(width)   {
          case 320:  if(height==200)  mode=0x10F; break;
          case 640:  if(height==480)  mode=0x112; break;
          case 800:  if(height==600)  mode=0x115; break;
          case 1024: if(height==768)  mode=0x118; break;
          case 1280: if(height==1024) mode=0x121; break;
          }
         break;
```

```
      }  // end of master case
    } // end of if graphics


    if (graphics==0) {  // do alphanumerics modes
        if (width==132) {
          if (height<25)  { mode=0x109; }  // use 25
           else   {
            if (height<30)  { mode=0x10A; }  // use 43
           else   {
            if(height<50)  { mode=0x10B; }  // use 50
             else {
              if(height<70) { mode=0x10C; }  // use 60
              }
            }
           }
         }
         if ((height==60) && (width==80)) mode=0x108;
      }
  if(mode!=-1) {
   // check if mode is present
   mode_ptr = VGA_Info.VideoModePtr;
   while ( (*mode_ptr != mode) && (*mode_ptr != -1)) {
        mode_ptr++;
        }

   if(*mode_ptr == -1) mode=-1;  //video mode not supported
   }
  return(mode);
}


/* (d) Function:  Check the VESA for a known id

Output Parameters:
  return    manufacturer id  -1= no match was made
Calling Protocol:
 VESA_id =  Check_VESA_for_ID(void); */


int Check_VESA_for_ID(void)
{ int ret_val;  char signature[256];
ret_val = Is_VESA_Present((char *)&VGA_Info);
if(ret_val) {
  if(Check_VESA("Chips"))    return(Which_Chips());
  if(Check_VESA("Cirrus"))   return(Which_Cirrus());
  if(Check_VESA("Diamond"))  return(Which_Diamond());
  if(Check_VESA("ITT"))      return(Which_ITT());
  if(Check_VESA("Western Digital"))  return(Which_Paradise());
```

(continued)

```
      if(Check_VESA("Paradise")) return(Which_Paradise());
      if(Check_VESA("NCR"))  return(Which_NCR());
      if(Check_VESA("Oak"))  return(Which_Oak());
      if(Check_VESA("S3"))        return(Which_S3());
      if(Check_VESA("Trident")) return(Which_Trident());
      if(Check_VESA("Tseng"))    return(Which_Tseng());
      if(Check_VESA("Video Seven")) return(Which_Video7());
      if(Check_VESA("Headland")) return(Which_Video7());
      if(Check_VESA("Weitek"))   return(Which_Weitek());
      }
   return(NO_ID_FOUND);
   }
```

15.15.1   Protected Mode VESA

The VESA drivers are non-protected mode drivers and consequently, it is necessary to provide an interface that is protected-mode compatible. Functions are provided in Listing 15.32 that get the VESA information, determine whether VESA is present, get the VESA mode capabilities, get the VESA mode information, and set the VESA mode.

LISTING 15.32 Access VESA in Protected Mode. (a) Access VESA in Real or Protected Mode (b) Data Declarations (b) Data Declarations (c) Get VESA Information (d) Get Whether VESA Is Present (e) Get VESA Mode Information (f) Set VESA Mode Through VESA (g) Get VESA Mode Through VESA

```
.MODEL LARGE,C
.286


; (a) Function:  Macro to access VESA BIOS

IFDEF     REAL_MODE                     ;;Real Mode
@VESA     MACRO     nSubFunc
          mov       ah,4FH              ;;VESA function number
          mov       al,nSubFunc         ;; sub-function number
          int       10H                 ;;Use INT 10h directly
          ENDM


ELSEIFDEF PHAR_LAP                      ;;Phar Lap extender


@VESA     MACRO     nSubFunc
          mov       ah,4FH              ;;VESA function number
          mov       al,nSubFunc         ;; sub-function number
          int       10H                 ;;Use INT 10h directly
          ENDM
```

```
        ELSE                                    ;;Other extenders

        @VESA      MACRO       nSubFunc
                   LOCAL       vmvregs,vmlocal       ;;Local symbols
                   EXTERN C    Vesa                  : FAR
                   vmvregs     equ <[bp - vrLEN]>    ;;PVREGS structure
                   vmlocal     equ vrLEN             ;;Total local space

                   push        bp                    ;;Set up stack frame
                   mov         bp,sp
                   sub         sp,vmlocal            ;; and local space

                   ;;Fill VESAREGS structure with
                   mov         vmvregs.vrbx,bx
                   mov         vmvregs.vrcx,cx       ;; register values
                   mov         vmvregs.vrdx,dx
                   mov         vmvregs.vrdi,di
                   mov         vmvregs.vres,es

                   push        nSubFunc    ;;VESA sub-function number
                   push        ss          ;;Pointer to PVREGS structure
                   lea         ax,vmvregs
                   push        ax
                   call        FAR PTR Vesa          ;;Call Vesa function

                   add         sp,6                  ;;Pop parameters

                   mov         bx,vmvregs.vrbx       ;;Copy register values
                   mov         cx,vmvregs.vrcx       ;; back from VESAREGS
                   mov         dx,vmvregs.vrdx       ;; structure
                   mov         di,vmvregs.vrdi
                   mov         es,vmvregs.vres

                   mov         sp,bp                 ;;Restore stack frame
                   pop         bp
                   ENDM
        ENDIF


; (b)  Data declarations


; VESA sub-function numbers
SVGAINFO    equ  00H              ;Return SVGA information
SVGAMODE    equ  01H              ;Return SVGA mode information
VSETMODE    equ  02H              ;Set current mode
VGETMODE    equ  03H              ;Get current mode
VSTATE      equ  04H              ;Get/Set video state
```

(continued)

```
VWINCTRL    equ   05H                 ;Get/Set memory window
VESAOK      equ   004FH               ;Successful VESA call status

;SVGAMODESTRUC structure
SVGAMODESTRUC       STRUC
smssig   db       4   dup (?) ;VESA signature string
smsver   dw       ?           ;VESA version number
smsoemptr dd      ?           ;Pointer to OEM string
smscap   db       4   dup (?) ;Capabilities of video system
smssmptr dd       ?           ;Pointer to supported SVGA modes
smsblocks dw      ?           ;Number of 64K memory blocks
smsfiller db      236 dup (?) ;Reserved for VESA
SVGAMODESTRUC      ENDS


;SVGAMODESTRUC structure size
smsLEN      equ        SIZE SVGAMODESTRUC

;Real Mode Translation registers structure  (DPMI)
RMTREGS            STRUC
rmtedi   dd       ?               ;EDI register  (32 bits regs)
rmtesi   dd       ?               ;ESI register
rmtebp   dd       ?               ;EBP register
rmtfiller dd      ?               ;Reserved
rmtebx   dd       ?               ;EBX register
rmtedx   dd       ?               ;EDX register
rmtecx   dd       ?               ;ECX register
rmteax   dd       ?               ;EAX register
rmtflags dw       ?               ;Flags register (16 bits regs)
rmtes    dw       ?               ;ES register
rmtds    dw       ?               ;DS register
rmtfs    dw       ?               ;FS register
rmtgs    dw       ?               ;GS register
rmtip    dw       ?               ;IP register
rmtcs    dw       ?               ;CS register
rmtsp    dw       ?               ;SP register
rmtss    dw       ?               ;SS register
RMTREGS           ENDS

rmtLEN      equ        SIZE RMTREGS   ;RMTREGS structure size

; VESAREGS structure
VESAREGS           STRUC
vrbx     dw       ?               ;BX register
vrcx     dw       ?               ;CX register
vrdx     dw       ?               ;DX register
vrdi     dw       ?               ;DI register
vres     dw       ?               ;ES register
VESAREGS           ENDS
```

```
vrLen       equ         SIZE VESAREGS       ;VESAREGS structure size

.DATA
EXTRN C  Seg0040              : WORD
EXTRN C  SegA000              : WORD
EXTRN C  SegB000              : WORD
EXTRN C  SegB800              : WORD
EXTRN C  SegC000              : WORD
EXTRN C  SegC800              : WORD
EXTRN C  SegF000              : WORD
EXTRN C  SelInc               : WORD


.CODE
EXTRN C  InitProtectedMode       : FAR
EXTRN C  VESA                    : FAR
EXTRN C  AllocDosMemory          : FAR
EXTRN C  FreeDosMemory           : FAR


PUBLIC    Get_VESA_Info
PUBLIC    Is_VESA_Present
PUBLIC    Get_VESA_Mode_Info
PUBLIC    Set_VESA_Mode
PUBLIC    Get_VESA_Mode


; (c) Function  Get VESA Information

;  Input with:
;      buf pointer to 256 byte buffer
;      &mode_bits    pointer to supported mode bits
; Output with
;      al = 4f hex function supported  al != NOT supported
;      ah = 00 hex function executed OK ah != 00 NOT OK
;  Calling Protocol:
;      result = Get_VESA_Info(buf,mode_bits)

Get_VESA_Info PROC FAR  USES ES DI, buf:FAR PTR, mode_bits:FAR
PTR
        les di,buf              ;get pointer to data vector ds:si
          @VESA      SVGAINFO
        les di,mode_bits        ;get pointer to data vector ds:si
        mov es:[di],bx          ;send back supported modes
        ret
Get_VESA_Info   endp


; (d) Function  Get whether VESA is present

;  Input with:
;      buf pointer to 256 byte buffer  (NOT USED but necessary)
```

(continued)

```
; Output with
;       result    1=VESA IS present    0=VESA NOT present
; Calling Protocol:
;       result = Is_VESA_Present(buf)

Is_VESA_Present PROC FAR  USES ES DI, buf:FAR PTR
        les   di,buf           ;get pointer to data vector ds:si
          @VESA      SVGAINFO
        cmp   ax,VESAOK         ;compare to vesa return
        jne   is1v
        mov   ax,01
        ret
is1v:   sub   ax,ax
        ret
Is_VESA_Present    endp


; (e) Function:  Get VESA Mode information

;  Input with:
;       mode    VESA Mode number
;       buf pointer to 256 byte buffer

; Output with
;       al  = 4f hex function supported  al != NOT supported
;       ah  = 00 hex function executed OK ah != 00 NOT OK

;  Calling Protocol:
;       result = Get_VESA_Mode_Info(mode,buf)

Get_VESA_Mode_Info PROC FAR    USES ES DI, mode, buf:FAR PTR
        les   di,buf       ;get pointer to data vector ds:si
        mov   cx,mode       ;mode number
          @VESA      SVGAMODE
        ret


Get_VESA_Mode_Info    endp

; (f) Function:  Set VESA Mode through VESA

; Input with:
;       mode        VESA Mode number
; Output with
;       al  = 4f hex function supported  al != NOT supported
;       ah  = 00 hex function executed OK ah != 00 NOT OK
; Calling Protocol:
;       result = Set_VESA_Mode(mode)
```

```
Set_VESA_Mode    PROC FAR   mode
        mov    bx,mode    ;mode number
          @VESA       VSETMODE
        ret
Set_VESA_Mode    endp

; (g)  Function: Get VESA Mode through VESA

; Input with:
;       mode        VESA Mode number
; Output with
;       ax  = current mode
; Calling Protocol:
;       result = Get_VESA_Mode()

Get_VESA_Mode    PROC FAR   mode
        mov    bx,mode    ;mode number
          @VESA       VGETMODE
        ret
Get_VESA_Mode    endp
```

Note that in these functions the VESA macro is called with a specific VESA command number. This macro provides the protected mode conversions when in a protected mode environment.

15.15.2   VESA Data Stuctures

There are two data structures that are filled by the VESA driver. These provide information regarding the state of the adapter and the VESA capabilities. These two data structures follow.

```
// VESA information structure
typedef struct {
    BYTEVESASignature[4];
    SHORT   VESAVersion;
    char *  OEMStringPtr;
    long    Capabilities;
    int *   VideoModePtr;
    SHORT   Memory;
    char    reserved[242];
    } VGA_Info_t;

// VESA Mode identification structure
typedef struct {
    SHORT   ModeAttributes;
    BYTE    WinAAttributes;
    BYTE    WinBModeAttributes;
    SHORT   WinGranularity;
```

```
        SHORT    WinSize;
        SHORT    WinASegment;
        SHORT    WinBSegment;
        char *   WinFuncPtr;
        SHORT    BytesPerScanLine;
        SHORT    XResolution;
        SHORT    YResolution;
        BYTE     XCharSize;
        BYTE     YCharSize;
        BYTE     NumPlanes;
        BYTE     BitsPerPel;
        BYTE     NumBanks;
        BYTE     BankSize;
        char     dummy[256];
    } VGA_Mode_Info_t;
```

15.16   IDENTIFYING THE CARD PRESENT

One needs to identify the card present in the system. You should determine
first if it is an EGA or a VGA; second, if it is a VGA or Super VGA; third, the
chip manufacturer; and fourth, which chip this is in the manufacturer's product
line. Optionally, it may be desirable to determine onto which board the specific
chip is loaded.

15.16.1   EGA or VGA Present

Two functions are provided in Listing 15.33 that determine if an EGA or a VGA
is present. One could first call Is_EGA_Present. If it reports negative, then you
have no information about what card is present. If it reports that an EGA is
present, next call the Is_VGA_Present. If this second function returns a positive response, then the card is a VGA; otherwise, it is an EGA.

LISTING 15.33 What Type of Card is Present. (a) Is an EGA Present (b) Is a VGA
Present

```
  ; (a) Function:  ;  Determine if an EGA is present

; Output with
;       ax=0 not present   ax=1 present
;  Calling Protocol:
;       EGA_Present = Is_EGA_Present()

Is_EGA_Present    PROC FAR
        mov     ah,12h ;Get EGA Status
        mov     bl,10h
```

```
        mov     bh,55h      ;dummy, it will change if EGA/VGA
        int     10h
        cmp     bh,55h
        jz      ega_not_there

        mov     ax,1        ;EGA/VGA present
        ret

ega_not_there:              ;EGA/VGA not present
        mov     ax,0
        ret
Is_EGA_Present endp


; (b)   Function:  Determine if a VGA is present

; Output with
;       ax=0 not present    ax=1 present
;  Calling Protocol:
;       VGA_Present = Is_VGA_Present()

Is_VGA_Present    PROC FAR
        mov     ah,1ah      ;Get VGA Configuration
        mov     al,00h      ;subfunction 0
        int 10h

        cmp     al,1ah      ; if still equal then no vga
        jnz     vga_not_there

        mov     ax,1        ;  VGA present
        ret

vga_not_there:              ; VGA not present
        mov     ax,0
        ret
Is_VGA_Present    endp
```

15.16.2 Checking BIOS for a Known ID

It is possible to check the BIOS for a known chip ID. This can sometimes provide useful information regarding which Super VGA card is present. It is not always useful, though, since the makers of the BIOS are not necessarily the chip manufacturers. Consequently, two chips can end up on two different cards with entirely different strings in BIOS. Some functions are provided in Listing 15.34 to help check BIOS for known strings.

LISTING 15.34 Check BIOS for Identification (a) Check the BIOS for a Known ID (b) Check the String for a Given String Match (c) Check the BIOS for a Given String Match (d) Return the BIOS ID

```
/* (a) Function:  Check the BIOS for a known id

Output Parameters:
  return   manufacturer id    -1= no match was made

Calling Protocol:
bios_id =  Check_BIOS_for_ID(void); */

int Check_BIOS_for_ID(void)
{ int ret_val;  char signature[256];

// check ATI
 if( (Check_BIOS("ATI Technologies")) || (Check_BIOS("MACH32")) )
    if(Is_It_ATI()) {
     if(Check_BIOS("MACH32")) return(ATImach32);
         else return(Which_ATI());
         }
// Check Chips
 if(Check_BIOS("Chips"))
    if(Is_It_Chips()) {
        return(Which_Chips());
    }
// check Cirrus
 if( (Check_BIOS("Cirrus")) || (Check_BIOS("GD540x/542x")) )
    if(Is_It_Cirrus()) {
        return(Which_Cirrus());
    }
 if(Check_BIOS("Genoa"))
    if(Is_It_Genoa()) {
        return(Which_Genoa());
    }
 if(Check_BIOS("Western Digital"))
    if(Is_It_Paradise()) {
        return(Which_Paradise());
    }
 if(Check_BIOS("NCR"))
    if(Is_It_NCR()) {
        return(Which_NCR());
    }
 if( (Check_BIOS("OAK VGA BIOS")) || (Check_BIOS("VGA67")) ||
        (Check_BIOS("VGA87")) )
    if(Is_It_Oak()) {
```

```
            return(Which_Oak());
        }
    if( (Check_BIOS("S3")) || (Check_BIOS("Fahrenheit 1280")) ||
            (Check_BIOS("86C801")) || (Check_BIOS("86C928")) ||
            (Check_BIOS("Stealth VRAM")) )
        if(Is_It_S3()) {
         if(Check_BIOS("86C801")) return(S3800);
         if(Check_BIOS("86C928")) return(S3928);
         if(Check_BIOS("Fahrenheit 1280")) return(S3911);
         if(Check_BIOS("Stealth VRAM")) return(S3911);
            else return(Which_S3());
        }
    if(Check_BIOS("Trident"))
        if(Is_It_Trident()) {
            return(Which_Trident());
        }
    // check for diamond stuff
    if(Check_BIOS("SpeedSTAR 24")) return(TsengS24);
    if(Check_BIOS("SpeedSTAR")) return(Tseng4000);
    if(Check_BIOS("Stealth VRAM")) return(S3911);
    if(Check_BIOS("Tseng"))
        if(Is_It_Tseng()) {
            return(Which_Tseng());
        }
    if( (Check_BIOS("Video Seven")) || (Check_BIOS("Headland")) )
        if(Is_It_Video7()) {
         if(Check_BIOS("VRAM II")) return(Headland209);
            else return(Which_Video7());
        }
    return(NO_ID_FOUND);
}


/* (b) Function:  Check the string for a given string match

Input Parameters:
        key     NULL terminated character string
        buf     buffer to check NOT NULL TERMINATED
        count   number of bytes to check

Output Parameters:
   return        return found code
                1= match was made
                0= no match was made
Calling Protocol:
 return =  Check_string(key,buf,count) */
```

(continued)

```
int Check_string(char *key,char *buf,int count)
 { int i,k,length,found=0;

length = strlen(key); // find length of match key
if(count>=length) {
 // find the first occurrence of key in buf
 for (i-0; i<=count-length; i++) {
   if(buf[i]==key[0]) {
     found=1;
     for (k=1; k<length; k++) if(buf[i+k]!=key[k]) found=0;
     if(found) return(1);
    }
  }
}
return(0);
}


/* (c) Function:  Check the BIOS for a given string match

Input Parameters:
  key        NULL terminated character string
Output Parameters:
  return    found code:  1= match  made 0= no match  made
Calling Protocol:
 error =  Check_BIOS(key) */

int Check_BIOS(char *key)
 { char buf[512];
   int i,k,length,found,offset_into_array,j;

 length = strlen(key);    // find length of match key
 for (j=0; j<10; j++) {   // look through BIOS 10*480 bytes
   offset_into_array = j * 480; // offset
   Get_BIOS_Key(buf,512,offset_into_array);

   // find the first occurrence of key in buf
   for (i=0; i<=512-length; i++) {
    if(buf[i]==key[0]) {   // case insensitive
     found=CHIP_FOUND;
     for (k=1; k<length; k++) {
       if(buf[i+k]!=key[k]) found=CHIP_NOT_FOUND;
         }
     if(found) return(CHIP_FOUND);
     }
   }
  }
 return(CHIP_NOT_FOUND);
}
```

```
; (d) Function: Return the BIOS ID.  The BIOS chips are
; identified by checking a string which is located at C000:0000.
; Output Parameters
;        length     length of array to read
;        offset     offset into array
;        signature character string should be 256 bytes long

; Calling Protocol:
;  Get_BIOS_Key(signature,length,offset)

Get_BIOS_Key PROC FAR   USES DS SI ES DI, arg1:FAR
PTR,len_buf,off_adr
        mov   ds,SegC000  ;set up source pointer
        mov   si,off_adr  ;location of signature
        les   di,arg1     ;set up destination "c" buffer signature

        mov   cx,len_buf  ;Get id  and move bytes
        rep   movsb
        ret
Get_BIOS_Key    endp
```

15.16.3 Determining Which Super VGA is Present

One technique for determining which Super VGA is present is to first check
VESA for an identification. If one is found, the card can be identified. If VESA
doesn't provide any information, you can check BIOS. If it doesn't provide information, the hardware can be interrogated. If the hardware returns a positive
for a given manufacturer, further interrogation can be used to determine the
specific chip. This process is illustrated in Listing 15.35.

LISTING 15.35 Which Super VGA is Present

```
/* Function:  Load the global VGA_ID  VGA identification flag

Output Parameters:
  VGA_IDglobal VGA identification flag
  return    return found code >0= identified a card
            NO_ID_FOUND = no known VGA detected
Calling Protocol:
 error =  Which_VGA() */

int  Which_VGA(void)
{
  int code;
code = Check_VESA_for_ID();
if(code==NO_ID_FOUND) {
 code = Check_BIOS_for_ID();
```

(continued)

```
if(code==NO_ID_FOUND) {
 if(Is_It_Paradise()) { code=Which_Paradise();
        Put_VGAid(code); return(code); }
 if(Is_It_ATI()) {  code=Which_ATI();
        Put_VGAid(code); return(code); }
 if(Is_It_Chips()) {  code=Which_Chips();
        Put_VGAid(code); return(code); }
 if(Is_It_Genoa()) {  code=Which_Genoa();
        Put_VGAid(code); return(code); }
 if(Is_It_Tseng()) {  code=Which_Tseng();
        Put_VGAid(code); return(code); }
 if(Is_It_Video7()) { code=Which_Video7();
        Put_VGAid(code); return(code); }
 if(Is_It_S3()) { code=Which_S3();
        Put_VGAid(code); return(code); }
 if(Is_It_Oak()) { code=Which_Oak();
        Put_VGAid(code); return(code); }
 if(Is_It_Cirrus()) { code=Which_Cirrus();
        Put_VGAid(code); return(code); }
 if(Is_It_NCR()) { code=Which_NCR();
        Put_VGAid(code); return(code); }
 if(Is_It_Trident()) { code=Which_Trident();
        Put_VGAid(code); return(code); }
 }
 }
Put_VGAid(code);
return(code);
 }
```

15.17   SPECIFIC VGA DISPATCH FUNCTION CALL TABLES

The specific functions that are most commonly called in the Super VGAs are bank swapping, setting the CRTC start address, and locating the cursor. The bank tables may be planar (16-color) or packed (256-color), and these may be either the read or write banks. Each of the entries in Listing 15.36 represent the code necessary to accomplish the given function on the specific Super VGA chip. "Unknown" refers to an unknown ID and it represents an error handler.

LISTING 15.36 Typical Call Table Used to Access Specific Functions

```
.DATA
write_bank_16_table LABEL WORD
DD      Unknown
DD      Load_Write_Bank_16_ATI_1          ; 1
DD      Load_Write_Bank_16_ATI_2          ; 2
DD      Load_Write_Bank_256_ATI_3         ; 3
DD      Load_Write_Bank_256_ATI_3         ; 4
```

```
DD          Unknown
DD          Load_Write_Bank_16_Chips_452        ; 6
DD          Load_Write_Bank_16_Chips_453        ; 7

DD          Unknown
DD          Unknown
DD          Unknown
DD          Unknown
DD          Unknown
DD          Unknown
DD          Unknown
DD          Load_Write_Bank_16_Genoa_5000       ; 15
DD          Load_Write_Bank_16_Genoa_GVGA       ; 16

DD          Unknown
DD          Unknown
DD          Load_Write_Bank_16_Par_PVGA         ; 19
DD          Load_Write_Bank_16_Par_PVGA         ; 20
DD          Load_Write_Bank_16_Par_PVGA         ; 21
DD          Unknown
DD          Load_Write_Bank_16_Par_PVGA         ; 23
DD          Load_Write_Bank_16_Par_PVGA         ; 24

DD          Load_Write_Bank_16_Trident_8800     ; 25
DD          Load_Write_Bank_16_Trident_8900     ; 26
DD          Load_Write_Bank_16_Trident_8900     ; 27
DD          Load_Write_Bank_16_Trident_8900     ; 28
DD          Load_Write_Bank_16_Trident_8900     ; 29

DD          Load_Write_Bank_16_Tseng_3000       ; 30
DD          Load_Write_Bank_16_Tseng_4000       ; 31
DD          Load_Write_Bank_16_Tseng_4000       ; 32
DD          Load_Write_Bank_16_Tseng_4000       ; 33

DD          Unknown
DD          Unknown
DD          Load_Wr_Bank_16_Video7_V7VGA        ; 36
DD          Load_Wr_Bank_16_Video7_208          ; 37
DD          Load_Wr_Bank_16_Video7_209          ; 38
DD          Load_Wr_Bank_16_Video7_216          ; 39

DD          Unknown
DD          Unknown
DD          Load_Wr_Bank_16_Oak_037             ; 42
DD          Load_Wr_Bank_16_Oak_067             ; 43
DD          Load_Wr_Bank_16_Oak_077             ; 44
```

(continued)

```
DD          Load_Wr_Bank_16_Oak_087                    ; 45

DD          Unknown
DD          Unknown
DD          Load_Wr_Bank_16_S3_911                     ; 48
DD          Load_Wr_Bank_16_S3_911                     ; 49

DD          Unknown                                    ; 50
DD          Unknown                                    ; 51
DD          Load_Wr_Bank_16_NCR_22                     ; 52

DD          Unknown                                    ; 53
DD          Unknown                                    ; 54
DD          Load_Wr_Bank_16_Cir_2                      ; 55
DD          Load_Wr_Bank_16_Cir_2                      ; 56
DD          Load_Wr_Bank_16_Cir_2                      ; 57
DD          Load_Wr_Bank_16_Cir_2                      ; 58
```

A typical table is shown in Listing 15.36. This table is located in a data segment. Each specific Super VGA is assigned a code number. These code numbers are provided in Listing 15.37.

LISTING 15.37 Specific Super VGA Chip Identification Codes

```
#define ATI18800      1      #define Trident8800 25
#define ATI28800      2      #define Trident8900 26
#define ATImach8      3      #define Trident9000 27
#define ATImach32     4      #define Trident9200 28
                            #define Trident9420 29
#define Chips451      5
#define Chips452      6      #define Oak037      42
#define Chips453      7      #define Oak067      43
#define Chips455      8      #define Oak077      44
#define Chips456      9      #define Oak087      45
#define Chips852      10     #define Oak107      46

#define Genoa5000     15     #define S3911       48
#define GenoaGVGA     16     #define S3924       48
                            #define S3928       49
#define PVGA1a        20     #define S3800       50
#define WD90C00       21
#define WD90C10       22     #define Cirrus5401  55
#define WD90C11       23     #define Cirrus5402  55
#define WD90C30       19     #define Cirrus5420  55
#define WD90C31       24     #define Cirrus5422  55
#define WD90C33       18     #define Cirrus5424  55
                            #define Cirrus5426  56
```

```
#define Tseng3000      30        #define Cirrus5428   57
#define Tseng4000      31        #define Cirrus5600   58
#define Tseng4000W32   32
#define TsengS24       33        #define NCR77c22     52
                                 #define NCR77c22e    52
#define Video7VEGA     35        #define NCR77c22ep   52
#define Video7V71_3    36
#define Video7V74      37
#define Headland208    38
#define Headland209    39
#define Headland216    40
#define Headland217    41
```

Each of the entries in Listing 15.36 represents the code necessary to accomplish the given function on the specific Super VGA chip. "Unknown" refers to an unknown ID and it represents an error handler.

15.18 USEFUL MACROS

Several useful macros are provided in Listings 15.38 through 15.41 for 4-bit color, 8-bit color, hi-color, and true-color, respectively. These macros determine the address of a pixel in a read mode, determine the address of a pixel in a write mode, read a pixel, write a pixel, and, for the case of 4-bit color, set up the bit mask register.

LISTING 15.38 16-color Macros (a) Determine the Address of a Pixel in a Read Mode 16-color (b) Determine the Address of a Pixel in a Write Mode 16-color (c) Read a Pixel in Mode 16 (d) Write a Pixel in Mode 16-color (e) Set up the Bit Mask Register in Mode 16-color

```
; (a)   Determine the address of a pixel in a read mode 16-color

; Input Parameters:
;  arg1: x      horizontal coordinate of point
;  arg2: y      vertical coordinate of point
;  arg3: bytes_per_row   display bytes_per_row = # of
;                        pixels per line
; Output Parameters:
;       si     address offset
;       bl     bank number
; Calling Protocol:
;       get_address_read_16

get_address_read_16   macro
; get the x index and divide by 8 for 16-color
```

(continued)

```
        mov    ax,arg1    ; get the x address
        shr    ax,1       ; divide by 8
        shr    ax,1
        shr    ax,1
        push   ax              ;save byte address for later

; determine the (long) address = ( y * bytes_per_row ) + x
; where the segment is in dx and the bytes_per_row is in ax
        mov    ax,arg3    ; get bytes_per_row in ax
        mov    bx,arg2    ; get y in bx
        mul    bx         ; y*bytes_per_row in dx:ax
        pop    cx         ; get the x byte address
        add    ax,cx      ; (y*bytes_per_row)+x lower 16 bits in ax
        mov    si,ax      ; load as display offset for es:di

;       determine bank register
        adc    dx,0       ; (y*bytes_per_row)+x upper n bits in dx
        movbl,dl            ;put page value into bl for port output
endm


; (b) Function:  Determine the address of a pixel in a write
  mode 16-color

; Input Parameters:
;  arg1: x      horizontal coordinate of point
;  arg2: y      vertical coordinate of point
;  arg4: bytes_per_row   display bytes_per_row = # of
                         pixels per line
; Output Parameters:
;       di      address offset
;       bl      bank number
; Calling Protocol:
;       get_address_write_16

get_address_write_16 macro

; get the x index and divide by 8 for 16-color
        mov    ax,arg1    ; get the x address
        shr    ax,1       ; divide by 8
        shr    ax,1
        shr    ax,1
        push   ax              save byte address for later

; determine the (long) address = ( y * bytes_per_row ) + x
; where the segment is in dx and the bytes_per_row is in ax
        mov    ax,arg4    ; get bytes_per_row in ax
        mov    bx,arg2    ; get y in bx
```

```
        mul    bx              ; y*bytes_per_row in dx:ax
        pop    cx              ; get the x byte address
        add    ax,cx           ; (y*bytes_per_row)+x lower 16 bits in ax
        mov    di,ax           ; load as display offset for es:di

;       determine bank register
        adc    dx,0            ; (y*bytes_per_row)+x upper n bits in dx
        mov    bl,dl           ;put page value into al for port output
endm
```

; (c) Function: Read a pixel in Mode 16.

```
; Input Parameters:
;       si          address offset
;       arg1: x     horizontal coordinate of point
; Output Parameters:
;       ax          output pixel (pixel in lower 4 bits of al)
; Calling Protocol:
;       read_pixel_16

read_pixel_16  macro
;       read the data from the display memory  once for each plane
        mov    ds,SegA000

;       set up the Read Plane Register
        mov    dx,3ceh    ;point to address port
        mov    ax,4
        out    dx,al      ;address read map mask
        inc    dx         ;DX points read map register data port

;       determine the number of bits to shift
        mov    ax,arg1    ;get x address
        and    ax,0007h   ;only want bit position
        mov    cl,07      ;bit mask
        sub    cl,al      ; 7-remainder = # bits to right shift
                         ; plane 0
        mov    bl,cl      ;save shift amount

;       read plane 0
        mov    al,0            ; read from plane 0
        out    dx,al
        mov    al,ds:[si]      ; read from display memory
        shr    al,cl
        and    al,01h          ;only want bit 0
        mov    ah,al           ;save in ah
```

(continued)

```
;          read plane 1
           mov    al,1          ; read from plane 1
           out    dx,al
           mov    al,ds:[si]    ; read from display memory
           mov    cl,bl         ; get shift count
           shr    al,cl
           and    al,01h        ;only want bit 0
           shl    al,1
           or     ah,al         ;save in ah

;          read plane 2
           mov    al,2          ; read from plane 2
           out    dx,al
           mov    al,ds:[si]    ; read from display memory
           mov    cl,bl
           shr    al,cl
           and    al,01h        ;only want bit 0
           shl    al,1
           shl    al,1
           or     ah,al         ;save in ah

;          read plane 3
           mov    al,3          ; read from plane 3
           out    dx,al
           mov    al,ds:[si]    ; read from display memory
           mov    cl,bl
           shr    al,cl
           and    al,01h        ;only want bit 1
           shl    al,1
           shl    al,1
           shl    al,1
           or     ah,al         ;save in ah

           mov    al,ah
           xor    ah,ah         ;send back in ax
endm

; (d) Function: Write a pixel in Mode 16-color.

; Input Parameters:
;       di          address offset
; Calling Protocol:
;       write_pixel_16

write_pixel_16 macro
; send the data to the display memory through set reset
           mov    es,SegA000
           mov    al,es:[di]    ; dummy read from display memory
```

```
        mov     es:[di],al     ; store color in display memory
                               ; through Set/Reset
endm


; (e) Function:  Set up the bit mask register in mode 16-color

; Input Parameters:
;  arg1: x      horizontal coordinate of point
; Calling Protocol:
;        load_bit_mask_16

load_bit_mask_16   macro
; set up the Bit Mask Register
        mov     dx,3ceh        ;point to address port
        mov     ax,8
        out     dx,al          ;address bit plane mask
        inc     dx             ;DX points to data port

;       load the Bit Mask Register
        mov     cx,arg1        ;get x address
        and     cx,0007h       ;only want bit position
        mov     ax,0080h       ;bit mask
        shr     al,cl          ;put bit mask into proper position
        out     dx,al          ;output bit plane mask
endm
```

LISTING 15.39 256-color Macros (a) Determine the Address of a Pixel in a Read Mode 256-color (b) Determine the Address of a Pixel in a Write Mode 256-color (c) Read a Pixel in Mode 256 (d) Write a Pixel in Mode 256-color (e) Write an XOR Pixel in Mode 256-color

```
; Listing 15.10.99.9 Determine the address of a pixel in a
; write mode 256-color

; (a) Function:
;  Determine the address of a pixel in a read mode 256-color

; Input Parameters:
;  arg1: x      horizontal coordinate of point
;  arg2: y      vertical coordinate of point
;  arg3: bytes_per_row   display bytes_per_row = # of
                         pixels per line

; Output Parameters:
;      si      address offset
;      bl      bank number
```

(continued)

```
; Calling Protocol:
;        get_address_read_256

get_address_read_256  macro

; determine the (long) address = ( y * bytes_per_row ) + x
; where the segment is in dx and the bytes_per_row is in ax
        mov     ax,arg3    ; get bytes_per_row in ax
        mov     bx,arg2    ; get y in bx
        mul     bx         ; y*bytes_per_row in dx:ax
        add     ax,arg1    ; (y*bytes_per_row)+x lower 16 bits in ax
        mov     si,ax      ; load as display offset for ds:si

;       determine page register
        adc     dx,0       ; (y*bytes_per_row)+x upper n bits in dx
        mov     bl,dl      ;put page value into al for port output

endm
```

```
; (b) Function: ;  Determine the address of a pixel in a write
  mode 256-color

; Input Parameters:
;  arg1: x      horizontal coordinate of point
;  arg2: y      vertical coordinate of point
;  arg4: bytes_per_row   display bytes_per_row = # of pixels per
line
; Output Parameters:
;       di      address offset
;       bl      bank number
; Calling Protocol:
;        get_address_write_256

get_address_write_256 macro

; determine the (long) address = ( y * bytes_per_row ) + x
; where the segment is in dx and the bytes_per_row is in ax
        mov     ax,arg4    ; get bytes_per_row in ax
        mov     bx,arg2    ; get y in bx
        mul     bx         ; y*bytes_per_row in dx:ax
        add     ax,arg1    ; (y*bytes_per_row)+x lower 16 bits in ax
        mov     di,ax      ; load as display offset for es:di

;       determine page register
        adc     dx,0       ; (y*bytes_per_row)+x upper n bits in dx
        mov     bl,dl      ;put page value into cl for port output

endm
```

```
; (c) Function:  Read a pixel in Mode 256-color.

; Input Parameters:
;        si          address offset
;        arg1: x   horizontal coordinate of point
; Output Parameters:
;        ax          output pixel (pixel in lower 8 bits of ax)
; Calling Protocol:
;        read_pixel_256

read_pixel_256 macro
; get the data from the display memory
        mov     ds,SegA000
        mov     al,ds:[si]    ; get color from display memory
        xor     ah,ah         ; clear ah just in case a word is
                              ; looked at
endm

; (d) Function: Write a pixel in Mode 256-color.

; Input Parameters:
;        di          address offset
;        arg3 : color  pixel color to write
; Calling Protocol:
;        write_pixel_256

write_pixel_256    macro
        mov     es,SegA000    ; send the data to the display memory
        mov  al,arg3          ; get color
        mov     es:[di],al    ; store color in display memory
endm

;   (e) Function: Write an XOR  pixel in Mode 256-color.

; Input Parameters:
;        di          address offset
;        arg3 : color  pixel color to write
; Calling Protocol:
;        write_Xpixel_256

write_Xpixel_256   macro
        mov     es,SegA000    ; send the data to the display memory
        mov     al,es:[di]    ; dummy read to get old data
        mov  al,arg3          ; get color
        mov     es:[di],al    ; store color in display memory
endm
```

LISTING 15.40 Hi-color Macros (a) Determine the Address of a Pixel in a Read Mode Hi-color (b) Determine the Address of a Pixel in a Write Mode Hi-color (c) Read a pixel in Mode Hi-color (d) Write a Pixel in Mode Hi-color (e) Write an XOR Pixel in Mode Hi-color

```
; (a) Function:  Determine the address of a pixel in a read
; mode Hi-color

; Input Parameters:
;  arg1: x       horizontal coordinate of point
;  arg2: y       vertical coordinate of point
;  arg3: bytes_per_row   display bytes_per_row = # of
;                        pixels per line
; Output Parameters:
;       si      address offset
;       bl      bank number
; Calling Protocol:
;       get_address_read_Hi

get_address_read_Hi    macro
; determine the (long) address = ( y * bytes_per_row ) + (2*x)
; where the segment is in dx and the bytes_per_row is in ax
        mov     ax,arg3  ; get bytes_per_row in ax
        mov     bx,arg2  ; get y in bx
        mul     bx       ; y*bytes_per_row in dx:ax
        mov     bx,arg1  ; (y * offset) + 2*x (lower 16 bits)
        shl     bx,1
        add     ax,bx
        mov     si,ax    ; load as display offset for ds:si

;       determine page register
        adc     dx,0     ; (y*bytes_per_row)+x upper n bits in dx
        mov     bl,dl    ;put page value into al for port output
endm

; (b) Function:  Determine the address of a pixel in a write
; mode Hi-color

; Input Parameters:
;  arg1: x       horizontal coordinate of point
;  arg2: y       vertical coordinate of point
;  arg4: bytes_per_row   display bytes_per_row = # of
;                        pixels per line
; Output Parameters:
;       di      address offset
;       bl      bank number
; Calling Protocol:
;       get_address_write_Hi
```

```
get_address_write_Hi  macro
; determine the (long) address = ( y * bytes_per_row ) + (2*x)
; where the segment is in dx and the bytes_per_row is in ax
        mov     ax,arg4    ; get bytes_per_row in ax
        mov     bx,arg2    ; get y in bx
        mul bx             ; y*bytes_per_row in dx:ax

        mov     bx,arg1    ; (y * offset) + 2*x (lower 16 bits)
        shl     bx,1
        add     ax,bx
        mov     di,ax      ; load as display offset for es:di

;       determine page register
        adc     dx,0       ; (y*bytes_per_row)+x upper n bits in dx
        mov     bl,dl      ;put page value into cl for port output
endm


; (c) Function: Read a pixel in Mode Hi-color.

; Input Parameters:
;       si              address offset
;       arg1: x         horizontal coordinate of point
; Output Parameters:
;       ax              output pixel (pixel in lower 8 bits of ax)
; Calling Protocol:
;       read_pixel_Hi

read_pixel_Hi  macro
        mov     ds,SegA000    ; get the data from the display memory
        mov     ax,ds:[si]    ; get color from display memory
endm


; (d)  Function: Write a pixel in Mode Hi-color.

; Input Parameters:
;       di              address offset
;       arg3 : color  pixel color to write
; Calling Protocol:
;       write_pixel_Hi

write_pixel_Hi macro
        mov     es,SegA000    ; send the data to the display memory
        mov     ax,arg3       ; get color
        mov     es:[di],ax    ; store color in display memory
endm
```

(continued)

```
; (e)  Function:  Write an XOR pixel in Mode Hi-color.

; Input Parameters:
;       di          address offset
;       arg3 : color pixel color to write
; Calling Protocol:
;       write_Xpixel_Hi

write_Xpixel_Hi    macro
        mov    es,SegA000   ; send the data to the display memory
        mov    ax,es:[di]   ; dummy read to get old data
        mov    ax,arg3      ; get color
        mov    es:[di],ax   ; store color in display memory
endm
```

LISTING 15.41 True-color Macros (a) Determine the Address of a Pixel in a Read Mode True-color (b) Determine the Address of a Pixel in a Write Mode True-color (c) Read a Pixel in Mode True-color (d) Read the First Byte of a Pixel in Mode True-color (e) Read the Two Second Bytes of a Pixel in Mode True-color (f) Read the First Two Bytes of a Pixel in Mode True-color (g) Read the Third Byte of a Pixel in Mode True-color (h) Write a Pixel in Mode True-color (m) Write an XOR Pixel in Mode True-color (i) Write the First Byte of a Pixel in Mode True-color (j) Write the Two Second Bytes of a Pixel in Mode True-color (k) Write the First Two Bytes of a Pixel in Mode True-color (l) Write the Third Byte of with a Pixel in Mode True-color (m) Write a Pixel in Mode True-color.

```
; (a) Function:  Determine the address of a pixel in a read
; mode True-color

; Input Parameters:
;  arg1: x      horizontal coordinate of point
;  arg2: y      vertical coordinate of point
;  arg3: bytes_per_row   display bytes_per_row = # of
;                        pixels per line
; Output Parameters:
;       si      address offset
;       bl      bank number
; Calling Protocol:
;       get_address_read_True

get_address_read_True macro
; determine the (long) address = ( y * bytes_per_row ) + (3*x)
; where the segment is in dx and the bytes_per_row is in ax
        mov    ax,arg3    ; get bytes_per_row in ax
        mov    bx,arg2    ; get y in bx
        mul    bx         ; y*bytes_per_row in dx:ax
```

```
        mov     bx,arg1    ; (y * offset) + 3*x (lower 16 bits)
        shl     bx,1
        add     bx,arg1    ;x times three

        add     ax,bx
        mov     si,ax      ; load as display offset for ds:si

;       determine page register
        adc     dx,0       ; (y*bytes_per_row)+x upper n bits in dx
        mov     bl,dl      ;put page value into bl for port output
endm


; (b) Function:  Determine the address of a pixel in a write
; mode True-color

; Input Parameters:
;  arg1: x      horizontal coordinate of point
;  arg2: y      vertical coordinate of point
;  arg4: bytes_per_row   display bytes_per_row = # of
;                        pixels per line
; Output Parameters:
;       di      address offset
;       bl      bank number
; Calling Protocol:
;       get_address_write_True

get_address_write_True    macro

; determine the (long) address = ( y * bytes_per_row ) + (3*x)
; where the segment is in dx and the bytes_per_row is in ax
        mov     ax,arg4    ; get bytes_per_row in ax
        mov     bx,arg2    ; get y in bx
        mul     bx         ; y*bytes_per_row in dx:ax

        mov     bx,arg1    ; (y * offset) + 3*x (lower 16 bits)
        shl     bx,1
        add     bx,arg1    ;x times three
        add     ax,bx

        mov     di,ax      ; load as display offset for es:di

;       determine page register
        adc     dx,0       ; (y*bytes_per_row)+x upper n bits in dx
        mov     bl,dl      ;put page value into cl for port output
endm
```

(continued)

```
; (c) Function:  Read a pixel in Mode True-color.

; Input Parameters:
;        si          address offset
;        arg1: x    horizontal coordinate of point
; Output Parameters:
;        ax          output pixel (pixel in lower 8 bits of ax)
; Calling Protocol:
;        read_pixel_True

read_pixel_True    macro
        mov     ds,SegA000  ; get the data from the display memory
        les     di,arg4   ;point to destination buffer for 3 bytes
        movsw             ;move 1'st and 2'nd byte
        movsb             ;move 3'rd byte
endm

; (d) Function: Read the first byte of a pixel in Mode
True-color.

; Input Parameters:
;        si      address offset
; Output Parameters:
;        arg4 : color  pixel color to read
; Calling Protocol:
;        read_pixel1a_True

read_pixel1a_True macro
        mov     ds,SegA000    ; send the data to the display memory
        les     di,arg4
        movsb
endm

; (e) Function: Read the two second bytes of a pixel in Mode
; True-color.

; Input Parameters:
;        si      address offset
; Output Parameters:
;        arg4 : color  pixel color to read
; Calling Protocol:
;        read_pixel1b_True

read_pixel1b_True macro
        mov     ds,SegA000    ;get the data from the display memory
        les     di,arg4
```

```
        inc     di              ;skip past the first byte
        movsw
endm
```

; (f) Function: Read the first two bytes of a pixel in Mode
; True-color.

; Input Parameters:
;   si   address offset
; Output Parameters:
;   arg4 : color pixel color to read
; Calling Protocol:
;   read_pixel2a_True

```
read_pixel2a_True       macro
        mov     ds,SegA000    ; send the data to the display memory
        les     di,arg4
        movsw
endm
```

; (g) Function: Read the third byte of a pixel in Mode
; True-color.

; Input Parameters:
;   si   address offset
; Output Parameters:
;   arg4 : color pixel color to read
; Calling Protocol:
;   read_pixel2b_True

```
read_pixel2b_True       macro
        mov     ds,SegA000    ; send the data to the display memory
        les     di,arg4
        inc     di
        inc     di              ;skip past the first two bytes
        movsb
endm
```

; (h) Function: Write a pixel consisting of three bytes in Mode
; True-color.

; Input Parameters:
;   di   address offset
;   arg3 : color pointer to first byte of pixel color to write

(continued)

```
; Calling Protocol:
;       write_pixel_True

write_pixel_True   macro


        mov     es,SegA000    ; send the data to the display memory
        lds     si,arg3
        mov     cx,3
        rep     movsb
endm

; (i) Function: Write the first byte of a pixel in Mode
; True-color.

; Input Parameters:
;       di          address offset
;       arg3 : color  pixel color to write
; Calling Protocol:
;       write_pixel1a_True

write_pixel1a_True    macro
        mov     es,SegA000    ; send the data to the display memory
        lds     si,arg3
        movsb
endm

; (j) Function:  Write the two second bytes of a pixel in Mode
; True-color.

; Input Parameters:
;       di          address offset
;       arg3 : color  pixel color to write
; Calling Protocol:
;       write_pixel1b_True

write_pixel1b_True     macro
        mov     es,SegA000    ; send the data to the display memory
        lds     si,arg3
        inc     si              ;skip past the first byte
        movsw
endm

; (k) Function:  Write the first two bytes of a pixel in Mode
; True-color.
```

```
; Input Parameters:
;       di          address offset
;       arg3 : color pixel color to write
; Calling Protocol:
;       write_pixel2a_True

write_pixel2a_Truemacro
        mov    es,SegA000    ; send the data to the display memory
        lds    si,arg3
        movsw
endm
```

```
; (l) Function: Write the third byte of a pixel in Mode
; True-color.
```

```
; Input Parameters:
;       di                  address offset
;       arg3 : color        pixel color to write
; Calling Protocol:
;       write_pixel2b_True

write_pixel2b_Truemacro
        mov    es,SegA000    ; send the data to the display memory
        lds    si,arg3
        inc    si
        inc    si            ;skip past the first two bytes
        movsb
endm
```

```
; (m) Function:  Write a pixel in Mode True-color.
```

```
; Input Parameters:
;       di          address offset
;       arg3 : color pixel color to write
; Calling Protocol:
;       write_Xpixel_True

write_Xpixel_True macro
        mov    es,SegA000    ; send the data to the display memory
        lds    si,arg3
        mov    ax,es:[di]    ; dummy read to get old data
        stosw
        mov    al,es:[di]    ; dummy read to get old data
        stosb
endm
```

Chapter 16

The Adapter Interface (AI)

16.1   INTRODUCTION

An adapter interface (AI) is a standardized set of commands that an application utilizes to communicate with an adapter. Common examples of graphics adapter interfaces are the BIOS graphics commands on the VGA, the Windows graphics device interface (GDI), the Texas Instruments (TIGA) interface, and the IBM adapter interface (AI). This chapter describes the IBM adapter interface commonly used with the 8514/A and the XGA cards.

I wish to extend my deepest thanks to ATI for providing much of the documentation and code examples provided in this chapter. The ATI Mach8 and Mach32 both emulate the 8514/A and, therefore, the AI interface can be used with either of their products.

16.1.1   Why an Adapter Interface?

An adapter interface provides a set of function calls that perform commonly used graphics operations. This middle manager sits between the application and the graphics adapter hardware. A set of calling protocols is provided for the application. These usually reside in either a terminate-and-stay-resident (TSR) or executable (COM or EXE) driver that can be loaded independently from the application program. Consequently, the AP driver can be distributed independently from the application. As long as a compatible AP driver is running in memory, the application will function properly. Thus, the application doesn't have to worry about which display adapter is present in the computer. This allows a single application to run under a wide variety of display adapters.

The advantages to an AI interface are clear. What about the disadvantages? Probably the most significant disadvantage is a speed degradation. There is an overhead imposed when calling the AI commands. The amount of calling overhead varies based on the way the interface was designed. For example, the VGA BIOS interface requires a software INT 10 hex interrupt to be generated every time a graphics operation is desired. This isn't so bad when setting a mode but it is intolerable when drawing pixels. The VESA interface also relies on interrupts. However, the VESA interface provides a faster means of accessing its commands. It is possible to acquire the address of the "switch memory bank" function. The application can then call this function directly, eliminating the interrupt overhead. The AI interface discussed in this chapter uses a similar technique providing a set of addresses for all commands. The Windows GDI interface is notorious for its speed penalties. Several graphics applications cannot run in Windows due to the speed penalties imposed by the GDI.

A second disadvantage involves the different capabilities of the adapters supported by the AI. I call this the LCD (Least Common Denominator) phenomena. For example, suppose that a card has a special feature that accelerates horizontal line segment drawing, especially designed for polygon filling. Because this feature might not have been anticipated when the AI spec was designed, it won't be optimally supported in the AI specification. In a case like this, there may be no way of invoking this important feature from the application. In order to use the feature, the application would have to utilize direct-to-adapter programming. This, of course, violates the whole reason for an AI.

The application developer has to determine the advantages and disadvantages of using an AI. This decision is based on the application's particular needs, the stability of the graphics adapters, and what other graphics adapters in the future will be supported by this interface.

16.1.2 The IBM Adapter Interface

IBM introduced two graphics cards after the VGA. These were the 8514/A and the XGA, both of which incorporated graphics accelerators. The 8514/A came first and IBM did not want developers to program it directly. Consequently, it introduced the adapter interface, AI. Most 8514/A or XGA cards include an AI driver. Several of the Super VGA cards discussed in this book are either 8514/A or XGA compatible. I am providing the details of this application for readers who want to program the AI interface.

16.1.3 Using the Adapter Interface

The AI is a software driver provided with the corresponding adapter. The 8514/A utilizes a TSR program called HDILOAD.EXE, and the XGA uses a driver called XGAAIDOS.SYS. The AI software must be installed before the application can use it. The application will then find its address at the interrupt vector 7F hex. The application must ensure that the AI is loaded and acquire its address before any commands can be issued. A typical programming flow chart is shown in Figure 16.1.

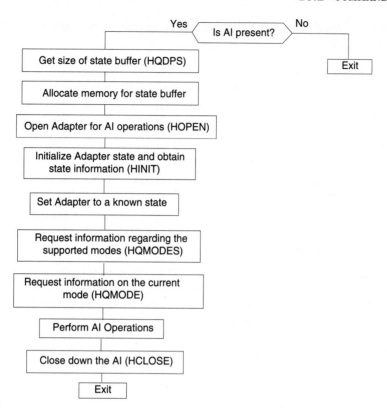

FIGURE 16.1 Programming Example Flow Chart

16.2 COMMANDS

There are 61 AI functions. Each requires a parameter block that must contain the size of the parameter block and any necessary parameters. A few functions do not require any parameters. The nine groups of commands in the AP interface can be roughly organized into setup, control, query, state control, line, image BitBlt, area, marker, and alphanumeric commands. A tenth group is specific to the XGA adapter. Eighteen commands are used specifically for the XGA.

16.2.1 Setup Commands

The setup commands, shown in Table 16.1, allow the application to engage and disengage the graphics hardware and software. Included are opening and closing the adapter and setting up the palette. This is necessary since the adapter may have a Super VGAs co-resident and it might be necessary to enable or disable the VGA.

TABLE 16.1 Setup Commands

Command	Section	Description
HOPEN	16.5.1	Open the adapter
HCLOSE	16.5.2	Close the adapter
HLDPAL	16.5.3	Load the palette
HSPAL	16.5.4	Save the palette
HRPAL	16.5.5	Restore the palette

16.2.2 Control Commands

The control commands, shown in Table 16.2, allow the application to control the graphics environment. Included are setting of interrupts, escape processing, the background and color comparison color, the foreground and background mix, and the assigning of text colors.

TABLE 16.2 Control Commands

Command	Section	Description
HINT	16.6.1	Initialize interrupt
HSGQ	16.6.2	Set graphics quality
HSCOORD	16.6.3	Set coordinate type
HESC	16.6.4	Escape and terminate processing
HSBPCOL	16.6.5	Set background color
HSBP	16.6.6	Set bit plane controls
HSCMP	16.6.7	Set color comparison value
HSCOL	16.6.8	Set color
HSHS	16.6.9	Set Scissors region
HSMX	16.6.10	Set mix
HXLATE	16.6.11	Assign multi-plane text color index table

16.2.3 Query Commands

The query commands, shown in Table 16.3, allow the application to determine the state of the graphics environment. Included are determining the current mode, the possible display modes, the coordinate types, the default palette, and the current position.

TABLE 16.3 Query Commands

Command	Section	Description
HQMODE	16.7.1	Query current mode
HQMODES	16.7.2	Query for all adapter modes
HQDPS	16.7.3	Query drawing process state size
HQDFPAL	16.7.4	Query default palette
HQCOORD	16.7.5	Query for coordinate type
HQCP	16.7.6	Query for current position

16.2.4 State Control Commands

The state control commands, shown in Table 16.4, initialize the state buffer, synchronize the adapter, and change the mode.

TABLE 16.4 State Control Commands

Command	Section	Description
HINIT	16.8.1	Initialize the state for a new task
HSYNC	16.8.2	Synchronize the adapter, switch task, and change state data
HSMODE	16.8.3	Change mode

16.2.5 Line Commands

Line commands, shown in Table 16.5, allow the drawing of lines, either absolute or relative, between two or more specified points. The starting point might be the current position or specified points. The application can also set the line type, the line width, and the line pattern count. Multiple lines can be drawn with a single command.

TABLE 16.5 Line Drawing Commands

Command	Section	Description
HLINE	16.9.1	Draw a line at a given position
HCLINE	16.9.2	Draw a line at the current position
HRLINE	16.9.3	Draw a relative line at a given position
HCRLINE	16.9.4	Draw a relative line at the current position
HSLT	16.9.5	Set line type
HSLW	16.9.6	Set line width

(continued)

TABLE 16.5 *(cont.)*

Command	Section	Description
HSLPC	16.9.7	Save line pattern count
HRLPC	16.9.8	Restore line pattern count

16.2.6   BitBlt Commands

The image BitBlt commands, shown in Table 16.6, allow the rapid movement of rectangular windows into and out of display memory. The read and write commands can be set up and then initiated by a chained data command. The current position or a specified position can act as the starting location of the rectangle.

TABLE 16.6 BitBlt Drawing Commands

Command	Section	Description
HBBW	16.10.1	BitBlt write image data
HBBR	16.10.2	BitBlt read image data
HCBBW	16.10.3	BitBlt write image data at current position
HBBCNH	16.10.4	BitBlt chained data Go
HBBC	16.10.5	BitBlt copy

16.2.7   Area Commands

Area commands, shown in Table 16.7, allow the application to build an off-screen image. An area-building session is defined by begin area and end area commands. Once opened, rectangles can be filled, patterns can be defined, and the screen can be erased.

TABLE 16.7 Area Commands

Command	Section	Description
HBAR	16.11.1	Begin area
HEAR	16.11.2	End area
HRECT	16.11.3	Fill rectangle
HSPATT	16.11.4	Set pattern
HSPATTO	16.11.5	Set pattern reference point
HEGS	16.11.6	Erase graphics screen

16.2.8 Marker Commands

Marker commands, shown in Table 16.8, set the current position, set multiple markers at given positions, and set the marker shape.

TABLE 16.8 Marker Commands

Command	Section	Description
HSCP	16.12.1	Set current position
HMRK	16.12.2	Set marker at given position
HCMRK	16.12.3	Set marker at current position
HSMARK	16.12.4	Set marker shape

16.2.9 Alphanumeric Commands

The alphanumeric commands, shown in Table 16.9, allow the specification of character sets, writing character strings, and erasing or scrolling alphanumeric regions. The string outputs can be to a specified location or to the current location. The alphanumeric data can be either one attribute per block or a different attribute per character. The alphanumeric cursor shape can also be defined.

TABLE 16.9 Alphanumeric Commands

Command	Section	Description
HSCS	16.13.1	Set character shape
HCHST	16.13.2	Write character string at given position
HCCHST	16.13.3	Write character string at current position
HSCELL	16.13.4	Define the character block size
ABLOCKMFI	16.13.5	Write character block (MFI format)
ABLOCKCGA	16.13.6	Write character block (CGA format)
AERASE	16.13.7	Erase a rectangle
ASCROLL	16.13.8	Scroll a rectangle
ACURSOR	16.13.9	Set alphanumeric cursor position
ASCUR	16.13.10	Set alphanumeric cursor shape
ASFONT	16.13.11	Set font
AXLATE	16.13.12	Assign alphanumeric colors

16.3 COMMAND FORMATS AND PROTOCOLS

Each command has an associated parameter block. The length of the parameter block varies from command to command. The address of the parameter block is sent to the AI by placing the address of the parameter block onto the stack (as a parameter) before calling the AI function. Each command has an associated number. This offset determines which function in the AI is called in order to satisfy the command. Each command is associated with a function. This number is an offset into a call table. Since each element in this table is a far pointer, each is four bytes long. Thus, the offset command number has to be multiplied by four before addressing the proper entry point into the AP driver.

16.3.1 Parameter Block Lengths

Each parameter block begins with a length field, designated LEN. This field is two bytes long, and is always included as the first two bytes of the parameter block. LEN contains the number of bytes that follow in the parameter block, but it does not include the two bytes used by the length field. For example, a parameter block might require eight bytes of data. The LEN field is two bytes. The parameter block passed to the interface is ten bytes long, but the LEN field indicates 8.

16.3.2 Zero Length Parameter Blocks

Certain commands are zero length, in which case the command LEN field contains a zero. These commands do not require any additional information.

16.3.3 Position Commands

Several commands involve position information. There are pairs of these commands that are identical except for the way that the first point is specified. The first command specifies the first point as a parameter, and the second command assumes that the first point is defined by the current position. For example, suppose the current position is at 10,10. This could be accomplished through the Set Current Position command, HSCP. One could define a set of marker points by the Set Marker Position command, HMRK, to be [10,10], [20,20], [30,30], and [40,40] by sending these four points as parameters in the HMRK command. Alternatively, the same marker points could be specified by sending the three points [20,20], [30,30], and [40,40] to the Set Markers at Current Position command, HCMRK. The first command used absolute references to the position, and the second used relative commands. The second is advantageous when the software doesn't know the value of current position.

16.3.4 Linking to the AI

The application is linked to the AI through a linkage vector. A table of pointers, called the function dispatch table, contains all of the entry points into the AI. The address of the function dispatch table is provided through the interrupt 7F, named AIVect. The service number is 105 hex, named RequestAddr. The code follows. The

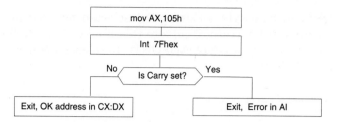

FIGURE 16.2 Acquiring the AI Vector

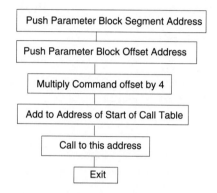

FIGURE 16.3 Calling the AI

program flow for acquiring the address of the call table is shown in Figure 16.2. The sequence required to actually call the AI is shown in Figure 16.3.

```
#define AIVect      0x7f    // AI linkage vector
#define RequestAddr 0x105   // Request the address of the
                            // function dispatch table address
```

16.3.5 Character Fonts

Neither the 8514/A nor the XGA include character fonts. The application is responsible for loading these fonts from disk and providing the address of the character set to the AI. It is necessary to load a font before any alphanumeric calls are made to the AI. Font files are either formatted as a bit-mapped font, in a single bit per pixel format, or as a short-stroke vector font. Typically, the 12x20, 8x14, and 7x15 fonts are provided with the 8514/A.

The code segment in Listing 16.1 loads a specified font file, which must be in short-stroke vector format. The structure returned contains two pointers. The first one points to the allocated memory area where the font file information is stored. If the memory can't be allocated or if an error occurs in this function, the pointer will be NULL. The second pointer points to the start of the short-stroke vector information within the allocated memory area. This pointer is used by the AI_SETFONT() function to set the font for AI use. If these function calls are successful, text can be displayed using the selected font set by calling the AI_TEXT() function. All successful calls to this function should have a corresponding call to the function UNLOADFONT() to release memory allocated to store the font set information.

LISTING 16.1 Load a Short-Stroke Font

```
FontSetInfo loadfont(char *name)
{
    unsigned int fontlen;                // Size of font to load
    int fonthdl;                         // Font file handle
    FontSetInfo fontinfo;

    // Open the font file
    if ((fonthdl = open(name, O_RDONLY|O_BINARY)) == -1) {
        fontinfo.fontaddr = NULL;
        return(fontinfo);
        }

    // Get size of font file by seeking to end of the file
    fontlen = (unsigned int)lseek(fonthdl, 0L, SEEK_END);

    // Allocate space to load font file contents
    fontinfo.fontaddr = (CharSetFileDef *)malloc(fontlen);
    if (fontinfo.fontaddr == NULL)  return(fontinfo);

    // rewind  to beginning of the font file and read font file
    //  into the allocated buffer
    lseek(fonthdl, 0L, SEEK_SET);
    read(fonthdl, (char *)(fontinfo.fontaddr), fontlen);

    // setup pointer
    (fontinfo.fontptr) = (CharSetDef *) (((char *)
    (fontinfo.fontaddr)) + (fontinfo.fontaddr)->
    pagearray[(fontinfo.fontaddr)->defaultpage].csdoffset);

    // setup all address fields with load font address
    (fontinfo.fontptr)->chardef1 = ((unsigned char far *)
      (fontinfo.fontaddr)) + ((long) (fontinfo.fontptr)->
      chardef1);
    (fontinfo.fontptr)->chardef2 = ((unsigned char far *)
      (fontinfo.fontaddr)) + ((long) (fontinfo.fontptr)->
      chardef2);
    (fontinfo.fontptr)->chardef3 = ((unsigned char far *)
      (fontinfo.fontaddr)) + ((long) (fontinfo.fontptr)->
      chardef3);
    (fontinfo.fontptr)->indextable = (int far *)
```

```
         (((unsigned char far *) (fontinfo.fontaddr)) + ((long)
         (fontinfo.fontptr)->indextable));
      (fontinfo.fontptr)->proptable = ((unsigned char far *)
         (fontinfo.fontaddr)) + ((long) (fontinfo.fontptr)->
         proptable);

      // close the font file handle
      close(fonthdl);

      // return address of stored font information
      return(fontinfo);
   }
```

The code segment provided in Listing 16.2 unloads the font memory previously allocated by a call to LOADFONT(), which returns a pointer in a structure that points to the allocated memory area. In order to reduce memory fragmentation to a minimum, the memory pointers returned from the LOADFONT() function should be freed in reverse order of their assignment. This applies to a situation where multiple font sets are being used as shown below:

```
fontset1 = loadfont(fontfile1); fontset2 = loadfont(fontfile2);
fontset3 = loadfont(fontfile3);
...
unloadfont(fontset3.fontaddr); unloadfont(fontset2.fontaddr);
unloadfont(fontset1.fontaddr);
```

LISTING 16.2 Load a Short-Stroke Font

```
void unloadfont(CharSetFileDef *fontaddr)
{
    if (fontaddr != 0)  free(fontaddr); // free memory allocated
                                        // by LOADFONT()
}
```

The code in Listing 16.3 sets a font for text usage using the information returned from the LOADFONT() function. This function must be called whenever a new font is used. It returns 1 if the call failed, and 0 if the call succeeded.

LISTING 16.3 Set a Font for Text Usage

```
int ai_setfont(CharSetDef *fontptr)
{
    HSCS_DATA setfont;

    //* inform AI about new font to use
    setfont.length = 4;
```

(continued)

```
            setfont.address = fontptr;
            if (!setfont.address)  return(1);

            HSCS(&setfont);
            return(0);
    }
```

16.3.6   Writing a Character

The code in Listing 16.4 draws text on the screen using short-stroke vector fonts. LOADFONT() and AI_SETFONT() must have been previously called successfully for this routine to work. If multiple font sets are being used, AI_SET-FONT() should be called prior to this function to tell the AI which font set to use.

LISTING 16.4 Writing a Character

```
    void    ai_text(unsigned int x, unsigned int y,
            unsigned char color, char *string)
    {
        HCHST_DATA(200)     textinfo;

        // protect data area from overflow
        if (strlen(string) > 200)    return;

        // set the desired foreground color
        ai_fcol(color);

        // set starting text position
        textinfo.position.x = x;    textinfo.position.y = y;

        // copy over the string to the AI parameter block
        strcpy(textinfo.string, string);
        textinfo.length = strlen(textinfo.string) + 4;

        HCHST(&textinfo);        // display the string
    }
```

16.3.7   The Palette

The palette registers for the 8514/A and the XGA are six bits per three colors, as is the case with the VGA. The difference is that the colors are left-justified into each byte for the 8514/A and the XGA while they are right-justified into each byte for the VGA. Thus, the VGA palette values have to be multiplied by four to provide the same values to the 8514/A and the XGA.

16.3.8 Setting up the AI

The code in Listing 16.5 opens the AI for use. The function ai_close() must be called before exiting the program.

LISTING 16.5 Open, Initialize, and Close the Adapter AI

```
unsigned char ai_open(unsigned char mode)
{
    HQDPS(&stateinfo);    // Obtain the size of the state buffer

    //  Allocate memory for the statebuffer with compensation
    //  for non-segment boundary alignment.
    statebuffer = (char *)malloc(stateinfo.datasize + 15);
    if (statebuffer == NULL)    return (1);
    stataddr = (char far *)statebuffer;

    //  Get the buffer segment with compensation for segment
    //  boundary alignment.
        statedata.segment = FP_SEG(stataddr) +
          ((FP_OFF(stataddr) + 15) >> 4);

    //  Initialize the parameters for the HOPEN command. The
    //   HOPEN command opens the AI for use.
    opendata.initflags = 0;
    opendata.mode = mode;
    HOPEN(&opendata);
     //  The return flags should always be checked for an error
     //  condition.
     if (opendata.retflags != 0)  {
        free(statebuffer);
        return(opendata.retflags);
       }

    HINIT(&statedata);       // Obtain the state information
    ai_context();      // set the AI context to a known state
    return(opendata.retflags);
}

// Set hardware to a known state through AI
void ai_context(void)
{
    ai_fcol(LIGHTGRAY);
    ai_bcol(BLACK);
    ai_mix(MIX_SRC, MIX_DST);
}
```

```
// Close down the AI. The function ai_open() must be called
// before this one.
void ai_close(void)
{
    HCLOSE(&closedata);        // Close the AI down
    // release the state buffer memory
    if (statebuffer != 0)    free(statebuffer);
}
```

16.3.9 Markers

A marker is a rectangular bit-mapped object, generally used in animation as sprite objects. Markers can be defined, or displayed at either the current or at an absolute display location. It is defined as a single bit pattern. If it is a monochrome bit-map, the typical foreground and background colors are used. If it is a color bit-map, an additional color table is provided where each pixel is represented with a color. The color table is a byte-per-pixel table for the 8514/A and it can be specified in a packed format. One marker can be current at a time.

The marker is first defined by the definition variables used in the Set Marker Symbol command, HSMARK. This includes the width and height, color, and flags. In addition, the bit pattern and color patterns are also defined. Next, the marker is displayed at a specified position using the HMRK command. This position may be generated by the mouse for interactive motion of the sprite.

16.3.10 Drawing Lines

Lines are specified by their width, color, and pattern. The patterns specify whether the line is solid or contains a pattern of dashes and dots. The line may be one, two, or three pixels wide.

16.3.11 BitBlts

Bit Block transfers can be from system memory to display memory, BitBlt Write, or from display memory to system memory, BitBlt Read. In addition, a BitBlt Copy transfers data from one location in display memory to another. The Copy command is a direct command while the Read and Write commands simply set up the parameters. It is necessary to issue a BitBlt Chain command to actually move the data.

16.3.12 Filling an Area

The AI provides services for filling polygons. However, it takes several commands to actually perform this operation. The Begin Area command, HBAR, begins the sequence. A figure is then defined by using a polyline type command. This is typically done in off-screen memory. This figure must be closed. If the

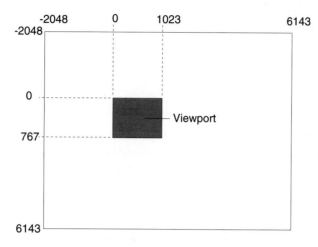

FIGURE 16.4 AI Coordinate System

application doesn't close it, the AI will. The Fill operation occurs when the End Area command, HEAR, is issued.

16.3.13 Coordinate System

The coordinate system ranges from −2048 to 6143 in each of the horizontal and vertical dimensions. A typical example is shown in Figure 16.4 when a 1024-by-768 screen resolution is active.

16.4 DATA STRUCTURES

Several data structures are associated with the command interface. The data structure associated with each command is provided with the command description in Sections 16.5 through 16.14. General data structures are listed in the following sections.

16.4.1 Specifying a Coordinate

A coordinate consists of a horizontal and vertical parameter specifying the point in X-Y space. This coordinate is commonly referred to as P0. It is two words wide. The first word specifies the X coordinate and the second word specifies the Y coordinate. Absolute and relative coordinates are specified in the following code.

```
// Data Structure for absolute coordinates
typedef struct  {
    unsigned int x;              // Absolute x and y values
    unsigned int y;
} coord;
```

```
// Data Structure for relative coordinates
typedef struct {
    char x;                         // Relative x and y values
    char y;
} rcoord;
```

16.4.2   Font Specifications

The font structures are described with four data structures. One is a pointer structure to two others. The other three describe the character set definitions, the character set file definitions, and the character set itself.

```
// Data structure defining the character set definition flags
typedef struct {
    int   reserved1    : 13; // reserved
    int   proportional : 1;  // 1 - proportional spaced
                             // 0 - fixed spaced
    int   color        : 1;  // 1 - color

                             // 0 - monochrome
    int   reserved2    : 1;  // reserved
} CharDefinitionFlags;
```

The font file header has five code pages, with character strings dedicated to each page as shown next. The actual font file header is also shown.

```
// Data structure defining the character set font file header
typedef struct  {
    short  npages;         // number of Code Pages
    short  defaultpage;    // index of the default code page
    short  altpage;        // index of the alternate default page
    struct    {
        char codepageid[4]; // code page id 4-character id
                            // string [0] = '437',0
                            //        [1]= '850',0 [2]= '860',0
                            //        [3]= '863',0 [4]= '865',0
        int csdoffset;    // offset within the disk file of this
                          // selected code page
        } pagearray[5];
} CharSetFileDef;

// Data structure that describes the character set definition
// block
typedef struct {
    unsigned char reserved1; // reserved
    unsigned char fonttype;  // font type 0 - Bitmapped
                             //           3 - Short stroke vector
    long reserved2;          // reserved
    unsigned char reserved3;    // reserved
```

```
    unsigned char cellwidth;        // width of character set
    unsigned char cellheight;       // height of character set
    unsigned char reserved4;        // reserved
    int bytesperchar;               // character area in bytes
    CharDefinitionFlags flags;      // flags - see above
    int far *indextable;            // index table offset
    unsigned char far *proptable;   // proportional table offset
    unsigned char firstchar;        // ascii value of first char
    unsigned char lastchar;         // ascii value of last char
    unsigned char far *chardef1;    // character definition 1
    int  reserved5;                 // reserved
    unsigned char far *chardef2;    // character definition 2
    int  reserved6;                 // reserved
    unsigned char far *chardef3;    // character definition 3
} CharSetDef;

// Data structure used to point to the font set
typedef struct  {
    CharSetDef *fontptr; // pointer to character set definition
                         // structure
    CharSetFileDef *fontaddr;  // pointer to character set file
                               // definition structure
} FontSetInfo;
```

16.4.3   Color Definitions

Commonly used 4- and 8-bit-per-pixel colors are defined in Table 16.10 and Table 16.11. These definitions are only applicable when the standard palette colors occupy the first sixteen locations of the palette.

TABLE 16.10   4-bit-per-color Character Attributes

Directive	Name	Value
#define	B4_RED	0x000CL
#define	B4_GREEN	0x000AL
#define	B4_BLUE	0x0009L
#define	B4_WHITE	(B4_RED | B4_GREEN | B4_BLUE)
#define	B4_CYAN	(B4_GREEN | B4_BLUE)
#define	B4_YELLO	(B4_RED | B4_GREEN)
#define	B4_MAGEN	(B4_RED | B4_BLUE)
#define	B4_R0	0x004L
#define	B4_B0	0x001L
#define	B4_G0	0x002L
#define	B4_IN	0x008L

TABLE 16.11 8-bit-per-color Character Attributes

Directive	Name	Value
#define	B8_RED	0x0049L
#define	B8_GREEN	0x0092L
#define	B8_BLUE	0x0024L
#define	B8_WHITE	(B8_RED | B8_GREEN | B8_BLUE)
#define	B8_CYAN	(B8_GREEN | B8_BLUE)
#define	B8_YELLO	(B8_RED | B8_GREEN)
#define	B8_MAGEN	(B8_RED | B8_BLUE)
#define	B8_R0	0x001L
#define	B8_R1	0x008L
#define	B8_R2	0x040L
#define	B8_B0	0x004L
#define	B8_B1	0x020L
#define	B8_G0	0x002L
#define	B8_G1	0x010L
#define	B8_G2	0x080L

The color data structure uses a 32-bit-per-pixel definition as follows:

```
typedef struct  {
    unsigned char red;          // red value
    unsigned char blue;         // blue value
    unsigned char green;        // green value
    unsigned char reserved;     // reserved (overlay)
} AI_RGB;
```

16.4.4 Character Attributes

The character attribute definitions are provided in Table 16.12. These can of course be ORed together to form combinations of attributes.

TABLE 16.12 Character Attributes

Directive	Name	Value	Description
#define	AI_FONT_NUM_M	0x03	// font selection mask
#define	AI_FONT_NUM_O	0x00	// offset
#define	AI_BG_TRANSPARENT_F	0x10	// background transparent
#define	AI_OVERSTRIKE_F	0x20	// over strike
#define	AI_REVERSE_F	0x40	// reverse video
#define	AI_UNDERLINE_F	0x80	// underline

16.4.5 Color Attributes

The definitions describing the foreground and offset masks are shown in Table 16.13.

TABLE 16.13 Color Attributes

Directive	Name	Value	Description
#define	FG_COLOR_M	0x0f	// foreground mask
#define	FG_COLOR_O	0x00	// offset
#define	BK_COLOR_M	0xf0	// background mask
#define	BK_COLOR_O	0x04	// offset

16.4.6 CGA Character Attribute Descriptions

The CGA character attributes rely on a 16-bit word for each character. The first byte is the ASCII code, and the second byte is the color.

```
typedef struct  {
    char        ascii; // ascii character code
    char    color; // color
} CGACharDescription;
```

16.4.7 MFI Character Attribute Descriptions

The MFI character attributes rely on a 32-bit word for each character. The first byte is the ASCII code, and the remaining three bytes are the color, character attribute, and a reserved byte.

```
typedef struct  {
    char          ascii;           // ASCII character code
    unsigned char color;           // color attributes
    unsigned char attr;            // character attributes
    unsigned char  reserved;       // reserved byte
} MFICharDescription;
```

16.5 SETUP COMMANDS

The setup commands allow the application to engage and disengage the graphics hardware and software. Included are opening and closing the adapter and setting up the palette. This is necessary since the adapter may have a Super VGAs co-resident and it might be necessary to enable or disable the VGA.

16.5.1 Open Adapter HOPEN

This opens the adapter for use with the adapter interface software and puts the adapter into a ready state allowing it to accept further commands. The parameters for this call are described in Table 16.14.

TABLE 16.14 Parameters for HOPEN Command

Name	Bytes	Description
Length	1,0	Length of parameter block
Flag	2	Initialization flags
		bit 7 Clear bit planes
		0 - no clear 1 - clear bit planes
		bit 6 Load default palette
		0 - load default palette 1 - don't load default
Mode	3	Mode definitions (See Table 16.15)
Return code	4	Return Code
		bit 7 driver hardware mismatch
		0 = adapter found 1 = no adapter

The alphanumeric cell size and the screen size are part of the screen mode names listed in Table 16.15. The initialization flags and the Return Code flag definitions are listed in Tables 16.16 and 16.17 respectively.

TABLE 16.15 Mode Definitions

Directive	Name	Bytes	Description
#define	AC12x20in1024x768	0	// 12x20 character set in 1024x768
#define	AC8x14in640x480	1	// 8x14 character set in 640x480
#define	AC8x14in1024x768	2	// 8x14 character set in 1024x768
#define	AC7x15in1024x768	3	// 7x15 character set in 1024x768

TABLE 16.16 Init Flags Definitions

Directive	Name	Bytes	Description
#define	AI_DEF_PALETTE_F	0x40	// 0 - load default palette
			// 1 - don't load default
#define	AI_CLR_PLANES_F	0x80	// 0 - no clear
			// 1 - clear bitplanes

TABLE 16.17 Return Flags Definitions

Directive	Name	Bytes	Description
#define	AI_MISMATCH_F	0x80	// 0 - adaptor // 1 - no adaptor

```
// Command Data Structure
typedef struct  {
    unsigned int  length;           // length of following data
    unsigned char initflags;        // caller setable flags
    unsigned char mode;             // mode
    unsigned char retflags;         // return flags
} HOPEN_DATA;     // Open the adapter for use.
```

16.5.2 Close Adapter HCLOSE

This closes out the adapter. It excludes usage of all subsequent AI commands, and puts the adapter into its quiescent state. The parameters for this call are described in Table 16.18.

TABLE 16.18 Parameters for HCLOSE Command

Name	Bytes	Description
Length	1,0	Length of parameter block
Return code	2	Return Code

```
// Command Data Structure
typedef struct {
    unsigned int  length;           // length of following data
    unsigned int  retflags;         // return flags
} HCLOSE_DATA;           // Close the adapter session.
```

16.5.3 Load Palette HLDPAL

This command loads a palette into the color lookup table. The palette may be specified to be the default palette or a user-defined palette. The starting index, number of entries, and address of the palette in system memory are provided. The parameters for this call are described in Table 16.19 and the palette definitions are provided in Table 16.20.

TABLE 16.19 Parameters for HLDPAL Command

Name	Bytes	Description
Length	1,0	Length of Parameter Block
Index	5,4	Starting palette number
Count	7,6	Number of entries to load
Address	11–8	Address of palette entries in system memory

TABLE 16.20 Palette Definitions

Directive	Name	Value	Description
#define	LOAD_USER_PALETTE	0	// load the user palette
#define	LOAD_DEFAULT_PALETTE	1	// load the default palette

```
// Command Data Structure
typedef struct  {
    unsigned int  length;          // length of following data
    unsigned char palid;           // palette id
    unsigned char reserved;        // reserved
    unsigned int  first;           // index of first entry
    unsigned int  nentries;        // the number of entries
    AI_RGB far *palette;           // palette table
} HLDPAL_DATA;    // Load a palette into the color lookup table.
```

16.5.4   Save Palette HSPAL

This command sets aside memory and saves the current color palette and display mask. The palette is saved from possible corruption. The palette can be restored using the HRPAL restore command. The size of the palette can be obtained if the palette needs to be used through the HQDPS call stored in the P_SIZE field. The parameters for this call are described in Table 16.21.

TABLE 16.21 Parameters for HSPAL Command

Name	Bytes	Description
LEN	1,0	Length of parameter block
DATA	770–2	Buffer containing the palette and display mask

```
// Command Data Structure
typedef struct  {
    unsigned int  length;          // length of following data
    AI_RGB palette[256];           // palette table
} HSPAL_DATA;        // Save the palette.
```

16.5.5   Restore Palette HRPAL

This command restores the palette and display mask as previously saved by the HSPAL command. The size of the palette can be obtained if the palette needs to be used through the HQDPS call stored in the P_SIZE field. The parameters for this call are described in Table 16.22.

TABLE 16.22 Parameters for HRPAL Command

Name	Bytes	Description
LEN	1,0	Length of parameter block
DATA	770–2	Buffer containing the palette and display mask

```
// Command Data Structure
typedef struct  {
    unsigned int  length;          // length of following data
    AI_RGB palette[256];           // palette table
} HRPAL_DATA;  //  Restore a previously saved palette
```

16.6   CONTROL COMMANDS

The control commands allow the application to control the graphics environment. Included are setting of interrupts, escape processing, the background and color comparison color, the foreground and background mix, and the assigning of text colors.

16.6.1   Interrupt HINT

This command synchronizes the adapter with a hardware event or interrupt and returns control to the application when the requested interrupt or event has occurred. The application should set bits in the interrupt/event identifier to indicate which events should cause the command to complete. The adapter is responsible for clearing all but the event bit after the event has occurred. This command is not widely supported due to the problems involving compatibility in the PC interrupt logic. The vertical blanking interrupt is stable. The parameters for this call are described in Table 16.23.

TABLE 16.23 Parameters for HINIT Command

Name	Bytes	Description
LEN	1–0	Length of parameter block
DATA	5–2	Interrupt/event identifier; the data block is four bytes long, consisting of 32 bits bit 31 Wait for vertical blanking

```
// Data structure
typedef struct  {
    unsigned reserved  : 15;   // reserved
    unsigned vertblank  : 1;   // 0 - !wait for vert Blank
                               // 1 - wait for vert blank
} AI_Interrupt;

// Command Data Structure
typedef struct  {
    unsigned int length;          // length of following data
    unsigned int reserved;        // reserved
    AI_Interrupt intselected;     // interrupt selection
} HINT_DATA;   // Wait for event or interrupt.
```

16.6.2 Set Graphics Quality HSGQ

This command sets the graphics parameters surrounding the quality of output to the display. There are two commands in this command. The first regards precision and the second involves the last PEL drawn. The precision portion of this command is not typically used. It was intended to allow the fast rendering of low-quality lines. Today, however, most adapters draw high-quality lines as fast as low-quality lines. Consequently, the quality portion of this command has little in any value. The parameters for this call are described in Table 16.24.

TABLE 16.24 Parameters for HSGQ Command

Name	Bytes	Description
LEN	1–0	Length of parameter block.
QUALITY	3–2	Quality settings bit 14 precision 0=low 1=high 12,11 Last pel code 0= last pel not drawn, 1=last pel drawn, 2=last pel conditional on overpainting and/or mixes. Polylines drawn in other mixes are adapter dependent approximations.

```
// Data structure describing the Graphics Quality
typedef struct {
    unsigned int  reserved1 : 10; // reserved
    unsigned int  closeflag  : 1; // area closure flag
                                   // 0 - close areas to be
                                   //    filled by drawing a line
                                   //    from the first point
                                   //    to the last point.
                                   // 1 - don't close areas to be
                                   //    filled.
    unsigned int  peltype    : 2; // pel
                                   // 0 - last PEL null (not drawn)
                                   // 1 - last PEL drawn
                                   // 2 - last PEL conditional on
                                   //    Overpaint/AND/OR mixes
    unsigned int  reserved2 : 1; // reserved
    unsigned int  precision : 1; // 0 - high precision
                                   // 1 - low precision
    unsigned int  reserved3 : 1; // reserved
} GraphicsQuality;

// Command Data Structure
typedef struct {
    unsigned int  length;          // length of following data
    GraphicsQuality quality;        // the graphics quality
} HSGQ_DATA;      // Set graphics quality information.
```

16.6.3 Set Coordinate Type HSCOORD

This sets the current coordinate type and number of dimensions for a point in coordinate space, including the number of bytes in each absolute or relative coordinate and the number of fraction bytes in each absolute or relative coordinate. The parameters for this call are described in Table 16.25.

TABLE 16.25 Parameters for HSCOORD Command

Name	Bytes	Description
LEN	1–0	Length of parameter block.
FORMAT	2	Coordinates format bits 7–4 Number of bytes in each coordinate bits 3–0 Number of fraction bytes in each coordinate
R_FORMAT	3	Relative coordinate format bits 7–4 Number of bytes in each relative coordinated bits 3–0 Number of fraction bytes in each relative coordinate
DIMEN	4	Number of dimension (2, 3 or 4).

```
// Command Data Structure
typedef struct  {
    unsigned int  length;        // length of following data
    unsigned char absolute;      // absolute coordinate format
    unsigned char relative;      // relative coordinate format
    unsigned char dimension;     // dimension:  2, 3 or 4
} HSCOORD_DATA;        //     Set coordinate type
```

16.6.4   Escape, Terminate Processing HESC

This command terminates any drawing operation that the graphics adapter is still executing. Some adapters stop immediately; others finish the current operation. The parameters for this call are described in Table 16.26.

TABLE 16.26 Parameters for HESC Command

Name	Bytes	Description
LEN	1–0	Length of parameter block = 0

16.6.5   Set Background Color HSBCOL

This command sets the background color index as specified by the INDEX color field. The parameters for this call are described in Table 16.27.

TABLE 16.27 Parameters for HSBCOL Command

Name	Bytes	Description
LEN	1–0	Length of parameter block
INDEX	5–2	Color index of background

```
// Command Data Structure
typedef struct  {
    unsigned int  length;        // length of following data
    unsigned long color;         // color index
} HSBCOL_DATA;  //  Set the background color.
```

16.6.6   Set Bit Plane Controls HSBP

This command selects and de-selects bit planes for future updating of the display. There are two types of bitmaps and they update and display bit masks. Bit masks are used for both graphics and alphanumeric modes. These specify which planes are updated under the drawing mix. Other planes are unmodified. Displaying bit masks specify which planes are enabled for display. The corresponding data is provided to the color output display section (Color DAC). All planes masked out provide a zero value to the DAC. The parameters for this call are described in Table 16.28.

TABLE 16.28 Parameters for HSBP Command

Name	Bytes	Description
LEN	1–0	Length of parameter block
G_MASK	5–2	Updating bit mask used for graphics modes
A_MASK	9–6	Updating bit mask used for alphanumerics modes
DACMASK	13–10	Display bit mask

```
// Command Data Structure
typedef struct {
    unsigned int  length;        // length of following data
    unsigned long graphics;      // planes selected for update
                                 // graphics mask
    unsigned long alphaNum;      // planes selected for update
                                 // alphanumerics mask
    unsigned long planesenable;  // planes enabled to index the
                                 // color palette
} HSBP_DATA;    // Enable/disable bit planes for updating and
                // displaying.
```

16.6.7 Set Color Comparison Register HSCMP

This command sets the color comparison register with the value in the CMPCOL field. It also sets the logic command associated with the comparison as indicated in the COMMAND field. The parameters for this call are described in Table 16.29.

TABLE 16.29 Parameters for HSCMP Command

Name	Bytes	Description
LEN	1–0	Length of parameter block.
CMPCOL	5–2	Comparison color
COMMAND	6	Logic command
		00 Always true 04 Always false
		01 Plane data > comparison 05 Plane data > = comparison
		02 Plane data = comparison 06 Plane data = comparison
		03 Plane data < comparison 07 Plane data < = comparison

TABLE 16.30 Definitions for the COMMAND Parameter

Directive	Name	Bytes	Description
#define	CMPOP_TRUE	0	// always TRUE
#define	CMPOP_GT	1	// Plane data > compare value
#define	CMPOP_EQ	2	// Plane data == compare value
#define	CMPOP_LT	3	// Plane data < compare value
#define	CMPOP_FALSE	4	// always FALSE
#define	CMPOP_GE	5	// Plane data >= compare value
#define	CMPOP_NE	6	// Plane data != compare value
#define	CMPOP_LE	7	// Plane data <= compare value

```
typedef struct   {
    unsigned int  length;          // length of following data
    unsigned long color;           // compare color
    unsigned char cmpop;            // compare operand
} HSCMP_DATA;      // Set Color compare information.
```

16.6.8   Set Color HSCOL

This command sets the foreground color index as specified by the INDEX color field. The parameters for this call are described in Table 16.31.

TABLE 16.31 Parameters for HSCOL Command

Name	Bytes	Description
LEN	1–0	Length of parameter block
INDEX	5–2	Color index of foreground

```
// Command Data Structure
typedef struct  {
    unsigned int  length;          // length of following data
    unsigned long color;           // color index
} HSCOL_DATA;   // Set the foreground color
```

16.6.9   Set Scissors HSHS

This command sets the scissors rectangle to the specified locations. If it is not specified, then the scissors rectangle is set to its default values. The parameters for this call are described in Table 16.32.

TABLE 16.32 Parameters for HSHS Command

Name	Bytes	Description
LEN	1–0	Length of parameter block
L_LIMIT	3–2	Left limit of rectangle
R_LIMIT	5–4	Right limit of rectangle
B_LIMIT	7–6	Bottom limit of rectangle
T_LIMIT	9–8	Top limit of rectangle

```
// Command Data Structure
typedef struct  {
    unsigned int  length;   // length of following data
    unsigned int  left;     // left limit of rectangle
    unsigned int  right;    // right limit of rectangle
    unsigned int  bottom;   // bottom limit of rectangle
    unsigned int  top;      // top limit of rectangle
} HSHS_DATA;  // Set the clipping rectangle (scissor setting).
```

16.6.10 Set Mix HMIX

This command sets the foreground and background current mix values. The AND/OR/XOR/NOT operations are bit-by-bit binary operations. The parameters for this call are described in Table 16.33.

TABLE 16.33 Parameters for HMIX Command

Name	Bytes	Description
LEN	1–0	Length of parameter block
F_MIX	2	Foreground mix
B_MIX	3	Background mix

The most common mixes for the foreground and background are listed in Table 16.34. In addition, some useful constants are defined in Table 16.35.

TABLE 16.34 Common Foreground and Mix Values

Value	Description
0	Retain previous mix
1	Source OR Destination

(continued)

TABLE 16.34 *(cont.)*

Value	Description
2	Select Source
4	Source AND Destination
5	Leave alone
6	Maximum of Source and destination
7	Minimum of Source and destination
8	Add Source + Destination (with clipping)
9	Subtract Destination − Source (with clipping to 0)
A	Subtract Source − Destination (with clipping to 0)
B	Average (Source + destination)/2
10	Zero all bits cleared
11	Source AND Destination

TABLE 16.35 Useful Foreground and Mix Constants

Directive	Name	Value	Description
#define	MIX_RETAIN	0	// retain previous mix
#define	MIX_SRC_OR_DST	1	// src | dst
#define	MIX_SRC	2	// src
#define	MIX_SRC_XOR_DST	4	// src ^ dst
#define	MIX_DST	5	// dst (leave alone)
#define	MIX_MAX_SRC_DST	6	// max(src, dst)
#define	MIX_MIN_SRC_DST	7	// min(src, dst)
#define	MIX_SRC_PLUS_DST	8	// src + dst
#define	MIX_DST_MINUS_SRC	9	// dst − src
#define	MIX_SRC_MINUS_DST	10	// src − dst
#define	MIX_AVG_SRC_DST	11	// (src + dst) / 2
#define	MIX_CLEAR	16	// dst = 0
#define	MIX_SRC_AND_DST	17	// src & dst
#define	MIX_SRC_AND_NOT_DST	18	// src & ~dst
#define	MIX_SRC_B	19	// src
#define	MIX_NOT_SRC_AND_DST	20	// src & ~dst
#define	MIX_DST_B	21	// dst (leave alone)
#define	MIX_SRC_XOR_DST_B	22	// src ^ dst

TABLE 16.35 *(cont.)*

Directive	Name	Value	Description
#define	MIX_SRC_OR_DST_B	23	// src | dst
#define	MIX_NOT_SRC_AND_NOT_DST	24	// ~src & ~dst
#define	MIX_NOT_SRC_XOR_DST	25	// ~(src ^ dst)
#define	MIX_NOT_DST	26	// ~dst
#define	MIX_SRC_OR_NOT_DST	27	// src | ~dst)
#define	MIX_NOT_SRC	28	// ~src
#define	MIX_NOT_SRC_OR_DST	29	// ~src | dst
#define	MIX_NOT_SRC_OR_NOT_DST	30	// ~src | ~dst
#define	MIX_ALL_ON	31	// dst = ~0 (all bits one)

```
// Command Data Structure
typedef struct  {
    unsigned int  length;          // length of following data
    unsigned char fgmix;           // foreground mix
    unsigned char bkmix;           // background mix
} HSMX_DATA;    // Set a mix type.
```

16.6.11   Assign Text Color HXLATE

This command provides a means for specifying a multi-plane text color. Thirty-two bytes of data specify the indexes. Three planes are involved (red, green, and blue). The table address is derived from the 3-bit code contained in planes 2–0. Each pixel is either a 0 or a 1 in each of the three planes. Thus, there are eight combinations for each pixel. This provides up to four bytes of color index value for each pixel. Table 16.36 illustrates the addressing. Table 16.37 contains the parameters to this command.

TABLE 16.36 Color Index Addressing into TABLE

Plane 2	Plane 1	Plane 0	Address	Byte
0	0	0	0	0
0	0	1	1	4
0	1	0	2	8
1	1	1	7	28

TABLE 16.37 Parameters for HXLATE Command

Name	Bytes	Description
LEN	1–0	Length of parameter block
TABLE	33-2	Color index table

```
// Command Data Structure
typedef struct  {
    unsigned int  length;          // length of following data
    unsigned char xlatetable[32];   // translate table
} HXLATE_DATA;  // Set a translation table for multicolor text
font.
```

16.7   QUERY COMMANDS

The query commands allow the application to determine the state of the graphics environment. Included are determining the current mode, the possible display modes, the coordinate types, the default palette, and the current position.

16.7.1   Get Current Mode HQMODE

This command returns data regarding the current adapter mode and configuration. The returned data is organized in the buffer included in the parameters. Table 16.38 contains the parameters to this command.

TABLE 16.38 Parameters for HQMODE Command

Name	Bytes	Description
LEN	1–0	Length of parameter block
MODE	2	Current display mode number
VERSION	4–3	Driver version number
TYPE	5	Adapter type
A_WIDTH	7	Character cell width
A_HEIGHT	8	Character cell height
PLANES	9	Number of bit planes
S_WIDTH	11–10	Screen width (PELS)
S_HEIGHT	13–12	Screen height (PELS)
H_RES	15–14	Horizontal resolution (PELS/INCH)
V_RES	17–16	Vertical resolution (PELS/INCH)
COLOR	18	00 hex = Monochrome or FF hex = Color
INTENSITY	19	Intensity levels

The MODE data is specified in Table 16.39.

TABLE 16.39 Mode Values

Mode	Cell Size	Resolution
0	12x20	1024x768
1	8x14	640x480
2	8x14	1024x768
3	7x15	1024x768

The VERSION information is specified in Table 16.40.

TABLE 16.40 VERSION Information

Bit	Description
6	1=80286/8086 CPU
5	0=4-plane minimum 1=8-planes
4–0	Current release number of adapter hardware

The supported Adapter Types are listed in Table 16.41.

TABLE 16.41 Supported Adapter Types

Directive	Name	Value	Description
#define	AI_8514_TYPE	3	// 8514 card
#define	AI_XGA_TYPE	4	// XGA card

```
// Command Data Structure
typedef struct  {
    unsigned int  length;       // length of following data
    unsigned char mode;         // current display mode
    unsigned int  drivercode;   // version information
    unsigned char adapter;      // adaptor type - should be set
    unsigned char displaytype;  // display type - reserved
    unsigned char cellwidth;    // horizontal size of character
    unsigned char cellheight;   // vertical size of character
    unsigned char nplanes;      // number of bit planes
    unsigned int  screenwidth;  // width of the screen
    unsigned int  screenheight; // height of the screen
    unsigned int  hres;         // PELs per inch - horizontally
```

```
    unsigned int  vres;          //  PELs per inch - vertically
    unsigned char color;         //  (0x00) mono or(0xFF) color
    unsigned char intensity;     //  intensity levels
} HQMODE_DATA;    // Query the current mode and configuration.
```

16.7.2   Get Adapter Modes HQMODES

This command returns information on the adapter and number of display modes supported. Data is returned to TYPE and INTENSITY fields in the parameter block. Up to 33 bytes should be reserved for returning data. The last byte is indicated by a FF hex. The parameters for this call are described in Table 16.42.

TABLE 16.42 Parameters for the HQMODES Command

Name	Bytes	Description
LEN	1–0	Length of parameter block
TYPE	2	Adapter type
MODES	34–3	Display modes available

```
// Command Data Structure
typedef struct  {
    unsigned int  length;        // length of following data
    unsigned char type;          // adapter type - should be set
                                 // to 3 after call returns
    unsigned char modes[32];     // display modes available
} HQMODES_DATA;                  // Query available modes.
```

16.7.3   Get Drawing Process State Size HQDPS

This command returns the size requirement of the task-dependent state data area. It includes the maximum sizes for data buffer, stack usage by the AI driver, and palette contents to be saved. The parameters for this call are described in Table 16.43.

TABLE 16.43 Parameters for the HQDPS Command

Name	Bytes	Description
LEN	1–0	Length of parameter block.
D_SIZE	3–2	Data buffer size in bytes
STACK	5–4	Stack size in bytes
P_SIZE	7–6	Save palette buffer size in bytes

```
// Command Data Structure
typedef struct  {
    unsigned int  length;          // length of following data
    unsigned int  datasize;        // data buffer size
    unsigned int  stacksize;       // stack size
    unsigned int  savepalettesize; // save palette buffer
} HQDPS_DATA;    // Query the task state and driver stack usage
                 // sizes.
```

16.7.4 Get Default Palette HQDFPAL

This command returns information including the sixteen color index entries. Each 4-byte entry is an index to a specified color in the default palette (also called Color Registers). Each returned value ranges between 0 and 255 indicating the specified colors in the default palette. The parameters for this call are described in Table 16.44.

TABLE 16.44 Parameters for the HQDFPAL Command

Name	Bytes	Description
LEN	1–0	Length of parameter block
DATA	65–2	Color index values

The default palette is repeated in Table 16.45 for convenience.

TABLE 16.45 Default Palette Colors

Index	Color	Index	Color
0	Black	8	Gray
1	Blue	9	Light blue
2	Green	A	Light green
3	Cyan	B	Light cyan
4	Red	C	Light red
5	Magenta	D	Light magenta
6	Brown	E	Yellow
7	White	F	High intensity white

```
// Command Data Structure
typedef struct  {
    unsigned int  length;            // length of following data
    unsigned char colorindextable[16];  // color index table
} HQDFPAL_DATA;   // Query the default palette.
```

16.7.5   Get Coordinate Type HQCOORD

This command verifies support for a coordinate type. It examines the contents of the input parameters FORMAT, R_FORMAT, and DIMEN and stores the test results in RESULT. The parameters for this call are described in Table 16.46.

TABLE 16.46   Parameters for the HQCOORD Command

Name	Bytes	Description
LEN	1–0	Length of parameter block
FORMAT	2	Coordinates format bits 7–4 Number of bytes in each coordinate bits 3–0 Number of fraction bytes in each coordinate
R_FORMAT	3	Relative coordinate format bits 7–4 Number of bytes in each relative coordinate bits 3–0 Number of fraction bytes in each relative coordinate
DIMEN	4	Dimensions (2, 3 or 4 dimensions)

RESULT	5	Returned test results
		bit 7 0=Coordinate format supported
		        1=Not supported
		bit 6 0=Relative coordinate format supported
		        1=Not supported
		bit 5 0=Specified dimension supported
		        1=Not supported

Some useful coordinate format values and results are provided in Table 16.47 and Table 16.48, respectively.

TABLE 16.47   Coordinate Format Definitions

Directive	Name	Value	Description
#define	AICOORD_FRAC_BYTES_M	0x0f	// fractional bytes
#define	AICOORD_FRAC_BYTES_O	0x00	
#define	AICOORD_NBYTES_M	0xf0	// number of bytes
#define	AICOORD_NBYTES_O	0x04	

TABLE 16.48   Coordinate Result Definitions

Directive	Name	Value	Description
#define	DIMENSION_F	0x20	// Specified dimension supported
#define	REL_COORD_F	0x40	// Relative coordinates supported
#define	ABS_COORD_F	0x80	// Absolute coordinates supported

```
// Command Data Structure
typedef struct  {
    unsigned int  length;        // length of following data
    unsigned char absolute;      // absolute coordinate format
    unsigned char relative;      // relative coordinate format
    unsigned char dimension;     // dimension:  2, 3 or 4
    unsigned char result;        // result of query
} HQCOORD_DATA;     //  Query the coordinate types.
```

16.7.6 Get Current Position HQCP

This command gets the current position coordinates. The parameters for this call are described in Table 16.49.

TABLE 16.49 Parameters for the HQCP Command

Name	Bytes	Description
LEN	1–0	Length of parameter block
PO	5–2	Coordinate data

```
// Command Data Structure
typedef struct   {
    unsigned int length;         // length of following data
    unsigned int x;              // current position returned
    unsigned int y;
} HQCP_DATA;    // Query the current position.
```

16.8 STATE CONTROL COMMANDS

The state control commands initialize the state buffer, synchronize the adapter, and change the mode.

16.8.1 Initialize State HINIT

This command initializes the task state buffer to an initial state. The initial state is defined by adapter implementation. The parameters for this call are described in Table 16.50.

TABLE 16.50 Parameters for the HINIT Command

Name	Bytes	Description
LEN	1–0	Length of parameter block
SEGMENT	3–2	Segment of the task buffer ??

```
// Command Data Structure
typedef struct  {
    unsigned int  length;              // length of following data
    unsigned int  segment;             // segment of task buffer
} HINIT_DATA;    //  Initialize task data area.
```

16.8.2   Synchronize Adapter HSYNC

This command sets the adapter state to match the task-dependent stated stored in the task state buffer as pointed to by ADDRESS. It is used to implement task switching in a multi-tasking environment. The parameters for this call are described in Table 16.51.

TABLE 16.51 Parameters for the HSYNC Command

Name	Bytes	Description
LEN	1–0	Length of parameter block
ADDRESS	3–2	Task state buffer

```
// Command Data Structure
typedef struct  {
    unsigned int length;               // length of following data
    unsigned int segment;              // task state buffer
} HSYNC_DATA;    // Synchronize the AI with a task.
```

16.8.3   Change Mode HSMODE

This command sets the adapter display mode. The parameters for this call are described in Table 16.52.

TABLE 16.52 Parameters for the HSMODE Command

Name	Bytes	Description
LEN	1–0	Length of parameter block
MODE	2	Desired adapter mode number

The MODE data is specified in Table 16.53.

TABLE 16.53 Mode Specifications

Mode	Char Cell	Screen Size
0	12x20	1024x768
1	8x14	640x480
2	8x14	1024x768
3	7x15	1024x768

```
// Command Data Structure
typedef struct  {
    unsigned int  length;          // length of following data
    unsigned int  mode;            // mode to set the adaptor
} HSMODE_DATA;   // Set a new mode.
```

16.9   LINE COMMANDS

Line commands allow the drawing of lines, either absolute or relative, between two or more specified points. The starting point might be the current position or specified points. The application can also set the line type, the line width, and the line pattern count. Multiple lines can be drawn with a single command.

16.9.1   Draw Line at Given Position HLINE

This command draws a set of connected lines (polyline) from a starting to a set of ending coordinates. The coordinates are absolute. Up to N lines can be specified in this single command. When all points have been drawn, the current position is then set to the last point specified in the command. Any number of points can be present.

The parameter block size is calculated by 4*(N+1) where N is the number of lines and each coordinate is four bytes long. Recall that there are N+1 points required to draw a N-sided polyline. The parameters for this call are described in Table 16.54.

TABLE 16.54 Parameters for the HLINE Command

Name	Bytes	Description
LEN	1–0	Length of parameter block
P0	5–2	First point
P1,P2,,,PN	6–9,10–13...	Second point, third point, N+1th point

```
// Command Data Structure macro
#define HLINE_DATA(n)                // n - number of points
  struct {
        unsigned int  length;       // length of following data
        coord points[n];            // points defining line
     }  // Draw a polyline starting at the specified position.
```

16.9.2   Draw Line at Current Position HCLINE

This command draws a set of connected lines (polyline) from the current position to a set of ending coordinates. The coordinates are absolute. Up to N lines can be specified in this single command. When all points have been drawn, the current position is then set to the last point specified in the command. Any number of points can be present.

The parameter block size is calculated by 4*N where N is the number of lines and each coordinate is four bytes long. Recall that there are N+1 points required to draw a N-sided polyline; no starting point is required. The parameters for this call are described in Table 16.55.

TABLE 16.55 Parameters for the HCLINE Command

Name	Bytes	Description
LEN	1–0	Length of parameter block
P1,P2,,,PN	2–5,6–9...	Second point, third point, N+1th point

```
// Command Data Structure macro
#define HCLINE_DATA(n)               // n - number of lines
    struct {
        unsigned int  length;       // length of following data
        coord points[n];            // each line's end point
     }  //  Draw a polyline starting at the current postion.
```

16.9.3   Draw Line Relative from Given Position HRLINE

This command draws a set of connected lines (polyline) from a starting to a set of ending coordinates. The coordinates are relative to the current point. These lines are often referred to as short-stroke lines. Each relative offset is a single byte that contains a direction (in increments of 45 degrees) and a length (up to sixteen pixels). Up to N lines can be specified in this single command. When all points have been drawn, the current position is then set to the last point specified in the command. Any number of points can be present.

The parameter block size is calculated by 4*(N+1) where N is the number of lines and each coordinate is four bytes long. Recall that there are N+1 points required to draw an N-sided polyline. The parameters for this call are described in Table 16.56.

TABLE 16.56 Parameters for the HRLINE Command

Name	Bytes	Description
LEN	1–0	Length of parameter block
P0	5–2	First point
OFF1,OFF2,,,OFFN	6–9,10–13...	Second point, third point, N+1th point

```
// Command Data Structure macro
#define HRLINE_DATA(n) struct {   // n - number of lines
    unsigned int  length;         // length of following data
    coord point;                  // start point of lines
    rcoord offsets[n];            // relative lines from first pt
}   // Draw a polyline starting at the specified position with
    // relative coordinates.
```

16.9.4 Draw Line Relative at Current Position HCRLINE

This command draws a set of connected lines (polyline) from the current position to a set of ending coordinates. The coordinates are relative to the current position. These lines are often referred to as short-stroke lines. Each relative offset is a single byte that contains a direction (in increments of 45 degrees) and a length (up to sixteen pixels). Up to N lines can be specified in this single command. When all points have been drawn, the current position is then set to the last point specified in the command. Any number of points can be present.

The parameter block size is calculated by 4+N where N is the number of lines and each coordinate is four bytes long. Recall that there are N+1 points required to draw a N-sided polyline; no starting point is required. The parameters for this call are described in Table 16.57.

TABLE 16.57 Parameters for the HCRLINE Command

Name	Bytes	Description
LEN	1–0	Length of parameter block
OFF1,OFF2,OFFN	2,3,4,...	Second point, third point, N+1th point

```
// Command Data Structure macro
#define HCRLINE_DATA(n)               // n - number of offsets
    struct {
```

```
        unsigned int  length;       // length of following data
        rcoord offsets[n];          // relative offsets
   }  // Draw a polyline starting at the current postion
with relative coordinates
```

16.9.5 Set Line Type HSLT

This command sets the current line type, also referred to as the line style. The parameters for this call are described in Table 16.58.

TABLE 16.58 Parameters for the HSLT Command

Name	Bytes	Description
LEN	1–0	Length of parameter block
TYPE	2	Line type
ADDRESS	7–4	Address of user line-type definition (if required)

The TYPE field codes are in Table 16.59.

TABLE 16.59 Parameters for the HSLT Command

Value	Line Type
0	Load user line type
1	Dotted line (1 pel on, 2 pel off then repeat)
2	Short dashed line (5 pel on, 3 pel off then repeat)
3	Dash-dot line (6 PEL on, 4 PEL off, 2 PEL on, 4 PEL off, then repeat)
4	Double dotted line (2 PEL on, 4 PEL off, 2 PEL on 8 PEL off, then repeat)
5	Long dashed line (9 PEL on, 3 PEL off then repeat)
6	Dashed-double-dot line (8 PEL on, 4 PEL off, 2 PEL on, 4 PEL off, 2 PEL on 4 PEL off, then repeat)
7	Solid line
8	Invisible line

Some useful Line Formats are provided in Table 16.60.

TABLE 16.60 Line Format Definitions

Directive	Name	Value	Description
#define	LOAD_USER_LINE	0	// load user line type
#define	DOTTED_LINE	1	// dotted line
#define	SHORT_DASH_LINE	2	// short dashed line

TABLE 16.60 *(cont.)*

Directive	Name	Value	Description
#define	DASH_DOT_LINE	3	// dash dot line
#define	DOUBLE_DOT_LINE	4	// double dotted line
#define	LONG_DASH_LINE	5	//dashed line
#define	DASH_DOUBLE_DOT_LINE	6	// dash double dot line
#define	SOLID_LINE	7	// solid line
#define	INVISBLE_LINE	8	// invisble line

```
// Data Structure for on-off sequence
typedef struct  {
    unsigned char npelson;        // number of pels on
    unsigned char npelsoff;       // number of pels off
} OnOffSequence;

// Data structure for line pattern
typedef struct  {
    unsigned int  size;           // number of pel Definitions
    OnOffSequence sequence[48];   // on off sequence
} LinePattern;

// Command Data Structure
typedef struct  {
    unsigned int  length;         // length of following data
    unsigned char linetype;       // line type
    unsigned char reserved;       // reserved
    LinePattern far *pattern;     // address of line pattern
} HSLT_DATA;    // Set the line-drawing type.
```

16.9.6   Set Line Width HSLW

This command sets the width of the line. Width values are assumed to be drawn such that the line is equally wide from the line drawn between the specified endpoints. Thus a 3-pixel-wide line drawn from 100, 100 to 200,100 would have lines drawn from 100,99 to 200,99, 100,100 to 200,100 and 100,101 to 200,101. The parameters for this call are described in Table 16.61.

TABLE 16.61 Parameters for the HSLW Command

Name	Bytes	Description
LEN	1–0	Length of parameter block
WIDTH	2	Width of line

```
// Command Data Structure
typedef struct  {
    unsigned int  length;          // length of following data
    unsigned char width;           // line width  <= 1 - width
set to 1  > 1 - width set to 3
} HSLW_DATA;  // Set the line-drawing width.
```

16.9.7   Save Line Pattern Count HSLPC

This command saves the line pattern count. This count enables line continuity of patterned lines that cross scissors boundaries. It uses a ZERO length parameter block since no parameters are required. The parameters for this call are described in Table 16.62.

TABLE 16.62 Parameters for the HSLPC Command

Name	Bytes	Description
LEN	1–0	Length of parameter block = 0

16.9.8   Restore Line Pattern Count HRLPC

This command restores the line pattern count as previously saved by the HSLPC command. This count enables line continuity of patterned lines that cross scissors boundaries. It uses a ZERO length parameter block since no parameters are required. The parameters for this call are described in Table 16.63.

TABLE 16.63 Parameters for the HRLPC Command

Name	Bytes	Description
LEN	1–0	Length of parameter block = 0

16.10   IMAGE BITBLT COMMANDS

The image BitBlt commands allow the rapid movement of rectangular windows into and out of display memory. The read and write commands can be set up and then initiated by a chained data command. The current position or a specified position can act as the starting location of the rectangle.

16.10.1   Write Image Data HBBW

This command defines the start of a rectangular image for bit block transfers (BitBlt) write operations. Data for the image is actually written to the display memory by the HBBCHN command. The transfer operation is terminated when an image command other than HBBCHN is called. It is possible to send a complete rectangle or a sub-rectangle. The sub-rectangle is defined within the main rectangle by the LEFT, TOP, B_WIDTH and B_HEIGHT parameters. The parameters for this call are described in Table 16.64.

TABLE 16.64 Parameters for the HBBW Command

Name	Bytes	Description
LEN	1–0	Length of parameter block
FORMAT	3–2	Format of data
P_WIDTH	5–4	Width of data rectangle
PHEIGHT	7–6	Height of data rectangle
P0	11–8	Left-top coordinates of rectangle in display memory
LEFT	13–12	Sub-rectangle left margin in PELS
TOP	15–14	Sub-rectangle top margin in PELS
M_WIDTH	17–16	Sub-rectangle width
M_HEIGHT	19–18	Sub-rectangle height

The FORMAT field describes whether the BitBlt is across-the-plane or through-the-plane. In the "Across-the-plane" mode, data is always confined to the selected plane. This is often referred to as Color Expansion. In the "Through-the-Plane" mode, data is transferred across the display planes. This field is described in Table 16.65.

TABLE 16.65 Across-the-Plane or Through-the-Plane Values

Value	Description
0	Across-the-plane copy. Data bits are extracted from the source as a monochrome bit map and expanded into the destination. A 1 in the input is expanded to the current color with the current color mix. A 0 in the input is expanded using the background color and background mix.
8	Through-the-plane copy. Data bits are copied from the source to the destination as packed pixels.

It should be noted that there are two forms of the parameter block. One is a short form, consisting of no sub-rectangle. This limits the parameter block to a length of 10. Remember to not count the two bytes of length. The long form includes the sub-rectangle and is eighteen bytes long. Constant definitions for these two forms are provided in Table 16.66.

TABLE 16.66 Parameter Block Length Definitions

Directive	Name	Value	Description
#define	HBBW_LS	10	// short form length
#define	HBBW_L	18	// long form length

```
// Data Structure
typedef struct {
    unsigned int  length;          // length of following data
    unsigned int  format;          // bit block format
    unsigned int  width;           // block width in pixels
    unsigned int  height;          // block height in lines
    unsigned int  destination_x;   // dst top left corner
    unsigned int  destination_y;
    unsigned int  source_x;        // src top left corner
    unsigned int  source_y;
    unsigned int  source_pitch;    // margin size of source
    unsigned int  source_height;
} HBBW_DATA;   // Write image data to board (BitBlt write).
```

16.10.2 Read Image Data HBBR

This command defines the start of a rectangular image for bit block transfers (BitBlt) read operations. Data for the image is actually read from the display memory by the HBBCHN command. The transfer operation is terminated when any image command other than HBBCHN is called. It is possible to read a complete rectangle or a sub-rectangle. The sub-rectangle is defined within the main rectangle by the LEFT, TOP, B_WIDTH and B_HEIGHT parameters. The parameters for this call are described in Table 16.67.

TABLE 16.67 Parameters for the HBBR Command

Name	Bytes	Description
LEN	1–0	Length of parameter block
FORMAT	3–2	Format of data
P_WIDTH	5–4	Width of data rectangle
PHEIGHT	7–6	Height of data rectangle
SRC_P_NO	8	Source bit plane number
P0	13–10	Left-top coordinates of rectangle in display memory
LEFT	15–14	Sub-rectangle left margin in PELS
TOP	17–16	Sub-rectangle top margin in PELS
M_WIDTH	19–18	Sub-rectangle width
M_HEIGHT	21–20	Sub-rectangle height

The FORMAT field describes whether the BitBlt is across-the-plane or through-the-plane. In the "Across-the-plane" mode, data is always confined to the selected plane. This is often referred to as Color Expansion. In the "Through-the-Plane" mode, data is transferred across the display planes. This field is described in Table 16.68.

TABLE 16.68 Across-the-Plane or Through-the-Plane Values

Value	Description
0	Across-the-plane copy. Data bits are extracted from the source as a monochrome bit map and expanded into the destination. A 1 in the input is expanded to the current color with the current color mix. A 0 in the input is expanded using the background color and background mix.
8	Through-the-plane copy. Data bits are copied from the source to the destination as packed pixels.

It should be noted that there are two forms of the parameter block. One is a short form, consisting of no sub-rectangle. This limits the parameter block to a length of 10. Remember to not count the two bytes of length. The long form includes the sub-rectangle and is eighteen bytes long. Constant definitions for these two forms are provided in Table 16.69.

TABLE 16.69 Parameter Block Length Definitions

Directive	Name	Value	Description
#define	HBBR_LS	12	// short form length
#define	HBBR_L	20	// long form length

```
// Data Structure
typedef struct {
    unsigned int  length;              //length of following data
    unsigned int  format;              //bit block format
    unsigned int  width;               //block width in pixels
    unsigned int  height;              //block height in lines
    unsigned char sourceplane;         //src plane for bit expand
    unsigned char reserved;            //reserved
    unsigned int  source_x;            //src top left corner
    unsigned int  source_y;
    unsigned int  destination_x;       //dst top left corner
    unsigned int  destination_y;
    unsigned int  destination_pitch;   //margin size of destination
    unsigned int  destination_height;
} HBBR_DATA;    //Read image data from board (BitBLT read).
```

16.10.3 Write Image Data at Current Position HCBBW

This command defines a rectangular image for BitBlt transfers (BitBlt) write operations at the current position. Data for the image is actually written to the display memory by the HBBCHN command. The transfer operation is terminated when an image command other than HBBCHN is called. It is possible to send a complete rectangle or a sub-rectangle. The sub-rectangle is defined within the main rectangle by the LEFT, TOP, B_WIDTH and B_HEIGHT parameters. The parameters for this call are described in Table 16.70.

TABLE 16.70 Parameters for the HCBBW Command

Name	Bytes	Description
LEN	1–0	Length of parameter block
FORMAT	3–2	Format of data
P_WIDTH	5–4	Width of data rectangle
PHEIGHT	7–6	Height of data rectangle
LEFT	9–8	Sub-rectangle left margin in PELS
TOP	11–10	Sub-rectangle top margin in PELS
M_WIDTH	13–12	Sub-rectangle width
M_HEIGHT	15–14	Sub-rectangle height

The FORMAT field describes whether the BitBlt is across-the-plane or through-the-plane. In the "Across-the-plane" mode, data is always confined to the selected plane. This is often referred to as Color Expansion. In the "Through-the-Plane" mode, data is transferred across the display planes. This field is described in the Table 16.71.

TABLE 16.71 Across-the-Plane or Through-the-Plane Values

Value	Description
0	Across-the-plane copy. Data bits are extracted from the source as a monochrome bit map and expanded into the destination. A 1 in the input is expanded to the current color with the current color mix. A 0 in the input is expanded using the background color and background mix.
8	Through-the-plane copy. Data bits are copied from the source to the destination as packed pixels.

It should be noted that there are two forms of the parameter block. One is a short form, consisting of no sub-rectangle. This limits the parameter block to a length of 6. Remember to not count the two bytes of length. The long form includes the sub-rectangle and is fourteen bytes long. Constant definitions for these two forms are provided in Table 16.72.

TABLE 16.72 Parameter Block Length Definitions

Directive	Name	Value	Description
#define	HCBBW_LS	6	// short form length
#define	HCBBW_L	14	// long form length

```
// Data Structure
typedef struct  {
    unsigned int  length;         // length of following data
    unsigned int  format;         // bit block format
    unsigned int  width;          // block width in pixels
    unsigned int  height;         // block height in lines
    unsigned int  source_x;       // src top left corner
    unsigned int  source_y;
    unsigned int  source_pitch;   // margin size of source
    unsigned int  source_height;
} HCBBW_DATA;  // Write image data to board at current position
               // (BitBLT write).
```

16.10.4   Chained Data Go HBBCHN

This command begins the BitBlt operation as specified by one of the BitBlt write (HBBW or HCBBW) or the BitBlt read (HBBR) commands. The system memory address of the subsequent data buffer and length of the data buffer are provided as parameters. The parameters for this call are described in Table 16.73.

TABLE 16.73 Parameters for the HBBCHN Command

Name	Bytes	Description
LEN	1–0	Length of parameter block
ADDRESS	5–2	Address of data buffer in system memory
LENGTH	7–6	Length of data transfer

```
// Data Structure
typedef struct   {
    unsigned int  length;        // length of following data
    unsigned char far *data;     // host buffer
    unsigned int  datalength;    // length of the data
} HBBCHN_DATA;  //   Chain BitBLT data for board-PC transfer.
```

16.10.5 Copy Data HBBC

This command defines all of the necessary parameters and begins a BitBlt transfer (BitBlt) that transfers data from one display memory location to another display memory location. Both the source and destination data address are provided. The parameters for this call are described in Table 16.74.

TABLE 16.74 Parameters for the HBBC Command

Name	Bytes	Description
LEN	1–0	Length of parameter block
FORMAT	3–2	Format of data
P_WIDTH	5–4	Width of data rectangle
P_HEIGHT	7–6	Height of data rectangle
SRC_B_PLANE	8	Bit plane in the case of Across-the-Plane transfers
P0	13–10	Left-top coordinates of source rectangle in display memory
P1	14–17	Left-top coordinates of destination rectangle in display memory

The FORMAT field describes whether the BitBlt is across-the-plane or through-the-plane. In the "Across-the-plane" mode, data is always confined to the selected plane. This is often referred to as Color Expansion. In the "Through-the-Plane" mode, data is transferred across the display planes. This field is described in Table 16.75.

TABLE 16.75 Across-the-Plane or Through-the-Plane Values

Value	Description
0	Across-the-plane copy. Data bits are extracted from the source as a monochrome bit map and expanded into the destination. A 1 in the input is expanded to the current color with the current color mix. A 0 in the input is expanded using the background color and background mix.
8	Through-the-plane copy. Data bits are copied from the source to the destination as packed pixels.

Constants are provided for the Across-the-Plane or Through-the-Plane operation definition. The Across-the-Plane operation can also be thought of as operations on a single plane. The Through-the-Plane operation can also be thought of as operations on all planes. These definitions are provided in Table 16.76.

TABLE 16.76 Operation on Single or all Planes

Directive	Name	Value	Description
#define	AI_SINGLE_PLANE	0x0000	// operation on one plane
#define	AI_ALL_PLANES	0x0008	// operation on all planes

```
// Data Structure
typedef struct   {
    unsigned int  length;            // length of following data
    unsigned int  format;            // bit block format
    unsigned int  width;             // block width in pixels
    unsigned int  height;            // block height in lines
    unsigned char sourceplane;       // src plane for bit expand
    unsigned char reserved;          // reserved
    unsigned int source_x;           // src top left corner
    unsigned int source_y;
    unsigned int destination_x;      // dst top left corner
    unsigned int destination_y;
} HBBC_DATA;       // BitBLT a rectangular region from one
location to another on the board.
```

16.11   AREA COMMANDS

Area commands allow the application to build off-screen images. An area-building session is defined by begin area and end area commands. Once opened, rectangles can be filled, patterns can be defined, and the screen can be erased.

16.11.1   Begin Area HBAR

This command sets the area drawing mode and indicates the beginning of a set of primitives that define the boundary of that area. The end of the set of primitives is indicated by the HEAR end area command.

Line drawing commands following BHR are drawn onto off-screen memory in a form required to construct a filled area. Pixels falling on the left and top boundaries are filled. Pixels falling on the right or bottom boundaries are left alone. Current attributes are used to draw the area when the HEAR is issued. The parameters for this call are described in Table 16.77.

This is a zero length parameter block. The following commands are not allowed between a HBAR and HEAR command sequence.

HOPEN	Open adapter
HCLOSE	Close Adapter
HSMODE	Set mode
HSHS	Set Scissors region

HSCMP	Set color comparison	
HSBP	Set bit plane control	
HCHST	Character string at given position	
HCCHST	Character string at current position	

TABLE 16.77 Parameters for the HBAR Command

Name	Bytes	Description
LEN	1–0	Length of parameter block = 0

16.11.2 End Area HEAR

This command indicates the end of a set of primitives that define the boundary of an area and fill the area defined by the primitives in the fill buffer. If FLAG is used, the specified area-fill algorithm also is applied. If the end point is not identical to the start point, a straight line is drawn to enclose the area automatically. The parameters for this call are described in Table 16.78.

TABLE 16.78 Parameters for the HEAR Command

Name	Bytes	Description
LEN	1–0	Length of parameter block
FLAGS	2	Area definition

The Area definitions, as defined in the FLAG field, are described in Table 16.79.

TABLE 16.79 Bits 7–6 of the FLAGS Area Definition Field

Bits 7–6	Description
00	Perform the fill operation
01	Suspend area definition
10	Stop area definition, by leaving the boundary definitions and not doing an area fill.

Some definitions are provided for the Area Commands in Table 16.80.

TABLE 16.80 Area Fill, Suspend, or Cancel Definitions

Directive	Name	Value	Description
#define	AI_FILL_AREA	0x00	// Complete & fill area defined
#define	AI_SUSPEND_AREA	0x01	// suspend area definition
#define	AI_CANCEL_AREA	0x02	// cancel the area definition

```
// Data Structure
typedef struct {
    unsigned int  length;          // length of following data
    unsigned char flags;           // see above for constants
} HEAR_DATA;  // End area definition.
```

16.11.3 Fill Rectangle HRECT

This command fills a rectangle with a specified pattern. The input data is a monochrome pattern; therefore, the fill utilizes color expansion. The rectangle is specified by the top-left corner, COORD, the width, WIDTH, and the height, HEIGHT. The fill utilizes the current pattern, color, and mix values. The rectangle is restricted into the hardware scissors rectangle. The current position is returned to the top-left corner at the end of the operation. This is a quicker fill command than is the HBAR or the HEAR operation. The parameters for this call are described in Table 16.81.

TABLE 16.81 Parameters for the HRECT Command

Name	Bytes	Description
LEN	1–0	Length of parameter block
COORD	5–2	Top-left corner of the rectangle
WIDTH	7–6	Width of the rectangle
HEIGHT	9–8	Height of the rectangle

```
// Data Structure
typedef struct {
    unsigned int length;          // length of following data
    unsigned int x;               // top left corner of rectangle
    unsigned int y;
    unsigned int width;           // size of the rectangle
    unsigned int height;
} HRECT_DATA;  // Draw a filled rectangle.
```

16.11.4 Set Pattern HSPATT

This command defines the shape of the current area fill pattern symbol as specified by the command. The image is a rectangular bit pattern. Description data is located by addresses in I_ADDR and in C_ADDR. The parameters for this call are described in Table 16.82.

TABLE 16.82 Parameters for the HSPATT Command

Name	Bytes	Description
LEN	1–0	Length of parameter block
WIDTH	7–6	Width of the rectangular pattern
HEIGHT	9–8	Height of the rectangular pattern
FLAGS	4	Flags
M_LEN	7–6	Length of the pattern symbol definition (byte)
I_ADDR	11–8	Address of the image definition data
C_ADDR	15–12	Address of the color definition data

The FLAGS field selects whether the pattern is to be drawn in monochrome or in multicolor. If monochrome is selected, the image is drawn with the current foreground color and mix and background color and mix. If multicolor is selected, the image is drawn in foreground color as defined in the pattern color definitions and background color as specified by the current background color and mix.

The image definition data, as pointed to by I_ADDR, defines a rectangular bit pattern, beginning with the PEL at the top-left corner of the marker with bit 7 of byte 0. The pattern is described from left to right, row by row, from top to bottom. There are no padding bits between rows; therefore, a row can begin in the middle of a byte.

The color definition data, as pointed to by the C_ADDR, consists of a 1-byte color index that defines both foreground and background colors of each PEL in the pattern rectangle as defined by the image data.

```
// Data Structure
typedef struct {
    unsigned int   length;           // length of following data
    unsigned char  cellwidth;        // cell width and height
    unsigned char  cellheight;
    MarkerFlags    flags;            // flags: see above
    unsigned char  reserved;         // reserved
    unsigned int   markerlength;     // marker symbol length
    unsigned char  far *imagedef;    // image definition data
    unsigned char  far *colordef;    // color definition data

} HSPATT_DATA;   //  Define an area pattern.
```

16.11.5 Set Pattern Reference Point HSPATTO

This command defines the origin (top-left corner of the pattern symbol rectangle) for area fill patterns by setting the reference point, P0, of the pattern cell as specified by the command. This allows the pattern to shift since the origin isn't constrained to the top-left corner. The parameters for this call are described in Table 16.83.

TABLE 16.83 Parameters for the HSPATTO Command

Name	Bytes	Description
LEN	1–0	Length of parameter block
P0	5–2	Reference point

```
typedef struct   {
    unsigned int length;           // length of following data
    unsigned int x;                // absolute coordinate
    unsigned int y;
} HSPATTO_DATA;    //  Set the pattern reference point.
```

16.11.6 Erase Graphics Screen HEGS

This command clears the screen. The current position is set to the top-left corner of the screen. Only bit planes that are enabled are cleared by this command. Screen clearing is limited to the hardware scissors region. The parameters for this call are described in Table 16.84.

TABLE 16.84 Parameters for the HEGS Command

Name	Bytes	Description
LEN	1–0	Length of parameter block = 0

16.12   MARKER COMMANDS

Marker commands set the current position, set multiple markers at given positions, and set the marker shape.

16.12.1   Set Current Position HSCP

Set the current position to the value specified in P0. The parameters for this call are described in Table 16.85.

TABLE 16.85 Parameters for the HSCP Command

Name	Bytes	Description
LEN	1–0	Length of parameter block
P0	5–2	The coordinate data

```
// Data Structure
typedef struct  {
    unsigned int length;          // length of following data
    unsigned int x;               // position
    unsigned int y;
} HSCP_DATA;  //  Set current position
```

16.12.2   Set Marker at Given Position HMRK

This command draws one or more marker symbols beginning at point P0. If more than one marker is specified, the second marker symbol is drawn at point P1, the third at P2, etc. After all points have been drawn, the current position is set to the last coordinate specified in the command. The current position is left at the last point at the end of this command. The parameters for this call are described in Table 16.86.

The marker cell is specified by a width=cx, a height=cy. The actual point is then drawn at Xpn – cx/2, Ypn – cy/2. This places the point at approximately in the middle of the point Pn.

TABLE 16.86 Parameters for the HMRK Command

Name	Bytes	Description
LEN	1–0	Length of parameter block.
P0	5–2	Coordinate data for first marker
P1,P2...	9–6,13–10	Optional Coordinate points

```
// Data Structure macro
#define HMRK_DATA(n)                 // n - number of markers
    struct {
        unsigned int  length;        // length of following data
        coord points[n];             // points markers are on
    }   //  Draw a marker at the specified positions.
```

16.12.3   Set Marker at Current Position HCMRK

This command draws one or more marker symbols beginning at the current position. If more than one marker is specified, the second marker symbol is drawn at point P1, the third at P2, etc. After all points have been drawn, the current position is set to the last coordinate specified in the command. The current position is left at the last point at the end of this command. The parameters for this call are described in Table 16.87.

The marker cell is specified by a width=cx, a height=cy. The actual point is then drawn at Xpn – cx/2, Ypn – cy/2. This places the point at approximately in the middle of the point Pn.

TABLE 16.87 Parameters for the HCMRK Command

Name	Bytes	Description
LEN	1–0	Length of parameter block
P1,P2...	5–2,9–6	Optional Coordinate points

```
// Data Structure macro
#define HCMRK_DATA(n)                  // n - number of markers
    struct {
        unsigned int  length;         // length of following data
        coord points[n];              // coord of lower left corner
    }  //  Draw a marker starting at the current position and
all others specified.
```

16.12.4   Set Marker Shape HSMARK

This command defines the shape of the current marker as specified by the command. The command is identical to the Set Current Area Fill Pattern Symbol command, HSPATT. The pattern is a rectangular bit pattern. Description data is located by addresses in I_ADDR and in C_ADDR. The parameters for this call are described in Table 16.88.

TABLE 16.88 Parameters for the HSMARK Command

Name	Bytes	Description
LEN	1–0	Length of parameter block
WIDTH	7–6	Width of the rectangular pattern
HEIGHT	9–8	Height of the rectangular pattern
FLAGS	4	Flags
M_LEN	7–6	Length of the pattern symbol definition (byte)
I_ADDR	11–8	Address of the image definition data
C_ADDR	15–12	Address of the color definition data

The FLAGS field selects whether the pattern is to be drawn in monochrome or in multicolor. If monochrome is selected, the image is drawn with the current foreground color and mix and background color and mix. If multicolor is selected, the image is drawn in foreground color as defined in the pattern color definitions and background color as specified by the current background color and mix.

The image definition data, as pointed to by I_ADDR, defines a rectangular bit pattern, beginning with the PEL at the top-left corner of the marker with bit 7 of byte 0. The pattern is described from left to right, row by row, from top to bottom. There are no padding bits between rows; therefore, a row can begin in the middle of a byte.

The color definition data, as pointed to by the C_ADDR, consists of a 1-byte color index that defines both foreground and background colors of each PEL in the pattern rectangle as defined by the image data.

```
// Data Structure for the marker flags
typedef struct   {
    unsigned int  reserved    : 7;    // reserved
    unsigned int  color        : 1;    // color  0 - color marker
                                       //        1 - monochrome
} MarkerFlags;

// Data Structure
typedef struct {
    unsigned int  length;          // length of following data
    unsigned char cellwidth;       // cell width and height
    unsigned char cellheight;
    unsigned char flags;           // flags: see above
    unsigned char reserved;        // reserved
    unsigned int  markerlength;    // marker symbol length
    unsigned char far *imagedef;   // image definition data
    unsigned char far *colordef;   // color definition data
} HSMARK_DATA;   //  Define a marker.
```

16.13   ALPHANUMERIC COMMANDS

The alphanumeric commands allow the specification of character sets, writing character strings, and erasing or scrolling alphanumeric regions. The string outputs can be to a specified location or to the current location. The alphanumeric data can be either one attribute per block or a different attribute per character. The alphanumeric cursor shape can also be defined.

16.13.1   Set Character Set HCHS

This command sets the current character set. The content of ADDRESS is a program address in system memory. The application must preserve the characters set buffer until a new HSCS is called and processed since the pointer is assumed to be current. The parameters for this call are described in Table 16.89.

TABLE 16.89 Parameters for the HCHS Command

Name	Bytes	Description
LEN	1–0	Length of parameter block
ADDRESS	5–2	Address of the character set definition block.

```
// Data Structure
typedef struct {
    unsigned int  length;          // length of following data
    CharSetDef far *address;       // character set
} HSCS_DATA;  // Define character set.
```

16.13.2   Write Character String at Given Position HCHST

This command draws a character string at the specified position. The current position is changed to the value specified in P0. The STRING contains one byte per character and does not need to be NULL terminated since the length of the string is implicitly defined in the parameter block size. The parameters for this call are described in Table 16.90.

TABLE 16.90 Parameters for the HCHST Command

Name	Bytes	Description
LEN	1–0	Length of parameter block
P0	5–2	Coordinate data of left-bottom corner of character string.
STRING	(6+n)–n	String of characters, n characters long.

The parameter block size is calculated by the length of the string + the size of a coordinate. A macro is provided in Table 16.91.

TABLE 16.91 Parameter Block Length Definitions

Directive	Name	Value	Description
#define	HCHST_LEN(s)	(strlen(s) + sizeof(coord))	// length of parameter block

```
// Data Structure macro
#define HCHST_DATA(n)                   // n - number chars in buffer
    struct {
```

```
        unsigned int  length;        // length of following data
        coord position;              // coord of lower left corner
        char string[n];              // the string buffer
  }  // Write a text string at a specified position
```

16.13.3   Write Character String at Current Position HCCHST

This command draws a character string at the current position. The current position is unchanged at the end of the command. The STRING contains one byte per character and does not need to be NULL terminated since the length of the string is implicitly defined in the parameter block size. The parameters for this call are described in Table 16.92.

TABLE 16.92 Parameters for the HCCHST Command

Name	Bytes	Description
LEN	1–0	Length of parameter block
STRING	(2+n)–n	String of characters, n characters long

```
// Data Structure macro
#define HCCHST_DATA(n)               // n - number chars in buffer
    struct {
        unsigned int  length;        // length of following data
        char string[n];              // the string buffer
    }  // Write a text string at the current position.
```

16.13.4   Set the Cell Size for Alphanumeric Text HSCELL

This command sets the width and height of the new character cell size. The parameters for this call are described in Table 16.93.

TABLE 16.93 Parameters for the ABLOCKMFI Command

Name	Bytes	Description
LEN	1–0	Length of parameter block
WIDTH	2	Width of new character cell
HEIGHT	3	Height of new character cell

```
// Data Structure
typedef struct  {
    unsigned int  length;            // length of following data
    unsigned char width;             // size of new character cell
    unsigned char height;
} ASCELL;  //  Set the cell size for alphanumeric text.
```

16.13.5 Write Character/Attribute Block ABLOCKMFI

This command writes a block of characters to the display buffer. Each character has its own foreground and background colors as well as its own attributes. The string of characters in the character block is specified by the *STR parameter. The first character is written to the buffer starting from the character cell coordinate specified by the TOPLEFT parameters. Subsequent characters are written in order of increasing column addresses. The parameters for this call are described in Table 16.94.

Writing continues row after row until the total number of characters written is equal to NCHARS. Each character is described in four bytes.

TABLE 16.94 Parameters for the ABLOCKMFI Command

Name	Bytes	Description
LEN	1–0	Length of parameter block
TOPLEFT	3–2	Top left coordinate of character block
SIZE	5–4	Width of the block
*STR	9–6	Address of the block of characters
NCHARS	10	Number of characters in the block

Each character is defined in a four byte description block as shown in Table 16.95.

TABLE 16.95 Character Description 32-bit Word

Bit	Description
9–8	Bits 0,1 of the font number (see ASFONT)
12	0=background opaque, 1=background transparent
13	Overstrike
14	Reverse video
15	Underscore
19–16	4-bit foreground color attribute
23–20	4-bit background color attribute
31–24	8-bit character code

```
// Data Structure
typedef struct {
    unsigned int  length;        // length of following data
    unsigned char col;           // initial column and row
    unsigned char row;
    unsigned char width;         // size in characters of box
```

```
        unsigned char height;
        unsigned char far *string;    // character block to write
        unsigned char pitch;          // pitch of block in PC memory
  } ABLOCKMFI_DATA; // Write a rectanglar block of characters
                    // to the display using an AI specific format.
```

16.13.6   Write Character Block ABLOCKCGA

This command writes a block of characters to the display buffer. Each character is sixteen bits long and contains a foreground and background color. The attributes of the character block are specified in the ATTRIB byte. The string of characters in the character block is specified by the *STR parameter. The first character is written to the buffer starting from the character cell coordinate specified by the TOPLEFT parameters. Subsequent characters are written in order of increasing column addresses. The parameters for this call are described in Table 16.96.

Writing continues row after row until the total number of characters written is equal to NCHARS. Each character is described in four bytes.

TABLE 16.96 Parameters for the ABLOCKCGA Command

Name	Bytes	Description
LEN	1–0	Length of parameter block
TOPLEFT	3–2	Top left coordinate of character block
SIZE	5–4	Width of the block
*STR	9–6	Address of the block of characters
NCHARS	10	Number of characters in the block
ATTRIB	11	Highlight attribute for block

Each character is defined in a 2-byte description block as shown in Table 16.97.

TABLE 16.97 Character Description 16-bit Word

Bit	Description
3–0	4-bit foreground color attribute
7–4	4-bit background color attribute
15–8	8-bit character code

The ATTRIB field is defined as shown in Table 16.98.

TABLE 16.98 Character Attribute 8-bit Word

Bits	Description
4	0=background opaque, 1=background transparent
5	Overstrike
6	Reverse video
7	Underscore

```
// Data Structure
typedef struct  {
    unsigned int  length;        // length of following data
    unsigned char col;           // initial column and row
    unsigned char row;
    unsigned char width;         // size in characters of box
    unsigned char height;
    unsigned char far *string;   // character block to write
    unsigned char pitch;         // pitch of block in PC memory
    unsigned char highlight_attribute; // attribute for char
                                       // block
} ABLOCKCGA_DATA;  // Write a rectanglar block of characters to
                   // the display using CGA-type attributes.
```

16.13.7 Erase Rectangle AERASE

This command erases a rectangle by setting the rectangle of character cells to the background color. The upper-left coordinate of the rectangle is R_START, CSTART. The size of the rectangle is defined by COLS and ROWS. The COLOR byte is defined as follows. The parameters for this call are described in Table 16.99.

TABLE 16.99 Parameters for the AERASE Command

Name	Bytes	Description
LEN	1–0	Length of parameter block
C_START	2	Starting column (0–n)
R_START	3	Starting row (0–n)
COLS	4	Number of character cells across
ROWS	5	Number of character cells down
COLOR	6	Background color bits 7–4 4-bit background color

```
// Data Structure
typedef struct  {
    unsigned int  length;          // length of following data
    unsigned char col;             // initial column and row
    unsigned char row;
    unsigned char width;           // size in characters of box
    unsigned char hcight;
    unsigned char color;           // background color
} AERASE_DATA;  // Erase a block of characters.
```

16.13.8   Scroll Rectangle ASCROLL

This command scrolls a rectangle of character cells. The upper-left coordinate of the source rectangle is R_STARTS and C_STARTS. The size of the rectangle is defined by COLS and ROWS. The rectangle is scrolled such that the new upper-left coordinate is R_STARTD and C_STARTD. The parameters for this call are described in Table 16.100.

TABLE 16.100 Parameters for the ASCROLL Command

Name	Bytes	Description
LEN	1–0	Length of parameter block
C_STARTS	2	Starting column (0–n) of source
R_STARTS	3	Starting row (0–m) of source
COLS	4	Number of character cells across
ROWS	5	Number of character cells down
C_STARTD	6	Starting column of destination
R_STARTD	7	Starting row of destination

```
// Data Structure
typedef struct  {
    unsigned int  length;          // length of following data
    unsigned char source_x;        // block to copy
    unsigned char source_y;
    unsigned char width;           // size of block to copy
    unsigned char height;
    unsigned char destination_x;   // new position for block
    unsigned char destination_y;
} ASCROLL_DATA;  // Scroll a rectangular block of characters
                 // on the display
```

16.13.9 Set Alphanumerics Cursor Position ACURSOR

This command sets the current alphanumeric cursor position. The cursor is moved from the previously marked character cell to the current cell to the current cell as specified by the coordinate AT. The parameters for this call are described in Table 16.101.

TABLE 16.101 Parameters for the ACURSOR Command

Name	Bytes	Description
LEN	1–0	Length of parameter block
AT	3–2	Column (0–n) and Row (0–m) of cursor

```
// Data Structure
typedef struct  {
    unsigned int  length;            // length of following data
    unsigned char x;                 // new position coordinates
    unsigned char y;
} ACURSOR_DATA;  //  Position the alphanumeric text cursor.
```

16.13.10 Set Alphanumeric Cursor Shape ASCUR

This command sets the cursor shape of the alphanumeric cursor. The cursor shape and attributes apply to the subsequent cursor operations. The parameters for this call are described in Table 16.102.

The alphanumeric cursor is hidden after every mode change. All interactions between characters and the cursor are handled by the adapter. The one exception is that the graphics coordinates are handled by the application. No cursor is drawn if START>STOP. The alphanumeric cursor must be within the bounds of a character cell. The arrow cursor must be between START+2 and the bottom of the cell. The current cursor shape is retained if START is FF hex.

TABLE 16.102 Parameters for the ASCUR Command

Name	Bytes	Description
LEN	1–0	Length of parameter block
START	2	Cursor start line (0–n, 0=top)
STOP	3	Cursor stop line (0–n)
ATTRIB	4	Cursor Attribute

The ATTRIB cursor attribute field is defined as shown in Table 16.103.

TABLE 16.103 Cursor Attribute Field 8-bit

Value	Description
0	Normal cursor
1	Hidden cursor
2	Left-arrow cursor
3	Right-arrow cursor

Definitions for the Cursor Attribute field are provided in Table 16.104.

TABLE 16.104 Cursor Attribute Definitions

Directive	Name	Value	Description
#define	NORMAL_CURSOR	0	// normal cursor
#define	HIDE_CURSOR	1	// hide cursor
#define	LEFT_ARROW_CURSOR	2	// left arrow cursor
#define	RIGIIT_ARROW_CURSOR	3	// right arrow cursor

```
// Data Structure
typedef struct {
    unsigned int   length;            // length of following data
    unsigned char  start_line;        // cursor start line
    unsigned char  stop_line;         // cursor stop line
    unsigned char  attribute_style;   // cursor attribute
} ASCUR_DATA;  // Set Cursor Shape.
```

16.13.11   Set Font ASFONT

This command selects an alphanumeric character set. The set is located at the address specified by ADDRESS. The set is either type 0 (bitmapped) or type 3 (short-stroke vector). See the Character set definition block format below. The parameters for this call are described in Table 16.105.

TABLE 16.105 Parameters for the ASFONT Command

Name	Bytes	Description
LEN	1–0	Length of parameter block
FONT	2	Font number (0–3)
ADDRESS	7–4	Address of the character set definition block

The Character Set Definition Block is defined in Table 16.106.

TABLE 16.106 Character Set Definition Block

Byte	Label	Content
0	BYTE	Reserved
1	TYPE	Type of character set 0=bitmapped 1=reserved 2=reserved 3=short stroke
2	BYTE	Reserved
6–3	DWORD	Reserved
7	BYTE	Cell width in PELS (cx)
8	BYTE	Cell height in PELS (cy)
9	BYTE	Reserved
11–10	WORD	Cell size = CEILING (cx*cy)/8
13–12	WORD	FLAGS (see Table 16.103)
17–14	ADDRESS	Address of index table
21–18	ADDRESS	Address of character width table
22	BYTE	Initial code point
23	BYTE	Final code point
27–24	ADDRESS	Address of character definition table
29–28	WORD	Reserved
33–30	ADDRESS	Address of 2nd character definition table
35–34	WORD	Reserved
39–36	ADDRESS	Address of 3rd character definition table

The FLAGS field is defined as shown in Table 16.107.

TABLE 16.107 Character Set Flags

Bits	Description
15	reserved =0
14	0=monochrome bitmap, 1=color bitmap
13	0=not proportional spacing, 1=proportional spacing

```
// Data Structure
typedef struct {
    unsigned int  length;        // length of following data
    unsigned char font;          // font number
    unsigned char reserved;      // reserved
    CharSetDef far *address;     // char set
} ASFONT_DATA;  // Set the character set for use with the
                // alphanumeric functions.
```

16.13.12 Assign Alphanumeric Color AXLATE

This command assigns a table that converts between alphanumeric attribute colors to color indexes. The two tables are defined in the parameter block, one for the character foreground and one for the character background. Each color index table entry is 32 bits wide. TBLF contains values for character foreground, and TBLB contains values for character background. Bits 7–4 of the ATTRIBUTE byte are used to address the TBLF, and bits 3–0 address the TBLB. The parameters for this call are described in Table 16.108.

TABLE 16.108 Parameters for the AXLATE Command

Name	Bytes	Description
LEN	1–0	Length of parameter block
TBLF	65–2	Translate table for the character foreground
TBLB	129–66	Translate table for the character background

```
// Data Structure
typedef struct  {
    unsigned int  length;          // length of following data
    unsigned long fg[16];          // foreground color table
    unsigned long bk[16];          // background color table
} AXLATE_DATA;  // Define alphanumeric color translation table.
```

Chapter 17

The 8514/A

17.1   8514/A OVERVIEW

The 8514/A, introduced in 1987 by IBM, incorporated the first popular graphics coprocessor. Although a good design, the 8514/A could never really compete against the VGA for several reasons. First, IBM kept its register definitions proprietary, which hampered software development. Second, IBM wanted to force everyone into the Adapter Interface (AI), as discussed in Chapter 16. Third, the 8514/A was designed for the micro channel, and IBM couldn't finesse the micro channel into the market at the numbers that they had originally intended.

17.1.1   8514/A Features

The 8514/A contains hardwired graphics functions including BitBlts, filled rectangles, and line drawing. Several of its features are provided in Table 17.1.

17.1.2   Data Streams

The drawing engine combines one color source, one monochrome source, and the destination data. The monochrome data may be supplied from the four sources shown in Table 17.2. The color data may be supplied from the three sources shown in Table 17.3.

17.1.3   The Pixel ALU

The pixel ALU provides sixteen Boolean and sixteen arithmetic functions operating on the data sources described in Section 17.1.2. The ALU can use two separate mixes, one for the foreground and one for the background. The foreground and background are selected by the pixel-by-pixel value of the monochrome data stream. These mixes are provided in Table 17.4.

TABLE 17.1 The 8514/A Features

Command FIFO	3-source pixel transfer ALU
High-speed line draw	Vector line draw
High-speed polygon fill	Short-stroke vector draw
Automatic rectangle fill	Polygon boundary draw
Color and monochrome BitBlts	Scissoring
BitBlts to and from Host	Destination color compare
BitBlts within display memory	

TABLE 17.2 Monochrome Data Streams

MONO_SRC Field	Monochrome Source
00	Always 1
01	Two 4-bit monochrome pattern registers
10	Host supplied Data
11	Selected Planes of the BitBlt Source

TABLE 17.3 Color Data Streams

COLOR_SRC Field	Color Source
00	Background color based on monochrome data=0
01	Foreground color based on monochrome data=1
10	Host supplied Data
11	The BitBlt Source

17.1.4 Filled Polygons

Arbitrary complex filled polygons may be drawn in three passes by using the Edge Flag polygon fill algorithms. The original pattern may be drawn into off-screen memory. Once filled, this polygon can be transferred to on-screen memory using a BitBlt.

17.1.5 Scissors Clipping

A rectangular clipping rectangle can be defined by the scissors region. All draw operations are clipped as they are drawn to this selected region.

TABLE 17.4 ALU Mix (S=source D=Destination)

Value	Operation	Value	Operation
00	NOT D	10	Min (S,D)
01	Zero	11	D – S
02	One	12	S – D
03	Leave alone	13	D + S
04	NOT S	14	Max (S,D)
05	D XOR S	15	(D–S)/2
06	NOT D (XOR S)	16	(S–D)/2
07	Overpaint	17	Average (D+S)/2
08	NOT (D OR (NOT S))	18	Subtract with limit Max (0,D–S)
09	D OR (NOT S)	19	Subtract with limit Max (0,D–S)
0A	(NOT D) OR S	1A	Subtract with limit Max (0,S–D)
0B	D OR S	1B	Min(255,D+S)
0C	D AND S	1C	Subtract with limit (Max (0,D–S)) /2
0D	(NOT D) AND S	1D	Subtract with limit (Max (0,D–S)) /2
0E	D AND (NOT S)	1E	Subtract with limit (Max (0,S–D)) /2
0F	(NOT D) AND (NOT S)	1F	if(255<S+D) then 255 else (S+D)/2

17.2   SETUP REGISTERS

The micro channel power-on setup registers are located at 0100, 0101, and 0102 hex. Bit 0 of the Setup Mode Option Select Register is used to enable or disable the card. If a 0 is written to Register 102, the card is disabled. A 1 enables the card. Register 0100 is the Setup Mode Identification Byte 1 Register. It returns a 7F hex for identification. Register 0101 is the Setup Mode Identification Byte 2 Register. It returns an EF hex for identification.

17.3   DAC CONTROLLER REGISTERS

The RAM DAC registers are located in the 8514/A at address 2EA hex through 2ED hex. In order to conform to the timing requirements of slower DACs, it is necessary to use instruction loops rather than REP OUTSB instructions when writing to the DACs. Otherwise, data may be lost.

The DAC registers at 2EA hex through 2ED hex are identical to the VGA DAC Registers described in Chapter 8 of this book. They are listed in Table 17.5.

The DAC mask determines which bits participate in the DAC lookup. The Read Color Index auto-increments after every third read from DAC_DATA. The Write Color Index auto-increments after every third write to the

TABLE 17.5   DAC Registers

Address	R/W	Name	Bits	Description
2EA	R/W	DAC_MASK	7–0	DAC Mask
2EB	R	DAC_R_INDEX	7–0	Current Color Index
2EB	W	DAC_R_INDEX	7–0	Read Current Color Index
2EB	R	DAC_W_INDEX	7–0	Current Color Index
2EB	W	DAC_W_INDEX	7–0	Write Current Color Index
2ED	R/W	DAC_DATA	5–0	6–bit Color data (R, G, or B)

DAC_DATA. It should be noted that the Current Color Index is the Current Write Index, if the DAC is in a write mode. If the DAC is in a read mode, it is the Current Read Index + 1.

Like the VGA, there are three 8-bit DAC registers assigned to each index—one each for red, green, and blue. Also, like the VGA, each color component is only six bits. It should be noted that the 8514/A DAC registers differ from the VGA in that the six bits are positioned in the most-significant bits of the word. The VGA uses the least-significant bits. Using the most significant bits is a much better solution in that it is compatible with an 8-bit color value (the lower 2-bits simply add more resolution).

17.4   CRT REGISTERS

The CRT registers determine the display resolution. The CRT Controller should be put into its reset state while CRT parameters are being changed using the sequence described in Table 17.6.

The CRT registers are listed in Table 17.7. The common values for three display modes are shown.

The relationship of these CRT Registers to the actual display is illustrated in Figure 17.1

TABLE 17.6   Changing the CRT Controller Registers

Step	Operation
1	Set the DISP_CNTL.ENABLE_DISPLAY to 2 (Reset condition)
2	Modify the CRT registers
3	Set the DISP_CNTL.ENABLE_DISPLAY to 1 (Enable condition)

TABLE 17.7 The CRT Registers

Register Name	Address	640x480 (512 K)	640x480 (1 Meg)	1024x768 (All)
DISP_CNTRL	22E8	21	23	33
ADVFUNC_CNTL	4AE8	3	3	7
H_TOTAL	02E8	63	63	9D
H_DISP	06E8	4F	4F	7F
H_SYNC_STRT	0AE8	52	52	81
H_SYNC_WID	0EE8	WC	2C	16
V_TOTAL	12E8	830	418	660
V_DISP	16E8	779	3BB	5FB
V_SYNC_STRT	1AE8	7A8	2D2	600
V_SYNC_WID	1EE8	22	22	08

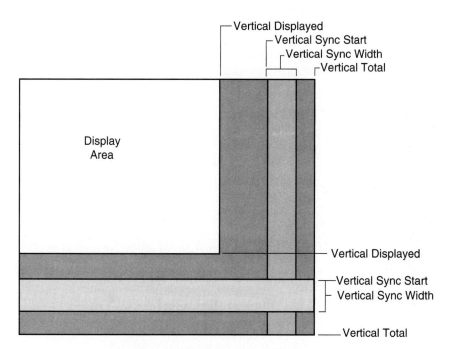

FIGURE 17.1 CRT Registers and the Display

17.5 INTERRUPT AND CONFIGURATION REGISTERS

The 8514/A can generate host interrupts during vertical blanking, whether an IO address is invalid, when the graphics coprocessor becomes idle, or when a draw is inside the scissors region. Four flags are used for each of these interrupts as listed in Table 17.8.

Each interrupt has corresponding ENA and ACK fields in the SUBSYS_CNTL Register and an INT field in the SUBSYS_STAT Register. Writing a 1 to the ACK field clears the INT field. The INT field generate an interrupt if the ENA field is a 1. The SUBSYS_CNTRL Register is described in Table 17.9.

TABLE 17.8 Interrupt Flags

Flag	Operation
VBLANK	Set at start of vertical blanking interval.
INVALID_IO	Set when either: (a) A host write to the command FIFO when the FIFO is full. (b) A host read from the pixel transfer ready when there is no data.
GP_IDLE	Set when the Graphics Processor becomes idle.
INSIDE_SCISSOR	Set when a draw command trajectory enters the scissors region.

TABLE 17.9 SUBSYS_CNTL Subsystem Control Register at 42E8 (Write Only)

Bit	Name	Description
15–14	GP_RESET	Control Processor 00=No change 01=Enable GP 02=Reset GP 03=Reset GP
13–12	HW_TEST	Hardware test 00=No change 01=switch to normal mode
11	GP_IDLE_ENA	1=enable 0=disable GP_IDLE interrupt
1–	INVALID_IO_ENA	1=enable 0=disable INVALID_IO interrupt
0	INSIDE_SCISSOR_ENA	1=enable 0=disable INSIDE_SCISSOR interrupt
9	VBLANK_ENA	1=enable 0=disable VBLANK interrupt
7–4		reserved
3	GP_IDLE_ACK	1=clear GP_IDLE interrupt
2	INVALID_IO_ACK	1=clear INVALID_IO interrupt
1	INSIDE_SCISSOR_ACK	1=clear INSIDE_SCISSOR interrupt
0	VBLANK_ACK	1=clear VBLANK interrupt

TABLE 17.10 SUBSYS_STAT Subsystem Status Register at 42E8 (Read Only)

Bit	Name	Description
15–8		reserved
7	MEM_SIZE	memory size 0=512 1=1meg
6–4	MONITOR_ID	Monitor type 2=8514, 5=8503,6=8513 or 8512 7=no monitor
3	GP_IDLE_INT	1=detected
2	INVALID_IO_INT	1=detected
1	INSIDE_SCISSOR_INT	1=detected
0	VBLANK_INT	1=detected

When a GP_RESET is set to 2 or 3, the reset operation, all interrupts are reset and the command FIFO is cleared. The system status register, SUBSYS_STAT, provides status about the display. The fields within this register are shown in Table 17.10.

17.6 MEMORY CONFIGURATION REGISTERS

The memory configuration register for several display modes is shown in Table 17.11. Also included are the values for the DAC_MASK Register and the WRT_MASK Register.

The 640-by-480 resolution with 512K memory is referred to as the SKIP1 mode. In this mode, the Y-addressing ignores Bit 1 of all Y-coordinate registers. The host must translate all Y-coordinates to the following value:

translated SKIP1 Y = (2*Y) + (Y&1)

In the 512K memory configuration, the 8514/A adapter works as a four plane device. In the SKIP1 mode, the two banks of four planes each are available. If

TABLE 17.11 Memory Configuration Registers

Memory	Resolution	# colors	MEM_CNTL	DAC_MASK	WRT_MASK
512K	640x480	bank 0 16	5002	0F	0F
512K	640x480	bank 1 16	5012	F0	0F
512K	640x480	256	5002/5012	FF	0F
512K	1024x768	16	5006	0F	0F
1 Meg	640x480	256	5006	FF	FF
1 Meg	1024x768	256	5006	FF	FF

TABLE 17.12   MEM_CNTL Memory Control Register at BEE8 (Write Only)

Bit	Name	Description
15–12	MF_INDEX	multi-function index = 5
11–5		reserved

4	PLANE_SELECT	Plane select (512 K memory only)
		    00=lower 4 planes (Bank 0)
		    01=upper 4 planes (Bank 1)

3–2	GP_Y_CONTROL	GP Memory control (512 K memory only)
		    00=SKIP1 (640x480x4)
		    01= all other resolutions (linear)

1–0	GP_X_CONTROL	reserved = 2

TABLE 17.13   Registers Affected by SKIP1

CUR_Y
DESTY_AXSTP
MULTIFUNC_CNTL SCISSORS_T
MULTIFUNC_CNTL SCISSORS_B

the DAC_MASK is set to FF hex, it is possible to display eight bits of color per pixel. In this case, the lower four bits come from Bank 0 and the upper four bits come from Bank 1. It is necessary to perform two writes, once each to bank 0 and to bank 1. The MEM_CNTL Register is described in Table 17.12.

In the SKIP 1 mode, the application must adjust the values it sends to the registers listed in Table 17.13.

17.7   COMMAND FIFO

The 8514/A has a command FIFO that allows it to buffer new commands while executing previous commands. This assists in the parallel processing capability of the 8514/A and the host. The 8514 uses an 8-word command FIFO. The Writable Graphics Processor registers, shown in Table 17.14, are all queued in the FIFO.

17.8   GRAPHICS PROCESSOR COMMAND/STATUS REGISTERS

The Command Register (CMD) is used to define and initiate draw commands. All other parameters should be loaded into other registers before the Command Register is loaded. This register defines the type of drawing operation (either line draws, rectangle fills, or BitBlts).

TABLE 17.14 Writable Registers that use the FIFO

Address	Name	Description
82E8	CUR_Y	Current Y Position
86E8	CUR_X	Current X Position
8AE8	DESTY_AXSTP	Destination Y Position/Axial Step Constant
8EE8	DESTX_DIASTP	Destination X Position/Diagonal Step Constant
92E8	ERR_TERM	Error Term
96E8	MAJ_AXIS_PCNT	Major Axis Pixel Count
9AE8	CND	Command
9EE8	SHORT_STROKE	Short Stroke Vector Transfer
A2E8	BKGD_COLOR	Background Color
A6E8	FRGD_COLOR	Foreground Color
AAE8	WRT_MASK	Write Mask
AEE8	RD_MASK	Read Mask
BEE8	COLOR_CMP	Color Compare
B6E8	BKGD_MIX	Background Mix
BAE8	FRGD_MIX	Foreground Mix
BEE8	MULTIFUNC_CNTL	Multifunction Control
E2E8	PIX_TRANS	Pixel Data Transfer

17.8.1 The Command Register

Details of the Command Register are provided in Table 17.15.

The OPCODE values determine the type of draw operation and are described in Table 17.16.

The PIXEL_MODE field in the CMD Register determines how the pixel data is organized in host memory. In the SNGLE pixel mode, one byte of host data is used for every pixel read or drawn. In the NIBBLE mode, one byte of host data is used for every nibble (or fraction of a nibble) read or drawn. A nibble is a horizontal group of four contiguous pixels. Table 17.17 further describes the effects of this field.

The DIR_TYPE field determines whether DEGREE or XY is used while the OCTANT specifies the direction of the trajectory as shown in Table 17.18.

The CPU_WAIT field commands the GP to wait for the MSB of the Host I/O. This is used for host-VRAM image transfers and for patterned draws.

17.8.2 Draw Modes

The OPCODE field determines the type of draw operation as listed in Table 17.16. Each of these codes is described below.

TABLE 17.15 CMD Command Register at 9AE8 (Write Only)

Bit	Name	Description
15–13	OPCODE	Draw function
12	LSB_FIRST	0 use MSB of host data first when DATA_WIDTH=1
		1 use LSB of host data first when DATA_WIDTH=1
11–10		reserved = 0
9	DATA_WIDTH	0 = 8-bit 1 = 16-bit
8	CPU_WAIT	0 = no wait for CPU 1= wait for CPU
7–5	OCTANT	Drawing direction
7	YPOS	0=negative Y direction 1= positive Y direction
6	YMAJOR	0 = Major Axis is X 1 = Major Axis is Y
5	XPOS	0=negative X direction 1= positive X direction
4	DRAW	0=no draw 1=draw
3	DIR_TYPE	0 = coordinate mode is (XY) 1 = degree mode (DEGREE)
2	LAST_PEL_OFF	0=draw last pixel 1=don't draw last pixel
1	PIXEL_MODE	0=draw last pixel (SINGLE) 1=nibble mode (NIBBLE)
0	RW	0=read (READ) 1=write (WRITE)

TABLE 17.16 OPCODE names and Description

Value	Name	Description
0	NO_OP	Short stroke setup
1	DRAW_LINE	Draw line
2	FILL_RECT_HOR	Fill Rectangle horizontal first
3	FILL_RECT_VPIX	Fill Rectangle vertical first
4	FILL_RECT_VNIB	Fill Rectangle nibbles up and down
5	DRAW_POLY_LINE	Draw Polygon Boundary line
6	BLIT	Copy screen area BitBlt
7		reserved

Short-Stroke Setup OP_CODE=0

This operation sets up the Short-Stroke Vector (SSV) draw operation. It is similar to the Draw Line operation described next, The parameters for the SSV are provided in the SHORT_STROKE Register. Table 17.19 describes the registers affected that differ from the Draw Line operation (listed below).

TABLE 17.17 Effects of the PIXEL_MODE field

PIXEL_MODE	RW	Color of data	Result
SINGLE	READ	monochrome	Don't use
SINGLE	WRITE	monochrome	Each pixel uses a separate byte
NIBBLE	READ	monochrome	Appropriate
NIBBLE	WRITE	monochrome	Each nibble uses a separate byte
SINGLE	READ	color	Appropriate
SINGLE	WRITE	color	Each pixel uses a separate byte
NIBBLE	READ	color	Don't use
NIBBLE	WRITE	color	Each nibble uses a separate byte

TABLE 17.18 Trajectory Drawing Direction

OCTANT	DEGREE	XY
0	0	Y neg, X major, X neg
1	45	Y neg, X major, X pos
2	90	Y neg, Y major, X neg
3	135	Y neg, Y major, X pos
4	180	Y pos, X major, X neg
5	225	Y pos, X major, X pos
6	270	Y pos, Y major, X neg
7	315	Y pos, Y major, X pos

TABLE 17.19 SSV Related Registers

Register	Effect
DRAW	No effect due to the move/draw field of the SHORT_STROKE Register.
DATA_WIDTH	The GP always processes two SSV commands per word.
CPU_WAIT	The first SSV or every pair should be NO_OP.
LSB_FIRST=1	LSB of SHORT_STROKE is processed first.
LSB_FIRST=0	MSB of SHORT_STROKE is processed first.
Side Effects	MAJOR_AXIS_PCNT is replaced by the LENGTH field in SHORT_STROKE.

Draw Line OP_CODE=1

Line draw, polygon boundary draw, and short-stroke vector share the same behavior. Table 17.20 describes the registers affected.

Draw Polygon OP_CODE=5

Drawing a polygon boundary uses a variant of DRAW_LINE described above. However, only one pixel is drawn or read per scan line. When the Scissors boundary is hit, the trajectory follows the Scissors boundary line. This ensures a closed polygon. Table 17.21 describes the registers affected.

Fill Rectangle Type FILL_RECT_HOR OP_CODE=2

Rectangles are filled using horizontal lines. Table 17.22 describes the registers affected.

TABLE 17.20 Draw Line Related Registers

Register	Effect
LAST_PEL_OFF=0	MAJ_AXIS_PCNT+1 pixels are drawn or read.
LAST_PEL_OFF=1	MAJ_AXIS_PCNT pixels are drawn or read. If CPU_WAIT=1, no host data is required for the last pixel.
DIR_TYPE=DEGREE	Lines are drawn in one of the specified OCTANT 8 directions.
DIR_TYPE=XY	Current Bressenham parameters are used in the specified OCTANT.
Side Effects	CUR_X = CUR_X + dx; CUR_Y = CUR_Y + dy, ERR_TERM is updated.

TABLE 17.21 Draw Polygon Boundary Related Registers

Register	Effect
RW=READ	In color, if pixels are skipped on the draw trajectory, they are read as FF hex.
RW=WRITE	CPU_WAIT=1, host data is used for skipped pixels.
LAST_PEL_OFF	For polygon fill operations, LAST_PEL_OFF should be set to 1 to disable the last scan line.

TABLE 17.22 Fill Rectangle Horizontal Lines Related Registers

Register	Effect
LAST_PEL_OFF	Last pixel in each scan line is ignored.
DIR_TYPE=XY	X and Y direction bits are observed, X,Y MAJOR bit is ignored. If OCTANT=0, the rectangle is drawn above and to the left of the CUR_X,CUR_Y.
DIR_TYPE=DEGREE	Quadrant is determined by OCTANT/2. i.e., 0 and 1 map to upper right quadrant. 2 and 3 map into upper left quadrant etc.
Side Effects	CUR_X = CUR_X + width; CUR_Y = CUR_Y + height.

TABLE 17.23 Fill Rectangle Horizontal Lines Related Registers

Register	Effect
PIXEL_MODE	Ignored. Always works in SINGLE pixel mode.
LAST_PEL_OFF	Last pixel in each column is ignored.
DIR_TYPE=XY	X and Y direction bits are observed, X,Y MAJOR bit is ignored. If OCTANT=0, the rectangle is drawn above and to the left of the CUR_X,CUR_Y.
DIR_TYPE=DEGREE	Quadrant is determined by OCTANT/2. i.e., 0 and 1 map to upper right quadrant. 2 and 3 map into upper left quadrant etc.
Side Effects	CUR_X = CUR_X + width; CUR_Y = CUR_Y + height.

Fill Rectangle Type FILL_RECT_VER OP_CODE=3

Rectangles are filled using vertical lines. Table 17.23 describes the registers affected.

Fill Rectangle Type FILL_RECT_VNIB OP_CODE=4

Rectangles are filled in a vertical trajectory in a nibble wide mode. Table 17.24 describes the registers affected.

Block Transfer BLIT OP_CODE =6

BitBlt copies data from a source rectangle at CUR_X,CUR_Y to a destination rectangle at DESTX_DIASTP, DESTY_AXSTP. For a color BitBlt to operate correctly, the foreground color source must be = BLIT. For a monochrome

TABLE 17.24 Fill Rectangle Nibble Wide Lines Related Registers

Register	Effect
PIXEL_MODE	Ignored. Always works in NIBBLE pixel mode.
LAST_PEL_OFF	No effect
DIR_TYPE=XY	X and Y direction bits are observed, X,Y MAJOR bit is ignored. If OCTANT=0, the rectangle is drawn above and to the left of the CUR_X,CUR_Y.
DIR_TYPE=DEGREE	Quadrant is determined by OCTANT/2. i.e., 0 and 1 map to upper right quadrant. 2 and 3 map into upper left quadrant etc.
DRAW	No effect
Side Effects	CUR_X,CUR_Y remain unchanged.

TABLE 17.25 BitBlt Related Registers

Register	Effect
RW=READ	PIXEL_MODE is ignored. NIBBLE mode always used.
LAST_PEL_OFF	No effect.
OCTANT,DIR_TYPE	Same as rectangle fill.
DRAW	No effect.
Side Effects	DESTX_DIASTP remains unchanged, DESTY_AXSTP = DESTY_AXSTP + dy; where dy = MIN_AXIS_PCNT + 1; Other registers remain unchanged.

BitBlt to operate correctly, the MONO_SCR field must be set to BLT Source. Table 17.25 describes the registers affected.

17.8.3 Status Register CP_STAT

The Status Register is located at 9AE8. It is a Read Only Register and is described in Table 17.26.

The FIFO-occupied bits (in bits 7–0) indicate the status of the eight FIFO entries. Thus, looking at the first occurrence of a 0 from bit 7 to bit 0 determines how many FIFO positions are available.

TABLE 17.26 GP_STAT Status Register at 9AE8 (Read Only)

Bit	Name	Description
15–10		reserved
9	GP_BUSY	1=GP is busy 0=GP is idle
8	DATA_READY	1= data is ready to be read by host 0= no data is ready for host
7	FIFO_OCCUPIED7	FIFO position 7 is occupied
6	FIFO_OCCUPIED6	FIFO position 6 is occupied
5	FIFO_OCCUPIED5	FIFO position 5 is occupied
4	FIFO_OCCUPIED4	FIFO position 4 is occupied
3	FIFO_OCCUPIED3	FIFO position 3 is occupied
2	FIFO_OCCUPIED2	FIFO position 2 is occupied
1	FIFO_OCCUPIED1	FIFO position 1 is occupied
0	FIFO_OCCUPIED0	FIFO position 0 is occupied

17.9 TRAJECTORY CONTROL REGISTERS

Each of the draw operations, including the line draws, rectangle fills or BitBlts, create a "trajectory," which is a path along which pixels are drawn. There are several parameters that influence the trajectory. These include the registers listed in Table 17.27.

The pixel sources that are drawn onto the trajectory include the foreground, the host CPU, or the BitBlt. The CPU_WAIT field of the Command Register (CMD) can be used to force the GP to wait for host CPU I/O data.

TABLE 17.27 Registers that Affect the Trajectory

Address	Name	Description	Effect
82E8	CUR_Y	Current Y Position	position
86E8	CUR_X	Current X Position	position
96E8	MAJ_AXIS_PCNT	Major Axis Pixel Count	size of line
BEE8	MULTIFUNC_CNTL	Multifunction Control	size of line
8AE8	DESTY_AXSTP	Axial Step Constant	slope
8EE8	DESTX_DIASTP	Diagonal Step Constant	slope
9AE8	CMD	Command	direction type, octant and last pel

17.9.1 Current Position

The Current Position Registers for the X and Y dimensions are named CUR_X and CUR_Y and are located at 86E8 and 8E28. Both are read/write registers. These registers specify the starting coordinates of all draw operations. When a BitBlt operation occurs, these registers specify the starting coordinates for the source rectangle. The lower eleven bits of each register indicate the current position for each respective dimension. The eleven bits are offset by 512 in value ranging from –512 to 1535, instead of the balanced –1024 to 1023. The two registers are shown in Table 17.28 and 17.29 respectively.

If the SKIP1 mode is active, the CUR_Y address is derived from the desired screen position by the following:

CUR_Y = (2 * Y) | (Y & 1);

17.9.2 Destination Position/Axial Step Constant

The Destination Position/Axial Step Constant Registers are named DESTX_AXSTP and DESTY_AXSTP and are located at 8EE8 and 8AE8. Both are write only registers. These registers specify the starting coordinates for the destination rectangle of BitBlt operations. The lower eleven bits of each register indicates the current position for each respective dimension. The eleven bits are offset by 512 in value ranging from –512 to 1535, instead of the standard –1024 to 1023.

TABLE 17.28 CUR_X Current X Position Register at 86E8 (Read/Write)

Bit	Name	Description
15—12		reserved
11		reserved = 0
10—0	CURRENT_X	Current X position (–512 to 1535)

TABLE 17.29 CUR_Y Current Y Position Register at 86E8 (Read/Write)

Bit	Name	Description
15–12		reserved
11		reserved = 0
10–0	CURRENT_Y	Current Y position (–512 to 1535)

TABLE 17.30 DESTX_DIASTP Destination Position X/Diagonal Step Constant Register at 8EE8 (Read/Write)

Bit	Name	Description
15–12		reserved
11		reserved = 0
10–0	CURRENT_X	Current X position (–512 to 1535) used during BitBlt
10–0	DIAGONAL_STEP	Diagonal step constant (–1024 to 1023) used during line draws

TABLE 17.31 DESTY_DIASTP Destination Position Y/Axial Step Constant Register at 86E8 (Read/Write)

Bit	Name	Description
15–12		reserved
11		reserved = 0
10–0	CURRENT_Y	Current Y position (–512 to 1535) used during BitBlt
10–0	AXIAL_STEP	Axial step constant (–1024 to 1023) used during line draws

There is another use of these registers when line draw operations occur. These registers are also used for the diagonal and axial step constants The two registers are shown in Table 17.30 and 17.31 respectively.

If the SKIP1 mode is active, the DESTY_DIASTP_Y address is derived from the desired screen position by the following:

DESTY_AXSTP = (2* (Y & ~1)) | (Y & 1);

Before a line draw operation, the DESTY_AXSTP Register should be set to two times the minimum of the absolute value of dx or dy as shown here:

2 * min (|dx| , |dy|);

Before a line draw operation, the DESTX_AXSTP Register should be set to two times the minimum of the absolute value of dx or dy minus the maximum of the absolute value of dx or dy as shown here:

2 * min (|dx| , |dy) − max (|dx| , |dy|);

17.9.3   Error Term

The Error Term Register, ERR_TERM, defines the initial Bresenham error term for the current line draw. Before starting a line draw, the ERR_TERM should be set to value in the DESTX_AXSTP Register or this value −1 as follows:

if starting x >= ending x: $2 * \min (|dx|, |dy|) - \max (|dx|, |dy|)$;

if starting x < ending x: $2 * \min (|dx|, |dy|) - \max (|dx|, |dy|) - 1$;

The Error Term register is described in Table 17.32.

17.9.4   Pixel Count

The Pixel Count registers for the major and minor axis are named MAJ_AXIS_PCNT and MAJ_AXIS_PCNT respectively. These registers define both rectangle width for a BitBlt or rectangle fill operation or they define the line length for a line draw. The Pixel Count registers are described in Table 17.33 and Table 17.34 respectively. Both are write-only registers.

For line draws, before starting, the MAJ_AXIS_PCNT register should be set to the following:

$\max (|dx|, |dy|)$;

For BitBlts or rectangle fills, before starting, the MAJ_AXIS_PCNT register should be set to the following:

horizontal rectangle dimension −1;

TABLE 17.32   ERR_TERM Error Term Register at 92E8 (Read/Write)

Bit	Name	Description
15–13		reserved
12–0	ERROR	Bresenham error term (−4096 to 4095)

TABLE 17.33   MAJ_AXIS_PCNT Major Axis Pixel Count Register at 96E8 (Write Only)

Bit	Name	Description
15–11		reserved
10–0	WIDTH	rectangle width/line length (0 to 2047)

TABLE 17.34 MIN_AXIS_PCNT Minor Axis Pixel Count
Register at BEE8 (Write Only)

Bit	Name	Description
15–12	MF_INDEX	Multi-function index = 0
11		reserved
10–0	HEIGHT	rectangle height (0 to 2047)

Note: The LAST_PEL_OFF field of the CMD Register has a one pixel effect on the width of the FILL_RECT_HOR rectangles.

The MIN_AXIS_PCNT register shares a function with the MULTI_FUNC_CNTL Register.

For BitBlts or rectangle fills, the MIN_AXIS_PCNT register should be set before starting to the following:

vertical rectangle dimension – 1;

Note: The LAST_PEL_OFF field of the CMD register has a one pixel effect on the height of the FILL_RECT_VPIX rectangles.

17.10   SCISSORS REGISTERS

The Scissors registers inhibit drawing outside a rectangular area of the screen. These registers only affect clipping when the graphics coordinates fall within the Graphics Processor coordinate system, which extends from (–512,–512) to (1535,1535). Any values falling outside of these coordinates will be aliased and will be interpreted incorrectly. The scissors rectangle can be used to generate interrupts when drawing operations fall inside the scissors rectangle.

The Top and Left Scissors Registers are 11-bit registers defining a signed number from (–1024 to 1023). The Right and Bottom Scissors Registers define an unsigned number from (0 to 2047). The X and Y coordinates are numbers ranging from (–512 to 1535) as described in Section 17.9.

When a point is to be written onto a trajectory, it is first compared against the Scissors registers; if it survives the test, it is plotted. Read operations always return an FF hex if the point is not contained in the Scissors region. During a BitBlt operation, the source rectangle is not affected by the scissors region. The BitBlt source wraps at 1024 in X and Y. The scissors region has no effect on monochrome reads.

If SKIP1 mode is active, the Y scissors registers must be set to the following equation:

$$Y = (2*N) + (N\&1);$$

The Top, Left, Bottom and Right Scissors Registers are described in Tables 17.35 through 17.38.

TABLE 17.35 MULTIFUNC_CNTL [SCISSORS_T] Top Scissors Register at BEE8 (Write Only)

Bit	Name	Description
15–12	MF_INDEX	Multifunction index = 1
11		reserved = 0
10–0	TOP_SCISSORS	top scissors value (−1024 to 1023)

TABLE 17.36 MULTIFUNC_CNTL [SCISSORS_L] Left Scissors Register at BEE8 (Write Only)

Bit	Name	Description
15–12	MF_INDEX	Multifunction index = 2
11		reserved = 0
10–0	LEFT_SCISSORS	left scissors value (−1024 to 1023)

TABLE 17.37 MULTIFUNC_CNTL [SCISSORS_B] Bottom Scissors Register at BEE8 (Write Only)

Bit	Name	Description
15–12	MF_INDEX	Multifunction index = 3
11		reserved = 0
10–0	BOTTOM_SCISSORS	bottom scissors value (0 to 2047)

TABLE 17.38 MULTIFUNC_CNTL [SCISSORS_R] Right Scissors Register at BEE8 (Write Only)

Bit	Name	Description
15–12	MF_INDEX	Multifunction index = 4
11		reserved = 0
10–0	RIGHT_SCISSORS	top scissors value (0 to 2047)

17.11 DATA TRANSFER REGISTERS

The two Data Transfer registers are the Short-Stroke Vector Transfer Register and the Pixel Transfer Data Register. Both registers, once loaded, cause actions to take place. All other registers containing parameters relevant to the operation should be loaded with the desired values before writing into these two registers.

17.11.1 The Short-Stroke Vector Transfer Register

The Short Stroke Vector Transfer Register specifies and initiates the drawing of two short-stroke vectors. Both short-stroke vectors, one in bits 15–8 called HI and the second in bits 7–0 called LO, are described in Table 17.39.

17.11.2 The Pixel Transfer Data Register

The Pixel Transfer Register is used when data is transferred between the host and adapter. For monochrome image transfers, read/write data is aligned by a nibble boundary on the screen. When the DATA_WIDTH field of the CMD Register is BIT16, then two nibbles of data can be transferred for each read or write. This also applies to 8-bit image transfers such that two pixels can be transferred for each read and write.

For a monochrome read, the bit value returned for each pixel follows the following rule:

1 if ((P | ~ RD_MASK) == 0xFF)   0 otherwise

For monochrome writes where the bit is zero, the COLOR_SRC field of the BKGD_MIX Register is used. If the bit is 1, the COLOR_SRC field of the FRGB_MIX Register is used. The exact usage of the high and low bytes of this register depends on the DATA_WIDTH and the LSB_FIRST field of the CMD Register as described in Section 17.1.1. Either monochrome or color source

TABLE 17.39 SHORT_STROKE S Short Stroke Vector Transfer Register at 9EE8 (Write Only)

Bit	Name	Description
15–13	DRAW_DIR_HI	Draw Direction
12	DRAW_HI	0=no draw (pen up) 1=draw (pen down)
11–8	LENGTH_HI	Stroke Length
7–5	DRAW_DIR_LO	Draw Direction
4	DRAW_LO	0=no draw (pen up) 1=draw (pen down)
3–0	LENGTH_LO	Stroke Length

TABLE 17.40 PIX_TRANS Pixel Transfer Register at E2E8 (Read/Write)

Bit	Name	Description
15–8	MSB_COLOR	MSB of Color DATA
7–0	LSB_COLOR	LSB of Color Data
15–13		not used for monochrome data
12–9	MSN_MONO	MS nibble of monochrome data
8		Reserved
7–5	LSN_MONO	not used for monochrome data
4–1		LS nibble of monochrome data
0		Reserved

should be selected as the source of data. The PIX_TRANS Register is described in Table 17.40.

17.12   PIXEL TRANSFER ALU CONTROL REGISTERS

The Pixel Transfer ALU (Arithmetic Logic Unit) is used to combine each pixel on a drawing trajectory with one or more sources of data. For each draw operation, one pixel from each of the color and monochrome data sources is combined with the destination pixel by the pixel transfer ALU. The ALU provides sixteen Boolean functions and sixteen arithmetic functions. The ALU uses one of two independent mixes (functions) depending on the value of the monochrome data streams. If the value of the monochrome data stream is one for the current pixel, the foreground mix is used; if the value is zero, the background mix is used.

17.12.1   Foreground and Background Color

The foreground and background color registers specify the foreground and background colors. These are currently 16-bit registers of which only eight bits are used. The foreground and background registers are enabled by selecting the FRGD_MIX or BKGD_MIX as the foreground and background mix respectively. The foreground and background registers are described in Tables 17.41 and 17.42.

17.12.2   Read and Write Mask

The read and write mask registers specify the bit planes that are used in read and write operations. These are shown in Tables 17.43 and 17.44. The read mask is used during monochrome reads and poly fills. It has no effect on color reads. For monochrome reads, the value of RD_MASK is the "true" mask rotated left one bit. That is, Bit 0 is the mask for Plane 7 while bits 1–7 are the masks for Planes 0–6 respectively.

TABLE 17.41 FRGD_COLOR Foreground Color at A2E8 (Write Only)

Bit	Name	Description
15–8		reserved
7–0	FRGD_C	Foreground Color

TABLE 17.42 BKGD_COLOR Foreground Color at A6E8 (Write Only)

Bit	Name	Description
15–8		reserved
7–0	BKGD_C	Background Color

The write plane specifies the bit-planes that are enabled for update. This register also participates in the two polygon fill modes. Planes that are masked out by the Write Mask Register do not participate in any arithmetic ALU operations.

17.12.3 Color Compare

The Color Compare Register specifies the destination comparison color. When a pixel on the draw trajectory is to be updated, it is compared to the value of COLOR_CMP using the function specified in the COLOR_CMP_FN field of the MULTIFUNC_CNTL [PIX_CNTL] Register. If the result is FALSE, the write

TABLE 17.43 RD_MASK Read Mask Register at AEE8 (Write Only)

Bit	Monochrome Reads	Poly Fills
15–8	reserved	reserved
7	Plane 6 Mask	Plane 7 mask
6	Plane 5 Mask	Plane 6 mask
5	Plane 4 Mask	Plane 5 mask
4	Plane 3 Mask	Plane 4 mask
3	Plane 2 Mask	Plane 3 mask
2	Plane 1 Mask	Plane 2 mask
1	Plane 0 Mask	Plane 1 mask
0	Plane 7 Mask	Plane 0 mask

TABLE 17.44 WR_MASK Write Mask Register at AAE8 (Write Only)

Bit	Name	Description
15–8		reserved
7		Plane 7 write enable
6		Plane 6 write enable
5		Plane 5 write enable
4		Plane 4 write enable
3		Plane 3 write enable
2		Plane 2 write enable
1		Plane 1 write enable
0		Plane 0 write enable

TABLE 17.45 COLOR_CMP Color Compare Register at B2E8 (Write Only)

Bit	Name	Description
15–8		reserved
7–0	CMP_COLOR	Destination Compare Color

succeeds; otherwise, the destination pixel is left alone. Color compares are masked through the WRT_MASK register described in Section 17.11.2. The comparison, therefore, ignores all unmasked planes. The Color Compare Register is described in Table 17.45.

The Color Comparison Type is determined by the COLOR_CMP_FN field of the Pixel Control Register described in Section 17.11.6. The possible values are provided in Table 17.46.

17.12.4 Color Sources

The Foreground and Background Mix Registers are used to specify the foreground and background color sources. In addition, the mix functions are used to combine source and destination data. Table 17.47 provides the COLOR_SRC values for these registers.

The Foreground and Background Mix Register are described in Table 17.48 and Table 17.49 respectively.

TABLE 17.46 Color Comparisons

COLOR_CMP_FN	Comparison Type
0	False (destination overwritten)
1	True (destination not overwritten)
2	Destination Color >= COLOR_CMP Register
3	Destination Color < COLOR_CMP Register
4	Destination Color != COLOR_CMP Register
5	Destination Color = COLOR_CMP Register
6	Destination Color <= COLOR_CMP Register
7	Destination Color > COLOR_CMP Register

TABLE 17.47 Color Sources

COLOR_SRC	Color Source Selected
0	BKGD_COLOR Register
1	FRGD_COLOR Register
2	PIX_TRANS Register (Host)
3	BLIT buffer (BitBlt)

TABLE 17.48 FRGD_MIX Background Mix Register at BAE8 (Write Only)

Bit	Name	Description
15–7		reserved
6–5	COLOR_SRC	Background Source Select
4–0	MIX_FN	Background Mix Value

TABLE 17.49 BKGD_MIX Foreground Mix Register at B6E8 (Write Only)

Bit	Name	Description
15–7		reserved
6–5	COLOR_SRC	Background Source Select
4–0	MIX_FN	Background Mix Value

17.12.5 Pattern Registers

The Pattern registers are described in the Fixed Pattern Low and Fixed Pattern High Registers, which contain the monochrome pattern for pixels 0–3. The monochrome pattern for all even-numbered nibbles in a trajectory is described in the MULTIFUNC_CNTL[PATTERN_L] Register when the Pattern registers are selected as monochrome source in the PIX_CNTL field of the MULTIFUNC_CNTL Register. Similarly, the monochrome pattern for all odd numbered nibbles in a trajectory is described in the MULTIFUNC_CNTL[PATTERN_H] Register. The Fixed Pattern Low and Fixed Pattern High Registers are described in Table 17.50 and Table 17.51 respectively.

TABLE 17.50 MULTIFUNC_CNTL[PATTERN_L] Fixed Pattern Low Register at BEE8 (Write Only)

Bit	Name	Description
15–8	MF_INDEX	Multifunction index = 8
11–5		reserved
4		Monochrome pattern for pixel 0
3		Monochrome pattern for pixcl 1
2		Monochrome pattern for pixel 2
1		Monochrome pattern for pixel 3
0		reserved

TABLE 17.51 MULTIFUNC_CNTL[PATTERN_L] Fixed Pattern Low Register at BEE8 (Write Only)

Bit	Name	Description
15–8	MF_INDEX	Multifunction index = 9
11–5		reserved
4		Monochrome pattern for pixel 0
3		Monochrome pattern for pixel 1
2		Monochrome pattern for pixel 2
1		Monochrome pattern for pixel 3
0		reserved

17.12.6   Pixel Control

The Pixel Control Register selects the monochrome source, destination color compare function, polygon fill type, monochrome read mode, and polygon fill mode as shown in Table 17.52.

The Fields in the Pixel Control Register are further described in Table 17.53.

TABLE 17.52   MULTIFUNC_CNTL[PIX_CNTL] Pixel Control Register at BEE8 (Write Only)

Bit	Name	Description
15–8	MF_INDEX	Multifunction index = A
11–8		reserved
7–6	MONO_SRC	Monochrome Source (See Table 17.2)
5–3	COLOR_CMP_FN	Color Compare Function
2	MONO_READ	Monochrome Read Enable
2	POLY_FILL_ENABLE	Enable Polygon Fill
1	POLY_FILL_TYPE	Select Polygon Fill Type 0=Polygon Fill Mode A 1=Polygon Fill Mode B
0		reserved

TABLE 17.53   Fields in the Pixel Control Register

Field	Description
MONO_SRC	Monochrome source. All write operations involve the FRGD_MIX, BKGD_MIX and a monochrome pattern. When mono patterns are not desired, the MONO_SRC is set to 00. This causes only the FRGD_MIX to be involved.
COLOR_CMP_FN	Specifies the Color comparison parameters. If TRUE, the destination is not overwritten. This field is specified in Table 17.46.
MONO_READ	This field is used during monochrome read operations. When 1, monochrome data is computed from the read/BLIT-source trajectory. Pixels are translated into bits. A pixel is set to 1 if all bits selected by the RD_MASK are high. Else, it is set to 0.
POLY_FILL_ENABLE	Enables polygon filling
POLY_FILL_TYPE	Bit 1 specifies whether Polygon fill mode A or B is selected.

17.12.7 Polygon Fill

Both types A and B of the polygon fill are used during a FILL_RECT_HOR Fill Rectangle operation. Both use monochrome reads to detect outlines. Whenever outlines are detected, the Fill State is toggled. During FILL_RECT_HOR Rectangle Fill and BLIT, the Fill State is set to 0 at the beginning of each scan line. The Polygon Fill Modes are only relevant to the FILL_RECT_HOR and the BLIT commands.

The Polygon Fill Mode A uses the RD_MASK for the monochrome outline detect. For a pixel to be classified as an outline, all bits selected by RD_MASK must be high. WRT_MASK selects the planes where the polygon will be written. Those planes for which both read and write masks are high are cleared. The right edges of the outline are not included in the fill, but the left edges are included. The following example illustrates the outline and fill result using a Polygon Fill Mode A.

Outline Plane   00000000100000000100000000010001000000100000

Fill Plane   00000000111111110000000000111100000000111111

The Polygon Fill Mode B selects both the outline and the fill planes. For a pixel to be classified as an outline, all bits selected by the WRT_MASK must be high and the RD_MASK must be non-zero. The RD_MASK is otherwise ignored. Both the left and right edges are included in the resultant filled area.

Before Outline   00000000100000000100000000010001000000100000

After Fill   00000000111111110000000000111100000000111111

The operation of the polygon fill modes is summarized in Table 17.54.

TABLE 17.54 Operation of the Polygon Fill

Fill State	Write Mask	Read Mask	Result Mode A	Result Mode B
0	0	0	Destination	Destination
0	0	1	Destination	Destination
0	1	0	Destination	Destination
0	1	1	0	Destination
1	0	0	Destination	Destination
1	0	1	Destination	Destination
1	1	0	ALU	ALU
1	1	1	0	ALU

17.13   USING THE 8514/A

Following are several examples that should help you use the 8514/A. These include setting up the 8514/A, initializing the graphics processor, using the FIFO, drawing a line drawing a short-stroke vector, performing a rectangle fill, writing to single pixels, a color BitBlt from the host to the adapter, a monochrome image transfer, the use of monochrome line patterns, a BitBlt copy, and a polygon fill.

17.13.1   Setting Up the 8514/A

It is necessary to first put the 8514/A through its reset/normal sequence by writing a 9000 hex and then a 5000 hex to the SUBSYS_CNTL register. The desired DAC color table should then be loaded into the DAC registers. The CRT Registers must be set according to the desired resolution, monitor type and memory configuration. The MULTIFUNC_CNTL[MEM_CNTL], the WRITE_MASK, and the DAC_MASK registers must be set according to the memory configuration, desired resolution, and bank configuration.

17.13.2   Initializing the Graphics Processor

It is often advisable to set up the Graphics Processor (GP) registers to a known state. One possible setup is shown in Table 17.55.

The following examples assume that the system is not in a SKIP1 mode and that all coordinates are within the adapter coordinate system and don't need to be pre-clipped.

17.13.3   Using the FIFO

The host is responsible for ensuring that the FIFO never overflows, since an overflow will cause the adapter to cease accepting further input. The preferred method is to read the GP_STAT Register to check if there is enough room for

TABLE 17.55   GP Register Initialization

Register	Value (hex)
FRGD_MIX	27 (paint FRGD_COLOR)
BKGD_MIX	03 (leave destination alone)
SCISSOR_T	0
SCISSOR_L	0
SCISSOR_B	3FF
SCISSOR_R	3FF
PIX_CNTL	A000 (overwrite destination)

the new parameters. For example, suppose that the next command requires five parameters. To check bit 3 to see if there were five available slots, one could use the following wait loop:

```
while (inp(GP_STAT) & 0x08 {};
```

It is also the host's responsibility to check for the DATA_READY field of the GP_STAT Register to go high before performing a read operation.

The FIFO must be empty before the host writes image or pattern data to PIX_TRANS. This indicates that the previous operations have completed. This can be accomplished as follows:

```
while (inp(GP_STAT) & 0x08 {};
```

17.13.4   Drawing a Line Drawing

Three types of line draw operations are shown in Table 17.56. This table supposes that the line is to be drawn from (start_x, start_y) to (end_x, end_y) and that dx and dy are the absolute value of the difference between the start and end coordinates as follows:

$$dx = abs (end\_x - start\_x); \quad dy = abs (end\_y - start\_y);$$

17.13.5   Short-Stroke Vector

The following code draws a diamond figure with edges that are ten pixels long and based at (100,100), using the Degree mode lines.

```
outpw(CUR_X,100);  outpw(CUR_Y,100);  outpw(MAJ_AXIS_PCNT,9);
outpw(CMD,0x203F);  outpw(CMD,0x207F);  outpw(CMD,0x20BF);
outpw(CMD,0x20FF);
```

The following code performs the same operation using the Short-Stroke Vector:

```
outpw(CUR_X,100);  outpw(CUR_Y,100);  outpw(CMD,0x100F);
outpw(SHORT_STROKE,0x7939);  outpw(SHORT_STROKE,0xF9B9);
```

17.13.6   Performing a Rectangle Fill

A rectangle fill of width vs. height starting at upper-left corner (100,100) is accomplished by the following code:

```
outpw(CUR_X,100);  outpw(CUR_Y,100);
outpw(MAJ_AXIS_PCNT,width-1);  outpw(MULTIFUNC_CNTL,height-1);
outpw(CMD,0x40F3);
```

TABLE 17.56 Three Different Line Types

Register	Pattern line	Normal line	Polygon Boundary
CUR_Y	start_x	start_x	(see Note 2)
CUR_X	start_y	start_y	min (start_y, end_y)
DESTY_AXSTP		$2 * \min(\,\lvert dx \rvert\,,\,\lvert dy \rvert\,)$	
DESTX_DIASTP		$2 * (\,\min(\,\lvert dx \rvert\,,\,\lvert dy \rvert\,) - \max(\,\lvert dx \rvert\,,\,\lvert dy \rvert\,)\,)$	
ERR_TERM		$2 * (\,\min(\,\lvert dx \rvert\,,\,\lvert dy \rvert\,) - \max(\,\lvert dx \rvert\,,\,\lvert dy \rvert\,)\,) - \text{fixup}$	
MAJ_AXIS_PCNT		$\max(\,\lvert dx \rvert\,,\,\lvert dy \rvert\,)$	
FRGD_MX	0x47	0x27	0x27 (see Note 2)
FRGD_COLOR	don't care	as appropriate	as appropriate
CND	0x3311+OCTANT	0x2013+OCTANT	0xA017+OCTANT
.OP_CODE	1 (DRAW_LINE)	1 (DRAW_LINE)	5 (DRAW_POLY_LINE)
.LSB_FIRST	1 (see Note 1)	don't care	don't care
.DATA_WIDTH	1 (see Note 1)	don't care	don't care
.CPU_WAIT	1	0	0
.OCTANT		see CMD.YPOS,CMD.YMAJOR,CMD.XPOS	
.YPOS		(start_y < end_y) ? 1 : 0) (see Note 2)	
.YMAJOR		$(\,\lvert dy \rvert < \lvert dx \rvert\,)$? 1 : 0)	
.XPOS		(start_x < end_x) ? 1 : 0) (see Note 2)	
.DRAW	1		
.DIR_TYPE	0 (XY Coding)		
.LAST_PEL_OFF	(see Note 3)	(see Note 3)	(see Note 2)
.PIXEL_MODE	0 (single)	1(nibble)	1 (nibble)
.RW	1 (write)	1 (write)	1 (write)
PIX_TRANS	pattern data	not used	not used

Notes:

1. Assumes that the REP OUTSW will be used to write to the PIX_TRANS.

2. The polygon fill requires that boundary lines be drawn from top to bottom with last pixel off and a NOT_D mix. These lines are typically drawn on a single plane in off-screen memory prior to the poly fill step.

3. The "last pel" should be off for lines that are part of a curve or outline made up of multiple line segments.

It should be noted that the same operation could be performed using the last pixel off and, consequently, avoiding a subtraction as follows:

```
outpw(CUR_X,100);  outpw(CUR_Y,100);
outpw(MAJ_AXIS_PCNT, width);  outpw(MULTIFUNC_CNTL,height-1);
outpw(CMD,0x40F7);
```

17.13.7   Writing to Single Pixels

Single pixels are written directly to 100,100 as follows. If a series of single points are written, it is only necessary to set the MAJ_AXIS_PCNT once.

```
outpw(CUR_X,100);  outpw(CUR_Y,100);
outpw(MAJ_AXIS_PCNT,0);  outpw(CMD,0x2013);
```

17.13.8   A Color BitBlt from the Host to the Adapter

A rectangular image of width vs. height can be transferred from the host to the adapter at upper-left corner (100,100) as follows. A block word write can then be transferred to the PIX_TRANS that is (width*height)/2 words long if the data is contiguously resident in host memory.

```
outpw(FRGD_MIX,0x47);
outpw(CUR_X,100);  outpw(CUR_Y,100);
outpw(MAJ_AXIS_PCNT,width-1);  outpw(MULTIFUNC_CNTL,height-1);
outpw(CMD,0x53F1);
```

17.13.9   A Monochrome Image Transfer

A rectangular image of width vs. height can be transferred from the host to the adapter at upper-left corner (100,100) as follows:

```
outpw(MULTIFUNC_CNTL, PIX_CNTL | 0x80);
outpw(CUR_X,100);  outpw(CUR_Y,100);
outpw(MAJ_AXIS_PCNT,width-1);  outpw(MULTIFUNC_CNTL,height-1);
outpw(CMD,0x41F3);
```

The monochrome image is transferred four bits (a nibble) at a time in bits 3–0 of the PIX_TRANS. This is illustrated in Figure 17.2. Figure 17.2a illustrates the data as written into display memory. Figure 17.2b illustrates the data as it resides in host memory.

A word has to be written at a time to transfer the four bits. If the CMD.DATA_WIDTH is set for 16-bit transfers, an extra four bits can be written in bits 13–10 of PIX_TRANS. A rectangular image of width vs. height can be transferred from the adapter to the host at upper-left corner (100,100) as follows:

```
outpw(MULTIFUNC_CNTL, PIX_CNTL | 0x04); outpw(RD_MASK,
source_plane);
```

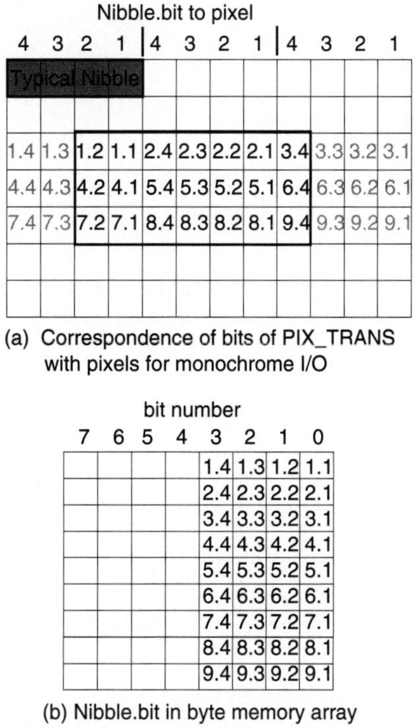

Nibble.bit to pixel

4 3 2 1 │ 4 3 2 1 │ 4 3 2 1

Typical Nibble										
1.4	1.3	1.2	1.1	2.4	2.3	2.2	2.1	3.4	3.3	3.2	3.1
4.4	4.3	4.2	4.1	5.4	5.3	5.2	5.1	6.4	6.3	6.2	6.1
7.4	7.3	7.2	7.1	8.4	8.3	8.2	8.1	9.4	9.3	9.2	9.1

(a) Correspondence of bits of PIX_TRANS
with pixels for monochrome I/O

bit number

7 6 5 4 3 2 1 0

				1.4	1.3	1.2	1.1
				2.4	2.3	2.2	2.1
				3.4	3.3	3.2	3.1
				4.4	4.3	4.2	4.1
				5.4	5.3	5.2	5.1
				6.4	6.3	6.2	6.1
				7.4	7.3	7.2	7.1
				8.4	8.3	8.2	8.1
				9.4	9.3	9.2	9.1

(b) Nibble.bit in byte memory array

FIGURE 17.2 Monochrome BitBlt. (a) Correspondence of bits and pixels (b) Correspondence of bits and nibbles

```
outpw(CUR_X,100); outpw(CUR_Y,100);
outpw(MAJ_AXIS_PCNT,width-1); outpw(MULTIFUNC_CNTL,height-1);
outpw(CMD,0x41F2);
```

After waiting for GP_STAT.DATA_READY to go high, the host can read from PIX_TRANS, unpacking four bits from bits 3–0 after each read.

17.13.10 Monochrome Line Patterns

Monochrome patterns are used with nibbles, but not pixels. It is therefore difficult to use monochrome patterns on lines. This is illustrated in Figure 17.3. In Figure 17.3a, the line is drawn in a nibble mode while in 17.3b, the line is drawn in a single mode. The pattern is stored in host memory as indicated in Figure 17.2b.

There are two ways to draw a patterned line:

1. Use a run-length encoding of the line pattern. The trajectory control registers for the desired line are set, except for MAJ_AXIS_PCNT. The host writes to MAJ_AXIS_PCNT and CMD to write the individual runs. The

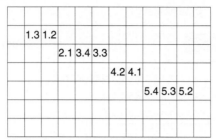

(a) Correspondence of PIX_TRANS bits with pixels for
a line drawn using monochrome nibble mode

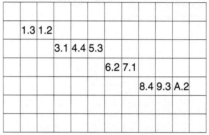

(b) Correspondence of PIX_TRANS bits with pixels for
a line drawn using monochrome single mode

FIGURE 17.3 Monochrome Patterns on Lines. (a) Correspondence of bits and pixels in nibble mode (b) Correspondence of bits and nibbles in single mode

CMD.DRAW bit alternates as 1 and 0 if the background mix is LEAVE_ALONE. The CMD.DRAW bit can remain set to 1, and the FRGD_MIX.COLOR_SRC and FRGD_MIX.MIX_FN can be manipulated to achieve the desired foreground and background effects.

2. In SINGLE mode, four pattern bits are used for every pixel, with the one bit corresponding to the pixel's position being used per nibble.

A line draw operation using monochrome host data is set up in SINGLE pixel mode, and for every pixel in the line the host writes either a 0xFF or a 0x00 to PIX_TRANS depending on whether the corresponding pattern bit is 1 or 0. Thus the single bit within the nibble is always either a correct 1 or a 0. This is shown in the following code:

```
outpw(MULTIFUNC_CNTL, PIX_CNTL | 0x80);
outpw(CUR_X,100);  outpw(CUR_Y,100);
outpw(DESTY_AXSTP,500);  outpw(DESTX_DIASTP,500);
outpw(MAJ_AXIS_PCNT,500-100);
outpw(CMD,0x2113 | octant | last_pel_off);
while (pixels_remain()) {
  bit = get_next_pattern_bit();
  outp(PIX_TRANS,bit ? 0xFF : 0x00);
  }
```

17.13.11 BitBlt Copy

The following code copies a width-by-height rectangle from upper-left-hand corner at (100,100) to upper-left-hand corner at (500,500):

```
outpw(CUR_X,100);  outpw(CUR_Y,100);
outpw(DESTY_AXSTP,500);  outpw(DESTX_DIASTP,500);
outpw(MAJ_AXIS_PCNT,width-1);  outpw(MULTIFUNC_CNTL,
MIN_AXIS_PCNT | height-1);
outpw(FRGD_MIX,0x67);
outpw(CMD,0xC0F3);  // sweep down and to the right
```

A second example occurs when the rectangles overlap as shown in the following code:

```
outpw(CUR_X,100+width-1);  outpw(CUR_Y,100+height-1);
outpw(DESTY_AXSTP,200+width-1);  outpw(DESTX_DIASTP,200+height-1);
outpw(MAJ_AXIS_PCNT,width-1);
outpw(MULTIFUNC_CNTL, MIN_AXIS_PCNT | height-1);
outpw(FRGD_MIX,0x67);
outpw(CMD,0xC013);   // sweep up and to the left.
```

17.13.12 Polygon Fill

The host must perform several steps to perform a polygon fill. A simple example is provided, assuming that the polygon is small enough to fit into off-screen memory, the bounding box of the polygon is known, and a solid fill is desired.

1. Allocate a scratch rectangle in off-screen memory the size of the polygon bounding box.

2. Clear the scratch rectangle and set the scissors rectangle to the scratch rectangle.

3. Set the FRGD_MIX = 0x20 (NOT_D) and the WRT_MASK = 0x02. (Plane 1)

4. Draw the polygon boundary using DRAW_POLY+LINE with last pel off. All edges must be drawn from top to bottom.

5. Set MULTIFUNC_CNTL[PIX_CNTL] to 0x04 to enable poly fill mode.

6. Set the RD_MASK=0x02 and the WRT_MASK to 0x01.

7. Invoke a FILL_RECT_HOR on the scratch rectangle. The result is a filled polygon in Plane 0 corresponding to the outline in plane 1.

8. Restore the scissors rectangle to its original state.

9. Set the MULTIFUNC_CNTL[PIX_CNTL] to 0x80. This will perform a color expansion using the monochrome source. Set FRGD_COLOR as desired

and FRGD_MIX to 0x27 (PAINT). Make sure that the BKGD_MIX is set to LEAVE_ALONE.

10. Invoke a BLIT operation using the scratch rectangle as the source and the original polygon bounding box as the target. The result is a filled polygon in FRGD_COLOR.

Chapter 18

The XGA

18.1 THE XGA

The XGA was an attempt by IBM to improve upon the VGA standard. It is a sound architecture adding a high-color display mode and a graphics coprocessor. It can be considered as another type of Super VGA; in fact, the IIT Super VGA chip emulates the XGA. Special thanks to IIT for providing documentation relating to the XGA standard. The XGA includes all VGA modes, a 132-column text mode, and enhanced modes up to 1024 by 768 in an 8-bit-per-color mode. A 16-bit-per-color mode is also available in a 640-by-480 display resolution.

The most notable feature of the XGA is the graphics coprocessor, which was equipped to be a bus master on the micro channel systems; however, this feature is currently not used on the ISA or VL bus architectures. It could become available when used on the PCI bus. The coprocessor can draw straight lines, perform BitBlts, and do rapid rectangle fills. Like most coprocessors, it can perform arithmetic and logical raster operations.

18.1.1 Memory-Related Registers

The XGA was designed to utilize VRAM memory in 1-, 2-, 4-, 8-, or 16-bits-per-pixel modes. The maximum memory supported by the XGA was 1 Mbyte; however, third party implementations often include up to 24-bit color, higher display resolutions, and support upwards to 4 Mbytes of memory. The memory aperture can be set up as a 1-Mbyte aperture, a 4-Mbyte aperture, or as 16 banks of 64 Kbytes VGA type memory. The 1- and 4-Mbyte linear mappings require an 80386 or above processor with an extended DOS operating environment. The XGA graphics coprocessor works in the 4-Mbyte memory aperture.

The registers associated with the memory access are the Aperture Control Register at 21x1, Aperture Index Register at 21x8, and the Memory Access

TABLE 18.1 VRAM System Aperture (Bits 1–0) of 21x1

Value	Function
0	No 64 Kbyte aperture
1	64 Kbyte aperture at A0000h
2	64 Kbyte aperture at B0000h
3	Reserved

TABLE 18.2 Pixel Size Field of the Memory Access Register

Field	Bits/Pixel
0	1
1	2
2	4
3	8
4	16

Mode Register at 21x9. The Aperture Control Register uses bits 1–0 as the VRAM system aperture with values as specified in Table 18.1.

The Aperture Index Register uses bits 4–0 as the aperture index providing up to sixteen banks of 64 Kbytes each. This aperture is used when the VRAM System Aperture (Bits 1–0) of 21x1 is either a 1 or a 2 and it would reside at either A0000h or B0000h respectively. Other implementations of the XGA that access more memory would use bits 7–5 to add additional banks. For example, a 2-Mbyte system would require bit 5 and a 4-Mbyte system would require bits 6–5.

The Memory Access Register determines the pixel format (bit 3) and the pixel size (bit 2–0). The Pixel Size field resides in bits 2–0. This field is described in Table 18.2.

The VRAM Pixel Format Register uses bit 3 of this register. A 0 indicates Intel memory format, and a 1 indicates Motorola memory format.

18.1.2 XGA Display Controller

The XGA display controller is memory mapped at a base address of 21x0 hex, where x is called the instance of the XGA adapter. In the micro channel, this default is 6; however, it may often reside at 0. More than one XGA can reside

TABLE 18.3 XGA Display Controller Registers

Address	Description	Usage
21x0	Operating Mode	Display mode
21x1	Aperture Control	What type of aperture
21x4	Interrupt Enable	Interrupt enables
21x5	Interrupt Status	Interrupt status
21x6	Video Memory Control	What type of video memory
21x8	Aperture Index	Which aperture index
21x9	Memory Access Mode	How is memory accessed
21xA	Index Register	Indexes other XGA registers including CRT, display control, hardware control, and sprite

TABLE 18.4 Operating Mode Register Display Mode Field

Field	Description
0	VGA mode (XGA address decode disabled)
1	VGA mode (XGA address decode enabled)
2	132-column mode (XGA address decode disabled)
3	132-column mode (XGA address decode enabled)
4	XGA Extended Graphics Mode

on a system at a time, due to the instance. The programmable registers range from 21x0 hex to 21xF hex as shown in Table 18.3.

18.1.3 Operating Mode Register

The Operating Mode Register contains an order field in bit position 3 and a mode control variable in bits 2–0 as shown in Table 18.4.

18.2 SETTING UP THE XGA

Due to the multiple-adapter capabilities of the XGA, the XGA requires several setup operations. The XGA is set up by first determining if a micro channel is present. If it is, you should check for a valid XGA ID. If one is present, it will reside at location 0 (motherboard) or slot (1–7) for an adapter card. Whether a motherboard or adapter card implementation is present, determines the operations that follow. The steps are illustrated in Figure 18.1.

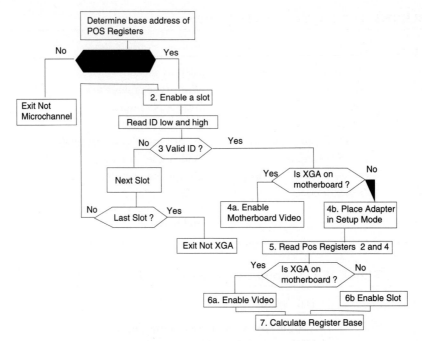

FIGURE 18.1 Setting up the XGA

Following are the code segments associated with Figure 18.1.

1. **Is Micro channel present. Returns –1 if not, else returns XGA_POS.**

```
Is_it_Microchannel proc far
    mov     ah,0C4h     ;service 196 of INT 15h
    mov     al,00h
    INT 15h
    jc      no
    mov     ax,dx       ;microchannel present return XGA_POS
    ret
no: mov     ax,-1
    ret
Is_it_Microchannel endp
```

2. **Enable slot for setup.**

```
enableSlot proc far XGA_POS
    mov     AH,0C4h
    mov     AL, 01h
    mov     CX,XGA_POS
    INT 15h
    ret
enableSlot endp
```

3. **Check for valid ID.**

```
int isValidId(int XGA_POS)
{  unsigned int value;
 value =   _inpw(XGA_POS);
 if( (value >= 0x8fd8) && (value <= 0x8fdb) )
  return(1);
 else
  return(-1);
}
```

4a. **Set up motherboard.**

```
setupMotherboardVideo proc far
    mov    al,0DFh
    mov    dx, 94h
    out    dx,al
    ret
setupMotherboardVideo endp
```

4b. **Set up Slot.**

```
setupSlotVideo proc far slot
    mov    ax,0C401h
    mov    bx,slot
    INT 15h
setupSlotVideo endp
```

5. **Get POS Registers 2 and 4.**

```
void  getPosValues(int XGA_POS, BYTE *pos2, BYTE *pos4)
{
*pos2 = _inp (XGA_POS+2);
*pos4 = _inp (XGA_POS+4);
 }
```

6a. **Enable motherboard video.**

```
enableMotherboardVideo proc far
    mov    al,0FFh
    mov    dx, 94h
    out    dx,al
    ret
enableMotherboardVideo  endp
```

6b. **Enable adapter card video.**

```
enableSlotVideo proc far slot
    mov    ax,0C402h
    mov    bx,slot
    INT 15h
enableSlotVideo   endp
end
```

7. Calculate register base.

```
// Instance is in POS 2 Register bits 3-1 <<3 for  21x0h
 int getXGAbase(int pos2)
 {
  return( ((pos2 & 0x0e)<<3) + 0x2100);
 }
```

18.3 SETTING UP THE COLOR REGISTERS

The XGA is similar to the VGA in that it has 256 color registers. However, these registers are different from the VGA in that there are no associated palette registers. The color registers are listed in Table 18.5 and loaded by the code in Listing 18.1.

There are two modes for setting the palette. The first is a mode similar to the VGA where a 3-byte sequence is used. This sequence, red followed by green followed by blue, is active if bit 2 of the Palette Sequence Register is 0. If this bit 2 is set, then a 4-byte sequence is used. This sequence is red followed by green followed by blue followed by a dummy byte.

Like the VGA, each of the color registers uses six bits for each color. However, unlike the VGA, these six bits are left-justified in the word. Consequently, a VGA color register would have to be shifted left two bits before being loaded into the XGA. This is actually a more flexible approach since it easily incorporates DACs with 8 bits per color.

LISTING 18.1 Code Segment to Load the Color Registers

```
Assume:  DX = Index Register is at XGA_BASE + 0ah
         DX = Data Register is at XGA_BASE + 0bh
         DS:[SI] points to the palette data. Note that the order
         is red followed by blue, followed by green.

; Disable Color Registers from Display
         mov    ax,64h ; Write 00 to Palette Mask Register
         out    dx,ax
         mov    ax,55h ; Write 00 to Border Color Register.
         out    dx,ax
; Select 4-color write mode (RGBx)
         mov    ax,466h
         out    dx,ax
; Select first register
         mov    ax,60h
         out    dx,ax
         mov    ax,61h
         out    dx,ax
```

```
; Select Data Register
        mov     ax,65h    ;select the data register
        out     dx,ax
        inc     dx        ;access data register
; Move 1024 bytes as pointed to by DS:[SI]
        mov     cx,1024  ; write to all 256 of the 4-color registers
perbyte:lodsb             ;get byte into ax from ds:[si] and inc si
        out     dx,al
        loop    perbyte
; Point back to select index register
        dec     dx
; Enable Color Registers for display
        mov     al,0FFh
        mov     ah,64h
        out     dx,ax
```

TABLE 18.5 Color Registers

Index	Description	Usage
55	Border Color Register	Border color
60	Palette Index Low	Low byte of index (0–1023)
61	Palette Index High	High byte of index (0–1023)
64	Palette Mask	Palette Mask bit=0 disables
65	Palette Data	Data Register for color registers
66	Palette Sequence	
67	Palette Red Prefetch	Red prefetch
68	Palette Green Prefetch	
69	Palette Blue Prefetch	

18.3.1 Hi-Color Color Registers

The color registers have to be loaded with a special set of values, as specified by IBM, for the hi-color mode to operate. All red and blue registers must be set to 0, and the green registers must increment by 8, providing eight sets of ramps each 32 long. The 256 registers are split into two banks of 128 registers each. The bank is selected by bit 7 of the Border Color Register. If bit 7 is set to 1, the first bank is selected (color registers 0–127). If bit 7 is a 0, the second bank is selected (color registers 128–255).

18.4 DISPLAY CONTROL REGISTERS

The Display Controller registers control aspects of the display, some of which are important to the programmer. The registers are provided in Table 18.6.

TABLE 18.6 Display Control Registers

Offset	Description	Usage
40h	Display Map Offset Low	Low-order eight bits of the start address
41h	Display Map Offset Middle	Middle-order eight bits of the start address
42h	Display Map Offset High	High-order one bit of the start address
43h	Display Map Width Low	Low-order eight bits of the width of the display
44h	Display Map Width High	High-order three bits of the width of the display
50h	Display Control 1	Various display parameters
51h	Display Control 2	Various display parameters including pixel size

TABLE 18.7 Standard Display Modes as Described by IBM

Mode	Resolution	Bits per Pixel
0	VGA Text Mode 3	
1	132-column Text	
2	1024 by 768	8 bits
3	1024 by 768	4 bits
4	640 by 480	8 bits
5	640 by 480	16 bits

The three Display Map Offset registers provide the start address of the on-screen display. Each value in these registers corresponds to an 8-byte granularity. Therefore, the seventeen bits translate to twenty bits providing the full-memory access.

The Display Map Width registers provide an 11-bit address allowing up to 2048 pixels per scan line. Each value in these registers corresponds to an 8-byte granularity. Therefore, the eleven bits translate to fourteen bits maximum width. The standard widths of the display modes are provided in Table 18.7.

18.5   HARDWARE SPRITE

The Hardware cursor (sprite) is a 64-by-64 pattern. This pattern is stored in a RAM chip not associated with display memory. This feature is often **not** used in XGA clones (see Chapter 23). The sprite is not mixed into the video stream until the DAC; therefore, its data does not overwrite image data. The sprite image can be smaller than 64 by 64. This is accomplished by using the Hotspot Registers and transparent codes in the sprite pattern. The Sprite Horizontal Start and Vertical Start Registers control the location of the sprite when displayed. Setting bit 0 of the Sprite Control Register to 1 enables the sprite for display. The horizontal and vertical hotspots determine the offset into the 64-by-64 sprite region where the visible sprite is shown.

The sprite image is stored as 64 pixels, one horizontal line at a time (top line first). These 64 pixels occupy 128 bits or 16 bytes. These 16 bytes are followed by the 64 pixels of the second to top line. Motorola ordering is used with the left-most pixel occupying the most significant two bits in a byte. The cursor is controlled through the cursor positioning registers and are indexed through the AGX index/data registers as listed in Table 18.8.

TABLE 18.8 Hardware Cursor Registers

Index	Description	Usage
31–30h	Cursor Position X	Sets the X-pixel position of the visible portion of the cursor in screen coordinates
34–33h	Cursor Position Y	Sets the Y-pixel position of the visible portion of the cursor in screen coordinates
32h	Cursor Hotspot X	Sets the X-offset pixel position of the visible portion of the cursor within the cursor pattern
35h	Cursor Hotspot Y	Sets the Y-offset pixel position of the visible portion of the cursor within the cursor pattern
36h	Cursor Control	Bit 0 turns on and off the cursor
38h	Cursor Color 0 Red	Red component of color 0
39h	Cursor Color 0 Green	Green component of color 0
3Ah	Cursor Color 0 Blue	Blue component of color 0
3Bh	Cursor Color 1 Red	Red component of color 1
3Ch	Cursor Color 1 Green	Green component of color 1
3Dh	Cursor Color 1 Blue	Blue component of color 1
60h	Sprite Index Low	Sprite index low
61h	Sprite Index High	Sprite index high
62h	Sprite Prefetch Low	Sprite prefetch low
63h	Sprite Prefetch High	Sprite prefetch high
6Ah	Sprite Data	Sprite data

TABLE 18.9 Sprite Image Bits

Bits	Function
0	Use sprite color 0
1	Use sprite color 1
2	Transparent (don't draw)
3	One's complement

The sprite image consists of two bits per pixel. These are described in Table 18.9.

18.6 CONTROLLING THE COPROCESSOR

The coprocessor is controlled through a simple control register and status register. A busy bit is in the Coprocessor Control Register. It is typically polled to determine when the coprocessor is ready for another command. A command is issued to generate a line, area fill, or BitBlt through the Pixel Operation Register. The Short-Stroke Register also issues a command to draw another (one to four) short-stroke vectors. The XGA can generate an interrupt on the occurrence of processor ready; however, this feature is rarely used due to the difficulties involved with using sharing interrupts in the DOS environment and the delays incurred when servicing interrupts in a Windows environment. Polling the coprocessor is accomplished by the code in Listing 18.2. Note that a delay loop is present so that the coprocessor is not constantly polled. Constant polling slows down the coprocessor.

LISTING 18.2 Determining if the Coprocessor Is Ready

```
rloop:  mov al,XGA_BASE + 11h
        test   al,80h test bit 7
        jz     ok
        mov    cx,100     ;wait a bit before retesting
wait:   jmp    $+2
        loop   wait
        jmp    rloop
ok:     ret
```

18.7 PIXEL MAPS

Image data is stored in rectangular regions defined by the address of the start of the rectangle, the width and height of the map, and the format of the data in the map. These regions may be used as the source or destination for operations. In addition, they can be used to hold the mask or pattern. The 8514/A and the

XGA, along with many Super VGAs, were defined with a graphics arithmetic processor capable of handling four inputs, corresponding to the source, destination, pattern, and mask. The pattern and mask are always 1-bit-per-pixel maps. Every operation has to have a destination map. The source of an operation can be either one of the maps or a constant stored in one or more registers. For example, a BitBlt and a Rectangular fill would require a destination bit map, where the first would have a source bit map and the second would use a constant as the source. The pattern mask is used to either augment source data or be the actual source of data. The mask map is used to clip on non-rectangular boundaries.

The XGA uses an indirect addressing scheme called pixel maps to specify the rectangular regions. There are three pixels maps called Map A, Map B, and Map C. Each of these three maps is specified by the four parameters. Each operation then refers to one of these three maps. Therefore, an operation doesn't have to specify the base, width, height, and format each time. It simply refers to either Map A, Map B, Map C.

The pixel maps are specified by the four parameters—base, width, height, and format—as shown in Table 18.10. The map is shown in Figure 18.2.

The four descriptive parameters that describe a map are located at offsets 14–1Ch. Only one map can be written to at a time. Therefore, the maps have to

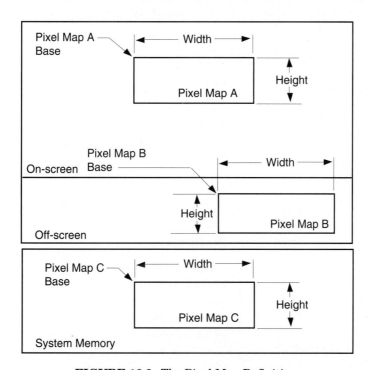

FIGURE 18.2 The Pixel Map Definition

TABLE 18.10 Pixel Map Parameters

Offset	Description	Usage
13–12h	Pixel Map Index	Defines the map selected for writing. Can be A,B,C, or the mask map.
17–14h	Pixel Map Base	Defines the linear start of the pixel map. This could be the physical address in real mode or it could be the virtual address in protected mode.
19–18h	Pixel Map Width	The horizontal pixel width of the map.
1B–1Ah	Pixel Map Height	The vertical pixel height of the map.
1Ch	Pixel Map Format	The number of bits/pixel and the Motorola or Intel ordering.

be indexed. This is accomplished by the Pixel Map Index Register. The maps are defined by the two bits in bit positions 1,0. The values for this register are described in Table 18.11.

The Pixel Map Format Register uses bits 2–0 for the bits/pixel and bit 3 for the pixel ordering. The pixel size is specified in Table 18.12. It should be noted that the format of the source and destination bit maps must be identical. Also,

TABLE 18.11 Pixel Map Index Register

Value	Description
0	Mask Map
1	Pixel Map A
2	Pixel Map B
3	Pixel Map C

TABLE 18.12 Pixel Size

Value	Description
0	1 bit per pixel (monochrome)
1	2 bit per pixel
2	4 bit per pixel
3	8 bit per pixel
4	16 bit per pixel

TABLE 18.13 Pixel Ordering

Value	Description
0	Intel ordering
1	Motorola ordering

the format for the mask or pattern must be 1 bit per pixel since these are inherently monochrome bit maps. The pixel ordering is shown in Table 18.13.

The pixel map width and height are 16-bit registers that define the width and height of the pixel map. These values should be loaded with one less than the actual desired width or height.

18.8 COPROCESSOR REGISTERS

The XGA coprocessor performs line draws, BitBlts, short-stroke lines, and scanline area fills. The coprocessor registers are listed Table 18.14.

AGX: The offset field of the coprocessor registers is relative to the coprocessor base register. This is set to either B1F00h or D1F00h, depending on the AGX Mode Register 3, bit 0.

TABLE 18.14 Coprocessor Registers

Offset	Register	Offset	Register
11h(W)	Coprocessor Control	50h	Pixel Bit Mask
11h (R)	Coprocessor Status	58h	Foreground Color
12h	Pixel Map Index	5Ch	Background Color
14h	Pixel Map Base	60h	Operation Dimension 1
18h	Pixel Map Width	62h	Operation Dimension 2
1Ah	Pixel Map Height	6Ch	Mask Map X
1Ch	Pixel Map Format	6Eh	Mask Map Y
20h	Bresenham Error Term	70h	Source Map Y
24h	Bresenham K1	72h	Source Map Y
28h	Bresenham K2	74h	Pattern Map X
2Ch	Short Stroke	76h	Pattern Map Y
48h	Foreground Mix Registers	78h	Destination Map X
49h	Background Mix Registers	7Ah	Destination Map Y
4Ah	Color Compare	7Ch	Pixel Operation
4Ch	Destination Compare Color		

18.8.1 Pixel Operation Register

The most important register is the Pixel Operation Register, which is located at offset 7Ch. This register sets up several important parameters and can start a line draw, BitBlt, short-stroke mode, and area fills. The fields of this register are shown in Table 18.15.

18.8.2 Foreground and Background Sources

The background and foreground sources can be either the background or foreground constant colors, or can be determined from the source map. If a pixel in the pattern map is a 1, then the foreground source will be selected. If it contains a 0, the background source will be selected. These sources are shown in Table 18.16.

TABLE 18.15 The Pixel Operation Register at Offset 7C

Bits	Description	Usage
31–30	Background Source	Background source of data [foreground or source]
29–28	Foreground Source	Foreground source of data [background or source]
27–24	Command	Command to issue [operation to perform]
23–20	Source Map	Source Pixel Map [A, B, or C]
19–16	Destination Map	Destination Pixel Map [A, B, or C]
15–12	Pattern Map	Pattern Pixel Map [A, B, or C]
11–8	Reserved	
7–6	Mask Mode	Enable masking
5–4	Drawing Mode	Draw all, not first, not last, or special area boundary
3	Reserved	
2–0	Octant	Direction of line draws

TABLE 18.16 Foreground and Background Sources (Bits 31–30 and 29–28)

Field	Description
0	Background (31–30) or foreground (29–28) color
1	Reserved
2	Source map
3	Reserved

18.8.3 Command Field

The Command field actually determines the nature of the operation and, with the exception of the short-stroke commands, actually initiates the function. The Command field is shown in Table 18.17.

18.8.4 Foreground and Background Mix Registers

The Foreground and Background Mix Registers are each byte-wide registers containing the code for the mix. The mix codes are shown in Table 18.18.

18.8.5 Color Comparison

The Color Compare Register contains the color condition code as shown in Table 18.19. The condition compares each destination pixel with a color value loaded in the Destination Compare Color Register. If the result of the comparison is False, the mix operation is used on the destination pixel. If it is true, the destination pixel is left unmodified. This is a destination compare; consequently, data in the destination is compared to the specified color and objects in the destination will be in the foreground (in front of objects written into the destination). This is the inverse of source compare operations.

NOTE: The Color Compare Register must be initialized to 100 = FALSE such that the destination pixels can be updated. The compare color is found in the 32-bit Color Compare Register.

TABLE 18.17 Command Field (bits 27–24)

Field	Description
0	Reserved
1	Reserved
2	Short Stroke Read
3	Bresenham Read
4	Short Stroke Write
5	Bresenham Write
6	Reserved
7	Reserved
8	BitBlt
9	Inverted BitBlt
A	Area Fill
F–B	Reserved

TABLE 18.18 Mix Fields for Foreground and Background Registers

Code	Mix	Code	Mix
0	All 0	B	S OR !D
1	S AND D	C	!S
2	S AND !D	D	!S OR D
3	S (opaque)	E	!S OR !D
4	!S AND D	F	All 1
5	D (transparent)	10	Max((S,D)
6	S XOR D	11	Min(S,D)
7	S OR D	12	S + D with saturation
8	!S AND !D	13	D – S with saturation
9	S XOR !D	14	S – D with saturation
A	!D	15	Average

TABLE 18.19 Color Compare Codes

Code	Condition
0	Always True
1	Dest > Color
2	Dest = Color
3	Dest < Color
4	Always True
5	Dest >= Color
6	Dest != Color
7	Dest <= Color

18.8.6 Pixel Bit Mask

The Pixel Bit Mask Register dictates which bits within a pixel are updated during a write operation. A 0 in a bit position in the pixel mask enables that bit position. The bit will then contribute to the outcome of the operation. A 1 in a bit position excludes a bit from being used in an operation.

18.8.7 Foreground and Background Colors

The Foreground Color and Background Color registers are used as a constant source of data. These registers are 32 bits wide and, like the bit mask, are least-significant-bit justified. Thus, a 4-bit color would be located in bits 3–0, and an 8-bit color would be in 7–0 respectively.

A 16-bit color value is coded such that a 5:6:5 color coding is used for the red, green, and blue color components respectively. Note that blue is in the least significant field. Twenty-four-bit color is stored in an 8:8:8 format with red followed by green followed by blue (Intel ordering). A 32-bit format for data is 8:8:8:8 with GBRx with green followed by blue followed by red followed by a dummy byte. This dummy byte is sometimes used as an alphanumeric overlay.

18.8.8   The Source, Destination, and Pattern Maps

The source, destination, and pattern maps are shown in Table 18.20. Note that the pattern map can also select the foreground or generated from source maps. The pattern can use a solid color from the foreground color or it can use the source data. This is a color compression, the opposite of a color expansion. The 1-bit pattern is generated from the source. This is an OR operation. Any plane in the source that is a 1 will cause a 1 pattern. All 0s generate a 0.

18.8.9   Mask Mode

The Mask Mode field allows two types of masking operations. The first uses the boundary of the map mask as a rectangular clipping mask. The second type allows for a non-rectangular clipping map region dictated by the pattern in the map mask. Either or both can be enabled as seen in Table 18.21.

18.8.10   Drawing Mode

The Drawing Mode field controls the way that pixels are drawn and is shown in Table 18.22. You can select to have all pixels drawn, all but the first and/or last pixel, or a special mode for drawing area boundaries. These modes are necessary when using the XOR type of lines and when drawing polylines. Since the

TABLE 18.20 Source (32–20), Destination (19–16), and Pattern Fields (15–12)

Field	Description
0	reserved
1	Pixel Map A
2	Pixel Map B
3	Pixel Map C
7–4	reserved
8	Foreground (Pattern Only)
9	Use source (Pattern Only)
F–Ah	reserved

TABLE 18.21 Mask Mode (7–6)

Field	Description
0	Mask Map
1	Mask Map Boundary Enabled
3–2	Reserved

TABLE 18.22 Drawing Mode (5–4)

Field	Description
0	Draw all pixels
1	Draw all but first pixel
2	Draw all but last pixel
3	Draw Area Boundary

XOR inverts a point and a polyline draws each vertex twice, some action has to take place so that the vertices don't do a double-invert (no change). When filling a polygon, a single point in a horizontal scan line can cause a problem. For example, the area-fill algorithm scans each scan line in a source map for alternating starting and ending points. Since the object to be filled does not touch the border of the map, the first boundary point encountered is considered to be the object and the fill algorithm fills until it reaches a second border point. This is considered the end of the object. A single boundary point on a horizontal scan line messes everything up since the algorithm will fill until the end of that scan line. Therefore, it is best not to draw these single points. This is illustrated in Figure 18.3.

18.8.11   Octant Field

The Octant field is used in the BitBlt, short-stroke, and the line draws to determine the direction of the transfer. It is three bits long describing the eight directions. The octant direction for BitBlts are shown in Figure 18.4a and for short-stroke vectors are shown in Figure 18.4b.

18.9   BITBLTS

BitBlts transfer data from one location in memory to another. They may be from host-to-display, display-to-host, or from display-to-display. They can handle a variety of cases such as overlapping areas and color expansion. Registers associated with BitBlts are shown in Table 18.23.

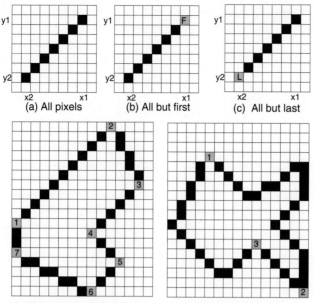

(a) All pixels (b) All but first (c) All but last

(d) XOR polylines with all pixels drawn. Note: vertex points are incorrect due to double inversion.

(e) Area-Fill lines showing single inflection points that must NOT be part of outline.

FIGURE 18.3 Drawing Modes (a) All Pixels (b) All but First (c) All but Last (d) Area Boundary

(a) Octant indices for pixel operations

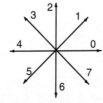

(b) Directions used as vector direction for short stroke vectors

FIGURE 18.4 Octant Directions. (a) BitBlts (b) Short-Stroke Vectors

TABLE 18.23 BitBlt Related Registers

Offset	Description	Usage
61–60h	Operating Dimension 1	The major axis for line draws or the width for BitBlts. The length of the line-1.
63–62h	Operating Dimension 2	The minor axis for BitBlts. The height of the BitBlt-1.
6D–6Ch	Mask Map X	X offset of the mask map relative to the origin of the destination map
6F–6Eh	Mask Map Y	Y offset of the mask map relative to the origin of the destination map
71–70h	Source Map X	X offset of the source map relative to the origin of the source map
73–72h	Source Map Y	Y offset of the source map relative to the origin of the source map
75–74h	Pattern Map X	X offset of the pattern map relative to the origin of the pattern map
77–76h	Pattern Map Y	Y offset of the pattern map relative to the origin of the pattern map
79–78h	Destination Map X	X offset of the destination map relative to the origin of the destination map
7B–7Ah	Destination Map Y	Y offset of the destination map relative to the origin of the destination map

A BitBlt operation from system memory to display memory is provided in Listing 18.3. It assumes that the coprocessor is ready and that the source image is 1 bit per pixel to be expanded into the 8-bit-per-pixel format on the screen.

LISTING 18.3 Color Expanded BitBlt from System to Display

```
; set up map A as destination
+12h PixelMapIndex = 01h ;select map A (destination)
+14h PixelMapBase = LongAddress ;32 bit display address
+18h PixelMapWidth=1023  ;destination width 1024-1
+20h PixelMapHeight=767  ;destination height 768-1
+1Ch PixelMapFormat=3 ;Intel Order, 8-bits/pixel

;  set up Map B as source
+12h PixelMapIndex = 02h ;select map B (source)
+14h PixelMapBase = LongAddress ;32 bit host address
(segment<<4)+offset
+18h PixelMapWidth=63 ;source width 64-1
```

```
+20h PixelMapHeight=31    ;source height 32-1
+1Ch PixelMapFormat=8 ;Motorola Order, 1-bit/pixel

;  set up the Mix as a transparent background with a color
expanded foreground
+48h ForegroundMix = 3h  ;source replaces destination (src_copy
or opaque) mix mode
+58h ForegroundColor = color;color to expand foreground into

;  set up the coordinates
+70h SourceX = 0   ; offset x is 0 of source
+72h SourceY = 0   ; offset y is 0 of source
+78h DestinationX = 199  ; destination x coordinate = 200-1
+7Ah DestinationY = 99    ; destination y coordinate = 100-1
+60h OpDimension 1 =  63 ;source width 64-1
+62h OpDimension 2 =  31 ;source height 32-1

;  set up the Pixel Operation
+7C PixelOperation=PixelCode;set up operation register and
begin operation

where PixelCode =
 BackgroundSource=0;  ForegroundSource=0; Command=8 (PixBlt);
 SourcePixelMap=2 (B);  DestinationPixelMap=1 (A);
 PatternPixelMap=2 (B);  MaskPixelMap=0 (disabled) Octant=0
(left-to-right/top-down)
```

18.10   LINE DRAWING

The coprocessor is capable of performing Bresenham line draws. The Bresenham parameters are described in three specific registers as shown in Table 18.24. All three values range from [−8192 to 8919].

The lines can be drawn with a solid single foreground color, with both the foreground and background constant colors based on a mask, or with a pattern. In addition, the line can be drawn using some logical operation based on the source, destination, pattern, or mask.

A line draw operation is started after the Bresenham parameters are loaded and the pixel operation is written to with a Line Draw command.

18.10.1   Short-Stroke Vectors

Short-stroke vectors are controlled differently than the BitBlt or line draws. The Pixel Operation Register is set up for short strokes; however, no operation occurs at this point. A short stroke occurs each time the Short-Stroke Register is written to after the coprocessor is alerted to expect this operation via the Command Register. This mode of operation is ended when a 00hex byte is

TABLE 18.24 The Bresenham Line Drawing Registers

Offset	Description	Usage
21–20h	Bresenham Error Term	Initial Error = 2 * (Y2–Y1) – (X2–X1).
25–24h	Bresenham Constant K1	Axial Step Constant K1 = 2 * (Y2–Y1).
29–28h	Bresenham Constant K2	Diagonal Step Constant K2 = 2 * (Y2–Y1) – 2 * (X2–X1).
61–60h	Operating Dimension 1	The major axis for line draws or the width for BitBlts. The length of the line-1.
63–62h	Operating Dimension 2	The minor axis for BitBlts; the height of the BitBlt-1.

written as a vector. Alternatively, another command value can be written to the Pixel Operation Register to end this mode.

Short-stroke vectors are defined by a 32-bit word in the Short Stroke Vector Register at offset 2C. This register is described in Table 18.25 and shown in Figure 18.4b. It is a write-only register containing four identical 1-byte fields describing a standard short-stroke vector. Writing a value of 00h to a byte causes the short stroke process to end.

A line draw operation is shown in Listing 18.4. It is assumed that the coprocessor is not busy and that the line will be drawn from (x1,y1) to (x2,y2).

TABLE 18.25 Short Stroke Register at Offset 2Ch

Bits	Description
31–24	Short-Stroke Vector 4
23–16	Short-Stroke Vector 3
15–8	Short-Stroke Vector 2
7–0	Short-Stroke Vector 1

LISTING 18.4 Line Draw Operation

```
; set up map A as destination
+12h PixelMapIndex = 01h ;select map A (destination)
+14h PixelMapBase = LongAddress ;32 bit display  address
+18h PixelMapWidth=1023  ;destination width 1024-1
+20h PixelMapHeight=767  ;destination height 768-1
+1Ch PixelMapFormat=3 ;Intel Order, 8-bits/pixel
```

```
;   set up the Mix as a transparent background with a color
;   expanded foreground
+48h ForegroundMix = 3h  ; source replaces destination (src_copy
                             ; or opaque) mix mode
+58h ForegroundColor = color;color to expand foreground into


; setup for Bresenham
Dy =abs (y2-y1);   Dx=abs(x2-x1)
if ((x2-x1)<0)    DX=0; else DX=1;
if ((y2-y1)<0)    DY=0; else DY=1;
if (Dy >= Dx) DZ=0; else DZ=1;


;  set up the coordinates
+78h DestinationX = x1   ; line x start coordinate
+7Ah DestinationY = y1   ; line y start coordinate
+60h OpDimension1 = LineLength ;line length = Dx
+20h ErrorTerm =  Error  ;Error = (2*Dy) - Dx
+24h K1Register =  K1 ;K1 = 2 * Dy
+ 28h K2Register = K2 ;K2 = 2 * (Dy-Dx)


; where PixelCode =
; BackgroundSource=0;  ForegroundSource=0; Command=5 (LineDraw);
; SourcePixelMap=1 (A);  DestinationPixelMap=1 (A);
; PatternPixelMap=8 (Foreground Fixed);
;   MaskPixelMap=0 (disabled) DrawingMode=0
; Octant=DX:DY:DZ


;  set up Pixel Operation
+7C PixelOperation=PixelCode   ; set up operation register and
                                ; begin operation
```

18.11   AREA FILL

The XGA is capable of performing area fill operations. The area must be totally enclosed by an outline with no single points on a single horizontal line. The area fill operation occurs on a horizontal line-by-line basis. The procedure for area fills is to draw an outline in a bit-map, set up the destination for the resultant closed area (typically in on-screen memory), and perform the area fill. This is shown in Example 18.1.

Example 18.1 Area Fill

Step	*Action*
1.	Create a monochrome bit map in off-screen memory such that the object will be completely enclosed.
2.	Clear this area to all zeros.

(continued)

Step	*Action*
3.	Draw the outline using the Line Draw command. The Drawing Mode field of the Pixel Operation Register must be set to Area Boundary Draw.
4.	Set up the destination area so that it's large enough to contain the resultant closed object.
5.	Set up the foreground mix and foreground source.
6.	Set up the background mix (most likely to destination).
7.	Fill the area with the Area Fill command with the Octant field of the Pixel Operation Register increasing values of X (left-to-right).

A Rectangular Fill is the simplest fill operation. It is actually a BitBlt with a constant color source. Code for a Rectangular Fill is provided in Listing 18.5.

LISTING 18.5 Rectangular Fill

```
;   set up map A as destination
+12h PixelMapIndex = 01h ;select map A (destination)
+14h PixelMapBase = LongAddress ;32 bit display  address
+18h PixelMapWidth=1023   ;destination width 1024-1
+20h PixelMapHeight=767   ;destination height 768-1
+1Ch PixelMapFormat=3     ;Intel Order, 8-bits/pixel

;   set up the Mix as a transparent background with a color
;   expanded foreground
+48h ForegroundMix = 3h  ;source replaces destination (src_copy
                         ; or opaque) mix mode
+58h ForegroundColor = color;color to expand foreground into

;   set up the coordinates
+78h DestinationX = 199  ; destination x coordinate = 200-1
+7Ah DestinationY = 99   ; destination y coordinate = 100-1
+60h OpDimension 1 =  63 ;source width 64-1
+62h OpDimension 2 =  31 ;source height 32-1

; PixelCode =
; BackgroundSource=0;  ForegroundSource=0; Command=8 (PixBlt);
; SourcePixelMap=1 (A);  DestinationPixelMap=1 (A);
; PatternPixelMap=8 (Foreground Fixed);
;   MaskPixelMap=0 (disabled) Octant=0 (left-to-right/top-down)

;   set up the Pixel Operation
+7C PixelOperation=PixelCode  ; set up operation register and
                              ; begin operation
```

18.12 IDENTIFYING THE XGA

There are several possibilities for the XGA. The first is that it resides on a microchannel system. In this case, the XGA might be on the motherboard (slot=0) or on an adapter slot (slot=0,7). If there is no microchannel system, the XGA might be on an adapter card in an ISA, VL, or PCI bus. The function in Listing 18.6 tests these possibilities. If it is not a microchannel system, the eight possible slots are tested using the function in Listing 18.7 calling upon the function in Listing 23.2. It calls upon an IIT specific chip since this is the only known XGA not on a microchannel.

LISTING 18.6 Is an XGA Present?

```
int Is_It_XGA(int *XGA_BASE)
{int Slot,i; BYTE pos2,pos4;

// first check if microchannel or not
if ((*XGA_BASE=Is_it_Microchannel())!=-1) {
  Slot=-1;  // assume no valid slot
  for (i=0; i<=8; i++) {
   enableSlot(*XGA_BASE);
   if( IsValidId(*XGA_BASE)) {
    Slot=i;
    break;
    }
   }
 if(Slot==-1) return(NOT_FOUND);  // microchannel but no XGA
 if(Slot==0) {  // motherboard microchannel
   setupMotherboardVideo();
   getPosValues(*XGA_BASE,&pos2,&pos4);
   enableMotherboardVideo();
   }
else {  // slot microchannel
   setupSlotVideo(*XGA_BASE);
   getPosValues(*XGA_BASE,&pos2,&pos4);
   enableSlotVideo(*XGA_BASE);
   }
 *XGA_BASE=getXGAbase(pos2);
  }
else {  // not microchannel
 if( Is_XGA_Card_Present(XGA_BASE)) return(IS_FOUND); // is
adapter
 else return(NOT_FOUND);  // not adapter
 }
return(IS_FOUND);
}
```

LISTING 18.7 Is an XGA card present at slot 0–7?

```
int Is_XGA_Card_Present(int *XGA_BASE)
{ int i;
  for (i=0; i<=8; i++) {
    // try for IIT XGA (See Chapter 23 Listing 23.2)
    if(Is_IIT_Slot_Valid(i)) {
      *XGA_BASE = 0x2100 + (i<<4);
      return(IS_FOUND);
      }
  }
  return(NOT_FOUND);
}
```

18.13   SETTING THE MODE

Setting the mode on the XGA requires loading the first register bank, initializing the palette, clearing video memory if desired, and initialing a second register group. The first register group is loaded with table values depending on the mode selected. There are more than 60 registers involved besides the 768 color registers. It is beyond the scope of this book to provide a detailed mode loading program. This software is included in the Super VGA Toolbox.

Chapter 19

ATI Technologies

19.1 INTRODUCTION TO THE ATI TECHNOLOGIES SUPER VGA CHIPS

ATI Technologies has several Super VGA chips. The first version of the first-generation 18800 chip version provided 1024-by-768 16-color and 4-color modes and up to 800-by-600 256-color modes. The 16-color, high-resolution mode utilized a packed format with two pixels per byte. This provided programmers with a challenge since it was not planar and consequently did not port easily to other 1024-by-768 16-color Super VGA cards. A later version added an additional display mode that did provide the planar 1024-by-768 16-color mode.

The VGA Wonder Card is based on the 18800 chip. Version 3 of this chip contained no clock chip. Version 4 was titled the 18800-1. It did not include a clock chip. Version 5 was titled the 18800-1 and it did contain a clock chip.

The VGA Wonder+ Card is based on the 28800 chip with a clock chip. The VGA Edge is based on the 18800-1 without a clock chip. The VGA Edge-16 has a clock chip. The EGA Wonder+ is based on the 18800-1 without a clock chip.

The second generation ATI Super VGA chip, the 28800, provides a fine-tuned VGA environment for high performance. Utilizing high-speed DRAMs and FIFO buffers, the 18800 provides nearly a two-to-one speed advantage over the 28800. From a programmer's perspective, the 28800 is nearly identical to the 18800.

The ATI cards also include non-volatile RAM. When used in conjunction with the VSetup program, the cards can be optimized for the desired system performance.

The graphics accelerator chips include the Mach-8 products and the Mach-32 products. Both are super-sets of the 8514 standard and include sophisticated graphics processors. Both support the IBM Adapter Interface as discussed in Chapter 16.

The Mach-8 is a separate chip from the VGA controller. The Mach-32 incorporates the VGA controller on the chip. In either case, the accelerator or the VGA are separate entities. One either programs to the VGA or the Mach-8. For example, some of the higher resolution modes are **only** supported by the Mach-8 and not the VGA portion of the chip.

19.1.1 Mach-8

The Mach-8 products include all boards with Ultra designations including the 8514-Ultra, the ISA Ultra, the ISA Vantage, MCA Ultra Graphics Ultra, and the Graphics Vantage. The Mach-8 is based on the 38800 chip families. The Mach-8 based cards therefore include a VGA controller, an 8514 engine, and additional graphics accelerator registers and features. The Mach-8 is completely downward compatible with the IBM 8514/A register set. It provides dramatic performance improvements over the 8514.

The 8514/A compatible features of the Mach-8 are described in Chapter 17. Reference should be made to this chapter regarding these registers and functions. The 8514/A compatible registers provide the following features:

High-speed line draw

High-speed two-pass polygon fill using edge flag polygon fill

Automatic rectangle fill

Automatic color and monochrome BitBlts to and from host and from VRAM to VRAM

Full-featured three-source rasterops

Support for short-stroke vectors

Post-clipped scissoring

The Mach-8 extended register set provides additional drawing operations and high-performance functions not available on other 8514/A products. These registers are described in this chapter. The extended ATI features of the Mach-8 include the following:

Alternate rectangular and non-rectangular fills, BitBlts, and polygon fill operations

Direct point-to-point vector line drawing

Direct horizontal line drawing

Alternate short-stroke vector drawing

Alternate degree and Bresenham line draw

Extended resolution display modes

The Mach-8 can combine the destination pixel with either one of the two color source data streams as determined by the monochrome source data stream. The monochrome and color source data streams provide the following:

8-bit-per-pixel packed host-supplied data

Selected planes of a source area

32 8-bit color pattern registers

32 1-bit monochrome pattern registers

Foreground or background color

19.1.2 Mach-32

The Mach-32 products are based on the ATI68800, 68800LX, 68800AX chips. There are several revision numbers of the 68800 family. Many of the differences have to do with supporting VRAM or DRAM or other hardware considerations. There are some software differences between the revision numbers that the programmer needs to be aware of and I will discuss these wherever possible.

Like the Mach-8, the Mach-32 supports the 8514/A standard and all references to these registers or functions will be found in Chapter 17. The Mach-32 either runs in the 8514/A-compatible mode or in the ATI-proprietary mode. In the 8514/A compatible mode, only resolutions up to 1024x768 in 8 bit/color are possible. The additional features supported by the Mach-32 are described in this chapter and include support for the following features:

Support of up to 4 Mbytes of display memory

Hi-color and true-color color resolutions

High-speed point-to-point line draw for hi-color modes

XGA function compatible hardware cursor

High-speed polygon fill

Hardware assisted line and polygon pre-clipping

Packed bitmap data transfers

Enhanced BitBlt transfers

Extended FIFO control

19.1.3 Non-Standard Display Modes

Using clever implementations, the version 1 18800 chip from ATI utilized uncommon high-resolution display modes. These modes incorporated a hybrid combination of planar and packed modes. A 4-color 1024-by-768 mode was introduced and was essentially the only 4-color non-CGA type mode available in the VGA. There are some clear advantages to 4-color modes, and it would be useful for the industry to standardize such a mode.

Many programmers favor the 16-color mode implemented in a packed format. Unfortunately, it is unique to ATI Technologies. Instead of a pixel spreading its bits across the four display planes, the four bits are packed into half of a byte. This packed 16-color technique is the standard 16-color technique on the Macintosh. Fortunately, the 18800 and the 28800 Super VGA chips also includes a planar (standard) 16-color high-resolution mode.

19.1.4   Locating the Extended Register Set

It is important to note where ATI Technologies locates the extended register set registers. The extended register set is based on indexed register pairs common to many VGA register sets. ATI has provided an indirect pointer to the location of the Index Register of this register pair (one less than the data register) in BIOS ROM at location C000:0010. To determine the address, a programmer must retrieve this address from BIOS memory. ATI warns against hard-coding the address of the extended register based on the company's stated prerogative to "change the location in future BIOS releases." It seems if there is a need to alter it, the change would be in future VGA chip versions and not BIOS releases.

Typically, this index address is loaded into the DX register for an output port instruction. To fetch this location without disrupting other registers, the following macro code is necessary. In the code examples that follow, it is assumed that this value is stored in a variable called *EXT* as shown in Listing 19.1.

LISTING 19.1 Get Extended Register Set Index Register Port Address Macro

```
; Function:
;  Returns the value of the extended register in the DX register
; Output Parameters:
;  dx        Extended Register Set Index Register Port Address
; Calling Protocol:
;  get_extended_ATI

get_extended_ATI  macro
        push    es
        push    bx        ;; save the two registers used in this code

        mov     es,SegC000 ;; load the BIOS ROM segment
        mov     bx,10h     ;; load the offset to the indirect
                           ;; pointer
```

```
        mov     dx,es:[bx]   ;; get the location of the extended
                             ;; registers

        pop     bx   ;; restore the two registers used in this code
        pop     es
endm
```

The extended registers are at the core of every Super VGA function and the above code can take a considerable amount of time. As a result, hard coding seems inevitable.

19.2 INQUIRING FOR THE ATI SUPER VGA CONFIGURATION

ATI provides information in BIOS memory regarding the VGA card ID, card definition, chip revision number, monitor type, and memory size as indicated in Table 19.1.

TABLE 19.1 Determining ATI Technologies Display Status

Function	Register Name	Port	Index	Bits	Value
Identify Card	9 Characters at C000:003–003A				
Card Definition	1 byte at C000:0042				
VGA Chip Revision Number	1 byte at C000:0043				
Monitor Type	Status	Ext	BB	0–3	0–15
Memory Size	Status	Ext	BB	5	0–1

19.2.1 Identifying the ATI VGA Card

The ATI card is identified by checking a string starting at C000:0031–003A for the following characters: 761295520. This can be accomplished through Listing 19.2.

Once an ATI chip is found, it is necessary to identify which ATI chip. This is accomplished by the code in Listing 19.3. Listing 19.4 contains several useful functions that acquire information from the ATI.

LISTING 19.2 Determine if the Chip is an ATI

```
/* Output Parameters:
        =1 chip is an ATI      =0 chip is NOT an ATI
```

(continued)

```
Calling Protocol:
  ATI= Is_It_ATI()   */

int Is_It_ATI(void)
{ char key[10],signature[10]; int result;

  strncpy(key,"761295520",9);   // put ATI key into string
  Get_ATI_Key(signature);    // get ATI key
  result = strncmp(key,signature,9);     // compare the two
strings
  if(result==0) return(CHIP_FOUND);
        else   return(CHIP_NOT_FOUND);
}
```

LISTING 19.3 Determine the ATI Card Version Number and Identification

```
/*  Output Parameters:
        chip_version   ATI chip version
Calling Protocol:
 version = Which_ATI()   */

int Which_ATI(void)

{ int version;

  //    first check for Mach8 or Mach32
  if(mach32_detect()) return(ATImach32);
  if(mach8_detect()) return(ATImach8);

  version =  Get_Version_ATI();
  if((version==0x31)||(version==0x32)) return(ATI18800);
  else if(version0x32) return(ATI28800);
  return(NO_ID_FOUND);
}
```

LISTING 19.4a Return the ATI Signature String

```
; Function:
;       Return the 16 bytes at C000:0040-4F
; Output Parameters
;       signature output string to load 16 characters into
; Calling Protocol:
;  Get_ATI_Stuff(signature)

Get_ATI_Stuff PROC FAR  USES ES DI DS SI, arg1:FAR PTR, arg2
        mov    ds,SegC000   ;set up source pointer
        mov    si,0040h     ;location of signature
```

```
;       set up destination pointer
        les     di,arg1


;       set up for number of bytes to transfer and transfer
        mov     cx,16
        rep     movsb
        ret
Get_ATI_Stuff  endp
```

LISTING 19.4b Get the BIOS Segment Address

```
; Function:
;       Returns the segment address of BIOS
; Input Parameters
;       mode        desired mode number
; Output Parameters:
;       return     BIOS Segment Address
; Calling Protocol:
;   BIOS_segment = Get_BIOS_Seg_ATI

Get_BIOS_Seg_ATI PROC FAR  USES SI DI ES DS, mode:BYTE
        push    bp              ;Preserve BP
        mov     al,mode
        mov     ah,12h          ;Function=Get VGA Status
        mov     bx,5506h        ;Subfunction = Get Parameter Table
        mov     bp,0FFFFh       ;Initialize BP and SI
        mov     si,0
        int     10h             ;Interrogate BIOS for Parameter Table
        mov     si,bp           ;Restore BP
        pop     bp
        cmp     si,0FFFFh        ;Check if function performed
        je      Not_ATI_BIOS     ;...No, go report error
        cmp     BYTE PTR es:[si],80 ;Check for valid data
                                    ;(#columns)
        je      BIOS_Found       ;...Yes, BIOS found, continue as
                                 ;normal

Not_ATI_BIOS:  ;If ATI BIOS was not found, report error and quit
        xor     ax,ax           ;Set returned address to NULL
        mov     dx,ax
        ret


        ;Fetch segment of ATI BIOS
BIOS_Found:
        mov     ax,es           ;by BIOS call
        ret
Get_BIOS_Seg_ATI   endp
```

LISTING 19.4c Return the ATI Signature String

```
; Function:
;       Return the 9 bytes at C000:0031 The ATI card is
;       identified by checking a string starting at
;       C000:0031-003A for the following characters "761295520".

; Output Parameters
;       signature output string to load 9 characters into

; Calling Protocol:
;   Get_ATI_Key(signature)

Get_ATI_Key PROC FAR  USES ES DI DS SI, arg1:FAR PTR, arg2
        mov     ds,SegC000    ;set up source pointer
        mov     si,0031h       ;location of signature

;       set up destination pointer
        les     di,arg1

;       set up for number of bytes to transfer and transfer
        mov     cx,9
        rep     movsb
        ret
Get_ATI_Key endp
```

LISTING 19.4d Return the ATI version and ID information

```
; Function:
;       Return the identification and chip version bytes.
; Output Parameters
;       version      chip version number
; Calling Protocol:
;   version = Get_Version_ATI()

Get_Version_ATI PROC FAR   USES DS SI
        mov     ds,SegC000   ; set up source pointer
        mov     si,0043h      ;location of identification

;       set up for number of bytes to transfer and transfer
        mov     al,ds:[si]    ;return c000:43 and return to caller
        xor     ah,ah
        ret
Get_Version_ATI     endp
```

LISTING 19.4e Return the ATI configuration

```
; Function:
;        Return the chip version bytes.
; Output Parameters
;        config     chip configuration

; Calling Protocol:
;   config = Get_Config_ATI()

Get_Config_ATI PROC FAR   USES DS SI
        mov     ds,SegC000    ;set up source pointer
        mov     si,0042h      ;location of identification

;       set up for number of bytes to transfer and transfer
        mov     al,ds:[si]    ;return c000:43 and return to caller
        xor     ah,ah
        ret
Get_Config_ATI endp
```

19.2.2 Handling the Monitor Type

The monitor is automatically sensed at power-up, and the card is configured accordingly. To determine the current monitor configuration, the Status Register can be read and the monitor values are contained in bits 0–3, denoted by the *MON* field in Figure 19.1. The memory size, denoted by *DEF* field, returns either a 0 in bit 5, indicating 256 Kbytes of memory, or a 1 in bit 5, indicating 512 Kbytes of memory. This is loaded into the upper byte of the return variable from Listing 19.5a.

The monitor configurations are listed in Table 19.2. These codes are returned in the lower byte of the return parameter from Listing 19.5a.

It is possible to set the monitor to a specific code through software as shown in Listing 19.5b. This function will work when switching between analog monitor types or digital monitor types. It cannot be used to switch between analog and digital monitor type.

Status Register

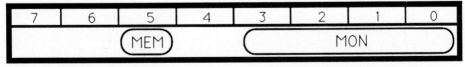

Index BB at Port EXT   Port EXT+1 Read/Write

FIGURE 19.1 ATI Status Register. The Monitor type resides in the MON field. The amount of memory is indicated in the MEM field.

TABLE 19.2 Monitor Configuration Codes

Status Register Bits 0–3	Monitor Type
0	EGA
1	PS/2 monochrome
2	TTL monochrome
3	PS/2 color
4	RGB color
5	Multisync
7	PS/2 8514
8	Seiko 1430
9	NEC Multisync 2A
A	Crystalscan 860/Tatung 1439
B	NEC Multisync 3D
C	TVM 3M
D	NEC MultiSync XL
E	TVM 2A
F	TVM 3A

LISTING 19.5a Get the Monitor ID

```
; Function:
;       get the monitor and memory configuration
; Calling Protocol:
;       monitor = Get_Monitor_ATI();

Get_Monitor_ATI PROC FAR
        get_Extended_ATI       ;load the extended port address in dx
        mov     al,0bbh        ;index of monitor/memory
        xor     ah,ah
        out     dx,ax          ;index monitor/memory port
        inc     dx
        in      al,dx          ;get monitor and memory configuration
        xor     ah,ah
        ret
Get_Monitor_ATI endp
```

LISTING 19.5b Load the Monitor ID

```
; Input Parameters:
;       code        monitor code
; Calling Protocol:
;       Load_Monitor_ATI(code);

Load_Monitor_ATI PROC FAR   arg1:byte
        get_Extended_ATI        ;load the extended port address in dx
        mov     al,0bbh         ;index of monitor/memory
        xor     ah,ah
        out     dx,ax           ;index monitor/memory port
        inc     dx
        in      al,dx           ;get monitor and memory configuration

;       now load up the monitor
        mov     ah,al           ;copy monitor into upper
        and     ah,0f0h         ;isolate monitor
        or      ah,arg1         ;monitor code( multisync X1 = 0d hex)
        mov     al,0bbh         ;index of monitor/memory

        dec     dx              ;point back to index
        out     dx,ax           ;output new monitor/memory

        ret
Load_Monitor_ATI endp
```

19.3 ATI TECHNOLOGY DISPLAY MODES

The Super VGA alphanumeric modes are 132 columns wide, from 25 to 44 lines. All operate in the standard 16-color mode. Four different display fonts are utilized. These are listed in Table 19.3.

TABLE 19.3 ATI Technologies Alphanumeric Modes

Mode	Rows	Columns	Font	Resolution	Colors	Chip
23	25	132	8x14*	1056 by 350	16	18800
27	25	132	8x14*	1056 by 350	2	18800
33	44	132	8x8	1056 by 352	16	18800
27	44	132	8x18	1056 by 352	2	18800

*8x16 on 1056-by-400 modes with analog monitor on a V5 VGA Wonder+

TABLE 19.4 ATI Technologies Graphics Modes

Mode	Resolution	Colors	Chip	Memory
53	800 by 600	16	18800	256 Kbytes
54	800 by 600	16	18800	256 Kbytes
55	1024 by 768	16 (planar)	18800–1	512 Kbytes
61	640 by 400	256	18800	256 Kbytes*
62	640 by 480	256	18800	512 Kbytes
63	800 by 600	256	18800	512 Kbytes
65	1024 by 768	16 (packed)	18800	512 Kbytes

The Super VGA graphics modes span the common 16- and 256-color display modes. Two unique modes are provided. These are modes 55 hex and 65 hex. The display modes 53 and 54 appear identical. Mode 53 is downwardly compatible to the ATI EGA Wonder Card which supported an 800-by-600 EGA display mode. These modes are listed in Table 19.4.

19.3.1 Display Mode 65 hex

Mode 65 hex is the 1024-by-768 16-color mode that utilizes packed memory organization. This was the first technique employed by ATI Technologies to implement a 1024-by-768 mode. Another 1024-by-768 16-color mode is mode 55h. This mode uses a planar memory organization common to all the other Super VGA chips. Older cards may not support the newer mode 55 hex.

The display memory is organized in a packed fashion, with a pair of pixels represented in each byte of display memory. A typical byte is displayed in Figure 19.2. Outside of the fact that there are two pixels per byte, the memory organization is identical to the packed display modes.

A major difference occurs between this mode and either the 256-color packed modes or the 16-color planar modes with respect to accessing the color palette. The 16-color planar modes utilize the sixteen palette registers located in the Attribute Registers at 3C0 as described in Section 10.6. The packed mode utilizes fifteen of the locations in the color registers. Thus, this mode could be considered a pseudo 31-color mode.

Two groups of registers within the 256 color registers are used in this display mode. The first set of color registers are indexed from 0–0F, incrementing by 1. These correspond to the pixel located in the lower nibble of the byte. This pixel is labeled *pixel n+1* in Figure 19.1. This is the standard way in which a 16-color mode accesses the color registers.

The second group of color registers is indexed from 0–F0 incrementing by 10 hex. These correspond to the pixel located in the upper nibble of the byte. This pixel is labeled *pixel n* in Figure 19.1. This is described in Table 19.5.

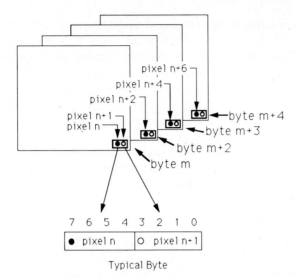

Typical Byte

FIGURE 19.2 Memory Organization for ATI Mode 65 Hex. Illustrates 16-color packed organization.

TABLE 19.5 Color Registers Used in Mode 65 Hex

Low Order Pixel Index	High Order Pixel Index	Default Color Value *1
00	00	black
01	10	blue
02	20	green
03	30	cyan
04	40	red
05	50	magenta
06	60	brown
07	70	white
08	80	dark gray
09	90	light blue
0A	A0	light green
0B	B0	light cyan
0C	C0	light red
0D	D0	light magenta
0E	E0	yellow
0F	F0	bright white

It should be noted that there is no way to distinguish between the 00 of the low order pixel and the 00 of the high order pixel. ATI recommends that this pixel be left at black because the 00 palette register controls the color of the border region. I agree, since the border regions are typically problematic, and it is a good idea to keep this color black. Many VGAs allow the border region to be assigned a specific color other that one in the color palette. This is the best approach since there are times one does not want to dedicate palette register 0 to black (or any fixed color for that matter).

The external color registers can be programmed directly or through the Set Color Register BIOS calls described in Section 11.11. One simply uses the indexes 00–0F or the indexes 00–F0.

19.3.2   Display Mode 67 Hex

Display mode 67 hex is a 1024-by-768 4-color mode. These four colors are reminiscent of the CGA modes. This mode can best be described as a planar mode utilizing odd-even bank switching. Each pixel is represented by two bits spread across two display planes. Even pixels are represented in planes 0 and 1; odd pixels are stored in planes 2 and 3. This is illustrated in Figure 19.3.

Locating a pixel is accomplished by first multiplying the vertical, y, coordinate by the number of bytes per display line. In this case, there are 1024 pixels per scan line and eight pixels per byte. Therefore, there are 128 bytes per scan line. Each plane is 64 Kbytes long—thus single precision unsigned arithmetic will suffice. This number, base_address, forms the base address of the byte containing the eight left-most pixels in the proper scan line. Next, the horizontal pixel number, x, is divided by eight. Both the whole and the fractional parts should be calculated. The whole part of the division provides the byte number byte_number, which contains the pixel in question. The fractional part, pixel_place, is saved for later. If this byte number, byte_number, is even, the pixel resides in a byte that is located in display planes 0 and 1. If the byte number is odd, the pixel resides in a byte that is located in display planes 2 and 3. Next, dividing the byte number, byte_number, by two provides the byte offset, byte_offset, within the selected pair of planes. Finally, the fractional part, pixel_place, is used to find the bit position within the selected byte. The pixel_place resulting from the division of x/8 is used to find the actual bit position of the pixel in question. This division is also a mod 8 operation. A mask can be formed by shifting the constant 01 hex left by the number pixel_place. This occurs because the most significant bit in each byte represents the right-most pixel when mapped to the display.

The two bits refer to one of four predefined colors in one of four color sets. The color sets are selected by setting bits 0 and 1 in the Color Select Register described in Section 10.6.7. The color selections possible are shown in Table 19.6.

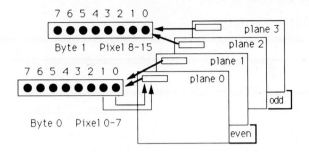

a) Planar Organization Showing 8 Pixels per Byte Resident
in 2 Planes Organized in an Odd/Even Fashion. Note: Reverse
pixel to display ordering. Pixel in bit 0 is left-most pixel on
display.

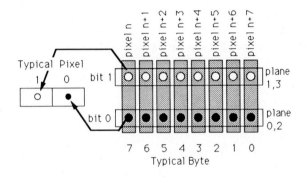

b) Memory Organization Showing a Pixel
Resident in Two Display Planes

FIGURE 19.3 Memory Organization for ATI Mode 67 Hex.
Illustrates 4-color planar odd-even addressing.

TABLE 19.6 4-color Mode Color Values

Color Set	C0=0,C1=0	C0=1,C1=0	C0=0,C1=1	C0=1,C1=1
0	black	white	gray	bright white
1	black	cyan	red	white
2	black	green	yellow	red
3	black	cyan	magenta	white

Typical Palette Register

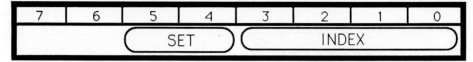

Index 0-15 at Port 3C0   Port 3C0 Read/Write

FIGURE 19.4 ATI Palette Registers in Mode 67 Hex. The palette index is stored in the INDEX field. The color set is stored in the SET field.

The palette registers are loaded with the standard index values allowing them to point to their respective color registers. The Set field, an additional field, is present in these sixteen palette registers as shown in Figure 19.4.

This SET field must contain the color set for each of the sixteen registers. Code that performs this function is provided in Listing 19.6.

LISTING 19.6 Setting up the Palette for a 4-color Color Set

```
; Inputs:
;       colorSet      color set number from  0-3
; Outputs:
;       Loads the palette Registers with the color set
; Calling Protocol:
;   Set_Palette_Mode_67(colorSet)

Set_Palette_Mode_67   PROC FAR  arg1:byte
        mov    dx,3dah       ;load input status register one

;       first wait for active period
wait_active:
        in     al,dx
        test   al,8          ;look for bit = 0
        jz     wait_active   ;wait for start of vertical retrace
                             ;period

;       now wait for retrace period
wait_retrace:
        in     al,dx
        test   al,8          ;look for bit 3=1
        jnz    wait_retrace  ;wait for start of vertical retrace
                             ;period
```

```
;           ;set up for transfer to palette registers
            mov     ah,arg1     ;get color set
            mov     cl,4
            shl     ah,cl       ;shift into the SET field bits 6-5
            mov     dx,3c0h     ;palette register address
            xor     bl,bl       ;start at zero
            mov     cx,16       ;load all 16 palette registers

; load the color index value in bits 6-5 of each index register
load_all: mov       al,bl       ;get the palette index
            out     dx,al       ;output index
            or      al,ah       ;put in the color set bits in ah

            out     dx,al       ;output to the palette register
            inc     bl          ;increment the index
            loop    load_all
            ret
Set_Palette_Mode_67   endp
```

The Mach-8 is capable of the modes shown in Table 19.7.

The Mach-32 is capable of the modes shown in Table 19.8.

A function that determines if the mode is supported is provided in Listing 19.7.

TABLE 19.7 Display Modes for Mach-8

Mode	Resolution	Bits/Colors
54	800 by 600	4 planar
55	1024 by 768	4 planar
	640 by 480	4 packed
	800 by 600	4 packed
	1024 by 768	4 packed
	1280 by 1024	4 packed
62	640 by 480	8
63	800 by 600	8
64	1024 by 768	8
23	132 by 25	text
33	132 by 44	text

TABLE 19.8 Display Modes for Mach-32

Mode	Resolution	Bits/Colors
54	800 by 600	4 planar
55	1024 by 768	4 planar
62	640 by 480	8
63	800 by 600	8
64	1024 by 768	8
62	640 by 480	8
63	800 by 600	8
64	1024 by 768	8
23	132 by 25	text
33	132 by 44	text
72	640 by 480	165
73	800 by 600	16
75	640 by 480	24

LISTING 19.7 Determining if a Mode Is Available BIOS Function

```
; Input Parameters:
;    mode            desired mode
;  BIOS setup
;    AH=12 hex       Extended VGA Control
;    BX=5506 hex
Get Mode information
;    BP=FFFF hex  Setup for return argument
;    AL= Mode        Desired mode number of which status is desired
; Output Parameters:
;    BP=return FFFFh=Mode not supported ! FFFFh= Mode supported.
;       Value returned is the offset into the CRTC table for
;       that mode.
;       The segment to this table is C000 hex.
; Calling Protocol:
; response=Is_ATI_Mode_Available(mode);

Is_ATI_Mode_Available PROC FAR  USES BP ES, arg1:byte
        mov     al,arg1    ;get desired mode value
        mov     ah,12h
        mov     bx,5506h
        mov     bp,0ffffh
        int     10h        ;is mode available?
        mov     ax,bp
        ret
Is_ATI_Mode_Available endp
```

19.4   ACCESSING THE ATI DISPLAY MEMORY

The ATI Technologies VGA chip maps display memory into host memory address space by using one or two bank registers. These are listed in Table 19.9. Each page maps a 64-Kbyte segment of display memory into the host address space. The values range from 0 to 19. Currently, only eight display pages are supported with the 512 Kbyte maximum memory configuration.

The 1-Mbyte of address space, currently limited to 512 Kbytes, can be mapped into the host address space through a single or dual bank mode. This feature is controlled by the E2B field in the ATI Technologies # Register. If this bit is zero, the single bank mode is selected. If one, the dual bank mode is selected. This register is shown in Figure 19.5.

In both cases, the registers are aligned to 4-Kbyte segments, providing a granularity of 4 Kbytes. The 20-bit memory address is formed by the 16-bit address generated by the CRT addressing (low order 16 bits) added to the four bits in the Bank Select Register (high order 4 bits) shown in Figure 19.6.

19.4.1   Single Bank Mode

In the single-bank mode, one bank field, Bank, in the Bank Register, is used to access the bank memory in 64-Kbyte banks. This register is shown in Figure 19.7.

The single-bank field, Bank, of the Bank Select Register, can be loaded through the macro code in Listing 19.8. The C-callable function is provided in Listing 19.9.

TABLE 19.9   Reading and Writing to ATI Technologies Display Memory

Function	Register Name	Port	Index	Bits	Value
Select Write Bank	Bank Select	Ext	B2	4–1	0–7
Select Read Bank	Bank Select	Ext	B2	7–5	0–7
Single/Dual Bank Mode	ATI Technologies Register E	Ext	BE	3	0,1

ATI Register E

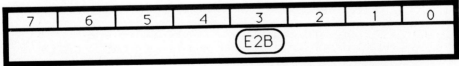

Index BE at Port EXT   Port EXT+1 Read/Write

FIGURE 19.5 ATI Register E. The E2B field enables the single or dual bank memory accessing modes.

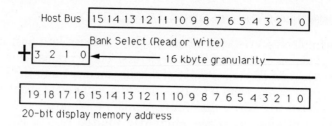

FIGURE 19.6 Creation of a 20-bit Address Using Bank Selection

Bank Register Single Bank Mode

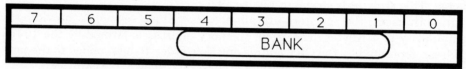

Index B2 at Port EXT   Port EXT+1 Read/Write

FIGURE 19.7 Bank Select Register in Single Bank Mode

LISTING 19.8 Set up for Single-bank Mode Macro

```
;     bank mode is single or dual based on bit 3 of ATI Extended E
;       bit 3=0   single bank   bit 3=1   dual bank

; Calling Protocol:
;   Set_Single_Bank_ATI();

Set_Single_Bank_ATI macro
        get_extended_ATI   ;;load the extended port address in dx
        mov    al,0beh      ;;index of dual paging enable
        xor    ah,ah
        out    dx,ax
        inc    dl
        in     al,dx        ;;input value from ATI Extended E
        mov    ah,al
        and    ah,0f7h      ;;set bit 3 to 0

;;      rewrite the new port
        dec    dl
        mov    al,0beh      ;;index of dual paging enable
        out    dx,ax        ;;output new value to ATI register E
endm
```

LISTING 19.9 Set up for Dual-bank Mode Macro

```
;  bank mode is single or dual based on bit 3 of ATI Extended E
;    bit 3=0  single bank   bit 3=1   dual bank
; Calling Protocol:
;  Set_Dual_Bank_ATI();

Set_Dual_Bank_ATI macro
         get_extended_ATI    ;;load the extended port address in dx
         mov     al,0beh     ;;index of dual paging enable
         out     dx,al
         inc     dl
         in      al,dx       ;;input value from ATI Extended E
         mov     ah,al
         or      ah,08h      ;;set bit 3 to 1

;;       rewrite the new port
         dec     dl
         mov     al,0beh     ;;index of dual paging enable
         out     dx,ax       ;;output new value to ATI register E
    endm
```

19.4.2 Dual-bank Mode

The dual-bank mode is only supported on the 18800–1 and 28800 chip sets. In the dual-bank mode, the Bank Select Register maps 64-Kbyte segments into the host memory address space. One field is dedicated to read operations and the second is dedicated to write operations. The write bank starting address field, WB, is located in bits 3–0; the read bank starting address field, RB, is located in bits 7–5 of the Select Bank Register as shown in Figure 19.8 and listed in Table 19.9. This register is located at Port Ext and index B2. Since each register is dedicated to a read or write operation, both can be mapped into the same host address space. An operation that writes anywhere between A0000–AFFFF will automatically use the WB field. Similarly, an operation that reads anywhere between A0000–AFFFF will automatically use the RB field.

The dual-bank registers provide a mechanism for transferring data from one display memory location to another. The read and write fields of the Bank Select Register need to be written to only once for every time a 64-Kbyte bank is crossed.

Suppose a programmer wants to move a bank from one location to another in the display memory. It is desirable to use the REP MOVSW instruction. It is only necessary to load the Bank Select Register, set up the segment registers to both point to A000, set up the offset registers to point to the source and desti-

Bank Register Dual Bank Mode

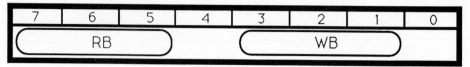

Index B2 at Port EXT   Port EXT+1 Read/Write

FIGURE 19.8 ATI Bank Register in a Dual-bank Mode. The write bank
pointer is in the WB field and the read bank pointer is in the RB field.

nation offset, and the CX Register with the number of words to move. This
setup is followed by the REP MOVSW instruction. The maximum number of
pixels that can be moved in one REP MOVSW sequence would be determined
by the distance to the next 64-Kbyte boundary. It is necessary to set up the
Bank Select Register before crossing these boundaries. This is illustrated in
Figure 19.9.

Code to load the write bank address would perform a read, modify, and write
operation putting the new write bank number into the Bank Select Register as
shown in Listing 19.10.

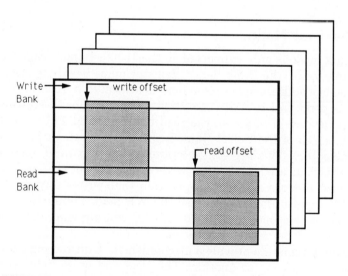

FIGURE 19.9 Display Memory Address Generation. Read/write
operations utilizing the read and write bank registers. A 20-bit
address is formed by the 4-bit bank value and the 16-bit offset value.

LISTING 19.10a Set the Write Bank in Single-bank Mode for the ATI 18800 or 28800 Ver 1

```
; supports the ATI 18800 or 28800 ver 1
; input with a 3-bit value in bl
Set_Write_ATI_1    macro
;;         set up index to Bank Select Register
           get_extended_ATI
           mov    al,0b2h
           out    dx,al          ;;output index

;;         Read...  read Bank Select Register
           inc    dl             ;;point to data
           in     al,dx          ;;read Bank Select Register
           mov    ah,al          ;;put Bank Select Register
           and    ah,0e1h        ;; zero out bits 4-1

;;         Modify...  put bank value and index into ax
           and    bl,7           ;; only want bits 2-0
           shl    bl,1           ;; put into positions 3-1
           or     ah,bl          ;;put Bank Value into high order byte

;;         Write....  output New Bank Register
           dec    dl             ;;point to extended index
           mov    al,0b2h        ;;put index into low order byte
           out    dx,ax          ;;output new Bank Value Register

           ret
endm
```

LISTING 19.10b Set the Write Bank in Dual-bank Mode for the ATI 28800 Ver 2+

```
;  supports the ATI  28800 ver 2+
; input with a 4-bit value in bl
Set_Write_ATI_2 macro
;;         set up index to Bank Select Register
           get_extended_ATI
           mov    al,0b2h
           out    dx,al          ;;output index

;;         Read...  read Bank Select Register
           inc    dl             ;;point to data
           in     al,dx          ;;read Bank Select Register
           mov    ah,al          ;;put Bank Select Register
           and    ah,0e1h        ;;zero out bits 4-1
```

(continued)

```
;;        Modify...  put bank value and index into ax
          and     bl,0fh          ;;only want 4 bits
          shl     bl,1            ;;put into bits 4-1
          or      ah,bl           ;;put Bank Value into high order byte

;;        Write....  output New Bank Register
          dec     dl              ;;point to extended index
          mov     al,0b2h         ;;put index into low order byte
          out     dx,ax           ;;output new Bank Value Register

          ret
endm
```

LISTING 19.10c Set the Read Bank in Dual-bank Mode for the Mach8 and Mach32

```
;; supports the Mach8 and Mach32
;; input with a 6-bit value in bl
Set_Read_ATI_3 macro
          mov     bh,bl
          Set_Read_ATI_2          ;;write out lower 4-bits
;;        MACH-32 extension
;;        write out the top two bits into bits positions 0-1 of
;;        index AE
          mov     al,0aeh         ;;extended index register
          out     dx,al           ;;output index

;;        Read...   read Extended Bank Select Register
          inc     dl              ;;point to data
          in      al,dx           ;;read Extended Bank Select Register
          mov     ah,al           ;;put Extended Bank Select Register
          and     ah,0f3h         ;;zero out bits 3-2

          shr     bh,1            ;;put from 6-5 into bit positions 1-0
          shr     bh,1
          and     bh,0ch          ;;only want bits 3-2
          or      ah,bh           ;;put bits 1-0 into high order byte

;;        write out the top two bits into bits positions 0-1 of
;;        index AE
          dec     dl              ;;point to extended index
          mov     al,0aeh         ;;extended index register
          out     dx,ax           ;;output index

          ret
endm
```

Code to load the read bank address would perform a read, modify, and write operation. It puts the new read bank number into the Bank Select Register as shown in Listing 19.11.

LISTING 19.11a Set the Read Bank in Single-bank Mode for the ATI 18800 or 28800 Ver 1

```
; supports the ATI 18800 or 28800 ver 1
; input with a 3-bit value in bl
Set_Read_ATI_1 macro
;;      set up index to Bank Select Register
        get_extended_ATI
        mov    al,0b2h
        out    dx,al          ;;output index

;;      Read...  read Bank Select Register
        inc    dl             ;;point to data
        in     al,dx          ;;read Bank Select Register
        mov    ah,al          ;;put Bank Select Register
        and    ah,0e1h        ;; zero out bits 4-1

;;      Modify...  put bank value and index into ax
        and    bl,7           ;; only want bits 2-0
        shl    bl,1           ;; put into positions 3-1
        or     ah,bl          ;;put Bank Value into high order byte

;;      Write....  output New Bank Register
        dec    dl             ;;point to extended index
        mov    al,0b2h        ;;put index into low order byte
        out    dx,ax          ;;output new Bank Value Register

        ret
endm
```

LISTING 19.11b Set the Read Bank in Dual-bank Mode for the ATI 28800 Ver 2+

```
;  supports the ATI  28800 ver 2+
; input with a 4-bit value in bl
Set_Read_ATI_2 macro
;;      set up index to Bank Select Register
        get_extended_ATI
        mov    al,0b2h
        out    dx,al          ;;output index

;;      Read...  read Bank Select Register
        inc    dl             ;;point to data
```

(continued)

```
        in      al,dx               ;;read Bank Select Register
        mov     ah,al               ;;put Bank Select Register
        and     ah,1eh              ;; zero out bits 6-4

;;      Modify...  put bank value and index into ax
        ror     bl,1
        ror     bl,1
        ror     bl,1
        or      ah,bl               ;;put Bank Value into high order byte

;;      Write....  output New Bank Register
        dec     dl                  ;;point to extended index
        mov     al,0b2h             ;;put index into low order byte
        out     dx,ax               ;;output new Bank Value Register

        ret
endm
```

LISTING 19.11c Set the Read Bank in Dual-bank Mode for the Mach8 and Mach32

```
;; supports the Mach8 and Mach32
;; input with a 6-bit value in bl
Set_Read_ATI_3 macro
        mov     bh,bl
        Set_Read_ATI_2      ;;write out lower 4-bits

;;      MACH-32 extension
;;      write out the top two bits into bits positions 0-1 of
;;      index AE
        mov     al,0aeh             ;;extended index register
        out     dx,al               ;;output index

;;      Read...  read Extended Bank Select Register
        inc     dl                  ;;point to data
        in      al,dx               ;;read Extended Bank Select Register
        mov     ah,al               ;;put Extended Bank Select Register
        and     ah,0f3h             ;; zero out bits 3-2

        shr     bh,1                ;;put from 6-5 into bit positions 3-2
        shr     bh,1
        and     bh,0ch              ;;only want bits 3-2
        or      ah,bh               ;;put bits 3-2 into high order byte

;;      write out the top two bits into bits positions 0-1 of
;;      index AE
```

```
        dec     dl                  ;;point to extended index
        mov     al,0aeh             ;;extended index register
        out     dx,ax               ;;output index


        ret
endm
```

19.5 CONTROLLING THE CRT ADDRESS GENERATION

19.5.1 Controlling the Start Address

The host cannot extend control of the start address of the display or of the cursor past the 64-byte segment controlled through the Start Address Low and Start Address High registers. The ATI start address can be loaded through the function in Listing 19.12.

LISTING 19.12a Set the Start Address for the ATI 18800 or 28800 Ver 1

```
; supports the ATI 18800 or 28800 ver 1
;; put bits 17-16 in bl into port at bits 7-6
Set_Start_ATI_1    macro
;;        set up index to Bank Select Register
          get_extended_ATI
          mov     al,0b0h
          out     dx,al        ;;output index


;;        Read...   read Bank Select Register
          inc     dl           ;;point to data
          in      al,dx        ;;read Bank Select Register
          and     al,3fh       ;;zero bit positions 7-6


          ror     bl,1
          ror     bl,1         ;;put bits 17-16 into bit positions 7-6
          and     bl,0c0h      ;;zero all but bits 17-16


          mov     ah,al        ;;put Bank Select Register
          or      ah,bl        ;;put in new 17-16 bits


          dec     dl           ;;point to extended index
          mov     al,0b0h
          out     dx,ax        ;;output new Register
          ret
endm
```

LISTING 19.12b Set the Start Address for the ATI 28800 Ver 2+

```
;  supports the ATI  28800 ver 2+
;; 2-bit start address in bl
Set_Start_ATI_2    macro
        get_extended_ATI

;;      set up for bit 16
        mov    al,0b0h    ;;output index to handle bit 16
        out    dx,al      ;;output index

;;      Read...
        inc    dl         ;;point to data
        in     al,dx      ;;read
        and    al,0bfh    ;;zero bit position 6

        mov    bh,bl      ;;save start bits 17-16 in bit
                          ;;positions 1-0
        ror    bl,1
        ror    bl,1       ;;put bit 16 into bit positions 6
        and    bl,040h    ;;zero all but bits 16 in bit position 6

        mov    ah,al
        or     ah,bl      ;;put in new 16 bits

        dec    dl         ;;point to extended index
        mov    al,0b0h    ;;put index back
        out    dx,ax      ;;output new Register

;;      set up index again
        mov    al,0a3h
        out    dx,al      ;;output index

;;      Output index to handle bit 17
        mov    al,0b0h
        out    dx,al      ;;output index

;;      Read...
        inc    dl         ;;point to data
        in     al,dx      ;;read
        and    al,0efh    ;;zero bit position 4

        shl    bh,1
        shl    bh,1
        shl    bh,1       ;;put bit 17 into bit position 4
        and    bh,10h     ;;zero all but bits 17 in bit position 4

        mov    ah,al
        or     ah,bh      ;;put in bit 17
```

```
        dec     dl              ;;point to extended index
        mov     al,0a3h
        out     dx,ax           ;;output new Register
        ret
endm
```

LISTING 19.12c Set the Start Address for the Mach8 and Mach32

```
;; supports the Mach8 and Mach32
;; 4-bit extended start address
Set_Start_ATI_3    macro
        push    bx              ;;save 4-bit input start address
        Set_Start_ATI_2
        pop     bx              ;;restore 4-bit input start address

;;      now take bits 19:18 in bit positions 1-0 and load
;;      into 3-2
;;      MACH-32 extension
;;      write out the top two bits into bits positions 6-5 of
;;      index AD
        mov     al,0adh         ;;extended index register
        out     dx,al           ;;output index

;;      Read...   read Extended Bank Select Register
        inc     dl              ;;point to data
        in      al,dx           ;;read Extended Bank Select Register
        mov     ah,al           ;;put Extended Bank Select Register
        and     ah,0f3h         ;; zero out bits 3-2

        shr     bl,1            ;;put from 6-5 into bit positions 3-2
        shr     bl,1
        and     bl,0ch          ;;only want bits 3-2
        or      ah,bl           ;;put bits 3-2 into high order byte

;;      write out the top two bits into bits positions 0-1 of
;;      index AE
        dec     dl              ;;point to extended index
        mov     al,0adh         ;;extended index register
        out     dx,ax           ;;output index
endm
```

16-color Modes Start Address

The memory is configured as four overlapped planes in the 16-color modes.
Each plane is 64 Kbytes long. There is one such set of planes in the 256-Kbyte
implementations and there are two groups of these planes in the 512 Kbyte
configurations. These groups are called pages. The sixteen bits of the Start

Address Low and High Registers, therefore, actually point to a pixel within the 256 Kbyte page of memory. The granularity of the start address is four bytes.

Two 16-color display modes extend into the second bank of memory. These are the 1024-by-768 16-color modes. Both of these modes, 55 hex and 65 hex, will automatically cross the page boundary during display cycles. It is not possible to set the start address beyond a location of the first page. Since the first page consists of 64 Kbytes and a single line requires 1024/8 = 128 bytes, a total of 512 scan lines can fit in the first page. Thus, the start address cannot extend beyond scan line 511.

256-Color Mode Start Address

The memory is physically divided among four display planes in the 256-color modes. However, unlike the 16-color modes, the memory is not logically split between these four display planes in the 256-color modes. Due to the memory organization (sequential locations being loaded across the four display pages), the 64-Kbyte span of the start addresses covers only 64 Kbytes. The 256-color modes include the 640-by-400, the 640-by-480 and the 800-by-600 resolutions. These require 256,000 bytes, 307,200 bytes and 480,000 bytes respectively. This means that the starting address cannot exceed scanlines 102 for the 640-pixel-wide display modes and scanline 81 for the 800-pixel-wide display mode.

19.5.2 Cursor Control

The alphanumeric modes do not have a problem with page crossing since none extend beyond the first 256-Kbyte page. The cursor can be controlled in the alphanumeric modes by using the 16-bit cursor start address contained in the Cursor Start Address High and Cursor Start Address Low Registers. These registers are discussed in Sections 10.4.15 and 10.4.16, respectively.

There is no hardware cursor capability in the ATI chip. Therefore, the hardware cursor has to be positioned through read/modify/write operations. Controlling the cursor can be done through the BIOS cursor control functions in Section 11.3.2 and 11.3.3. In addition, the programmer can use the same techniques used in accessing the memory to draw the cursor anywhere on the screen. The cursor can be positioned through the function in Listing 19.13 using the "set_cursor_position" macro found in Listing 14.33.

LISTING 19.13a Set the Cursor Address for the ATI 18800 or 28800 Ver 1

```
; supports the ATI 18800 or 28800 ver 1
; NOTE:  no extended start addresses
Set_Cursor_ATI_1  macro
endm
```

LISTING 19.13b Set the Cursor Address for the ATI 28800 Ver 2+

```
;   supports the ATI  28800 ver 2+
Set_Cursor_ATI_2  macro
;;        set up for bit 16
          get_extended_ATI
          mov     al,0b0h
          out     dx,al       ;;output index

;;        Read...  read Bank Select Register
          inc     dl          ;;point to data
          in      al,dx       ;;read Bank Select Register
          and     al,0fbh     ;;zero bit position 2

          mov     bh,bl       ;;save bits 17-16 in bit positions 1-0
          shl     bl,1
          shl     bl,1        ;;put bit 16 into bit positions 6
          and     bl,040h     ;;zero all but bits 16

          mov     ah,al
          or      ah,bl       ;;put in new 16 bits

          dec     dl          ;;point to extended index
          mov     al,0b0h     ;;put index back
          out     dx,ax       ;;output new Register

;;        set up index for bit 17
          mov     al,0a3h
          out     dx,al       ;;output index

;;        Read...
          inc     dl          ;;point to data
          in      al,dx       ;;read Bank Select Register
          and     al,0f7h     ;;zero bit position 3

          shl     bh,1
          shl     bh,1        ;;put bits 17 into bit positions 7
          and     bh,80h      ;;zero all but bits 17

          mov     ah,al       ;;put Bank Select Register
          or      ah,bh       ;;put in new 17-16 bits

          dec     dl          ;;point to extended index
          mov     al,0a3h     ;;put index back
          out     dx,ax       ;;output new Register
          ret
endm
```

LISTING 19.13c Set the Cursor Address for the Mach8 and Mach32

```
; input with cursor position in bl
;; supports the Mach8 and Mach32
Set_Cursor_ATI_3   macro

         push   bx          ;;save for extended bits
         Set_Cursor_ATI_2
         pop    bx          ;;restore extended bits

;;       now take bits 19:18 in bit positions 6-5 and load
;;       into 1-0
;;       MACH-32 extension register 2D
;;       write out the top two bits into bits positions 0-1 of
;;       index AD
         mov    al,0adh     ;;extended index register
         out    dx,al       ;;output index

;;       Read... read Extended Bank Select Register
         inc    dl          ;;point to data
         in     al,dx       ;;read Extended Bank Select Register
         mov    ah,al       ;;put Extended Bank Select Register
         and    ah,0fch     ;; zero out bits 1-0

         shr    bl,1        ;;put from 6-5 into bit positions 1-0
         shr    bl,1
         shr    bl,1
         shr    bl,1
         and    bl,03h      ;;only want bits 1-0
         or     ah,bl       ;;put bits 1-0 into high order byte

;;       write out the top two bits into bits positions 0-1 of
;;       index AE
         dec    dl          ;;point to extended index
         mov    al,0aeh     ;;extended index register
         out    dx,ax       ;;output index

         endm
```

19.5.3   Controlling the Display Offset

The display offset determines the size of the virtual image. The 8-bit value stored in the Offset Register in the CRTC register group, is described in Section 10.4.22. In the word mode, which is typically the case, display offsets up to 1024 bytes can be defined.

TABLE 19.10 ATI Technologies Super BIOS

Function	AH	Feature
Is Mode Available	12	Returns whether mode is supported
Scroll Active Page Up	06	Not supported in modes 61, 62, 63, 65, 67
Scroll Active Page Down	07	Not supported in modes 61, 62, 63, 65, 67
Read Character at Cursor	0C	Not supported in modes 65, 67
Write Dot	0D	Not supported in modes 65, 67
Read Dot	0D	Not supported in modes 65, 67
Write TTX	0E	Not supported in modes 65, 67

19.6 ATI TECHNOLOGY BIOS EXTENSIONS

One new BIOS call provided is called Is Mode Available?. Several modes do not support certain alphanumeric functions. Most notably, there are no graphics BIOS calls for the extended and non-standard 1024-by-768 modes. These BIOS differences are listed in Table 19.10.

The new BIOS call is accessed through AH=12 hex. This mode returns a coded value indicating whether the desired mode is available.

19.6.1 Is Mode Available?

```
Inputs:
        AH=12 hex      Extended VGA Control
        BX=5506 hex    Get Mode information
        BP=FFFF hex    Setup for return argument
        AL= Mode       Desired mode number of which status is
                       desired

Output Parameters:
        BP=return      Return argument
        FFFF hex       Mode not supported
        Not FFFF hex   Mode is supported and value returned is the
                       offset into the CRTC table for that mode.
                       The segment to this table is C000 hex.
```

19.7 CONTROLLING THE GRAPHICS ENGINES OF THE MACH-8 AND MACH-32

The Mach-8 and Mach-32 are very similar and both have extensions beyond the 8514 and VGA standards. The Mach-32 has a set of VGA extension registers internal to the chip; the Mach-8 is co-resident with a VGA controller. The Mach-32 adds the important feature of hi-color support and true-color support. However, true-color support is limited when using the graphics engine.

TABLE 19.11 FIFO Options Register

Bit	Name	Description
0	W_STATE_EN	0=wait state disable unless FIFO full; 1=wait state enable
1	HOST_8_ENA	0=16-bit host data I/O; 1=8-bit

19.7.1 Setup

One register used to set up the Graphics Engine is the write-only FIFO Options Register at 36EEh for the Mach-8 and Mach-32 as shown in Table 19.11.

Wait states are disabled unless the FIFO is full if the W_STATE_EN bit is 0. If it is set to 1, wait states are generated if the FIFO is at least half full. Wait states are always generated if the FIFO is full.

19.7.2 Graphics Engine Control

The graphics engine control functions select the following:

ROM page selection

Control and handling of interrupts and flags

Subsystem control

Wait states

FIFO control/status

Host I/O bus width

Base address select for the drawing buffer

19.7.3 Configuration Registers

The Graphics Engine Configuration registers are shown in Table 19.12. The Subsystem Control Register is detailed in Table 19.13. The Maximum Wait State Register is detailed in Table 19.14.

The Read Extended Graphics Configuration Register at 8EEE is a read-only register available on the Mach-32 only. It has an identical format to the Extended Graphics Engine Configuration Register at 7AEE and therefore provides read access to the important fields in this register.

The Display Pitch is preset to 128 (1024/8) for the Mach-8 only on power up and whenever MEM_CNTL at BEE8 bit 5 or the ADVFUNC_CNTL at 4AE8 is updated. The value of the pitch is not necessarily the same as the CRT_PITCH at 26EE. For the Mach-32, it specifies the length of each line in the display buffer specified in units of eight pixels.

TABLE 19.12 Graphics Configuration Registers

I/O	Name	R/W
42E8	Subsystem Control	W
46E8	ROM page selection	W
36EE	FIFO Option	W
6AEE	Max Wait States	R/W
6EEE	Engine Video Buffer Offset Low	W
72EE	Engine Video Buffer Offset High	W
76EE	Engine Display Pitch	W
7AEE	Extended GE Configuration	W
8EEE	Read Extended Graphics Config	R

TABLE 19.13 Subsystem Control Register at 42E8h (Write Only)

Bits	Name	Description
15–14	GP_RESET	0=no change; 1=normal operation; 2=reset processor and FIFO
11	GP_IDLE_ENA	(when processor idle) 0=disable interrupt; 1=enable
10	INVALID_IO_ENA	if invalid I/O 0=disable interrupt; 1=enable
9	INSIDE_SCISSOR_ENA	if inside scissors region 0=disable interrupt; 1=enable
8	VBLANK_ENA	0=disable interrupt; 1=enable
3	GP_IDLE_ACK	0=no change; 1=clear associated interrupt status bit
2	INVALID_IO_ACK	0=no change; 1=clear associated interrupt status bit
1	INSIDE_SCISSOR_ACK	0=no change; 1=clear associated interrupt status bit
0	VBLANK_ACK	0=no change; 1=clear associated interrupt status bit

For the Mach-8, the Graphics Engine Video Buffer Offset is an 18-bit field with sixteen bits in the Engine Video Buffer Offset Low and two bits in bit positions 1–0 of the Engine Video Buffer Offset High Register. This address is 18-bit precision in linear format. It is specified in pixels divided by 4 or 8 depending on the setting of the Y_CONTROL field in the 8514/A MULTI_FUNC_CNTL[MEM_CNTL] Register.

TABLE 19.14 Maximum Wait State at 6AEEh (Read-Write)

Bits	Name	Description
10	PASSTHROUGH_OVERRIDE	Leave alone
9	IOR16_ENA	1=16 bit I/O 0 for DRAM monochrome reads
8	LINE_OPT_ENA	0 for horizontal degree-mode line draws

For the Mach-32, the Graphics Engine Offset High and Low Register specifies the 20-bit graphics engine video buffer address offset. The Low Registers field GE_OFFSET_LO is the 16 bits of the Graphics Engine Low Register at 6EEE. The High Register field GE_OFFSET_HI is in bits 3–0 of the Graphics Engine Offset High Register at 72EE.

The Graphics Engine Pitch is eight bits loaded into bits 7–0 of the Engine Pitch Register. The pitch field is specified in pixels divided by 8. The contents determine the number of pixels on each line of the display buffer.

The Extended Graphics Engine Configuration Register is shown in Table 19.15. Note that certain bits are available on the Mach-32 only

TABLE 19.15 Extended Graphics Engine Register at 7AEEh (Write Only)

Bits	Name	Description
15	DRAW_PIXEL_SIZE	Drawing pixel size to be written (ATI6800–6 only)
14	DAC_8_BIT_EN	0=6-bit DAC; 1=8-bit DAC (Mach-32 only)
13–12	DAC_EXT_ADDRESS	DAC address inputs RS(3:2) control (Mach-32 only)
11	DISPLAY_PIXEL_SIZE	Display pixel size to be written (ATI68800–6 only)
10	24-BIT_COLOR_ORDER	0=RGB(8,8,8); 1=BGR (8,8,8) (Mach-32 only)
9	24_BIT_COLOR_CONFIG	Bytes per pixel 0=3; 1=4 (Mach-32 only)
8	MULTIPLEX_PIXELS	1=Four pixels processed by the DAC in parallel (Mach-32 only)
7–6	16_BIT_COLOR_MODE	16-bit-per-color word format (Mach-32 only)
5–4	PIXEL_WIDTH	Number of bits per pixel (Mach-32 only)
3	ALIAS_ENA	0-reports actual monitor; 1=reports monitor alias
2–0	MONITOR_ALIAS	Alternate Monitor ID

The color depth is controlled by the PIXEL_WIDTH field as shown in Table 19.16. The 16- and 24-bit color modes require installation of the proper DAC. The 24-bit format flexibility is shown in Table 19.17. The hi-color mode format flexibility is controlled through the 16_BIT_COLOR_MODE field as shown in Table 19.18.

TABLE 19.16 Pixel Width Field

PIXEL_WIDTH	Bits/pixel
0	4
1	8
2	16
3	14

TABLE 19.17 True-Color Formats

24_BIT_COLOR_ORDER	24_BIT_COLOR_CONFIG	Format
0 (RGB)	0 (3 bytes/pixel)	Red (23–16) Green (15–8) Blue (7–0)
0 (RGB)	1 (4 bytes/pixel)	Red (31–24) Green (23–16) Blue (15–8) x (7–0)
1 (BGR)	0 (3 bytes/pixel)	Red (23–16) Green (15–8) Blue (7–0)
1 (BGR)	1 (4 bytes/pixel)	x (31–24) Red (23–16) Green (15–8) Blue (7–0)

TABLE 19.18 Hi-Color Formats

16_BIT_COLOR_MODE	(R,G,B)	Format
0	(5,5,5)	Red (14–10) Green (9–5) Blue (4–0)
1	(5,6,5)	Red (15–11) Green (10–5) Blue (4–0)
2	(6,5,5)	Red (15–10) Green (9–5) Blue (4–0)
3	(6,6,4)	Red (15–10) Green (9–4) Blue (3–0)

19.8 DRAWING CONTROL REGISTERS

19.8.1 General Drawing Control Registers

The general drawing controls include data paths, current X/Y Positions, foreground/background, and color/monochrome source and destination information. These features are used for various drawing operations. The General Drawing Control registers are provided in Table 19.19. Note that the Source Y/Destination Y and Axial Step Registers are the same address but are used for two different functions. The same holds for the Source X/Destination X and the Diagonal Step Registers.

19.8.2 Datapath Configuration Register

The Datapath Configuration Register is shown in Table 19.20

19.8.3 Data Source

The Foreground Color, Background Color, and Monochrome Data Source choices are provided in Table 19.21. If the Pixel Transfer Register is selected (2), then the graphics processor will wait for data from the Pixel Transfer Register as required. If the Pixel Transfer Register is selected as the monochrome source, then color sources involving the Pixel Transfer Register may not be used. If the VRAM BitBlt Source register is selected, then the graphics processor will automatically fetch data from the BitBlt Source Area. The Color Pattern Shift Register is up to 32 pixels long.

If the Mono Pattern Register is selected, then the graphics engine will wait for data from the Mono Pattern Register. If the VRAM BitBlt Source is selected, then selected planes of this area are used to determine whether the foreground or background source and mix are to be used. An AND operation is used

TABLE 19.19 General Drawing Control Registers

Port	Name	Function	R/W
CEEE	DP_CONFIG	Datapath Configuration	W
82E8	CUR_Y	Current Y Position	R/W
86E8	CUR_X	Current X Position	R/W
8AE8	SRC_Y/DESTY_AXSTP	Source Y/Destination Y	W
8AE8	SRC_Y/DESTY_AXSTP	Axial Step	W
8EE8	SRC_X/DESTX_DIASTP	Source X/Destination X	W
8EE8	SRC_X/DESTX_DIASTP	Diagonal Step	W

TABLE 19.20 Datapath Configuration Register

Bits	Name	Description
15–13	FG_COLOR_SCR	Foreground Color Source
12	LSB_FIRST	0=most-significant byte first; 1=least
9	DATA_WIDTH	0=8 bits; 1=16 bits
8–7	BG_COLOR_SRC	Background Color Source
6–5	MONO_SRC	Monochrome Data Source
4	DRAW	0=disable draw; 1=enable draw
2	READ_MODE	0=read monochrome data; 1=read color data
1	POLY_FILL_MODE	0=Disable Polygon-Fill BitBlt; 1=Enable Polygon BitBlt
0	READ_WRITE	0=Read Data from Drawing Trajectory; 1=Write Data to Drawing Trajectory

TABLE 19.21 Data Sources

Value	Foreground	Background	Monochrome
0	Background Color Rgtr	Background Color Rgtr	Always 1
1	Foreground Color Rgtr	Foreground Color Rgtr	Mono Pattern Rgtr
2	Pixel Transfer Rgtr	Pixel Transfer Rgtr	Pixel Transfer Rgtr
3	VRAM BitBlt Source	VRAM BitBlt Source	VRAM BitBlt Source
5	Color Pattern Shift Rgtr	—	—

across all planes. The Source Pixel is logically ORed with the RD_MASK. If all bits are 1, (= FFh), then use the foreground and mix. Otherwise, use the background source and mix.

19.8.4   Data Ordering

The LST_FIRST field determines the byte ordering of the Host Data Register and the Short-Stroke Vector Register. If in an 8-bit ATI mode, 0 reads the most-significant byte first (D8–D15); a 1 reads the least-significant byte first (D78–D0). For 8514 operation, the lower byte (D7–D0) is always read first.

For monochrome data, bit ordering is determined by the graphics operation taking place at the time the data is transferred. Normally the most-significant bit is transferred to the screen first (left-most). On right-to-left fills, the least-significant bit is transferred first.

19.8.5   Drawing Trajectory

The DRAW bit allows for data to be drawn or ignored. If drawn, then each pixel along the trajectory is written to the display consistent with the current drawing parameters. If drawing is disabled, each pixel is subject to clipping and drawing tests but no data will be transferred during the operation.

Data may be read READ_WRITE=0 or written READ_WRITE=1 to the display along the drawing operation.

19.8.6   Polygon Fill

If POLY_FILL_MODE is set, the BitBlt source is automatically used as polygon mask data when performing the BitBlts. At the start of each row of the BitBlt destination area, an internal polygon fill flag is cleared. Each pixel of the source data is ORed with the contents of the inverted RED_MASK Register. If the result is equal to FFh, the source pixel is considered as a polygon outline boundary. Upon each encounter of a polygon boundary, the polygon fill flag is inverted. If the polygon fill flag is cleared, the destination pixel will **not** be updated. If it is set, the destination pixel will be updated.

The ATI Extended Polygon fill differs from the 8514 polygon fill as shown in Table 19.22.

19.8.7   Current Position

The Current X and Current Y Positions are 11-bit fields that are used to determine the destination starting point of most drawing operations. Values range from -512 to 1535 (in a signed 11-bit word).

The SRC_X/DESTX and the SRC_Y/DESTY Registers are 11-bit fields that are used to determine the starting point of the BitBlt Source. These registers share the responsibility for being the AXSTP and the DIASTP Bresenham line registers during line draw operations.

TABLE 19.22   Differences in ATI versus 8514 Polygon Fill

Feature	ATI Extended	8514
Data Source	Taken from BitBlt Source	Taken from BitBlt Destination
WRT and RD_MASK	Do **not** interact	Interact with Polygon Fill Mode A
Left Edge of Polygon	Included in fill area	**Not** included

19.8.8 Line Draw Options Register

The Line Draw Options Register, LINEDRAW_OPT, is located at a read-write register located at an address of A2EE. It is described in Table 19.23.

The CLIP_MODE determines the type of clipping as shown in Table 19.24.

The OCTANT field determines the option direction. This field applies when drawing the Bresenham lines and **not** the direct draw lines. The values in this field depend on the DIR_TYPE bit. If DIR_TYPE is 0, the function of this OCTANT field is described in Table 19.25. If DIR_TYPE is 1, the function of this OCTANT field is described in Table 19.26.

TABLE 19.23 Line Draw Options Register at A2EE

Bits	Name	Description
10–9	CLIP_MODE	Clipping mode
8	BOUNDS_RESET	1=reset the four Bounds Accumulator Registers
7–5	OCTANT	Direction field for BitBlts or line draws
3	DIR_TYPE	0=Bresenham/Octant; 1=Line–length/degree
2	LAST_PEL_OFF	0=draw last pixel; 1=do **not** draw last pixel
1	POLY_MODE	0=normal line draw; 1=polyline draw

TABLE 19.24 Clipping Modes

Value	Function
0	Disable Clip Exception
1	Do Stroked Plain Lines
2	Do Polygon Boundary Lines
3	Do Patterned Lines

TABLE 19.25 OCTANT field DIR_TYPE=0

Bit	Value	Axis	Direction
7	0	YDIR	Decrement Y
6	0	YMAJOR	X is major Axis
5	0	XDIR	Decrement X
7	1	YDIR	Increment Y
6	1	YMAJOR	Y is major Axis
5	1	XDIR	Increment X

TABLE 19.26   OCTANT field DIR_TYPE=1

Value	Direction
0	0 degrees
1	45 degrees
2	90 degrees
3	135 degrees
4	180 degrees
5	225 degrees
6	270 degrees
7	315 degrees

The DIR_TYPE field affects the operation of raw Bresenham line-draw operation and short-stroke vector operations. If DIR_TYPE is 0, the lines are based on Bresenham parameters and the octant in which the lines will be drawn is determined by OCTANT (see Table 19.13). If DIR_TYPE is 1, the lines are based on the line-length/degree; the Bresenham Count Register determines the line length and the OCTANT field determines the line direction.

19.8.9   Bounds Accumulator Registers

The bounds accumulator registers accumulate the bounding box of all points written through the Line Draw Register. These four registers are read-only registers and are described in Table 19.19. These registers have an accumulation range of -2048 TO 2047. Even though comparisons use the full sixteen bits, saturation occurs at either -2048 or 2047. Writing to one of the BOUNDS_RESET fields of the Linedraw Options Register resets the field as shown in Table 19.27.

TABLE 19.27   Bounds Accumulator Registers

Address	Name	Reset Value	R/W
72EE	BOUNDS_LEFT	2047	R
76EE	BOUNDS_TOP	2047	R
7AEE	BOUNDS_RIGHT	−2048	R
7EEE	BOUNDS_BOTTOM	−2048	R

TABLE 19.28   Differences in ATI versus 8514 Scissors

Feature	ATI Extended	8514
Range X	−2048 to 2047	−1024 to 1023
Range Y	−2048 to 2047	0 to 2047

TABLE 19.29   Scissors Registers

Port	Name	R/W
DAEE	SCISSOR_LEFT	W
DEEE	SCISSOR_TOP	W
E2EE	SCISSOR_RIGHT	W
E6EE	SCISSOR_BOTTOM	W

19.9   SCISSORS

Scissors registers are used to inhibit drawing outside a rectangular area. This is called *post-clipping*. The Clipping registers do not perform correctly outside of the (-512,-512) to (1535,1535) region. They can generate interrupts when a drawing occurs inside the scissors region and are used for high-speed pick operations.

The ATI scissors registers differ from the 8514 registers as shown in Table 19.28.

A value is inside the scissors region based on the following equations:

SCISSOR_LEFT <= CUR_X <= SCISSOR_RIGHT

SCISSOR_TOP <= CUR_Y <= SCISSOR_BOTTOM

Each of the scissors registers is a 12-bit field, located as shown in Table 19.29.

19.10   PRE-CLIP MODES

Pre-clipping is supported by hardware in the Mach-8. Pre-clip modes are set in the Linedraw Options Register. Four pre-clipping modes are shown in Table 19.30. The pre-clipping allows arbitrary lines to be drawn quickly with little intervention by the host processor.

19.10.1   Clip Mode 1: Line Segment

Pre-clipping of line segments uses the modified version of the Cohen-Suther-land algorithm. Each line is examined to determine whether the drawing engine must actually draw the line pixel-by-pixel or whether the line can be

TABLE 19.30 Pre-Clip Modes

Clip_Mode	Description
0	Disable clip exceptions
1	Enable clipping of stroked plain lines
2	Pre-clip polygon boundary lines
3	Pre-clip patterned lines

trivially rejected. These are shown in Figure 19.10. Lines are categorized as either trivially rejected, trivially accepted, or exception. Exception lines may fall into the scissors region but are not drawable by the graphics engine because one or both endpoints lie outside the device coordinate space.

When the graphics engine encounters exception lines, a clip exception condition occurs and the engine stops drawing the current line until the clip exception condition has been cleared by the host processor. The host can then back up and determine the exception line. In practice, few lines are exception lines.

When a clip exception occurs, the CLIP_OVERRUN field of the EXT_GE_STATS is set to 1. All subsequent attempts to write to the Line End

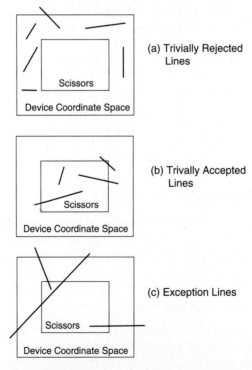

(a) Trivially Rejected Lines

(b) Trivially Accepted Lines

(c) Exception Lines

FIGURE 19.10 Line Segment Clipping

Y through the Linedraw register are rejected by the engine. Each attempt is recorded in the CLIP_OVERRUN counter. This is reset to zero when the CLIP_MODE is set to zero and when Y is written from LINEDRAW. The CLIP_OVERRUN count can be used by the host to find the offending line.

19.10.2 CLIP MODE 2: Polygon Boundary Lines

The Polygon Boundary Lines Clipping method is almost identical to the Line Segment Clip except that lines outside the scissors rectangle are trivially accepted provided they are polygon boundary lines and their endpoints are neither above nor below the scissors. The lines are clamped to the edge of the device coordinate systems and the normal line draw procedure clamps the line to the edge of the scissors region. This is shown in Figure 19.11.

Since endpoint clamping alters the angle to the affected lines, lines for which one endpoint lies to the left and the other to the right of the left edge must generate exceptions.

19.10.3 Clip Mode 3: Pattern Lines

Patterned lines that are inside the device coordinate space are drawn. Patterned lines that are outside or partially outside the device coordinate space generate exceptions. The graphics engine attempts to draw all lines that would have been trivially rejected. The graphics engine updates the PATTERN_INDEX. Exception lines that are outside or partially outside the device coordinate space have to be handled by the host. Typical lines are shown in Figure 19.12.

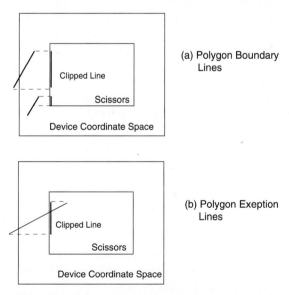

FIGURE 19.11 Polygon Boundary Lines Clipping

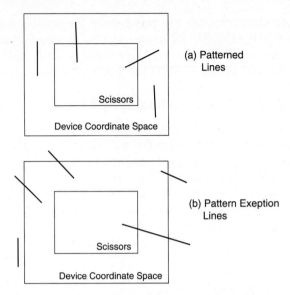

FIGURE 19.12 Patterned Lines Clipping

19.11   DIRECT LINE DRAWING

Direct line draw registers provide for high-speed line drawing. Instead of drawing lines based on the Bresenham parameters, the programmer can set beginning and ending points into the line drawing engine. This provides a fast way of drawing lines, especially polylines. For example, suppose you want to draw a set of polylines beginning at the current point. You would set the End X and End Y values and then issue the Line Draw command. Repeating this would draw each subsequent line since each line would begin where the previous line ended.

The direct line draw registers are indexed through the Linedraw Index Register. This register is a write-only register located at 9AEE and has a 3-bit LINEDRAW_OPERATION field as shown in Table 19.31.

TABLE 19.31   Linedraw Index Register LINEDRAW OPERATION FIELD at 9AEE

Value	Description
0	Set Current X
1	Set Current Y
2	Set Line End X
3	Set Line End Y, Draw Line and Reset Index to 2
4	Set Current X (The graphics engine performs MOVES instead of DRAWS)
5	Set Current Y and Reset Index to 4

The polyline example can be issued from the current point by setting the value of the LINEDRAW OPERATION FIELD to 2, sending the Line End X value, setting the LINEDRAW OPERATION FIELD to 3, sending the Line End Y value. Note that the hardware automatically draws the line and indexes 2 again in anticipation of the next END X and END Y points. A move could be issued by setting the Current X to 4, writing the current X value, setting the index to 5, writing the current Y value.

The values for these starting or ending points are loaded into the Direct Line-draw Register, which is a 16-bit field at address FEEE. It is a write-only register that should be loaded with one of the following values:

Set Current X

Set Current Y

Set Line End X

Set Line End Y and draw

19.12 SHORT-STROKE VECTOR

The extended short-stroke vector is different from the 8514 in that monochrome data must be supplied in packed-bit format as opposed to the 8514 nibble format. It also supports color patterns. The Short-Stroke Vector Register is a write-only register at C6EE containing the two short-stroke 8514 format fields.

19.13 BRESENHAM LINE DRAW REGISTERS

The Bresenham line draw registers perform similarly to the 8514 and are provided in Table 19.32.

TABLE 19.32 Bresenham Line Draw Registers

Address	Name
86E8	CUR_X
82E8	CUR_Y
8AE8	SRC_Y/DESTY_AXSTP
8EE8	SRC_X/DESTX_DIASTP
92E8	ERR_TERM
96EE	BRES_COUNT
A2EE	LINEDRAW_OPT

19.14 BITBLT

The ATI Extended BitBlt operations support rectangle fills, polygon fills, and data transfers between the host and the graphics engine. Unlike the 8514, the exact operation is determined by the DP_CONFIG Register. Extended BitBlts allow more flexible specifications between the shapes of the source and destination area. Packed monochrome data can be supplied directly to the drawing engine.

If a BitBlt region is selected as the data source in the Datapath Configuration Register, or if the POLY_FILL_MODE is selected, the BitBlt source operations will activate. If the Pixel Transfer Register is selected as the data source, then the graphics processor will automatically wait for data to be transferred by the host.

The registers associated with the BitBlts are provided in Table 19.33.

19.14.1 Source Data Pointer

The extent and direction of motion of the source data pointer are determined by the following BitBlt Parameter registers in Figure 19.13a.

If the BitBlt Source X Row Start Register is equal to the BitBlt Source X Row End Register at the time that the BitBlt source is activated, the engine will abort the drawing routing immediately. The graphics controller has an internal BitBlt-Source Data FIFO build-in. This is used to speed up the process; however, it causes the BitBlt Source Current X and Y Registers to have an indeterminate value at the end of an operation.

19.14.2 Data Pointer

The extent and direction of motion of the source data pointer are determined by the following BitBlt Parameter Registers are defined in Figure 19.13b.

TABLE 19.33 BitBlt Related Registers

Address	Name	Function	R/W
8EE8	SRC_X	Source X	W
8AE8	SRC_Y	Source Y	W
B2EE	SRC_X_START	Source X Row Start	W
BEEE	SRC_X_END	Source X Row End	W
C2EE	SRC_Y_DIR	Source Y Direction	W
86E8	CUR_X	Current X Position	R/W
82E8	CUR_Y	Current Y Position	R/W
A6EE	DEST_X_START	Destination X Row Start	W
AAEE	DEST_X_END	Destination X Row End	W
AEEE	DEST_Y_END	Destination Y Row End	W

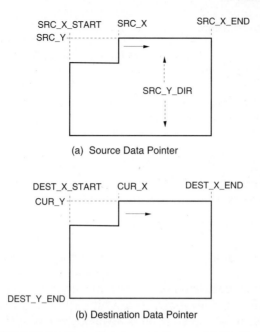

(a) Source Data Pointer

(b) Destination Data Pointer

FIGURE 19.13 Data Pointers (a) Source (b) Destination

19.14.3 BitBlt Direction

The first row of the BitBlt starts at CUR_X and ends at DEST_X_END. All subsequent rows start at DEST_X_START and end at DEST_X_END. Generally, the left-edge is inclusive and the right edge is exclusive.

If the DEST_X_START is greater than the DEST_X_END, the BitBlt is performed in a right-to-left order. In this case, the CUR_X and DEST_X_ROW_START are exclusive and DEST_X_ROW_END is inclusive. If the DEST_X_START is less than the DEST_X_END, the BitBlt is performed in a left-to-right order. In this case, the CUR_X and DEST_X_ROW_START are inclusive and DEST_X_ROW_END is exclusive. If the starting X equals the ending X no operation takes place. The source data behaves similarly.

If the DEST_Y_START is greater than the DEST_Y_END, the BitBlt is performed in a top-to-bottom order. In this case, the CUR_X and DEST_Y_END is inclusive. If the DEST_Y_START is less than the DEST_Y_END, the BitBlt is performed in a bottom-to-top order. In this case, the DEST_Y_END is exclusive. If the starting Y equals the ending Y, no operation takes place. The SRC_Y_DIR determines the source Y direction.

19.14.4 Data Transfers

Data is transferred from the host to the Pixel Transfer Register if the register is designated as a color or monochrome source. The engine waits for the host to supply the data. When reading data from the Pixel Transfer Register during

TABLE 19.34   Data transfers

R/W	Direction	Bits/Transfer	DATA_WIDTH	LSB_FIRST	Code
Write	Left-to-right	16	1	1	Listing 29.1a
Write	Left-to-right	8	0	0	Listing 29.1b
Read	Left-to-right	16	1	1	Listing 29.1c
Read	Left-to-right	8	0	0	Listing 29.1d
Write	Right-to-left	16	1	0	Listing 29.1e
Write	Right-to-left	8	0	0	Listing 29.1f
Read	Right-to-left	16	1	0	Listing 29.1g
Read	Right-to-left	8	0	0	Listing 29.1h

BitBlts, data is read from the destination trajectory. The 8514 reads from the source trajectory. Several functions are provided in Listing 19.14.

When monochrome data is read, it is organized most-significant byte first for left-to-right transfers and least-significant bit first for right-to-left transfers. In either case, the left-most screen pixel is always present in the most-significant bit of the Pixel Transfer Register.

If 16-bit monochrome data is read, the data is expected to be in least-significant-byte-left order, although byte ordering is independently selected by the LSB_FIRST field of the Datapath Configuration Register. Thus, in a right-to-left transfer, the data is transferred to the host D15–D8 followed by D7–D0. In a left-to-right transfer, the data is transferred to the host D7–D0 followed by D15–D8. This is summarized in Table 19.34.

LISTING 19.14   Code Segments for Data Transfers

Listing 19.14.a   Left-to-Right Word Transfer

```
mov     dx,PIX_TRANS
std
rep     outsw
```

Listing 19.14.b   Left-to-Right Byte Transfer

```
mov     dx,PIX_TRANS+1
std
rep     outsb
```

Listing 19.14.c   Left-to-Right Word Transfer

```
mov     dx,PIX_TRANS
std
rep     insw
```

Listing 19.14.d Left-to-Right Byte Transfer

```
mov      dx,PIX_TRANS+1
std
rep      insb
```

Listing 19.14.e Right-to-Left Word Transfer

```
mov      dx,PIX_TRANS
cld
rep      outsw
```

Listing 19.14.f Right-to-Left Byte Transfer

```
mov      dx,PIX_TRANS+1
cld
rep      outsb
```

Listing 19.14.g Right-to-Left Word Transfer

```
mov      dx,PIX_TRANS
cld
rep      insw
```

Listing 19.14.h Right-to-Left Byte Transfer

```
mov      dx,PIX_TRANS+1
cld
rep      insb
```

Monochrome data is row-packed. Therefore, the last bit of a row is followed immediately by the first bit of the next row, regardless of byte boundaries. It is row-packed consistent with the direction of the transfer. For right-to-left transfers, the first bit of a row will be followed immediately by the last bit of the next row of data. Bitmap data is byte-aligned in a row format. The right edge of the destination can be shifted and extraneous bits can be scissored.

The Pattern Index Register is updated when a pattern is used as the source. It is post-incremented if the BitBlt is left-to-right and pre-decremented if it is right-to-left. In addition, the Pattern Index is reset to the previous value whenever the CUR_X becomes equal to the BitBlt_X_End.

The source BitBlt parameters registers are modified during a BitBlt or Fill operation only if the BitBlt source is named as a monochrome source, color source, or if the Polygon-Fill is enabled. The Pattern Index Register is modified only if the monochrome or color pattern register are selected as the source.

19.15 MISCELLANEOUS COMMAND REGISTER

The Miscellaneous Command Register provides an 11-bit field used to perform fast polygon scan conversion under processor control. It is a write-only register located at CAEEh. The Current X and Current Y Registers will be set to the address of the first point in the active edge table. Writing to the Current X Register clears the internal Scan-to-X State Register. Subsequent points are block copied to the Scanline Draw to X Register. Each write to the register will produce the following action.

If the Scan-to-X State Register is cleared, a horizontal line will be drawn from the current X to the Specified X. If the Scan-to-X State Register is set, the pixel mask bit for each pixel in the draw will be set causing a move operation. The value of the Scan-to-X State Register is toggled after each draw. If the value written to the Scanline Draw to X Register is less than the Current X value, the scanline will be drawn in the reverse direction. The Current X will be considered exclusive and the supplied X will be considered inclusive. For left-to-right direction, the CUR_X is inclusive; the SCAN_TO_X is exclusive.

19.16 PATTERN REGISTERS

A 32-pixel color and a 32-pixel monochrome pattern register are provided. Each of these can be selected as data sources. They are accessed through a write-only index register at 82EEh. There are eighteen color pattern registers. The index register is auto-incremented after each write. The registers are listed in Table 19.35.

The sixteen color registers provide a 32-byte color pattern as selected by the FG_COLOR_SRC field in the Datapath Configuration Register. Each word contains the least-significant byte first. The color pattern may be used as a color source during pixel transfers. The Pattern Length Register (a 5-bit field) determines the length (in pixels) of the pattern. The Pattern Index Register determines the first pixel to be used in the pattern. Note that these registers may be used as scratch area for BitBlt operations that do not use the pattern registers.

TABLE 19.35 Pattern Registers

Address	Name	Function	R/W
82EE	PATT_DATA_INDEX	Pattern Index	W
8EEE	PATT_DATA[0–F]	Color Patterns 0–F	W
8EEE	PATT_DATA[10–11]	Mono patterns 10–11	W
D2EE	PATT_LENGTH	Pattern Length	W
D6EE	PATT_INDEX	Pattern Index	R/W

The two monochrome registers contain 32-bits of monochrome pattern. The Pattern Length Register determines the number of bits used. The Pattern Index Register determines the first pixel to participate in the mix. The order of the bits is least-significant byte first, most-significant bit first.

19.17 PIXEL TRANSFER CONTROL REGISTERS

This collection of registers is provided in Table 19.36.

19.17.1 Colors

The Background and Foreground Color registers are sixteen bits wide for the Mach-32, but are restricted to eight bits for the Mach-8. This is consistent with the lack of support for hi-color mode on the Mach-8 and the fact that the graphics accelerator of the Mach-32 does not support true-color mode.

19.17.2 Pixel Transfer Functions

The lower four bits of the Foreground and Background Function Registers (ALU_FG_FN and ALU_BG_FN) contain the foreground and background function codes as shown in Table 19.37. The Write Mask Register affects all arithmetic/boolean operations. Planes that are masked out by the Write Mask Register do not participate in any ALU Operation. All unmasked planes are treated as if they were contiguous. During add and subtract operations, carries or borrows entering into a bit position that are masked by the plane mask are passed through, unmodified to the next most-significant bit.

TABLE 19.36 Pixel Transfer Control Registers

Address	Name	Function	R/W
A2E8	BKGD_COLOR	Background Color	W
A6E8	FRGD_COLOR	Foreground Color	W
AAE8	WRT_MASK	Write Mask Register	W
AEE8	RD_MASK	Read Mask Registers	W
EEEE	DEST_CMP_FN	Destination Compare Function	W
92EE	SRC_CMP_FN	Source Compare Function	W
B2E8	DEST_CMP_COLOR	Destination Compare Color	W
EAEE	SRC_CMP_COLOR	Source Compare Color	W
BAEE	ALU_FG_FN	Foreground Raster Operation	W
B6EE	ALU_BG_FN	Background Raster Operation	W
E2E8	PIX_TRANS	Pixel Transfer	R/W

TABLE 19.37 Foreground and Background Function Codes

Value	Function	Value	Function
0	!D	10	MIN (S,D)
1	0	11	D – S
2	1	12	S – D
3	D	13	S + D
4	!S	14	MAX (S,D)
5	S XOR D	15	(D–S) /2
6	! (S XOR D)	16	(S–D) /2
7	S	17	(S+D) /2
8	!(S AND D)	18	MAX (0,D–S)
9	D OR !S	19	MAX (0,D–S)
A	!D OR S	1A	MAX(0,S–D)
B	S OR D	1B	MIN(FFh,S+D)
C	S AND D	1C	MAX (0,D–S)/2
D	S AND !D	1D	MAX (0,D–S)/2
E	!S AND D	1E	MAX(0,S–D)/2
F	!(S OR D)	1F	FFh if (S+D > FFh) else (S+D)/2

Formulas for add and subtract are as follows:

subtract: result = (X AND PlaneMask) - (Y AND PlaneMask)

add: result = ((X AND PlaneMask) + (Y OR !PlaneMask)) XOR !PlaneMask

The divide-by-two (/2) operation is performed by shifting the result of the previous operation (add or subtract, saturate or unsaturated, right by 1. The carry or borrow from the preceding operation is shifted into the most-significant bit of the result.

The average operation produces an arithmetic average for any contiguous set of unmasked planes. The Max and Min operations are unsigned comparisons. The plane mask affects the comparison between source and destination data. The decision on whether the source data or destination data is passed as a result is based on whether a SUBTRACT (D,S) operation would produce a borrow from the most-significant bit position.

19.18   SOURCE AND DESTINATION COMPARE

The Source Compare Function Codes are three bits located in bit positions 5–3 of the Source Color Compare Function Register. The Source Compare Color Register contains the 8-bit value used for the comparison (SCC) along with the

TABLE 19.38 Source and Destination Comparison Codes

Value	Destination	Source
0	0=False	0=False
1	1=True	1=True
2	DP >= DCC	SP >= SCC
3	DP < DCC	SP < SCC
4	DP !+ DCC	SP !+ SCC
5	DP = DCC	SP = SCC
6	DP <= DCC	SP <= SCC
7	DP > DCC	SP > SCC

source pixel (SC). This value occupies the lower eight bits of the Source Compare Color Register. The Destination Compare Function Codes are four bits located in bit positions 6–3 of the Destination Color Compare Function. The Destination Compare Color Register (DCC) contains the 8-bit value used for the comparison along with the destination pixel (DP). This value occupies the lower eight bits of the Destination Compare Color Register. These function codes are shown in Table 19.38.

Comparisons are unsigned. Only planes that have been enabled by the write mask participate in the comparison. Both source and destination pixel values are ANDed with the write plane mask before comparison. For destination comparisons, if the result is TRUE, the pixel will not be overwritten. If the result is FALSE, the pixel will be overwritten. For source comparisons, if the result is TRUE, the pixel processor will use the background ALU function to perform the source and destination mix regardless of the current monochrome input. If the result is FALSE, the monochrome input value for the current pixel will be used to select the ALU function.

19.19   MASK REGISTERS

The Write Mask bits occupy the lower eight bits of the Write Mask Register. A 0 in a bit position disables writing to the plane; a 1 enables writing. The Read Mask bits occupy the lower eight bits of the Read Mask Register. A 0 in a bit position disables using the plane in comparisons; a 1 enables the plane for comparison. The read mask selects one or more planes to be used for comparison during monochrome reads or during VRAM to VRAM BitBlts if a monochrome source is selected. The following formula is used for the read mask:

    if (SrcColor OR !ReadPlaneSelect == 0xFF)
        the monochrome result is set to 1 (foreground selected)
    else
        the monochrome result is set to 0 (background selected)

NOTE: The read mask is **never** rotated for the Extended ATI operations as it is for certain 8514/A operations.

19.20 PIXEL TRANSFER REGISTER

The Pixel Transfer Register supports data transfers to and from the graphics engine. It is a read/write register located at E2E8. On a read, data is from the BitBlt Destination Trajectory. It is the responsibility of the host to read this data from the Pixel Transfer Register. On a write, data is from the Pixel Transfer Register to the graphics engine.

If monochrome data is to be read, PIX_CNTL=1, and data will be read as packed 1-bit monochrome (across the plane) data. The Read Mask Register will be used to convert each byte of color data from the video buffer to a single bit.

If color data is to be read, PIX_CNTL=0, and data will be read as 8-bit color data. In 4-bit-per-color resolutions, the most-significant four bits will be masked to zero.

On a read, if data is still not ready after time-out, an INVALID_IO exception will occur and invalid data will be returned. On a write, if an entry in the command FIFO is still not available after time-out, an INVALID_IO exception will occur and the graphics processor will ignore the data that caused the exception.

19.21 STATUS REGISTERS

The status registers are shown in Table 19.39. These registers provide the status information necessary for the programmer to control the graphics engine.

The Extended FIFO Register contains the sixteen entry status bits in Bits 0–15 respectively. A bit indicates that the respective FIFO Entry is empty (bit=0) or full (bit=1). The Subsystem Status Register at 42E8 is shown in Table 19.40.

TABLE 19.39 Status Registers

Address	Name	Register	R/W
9AEE	EXT_FIFO_STATUS	Extended FIFO Status	R
42E8	SUBSYS_STAT	Subsystem Status	R
62EE	EXT_GE_STATUS	Extended Graphics Status	R
12EE	CONFIG_STATUS_1	Configuration Status 1	R
16EE	CONFIG_STATUS_2	Configuration Status 2	R

TABLE 19.40 Subsystem Status Register

Bit	Name	Function
7	MEM_CONFIG	Memory Configuration 0=512K; 1=1 Meg
6–4	MONITOR_ID	Monitor ID
3	GP_IDLE_INT	0=not detected; 1=detected empty FIFO and idle processor
2	INVALID_IO_INT	0=not detected; 1=detected overflowed FIFO or data not ready when Pixel Transfer Register is read
1	INSIDE_SCISSOR_INT	0=not detected; 1=detected destination (CUR_X,CUR_Y) inside scissors
0	VBLANK_INT	0=not detected; 1=detected start of vertical blanking interval

TABLE 19.41 Extended Graphics Engine Status Register

Bit	Name	Function
15	POINTS_OUTSIDE	Point outside device coordinate system
14	EE_DATA_IN	Current data output of EEPROM
13	GE_ACTIVE	0=Graphics engine idle; 1=Graphics engine busy
12–9	CLIP_FLAGS	Result of clip
8	CLIP_INSIDE	Point potentially in scissors rectangle
7	EE_CRC_VALID	EEPROM CRC was correct after last hardware reset
3–0	CLIP_OVERRUN	Number of lines attempted since a clip operation

The Extended Graphics Engine Status Register at 62EE provides additional status information as shown in Table 19.41.

The POINTS_OUTSIDE field indicates that a point fed through the Line Draw Register was outside the device coordinate system (-512,-512) to (1535,1535). This field is set/reset after CUR_Y is written to through the Line Draw Register. This field is set if any one or more lines that have been written to the Line Draw Register, including the starting point, fell outside the device coordinate system.

The CLIP_FLAGS field provides the relationship between the values of the Destination Current X and Y Registers to the values of the Scissors Register. NOTE: The CUR_X and CUR_Y are normally used, but the DESTX_DIASTP

TABLE 19.42   Clip Flags

Bit	Clip Result
12	Point above the rectangle
11	Point below the rectangle
10	Point left the rectangle
9	Point right the rectangle

and DESTY_AXSTP are used during the 8514 compatible BitBlts. Each bit is set/reset according to the specified relationship of the current point to the current scissors as shown in Table 19.42. If the point is outside the current scissors, then the bits in the CLIP_FLAGS field are set to 1. If the point is inside, it is set to 0.

The CLIP_INSIDE field indicates whether one or more lines are potentially inside a scissors region. If it is 0, then none of the line segments in the most recent line drawing sequence are inside the scissors. If it is 0, then a move to operation is performed through the Line Draw Register. The bit becomes set (and remains set) if any line segment in the sequence is not trivially determined to be outside the scissors.

The CLIP_OVERRUN counter field indicates whether a line segment in a Line Draw Register line draw sequence needs to be clipped. It is reset to 0 when an operation is performed through the Line Draw Register. It is set to 1 when a line segment is detected as a candidate for clipping. Once set, all further line draw operations will be rejected, and this field becomes a counter, incrementing each time an attempt is made to draw a line.

19.22   MISCELLANEOUS REGISTERS

These registers are used to store the adapter ID, power-on start-up setup options. These are compatible with Micro Channel Systems. They are provided in Table 19.43.

19.23   MEMORY APERTURE INTERFACE ON THE MACH-32

The Mach-32 can access display memory through the graphics accelerator or through its aperture interface directly as a frame buffer for any but the 24-bit color modes. The 24-bit color modes must use the aperture interface. When the aperture interface is disabled, the memory is **not** mapped into the host address space.

Two registers provide access to the aperature size, location, and control. The Memory Boundary Register at 42EEh is a read-write register and it controls the memory divider that separates available display memory between the VGA and the accelerator. This register is shown in Table 19.44. The Video Memory Boundary Register separates the video memory. Any memory above the boundary can be accessed only by the 8514; any memory below the boundary can be accessed only by the VGA. The Partition Enable flag enables this boundary. If it is 0, both the 8514 and the VGA can write anywhere in video memory. If it is a 1, then the boundary conditions hold.

The Memory Aperture Configuration Register is shown in Table 19.45. The aperture interface is enabled through the Bit 1–0 field. It is enabled as either a 1 Mbyte or a 4 Mbyte aperture. If it is a 1 Mbyte aperture, then the page number field selects which Mbyte is currently selected within the 4 Mbyte address space. The memory aperture may be aligned to any 1 Mbyte boundary between 0 and 127 Mbytes in the host memory address space.

TABLE 19.43 Miscellaneous Registers

Address	Name	Register	R/W
0100	SETUP_ID1	POS ID 1	R = 80h
0101	SETUP_ID2	POS ID 2	R = 88h
0102	SETUP_OPT	POS Setup Options	R/W
52EE	ROM_ADDR_1	EPROM Address Select 1	R/W
562EE	ROM_ADDR_2	EPROM Address Select 2	R/W

TABLE 19.44 Memory Boundary Register at 42EE

Bit	Function
3–0	Video Memory Boundary (in 256-Kbyte pages)
4	Video Memory Partition enable

TABLE 19.45 Memory Aperture Configuration Register

Bit	Function
1–0	Direct Memory Interface. 0=direct interface disabled; 1=1 Mbyte aperture; 2=4 Mbyte.
3–2	1 Mbyte Page Select Page Number (0–3).
15–8	Memory aperture location (on 1 Mbyte boundaries).

19.24 MODE SETTING WITH THE MACH-32

The Mach-32 ROM contains functions to easily set a mode on the Mach-32 without the need for low-level initializations. The functions are accessible by absolute calls to specific addresses in the Mach-32 ROM. The base ROM address is determined from the ROM Address Register called ROM_ADDR_1 at 52EEh, as shown in Listing 19.15. Typically, the Mach-32 segment value is C000h with VGA controller enabled and C800h if the VGA is disabled.

LISTING 19.15 Accessing the Extended Mach-32 Display Modes

```
; Calling Protocol
        RomFunctionAddress=getModeAddress();
getRomSegment  proc far

        ;retrieve the segment of the Mach-32 ROM in ax
        mov    dx,ROM_ADDR_1    ;this register 52EE is loaded by
                                ;the Mach32 boot ROM
        in     al,dx      ;read the register
        and    al,7Fh     ;only want bits 6-0
        xor    ah,ah      ;zero ah
        mov    cl,7       ;want bits 6-0 into positions 13-7
        shl    ax,cl
        add    ax,0C000h ;add in C = 11 in bits 15-14 for address
        ret
getRomSegment  endp
```

Typically, two ROM calls are required to set a mode on the Mach-32. The first call, Load Shadow Set, initializes one of the Mach-32's two shadow sets. A shadow set contains information such as resolution, color depth, and pitch for a specific mode. The second call, Set Mode, invokes the mode initialized by a previous call to Load Shadow Set. The input parameters for the two functions are shown next. The first call, Load Shadow Set, is shown in Listing 19.16. The second call, which actually sets the mode, is shown in Listing 19.17.

LISTING 19.16 Load Shadow Set at Address Rom_Segment=0064h

```
Input Parameters:
        ah = 0     bits per pixel for Mach-8 compatibility.
or
        ah = DEEP_COLOR_OPTIONS (Mach 32)
           bit 0      ;set to 1
           bts 2-1    ;PIXEL_WIDTH  0=4, 1=8, 2=16, 3=24
           bits 4-3   ;16_BIT_COLOR_WIDTHINGS 0=555, 1=565, 2=655,
                      ;3=664
           bit 5      ;set to 0
```

```
    bit 6        ;24_BIT_COLOR_CONFIG   0=3 bytes/pixel
                 ;1=4 bytes/pixel
    bit 7        ;24_BIT_COLOR_ORDER 0=RGB 1=BGR

al = RESOLUTION and SHADOW_SET
   0h    ; default (shadow set 1=640x480x8  2=1024x768x8
   1h    ; load 800 by 600 into shadow set 1
   2h    ; load 800 by 600 into shadow set 2
   11h   ; load 1280 by 1024  into shadow set 1
   12h   ; load 1280 by 1024  into shadow set 2
   21h   ; load 640 by 480 into shadow set 1
   22h   ; load 640 by 480 into shadow set 2
   41h   ; load 1024 by 768 into shadow set 1
   42h   ; load 1024 by 768 into shadow set 2
   81h   ; load alternate mode into shadow set 1
   82h   ; load alternate mode into shadow set 2
bx = PITCH
   0h    ; pitch of 1024
   1h    ; pitch of mode rounded to nearest multiple of 128
   2h    ; pitch of 1536
   3h    ; do not modify pitch

Output Parameters:
        carry flag    ; return status
          clear       ; shadow set load completed without errors
          set         ; shadow set load failed; requested mode
                      ; not supported
```

LISTING 19.17 Set Mode at Address Rom_Segment=0068h

```
Input Parameters:
        al = SHADOW_SET
           0h   ; VGA pass through
           1h   ; shadow set 1
           2h   ; shadow set 2

Output Parameters:
        carry flag ; return status
        clear      ; shadow set load completed without errors
        set        ; shadow set load failed;  requested mode
                   ; not supported
```

Setting a mode successfully depends on two basic factors. These are the Mach-32's hardware, including the memory and DAC type, and its configuration by the INSTALL program. For example, attempting to set an 800-by-600 mode will fail if the Mach-32 is configured for a PS2 VGA monitor whose max resolution is 640 by 480.

The code in Listing 19.18 illustrates the setting of a mode on the Mach-32:

LISTING 19.18 Setting a Mode on the Mach-32

```
rom_offset  dw ?
row_segment dw ?

            ; get the segment of the Mach32 ROM in ax
            call    getRomSegment ; see listing 19.15

            ;load Shadow Set 1 with 640 by 480 x 16-bits/color in a
            ;565 color weighting
            mov     rom_segment,ax   ; put segment from 19.15 into
                                     ; rom_segment
            mov     ax,64h           ;offset is 64 + rom_segment
            mov     rom_offset,ax    ; save as address
            mov     al,21h           ; 640 by 480 into shadow set 1
            mov     ah,00001101h     ; 16-bit/color, 555 RGB
            mov     bx,1             ; pitch of mode resolution to
                                     ; nearest 128 (=640)
            call    DWORD PTR rom_offset    ;see listing 19.16
            jnc     no_error         ; if no error go on to attempt
                                     ; to set mode
            jmp     set_error        ; if error exit
no_error:
            ;set Mode using shadow set 1
            mov     ax,68h           ; set up call pointer offset
            mov     rom_offset,ax    ; put into offset
            mov     ax,1             ; use shadow set 1
            call    DWORD PTR rom_offset    ; see Listing 19.17
            jnc     success          ; if no error mode is set
            jmp     set_error        ; if error then exit
success:
            mov     ax,0   ;return 0 for no error
            ret
set_error
            mov     ax,1   ;return 1 for error
            ret
```

19.25   MACH-32 EXTENDED VGA REGISTERS

The Mach-32 contains an internal VGA with extended VGA features. The Mach-8 requires a separate VGA.

19.25.1 Configuraing the VGA Extended Registers

The I/O address and offset for the VGA extended registers are user-selectable. This feature allows users to pick whatever I/O address is desired. At system reset, the BIOS writes the values for the I/O Address (A11–A0) and the Offset (O1–O0) to locations 3CEh offset 50h and 51h. These are write-only registers. The default value for this address is 1CEh and for the offset is 2. The code in Listing 19.19 performs this operation. This default address will be assumed during the remaining examples.

LISTING 19.19 Writing the Default Values to 3CEh Offset 50 and 51

```
mov     dx,3ceh
mov     ax,0ce50h ; CE = address bits A7-A0  50 is register index
out     dx,ax
mov     ax,8151h  ; 81 = offset bits O1-O0  51 is register index
out     dx,ax
```

19.25.2 Accessing the ATI Extended Registers

Once the locations of the registers are known, follow these steps for writing to a register:

Step 1. Obtain the offset for the desired register by concatenating the index offset 2 into bit positions 7–6 with the register index in bits 5–0. For example, ATI3E has an index of 3Eh. Thus, the result is 80h or 3Eh. This results in a value of BEh.

Step 2. Write the desired value to the extended register by outputing the desired value to the resultant concatenated index of Step 1. For example, the code in Listing 19.20 will write an FFh to ATI3E. (We are assuming the 1ceh default address).

LISTING 19.20 Writing an FFh to ATI3E Register

```
mov     dx,1ceh
mov     ax,0ffbeh ; ff = adesired value  be = concatenated index
out     dx,ax
```

19.25.3 VGA Extended Registers

The VGA extended registers are listed in Table 19.46. Table 19.47 contains the fields in these registers that are relevant to the programmer.

The index register is loaded with the offset concatenated with the index of the desired register as just discussed. Registers 0–4 are scratch pad registers.

TABLE 19.46 VGA Extended Registers

Name	Offset	Description	R/W
ATIx	x	Index	R/W
ATI0	0	ATI Register 0	R/W
ATI1	1	ATI Register 1	R/W
ATI2	2	ATI Register 2	R/W
ATI3	3	ATI Register 3	R/W
ATI4	4	ATI Register 4	R/W
ATI5	5	ATI Register 5	R/W
ATI6	6	ATI Register 6	R/W
ATI20	20	ATI Register 20	R/W
ATI23	23	ATI Register 23	R/W
ATI24	24	ATI Register 24	R/W
ATI25	25	ATI Register 25	R/W
ATI26	26	ATI Register 26	R/W
ATI27	27	ATI Register 27	R/W
ATI28	28	ATI Register 28	R
ATI29	29	ATI Register 29	R
ATI2B	2B	ATI Register 2B	R/W
ATI2D	2D	ATI Register 2D	R/W
ATI2E	2E	ATI Register 2E	R/W
ATI30	30	ATI Register 30	R/W
ATI31	31	ATI Register 31	R/W
ATI32	32	ATI Register 32	R/W
ATI33	33	ATI Register 33	R/W
ATI34	34	ATI Register 34	R/W
ATI35	35	ATI Register 35	R/W
ATI36	36	ATI Register 36	R/W
ATI37	37	ATI Register 37	R
ATI38	38	ATI Register 38	R/W
ATI39	39	ATI Register 39	R/W
ATI3A	3A	ATI Register 3A	R/W
ATI3B	3B	ATI Register 3B	R/W
ATI3C	3C	ATI Register 3C	R
ATI3D	3D	ATI Register 3D	R/W
ATI3E	3E	ATI Register 3E	R/W
ATI3F	3F	ATI Register 3F	R/W

TABLE 19.47   Interesting Fields in the Extended VGA Registers

ATI Register	Bit	Function
5	7	Cursor rate 0=normal; 1=twice normal
23	3	Display Start Address bit 17
23	4	Display Start Address bit 17
26	6	0=dashed; 1=solid underline in monochrome text
2D	1–0	Cursor Start Address bits 19–18
2D	3–2	Display Start Address bits 19–18
2D	5–4	Character Map Address bits 19–18
2E	1–0	CPU Write Page Pointer bits 5–4
2E	3–2	CPU Read Page Pointer bits 5–4
30	2	Display Start Address bit 17 in ATI extended modes
30	3	1=1 Mbyte for VGA
30	4	0=256 Kbytes for VGA 1=512 Kbytes
30	5	1 enables 8-bit-per-color mode in ATI extended modes
30	6	Display Start Address bit 17 in ATI extended modes
32	0	CPU Read Address Paging bit 3; must =0
32	4–1	CPU Write Address Paging bits 3–0
32	7–5	CPU Read Address Paging bits 2–0
34	2	Write protect CRT0 bits 7 and 4–0
34	3	Write protect CRT vertical timing registers
34	4	Write protect CRTa–b
34	5	Write protect CRT8–14
34	6	Write protect CRT0–7
34	7	Ignore Write Protect bit 7 of CRT11
35	5	1 disables cursor blinking
36	2	Linear addressing, 8-bit-per-color modes
36	4	Enable 4-bit-per-color high resolution modes
36	5	Enable vertical interrupt
36	6	Linear addressing, text modes
38	0	Write protect ATTR00–0F
38	1	Write protect ATTR11
38	2	Write protect VGA Registers CRTC0A–0D
38	3	Write protect I/O 3c2h
39	7	Write protect CRT 18
3D	2	Enable 128 Kbyte bank from A0000h–BFFFFh
3E	3	Read/Write Paging Select bit 0=single; 1=dual read/write paging

19.25.4 Bank Switching

The CPU Read and Write Address Paging bits indicated the desired 64 KByte block or the 128 Kbyte block. If ATI extended register 3D bit 2 is set to 1, then 128 Kbyte bank switching is enabled. If it is a 0, then 64 Kbyte bank switching is enabled.

If ATI Extended Register 3E bit 3 is set to 0, bits 3–1 are used to control both CPU reads and writes; otherwise, dual paging is enabled. The extended registers related to bank switching are provided in Table 19.48.

TABLE 19.48 Registers Related to Bank Switching

ATI Register	Bit	Function
2E	1–0	CPU Write Page Pointer bits 5–4
2E	3–2	CPU Read Page Pointer bits 5–4
32	0	CPU Read Address Paging bit 3; must = 0
32	4–1	CPU Write Address Paging bits 3–0
32	7–5	CPU Read Address Paging bits 2–0
3D	2	Enable 128 Kbyte bank from A0000h–BFFFFh
3E	3	Read/Write Paging Select bit 0=single; 1=dual read/write paging

Chapter 20

Chips and Technologies

20.1 INTRODUCTION TO THE CHIPS AND TECHNOLOGIES CHIP SET

Chips and Technologies manufactures five Super VGA chips as listed in Table 20.1. The low-end 82c451 is intended for minimum Super VGA configurations. The 82c452 is designed for demanding graphics applications. The high-resolution 82c453 is capable of driving VRAM. Finally, the 82c455 and 82c456 are meant for the flat-panel displays.

For the most part, the chips are compatible at the register level. Unless otherwise noted, the reader may assume that documentation in this section refers to all chips in Table 20.16. Chip-specific features are indicated and multiple definitions are provided when differences occur. The 82c451 provides the core for these registers.

Chips and Technologies offers a generous set of extension registers. These allow functions to remain isolated in specific registers. Thus, the programmer is not faced with the constant problem of having to read/modify/write everything, and constantly having to shift around bit fields.

The Chips and Technologies chips provide the greatest number of functions and special features of any of the Super VGAs. The 82c451 provides the basic Super VGA format and forms the foundation for the later generation of chips. The 82c455 and 82c456 are based on the 82c451 and are specially designed to interface to flat-panel displays.

The 82c452 is the second-generation Super VGA with an impressive array of features. It contains just about everything that one could hope for in a Super VGA. The only major drawback is that it cannot support VRAM, nor display resolutions much greater than 640 by 480 in the 256-color modes.

The 82c453 was designed to be very fast. It is meant specifically for VRAM. It supports the high-resolution, 256-color modes.

TABLE 20.1 Chips and Technologies Super VGA Product Line

Chip	Memory	Features
82c451	256 Kbytes DRAM	Low cost
82c452	1 Mbyte DRAM	Lots of features; 640x480 maximum 256-color modes
82c453	1 Mbyte VRAM	Fast VRAM, high resolution 256-color modes
82c455	256 Kbytes DRAM	Flat Panel Display Compatible
82c456	256 Kbytes DRAM	Enhanced Flat Panel Display Compatible

These processors provide a high level of integration when interfaced to the PC/AT or to the microchannel bus. All processors are configured with the ability to eloquently coexist in a system with multiple Super VGAs of the same product line. Each can operate in a variety of 8- or 16-bit bus width modes.

20.1.1 Emulation

Downward compatibility is provided to the MDA, Hercules, CGA, and EGA through BIOS calls or direct access to the emulation registers. The programmer can choose to protect a wide variety of registers through a sophisticated selection of Write Protect fields within several Write Protect registers. Trap registers are also provided for generating traps or access to specific registers. Compatibility is also enhanced by the provision of an alternate set of CRTC registers, providing display timing control. When an emulation mode is engaged, these registers can contain the relevant timing for the specified emulation mode without disrupting the VGA timing registers.

The general trend in Super VGAs is to move away from the non-maskable interrupts and their associated traps. One problem that plagues these implementations occurs in a program like Microsoft Word. This application queries to see what adapter is present. The only way to find out if an adapter is present is to try and access a register in the questioned adapter. As soon as this query occurs, the auto-sensing VGA detects the access to the register and flags it in an attempt to access a non-VGA card. The VGA then traps and sets itself up to emulate that adapter.

The newer generation Super VGAs have implemented downward compatibility through the use of registers and special software. By using a second set of timing registers and exhaustive write protection, it is possible to emulate the other adapters without generating traps. However, this precludes auto-emulation.

20.1.2 Processing Speed

Each new chip has increased display memory. Consequently, there is need for speed in graphics processing. Hardware assist on frequently used graphics functions, VRAM support, and fast host interfaces have dramatically improved the performance of the Super VGAs.

These chips sport several levels of pipelining and cache memories. They provide a fast interface to the host interface and to the graphics memory. The 82c453 claims to operate at the AT 8 mHz bus rates.

20.1.3 82c451 Chip

The 82c451 is the first generation Super VGA. It provides the basic platform for the chips of a later generation. The 82c451 can support downward emulation, bank switching 132-column text modes, and up to 800-by-600 16-color modes. The VGA-standard bus interface is provided for either 8- or 16-bit transfers to the PC/AT bus and 16-bit transfers to the PS/2 via the motherboard or microchannel. The 82c451 includes a single bank register for bank switching (paging). The flat-panel controllers, the 82c455 and 82c456, are based on this 82c451 engine.

20.1.4 82c452 Chip

The 82c452 is the second generation Super VGA chip designed to access up to one Mbyte of DRAM and to display 1024-by-768 16-color non-interlaced graphics modes. The 82c452 chip has many features not present in any of the other VGA chips. However, the 82c452 cannot support interlaced display modes.

One of the most important new features of this chip set is the ability to do non-byte-aligned data transfers. This applies only to the planar modes where multiple pixels reside in each byte. The traditional technique shifts data to get it to byte align, read the data from display memory, mask off the appropriate bits, and write the data byte aligned. If eight pixels were to be written, beginning at pixel 4 of one byte and ending in pixel 3 of the next byte, these operations would have to be performed twice.

Chips and Technologies allows the programmer to do non-byte-aligned transfers transparently. The programmer merely loads a direction and shift count before the transfer. From then on, subsequent read and write operations act as if there were no byte boundaries. Using the previous example, a single write would suffice to send four bits to the first byte and four bits to the second byte, without disrupting the undesired bits.

Another feature is the ability to generate interrupts during vertical refresh cycles with frame interrupt counting. By using this feature, the VGA can interrupt the host processor only after a preset number of vertical refresh cycles have occurred. Other processors that allow the generation of vertical interrupts require that one interrupt be generated at each vertical refresh cycle.

20.1.5   82c453 Chip

The 82c453 is the "hot rod" of the Chips and Technologies family of Super VGA chips. It is designed specifically for VRAM memory and utilizes the VRAM capabilities better than any other implementation. Several features were sacrificed in order to fit this into silicon. The hardware cursor present in the 82c452 is one example. Chips and Technologies claims that the speed of the 82c453 allows adequate control of a programmable cursor through standard read/write operations. The 82c453 has extended its banking to provide a quadruple improvement in granularity. The granularity of the bank addressing is now 4 Kbytes as opposed to the 16 Kbytes in the 82c451 and 82c452.

Certain other features were not carried over from the 82c452. These include interrupt skipping, sliding data transfers, and the hardware cursor. In many instances, the speed advantages of the 82c453 accomplish the same tasks in comparable amounts of time. For example, standard memory accessing techniques can be used to implement the non-byte-aligned transfers and the hardware cursor.

Features in the 82c453 that provide the speed enhancements include uncompromised VRAM control, hardware bit masking to the display memory, and enhanced character manipulations in the 256-color graphics modes. In addition, internal data paths are filled with caches and FIFOs. The host interface has also been improved. Together, these enhancements provide a remarkably fast graphics processor.

20.1.6   82c455 Chip

Displaying VGA to a flat panel requires special implementation due to the feature differences and hardware variations between the CRT monitor and the flat panels. Supported flat panels include LCD, plasma, and electroluminescent panels of varying resolutions. In addition, the 82c455 can control analog or digital CRT monitors. The 82c455 is the first generation flat-panel controller, and it is based on the 82c451 register set. Several additional registers are incorporated to assist in the control of the flat-panels. Other registers and features are included to handle the mapping of colors from the VGA color modes to the flat-panel displays. The flat-panel displays are either black and white or have limited color capabilities. The 82c455 cannot drive either.

Features in the 82c455 include sixteen gray scales, text enhancements, and vertical compensation for EGA modes. The 256-color Mode 13 display mode is not directly supported. Instead, it requires a special software driver.

The 82c455 can produce gray scales on panels that do not support gray levels directly, for example, LCD panels. This is accomplished through the use of linear Frame Rate Control (FRC). The 82c455 can produce gray scales on panels that do support gray levels directly, for example, on most plasma panels. This is accomplished through the use of Pulse Width Modulation (PWM).

20.1.7 82c456 Chip

The 82c456 is the second-generation flat-panel Controller and is based on the 82c455. It differs from the 82c455 in several ways. It produces a true 64 gray-scale representation of color, has hardware support for the 256-color mode, Mode 13, and produces 64 colors for the Super Twist (STN) color flat panels. The 82c456 can support resolutions up to 800 by 600 in the 16-color modes. Extended BIOS tables are provided, which allow special control parameters to accommodate the wide variety of flat-panel displays.

The 82c456 is equipped with two additional registers to handle the color mapping on panels that do not directly support gray scale, for example, LCDs. The 82c456 enhances this by the use of polynomial-based FRC counters, in addition to the linear-based FRC counters in the 82c455.

20.2 CONFIGURING THE CHIPS AND TECHNOLOGIES SUPER VGA

The Chips and Technologies Super VGA chips can be configured in a variety of ways, depending on the particular chip. Most of the configuration features either speed up the graphics operation or provide additional flexibility.

Speed enhancements include 16-bit data and program transfers and fast address decoding. Additional flexibility allows the system to be used in a PC/AT or PS/2 , on a motherboard or adapter card, with other VGAs, and in lower one Mbyte memory or upper memory.

20.2.1 Configuring the Chips and Technologies VGAs

Two registers contain the bit fields necessary to configure the VGA with respect to 8- or 16-bit transfers. These include 8/16-bit I/O or memory transfers and the ability to enable or disable the on-card BIOS ROM as shown in Table 20.2.

The CPU Interface Register for the 82c451, 2, 4 and 5 controls the data bus width as shown in Figure 20.1. If the I16 field is set to 1, 16-bit I/O transfers are enabled. If 0, 8-bit I/O transfers are enabled. If the M16 field is set to 1, 16-bit memory transfers are enabled; if 0, 8-bit memory transfers are enabled. The ATR field provides readback information on the status of the Attribute Register flip-flop and is discussed in Section 20.4.3.

The I/O addressing can include all sixteen address bits or it can include only ten address bits. The EGA/VGA can be accessed by ten bits for addresses under 3FF hex. If the I/O field is set to 1, only ten bits are used. If the I/O field is set to 0, all sixteen bits are used.

TABLE 20.2 Configuring the Chips and Technologies Super VGAs

Function	Register Name	Port	Index	Bits	Value
Slow Decoding	CPU Interface	3D6	2	2	0
Fast Decoding	CPU Interface	3D6	2	2	1
Select 8-bit I/O	CPU Interface	3D6	2	1	0
Select 16-bit I/O	CPU Interface	3D6	2	1	1
Select 8-bit Data Path	CPU Interface	3D6	2	0	0
Select 16-bit Data Path	CPU Interface	3D6	2	0	1
Enable on-card ROM	ROM Interface	3D6	3	0	0
Disable on-card ROM	ROM Interface	3D6	3	0	1
Attribute Port Pairing	CPU Interface 82c453	3D6	2	4–3	0–3
16-bit I/O Decoding	CPU Interface 82c453	3D6	2	5	0
10-bit I/O Decoding	CPU Interface 82c453	3D6	2	5	1
Pel Panning Control	CPU Interface 82c453	3D6	2	6	0,1

CPU Interface

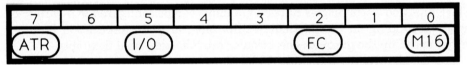

Index 02 at Port 3D6   Port 3D7 Read/Write

FIGURE 20.1 CPU Interface Register. The M16 and I16 fields
select 8- or 16-bit memory cycles respectively. The FC field enables
proprietary fast cycles for MCA interface only. The ATR field is a
read-only field containing the attribute flip-flop status.

20.2.2 Configuring the Flat Panel VGAs

There are several configuration fields necessary to control the flat panels. The
Display Type Register shown in Figure 20.2 contains five such fields as indicated in Table 20.3.

The PD field configures the VGA to interface to a single- or double-drive flat
panel. If the PD field is set to 1, the VGA is configured for a double drive. If it
is 0, a single drive is expected. A double-drive system requires two distinct data
ports; a single-drive system requires one port to access both panels. There is no
such thing as a single-panel, dual-drive system. The PO field configures the
VGA to control a single- or dual-panel display. The PO field is set to 0 for a
single panel and 1 for a double panel. The Type field configures the VGA for the

Panel Type 82c455/6

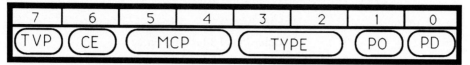

Index 51 at Port 3D6   Port 3D7 Read/Write

FIGURE 20.2   Panel Type Register for 82c455/456. The PD field configures the single/dual drive. The PO field configures for single/dual panels. The TYPE field configures for the type of display. The MCP configures for the mono/color panels. The CE controls the compatibility Mode Enable. The TVP controls the text video output polarity.

TABLE 20.3   Configuring the Chips and Technologies Flat-panel Super VGAs

Function	Register Name	Port	Index	Bits	Value
Single/Dual Drive	Display Type	3D6	51	0	0–1
Single/Dual Panel	Display Type	3D6	51	1	0–1
Panel Type	Display Type	3D6	51	3–2	0–3
Mono/Color Type	Display Type	3D6	51	5–4	0–3
Horizontal Panel Size	Panel Size	3D6	52	2–0	0–7
Vertical Panel Size	Panel Size	3D6	52	4–3	0–7

type of display. A TTL or analog display is the reset default. Table 20.4 lists the display types.

The MCP field configures the VGA for a monochrome or color panel. Table 20.5 lists the possible monochrome or color selections for the MCP field. The TVP field configures the system for the proper polarity of video data in the text mode. This field is relevant only to flat panels and determines whether normal or inversed video is displayed (that is, white on black or black on white).

TABLE 20.4   Display Types

TYPE	Display Type
0	LCD
1	CRT (default)
2	Plasma, Electroluminescent

TABLE 20.5   Monochrome or Color Panel Select

TYPE	Display Type
0	Color Panel 3-bit data pack
1	Color Panel 1-bit data pack
2	Monochrome panel

The VGA is alerted to the size of the flat panel through the Panel Size Register shown in Figure 20.3. The horizontal size is reported in the HSIZE field, and the vertical size field is reported in the VSIZE field. The supported horizontal and vertical sizes are listed in Tables 20.6 and 20.7, respectively.

TABLE 20.6   Flat Panel Horizontal Size

HSIZE	Horizontal Size
1	640 pixels
2	720 pixels

TABLE 20.7   Flat Panel Vertical Size

VSIZE	Vertical Size
1	200 lines
2	350 lines
4	400 lines
8	480 lines

Panel Size 82c455/6

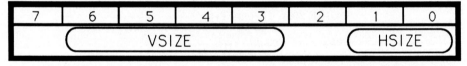

Index 51 at Port 3D6   Port 3D7 Read/Write

FIGURE 20.3   Panel Size Register for 82c455/456. The HSIZE field controls the panel horizontal resolution. The VSIZE field controls the vertical resolution.

ROM Interface

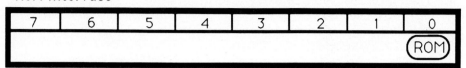

Index 03 at Port 3D6   Port 3D7 Read/Write

FIGURE 20.4 ROM Interface Register. The ROM
field enables the on-card ROM.

20.2.3 On-Card ROM

The on-card can be enabled or disabled through the ROM field of the ROM
Interface Register as displayed in Figure 20.4. If the ROM field is 1, the on-card
ROM is enabled. If 0, the on-card ROM is disabled. In the PC/AT the default
condition enables the on-card ROM. In the PS/2 microchannel interface, the
default condition disables the on-card ROM.

20.3 CONTROLLING THE CHIPS AND TECHNOLOGIES SUPER VGAS

20.3.1 Setup Mode

The Chips and Technologies VGA can be controlled by several registers as
listed in Table 20.8. These chips are equipped with the industry-standard 46E8
and 3C3 hex registers, which enable or disable the VGA and allow it to be put
into a setup mode. If the VGA resides on a PC/AT adapter card, the port
address for the Setup Control Register is at 46E8 hex. If the VGA resides on the
motherboard, presumably in a microchannel system, it resides at port address
3C3 hex. The Setup Control Register is shown in Figures 20.5 and 20.6 for the
PC/AT and motherboard respectively.

The Setup Mode can be entered and exited through Listings 20.3 and 20.4
respectively. It should be noted that no other registers in the Chips VGA register set can be accessed when the VGA is in the Setup Mode. Listings 20.1 and
20.2 perform the same functions implemented as assembly language macros.

LISTING 20.1 Entering into the Setup Mode

```
; Function:
; Entering into the setup mode

; Calling Protocol:
; Into_Setup_Chips()
```

(continued)

```
Into_Setup_Chips proc far
        into_setup
        ret
Into_Setup_Chips endp
```

Setup Control PC/AT Register

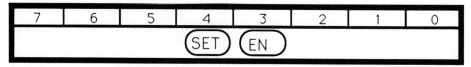

Port 46E8 Read Only

FIGURE 20.5 Setup Control PC/AT Register. Adapter Card
Implementation at Port 46E8 hex. The EN field enables or disables
the VGA. The SET field enters or exits the Setup mode.

Setup Control PS/2 Register

Port 3C3 Read/Write

FIGURE 20.6 Setup Control PS/2 Register. Motherboard
Implementation at Port 3C3 hex. The EN field enables or disables
the VGA. The SET field enters or exits the Setup mode.

TABLE 20.8 Resetting and Enabling the Chips and Technologies Super VGAs

Function	Register Name	Port	Index	Bits	Value
Index Extended Registers	Extended Index	3D6			0–FF
Enable VGA PC/AT	Setup Control	46E8		3	1
Disable VGA PC/AT	Setup Control	46E8		3	0
Enable VGA Microchannel	Setup Control	3C3		0	1
Disable VGA Microchannel	Setup Control	3C3		0	0
VGA Awake	Global Enable	102		0	1
VGA Asleep	Global Enable	102		0	1
Enter Setup PC/AT	Setup Control	46E8		4	1
Exit Setup PC/AT	Setup Control	46E8		4	1
Enter Setup Microchannel	Setup Control	3C3		4	1
Exit Setup Microchannel	Setup Control	3C3		4	1
Multiple VGA Enable	Extended Enable	103		4–0	0–31

LISTING 20.2 Exit from Setup Mode

```
; Function:
; Exit into the setup mode
; Calling Protocol:
; Exit_Setup_Chips()
Exit_Setup_Chips proc far

        out_of_setup
        ret
Exit_Setup_Chips endp
```

LISTING 20.3 Going into Setup Mode Macro

```
; Function:
;        Going into setup mode
; Calling Protocol:
;        into_setup

into_setup macro
        mov     dx, 46e8h
        mov     al, 1eh
        out     dx, al
endm
```

LISTING 20.4 Going Out of Setup Mode Macro

```
; Function:
;        Going out of setup mode
; Calling Protocol:
;        out_of_setup

out_of_setup macro
        mov     dx, 46e8h
        mov     al, 0eh
        out     dx, al
endm
```

20.3.2 Enabling and Resetting the Super VGAs

The VGA can be enabled through the EN field, bit 3, of the Setup Control Register at 46E8 or through the EN field, bit 0, at 3C3. The VGA can also be put into the setup mode through the SET field of either the 46E8 or 3C3 implementation. In either implementation, the setup registers, xx2, 103, and 104 hex, can be accessed only when the setup mode is active. Once in the setup mode, only the setup registers can be accessed.

The extended registers are normally locked and must be turned on if access is desired. The extended registers all reside at the 3C6/3C7 indexed address pair. These can be enabled or disabled through the macros in Listings 20.5 and 20.6 respectively.

LISTING 20.5 Enabling Extensions Macro

```
; Function:
;       Enabling Extensions

; Calling Protocol:
;       enable_extensions

enable_extensions macro
        into_setup
        mov     dx,103h
        mov     al,80h
        out     dx,al
        out_of_setup
endm
```

LISTING 20.6 Disable Extensions Macro

```
; Function:
;       Disable Extensions

; Calling Protocol:
;       disable_extensions

disable_extensions macro
        into_setup
        mov     dx,103h
        mov     al,00h
        out     dx,al
        out_of_setup

endm
```

The extended registers can be turned on or off through a C function provided in Listings 20.7 and 20.8 respectively.

LISTING 20.7 Enabling the Extended Registers

```
; Function:
; Enabling the extended registers
```

```
; Calling Protocol:
;       Extended_On_Chips();
Extended_On_Chips proc far arg1:byte

        into_setup
        enable_extensions
        out_of_setup

        ret
Extended_On_Chips endp
```

LISTING 20.8 Disable the Extended Registers

```
; Function:
; Disable the extended registers

; Calling Protocol: */
; Extended_Off_Chips()

Extended_Off_Chips proc far arg1:byte

        into_setup
        disable_extensions
        out_of_setup

        ret
Extended_Off_Chips endp
```

20.3.3 Setup Registers

The setup registers include the Global Enable Register, the Extended Enable Register and the Global ID Register, as shown in Figures 20.7 through 20.9, respectively.

Global Enable (Setup)

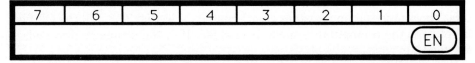

Port xx2 and Setup Mode Read/Write

FIGURE 20.7 Global Enable Register, accessed only in Setup Mode at port address xx2, indicates that any address ending in 2 within the setup registers will access this register. Allows enabling and disabling the VGA through EN.

Extended Enable (Setup)

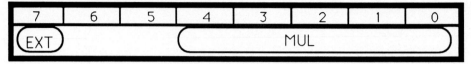

Port 103 and Setup Mode Read/Write

FIGURE 20.8 Extended Enable Register, accessed only in Setup Mode at port address 103. Allows use of multiple VGAs through MUL and access to extended registers through EXT.

Global ID (Setup)

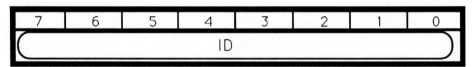

Port 104 and Setup Mode Read Only

FIGURE 20.9 Global ID Register, accessed only in Setup Mode at port address 104. The Chips I/D number resides in the ID field.

The two principal functions of these setup registers are to enable the extended registers and to determine the ID of the VGA. The extended registers are an extensive set of registers that surpass the standard VGA register set as discussed in Chapter 10. These extended registers may be enabled through the EXT field of the Extended Enable Register.

20.3.4 Controlling the Flat Panel VGAs

There are several control functions specific to the flat-panel controllers. These are listed in Table 20.9. A compatibility mode can be enabled through the CE field of the Panel Type Register shown in Figure 20.2 above. When compatibility is enabled, the display is adjusted according to three factors. These are the panel size, current display mode, and the contents of the compensation registers. The compensation registers are discussed in Section 20.3.4. If the CE field is set to 1, the compatibility mode is enabled. If 0, the compatibility mode is disabled.

It is possible to produce gray scales using flat panels. Some panels have inherent gray scale or color capabilities while others do not. The Panel Format Register, shown in Figure 20.10, controls the type of gray scale. If the panel does not support gray levels, internally gray scale is achieved through FRC. In the 82c455, linear FRC is available. In the 82c456, both linear and polynomial FRCs are possible. If the flat panel does internally support gray levels, Pulse Width modulation (PWM) is used to produce the gray scale.

TABLE 20.9 Controlling the Chips and Technologies Flat-panel Super VGAs

Function	Register Name	Port	Index	Bits	Value
Compatibility	Display Type	3D6	51	6	0–1
Frame Rate Control	Panel Format	3D6	50	1–0	0–1
Pulse Width Mod. Control	Panel Format	3D6	50	3–2	0–1
Color Threshold	Color Mapping	3D6	63	3–0	0–1
256 Color mapping	Color Mapping	3D6	63	4	0,1
Color Lookup Enable	Color Mapping	3D6	63	5	0,1
Color Lookup Protect	Color Mapping	3D6	63	6	0,1
Graphics Output Polarity	Color Mapping	3D6	63	7	0,1
Text Video Polarity	Display Type	3D6	51	7	0–1
Blink Rate	Blink Rate Control	3D6	60	5–0	0–63
Blink Cycle	Blink Rate Control	3D6	60	7–6	0–3

Panel Format 82c455/6

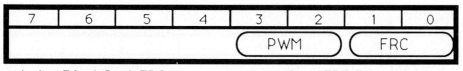

Index 50 at Port 3D6   Port 3D7 Read/Write

FIGURE 20.10 Panel Format Register for 82c456. The FRC field controls the frame rate control. The PWM controls the pulse width modulation.

The Frame Rate Control (FRC) is controlled through the FRC field of the Panel Format Register. Table 20.10 lists the possible frame rate control options. FRC performs the same function as Pulse Width Modulation. A pixel is allowed to be on or off during five cycles. For example, a pixel can be on 0, 20, 40, 60, 80 or 100 percent of the time.

The Pulse Width Modulation (PWM) is controlled through the PWM field of the Panel Format Register. Table 20.11 lists the possible pulse width modulation options.

20.3.5 Gray Levels and Color Attributes for Flat Panel VGAs

The Graphics Color Mapping Control Register shown in Figure 20.11 and the Panel Type Register shown in Figure 20.2 control the color and gray scale mapping for the flat panels.

TABLE 20.10 Frame Rate Control

FRC	Meaning
0	No gray scale simulated for monochrome systems. Eight colors for color displays.
1	Four simulated colors for color panels only (64 colors are displayed).
2	64 gray levels simulated on monochrome panels only.

TABLE 20.11 Pulse Width Modulation

PWM	Meaning
0	No gray scales for monochrome or color systems.
1	Four colors supported by the color panels only (64 colors are displayed).
2	Sixteen gray levels supported by the monochrome panels only.
3	256 gray levels supported by the color single panels only.

Graphics Color Mapping Control 82c455/6

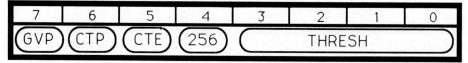

Index 63 at Port 3D6   Port 3D7 Read/Write

FIGURE 20.11 Graphics Color Mapping Control Register for 82C455/6. The THRESH field contains the graphics threshold value. The 256 field controls which nibble to use for the 8-bit color. The CTE field enables the color table lookup. The CTP field write protects the color lookup table. The GVP field controls the graphics video polarity.

The Text Mode Video Polarity is controlled in the TVP field of the Display Type Register. The analogous polarity for the graphics modes is controlled by the GVP field of the Graphics Color Mapping Control Register.

When no gray levels are supported, the display is bistable. This is the case when the FRC and PWM fields in the Panel Format Register are set to 0. In a bistable display, it is necessary to threshold a color so all values less than that threshold are mapped to a 0, and all values equal or above the threshold are mapped to a 1. The Color Threshold Value is controlled through the Thresh field of the Graphics Color Mapping Control Register.

When the VGA is in a 256-color mode, either the low four bits or the upper four bits of the 8-bits-per-pixel value can be used to generate a four-bit value. If the 256 field of the Graphics Color Mapping Control Register is set to 1, the upper four bits are used to generate a 16-level color. If the 256 field is set to 0, the lower four bits are used.

The internal color lookup table can be enabled or disabled through the CTE field. If the CTE field is set to 1, the internal color table is enabled. If 0, the internal color table is disabled. The internal color table can be write protected through the CTP field. If the CTP field is set to 1, the internal color table is enabled. If 0, the color table is disabled. Write protecting the internal color lookup table is contingent on the attribute registers being write-protected.

The blink rate of the the cursor, characters, and pixels can be controlled though the Blink Rate Control Register shown in Figure 20.12.

The cursor blink rate determines the frequency of the character and dot blink rates. The blink rate is determined by the number of vertical sync periods during which the cursor will be on and off. The cursor blink duty cycle is fixed at a 50 percent duty cycle. The character and blink period will be twice that of the cursor blink period. This means it will blink twice as slow. The equation used to determine the blink rate uses the value in the Rate field as follows:

```
Cursor Blink Frequency = Vertical Sync Frequency * 2 * (RATE+1)
```

The blink duty cycle determines the brightness of the character or pixel that is blinking. The duty cycle is controlled through the Cycle field as shown in Table 20.12. Note that the cursor is restricted to a 50 percent duty cycle.

Blink Rate Control 82c455/6

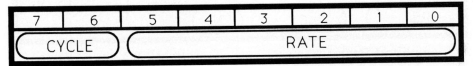

Index 60 at Port 3D6   Port 3D7 Read/Write

FIGURE 20.12 Blink Rate Control Register for 82c455/6. The RATE field controls the blink rate. The CYCLE field controls the blink duty cycle.

TABLE 20.12 Attribute Blink Duty Cycle

CYCLE	Duty Cycle
1	25 percent
2	50 percent
3	75 percent

20.3.6 Frame Rate Control in the 82c456

The 82c456 can use either linear or polynomial-based FRC to generate gray scales on flat panel displays that do not have internal gray levels. FRC is based on time sharing the pixel. This is identical to the PWM features of the internal gray scale panels. Time sharing is sufficient for the 16-color modes.

In addition to time sharing, it is possible to dither the image to produce subjective gray scale. Since mode 13 hex is 320 by 200 pixels, dithering can be used to zoom this resolution to 640 by 400. Each pixel in the Mode 13 space can be represented by four pixels in the 640 by 400 space. The pattern generator that produces the dither is controlled through the polynomial generator.

The FRC and Palette Control Register, shown in Figure 20.13, controls the type of frame rate control and selects the palette. If the EN field of the FRC and Palette Control Register is set to 1, the polynomial FRC counters are used. If the EN field is set to 0, the linear FRCs are used.

If the polynomial-based FRC option is engaged, the polynomial N and M values determine the offset in row and columns of the FRC count. The N and M values are controlled through the PN and PM fields respectively of the Polynomial FRC Control Register shown in Figure 20.14. Trial and error can produce a variety of effects. Programmers are encouraged to experiment with different values of N and M.

FRC and Palette Control 82c456

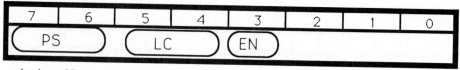

Index 6D at Port 3D6   Port 3D7 Read/Write

FIGURE 20.13 FRC and Palette Control Register for 82c456. The EN field enables the FRC mode. The LC field controls the maximum number of gray levels. The PS field selects the Palette.

Polynomial FRC Control 82c456

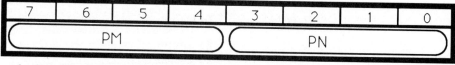

Index 6E at Port 3D6   Port 3D7 Read/Write

FIGURE 20.14 Polynomial FRC Control Register for 82c456. The PN and PM fields control the values in the polynomial counters.

TABLE 20.13 Flat Panels Palette

PS	External Palette	16-color Modes	256-color Modes
0	Bypass	Bypass	Bypass
1	Conditional	Bypass	Use
2	Use	Use	Use
3	Use	16 gray levels	64 gray levels

20.3.7 Flat Panel Palette

To produce the color or gray level, the 82c456 can bypass the external palette, always use the external palette, utilize the external palette only during 256-color modes, or always employ 64 gray levels for the 256-color modes and 16 gray levels for all other modes. This ability is controlled through the PS field. The PS field is described in Table 20.13. The 82c455 always bypasses the external flat-panel palette.

20.3.8 Flat Panel SmartMap

The compression from the 16-color modes to gray scale requires an intelligent algorithm. The algorithm used by the 82c455 and 82c456 is called Smartmap. The Smartmap feature is used when sixteen gray levels are supported. This is indicated by the FRC=2 and PWM=2 values in the Panel Format Register. It is controlled through the Smartmap Control Register shown in Figure 20.15. The Smartmap feature is enabled by setting the EN field of this register to 1. If 0, the Smartmap feature is disabled. If the Smartmap feature is disabled, the color-lookup table is used. If the Smartmap feature is enabled, the color-lookup table is bypassed.

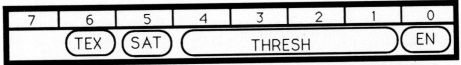

Smartmap Control 82c455/6

Index 61 at Port 3D6   Port 3D7 Read/Write

FIGURE 20.15 Smart Map Control Register for 82c455/6. The EN field enables or disables the Smartmap function. The THRESH field contains the background and foreground color difference threshold. The SAT field contains the Smartmap saturation value. The TEX field enhances the text by reversing the 7 and F text attributes on the 82c456.

Smartmap Shift Parameter 82c455/6

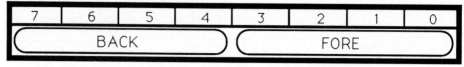

Index 62 at Port 3D6   Port 3D7 Read/Write

FIGURE 20.16 Smartmap Shift Parameter Register for 82c455/6. The FORE field contains the number of levels to shift the foregound color. The BACK field contains the number of levels to shift the background color.

The Smartmap threshold defines the minimum difference between the foreground and background colors. If the difference is zero, it may not be possible to differentiate the colors. It is desirable to spread apart the foreground and background colors to achieve a sufficient contrast. The amount of desirable contrast depends on the application.

The THRESH field of the Smartmap Control Register defines the minimum difference between the foreground and background colors before they are spread apart. If the threshold is not crossed, the foreground and background colors are spread apart. These are spread by an amount indicated in the FORE and BACK fields of the Smartmap Shift Parameter Register shown in Figure 20.16.

The FORE field controls the number of levels to shift the foreground color when the THRESH value is not crossed. If the foreground color is greater than the background color, the FORE field is added to the foreground color. If the foreground color is less than the background color, the FORE field is subtracted from the foreground color.

The BACK field controls the number of levels to shift the background color when the THRESH value is not crossed. If the foreground color is greater than the background color, the BACK field is subtracted from the background color. If the foreground color is less than the background color, the BACK field is added to the background color.

The text attributes can be enhanced by the TEX field of the Smartmap Control Register. If the TEX field is set to 1, the text attributes 07 and 0F hex are reversed. The text attribute 07 hex is normally bright gray while the attribute 0F hex is darker gray. If the TEX field is 0, the text attributes are not altered.

20.3.9   Flat Panel Compensation

When controlling a CRT, the VGA provides the master timing. If the CRT can accommodate the scan rates and bandwidth, the VGA can produce a wide variety of pixel resolutions on the screen. The VGA also controls the timing of the display data, which allows the image to be moved on the screen. Positioning, centering, and filling the screen with the image are relatively straightforward tasks.

Unlike the continually variable CRTs, the flat-panel displays have a fixed number of horizontal and vertical pixels. The VGA has few options regarding positioning the image on the display. A pixel can be written to or skipped. Similarly, a scan line can be written to or skipped.

This presents difficulties when a VGA controller has to provide multiple resolutions. The flat panels are typically 640 pixels wide. This works out very well since the common widths are 320 and 640. Obviously, one would not want to use an 800- or 1024-wide scan line. The 320-pixel width is accommodated by simply writing each pixel twice to fill the 640 flat-panel width. The MDA modes use 720 pixels wide with 9-pixel-wide characters. This can be rectified by dropping the resolution to 640 pixels and utilizing 8-pixel wide characters. If all display accesses go through the BIOS, this works out well. However, graphics modes that utilize the Hercules standard will have problems fitting the 720 pixels into the 640 flat-panel width.

A common height for flat panels is 240 scan lines. Placing two flat panels together provides 480 scan lines. This is a good match for the 480 scan line modes. However, the VGA commonly uses the 350 and 400 scan line modes. To fit the 350 or 400 lines into the 480 scan-line display, the 82c455 and 82c456 use compensation.

There are two types of compensation—text-mode and graphics-mode compensation. It is possible to disable text and use graphics-mode compensation even if the VGA is in a text mode.

Compensation either compresses or stretches the image to fit the image into the flat-panel display space. In a text mode, only compression is allowed. An example of text-mode compensation is shown in Figure 20.17.

In a graphics mode, either compression or stretching is allowed. Compression is illustrated in Figure 20.18, and stretching is illustrated in Figure 20.19. Programmers should recall that graphics-mode compensation can be used in a text mode.

Text-mode compensation is controlled by three registers. One register corresponds to 350 line modes when the number of scan lines per character row is

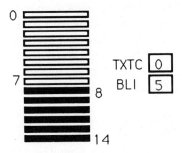

FIGURE 20.17 Text-mode Compressing Compensation. For example, a 200-line mode on a 350-line panel.

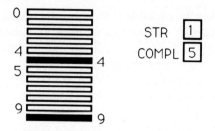

FIGURE 20.18 Graphics-mode Vertical Compensation.
For example, 350 lines on a 380-line panel.

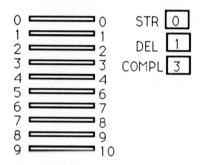

FIGURE 20.19 Graphics-mode Stretching Compensation. For example,
program every line except fourth to repeat. 200 lines on a 350-line panel.

greater than 8. A second corresponds to 350 line modes when the number of scan lines per character row is less than or equal to 8. The third corresponds to 400 line modes. Text-mode compensation can insert a programmable amount of blank lines in between each displayed row of data.

The three registers that control text-mode compensation are identical in operation. When there are 350 scan lines and a character is represented by greater than eight lines, text mode compensation is controlled through the Text Mode 350_A Compensation Register shown in Figure 20.20. When there are 350 scan lines and a character is represented by eight or fewer scan lines, text-mode compensation is controlled through the Text Mode 350_B Compensation Register shown in Figure 20.21. When there are 400 scan lines, text-mode compensation is controlled through the Text Mode 400 Compensation Register shown in Figure 20.22.

In each of these three registers, the type of compensation is controlled through the TXTC field. If the TXTC field is set to 0, text-mode compensation is enabled and blank lines are inserted after each row. The inserted blank lines are the color of the border color. If the TXTC field is set to 1, the text-mode compensation is disabled and graphics compensation will be used if it is enabled.

Text Mode 350_A 82c455/6
7
6
5
4
3
2
1
0
TXTC
BLI
Index 55 at Port 3D6
Port 3D7 Read/Write

FIGURE 20.20 Text Mode 35O_A Register for 82c455/6. The BLI field controls the number of blank lines+ 1 inserted after each row. The TXTC field is the compensation type for fonts larger than eight lines.

Text Mode 350_B 82c455/6
7
6
5
4
3
2
1
0
TXTC
BLI
Index 56 at Port 3D6
Port 3D7 Read/Write

FIGURE 20.21 Text Mode 350_B Register for 82c455/6. The BLI field controls the number of blank lines+ 1 inserted after each row. The TXTC field is the compensation type for fonts eight lines or smaller.

Text Mode 400 82c455/6
7
6
5
4
3
2
1
0
TXTC
BLI
Index 57 at Port 3D6
Port 3D7 Read/Write

FIGURE 20.22 Text Mode 4000_B Register for 82c455/6. The BLI field controls the number of blank lines+ 1 inserted after each row. The TXTC field is the compensation type.

The number of blank lines inserted is controlled through the BLI field. The BLI field contains the number of blank scan lines + 1 to insert after each row. This field is effective only when the text-mode compensation is enabled, TXTC=0.

Graphics mode compensation is controlled through two registers. One corresponds to 350 line graphics modes, and the second register corresponds to 400 scan line modes. Three techniques may be used. One technique allows a blank scan line to be interjected after a programmable number of displayed scan lines. A second technique allows a scan line to be periodically replicated after a programmable number of scan lines. A third allows a scan line to be

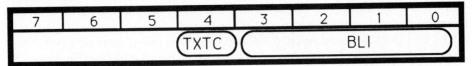

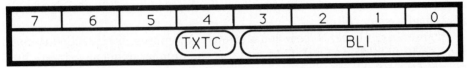

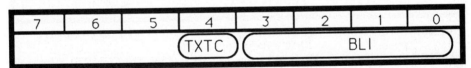

periodically deleted after a programmable number of scan lines. A qualifier to all these modes allows the programmable number, used in the three described techniques, to be incremented every other period.

The two graphics compensation registers are identical in their functioning. The Graphics Mode 350 Compensation Register shown in Figure 20.23 is used when a 350-line graphics mode is active. The Graphics Mode 400 Compensation Register shown in Figure 20.24 is used when a 400-line graphics mode is active.

The two types of compensation allow stretching or compressing the vertical display. The stretch feature is controlled through the STR field. If the STR field is set to 1, vertical stretching is enabled and a scan line is replicated periodically every N lines. The compress feature is enabled through the DEL field. If the DEL field is set to 1, vertical deletion is enabled and a scan line is deleted periodically every N lines.

The number of lines, N, between a stretch or compress is controlled through the COMP field. The COMP field contains the number of displayed scan lines between a stretch or compress. In addition, double scanning can represent a single line by two displayed scan lines.

Graphics Mode 350 82c455/6
7
6
5
4
3
2
1
0
COM
DEL
STR
COMP
Index 58 at Port 3D6
Port 3D7 Read/Write

FIGURE 20.23 Graphics Mode 350 Register for 82c455/6. The COMP field controls the number of displayed scan lines between replication or skip. The STR field enables the vertical stretch function. The DEL field enables the vertical delete function. The COM field controls an increment of the COMP field every other period.

Graphics Mode 400 82c455/6
7
6
5
4
3
2
1
0
COM
DEL
STR
COMP
Index 59 at Port 3D6
Port 3D7 Read/Write

FIGURE 20.24 Graphics Mode 400 Register for 82c455/6. The COMP field controls the number of displayed scan lines between replication or skip. The STR field enables the vertical stretch function. The DEL field enables the vertical delete function. The COM field controls an increment of the COMP field every other period.

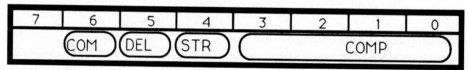

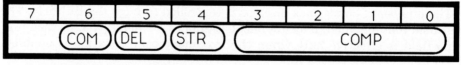

20.4 INQUIRING ABOUT THE CHIPS AND TECHNOLOGIES CONFIGURATION

The programmer can acquire information about the Super VGA chips. The chip identification, amount of memory, and card ID can be identified as indicated in Table 20.14.

TABLE 20.14 Determining Chips and Technologies Display Status

Function	Register Name	Port	Index	Bits	Value
Chip Version	Chip Version	3D6	0	7–0	0–255
Memory Map	Memory Mapping	3D6	4	1–0	0–3
Card ID Microchannel	Microchannel ID High	101		7–0	0–255
Card ID Microchannel	Microchannel ID Low	100		7–0	0–255
PC/AT Bus	Configuration	3D6	26	0	1
PS/2 Bus	Configuration 82c453	3D6	26	0	0
VRAM Memory	Configuration 82c453	3D6	26	2–1	0–3

TABLE 20.15 Chips and Technologies Identification Numbers

ID Field	Meaning
A5 hex	Chips and Technologies Chip

20.4.1 Identifying the Chips and Technologies VGA

The VGA ID can be found through the ID field of the Global ID Register. This field can be used to identify the chip as indicated in Table 20.15.

A Chips and Technologies Super VGA can be identified through the code in Listing 20.9.

LISTING 20.9 Determining if the Chip is a Chips and Technologies Super VGA

```
/*
Function:
 Determining if the chip is a Chips and Technologies Super VGA

Output Parameters:
 1 card is a Chips
 0 card is NOT a Chips
```

(continued)

```
Calling Protocol:
 Chips= Is_It_Chips() */

int Is_It_Chips()
{ unsigned char value; int flag;
into_setup();

value = inp(0x104); /* input Global ID register */
if(value==0xa5) flag=1;
        else flag=0;

exit_setup();
return(flag);
}
```

20.4.2   Identifying Which Chips and Technologies VGA

The chip version can be found in the Chip field of the Chip Version Register shown in Figure 20.25. The first version is Number 11 hex. This number increments for every revision. The chip number may be an 82c451, 452, 453, 455, or 456. Which Chips and Technologies Super VGA is in place can be identified through Listing 20.10. The chip number can be identified by the returned identity through the codes in Table 20.16.

TABLE 20.16   Identifing the Chips and Technologies Chip Number

Code	Chip Number
1	82c451
2	82c452
3	82c453
5	82c455
6	82c456

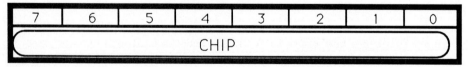

Chip Version

7	6	5	4	3	2	1	0
CHIP							

Index 00 at Port 3D6   Port 3D7 Read/Write

FIGURE 20.25   Chip Version Register. The chip version number is located in the CHIP field.

LISTING 20.10 Determining Which Chips and Technologies Super VGA Chip

```
/*
Function:
 Determining the Chips and Technologies chip Number

Output Parameters:
identity    integer containing chip code. The version register
            contains two hex characters. The hex character in
            the upper nibble is a chip code.
                  1 = 82c451
                  2 = 82c452
                  3 = 82c453
                  5 = 82c455
                  6 = 82c456
            The hex character
            in the lower byte is the version number.

Calling Protocol:
identity = Which_Chips() */

int Which_Chips()

{ int answer; unsigned char old_value,value,version;

Extended_On_Chips(); /* turn on extensions */

outp(0x3d6,00); /* Chip Version Register */
version = inp(0x3d7)&0xf0;   /* get chip id but remove version */

switch(version)
{
 case 0x10: /* must differentiate between 451 and 452 */
 outp(0x3D6,0x3a); /* see if Graphics Cursor Color 1 is there */
 old_value = inp(0x3D7);
 outp(0x3d7,0xaa); /* modify register */
 value = inp(0x3D7); /* read back register */
 outp(0x3d7,old_value); /* restore register */
 if(value==0xaa) answer=2;
            else answer=1;

 break;
 case 0x20: answer=5; break;
 case 0x30: answer=3; break;
 case 0x50: answer=6; break;
 }
```

(continued)

```
Extended_Off_Chips();
return(answer);
}
```

20.4.3   Determining the Attribute Flip-Flop Status

Accessing the Attribute Index Register, as described in Section 10.6, controls a flip-flop that determines whether the port address 3C0 is an Index or Data register. The status of this flip-flop can be read in the ATR field of the CPU Interface Register shown in Figure 20.1. This field is the same for the 82c451,2,3,5 and 6.

20.4.4   Addressing the Attribute Registers

The I/O addressing of the attribute registers is strange due to the internal flip-flop. This can be rectified through the ACM field of the CPU Interface Register shown in Figure 20.1. If the ACM field is set to 1, the attribute register index/data pair is accessed through 3C0 and 3C1 respectively. This works for either 8-bit or 16-bit port accesses. If the ACM field is set to 2, the attribute register index/data pair is also accessed through 3C0 and 3C1 respectively. However, this works only for 8-bit port accesses. This is non-standard and will not work for all of the other Super VGAs. On the other hand, it is simpler and faster to use. Several Super VGAs have such a feature. If the ACM field is set to 0, normal addressing at 3C0 for both the index and data occurs.

20.4.5   VRAM Memory 82c453

The 82c453 supports VRAM memory. The amount and configuration of this memory can be determined through the MEM field of the Configuration Register for the 82c453 shown in Figure 20.26. The MEM field is described in Table 20.17.

Configuration 82c453

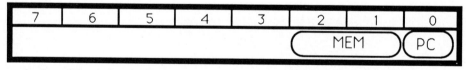

Index 26 at Port 3D6   Port 3D7 Read/Write

FIGURE 20.26 Configuration Register for 82c453. The PC field describes whether the 453 is in a PC/AT or Microchannel. The MEM field describes the VRAM memory configuration.

TABLE 20.17   VRAM Memory

MEM field	Amount of memory	# Chips	Chip Configuration
0	512 Kbytes	16	64 Kbyte x 4
1	512 Kbytes	4	256 Kbyte x 4
2	1 Mbyte	8	256 Kbyte x 4
3	512 Kbytes	8	64 Kbyte x 4

20.4.6   82453 on a PC or AT

The host computer can be determined through the PC field of the Configuration Register for the 82c453 shown in Figure 20.26. If the host computer is a PC/AT the PC field will return a 1. If the host computer is a PS/2, the PC field will return a 0.

20.5   CHIPS AND TECHNOLOGIES DISPLAY MODES

Chips and Technologies supports all of the standard Super display modes as shown in Tables 20.18 and 20.19. The alphanumeric modes support 132 column displays; the graphics modes go up to 1024x768 256-color. All 16-color display modes operate in the Planar Display Mode. All 256-color modes operate in the Packed Display Mode.

20.6   ACCESSING CHIPS AND TECHNOLOGIES DISPLAY MEMORY

The Chips and Technologies' solution to accessing the extended memory is simple and effective. It should be clear by now that the objective is to map the display memory into a 64-Kbyte host memory address segment. Control of the memory access is accomplished through manipulation of the extended registers.

The bank registers described in the following sections provide three distinct granularities as shown in Table 20.20.

TABLE 20.18   Chips and Technologies Alphanumeric Modes

Mode	Rows	Columns	Font	Resolution	Chip
60	25	132	8x8	1056x400	451/452/453
61	50	132	8x8	1056x400	451/452/453

TABLE 20.19 Chips and Technologies Graphics Modes

Mode	Resolution	Colors	Chip	Memory Organization
25	640x480	16	451/452/453	Planar
6A	800x600	16	451/452/453	Planar
70	800x600	16	451/452/453	Planar
71	960x720	16	452	Planar
72	1024x768	16	452/453	Planar
78	640x400	256	451/452/453	Packed
79	640x480	256	452/453	Packed
7A	768x576	256	452	Packed
7C	800x600	256	453	Packed
7E	1024x768	256	453	Packed

TABLE 20.20 Bank Granularity

Chip	Memory	Mode	Granularity
82c451,5,6	256 Kbytes	Packed	64 Kbytes
82c451,5,6	256 Kbytes	Planar	Not applicable
82c452	1 Mbyte	Packed	16 Kbytes
82c452	1 Mbyte	Planar	4 Kbytes
82c453	1 Mbyte	Packed	4 Kbytes
82c453	1 Mbyte	Planar	1 Kbytes

The bank granularity for the 451, 455, and 456 relates only to the Packed Display Mode due to the 256-Kbyte memory limit. The planar modes are organized as four planes, each 64 Kbytes long. The only packed mode that fits into the 256 Kbytes is Mode 13 hex. Mode 13 hex is a 320-by-200 display mode requiring 64 Kbytes. The bank selection therefore allows Mode 13 hex to access all 256 Kbytes of memory.

The bank granularity for the 452 is 16 Kbytes for the Packed Display Modes and 4 Kbytes for the Planar Display Modes. The factor of four difference is again based on the four overlapped display planes.

The bank granularity for the 453 is 4 Kbytes for the Packed Display Modes and 1 Kbyte for the Planar Display Modes. The factor of four difference is again based on the four overlapped display planes. The factor of four improvement over the 452 is due to the two additional bits in the bank registers.

20.6.1 Accessing 82c451 Display Memory

The 82c451 is configured with 256 Kbytes of display memory. The registers relevant to memory accessing are listed in Table 20.21. The memory mapping register has one field in the 82c451, shown in Figure 20.27 The MEM field of Figure 20.11 controls the memory addressing. If 0, the memory is VGA compatible. If 1, the extended memory is mapped as four pages of 64 Kbytes each or two pages of 128 Kbytes each.

Either the 64-Kbyte or 128-Kbyte addressing is in effect, based on the page number field, PN field, 82c451 CPU Paging Register as show in Figure 20.28. This two-bit page number defines which of the 64-Kbyte banks of display memory is to be mapped into CPU address space. Thus, all 256 Kbytes of memory on the 82c451 can be accessed.

TABLE 20.21 Accessing Chips and Technologies Display Memory in the 82c451

Function	Register Name	Port	Index	Bits	Value
Select VGA Compatibility	Memory Mapping	3D6	4	2	0
Memory Quad Mode	Memory Mapping	3D6	4	2	0
Memory Map Mode	Miscellaneous	3CE	6	3–2	0–3
Bank Switching	CPU Paging	3D6	B	1–0	0–3

Memory Mapping 82c451, 455, 456

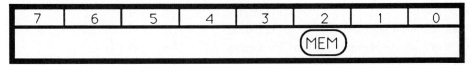

Index 04 at Port 3D6   Port 3D7 Read/Write

FIGURE 20.27 Memory Mapping Register for the 82c451 allows access to extended memory through the MEM field.

CPU Paging 82c451, 455, 456

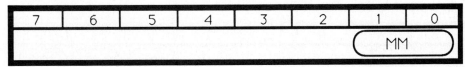

Index 0B at Port 3D6   Port 3D7 Read/Write

FIGURE 20.28 CPU Paging Register for the 82c451 selects one of four 64-Kbyte segments to be mapped into CPU address space through the MEM field.

20.6.2 Accessing 82c452/453 Display Memory

The 82c452 and 82c453 provide the programmer with a great deal of flexibility and control over the display memory. The relevant registers used to map the display memory into the host memory space are listed in Table 20.22.

In the 82c452/453 implementations, the host CPU can access the display memory through bank switching. The programmer can select to utilize one or two bank registers. Three registers permit utilization of the bank facility. These are the CPU Paging, the Single/Low Map, and the High Map registers as shown in Figures 20.29 to 20.31.

The CPU Paging Register controls memory compatibility mapping through the MM field, whether the system is in a single- or dual-bank (paging) mode through the "S/D" field. It also controls how the CPU should access memory in display mode 13 hex.

If the MM field is a 0, the memory is configured as 256 Kbytes of VGA-compatible memory. If 1, the memory is configured for the extended modes and enables access to the 512 Kbyte- or 1 Mbyte-memory configurations. If the S/D field is 0, only the Single/Low Map Register is used to page through the memory. If 1, two bank registers can be used in parallel. These are both the Single/Low Map and the High Map Registers. If the CPU field is 0, no divide by

TABLE 20.22 Reading and Writing to Chips and Technologies Display Memory

Function	Register Name	Port	Index	Bits	Value
Single Bank	CPU Paging	3D6	B	1	0
Dual Banks	CPU Paging	3D6	B	1	1
VGA Standard Memory	CPU Paging	3D6	B	0	0
512k or 1 Mbyte Memory	CPU Paging	3D6	B	0	1
Display Address Don't Divide	CPU Paging	3D6	B	2	0
Display Address Divide by 4	CPU Paging	3D6	B	2	1
Single/Low Bank Start Adr.	Single/Low Map	3D6	10	5–0	0–63
High Bank Start Address	High Map	3D6	11	5–0	0–63

CPU Paging 82c452,453

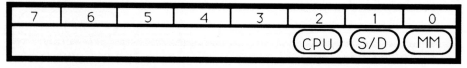

Index 0B at Port 3D6   Port 3D7 Read/Write

FIGURE 20.29 CPU Register for the 82c453. The divide by 4 mode is enabled by CPU. The Single/Dual mode is controlled by S/D and the Extended Memory is controlled by MM.

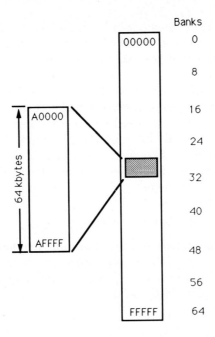

FIGURE 20.30 Single Map Single/Low Map = 100 addressing a 64-byte segment from 64000 to 73FFF.

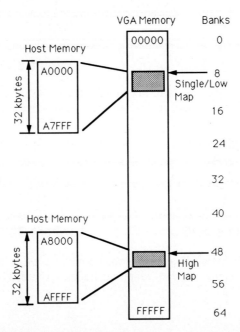

FIGURE 20.31 Dual Map Single/Low = 32 to address a 32-Kbyte segment from 20000–27FFF and High Map=192 to address 32-Kbyte segment from C0000 to C7FFF.

four occurs, and the display memory in Mode 13 hex is accessed as normal. If 1, the CPU addresses are divided by four. This allows access to all of the display memory in Mode 13 hex and permits display memory to be accessed sequentially.

The bank (page) registers of Figures 20.32 and 20.33 control the bank selection of the display memory. The Single/Low Register contains the bank starting address when the system is configured for one bank register when the S/D field is set to 0. It also controls the bank starting address of the lower 32 Kbytes of display memory when the S/D field is set to 1. If the S/D field is set to 1, the upper 32 Kbytes of display memory are accessed through the bank start address in the High Map Register.

20.6.3   Accessing 82c453 Display Memory

The 82c453 handles bank switching in a similar fashion as the 82c452. The major difference is that the 453 provides finer granularity. As can be seen in Figures 20.34 and 20.35, the BANK fields are each eight bits wide. This provides a 1 Kbyte granularity in the planar display modes and a 4 Kbyte granularity in the packed modes.

Single/Low Map 82c452

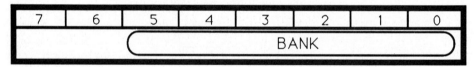

Index 10 at Port 3D6   Port 3D7 Read/Write

FIGURE 20.32   Single/Low Map Register for the 82c452. Contains bank starting address for full single or dual mapping modes in the BANK field.

High Map 82c452

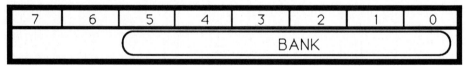

Index 11 at Port 3D6   Port 3D7 Read/Write

FIGURE 20.33   High Map Register for the 82c452. Contains bank starting address for full single or dual mapping modes in the BANK field.

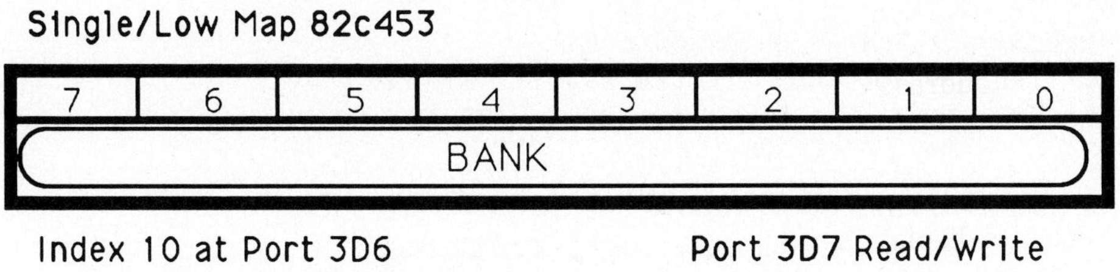

Single/Low Map 82c453

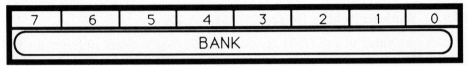

7	6	5	4	3	2	1	0
BANK							

Index 10 at Port 3D6   Port 3D7 Read/Write

FIGURE 20.34 Single/Low Map Register for the 82c452. Contains bank starting address for full single or dual mapping modes in the BANK field.

High Map 82c453

7	6	5	4	3	2	1	0
BANK							

Index 11 at Port 3D6   Port 3D7 Read/Write

FIGURE 20.35 High Map Register for the 82c452. Contains bank starting address for full single or dual mapping modes in the BANK field.

20.6.4   Single Paging

The 82c451, 455, and 456 are always in a single-paging mode. The 82c452 and 82c453 can be put into a dual-paging mode. If the system is configured in a single map mode, the Single/Low Map Register contains the bank start address. The value in the Map field ranges from 0 to 63. It indicates the 4-Kbyte starting boundary. For example, a 1 in the Map field causes the host 64-Kbyte memory beginning at A0000 to be mapped into display memory, beginning at memory address 4096. This is illustrated in Figure 20.30. The granularity of the bank mapping is 4 Kbytes.

Single-mode paging is enabled through the code in Listing 20.11.

LISTING 20.11 Setting up for Single-mode Paging

```
; Function:
;       Setting up for single-mode paging

; Calling Protocol:
;       Set_Single_Paging_Chips();
```

(continued)

```
Set_Single_Paging_Chips proc far
;          set up index to CPU Paging Register
           mov     dx,3d6h     ;point to CPU Paging Register
           mov     al,0bh
           out     dx,al

;          input the current value for non-destructive output
           in      al,dx   ;input CPU Paging Register
           and     al,0fdh    ;zero bit 1 for single page
           out     dx,al   ;output control
           ret
Set_Single_Paging_Chips endp
```

20.6.5   Bank Switching for the 82c451,455,456

A macro provided in LISTING 20.12 loads the Single Bank Register for the
82c451,455 or 456. These chips can access only 256 Kbytes of memory. The
bank field can be 0–3, providing a 64-Kbyte granularity. It allows access to the
entire 256 Kbytes of memory during Mode 13 hex.

LISTING 20.12   Loading the Bank Register for the 82c451, 455, and 456

```
; Function:
;       Loading the Single Bank with a new start address for
;       256-color modes

; Input with:
;       bl Single Bank_Number
;          0-3 bank number indicating desired 64-kbyte bank

; Calling Protocol:
;       Load_Bank_Chips

Load_Bank_Chips macro

;          set up index to Bank Select Register
           mov     dx,3d6h     ;point to CPU Paging Register
           mov     al,0bh
           mov     ah,bl
           out     dx,ax   ;output bank

endm
```

Listings 20.13 and 20.14 load the Single Bank Register with a bank value
that assumes a granularity of 64 Kbytes. These functions are called when a
16-bit planar mode is active. Since the Single Bank Register does not differentiate between reading and writing, the two listings are identical. They are both

provided to facilitate code calling protocol compatibility with the listings in the other Super VGA chapters.

LISTING 20.13 Loading Write Bank Number for the 82c451, 455, and 456

```
; Function:
;       Loading the Write Bank with a new start address for the
;       82c451,455 and 456

; Input with:
;       write_bank    Write Bank_Number
;               0-3 bank number indicating desired 64-kbyte bank

; Calling Protocol:
;       Set_Write_Bank_Chips(write_bank);

Set_Write_Bank_Chips proc far arg1:byte

        mov     bl,arg1    ;get argument
        Load_Bank_Chips


        ret
Set_Write_Bank_Chips endp
```

LISTING 20.14 Loading Read Bank Number for the 82c451, 455, and 456

```
; Function:
;       Loading the Read Bank with a new start address for the
;       82c451,455 and 456

; Input with:
;       read_bank Read Bank_Number
;               0-3 bank number indicating desired 64 Kbyte bank

; Calling Protocol:
;       Set_Read_Bank_Chips(read_bank);
;       Set_Read_Bank_Chips proc far arg1:byte

        mov     bl,arg1    ;get argument
        Load_Bank_Chips
        ret
Set_Read_Bank_Chips endp
```

20.6.6 Bank Switching for the 82c452 and 82c453

Two macros provided for the 82c452 load the Single Bank Register depending on whether a Planar or Packed Display Mode is active. The Bank Register has a different granularity, depending on whether the display mode is a 16-bit planar or a 256-color packed mode.

Listing 20.15 contains a macro to load the Single Bank Register with a value in a 16-bit planar mode. Listing 20.16 contains a macro to load the Single Bank Register with a value in a 16-bit packed mode.

LISTING 20.15 Loading the Single Bank Register Bank Number 16-color modes 82c452/3 Macro

```
; Function:
;       Loading the Single Bank with a new start address for
;       16-color modes for the 82c452/3

; Input with:
;       bl Single Bank_Number
;           0-63 bank number indicating desired 16-kbyte bank

; Calling Protocol:
;       Load_Single_Bank_16_Chips

Load_Single_Bank_16_Chips macro
;       set up index to Bank Select Register
        mov     dx,3d6h    ;point to Single/Low Map Register
        mov     al,10h
        mov     ah,bl
        shl     ah,1
        shl     ah,1
        shl     ah,1
        shl     ah,1    ;shift left 4 for 64 kbyte banks
        out     dx,ax   ;output bank

    endm
```

LISTING 20.16 Loading the Single Bank Register Bank Number 256-color modes 82c452/3 Macro

```
; Function:
;       Loading the Single Bank with a new start address for
;       256-color modes 82c452/3

; Input with:
;       bl Single Bank_Number
;           0-63 bank number indicating desired 16-kbyte bank

; Calling Protocol:
;       Load_Single_Bank_256_Chips
```

```
Load_Single_Bank_256_Chips macro
;       set up index to Bank Select Register
        mov     dx,3d6h    ;point to Single/Low Map Register
        mov     al,10h
        mov     ah,bl
        shl     ah,1
        shl     ah,1   ;shift left 2 for 64 kbyte banks
        out     dx,ax  ;output bank

endm
```

Listings 20.17 and 20.18 load the Single Bank Register with a bank value that assumes a granularity of 64 Kbytes. These functions are called when a 16-bit Planar Mode is active. Since the Single Bank Register does not differentiate between reading and writing, the two listings are identical. They are both provided to facilitate code-calling protocol compatibility with the listings in the other Super VGA chapters.

LISTING 20.17 Loading the Write Bank Number 256-color Modes for the 82c452/3

```
; Function:
;       Loading the Write Bank with a new start address 256-color
;       modes for the 82c452/3

; Input with:
;       write_bank   Write Bank_Number
;              0-63 bank number indicating desired 64-kbyte bank

; Calling Protocol:
;       Set_Write_Bank_256_Chips(write_bank);

Set_Write_Bank_256_Chips proc far arg1:byte
        mov    bl,arg1   ;get argument
        Load_Single_Bank_256_Chips

        ret
Set_Write_Bank_256_Chips endp
```

LISTING 20.18 Load Read Bank Number 256-color modes for the 82c452/3

```
; Function:
;       Load the Read Bank with a new start address 256-color
;       modes for the 82c452/3

; Input with:
;       read_bank Read Bank_Number
;              0-63 bank number indicating desired 64-kbyte bank
```

(continued)

```
; Calling Protocol:
;        Set_Read_Bank_256_Chips(read_bank);

Set_Read_Bank_256_Chips proc far arg1:byte

        mov    bl,arg1    ;get argument
        Load_Single_Bank_256_Chips

        ret
Set_Read_Bank_256_Chips endp
```

Listings 20.19 and 20.20 load the Single Bank Register with a bank value that assumes a granularity of 64 Kbytes. These functions are called when a 16-bit planar mode is active. Since the Single Bank Register does not differentiate between reading and writing, the two listings are identical. They are both provided to facilitate code calling protocol compatibility with the listings in the other Super VGA chapters.

LISTING 20.19 Loading Write Bank Number 16-color modes for the 82c452/3

```
; Function:
;        Loading the Write Bank with a new start address 16-color
;        modes for the 82c452/3

; Input with:
;        write_bank    Write Bank_Number
;                0-63 bank number indicating desired 64-kbyte bank

; Calling Protocol:
;        Set_Write_Bank_16_Chips(write_bank);

Set_Write_Bank_16_Chips proc far arg1:byte

        mov    bl,arg1    ;get argument
        Load_Single_Bank_16_Chips

        ret
Set_Write_Bank_16_Chips endp
```

LISTING 20.20 Loading Read Bank Number 16-color modes for the 82c452/3

```
; Function:
;        Loading the Read Bank with a new start address 16-color
;        modes for the 82c452/3
```

```
; Input with:
;       read_bank Read Bank_Number
;               0-63 bank number indicating desired 64-kbyte bank

; Calling Protocol:
;       Set_Read_Bank_16_Chips(read_bank);

Set_Read_Bank_16_Chips proc far arg1:byte

        mov     bl,arg1    ;get argument
        Load_Single_Bank_16_Chips

        ret
Set_Read_Bank_16_Chips endp
```

20.6.7 Dual Paging

The 82c452 and 82c453 can be placed into a dual-paging mode. In the Dual-paging Mode, the bank-switching operation is a bit more complex. Two bank start address registers are provided. The VGA hardware knows which one to use based on the memory addressing. In a typical scenario, the display memory is mapped into the host through a 64-Kbyte segment at A0000. This 64-Kbyte segment is split into a lower portion (A0000–A7FFF) and an upper portion (A8000–AFFFF), each 32 Kbytes long. If a memory transfer is addressed within the A0000–A7FFF range, the Single/Low Map Register is engaged. Similarly, if the A8000–AFFFF range is addressed, the High Map Register is engaged.

Dual-mode paging is enabled through the code in Listing 20.21.

LISTING 20.21 Setting up for Dual-paging Mode for the 82c452/3

```
; Function:
;       Set up for dual-paging mode for the 82c452/3

; Calling Protocol:
;       Set_Dual_Paging_Chips();

Set_Dual_Paging_Chips proc far

;       set up index to CPU Paging Register
        mov     dx,3d6h    ;point to CPU Paging Register
        mov     al,0bh
        out     dx,al

;       input the current value for non-destructive output
        in      al,dx  ;input CPU Paging Register
```

(continued)

```
        or      al,02h ;set bit 1 for dual page
        out     dx,al  ;output control
        ret
Set_Dual_Paging_Chips endp
```

The values in the BANK fields of these registers range from 0–63. These indicate a 4-Kbyte increment within one of the four display planes.

In the planar display modes, the display memory address of a pixel, within a plane, is pointed to by this register. The address is determined by multiplying the bank number by 4 Kbytes. This accounts for the 4-Kbyte granularity.

In the packed display modes, the display memory address of a pixel in plane 0 is pointed to by this register. The memory in display planes 1–3 follows sequentially and cannot be accessed by the bank register. The address is determined by multiplying the bank number by 16 Kbytes. This accounts for the 4-Kbyte granularity and four display planes. Note that although the bank is 64 Kbytes long, only 32-Kbyte transfers can occur in one transfer. This limitation occurs because the boundary at A8000 must be crossed. Otherwise, a wraparound would occur.

Dual-paging is accomplished using the same functions used in Section 20.6.6. The Single Bank Register is used for the low address map, which is 32 Kbytes long, ranging from A0000–A7FFF hex. The High Bank Register is used for the high address map, which is 32 kbytes long, ranging from A8000–AFFFF hex. Accessing these registers is accomplished through Listings 20.22 and 20.23. These are identical to the listings in Section 20.6.6 with the exception that the Single/Low Map Bank Select Register is located at index 10 hex and the High Map Bank Select) Register is located at 11 hex.

LISTING 20.22 Loading the High Map Bank Register in 16-color Modes for the 82c452/3 Macro

```
; Function:
;       Loading the High Map Bank with a new start address for
;       16-color modes for the 82c452/3

; Input with:
;       bl Single Bank_Number
;           0-63 bank number indicating desired 16-kbyte bank

; Calling Protocol:
;       Load_High_Bank_16_Chips

Load_High_Bank_16_Chips macro
```

```
;          set up index to Bank Select Register
           mov    dx,3d6h    ;point to Single/Low Map Register
           mov    al,11h
           mov    ah,bl
           shl    ah,1
           shl    ah,1
           shl    ah,1
           shl    ah,1    ;shift left 4 for 64 kbyte banks
           out    dx,ax   ;output bank

    endm
```

LISTING 20.23 Loading High Map Bank Register in 256-color for the 82c452/3

```
; Function:
;       Loading the High Bank with a new start address for
;       256-color modes for the 82c452/3

; Input with:
;       bl Single Bank_Number
;          0-63 bank number indicating desired 16-kbyte bank

; Calling Protocol:
;       Load_High_Bank_256_Chips

Load_High_Bank_256_Chips macro

;          set up index to Bank Select Register
           mov    dx,3d6h    ;point to Single/Low Map Register
           mov    al,11h
           mov    ah,bl
           shl    ah,1
           shl    ah,1    ;shift left 2 for 64 kbyte banks
           out    dx,ax   ;output bank

    endm
```

Listings 20.24 and 20.25 load the Single Bank Register with a bank value that assumes a granularity of 64 Kbytes. These functions are called when a 16-bit planar mode is active. Since the Single Bank Register does not differentiate between reading and writing, the two listings are identical. They are both provided to facilitate code calling protocol compatibility with the listings in the other Super VGA chapters.

LISTING 20.24 Loading Write Bank Number 256-color Dual-paging Modes for the 82c452/3

```
; Function:
;       Load the Write High Bank with a new start address
;       256-color dual-paging modes

; for the 82c452/3
; Input with:
;       write_bank    Write Bank_Number
;               0-63 bank number indicating desired 64-kbyte bank

; Calling Protocol:
;       Set_Write_High_Bank_256_Chips(write_bank);

Set_Write_High_Bank_256_Chips proc far arg1:byte

        mov    bl,arg1    ;get argument
        Load_High_Bank_256_Chips

        ret
Set_Write_High_Bank_256_Chips endp
```

LISTING 20.25 Load Read High Bank Number 256-color dual-paging modes for the 82c452/3

```
; Function:
;       Load the Read High Bank with a new start address
;       256-color dual-paging modes for the 82c452/3

; Input with:
;       read_bank Read Bank_Number
;               0-63 bank number indicating desired 64-kbyte bank

; Calling Protocol:
;       Set_Read_High_Bank_256_Chips(read_bank);

Set_Read_High_Bank_256_Chips proc far arg1:byte
        mov    bl,arg1    ;get argument
        Load_High_Bank_256_Chips

ret
Set_Read_High_Bank_256_Chips endp
```

Listings 20.26 and 20.27 load the single bank register with a bank value that assumes a granularity of 64 Kbytes. These functions are called when a 16-bit planar mode is active. Since the Single Bank Register does not differentiate between reading and writing, the two listings are identical. They are both provided to facilitate code calling protocol compatibility with the listings in the other Super VGA chapters.

LISTING 20.26 Load Write High Bank Number 16-color Dual-paging Modes for the 82c452/3

```
; Function:
;       Load the Write High Bank with a new start
;       address 16-color dual-paging modes for
;       the 82c452/3

; Input with:
;       write_bank    Write Bank_Number
;                 0-63 bank number indicating desired 64-kbyte bank

; Calling Protocol:
;       Set_Write_High_Bank_16_Chips(write_bank);

Set_Write_High_Bank_16_Chips proc far arg1:byte
        mov    bl,arg1    ;get argument
        Load_High_Bank_16_Chips

        ret
Set_Write_High_Bank_16_Chips endp
```

LISTING 20.27 Load Read Bank Number 16-color Dual-paging Modes for the 82c452/3

```
; Function:
;       Load the Read Bank with a new start address
;       16-color modes in dual-paging modes for
;       the 82c452/3

; Input with:
;       read_bank Read Bank_Number
;                 0-63 bank number indicating desired 64-kbyte bank

; Calling Protocol:
;       Set_Read_High_Bank_16_Chips(read_bank);

Set_Read_High_Bank_16_Chips proc far arg1:byte
        mov    bl,arg1    ;get argument
        Load_High_Bank_16_Chips

        ret
Set_Read_High_Bank_16_Chips endp
```

20.6.8 Hardware Bit Masking 82c453

In the planar configurations, a pixel is represented by data that resides in more than one display plane. In addition, the data associated with more than one pixel is stored in a single byte of display memory within a plane. Bit masking is required when writing to one or more pixels without affecting the other pixels in a given byte. A hardware bit mask feature in the 82c453 provides a very fast technique for bit masking.

In the standard VGA, a Bit Mask Register is provided to facilitate this bit-masking operation. However, this requires a read/modify/write to display memory, and the read operations are typically very slow. The Bit Mask Register is described in Section 10.5.11.

In the 82c453, two registers are provided to facilitate fast bit masking. These utilize the organization of the video RAM memory to provide bit masking without requiring read/modify/writes. The Write Bit Mask Control Register, shown in Figure 20.36, controls the bit masking operation.

The EM field of this register enables the Bit Mask Function. If the EM field is set to a 1, the hardware bit masking is enabled. If 0, this feature is disabled. If the feature is enabled, the SRC field controls the source of the bit-mask pattern. The SRC field is described in Table 20.23.

As shown in Figure 20.37, the Bit Mask Pattern Register is used to provide the mask if the SRC field is 0. If the SRC field is 1, the Bit Mask Register

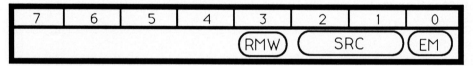

Write Bit Mask Control 82c453

Index 23 at Port 3D6   Port 3D7 Read/Write

FIGURE 20.36 Write Bit Mask Control Register for 82c453. The EM field enables or disables the VRAM write mask function. The SRC field controls the source of the pattern for the write mask function. The RMW field enables the fast read/modify/write function.

TABLE 20.23 The Source of Bit Mask Patterns

SRC	Source
0	Write Bit Mask Pattern Register
1	Graphics Controller Bit Mask Register
2	Rotated CPU byte

Write Bit Mask Pattern 82c453

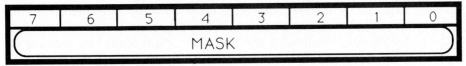

Index 24 at Port 3D6   Port 3D7 Read/Write

FIGURE 20.37 Write Bit Mask Pattern Register for 82c453. The MASK field contains the mask pattern for the write bit mask function when enabled by the SRC field of the Write Bit Mask Pattern Register.

described in Section 10.5.11 provides the mask pattern. This is very useful when older code is converted since it provides a simple porting task. If the SRC field is a 2, the rotated CPU byte is used as the mask. This is useful for character generation.

20.6.9 Hardware Read/Modify/Write Cycles 82c453

The 82c453 also provides a hardware assist for read/modify/write cycles. This is enabled through the EM field in the Write Bit Mask Control Register. If the EM field is set to 1, the hardware read/modify/write cycle feature is enabled. It must be pointed out that a CPU read operation cannot be performed when this hardware read/modify/write cycle is enabled.

This feature reduces the time to perform the read/modify/write cycles by 50 percent. This feature is very effective for logical operations. It is possible to perform a read/modify/write using this hardware assist at the same time that the hardware Bit Mask function is enabled.

20.6.10 Hardware Fast Font Paint 82c453

The 82c453 supports the high resolution 1024-by-768 256-color mode. This powerful mode contains 3/4 of a Mbyte of memory. If this mode is displaying alphanumerics, a simple screen scroll involves moving 3/4 Mbyte of memory! This, of course, is due to the fact that in a graphics mode each character is stored as a bit pattern. Fortunately, the 82c453 has provided an eloquent path for speeding up alphanumeric processing in the high resolution graphics modes.

The actual bit pattern for the character font is not stored in display memory. The bit patterns are interjected into the video data path further down stream. A typical character is 8 bits wide by 16 scan lines high. This requires 16 bytes of data for a single character.

In the packed pixel graphics modes, the 82c453 makes it possible to display alphanumeric characters as character codes. In the Packed Pixel Mode, four bytes are consecutively loaded into the four display planes. These four bytes produce a 32-bit display memory word that resides in the display latches. In a 256-color mode, an 8x16 pixel character is represented by 128 bytes of information corresponding to the 128 pixels covered by the character.

The technique implemented in the Fast Font Paint Mode can increase the graphics character map painting by a factor of four or eight. Early versions of the 82c453 require two write operations per byte of character font. Since a byte of character font contains eight pixels, a 4:1 enhancement is achieved. Later versions of the 82c453 require one write operation per byte of character font. This provides an 8:1 enhancement.

The Fast Font Paint Mode is enabled through the FFP field of the CPU Interface Register for the 82c453 shown in Figure 20.38. If the FFP field is set to 1, the Fast Font Paint Mode is enabled. If it is set to 0, the mode is disabled.

In the early 82c453 versions, if the Fast Font Paint Mode is enabled, the byte written to display memory consists of a nibble of information. This nibble corresponds to the left-most or right-most four pixels in the particular character scan line. Four memory-write operations to display memory are accomplished by this one host write operation. Instead of the four bits being written into display memory, the foreground color is written to all pixels that correspond to a 1 in the nibble. Similarly, the background color is written to all pixels that correspond to a 0 in the nibble.

In the later 82c453 versions, the entire byte can be written in one host write operation, causing the foreground and background colors to be written to eight consecutive pixel locations. This is illustrated in Figure 20.39.

Figure 20.39a illustrates the mapping of a single scan line of a character into the four display memory planes. Since a horizontal scan line contains eight pixels, two pixels are shown in each plane. In Figure 20.39b a typical character font pattern is shown. In Figure 20.39c the corresponding display shows the foreground and background colors for each pixel.

The attribute of the pixel consists of a foreground color and a background color. Since a 256-color Packed Display Mode is active, both the foreground and background color are eight bits. The foreground color is stored in the Scratch

CPU Interface 82c453

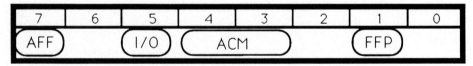

Index 02 at Port 3D6   Port 3D7 Read/Write

FIGURE 20.38 CPU Interface Register for 82c453. The FFP field enables the Fast Font Paint function. The ACM field controls the Attribute Controller Mapping. The I/0 field selects either 1O-bit or 16-bit I/0 address decoding. The AFF field contains the Attribute Flip-Flop Status.

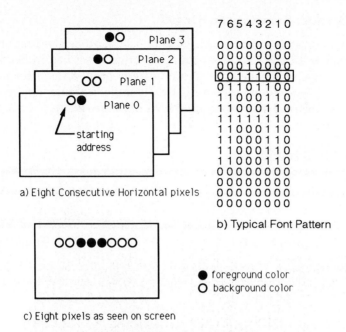

76543210
00000000
00000000
00010000
00111000
01101100
11000110
11000110
11111110
11000110
11000110
11000110
11000110
00000000
00000000
00000000
00000000
b) Typical Font Pattern
Plane 3
Plane 2
Plane 1
Plane 0
starting address
a) Eight Consecutive Horizontal pixels
c) Eight pixels as seen on screen
foreground color
background color

FIGURE 20.39 Fast Font Paint

#1/Foreground Color Register shown in Figure 20.40. If the fast font painting mode is disabled, this register can be used as scratch storage.

The background color is derived from the values in the display latch registers. There are four display latch registers corresponding to the four display planes. In the 256-color modes, these four display planes translate into four horizontal consecutive pixels. If all four display latch registers are loaded with the same value, all four consecutive pixels will have the same background color. This would be used in an opaque character paint operation. If the four display latches are loaded with the current colors of the four consecutive pixels, a transparent character map will result since only the pixels corresponding to the foreground of the character will be changed.

Scratch *1/Foreground Color 82c453
7
6
5
4
3
2
1
0
SOF
Index 45 at Port 3D6
Port 3D7 Read/Write

FIGURE 20.40 Scratch #1/Foreground Color Register for 82c453. The SOF field contains either the scratch value that can be used as a scratchpad or the foreground color when in the Fast Font Paint Mode.

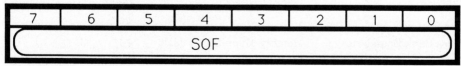

20.6.11 Scratch Registers on 82c453

There are two scratch registers available on the 82c453. The first is discussed in conjunction with the Fast Font Paint function described in Section 20.6.8. This scratch register is called the Scratch #1/Foreground Color Register shown in Figure 20.41. The second register is totally undedicated and may be used by application software. This register is shown in Figure 20.40.

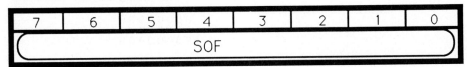

Index 44 at Port 3D6   Port 3D7 Read/Write

FIGURE 20.41 Scratch #0 Register for 82c453. The SCRATCH field contains the scratch value that can be used by application software.

20.7 CONTROLLING THE CRT ADDRESS GENERATION

20.7.1 Controlling the Display Start Address

The manner in which the display memory is mapped to the screen is controlled through the CRT address generation circuitry. The operating characteristics of this memory are controlled through the Memory Mapping Register. Added addressing bits are provided for the start address, cursor, and offset as listed in Table 20.24.

The Memory Mapping Register is shown in Figure 20.42. The Mem field in the Memory Mapping Register indicates the amount of memory present as listed in Table 20.25. The three popular configurations are provided with one field available for future expansion (more memory hopefully). If 256 Kbytes are

TABLE 20.24 Chips and Technologies Display Address Control

Function	Register Name	Port	Index	Bits	Value
Wrap Around	Memory Mapping	3D6	4	2	0
Cross Bank Boundaries	Memory Mapping	3D6	4	2	1
Start Address Bits 17–16	Start Address Top	3D6	C	1–0	0–3
Cursor Address Bits 17–16	Cursor Address Top	3D6	A	1–0	0–3
Fine Granularity for Offset	Auxiliary Offset Register	3D6	D	0	0–1

TABLE 20.25 Memory Size as Found in the Memory Mapping Register

MEM field	Display Memory Size
00	256 Kbytes
01	512 Kbytes
10	1 Mbyte
11	Not Used

present, the memory is organized into four planes of 64 Kbytes each. If 512 Kbytes is present, the memory is organized into two banks and four planes of 64 Kbytes each. If 1 Mbyte is present, the memory is organized into four planes, 256 Kbytes each. Each plane can either be divided into 64-Kbyte banks in planar modes, or the entire 1 Mbyte can be divided into 64-Kbyte banks in packed modes.

The WRP field controls wrap around. If this bit is set to 0, the CRT address generation will wrap around at the 64-Kbyte boundary. The CRT address generation controls what is seen on the display. If the WRP bit is 0, the CRT address will wrap around since the display memory address bits 17 and 16 will be generated by the CRT address counter. If the WRP field is 1, the CRT address will cross banks since the address bits 17 and 16 will be generated by the TOP field of the Top Address Register.

Due to 1 Mbyte of display memory space, additional address bits are required for the display start address, cursor start address, and display offset. The Start Top Address Register provides the additional address bits 16 and 17 as shown in Figure 20.43.

The extended memory beyond 256 Kbytes must be enabled if it is to be accessed by the CRT controller. If it is disabled, wrap around on the display will occur at the 256-Kbyte boundary. It can be enabled or disabled through Listings 20.28 and 20.29, respectively.

Memory Mapping 82c452

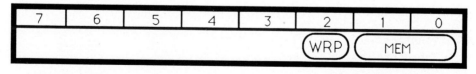

Index 04 at Port 3D6   Port 3D7 Read/Write

FIGURE 20.42 Memory Mapping Register for the 82c452 provides access to the amount of display memory through the "MEM" field and controls CRT wrap around through the "WRP" field.

Start Address Top 82c452, 82c453

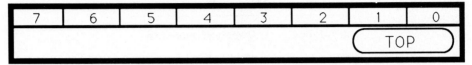

Index 0C at Port 3D6   Port 3D7 Read/Write

FIGURE 20.43 Start Address Top. The display start address bits 17–16 are located in the TOP field.

LISTING 20.28 Enabling Extended Memory Addressing

```
/*
Function:
 Enabling extended memory CRT addressing. Memory above 256
 kbytes can be displayed.

Calling Protocol: */
 Enable_Ext_Memory_Access()

{ unsigned char value;
 Extended_On_Chips();

outp(0x3d6,0x04); /* memory map register */
value = inp(0x3d7);   /* read register */
value |= 0x04; /* set bit 2=1 for extended memory addressing */
outp(0x3d7,value);

 Extended_Off_Chips();
}
```

LISTING 20.29 Disable Extended Memory addressing casuing wrap around

```
/*
Function:
 Disable extended memory CRT addressing. Memory above 256
 kbytes cannot be displayed. Wrap around will occur.

Calling Protocol: */
 Disable_Ext_Memory_Access()

{ unsigned char value;
 Extended_On_Chips();

outp(0x3d6,0x04); /* memory map register */
value = inp(0x3d7);   /* read register */
```

```
value &= 0xfb; /* reset bit 2=0 for extended memory addressing */

outp(0x3d7,value);

 Extended_Off_Chips();
}
```

The 20-bit start address is loaded by sending the lower sixteen bits to the Start Address High and Low Registers and the upper two bits to the Start Address Top Register as shown in Listing 20.30. This function utilizes the Load_Start_Chips function in Listing 20.31.

LISTING 20.30 Loading the Display Start Address

```
; Function:
;       Loading the 20-bit Display Start Address

; Input Parameters

;       address     unsigned integer starting address
;       top top     two bits of address

; Calling Protocol:
;       Load_Start_Chips(address,top)

Load_Start_Chips  proc far  arg1,arg2:byte
        mov    bx,arg1
        set_start_address     ;load the lower 16-bits of the start
                              ; address

;       send out top address
        enable_extensions  ; enable extensions
        mov    dx,3d6h
        mov    al,0ch        ;index Extended Start Address
        mov    ah,arg2
        out    dx,ax
        disable_extensions ; disable extensions

        ret
Load_Start_Chips  endp
```

20.7.2 Controlling the Cursor Start Address

Due to the 1 Mbyte of display memory space, additional address bits are required for the display start address, cursor start address, and display offset. The Cursor Address Top Register provides the additional address bits 16 and 17 as shown in Figure 20.44.

Cursor Address Top
7
6
5
4
3
2
1
0
TOP
Index 0A at Port 3D6
Port 3D7 Read/Write

FIGURE 20.44 Cursor Address Top. The cursor display start address bits 17–16 are located in the TOP field.

Auxiliary Offset Register
7
6
5
4
3
2
1
0
A09
09
Index 0D at Port 3D6
Port 3D7 Read/Write

FIGURE 20.45 Auxiliary Offset Register. Offset address bit located in 09 and alterate emulation offset bit in A09.

The term *offset* determines the virtual width of the display. The standard VGA Offset Register is eight bits and can handle virtual display widths of up to 1024. To provide for wider virtual images up to 2048 pixels, an additional bit is provided as shown in Figure 20.45. This bit, field O8, acts as the ninth offset address bit. Also included in this register is an analogous bit for the alternate offset register used during emulation.

The 20-bit cursor address is loaded by sending the lower 16-bits to the Cursor Address High and Low Registers and the upper two bits to the Cursor Address Top Register as shown in Figure 20.44 and Listing 20.31.

LISTING 20.31 Position the Cursor

```
; Function:
;        Load the 20-bit Cursor Position

; Input Parameters

         position  unsigned integer position
;        top       top two bits of address
```

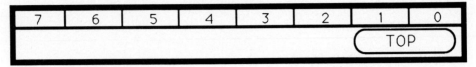

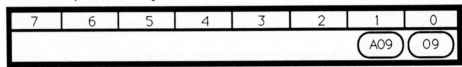

```
; Calling Protocol:
;         Position_Cursor_Chips(position,top)

Position_Cursor_Chips proc far  arg1,arg2:byte

        mov    bx,arg1
        position_cursor  ;position cursor

;       send out top cursor address
        enable_extensions    ; enable extensions
        mov    dx,3d6h
        mov    al,0ah         ; index Cursor Address Top
        mov    ah,arg2
        out    dx,ax
        disable_extensions   ; disable extensions

        ret
Position_Cursor_Chips endp
```

20.7.3   Controlling the Display Offset

The display offset determines the size of the virtual image. The 8-bit value stored in the Offset Register of the CRTC Register Group is the only control for the display offset. This register is described in Section 10.4.22.

20.8   CHIPS AND TECHNOLOGIES BIOS EXTENSIONS

Extended BIOS calls are accessed through the AH=5F code as listed in Table 20.26.

20.8.1   Get Controller Information

This provides the programmer with information about the graphics chip and memory configuration.

TABLE 20.26 Chips and Technologies Extended BIOS Calls

Function	AH	AL	Feature
Get Controller Information	5F	00	Returns Chip Information
Set Emulation Mode	5F	01	Set Emulation Mode
Auto Emulation Control	5F	02	Enable/Disable Auto Emulation
Power-On Video Conditions	5F	03	Sets Power-on Conditions
Enhanced Save/Restore State	5F	90–92	Handles Standard and Super States

Inputs:

AH=5F	Extended VGA Control
AL=00	Get Controller Information

Outputs:

AL=5F	Extended VGA control function supported
BL= Chip Type	bits 7–4 Chip Type
	0 = 82c451
	1 = 82c452
	2 = 82c455
	? = 82c453
	bits 3–0 Revision Number
BH= Memory Size	video memory size
	0 = 256 Kbytes
	1 = 512 Kbytes
	2 = 1 Mbyte
CX=Miscellaneous	Miscellaneous Information
	15–2 = reserved
	1 = System Environment
	0=PC/AT
	1=PS/2
	2 = Dac Size
	0=6-bit
	1=8-bit

20.8.2   Set Emulation Mode

This allows the programmer to set up emulation modes.

Input:

AH=5F	Extended VGA Control
AL=00	Get Controller Information
BL=Operation Mode	Operation Mode
	0–1=reserved
	2 =Enable CGA Emulation
	3 =Enable MDA Emulation
	4 =Enable Hercules Emulation
	5 =Enable EGA Emulation
	6 =Enable VGA Emulation

Outputs:

AL=5F	Extended VGA control function supported
AH=Return Status	Return Status
	0=Function Unsuccessful
	1=Function Successful

20.8.3   Auto Emulation Control

Auto Emulation Control makes it possible to enter into an emulation mode automatically. Thus, any application that attempts to access non-VGA registers will cause the VGA chips to generate non-maskable interrupts causing the system to jump into an emulation mode.

Inputs:

AH=5F	Extended VGA control
AL=2	Auto emulation control
BL=selection	Enable or disable auto emulation
	0=enable auto emulation
	1=disable auto emulation

Outputs:

AL=5F	Extended VGA control function supported
AH=Return Status	Return Status
	0=Function Unsuccessful
	1=Function Successful

20.8.4   Set Power-on Video Conditions

Set Power-on Video Conditions permits the saving of start-up parameters for automatic installation during power up. The VGA implementation requires non-volatile storage for the memory associated with these selections. If this feature is available, the bits 13–10 of the Miscellaneous Information 0 data would be set.

Inputs:

AH=5F	Extended VGA control
AL=3	Set Power-on video conditions
BL=Configuration	Configuration selection
	0=Set display mode as specified in the cx register to boot up at power-up.
	1=Set emulation mode as specified in the cx register to boot up at power-up.
if(BL==0)	
CL=mode	Display Mode
CH=mode	Options
	Bits 1–0 = Scanlines
	0=200
	1=350
	2=400
	Bit 7 = Performance

0=Reset after next boot
1=Set until changed

if(BL==1)
  CL=mode   Emulation Mode (See extended BIOS emulation
                             call above)
  CH=mode   Options
                               Bit 7 = Performance
                                 0=Reset after next boot
                                 1=Set until changed

Outputs:
  AL=5F   Extended VGA control function supported
  AH=Return Status   Return Status
                               0=Function Unsuccessful
                               1=Function Successful

20.8.5 Enhanced Save/Restore Video State Function

This function is similar to the Save/Restore BIOS function 1C described in Sections 11.16.3 and 13.7.7. The capacity to store the Super VGA state has been added to this function through bit 15 of the CX input parameter. This BIOS function is split into three sub-functions. One returns the amount of storage necessary or expected for the save/restore functions respectively. The other two sub-functions actually perform the Save or Restore functions.

Subfunction 90   Determine size of buffer

Inputs:
  AL=5F hex   Extended VGA control function
  AL=90 hex   Return Save/Restore buffer size
  CX=Mask State   States of Save/Restore
                               bit 0 = save/restore video hardware
                               bit 1 = save/restore BIOS data state
                               bit 2 = save/restore DAC state
                               bit 15 = save/restore type
                                 0 = save/restore all state information
                                 1 = save/restore super state only

Outputs:
  AL=5F   Extended VGA control function supported
  bx = blocks required   Number of 64-byte blocks required for the save or
                             expected for the restore.

Subfunction 91	*Save the State*
Inputs:	
AL=5F hex	Extended VGA control function
AL=91 hex	Save state
CX=Mask State	States to Save
	bit 0 = save video hardware
	bit 1 = save BIOS data state
	bit 2 = save DAC state
	bit 15 = save type
	0 = save all state information
	1 = save super state only
ES:BX	Segment:Offset pointer to buffer which will contain the state information at the successful conclusion of this call.

Outputs:	
AL=5F	Extended VGA control function supported
Subfunction 90	Determine size of buffer

Inputs:	
AL=5F hex	Extended VGA control function
AL=92 hex	Restore state
CX=Mask State	States to Restore
	bit 0 = restore video hardware
	bit 1 = restore BIOS data state
	bit 2 = restore DAC state
	bit 15 = restore type
	0 = restore all state information
	1 = restore super state only
ES:BX	Segment:Offset pointer to buffer which should contain the state information for the restore function.

Outputs:	
AL=5F	Extended VGA control function supported

20.9 CHIPS AND TECHNOLOGIES SPECIAL FEATURES

Several special features available on the Chips and Technologies chip are listed in Table 20.27.

20.9.1 Anti-Aliased Display Fonts

The 82c452 and 82c453 support a font mode that utilizes 2 bits/pixel. The fonts are stored in corresponding addresses in display planes 2 and 3. The most sig-

TABLE 20.27 Chips and Technologies Special Features

Feature	Supporting Chips	Description
Anti-Aliased Fonts	452	Allows gray scale alphanumeric fonts
Downward Emulation	451,452,453,455,456	Emulates MDA, Hercules, CGA,EGA
Interrupt Skipping	452	Interrupts after n vertical cycles
Hardware Cursor	452	Hardware cursor
Hardware Write Mask	453	Hardware write mask
Hardware Fast Font	453	Hardware fast font drawing

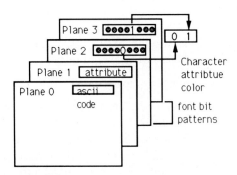

FIGURE 20.46 Anti-aliased Font Storage

nificant bit is stored in display plane 2 and the least in display plane 3 as shown in Figure 20.46.

The anti-aliased fonts are controlled by the Text Mode Register shown in Figure 20.47. The 2BP field of this register enables (2BP=1) or disables (2BP=0) the anti-aliased font feature. If 2BP is set to 0, the feature is disabled and normal font patterns are utilized. The font bit patterns are stored in bit plane 2 under normal VGA conditions. Each pixel in the foreground of a character is represented by a 1; the background pixels in the rectangular pixel pattern box are represented by 0.

If the anti-aliased fonts are enabled, each pixel in the rectangular character box is represented by two bits instead of the standard one bit per pixel. The font bit pattern for each character is stored with one bit of each pixel in bit plane 2 and one bit in bit plane 3. The lower order bit is stored in bit plane 3, and the higher order bit is stored in bit plane 2. The meaning of the four possible colors are described in Table 20.28. A typical character pattern is shown in Figure 20.48.

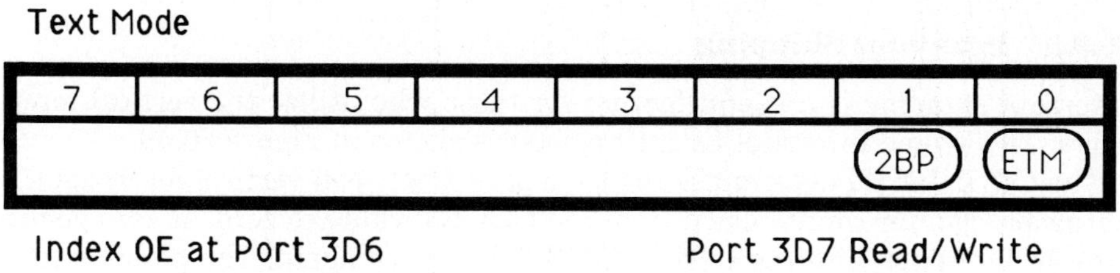

Text Mode

7	6	5	4	3	2	1	0
						(2BP)	(ETM)

Index OE at Port 3D6   Port 3D7 Read/Write

FIGURE 20.47 Text Mode Register, Extended Text Mode
Controlled by ETM and 2 bits/pixel enable by 2BP.

TABLE 20.28 Anti-Aliased Bit Colors

Bit Plane 2	Bit Plane 3	Color	Percent Foreground
0	0	0 Background	$0 <= x < .25$
0	1	1 Foreground 1	$.25 <= x < .50$
1	0	2 Foreground 2	$.50 <= x < .75$
1	1	3 Foreground 3	$.75 <= x < 1.0$

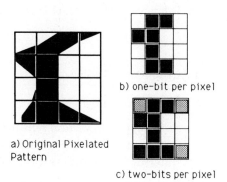

a) Original Pixelated Pattern

b) one-bit per pixel

c) two-bits per pixel

FIGURE 20.48 Anti-aliased Four-color Font

20.9.2   Downward Emulation

The 82c450 family can emulate the MDA, Hercules, CGA, and EGA cards
through BIOS calls or through several extended registers. It is beyond the
scope of this book to detail the many registers involved in this complex project.
The registers include the emulation control, alternate timing, and trap status
registers. It is useful to reference the Set Emulation BIOS call detailed in Section 20.3.6.

20.9.3 Interrupt Skipping

Interrupt skipping is a useful feature for those who utilize the vertical interrupts. The Frame Interrupt Count Register is shown in Figure 20.49.

The COUNT field determines the time period between vertical interrupts. A hardware counter counts down from the COUNT value to zero, at zero generates an interrupt, and resets the COUNT field once again. The possible time periods are listed in Table 20.29. If the vertical refresh period occurs at 30 frames a second, the maximum value of 31 in the COUNT field will cause an interrupt approximately every second.

Frame Interrupt Count

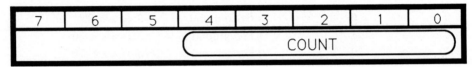

Index 2A at Port 3D6   Port 3D7 Read/Write

FIGURE 20.49 Frame Interrupt Count. COUNT vertical refresh cycles occur before vertical interrupt is generated.

TABLE 20.29 Interrupt Count Timing

Count field	Interrupt Timing
0	Interrupt every vertical refresh cycle
1	Interrupt every other vertical refresh cycle
31	Interrupt every 32nd vertical refresh cycle

20.9.4 Hardware Cursor

The Hardware Cursor is available on the 82c452. It provides an excellent cursor compatible to the Windows Presentation Manager standards. Its features are outlined in Table 20.30. Details of the eleven registers and memory location of this cursor are beyond the scope of this book.

TABLE 20.30   Hardware Cursor Features

Feature	Description
Size	32 pixels wide and 512 pixels high
Positioning	Pixel resolution anywhere on the screen
Zoom	Horizontally zoomed by factor of 2
Colors	Foreground color, background color, transparencies
Color Resolution	2 bits/pixel
Attributes	Blink at 8 or 16 blinks frames per on-and-off period

Chapter 21

Cirrus Logic

21.1 THE 542X SUPER VGA CONTROLLERS

The 542x series range from the 5420 through the 5428/29. All are dynamic ram (DRAM) controllers supporting up to 2 Mbytes of memory. The 5426 includes a BitBlt engine, and the 5428 has an enhanced BitBlt engine. The 5429 is identical to the 5428 with addition of memory-mapped I/O registers for the BitBlt engine and with VESA VAFC baseline support. A 32-by-32 hardware cursor is supported on the 5420; up to a 64-by-64 hardware cursor is supported on all other chips. A 32-bit memory bus is present for all chips. All but the 5420 support video overlay and color keying. The 542x display modes based on the different controllers are shown in Table 21.1.

21.2 THE 543X SUPER VGA CONTROLLERS

The 543x series is mostly downward compatible to the 5428 and 5429. The basic differences include faster throughput due to the 64-bit DRAM bus, the 32-bit CPU bus, and the 64-bit BitBlt engine. It supports resolutions up to 1024 by 768 in (non-interlace) and 1280 by 1024 (interlaced) in the 4-bit-per-color, 8-bit-per-color, and hi-color modes and 800 by 600 in true-color modes. The true-color modes include both 24-bit and 32-bit-per-color modes. The "alpha-channel" 8-bit bus can be used for overlays or for color keying to external video sources.

  The 543x series registers are almost identical, with the most notable difference being the 24-bit foreground and background registers. These are necessary since the color expansion supports the high-color and true-color modes.

21.3 THE 545X SUPER VGA CONTROLLERS

The 545x series is downward compatible to the 543x and the 5428 and 5429 processors. It is considerably faster than the 543x series due to its VRAM inter-

TABLE 21.1 Cirrus Logic Super VGA Controllers

Chip	4-bit	8-bit	16-bit	24-bit	Coprocessor
5420	1024 by 768	1024 by 768	None	None	No
5422/24	1280 by 1024	1024 by 768	800 by 600	640 by 480	Yes
5426/28/29	1280 by 1024	1280 by 1024	1024 by 768	640 by 480	Enhanced

face. It includes a styled line draw engine and dynamic video overlay. It can support 1600 by 1200 (interlaced) in the 8-bit-per-color mode, 1280 by 1024 (non-interlaced) in the 4-bit-per-color, 8-bit-per-color, and hi-color modes and 1024 by 768 in true-color modes.

The dynamic video overlay logic allows video data to be overlaid onto the display stream. The selection of where to place the data can be either from a color key value or an internal or external timing generator. The line draw engine can be programmed with either the standard Bresenham constants or the end-point technique.

21.4 DISPLAY MODES

The Cirrus Logic family of controllers supports the display modes shown in Table 21.2.

TABLE 21.2 Cirrus Logic Display Modes

Mode	Resolution	Bits/Pixel	Chips
54h	132 by 43	alpha	all
55h	132 by 25	alpha	all
58h	800 by 600	4	all
5Ch	800 by 600	8	all
5Dh	1024 by 768	4	all
5Fh	640 by 480	8	all
60h	1024 by 768	8	all
64h	640 by 480	16	not 5420
65h	800 by 600	16	not 5420
66h	640 by 480	mixed	not 5420, 5422
67h	800 by 600	mixed	not 5420
6Ch	1280 by 1024	4	not 5420
6Dh	1280 by 1024	8	not 5420, 5422
6Fh	320 by 200	16	not 5420
70h	320 by 200	24	not 5420
71h	640 by 480	24	not 5420

TABLE 21.2 *(cont.)*

Mode	Resolution	Bits/Pixel	Chips
71h	1024 by 768	16	not 5420, 5422, 5424
72h	800 by 600	32	543x,545x
73h	1024 by 768	32	543x,545x
74h	1024 by 768	16	543x,545x
75h	1280 by 1024	16	543x, 545x
76h	640 by 480	32	543x, 545x
77h	1280 by 1024	24	545x
78h	1600 by 1200	8	545x

21.5 EXTENSION REGISTERS

There are several sets of extended registers in the Cirrus Logic chip family. These are provided in Table 21.3 through Table 21.6. Registers relevant to the programmer are described in detail in the following sections.

TABLE 21.3 Extended Registers at Port 3C4/3C5

Index	Name	Usage
2	Enable Writing Pixel Extension	SR2
6	Unlock All Extension Registers	SR6
7	Extended Sequencer Mode	SR7
8	EPROM Control	SR8
9	Scratch Pad 0	SR9
A	Scratch Pad 1	SRA
B	VCLK0 Numerator	SRB
C	VCLK1 Numerator	SRC
D	VCLK2 Numerator	SRD
E	VCLK3 Numerator	SRE
F	DRAM Control	SRF
10	Graphics Cursor Y Position	SR10
11	Graphics Cursor X Position	SR11
12	Graphics Cursor Attributes	SR12
13	Graphics Cursor Pattern Address	SR13
14	Scratch Pad 2 (26/28)	SR14
15	Scratch Pad 3 (26/28)	SR15
16	Performance Tuning	SR16

(continued)

TABLE 21.3   *(cont.)*

Index	Name	Usage
17	Config. Read and Extended Control (28)	SR17
18	Signature Generator Control (!20)	SR18
19	Signature Generator Result Low (!20)	SR19
1A	Signature Generator Result High (!20)	SR1A
1B	VCLK0 Denominator ad Post-Scalar	SR1B
1C	VCLK1 Denominator ad Post-Scalar	SR1C
1D	VCLK2 Denominator ad Post-Scalar	SR1D
1E	VCLK3 Denominator ad Post-Scalar	SR1E
1F	BIOS ROM Write Enable	SR1F

TABLE 21.4   Extended Registers at Port 3CE/3CF

Index	Name	Usage	
0	Write Mode 5/Background Extension	GR0	
1	Write Mode 4.5/Foreground Low (Byte 0)	GR1	
9	Offset Register 0	GR9	
A	Offset Register 1	GRA	
B	Mode Extensions	GRB	
C	Color Key (!20)	GRC	
D	Color Key Mask (!20)	GRD	
E	Miscellaneous Control (28)	GRE	
10	16-bit Pixel Background High (!20)	GR10	
11	16-bit Pixel Foreground High (!20)	GR11	
12	Background Color Byte 2	GR12	543x, 545x
13	Foreground Color Byte 2	GR13	543x, 545x
14	Background Color Byte 3	GR14	543x, 545x
15	Foreground Color Byte 3	GR15	543x, 545x
19	GD5453 Mode	GR19	545x
20	BLT Width Low	GR20	
21	BLT Width High	GR21	
22	BLT Height Low	GR22	
23	BLT Height High	GR23	
24	BLT Destination Pitch High	GR24	
25	BLT Destination Pitch Low	GR25	
26	BLT Source Pitch High	GR26	
27	BLT Source Pitch Low	GR27	

TABLE 21.4 *(cont.)*

Index	Name	Usage	
28	BLT Destination Start Low	GR28	
29	BLT Destination Start Mid	GR29	
2A	BLT Destination Start High	GR2A	
2C	BLT Source Start Low	GR2C	
2D	BLT Source Start Mid	GR2D	
2E	BLT Source Start High	GR2E	
30	BLT Mode	GR30	
31	BLT Start/Status	GR31	
32	BLT Raster Operation	GR32	
34	Transparent Color Select Low	GR34	26, 28 only
35	Transparent Color Select High	GR35	26, 28 only
38	Source Transparent Color Mask Low	GR38	26, 28 only
39	Source Transparent Color Mask High	GR39	26, 28 only
40	Linedraw Start X Byte 0	GR40	545x
41	Linedraw Start X Byte 1	GR41	545x
42	Linedraw Start Y Byte 0	GR42	545x
43	Linedraw Start Y Byte 1	GR43	
44	Linedraw End X Byte 0	GR44	
45	Linedraw End X Byte 1	GR45	
46	Linedraw End Y Byte 0	GR46	
47	Linedraw End Y Byte 1	GR47	
50	Linedraw Line Style Increment	GR50	
51	Linedraw Line Style Rollover	GR51	
52	Linedraw Line Style Mask	GR52	
53	Linedraw Line Style Accumulator	GR53	
54	Bresenham K1 Byte 0	GR54	
55	Bresenham K1 Byte 1	GR55	
56	Bresenham K3 Byte 0	GR56	
57	Bresenham K3 Byte 1	GR57	
58	Bresenham Error Byte 0	GR58	
59	Bresenham Error Byte 1	GR59	
5A	Bresenham Delta Major Byte 0	GR5A	
5B	Bresenham Delta Major Byte 1	GR5B	
5C	Bresenham Direction	GR5C	
5D	Linedraw Mode	GR5D	

TABLE 21.5 Extended Registers at Port 3C4/3C5

Index	Name	Usage
19	Interlace End	CR19
1A	Interlace Control	CR1A
1B	Extended Display Controls	CR1B
25	Part Status Register	CR25
27	ID Register	CR27

TABLE 21.6 Hidden DAC Register

Bit	Field	Name
—	Hidden DAC Register at 3C6	HDR

21.5.1 Mode Extensions Register, GRB

The Mode Extensions Register, GRB, is an important register and it is described in detail in Table 21.7. It is used to control the color expansion and it can be used on any of the processors. Color expansion can also be controlled through the BitBlt engine. The color expansion can be 8 or 16 bits per pixel as determined by the values in this register.

21.5.2 Enable Extended Write Modes

If this bit is a 1, extended write modes are enabled. The enhanced extended write modes are controlled by the fields listed in Table 21.8; 16-bit expansion transfers are controlled by the fields in Table 21.9.

21.5.3 Enable by 8 Addressing

This bit enables 8-byte transfers for color expansion. Up to eight bytes can be written into display memory for each CPU byte transferred. If GRB bit 4 is programmed to a 1, up to sixteen bytes can be written for color expansion.

21.5.4 Color Keying

Color keying allows data to be switched in on a pixel-by-pixel level from the feature connector. This is done using the Color Key Compare Register and the Color Key Mask Register at GRC and GRD. Any color in the display memory that matches the masked color key compare color causes that pixel to be replaced with data from the feature connector. Any bit that is 1 in the mask enables that bit in the key color for comparison.

TABLE 21.7 Mode Extension Register

Bit	Field	Description
0	Enable Offset Register 1	If 1, SA15 is used to choose between Offset Register 0 and 1. If 0, Offset Register 0 is always selected. Must be 0 for linear addressing.
1	Enable by 8 Addressing	System address is shifted by 3 relative to true packed-pixel addressing. If enabled, each system byte addresses a different 8-byte block in display memory.
2	Enable Extended Write	If 1, extended write modes are enabled.
3	Enable Eight Byte Data Latches	If 1, the display memory latches are 8 bytes wide rather than 4.
4	Enable Enhanced Writes 16-bit	Execute enhanced writes for 16-bit pixels.
5	Offset Granularity	If 1, Offset Registers are 16 Kbyte granularity.

TABLE 21.8 Enabled Enhanced Writes

Field	Description
GR5 bit 2	Extended write modes 4 and 5 can be enabled.
GR0	Extended from 4 bits to 8 bits.
GR1	Extended from 4 bits to 8 bits.
SR2	Extended from 4 bits to 8 bits.
GRB bit 4	GRB bit 2 must be programmed to a 1 to enable 16-bit color extended write modes.

TABLE 21.9 Enabled Enhanced Writes for 16-bit Pixels

Field	Description
By 16	System address is shifted by 4 relative to true packed-pixel addressing so that each system byte points to a different 16-byte block.
16-byte transfer	Up to 16 bytes can be written into display memory per access.
GR10 & GR11	Foreground and background color extensions.
SR2	Doubling enabled.

TABLE 21.10 Foreground and Background Colors

Field	Description
GR0	Background Low
GR1	Foreground Low
GR10	Background High
GR11	Foreground High

21.5.5   Foreground and Background Colors

The foreground and background color registers are sixteen bits wide. Depending on whether sixteen bits are enabled, either the lower eight bits or all sixteen bits will be used. These 16-bit values are located in four registers as shown in Table 21.10. These are used when the display is put into a write mode 4 or 5.

21.6   BITBLTS

The BitBlt Engine is used to transfer data from host-to-screen, screen-to-host, or screen-to-screen. The BitBlts require a source area, a destination area, and an operation to perform on the data during the transfer operation. The source and destination areas can be affected by masking or scissoring.

21.6.1   Source Area

The source area of a BitBlt is the area from which the data are copied. The source area may be in display or host memory. It may contain an image of any pixel-depth supported by the BitBlt engine. If it is a monochrome image, 1 bit per pixel, it might be copied directly or color expanded to the color resolution of the screen. It might be a single 8-by-8 pattern that is replicated to fill a larger area.

21.6.2   Destination Area

The destination area of a BitBlt is the area into which the data are written. The destination memory might be in host or display memory. If the source area is in host memory, then the destination memory **cannot** be in host memory.

21.6.3   Width

The width of a BitBlt is the number of bytes (not pixels) of destination that are processed before adding the pitch value to the address. If the destination area, source area, or both are actually in, or potentially in, the on-screen portion of display memory, the width is the number of bytes in each scanline (of the source or destination area). In this case, the data exists in a two-dimensional space (not linear). If neither the source nor destination is in display memory, the width has no special meaning. The number actually written into the GR20/GR21 registers is the width –1.

21.6.4 Height

The height of the BitBlt is the number of times the pitch values are added to the address. If the destination area, source area or both are in, or potentially in, the on-screen portion of display memory, the height is the number of scanlines in that area. If not, height has no special meaning. The number of bytes in the destination is determined by multiplying the width by the height. The number actually written into the GR22/GR23 registers is the height –1.

21.6.5 Pitch

The source pitch and destination pitch are the values that are added to the respective addresses after the number of bytes equal to the destination width have been processed. Destination and source pitch are specified separately. When in a two-dimensional space, the pitch is the number of bytes between the first pixel of a scanline and the first pixel of the next scan line. This is the case if the destination area, source area, or both are actually in, or potentially in, the on-screen portion of display memory. If the space is a one-dimensional space, like off-screen display memory, the data is stored in contiguous locations (linear). In this case, the pitch is equal to the width. When host memory is used, the pitch has no meaning. When executing pattern copies or color expansion, the source area is taken to be linear and the source pitch has no meaning. The source pitch is specified in register pair GR26 and GR27. The destination pitch is specified in register pair GR24 and GR25.

21.6.6 BitBlt Registers

The BitBlts Registers that specify the dimensionality of the BitBlt are listed in Table 21.11 and are described in this section.

21.6.7 BLT Mode Register

This register controls various BitBlt fields as indicated in Table 21.12.

When the source is expanded, the most significant bit of the first source byte will become the first pixel in the screen destination. Either system or display memory may be the source of the transfer. Each logical line must be filled out to an even byte. "Dummy" bits might be necessary. If the source is display memory, then the source starting address must be on a 4-byte boundary and the source pitch is linear (source pitch is ignored).

The BLT direction is controlled by bit 0. This bit determines if the address is incremented (if 0) or decremented (if 1). If 0, then the BLT start address should

TABLE 21.11 BLT Width and Height

Name	Register	Name	Register
GR20	Width Low	GR29	BLT Destination Start Mid
GR21	Width High	GR2A	BLT Destination Start High
GR22	Height Low	GR2C	BLT Source Start Low
GR23	Height High	GR2D	BLT Source Start Mid
GR24	Destination Pitch Low	GR2E	BLT Source Start High
GR25	Destination Pitch High	GR30	BLT Mode
GR26	Source Pitch Low	GR31	BLT Start/Status
GR27	Source Pitch High	GR32	BLT Raster Operation
GR28	BLT Destination Start Low		

TABLE 21.12 BLT Mode Register GR30

Bit	Field	Description
0	BLT Direction	If 1, the source and destination address are decremented. If 0, they are incremented.
1	BLT Destination Display/System	If 1, the BLT destination will be system memory rather than display memory.
2	BLT Source Display/System	If 1, the BLT source will be system memory rather than display memory.
3	Enable Transparency Compare	If 1, the result of the raster op is compared with the Transparent Color Register for each pixel to determine if the destination pixel should be left alone.
4	Color Expand/Transparency Width	Controls the width of the color expansion.
5	Reserved	
6	Enable 8-by-8 Pattern Copy	If 1, the source pattern will be copied repeatedly to the destination rectangular area.
7	Enable Color Expand	If 1, the ROP source is the expanded result from the binary bit-mapped source. This enables Write Mode 4/65.

be the lowest address. If 1, the BLT start address should be the highest address.

The BLT destination can be display memory or system memory, as controlled by the BLT Destination Display/System field. Similarly, the BLT source can be display memory or system memory, as controlled by the BLT Source Display/System field. It should be noted that system-to-system transfers are not allowed. Since these chips are not bus masters, it is necessary for the host to issue the write commands, even in the case of display-to-display transfers. Therefore, in display-to-system BLTs the host would perform the correct number of read operations. In system-to-display BLTs the host would perform the correct number of write operations. In either case, when the system memory is involved, the CPU transfers data in increments of four bytes. Extra "dummy" bytes must be written if the transfer is not an even multiple of four. In display-to-display transfers, the CPU must issue 16-bit transfers.

Transparency BitBlts do not write to the destination for every pixel that corresponds to a background (source) color. For example, suppose that the source data is a red circle on a blue background and it is desired to BitBlt only the red circle. One would set the Transparent Color Compare Register value to blue and enable the Enable Transparency Compare field. This feature must be used, and the transparent color set to the background color, if the color expand BLT is to be used with an opaque foreground and a transparent background. This is similar to Extended Write Mode 4.

It is necessary to specify the width of the operations when dealing with color expansion or with transparency. Either 8- or 16-bit operations could be desired. The combinations are provided in Table 21.13.

The Pattern Copy field repeatedly copies an 8-by-8 pattern to the destination if the Enable 8x8 Pattern bit is set. This pattern must be aligned on a 4-byte

TABLE 21.13   Color Expansion and Transparency Width

Color Expand / Transparency Width	GR30 bit 7	GR30 bit 5	Operation
1	1	x	Bit-mapped source will be expanded to 16 bits per pixel.
0	1	x	Bit-mapped source will be expanded to 8 bits per pixel.
1	x	1	Transparency compare done on 16 bits per pixel.
1	x	0	Transparency compare done on 8 bits per pixel.

TABLE 21.14 8-by-8 Pattern Copy Arrangements

Color Expansion	Bits / Pixel	Arrangement
Enabled	x	8 bytes of Monochrome bitmap for the 8-by-8 pattern
Disabled	8	64 bytes of color data for the 8-by-8 pattern
Disabled	16	128 bytes of color data for the 8-by-8 pattern

boundary. The source will be linear addressed data in one of the three arrangements as shown in Table 21.14.

Color expansion is enabled by the Enable Color Expand bit. If 1, the result of the raster operation will be the expanded result from the bit-mapped source. Color expansion requires a destination of screen memory and the direction must be incrementing. Color expansion involves the 8- or 16-bit foreground and background values in GR0, GR1, GR10, and GR11.

21.6.8 BitBlt Control

The BitBlt engine is controlled by the Start/Status Register. The programmer can reset the BLT engine to a known start state, suspend an operation, or restart an operation. In order to suspend an operation, it is necessary to test bit 0, the BLT status bit, to actually know when the BLT is suspended. The BLT stops at the end of a scan line. Its progress can be monitored by the BLT Height Registers, which reflect the line count for the last completed line. This register is described in Table 21.15.

BitBlts transfer data from system-to-display, display-to-system, or from display-to-display memory. The registers affecting a BitBlt are shown in Table 21.16.

The Bit BLT parameters are illustrated in Figure 21.1.

Example 21.1 Copy a 64-by-64 region from display memory to display memory in a 1024-by-768 16-bit-per-pixel display mode.

GR20/21 =	127	width = (64 * 2) −1
GR22/23 =	63	height = 64 − 1
GR24/25 =	2048	Destination pitch = 1024 * 2
GR26/27 =	128	Source pitch linear (64*64)
GR28/29/2A =	1000	on-screen
GR2C/2D/2E =	1,000,000	off-screen
GR30 =	0	Direction = +, display-to-display, no pattern, no transparency no color expand

GR32 =	0Dh	Raster Op = SRCCOPY
GR34/35 =	—	no color transparency
GR38/39 =	—	no color transparency
GR31 =	2	Start BLT

TABLE 21.15 BitBlt Control

Bit	Name	Description
0	BLT Status (read only)	If 1, the BLT is in progress. If 0, the BLT is complete.
1	BLT Start/Suspend	If 1, the BLT will resume operation at the next available display memory cycle. If set to 0, the BLT will be suspended at the end of the current scanline.
2	BLT Reset	If set to 1, the BLT engine is immediately reset and any operation in progress will be terminated.
3	BLT Progress Status (read only)	Is set to 1 at the start of a BLT and is reset to 0 when the entire operation completes.

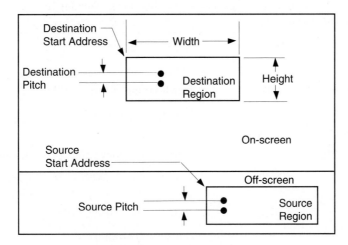

FIGURE 21.1 BitBlt Definitions

TABLE 21.16 Registers Affecting a BitBlt

Name	Register	Bit	Value	Function
GR20/21	BLT Width Low/High	10–0	0–2047	Sets width-1
GR22/23	BLT Height Low/High	9–0	0–1023	Sets height-1
GR24/25	BLT Destination Pitch Low/High	11–0	0–4095	Destination pitch
GR26/27	BLT Source Pitch Low/High	11–0	0–4095	Source pitch
GR28/29/2A	BLT Destination Start Low/Mid/High	20–0	0–2 Meg	Destination start
GR2C/2D/2E	BLT Source Start Low/Mid/High	20–0	0–2 Meg	Destination end
GR30	BLT Mode Register	7–0	misc.	Desired mode
GR32	BLT Raster Op	7–0	0–255	Raster operation
GR34/35	BLT Transparent Color Low/High	15–0	8 or 16 bits	Transparent color
GR38/39	BLT Transparent Color Mask Low/High	15–0	8 or 16 bits	Transparent mask
GR31	BLT Start/Status	0	Read 1	Bit BLT is Busy
GR31	BLT Start/Status	1	1	Start BLT

Example 21.2 Copy a text string from system memory to display memory. The string is organized in linear array left-to-right, top-down. The destination area is 150 by 25 pixels. The display is in a 1024-by-768 8-bit-per-pixel display mode.

GR20/21 =	149	width = 150 –1
GR22/23 =	24	height = 25 – 1
GR24/25 =	1024	Destination pitch = 1024
GR26/27 =	—	Source pitch ignored
GR28/29/2A =	1000	on-screen
GR2C/2D/2E =	—	system memory, host provides data
GR30 =	8Ch	Direction = +, system-to-display, no pattern, no transparency, color expand
GR32 =	0Dh	Raster Op = SRCCOPY
GR34/35 =	—	no color transparency
GR38/39 =	00	no color transparency, must be 0
GR31 =	2	Start BLT

21.7 RASTER OPERATIONS

The pixel processing takes two inputs, the source and destination, and combines them in sixteen ways as enumerated in Table 21.7. The Raster Operation register contains the raster operation code.

21.8 TRANSPARENCY COLOR

The transparency color registers provide up to a 16-bit word in the Transparent Color Low (GR34) and Transparent Color High (GR35) Registers. These registers are available in only the 5426 and 5428. The high (GR35) is used if the GR30 bit 3 is set to a 1. Otherwise, only the low (GR34) is used. In order for this to work, GR35 must be equal to GR34 if in an 8-bit mode.

Only selected bits (planes) in the Transparent Color Low and Transparent Color High Registers are used. These bits correspond to the bit positions set to 0 in the Transparent Color Mask Low (GR36) and High (GR37) Registers. Any bits in these two registers set to a 1 result in that corresponding bit position being considered a don't care.

TABLE 21.17 Raster Operations

Value	Operation	Microsoft Name
00	always 0	BLACKNESS
0E	always 1	WHITENESS
0D	S	SRCCOPY
06	D	
D0	!S	NOTSRCCOPY
0B	!D	DSTINVERT
05	S AND D	SRAND
09	S AND !D	SRCERASE
50	!S AND D	
90	!S AND !D	NOTSRCERASE
6D	S OR D	SRCPAINT
AD	S OR !D	
D6	!S OR D	MERGEPAINT
DA	!S OR !D	
59	S !+ D	SRCINVERT (XOR)
95	S = D	– (XNOR)

21.9 EXTENDED DISPLAY CONTROLS REGISTER

Several extended fields are present in the Extended Display Controls Register. Several of these are relevant to the programmer and are listed in Table 21.18.

21.10 COLOR MODES

The Cirrus chips provide support for the standard 4-bit and 8-bit color modes along with the high color (15-bit and 16-bit) modes, the true-color 24-bit or 32-bit modes, and a novel mixed mode (15-bit and 8-bit combined).

The multi-mode DACs support the modes shown in Table 21.19. These include the 8-bit, 15-bit, 16-bit, 24-bit, and 32-bit color modes (with and without Gamma correction. The Hidden DAC Register at I/O Port 3C6h is used to enable the extended color modes. At reset, this register is loaded with a 00h, so the DAC is initialized in an 8-bit color mode. By writing the appropriate code to the register, the palette DAC can be programmed. The Select High Resolution Extended Mode field in SR7 bits 3–1 is also shown in this table.

In order to talk with the Hidden DAC Register, the following two steps must be followed:

1. Read from the Pixel Mask Register at 3C6h four times in succession. Discard the data read. No intervening I/O reads or writes can take place without forcing a repeat of this step.

2. After the fourth read, the Pixel Mask Register will point to the Hidden DAC Register. Now the Hidden DAC Register can be programmed by writing a value to it at 3C6h. Any other I/O read or write to any address other than 3C6h will reset the internal counter and the two steps will have to be repeated.

21.10.1 Hi-color Modes

The 15-bit color positions bits 4–0 as blue, 9–5 as green, and bits 14–10. It also supports 16-bit color with blue in bits 4–0, green in bits 10–5, and red in bits 15–11.

TABLE 21.18 Extended Display Control Register

Bit	Value	Description
4	Offset Register Overflow 8	Bit 8 of the Offset Register
3	Extended display start address bit 18	Bit 18 of the start address
2	Extended display start address bit 17	Bit 17 of the start address
0	Extended display start address bit 16	Bit 16 of the start address

TABLE 21.19 The Multimode Palette DAC

Function	7	6	5	4	3	2	1	0	SR7[3–1]
VGA Compatibility	0	0	0	0	0	0	0	0	000
5-5-5	1	0	0/1	0	x	x	x	x	011
5-5-5	1	1	0/1	0	0	0	0	0	011
5-5-5 Mixed	1	1	0/1	1	0	0	0	0	011
5-6-5 XGA	1	1	0/1	0	0	0	0	1	011
8-8-8	1	1	0	0	0	1	0	1	111
8-8-8-Alpha	1	1	0	0	0	1	0	1	101
8-8-8-Alpha (with Gamma)	1	1	0	0	0	1	0	1	101
Palette Power Down	1	1	0	x	0	1	1	x	000
8-bit Gray	1	1	0	x	1	0	0	0	000
3-3-2 8-bit RGB	1	1	0	x	1	0	0	1	000
DAC Power down	1	1	1	1	1	1	1	1	xxx

21.10.2 True-color Modes

The true-color modes must have 2048 bytes per row for the 640-by-480 mode. Three bytes per pixel are stored in the TARGA compatible with blue, followed by green, followed by red. Each pixel is packed with 24-bits per pixel. The 640x3=1920 means that there are 2048–1920 = 128 extra bytes at the end of each display line. These 128 extra bytes can be considered as off-screen memory or can be used for panning.

21.10.3 Mixed-Mode Programming

The Cirrus chips have an interesting mode based on their palette called mixed mode. This mode mixes a 15-bit-per-pixel mode with an 8-bit-per-pixel mode on the same page, where each pixel is switched dynamically. Since the 15-bit-per-pixel mode leaves 1 bit extra (bit 15), this bit can be used for switching. If this bit is a 1, then bits 7–0 of the word are considered as an index into the color table (8-bit color). On the other hand, if this bit is reset to 0, the lower 15 bits are used as a standard 15-bit color. Thus, each pixel can switch between the palette and 15-bit color.

21.11 EXTENDED WRITE MODES

There are two important extended write modes that allow access to color expansion. These write modes are called write modes 4 and 5. Remember that the VGA has write modes 0–3. Write mode 4 allows for a transparent color expansion; write mode 5 is an opaque expansion. Either mode can operate in an 8- or 16-bit-per-pixel mode.

These write modes are controlled using the Graphics Controller Mode Extensions Register. They are enabled by the bit 2, Enable Extended Write Modes Bit. Bit 2 of the Mode Register GR5 selects either write mode 4 or write mode 5. It extends GR0, Set/Reset Register for Write Mode 5 Background Color and GR1, Enable Set/Reset Register for Write Mode 4 and 5 Foreground Color. It also extends SR2, Map Mask Register to bits 7–0 for Write Modes 4 and 5.

The Enable BY8 Addressing, Bit 1 of the Graphics Controller Mode Extension Register, enables up to eight bytes for every CPU byte transfer. The Enable Enhanced Writes 16-bits field, Bit 4, in conjunction with Bit 2, of this register selects x16 addressing. In this case, the CPU address is shifted by four and each access points to a different 16-byte block (eight pixels). Therefore, sixteen bytes can be transferred per CPU byte cycle. It enables GR10 and GR11 as the high bytes of the foreground and background color extensions. It also enables each bit of SR2 to be used as a pixel write mask.

When using the transparent modes, the read back data latches are used. If the Enable 8-byte Data Latches bit is set, bit 3, eight bytes are latched instead of four. This is also useful when using write mode 1.

21.11.1   Write Mode 4

Write Mode 4 writes the foreground color bits for each pixel in display memory corresponding to a CPU data bit set to 1 and the corresponding bit in the Map Mask Register is set to a 1. If either is 0, the pixel in display memory remains unchanged. This creates a transparent write.

21.11.2   Write Mode 5

Write Mode 5 writes the foreground color similar to Write Mode 4; however, if the pixel is a 0 and the map mask bit is a 1, then the pixel is overwritten with the background color. If the map mask bit is a 0, the display pixel remains unchanged.

21.12   COLOR EXPANSION

Color expansion can be controlled with or without the BitBlt engine. Color expansion can greatly relieve the host memory bandwidth limitations when sending data to the display.

21.12.1   Color Expansion Without the BitBlt Engine

The registers that affect color expansion without the BitBlt Engine are listed in Table 21.20.

TABLE 21.20 Registers Affecting Color Expansion

Name	Register	Bit	Value	Function
SR2	Enable Writing Pixel Extensions	7–0	0–255	Enable Writing Pixels
GRB	Mode Extensions	2	1	Enable Extended Write Modes
GRB	Mode Extensions	4	1	16 bit-per-pixel
GR5	Mode Register	2–0	4	Write Mode 4
GR5	Mode Register	2–0	5	Write Mode 5
GR0	Set/Reset	7–0	0–255	Write Mode 5 Background Low
GR1	Enable Set/Reset	7–0	0–255	Write Mode 4/5 Foreground Low
GR10	Background Color High	7–0	0–255	Write Mode 5 Background High
GR11	Background Color High	7–0	0–255	Write Mode 4/5 Foreground High

21.12.2 Color Expansion With the BitBlt Engine

The data to be expanded is always in a 1-bit-per-pixel format. The BitBlt engine can color expand data in the host or in the display memory. The destination must always be the display memory. The data can also be a pattern that is repeatedly expanded. Pattern copies are supported only for screen-to-screen BitBlts.

The Foreground and Background Color Registers for the 542x registers are 16 bits as stored in GR0, GR1, GR10, and GR11. The Foreground and Background Color Registers for the 543x and 545x registers are 32 bits as stored in GR0, GR1, GR10, and GR11 and in GR12, GR13, GR14, and GR15. The format is shown in Table 21.21.

TABLE 21.21 Color Expansion Foreground and Background Register Format

Bits/pixel	Foreground				Background			
	GR0	GR10	GR12	GR14	GR1	GR11	GR13	GR15
8	data	x	x	x	data	x	x	x
16	low	high	x	x	low	high	x	x
32	blue	green	red	alpha	blue	green	red	alpha

TABLE 21.22 ID Register

Value	Chip
22h	5420
23h	5422
25h	5424
24h	5426
26h	5428
A4h	543x
B0h	545x

21.13 IDENTIFYING THE CIRRUS LOGIC CHIPS

The current Cirrus chip can be accessed from the ID Register as shown in Table 21.22. The code in Listing 21.1 determines if a Cirrus chip is present. The code in Listing 21.2 determines which Cirrus chip is present.

LISTING 21.1 Determine if the Chip is a Cirrus Logic

```
/* Output Parameters:
        1 card is a Cirrus   0 card is NOT a Cirrus
     Calling Protocol:
       Cirrus= Is_It_Cirrus()   */

int Is_It_Cirrus(void)
{ BYTE in_value_1,in_value_2;

// first unlock the Cirrus
   Extended_On_Cir();

// now lets see if 3ce=9,A are read/write
outp(0x3ce,0x09);
outp(0x3cf,0x55); in_value_1=inp(0x3cf);
outp(0x3cf,0xAA); in_value_2=inp(0x3cf);
if((in_value_1!=0x55)||(in_value_2!=0xAA))
return(CHIP_NOT_FOUND);

outp(0x3ce,0x0A);
outp(0x3cf,0x55); in_value_1=inp(0x3cf);
outp(0x3cf,0xAA); in_value_2=inp(0x3cf);
if((in_value_1!=0x55)||(in_value_2!=0xAA))
return(CHIP_NOT_FOUND);
```

```
// now see if we read anything from 3ce=f. if nothing at 3cf =ff
// then it is a CIRRUS (and not a Paradise)
outp(0x3ce,0x0f); in_value_1=inp(0x3cf);
if(in_value_1==0xff) return(CHIP_FOUND);

return(CHIP_NOT_FOUND);
}
```

LISTING 21.2 Determine Which Cirrus Chip

```
Output Parameters:
        identity        integer containing chip code

Calling Protocol:
 identity = Which_Cirrus()   */

int  Which_Cirrus(void)
  {
  unsigned int result,value,value2,chiptype=NO_ID_FOUND;

  outp (0x3c4,6);   // Check for change in 5402 extended
register lock
  outp (0x3c5,0x12);
  result = inp (0x3c5);   // See if 12h is there and not 0Fh
  if (result == 0x12) {
        chiptype = Cirrus5402;
        outp (0x3c4,6);   // try to unlock 5422 extended registers
        outp (0x3c5,0x12);
        outp (0x3d4,0x27);
        value = inp (0x3d5);   value = value >> 2;
        switch(value) {
                case 0x22: chiptype = Cirrus5420; break;
                case 0x23: chiptype = Cirrus5422; break;
                case 0x25: chiptype = Cirrus5424; break;
                case 0x24: chiptype = Cirrus5426; break;
                case 0x26: chiptype = Cirrus5428; break;
                case 0xA4: chiptype = Cirrus543x; break;
                case 0xB0: chiptype = Cirrus545x; break;
                }
        }
    else chiptype = Cirrus5401;
  return(chiptype);
  }
```

21.14 ENABLING THE EXTENDED REGISTERS

The Unlock ALL Extensions Register at Index 6 of 3C5 contains a lock pattern in Bits 4, 2, 1, and 0. The Extension Registers will be enabled for read and write operations if this field is loaded with xxx1x010. It will be read as 00010010. The Extension Registers will be locked if any other pattern is written to this register. In this case, it will be read as 00001111. This is summarized next:

To Unlock Extension Registers   Write 12h to SR2. Read as 12h.

To Lock Extension Registers   Write any value but 12h to SR2.
                                       Read as 0Fh.

The Cirrus Logic family requires you to unprotect the extended registers, and in our case, enable the single bank swapping mechanism before usage. This is conveniently done after a mode set. The extensions are turned on or off as shown in Listings 21.3 and 21.4.

LISTING 21.3 Enabling the Cirrus Extended Registers

```
Extensions_On_Cir macro
        mov     dx,3c4h         ;select extended Register SR6
        mov     ax,1206h        ;send 12h xxx1x010 to 06 index
        out     dx,ax
endm
```

LISTING 21.4 Disable Cirrus Extensions Macro

```
Extensions_Off_Cir macro
        mov     dx,3c4h         ;select extended Register SR6
        mov     ax,0006h        ;send 00 to 06 index
        out     dx,ax
endm
```

21.15 ACCESSING THE CIRRUS DISPLAY MEMORY

The Cirrus logic display memory is accessed in a paged VGA mode or by using linear adddressing.

21.15.1 Memory Addressing

The Cirrus chips allow memory to be organized as VGA memory-mapped memory residing at A0000h–BFFFFh or as linear memory residing in upper memory. The registers that affect the memory mapping are shown in Table 21.23. Remember that the words segment, page, or offset often mean the same thing.

TABLE 21.23   Registers that Affect Memory Mapping

Name	Register	Bit	Value	Function
GRB	Graphics Controller Mode Extension	0	0	Single Page
GRB	Graphics Controller Mode Extension	0	1	Dual Page
GRB	Graphics Controller Mode Extension	5	0	4 Kbyte Granularity
GRB	Graphics Controller Mode Extension	5	1	16 Kbyte Granularity
SR7	Extended Sequencer Mode Extension	7–4	15–1	Linear Addressing
SR7	Extended Sequencer Mode Extension	0	0	VGA Mapping
GR9	Offset Register 0	7–0	0–255	Segment Page
GRA	Offset Register 1	7–0	0–255	Segment Page

21.15.2   Single Page VGA Memory Map

If the display memory is mapped as VGA memory, the host can access the memory through either a single register (single-page) or two registers (dual-page) register. If a single register is used, a 64 Kbyte window can be aligned in the display memory space using the GR9 Offset Register 0.

21.15.3   1-Mbyte Memory

The eight bits from this register are added to the address bits 15–12 (19–16 are 0) of the host address creating a 20-bit address. Since the lower twelve bits of the address are not modified, the page can start on a 4 Kbyte boundary (granularity).

21.15.4   2-Mbyte Memory

The eight bits from this register are added to the address bits 15–14 (19–16 are 0) of the host address creating a 21-bit address. Since the lower fourteen bits of the address are not modified, the page can start on a 16 Kbyte boundary (granularity).

21.15.5   Dual-Page

If two mapping registers are desired, the host memory address is split into two sections, one from A0000h–A7FFFh and the second from A8000h–AFFFFh. The Offset Register 0 is used for all addresses in the lower 32 Kbyte range; the Offset Register 1 is used for all addresses in the upper 32-Kbyte range. The eight bits from this register are added to the address bits 15–12 (19–16 are 0) of the host address creating a 20-bit address. Since the lower twelve bits of the address are not modified, the page can start on a 4-Kbyte boundary (granularity).

21.15.6   Linear Addressing

Linear addressing is accessed through the SR7: Extended Sequencer Mode Register. The Memory Select field in Bits 7–4 enable linear addressing. Standard VGA addressing at A0000h–BFFFFh is the default condition and is enabled by writing a 0 to this field. Linear addressing is enabled by writing any value other than 0 to this register. In this case, a 1-Mbyte linear window is enabled. The memory will respond to any memory address from the host whose address bits 23:20 match the Memory Segment field. For example, programming this field to a 3 will cause the 1-Mbyte address to reside between 300000h–3FFFFFh in the host address space.

21.15.7   Accessing Display Memory

Display memory can be accessed through the Offset Register 0 at GR9 and Offset Register 1 at GRA. It uses a 4-Kbyte granularity. The contents of this 8-bit field are added to address bits 19:12 when Extension Registers GRB bit 0 is programmed to a 0. If GRB bit 0 is programmed to a 1, bits 6:0 are added to address bits 20:14 to provide access to 2 Mbytes of memory with a 16-Kbyte granularity. Offset Register 0 is enabled when GRB bit 0 is programmed to a 0 and SA15=0. Offset Register 1 is enabled when GRB bit 0 is programmed to a 1 and SA15=1.

The display memory can be banked switched as single or dual banks. Single bank switching is accomplished when the Set_Single_Cir macro is called in Listing 21.5. Dual bank switching is accomplished when the Set_Dual_Cir macro is called in Listing 21.6.

Single Bank switching has all memory accesses to the 64-Kbyte memory A0000h–AFFFFh to use the Extension Offset Register 0 for its bank extended addresses. Dual bank switching has all accesses to the 32-Kbyte memory A0000h–A7FFFh go through Extension Offset Register 0 and all accesses to the 32-Kbyte memory A8000h–AFFFFh go through Extension Offset Register 1.

LISTING 21.5 Enable Single Bank Switching

```
Set_Single_Cir macro
        mov     dx,3ceh    ;select GRB extension
        mov     al,0bh ;GRB
        out     dx,al
        inc     dx
        in      al,dx  ;read data
        and     al,0feh   ;apply mask to set GRB[0]=0
        out     dx,al  ;write port with new value
endm
```

LISTING 21.6 Enable Dual Bank Switching

```
Set_Dual_Cir macro
        mov     dx,3ceh     ;select GRB extension
        mov     al,0bh ;GRB
        out     dx,al
        inc     dx
        in      al,dx  ;read data
        or      al,01h ;apply mask to set GRB[0]=1
        out     dx,al  ;write port with new value
endm
```

Once set up for single bank switching, the code in Listing 21.7 can be used. In this case, a granularity of 64 Kbytes is desired so the bank value, entered in bl, is multiplied by 16 before being loaded into GR09.

LISTING 21.7 Writing a Single Bank

```
; enter with bank value (64Kbyte granularity) in bl register
Set_Bank_Cir_2 macro
        mov     dx,3ceh         ;access GR09 extension
        mov     al,09h
        shl     bl,1
        shl     bl,1
        shl     bl,1      ;* 16
        shl     bl,1      ;move to 64K granularity
        mov     ah,bl     ;get bank
        out     dx,ax     ;output bank (0-255)
endm
```

21.16 CONTROLLING THE CRT ADDRESS GENERATION

The display start address is controlled by the extended address bits 18, 17 and 16 as found in the CR1B Register. This is accomplished by the code in Listing 21.8.

LISTING 21.8 Load the Display Start Address

```
; Input Parameters:
;       bl           top two bits of address
; Calling Protocol:
;       Load_Start_Top_Cir_2
Load_Start_Top_Cir_2

; first get the 0-7 value in bits 0-2 of the input bl into
; bits 3,2,0
        mov     bh,bl      ;save for now
        and     bh,01h     ;only save bit 0

        shl     bl         ;put start bits 2-1 into bit positions 3-2
        and     bl,0ch     ;only keep bits 3-2
        or      bl,bh      ;put back in bit 0

        mov     dx,3ceh    ;access CR1B extended display control
        mov     al,1Bh
        out     dx,al      ;output index to CR1B
        inc     dx
        in      al,dx      ;get current value
        and     al,0f2h    ;0 bits 3,2,0 (old extended start address)
        or      al,bl      ;put in new bits 3,2,0 for new extended
                           ;start address
        out     dx,al      ;output
endm
```

21.17 GRAPHICS CURSOR

The hardware cursor on the 542x family supports the 4-, 8-, 15-, and 16-bit-per-pixel modes. The 543x and 545x series supports the hardware cursor in the 24-bit-per-pixel mode as well. The graphics cursor is positioned by the Graphics Cursor X and Graphics Cursor Y Registers. These are 8-bit registers providing address bits 10–3. Bits 7–5 of the index are used as the lower-order three bits. The index of this register is 10h for the Cursor X and 11 for the Cursor Y. One can index these registers at 10, 30, 50, 70, 90, B0, D0, and F0 or at 11, 31, 51, 71, 91, B1, D1, and F1. These correspond to address bits 0, 1, 2, 3, 4, 5, 6, and 7.

The Graphics Cursor Attributes Register controls the graphics cursor. Setting bit 0 to a 1 enables the cursor displaying it on-screen. Bit 1 allows access to the DAC Extended Colors Register providing two additional colors for the

TABLE 21.24 Graphics Cursor Related Registers

Name	Register	Bit	Value	Function
SR12	Graphics Cursor Attributes	0	1	Enable Cursor
SR12	Graphics Cursor Attributes	1	1	Access Graphics DAC
SR12	Graphics Cursor Attributes	2	0	32-by-32 pattern
SR12	Graphics Cursor Attributes	2	1	64-by-64 pattern
SR13	Graphics Cursor Pattern Address	5–0	0–63	Pattern Offset
SR10...F0	Graphics Cursor X Position (& index)	7–5:7–0	0–2047	X Position
SR11...F1	Graphics Cursor Y Position (& index)	7–5:7–0	0–2047	Y Position

foreground and background of the cursor. If set to a 1, DAC entries 256 (background) and 257 (foreground) are accessible at locations x0h and xFh. Note that bit 1 of this register provides index 258 accessed at x2h for an additional border color. Bit 2 selects the cursor size. A 0 selects a 32-by-32 pixel pattern; a 1 selects a 64-by-64 pattern.

The bits 5–0 of the Graphics Cursor Pattern Address Offset Register select one of 64 possible 32-by-32 cursor patterns from memory. If a 64-by-64 cursor is used, bits 3–0 select one of sixteen possible 64-by-64 cursor patterns from memory. Each is located at an 8 Kbyte-granularity from the highest available display address. The registers that affect the hardware cursor are shown in Table 21.24.

21.17.1 Cursor Pattern

The cursor pattern is in a 2-bit-per-pixel format where the two bits determine the color of the pixel as shown in Table 21.25.

TABLE 21.25 Cursor Planes

Plane 0	Plane 1	Display State
0	0	Transparent
0	1	Inverted VGA Display Data
1	0	Cursor Color 0
1	1	Cursor Color 1

Cursor Color 0 and Cursor Color 1 are supplied by the palette DAC extra LUT locations 00h and FFh as described above. This allows the hardware cursor colors to be independent of the palette DAC table 0 to 255 locations.

21.17.2   Hardware Cursor Data

The Hardware Cursor Data is stored in the upper 16 Kbytes of display memory. This can also be considered to be the upper 4 Kbytes of each logical memory plane. Based on the cursor size selected, the number of cursor patterns that can be loaded into display memory varies. For a 32-by-32 cursor, 64 cursors can be present; for a 64-by-64 cursor, only 16 can be co-resident.

21.17.3   Cursor Position

The cursor position is controlled by programming the Graphics Cursor X and Y Position Registers. The 11-bit cursor address is in bits 15–5 of the 16-bit word. The lower bits 7–5 of the word are actually the index value of the register, in this case 10h for X and 11h for Y.

21.18   MEMORY MAPPED I/O

The 5489, the 543x, and the 545x family of controllers allow the BitBlt Registers to be memory mapped. The BLT control registers can be mapped into memory locations. This can be up to four times faster than using I/O accesses, particularly when multiple registers must be changed at once. The register address is implied in the address of the write operation rather than as an index value.

Memory-mapped I/O is enabled when SR17 bit 2 is programmed to a 1. In addition GR6, bits 3 and 2 must be programmed to a 1 and 1 respectively. If linear addressing is **not** programmed, the window into display memory is 64 Kbyte from A0000–AFFFF.

If SR17 bit 6 is programmed to a 0, a block of 256 bytes of memory is reserved beginning at B8000. If SR17 bit 6 is programmed to a 1 and linear addressing is enabled, a 256-byte block of memory is reserved at the end of the 2-Mbyte linear address space, regardless of the amount of DRAM actually installed.

Memory-mapped I/O can be done using BYTE, WORD, or DWORD cycles. Memory-mapped reads are allowed only for the BLT Status Registers at GR31. The address offsets of the memory-mapped registers are shown in Table 21.26. Each group of four registers, for example offset 0, 1, 2, and 3, represent one double word. Thus the 543x and 545x processors can load the 32-bit foreground and 32-bit background values in two DWORD bus transfers. The memory-mapped I/O registers are provided in Table 21.26.

TABLE 21.26   Memory Mapped I/O Registers

Offset	Register	Description	Chips
0	GR0	Write Mode 5/Background Low (Byte 0)	
1	GR10	Background Color High (Byte 1)	
2	GR12	Background Color Byte 2	543x, 545x
3	GR14	Background Color Byte 3	543x, 545x
4	GR1	Write Mode 4.5/Foreground Low (Byte 0)	
5	GR11	Foreground Color High (Byte 1)	
6	GR13	Foreground Color Byte 2	543x, 545x
7	GR15	Foreground Color Byte 3	543x, 545x
8	GR20	Blt Width Low	
9	GR21	Blt Width High	
A	GR22	Blt Height Low	
B	GR23	Blt Height High	
C	GR24	Blt Destination Pitch Low	
D	GR25	Blt Destination Pitch High	
E	GR26	Blt Source Pitch Low	
F	GR27	Blt Source Pitch High	
10	GR28	Blt Destination Address Low	
11	GR29	Blt Destination Address Mid	
12	GR2A	Blt Destination Address High	
13	GR2B	Reserved	
14	GR2C	Blt Source Address Low	
15	GR2D	Blt Source Address Mid	
16	GR2E	Blt Source Address High	
17	GR2F	Blt Destination Write Mask	
18	GR30	Blt Mode	
19		Reserved	
1A	GR32	Blt Raster Op	
24	GR40	Linedraw Start X byte 0	545x
25	GR41	Linedraw Start X byte 1	545x
26	GR42	Linedraw Start Y byte 0	545x
27	GR43	Linedraw Start Y byte 1	545x
28	GR44	Linedraw End X byte 0	545x
29	GR45	Linedraw End X byte 1	545x
2A	GR46	Linedraw End Y byte 0	545x
2B	GR47	Linedraw End Y byte 1	545x
2C	GR50	Linedraw Line style Increment	545x
2D	GR51	Linedraw Line Style Rollover	545x

(continued)

TABLE 21.26 *(cont.)*

Offset	Register	Description	Chips
2E	GR52	Linedraw Line Style Mask	545x
2F	GR53	Linedraw Line Style Accumulator	545x
30	GR54	Bresenham K1 byte 0	545x
31	GR55	Bresenham K1 byte 1	545x
33	GR56	Bresenham K3 byte 0	545x
33	GR57	Bresenham K3 byte 1	545x
34	GR58	Bresenham Error byte 0	545x
35	GR59	Bresenham Error byte 1	545x
36	GR5A	Bresenham Delta Major Byte 0	545x
37	GR5B	Bresenham Delta Major Byte 1	545x
38	GR5C	Bresenham Direction	545x
39	GR5D	Linedraw Mode	545x
40	GR31	Blt Start/Status (read/write)	

21.19 HARDWARE ASSISTED LINE DRAWS

The 545x series of processors is equipped with a line draw engine, which is programmed in a similar fashion as the BitBlt engine and draws both solid and styled zero-width lines. The application can specify either the end points of the line or the Bresenham parameters. There is no time penalty to the end-point lines, so typically this will be the method of preference. Any raster op can be used. The line draw registers are very straightforward. The end-point method requires the starting X and Y coordinates and the desired colors, styles, and masking.

21.19.1 Line Coordinates

The registers associated with the line coordinates are provided in Table 21.27. Either the end-point or the Bresenham Registers can be used.

It should be noted that when an end-point specification is active, the Start X and Start Y Registers will reflect the End X and End Y values at the end of a line. This is useful when drawing polylines. The BLT Width, the BLT Height, and the BLT Destination Start Address will be modified as an effect of executing a line draw.

21.19.2 Line Colors and Styles

Line colors include the foreground color for solid lines, or the foreground and background colors for styled lines. Styled lines include dotted, dashed,

TABLE 21.27 Memory-Mapped Line Coordinate Registers

Offset	Register	Description	Line Type
C	GR24	Blt Destination Pitch Low	both
D	GR25	Blt Destination Pitch High	both
18	GR30	Blt Mode	both
1A	GR32	Blt Raster Op	both
24	GR40	Linedraw Start X byte 0	end-point
25	GR41	Linedraw Start X byte 1	end-point
26	GR42	Linedraw Start Y byte 0	end-point
27	GR43	Linedraw Start Y byte 1	end-point
28	GR44	Linedraw End X byte 0	end-point
29	GR45	Linedraw End X byte 1	end-point
2A	GR46	Linedraw End Y byte 0	end-point
2B	GR47	Linedraw End Y byte 1	end-point
30	GR54	Bresenham K1 byte 0	Bresenham
31	GR55	Bresenham K1 byte 1	Bresenham
33	GR56	Bresenham K3 byte 0	Bresenham
33	GR57	Bresenham K3 byte 1	Bresenham
34	GR58	Bresenham Error byte 0	Bresenham
35	GR59	Bresenham Error byte 1	Bresenham
36	GR5A	Bresenham Delta Major Byte 0	Bresenham
37	GR5B	Bresenham Delta Major Byte 1	Bresenham
38	GR5C	Bresenham Direction	Bresenham
39	GR5D	Linedraw Mode	both

and dashed dotted lines. The registers that control the color are shown in Table 21.28.

21.19.3 Line Styles

The registers associated with line styles are shown in Table 21.29.

The Line Style Mask Register at GR52 contains the mask that actually defines whether the current pixel should be drawn in the foreground or background color (or not drawn at all). It contains eight bits.

The Line Draw Mode Register contains several fields as shown in Table 21.30.

In several cases, it is not desirable to draw the end point or starting point of a line. This is especially true when drawing polylines in an XOR mode. Bits 4 and 5 control whether the first or last points are drawn. The Direct Specification Mode field determines whether the Bresenham or the end-point method.

TABLE 21.28   Memory-Mapped Color and Line Style Registers

Offset	Register	Description
0	GR0	Write Mode 5/Background Low (Byte 0)
1	GR10	Background Color High (Byte 1)
2	GR12	Background Color Byte 2
3	GR14	Background Color Byte 3
4	GR1	Write Mode 4.5/Foreground Low (Byte 0)
5	GR11	Foreground Color High (Byte 1)
6	GR13	Foreground Color Byte 2
7	GR15	Foreground Color Byte 3
18	GR30	Blt Mode
1A	GR32	Blt Raster Op

TABLE 21.29   Memory-Mapped Line Style Registers

Offset	Register	Description
2C	GR50	Line draw Line Style Increment
2D	GR51	Line draw Line Style Rollover
2E	GR52	Line draw Line Style Mask
2F	GR53	Line draw Line Style Accumulator
39	GR5D	Line draw Mode

TABLE 21.30   Line Draw Mode Register

Bit	Name	Function
5	Draw Start Point	If 1, the first point is drawn.
4	Draw End Point	If 1, the last point is drawn.
3	Direct Specification Mode	0=Bresehnam; 1=End-Point.
2–0	Line Style	The bit in the Line Style Mask where the line begins.

The Line Style Index field specifies the bit in the Line Style Mask Register where the line begins. This is the phase of the Line Style.

If the bit in the Line Draw Mode Register, as pointed to by the Line Style Field, is a 1, then the pixel is drawn in the foreground color. If the bit in the Line Draw Mode Register, as pointed to by the Line Style Field, is a 0, the pixel

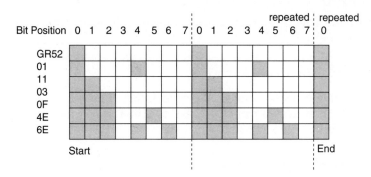

FIGURE 21.2 Simple Pixel Map Representation of GR52

will not be written (transparent) if bit 3 of the GR30 Register is a 1. It will be drawn in the background color if GR30 bit 3 is a 0.

The Line Style Field is not static. It can be modified directly by the line drawing engine. For example, it can be incremented after some number of pixels. This number might be less than 1, greater than one, not at all, or after every pixel. In a simple line, this would be incremented after every pixel. This is illustrated in Figure 21.2. If the Line Style Index is incremented for every pixel, the lines would be drawn with the patterns shown.

21.19.4 The Line Draw Numerator, Denominator, and Accumulator Registers

In two cases, it is not desirable to increment the pixel after every pixel. The first reason is when the elements in the line would be too small to see. For example, an on-off pattern of 1 pixel would be difficult to distinguish on a high-resolution monitor. In order to compensate for this effect, fractional incrementing is allowed. This elongates the elements to a readable format.

The second reason is that the style elements will appear to be elongated for lines drawn at an angle. A 45-degree line with an aspect ratio of 1:1 would show an on-off pattern of 1 pixel to be an on-off pattern of 1.4 pixels. Incrementing the index by a fractional number can compensate for this effect. For example, the 45-degree line would have the same apparent pattern to a horizontal or vertical line if it was incremented by 71/100 pixels as opposed to every pixel for the horizontal or vertical line.

The technique is as follows: After the pixel is drawn, the numerator is added to the accumulator. If the accumulator is greater than the denominator, then the index is incremented and the denominator is subtracted from the accumulator. If the accumulator is less than or equal to the denominator, no action is taken.

It is not intended for the numerator to be larger than the denominator. Setting them equal will have the same effect. The accumulator can be started at a value other than zero, but should never be greater than the denominator. Since the numbers in these three registers are unsigned integers, there will be truncation errors.

21.19.5   Solid Line Draw Example

A simple example draws a solid line of color Index 4, onto a 1024-by-768 8-bit-per-color mode. It is drawn from [512,384] to [1023,767]. The line is drawn following the steps in Table 21.31.

21.19.6   Dashed Line Example

A more complicated line example draws a dashed line of color Index 0fh, onto a 1024-by-768 8-bit-per-color mode. It is drawn from [0,767] to [1023,0]. The line style is sixteen pixels long (twelve are drawn and four are not), and is drawn following the steps in Table 21.32.

TABLE 21.31   Solid Line Draw

Registers [GRx]	Contents	Field	Description
0,10,12,14	x x x x	Background Color	Only for styled lines
1,11,13,15	04h x x x	Foreground Color	Index 4
24,25	1024	Destination Pitch	
30	00	Mode	8-bit-per-pixel color expansion
32	0Dh	RasterOp	Draw foreground color
40,41	512	Start X	
42,43	384	Start Y	
44,45	1023	End X	
46,47	767	End Y	
52	FFh	Line Style	Solid line
5D	30h	Line Draw Mode	Draw start and end, use end point
31	22h	Start/Status	Linedraw operation and start

TABLE 21.32 Dashed Line Draw

Registers [GRx]	Contents	Field	Description
0,10,12,14	x x x x	Background Color	Transparency will be enabled
1,11,13,15	04h x x x	Foreground Color	Index 0F
24,25	1024	Destination Pitch	
30	38h	Mode	32-bit pixel color expansion
32	0Dh	RasterOp	Draw foreground color
40,41	512	Start X	
42,43	384	Start Y	
44,45	1023	End X	
46,47	767	End Y	
50	01	Line Style Numerator	
51	02	Line Style Denominator	Fraction is 1/2
52	FFh	Line Style	Solid line
53	00	Line Style Accumulator	Start at 0
5D	32h	Line Draw Mode	Draw start and end, End-point, start at 2
31	22h	Start/Status	Linedraw operation and Start

Chapter 22

The Video7 Super VGA Chip Sets

22.1 INTRODUCTION TO THE VIDEO7/HEADLAND TECHNOLOGIES VGA

Video7/Headlands Technologies manufacturers the V7VGA Super VGA chip and uses it in several of its Super VGA cards. The V7VGA chip is very powerful and supports several special effects. Depending on the implementation, the chip can support resolutions up to 1024 by 768 in the 16-color mode and 800 by 600 in the 256-color modes. The chip can access up to 1 Mbyte of display memory. A wide variety of display modes are available. The chip can support DRAM or VRAM implementations

Following the V7VGA, Headland Technologies introduced the HT208 and HT209 processors. These added resolutions up to 1024 by 256 in 8-bit-per-color modes, up to 1 Mbyte of linear addressing, color expansion, and a hardware cursor. More recently, two graphics accelerator chips, the HT216 and HT216-32, were also introduced. These provide an ISA or VL bus interface.

22.1.1 V7VGA

Dual-bank selection is provided with separate Read and Write Bank Select Registers. In Version 3 of the V7VGA chip, the implementation was very poor. The bits of these read and write banks were spread across three registers. In addition, the Read and Write Bank Registers shared the same two low-order bits, so read and write windows had to be separated by 16 Kbytes. In Version 4 of the V7VGA chip, this was rectified by putting the read and write banks into separate registers with no bits in common. In addition, all four bits of each bank are contiguous.

Several extended BIOS functions are provided, which give information about the system, set up the extended display modes, and handle emulation modes.

The V7VGA is known for its special features, which include masked bit-plane writing, hardware cursor, foreground and background color control for drawing characters, and dithering.

22.1.2 HT208/HT209

The HT208 and HT209 are nearly identical from a programmer's perspective. These were used in the VGA 1024i and the VRAM II cards respectively. Because of their similarity, they will be referred to as the 208/209. The HT208 supports up to 1024 by 768 in 4-bit-per-color and up to 800 by 600 in 8-bit-per-color. The HT209 includes a 1024 by 768 8-bit-per-color mode. Both support a 132-by-28 text mode.

22.1.3 HT216

The 216 chip supports the 1024-by-768 8-bit-per-color mode, a 132-by-28 text mode, and a 1280-by-1024 4-bit-per-color mode. The graphics accelerator is highly integrated into the 216 providing the standard accelerator features of BitBlt, raster operations, masking, hardware cursor, and color expansion.

22.2 CONTROLLING THE VIDEO7 VGA

The Video7 VGA can be controlled by several registers, as listed in Table 22.1. Note that the port address 3x5 refers to either 3D5 or 3B5, depending on whether the system is configured in a color or monochrome mode. These chips are equipped with the industry standard 46E8 and 3C3 registers, which enable or disable the VGA and which allow the VGA to be put into a setup mode. The 46E8 register is non-standard in the sense that it also contains a ROM Bank Control field, RBC.

22.2.1 Enabling the VGA

If the VGA resides on a PC/AT adapter card, the register used to enable and disable the video adapter is the ROM Map and Video Subsystem Register, located at port address 46E8 hex. This register is illustrated in Figure 22.1.

If the VGA resides on the motherboard, presumably in a microchannel system, the register used to enable and disable the video adapter is the Video Subsystem Enable Register, located at port address 3C3 hex. This register is illustrated in Figure 22.2.

A third register for enabling and disabling the card is the Alternate Video Subsystem Enable Register, shown in Figure 22.3. This register is located at port address 102 hex.

The VGA can be enabled through the EN field of the Video Subsystem Enable Register, the Alternate Video Subsystem Enable Register, or the ROM

TABLE 22.1 Resetting and Enabling the Video7 Super VGAs

Function	Register Name	Port	Index	Bits	Value
Enable Video Microchannel	Video Subsystems Enable	3c3	0	1	
Disable Video Microchannel	Video Subsystems Enable	3c3	0	0	
Enable VGA PC/AT	ROM Map & Video Subsystem	46E8	3	1	
Disable VGA PC/AT	ROM Map & Video Subsystem	46E8	3	0	
Enable Video	Alt Video Subsystems Enable	102	0	1	
Disable Video	Alt Video Subsystems Enable	102	0	0	
Enter Setup Mode PC	ROM Map & Video Subsystem	46E8	4	1	
Exit Setup Mode PC	ROM Map & Video Subsystem	46E8	4	0	
Disable Video	Clear Vertical Display	3x5	30-3F	0	0,1
Enable Extensions	Extensions Control	3C5	6	—	EA
Disable Extensions	Extensions Control	3C5	6	—	AE

ROM Mapping and Video Subsystem Control

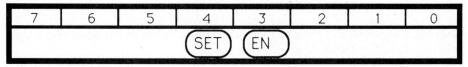

Port 46E8

Port 46E8 Write Only
Typically PC/AT

FIGURE 22.1 ROM Mapping and Video Subsystem Control Register. The video system can be enabled through the EN field. The setup mode can be entered through the SET field.

Video Subsystem Enable

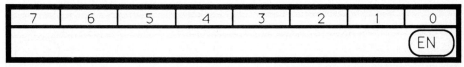

Port 3C3

Port 3C3 Read/Write
Typically PS/2

FIGURE 22.2 Video Subsystem Enable Register. The EN field enables the VGA card when the ARM field of the Compatibility Control Register is armed.

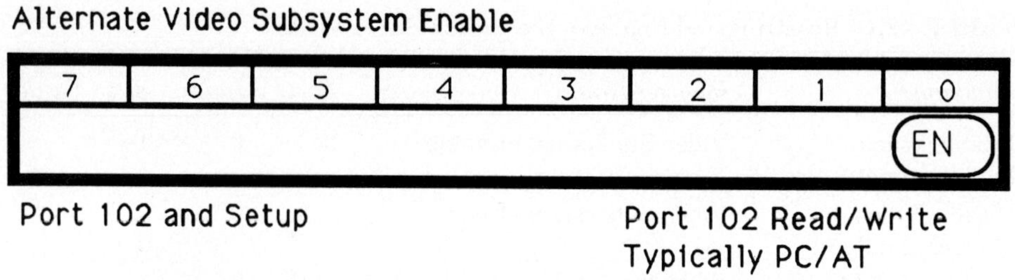

Alternate Video Subsystem Enable

7	6	5	4	3	2	1	0
							EN

Port 102 and Setup   Port 102 Read/Write
                                        Typically PC/AT

FIGURE 22.3 Alternate Video Subsystem Enable Register. The EN field enables the VGA card. The system must be in the setup mode for the host to access this register.

TABLE 22.2 Enabling the VGA

Register	Platform	Constraints
ROM Mapping and Video Subsystem	PC/AT	None
Video Subsystem Enable	PS/2	Must be armed
Alternate Video Subsystem Enable	PC/AT PS/2	Must be in Setup mode or armed

Mapping and Video Subsystem Register. The differences between these three fields are listed in Table 22.2.

The setup mode is enabled in the PC/AT systems by setting the SET field of the ROM Mapping and Video Subsystem Register to 1. Once in the setup mode, only ports 102 hex, 3C3 hex and 46E8 hex will be active.

Arming of the enable function occurs in the Arm field of the Compatibility Control Register. This register is illustrated in Figure 22.4. If the Arm field is set to 1, the enable field in either the Video Subsystem Enable Register or the

Compatibility Control

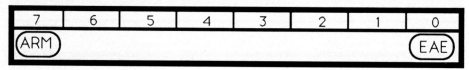

7	6	5	4	3	2	1	0
ARM							EAE

Index FC at Port 3C4   Port 3C5 Read/Write

FIGURE 22.4 Compatibility Control Register. The ARM field controls whether the VSE field of the Video Subsystem Enable register is armed. The EAE field controls the extended attribute function.

Extensions Control

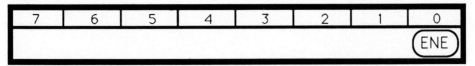

Index 06 of Port 3C4   Port 3C5 Read/Write

FIGURE 22.5 Extensions Control Register. The ENE field enables
access to the extension registers. The extension registers are located at
indexes 80–FF of the indexed register pair 3C4/3C5.

Alternate Video Subsystem Enable Register is active. If the Arm field is set to
0, these EN fields are inactive.

22.2.2   Enabling the Extended Registers

The Video7 extended registers must be enabled before access will be granted.
They are enabled through the Extensions Control Register. The Extensions
Control Register does not reflect the data written to it. It is a read-only register.
It has one field that returns the status of whether the extensions are enabled
or not. The ENE field returns a 0 if the extensions are disabled, or a 1 if the
extensions are enabled.

Writing a code of EA hex to this register enables extensions. Writing a code
of AE hex disables extensions. All other writes to this register are ignored. The
Extensions Control Register, displayed in Figure 22.5, is in fact a read-only
register; however, writing to this register does casue extensions to be enabled
or disabled.

The extensions can be enabled or disabled through the macros provided in
Listings 22.1a and 22.1b.

LISTING 22.1a   Enable Video 7 Extensions Macro

```
; Calling Protocol:
;       Extensions_On_Video7

Extensions_On_Video7 macro
        mov     dx,3c4h         ;address Extensions Control Register
        mov     al,6
        mov     ah,0eah         ; turn on extensions
        out     dx,ax
    endm
```

LISTING 22.1b Disable Video 7 Extensions Macro

```
; Calling Protocol:
;       Extensions_Off_Video7

Extensions_Off_Video7 macro
        mov     dx,3c4h         ;address Extensions Control Register
        mov     al,6
        mov     ah,0aeh         ; turn off extensions
        out     dx,ax
endm
```

22.3   INQUIRING FOR THE VIDEO7 SUPER VGA CONFIGURATION

The V7VGA has made identification very easy and thorough as shown in Table 22.3. Note that the port address 3x5 refers to either 3D5 or 3B5, depending on whether the system is configured in a color or monochrome mode. The microchannel ID value is available at the Card ID Microchannel High and Low Registers as per the PS/2 microchannel standard.

22.3.1   Chip Identification

The chip identification code is available in the Identification Register, as illustrated in Figure 22.6. A unique and clever technique was designed by Video7 to allow the programmer to identify the chip, regardless of the chip's mode.

TABLE 22.3   Determining Video 7 Display Status

Function	Register Name	Port	Index	Bits	Value
Card ID Microchannel	Microchannel ID High	101		7–0	0–255
Card ID Microchannel	Microchannel ID Low	100		7–0	0–255
Identification	Identification	3x5	1F	7–0	0–255
Chip Revision	Chip Revision	3C5	8E	7–0	0–255
Bus Status	16–bit Interface	3C5	FF	3	0,1
Copy the switches	Switch Strobe	3C5	EA	—	—
Location of switches	Switch Readback	3C5	F7	7–0	0–255
Attribute Index	Graphics Controller Data	3x5	24	4–0	0–31
Palette Source	Graphics Controller Data	3x5	24	5	0,1
Index or Display	Graphics Controller Data	3x5	24	7	0,1
Extensions Enabled	Extensions Control	3C5	6	0	1
Extensions Disabled	Extensions Control	3C5	6	0	0

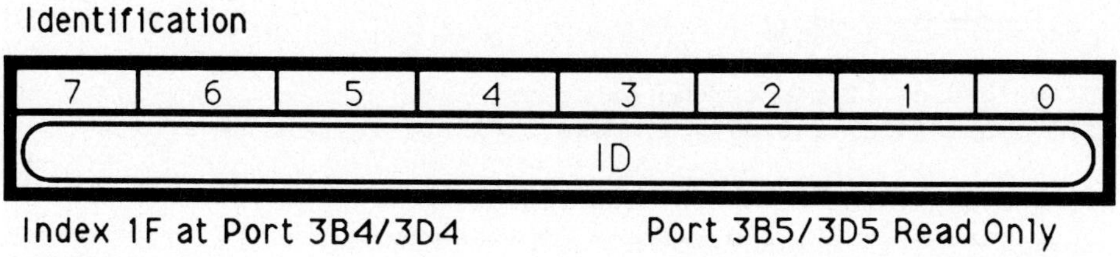

Identification

Index 1F at Port 3B4/3D4   Port 3B5/3D5 Read Only

FIGURE 22.6 Identification Register. The V7VGA is identified through the ID field. The ID field is EA hex XORed with the SAH field of the Start Address High Register.

TABLE 22.4 Exclusive OR operation

Input	Input	Output
0	0	0
0	1	1
1	0	1
1	1	0

The Start Address High Register, described in Section 10.4.13, and its associated CRTC Index Register are available in any configuration (that is, EGA, VGA, CGA, and MDA). This register can be read in any situation without causing damage to the current mode. The technique used to identify the V7VGA is to read the value of the Start Address High Register and to read in the Identification Register. The Identification Register contains an ID field, the result of the logical XOR function taking on the value in the Start Address High Register and the constant value EA. The XOR function is an exclusive-OR operation, as described in Table 22.4. If the inputs are different, the output is a 1. Similarly, if the inputs are the same, the output is a 0.

Suppose that the value in the Start Address High Register is 8F hex. If the 8F hex value is exclusive ORed with the constant EA hex from Figure 22.6, the result is 65 hex. This value should show up in the Identification Register.

The Video7 VGA can be identified through the code in Listing 22.2.

LISTING 22.2 Determine if the Chip Is a Video7

```
/* Output Parameters:
         1   card is a Video7      0   card is NOT a Video7
Calling Protocol:
  value = Is_It_Video7()   */

int Is_It_Video7(void)
{ unsigned char new_value,old_value,id;
  int base;
```

```
    Extended_On_Video7();

// determine if monochrome or color
if( (inp(0x3CC) & 0x01)==1) base = 0x3D0;  else base = 0x3B0;

// get old value of start high register
outp(base+4,0x0C); old_value = inp(base+5);

// change value
outp(base+5,0x55); // new_value = inp(base+5);

// read the ID register
outp(base+4,0x1f); id = inp(base+5);  // read the ID Register

// restore old value
outp(base+4,0x0C); outp(base+5,old_value);

    Extended_Off_Video7();

// ID = (Start_High XOR EA hex)
  if(id==(0x55^0xEA)) return(CHIP_FOUND);
        else   return(CHIP_NOT_FOUND);
}
```

22.3.2 Which Video7 VGA

The specific VGA chip can be determined through the chip-revision number in the CHIP field of the Chip Revision Register, as illustrated in Figure 22.7. The chip name can be accessed through the code in Listing 22.3.

Chip Revision

7	6	5	4	3	2	1	0
CHIP

Index 8E-8F at Port 3C4   Port 3C5   Read Only

FIGURE 22.7 Chip Revision Register. The chip revision level is returned in the CHIP field.

LISTING 22.3 Which Headland Video7 Chip

```
/* Output Parameters:
        identity       integer containing chip code
Calling Protocol:
  identity = Which_Video7()   */
```

```
int  Which_Video7(void)

{ int result;
 unsigned char value;

Extended_On_Video7();

 outp(0x3C4,0x8E);  // Version Register
 value = inp(0x3C5);  // read version

Extended_Off_Video7();

if((value<0xFF) && (value>=0x80)) result=Video7VEGA;// vega
if((value<0x7F) && (value>=0x70)) result=Video7V74; // V7-vga 4
if((value<0x4F) && (value>=0x40)) result=Headland208;// 208
if((value<0x5F) && (value>=0x50)) result=Headland209;// 209
if((value<0x6F) && (value>=0x60)) result=Headland216; // 216

return(result);
}
```

22.3.3 Inquiring through BIOS

Four extended BIOS functions are provided for assisting the programmer in acquiring information from the VGA. These are listed in Table 22.5 and are described in Section 22.7.

Information relevant to the active display mode can be acquired through the Get Information BIOS call as provided in Listing 22.4.

TABLE 22.5 Acquiring Information through Extended BIOS Functions

BIOS Function Name	Section
Inquire into Super Condition	20.7.1
Get Information	20.7.2
Get Mode/Screen Resolution	20.7.3
Get Video Memory Configuration	20.7.4

LISTING 22.4 Get Information About the Current Active Display Mode

```
; Output Parameters:
;       buf[0]    active display page
;       buf[1]    active display mode
;       buf[2]    number of character columns per row
;       buf[3]    number of rows per screen
```

(continued)

```
; Calling Protocol:
;   Get_Status_Video7(buf);

Get_Status_Video7 proc far USES ES DI, arg1:FAR PTR
        les     di,arg1     ;point to output array

        mov     ah,0fh      ;get current video state for page
        int     10h         ;interrupt 10
        xor     bl,bl
        mov     ax,bx
        stosw               ;store active page in BUF[0]

        mov     ax,6f04h    ;extended G2 function
        int     10h         ;to get status
        xor     ah,ah
        stosw               ; store mode in BUF[1]
        mov     ax,bx       ;store horizontal columns in BUF[2]
        stosw
        mov     ax,cx       ; store vertical rows in BUF[3]
        stosw

        ret
Get_Status_Video7 endp
```

22.3.4   Inquiring About Attribute Status

One of the problematic areas when trying to acquire the state of the VGA has been the attribute controller. The Attribute Controller Index Register, described in Section 10.6.1, has several functions, one of which is that it acts as both the Index Register and the Data Register. An internal switch is toggled each time the register is written to, switching it from the Index Register to the Data Register. Reading the complete state of the VGA would require reading the state of this internal switch.

Graphics Controller Data Latch

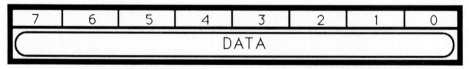

Index 22 at Port 3B4/3D4   Port 3B5/3D5 Read Only

FIGURE 22.8 Graphics Controller Data Latch Register. The DATA field contains one of the four bit- plane data latches. The latch is selected through the RMS field of the Read Map Select Register.

Video7 provides the ability to read this switch through the I/D field of the Graphics Controller Data Latch illustrated in Figure 22.8.

The INDEX field represents the index value, which points to one of the palette or attribute registers. The PAS field indicates whether the palette registers are pointing to the index or to the display memory. Both the INDEX and PAS fields mimic the same fields in the actual Attribute Controller Index Register, which can be read at Port 3C0 hex.

22.4   VIDEO7 DISPLAY MODES

The V7VGA is equipped with the Super VGA standard, 132-column alphanumeric modes, along with several 80- and 100-column modes. The Super VGA graphics modes include 2-, 4-, 16- and 256-color modes, spanning to 1024 by 768 in the 16-color mode, and 800 by 600 in the 256-color mode. Only the VRAM supports the 800-by-600 256-color mode. The VRAM is non-interlaced at the 1024-by-768 resolution. The 1024 is interlaced at the 1024-by-768 resolution. The alphanumeric and graphics modes are listed in Tables 22.6 and 22.7, respectively. It should be noted that these extended display modes cannot be entered through the standard AH=00 Set Mode BIOS call. Rather, a special function is provided to set the extended modes. The calling protocol of this BIOS call is presented in Section 22.7.4. An example of its usage is provided in Listing 22.5.

LISTING 22.5   Set a Video7 Extended Display Mode

```
; Function:
;  Set Video-7 extended display mode

; Input Parameters:
;       mode       desired extended display mode

; Calling Protocol:
;   Set_Mode_Video7(mode);

Set_Mode_Video7 proc far arg1
        mov    bx,arg1
        mov    ax,6f05h
        int    10h
        ret
Set_Mode_Video7 endp
```

The 208/209 and 216 chips support the text and graphics modes listed in Table 22.7.

TABLE 22.6 Video7 Alphanumerics Modes

Mode	Rows	Columns	Font	Resolution	Colors	Chip
40	43	80	8x8	640 by 344	2	V7VGA
41	25	132	8x14	1056 by 350	2	V7VGA
42	43	132	8x8	1056 by 344	2	V7VGA
43	60	80	8x8	640 by 480	16	V7VGA
44	60	100	8x8	800 by 480	16	V7VG
45	28	132	8x14	1056 by 392	16	V7VGA

TABLE 22.7 Display Modes

Mode	Resolution	Bits/color	Chip
60	752 by 410	4	
61	720 by 540	4	
62	800 by 600	4	
63	1024 by 768	1	
65	1024 by 768	4	
66	640 by 400	8	
67	640 by 480	8	
68	720 by 540	8	
69	800 by 600	8	
6A	1024 by 768	8	209,216
70	1280 by 1024	8	216

22.5   ACCESSING THE VIDEO7 DISPLAY MEMORY

Unfortunately, accessing the Video7 display memory in Version 3 is complex and time-consuming. The functions that control the process are based on several fields dispersed between several registers. In addition, certain differences exist, depending on whether DRAM or VRAM memory is installed. Enabling the high-resolution modes can be accomplished through mode sets, so the control functions do not really need to be considered. The registers involved in accessing the display memory are listed in Table 22.8.

Fortunately, Version 5 of the V7VGA chip rectifies this problem. A single field exists for the bank address. In addition, a dual-bank mode can be engaged, providing separate bank selection for read and write operations.

TABLE 22.8 Reading and Writing to Video 7 Display Memory

Function	Register Name	Port	Index	Bits	Value
Write Bank Start Address	1 Mbyte RAM Bank Select	3C5	F6	1–0	0–3
Read Bank Start Address	1 Mbyte RAM Bank Select	3C5	F6	3–2	0–3
Select Page	Page Select	3C5	F9	0	0,1
Enable Bank Selection	16–bit Interface Control	3C5	FF	4	0,1
Dual Bank Selection	Dual Bank Select (Ver 4)	3C5	E0	7	0,1
Single/Write Bank	Write Bank (Ver 4)	3C5	E8	7–4	0–15
Read Bank	Read Bank (Ver 4)	3C5	E9	7–4	0–15

22.5.1 Reading and Writing to the Display Memory

The Video7 display memory is accessed through the standard bank selection techniques. Up to 1 Mbyte of display memory can be accessed through a 64-Kbyte segment mapped into the host address space at A0000-AFFFF hex. In 512-Kbyte configurations, there are eight 64-Kbyte banks; in the 1-Mbyte configuration, there are sixteen such banks.

In either the 512-Kbyte or 1-Mbyte configurations, the field is split between three separate registers. This provides for slow bank switching. The three fields involved in this bank switching are listed in Table 22.9 and displayed in Figure 22.9.

22.5.2 V7VGA Versions 1-3

The least significant bit in the bank pointer, bit 0, is the PS field of the Page Select Register, shown in Figure 22.10. This field determines the 4-Kbyte granularity. Currently, no other fields share this register; consequently, no read/modify/write operation is required.

TABLE 22.9 Bank Selection

Bank Bit	Register	Field	
0	Page Select Register	PS	Figure 22.10
1	Miscellaneous Output	PB	Section 10.2.1
2-3 (Write)	Bank Select	WB	Figure 22.11
2-3 (Read)	Bank Select	RB	Figure 22.11

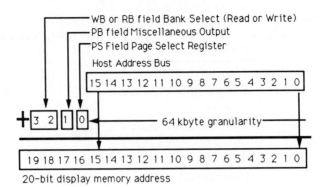

FIGURE 22.9 Creation of a 20-bit Address using Bank Selection.

The second, least significant bit in the bank pointer, bit 1, is in the PB field of the Miscellaneous Output Register. This register is described in Section 10.2.1 and the PB field resides in bit position 5. A read/modify/write operation will be required to preserve the other bit fields in this register.

Bits 0 and 1 are the same, whether a read or write operation is in effect. Thus, the display memory location must be separated by a minimum of 16 Kbytes.

The two most significant bits of the bank pointer, bits 3-2, reside in the Bank Select Register, illustrated in Figure 22.11. Two bank selection fields are provided in this register. The WB field of this register contains the two-bit fields for write operations, and the RB field contains the two-bit fields for the read operations. Writing to either of these fields requires read/modify/write operations to preserve the other fields.

The values loaded into the respective fields in the Bank Select Register are always used to access the display memory when 1 megabit, DRAM memory chips are used. The host read, host write, and CRTC addresses use these fields. The BE field of the 16-bit Interface Register typically enables bank selection; however, it has no effect when DRAM memory is used.

Page Select

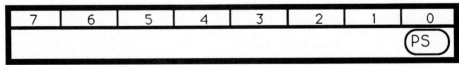

Index F9 at Port 3C4   Port 3C5 Read/Write

FIGURE 22.10 Page Select Register. The PS field controls the linear address mapping of the 256-color high-resolution modes into a single 64-Kbyte address space.

Bank Select

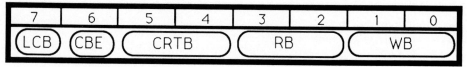

Index F6 at Port 3C4   Port 3C5 Read/Write

FIGURE 22.11 Bank Select Register. The WB field controls the Write Bank. The RB field controls the Read Bank and the CRTB controls the CRT bank. The WRP field controls bank wrap-around. The LCB field contains the enable bit allowing bank control of the line compare function.

When the VGA is equipped with VRAM, the bank selection process is activated when the BE field of the 16-bit Interface Register is set to 1. If the BE field is set to 0, the fields in the Bank Register have no effect. If the BE field is 0, up to four virtual VGA screens can be loaded in the 1 Mbyte of address space.

Loading the read and write banks is accomplished differently for the 16-color and 256-color modes. The Read Bank and write bank fields for the 16-color modes are loaded through the code in Listings 22.6 and 22.7, respectively.

LISTING 22.6 Setting up the Write Bank for 16-color Mode for V7VGA

```
; input parameters:
;       bl write bank number

Set_Wr_Bank_16_Video7 macro
;       set up the Bank Select Register bits 0  with address
;       bits 17 non-destructively
        mov     dx,3c4h    ;access Bank Select Register
        mov     al,0f6h
        out     dx,al      ;index Bank Select Register
        inc     dx
        in      al,dx      ;get its current value

;       put bits 17 into bit 0 of Bank Select Register
        and     al,0fch    ;zero bit 0-1
        and     bl,1       ;only want bit 0 of bank
        or      al,bl
        out     dx,al      ;load Bank Select Register
        ret
endm
```

LISTING 22.7 Setting up the Read Bank for 16-color Mode for V7VGA

```
; input parameters:
;       bl read bank number

Set_Rd_Bank_16_Video7 macro
;       set up the Bank Select Register bits 0  with address
;       bits 17 non-destructively
        mov    dx,3c4h   ;access Bank Select Register
        mov    al,0f6h
        out    dx,al     ;index Bank Select Register
        inc    dx
        in     al,dx     ;get its current value

;       put bits 17 into bit 2 of Bank Select Register
        and    al,0f3h   ;zero bit 3-2
        and    bl,1      ;only want bits 1
        shl    bl,1
        shl    bl,1      ;put into bit position 2
        or     al,bl
        out    dx,al     ;load Bank Select Register
        ret
endm
```

The Read Bank and Write Bank fields for the 256-color modes are loaded through the code in Listings 22.8 and 22.9 respectively.

LISTING 22.8 Setting up the Write Bank for 256-color Mode for V7VGA

```
; input parmaeters:
;       bl write bank number

Set_Wr_Bank_256_Video7 macro
;       set up the Extended Page Select Register for bit 16
        mov    dx,3c4h   ;bank bit 0
        mov    ah,bl
        and    ah,1      ;only concerned with bit 16 (bank bit 0)
        mov    al,0f9h   ;index Extended Page Select
        out    dx,ax     ;load bit 0

;       set up the Miscellaneous Output  Register with bit 21.
;       Load it into bit 5 without disrupting other values
        mov    ah,bl     ;bank bit 1
        and    ah,2      ;bit 1 contains bit 17
        shl    ah,1      ;bit 2 "   "   "
        shl    ah,1      ;bit 3 "   "   "
        shl    ah,1      ;bit 4 "   "   "
```

```
        shl    ah,1        ;bit 5 "   "   "
        mov    dx,3cch     ;address Miscellaneous Register
        in     al,dx       ;read value
        and    al,0dfh     ;zero bit 5
        mov    dx,3c2h     ;address Miscellaneous Register
        or     al,ah       ;load the page bit (bit 5)
        out    dx,al       ;output page bit 17

;       set up the Bank Select Register bits 0 and 1 with
;       address bits 18
;       and 19 non-destructively
        mov    dx,3c4h     ;access Bank Select Register
        mov    al,0f6h
        out    dx,al       ;index Bank Select Register
        inc    dx
        in     al,dx       ;get its current value

;       put bits 19-18 into bits 1-0 of Bank Select Register
        mov    ah,al
        and    ah,0fch     ;zero bits 1-0
        shr    bl,1        ;put address bits 19-18 into bits 1-0
        shr    bl,1
        and    bl,3        ;only want bits 1-0
        or     ah,bl
        mov    al,ah
        out    dx,al       ;load Bank Select Register
        ret
endm
```

LISTING 22.9 **Setting up the Read Bank for 256-color Mode for V7VGA**

```
; input parameters:
;       bl read bank number

Set_Rd_Bank_256_Video7 macro
;       set up the Extended Page Select Register for bit 16
        mov    dx,3c4h     ;bank bit 0
        mov    ah,bl
        and    ah,1        ;only concerned with bit 16 (bank bit 0)
        mov    al,0f9h     ;index Extended Page Select
        out    dx,ax       ;load bit 0

;       set up the Miscellaneous Output  Register with bit 21.
;       Load it into bit 5 without disrupting other values
        mov    ah,bl       ;bank bit 1
        and    ah,2        ;bit 1 contains bit 17
        shl    ah,1        ;bit 2 "   "   "
```

(continued)

```
        shl    ah,1       ;bit 3 "    "    "
        shl    ah,1       ;bit 4 "    "    "
        shl    ah,1       ;bit 5 "    "    "
        mov    dx,3cch    ;address Miscellaneous Register
        in     al,dx      ;read value
        and    al,0dfh    ;zero bit 5
        mov    dx,3c2h    ;address Miscellaneous Register
        or     al,ah      ;load the page bit (bit 5)
        out    dx,al      ;output page bit 17

;       set up the Bank Select Register bits 0 and 1 with
;       address bits 18
;       and 19 non-destructively
        mov    dx,3c4h    ;access Bank Select Register
        mov    al,0f6h
        out    dx,al      ;index Bank Select Register
        inc    dx
        in     al,dx      ;get its current value

;       put bits 19-18 into bits 3-2 of Bank Select Register
        and    al,0f3h    ;zero bits 3-2
        and    bl,0ch     ;only want bits 3-2
        or     al,bl
        out    dx,al      ;load Bank Select Register
        ret
endm
```

22.5.3   V7VGA Version 4

The default condition for the Version 4 V7VGA chip is the single-bank mode. In the single-bank mode the Single/Write Bank Register, shown in Figure 22.12, provides the bank address. In the dual-bank mode, the Read Bank Register, shown in Figure 22.13, provides the bank address. The BANK field in each register is four bits wide, providing a 16-Kbyte granularity.

Single/Write Bank Register (Version 5+)

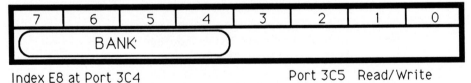

Index E8 at Port 3C4   Port 3C5   Read/Write

FIGURE 22.12   Single/Write Bank Register. The BANK field contains the four-bit bank value providing 16-Kbyte granularity.

Read Bank Register (Version 4+)

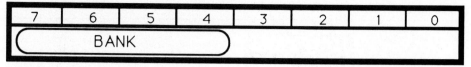

Index E8 at Port 3C4   Port 3C5   Read/Write

FIGURE 22.13 Read Bank Register. The BANK field contains the 4-bit bank value providing 16-Kbyte granularity for read operations when in split-bank mode.

Miscellaneous Control Register (Version 4+)

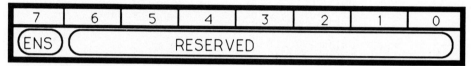

Index E8 at Port 3C4   Port 3C5   Read/Write

FIGURE 22.14 Miscellaneous Control Register. The ENS field enables split-bank mode.

The single- or dual-bank mode, is selected by the ENS field of the Miscellaneous Control Register shown in Figure 22.14. If the ENS field is set to 1, the split-bank mode is enabled. If it is set to 0, the single-bank mode is selected.

The Read Bank and Write Bank fields for the Version 4 V7VGA chip and above are loaded through the code in Listings 22.10 and 22.11, respectively.

LISTING 22.10 Setting up the Write Bank for 16- or 256-color Mode for V7VGA-4 208,209,216

```
; input parameters:
;       bl      write bank number

Set_Wr_Bank_Video7_4 macro
        mov     ah,bl
        shl     ah,1            ;put bank into bits 7-4
        shl     ah,1
        shl     ah,1
        shl     ah,1
        mov     al,0e8h         ;point to write bank register
        mov     dx,3c4h         ;in extended registers
        out     dx,ax
        ret
endm
```

LISTING 22.11 Setting up the Read Bank for 16- or 256-color Mode for V7VGA-4
208,209,216

```
; input parameters:
;       bl      read bank number

Set_Rd_Bank_Video7_4 macro
        mov     ah,bl
        shl     ah,1        ;put bank into bits 7-4
        shl     ah,1
        shl     ah,1
        shl     ah,1
        mov     al,0e9h     ;point to read bank register
        mov     dx,3c4h     ;in extended registers
        out     dx,ax
        ret
endm
```

The single- or dual-bank modes for the Version 4 V7VGA chip are enabled
through the code in Listings 22.12a and 22.12b, respectively.

LISTING 22.12a Enable Dual Bank Mode (Version 4)

```
;   Calling Protocol:
;       Enable_Dual_Bank_Video7_V7VGA_4();

Enable_Dual_Bank_Video7_V7VGA_4   proc far
        Extensions_On_Video7
        mov     dx,3c4h    ;point to extension registers
        mov     al,0e0h    ;point to Miscellaneous Control
        out     dx,al
        inc     dx
        in      al,dx      ;don't disturb other bits

        or      al,80h     ;set bit 7=1
        out     dx,al
        Extensions_Off_Video7
        ret
Enable_Dual_Bank_Video7_V7VGA_4   endp
```

LISTING 22.12b Enable Single Bank Mode (Version 4)

```
;   Calling Protocol:
;       Enable_Single_Bank_Video7_V7VGA_4();

Enable_Single_Bank_Video7_V7VGA_4   proc far
        Extensions_On_Video7
```

```
        mov    dx,3c4h       ;point to extension registers
        mov    al,0e0h       ;point to Miscellaneous Control
        out    dx,al
        inc    dx
        in     al,dx        ;don't disturb other bits

        and    al,7fh       ;set bit 7=0
        out    dx,al
        Extensions_Off_Video7
        ret
   Enable_Single_Bank_Video7_V7VGA_4    endp
```

22.6 CONTROLLING THE CRT ADDRESS GENERATION

The CRT address generation handles the transferring of display memory to the monitor. The register fields associated with the CRT address generation are listed in Table 22.10.

22.6.1 CRT Display and Cursor Address Generation

When enabled, the CRTB field of the Bank Select Register contains the upper order address bits, bits 17 and 16, for the CRT address generation. While reading and writing to single Mbytes of display memory requires twenty bits, only eighteen bits are required for displaying the data on the screen. The lower-order sixteen bits are found in the Start Address High and Low Registers and in the Cursor Location High and Low Registers. These registers are described in Sections 10.4.13 through 10.4.21. The upper-order two bits, bits 17 and 16, are contained in the CRTB field of the Bank Select Register. The selection of bits 17 and 16 is illustrated in Figure 22.15.

Enabling the CRTB field and bank selection is accomplished through the CBE and LCB fields, which enable the bank selection process. Wraparound occurs when these fields are disabled and a maximum of 256 Kbytes of display memory is displayed.

TABLE 22.10 Video 7 Display Address Control

Function	Register Name	Field	Port	Index	Bits	Value
Enable Bank Selection	16-bit Interface	BE	3C5	FF	4	1
Disable Bank Selection	16-bit Interface	BE	3C5	FF	4	0
Write Bank Start Address	Bank Select	CRTB	3c5	F6	5–4	0–3
Bank Wrap Around	Bank Select	CBE	3c5	F6	6	1
Cross Bank Boundaries	Bank Select	CBE	3c5	F6	6	0
Line Compare Wrap	Bank Select	LCB	3c5	F6	7	1
Line Compare Cross Banks	Bank Select	LCB	3c5	F6	7	0

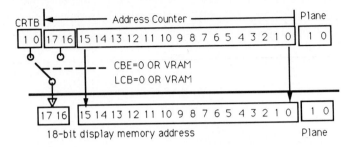

FIGURE 22.15   Creation of an 18-bit CRT address. If VRAM is present, CRTB is always selected. If DRAM is present, the CBE and LCB fields control whether CRTB or the Address Counter is selected for bits 17–16. The Address Counter always is selected for bits 15–0.

The Counter Bank Enable field, CBE, determines where bits 16 and 17 of the generated display address, used during CRT operations, come from. It can either come from the memory address counter or from the bank select field, CRTB in this register.

If the CBE field is set to 1, the bank memory addressing mode is disabled and the address bits 17 and 16 are generated by the memory address counter. In this case, wraparound occurs and the bank pointer has no effect. If the CBE field is set to 0, the bank address bits 17 and 16 are generated by the CRTB field of this register. In this case, bank selection is engaged.

Fonts cannot cross bank boundaries; thus, the bank select field, CRTB, associated with CRT operations should always be engaged. The address counter will simply wraparound at 64 Kbytes. The CBE field should be set to 0 in text modes so that the font and character/attribute pairs are guaranteed to come from the same bank.

The LCB field similarly enables the bank registers for the line compare function. If the LCB field is set to 0, the bank memory addressing mode is enabled. Thus, address bits 16 and 17 will be generated by the CRTB field. When the scan line number is reached and the split screen needs to be refreshed, the top line displayed will come from the top of the current bank, as indicated in the CRTB field.

If the LCB field is set to 1, the bank pointers have no effect and the split screen function displays data from the top of display memory. In this case, the address bits 16 and 17 are reset to 0.

22.6.2   Display Starting Address

The display starting address can be controlled through the code in Listing 22.13.

LISTING 22.13 Load the Display Start Address for the Video7

```
; Input Parameters:
;      top         top two bits of address
; Calling Protocol:
;      Load_Start_Top_Video7

Load_Start_Top_Video7     proc far top:BYTE

        Extensions_On_Video7    ;turn on extensions
        mov     bl,top
        mov     dx,3c4h
        mov     al,0f6h           ;Bank Select Register
        out     dx,al

;       read current value
        inc     dx
        in      al,dx      ;get value
        and     al,0cfh    ;zero out start address 17-16 bit 5-4

;       or in new start address
        and     bl,03h     ;only want 2 bits
        mov     cx,4
        shl     bl,cl      ;shift left 4 to get bit 5-4
        or      al,bl
        out     dx,al      ;output top address
        ret
Load_Start_Top_Video7     endp
```

22.6.3 Positioning the Cursor

The cursor position can be controlled through the code in Listing 22.14.

LISTING 22.14 Position the Cursor for the Video7

```
; Input Parameters:
;      top         top two bits of address
; Calling Protocol:
;      Position_Cursor_Top_Video7 (top)

Position_Cursor_Top_Video7  proc far top:BYTE

        Extensions_On_Video7     ;turn on extensions
        mov     bl,top     ;get top address
```

(continued)

```
        mov     dx,3c4h
        mov     al,0f6h     ;Bank Select Register
        out     dx,al

;       read current value
        inc     dx
        in      al,dx       ;get value
        and     al,0cfh     ;zero out start address 17-16 bit 5-4

;       or in new start address
        and     bl,03h      ;only want 2 bits
        mov     cx,4
        shl     bl,cl       ;shift left 4 to get bit 5-4
        or      al,bl
        out     dx,al       ;output top address
        ret
Position_Cursor_Top_Video7    endp
```

22.6.4 Controlling the Display Offset

No additional bits are provided for the offset address, beyond the eight bits provided in the Offset Register as described in Section 10.4.22. With word addressing, these eight bits can cover 1024 pixels. Having no additional offset bits limits the virtual display width to 1024 pixels.

22.7 VIDEO7 BIOS EXTENSIONS

The Video7 cards are equipped with six extended BIOS functions listed in Table 22.11. These assist the programmer in setting the extended display modes, setting up emulation, and returning display status.

22.7.1 Inquire into Super Condition

Returns whether the Video7 extensions are enabled.

Inputs:
AH=6F hex	Extended BIOS Functions
AL=00 hex	Inquire into super condition

Outputs:
BX=return parameter	Return parameter
	'V7' = indicates Video7 extensions are available
	Not 'V7' = No Video7 extended functions

TABLE 22.11 Video7 Super BIOS

Function	AH	AL	Feature
Inquire into Super Condition	6F	00	Returns whether extensions are enabled
Get Information	6F	01	Returns video information
Get Mode/Screen Resolution	6F	04	Returns mode and screen size
Set Super Mode State	6F	05	Allows setting of super modes
Select Autoswitch Mode	6F	06	Automatically enters emulation mode
Get Video Memory Configuration	6F	07	Returns memory configuration

22.7.2   Get Information

Returns video information regarding the diagnostic bits, display type, monitor resolution, vertical sync, light pen, and display enabled. It should be noted that the last four values in positions 0–3 can be read directly from the Input Status #1 Register, as discussed in Section 10.2.4. These fields tend to be temporal and would likely change state before the BIOS could return. The programmer should not use this BIOS call for determining the status of these fields but rather should interrogate Input Status #1 directly.

Inputs:

AH=6F hex	Extended BIOS Functions
AL=01 hex	Get Information

Outputs:

AH=return parameter	Return parameter. See Table 22.12
	Valid Byte returned.
	2 = Invalid BIOS call

22.7.3   Get Mode/Screen Resolution

Returns current video mode and screen size in either columns versus rows or pixels versus pixels depending on whether the current mode is a text or graphics mode respectively.

Inputs:

AH=6F hex	Extended BIOS functions
AL=04 hex	Get current mode and screen resolution

TABLE 22.12 Get Information Return Status

Bit	Meaning	0	1
7–6	Diagnostic Bits		
5	Display Type	Color	Monochrome
4	Monitor Resolution	>200 lines	<=200 lines
3	Vertical Sync	Display	Retrace
2	Light Pen Switch	Active	Not Active
1	Light Pen Flip Flop	Not Set	Set
0	Display Enabled	Enabled	Retrace

Outputs:

AL=current video mode	Mode number
BX=horizontal resolution	Columns if alphanumeric mode, Pixels if graphic mode
CX=vertical resolution	Rows if alphanumeric mode, Pixels if graphic mode
AH=return parameter	Return parameter.
	!2 = Valid BIOS call
	2 = Invalid BIOS call

22.7.4 Set Super Mode State

Allows the setting of one of the Super VGA modes. The standard AH=0 Set Mode BIOS function will not handle these extended modes. This function, however will handle the standard VGA calls.

Inputs:

AH=6F hex	Extended BIOS functions
AL=05hex	Set Mode
BL=mode value	

Outputs:

AH=return parameter	Return parameter.
	!2 = Valid BIOS call
	2 = Invalid BIOS call

22.7.5 Select Autoswitch Mode

Selects the type of emulation autoswitched and bootup modes. This function can be invoked repeatedly to enable and disable different functions. More than one selection can be enabled at a time.

Inputs:

AH=6F hex	Extended BIOS functions
AL=06hex	Enter emulation mode
BL=autoswitch mode	Selection
	00 = Select EGA/VGA only modes
	01 = Select Autoswitched VGA/EGA/CGA/MDA
	02 = Select 'Bootup' CGA/MDA
BH=function	Function to perform on selection
	0 = enable selection
	1 = disable selection

Outputs:

AH=return parameter	Return parameter.
	!2 = Valid BIOS call
	2 = Invalid BIOS call

22.7.6   Get Revision Code/Video Memory Configuration

Returns memory configuration as DRAM or VRAM, amount of memory present, and chip revision. The chip revision code can also be determined directly through the chip revision registers at Index 8E and 8F hex of the extended register 3C4/3C5 port. The chips are described in Table 22.13. The VEGA VGA is the older Video7 card and can be identified by a revision code between 80–8F hex. The Fast Write and VRAM card can be identified by revision codes between 70–79 hex. They can be differentiated by the memory code. If bit 7 of the memory configuration is 1, the memory is VRAM and the card must be a VRAM card. If bit 7 is a 0, the card must be a Fast Write card. The 1024i card can be identified by a revision code of 42 hex. In addition, the V7VGA version 5 chips will be identified by a code of 50 to 5F hex.

Inputs:

AH=6F hex	Extended BIOS functions
AL=07hex	Return Memory Configuration

Outputs:

AH=Memory configuration	Memory configuration
	Bit 7=0 DRAM
	Bit 7=1 VRAM
	Bit 6–0 # of 256 Kbyte blocks of memory
BH=Chip Revision	Revision code for S/C chip
BL=Chip Revision	Revision code for G/A chip

TABLE 22.13 Chip Revisions

Code	Chip
00–41	Reserved for future chips
40–49	1024i card
50–59	V7VGA Version 5.0
70–7F	V7VGA Chip revision 3
80–FF	VEGA VGA chip

22.8   VIDEO7 SPECIAL FEATURES

The Video7 processor is rich in extended features. These features include extended alphanumeric underlining, enhanced graphics operations, hardware cursor and fast character drawing.

22.8.1   Alphanumerics Extended Attributes

Extended attributes allows for underlining to occur regardless of the attribute byte of a character. This is accomplished by providing for a character attribute code to be represented by a 16-bit value. Any texture of underlining is possible since any bit in the 8-bit extended attribute byte can be set or reset.

Typically, the attribute code is eight bits and is stored in display memory plane 1. Its analogous ASCII code is stored in display memory plane 0. Extended attribute codes are stored at the same address in display memory plane 3. This extended attribute feature allows any attribute to be underlined. Any bit that is set to 1 in the extended attribute byte will result in the corresponding character. Any bit that is 0 will not cause an underline. If the byte is set to FF hex, the entire eight bits of the character pattern will be underlined.

The extended attributes function is enabled through the EAE field of the Compatibility Control Register illustrated in Figure 22.4. If the EAE field is set to 1, the extended text attributes are enabled. If it is set to 0, the extended attributes are disabled. Each character can have its own extended attribute byte. This is accomplished by writing the extended attribute code to display plane 3. The Map Mask Register, described in Section 10.3.3, can be used to enable only plane 3. The address of the attribute byte would correspond to the attribute of the character code.

22.8.2   Masked Writes

It is often desirable to write to selected bit positions within a selected byte without disturbing other bit positions within the same byte. This is possible in a standard VGA by using Bit Mask Register as described in Section 10.5.11. However, this requires a read cycle followed by a write cycle. This is very time-consuming due to the burden of wait-states placed on write operations that immediately follow read operations. If the VGA configuration includes VRAM memory, it is possible to perform masked write operations without using read instructions. Masked write operations are accomplished by using the Masked Write Control Register and the Masked Write Mask Register illustrated in Figures 22.16 and 22.17, respectively.

The MWE field of the Masked Write Control Register enables or disables the masked write function. If the MWE field is set to 1, the masked writes are enabled. If it is set to 0, the masked writes are disabled and all bit positions will be affected. The MWS field selects the source for the masked write mask. The mask is eight bits wide. If a bit in the mask is set to 1, the corresponding bit in display memory will be affected by the write operation. If a bit in the mask is a 0, the corresponding bit in display memory will not be affected. If the MWS field is set to 1, the rotated CPU byte is selected as the source for the masked write mask. If the MWS field is set to 0, the mask value present in the Masked Write Mask Register is selected as the source for the mask. Both of these can be very useful depending on the application.

Masked Write Control VRAM Only

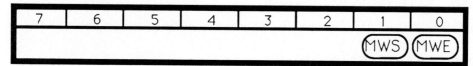

Index F3 at Port 3C4   Port 3C5 Read/Write

FIGURE 22.16 Masked Write Control Register. The write masking function is enabled through the MWE field. When enabled, the MWS field selects whether the rotated CPU bit is selected or the MASK field of the Masked Write Mask Register is used for the mask.

Masked Write Mask VRAM Only

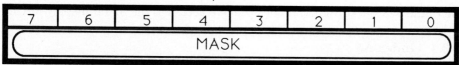

Index F4 at Port 3C4   Port 3C5 Read/Write

FIGURE 22.17 Masked Write Mask Register. The write mask is controlled through the MASK field.

22.8.3   Fast Character Drawing

It is often desirable to draw characters onto a colored background. This can be accomplished by specifying a foreground color and a background color. Any bit in the character pattern that is set to a 1 (foreground) will be written into display memory with the foreground color. Similarly, any character pattern set to a 0 (background) will be written into display memory with the background color.

Video7 provides several alternate techniques to perform this task through a set of several foreground/background registers. It is beyond the scope of this book to describe this process. The V7VGA technical reference manual can be consulted for more details.

22.8.4   Hardware Cursor

The hardware cursor provides a fast technique for non-destructive cursor placement. The cursor can be any pattern or color and can be positioned anywhere on the screen. It is beyond the scope of this book to describe this hardware cursor. The V7VGA technical reference manual can be consulted for more details.

22.9   EXTENSION REGISTERS

The 208/209 and 216 chips use the extension registers listed in Table 22.14.

22.9.1   8E and 8F

The product revision and identification codes are provided in product revision and product identification registers.

22.9.2   Index 94

The Pointer Pattern Address Register is used in combination with bits 6–5 of Register FF to determine the hardware cursor pattern in display memory.

22.9.3   Index A0–A3

The Plane 0–3 Background Latches provide access to the 32-bit display latch.

22.9.4   Index A5

The Cursor Attributes Register is used to turn on and off the hardware cursor. It also controls attributes of the text cursor, blinking, and transparency.

TABLE 22.14 Extension Registers

Index	Register	R/W	Chip
83	Attribute Controller Index	R/W	
8E	Chip Revision	R	
8F	Chip Family	R	
94	Pointer Pattern	R/W	
9C	Pointer Horizontal Position High	R/W	
9D	Pointer Horizontal Position Low	R/W	
94	Pointer Pattern Address	R/W	
9F	Pointer Vertical Position Low	R/W	
A0	Plane 0 Background Latch	R/W	
A1	Plane 1 Background Latch	R/W	
A2	Plane 2 Background Latch	R/W	
A3	Plane 3 Background Latch	R/W	
A4	Extended Clock Select	R/W	
A5	Cursor Attributes	R/W	
B3	Scratch RAM	R/W	
B4	Power On Reset 0	R	216
B5	Power On Reset 1	R	216
B6	Power On Reset 2	R	216
B7	Power On Reset 3	R	216
C0	Monochrome Lock	R/W	
C8	Miscellaneous Control 2	R/W	
C9	Extended Linear Address offset	R/W	
CA	Horizontal Overflow	R/W	216
CB	Low Water Mark	R/W	216
CC	DM Function Control	R/W	216
CD	Extended ALU Function Control	R/W	216
CE	Extended ALU Function Select	R/W	216
CF	Extended Linear Addr Offset High	R/W	216
E0	Miscellaneous Control 1	R/W	
E1	Interlace Value	R/W	
E2	Extended Character Width Enable	R/W	
E3	High Water Mark	R/W	
E8	Low Split Bank Address Value	R/W	
E9	Upper Split Bank Address Value	R/W	
EA	Switch Strobe	W	

(continued)

TABLE 22.14 *(cont.)*

Index	Register	R/W	Chip
EB	Overstrike Row Scan Match	R/W	
EC	Foreground Latch Plane 0	R/W	
ED	Foreground Latch Plane 1	R/W	
EE	Foreground Latch Plane 2	R/W	
EF	Foreground Latch Plane 3	R/W	
F3	Masked Write Control	R/W	208/209
F4	Masked Write Mask	R/W	208/209
F5	Foreground/Background Pattern	R/W	
F6	1 Mbyte Ram Bank Select	R/W	
F7	Switch Readback	R	
F8	Extended Clock Control	R/W	
F9	Extended Page Select	R/W	
FA	Extended Foreground Color	R/W	
FB	Extended Background Color	R/W	
FC	Compatibility Control	R/W	
FD	Display Memory Controller Timing	R/W	
FE	Foreground/Background Control	R/W	
FF	16-bit Interface Control	R/W	

22.9.5 Index C8

The Miscellaneous Control 2 Register enables and disables important features including the extended linear addressing mode.

22.9.6 Index C9

The Extended Linear Address Offset Register provides the extended linear address base address.

22.9.7 Index CC

The DM Function Control Register contains bits to enable various features including split bank addressing and display memory width.

22.9.8 Index CD

The Extended ALU Function Control Register controls several aspects of the ALU. Bits 3–2 specify the bit mask source. The remaining bits control planar color expansion, packed-pixel color expansion, word background latch, read-modify-write mode, auto alignement of source to destination, and enable all extended ALU functions.

22.9.9   Index CE

The Extended ALU Function Select Register selects the raster operation for the ALU.

22.9.10   Index CF

The Extended Linear Address Offset High Register provides bits 31–24 of the extended linear address base address.

22.9.11   Index E8 and E9

The Lower and Upper Split Bank Address Value Register defines the split bank address.

22.9.12   Index F5

The Foreground/Background Pattern Register provides the foreground/background patterns used in the ALU functions.

22.9.13   Index F6

The 1 Mbyte RAM Bank Select Register is used in bank selection for the various modes.

22.9.14   Index F9

The Extended Page Select Register is used as bit 16 of the display memory address.

22.9.15   Index FA and FB

The Foreground and Background Color Registers are used in solid color expansion.

22.9.16   Index FE

The Foreground/Background Control Register has several fields. Bits 3–2 select the foreground/background mode to be either solid or dithered foreground. Bits 5–4 specifiy the source of the operands to the raster operation. Bit 0 specifies the source of the color expansion data.

22.10 EXTENDED LINEAR ADDRESSING

The HT216 linear addressing mode provides a flat 1 Mbyte address space. It is available only on systems with a 32-bit address (or above). The technique involved in setting up the linear address is shown in Table 22.15

22.10.1 Linear Addressing in a Packed Display Mode.

In a packed display mode, 1 Mbyte of display memory is addressed with a CPU address within the range of 1 to 16 Mbytes starting at the display memory base address programmed into the lower four bits of Extended Register C9.

TABLE 22.15 Steps to Set Up Linear Addressing

Step	Function
1	Turn off 64 Kbyte Split Bank Register by writing a 0 to bit 0 of the DM Function Control Register at CCh and by writing a 0 to bit 7 of the Miscellaneous Control 1 Register at EEh.
2	Write a 0 to all bank select bits. This includes the Upper Split Bank Register at E9h, the Lower Split Bank Register at E8, and bits 5–0 of the 1 Mbyte RAM Bank Select Register at F6h.
3	Write a 0 to bit 0 of the Extended Page Select Register at F9.
4	Write a 0 to bit 5 of the Miscellaneous Output Register at port 3C2h.
5	Specify video memory base address. Write a 4-bit value to lower nibble of the Extended Linear Address Offset Low Register at C9h. The lower four bits of Register C9 determine the upper four bits of the linear address (bits 23–20). If bits (A23–A20) of the CPU address match the value in Register C9, the HT216 decodes the address as a display memory access; bits A19–A0 select a specific byte in display memory. In a 386/486DX local bus configuration, the 8-bit value in the Extended Linear Address High Offset Register at CFh is used in conjunction with Register C9 for address decoding. This selects one 16 Mbyte window out of the total 386/486 address space of 4 Gbyte. If the eight bits in CF match CPU address bits (A31–A24) and the lower four bits in C9 match CPU address (A23–A20), the HT216 decodes the address as s display memory access. In this case, bits A19–A0 select a specific byte in display memory.
6	Write a 1 to bit 6 of the Miscellaneous Control 2 Registers at C8h to turn on extended linear addressing mode.

22.10.2 Linear Addressing in a Planar Display Mode

In a planar display mode, each 64 Kbyte memory bank wraps around at the 64 Kbyte boundary repeating four times. The memory is accessed as shown in Table 22.16.

Display memory can be accessed through contiguous memory addresses by modifying the system page tables in the 80386/486 protected mode. Memory addresses should be re-mapped as shown in Table 22.17.

22.11 RASTER OPERATIONS

The raster operations feature a bit-wise Boolean logical function to the two operands. The two operands are determined by bits 3–2 of Register FE (input A) and bit 5 of Register CD (input B). To enable raster operations, set Register CD bit 7 to 1. This enables the extended ALU functionality. Program the desired logical operation into Register CE. The available operations are shown in Table 22.18. Whenever the Extended ALU Functionality is enabled, raster operations are in effect. To disable raster operations, in effect, program a value of A to write the A inputs as the output.

TABLE 22.16 Linear Memory Mapping in a Planar Mode

Address	DM Bank	Address	DM Bank
0	0	512K	2
64K	0	576K	2
128K	0	640K	2
192K	0	704K	2
256K	1	768K	3
320K	1	832K	3
384K	1	896K	3
448K	1	960K	3
		1MB	–

TABLE 22.17 Re-mapping Address for Planar Mode

Bank	Mapping	Re-mapped to
0	0K – 64K-1	Not Re-mapped
1	64K – 128K-1	320K – 384K-1
2	128K – 192K-1	512K – 576K-1
3	192K – 256K-1	768K – 832K-1

TABLE 22.18 Raster Operations in Extended
ALU Function Select Register at CEh

Value	Operation
0	Set to 0
1	!(A OR B)
2	!B AND A
3	!B
4	BA AND B
5	!A
6	A XOR B
7	!(A AND B)
8	A AND B
9	A XNOR B
A	A
B	A OR !B
C	B
D	!A OR B
E	A OR B
F	Set to 1

22.12 SINGLE OPERATION READ/MODIFY/WRITE

To enable read/modify/write, write a 1 to bit 5 of Register CD. A read always precedes a write operation and the pixel mask is used to determine which bits are involved in the operation.

22.13 SOURCE-TO-DESTINATION ALIGNMENT IN PACKED PIXEL MODES

Source-to-destination alignment is enabled by writing a 1 to bit 6 of Register CD. Other settings are required to set color expansion in packed pixel modes. The HT216 accesses eight bytes at a time. CPU addresses to display memory are divided by 8. An 8-byte read from display memory must begin on an 8-byte boundary. By using source-to-destination alignment during CPU reads, the HT216 can rotate the eight adjacent pixels before storing them sequentially in the 64-bit background latch. When used in combination with masking, a memory transfer with color expansion can occur between any desired source and destination pixel location. In this mode, the number of bytes to rotate the source data is programmed into bits 2–0 of the Data Rotate Register. In this mode, the rotate value (0 to 8) is used as a byte rotate. Rotation is always to the right.

22.14 COLOR EXPANSION

When color expansion is enabled, a 1 in the source is expanded to the foreground color at FA. A 0 in the source is expanded to the background color at FB. The source is selected by Register FE bit 1. It can be either the rotated CPU byte or the contents of the Foreground/Background Pattern Register at F5. Color expansion is controlled by the Foreground/Background Control Register at FE bits 3–2 as shown in Table 22.19.

In Solid Color Expansion, the foreground and background colors are used. In dithered foreground mode, the contents of the four foreground latch registers at EC, ED, EE, and EF are used as inputs to the ALU for each corresponding plane. This provides a patterned foreground. The background, if required, is stored in the background latches. The source of the data to be color expanded is controlled by bit 1 of Register FE as shown in Table 22.20.

Bits 0 and 1 of the Extended ALU Function Control Register at CD selects planar or packed pixel color expansion. These are set according to a planar or packed mode as described in Table 22.21.

TABLE 22.19 Color Expansion Control Register FE Bits 3–2

Bits 3–2	Select Color Expansion Mode
0	Set/Reset Output Mode (Normal VGA)
1	Solid Color Expansion
2	Dithered Foreground Color
3	Uses Background latch (transparent)

TABLE 22.20 Foreground/Background Control Register FE Bit 1

Bit 1	Data Source
0	Select Foreground/Background Pattern Register
1	Select Rotated CPU Byte

TABLE 22.21 Extended ALU Function Control Register at CD Bits 1–0

Bit 1	Bit 0	Function
0	0	HT216 operates in VGA-compatible mode.
0	1	Selects packed pixel 8-plane color expansion.
1	0	HT216 operates in VGA-compatible mode.
1	1	Selects planar color expansion mode.

TABLE 22.22 Steps to Packed Pixel Select Color Expansion

Step	Function
1	Select the color expansion mode by writing the appropriate value to bit 3–2 of the Register FE
2	Select the data source by writing the appropriate value to bit 1 of Register FE
3	Select packed pixel color expansion by writing a value of 0 to bit 1 and a value of 1 to bit 0 of Register CD.
4	Enable align-source-to-destination mode by writing a value of 1 to bit 6 of Register CD.

22.14.1 Packed Pixel Color Expansion Mode

To select the packed pixel color expansion mode, follow the steps in Table 22.22.

In packed pixel color expansion mode, each byte from the source represents eight adjacent pixels in display memory. Each bit is expanded into an 8-bit pixel before the raster operation is performed. Each bit in the bit mask is expanded to a byte to serve as the mask for the 8-bit pixel. Each bit in the A and B inputs to the ALU are also expanded to a byte. The eight bytes in the extended background latch represent eight adjacent pixels. The raster operation is applied to all eight pixels concurrently. In this mode, each bit in the bit mask is replicated to eight bits and used as the mask for the corresponding 8-bit pixel. For each ALU operation, there must be two inputs to the ALU. In this mode, each input is made up of a set of eight 8-bit pixels (64 bits total). The output of the ALU is a set of eight 8-bit pixels.

22.14.2 Planar Pixel Color Expansion Mode

To select the planar pixel color expansion mode follow the steps in Table 22.23.

In planar color expansion mode, each word from the CPU represents sixteen adjacent pixels in display memory. The HT216 operations on sixteen pixels simultaneously when the CPU writes a 16-bit word to display memory. In this mode, all registers and ALU functions, except the Extended Background Latch, are used in the same way for each byte in the word. Bit 7 of the most significant byte represents the left-most pixel and bit 0 of the least significant byte represents the right-most displayed pixel.

22.15 BIT MASK SOURCE

Bits 3–2 of the Register CD specify the source of the extended bit mask. A 0 value in a bit position of the mask preserves the contents of the corresponding display memory location during CPU writes into display memory. There are

TABLE 22.23   Steps to Select Color Expansion

Step	Function
1	Select the color expansion mode by writing the appropriate value to bit 3–2 of the Register FE
2	Select the data source by writing the appropriate value to bit 1 of Register FE
3	Select planar pixel color expansion by writing a value of 0 to bit 1 and a value of 1 to bit 0 of Register CD.
4	Enable word background latch by writing a 1 to bit 4 of Register CD.

TABLE 22.24   Extended Bit Mask Source Bits 3–2 of Register CD

Bits 3–2	Function
0	Bit mask from Graphics Controller Register 8
1	Bit mask from CPU byte
2,3	Bit mask from contents of Register F5

three sources as shown in Table 22.24. In packed pixel color expansion mode, each bit in the bit mask is replicated to eight bits and used as the mask for the corresponding 8-bit pixels.

22.16   HARDWARE CURSOR

The hardware cursor is a 32-by-32 bit pattern represented by two bit masks (AND and XOR) stored in off-screen display memory. The base address (bits 13–6) of the cursor pattern is set by the Pointer Pattern Address Register at 94h. The memory bank location (address bits 17–16) of the cursor pattern is set by bits 6–5 of the 16-bit Interface Control Register at FFh. Bits 15–14 are always set to 1.

The resultant operation on the destination pixel is based on the value in the 2-bit-per-pixel cursor pattern as shown in Table 22.25.

The cursor position is determined by the registers in Table 22.26. The Cursor X and Y screen coordinates are an 11-bit value ranging from 0 to 2047. The values loaded into these registers determine the position of the upper-left corner of the cursor pattern (also called the hot spot). There are no programmable hot spot hardware registers. The cursor position can be read from these registers as well.

The hardware cursor is turned on (set to 1) or off (set to 0) by writing to bit 7 of the Register A5. The other bits in this register must be preserved.

TABLE 22.25 Cursor Pattern Function

AND	XOR	Result
0	0	Black (set to 0)
0	1	White (set to 1)
1	0	Transparent (screen data)
1	1	Inverse screen data

TABLE 22.26 Registers Involved in the Cursor Position

Offset	Register
9C	Pointer Horizontal Position High
9D	Pointer Horizontal Position Low
9E	Pointer Vertical Position High
9F	Pointer Vertical Position Low

Chapter 23

IIT

23.1 THE IIT SUPER VGA CONTROLLERS

Integrated Information Technology (IIT) developed the AGX14 and AGX15 as
XGA clones. The AGX14 and AGX15 can be considered as super-sets of the
XGA. The AGX14 and AGX15 are functionally equivalent; the difference is that
the AGX14 is an ISA bus device, and the AGX15 is a local bus device. Except for
a few instances that are outlined in this chapter, these chips can be programmed as XGA chips (see Chapter 18).

Special thanks to Greg Tupper for the technical information provided on the
IIT chips and to Orchid Technologies for providing the XGA15-based card.

23.2 IIT REGISTERS

There are a few additional display modes and features with control conveniently located in a set of seven mode registers. Since most of the mode registers
pertain to hardware, only those fields pertaining to software will be described.

23.2.1 Virtual Memory Registers

The XGA included two I/O registers and two memory-mapped coprocessor registers that were used for virtual memory address translation. These are not
commonly supported; consequently, they are not included in the AGX products.

23.2.2 AGX Index Register

The AGX Index Register is located at I/O address 21xA, where x is typically 0
for single card systems. This Read/Write Index Register provides access to the
XGA display control and sprite registers. The relevant registers are described
in Chapter 18.

TABLE 23.1 AGX Mode Registers

Index	Description	Usage
77h	AGX Mode Register 1	Controls the clocks, interlace CPU bus and wait states, interlace, and clock frequency. Mode Register 2.
76h	AGX Mode Register 2	Controls the DAC, bus mastership, engine clock and VRAM frequency.
75h	AGX Mode Register 6	Not used.
70h	Clock Frequency Select 2	Not used.
6Fh	AGX Mode Register 5	Controls DAC clock frequency, engine delay, and sprite base address high.
6Eh	AGX Mode Register 4	Controls sprite base address low.
6Dh	AGX Mode Register 3	Controls 24-bit timing and enable, screen refresh, coprocessor base select, and source map power of 2 adjust.
6Ch	AGX Mode Register 7	AGX-15, local bus, and memory buffer enable.

23.2.3 AGX Data Registers

The actual registers are reached through the AGX data registers located at 21xBh–21xFh. These are one, two, or four bytes long and are read/write. First the index is written to 21xAh, and then the data to 21xBh through 21xFh as either a single byte, word, or double word. As is the case with the VGA, a word write to 21xAh will treat the lower byte as index and the upper byte as data.

23.2.4 AGX Mode Registers

The eight AGX mode registers are listed in Table 23.1. As the table shows, only the sprite-related registers will perhaps be useful to programmers.

23.3 HARDWARE CURSOR SPRITE

The hardware cursor is similar to the XGA, yet the actual pattern is stored in off-screen memory in the AGX products as opposed to in a special static RAM in the XGA. Therefore, an additional address has to be provided in the AGX products indicating where the cursor pattern is located. This is similar to other Super VGAs. In addition, a means of writing the cursor pattern to display memory is provided in the Cursor Index and Cursor Data Registers, which are described in Table 23.2.

The Hardware Cursor Registers are further defined in Figure 23.1.

TABLE 23.2 Hardware Cursor Registers

Index	Description	Usage
61–60h	Cursor Index	Index into the cursor definition pattern when writing a cursor pattern (see Cursor Data in next item).
6Ah	Cursor Data	Four pixels are sent to the cursor data buffer at the offset of the Cursor Base Register + the value in the Cursor Index Register.
6F–6Eh	Cursor Base Address	Bits 7–0 of 6Eh and bits 1,0 of 6Fh contain the 10-bit base address of the hardware cursor pattern.

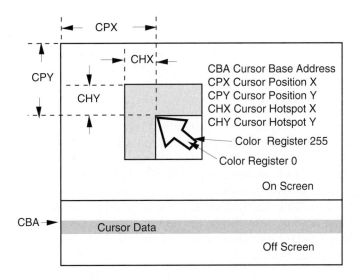

FIGURE 23.1 Hardware Cursor Definitions

23.3.1 Hardware Cursor Base Address

The hardware cursor address defines where the cursor pattern resides. This is shown in Figure 23.1 as CBA. The cursor base address is a 10-bit address in AGX Mode Registers 4 and 5. This address is calculated by the following formula:

CBA = (VRAMoffset / BufferSize) XOR 1DFh

where:

    BufferSize = 32x32x2 = 800 hex bytes
    there are 10000h bytes per aperture
    suppose we desire the cursor to reside in aperture F
    VRAMoffset = 0Fh * 10000h = F00000h

therefore:

    F0000h / 800h = 1E0h
    CBA = 1E0h XOR 1DFh = 3Fh

23.3.2   Hardware Cursor Data Pattern

The hardware cursor data pattern follows the XGA format described in Chapter 18.

23.3.3   Hardware Cursor Colors

The colors are **not** the same as the XGA. Rather, Cursor Color 0 is gotten from the Color Register 0, and Cursor Color 1 is gotten from the Color Register 255.

23.4   DISPLAY MODES

The IIT implementation uses a different set of display modes than are described by IBM for the XGA. These include a 24-bit-per-color display mode along with higher resolution 4-, 8-, and 16-bits-per-color modes than are present on the XGA. These modes are provided in Table 23.3.

Display modes require a width of either a power of 2, (512,1024, 2048) or a power of 2 + 256 (640, 1280). This is accomplished by setting the AGX Mode Register in the AGX15 to facilitate the add 256.

The Display Control 2 Register contains the Pixel Size field in bits 2–0. This field is described in Table 23.4.

23.5   PIXEL SIZE

As shown in Table 23.3, the IIT XGA implementation includes a 24-bit-per-color display format. The color formats are provided in Table 23.4.

23.6   IDENTIFYING THE AGX CHIPS

The best way to identify the AGX chips is to use the AGX Mode Registers, which are described in Table 23.1. The technique uses checks for AGX Mode Register 4 at index 6eh. This is a read/write register containing the sprite base address low. The code in Listing 23.1 calls upon the slot specific test of Listing 23.2.

TABLE 23.3 Standard Display Modes for IIT

Mode	Resolution	Bits/Pixel	Map Width
1	640 by 480	8	1024
2	640 by 480	16	2048
3	640 by 480	24	2048
4	800 by 600	8	1024
5	800 by 600	16	1600 (not a coprocessor mode)
6	1024 by 768	8	1024
7	1152 by 900	4	640
8	1280 by 960	8	2048
9	1280 by 1024	4	640
A	640 by 400	8	1024
B	1024 by 768	16	2048
C	1280 by 1024	8	1280

TABLE 23.4 Pixel Size Field of Display Control 2 Register

Field	Bits/Pixel
0	1
1	2
2	4
3	8
4	16
5	24

LISTING 23.1 Is an IIT Chip Present

```
int Is_It_IIT(void)
 {
 if(Is_IIT_Slot_Valid(6)) return(IS_FOUND);
        else return(NOT_FOUND);
 }
```

LISTING 23.2 Is an IIT Chip Present at Provided Slot

```
int Is_IIT_Slot_Valid(int slot)
{ unsigned char old_value,new_value;
   int index_reg,data_reg,XGA_BASE;

   XGA_BASE = 0x2100 + (slot<<4);
   index_reg = XGA_BASE+0x0a;  // point to index register
   data_reg = XGA_BASE+0x0b;// point to data register
   outp(index_reg,0x6e);  // output index of AGX Mode Register 4
   old_value = _inp(data_reg);  // read AGX Mode Register 4 and
save for later

    outp(data_reg,0xAA);  // try AA pattern
    new_value = _inp(data_reg);  // read AGX Mode Register 4
    if(new_value==0xAA) {
    outp(data_reg,old_value);  // restore
    return(IS_FOUND);
    }
  return(NOT_FOUND);
}
```

Chapter 24

NCR

24.1 THE NCR CHIPS

NCR has entered the SuperVGA marketplace with its 77C22, 77C22E, 77C22E+ processors, and the powerful 77C32BLT processor. The 77C22 series includes hardware-assisted graphics operations including color expansion and a hardware cursor. These support modes up to 1280 by 1024 in 4- and 8-bit color modes (8-bit is interlaced) as well as in 800-by-600 hi-color mode and a 640-by-480 true-color mode.

The 7C32BLT chip supports resolutions up to 1280 by 1024 in both 4- and 8-bit-per-color modes, 1024 by 768 in hi-color modes, and 800 by 600 in true-color modes. This chip is downward compatible to the 88C22E+ drivers. It includes a VL interface, linear memory addressing, a BitBlt engine, memory-mapped control registers, step addressing for high-speed Text BitBlts, transparency control, a writeable BIOS, and a Microsoft compatible 64-by-64 or 128-by-128 hardware cursor.

24.2 IDENTIFYING THE NCR CHIPS

Code to identify the NCR chip family is provided in Listing 24.1. Code to distinguish which NCR chip is present is provided in Listing 24.2.

LISTING 24.1 Determine If the Chip Is an NCR

```
/* Output Parameters:
        1=card is an NCR   0=card is NOT an NCR
Calling Protocol:
  NCR= Is_It_NCR()   */

int Is_It_NCR(void)
{ unsigned char new_code,code; int i;
```

(continued)

```
        Extended_On_NCR();   // turn on NCR Extended Registers

    // read the Chip ID extended register 3c4/3c5 index 8
            outp(0x3c4,0x08); // send index 8
            code = inp(0x3c5);   // read value

            outp(0x3c5,0xff);   // try setting to ffs to check for
                                // read only
            delay_a_bit(1);
            new_code = inp(0x3c5); // read value
            if(new_code!=code)      return(CHIP_NOT_FOUND);

            outp(0x3c5,0x00);   // try setting to 00s to check for
                                // read only
            delay_a_bit(1);
            new_code = inp(0x3c5); // read value
            if(new_code!=code)      return(CHIP_NOT_FOUND);

    //  now try to read/write to 13-1d which should be read/write
        for (i=0x15; i<0x1a; i++) {
            outp(0x3c4,i); // send index
            outp(0x3c5,0xAA); // send value
            delay_a_bit(1);
            if(inp(0x3c5)!=0xAA) return(CHIP_NOT_FOUND);

            outp(0x3c5,0x55); // send value
            delay_a_bit(1);
            if(inp(0x3c5)!=0x55) return(CHIP_NOT_FOUND);
            }

return(CHIP_FOUND);
}
```

LISTING 24.2 Determine Which NCR Chip Is Present

```
/* Output Parameters:
 identity   integer containing chip code
            1 = 77c22, 2 = 77c22e and e+,  3 = 77c32BLT
Calling Protocol:
 identity = Which_NCR()   */

int  Which_NCR(void)

{ unsigned char code,rev_code,chip_code;

 // read the Chip ID extended register 3c4/3c5 index 8
        outp(0x3c4,0x08);  // send index 8
        code = inp(0x3c5);  // read value
```

```
    // it is a read only register so see if the values are okay
        chip_code = (code>>4)&0x0f;
        switch(chip_code) {

        case 0: return(NCR77c22);   // was 77c22
        case 2:
            rev_code = code&0x0f;
            if(rev_code<8) return(NCR77c22e);   // was 77c22e
          return(NCR77c22ep);   // was 77c22e+
        }
   return(NO_ID_FOUND);   // couldn't detect it
 }
```

24.3   DISPLAY MODES

The 77C22 series supports the display modes shown in Table 24.1. After the SetMode function is called to set the mode, the extended registers should be enabled. The VESA compatible modes are provided in Table 24.2.

TABLE 24.1   Extended Display Modes

Mode	Resolution	Bits / Color	Chip
50	640 by 480	24	C32
51	800 by 600	24	C32
54	132 by 50	4	
55	132 by 25	4	
56	132 by 50	2	
57	132 by 25	2	
58	800 by 600	4	
59	800 by 600	1	
5A	1024 by 768	1	
5B	1024 by 768i	4	
5C	800 by 600	8	
5D	1024 by 768	4	
5E	640 by 400	8	
5F	640 by 480	8	
61	1024 by 768i	8	
62	1024 by 768	8	
69	1280 by 1024i	8	
6A	1280 by 1024	8	C32
6C	1280 by 1024	4	
70	640 by 480	15	

(continued)

TABLE 24.1 *(cont.)*

Mode	Resolution	Bits / Color	Chip
71	800 by 600	15	
78	640 by 480	16	
79	800 by 600	16	
7A	1024 by 768	16	C32

TABLE 24.2 VESA Compatible Extended Display Modes

Mode	Resolution	Bits / Color	Chip
100	640 by 400	8	
101	640 by 480	8	
102	800 by 600	4	
103	800 by 600	8	
104	1024 by 768	4	
105	1024 by 768	8	
106	1280 by 1024	4	
107	1280 by 1024	8	C32
110	640 by 480	15	
111	640 by 480	16	
112	640 by 480	24	C32
113	800 by 600	15	
114	800 by 600	16	
115	800 by 600	24	C32
116	1024 by 768	15	C32
117	1024 by 768	16	C32

24.4   EXTENDED REGISTERS

The extended registers are provided in Table 24.3. Note that these are indexed registers found at the 3C4h/3C5h I/O indexed register pair for the SeqXX registers and at the 3D4h/3D5h (color) I/O indexed register pair for the CrtcXX registers.

24.4.1   Accessing the Extended Registers

The NCR extended registers can be enabled through the Extensions Control Register at SEQ 5 as shown in the macros provided in Listing 24.3 and Listing

TABLE 24.3 Extended Registers

Index	Name	R/W	Chip
Seq05	Extended Function Enable	R/W	
Seq08	Chip ID	R	
Seq18	Primary Host Offset High	R/W	
Seq19	Primary Host Offset Low	R/W	
Seq1A	Linear Address Register 0	R/W	C32
Seq1B	Linear Address Register 1	R/W	C32
Seq1C	Secondary Host Offset High	R/W	
Seq1D	Secondary Host Offset Low	R/W	
Seq1E	Extended Memory Enable	R/W	
Seq1F	Extended Clocking Mode	R/W	
Seq20	Extended Video Memory Addressing	R/W	
Seq21	Extended Pixel Control	R/W	
Seq22	Bus Width Feedback	R/W	
Seq23	Performance Select	R/W	
Seq24	Color Expanded Foreground	R/W	
Seq25	Color Expanded Background	R/W	
Seq26	Extended Read/Write Control	R/W	
Seq27	Misc. Feature Select	R/W	
Seq28	Color Key Control	R/W	
Seq29	Color Key Match Value 0	R/W	
Seq2A	Color Key Match Value 1	R/W	C32
Seq2B	Color Key Match Value 2	R/W	C32
Seq2C	—Reserved		
Seq2D	CRC Control	R/W	
Seq2E	CRC Data Low	R	
Seq2F	CRC Data High	R	
Seq30	Memory Mapped Register Control	R/W	C32
Seq31	ACM Aperture Register 1	R/W	C32
Seq32	ACM Aperture Register 2	R/W	C32
Seq33	ACM Aperture Register 3	R/W	C32
Seq3E	BIOS Utility Register 0	R/W	C32
Seq3F	BIOS Utility Register 1	R/W	C32
Crtc30	Extended Horizontal Timings One	R/W	
Crtc31	Extended Start Address	R/W	
Crtc32	Extended Horizontal Timings Two	R/W	
Crtc33	Extended Vertical Timings	R/W	
Crtc34	Monitor Power Management	R/W	C32

24.4. Note that the Extensions_On_Macro also sets up for write-on primary and read-on secondary dual-bank swapping.

LISTING 24.3 Enable NCR Extensions Macro

```
; Function:
;    Enable the NCR Extensions registers, enable extended memory
;    and set up for write on primary and read on secondary
; Calling Protocol:
;    Extensions_On_NCR

Extensions_On_NCR macro
        mov     dx,3c4h     ;address Extensions Control Register
        mov     al,5
        out     dx,al       ;output index

        inc     dx
        in      al,dx       ;get value
        or      al,01h      ;set bit 1=1
        out     dx,al

        mov     dx,3c4h     ;address Extensions Control Register
        mov     al,1eh
        out     dx,al       ;output index
        inc     dx
        in      al,dx       ;get value
        and     al,0bh      ;zero all but bits 3,1,0
        or      al,14h      ;set bits 4,2=1
        out     dx,al       ;output to extended memory enable
endm
```

LISTING 24.4 Disable NCR Extensions Macro

```
; Function:
;        Disable NCR extensions
; Calling Protocol:
;        Extensions_Off_NCR

Extensions_Off_NCR macro
        mov     dx,3c4h     ;address Extensions Control Register
        mov     al,5
        out     dx,al       ;output index
        inc     dx
        in      al,dx       ;get value
        and     al,0feh     ;zero bit 1=0
        out     dx,al
endm
```

TABLE 24.4 Extended Memory Registers

Index	Description	R/W	Chip
Seq18	Primary Host Offset High	R/W	
Seq19	Primary Host Offset Low	R/W	
Seq1A	Linear Address Register 0	R/W	C32
Seq1B	Linear Address Register 1	R/W	C32
Seq1C	Secondary Host Offset High	R/W	
Seq1D	Secondary Host Offset Low	R/W	
Seq1E	Extended Memory Enable	R/W	

24.5 DISPLAY MEMORY

The extended memory registers provide access to the 4 Mbytes of display memory. They are listed in Table 24.4.

24.5.1 Bank Swapping

The primary offset (high and low) registers provide a 16-bit offset into display memory. This offset is added to all host accesses if extended memory is enabled. This offset allows selection of additional banks of video memory. The secondary offset (high and low) registers provide a 16-bit offset into display memory. This offset is added to all host accesses if extended memory is enabled. This offset allows selection of additional banks of video memory. The primary and secondary offsets are used according to the secondary offset enable bit in the Extended Memory Enable Register. The switching between these two offset registers is determined by the Primary/Secondary Read/Write Select Field of the Extended Memory Enable Register.

Bank swapping is accomplished through the macros in Listing 24.5. The secondary registers at SEQ 1Ch and 1Dh are used for the read macro. The primary registers at SEQ 18h and 19h are used for the write macro. Macros are provided for both the 4-bit-per-color planar modes and the packed modes. Note that the 4-bit-per-color modes multiply the bank value by 4 to maintain a 64 Kbyte bank.

LISTING 24.5 Setting the Read and Write Bank

```
;Input Parameters
;       bl 64 Kbyte bank value

Set_Bank_Rd_NCR_22 macro
        shl    bl,1
        shl    bl,1        ;put into bits 7-2
        and    bl,0fch     ;zero bits 1-0 for 6 bits of bank
```

```
        mov     dx,3c4h     ;access secondary high
        mov     al,1ch
        out     dx,al       ;output index

        inc     dx          ;bank high
        mov     al,bl
        out     dx,al       ;output read bank

        mov     dx,3c4h     ;access secondary low
        mov     al,1dh
        out     dx,al       ;output index

        inc     dx          ;bank low
        xor     al,al
        out     dx,al       ;output read bank low = 0
    endm

Set_Bank_Wr_NCR_22 macro
        shl     bl,1
        shl     bl,1        ;put into bits 7-2
        and     bl,0fch     ;zero bits 1-0 for 6 bits of bank

        mov     dx,3c4h     ;access primary high
        mov     al,18h
        out     dx,al       ;output index

        inc     dx          ;bank high
        mov     al,bl
        out     dx,al       ;output write bank

        mov     dx,3c4h     ;access primary low
        mov     al,19h
        out     dx,al       ;output index

        inc     dx          ;bank low
        xor     al,al
        out     dx,al       ;output write bank low = 0
endm

Set_Wr_Bank_256_NCR_22 macro
        Set_Bank_Wr_NCR_22
        ret
endm

Set_Rd_Bank_256_NCR_22 macro
        Set_Bank_Rd_NCR_22
        ret
endm
```

```
Set_Wr_Bank_16_NCR_22 macro
        shl    bl,1       ; multiply by 4
        shl    bl,1       ; multiply by 4
        Set_Bank_Wr_NCR_22
        ret
endm


Set_Rd_Bank_16_NCR_22 macro
        shl    bl,1       ; multiply by 4
        shl    bl,1       ; try multiply by 4
        Set_Bank_Rd_NCR_22
endm
```

The Extended Memory Enable Register controls the primary/secondary address selection and the enable for extended memory. This is shown in Table 24.5. If the extended memory is enabled, the extended memory controls are enabled. If disabled, the Primary Host Offset Register is set to 0. If the Secondary Offset Enable register is 1, then the Secondary Offset Address Register is used to access memory as selected by the Primary/Secondary Read/Write Select Field.

The Primary/Secondary Read/Write Select Field provides dual bank switching and is described in Table 24.6. A value of 0 is the standard read/write selection mechanism. A value of 2 is based on the host memory address. The 128 Kbyte range from A0000–BFFFFh is used. Accesses to A0000h–AFFFFh use the primary offset; accesses to B0000h–BFFFFh use the secondary offset. A value of 1 uses a read operation to switch from secondary to primary.

TABLE 24.5 Extended Memory Enable

Bits	Function
7–5	Primary/Secondary Read/Write Select
4	Extended Memory Enable; 1=enable extended memory
2	Secondary Offset Enable; 1=enable

TABLE 24.6 Primary/Secondary Read/Write Select

Value	Function
0	Write to Primary, Read from Secondary
1	Write to Primary, Read Toggles from Secondary to Primary
2	Read/Write on Address A0, Secondary of B0
3	Read/Write on Secondary Only

TABLE 24.7 Linear Address Register 0 and 1

Bit	Description	Register
7–0	Aperture Location bits 31–24	Linear Address Register 1
7–4	Aperture Location bits 2319620	Linear Address Register 0
1–0	Aperture Size	Linear Address Register 1

TABLE 24.8 Aperture Size

Value	Aperture Size	Aperture Location
0	1 Mbyte	A32–A20
1	2 Mbyte	A32–A21
2	4 Mbyte	A32–A22

24.5.2 Linear Addressing

The Linear Address Register 0 and Linear Address Register 1 control the linear addressing, if the Linear Address Enable field of the Extended Function Enable Register selects linear addressing. Linear Address Register 0 provides control fields and the lower four bits of the aperture location. Linear Address Register 1 provides the upper eight bits of the linear address. Together, these twelve bits form the address bits 20–31 for the aperture location. The aperture size is selected in bit locations 1–0 of the Linear Address Register 0 as shown in Table 24.7. If 0, a 1 Mbyte aperture is selected. If 1, a 2 Mbyte aperture, if 3 a 4 Mbyte aperture, as shown in Table 24.8. In order to enable linear addressing, it is necessary to set bit 0, the Host Address Bit 16 to a 1.

24.6 MEMORY MAPPED REGISTERS

The control registers can be accessed as memory-mapped registers. The Memory Mapped Register Control Register, shown in Table 24.9, determines whether the primary/secondary offset registers, the cursor registers, or the accelerator registers are memory mapped through the ACM Aperture Registers 1–3.

The Enable Primary/Secondary Offset Register access allows the SEQ 18h, 19h, 1Ch, and 1Dh registers to be accessible through the ACM. The Enable Cursor Register access allows access to the Cursor X and Y Position registers at SEQ ODh, OEh, OFh, and 10h. These become available at Index 0Ch. The Enable Accelerator Control menu allows access to the Accelerator Control menu.

The aperture registers 1–3 provide the upper 24 bits of a 32-bit aperture address as shown in Table 24.10. Together, these provide an address where the Control Menu can be accessed.

TABLE 24.9 Memory Mapped Register Control Register

Bit	Function
2	Enable Primary/Secondary Offset Register access
1	Enable Cursor Register access
0	Enable Accelerator Control menu

TABLE 24.10 Aperture Registers

Register	Bits
Aperture Reg 1	15–8
Aperture Reg 2	23–16
Aperture Reg 3	31–24

24.7 GENERAL CONTROL REGISTERS

The Extended Pixel Control Register is shown in Table 24.11. The Pixel Depth field controls the number of bytes used for each pixel. A 0 selects one byte, a 1 selects two bytes, and a 2 selects three bytes. The Packed Nibble to Targa Convert field is an interesting field that, when enabled, converts from packed nibble to Targa format. The Targa format is the standard 15-bit hi-color format with red in bits 0–4, green in bits 5–9, and blue in bits 14–10. The packed nibble format is a 12-bit Hi-Color format with red in bits 0–3, green in bits 7–4, and blue in bits 11–8. The Enable Graphics Byte Path selects 8-bit color.

The Color Expanded Write Foreground and Background Registers provide eight bits of foreground and background color information. The lower four bits are used if the system is in a 16-color expansion mode.

The Extended Read/Write Control Register is shown in Table 24.12. The Color Transparency Enable bit enables color transparency when used in conjunction with the Foreground/Background Color Expansion Enable bit that enables color expansion.

TABLE 24.11 Extended Pixel Control Register

Bit	Function
5–4	Pixel Depth
2	Packed Nibble to Targa Convert Enable
1	Enable 12-bit Hi-Color Packed Format
0	Enable Graphics Byte Path

TABLE 24.12 Extended Read/Write Control Register

Bit	Function
7	Color Transparency Enable
6	64-bit Read Latch for Writes
5	Packed Pixel Color Compare
4	Packed Pixel Mask Enable
3	Planar to packed Pixel Conversion Enable
1	256-Color Expansion Enable
0	Foreground/Background Color Expansion Enable

The 64-bit Read Latch for Writes causes the 64 bits of the data latch to be used when a 16-bit write operation occurs in Write Mode 1. The Packed Pixel Color Compare field enables color compare logic to operate on packed pixel data. It is used in conjunction with the 256-Color Expansion Enable bit. This bit should be set to 1 to enable 256-color expansion If 0, then it is possible to have 16-color expansion. The Packed Pixel Mask Enable enables pixel masking when in a 256-color mode.

24.8 START ADDRESS

The CRTC is controlled by the Extended Start Address Register as shown in Table 24.13. Bits 16 through 18 of the 19-bit start address are found in bit positions 3–0 of this register. Bit 4 contains the bit 8 of the 9 bit display offset.

A macro that sets the CRTC start bank is provided in Listing 24.6. This sets the CRTC 31h port with the extended start address bits.

TABLE 24.13 Extended Start Address Register

Bits	Function
4	Bit 8 of the Address Row Offset
3–0	Display Start Address Bits 18–16.

LISTING 24.6 Setting the extended start address

```
;Input Parameters:
;       bl      start

Set_CRTC_Bank_NCR_22 macro
        and     bl,0fh    ;only want 4 bits of bank
```

```
        mov     dx,3d4h          ;access CRT Extended Start Address
        mov     al,31h
        out     dx,al            ;output index

        inc     dx               ;non-destructive write bank
        in      al,dx
        and     al,0f0h          ;zero bits 3-0

        or      al,bl
        out     dx,al
endm
```

24.9 HARDWARE CURSOR

The 77C22E+ and the 77C32BLT includes a hardware cursor as shown in Table 24.14.

The Cursor Color One and Cursor Color Zero Registers provide two 8-bit colors for the hardware cursor. The cursor pattern is 2-bits-per-pixel, like all hardware cursors. If the cursor pattern is 2, the Cursor Color One is used. If the cursor pattern is 0, the Cursor Color Zero is used.

Note: At the writing of this chapter, there were certain idiosyncrasies regarding the copying of the Cursor Y High and Low Registers into the Cursor X High and Low Registers.

The Cursor Control Register is described in Table 24.15.

TABLE 24.14 Hardware Cursor Registers

Index	Name	R/W
Seq0A	Cursor Color One	R/W
Seq0B	Cursor Color Zero	R/W
Seq0C	Cursor Control	R/W
Seq0D	Cursor X Location High	R/W
Seq0E	Cursor X Location Low	R
Seq0F	Cursor Y Location High	R
Seq10	Cursor Y Location Low	R/W
Seq11	Cursor X Index	R/W
Seq12	Cursor Y Index	R/W
Seq13	—	R/W
Seq14	Cursor Storage Low	R/W
Seq15	Cursor Storage High	R/W
Seq16	Cursor Storage Middle	R/W
Seq17	Cursor Pixel Mask	R/W

TABLE 24.15 Cursor Control Register

Bit	Function
7	Cursor Width Select; 0=32, 1=64
6–5	Repeat Count; 0=1, 1=2, 2=3, 3=4 bytes
4	Blink Enable 1=on
3	Blink Frequency Select; 0=every 8 frames, 1=every 16 frames
2–1	Cursor Height; 0=16, 1=32, 2=64, 3=128
0	Cursor Enable; 1=on, 0=off

The Repeat Count field controls the number of bytes allotted per pixel for cursor image overlay. The cursor pixel is clocked out for one to four display bytes.

The Cursor X Location and Cursor Y Location are 11-bit addresses that locate the cursor with respect to the display. The Cursor X and Cursor Y Index provide a 6-bit hot spot and a 7-bit hot spot respectively. These index values are referenced to the top-left corner of the cursor pattern.

The Cursor Storage Low, Middle, and High Registers provide a 20-bit address that points to the top of the cursor pattern.

The Cursor Pixel Bit Mask Register is an 8-bit binary pattern representing a mask for each of eight pixels. A 1 in a bit allows the corresponding bit of the 8-bit cursor pixel word to form the final pixel value. A 0 prohibits the corresponding bit of the 8-bit cursor pixel word from forming the final pixel value, thereby allowing the original pixel data through (transparent).

24.10 GRAPHICS COPROCESSOR

The 77C32BLT drawing engine is accessed through a memory-mapped command menu called the Accelerator Control menu (ACM). These registers are listed in Table 24.16. This group of memory-mapped registers can be placed at any 256-byte boundary in the system's 32-bit address space. The command menu is organized such that decreasing address represent most frequently updated registers. Thus, simple BLTs can be set up with a minimum of overhead. The address location of this ACM is found in the SEQ 31h, 32h, and 33h Aperture Registers.

The Primary and Secondary Offset Registers are sixteen bits and provide memory mapping for the SEQ Register 18h and 19h, 1Ch and 1Dh. Access is provided to the Primary and Secondary Registers when bit 2 of the Memory Map Control Register (SEQ 30h) is set to 1.

The Mode Control Register provides memory-mapped access to the bits 7–0 of the Extended Memory Enable Register located at SEQ 1Eh.

TABLE 24.16 Accelerator Control Menu Memory Mapped Registers

Offset	31–24	23–16	15–8	7–0
50	—	Background Color	Background Color	Background Color
4C	—	Foreground Color	Foreground Color	Foreground Color
48	—	Pattern	Pattern	Pattern
44	—	Source Address	Source Address	Source Address
40	—	Destination Address	Destination Address	Destination Address
3C	Height	Height	Width	Width
38	—	Raster Op	Y Rotation	X Rotation
34	—	BLT Control	BLT Control	BLT Control
30	—	BLT Status	—	BLT Start
0C	Cursor Y High	Cursor Y Low	Cursor X High	Cursor X Low
08	—	—	Mode Control	—
04	—	—	Secondary High	Secondary Low
00	—	—	Primary High	Primary Low

The Cursor X, Cursor Y registers provide memory-mapped access to the Cursor Position Registers at SEQ 0D, 0E, 0F and 10h.

24.11   BITBLT

The BitBlt registers include the Start and Status Registers, the Control Registers, the Height and Width Registers. The BLT Start Register is shown in Table 24.17.

Bit 0 of this register starts the BitBlt. It is necessary to run a short BitBlt in order to clear the address pipeline before actually attempting BitBlts. You can perform this to off-screen memory.

TABLE 24.17 BLT Start Register

Bit	Function
3	Write FIFO empty Interrupt
2	BLT Completed Interrupt
1	Text BLT
0	Start/Stop

24.11.1 Start and Status

The Start/Stop field is used to start and stop the BLT engine. Setting this bit to a 1 instructs the drawing engine to begin an operation. Setting this bit to a 0 causes the present BLT operation to end gracefully and to stop the drawing engine.

The Text BLT, when set to 1, enables the Text BLT function. If 0, a standard BLT is performed. The Ready bit has to be checked for 0 before changing out of Text BLT mode.

The BLT Completed Interrupt enables IRQ to go active when the Accelerator engine has completed a task. Setting this bit to a 0 resets the interrupt.

The Write FIFO Empty Interrupt enables IRQ to go active when the FIFO Empty condition occurs. Setting this bit to a 0 resets the interrupt.

The BLT Status Register is shown in Table 24.18. It provides the status necessary to control the BLT engine.

The Ready bit is a read-only bit. When it is read as a 1, it indicates that the drawing operation has been completed. If 0, the drawing engine is still operating. If in text BLT mode, this bit must be 0 before changing out of text mode.

The Error bit indicates that an illegal BLT operation has been entered. This bit is automatically reset at the Start Command of every operation.

The BLT Done Interrupt Status Bit is a read-only bit. It indicates that an interrupt has been generated due to a done condition. This bit is reset when the interrupt is cleared.

The BLT Write FIFO Near Empty Interrupt Status Bit is a read-only bit. It indicates that an interrupt has been generated due to a near empty write FIFO condition. It indicates that seven levels are available in the FIFO. This bit is reset when the interrupt is cleared.

The Write FIFO Full bit is a read-only bit and, when 1, indicates that all locations of the Write FIFO are occupied.

TABLE 24.18 BLT Status Register

Bit	Function
20	Write FIFO Full
19	Write FIFO Empty
18	BLT Done Interrupt Status
17	Error
16	Ready

24.11.2 BLT Control

The BLT control registers are shown in Table 24.19.

The Source Location Bit, when set to a 0, indicates that the source data will be supplied by the system. If it is set to a 1, the source data is frame buffer resident.

The Destination Location Bit, when set to a 1, indicates that the Destination address is in frame buffer memory. If it is set to a 0, the destination data will be transferred to system memory. The data is placed into the Read FIFO and it is the obligation of the host to read it out.

The Source Address Mode Bit, when set to a 1, indicates that the data is stored in a linear format. If 0, the bit-map data is in rectangular format.

The Destination Address Mode Bit, when set to a 1, indicates that the data is stored in a linear format. If 0, the bit-map data is in rectangular format.

The Color Expand Enable bit, when set to a 1, indicates monochrome source data is replaced with full depth foreground and background color data. When this bit is 0, source data is not color expanded.

The Color Compare Enable bit, when set to a 1, indicates that the color comparison is for color data. If 0, the comparison is for monochrome data. Screen-to-memory operations, when data is retrieved from the screen memory, are subject to color comparison.

The Color Fill Enable bit, when set to a 1, indicates that the pattern is a vertically solid color and need only be retrieved once. If 0, it is assumed that the pattern is based on a scan line at a time basis for textured patterns.

TABLE 24.19 BLT Control Registers

Bit	Function
15	Source Location
14	Destination Location
13	Source Address Mode
12	Destination Address Mode
11	Color Expand Enable
10	Color Compare Enable (reserved at time of writing)
9	Color Fill Enable
7	Horizontal Direction
6	Vertical Direction
5	Transparency Enable
4	Large Pattern Enable
3	Map Width
1	Color Compare Invert (reserved at time of writing)

The Horizontal Direction bit, when set to a 1, indicates that the direction is left-to-right. If 0, it is right-to-left.

The Vertical Direction bit, when set to a 1, indicates that the direction is top-to-bottom. If 0, it is bottom-to-top.

The Transparency Enable bit, if set to 1, enables background transparency for color expansion operations. If 0, the operation is opaque.

The Large Pattern Enable bit, if set to a 1, selects a pattern width of 16. This is supported for 256-color modes. If 0, a pattern width of 8 is selected and applicable to all color depths.

The Map Width bit, if set to 1, specifies that the bit-map width is an odd number of words. This allows double word transfers to be used. The BLT will discard the extra data on writes and pad the extra data on reads. Thus data is always word-aligned as defined in the Microsoft Windows specifications. This applies if either the source or destination data is in system memory. If 0, no padding or discarding is performed.

The Color Compare Invert bit, if set to 1, causes the returned color compare value to show a one value when the colors do **not** match, and a zero value in the pixel positions when the colors match. If 0, a color match operation returns a one in pixel positions where the pixel color matches the reference color and a zero value when the colors do **not** match.

24.11.3 Raster Opcode and Rotate Registers

The raster opcode and rotate registers are shown in Table 24.20.

The Raster OpCode field specifies the logical combination of source, destination, and pattern to be used for drawing operations. This OpCode is specified using the 8-bit Microsoft Raster OpCode list.

The Pattern Y Rotation field specifies the vertical pixel alignment of the pattern to be used for the drawing operation. The pattern is typically eight pixels high. It is possible to have 16-pixel-high patterns as supported in the 256-color formats via bit 4 of the Control Register.

The Pattern X Rotation field specifies the horizontal pixel alignment of the pattern to be used for the drawing operation. The pattern is typically eight pixels high. It is possible to have 16-pixel-high patterns as supported in the 256-color formats via bit 4 of the Control Register.

TABLE 24.20 Raster Opcode and Rotate Registers

Bit	Function
23–16	Raster Opcode (RasterOp)
11–8	Pattern Y Rotation
3–0	Pattern X Rotation

24.11.4   BitMap Dimension Registers

The BitMap Height and Width Dimension Registers are 12-bit registers that specify the height and width of the source and destination bit-maps. The Bit-Map Width Register also specifies the character cell height for Text BitBlt Mode. These registers are shown in Table 24.21.

24.11.5   Source, Destination, and Pattern Registers

The source address is a 24-bit address and specifies the bit address of the starting corner of the source bit map. This corner is relative to the direction indicated by bits 6 and 7 of the Control Register at ACM Index 34h. The three least significant bits of this address specify alignment for monochrome bitmaps. These monochrome bit maps may be color expanded. For full color depth color, SRC data, the three least significant bits of the source address are not used. For Color Expand BitBlts, where a monochrome SRC bitmap is used, either supplied by the system or resident in video memory, the LSBs of this register are required to specify initial bit alignment. All adresses are bit addresses.

The pattern address is a 24-bit address and specifies the starting address of the pattern to be used. This address is BLT direction specific and identifies which line of the pattern is to be used with the first line of the BLT. This allows for pattern offset. Note that the pattern must be loaded to a 32-bit address boundary such that bits 4–0 are zero. The writes must be on the boundaries shown in Table 24.22.

The destination address is a 24-bit address and specifies the bit address of the starting corner of the destination bit map. This corner is relative to the direction indicated by bits 6 and 7 of the Control Register at ACM Index 34h. For full color depth color, DST data, the three least significant bits of the source

TABLE 24.21   BitMap Dimension Registers

Bits	Format
27–16	Bitmap Height
11–0	Bitmap Width

TABLE 24.22   Pattern Address Boundaries

Bits/Color	Boundary
8	Modulo 2 dword
15/16	Modulo 4 dword
24	Modulo 6 dword

address are not used. For color comparison screen-to-memory BitBlts, where a monochrome SRC bitmap is used, either supplied by the system or resident in video memory, the LSBs of this register are required to specify initial DST bit alignment.

24.11.6 Foreground and Background Color Registers

These 24-bit registers specify the foreground and background colors that will be used for color expansion of a monochrome source. The pixel depth is specified through bits 5–4 of the Extended Pixel Control Register at SEQ 21h. In addition, the Background Color Register is used to hold the compare color for full depth Source Transparency functions.

24.12 THE BLT ENGINE SOFTWARE INTERFACE

There are two ways of communicating with the BLT engine. These are by processing one BLT at a time or by building an instruction queue. An instruction template is used in either case. It consists of three items as shown in Table 24.23. The terminology MS (system Memory to Screen) is used when the source address of a BLT is not in video memory. The terminology SM (Screen to system Memory) is used when the destination address of a BLT is not in video memory. Both MS and SM transfers are called autonomous. Non-autonomous transfers are Screen-to-Screen (SS).

24.12.1 Single Instruction Operation

When loading one instruction at a time, it is necessary to follow the steps listed in Table 24.24.

24.12.2 Instruction Queue

If an instruction queue is required, the steps would occur as shown in Table 24.25. In this case, an interrupt handler is required such that an interrupt will be generated upon completion of an autonomous BLT call. The interrupt

TABLE 24.23 Instruction Template

Field	Description
Control Word	Contains information on whether this BLT is MS or SM and whether a pattern is used and needs to be loaded.
Array of Parameters	Values to be loaded into registers.
Pointers	Pointing to system memory bitmaps, if necessary, patterns, source or destination for SM Bit Maps.

TABLE 24.24 Steps Involved in Single Instruction Control of the BLT

Step	Operation
1	Process parameters into the instruction template.
2	Wait for any previous autonomous BLT drawing to finish.
3	Load any pattern data into the frame buffer, if necessary.
4	Load the BLT Registers from the template using rep outs or movs instructions.
5	Transfer data into or out of video memory.

TABLE 24.25 Steps Involved in Queued Instruction Control of the BLT

Step	Operation
1	Process parameters into the instruction template.
2a	If BLT is busy, put the instruction template onto the queue.
2b	If BLT is not busy proceed with steps 3–5.
3	Load any pattern data into the frame buffer, if necessary.
4	Load the BLT registers from the template using rep outs or movs instructions.
5	Transfer data into or out of video memory.

handler should take the first instruction off of the instruction queue, adjust the queue pointers, and follow steps 3-5 in Table 24.25.

24.13 DATA TRANSFERS INVOLVING THE HOST

The BLT can do data alignment, color expansion, operand fetches, and masking as the CPU pushes SRC data into the chip. All bitmap data transfers to and from video memory with the BLT turned on should use the REP MOVSD instruction. This moves double words into the engine. Text is an exception to this rule. The BLT should be turned on with appropriate information regarding the type of BLT and the operand locations before the bitmaps are sent to the engine. For MS BitBlts, the CPU address sent by the host on the address bus is ignored. However, they must be sent into the A0000h–AFFFFh 64 Kbyte aperture.

24.13.1 Source and Destination Initial Alignment

The least significant byte of the address found in the source and destination address registers will be initial alignment information. For MS BLT calls, the source is in system memory. The driver code needs to load this least significant byte into the SRC Address Register even though the source is not in video memory. This byte is used to specify the initial alignment of the source data in the system memory. The DST Address Register needs to be loaded with the address of the first pixel of the destination. This would be the upper-left corner for left-right, top-down BLTs. The DST, SRC, and PAT Address Registers contain a linear address pointing into the display memory. None of the other extended registers affect this address.

One REP MOVSD instruction should be used per scan line. The CPU SI Register should be loaded with the first source pixel address in host memory. However, this word has to be double-word aligned. A double-word-aligned address has the two least significant bits set to 0. The DI Register can be set to any address in the A0000h–AFFFFh 64 Kbyte aperture. It is typically set to A0000h. The DI Register must also be double-word aligned. The BLT engine expects a integer number of double word transfers for each scan line. Once again, text BLTs are the exception. The first and last double word are special cases. They may or may not contain real data, depending on the initial alignment and the X-extent. It is a good habit to reload the SI and DI Registers after every scan line transfer.

24.13.2 Color Expansion

Color expansion works in the same manner. Initial alignments point to the individual pixels of the source of the color expansion data. The SRC address registers, bits 4–0, refer to which of the 32 bits (pixels) in the double word represent the first valid pixel. Color expansion, alignment, and masking are accomplished in hardware. Thus, the software need only generate the REP MOVSD instruction.

24.13.3 Source and Address Registers

Source and destination address registers are linear addresses that point into the display memory. Each must be loaded with a pointer to the first pixel involved in the operation. When performing a MS or SM BLT, the data can never overlap and consequently, the left-to-right and top-down direction is typically used. In this case, the top-left corner should be loaded as the starting address. In the case of a left-to-right and down-up BLT, the lower-right corner is loaded into the source or destination addresses.

NOTE: The source and destination address registers are BIT addresses. They point to bits as opposed to bytes, words, or double words. This is necessary when dealing with monochrome, 1-bit-per-color bit maps. When performing full-color bitmaps, the three least significant bits of the low-order byte of both the source and destination address registers are meaningless and can be set to 0.

The five least significant bits of an address register must be used to determine the initial alignment in system memory. Bits 4–3 are used for full color byte alignment. Bits 4–0 are used for monochrome bit alignment. If the bitmap does not start on a double word boundary, the starting alignment should be loaded into bits 4–0.

For system memory-to-screen (MS) full-color transfers, the source address bits 4–3 will point to the initial source byte alignment. This occurs since bits 2–0 point to one-of-eight pixels per byte. Bits 4–3 point to each 4-bytes-long double word. For the color expansion of monochrome data, the source address bits 4–0 contain the starting bit within the first double word. For full-color screen-to-system memory (SM) transfers, the destination register bit 4–3 point to the starting byte alignment expected in system memory. When performing color comparisons, the SM BLT requires that the destination address bits 4–0 should be loaded with a bit alignment indicating where the position of the first color comparison.

24.13.4   Screen to Screen BLT

Some system memory-to-screen transfers can be performed autonomously as SS BLTs if the appropriate operands are first loaded into the registers and the appropriate data loaded into the display memory. For example, pattern copies should be done as SS BLTs. First the pattern is loaded into memory using the MS BLT. Repetitive BLTs can then be accomplished using the screen-to-screen transfers. A rectangle fill operations such as whiteness and blackness, may be referred to as a MS BLT in certain documentation. However, it is always done as an SS BLT.

An example is provided that performs a screen-to-screen BitBlt copy operation. The steps are illustrated in Table 24.26.

The ACM template is typically set up by defining a structure in system memory and then using REP MOVSD with decrementing address to transfer the values to the 32BLT ACM. The BitBlt control section of the ACM ranges from index 50h to index 30h such that the decrementing REP MOVSD ends with

TABLE 24.26   Screen-to-Screen Copy

Step	Function
1	The linear address of the source starting corner is calculated and loaded into the Index 44h Register of the template.
2	The linear address of the destination is written to template Index 40h.
3	The width of the source (in pixels) is located to template Index at 3Ch.
4	The height of the source in scan lines is written to template Index 3Eh.
5	The raster op is written to template Index 3Ah.
6	The "GO" bit is set in template Index 30h.
7	The template is MOVSD to the ACM aperture.

ACM index 30h, which is the start/status register. In the template, the registers associated with each template location are equated to the name of that register, such that offset 40h is named Dest.

The example provided in Listing 24.7 is a screen-to-screen copy where the source and destinaion maps do not overlap and all drawing is done to the right-and-down. For overlapping bitmaps, the x values of the source and destination are compared and then the BLT is performed left-to-right if the destination lies to the left of the source. Similarly, if the destination lies below the source, then the vertical direction is from bottom-to-top.

The information provided to this section of code are the X and Y coordinates of the top-left corner of the source and destination, the width of the source in pixels, the height of the source in scan lines, and the raster op.

LISTING 24.7 Screen-to-Screen BitBlt

```
;     calculate the linear address of the source starting corner
      movzx   eax,SRC_Y      ; SRC starting corner Y
      movzx   ebx,SCRN_WID   ; Screen width in pixels
      mul     ebx            ; linear pix to reach this scan line
      add     eax,SRC_X      ; SRC starting corner X
      movzx   ebx,PIX_DEPTH  ; Number of bytes per pixel
      mul     exb            ; linear byte address of SRC corner
      shl     eax,3          ; linear bit address of SRC corner
      mov     SRC,eax        ; write to source location in template

;     calculate the linear address of the destination starting
;     corner
      movzx   eax,DST_Y      ; DST starting corner Y
      movzx   ebx,SCRN_WID   ; Screen width in pixels
      mul     ebx            ; linear pix to reach this scan line
      add     eax,DST_X      ; DST starting corner X
      movzx   ebx,PIX_DEPTH  ; Number of bytes per pixel
      mul     exb            ; linear byte address of DST corner
      shl     eax,3          ; linear bit address of DST corner
      mov     DST,eax        ; write to destination location in template

;     specifiy rotation (none) and RasterOp
      mov     ax,0CCh        ;SRCCOPY
      mov     ROT_ROP,ax     ;store in template

;     Specify the BLT type as screen-to-screen and full color
      mov     ax,0B000h      ;specify screen to screen full color
      mov     CNTL,ax        ;put in template

;     Set the start bit in the start/status reg
      mov     ax,1           ;start code
```

```
        mov     STRT_STAT,ax  ;put into template

;   Transfer template data to the 32BLT ACM
        mov     cx,6          ;repeat count double words
        mov     di,ACM_LOC    ACM location
        mov     si,TEMP_LOC   ; template location
        std                   ;decrement direction
        rep     movsd         ;send template to 32BLT
```

Depending on the type of BLT, some template values may or may not need to be loaded and transferred to the ACM. Of course, the fewer values transferred, the faster the operation. Thus, the starting index for the ACM_LOC may point to a starting index less than 50h. The transfer in Listing 24.7 moves data from 44h to 30h. Note that this is 6 (double words) * 4 (bytes/double word) = 24 bytes.

24.14   PATTERNS

24.14.1   Loading Patterns into Screen Memory

Patterns are loaded into the screen memory as linear bitmaps, not as two-dimensional data. The terminology is confusing here. Screen memory or display memory can be off-screen, which is linear, or on-screen, which is rectangular. Off-screen memory is also referred to as frame buffer memory. The first scan line, scan line 0, of a pattern should be loaded first, beginning with the lowest address. A pattern remains loaded until some other data overwrites it. Therefore, some type of off-screen memory management is required to maintain control of the patterns and other data that might reside there. This off-screen memory is valuable real estate. Patterns need to be started at certain boundaries in the off-screen memory. For 8-bit-per-color modes, the condition for the boundary is the first double word address must be even, called modulo 2. For the hi-color modes, 16-bit-per-color modes, the alignment must be modulo 4. For true-color modes, 24-bit-per-color, the boundary is modulo 6. Remember, these modulos are with respect to double-word addresses. An even double word means that the three least significant bits of the address are 0, not just the least significant bit. These are provided in Table 24.27.

An 8-by-8 pattern in an 8-bit-per-color mode would therefore require its first pixel to be on an even boundary, say 4002h. A double-word address consists of four bytes, put into maps 0–3. This is illustrated in Table 24.28. In this table, L refers to the line of the pattern, 0–7, and P refers to the pixel within that line.

24.14.2   Pattern Address Calculations

The Pattern Address Register is loaded with a new calculation each BLT call. This is because the register is **not** loaded with the starting address as indicated in Table 24.25. Rather, it is loaded with the location of the first scan line that

TABLE 24.27 Pattern Alignment

Bits/color	Modulo	Bytes/pixel	Alignment (bytes)
8	2	1	2 double words = 8 bytes
16	4	2	4 double words = 16 bytes
24	6	3	6 double words = 24 bytes

TABLE 24.28 Loading an 8-by-8 Pattern in an 8-bit-per-color Mode

Double-word Address (hex)	Map 3		Map 2		Map 1		Map 0	
	L	P	L	P	L	P	L	P
4002	0	3	0	2	0	1	0	0
4003	0	7	0	6	0	5	0	4
4004	1	3	1	2	1	1	1	0
4005	1	7	1	6	1	5	1	4
4006	2	3	2	2	2	1	2	0
4007	2	7	2	6	2	5	2	4
4008	3	3	3	2	3	1	3	0
4009	3	7	3	6	3	5	3	4
4010	7	3	7	2	7	1	7	0
4011	7	7	7	6	7	5	7	4

is fetched by the BLT. The BLT engine cannot currently compute the offset into the pattern address; consequently, this must be done by the software. The direction of the pattern fetches also affects this address. If the Direction_Down bit is reset, the address of the last double word of that scan line must be loaded into the Pattern Address Register. The appropriate scan line of the pattern must be used for the starting destination corner. If the Direction_Down bit is reset, the address of the last double word (not the first) of that scan line is issued.

Suppose that the pattern loaded in Table 24.25 is to be used as the source of a pattern copy BLT and that the upper-left corner of the destination rectangle has a Y coordinate of 3 and X coordinate of 6. In addition, suppose that the BLT direction can be done left-to-right and top-down. The BLT will start in the upper-left corner of the destination rectangle at (6,3). Note from Table 24.25 that the Y=3 refers to the third scan line. Since the pattern has scan line 3 beginning at 4008, the value of 4008 would be loaded into the Pattern Address Register. Note that the X=3 coordinate is ignored.

A second example supposes that the same pattern is used but the BLT is a two operand SRC and PAT combination and that the source and destination overlap such that the BLT needs to start in the lower-right corner for a right-to-left, top-down BLT. In addition, suppose that the lower-right corner is at Y=3 and X=6. Once again, the X=6 is ignored, and the Y=3 is used. Since the pixel P=7 resides at double-word address 4009, the value of 4009 is loaded into the Pattern Address Register. Note that the address value calculated for PAR is a double-word address; therefore it would be loaded into bits PAR [24"5].

PAR[24-5] = Pattern Start Address + rotation + offset

where:

The rotation is equal to the starting PAT Y rotation * modulo.
where the modulo is 2, 4 or 6 depending on the bits/color of 8, 16, or 24 respectively.

The offset is equal to 0 if it is a left-to-right, top-down BLT or

is equal to 1,3 or 5 if it is a right-to-left, down-up BLT depending on the bits/color of 8, 16, or 24 respectively.

Consequently, it can be seen that the destination of the transfer affects the starting address of the pattern offset.

24.14.3   The PAT Starting X and Y Rotation Registers

These registers are modulo 8 for an 8-by-8 pattern. These are used to load the starting PAT X and Y rotation values. If a corner other than the upper-left is used, the starting rotation for the corner used must be loaded. The X rotation is used only in the 24-bit-per-color true-color modes. Instead of the X rotation, the Destination Address Register is used when in the 8- or 16-bit-per-color modes.

24.14.4   Loading an 8-by-8 Pattern

You can use the BLT engine to perform an 8-by-8 copy, or you can use the REP MOVSD instruction to move the same data keeping the BLT engine turned off. It takes approximately eight to ten 32-bit registers to turn the BLT engine on. This is about 40 bytes. An 8-by-8 pattern in a 8-bit-per-color mode occupies 64 bytes. Thus, an extra 40 bytes of transfer are required if the BLT engine is to be used. Since the original pattern resides in system memory, it can be constrained to be double-word aligned. Similarly, patterns are forced to be double-word aligned in the screen memory. Consequently, the REP MOVSD instruction can be very fast.

24.15 SIMULTANEOUS OPERATION

It is possible to load data from the host into the screen memory while a screen-to-screen BLT is in progress. This parallel processing can be used to an advantage. However, it is not possible to perform non-BLT writes to the screen when a system memory-to-screen BLT is in progress.

24.16 TEXT BLT

Fonts are typically eight pixels wide residing in consecutive bytes in system memory. These fonts are in a 1-bit-per-pixel data format. With the BLT turned on in a text mode, the data transfer should occur using the REP MOVSB command. The repeat count in the CX Register is equal to the character height. The SI Register contains the address of the font in system memory, and the DI Register contains the pixel address. The address of the first byte of each font will be used as the address of the upper-left corner of the character box. This address will be affected by the extended memory registers and will be captured by the BLT and used as a base address to complete the drawing of the character. Each byte received is color expanded, aligned, and written with the appropriate masking. Each byte is written on consecutive scan lines based on the offset value in the CRTC Offset Register.

24.16.1 Clipping

Non-clipped characters should be programmed with an Xextent of 8 since these are eight pixels wide. If a character is clipped on the right side only, the Xextent register is changed to the actual number of pixels to be written. If the character is clipped on the left side, both the Xextent and the initial source alignment in the SRC Address Register bit 4–0 must be changed to reflect the initial alignment.

24.16.2 Character Strings

The Text Blt operation is reenabled at the completion of each repeat count. A string of text with the same character height need not reload the BLT registers. Only the address of the first memory write operation is important as a pointer to the new character box.

24.16.3 Stopping a Text BLT

Since text BLTs are reenabling, the BLT must be stopped with a write to the Mode/Control/Status Register.

24.16.4 Transparency

Text BLTs can be opaque or transparent. The foreground and background colors are used for the color expansions for opaque transfers; only the foreground color is used if transparent. To stop a text BLT, the CPU must write the GO bit and Text BLT field to 0 when the BLT is not busy. Not busy is sensed by reading bit 5 of this register. For text BLTs, the busy bit indicates when the previous font is finished, the BLT is idle, and the registers can be changed for the next font.

24.17 STARTING AND STOPPING THE BLT

The Mode/Status Register is used to start and stop the BLT engine. After all of the appropriate registers are loaded, the Mode/Status Register should be loaded with the GO bit active. The GO bit is in bit position 2. This starts the BLT. At the completion of the BLT, the GO bit is reset by the BLT engine. The text BLT is the exception as shown in Section 24.6.3. The BLT can generate an interrupt.

To stop a scan left/right BLT, comparing for boundary, the CPU must stop the BLT by clearing the GO and Text BLT bits to 0. The CPU should not wait for the busy state by reading the busy bit since this may never occur. Otherwise, the busy bit should be checked before writing to any of the BLT registers. For non-text BLTs, the busy bit indicates when the BLT operation is finished.

24.18 BLT TYPES

There are several types of BLT operations as indicated in Table 24.29. Table 24.30 further illustrates the values that would be loaded into the various registers to create these BLTs.

24.18.1 Raster Operations

Some useful raster operations are shown in Table 24.31.

24.19 WRITABLE BIOS

The 32BLT also supports writable BIOS through redirecetd frame buffer addressing. This is enabled through the setting of bit 7 of the Miscellaneous Select Register at SEQ 27h. When this bit is set, writes to display memory are written to the BIOS location at C0000–C7FFF. Display memory addresses are located at the 32 Kbyte segment at A0000–A7FFFh in graphics modes or B8000–BFFFFh in text modes. This eliminates the need for BIOS shadowing, typically selected through the CMOS setup.

TABLE 24.29 Types of BLT operations

Type	Description
1	Screen to screen (SS)
2	Screen to screen (SS) with color expansion
3	Color fill solid color rectangle or a limited pattern rectangle
4	System memory-to-screen (MS)
5	System memory-to-screen (MS) with color expansion
6	Text BLT font in system memory, color expansion, step addressing
7	Screen-to-system memory (SM) full color
8	Screen-to-system memory (SM) with color comparison used on monochrome data in screen
9	Scan right; similar to 8 for 1 scan line
10	Scan left; similar to 8 for 1 scan line
11	Screen-to-screen with magic color transparency
12	Push box; save area of screen in linear off-screen memory (see 13)
13	Pop box; restore linear area back to display memory (see 12)
14	16-by-16 pattern Blt
15	System memory-to-screen (MS) full color with linear CPU data and an odd bit map width
16	Same as 15 with mono source data and color expansion
17	Screen-to-screen (SS) text storing fonts in video memory

TABLE 24.30 Register Programming for BLTs

Blt type	15–12	11–8	7–4	3–0	Register Program
1	1100	0000	aa00	0000	C0U0 – C0C0
2	1110	1000	11a0	0000	E8U0 – E8C0
3	1100	0010	1100	0000	C2C0
4	0100	0000	1100	a000	40CU – 40C0
5	0100	1000	11a0	a000	48UU – 48C0
6	0100	1000	11a0	0000	48U0 – 48E0
7	1000	0000	1100	a000	80CU – 80C0
8	1000	0100	1100	a000	84CU – 84C0
9	1000	0100	1100	0000	84C0
10	1000	0100	0100	0000	8440

TABLE 24.31 Raster Operations

Ropcode	Function	Name
00	0	Blackness
11	DSon	NotSRCcopy
44	SDna	SRCerase
5A	DPx	PATinv
66	DSx	SRCinv
88	DSa	SRCand
BB	DSno	Mergepaint
C0	PSa	Mergecopy
CC	S	SRCcopy
F0	P	PATcopy
FB	DPSnoo	PATpaint
FF	1	Whiteness
FE	DPSoo	3 operands ORed together
FC	PSo	Pat OR Source
FA	DPo	Dst OR Pat
EE	DSo	(SRCPAINT)
55	Dn	Invert destination
96	DPSxx	3 operands XORed together

Chapter 25

Oak

25.1 OAK SUPER VGA CHIPS

Oak has produced a series of VGA and Super VGA chips including the O37, O67, O77, O87, and the O107. The O37 is a single-chip VGA graphics controller capable of 800 by 600 in a 4-bit-per-color mode display mode supporting 132-column text. The O67 supports up to 1024 by 768 in 4-bit-per-color modes, 800 by 600 in 8-bit-per-color modes and 132 column text modes. In addition, the O67 supports a 768 by 1024 2-bit-per-color portrait mode.

25.1.1 OTI O87

The O87 supports 1280 by 1024 in 4 and 8-bit-per-color modes, 800 by 600 in 15- or 16-bit-per-color modes and 640 by 480 in 24-bit-per-color modes. It also supports the 132 column text modes and a portrait mode of 768 by 1024 with 4-bits-per-color mode. The O87 includes a VL bus interface, hardware cursor, read and write cache, and linear addressability. The O87 includes color expansion, 256 color patterns and fills, and a 16-bit graphics latch.

25.1.2 Spitfire OTI 64107, OTI 64105

These two chips are compatible high performance 654-bit DRAM GUI accelerators. These chips are **not** downwardly compatible to any other Oak chips. Several of the techniques used are similar; in fact, several registers are identical. However, they cannot be programmed with the same software. The OTI 64017 includes integrated multimedia support with a 16-bit interface and a shared video memory architecture. This multimedia architecture allows the simultaneous display of two overlapping video and graphics windows. Both chips talk to the ISA, VL, or PCI bus and support four operand raster ops, as called for by the Windows NT specifications. In addition, both support resolutions up to

1280 by 1024 in the 8-bit-per-color modes and 1024 by 768 in the true-color modes. True-color modes can be either 24 bit or 32 bit per color.

25.2 DISPLAY MODES

The Oak series of chips can support the standard extended display modes with the additional 768-by-1024 portrait mode. These modes are provided in Table 25.1.

25.2.1 Hi- and True-Color Modes

It is necessary to set the Oak DAC up to support the hi-color and true-color display modes. This is accomplished by the code segment in Listing 25.1, which calls upon the function in Listing 25.2.

TABLE 25.1 Display Modes

Mode	Resolution	Colors
52h	800 by 600	4
53h	640 by 480	8
54h	800 by 600	8
55h	1024 by 768	2
56h	1024 by 768	4
57h	768 by 1024	4
58h	1280 by 1024	4
59h	1024 by 768	8
5Ah	640 by 480	16
5Bh	640 by 400	15,16
5Ch	640 by 480	15
5Dh	800 by 600	15
5Eh	1280 by 1024	8
5Fh	640 by 480	24
60h	800 by 600	16
61h	640 by 400	8
h	640 by 480	32
h	800 by 600	32
h	1024 by 768	32

LISTING 25.1 After a Mode Set, Set Up the Oak DAC

```
case Oak087:  case Oak107:
        switch(Pixel_Bits) {
          case c15_bit: dac_value=0xa0;  break;
          case c16_bit: dac_value=0xc0;  break;
          case c24_bit: dac_value=0xe0;  break;
          default:              dac_value=0x00;  break;
            }
        Set_Oak_DAC(dac_value);
        break;
```

LISTING 25.2 Set the Oak DAC to Support Hi-color or True-color DACs

```
; Function:
;  It is necessary to manually control the true-color DAC in
;  order to achieve correct hi-color and true-color operation.
; Input Parameters
;       Dac_Value
;           00 to reset DAC disabling high or true color
;           A0 for hi-color 32K colors (15-bit)
;           C0 for hi-color 64K colors (16-bit)
;           E0 for hi-color 32K colors (24-bit)
; Calling Protocol:
;  Set_Oak_DAC(Dac_Value)

Set_Oak_DAC PROC FAR  , Dac_Value:BYTE
        mov     dx,3C8h
        in      al,dx   ;input to reset counter and point to index
        mov     dx,3c6h ;mask/command register
        in      al,dx
        in      al,dx
        in      al,dx ;must read 4 times for 3C6 to become command
        in      al,dx   ;register
        mov     al,Dac_Value
        out     dx,al   ;Set mode of DAC

        mov     dx,3c8h ;just for protection
        in      al,dx   ;reset 3c6h to mask
        ret
Set_Oak_DAC endp
```

25.3   EXTENSION REGISTERS

25.3.1   Extension Registers for the O87 and Below

The extension registers for the Oak chips including up to the O87 chip are located at 3DEh/3DFh indexed through the address registers at 3DEh. These are listed in Table 25.2. The extension registers are different for the OTI-64107 and are provided in Section 25.11.

TABLE 25.2   Extension Registers

Index	Register	R/W
—	Extension Address	R/W
0	Product Number	R
2	Status Register	R/W
3	Oak Test Register	R/W
4	Local Bus Control	R/W
5	Video Memory Mapping	R/W
6	Clock Select	R/W
7	Configuration Reg 1	R
8	Configuration Reg 2	R
9	Scratch Reg 1	R/W
A	Scratch Reg 2	R/W
B	Scratch Reg 3	R/W
C	CRT Control	R/W
D	Oak Miscellaneous	R/W
E	Backward Compatibility	R/W
F	NMI Data Cache	R
10	Dip Switch Read	R
11	Segment	R/W
12	Configuration	R
13	Bus Control	R/W
14	Oak Overflow	R/W
15	HSYNC/2 Start	R/W
16	OTI Overflow Reg 2	R/W
17	Extended CRTC Reg	R/W
18	EEPROM Control	R/W
19	Extended Color Palette Address	R/W
20	FIFO Depth	R/W
21	Mode Select	R/W
22	Feature Select	R/W
23	Extended Read Segment	R/W

TABLE 25.2 *(cont.)*

Index	Register	R/W
24	Extended Write Segment	R/W
25	Extended Common Read/Write	R/W
30	Color Expansion	R/W
31	Foreground Color	R/W
32	Background Color	R/W
33	Color Pattern	R/W
34	Word Mode Pixel Mask	R/W
35	CPU Latch Index	R/W
36	CPU Latch Data	R/W

25.3.2   The Extension Registers in the OTI 64105/107

The extension registers for the OTI 64105 and 64107 are provided in Section 25.11. Since these registers are not downwardly compatible in all cases to the O87 and below chips, they are provided in their own section.

25.4   IDENTIFYING THE OAK CHIP

The Product Identification Register returns a 1 if the chip is a O87 chip. The Status Register returns information regarding the system. It is set at hardware reset and is shown in Table 25.3. The Status Register provides information that may be useful to the programmer as shown in Table 25.3.

Code to identify if an Oak chip is present is provided in Listing 25.3. Code to identify which Oak chip is provided in Listing 25.4.

TABLE 25.3   Status Register

Bit	Description	
0	Status	0=286, 1=386/486 Read Only
2–1	Memory Size	0=256K, 1=512K, 2=1Meg, 3=2Meg

LISTING 25.3   Determine if the Chip Is an Oak

```
/* Output Parameters:
        1   card is a Oak
        0   card is NOT a Oak
Calling Protocol:
  Oak= Is_It_Oak()   */
```

(continued)

```
int Is_It_Oak(void)
{ int i;
  unsigned char in_value,out_value;

  // try and write to the 3DE/3DF pair. see if 3DE exists
  for(i=0; i<32; i++) {
  out_value = i;   outp(0x3DE,out_value);
  in_value = inp(0x3DE)&0x1f;
  if(in_value!=out_value) return(CHIP_NOT_FOUND);
  }
return(CHIP_FOUND);
}
```

LISTING 25.4 Determine Which Oak Chip

```
/* Output Parameters:
        identity        integer containing chip code
Calling Protocol:
 identity = Which_Oak()   */

int  Which_Oak(void)
{ int i;
  unsigned char in_value,out_value,old_value;

 outp(0x3DE,0x11);   // first figure out if it is an 037 by
                     // seeing if 3DE index 11h exists
 // try and write to the 3DE/3DF pair. see if 3DE exists
 for(i=0; i<8; i++) {
        out_value = i;   outp(0x3DF,out_value);
        in_value = inp(0x3DF);
        if(in_value!=out_value) return(Oak037);   // it is 037
        }

 out_value=0x00;  outp(0x3DF,out_value);   // restore to 0

// check if it is an 087 by programming an A into index 24 and
// reading it in 25.  If it reads back then it is a 087
 outp(0x3DE,0x24);   // try programming an A into the index
register 24
 outp(0x3DF,0x0a);
 outp(0x3DE,0x25);   // try reading index register 25
 in_value = inp(0x3DF);
 if(in_value==0x0A) return(Oak087);   //it is an 087

// check here for 107 see if the Scratch Register exists at
// index F0
outp(0x3DE,0xF0);
```

```
in_value=inp(0x3DF);
outp(0x3DF,0xAA);
outp(0x3DF,in_value);   // replace the original value
if(in_value==0xAA)  {
  // now see if index 29 exists for the Hardware Window
Arbitration Register
   return(Oak105) else return(Oak107);
   }

// check if it is an 067/077 by programming the index 16 register
// with a 0-3 in bits position 4-3.  If they can be read back
// then 077 (since not 87 or 107) else it is a 67
 outp(0x3DE,0x16);
 old_value = inp(0x3DF);

 // see if we can write a 00
 out_value=(old_value & 0xe7);   // don't touch bits 7,6,5,2,1,0
 outp(0x3DF,out_value);  // send out 0's in bits 4-3
 in_value = inp(0x3DF);

 if(in_value!=out_value) return(Oak067);   // must be 067 since
                                           // no index 16

 // see if we can write 1's into bits 4-3
 out_value |= 0x18;  outp(0x3DF,out_value);
 in_value = inp(0x3DF);
 if(in_value!=out_value) return(Oak067);   // must be 067

 outp(0x3DF,old_value);
 return(Oak077);  // must be a 077 since can successfully write
bits
 }
```

25.5 MEMORY ADDRESSING

The Video Memory Mapping Register, which is described in Table 25.4, is used to enable linear mapping. If bit 0 is set to 1, linear addressing is in effect. If the linear mapping is to extend beyond the 16 Mbyte space, DMA has to be turned off. This is accomplished by setting bit 1. The memory address aperture select field selects the size of the aperture as per Table 25.5. The starting address is described in Table 25.6.

The Segment Register controls the Read and Write Segments as shown in Table 25.7. The Write Segment controls all CPU Memory writes, and the Read Segment controls all CPU Memory reads. This register is provided for downward compatibility to other Oak products. The Extended Read, Write, and Common Read/Write Registers should be used in new applications.

TABLE 25.4 Video Memory Mapping Register

Bit	Description
0	Enable Oak Address Mapping; 0=A0000,B8000, 1=Oak Memory (see bit 2–3)
1	DMA Access disable; 0=normal, 1=Disable DMA to video memory
3–2	Memory address aperture select
7–4	Starting address

TABLE 25.5 Memory Address Aperture Select

0	x00000–x3FFFF 256 Kbyte aperture
1	x00000–x7FFFF 512 Kbyte aperture
2	x00000–xFFFFF 1 Mbyte aperture
3	x00000–1FFFFF 2 Mbyte aperture

TABLE 25.6 Starting Address

Value	Start Address
0	000000h
1	100000h
—	–
15	F00000h

TABLE 25.7 Segment Register

Bit	Description
7–4	Write Segment
3–0	Read Segment

The Extended Read Segment register uses the lower five bits for all read operations. The Extended Write Segment Register uses the lower five bits for all write operations. The Extended Read/Write Segment Register uses the lower five bits for all common read and write operations.

The macros found in Listing 25.5 can be used to set the read or write banks for the Oak chips. Although the registers in the OTI64105/107 are not generally compatible to the other Oak chips, the bank select mechanisms are identical.

LISTING 25.5 Macros to Set the Read and Write Banks

```
Input Parameters:
        bl desired bank number (64 Kbyte)

set_oak_write_bank    macro
        mov     dx,3deh       ;point to INDEX 11 Register
        mov     al,11h
```

```
        out    dx,al
        inc    dx
        in     al,dx       ;get the current value
        and    al,0fh      ;zero current write bank

        and    bl,0fh      ;make sure bank contains 0-15 only
        shl    bl,1        ;put into bits 4-7
        shl    bl,1
        shl    bl,1
        shl    bl,1
        or     al,bl
        out    dx,al       ;output bank
endm


; macro to read to read bank select for 037,067,077 bits 0-3
get_oak_read_bank    macro
        mov    dx,3deh     ;point to INDEX 11 Register
        mov    al,11h
        out    dx,al
        inc    dx
        in     al,dx       ;get the current value
        and    al,0f0h     ;zero current read bank
        and    bl,0fh      ;make sure bank contains 0-15 only
        or     al,bl
        out    dx,al       ;output bank
endm


; macro to write to separate write bank select for 087
set_oak_writes_bank  macro
        mov    dx,3deh     ;point to INDEX 24 Register
        mov    al,24h
        mov    ah,bl
        out    dx,ax       ;output bank
endm


; macro to write to separate read bank select for 087
set_oak_reads_bank   macro
        mov    dx,3deh     ;point to INDEX 23 Register
        mov    al,23h
        mov    ah,bl
        out    dx,ax       ;output bank
endm
```

25.6 START ADDRESS

The Oak Overflow Register contains bit 8 of the High Order Start Address in bit position 3. This high order start address bit 8 can also be controlled through the Extended CRTC Register. Bits 2–0 of this register contain bits 10–8. Three functions that load the start address for the O67, O77, and O87 processors are provided in Listing 25.6.

LISTING 25.6 Loading the Start Address on an O67

```
; Input Parameters:
;       start          top two bits of the start address
; Calling Protocol:
;       Load_Start_Top_Oak_0x7(cursor);

Load_Start_Top_Oak_067   proc far   cursor:BYTE
        mov    bl,start
        mov    dx,3deh    ;access bit 8 of the start address
        mov    al,14h     ;index Overflow Reg
        out    dx,al

;       read current value
        inc    dx
        in     al,dx      ;get value
        and    al,0f7h    ;zero out bit 3

;       or in new start address
        and    bl,01h     ;only want 1 bit in bit position 0
        mov    cx,3
        shl    bl,cl      ;shift left 3 to get bit in proper position
        or     al,bl
        out    dx,al      ;output bit 8 address
        ret
Load_Start_Top_Oak_067   endp

Load_Start_Top_Oak_077   proc far   cursor:BYTE
        mov    bl,start
        mov    dx,3deh    ;access bit 8 of the start address
        mov    al,14h     ;index Overflow Reg
        out    dx,al

;       read current value
        inc    dx
        in     al,dx      ;get value
        and    al,0f7h    ;zero out bit 3

;       or in new start address
        and    bl,01h     ;only want 1 bit in bit position 0
        mov    cx,3
        shl    bl,cl      ;shift left 3 to get bit in proper position
        or     al,bl
        out    dx,al      ;output bit 8 address
```

```
;       access bit 9 of the start address
        mov     dx,3deh
        mov     al,16h      ;index the Overflow Reg II
        out     dx,al

;       read current value
        inc     dx
        in      al,dx       ;get value
        and     al,0f7h     ;zero out bit 3

;       or in new start address
        and     bl,02h      ;only want 1 bit in bit position 1
        mov     cx,2
        shl     bl,cl    ;shift left 2 to get bit in proper position
        or      al,bl
        out     dx,al       ;output bit 9 address

        ret
Load_Start_Top_Oak_077   endp

Load_Start_Top_Oak_087   proc far  cursor:BYTE
        mov     bl,start
        mov     dx,3deh     ;access bit 8-10 of the start address
        mov     al,17h      ;index Overflow Reg

        mov     ah,bl
        out     dx,ax       ;output bit 8-10 address
        ret
Load_Start_Top_Oak_087   endp

Load_Start_Top_Oak_107   proc far  cursor:BYTE
        mov     bl,start
        mov     dx,3deh     ;access bit 8-10 of the start address
        mov     al,31h      ;index CRT Start Address Hi Reg

        mov     ah,bl
        out     dx,ax       ;output bit 22-16 address
        ret
Load_Start_Top_Oak_107   endp
```

25.7   64-BIT CPU LATCH

The CPU latch index/data registers select which of the eight bytes in the 64-bit graphics latch are read back. The 3-bit field in bits 2–0 of the CPU latch index latch select the desired byte. The byte can then be read or written to using the CPU Latch Data Register.

TABLE 25.8 Feature Select Register

Bit	Description
0	Enable content addressable for 64-bit graphics latch
4	Enable the 64-bit graphics latch
5	CPU latch swap

The Feature Select Register is shown in Table 25.8 It controls the 64-bit graphics latch.

If bit 4 is 0, the 64-bit graphics latch is disabled and this bit is high, the content of the 64-bit graphics latch can be selected from system address to be written out to video memory.

The CPU Latch Swap bit, if set, reverses the order to the high and low CPU latch during CPU write operations. This is useful when the CPU write address and the CPU read address are unaligned.

25.8 COLOR EXPANSION

The Color Expansion Control Register is used to control the color expansion feature. It is described in Table 25.9.

If the Enable Color Expansion bit is set to 1, color expansion is enabled. Memory data written to the video memory depends on the contents of the foreground color register, the contents of the background color register, and the contents of the color pattern register.

If the Select Pattern Register for color expansion bit is set, the color pattern register is used to select the foreground and background register. If 0, the CPU data bus is used to select the foreground or background register.

If the pixel ordering bit is 0, bit 7 correlates to pixel 7 of the character. If it is 1, bit 7 correlates to pixel 0 of the character.

TABLE 25.9 Color Expansion Control Register

Bit	Description
0	Enable Color Expansion 1=enable
1	1=Planar/0=Packed pixel color expansion mode select
2	Select Pattern Register for color expansion
3	Pixel Mask Enable
4	Pixel Mask Ordering

The foreground and background color registers are all 8-bit registers, containing an 8-bit color value. The Pattern Register is also eight bits; however, it contains eight individual binary bits for eight associated pixels.

25.9 PIXEL MASK

The Pixel Mask Register is also 8-bits containing eight individual bit-fields. In this case, each bit masks a pixel data. A 0, masks the data while a 1 allows the data through for the eight associated pixels. In Packed Pixel Modes, this register is used to mask individual pixels of a character, with bit 0 being the first pixel in a character. For planar modes, this register can be used as the Map Mask Register. The least-significant four bits are used as the map mask bits when the video memory address is odd and the most-significant four bits are used when the address is even.

25.10 STANDARD CURSOR

The standard cursors found on the O67, O77, and O87 are controlled using the code in Listing 25.7.

LISTING 25.7 Position the Cursor for the Oak O67, O77 or O87

```
; Input Parameters:
;       cursor          top two bits of address
; Calling Protocol:
;       Position_Cursor_Top_Oak_0x7(cursor);

Position_Cursor_Top_Oak_067 proc far  cursor:BYTE
        mov     bl,cursor
        mov     dx,3deh    ;access bit 8 of the cursor address
        mov     al,14h     ;index Overflow Reg
        out     dx,al

;       read current value
        inc     dx
        in      al,dx      ;get value
        and     al,0efh    ;zero out bit 4

;       or in new cursor address
        and     bl,01h     ;only want 1 bit in bit position 0
        mov     cx,4
        shl     bl,cl      ;shift left 4 to get bit in proper position
        or      al,bl
        out     dx,al      ;output bit 8 address

        ret
Position_Cursor_Top_Oak_067 endp
```

(continued)

```
Position_Cursor_Top_Oak_077 proc far   cursor:BYTE
        mov     bl,cursor
        mov     dx,3deh     ; access bit 8 of the cursor address
        mov     al,14h      ;index Overflow Reg
        out     dx,al

;       read current value
        inc     dx
        in      al,dx       ;get value
        and     al,0efh     ;zero out bit 4

;       or in new cursor address
        and     bl,01h      ;only want 1 bit in bit position 0
        mov     cx,4
        shl     bl,cl       ;shift left 4 to get bit in proper position
        or      al,bl
        out     dx,al       ;output bit 8 address

;       access bit 9 of the cursor address
        mov     dx,3deh
        mov     al,16h      ;index the Overflow Reg II
        out     dx,al

;       read current value
        inc     dx
        in      al,dx       ;get value
        and     al,0efh     zero out bit 4

;       or in new cursor address
        and     bl,02h      ;only want 1 bit in bit position 1
        mov     cx,3
        shl     bl,cl       ;shift left 3 to get bit in proper position
        or      al,bl
        out     dx,al       ;output bit 9 address

        ret
Position_Cursor_Top_Oak_077 endp

Position_Cursor_Top_Oak_087 proc far   cursor:BYTE
        mov     bl,cursor
        mov     dx,3deh     ;access bit 8-10 of the start address
        mov     al,17h      ;index Overflow Reg

        mov     ah,bl
        out     dx,ax       ;output bit 8-10 address
        ret
Position_Cursor_Top_Oak_087 endp
```

```
Position_Top_Oak_107 proc far   cursor:BYTE
        mov     bl,start
        mov     dx,3deh    ;access bit 8-10 of the start address
        mov     al,31h     ;index CRT Start Address Hi Reg

        mov     ah,bl
        out     dx,ax      ;output bit 22-16 address
        ret
Position_Start_Top_Oak_107   endp
```

25.11 HARDWARE CURSOR FOR UP TO THE O87 CHIP

The hardware cursor is controlled by the extension registers listed in Table 25.10.

The hardware cursor is controlled by the sixteen bits of the Horizontal Start Register (High and Low) and the sixteen bits of the Vertical Start Register (High and Low). The Horizontal and Vertical Preset Register define where the start of the cursor pattern resides within the 64-by-64 cursor pattern. The 24-bit start address of the cursor pattern is stored in the start address.

The foreground color and background color represent the colors selected by the cursor pattern.

The Control Register is described in Table 25.11

TABLE 25.10 Hardware Cursor Registers

Index	Register	R/W
—	Extension Address	R/W
40	HC Horizontal Start High	R/W
41	HC Horizontal Start Low	R/W
42	HC Vertical Start High	R/W
43	HC Vertical Start Low	R/W
44	HC Horizontal Preset	R/W
45	HC Vertical Preset	R/W
47	HC Start Address High Low	R/W
48	HC Start Address Low High	R/W
49	HC Start Address Low Low	R/W
4A	HC Foreground Color	R/W
4B	HC Background Color	R/W
4C	HC Control Register	R/W

TABLE 25.11 HC Control Register

Bit	Description
0	Enable Hardware Cursor; 1=on, 0=off
1	Display Selection; 0 is overscan, 1=displayed over the overscan
2	Data Format of Cursor; 0= bit 0 is first, 1=bit 7 is first
3	Blink Rate Enable; 1=enable blinking
5–4	Blink Rate; 0=4 frames/sec, 1=8, 2=16, 3=32

25.12 THE 64105/107 EXTENDED REGISTERS

The 64105/107 extended registers are provided in Tables 25.12.

TABLE 25.12 64105/107 Extended Registers at 3DE/3DF

Index	Register	R/W
—	Extension Address	R/W
2	Status	R/W
3	OTI Test Reg 1	R/W
4	OTI Test Reg 2	R/W
6	Clock Select/Scratch	R/W
7	Configuration Reg 1	R
8	Configuration Reg 2	R
9	Configuration Reg 3	R
C	I2C Control	R/W
D	Dip Switch Read	R
E	EPROM Control	R/W
F	Power Saving	R/W
10	Local Bus Control	R/W
11	Compatible Segment	R/W
13	ISA Bus Control	R/W
14	Memory Mapping	R/W
15	Mem & I/O Map Enable	R/W
19	Config/Aux/DAC Address	R/W
20	FIFO Depth	R/W
21	Mode Select	R/W
22	Feature Select	R/W
23	Extended Read Segment	R/W
24	Extended Write Segment	R/W

TABLE 25.12 *(cont.)*

Index	Register	R/W
25	Extended Common Read/Write Seg	R/W
26	RASn Control	R/W
27	CASn Control	R/W
28	Refresh Control	R/W
29	Hardware Window Arbitration	R/W
30	OTI CRT Overflow	R/W
31	CRT Start Address Hi	R/W
32	HSYNC/2 Start	R/W
33	CRT Address Compatibility	R/W
38	Pixel Interface	R/W
F0	Scratch Reg 0	R/W
F1	Scratch Reg 1	R/W
F2	Scratch Reg 2	R/W
F3	Scratch Reg 3	R/W
F4	Scratch Reg 4	R/W
F5	Scratch Reg 5	R/W
F6	Scratch Reg 6	R/W
F7	Scratch Reg 7	R/W

25.12.1 The Memory & Memory Mapping I/O Enable Register

The Memory & Memory Mapping I/O Enable Register is shown in Table 25.13. Bits 6 and 7 are necessary when the graphics memory base address is the same or in the same range as the memory-mapped I/O base address. If the memory spaces are not the same, both bits should be set to 1. This register defaults to 40h, with graphics memory enabled and memory-mapped I/O disabled.

TABLE 25.13 Memory & Memory Mapping I/O Enable Register

Bits	Description
6	Enable Graphic Memory Response; 1=enable access to graphics memory, 0=disable
7	Enable Memory Mapped I/O; 1=enable access to memory mapped I/O, 0=disable

TABLE 25.14 Configuration/DAC/Auxiliary Register Range

Bits	Description
3–0	I/O address range for special registers
4	Enable DAC address space; 0=3C6–3C9, 1=3C6–3C9, and 2x80–2x9F
5	Enable auxiliary DAC address space; 0=disable decoding for Auxiliary Registers, 1=enable

TABLE 25.15 I/O Address Range

Source	Address Range
Configuration Registers	3x00–2x3C
DAC Registers	2x80–2x9F
Auxiliary Registers	2xA0–2xBF

25.12.2 Configuration/DAC/Auxiliary Register Range

This register defines the address range for special registers as shown in Table 25.14.

Special registers controlled by bits 3–0 include the PCI-compatible configuration registers on the ISA and VL buses, DAC register address range in addition to the VGA DAC address range 3C6–3C9h, and auxiliary register address range for other devices in the graphics sub-system. The I/O range can be programmed to be from 2x00 to 2xBF where x is defined by the four bits in bits 3–0 and is shown in Table 25.15.

Bit 5 of the Feature Select Register enables write mode 4. Write mode 4 is used in unpacked pixel mode only. When this bit is set to 1, system data is routed directly to the display memory, bypassing the barrel shifter and the ALU. This provides for quicker system memory-to-screen source copies.

25.12.3 Extended CRT Controller Registers

The OTI CRT Overflow Register at index 30h bit 3 controls the CRT address offset bit 9 as required for large screen offsets.

The CRT Start Hi Register at index 31h contains the height order start address bits 22–16 in bits 6–0.

25.12.4 Extended Attribute Control Registers

The Pixel Interface Register at index 38h controls the pixel formatting as shown in Table 25.16.

TABLE 25.16 The Pixel Interface Register

Bits	Description
3–0	Pixel Mode
4	Color Ordering
6–5	Bits/pixel

The pixel mode defines nine modes that control the data routing. Only in mode 0 is memory data routed through the attribute controller data path. For modes 1–8, memory data is routed directly to the display memory bypassing the internal palette and PEL panning logic. This is shown in Table 25.17 where X represents the 8-bit pixel data.

The color ordering applies only to the 16- and 24-bits-per-pixel modes as shown in Table 25.18.

TABLE 25.17 Pixel Modes

Bits 2–0	Bits/pixel	Pixel Bus Width	Pixel Bus Ordering
0	VGA	8	25. P[7–0]
1	4	8	25. P1[3–0] P0[3–0]
2	8	8	25. P[7–0]
2	16	8	25. P0[7–0] 25. P0[15–8]
2	24	8	25. P0[7–0] 25. P0[15–8] 25. P0[23–16]
3	24	16	XP0[15–0] XP0[23–16]P1[7–0]
4	8	16	XP1[7–0]P0[7–0]
5	16	16	XP[15–0]
6	32	16	XP0[15–0]XP0[31–16]
7	24	24	P[23–0]
8	32	24	P[23–0]

TABLE 25.18 Color Ordering

Bits/pixel	Bit 4	Pixel[23–16] Byte 2	Pixel[15–8] Byte 1	Pixel[7–0] Byte 0
16	0	GGGRRRRR	BBBBBGGG	GGGRRRRR
24	0	BBBBBBBB	GGGGGGGG	RRRRRRRR
16	1	GGGBBBBB	RRRRRGGG	GGGBBBBB
24	1	RRRRRRRR	GGGGGGGG	BBBBBBBB

TABLE 25.19 Bits/Pixel

Bits 6–5	Bits/pixel
0	8
1	16
2	24
3	32

The Bits/Pixel field is shown in Table 25.19. The 32-bit-per-pixel mode using RGB swapping involves only the lower three bytes with the most significant byte left alone. For pixel mode 8, the lower three bytes are sent out to the DAC ad the most significant byte is ignored. Thus, pixel mode 8 is really a 24-bit-per-pixel mode using four bytes per pixel for improved ease of addressing.

25.12.5   Hardware Cursor/Hardware Window Registers

Either the hardware cursor or the hardware window registers can be active at a time, but never both at once. These registers are provided in Table 25.20.

The Horizontal and Vertical Start Registers provide the start of the HC/HW display area with respect to the start of the display are in pixel units. These numbers can be negative.

TABLE 25.20   Hardware Cursor/Hardware Window Registers

Offset	Register	R/W
81–80	HC/HW Horizontal Position Start	R/W
83–82	HC/HW Vertical Position Start	R/W
84	HC Horizontal Preset/HW Width Low	R/W
85	HW Width High	R/W
86	HC Vertical Preset Low	R/W
87	HW Height High	R/W
8A–88	HC Start Address	R/W
8F–8C	HC Color 0	R/W
93–90	HC Color 1	R/W
94	HC Control	R/W
96	HW Control	R/W
9A–98	HW Mask Map Start Address	R/W
9E–9C	HW Start Address	R/W
9F	HW Address Offset	R/W

TABLE 25.21 HC Control Register

Bit	Description
0	0=disable color HC 1=enable color HC
1	0=HC display is under overscan 1=HC display is over overscan
2	HC Data format 1=Motorola 0=Intel
3	HC Blink 0=disable blinking 1=enable blinking
5–4	Blink Rate: 0=4 1=8 2=16 3=32 frames on and off

The HC Horizontal Preset/HW Width Low Register provides the starting horizontal position of the HC within the 64-by-64 area in pixel units. The HC always ends at 63. For the HW Width, it provides the lower eight bits of the hardware window width in double-word increments. The HW Width High Register provides the upper eight bits of the HW width.

The IIC Vertical Preset Low and HW Height Low Registers provide the starting vertical position of the HC within the 64-by-64 area in scan line units. The HC always ends at position 63. The HW Height Register provides the lower eight bits of the HW height. The HW Height High Register provides the upper eight bits of the HW height.

The Start Address is a 24-bit starting address of the hardware window or cursor within display memory. TIT is programmed to the system linear address divided by 4 when in planar modes and divided by 8 when in packed display modes.

The HC Color 0 and Color 1 registers provide up to 32 bits of color for each color state. It follows the color format of the display mode.

The Hardware Cursor HC Control Register is described in Table 25.21.

25.12.6 HW Control Register

The Hardware Window HW Control Register is described in Table 25.22.

The HW Mask Map Start Address Register contains the 24-bit linear starting address of the image mask map buffer within the display memory. The value to be programmed is the system linear address and it must begin on word boundary.

The HW Start Address Register contains the 24-bit linear starting address of the buffer used by the input and output port within the display memory. The value to be programmed is the system linear address and it must begin on word boundary.

The HW Address Offset Register contains the display offset address in word units used to calculate the start of the next line in the window.

TABLE 25.22 HW Control Register

Bit	Description
0	1=Enable Hardware Window; 0=Enable Hardware Cursor
2–1	Horizontal scaling factor; 0=none, 1=/2, 2=/4, 3=/8
4–3	Vertical scaling factor; 0=none, 1=/2, 2=/4, 3=/8
5	Select odd/even lines for scaling; 0=select even, 1=select odd
6	YUV or RGB for scaling; 0=incoming data from Multimedia port is YUV, 1=RGB
7	Enable Mask Map for Multimedia Port with the Multimedia Mask Map

25.13   CO-PROCESSOR REGISTERS

The co-processor registers control all aspects of the graphics co-processor. These are memory-mapped registers as shown in Table 25.23.

25.13.1   Co-Processor Status Register

The Co-Processor Status Register is described in Table 25.24.

The bits 1–0 are read-only. They are used in CPU-assisted mode, where the software can find out which map the co-processor would need data to be fetched (memory-to-screen) by the CPU or which map would need data to be written to (screen-to-memory). The display map is shown in Table 25.25.

The bit 2 is used to indicate whether the map indicated by bits 1–0 needs to be written to (if 1) or read from (if 0).

The bit 3 is a read-only bit used to indicate whether bits 1–0 map are valid or not. When not valid, the software should reread bits 1–0 until this bit is valid. This bit acts like a ready status bit.

The bit 4 indicates that the address of the next access needs to be reset (if 1) or incremented (if 0) at the beginning of the map.

25.13.2   Co-Processor Control Register

The Co-Processor Control Register is shown in Table 25.26.

25.13.3   Pixel Map Registers

The Pixel Map Select Register selects the pixel map being accessed as shown in Table 25.27.

The Pixel Map n Width Register contains the value –1 in pixel units of the width of the pixel map. The Pixel Map n Height Register specifies the pixel map height –1 in pixel units.

TABLE 25.23 Co-Processor Registers

Offset	Register	R/W
10	Co-Processor Status	R/W
11	Co-Processor Control	R/W
12	Pixel Map Select	R/W
17–13	Pixel Map n Width	R/W
19–18	Pixel Map n Height	R/W
1B–1A	Pixel Map n Height	R/W
1C	Pixel Map n Format	R/W
21–20	Bresenham Error Term	R/W
25–24	Bresenham K1	R/W
29–28	Bresenham K2	R/W
2F–2C	Direction Steps	R/W
48	ROP	R/W
4A	Destination Color Compare Condition	R/W
4F–4C	Destination Color Compare Value	R/W
53–50	Pixel Bit Mask	R/W
5B–58	Foreground Color	R/W
5F–5C	Background Color	R/W
61–60	Operation Dimension 1	R/W
63–62	Operation Dimension 2	R/W
6D–6C	Mask Map Origin X Offset	R/W
6F–6E	Mask Map Origin Y Offset	R/W
71–70	Source X Pointer	R/W
73–72	Source Y Pointer	R/W
75–74	Pattern X Pointer	R/W
77–76	Pattern Y Pointer	R/W
79–78	Destination X Pointer	R/W
7B–7A	Destination Y Pointer	R/W
7F–7C	Pixel Operations	R/W

The Pixel Map n Format Register contains format information as seen in Table 25.28.

The number of bits per pixel field is described in Table 25.29.

The System Memory Indication field indicates where the selected pixel map resides. The source and destination pixel maps can have either 1, 8, 16, or 32 bits per pixel. Pattern pixel map can only have 1 bit per pixel. Programming

TABLE 25.24 Co-Processor Status Register

Bit	Description
1–0	Indicates which map needs data next.
2	Map needs read or write.
3	Map status valid.
4	0=Reset address to beginning of map, 0=increment address for next access.
5	0=Remain on current line, 1=advance to next line.
7	Co-Processor busy status bit; 0=idle, 1=busy. Read only.

TABLE 25.25 Display Map That Needs Data Next Field

Bits 1–0	Map
0	Pattern
1	Mask
2	Source
3	Destination

TABLE 25.26 Co-Processor Control Register

Bit	Description
0	Enable interrupt; 1=VGA interrupt to CINTn, 1=Co-processor interrupt to CINTn.
1	Enable Master Mode; 0=CPU assisted, 1=Bus Master.
4	Interrupt status; 1=interrupt pending. Writing a zero to this bit clears interrupt.
5	Terminate Co-processor operation; 0=allow coprocessor to finish, 1=abort.
6	Enable Turbo Co-processor data path; 0=default, 1=delete extra clock for datapath delay.

the pattern pixel map to be anything other than 1 bit per pixel will produce undefined results. The Mask Map Format Register cannot be programmed at all because it is assumed to be 1 bit per pixel. However, one should still program it to be 1 bit per pixel to ensure future compatibility.

TABLE 25.27 Pixel Map Select Register

Bits 1–0	Pixel Map
0	Mask
1	Pixel Map A
2	Pixel Map B
3	Pixel Map C

TABLE 25.28 Pixel Map n Format

Bit	Description
2–0	Number of bits per pixel
3	0=Intel format, 1=Motorola format
7	System Memory Indication; 0=local frame buffer, 1=system memory

TABLE 25.29 Number of Bits Per Pixel

Bits 1–0	Bits per pixel
0	1 bit
3	8 bits
4	16 bits
5	32 bits

25.13.4 Destination Color Comparison

The Destination Color Compare Condition Register contains a code in Bits 2–0 as shown in Table 25.30.

The Destination Color Compare Value Register is a 32-bit register that contains the color value to be compared to destination pixels when the color compare is enabled. Only the corresponding number of bits per pixel in the destination are required. If the Destination is 8 bits per pixel, only the low-order eight bits are used.

The Pixel Bit Mask Register is a 32-bit register that contains the enable (if 1) or disable (if 0) code for each pixel. If enable, the corresponding pixel is subject to change. Again, only the number of bits per pixel in this register are relevant.

The Foreground and Background Color Registers are each 32 bits long and contain the foreground and background colors.

TABLE 25.30 Destination Color Compare Condition Register

Bits 2–0	Condition
0	Always true disable update
2	Dest = color compare value
4	Dest != color compare value
6	Always false (enable update)

The Operation Dimension 1 and 2 Registers use the lower 12 bits to specify the width and height respectively of the rectangle to be drawn by the PxBlt function. In each case, the number should be one less than the desired value.

The following registers, from offsets 6C to 7Bh, have two stages. The first stage of each register is where data is written to. The second stage is the actual counter where data can be read from. The counters are not loaded until a co-processor start is issued. These registers can therefore **not** be read immediately after they are written.

The Mask Map Origin X and Y Offset Registers provide the 13-bit X and Y offset to the mask map relative to the origin of the destination map.

The Source X and Source Y Pointer Registers contain the 12 bits of the X and Y coordinate of the source map. The Pattern X and Pattern Y Pointer Registers contain the 12 bits of the X and Y coordinates of the pattern map. The Destination X and Destination Y Pointer Registers contain the 12 bits of the X and Y coordinates of the destination map.

25.13.5 Pixel Operations Register

The Pixel Operations Register is described in Table 25.31.

TABLE 25.31 Pixel Operations Register

Bit	Description
2–0	Direction of the PxBlt or Line Draw
5–4	Drawing Mode
7–6	Mask Pixel Map
15–12	Pattern Pixel Map
19–16	Destination Pixel Map
23–20	Source Pixel Map
27–24	Co-Processor Function Control
29–28	Foreground Source
31–30	Background Source

The Direction of the PxBlt or Line Draw field specifies the direction octant for PxBlt and line draw operations as shown in Table 25.32. Note that if the direction refers to a line, the value in bits 2–0 is the octant 0–7 respectively. If it is the bit-Blt, only bits 2 and 1 are relevant.

The Drawing Mode field contains the bits that determine the attributes of line draw and draw and step operations as shown in Table 25.33.

The Mask Pixel Map Control field controls the enabling of the Mask Pixel Map as shown in Table 25.34.

The Pattern Pixel Map contains information regarding the pattern pixel map as shown in Table 25.35.

The Destination Pixel Map contains information regarding the destination map as shown in Table 25.36.

TABLE 25.32 Direction of the PxBlt

Bit 2–0	Direction Octant
00x	Start at top-left corner, increasing right and down
01x	Start at bottom-left corner, increasing right and up
10x	Start at top-right corner, increasing left and down
11x	Start at bottom-right corner, increasing left and up

TABLE 25.33 Drawing Mode

Bits 5–4	Drawing Mode
0	Draw all pixels
1	Draw first pixel null
2	Draw last pixel null
3	Draw area boundary

TABLE 25.34 Mask Pixel Map

Bits 7–6	Mask Functions
0	Mask Map disabled
1	Mask Map boundary enabled
2	Mask Map enabled
3	Reserved

TABLE 25.35 Pattern Pixel Map Control

Bits 15–12	Pattern Map Control
1	Use Pixel Map A
2	Use Pixel Map B
3	Use Pixel Map C
8	Use Foreground ROP
9	Generate Pattern From Source

TABLE 25.36 Destination Pixel Map Control

Bits 19–16	Destination Map Control
1	Use Pixel Map A
2	Use Pixel Map B
3	Use Pixel Map C

The Source Pixel Map contains information regarding the Source Pixel Map as shown in Table 25.37.

The Co-Processor Function Control Field contains control information for the Coprocessor as shown in Table 25.38.

The mode is designed to enhance text output. In order to use this mode, the following conditions must be met. The monochrome font must be stored as a pattern map. The font (pattern) map base address plus map width must always be within one quad word (64 bits). The operation dimension 1 must be less than or equal to map width (no tiling). For example, if the base address is 0, the map width can be any size up to 64. If the base address is 38 hex, the map width can only be up to 8.

The foreground source contains the source of the foreground data that will be combined with the destination when the pattern pixel is a 1 as shown in Table 25.39.

TABLE 25.37 Source Pixel Map Control

Bits 23–20	Source Map Control
1	Use Pixel Map A
2	Use Pixel Map B
3	Use Pixel Map C

TABLE 25.38 Co-Processor Function Control

Bits 27–24	Function
2	Draw and Step Read
3	Line Draw Read
4	Draw and Step Write
5	Line Draw Write
8	PxBlt
9	Inverting PxBlt
10	Area Fill PxBlt
11	TextBlt

TABLE 25.39 Foreground Source

Bits 29–28	Foreground Source
0	Use Foreground Color Register
2	Use Source Pixel Map

TABLE 25.40 Background Source

Bits 29–28	Background Source
0	Use Background Color Register
2	Use Source Pixel Map

The background source contains the source of the background data that will be combined with the destination when the pattern pixel is a 0 as shown in Table 25.40.

25.14 MULTIMEDIA INTERFACE

Multimedia support consists of the multimedia input port (MMI) and a multimedia output port (MMO) pair connected directly to the graphics frame buffer memory. This is also referred to as the display memory or the video memory.

25.14.1 MMI Port

The MMI port accepts live video data in a continuous input data stream from any source and stores it into the graphics frame buffer, eliminating the need of a system bus data path and a dual-frame-buffer memory scheme. The video data coming into the MMI port can be either in an RGB or in a YUV data format. Once the video data is stored into the graphics frame buffer it can be displayed on the screen via the MMO port.

25.14.2 MMO Port

The MMO port consists of a hardware window logic section that displays the stored video data, as opposed to the graphics data, on the screen. The hardware window fetches the video data directly from the graphics frame buffer and sends the video data to the DAC.

25.14.3 Chroma-keying

Video data can be displayed using chroma-keying. This involves storing the video data into a non-displayed area of the graphics frame buffer. In this case, a key code is placed in the display area of the graphics frame buffer at the point at which the video data is to be displayed on the screen. As the data from the graphics frame buffer is sent to the DAC, the DAC scans the incoming data for the key code. When the key code is encountered, the DAC will fetch the data from the non-displayed area of the graphics frame buffer. This non-displayed area is referred to as the video data, and the displayed area is referred to as the graphics area. The DAC multiplexes the data between the display area and the non-displayed area each time the key code is encountered. Chroma keying uses a pre-defined byte for the key. The switch is always done on a pixel boundary.

The window size for the video data is displayed on the screen. For each scan line, chroma-keys are placed in the graphics frame buffer to indicate the points at which the data multiplexing between the video and graphics data is to occur. A key is placed in the display area to indicate the beginning of the video image. Another key is placed in the video data itself to indicate the end of the video image. The window size of the video image is defined in this manner. The advantage of chroma-keying is that the color depth of the video data and format can be different from the graphics data. While this scheme provides color depth flexibility, it requires the use of an intelligent AC and external support logic used for switching.

In order to provide adequate bandwidth from memory, the graphics data is fetched during the display time while the video data is sent out during the non-display time. This scheme effectively limits the size of the video data window to the ration of display versus non-display time. This is typically 20–25 percent.

25.14.4 Video Masking

A second method called video masking or alpha channel masking is used to eliminate these switching problems. In this case, the color depth of the video data must be the same as the color depth of the graphics data and the input format must be RGB. This may limit the kind of video data that can be displayed. An inexpensive DAC can be used. Additional display memory is not required, and larger display windows can be used.

No special keying codes are required. The contents of the graphics frame buffer are sent to the AC, regardless of the data type. In order to support overlapping windows, a multimedia mask map is utilized to mask the video data that is stored in the graphics frame buffer. The multimedia mask map is a 1-bit-per-pixel map used to prevent the incoming video data from updating current graphics at on the screen, thereby preserving the contents of any graphics data that overlaps the video data. Each bit in the mask corresponds to one pixel in the display memory. Only incoming pixels of the video data corresponding to bits set to 1 in the mask will be stored into the graphics frame buffer. Because the video data occupies a portion on the displayed area, the video data is sent to the DAC in the same manner as graphic data. The driver must determine the size and shape requirement of the video windows and set up the multimedia mask map to simulate window overlap.

The multimedia mask map is read and written as bytes in the graphics frame buffer memory address space. Only whole bytes can be manipulated for each read or write to the mask. Each bit in the mask corresponds to one pixel in the displayed area of the screen. The software is responsible for "masking" the write to the mask map, so that only desired pixels are affected. The mask can reside anywhere in the non-display area and is programmable through the Multimedia Mask Map Start Address Register. This map is assumed to be continuous and has no offset. There is no alignment hardware for this map. All unused bits should be filled with 0 so that undesired pixels won't appear on the screen.

The 64107 supports video masking. There are two sets of memory-mapped registers that affect video masking . The first set, which controls the video data window, contains the WH Start Address Registers at offsets 9Ch–9Eh and the HW Address Offset Register at offset 9Fh. The Start Address Registers define the address within the graphics frame buffer at which the input data will be stored. The Address Offset Register defines the starting address of the next scan line of the video data. The value in the Offset Register is the scan line length of the displayable area on the screen. This may not be the same as the total scan line length. Once these registers are set up, the video data is automatically written into the graphics frame buffer for each cycle on the MMI port. In the case of outputs, the video data is fetched from the frame buffer for each cycle on the MMO port.

A second set of registers control the multimedia mask map. These are the HW Mask Map Start Address Registers at 3DF index 98–9Ah and the HW Control Register at 3F index 96h. The Mask Map Start Address Registers define the address within the frame buffer at which the multimedia mask map begins. The Control Register enables the use of the mask. When the video data is stored directly into the display area of the frame buffer, the multimedia mask

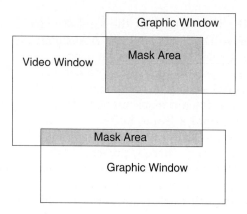

FIGURE 25.1 Video Windows and Image Masking on the 64107

map can prevent live video data from updating the existing contents of the frame buffer. First, masking has to enabled in the Multimedia Control Register; second, the corresponding bit in the mask has to be 0. They are defined by the video data window control registers must be greater than or equal to the area masked by the multimedia mask map. This is illustrated in Figure 25.1.

25.15 THE PCI INTERFACE

The PCI registers conform to the PCI specification with several manufacturer-specific fields as shown in Table 25.41.

25.15.1 Vendor ID Register

This register contains the vendor identification for the PCI bus. The value is 104E.

25.15.2 Device ID Register

This register contains the device identification. The OTI–107 is ID as 0107h.

25.15.3 System Bus Command Register

This register is configured at space address 04. It provides undefined control over a device's capability to generate and respond to PCI cycles. A zero written to this register disconnects a device from the PCI bus except for configuration accesses. Bits that do not pertain to the device's functionality may not be used. For example, if a device does not implement an I/O space, it is not likely to implement a writable element at bit location 0. The System Bus Command Register is a read/write register as described in Table 25.42.

TABLE 25.41   64105/107 PCI Registers

Address	PCI Registers	R/W
2x00	Vendor ID	R
2x02	Device ID	R
2x04	System Bus Command	R/W
	System Bus Status	R
2x08	Revision ID	R
	Programming Interface	R
	Cache Line Size	R/W
	Header Type	R
	Built-In Self Test	R/W
2x10	Mem Mapped I/O Base Address	R/W
2x14	Mem Base Address	R/W
	Aux & DAC I/O Base Address	R/W
	Base Address Reg 5–3	R/W
	Reserved	R
2x30	BIOS ROM Base Address	R/W
	Reserved	R
2x3C	Interrupt Line	R/W
	Interrupt Pin	R
	Min_Gnt	R
	Max_Lat	R

TABLE 25.42   System Bus Command Register

Bit	Description	Access	Function
9	Back to Back Cycle	R/W	1=no idle cycles between requests.
8	System Error Driver		1=error driver reporting address parity errors, 0=system error driver is disconnected.
7	Wait Cycle Control	R/W	1-address/data stepping is enabled, 0-disabled.
6	Parity Error	R/W	1=device set to respond to parity errors, 0=device ignores parity errors. Must be reset to 0. Devices must generate parity even if parity errors are disabled.
5	VGA Palette Snoop	R/W	1=Special snooping behavior is enabled. The device must not respond to DAC write operations. 0=Palette accesses are not treated specially.

(continued)

TABLE 25.42 *(cont.)*

Bit	Description	Access	Function
4	Reserved		
3	Special Cycles	R/W	1=device is allowed to monitor special cycle operations.
2	Reserved		
1	Memory Space	R/W	1=device is allowed to respond to memory space accesses. 0=device response is disabled.
0	I/O Space	R/W	1=device is allowed to respond to I/O space accesses. 0=device response is disabled.

The Back-to-Back Cycle bit is used when the controller is on the PCI bus and is capable of going into the bus master mode. Back-to-back cycles are transactions from one master to the same target without IDLE cycles in between the consecutive requests.

The Wait Cycle Control bit, if set to 1, allows the address/data to be driven out in more than one clock. If 0, the address/data stepping is disabled.

The VGA Palette Snoop bit is required in order to write to the DAC on the ISA bus. It writes to the palette register assert DEVSELn (LBSELn), allowing the write cycle to propagate out to the standard ISA bus for other devices to shadow these registers.

Memory space accesses are allowed to both memory and memory-mapped I/O when both the Memory Space bit and bit 1 of 3C2 are set to 1.

25.15.4   System Bus Status Register

The Device Status Register is at configuration space address 06h. The status of the PCI bus-related events are recorded in the Device Status Register. Bits that do not pertain to the device's functionality may not be used. As an example, a device that acts as a target but will never signal target-abort would not implement bit 11. Reads to this register are handled normally; writes differ in that bits can be reset but not set. Bits are reset whenever the register is written with data in the corresponding bit location. For example, writing the value 4000 clears bit 14 without affecting other bits. The Device Status Register is shown in Table 25.43.

The Master Abort Status bit is issued whenever the 107 is a bus master. It terminates its transaction (except for Special cycle) with a master-abort.

TABLE 25.43 Device Status Register

Bit	Description	Access	Function
15–14	Reserved		
13	Master Abort Status	RR	Set whenever 107 as master issues master abort
12	Received Target-abort	RR	Set whenever 107 as master receives target abort
11	Device Target-abort	RR	Set whenever 107 as target tissues target abort
10–9	Device Select Timing	RO	Timing of DEVSEL# 0=fast 1=medium 2=slow
8	Bus Master=0		Implemented by bus masters only
7	Fast back-to-back	RO	0=not capable of fast back-to-back, 1=capable

The Received Target Abort is set to 1 whenever the 107 is a target device. It receives a terminate transaction message with a target abort.

The Signaled Target Abort is set to 1 whenever the 107 is a target device. It terminates a transaction with a target abort.

The Device Select Timing field selects the speed of device selection. 0 is the fastest speed, 1 is medium, and 2 is slow.

The fast back-to-back transfers indicates whether the device is capable of fast back-to-back cycles. A 1 in this field indicates that fast back-to-back transfers are supported.

25.15.5 Revision ID Register

This register contains the chip revision. It changes only when there are functional differences between the revisions.

25.15.6 Class Code Register

This register provides the class encoding for backwards compatibility. The value of 0 in bits 23–0 represent all currently implemented devices except for VGA compatible devices. The value of 30000h indicates VGA compatible devices.

25.15.7 Cache Line Size Register

This register is currently reserved.

25.15.8 Latency Timer Register

This register specifies in units of the PCI bus clocks the value of the Latency Timer for OTI-107 while being bus master. Bits 7–3 are R/W. Bits 2–0 are read-only.

25.15.9 Header Type Register

Bits 6–0 are set to 0 and indicate the current offset for the configuration register. Bit 7 is a multi-function device indicator. This bit is read-only, but is configurable based on the board implementation. 0 indicates a single function device, and 1 indicates a multi-function device.

25.15.10 Built-in Self Test Register

This registers is currently reserved.

25.15.11 Memory-Mapped I/O Register

This register is described in Table 25.44.

The Locatable Area field indicates where memory resides as shown in Table 25.45.

25.15.12 Graphic Memory Base Address (1) Register

This register provides information regarding the memory and I/O addressing as seen in Table 25.46.

The Address Block Size field is set to 0 to occupy at least 8 Mbyte of memory address space on the PCI bus. On VL and ISA buses, however, these bits are R/W so that the display memory can be located at 1-Mbyte increments.

TABLE 25.44 Memory Mapped I/O Register

Bit	Description	Access	Function
31–8	Memory-Mapped I/O Base	R/W	Upper 24 bits of the base address for memory-mapped I/O.
7–4	Address space size	R	0 indicates 256 bytes of address space.
3	Pre-fetchable	R	0 if memory is not pre-fetchable (cacheable), 1 if cacheable.
2–1	Locatable area	R	Provides where address space resides.
0	Memory or I/O	R	Indicates 0 if memory mapped or 1 if I/O mapped.

TABLE 25.45 Locatable Area

Bits 2–1	Locatable area
0	Locate anywhere in the 32-bit address space
1	Locate below 1 Mbyte
2	Locate anywhere in the 64-bit address space
3	Reserved

TABLE 25.46 Graphic Memory Base Address (1) Register

Bit	Description	Access	Function
31–23	Base address	R/W	Upper 9 bits of base address for graphics memory
22–20	Address block size	R	0 Address block size
19–4	Address space size	R	0 indicates at least 1 Mbyte of address space
3	Pre-fetchable	R	0 if memory is not pre-fetchable (cacheable), 1 if cacheable
2–1	Locatable area	R	Provides where address space resides
0	Memory or I/O	R	Indicates 0 if memory mapped, 1 if I/O mapped

25.15.13 Extended I/O Base Address (2) Register

This register provides information regarding the memory and I/O addressing as seen in Table 25.47.

25.15.14 Base Address 5–3 Registers

These registers are reserved.

25.15.15 BIOS ROM Base Address Register

This register is reserved.

The ROM BIOS Address Decode Enable Register controls the ROM Address as shown in Table 25.48.

The BIOS ROM Size field may be a read-only field, depending on the values in the Configuration Register 2 bits 4 and 3. Otherwise, it is R/W. It indicates the size of the field as shown in Table 25.49.

TABLE 25.47 Extended I/O Base Address (1) Register

Bit	Description	Access	Function
31–8	Base address	R/W	Upper 24 bits of base address for extended I/O Registers
7–4	Address space size	R	0 indicates 256 bytes of address space
3	Pre-fetchable	R	0 if memory is not pre-fetchable (cacheable), 1 if cacheable
0	Memory or I/O	R	Indicates 0 if memory mapped or 1 if I/O mapped

TABLE 25.48 ROM BIOS Address Decode Enable Register

Bit	Description	Access	Function
31–18	BIOS ROM Address	R/W	Upper 14 bits of the base address for BIOS ROM
17–15	BIOS ROM Size	R/W	Size of BIOS ROM
14–11	BIOS ROM Min Size	R	0=BIOS ROM is minimally 32 Kbytes
0	BIOS ROM Decode	R/W	1=enable address decode for BIOS, 0=disable

TABLE 25.49 BIOS ROM Size Field

ER8[4–3]	ROM Size	R/W
0	32 K	Bits 17–15 are R/W
1	64 K	Bits 17–16 are R/W
2	128 K	Bit 17 is R/W
3	256 K	Bit 17–15 are always 0 and Read-only

25.15.16 Interrupt Line Register

The Interrupt Line Register is a scratch pad for POST software to write the interrupt line routine information during initialization and configuration of the system (PCI bus). Device drivers and operation systems can use this information to determine priority and vector information. Non PCI BIOS may use this register as a general purpose scratch register in addition to registers 3DF index 9, A and Bh.

25.15.17 Interrupt Pin Register

This register is at configuration space address 10h. It tells which interrupt pin a device uses. This register bit 0 is permanently set to the value of 1.

25.15.18 Minimum Grant (Min_Gnt) Register

The Minimum Grant Register is used to indicate to the system how long a burst period is required. The value of this register is FF (maximum allowed).

25.15.19 Max_Lat Register

The Maximum Latency Register is used to indicate to the system how often the device gets access to the PCI bus. The value of this register is 01, which indicates frequent access.

25.15.20 Base Address Register

The bits 24–31 of this register are written to by the system BIOS to indicate where in the 32-bit address space to map a 16 Mbyte linear address space to be used when the W32p is put into system linear mode. Bits 31–30 will be compared with address lines 31–30 in PCI mode when the CRTC Indexed Register 36 bit 4 is set to 1. In Revision B, bits 31–30 are not physically compared with address lines 31–30.

25.15.21 Expansion ROM Base Address Register

This register is at configuration space address 30h and handles the base address and size information for expansion ROM. In revisions prior to C, bits 31–1 are hardwired to the VGA compatible C0000h. Bit 0 is a read/write bit and is used to control whether or not the device accepts access to its expansion ROM.

In Revisions C and greater, bits 21–28 are read/write with a power up condition of 0. If the DISB PORI bit is set, then writes to these bits will have no effect. All zeros in this register locate the address at C0000h. When any other value is written to these registers, the ROM is remapped to a 256-Mbyte space which is designated by these bits 31–28. The actual ROM appears replicated at each 32 Kbyte boundary within this space.

Bits 27–1 are read-only and are hardwired to 0. Bit 0 is a read/write register used to control whether the device accepts accesses to its expansion ROM. When reset, the expansion ROM address space is disabled. When set, address decoding is enabled using the parameters in the other bits of this register. The memory space bit in the Command Register has precedence over this bit.

NOTE: Unlike the local bus implementation, moving the memory address range from A0000–BFFFF to any other location will not automatically disable the ROM. Disabling the ROM should be handled through bit 0 of this register.

Chapter 26

S3 Incorporated

26.1 S3 SUPER VGA CHIPS

S3 introduced the 86c911 GUI accelerator and created an instant success in the market place. Since then, they have introduced several other processors including the 86c914, the 86c801/86c805, and the 86c928. S3 incorporated several important graphics functions into the graphics accelerator while still maintaining a VGA-compatible platform. In addition, the chip was price competitive with other chips. The 911/924/928 drive VRAM while the 801/805 drive inexpensive DRAM memory. The fourth generation products from S3 include the Vision 864 and Vision 943.

26.2 PRODUCT LINE

S3 has introduced several graphics processors since the 911. These include the 924, 801/805, and the 928. Both the 911 and 924 are VRAM products, and the 801/805, which are functionally equivalent, are DRAM products. The 928 can support DRAM off-screen memory. The display resolutions increase up the chain from the 911, 924, 801, 805, to 928, as does the amount of addressable memory.

The chips power up in a VGA mode providing the VGA compatibility. It is kicked into the enhanced modes by setting bit 0 of the Advanced Function Control Register. The chip, like most VGAs, is backward compatible to the CGA, MDA, and HGC graphics chips.

The advanced modes provide hardware line drawing, BitBlt, rectangular fill, and image transfer between system and display memory. When in an advanced mode, operations are selected through a Drawing Command Register. Also available is a wide selection of data manipulation functions such as hardware clipping, color expansion, data source selection, and read/write bitplane control.

26.2.1   86C911/86C924

These two chips are very similar. Most differences are made up in the BIOS. Software can detect the difference in the S3R0 Register. An 81h indicates a 911, and an 82h indicates a 924. Both chips are designed for VRAM memory. Both are capable of driving up to 1024-by-768 8-bit color, 1280-by-1024 4-bit color, and 640-by-480 16-bit color modes. Alphanumeric modes include the 132-by-43 character mode.

26.2.2   86c801/86c805

These two chips are the DRAM versions of the 911/924. They have some additional capabilities including support for up to 2 Mbytes of memory and additional display modes up to 1280-by-1024 8-bit color, 800-by-600 16-bit color, and 640-by-480 24-bit color. The 801/805 are functionally equivalent, except for their bus interfaces. The 801/805 is downward compatible to the 911 and 924.

26.2.3   86c928

The 928 drives VRAM on-screen memory and can drive DRAM off-screen memory. It can directly access up to 4 Mbytes of memory. It supports modes up to 1600-by-1200 4- and 8-bit color, 1280-by-1024 16-bit color, and 1024-by-768 24-bit color. The 928 is downward compatible to the 924, 801/805.

26.2.4   The Vision864 and Vision964

The Vision864 and Vision964 processors are 64-bit graphic engines. The only difference is the 864 controls DRAM and the 964 controls VRAM. Because the 964 supports the higher bandwidth VRAM, it is capable of some higher resoluton display modes. Both parts are completely downward compatible to the 928 processor and can interface to the ISA, VL, or PCI bus. There are some different addtional features. The 864 can support up to 4 Mbytes of DRAM; the 964 can support up to 8 Mbytes. The 864 can provide resolutions up to 1600 by 1200 in 4 and 8 bits interlaced; the 964 can handle these resolutions non-interlaced. The 864 can support up to 1280 by 1024 in 4-, 8- and 16-bit color modes non-interlaced; the 964 can support up to 1600 by 1200 non-interlaced in the 4-, 8-, 16- and 32-bit display modes. The 864 supports a hardware cursor; the 964 relies on the hardware cursor capabilities of the resident DAC.

26.2.5   BIOS

At startup, the 911 enables the ROM region C6000h–C5FFFh. The BIOS then enables the extended ROM region from C6800h–C7FFFh. Note there is a 2-Kbyte gap from C6000h–C67FFh. The 924 enables the entire region from C6000h–C7FFFh.

26.2.6 864/964 BIOS Sets Default Linear Address Window

The S3 BIOS for the 864/964 sets default values in the Linear Address Window Position Registers during a graphics mode switch. This default value will be set to some position in the upper part of the lower 2 Gbytes of address space for VL Bus. On PCI systems, the base address specified in the Base Address 0 Register will automatically appear as the linear address specified in the Base Address 0 register and will also automatically appear as the linear address window position.

26.2.7 864/964 Pattern BLTs in 4-Bits-Per-Pixel Modes

The Pattern BLT function is not supported in the 4-bits-per-pixel modes. To duplicate this function, use another graphics engine feature by writing the pattern into off-screen memory and using the BitBlt function to copy the pattern to on-screen memory.

26.3 CONTROLLING THE S3 CHIPS

The S3 chips require extensive locking and unlocking before access to the extended registers is possible.

26.3.1 Locking and Unlocking the S3 Chips

It is necessary to unlock the S3 chips before extended mode programming. Functions that lock and unlock these chips are provided in Listings 26.1 and 26.2 respectively.

LISTING 26.1a Lock the S3 Registers by setting S3R8 to 0

```
; Calling Protocol:
;       Lock_S3();
Lock_S3  PROC FAR
         mov    dx,3d4h
         mov    al,38h
         out    dx,al  ;write 38 hex for S3 Register Lock 1 Register

         inc    dx     ;don't write pattern 48h
         mov    al,00h
         out    dx,al  ;input code

         dec    dx
         mov    al,39h
         out    dx,al  ;write 39 hex for S3 Register Lock 2 Register

         inc    dx     ;don't write pattern A0h
         mov    al,00h
```

(continued)

```
        out    dx,al  ;input code
        ret
Lock_S3 endp
```

LISTING 26.1b Unlock the S3 Registers in the 864/964

```
; Calling Protocol
;       Lock_S3x64();
Lock_S3x64  PROC FAR

; write code to CR38 to provide access to the S3 VGA registers
        mov    dx,3d4h
        mov    al,38h    ;index to CR38
        out    dx,al
        inc    dx
        mov    al,00h    ;locking code of 00 will do
        out    dx,al     ;write the unlocking code
        dec    ax        ;point back to index

; write code to CR39 to provide access to the System Control
; and System Extension Registers
        mov    al,39h    ;index to CR39
        out    dx,al
        inc    dx
        mov    al,00h    ;locking code of 00 will do
        out    dx,al
        dec    dx

; set bit 0 in CR40 to enable access to the Enhanced Commands
; Registers
        mov    al,40h    ;index to CR40
        out    dx,al
        inc    dx
        in     al,dx     ;get CR40
        and    al,0feh   ;clear bit 0
        out    dx,al
        dec    dx

        ret
Lock_S3x64  endp
```

LISTING 26.2a Unlock the S3 Registers by Setting S3R8 to 48h

```
; Calling Protocol
;       Unlock_S3();
Unlock_S3  PROC FAR
        mov    dx,3d4h
        mov    al,31h    ;set bit 0 of the Enable Base Address
                         ;Offset S3R1
```

```
        out     dx,al

        inc     dx
        in      al,dx       ;get old value
        or      al,01h      ;set bit 1 and bit 3
        out     dx,al       ;output code

        dec     dx
        mov     al,38h
        out     dx,al       ;write 38 hex for S3 Register Unlock 1
                            ;Register
        inc     dx          ;write pattern 48h
        in      al,dx       ;get old value
        mov     bh,al       ;save 38 in BH

        mov     al,48h
        out     dx,al       ;output code

        dec     dx
        mov     al,39h
        out     dx,al       ;write 39 hex for S3 Register Unlock 1
                            ;Register
        inc     dx          ;write pattern A0h
        in      al,dx       ;get old value
        mov     bl,al       ;save 39 in BL

        mov     al,0A0h
        out     dx,al       ;output code

        mov     ax,bx       ;AL=39 AH=38
        ret
Unlock_S3   endp
```

LISTING 26.2b Unlock the S3 Registers in the 864/964

```
; Calling Protocol
;       Unlock_S3x64();
Unlock_S3x64    PROC FAR

; write code to CR38 to provide access to the S3 VGA registers
        mov     dx,3d4h
        mov     al,38h      ;index to CR38
        out     dx,al
        inc     dx
        mov     al,48h      ;unlocking code 01xx10xx
        out     dx,al       ;write the unlocking code
        dec     ax          ;point back to index
```

(continued)

```
; write code to CR39 to provide access to the System Control
; and System Extension Registers
        mov     al,39h      ;index to CR39
        out     dx,al
        inc     dx
        mov     al,0a5h     ;unlocking code is A5
        out     dx,al
        dec     dx


; set bit 0 in CR40 to enable access to the Enhanced Commands
; Registers
        mov     al,40h      ;index to CR40
        out     dx,al
        inc     dx
        in      al,dx       ;get CR40
        or      al,1        ;set bit 0
        out     dx,al
        dec     dx


        ret
Unlock_S3x64    endp
```

26.3.2   Locking/Unlocking other Registers

It is possible to lock and unlock the green PC register at SRD as shown in
Listing 26.3.

LISTING 26.3a Lock the S3 Register to Block Access to Power Management in the
864/964

```
; Calling Protocol
;       Lock_S3green();
Lock_S3green    PROC FAR

; lock the extended Sequencer Register SRD to access power
; management
        mov     dx,3c4h
        mov     al,08h      ;index SRD Extended Sequencer Register
        mov     ah,00h      ;0 will suffice as lock key
        out     dx,ax
        ret
Lock_S3green    endp
```

LISTING 26.3b UnLock the S3 Register to Provide Access to Power Management in the 864/964

```
; Calling Protocol
;        Unlock_S3green();
Unlock_S3green PROC FAR

; unlock the extended Sequencer Register SRD to access power
; management
        mov    dx,3c4h
        mov    al,08h      ;index SR8 Extended Sequencer Register
        mov    ah,06h      ;unlock key
        out    dx,ax
        ret
Unlock_S3green endp
```

TABLE 26.1 provides additional VGA registers that control access through locking and unlocking.

TABLE 26.1 VGA Register Access Control Extensions

Register	Bit	Controls Access To:	Code
CR33	1	CR7 bits 1 and 6	1=disable write protect setting of CR11 bit 7
CR33	4	RAMDAC Register	1=disable writes
CR33	6	Palette/Overscan registers	1=lock
CR34	5	SR1 bit 5	1=lock
CR34	7	3C2h bits 3-2	1=lock
CR35	4	Vertical Timing Registers	1=lock
CR35	5	Horizontal Timing Registers	1=lock

26.3.3 Identifying the S3 Chips

The S3 chips are identified by first unlocking the chips, then testing if 3D4 index 47 is read/write capable. This is accomplished by the function in Listing 26.4. If an S3 chip is identified, the specific chip can be found by the code in Listing 26.5.

LISTING 26.4 Determine if the chip is an S3

```
/* Calling Protocol:
  S3= Is_It_S3()  */

int Is_It_S3(void)
{ int old_value;  BYTE new_value_1,new_value_2;

  Unlock_S3();    // first unlock S3 registers

  outp(0x3d4,0x47);
  outp(0x3d5,0xff);  new_value_1=inp(0x3d5);
  outp(0x3d5,0x00);  new_value_2=inp(0x3d5);

  if((new_value_2==0x00) && (new_value_1==0xff))
return(CHIP_FOUND);
    else return(CHIP_NOT_FOUND);
}
```

LISTING 26.5 Determine Which S3 Chip

```
/* Determine the S3 chip
Output Parameters:
  identity     integer containing chip code in CR30

Calling Protocol:
 identity = Which_S3()  */

int  Which_S3(void)

{  BYTE value;

  outp(0x3d4,0x30);
  value = inp(0x3d5) & 0xf0;    only want bits 7-4
  switch(value) {
  case 0x80: case 0x81: case 0x91:  //911
       return(S3911);
  case 0x82:  //924
       return(S3924);
  case 0x90: case 0x94: case 0x95: case 0xB0: //928
       return(S3928);
  case 0xA0: case 0xA2: case 0xA3: case 0xA4:
  case 0xA5: case 0xA8:  //801-805
       return(S3800);
   case 0xC0:  return(S3864);
   case 0xC0:  return(S3964);
   }
return(NO_ID_FOUND);
}
```

26.3.4 Display Modes on the S3 Chips

The S3 chips support the display modes that are typically VESA compatible.

26.4 DISPLAY MEMORY

The VGA and the graphics accelerator share the display memory. Thus, in graphics modes, if the processor is switched between VGA to the graphics accelerator, the information in display memory will be likely overwritten. One exception is when the VGA is in an alphanumeric mode. A special 64-Kbyte region of off-screen memory is reserved for the alphanumeric data. Consequently, rapid switching is possible between the alphanumeric and graphics display modes. Display memory can be accessed directly through memory transfer instructions such as MOVSB, or through I/O instructions. If I/O mapped, then all CPU data is transferred to the display memory through the Image Transfer Register.

26.4.1 Direct Memory Access

The CPU can access display memory directly while the chip is in either the VGA or the enhanced mode. This direct access is enabled or disabled through the Miscellaneous Output Control VGA Register. If enabled, all accesses to VGA memory space are mapped into display memory. A base address offset into display memory is provided in the CRT Register Lock Register. When direct access is enabled through the Memory Configuration Register, this offset is added to the lower sixteen bits of address provided by the CPU. Either linear mapping or standard VGA memory mapping is possible through the S3R1 Register.

The 8-bit color modes always configure memory to be 1024 pixels wide, corresponding to a display bytes_per_row of 1024 bytes. All 1-Mbyte systems consequently are configured as 1024 by 1024. The 512 Kbyte memory configuration is 1024 by 512.

In all 4-bit color modes, the display memory is organized as 2048 by 1024 for the 1-Mbyte cards and 1024 by 1024 for the 512-Kbyte cards. Since there are two pixels per byte, the bytes_per_row is either 512 or 256 respectively. Display memory can be accessed in either a packed or planar display mode (through or across the plane).

26.4.2 64-Kbyte VGA Memory Mapping

Set bit 3 of the Memory Configuration Register to enable 64-Kbyte mapping. The base address offset is written into bits 3–0 of the CRT Register Lock Register. In addition, bit 2 of the Extended System Control 2 Register is used when accessing the second megabyte of display memory. Set bit 0 of the Memory

Configuration Register to force this offset to be added to the lower sixteen bits of the CPU address.

26.4.3 Accessing Memory through the Graphics Engine

All CPU data must move through the Pixel Data Transfer Register for 16-bit transfers. The 32-bit transfers can be enabled by memory mapping this register to a 64-Kbyte memory address space in the typical VGA display memory region from A0000h–AFFFFFh by setting bit 4 of the Extended Memory Cont 1 Register. The 805 also allows I/O 32-bit transfers through the Pixel Data Transfer Extension Register.

26.4.4 801/805 Fast Linear Addressing Memory Access

The 801/805 can access memory in a linear fashion. Of course, a protected mode is required. The hardware busy flag, bit 9 of the Input/Output Status register should be not busy before attempting fast addressing. Set bit 4 of the Linear Address Window Control Register to 1 to enable fast access. Video memory is mapped into the CPU memory address space using the Linear Address Window Control and the Linear Address Window Position Registers.

26.4.5 864/964 Linear Addressing

Enhanced mode operation must be enabled before linear addressing is enabled. Bit 0 of the 4AE8h Register must be set to 1 to enabled the enhanced mode functions. Bit 3 of CR31 must be set to 1 to specify enhanced mode memory mapping.

The 864 and 964 provides linear addressing up to 4 or 8 Mbytes of display memory respectively. Linear addressing of more than 64 Kbytes requires a 386 or above protected mode environment.

The Graphics Engine busy flag, bit 9 of 9AE8h, should be verified to be 0 indicating NOT BUSY before linear addressing is enabled. Linear addressing is enabled by setting bit 4 of CR58 or bit 4 of 4AE8h to 1. The size of the linear address window is set via bits 1–0 of CR58. The base address of the linear addressing window is set through CR59 and CR5A. For PCI systems, it is set in the PCI Configuration Register at Base Address 0, index 10h.

In Real Mode, the linear addressing window size can be set to 64 Kbytes. The base address for the window is set by programming bits 31–16 of the window position in CR59–CR5A. This allows the CPU to be operated in real mode. If bit 0 of CR31 is set to 1, the memory page offset at the 64-Kbyte bank is specified in bits 5–0 of CR6A. This is then added to the linear addressing window position base address to bank switch the 4 or 8 Mbytes of memory into the 64-Kbyte window.

26.4.6   Enhanced Mode Registers

The enhanced mode registers are I/O registers that can be mapped at either X2E8h, X6E8h, XAE8h, or EEE8h. Alternately, they can be remapped to locations X148h, X548h, X948h, and XD48h through the Extended Mode Register.

26.4.7   Two-page Mode

Enhanced mode memory can be configured as two pages through the Memory Configuration Register. Setting this bit to a 1 enables a 2 Kbyte by 1 Kbyte by 4 map image. Once in two-page mode, the graphics engine treats memory as one 2 Kbyte-by-1 Kbyte map. Display from the upper page is eanbled through the Display Start Address Register of the CRTC. The display memory is configured as a single page in the 1280-by-1024 4-bit-per-color mode.

26.4.8   86c928 Enhanced Register Memory Mapping

The I/O registers of X2E8 and so on can be memory mapped by setting bit 4 of the Extended Memory Control Register or bit 5 of the Advanced Function Control Register. Image transfers normally made by accessing I/O addresses to the Pixel Data Transfer Registers at E2E8h and E2EAh can be made by accessing any memory location in the 32-Kbyte address space from A0000h–A7FFFh (normal VGA display memory). Write-only accesses to the Enhanced Command Registers are made to particular locations in the A8000h–AFFFFh range as shown in Table 26.2. Note that the Read Register Select Register cannot be accessed as a memory-mapped register.

26.4.9   Accessing the Display Memory

The display memory is accessed via 64-Kbyte banks. This bank value is stored in the lower three bits of the CRT Register Lock Register (S3R5). This register can be loaded by the code in Listing 26.6. Note that the 4-bit color modes shift the bank by 4 to maintain a 64 Kbyte bank.

TABLE 26.2 Memory Mapping the Enhanced Command Registers

I/O Address	Memory Address
8xE8h	A8xE8h
9xE8h	A9xE8h
AxE8h	AAxE8h
BxE8h	ABxE8h

LISTING 26.6 Setting the S3 Bank Register

```
; enter with the bank in bl
Set_Bank_S3 macro
          and    bl,0fh     ;only want 4 bits of bank
          mov    dx,3d4h    ;access CRT Register Lock S3R5
          mov    al,35h
          out    dx,al      ;output index
          inc    dx         ;non-destructive write bank
          in     al,dx
          and    al,0f0h    ;zero bits 0-3
          or     al,bl
          out    dx,al
          in     al,dx      ;read from 3D5 for first generation S3911
endm


Set_Wr_Bank_256_S3 macro
          Set_Bank_S3
          ret
endm


Set_Rd_Bank_256_S3 macro
          Set_Bank_S3
          ret
endm


Set_Wr_Bank_16_S3 macro
          shl    bl,1       ; multiply by 4
          shl    bl,1       ; multiply by 4
          Set_Bank_S3
          ret
endm


Set_Rd_Bank_16_S3 macro
          shl bl,1          ; multiply by 4
          shl bl,1          ; try multiply by 4
          Set_Bank_S3
endm
```

26.4.10   864/964 Image Reads

The 924, 800 series, and 928 accelerators could be used to read information
from the bitmap through an I/O port. This functionality is not available with
the 864/964. All graphics engine commands are restricted to writes directly to
the bitmap.

26.4.11   864/964 Image Reads in 4-Bits-per-pixel Modes

When reading from display memory in the 4-bit-per-pixel modes, the lower and upper four bits of each byte are swapped. The nibbles must be swapped again to reproduce the original memory data. This applies to all read-modify-write instructions. For example, one would read the information, swap nibbles in each byte, perform the desired operation, and then rewrite the data to the display memory. The nibbles are **not** swapped during writes.

26.5   ACCESSING THE GRAPHICS ACCELERATOR

Once enabled, graphics functions can be initiated by first setting up the required parameters located in the I/O space, and then issuing the command to the Command Register. All parameters and commands are entered into a command FIFO that is eight commands deep. Commands are picked up from the FIFO sequentially in the FIFO format. A Status Register is provided so that software can check on the state of the FIFO and write ahead if desired. The FIFO accumulates data when the graphics accelerator is full. An empty FIFO can be determined through the busy flag at 9AE8h or bit 0 of the 9AE8h register.

26.6   COLORS, COLOR SOURCES, AND COLOR MIXES

26.6.1   Color Source and Mix Source

The Color Source and Mix Source are selected through the Data Extension bits in the Pixel Control and Data Extension Registers. A mask bit is generated based on the settings in these registers. A mask bit of 1 indicates the Foreground Mix Register is used and the color source is determined by the settings in that register. A mask bit of 0 indicates the Background Mix Register is used and the color source is determined by the settings in that register. The mask source is selected by programming the Data Extension bits in the Pixel Control and Data Extension Registers.

Mask Selection is 0

Always selects a mask of 1. All drawing updates to the display bitmap use the Foreground Mix field, and the Color Source field is bits 6,5 of the Foreground Mix Register. It is used to draw solid lines, through plane image transfers and BitBlts.

Mask Selection is 2

The mask source is the CPU. Data is transferred via the Pixel Data Transfer Register. After the command is issued through the Command Register, mask bits are written into the Pixel Data Register. A mask bit corresponds to every pixel drawn on the display. It is used to transfer monochrome images using color expansion. All pixels corresponding to a 1 use the Foreground Mix field and the Color Index from the Color Source indicated in the Foreground Mix Register. All pixels corresponding to a 0 use the Background Mix field and the Color Index from the Color Source indicated in the Background Mix Register.

Mask Selection is 3

The display memory is used as the mask source. The mask is defined as a rectangle. The Read Mask Register is used to indicate the active planes that make up the mask source. An AND operation is used among the read enable plane bits. If all bits are set to a 1, then the mask is 1. If any are a 0, then the mask is a 0. The mask bits determine the mix and the color source. Used with BitBlt patterns and character images.

26.6.2 Color Source

The color source for drawing is selected in the color source selection bits of the Foreground and Background Registers. Table 26.3 illustrates the possibilities.

When the CPU provides the color source and after the command is issued through the Command Register, color indices are written into the Pixel Data Register corresponding to every pixel drawn on the display.

26.6.3 Hi-color Mode

Two-page mode must be enabled for the hi-color (16-bits-per-color modes). Each page holds half of the data (8 bits). Therefore, it is necessary to draw two lines for each line desired, one for each of the 8-bit halves. The lower page holds the least significant eight bits; the upper page holds the most significant eight bits. The memory is configured as one would suspect when accessed from the CPU. Thus, each two consecutive bytes represents one 16-bit word.

TABLE 26.3 Color Source

Bit	Description
0	Background Color Register color source
1	Foreground Color Register color source
2	CPU provides color source
3	The color source is the display memory

TABLE 26.4 Dual-display mode BIOS Calls

Call	Description
Int 10h ax=4fffh bx=2	Set up for dual-display mode reserving 64 Kbytes of text memory.
Int 10h ax=4fffh bx=1	Set up for dual-display mode reserving 32 Kbytes of text memory.
Int 10h ax=4fffh bx=0	Disable dual-display mode.

TABLE 26.5 Top Memory Access

CPU/CRTC	Memory Selected
A17=0	Select top of 512-Kbyte memory.
A17=1	Select top of 1-Mbyte memory. A16–A14=1.
A13=1	Select upper 32 Kbytes of the 64-Kbyte area.
A13=0	Select lower 32 Kbytes of the 64-Kbyte area.

26.7 DUAL-DISPLAY MODE

A portion of off-screen memory, in the enhanced mode, can be reserved for VGA text mode. This dual-display mode facilitates two independent displays. Switching between modes leaves both memory areas independent. This is accomplished by first selecting an enhanced mode, then performing a BIOS call to reserve the 64 Kbytes. An image can then be drawn into the enhanced display. The VGA text mode is then selected. You can go back to an enhanced mode using a mode set **without** clearing display memory.

The three relevant BIOS calls follow in Table 26.4.

The top 64 Kbyte of memory is called the *top memory*. It is accessed when the chip is in the top memory access mode. Addressing is described in Table 26.5.

26.8 S3 EXTENDED REGISTERS

The S3 extended registers are indexed registers located at either 3Bx for monochrome systems or 3Dx for color systems. These registers provide extended control and register locking to the S3 chip. These registers are protected by a software key. The extended registers are described in Table 26.6.

1340 S3 INCORPORATED

TABLE 26.6 S3 Extended Registers

Index	R/W	Register Name	Mnemonic
30	R/W	Chip ID/Rev	S3R0
31	R/W	Memory Configuration	S3R1
32	R/W	Backward Compatibility 1	S3R2
33	R/W	Backward Compatibility 1	S3R3
34	R/W	Backward Compatibility 1	S3R4
35	R/W	CRT Register Lock	S3R5
36	R	Reset State Read 1	S3R6
37	R	Reset State Read 2	S3R7
38	R/W	S3 Register Lock 1	S3R8
39	R/W	S3 Register Lock 2	S3R9
3A	R/W	S3 Miscellaneous 1	S3R0A
3B	R/W	Data Transfer Execute Position	S3R0B
3C	R/W	Interlace Retrace Start	S3R0C

26.8.1 System Control Registers

The S3 System Control Registers are indexed registers located at either 3Bx for monochrome systems or 3Dx for color systems. These registers provide control, mode, and status access along with the descriptive registers for the hardware cursor. These registers are protected by a software key. The system control registers are described in Table 26.7.

TABLE 26.7 System Control Registers

Index	R/W	Register Name	Mnemonic
40	R/W	System Configuration	SYS-CNFG
42	R/W	Mode Control	MODE-CTL
43	R/W	Extended Mode	EXT-MODE
45	R/W	Hardware Cursor Mode	HGC-MODE
47–46	R/W	Hardware Cursor Origin X	HGC-ORGX
49–48	R/W	Hardware Cursor Origin Y	HGC-ORGY
4D–4C	R/W	Hardware Curosr	HGC-STADR
4E	R/W	Hardware Cursor Pattern Start X	HGC-DX
4F	R/W	Hardware Cursor Pattern Start Y	HGC-DY

26.8.2 S3 Enhanced Command Registers

The S3 enhanced command registers provide command and status access to the graphics accelerator along with the parameter registers necessary for the accelerator operations. These registers are enabled only if the Enable Enhanced Drawing Functions bit is set. The enhanced commands are described in Table 26.8.

TABLE 26.8 Enhanced Command Registers

I/O	R/W	Register Name	Mnemonic
42E8	R/W	Subsystem Status	SYBSYS-STAT
42E8	R/W	Advanced Function Control	SYBSYS-CNTRL
4AE8	R/W	Current Y Position	ADVFUNC-CNTL
82E8	R/W	Current X Position	CUR-Y
86E8	R/W	Destination Y Pos/Axial Step Constant	CUR-X
8AE8	R/W	Destination X Pos/Diagonal Step Constant	DESTY-AXSTP
8EE8	R/W	Error Term	DESTX-DIASTP
92E8	R/W	Major Axis Pixel Count	ERR-TERM
96E8	R/W	Graphics Processor Status	MAJ-AXIS-PCNT
9AE8	R/W	Command	GP-STAT
9AE8	R/W	Short Stroke	CMD
9EE8	R/W	Vector Transfer	SHORT-STROKE
A2E8	R/W	Background Color	BKGD-COLOR
A6E8	R/W	Foreground Color	RGD-COLOR
AAE8	R/W	Write Mask	WRT-MASK
AEE8	R/W	Read Mask	RD-MASK
B6E8	R/W	Background Mix	BKGD-MIX
BAE8	R/W	Foreground Mix	GRGD-MIX
BEE8	R/W	Multi-Function Control	MULTIFUNC-CNTL
BEE8-0	R/W	Minor Axis Pixel Count	MIN-AXIS-PCNT
BEE8-1	R/W	Top Scissors	SCISSORS-T
BEE8-2	R/W	Left Scissors	SCISSORS-L
BEE8-3	R/W	Bottom Scissors	SCISSORS-B
BEE8-4	R/W	Right Scissors	SCISSORS-R
BEE8-A	R/W	Data Manipulation Control	DT-MP-CNTL

26.8.3 32-bit I/O for the 864/964

The 864/964 allows several of the graphics engine registers to be accessed directly with 32-bit I/O instructions. The Select 32-bit Command Registers bit 9 at BEE8h index Eh now enables and requires 32-bit accesses to command registers A2E8h, A6E8H, AAE8H, and B2E8H. Setting this bit with memory-mapped I/O allows 32-bit memory-mapped reads and writes to the registers.

26.9 COPROCESSOR PROGRAM EXAMPLES

The FIFO has to be checked before outputing any commands or parameters to the accelerator. Any instruction to the enhanced mode register must be one byte wide. Several examples follow.

26.9.1 Draw a Solid Line

Example 26.1 Draw a solid line from [x1,y1] to [x2,y2] using the mix OVERWRITE and color index 2.

1. Compute line constants

```
MAX = maximum (ABS(x2-x1), ABS(y2-y1));
MIN = minimum (ABS(x2-x1), ABS(y2-y1));
X is positive if x1<x2 else X is negative.
Y is positive if y1<y2 else Y is negative.
Major axis is X if ABS(x2-x1) > ABS(y2-y1) else Major axis
is Y
```

2. Wait for the FIFO bit 3 empty since three parameters are required

3. Set up the parameters

```
FRGD_MIX_REG = 27h;  // use FRGD_COLOR, overwrite
FRGD_COLOR_REG = 2;
MULTIFUNC_CNTL = A000H;  // A=Data Extension Register,
                        // 0=no extension, don't pack.
```

4. Wait for FIFO 7 empty since 7 locations are required

5. Send Parameters and Go Command

```
CUR_X = x1;    CUR_Y = y1;
MAJ_AXIS_PCNT = MAX;
DESTX_DIASTP = 2 * (MIN-MAX);    DESTY_AXSTP = 2 * MIN
if (X>=0) ERR_TERM = 2 * (MIN-MAX) ;
   else   ERR_TERM = 2 * (MIN-MAX) -1
```

6. Send Go Command

```
CMD_REG = 00100000DDD10011B Draw line, multi-pixel, write
operation
```

26.9.2 Draw a Textured Line

Example 26.2 Draw a textured line from [x1,y1] to [x2,y2] using the mix OVERWRITE for foreground mix and EXCLUSIVE OR for background mix. foreground color index 2, background color index=4. Texture pattern is 0011000011110011B. This is sent by the CPU after the Command Register is loaded.

1. Compute line constants (same as 26.1).

2. Wait for the FIFO bit 5 empty since five parameters are required.

3. Set up the parameters

```
FRGD_MIX_REG = 27h;    //color souce FRGD_COLOR, overwrite
FRGD_COLOR_REG = 2
BKGD_MIX_REG = 5h;     //color souce BKGD_COLOR, XOR
BKGD_COLOR_REG = 4
MULTIFUNC_CNTL = A080H;  // A=Data Extension Register,
2=from CPU, don't pack.
```

4. Wait for FIFO 7 empty since 7 locations are required

5. Send Parameters (same as 26.1)

6. Send Go Command

```
CMD_REG = 00100011DDD10011B Draw line, multi-pixel, write
operation, CPU Data
```

26.9.3 Draw a Rectangle

Example 26.3 Draw a rectangle with top-left corner at [x1,y1], with [HEIGHT,WIDTH] using the mix OVERWRITE color index 2, background color index=4. DDD= X positive, X major, Y positive.

1. Wait for the FIFO bit 8 empty since five parameters are required.

2. Set up the parameters

```
FRGD_MIX_REG = 27h;    // color souce FRGD_COLOR, overwrite
FRGD_COLOR_REG = 2
MULTIFUNC_CNTL = A000H;  // A=Data Extension Register, no
                         // extension, don't pack.
CUR_X = x1;    CUR_Y = y1;
RWIDTH_REG = WIDTH-1;   RHEIGHT_REG=HEIGHT-1;
```

3. Send Go Command

```
CMD_REG = 01000011DDD10011B Draw rectangle, multi-pixel,
write operation,
```

26.9.4   BitBlt Through Plane from Host to Display

Example 26.4 Transfer a rectangular image THROUGH PLANE with top-left corner at [x1,y1], with [HEIGHT,WIDTH] using the mix OVERWRITE from the host to the display, background color index=4. DDD= X positive, X major, Y positive. Note: The number of bytes per row must be even. A dummy byte must be added at the end of each row if the width is odd.

1. Wait for the FIFO bit 7 empty since five parameters are required.

2. Set up the parameters

   > FRGD_MIX_REG = 27h;   // color souce FRGD_COLOR, overwrite
   > MULTIFUNC_CNTL = A000H;   // A=Data Extension Register, no
   >   // extension, don't pack.
   > CUR_X = x1;   CUR_Y = y1;
   > RWIDTH_REG = WIDTH–1; RHEIGHT_REG=HEIGHT–1;

3. Send Go Command

   > CMD_REG = 01010011D0110001B Draw rectangle, CPU DATA,
   > write operation, Swap ON, X Major, X Positive

4. Transfer_Words = ((WIDTH+1)/2) * HEIGHT. Output Transfer_Words to PIX_TRANS_REG;

NOTE: In a 4-bit color mode, the image has to be packed so a single byte stores two pixels. The nigh-nibble contains pixel n while low contains n+1. The row width has to be a multiple of 4, so padding may be necessary. Count is ((WIDTH+3)/4)*HEIGHT words.

26.9.5   BitBlt Across Plane from Host to Display

Example 26.5 Transfer a rectangular image ACROSS PLANE with top-left corner at [x1,y1], with [HEIGHT,WIDTH] using the mix OVERWRITE from the host to the display. The image is stored as a monochrome bit image, each byte containing eight pixels. background color index=4. DDD= X positive, X major, Y positive. Note: The number of bytes per row must be a multiple of 16. Dummy bits may be necessary at the end of each word. Color expand such that 0=color index 0 and 1=color index 4.

1. Wait for the FIFO bit 5 empty since five parameters are required.

2. Set up the parameters

   ```
   FRGD_MIX_REG = 27h;  //color souce FRGD_COLOR, overwrite
   FRGD_COLOR_REG=4;  // foreground color index = 4
   BKGD_MIX_REG=7;  // color source BKGD_COLOR, overwrite
   ```

```
BKGD_COLOR_REG=0;  // background color index = 0
MULTIFUNC_CNTL = A000H;  // A=Data Extension Register, no
                         // extension, don't pack.
```

3. Wait for the FIFO bit 5 empty since five parameters are required

```
CUR_X = x1;    CUR_Y = y1;
RWIDTH_REG = WIDTH-1;  RHEIGHT_REG=HEIGHT-1;
```

4. **Send Go Command**

```
CMD_REG = 01010011D0110011B  Draw rectangle, CPU DATA,
multiple pixel, write operation, Swap ON, X Major, X
Positive
```

5. Transfer_Words = ((WIDTH+15)/16) * HEIGHT. Output
   Transfer_Words to PIX_TRANS_REG;

NOTE: In a 8-bit color mode, the number of bits per row must be a multiple of 8, so padding may be necessary. Count is ((WIDTH+7)/8)*HEIGHT words. If it is desired to write to a single plane, set the Foreground mix to all 1's. (0002H), Background Mix to all 0's (0001H) and set the WRITE MASK Register to the desired single plane.

26.9.6 BitBlt Through Plane from Display to Host

Example 26.6 Transfer a rectangular image THROUGH PLANE with top-left corner at [x1,y1], with [HEIGHT,WIDTH] from the display to the host, background color index=4. DDD= X positive, X major, Y positive. Note: The number of bytes per row must be even. A dummy byte will be inserted at the end of each row if the width is odd.

---

1. Wait for the FIFO bit 6 empty since five parameters are required.

2. Set up the parameters

```
MULTIFUNC_CNTL = A000H;  // A=Data Extension Register, no
                         // extension, don't pack.
CUR_X = x1;    CUR_Y = y1;
RWIDTH_REG = WIDTH-1;  RHEIGHT_REG=HEIGHT-1;
```

3. Send Go Command

```
CMD_REG = 01010011D0110000B  Read rectangle, CPU DATA,
write operation, Swap ON, X Major, X Positive
```

4. Wait for data available

5. Transfer_Words = ((WIDTH+1)/2) * HEIGHT. Input Transfer_Words
   to PIX_TRANS_REG;

26.9.7 BitBlt Across Plane from Display to Host

Example 26.7 Transfer a rectangular image ACROSS PLANE with top-left corner at [x1,y1], with [HEIGHT,WIDTH] from the display to the host. The image is stored as a monochrome bit image, each byte containing 8 pixels. background color index=4. DDD= X positive, X major, Y positive. Note: The number of bytes per row must a multiple of 16. Dummy bits may be inserted at the end of each word.

1. Wait for the FIFO bit 7 empty since seven parameters are required.

2. Set up the parameters

   ```
   MULTIFUNC_CNTL = A000H;   // A=Data Extension Register, no
                             // extension, don't pack.
   BRM_MASK_REG=1;  // read from plane 0
   CUR_X = x1;     CUR_Y = y1;
   RWIDTH_REG = WIDTH-1;   RHEIGHT_REG=HEIGHT-1;
   ```

3. Send Go Command

   ```
   CMD_REG = 01010011D0110010B  Read rectangle, CPU DATA,
   multiple pixel, write operation, Swap ON, X Major, X
   Positive
   ```

4. Wait for Data Available

5. ```
   Transfer_Words = ((WIDTH+15)/16) * HEIGHT. Input
   Transfer_Words to PIX_TRANS_REG;
   ```

NOTE: In a 8-bit color mode, the number of bits per row must be a multiple of 8, so padding may be necessary. Count is ((WIDTH+7)/8)*HEIGHT words. With more than one plane enabled for read, a 1 is read for each pixel if all planes enabled are a 1. (AND operation).

26.9.8 BitBlt Through Plane from Display to Display

Example 26.8 Transfer a rectangular image THROUGH PLANE with top-left corner at [x1,y1], with [HEIGHT,WIDTH] using the mix OVERWRITE from the display to the display.

If source and destination do not overlap

```
X=+, Y=+, Srcx=x1; Srcy=y1; Destx=x2; Desty=y2;
```

else

```
if (x1>x2) X=+; Srcx=x1; Destx=x2;
else X=-; Srcx=x1-WIDTH-1; Desty=x2-WIDTH-1;
if (y1>x2) Y=+; Srcy=y1; Srcy=y1;
else Y=-; Srcy=y1-HEIGHT-1; Desty=y2-HEIGHT-1;
```
```

1. Wait for the FIFO bit 2 empty since two parameters are required.

2. Set up the parameters

```
FRGD_MIX_REG = 67h;    // color souce display, overwrite
MULTIFUNC_CNTL = A000H;  // A=Data Extension Register, no
                         // extension, don't pack.
CUR_X = x1;    CUR_Y = y1;
RWIDTH_REG = WIDTH-1;  RHEIGHT_REG=HEIGHT-1;
```

3. Wait for the FIFO bit 7 empty since seven parameters are required.

4. Set up the parameters

```
CUR_X = x1;    CUR_Y = y1;
DESTX_DIASTP_REG=destx;  DESTY_AXSTP_REG=Desty;
RWIDTH_REG = WIDTH-1;  RHEIGHT_REG=HEIGHT-1;
```

5. Send Go Command

```
CMD_REG = 11000000D0D10011B  BitBlt, write operation, Swap
ON, X Major, Multiple pixel
```

26.9.9   BitBlt Across Plane from Display to Display

Example 26.9 Transfer a rectangular image ACROSS PLANE with top-left corner at [x1,y1], with [HEIGHT,WIDTH] from the display to the display. The image is stored as a monochrome bit image, each byte containing 8 pixels. The bits corresponding to a single plane, as specified by the Read Mask Register are transferred. If more than one plane is enabled, an AND operation is used (see above). Read from plane 0 to plane 2. Use same setup as Example 26.8.

1. Wait for the FIFO bit 5 empty since five parameters are required.

2. Set up the parameters

```
MULTIFUNC_CNTL = A0C0H;  // A=Data Extension Register,
                         // from display.
FRGD_MIX_REG = 2h;    //all 1's
BKGD_MIX_REG=1h;  // all 0's
BRM_REG=1;  // read from plane 0
WRT_MASK_REG=4;  // plane 2 enabled for write
```

3. Wait for the FIFO bit 7 empty since seven parameters are required

```
CUR_X = x1;    CUR_Y = y1;
RWIDTH_REG = WIDTH-1;  RHEIGHT_REG=HEIGHT-1;
DESTX_DIASTP_REG=destx;  DESTY_AXSTP_REG=Desty;
```

4. Send Go Command

```
CMD_REG = 11010000D0D10011B  BitBlt, multiple pixel, write
operation, Swap ON, X Major, X Positive
```

26.9.10   Short-Stroke Vector

Example 26.10   Draw short-stroke vectors with color 2. The current [x1,y1] and a NOP is issued. The short-stroke vectors are loaded into the SHORT_STROKE_REG. Two vectors can be defined at a time.

1. Wait for the FIFO bit 6 empty since six parameters are required

2. Set up the parameters

```
FRGD_MIX_REG = 27h;   // use FRGD_COLOR, overwrite
FRGD_COLOR_REG = 2;
MULTIFUNC_CNTL = A000H;   // A=Data Extension Register,
                          // 0=no extension, don't pack.
CUR_X = x1;    CUR_Y = y1;
```

3. Send Go (NOP) Command

```
CMD_REG = 00010010XXX11111B  NOP, multi-pixel, write
operation, Swap ON, RadialDir, LPixelOff
```

4. While space is available in the FIFO write the vectors

```
SHORT_STROKE_REG=SSVD1<<8 + SSVD0
SHORT_STROKE_REG=SSVD3<<8 + SSVD2     etc.
```

26.9.11   Pattern Fill Through Plane

Example 26.11   Pattern Fill Through Plane. Fill a rectangle with a repeated 8-by-8 pattern. The 8-by-8 pattern is initially copied into video memory using an Image Transfer operation. Each 8-by-8 region is aligned to an 8-pixel boundary. The current foreground mix is used.

1. Wait for the FIFO bit 2 empty since two parameters are required

2. Set up the parameters

```
FRGD_MIX=67;   // source in video memory, mix type is new
MULTIFUNC_CNTL = A000H;   // A=Data Extension Register,
                          // 0=no extension, don't pack.
```

3. Wait for the FIFO bit 7 empty since seven parameters are required

4. Set up the parameters

```
CUR_X = x1;    CUR_Y = y1;
DESTX_DIASTP_REG=x2;   DESTY_AXSTP_REG=x1;
MAJ_AXIS_PCNT=WIDTH-1;   MIN_AXIS_PCNT=HEIGHT-1;
```

5. Send Go (NOP) Command

```
CMD_REG = 11100000D0D10011B  Pattern Fill, multi-pixel,
write operation, Swap ON, X Major
```

26.9.12   Pattern Fill Across Plane

Example 26.12   Pattern Fill Across Plane. Fill a rectangle with a repeated 8-by-8 pattern. The 8-by-8 pattern is initially copied into video memory using an Image Transfer operation. Each 8-by-8 region is aligned to an 8-pixel boundary. The bits corresponding to a single plane specified by the Read Mask Register are transferred. The AND operation is used when more than one plane is enabled. The image is read from plane 0 and written to plane 2.

1. Wait for the FIFO bit 5 empty since five parameters are required

2. Set up the parameters

```
FRGD_MIX=67;   // source in video memory, mix type is new
MULTIFUNC_CNTL = A0C0H;   // A=Data Extension Register,
                         // 3=video memory selects mix.
FRGD_MIX=2;   // always 1
BKGD_MIX=1;   // always 0
RD_MASK=1  // read from plane 0
WR_MASK=4; // write to plane 4
FRGD_MIX=2;   // always 1
BKGD_MIX=1;   // always 0
RD_MASK=1  // read from plane 0
WR_MASK=4; // write to plane 2
```

3. Wait for the FIFO bit 7 empty since seven parameters are required

4. Set up the parameters

```
CUR_X = x1;     CUR_Y = y1;
DESTX_DIASTP_REG=x2;  DESTY_AXSTP_REG=x1;
MAJ_AXIS_PCNT=WIDTH-1;   MIN_AXIS_PCNT=HEIGHT-1;
```

5. Send Go (NOP) Command

```
CMD_REG = 11100000D0D10011B  Pattern Fill, multi-pixel,
write operation, Swap ON, X Major
```

26.10   PROGRAMMING THE START ADDRESS

The start address upper bits are programmed via the macro in Listing 26.7. This function can be used to program both the start address and the cursor address.

LISTING 26.7 Programming the CRTC Start Address

```
; input with the CRTC bank in bl
Set_CRTC_Bank_S3 macro
        and     bl,0fh      ;only want 4 bits of bank

        mov     dx,3d4h     ;access CRT Register Lock S3R5
        mov     al,31h
        out     dx,al       ;output index

        inc     dx          ;non-destructive write bank
        in      al,dx
        and     al,0cfh     ;zero bits 5-4

        shl     bl,1        ;move bl into bits 5-4
        shl     bl,1
        shl     bl,1
        shl     bl,1
        and     bl,30h      ;only 2 bits
        or      al,bl
        out     dx,al
endm
```

26.11   HARDWARE CURSOR

A programmable hardware cursor is compatible with the Microsoft Windows and X11 cursor definitions. The relevant control registers are shown in Table 26.9.

The cursor is operational only in the S3 Enhanced Mode. The cursor crosses 64 by 64 pixels and is stored in an off-screen portion of display memory. The pattern is the standard 2 bits per pixel requiring 512 bytes per pattern. The pattern is stored with the AND mask first followed by the XOR mask. The values in the two masks are combined for the effect shown in Table 26.10.

The Cursor Location High Register at 3D5h index 0Eh is used to hold the hardware cursor foreground color when in the enhanced mode. Similarly, the Cursor Location Low Registers at 3D5 index 0Fh are used to hold the hardware cursor background color. When using a hi-color or true-color mode, the foreground and background colors are programmed into the Hardware Graphics Cursor Foreground Stack Registers at 3D5 index 4Ah and the Hardware Graphics Cursor Background Stack Registers at 3D5 index 4Bh. Each of these is a stack of three 8-bit registers. The stack pointers are reset to 0 by reading the Hardware Graphics Cursor Mode Register at 3D5 index 45h. The color value is then programmed by 2 (16-bit) or 3 (24-bit) consecutive write operations (low, mid, and high byte) to the appropriate foreground or background register.

TABLE 26.9 Hardware Cursor Registers

Index	Name	Register
45	CR45	HGC Mode
47–46	CR47–CR46	HGC Origin X
49–48	C4R9–CR48	HGC Origin Y
4A	CR4A	HGC Foreground Stack
4B	CR4B	HGC Background Stack
4D–4C	CR4D–CR4C	HGC Start Address
4E	CR4E	HGC Pattern Display Start X
4F	CR4F	HGC Pattern Display Start Y

TABLE 26.10 Hardware Cursor Pixel Values

AND	XOR	Windows	X11
0	0	Cursor Background	Current Screen Pixel
0	1	Cursor Foreground	Current Screen Pixel
1	0	Current Screen Pixel	Cursor Background
1	1	! Current Screen Pixel	Cursor Foreground

26.11.1 Enabling and Disabling the Cursor

The cursor is automatically disabled when a VGA-compatible mode is in use. It is enabled or disabled as follows in Listing 26.8.

LISTING 26.8a Enabling the Hardware Cursor

```
S3R9 Register is set to A0h ;unlock System Control Registers
HGC_MODE bit 0 set to 1  // enable the hardware cursor
S3R9 Register is set to 0  // lock the System Control Registers
```

LISTING 26.8b Disabling the Hardware Cursor

```
S3R9 Register is set to A0h ;unlock System Control Registers
HGC_MODE bit 0 set to 0  // enable the hardware cursor
S3R9 Register is set to 0  // lock the System Control Registers
```

26.11.2 Positioning the Cursor

The cursor is positioned at any point on the display with the X,Y coordinates ranging from 0–20247. This enables the full cursor images to be displayed on the screen and partial cursor images to be displayed at the right and bottom of the screen. The cursor offset OX,OY has to be set to 0,0 for a 1024-by-768 resolution. If X is less than 1024–64, or Y is less than 768–64, then a partial cursor is visible.

A partial cursor can be displayed at the left or top edges of the screen. To enable partial cursor display at the top of the screen, Y is set to 0 and the Y Offset Register is set to OY. This displays the bottom 64–OY cursor rows of the cursor pattern. Similarly, a partial cursor off the left edge is accomplished by setting the X cursor position to 0 and the X Offset Register to OX. This displays the 64–OX pixel of the cursor. Listing 26.9 illustrates the process of positioning the cursor.

LISTING 26.9 Positioning the Cursor

```
S3R9 Register is set to A0h ;unlock System Control Registers

HWGC-CX(H) is set to most significant 3 bits of the X cursor
position
HWGC-CX(L) is set to least significant 3 bits of the X cursor
position
HWGC-CY(L) is set to least significant 3 bits of the Y cursor
position
HWGC-DX(H) is set to the X cursor offset
HWGC-DY(H) is set to the Y cursor offset
HWGC-CY(H) is set to most significant 3 bits of the Y cursor
position

S3R9 Register is set to 0  // lock the System Control Registers
```

26.11.3 Programming the Cursor Shape

The AND and the XOR images are 512 bytes each. The cursor-image bitmaps are loaded into the off-screen memory at some Y location (YI). This location must be aligned to a 1024-byte boundary. If the bitmap width is 1024, then set X=0 at some Y location. The cursor pattern load is accomplished by performing an image transfer operation with the destination rectangle on the display set to 0,Y1, the width set to 1024, and the height set to 1 (2 if the 4-plane option is used). The AND and XOR image bitmaps are transferred to the video memory via the Pixel Data Transfer Registers at E2E8h. The image is loaded into the register as a sequence of AND image mask words followed by a word of the XOR image mask. This alternation is continued until the entire cursor pattern is loaded. The hardware graphics cursor at 3D5 index 4C and 4Dh are programmed to YI so that the controller knows the start of the cursor definition in video memory. The X location is always assumed to be 0. This is illustrated in Listing 26.10.

LISTING 26.10 Loading the Cursor Shape

```
S3R9 Register is set to A0h  ;unlock System Control Registers
HWGC-STA(H) set to most-significant 4 bits of the cursor Y
start = YI bits 11-8
HWGC-STA(L) set to least-significant 8 bits of the cursor Y
start = YI bits 7-0

S3R9 Registers is set to 0  // lock the System Control Registers

Wait for FIFO 7 empty
MUTLIFUNC_CNTL set to A000h  // Foreground Mix Register is
source of color and mix
FRGD_MIX is set to 47h  // color source is CPU mix type NEW

Draw Operation:

CUR_X set to 0  // set starting horizontal position
CUR_Y is set to Y1  // off-screen area

MAJ_AXIS_PCNT is set to 1024-1
MIN_AXIS_PCNT = (1-1)
CMD = 0101001111010001  // Rectangle Fill (bits 15-13), Byte
                        // swap bit 12, 16-bit bus bit 9, Draw
                        // bit 4, Write bit 0

While FIFO space available
PIX_TRANS set to ANDword0,XORword0
PIX_TRANS set to ANDword1,XORword1
........
........
PIX_TRANS set to ANDword255,XORword255
```

26.11.4 Notes Regarding the Hardware Cursor

I/O operations to the registers used to program the cursor and set up extended mode are byte transactions. To write to the registers, an index is written at the I/O port at 3D4 and the data is written to I/O port 3D5.

If the cursor is not 64 bits, the given images should be padded to make the cursor image 64-by-64 bits. The padded area should be made transparent by padding the extra AND mask bits with 1 and the extra XOR bits by 0.

For the 4-plane mode with .5 Mbyte memory option, the cursor pattern is stored in the off-screen video memory in a rectangle of width 1024 and height

2. For the 4-plane mode, with 1 Mbyte memory option, the cursor pattern is stored in the off-screen video memory in a rectangle of width 2048 and height 1. In all cases, the clipping rectangle should be set to include the cursor definition rectangle prior to loading the cursor image.

The cursor can be programmed to 64-by-64 bits in all modes, including the 16- and 24-bit-per-pixel modes. When a 2x or 3x zoom is selected by setting bit 2 or bit 3 respectively in the hardware graphics cursor mode at 3D5, Index 45h. The colors are automatically taken from the hardware graphics cursor foreground stack at 3D5, index 4A and the hardware graphic cursor background stack at 3D5, index 4Bh.

When loading the cursor image bitmap into the off-screen memory, if the bitmap width is not 1024 bytes in a particular mode, calculate the X and Y coordinates corresponding to a 1024-byte boundary on this bitmap and copy the pattern starting at this location. For some bitmap widths, such as 640 bytes, the pattern will wrap to more than one scan line.

26.11.5   Programming the Hardware Cursor in the 864

The 864 hardware cursor can be used for all modes. The width of the pixel port can be determined by reading register bits CR67 bits 7–4. Values of 0000, 0010, 0101, or 0111 indicate that a 16-bit pixel port is in use.

Once the width of the pixel port is determined, the hardware Cursor Color Select Bits CR54 bits 3–2 must be set correctly based on Table 26.11.

The cursor color information for 4 and 8 bits per pixel for an 8-bit pixel port is stored in CRE and CRF. The cursor color information is stored in CR4A and CR4B for all configurations.

26.12   864/964 SYSTEM EXTENDED REGISTERS

The 864/964 contain additional system extended registers as shown in Table 26.12.

The display start address bits 19–16 are found in the Extended System Control 3 Register at CR69.

TABLE 26.11   8-bit Pixel Port Mode

CR54 bits 3–2	Pixel Port Mode	Cursor Colors Bits Per Pixel
0	8	4 or 8
1	8	16
2	8	24
3	8	32
0	16	4, 8 or 16
1	16	24 or 32

TABLE 26.12   Additional System Extended Registers in the 864/964

Index	Name	Register
60	CR60	Extended Memory Control 3
61	CR61	Extended Memory Control 4
62	CR62	Extended Memory Control 5
63	CR63	External Sync Delay Adjust High
64	CR64	Genlocking Adjustment
65	CR65	Extended Miscellaneous Control
66	CR66	Extended Miscellaneous Control 1
67	CR67	Extended Miscellaneous Control 2
68	CR68	Configuration 3
69	CR69	Extended System Control 3
6A	CR6A	Extended System Control 4
6B	CR6B	Extended BIOS Flag 3
6C	CR6C	Extended BIOS Flag 4
6D	CR6D	Extended Miscellaneous Control

26.13   THE PCI CONFIGURATION SPACE REGISTERS

The PCI Configuration Space Registers are shown in Table 26.13.

26.13.1   Vendor ID Register

The Vendor ID Register is hardwired to 5333h.

TABLE 26.13   The PCI Configuration Space Registers

Address	Register
0	Vendor ID
2	Device ID
4	Command
6	Status
8	Revision ID
A	Programming Interface
10	Base Address 0
30	BIOS Base Address

26.13.2 Device ID Register

The Device ID Register is hardwired to 88C0h.

26.13.3 Command Register

The Command Register is a read/write register as described in Table 26.14.

26.13.4 Status Register

The Status Register timing field in bits 10–9 is hardwired to select the minimum device select timing.

26.13.5 Revision ID Register

The Revision ID Register is hardwired to the revision level of the chip in stepping mode.

26.13.6 Programming Interface Register

The Programming Interface Register is hardwired to support the standard VGA programming.

26.13.7 Base Address 0 Register

The Base Address 0 Register is a read/write register as described in Table 26.15.

TABLE 26.14 Command Register

Bit	Function
0	Response to I/O space accesses enabled
1	Response to memory space accesses enabled
5	No response to RAMDAC register access

TABLE 26.15 Base Address 0 Register

Bit	Function
0	Hardwired to indicate base registers map into memory space
2–1	Hardwired to allow mapping anywhere in 32-bit address space
3	Hardwired to indicate does not meet pre-fetchable requirements
31–23	Base Address 0

26.13.8 BIOS Base Address Register

The BIOS Base Address Register is a read/write register as described in Table 26.16.

26.14 MEMORY MAPPING OF ENHANCED MODE REGISTERS

The 864/964 are capable of memory mapping of the enhanced registers. This function can be enabled by setting bit 4 of the CR53 Register (or bit 5 of the 4AE8h Register) to 1. Image writes normally made by accessing the Pixel Data Transfer Registers at I/O addresses E2E8 and E2EAh are made instead by accessing any memory location in the 32-Kbyte address space from A0000h–A7FFFh. Accesses to the enhanced command registers are write only. These are made to particular locations in the A8000–AFFFFh address range as shown in Table 26.17. The only exception is the Read Register Select Register at BEE8h, index 0fh. This cannot be accessed as a memory-mapped register.

TABLE 26.16 BIOS Base Address Register

Bit	Function
0	Enable access to BIOS ROM address space
31–16	Upper 16 bits of BIOS ROM Address

TABLE 26.17 Memory Mapped I/O Addresses for Enhanced Command Registers

I/O Address	Memory Addresses
8xE8h	A8xE8h
9xE8h	A9xE8h
AxE8h	AAxE8h
BxE8h	ABxE8h

Chapter 27

The Trident Super VGA Chip Sets

27.1 INTRODUCTION TO THE TRIDENT VGA

The Trident Super VGA chips include the TVGA 8800, 8900, 8900C, 9000, 9200, and 9400. The 8900 is very similar to the 8800 with a few minor differences. Most notable is the different default condition used for accessing the display memory. The 8800 default maps the display memory into host address space A0000–BFFFF hex through a 128-Kbyte bank-selection technique. The 8900 default maps the display memory into host address space A0000–AFFFF hex through a 64-Kbyte bank selection technique. In either case, the chip can be controlled such that either a 64-Kbyte or 128-Kbyte mapping is used. In addition, the 8800 can access only 512 Kbytes of memory, but the 8900 can access 1 Mbyte of display memory.

The 8800 can accommodate 1024-by-768 16-color display resolutions and 640-by-480 256-color display modes. The 8900 can accommodate 1024-by-768 in both the 16-color and 256-color modes. Neither chip can support VRAM implementations.

The 8900 supports emulation of the MDA, CGA, and Hercules standards. The 8800 supports a unique feature called super fonts, which allow up to 16 Kbytes of character codes to be stored in display memory. Each character can be up to 32 bytes, supporting 16-by-16 character sets.

Older versions of the Trident 8800 chip, called the BR version, do not support 64 Kbyte segments. These chips are rare and they can, for all intents and purposes, be ignored.

The 9000 is an inexpensive single-chip solution that includes the clock generator and DAC. It is capable of 1024 by 768 in 4-bit-per-color modes and 132 column text modes. The 9200CX family can access up to 2 Mbytes of display memory with display modes up to 1280 by 1024 in 4- and 8-bit-per-color modes, 800 by 600 in hi-color modes, and 640 by 480 in true-color modes.

The 9420 and 9430 chips provide a graphics accelerator capable of BitBlts, area fills, line drawing, and short-stroke vectors. In addition, the 9430 supports a hardware cursor, display modes up to 1024 by 768 in 4- or 8-bit-per-color modes, a 768-by-1024 portrait mode in 4- or 8-bit-per-color modes, up to 800 by 600 in hi-color modes, and up to 640 by 480 in true-color modes.

27.2 CONTROLLING THE TRIDENT 8800 AND 8900

The Trident chips can be enabled and disabled in either the PC/AT or the PS/2 microchannel implementations. The techniques are compatible with the IBM standard and are listed in Table 27.1.

The PC/AT implementation utilizes the EN field of the Display Adapter Enable shown in Figure 27.1. The PS/2 microchannel implementation utilizes the EN field of the Video Subsystem Enable Register, shown in Figure 27.2.

TABLE 27.1 Resetting and Enabling the Trident 8900

Function	Register Name	Port	Index	Bits	Value
Enable VGA adapter	Display Adapter Enable	46E8		3	0
Disable VGA adapter	Display Adapter Enable	46E8		3	1
Enable VGA motherboard	Video Subsystem Enable	3C3		0	0
Disable VGA motherboard	Video Subsystem Enable	3C3		0	1

Display Adapter Enable Register

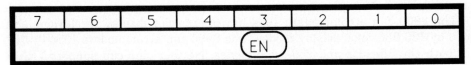

Port 46E8 Read Only

FIGURE 27.1 Display Adapter Enable Register. Adapter Card implementation at Port 46E8. Allows enabling and disabling of VGA through the EN field.

Video Subsystem Enable Register

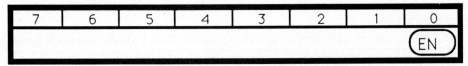

Port 3C3 Read/Write

FIGURE 27.2 Video Subsytem Enable Register. Motherboard implementation at Port 3C3. Allows enabling and disabling of VGA through the EN field.

TABLE 27.2 Determining Trident Display Status

Function	Register Name	Port	Index	Bits	Value
Chip Version	Hardware Version	3C4	B	3–0	0–15
Card ID Microchannel	Microchannel ID high	101		7–0	0–255
Card ID Microchannel	Microchannel ID low	100		7–0	0–255
Bus Type	Power-Up Mode #2	3C4	F	4	0–1
Switch Settings	Power-Up Mode #2	3C4	F	3-0	0–15

27.3 DETERMINING THE STATUS OF THE TRIDENT SUPER VGAS

The status of the Trident Super VGAs can be determined by reading the BIOS identification or writing and reading from the extended registers. In the case of the 8900, a Chip Version Register is provided. The 8800 can be identified through the Trident trademark in the BIOS area or through the Hardware Version Register value. The 8900 and beyond provides the chip identification in a CHIP field of the Chip Version Register or through the microchannel ID registers as shown in Table 27.2.

27.3.1 Identifying the Trident VGA

The Trident chips can be identified by the presence of an inverting bit field in the Mode Control #1 Register. The Page field at bit position 1 in this register is unique in that it inverts the data written into it when the data is read out. In other words, writing a 1 into the Page field will result in a 0 being read. All of the VGA manufacturers are rapidly filling the space in the 3B0–3DF port range and it is typically not safe to rely on a register as the sole source of evidence to indicate the presence of the VGA card. In this case, however, the probability that another manufactuer will have an inverting bit in this location is very small.

The Trident chips can be identified through the code in Listing 27.1. The Hardware Version Register can also be used to identify the chips. The register should be read twice to avoid changing the *old* and *new* definitions of other registers.

LISTING 27.1 Determine if the VGA Chip Is a Trident

```
Output Parameters:
      1=chip is a Trident  0=chip is NOT a Trident

Calling Protocol:
  Trident= Is_It_Trident()  */
```

(continued)

```
int Is_It_Trident(void)
{
    unsigned char old_value,old_misc_value,value,misc_value,
        power_up_value;

    // set Miscellaneous Register so MM (Memory MAP) field is set
    // to 01.
    outp(0x3CE,0x06);  // read the Miscellaneous Register
    old_misc_value = inp(0x3CF);
    misc_value = old_misc_value & 0x03;  // zero bits 3 and 3
    misc_value |= 0x04;  // set bits 3 and 2 to 01
    outp(0x3CF,misc_value);  // write the Miscellaneous Register

    outp(0x3C4,0x0E);  // read the Mode Control #1 Register
    old_value = inp(0x3C5);

    outp(0x3C5,0x00);  // write a new value bit 1=1 all other bits 0

    value = inp(0x3C5)&0x0F;  // read the new value

    outp(0x3C5,old_value);  // write the old value

    outp(0x3CE,0x06);  // fix the Miscellaneous Register
    outp(0x3CF,old_misc_value);  // write the Miscellaneous Register

    if(value>=0x02) return(1);  // check for bit 1=1 and all other
                                // bits 0
    // check for power up mode register
    outp(0x3C4,0x0F);  // read the Power up Register
    outp(0x3c5,0x00);  // try writting 00s
    power_up_value = inp(0x3C5);
    if(power_up_value!=00) return(CHIP_FOUND); // is older version
                                               // of 8800
    else return(CHIP_NOT_FOUND);  // none found

}
```

27.3.2 Determining Which Trident Chip

The chip identification is located in the CHIP field of the Hardware Version Register as illustrated in Figure 27.3. The chip number can be determined through the code in Listing 27.2.

Hardware Version Register

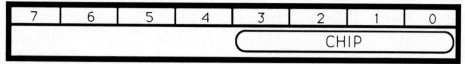

7	6	5	4	3	2	1	0
				CHIP			

Index 0B at Port 3C4   Port 3C5 Read/Write

FIGURE 27.3 Hardware Version Register. The chip version resides in the CHIP field. The mode control registers assume their "old" definitions when a write occurs to this register. The mode control registers toggle definitions when a read occurs.

LISTING 27.2 Determining Which Trident Chip

```
/* Output Parameters:
   identity    integer containing chip code
NOTE:  A subsequent consequence of this call is that the mode
       control registers are put into their new state.
Calling Protocol:
 identity = Which_Trident()  */

int Which_Trident(void)
{
 unsigned char value;
 outp(0x3C4,0x0B);  /* Version Register */
 outp(0x3c5,0);  /* dummy write to put system into old
definitions */
 value = inp(0x3C5);  /* read causes new definitions */

switch(value) {
  case 0x03:  case 0x04: return(Trident8900);
  case 0x13:  case 0x23:  case 0x93: return(Trident9000);
  case 0x53: case 0x83:  return(Trident9200);
  case 0x73:  return(Trident9420);
  default: return(Trident8800);
  }
}
```

27.4   TRIDENT DISPLAY MODES

The Trident Super VGAs support a wide variety of high-resolution display modes. The 8800 can display up to 1024 by 768 in the 16-color modes and 640 by 480 in the 256-color modes. The 8900 can display up to 1024 by 768 in both the 16- and 256-color modes interlaced or non-interlaced. In addition, the 8800

TABLE 27.3 Trident Alphanumeric Modes

Mode	Rows	Columns	Font	Resolution	Colors	Chip
50	30	80	8 by 16	640 by 480	16	8800,8900
51	43	80	8 by 11	640 by 480	16	8800,8900
52	60	80	8 by 8	640 by 480	16	8800,8900
53	25	132	8 by 14	1056 by 350	16	8800,8900
54	30	132	8 by 16	1056 by 480	16	8800,8900
55	43	132	8 by 11	1056 by 473	16	8800,8900
56	60	132	8 by 8	1056 by 480	16	8800,8900
57	25	132	9 by 14	1188 by 350	16	8800,8900
58	30	132	9 by 16	1188 by 480	16	8800,8900
59	43	132	9 by 11	1188 by 473	16	8800,8900
5A	60	132	9 by 8	1188 by 480	16	8800,8900

TABLE 27.4 Trident Graphics Modes

Mode	Resolution	Bits/color	Chip	Alpha	Character
5B	800 by 600	4	all	100 by 75	8 by 8
5C	640 by 400	8	all	80 by 25	8 by 16
5D	640 by 480	8	all	80 by 30	8 by 16
5E	800 by 600	8	not 8800	100 by 75	8 by 8
5F	1024 by 768	4	all	128 by 43	8 by 16
61	768 by 1024	8	all	96 by 64	8 by 16
62	1024 by 768	8	not 8800	128 by 48	8 by 16
60	1024 by 768 I	2	9200,9400	128 by 48	8 by 16
63	1280 by 1024	4	9200	160 by 64	8 by 16
64	1280 by 1024	8	9200	160 by 64	8 by 16
6C	640 by 480	24	9200,9400	–	–
70/71	512 by 480	15,16	9200,9400	–	–
74/75	640 by 480	15,16	9200,9400	–	–
76/77	800 by 600	15,16	9200,9400	–	–

and 8900 have a unique mode that displays 768 by 1024 in the 16-color mode. The 1024 raster lines require a special monitor capable of keeping up with the high bandwidth. The alphanumeric display modes are listed in Table 27.3, and the graphics display modes are listed in Table 27.4.

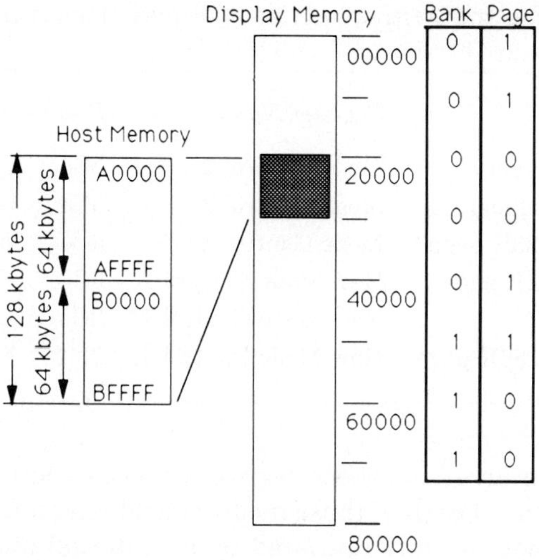

FIGURE 27.4 128-Kbyte Bank Memory Map.
Segment ranges from A0000–BFFFF. Page = 0, Bank = 0.

27.5 ACCESSING THE TRIDENT DISPLAY MEMORY

The Trident chips are mapped into the host address space through a bank over-lapped system. The 9200 and 9400 can alternately be linear mapped into the host address space. These chips can be configured to operate in a 128-Kbyte bank mode or a 64-Kbyte bank mode. The 8800 defaults to a 128-Kbyte bank map at power up. The others default to a 64-Kbyte bank map at power up. A 128-Kbyte bank memory map is shown in Figure 27.4.

Most likely, the chips the programmer will choose to configure the memory into 64-Kbyte segments are in the host address space from A0000–AFFFF. This is a much simpler technique than was involved in the 128-Kbyte memory map. The 8800 can access only 512 Kbytes of memory, and the others can access 1 Mbyte of display memory. The 512 Kbytes of display address space are mapped into eight of these 64-Kbyte banks (segments). The 1 Mbyte of display address space is mapped into sixteen of these 64-Kbyte banks (segments). The registers involved involved in accessing display memory are listed in Table 27.5.

27.5.1 Old Mode/New Mode

The register terminology, as defined by Trident, is called Old Mode Control #1 and Old Mode Control #2, or New Mode Control #1 and New Mode Control #2. A 64-Kbyte memory map is illustrated in Figure 27.5.

TABLE 27.5 Reading and Writing to Trident Display Memory in a 64-Kbyte Memory Map

Function	Register Name	Port	Index	Bits	Value
Enable Extended Memory	Mode Control 2	3C4	D	4	1
Disable Extended Memory	Mode Control 2	3C4	D	4	0
Select 256K Bank, 128K page	Mode Control 1	3C4	E	2–1	0–3
Select 256K Bank, 64K page	New Mode Control 1	3C4	E	3–2	0–3
Select 128K Page	New Mode Control 1	3C4	E	1	0–1
Select 64K Segment, 64K page	New Mode Control 1	3C4	E	0	0–1

The technique for accessing these registers creates additional problems. The old and new versions of each of these mode control registers reside at the same port addresses. They are differentiated by an internal switch. The switch is initialized and activated by reading and writing to a completely separate register. This could lead to problems if the exact state needs to be saved and restored. Figure 27.6 illustrates this internal switching.

Additional Trident registers provide the value of the attribute index and attribute state. Recall that the attribute registers are controlled in a similar fashion. The attribute registers are described in Section 10.6.

The technique used to access the old or new registers involves writing to and reading the Hardware Version Register, shown in Figure 27.3. The CHIP field of this register provides information as to the chip version number. This would normally be considered a read-only field, and indeed it is. Writing to this register does not affect the bits in any way.

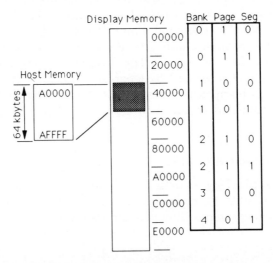

FIGURE 27.5 64-Kbyte Bank Memory Map. Segment = 0, Page = 0, Bank = 1

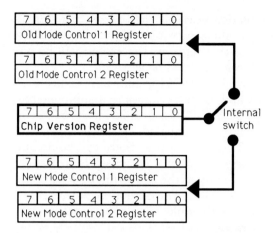

FIGURE 27.6 Old/New Internal Switch. Reading and writing to the chip version registers controls access to the old or new mode control registers.

The switch can be toggled between the old and new states through the code in Listings 27.3 and 27.4 respectively. This is illustrated in Figure 27.6.

LISTING 27.3 Enable Old Definition of Mode Registers

```
;   Calling Protocol:
;       Old_Mode_Trident();

Old_Mode_Trident PROC FAR
        mov     dx,3c4h
        mov     ax,000bh   ;index the Version Register
        out     dx,ax      ;perform write to cause old definition
        ret
Old_Mode_Trident endp
```

LISTING 27.4 Enable New Definition of Mode Registers

```
;   Calling Protocol:
;       New_Mode_Trident();

New_Mode_Trident PROC FAR
        mov     dx,3c4h
        mov     ax,000bh   ;index the Version Register
        out     dx,ax      ;perform write to cause old definition

        in      ax,dx      ;read to cause new definitions
        ret
New_Mode_Trident endp
```

When a read instruction accesses the version register, the internal switch that accesses either the old or new Mode Control 1 and 2 Registers will toggle. When a write occurs to this register, the switch will be positioned so the old Mode Control 1 and 2 registers will be accessed.

The Old Mode Control Register #1 is shown in Figure 27.7. It contains fields that control the VGA and provides access to display memory. The 512 field is used as address bit 17 of the CRTC controller. If the 512 field is 0, the lower 512 Kbytes of display memory are enabled. If 1, the upper 512 Kbytes of display memory are enabled. This implies that there can be no automatic crossing of this 512-Kbyte boundary. Thus, it is not possible to display part of the lower 512 Kbytes of display memory at the same time as part of the upper 512 Kbytes of memory are being displayed. The exception to this rule is the 1024-by-768 256-color display mode. Both banks of memory are required to display a single image in this display mode.

The Bank field of the Old Mode Control Register #1 selects one of four banks of 256 Kbytes of display memory for CPU operations. This page switching mechanism is relevant to the 128-Kbyte paging scheme that is activated when the internal switch is in the old position.

The Old Mode Control Register #2 is shown in Figure 27.8. It contains fields that control the VGA. The emulation modes are selected through the EMU field of Old Mode Control Register #1 as listed in Table 27.6. The Bank Selection (paging) mode can be enabled or disabled through the ENP field. If the ENP

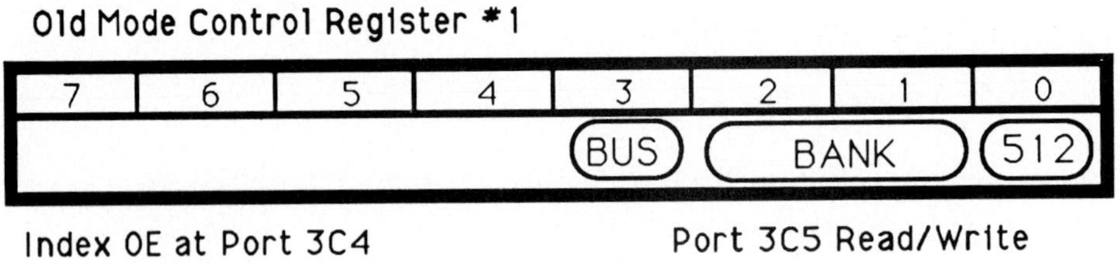

Old Mode Control Register #1

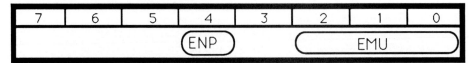

Index OE at Port 3C4   **Port 3C5 Read/Write**

FIGURE 27.7 Old Mode Control Register #1. The old definition of the Mode Control Register #1. Extended CRT Display Addressing in the 512 field. The Memory bank addressing is controlled through the BANK field. The 8- or 16-bit host bus is selected through the bus field.

Old Mode Control Register #2

7	6	5	4	3	2	1	0
			ENP		EMU		

Index OD at Port 3C4   **Port 3C5 Read/Write**

FIGURE 27.8 Old Mode Control Register #2. The old definition of the Mode Control Register #2 enables emulation through the EMU field. It also enables or disables the page switching mode through the ENP field.

TABLE 27.6 Emulation Mode Control

EMU field	Emulation
0	VGA
3	EGA
5	CGA, MDA, Hercules

New Mode Control Register #1

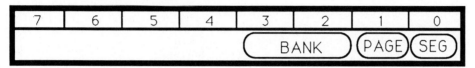

Index OE at Port 3C4   Port 3C5 Read/Write

FIGURE 27.9 New Mode Control Register #1. The new definition of the Mode Control Register #1 provides a three-bit bank start address through the SEG, PAGE, and BANK fields. Note that the PAGE field is inverted.

field is 0, the paging is disabled, and the memory is compatible with the standard VGA. If the ENP field is 1, the paging mode is enabled and access to the display memory above 256 Kbytes is enabled.

The New Mode Control Register #1 is shown in Figure 27.9. It is active when the system is in a 64-Kbyte paging scheme. The four bits necessary to access the sixteen 64-Kbyte pages are resident in this register. The segment selection accesses 64-Kbyte segments and is found in the Seg field. The page selection accesses 128-Kbyte segments and is found in the PAGE field. (NOTE: Like the 8800, the page field is inverted. A 0 in the PAGE field would access the upper 128-Kbyte page, and a 1 would access the lower 128-Kbyte page for write operations. Read operations are not inverted.) The 256-Kbyte banks (0–3) are located in the Bank field of this register. These three fields can be considered as one bank address field. This register can be programmed in a fashion compatible to other VGA systems that use 64-Kbyte segments. However, before the 64-Kbyte bank number can be loaded into this register, the bit value in the bit 1 position must be inverted.

The New Mode Control Register #2 contains clock control information that is not relevant for this book.

27.5.2 Bank Selection

Bank selection typically occurs through the New Mode Control Register #1. The bank value is different depending on whether the host operation reads or writes to display memory. If the operation is a write, the PAGE field of this register should be inverted. This can be seen in Listing 27.5a in the XOR BL,2 instruction. If the operation is a read, the PAGE field should not be inverted. Two macros are provided in Listings 27.5a and 27.5b to perform the loading of the bank value.

LISTING 27.5a Load the Write Bank for the Trident

```
;   Input with:
;   bank  Write Bank_Number 0-7 bank number indicating desired
;         64-Kbyte bank
;   Calling Protocol:
;     Load_Write_Bank_Trident(bank)

Load_Write_Bank_Trident   Proc far   bank:BYTE
;        set up index to Bank Select Register
         mov     dx,3c4h    ;point to Mode Control #1 Register
         mov     al,0eh
         mov     ah,bank
         xor     ah,02      ;adjust page bit
         out     dx,ax      ;output bank
         ret
Load_Write_Bank_Trident endp
```

LISTING 27.5b Load the Read Bank for the Trident

```
;   Input with:
;   bank  Read Bank_Number 0-7 bank number indicating desired
;         64-Kbyte bank
;   Calling Protocol:
;         Load_Read_Bank_Trident(bank)

Load_Read_Bank_Trident    Proc far   bank:BYTE
         mov     dx,3c4h    ;point to Mode Control #1 Register
         mov     al,0eh
         mov     ah,bank
         xor     ah,02      ;adjust page bit (invert bit 1)
         out     dx,ax      ;output bank
         ret
Load_Read_Bank_Trident endp
```

27.5.3   Page Modes

Page Mode is controlled by the register at 3CF index 6. If bits 3 and 2 are set to 00, this puts the chip into a 128-Kbyte mode. Setting these bits to 01 puts the chip into a 64-Kbyte mode. It is important to note that it is necessary to read from register 3C5 at index B, which sets 3C5 at index E to a 64-Kbyte mode. Writing to 3C5 index B sets 3C5 index E to a 128-Kbyte mode. The 64-Kbyte page mode is strongly recommended. The 2 Mbyte of display memory requires a 20-bit address as shown in Figure 27.10.

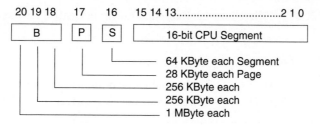

FIGURE 27.10 Addressing Scheme

The 64 Kbyte page mode can access the full 2 Mbytes of display memory. There are two means of accessing this memory—through the paging registers through the New Source and Destination Address Registers or through the Alternate Segment Selection Registers.

27.5.4 Addressing through the New Source and Destination Address Register

The New Source Address Register is located at port 3CF index E. It is described in Table 27.7.

The Page Select field is a bit complicated due to an inversion during writes as shown in Table 27.8.

A similar register is the New Mode Control Register with identical fields as the New Source Address Register shown in Tables 27.7 and Tables 27.8. It is located at Port 3C5 index E.

The Miscellaneous Extended Function Control Port at 3CF index F uses bit 0 and bit 2 for paging as shown in Table 27.9. The DUAL field in bit 0 enables

TABLE 27.7 New Source Address Register at port 3CF index E

Bits	Function
0	Segment Select 0=lower segment of a page, 1=upper segment
1	Page Select
3–2	Bank Select Bank 0–3

TABLE 27.8 The Page Select Field

Value	R/W	Function
0	R	Select lower page
0	W	Select higher page
1	R	Select higher page
1	W	Select lower page

TABLE 27.9 Miscellaneous Extended Function Control Port at 3CF index F

Bits	Function	
0	DUAL	Enables single=0 or dual=1 bank registers
2	ENALTP	Enables alternative registers for bank select

single or dual bank switching. It defaults to single. During single bank selection, the Source Segment Register is disabled and the Destination Segment Register is used for all accesses. The Destination Register is called the New Mode Control Register in one case or the Destination Segment Register. The Source Register is called the New Source Address Register or the Source Segment Register.

The ENALTP field selects which of these register pairs should be used. If this field is set to 0, the Source Segment Register and Destination Segment Registers at 3D9 and 3D8 are disabled and the New Source Address Register and the New Mode Control Register are used. If the ENALTP field is set to 1, both sets of registers are active. The memory addressing schemes are shown in Figure 27.11 for both the 1-Mbyte and the 2-Mbyte addressing scheme. It should be noted that the ENALTP bit should always be set if 2 Mbytes of memory are to be addressed.

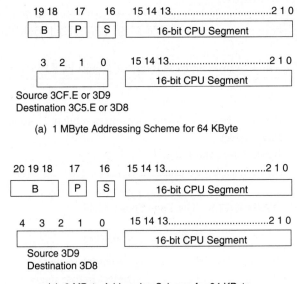

FIGURE 27.11 Memory Addressing for 1- and 2-Mbyte Systems

27.5.5   Alternate Segment Selection

The 9200 and 9400 series includes an alternate means of segment selection that is far superior to the means discussed in Section 27.5. These provide dual bank selection, one for reads and one for writes from the CPU.

The Source Segment Register is located at ports 3D9h. It is used during host read operations. The Destination Segment Register is located at 3D8h. It is used during host write operations. Both registers are described in Table 27.10.

It should be noted that there is no inversion necessary on any bits in these registers, as was the case in the New Source Address Register and the New Mode Control Registers.

These registers are valid only if the ENALTP bit, bit 2 of the Miscellaneous Extended Function Control Port at 3CF index 0Fh, is set to 1.

27.5.6   Linear Addressing

Both the 9200 and 9400 series chips are capable of linear addressing. The Configurable Linear Addressing Register is located at 3D5 index 21h. It controls the linear addressing as shown in Table 27.11. The address bits determine the 1- or 2-Mbyte boundary location of the linear addressing window. As is always the case, a protected mode environment is required to use linear addressing.

TABLE 27.10   Source Segment Register at 3D9 and Destination Segment Register at 3D8

Bit	Name	Function
0	SRCSEG/DESSEG	Shares bit 0 of the New Source Address Register
1	SRCPAGE/DESPAGE	Shares bit 1 of the New Source Address Register
2	SRCBNK0/DESBNK0	Shares bit 2 of the New Source Address Register
3	SRCBNK1/DESBNK1	Shares bit 3 of the New Source Address Register
4	SRCMEG/DESMEG	

TABLE 27.11   Configurable Linear Addressing Register at 3D5 index 21h

Bit	Name	Function
0	LAWB0	Address bit A20
1	LAWB1	Address bit A21
2	LAWB2	Address bit A22
3	LAWB3	Address bit A23
4	LAWS	Aperture Size 0=1 Mbyte 1=2 Mbyte
5	ENLA	1=Enable Linear Addressing

27.6   CONTROLLING THE CRT ADDRESS GENERATION

27.6.1   Controlling the Display Start Address

To display the 1 Mbyte onto the screen, it is necessary to utilize the Old Mode Control 1 Register and the CRTC Module Testing Register. These registers are described in Table 27.12.

The CRTC Module Testing Register, shown in Figure 27.12, contains two fields that augment the 16-bit start addresses provided in the CRTC registers. The 16-bit addressing can be enabled through the A16 field of this register. If the A16 field is a 0, the address bit 16 function is disabled. This is the standard VGA implementation and will cause wrap around at the 64-Kbyte segment. If the A16 field is a 1, the address bit 16 function is enabled.

The address bit 16 is provided to the CRT addressing through the S16 field of this register. This allows access to 128 Kbytes of display memory. The display start address can be loaded through the code in Listing 27.6.

LISTING 27.6   Load the Display Start Address for the Trident

```
; Input Parameters:
;       top         top two bits of address
; Calling Protocol:
;       Load_Start_Top_Trident(top)

Load_Start_Top_Trident   proc far   top:BYTE
        mono_or_color
        add    dx,4
        mov    al,1eh      ;index Module Testing Register
        out    dx,al

;       read current value
        inc    dx
        in     al,dx       ;get value
        and    al,0dfh     ;zero out start address-16 bit 5

;       or in new start address
        mov    bl,top
        and    bl,01h      ;only want 1 bit
        mov    cx,5
        shl    bl,cl       ;shift left 5 to get bit in proper position
        or     al,bl
        or     al,80h      ;set bit 1 for enable bit 16
        out    dx,al       ;output top address
        ret
Load_Start_Top_Trident   endp
```

TABLE 27.12 8900 Trident Display Address Control

Function	Register Name	Port	Index	Bits	Value
Select lower 512K Bank	Old Mode Control 1	3C4	E	0	0
Select higher 512K Bank	Old Mode Control 1	3C4	E	0	1
Start Address Bit 16	CRTC Module Testing	3D4	1E	5	0–1
Address Bit 16 Enable	CRTC Module Testing	3D4	1E	7	0–1

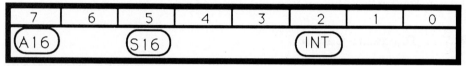

Module Testing Register

7	6	5	4	3	2	1	0
A16		S16			INT		

Index 1E at Port 3C4   Port 3C5 Read/Write

FIGURE 27.12 Module Testing Register. The interlaced mode is controlled through the INT field. The CRT starting address bit-16 is controlled through the S16 field. The host address bit-16 is controlled through the A16 field (8900only).

27.6.2 Controlling the Cursor Start Address

The cursor start address cannot be extended beyond the 16-bit cursor address contained in the Cursor Start Address High and Low Registers. This does not create a problem since the alphanumeric modes do not extend beyond the first 64-Kbyte segment. The graphics modes require read/modify/write memory accesses as described in Section 27.4.

27.6.3 Controlling the Display Offset

The display offset determines the virtual image size. The 8-bit value is stored in the Offset Register in the CRTC register group, described in Section 10.4.22. In the word mode, which is typically the case, display offsets up to 1024 bytes can be defined.

27.7 GRAPHICS ENGINE EXTENDED REGISTERS

The Graphics Engine extended registers control all hardware drawing functions. At RESET condition, these registers are I/O mapped. They may also be memory mapped in addition to I/O mapping. If they are I/O mapped, an indexed scheme is used. The index register is located at 21xA. The data is written or read through a Data Port Register located at 21xC through 21xF. Each register is 32 bits long and the bytes 0 through 3 can be accessed through the ports 21xC throught 21xF respectively. In this case, the x is the instance and it defaults to 0 at RESET. It may be programmed to another value through power-on strapping of bits. I will refer to these registers as if they were the default condition.

Memory mapping is enabled by writing a 0 to bit 4 of the Configuration Register at I/O index 90h, byte 0. In this case, the parameters are offset from a base address that is located in the Parameter Block Base Address Register at index 7Ch. This 256-byte block can be located anywhere in the 32-bit memory address space. It is typically put at B8000h , thereby overwritting the CGA space. This ensures that no memory conflicts occur.

The Graphics Engine extended registers are 32-bit registers found on the Trident 9400 series chips, and they are provided in Table 27.13. Field names preceded and followed by dashes are either 16 bits or 32 bits long.

27.7.1 Hardware Cursor

The hardware cursor is not available on the 9420. The registers associated with the hardware cursor are shown in Table 27.14. Both the horizontal and vertical start registers are with respect to the active display area.

27.7.2 Configuration Register

The Configuration Register is located at index 90 byte 0. It is described in Table 27.15.

27.7.3 Source and Destination Memory Maps

The source and destination maps each contain a 32-bit start address, a width, height, and format. These registers are shown in Table 27.16.

The Source Map Format Register contains the bits/pixel as shown in Table 27.17.

27.7.4 Background and Foreground Colors

The registers associated with colors are shown in Table 27.18. The use of the foreground and background registers are controlled in the Pixel Operation Register described in Section 27.7.5. The mix functions are shown in Table 27.19.

27.7.5 Pixel Operation Register

The Pixel Operation Register is the general purpose control register. A write to byte 3 starts the graphics engine. It is described in Table 27.20. The Direction of the Pixel Operation is shown in Table 27.21 while the Graphics Engine Functions are shown in Table 27.22.

TABLE 27.13 Graphics Engine Extended Registers

Index	Byte 3	Byte 2	Byte 1	Byte 0
30	Cursor V Start Low	—	Cursor H Start High	Cursor H Start Low
34	—	Cursor Enable	—	Cursor V Start High
38	Cursor Color 1	—	—	Cursor Color 1
74	Hardware Cursor Bitmap Base Address			
78	—	Cursor Height	—	Cursor Width
7C	Parameter Block Base Address			
90	—	—	—	Configuration
94	Source Map Base Address			
98	Source Map Height		Source Map Width/Line Draw Constant 1	
9C	—	—	—	Source Map Format
AC	Direction Step Register			
B8	Destination Map Height		Destination Map Width	
BC	—	—	—	Destination Format
C0	Image Data			
C4	—	—	Sytle Pattern	
C8	—	—	Background Mix	Foreground Mix
D8	—	—	Foreground Color	
DC	—	—	Background Color	
E0	Operation Height/Line Draw Error Term		Operation Width / Line Length	
E4	Destination Line Start Position			
E8	Source Line Start Position/Line Draw Constant 2			
F0	Source Start Y Corrdinate/Minor Axis Incr		Source Start X Corrdinate/Major Axis Incr	
F8	Destination Start Y Coordinate		Destination Start X Coordinate	
FC	Pixel Operation			

27.7.6 Image Data Register

Image data can be transferred from system memory through this port. Writing to byte 3 of this register initates the data transfer operation from the image data buffer into the display memory. An 8-bit operation should perform four

TABLE 27.14 Hardware Cursor Registers

Register	Function
Cursor Horizontal Start	Provides 16 bits of cursor horizontal position start address (pixels).
Cursor Vertical Start	Provides 16 bits of cursor vertical position start address (scan lines).
Cursor Enable	Bit 0=1 to enable. Bit 0=0 to disable.
Cursor Color 0	8-bit background color for cursor pattern.
Cursor Color 1	8-bit foreground color for cursor pattern.
Hardware Cursor Bitmap Address	Base address of cursor pattern with respect to display memory.
Cursor Width	Width −1 of Cursor (up to 64).
Cursor Height	Height−1 of cursor (up to 64).

TABLE 27.15 Configuration Register at Index 90 Byte 0

Bits	Name	Function
5	STOP	0=Normal operation. 1=terminate current operation immediately.
6	IMGI	0=Image Data buffer is empty. 1=Image data buffer is full.
7	BUSY	0=Engine is idle. 1=Engine is full.

TABLE 27.16 Memory Map Registers

Register	Function
Source Map Base Address	32-bit address of source data in display memory
Source Map Height	Height−1 of source
Source Map Width	Width−1 of source
Source Map Format	Format of data (see Table 27.12)
Destination Map Base Address	32-bit address of destination data in display memory
Destination Map Height	Height−1 of source
Destination Map Width	Width−1 of source
Destination Map Format	Format of data (see Table 27.12)

TABLE 27.17 Source Map Format Register

Value	Format
0	1 bits per pixel
1	2 bits per pixel
2	4 bits per pixel
3	8 bits per pixel
4	16 bits per pixel

TABLE 27.18 Color-Related Registers

Register	Function
Foreground Mix Register	Foreground Mix (see Table 27.19)
Background Mix Register	Background Mix (see Table 27.19)
Foreground Color Register	Foreground Color
Background Color Register	Background Color

TABLE 27.19 Foreground Mix and Background Mix

Value	Mix
0	All zero
1	S AND D
2	S AND !D
3	S
4	!S AND D
5	D
6	S XOR D
7	S OR D
8	!S AND !D
9	S XOR !D
A	!D
B	S OR !D
C	!S
D	!D OR D
E	!S OR !D
F	All one

TABLE 27.20 Pixel Operation Register

Bits	Name	Function
3–0	Pixel Operation Direction	Determines direction of operation (see Table 27.21).
27–24	Graphics Engine Function	Function to be performed (see Table 27.22).
30	Foreground Source	0=use foreground color. 1=use source map pixel.
31	Background Source	0=use background color. 1=use source map pixel.

TABLE 27.21 Direction of the Pixel Operation

Value	Start	Direction
0,1	Top-left	Right and Down
2,3	Bottom-left	Right and Up
4,5	Top-right	Left and Down
6,7	Bottom-right	Left and Up

TABLE 27.22 Graphics Engine Function

Value	Function
0	No Op
4	Short-Stroke Vector
5	Line Draw
8	Pixel Transfer
A	Area Fill
C	Image Transfer

writes to the Image Data Register, with byte 3 being the last. A 16-bit operation should perform two writes to the Image Data Register, with the high byte being the last. This ensures that the 32 bits are actually written. Bit 6, IMGI of the Configuration Register, should be queried as to whether the Image Data Buffer is empty or full before attempting a write operation. The Image Data Register is a 32-bit register.

27.7.7 Style Pattern Register

The Style Pattern Register is a 16-bit register containing a 16-bit pattern used for area fill, line draw, and short-stroke vector operations. A 1 in this pattern means that the foreground color should be used; a 0 means the background color should be used.

27.7.8 Line Drawing

Registers associated with line drawing are shown in Table 27.23. Note that the Line Draw Constant 1, the Line Length and the Line Draw Error Term share other functions.

   The programming of these Bresenham-related registers is shown in Listing 27.7a when x is the major axis and 27.7b when y is the major axis. NOTE: The Line Draw Constant Register #2 and the Major and Minor Axis Increment Registers are programmed in 2's complement form.

LISTING 27.7a X is the Major Axis abs(x2-x1) > =abs(y2-y1)

```
Line Draw Constant 2 = - ( abs(x2-x1) * 2 );

if (x1<=x2) Major Axis Increment = 1;
   else Major Axis Increment = -1;

if (y1<=y2) Minor Axis Increment = Destination Map Width;
   else Minor Axis Increment = -Destination Map Width;

if (x1<=x2) Line Draw Error Term = - (abs(x2-x1) + 1);
   else Line Draw Error Term = - abs(x2-x1);
```

TABLE 27.23 Registers Associated with Line Drawing

Register	Function
Line Draw Constant 1	Bresenham constant 1
Direction Step	Step direction and draw enable
Line Length	Length of line −1
Line Draw Error Term	Bresenham error term
Destination Line Start	Start position of line in linear coordinates
Line Draw Constant 2	Bresenham constant 2
Major Axis Increment	Major axis increment
Minor Axis Increment	Minor axis increment

LISTING 27.7b   Y is the Major Axis abs(y2-y1) > abs(x2-x1)

```
Line Draw Constant 2 = - ( abs(y2-y1) * 2 );

if (y1<=y2) Major Axis Increment = Destination Map Width;
   else Major Axis Increment = -Destination Map Width;

if (x1<=x2) Minor Axis Increment = 1;
   else Minor Axis Increment = -1;

if (x1<=x2) Line Draw Error Term = - (abs(y2-y1) + 1);
   else Line Draw Error Term = - abs(y2-y1);
```

27.7.9   Direction Step

The Step Direction Register contains the direction step code in bits 7–0 and the Draw Enable command in bits 32–24 as shown in Table 27.24. The step code is a non-standard short-vector step shown next.

```
3   2   1
4   x   0
5   6   7
```

Writing to byte 3 draws one line as a short-stroke vector at the starting location and then updates the current position according to the direction code.

27.7.10   Position Registers

The registers associated with the position of data transfers are shown in Table 27.25.

The Operation Width and Height Registers provide the width–1 and height–1 of the destination block for area fill, PxBlt, pattern block tansfers with variable size source, and color expanded block transfers. For PxBlt operations, this contains the width and height of both the source and destination blocks.

The Source Line Start Position Register is the linear address obtained by the following equation. NOTE: This is a redundant but necessary operation since the silicon does not perform the arithmetic for you.

Source Line Start Position Register = (Source Start Y Coordinate *
    Source Map Width) + Source Start X Coordinate;

The Source Start X Coordinate and Source Start Y Coordinates are the offsets into the source block within the source map. The Destination Start X Coordinate and Destination Start Y Coordinates are the offsets into the destination block within the destination map.

TABLE 27.24 Step Code

Bits	Function
7–5	Direction Code as seen in Figure 27.13
4	reserved
3–0	Vector Length –1

TABLE 27.25 Registers Associated with Position

Register	Function
Source Start X Coordinate	Start X coordinate within the source map
Source Start Y Coordinate	Start Y coordinate within the source map
Destination Start X Coordinate	Start X coordinate within the destination map
Destination Start Y Coordinate	Start Y coordinate within the destination map
Source Line Start Position	Linear starting position
Operation Width	Width – 1 in pixels of the destination block
Operation Height	Height – 1 in pixels of the destination block

27.8 COLOR FORMATS

The 4-bit and 8-bit color formats are identical for the Trident products. The 9400 series offers both 15-bit-per-color and 16-bit-per-color hi-color modes. The organization for the hi-color modes is shown in Table 27.26. In addition, a true-color mode is provided where the color data format is also shown in Table 27.26.

27.9 GRAPHICS ENGINE PROGRAMMING EXAMPLES

Several programming examples are provided. In each case, the foreground and background color mixes and styles are programmed, even though they need not change for each operation. It has been assumed that the destination map is already defined. The destination map is usually on-screen display memory

TABLE 27.26 Hi-Color and True-Color Data Formats

Bits/Color	Red	Green	Blue
15	14–10	9–5	4–0
16	15–11	10–5	4–0
24	23–16	15–8	7–0

defined by the Destination Map Base Address, the Destination Map Height, Destination Map Width, and the Destination Map Pixel Format Registers.

The graphics engine must be checked to ensure that previous operations have completed. The Configuration Register, bit 7, contains the busy flag. Reading a 1 in this bit position indicates busy, and a 0 indicates ready.

27.9.1 Area Fill

Draw an 8-bit-per-pixel filled area of 25 by 30 pixels in the upper-left corner of the display using the Style Pattern Register. Assume the destination map is 1024 by 768.

Example 27.1 Area Fill

Step 1. Set up Destination map

```
Destination Map Width           = 03ffh  // 1024 -1
Destination Map Height          = 02ffh  // 768 -1
Destination Map Format          = 03h    // 8 bits per pixel
Destination Start X Coordinate  = 0000h  // start at 0
Destination Start Y Coordinate  = 0000h  // start at 0
Destination Line Start Position = 0000h  // (0 * 1024) + 0
```

Step 2. Set up operation size for area fill

```
Operation Width  = 01dh  //25-1
Operation Height = 018h  //30-1
```

Step 3. Set up colors

```
Foreground Mix    = 03h    //Color Mix = source into
destination
Background Mix    = 03h    //Color Mix = source into
destination
Foreground Color  = 0036h  // foreground color
Background Color  = 002ah  // background color
Style Pattern     = aaaah  // on-off pattern
```

Step 4. Pixel Operation Register set to Area Fill; use foreground and background colors, start at top-left corner of fill area increasing right and down

```
Pixel Operations Register = 0A000000h
```

27.9.2 Pixel Block Transfer (PxBlt)

Transfer a source to destination area in display memory. Assume the source and destination maps are 1024 by 768. Source and destination blocks will be 25 by 30 pixels wide and high. The upper-left corner of the source block will be at pixel location (50,40) and the destination block will be at (120,90). Source block data will be ANDed with destination block data before being written into the destination.

Example 27.2 PixBlt

Step 1. Set up Destination Map

```
Destination Map Width            = 03ffh  // 1024 -1
Destination Map Height           = 02ffh  // 768 -1
Destination Map Format           = 03h    // 8 bits per pixel
Destination Start X Coordinate   = 0032h  // start at 50
Destination Start Y Coordinate   = 0028h  // start at 40
Destination Line Start Position  = 0000A032h  // (40*1024)+50
```

Step 2. Set up source map

```
// beginning of display memory
Source Map Base Address Register = 00000000h
Source Map Width                 = 03ffh  // 1024 -1
Source Map Height                = 02ffh  // 768 -1
Source Map Format                = 03h    // 8 bits per pixel
Source Start X Coordinate        = 0078h  // start at 120
Source Start Y Coordinate        = 005Ah  // start at 90
Destination Line Start Position  = 00016878h // (90*1024)+120
```

Step 3. Set up operation size for area fill

```
Operation Width  = 01dh  //25-1
Operation Height = 018h  //30-1
```

Step 4. Set up colors

```
Foreground Mix  = 01h  //Color Mix = source AND destination
```

Step 5. Pixel Operation Register set to PixBlt; start at top-left corner of fill area increasing right and down. Use source map for colors.

```
Pixel Operations Register  =  0A800000h
```

27.9.3 PxBlt Transfer Repeating Pattern (PxBlt)

Transfer a source to destination area in display memory. This time the source is a rectangle of only 4 by 8 pixels. It will be stored in off-screen memory and pattern copied into the destination. Assume the source and destination maps are 1024 by 768. Source and destination blocks will be 25 by 30 pixels wide and high. The upper-left corner of the destination block will be at pixel location (120,90). Source block data will be ANDed with destination block data before being written into the destination.

Example 27.3 PxBlt with Small Off-Screen Display Pattern

Step 1. Set up destination map

```
Destination Map Width            = 03ffh  // 1024 -1
Destination Map Height           = 02ffh  // 768 -1
Destination Map Format           = 03h     // 8 bits per pixel
Destination Start X Coordinate   = 0078h  // start at 120
Destination Start Y Coordinate   = 005ah  // start at 90
Destination Line Start Position  = 00016878h  // (90*1024)+120
```

Step 2. Set up source map

```
//off-screen display memory
Source Map Base Address Register = 00180000h
Source Map Width                 = 03h   // 4 -1
Source Map Height                = 07h   // 8 -1
Source Map Format                = 03h   // 8 bits per pixel
Source Start X Coordinate        = 000h  // start at 0
Source Start Y Coordinate        = 000h  // start at 0
Destination Line Start Position  = 00000000h  // (0*1024)+0
```

Step 3. Set up operation size for area fill

```
Operation Width   = 01dh  //25-1
Operation Height  = 018h  //30-1
```

Step 4. Set up colors

```
Foreground Mix  = 01h   //Color Mix = source AND destination
```

Step 5. Pixel Operation Register set to PixBlt; start at top-left corner of fill area increasing right and down. Use source map for colors.

```
Pixel Operations Register  =  0A800000h
```

27.9.4   Color Expanded BitBlt Transfer (PxBlt)

Transfer a source to destination area in display memory. This time the source is a rectangle of only 4 by 8 pixels. It will be stored in off-screen memory and the pattern copied into the destination. The source map is treated as 1-bit-per-color monochrome map. Assume the source and destination maps are 1024 by 768. Source and destination blocks will be 25 by 30 pixels wide and high. The upper-left corner of the destination block will be at pixel location (120,90). Source block data will be color expanded into the foreground and background colors before being written into the destination.

Example 27.4 Color Expanded PxBlt with Small Off-Screen Display Pattern

Step 1. Set up destination map

```
Destination Map Width           = 03ffh  // 1024 -1
Destination Map Height          = 02ffh  // 768 -1
Destination Map Format          = 03h    // 8 bits per pixel
Destination Start X Coordinate  = 0078h  // start at 120
Destination Start Y Coordinate  = 005ah  // start at 90
Destination Line Start Position = 00016878h  // (90*1024)+120
```

Step 2. Set up source map

```
//off-screen display memory
Source Map Base Address Register = 00180000h
Source Map Width                 = 03h    // 4 -1
Source Map Height                = 07h    // 8 -1
Source Map Format                = 00h    // 1 bit per pixel
Source Start X Coordinate        = 000h   // start at 0
Source Start Y Coordinate        = 000h   // start at 0
Destination Line Start Position  = 00000000h // (0*1024)+0
```

Step 3. Set up operation size for area fill

```
Operation Width   = 01dh  //25-1
Operation Height  = 018h  //30-1
```

Step 4. Set up colors

```
Foreground Mix   = 03h  // Color Mix = copy source into
                        // destination
```

Step 5. Pixel Operation Register set to PxBlt; start at top-left corner of fill area increasing right and down. Use foreground and background colors.

```
Pixel Operations Register = 0A000000h
```

27.9.5   Image Transfer from CPU (BitBlt)

Transfer a source to destination area in display memory. This time the source comes from the host. Assume the destination map is 1024 by 768. Source and destination blocks will be 20 by 20 pixels wide and high. The upper-left corner of the destination block will be at pixel location (120,90). Source block data will be copied into the destination.

Example 27.5 BitBlt from Host to Display Memory

Step 1. Set up destination map

```
Destination Map Width         = 03ffh  // 1024 -1
Destination Map Height        = 02ffh  // 768 -1
Destination Map Format        = 03h    // 8 bits per pixel
Destination Start X Coordinate = 0078h  // start at 120
Destination Start Y Coordinate = 005ah  // start at 90
Destination Line Start Position = 00016878h  // (90*1024)+120
```

Step 2. Set up source map

```
Source Map Width          = 03FFh  // 1024-1
Source Map Height         = 02ffh  // 768 -1
Source Map Format         = 03h  // 8 bits per pixel
Source Start X Coordinate = 000h   // start at 0
Source Start Y Coordinate = 000h   // start at 0
Destination Line Start Position = 00000000h  // (0*1024)+0
```

Step 3. Set up operation size for area fill

```
Operation Width  = 013h  //20-1
Operation Height = 013h  //20-1
```

Step 4. Set up colors

```
Foreground Mix = 03h  // Color Mix = copy source into
                      // destination
```

Step 5. Pixel Operation Register set to Image Transfer; start at top-left corner of fill area increasing right and down.

```
Pixel Operations Register = 0C000000h
```

Step 6. Repeat exactly (20*20) = 400 times.

```
Image Data Register = 400 bytes of data.
```

27.9.6   Color Expanded Text BitBlt Transfer (BitBlt)

Transfer a source to destination area in display memory. This time the source is in the host. It will be stored in off-screen memory and pattern copied into the destination. The Source map is treated as 1-bit-per-color monochrome map. Assume the Destination Map is 1024 by 768. Source and destination blocks will be 20 by 20 pixels wide and high. The upper-left corner of the destination block will be at pixel location (120,90). Source block data will be color expanded into the foreground and background colors before being written into the destination.

Example 27.6 Color Expanded BitBlt from Host to display

Step 1. Set up destination map

```
Destination Map Width          = 03ffh  // 1024 -1
Destination Map Height         = 02ffh  // 768 -1
Destination Map Format         = 03h    // 8 bits per pixel
Destination Start X Coordinate = 0078h  // start at 120
Destination Start Y Coordinate = 005ah  // start at 90
Destination Line Start Position = 00016878h  // (90*1024)+120
```

Step 2. Set up source map

```
Source Map Width          = 03ffh      // 4 -1
Source Map Height         = 02ffh      // 8 -1
Source Map Format         = 00h        // 1 bit per
pixel
Source Start X Coordinate = 000h       // start at 0
Source Start Y Coordinate = 000h       // start at 0
Destination Line Start Position = 00000000h  // (0*1024)+0
```

Step 3. Set up operation size for area fill

```
Operation Width  = 013h  //20-1
Operation Height = 013h  //20-1
```

Step 4. Set up colors

```
Foreground Mix   = 03h  // Color Mix = copy source into
                        // destination
Background Mix   = 03h  // Color Mix = copy source into
                        // destination
Foreground Color = e6h  // foreground color
Background Color = 5ah  // background color
```

Step 5. Pixel Operation Register set to Image Transfer; start at top-left corner of fill area increasing right and down. Use foreground and background colors.

```
Pixel Operations Register = 0C000000h
```

Step 6. Repeat exactly (20*20) = 400 times.

```
Image Data Register = 400 bits = 50 bytes of data.
```

27.9.7 Line Draw

Draw a solid line from (15,35) to (55,20). Assume the destination map is 1024 by 768. Draw the line source into destination.

Example 27.7 Line Draw

Step 1. Set up destination map

```
Destination Map Width          = 03ffh  // 1024 -1
Destination Map Height         = 02ffh  // 768 -1
Destination Map Format         = 03h    // 8 bits per pixel
Destination Start Y Coordinate = 0023h  // start at 35
Destination Start X Coordinate = 000Eh  // start at 15
Destination Line Start Position = 3c23h // (35 * 1024) + 15
```

Step 2. Set up operation size for area fill

```
Line Draw Constant 1 = 30      // abs(20 - 35 ) * 2
Line Draw Constant 2 = -80     // abs(55-15) * 2
Major Axis Increment = 01dh    // 2's compliment
Minor Axis Increment = -1024   // Destination Map width +1 in
                               // 2's compliment
Operation Height     = 018h    // 30-1
Line Length          = -43     // 2's compliment
Line Draw Error Term = -41     // - abs(55-15) + 1 in 2's
                               // compliment
```

Step 3. Set up colors

```
Foreground Mix    = 03h    // Color Mix = source into
                           // destination
Background Mix    = 03h    // Color Mix = source into
                           // destination
Foreground Color  = 0036h  // foreground color
Background Color  = 002ah  // background color
Style Pattern     = ffffh  // no pattern
```

Step 4. Pixel Operation Register set to Line Draw; use foreground and background colors.

```
Pixel Operations Register = 05000000h
```

27.9.8 Short-Stroke Vector

Draw two solid color lines starting at (15,35). Draw a 3-pixel line up and right to pixel (13,38) and draw a second 5-pixel line straight down. Assume the destination map is 1024 by 768. Draw the line source into destination.

Example 27.8 Short-Stroke Vector Draw

Step 1. Set up destination map

```
Destination Map Width         = 03ffh  // 1024 -1
Destination Map Height        = 02ffh  // 768 -1
Destination Map Format        = 03h    // 8 bits per pixel
Destination Start Y Coordinate = 0023h  // start at 35
Destination Start X Coordinate = 000Eh  // start at 15
Destination Line Start Position = 00003c23h  // (35*1024)+15
```

Step 2. Set up colors

```
Foreground Mix   = 03h // Color Mix = source into destination
Foreground Color = 0036h // foreground color
Style Pattern    = ffffh
```

Step 3. Pixel Operation Register set to short-stroke vector draw; use foreground color.

```
Pixel Operations Register = 04000000h
```

Step 4. Draw the lines

```
Direction Step = 00100010B  // Draw the first line
Direction Step = 11000100B  // Draw the second line
```

Chapter 28

The Tseng Labs Super VGA Chips

28.1 INTRODUCTION TO THE TSENG LABS VGA

Tseng Labs has manufactured three Super VGA Chips named the ET3000, ET4000, and ET4000W32. As one would expect, the ET4000 is an advanced version of the ET3000. Its features include faster processing, the ability to handle VRAM memory, a generous helping of caches and FIFOs to speed up graphics operations, and the capacity to access more display memory. Both the ET3000 and ET4000 are simple processors to program.

The ET4000W32 includes a higher throughput graphics interface capable of sustaining high bandwidth 32-bit transfers from the host. It has been clocked at five times the host-interface speed of the ET4000. In addition, the W32 contains a powerful graphics coprocessor and multimedia interface.

Along with the capacity to access more display memory comes the higher resolution display modes. The ET3000 is capable of 1024-by-768 16-color and 800-by-600 256-color, the ET4000 is capable of 1024-by-768 16-color and 1024-by-768 256-color modes. With the proper DAC chips, the ET4000 is also capable of limited hi-color and true-color modes. The W32 supports up to 1280-by-1024 modes in the 4-bit-per-color modes, 1024-by-768 in the 8-bit-per-color modes, 800-by-600 in the hi-color modes, and 640-by-480 in the true-color modes. The ET4000 can emulate the MDA, Hercules, CGA, and EGA graphics cards. Either can reside in the PC/AT bus or on a microchannel bus and both can generate interrupts to the host.

One major difference between the ET3000 and ET4000 is the field locations for the Read and Write Bank Selection registers. The need to provide additional banks for the higher resolution display modes in the ET4000 forced the redefinition of the read and write bank. Thus, software that utilizes the dual-bank configuration must determine whether an ET3000 or ET4000 is present before setting the Read Bank Register. The hardware zoom window available on the ET3000 is not available on the ET4000.

The ET4000W32 adds a graphics coprocessor, a high-speed host interface, a second simultaneous display window, enhanced display modes, and a high-speed direct-to-display memory interface. The ET4000W32p supports both the VL and PCI bus.

28.1.1 ET3000 Chip

The ET3000 is the first-generation Super VGA from Tseng Labs. Table 28.1 describes the different versions of the ET3000. The ET3000-AX and ET3000-BX versions are discussed in this chapter. Both are register-level compatible to the standard VGA and are downwardly compatible to the MDA/Hercules and CGA. Each supports 132-column alphanumeric display modes, multiple windows, and multiple simultaneous soft fonts. In addition, both support hardware pan and zoom in graphics and text modes.

The hardware, zoom feature is an interesting special effect, which allows the creation of an independent window on the screen. This window contains a zoomed representation of a portion of display memory. The starting x and y location of the zoomed window is programmable. Its size is determined by the data that is to be zoomed. A rectangular region within the display memory is targeted as the window to zoom. Finally, a horizontal and vertical zoom factor, one to eight, is specified. At this point, the system is primed, and all that remains is to enable the zoom function. The zoom window overlays the normal display window.

28.1.2 ET4000 Chip

The ET4000 is the second-generation Super VGA chip from Tseng Labs. The major improvement of the ET4000 over the ET3000 is speed and resolution. The improved data paths, fast cache and fifo memories, and VRAM control all lead to faster graphics processing. The hardware, zoom feature of the ET3000 was not included in the ET4000. Additional registers are provided in the ET4000 for enhanced control.

The ET4000 is extremely fast. It supports VRAM memory and has highly optimized memory control for the DRAM memory. Speed tests have shown that

TABLE 28.1 ET3000 Versions

Chip Name	Capabilities	Host Bus	16-bit Resolution	256-bit Resolution
ET3000-AX	Most powerful	8/16	1024 by 768	800 by 600
ET3000-BX	Less powerful	8	800 by 600	640 by 480
ET3000-Bp	Basic VGA chip	8	800 by 600	320 by 200

the DRAM memory configuration can run nearly the speed of the 8 MHz PC/AT bus. This, of course, is based on the wait-states imposed on the PC/AT bus. Tseng recommends the DRAM configuration on cards that plug into this bus. When the ET4000 is mounted on a motherboard, it does not have the forced wait-states imposed upon it from the host. The VRAM memory configuration is recommended in this application.

The ET4000 takes full advantage of the VRAM dual-ported memory. One port is used for data input while the second port is used for data output. The memory is configured with a 16-bit wide data bus from the ET4000 to the display memory. The display memory can consist of two chips totaling 256 Kbytes, four chips totaling 512 Kbytes, or eight chips totaling 1 Mbyte of memory. The VRAM chips are 256K by 4 bits each. Four chips comprise a bank. Each bank utilizes a 16-bit data bus in and out to the host and a 16-bit data bus out to the video refresh circuitry. The 16-bit bus is not extended to 32 bits when eight chips are used. Rather, a second bank is placed in parallel to the first bank. This limits the bandwidth to the 16-bit bus rate instead of increasing the bandwidth to a 32-bit bus rate.

The ET4000 dedicates 25 percent of its silicon to FIFO memory, cache memory, and memory management. This silicon is well used and translates into very fast graphics.

28.1.3 ET4000 W32 Chip

The ET4000W32 is downward compatible to the ET4000. The W32 supports up to 4 Mbytes of DRAM display memory. A zero-wait state 32-bit interface exists between the host and the graphics coprocessor providing high-speed BitBlts, raster operations, and hardware cursor. A second simultaneous display window is included in the W32 providing a second window. This second window (CRTCB) may be overlaid and resized up to the size of the display creating an effective second simultaneous dual-window display. The 4 Mbytes of display memory become useful in this application. The W32 also supports linear memory addressing. The W32 also includes an Image Memory Access port (IMA) that allows direct access to the frame buffer at high speeds. This 8-bit port can be opened allowing images to be displayed on the screen in real-time at all display resolutions and color depths.

28.1.4 ET4000W32p Chip

The ET4000W32p chip is also downward compatible to the ET4000W32 with some nice improvements. Several new registers are provided that support a hardware line draw. It is a DRAM controller with advanced memory management capabilities. It interfaces to both the VL bus and the PCI bus.

28.2 CONFIGURING THE TSENG LABS VGA

The ET4000 provides the standard capabilities for configuring the card as shown in Table 28.2.

28.2.1 8- or 16-bit Bus Interface

Both the memory and I/O data paths are designed to be either 8 or 16 bits wide through the Video System Configuration #1 Register. The I/O bus width is controlled through the I16 field. The display memory bus width is controlled through the D16 field. This register is shown in Figure 28.1.

The on-card ROM can be configured for 8- or 16-bit operation through the R16 field of the Video System Configuration #2 Register shown in Figure 28.2. If the R16 field is set to 1, 16-bit ROM accesses will be enabled. If the R16 field is 0, 8-bit ROM accesses will be enabled. Typically, this field would not be modified by the programmer. Other hardware on the VGA card would have to be configured for the 8- or 16-bit ROM accesses. This might be in the form of jumpers or switches. The programmer may find it useful to determine whether 8- or 16-bit accesses are currently being used.

All other fields within the Video System Configuration #2 Register are related to hardware configuration. As with the R16 field, these should not be modified. The Mem field controls whether DRAM or VRAM is installed. If the

TABLE 28.2 Configuring the Tseng Labs Super VGAs

Function	Register Name	Port	Index	Bits	Value
Enable segment addressing	Video System Config. 1	3D4	36	4	0
Enable linear addressing	Video System Config. 1	3D4	36	4	1
Select 8-bit I/O	Video System Config. 1	3D4	36	7	0
Select 16-bit I/O	Video System Config. 1	3D4	36	7	1
Select 8-bit data path	Video System Config. 1	3D4	36	6	0
Select 16-bit data path	Video System Config. 1	3D4	36	6	1
Enable 8-bit ROM	Video System Config. 2	3D4	37	4	0
Enable 16-bit ROM	Video System Config. 2	3D4	37	4	1
Read Speed Performance	RAS/CASVideo Config.	3D4	32	7–0	0–255
Vertical NON-Interlace	Overflow High	3D4	35	7	0
Vertical Interlace	Overflow High	3D4	35	7	1
Disable On-Card ROM	TS Auxiliary Mode	3C4	7	3	0
Disable On-Card ROM	TS Auxiliary Mode	3C4	7	5	1
Enable VGA compatibility	TS Auxiliary Mode	3C4	7	7	1
Enable EGA compatibility	TS Auxiliary Mode	3C4	7	7	0

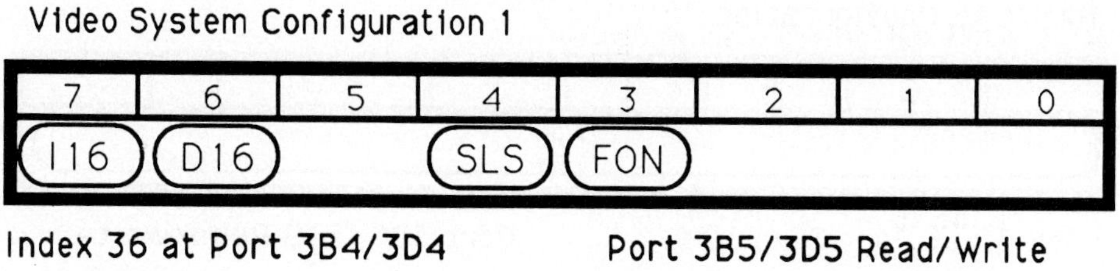

Video System Configuration 1

Index 36 at Port 3B4/3D4   Port 3B5/3D5 Read/Write

FIGURE 28.1 Video System Configuration Register #1. The 8- or 16-bit bus selection for display memory resides in the D16 field and for I/O memory in the I16 field. The addressing scheme can be linear or segmented controlled by the SLS field. The font width is controlled through the FON field.

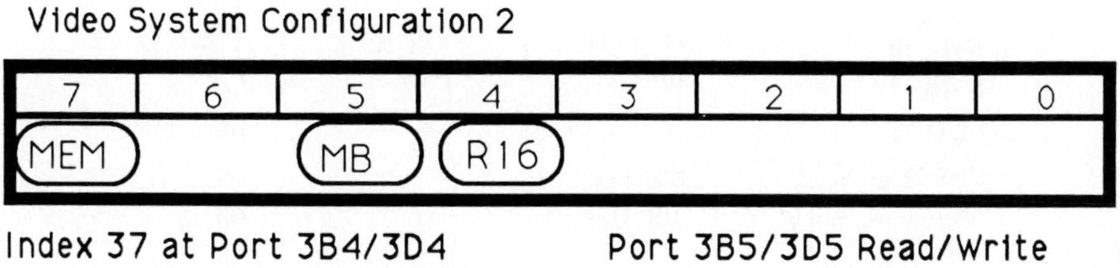

Video System Configuration 2

Index 37 at Port 3B4/3D4   Port 3B5/3D5 Read/Write

FIGURE 28.2 Video System Configuration Register #2. The R16 field controls whether a 16-bit BIOS is installed. The MB field optimizes memory bandwidth and the MEM field selects either VRAM or DRAM.

Mem field is 1, VRAM is installed. If Mem is set to 0, DRAM is installed. The MB field controls memory bandwidth. A 0 value in the MB field indicates better performance than if the MB field is set to 1.

The RAS/CAS Configuration Register can provide information regarding the bandwidth of the system. This field should not be altered by the programmer. It is likely that it is already optimized for the specific card. The TIME field is really a combination of six fields that reside in this register. It is beyond the scope of this book to describe each field but suffice it to say that a 1 in any bit position in the TIME field will degrade performance. The RAS/CAS Configuration Register is displayed in Figure 28.3. Table 28.3 lists some common configurations and their respective TIME fields. Each bit in the TIME field affects memory in a unique way. Calculating memory performance is complex. The fewer 1s in this TIME field the better.

One caveat regarding Table 28.3 concerns the relationship between the TIME field and the video boards system clock. If the system clock is slow, this value will be smaller than if the system clock is fast. Table 28.3 lists two entries, one for 28 MHz system clock and a second for a 36 MHz system clock. The 28 MHz system clock hasa smaller value in the TIME field. However, the 36 MHz version is likely to run faster.

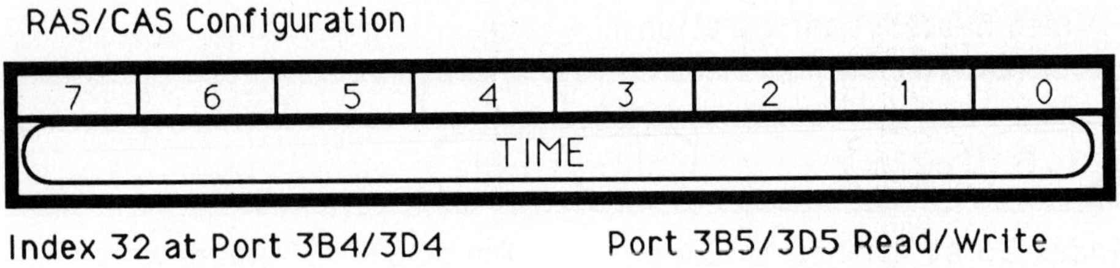

RAS/CAS Configuration

7	6	5	4	3	2	1	0
TIME

Index 32 at Port 3B4/3D4   Port 3B5/3D5 Read/Write

FIGURE 28.3   RAS/Configuration Register. The TIME field is a composite field that configures memory speed performance.

TABLE 28.3   RAS/CAS Configuration Register Typical Values

Memory Type	Memory Speed	System Clock	TIME Field
Ideal			00
VRAM memory	80 nsec		00
VRAM memory	100 nsec		09
VRAM memory		28 MHz	00
VRAM memory		36 MHz	08
DRAM memory		40 MHz	70

The memory speed certainly affects processing speed and the value in the TIME field. Typically, memory comes in either 80 or 100 nanosecond access-time versions. If the DRAM of VRAM memory is 80 nanosecond memory, the value in the TIME field is likely to be smaller than if the memory is 100 nanosecond memory. This occurs because the memory has added headroom. If the values in the TIME field are the same, it is likely that the faster 80 nanosecond memory is not being utilized. In Table 28.3, a VRAM entry with 80 nanosecond memory has a Time value of 0 (ideal); the 100 nanosecond memory has a value of 09.

28.2.2   On-Card ROM

The on-card BIOS ROM can be enabled or disabled through the R0 and R1 fields of the TS Auxiliary Mode ET3000 Register and TS Auxiliary Mode ET4000 Register shown in Figure 28.4 and Figure 28.5 respectively. These two fields combine to form a two-bit control code that configures the ROM, as shown in Table 28.4. The combination R1=0 and R0=1 disables the ROM. The power-on default is R1=1, R0=1. The ET3000 or ET4000 can also be placed into a VGA emulation or into an EGA emulation mode through the VGA field. If the VGA field is 1, the VGA compatibility is enabled; if 0, the EGA compatibility is enabled. The power-on default condition is VGA emulation.

TS Auxiliary Mode ET3000
7
6
5
4
3
2
1
0
VGA
R0
MSF
R1
CS
CZ
CN
Index 7 at Port 3C4
Port 3C5 Read/Write

FIGURE 28.4 TS Auxiliary Mode Register. The VGA field enables VGA or EGA compatibility. The R1,R0 fields select the ROM BIOS address space. The CN, CZ, and CX fields complement the function of the three possible windows. These are the normal, zoom, and split screen windows respectively. The MSF field enables multiple soft fonts.

TABLE 28.4 Configuring the BIOS ROM

R1	*R0*	*ROM BIOS Addresses*	*Total Memory*
0	0	C0000–C3FFF	16 Kbytes
0	1	ROM disabled	0 Kbytes
1	0	C0000–C5FFF; C6800–C7FFF	30 Kbytes
1	1	C0000–C7FFF	32 Kbytes

TS Auxiliary Mode ET4000
7
6
5
4
3
2
1
0
VGA
R0
R1
Index 7 at Port 3C4
Port 3C5 Read/Write

FIGURE 28.5 TS Auxiliary Mode ET4000 Register. TheVGA field enables VGA or EGA compatibility. The R1,R0 fields select the ROM BIOS address space.

28.2.3 Linear or Segmented Addressing

The VGA can be configured to access memory in a linear or in a segmented fashion through the SLS field. The linear addressing mode forces all display memory to be continuous. This is a much more efficient way to utilize the ET4000. If the SLS Field is 1, this linear mapping scheme is enabled. If 0, the standard VGA segmented memory mapping scheme is enabled.

In extended DOS or OS/2 applications, it is possible to place the VGA into high memory where there is room to place 1 Mbyte of display memory into a contiguous address space. This allows the ET4000 to ignore the bank selection registers. There are two advantages to this approach. The first ensures faster

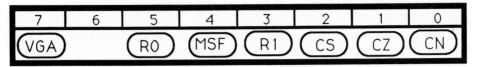

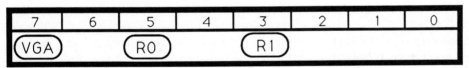

programs; the second ensures continuous high-speed operation from a hardware perspective.

The software advantage requires an extended operating system and access to the memory through the 80286, 80386, or 80486 processors. The software advantage becomes pronounced when 32-bit instructions can handle the 1 Mbyte without segment registers.

The hardware advantage is primarily aimed at video frame-grabbers where the hardware has a continuous stream of data coming at the ET4000 display memory, and the ET4000 cannot afford to perform bank switching.

28.2.4 Interlaced or Non-interlaced Control

The ET3000 and ET4000 can interface to either interlaced or non-interlaced monitors. This is accomplished through the Overflow High Register for the ET3000 and ET4000. This register contains several extended address and control fields as shown in Figures 28.16 and 28.17. The ET3000 and ET4000 can control either an interlaced or a non-interlaced monitor through the INT field of the Overflow High Register. If the INT field is 1, the interlaced mode is engaged. If 0, the non-interlaced mode is engaged.

28.2.5 Extended Vertical Timing

The extended address bits extend the address range of the Vertical Blank, Vertical Total, Vertical Display End, Vertical Sync Start, and the Line Compare registers. These five fields, located in the Overflow High Register, are described in Table 28.5. The Overflow High Register for the ET3000 and ET4000 are shown in Figures 28.16 and 28.17, respectively. Each acts as bit 10 of the respective field. Note that bit 8 of these registers resides in the same bit positions of the Overflow Low Register. The Overflow Low Register is described in Section 10.4.8. Also in the Overflow Low Register is bit 9 of the Vertical Total,

TABLE 28.5 Overflow High Register Fields

Bit	Field	Feature	Usage
7	INT	Vertical Interlace	1=vertical interlace
6	RMW	Read/Modify/Write	1=enable Read/Modify/Write
5	GL	Gen-lock	1=enable gen-lock
4	LC10	Line Compare Bit 10	
3	VS10	Vertical Sync Start Bit 10	
2	VD10	Vertical Display End Bit 10	
1	VT10	Vertical Total Bit 10	
0	VB10	Vertical Blank Start Bit 10	

Vertical Display End, and Vertical Sync Start. Bit 9 of the Vertical Blank Start and Line Compare Register is found in the Maximum Row Address Register described in Section 10.4.10.

These extended address bits in bit positions 0–4 extend the address range for the vertical timing to eleven bits. The standard VGA representations of these vertical timing functions are ten bits thereby allowing access of up to 1024 scan lines. Extending this to eleven bits allows accessing of up to 2048 scan lines.

28.3 CONTROLLING THE TSENG LABS VGA

The ET4000 uses the VGA-compatible control registers located at port address 46E8 for the PC/AT systems and 3C3 for the PS/2 motherboard microchannel systems. The EN field enables the VGA if set to 1 and disables the VGA if set to 0 as illustrated in Table 28.6 and in Figures 28.6 and 28.7.

TABLE 28.6 Resetting and Enabling the Tseng Super VGAs

Function	Register Name	Port	Index	Bits	Value
Enable VGA PC/AT	Video Subsystem Enable	46E8		3	1
Disable VGA PC/AT	Video Subsystem Enable	46E8		3	0
Enable VGA Microchannel	Video Subsystem Enable	3C3		0	1
Disable VGA Microchannel	Video Subsystem Enable	3C3		0	0
Enable Card Microchannel	Setup Control	102		0	0
Disable Card Microchannel	Setup Control	102		0	1
Switch Normal Window	TS Auxiliary Mode ET3000	3C5	7	0	1
Same Normal Window	TS Auxiliary Mode ET3000	3C5	7	0	1
Switch Zoom Window	TS Auxiliary Mode ET3000	3C5	7	1	1
Same Zoom Window	TS Auxiliary Mode ET3000	3C5	7	1	1
Switch Split Window	TS Auxiliary Mode ET3000	3C5	7	2	1
Same Split Window	TS Auxiliary Mode ET3000	3C5	7	2	1

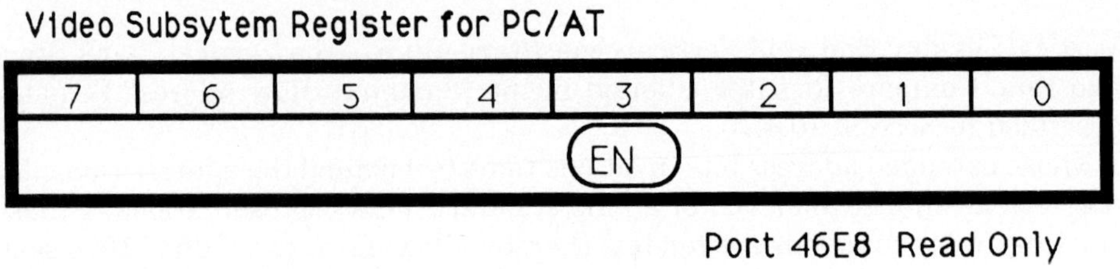

Video Subsytem Register for PC/AT

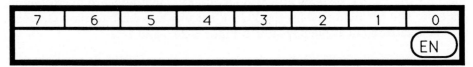

Port 46E8 Read Only

FIGURE 28.6 Display Adapter Enable Register. Adapter card implementation at port 46E8. Allows enabling and disabling of VGA through the EN field.

Video Subsystem Register for PS/2 Microchannel

Port 3C3 Read/Write

FIGURE 28.7 Video Subsystem Enable Register. Motherboard implementation at port 3C3. Allows enabling and disabling of VGA through the EN field.

28.3.1   Enabling the VGA

Only one of these two Video Subsystem Enable registers is enabled at a time. This is controlled through the ENVS field of the Compatibility Control Register shown in Figure 28.8. If the ENVS field is 1, the system is configured so that this register will reside at the 46E8 port address. If 0, the system is configured for the 3C3 port address. This is the power-up default position so that the Video Subsystem Enable Register is located at port address 3C3.

28.3.2   Switching Alphanumeric/Graphic Modes

The ET3000 provides a technique for switching the mode of each of three independent windows. The ET3000 can have a normal display window, split screen display window, and zoom window. These windows do not have to be displayed

Compatibility Control Register

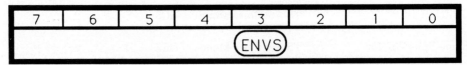

Index 34 at Port 3B4/3D4   Port 3B5/3D5 Read/Write

FIGURE 28.8 Compatibility Register. The ENVS field controls whether the Video Subsystem Enable Register is mapped to 3C3 or 46E8.

in the same fashion as the current display mode. Since each window is independent, it can be programmed to be in either a graphics or a text mode. This is accomplished through the CN, CZ, and CS fields in the TS Auxiliary Mode ET3000 Register as shown in Figure 28.4. It should be noted that these fields have different functions in the corresponding TS Auxiliary Mode ET4000 Register as shown in Figure 28.5. If the CN field is 1, the mode in the normal display window is changed from text to graphic or vice versa. If the CN field is 0, no change occurs. The CZ and CS fields operate similarly for the zoom and split screen windows respectively.

28.4 INQUIRING ABOUT THE TSENG CONFIGURATION

Other than the standard VGA registers and the extended registers described in this chapter, there are no additional register fields dedicated to Tseng configuration. The microchannel Card ID registers can be accessed only when the system is in a setup mode. Table 28.7 lists some registers used to acquire information.

28.4.1 Identifying the Tseng Chips

The Tseng chip family can be identified by accessing the Miscellaneous Register shown in Figure 28.9. This register is located in the Attribute Register group at index 16 hex. Bits 4 and 5, the High field of this register, are used to select the high-resolution timings. The programmer can read this High field, re-write it with a different value, then read it and verify that the re-write

TABLE 28.7 Inquiring about the Tseng Configuration

Function	Register Name	Port	Index	Bits	Value
Identify Card	Microchannel Id. Low	POS 100		7–0	0–255
Identify Card	Microchannel Id. High	POS 101		7–0	0–255
Identify Tseng	Miscellaneous	3C0	16	4	0,1
Identify Chip	Extended Start	3x4	33	0–3	0–15

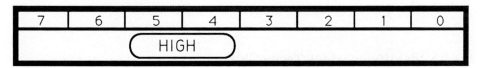

ATC Miscellaneous

Index 16 at Port 3C0   Port : Write 3C0 Read 3C1

FIGURE 28.9 ATC Miscellaneous Register. The high resolution and high-color mode resides in the HIGH field.

operation was successful. If it was successful, the card is based on a Tseng Labs chip. At this point, the original value in the High field should be restored.

The Tseng chip family can be identified through the code in Listing 28.1.

LISTING 28.1 Determine if the VGA Is a Tseng Labs Super VGA */

```
/*
Calling Protocol:
  Tseng= Is_It_Tseng()   */

int Is_It_Tseng(void)
{ unsigned char value,save,new_value;

  Set_Key_Tseng();    // set the key

  // Read the miscellaneous functions register at 36hex
  inp(0x3da); // set toggle to index

  outp(0x3c0,0x36);   //index 36 = index 16 + 20hex
  save = value = inp(0x3c1);
  value ^= 0x10;   // invert bit 4

  // write out the new value
  inp(0x3da); // set toggle to index
  outp(0x3c0,0x36);   //index 36 = index 16 + 20hex
  outp(0x3c0,value); //re-write the inverted bit 4

  inp(0x3da); // set toggle to index
  outp(0x3c0,0x36);   //index 36 = index 16 + 20hex

  // Read the miscellaneous functions register at 36hex
  new_value = inp(0x3c1);

// write out the old value
  inp(0x3da); // set toggle to index
  outp(0x3c0,0x36);   //index 36 = index 16 + 20hex
  outp(0x3c0,save); //re-write with the old value

  if(value==new_value) return(CHIP_FOUND); else
return(CHIP_NOT_FOUND);
}
```

28.4.2   Identifying which Tseng Chips

The ET4000 can be distinguished from the ET3000 by the availability of the Extended Start Address Register shown in Figure 28.15. This register is located in the CRTC register group at port address 3x4/3x5 index 33 hex. The x refers to D if a color mode is active and B if a monochrome mode is active. The programmer can read this register, re-write it with a different value, then read it and verify that the re-write operation was successful. If it was successful, the card is based on an ET4000 chip. If it was unsuccessful, the card is based on an ET3000 chip. At this point, the original value in the register should be restored.

The ET3000, ET4000, and ET4000W32 can be differentiated by the code in Listing 28.2.

LISTING 28.2 Determining which Tseng Labs Super VGA Chip

```
/*
Output Parameters:
        identity       integer containing chip code
Calling Protocol:
 identity = Which_Tseng()  */

int  Which_Tseng(void)

{ unsigned char value,save[6],found_3000,new_value;
  int base,i,ret_val;

 if( (inp(0x3CC) &0x01)==1) base = 0x3D0;  else base = 0x3B0;

// process the et3000
for (i=0; i<6; i++) {
  outp(base+4,0x1b+i); save[i] = inp(base+5);
  }

found_3000 = 1;  // assume it is an ET3000

for (i=0; i<6; i++) {
 outp(base+4,0x1b+i);
 new_value = (save[i]&0xf0) + i+8;
 outp(base+5,new_value); value = inp(base+5)&0x0f;
 if(value!=i+8) found_3000=0;
 }

for (i=0; i<6; i++) {
 outp(base+4,0x1b+i); outp(base+5,save[i]);
 }

if(found_3000) return(Tseng3000);

// now discriminate between the ET4000 and the ET4000-W32
 Set_Key_Tseng();

  outp(0x217A,0xE0); outp(0x217B,0xAA);
```

(continued)

```
  if(inp(0x217B)==0xAA) return(Tseng4000W32);
   else  return(Tseng4000);
}
```

The ET4000W32 can be differentiated from the ET4000 by writing to the register at 217Ah. Note that the ET4000 uses an XGA-type interface by mapping some of its registers at 21xAh and 21xBh. The "x" is the instance and the W32 typically forces a single instance and the x=7. This differs from the XGA where the instance often defaults to 6. The index E0 is the CRTCB/Sprite Horizontal Pixel Position Register and it should be a read/write register. If it can be loaded with a pattern, in this case AAh, then the chip is a W32; otherwise, it is a standard ET4000.

The ET4000W32 can be further identified by use of the upper four bits of the CRTCB Sprite Row Offset High Register at Index EC as shown in Table 28.8. The fields in this register are described in Table 28.8.

TABLE 28.8 Identifying the W32 Chips

Value (bits 7–4)	Chip / Revision
0	W32
1	W32i
2	W32p rev A
3	W32i rev B
4	W32i rev B
5	W32p rev B
7	W32p rev C

28.5   TSENG LABS DISPLAY MODES

The ET4000 supports the standard alphanumeric modes, which incorporate a variety of 132-column display modes. In addition, two alphanumeric modes allow 60-by-80 and 40-by-100 character resolutions. These modes are described in Table 28.9.

The ET4000 supports the standard graphics modes, which extend to 1024 by 768 in both the 16-color and 256-color modes. These modes are described in Table 28.10.

The ET4000 has been implemented in several different ways. The proper way to set the display mode depends on the specific chip (3000, 4000, or W32) as well as the manufacturer's implementation. In addition, the hi-color and true-color display modes require special handling. The code provided in Listing 28.3 is a segment of a mode set function that will handle most of the cases.

TABLE 28.9 Tseng Labs Alphanumeric Modes

Mode	Rows	Columns	Font	Resolution	Colors	Chip
18	44	132	8 by 8	1056 by 352	2	4000
19	25	132	9 by 14	1188 by 350	2	4000
1A	28	132	9 by 13	1188 by 364	2	4000
22	44	132	8 by 8	1056 by 352	16	4000
23	25	132	8 by 14	1056 by 350	16	4000
24	28	132	8 by 13	1056 by 364	16	4000
26	60	80	8 by 8	640 by 480	16	4000
2A	40	100	8 by 15	800 by 600	16	4000

TABLE 28.10 Tseng Graphics Modes

Mode	Resolution	Bits/Color	Chip
25	640 by 480	4	4000
29	800 by 600	4	4000
2D	640 by 350	8	4000
2E	640 by 480	8	4000
2F	640 by 400	8	4000
30	800 by 600	8	4000
37	1024 by 768	4	4000
38	1024 by 768	8	4000
3D	1024 by 768	4	4000
Hi-Color (15 and 16 bit)			
2D	640 by 350	15,16	4000
2E	640 by 480	15,16	4000
2F	640 by 400	15,16	4000
30	800 by 600	15,16	4000
True-Color			
2E	640 by 480	24	4000

LISTING 28.3 Segment of Code to Handle Specific Chips and Display Modes

```
case Tseng3000:
        if(mode>0x13) Set_64k_Tseng_3000();
        break;
```

(continued)

```
    case Tseng4000:  case TsengS24:  case Tseng4000W32:
        if(mode>0x13) Set_Key_Tseng();  /* set key if extended */
        break;

    case TsengS24:  // DIAMOND SPEEDSTAR 24
        if((Pixel_Bits==c15_bit)||(Pixel_Bits==c24_bit)) {
         switch(mode) {
          case 0x2e: SetModeHi_D24(0x2e); break;
          case 0x2f: SetModeTrue_D24(0x2e); break;
          case 0x30: SetModeHi_D24(0x30); break;
          }
      }
        else
        SetMode(mode);
        break;

    case Tseng4000W32:
        if((Pixel_Bits==c15_bit)||(Pixel_Bits==c16_bit)||
(Pixel_Bits==c24_bit)) {
          switch(mode) {
          case 0x50: retval=SetModeHi_W32(0x2e,f5r5g5b); break;
          case 0x60: retval=SetModeHi_W32(0x2e,f5r6g5b); break;
          case 0x70: retval=SetModeTrue_W32(0x2e,f8r8g8b); break;
         // 800x600
          case 0x51: retval=SetModeHi_W32(0x30,f5r5g5b); break;
          case 0x61: retval=SetModeHi_W32(0x30,f5r6g5b); break;
          case 0x71: retval=SetModeTrue_W32(0x30,f8r8g8b); break;
          }
      }
        else
          SetMode(mode);
    break;
```

The ET4000 has combined different color resolutions into the same display mode numbers. For example, mode 2Eh is a 640-by-480 display mode. It can be either be an 8-bit, 15-bit, 16-bit, or 24-bit per color display mode! Similarly, mode 30h is a 800-by-600 display mode. It can also be either be an 8-bit, 15-bit, 16-bit, or 24-bit per color display mode. It may be useful to create some pseudo-mode numbers in order to differentiate these modes. This is evident in Listing 28.3 with the mode numbers as shown in Table 28.11 and the display formats shown in Table 28.12. The functions to actually set the display mode are provided in Listing 28.4.

TABLE 28.11 Pseudo-mode Numbers

Pseudo-Mode	Tseng Mode	Color Depth
2eh	2eh	8-bit
50h	2eh	15-bit
60h	2eh	16-bit
70h	2eh	24-bit
30h	30h	8-bit
51h	30h	15-bit
61h	30h	16-bit
71h	30h	24-bit

TABLE 28.12 Hi-Color and True-Color formats

Code	Format
f5r5g5b	15-bit
f5r6g5b	16-bit
f8r8g8b	24-bit

LISTING 28.4 Functions that Set the ET4000 Modes

```
; Function:
; Set the display mode for hi-color Diamond 24

; Input parameters
;   mode    desired display mode

; Calling protocol
; ok= SetModeHi_D24(mode);

SetModeHi_D24 PROC FAR  arg1:byte
        mov    ax,10F0h  ;Hi-color mode set
        mov    bl,arg1   ;set desired mode
        int    10h       ;interrupt 10
        ret
SetModeHi_D24 endp

; Function:
; Setting the Active Display Mode for Hi-Color for the W32
```

(continued)

```
; Input parameters
;   mode    desired display mode
;   format 1=5,5,5  2=5,6,5

; Output parameters
;         ok 0=failure, 1=format 5,5,5 2=format 5,6,5 3=8R-8G-8B
;            4=8B-8G-8R

; Calling protocol
; ok= SetModeHi_W32(mode,format);

SetModeHi_W32 PROC FAR  mode:byte, format:byte
        mov     ax,10F0h  ;Hi color mode set
        mov     bl,mode
        int     10h

        mov     ax,10F2h  ;Hi color mode set
        mov     bl,format ;set desired format
        int     10h ;interrupt 10

        mov     al,bl     ;return status where ah=0 if ok and
                          ;<>0 if failure
        ret
SetModeHi_W32 endp

; Function:
;  Setting the Active Display Mode for Hi-Color for the W32

; Input parameters
; mode  desired display mode  format 1=5,5,5  2=5,6,5

; Output parameters
;         ok 0=failure, 1=format 5,5,5 2=format 5,6,5 3=8R-8G-8B
;            4=8B-8G-8R

; Calling protocol
; format= GetFormatHi_W32();

GetFormatHi_W32 PROC FAR
        mov     ax,10F2h  ;Hi color Format set
        mov     bl,0
        int     10h ;interrupt 10

        mov     al,bl     ;return status where ah=0 if ok and
                          ;<>0 if failure
        ret
GetFormatHi_W32 endp
```

```
; Function:
; Setting the Active Display Mode for TrueColor using mode 2eh
; for the Diamond 24

; Input parameters
; mode   desired display mode

; Calling protocol
;   SetModeTrue_D24(mode);

SetModeTrue_D24 PROC FAR   arg1:byte
        mov     ax,10E0h  ;True color mode set
        mov     bl,2Eh ;set desired mode for true color
        int     10h ;interrupt 10
        ret
SetModeTrue_D24 endp


; Function:
; Setting the Active Display Mode for TrueColor for the W32

; Input parameters
; mode   desired display mode   format FF=8R-8G-8B, FE=8B-8G-8R

; Calling protocol
;   SetModeTrue_W32(mode,format);

SetModeTrue_W32 PROC FAR   mode:byte,format:byte
        mov     ax,10F0h   ;True color mode set
        mov     bl,format  ;set desired format for true color
        mov     bh,mode    ;set desired mode for true color
        int     10h        ;interrupt 10

        mov     ax,10F2h   ;Get color format
        mov     bl,0       ;get format
        int     10h

        mov     al,bl      ;return status where ah=0 if ok and
                           ;<>0 if failure
        ret
SetModeTrue_W32 endp
```

In addition, there are several functions that are useful when determining what environment is present. These include determining the DAC present when the ET4000 is on a Diamond 24 or is a W32.

LISTING 28.5 Useful Tseng Related Functions

```
; Function:
; Get the DAC type for the Diamond 24

; Output parameters
;   type    current dac type
;           1=Sierra Hi Color DAC
;           2=Diamond 24-bit DAC

; Calling protocol
;   type = GetDacType_D24();

GetDacType_D24 PROC FAR  arg1:byte
        mov     ax,10F1h  ;Hi color mode set
        int     10h ;interrupt 10
        xor     ah,ah
        mov     al,bl  ;send back dac type
        ret
GetDacType_D24 endp


; Function:
; Get the DAC type for the W32

; Output parameters
;   type    current dac type
;           1=Sierra Hi Color DAC  SC11485, SC11486, SC11488
;           2=Sierra Hi Color DAC  SC11485, SC11487, SC11489
;           3=ATT ATT20c491 DAC
;           4=Cirrus CL-GD5200 ACUMOS ADAC1 DAC
;           5=Sierra SC15025, SC15026 DAC
;           6=INMOS IM5G174 DAC
;           7=Music MU9C1880
;
; Calling protocol
;   type = GetDacType_W32();

GetDacType_W32 PROC FAR  arg1:byte
        mov     ax,10F1h  ;Hi color mode set
        int     10h ;interrupt 10
        xor     ah,ah
        mov     al,bl  ;send back dac type
        ret
GetDacType_W32 endp
```

```
; Function:
;       Set the Tseng key to enable access to extended registers

; Calling Protocol:
;       Set_Key_Tseng();

Set_Key_Tseng  PROC FAR
        mov    dx,3bfh
        mov    al,3
        out    dx,al   ;write 03 hex to Hercules Compatibility Reg
        mov    dx,3d0h   ;assume color
        add    dx,08   ;access 3d8
        mov    al,0a0h
        out    dx,al      ;write A0 hex to Mode Control Register
        ret
Set_Key_Tseng  endp
```

28.6   ACCESSING THE TSENG LABS DISPLAY MEMORY

The ET3000 can access up to 512 Kbytes of display memory; the ET4000 can access up to 1 Mbyte of display memory. Tseng Labs implemented the traditional technique of overlaying the display memory into 64-Kbyte banks. To provide rapid transfers of data from display memory to display memory, dual-bank registers are implemented. One bank register is dedicated to write operations, and the other is dedicated to read operations. This allows both to be mapped into the same memory space. The optimum size with respect to the host is 64 Kbytes. The PC standard dictates that this should reside between A0000 and AFFFF hex.

Tseng wanted to provide a granularity of 16 Kbytes. This requires a 3-bit bank field for the fully populated ET3000 and a 4-bit bank field for the fully populated ET4000. Unfortunately, when the field was defined for the ET3000, only three bits were allocated for the Write Bank Select Register, immediately adjoined by the three bits of the Read Bank Select Register. When it was time to extend the memory for the ET4000, there was no adjacent bit in the register for the fourth bit required for the field. The two extra bits in the register were located in bit positions 6 and 7.

Fortunately, Tseng Labs reacted with the correct decision. They chose to move the read field over one bit to the left, thereby providing the additional bit position. While this causes compatibility problems, it means that programs that access the heavily-utilized Write Bank Select Register are not split up by the Write Bank value. One can simply load the 64-Kbyte bank value into the register as opposed to shifting the lone bank bit to the proper position.

An important feature of the ET4000 is its ability to map its display memory into a linear address space instead of a segmented address space. The 1 Mbyte of display memory is mapped into a linear 1 Mbyte address space in the host. Obviously, this would be placed above the lower 1 Mbyte memory space currently used by DOS. A protected mode-operating system must be used to utilize this mode. The performance of the graphics system based on the linear addressing mode, a 32-bit addressing processor (80386, 80486), zero wait-state video ram, and a motherboard implementation of the chip would be outstanding. In addition, software would be easy to write and highly compatible across different display adapters, given that the 1 Mbyte of host address space was standardized.

28.6.1 Reading and Writing to the Display Memory

There are two extended VGA registers relevant to reading and writing to the display memory as shown in Table 28.13.

The Video System Configuration #1 Register is illustrated in Figure 28.1. The bank-selection techniques are described in the following section.

28.6.2 ET3000 Bank Addressing

A Bank (segment) Selection register, called the GDC Segment Select Register, contains two bank-selection fields. One field, WSP, is the Write Bank field; the other, RSP, is the Read Bank field. The WSP field controls the upper three bits of address, which are provided to the display memory by the host during write operations. The RSP field controls the upper three bits of address, which are provided to the display memory by the host during read operations. This register is shown for the ET3000 in Figure 28.10.

The Write and Read banks can be loaded non-destructively through the macro code in Listing 28.6.

TABLE 28.13   Reading and Writing to Tseng Labs Display Memory

Function	Register Name	Port	Index	Bits	Value
Enable Segment Addressing	Video System Config. 1	3D5	36	4	0
Enable Linear Addressing	Video System Config. 1	3D5	36	4	1
Write Bank ET3000	GDC Segment Select	3CD		2–0	0–7
Read Bank ET3000	GDC Segment Select	3CD		5–3	0–7
Write Bank ET4000	GDC Segment Select	3CD		3–0	0–15
Read Bank ET4000	GDC Segment Select	3CD		7–4	0–15

Segment Select ET3000

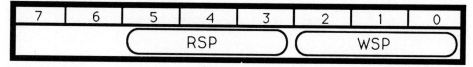

Port 3CD Read/Write

FIGURE 28.10 Segment Select Register ET4000. The Write Bank (segment) pointer resides in the WSP field. The Read Bank (segment) pointer resides in the RSP field.

LISTING 28.6 Load the Read and Write Banks for the ET3000

```
;   Function to load the Write Bank with a new start address for
;   the ET3000
;   Input with:
;        bank   Write Bank_Number
;               0-7 bank number indicating desired 64-kbyte bank
;   Calling Protocol:
;        Load_Write_Bank_16_Tseng_3000(bank);

Load_Write_Bank_16_Tseng_3000    PROC FAR bank:BYTE
        mov     bl,bank    ;get bank
        mov     dx,3cdh    ;point to memory Segment Register

;       input value so Read Bank is preserved
        in      al,dx      ;input value
        and     al,038h    ;zero write bank bits 2-0 and bits 7-6

;       load in the new bank value
        and     bl,07h     ;only want 3 bits of bank
        or      bl,40h     ;set bits 7=0 6=1 for 64 k memory map
        or      al,bl      ;or in write bank
        out     dx,al      ;output bank
        ret
Load_Write_Bank_16_Tseng_3000 endp

;   Function to load the Read Bank with a new start address for
;   the ET3000
;   Input with:
;        bank   Read Bank_Number
;               0-7 bank number indicating desired 64-kbyte bank
;   Calling Protocol:
;        Load_Read_Bank_16_Tseng_3000(bank);
```

(continued)

```
Load_Read_Bank_16_Tseng_3000    PROC FAR bank:BYTE
        mov     bl,bank     ;get bank
        mov     dx,3cdh     ;point to memory Segment Register

;       input value so Write Bank preserved
        in      al,dx       ;input value
        and     al,07h      ;zero read bank bits 5-3 and bits 7-6

;       load in the new bank value
        and     bl,07h      ;only want 3 bits
        shl     bl,1        ;put desired write bank into bits 5-3
        shl     bl,1
        shl     bl,1
        or      bl,40h      ;set bits 7=0 6=1 for 64 k memory map
        or      al,bl       ;or in read bank
        out     dx,al       ;output bank
        ret
Load_Read_Bank_16_Tseng_3000 endp

;   Function to load the Write Bank with a new start address for
;   the ET3000
;   Input with:
;       bank    Write Bank_Number
;               0-7 bank number indicating desired 64-kbyte bank
;   Calling Protocol:
;       Load_Write_Bank_256_Tseng_3000(bank);

Load_Write_Bank_256_Tseng_3000    PROC FAR bank:BYTE
        mov     bl,bank     ;get bank
        mov     dx,3cdh     ;point to memory Segment Register

;       input value so Read Bank is preserved
        in      al,dx       ;input value
        and     al,0f8h     ;zero write bank bits 2-0

;       load in the new bank value
        and     bl,07h      ;only want 3 bits of bank

        or      al,bl       ;or in write bank
        out     dx,al       ;output bank
        ret
Load_Write_Bank_256_Tseng_3000 endp


;   Function to load the Read Bank with a new start address for
;   the ET3000
```

```
; Input with:
;       bank    Read Bank_Number
;               0-7 bank number indicating desired 64-kbyte bank
; Calling Protocol:
;       Load_Read_Bank_256_Tseng_3000(bank);

Load_Read_Bank_256_Tseng_3000    PROC FAR bank:BYTE
        mov     bl,bank     ;get bank
        mov     dx,3cdh     ;point to memory Segment Register

;       input value so Write Bank preserved
        in      al,dx       ;input value
        and     al,0c7h     ;zero read bank bits 5-3

;       load in the new bank value
        and     bl,07h      ;only want 3 bits
        shl     bl,1        ;put desired write bank into bits 5-3
        shl     bl,1
        shl     bl,1
        or      al,bl       ;or in read bank
        out     dx,al       ;output bank
        ret
Load_Read_Bank_256_Tseng_3000 endp
```

28.6.3   ET4000 Bank Addressing

A Bank (segment) Selection register, called the GDC Segment Select Register, contains two bank selection fields. One field, WSP, is the Write Bank field while the other, RSP, is the Read Bank field. The WSP field controls the upper four bits of address, which are provided to the display memory by the host during write operations. The RSP field controls the upper four bits of address, which are provided to the display memory by the host during read operations. This register is shown for the ET4000 in Figure 28.11.

The Read and Write banks are set with the code in Listing 28.7.

Segment Select ET4000

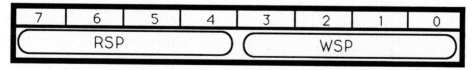

Port 3CD Read/Write

FIGURE 28.11 Segment Select Register ET4000. The Write Bank (segment) pointer resides in the WSP field. The Read Bank (segment) pointer resides in the RSP field.

LISTING 28.7 Functions to Load the Read and Write Banks for the ET4000

```
;   Function: to load the write banks with a new start address
;   for the ET4000.
;   Input with:
;         bank    Write Bank_Number
;                 0-15 bank number indicating desired 64-kbyte bank
;   Calling Protocol:
;         Load_Write_Bank_16_Tseng_4000(bank);

Load_Write_Bank_16_Tseng_4000     PROC FAR
          mov     bl,bank        ;get bank
          mov     dx,3cdh        ;point to memory Segment Register

;         input value so Write Bank preserved
          in      al,dx      ;input value
          and     al,0f0h    ;zero write bank bits 3-0

;         load in the new bank value
          and     bl,0fh     ;only want 4 bits
          or      al,bl      ;or in read bank
          out     dx,al      ;output bank
          ret
Load_Write_Bank_16_Tseng_4000 endp


;   Function to load the Read Bank with a new start address for
;   the ET4000
;   Input with:
;         bank    Read Bank_Number
;                 0-15 bank number indicating desired 64-kbyte bank
;   Calling Protocol:
;         Load_Read_Bank_16_Tseng_4000(bank);

Load_Read_Bank_16_Tseng_4000     PROC FAR
          mov     bl,bank    ;get bank
          mov     dx,3cdh    ;point to memory Segment Register

;         input value so Write Bank preserved
          in      al,dx      ;input value
          and     al,0fh     ;zero read bank bits 7-4

;         load in the new bank value
          and     bl,0fh     ;only want 4 bits
          shl     bl,1       ;put desired write bank into bits 5-3
          shl     bl,1
          shl     bl,1
```

```
        shl     bl,1
        or      al,bl       ;or in read bank
        out     dx,al       ;output bank
        ret
Load_Read_Bank_16_Tseng_4000 endp


; Function to load the read and write banks with a new start
; address for the ET4000.
;   Input with:
;       bank    Write Bank_Number
;               0-15 bank number indicating desired 64-kbyte bank
;   Calling Protocol:
;       Load_Write_Bank_256_Tseng_4000(bank);

Load_Write_Bank_256_Tseng_4000    PROC FAR
        mov     bl,bank     ;get bank
        mov     dx,3cdh     ;point to memory Segment Register
        mov     al,bl
        out     dx,al       ;output bank
        ret
Load_Write_Bank_256_Tseng_4000 endp


;   Function to load the Read Bank  for the ET4000
;   Input with:
;       bank    Read Bank_Number
;               0-15 bank number indicating desired 64-kbyte bank
;   Calling Protocol:
;       Load_Read_Bank_256_Tseng_4000(bank);

Load_Read_Bank_256_Tseng_4000    PROC FAR bank:BYTE
        mov     bl,bank     ;get bank
        mov     dx,3cdh     ;point to memory Segment Register

;       input value so Write Bank preserved
        in      al,dx       ;input value
        and     al,0fh      ;zero read bank bits 7-4

;       load in the new bank value
        and     bl,0fh      ;only want 4 bits
        shl     bl,1        ;put desired write bank into bits 5-3
        shl     bl,1
        shl     bl,1
        shl     bl,1
        or      al,bl       ;or in read bank
        out     dx,al       ;output bank
        ret
Load_Read_Bank_256_Tseng_4000 endp
```

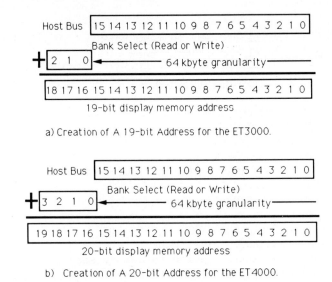

a) Creation of A 19-bit Address for the ET3000.

b) Creation of A 20-bit Address for the ET4000.

FIGURE 28.12 Creation of an Address Using Bank Selection for the ET3000 and ET4000

28.6.4 Granularity

The granularity of these Read and Write Bank fields in the GDC Segment Select Register is 64 Kbytes. In both the ET3000 and ET4000 implementations, the display memory is split into four display planes. A granularity of 64 Kbytes was selected to map this 512 Kbytes of memory into the 64-Kbyte host segment. Eight banks are required for this granularity. In the 1 Mbyte configuration, each plane is 256 Kbytes long. A granularity of 64 Kbytes was selected to map this 1 Mbyte of memory into the 64-Kbyte host segment. Sixteen banks are required for this granularity. Consequently, a 3-bit bank field is required for the fully populated ET3000 and a 4-bit bank field is required for the fully populated ET4000. The 20-bit address presented to the display memory is illustrated in Figure 28.12.

28.6.5 Dual Bank Selection

The dual-bank registers provide a mechanism for transferring data from one display memory location to another. The Read and Write fields of the GDC Segment Select Register need to be written to only once for every time a 64-Kbyte bank is crossed.

To move a bank from one location to another in the display memory, use the REP MOVSW instruction. It is only necessary to load the GDC Segment Select Register, set up the segment registers to both point to A000, set up the offset registers to point to the source and destination offset, and the cx register with the number of words to move. This setup would be followed by the REP MOVSW instruction. The maximum number of pixels that can be moved in one

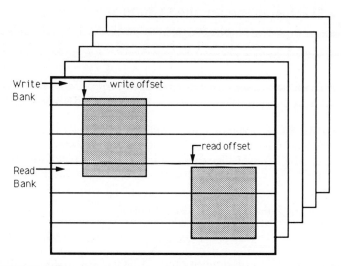

FIGURE 28.13 Display Memory Addressing. Read/write operations utilizing the Read and Write Bank registers. A 20-bit address is formed by the four-bit bank value and the 16-bit offset value.

REP MOVSW sequence would be determined by the distance to the next 64-Kbyte boundary. It is necessary to set up the GDC Segment Select Register before crossing these boundaries. This is illustrated in Figure 28.13.

28.7 CONTROLLING THE CRT ADDRESS GENERATION

Both the ET3000 and the ET4000 allow for extended CRT address control through the Extended Start Address Registers shown in Figures 28.14 and 28.15 respectively. Note that both are contained in the CRTC register group. However, each has a different CRTC index value. Since the ET3000 can access only half of the memory that the ET4000 can access, only one bit is required for the ET3000, while two are required for the ET4000. Also, there is no hardware zoom in the ET4000. Thus, there are no zoom-extended bits. Registers used for address control are listed in Table 28.14.

Extended Start Address for the ET4000

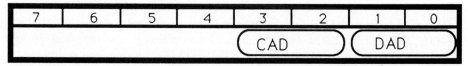

Index 33 at Port 3B4/3D4   Port 3B5/3D5 Read/Write

FIGURE 28.14 Extended Start Address Register for the ET4000. Contains bits 17-16 for the CRT addressing. These display start address bits reside in the DAD field and the cursor start address bits reside in the CAD field.

Extended Start Address for the ET3000

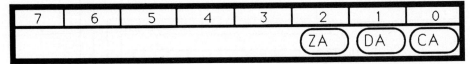

Index 23 at Port 3B4/3D4   Port 3B5/3D5 Read/Write

FIGURE 28.15 Extended Start Address Register for the ET3000. Contains bits 16 for the CRT addressing. The display start address bits resides in the DA field. The cursor start address bit resides in the CA field. The zoom start address bit resides in the ZA field.

TABLE 28.14 Tseng Labs' Display Address Control

Function	Register Name	Port	Index	Bits	Value
Start Address Bit 16	Extended Start ET3000	3x4	23	0	0,1
Cursor Address Bit 16	Extended Start ET3000	3x4	23	1	0,1
Zoom Address Bit 16	Extended Start ET3000	3x4	23	2	0,1
Start Address Bits 17–16	Extended Start ET4000	3x4	33	1–0	0–3
Cursor Address Bits 17–16	Extended Start ET4000	3x4	33	3–2	0–3
Bit 10 of CRT Address High	Overflow High ET3000	3x4	25	4–0	0–31
Bit 10 of CRT Address High	Overflow High ET4000	3x4	35	4–0	0–31

Overflow High Register ET3000

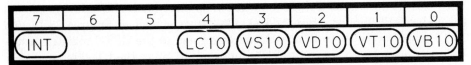

Index 25 at Port 3B4/3D4   Port 3B5/3D5 Read/Write

FIGURE 28.16 Overflow High Register. Bits 10 of the Vertical Bank Start, Vertical Total, Vertical Display End, Vertical Sync Start, and Line Compare fields are contained in the VB10, VT10, VD10, VS10, and LC10 fields respectively. Vertical interlace is enabled through the INT field.

It should be noted that the Overflow High Registers for the ET3000 and ET4000, shown in Figures 28.16 and 28.17 respectively, are accessed through different indexes. It is indexed in the ET3000 at 25 hex, while it is indexed at 35 hex in the ET4000. The Vertical Bank Start Bit 10 is contained in the VS10 field. The Vertical Total Bit 10 is contained in the VT10 field. The Vertical Display End Bit 10 is contained in the VD10 field. The Vertical Sync Start Bit 10 is contained in the VS10 field. The Line Compare Bit 10 is contained in the

Overflow High Register ET4000

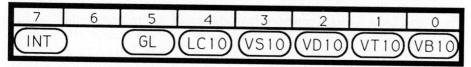

Index 35 at Port 3B4/3D4   Port 3B5/3D5 Read/Write

FIGURE 28.17 Overflow High Register. Bits 10 of the Vertical Blank Start, Vertical Total, Vertical Display End, Vertical Sync Start, and Line Compare fields are contained in the VB10, VT10, VD10, VS10, and LC10 fields respectively. Vertical interlace is enabled through the INT field. External syncing for gen-lock is enable through the GL field.

LC10 bit. The ET4000 has an additional high speed read/modify write bit in the RMW field. This feature is currently not supported.

28.7.1 ET3000 Display Start Address

The Tseng Labs ET3000 provides one additional bit of addressing to set up the CRT Addressing. The lower sixteen bits of the display start address are controlled through the Display Start Address registers in the standard VGA register set. These are described in Sections 10.4.13 and 10.4.14. Code that loads the display start address for the ET3000 is provided in Listing 28.8.

LISTING 28.8 Load the Display Start Address for the Tseng 3000

```
; Input Parameters:
;       start            top two bits of address
; Calling Protocol:
;       Load_Start_Top_Tseng_3000(start);

Load_Start_Top_Tseng_3000    PROC FAR start:BYTE
        mov     bl,start    ;start address top
;       load top address
        mov     dx,3D4h
        mov     al,23h      ;index Extended Start Address
        out     dx,al

;       read current value
        inc     dx
        in      al,dx       ;get value
        and     al,0fdh     ;zero out start address bit 1

;       or in new start address
        and     bl,01h      ;only want one bit
        shl     bl,1        ;put into bit position 1
        or      al,bl
        out     dx,al       ;output top address
        ret
Load_Start_Top_Tseng_3000    endp
```

28.7.2   ET4000 Display Start Address

The Tseng Labs ET4000 provides two additional bits of addressing, similarly provided to set up the Display Start Address. The lower sixteen bits of the display start address are controlled through the Display Start Address registers in the standard VGA register set. These are described in Sections 10.4.13 and 10.4.14. Two additional bits, bits 16 and 17, are provided in the DAD field of the Extended Start Address Register. This register is displayed in Figure 28.14. Code to load the start address for the ET4000 is provided in Listing 28.9.

LISTING 28.9   Load the Display Start Address for the Tseng 4000

```
; Input Parameters:
;       start  top two bits of address
; Calling Protocol:
;       Load_Start_Top_Tseng_4000(start);

Load_Start_Top_Tseng_4000    PROC FAR start:BYTE
        mov    bl,start   ;get start address
;       load top address
        mov    dx,3d4h    ;access 3x4/3x5
        mov    al,33h     ;index Extended Start Address
        out    dx,al

;       read current value
        inc    dx
        in     al,dx      ;get value
        and    al,0fch    ;zero out start address

;       or in new start address
        and    bl,03h     ;only want two bits
        or     al,bl
        out    dx,al      ;output top address
        ret
Load_Start_Top_Tseng_4000    endp
```

28.7.3   ET3000 Cursor Start Address

The Tseng Labs ET3000 provides one additional bit of addressing to set up the CRT Addressing. The lower 16 bits of the cursor start address are controlled through the Cursor Address registers in the standard VGA register set. These are described in Sections 10.4.15 and 10.4.16.

Since the display memory is split into four display planes, only 17 address bits are required for the CRT addresses as shown in Listing 28.10.

LISTING 28.10 Position the Cursor for the Tseng 3000

```
; Input Parameters:
;       start           top two bits of address
; Calling Protocol:
;       Position_Cursor_Top_Tseng_3000(start);

Position_Cursor_Top_Tseng_3000  PROC FAR start:BYTE
        mov     bl,start
        mov     dx,3d4h     ;access 3x4/3x5
        mov     al,23h      ;index Extended Start Address
        out     dx,al

;       read current value
        inc     dx
        in      al,dx       ;get value
        and     al,0feh     ;zero out cursor address bit 0

;       or in new start address
        and     bl,01h      ;only want one bit
        or      al,bl
        out     dx,al       ;output top address
        ret
Position_Cursor_Top_Tseng_3000 endp
```

28.7.4 ET4000 Cursor Start Address

The Tseng Labs ET4000 provides two additional bits of addressing, similarly provided to set up the Cursor Start Address. The lower sixteen bits of the cursor start address are controlled through the Cursor Start Address registers in the standard VGA register set. These are described in Sections 10.4.15 and 10.4.16. Two additional bits, bits 16 and 17, are provided in the CAD field of the Extended Start Address Register. This register is displayed in Figure 28.14. Code to position the cursor for the ET4000 is provided in Listing 28.11.

LISTING 28.11 Position the Cursor for the Tseng ET4000

```
; Input Parameters:
;       start           top two bits of address
; Calling Protocol:
;       Position_Cursor_Top_Tseng_4000(start);

Position_Cursor_Top_Tseng_4000  PROC FAR
        mov     bl,start
        mov     dx,3d4h     ;access 3x4/3x5
```

(continued)

```
        mov    al,33h      ;index Extended Start Address
        out    dx,al

;       read current value
        inc    dx
        in     al,dx         ;get value
        and    al,0fch       ;zero out cursor address

;       or in new start address
        and    bl,03h      ;only want two bits
        shl    bl,1           ;put into bit positions 3-2
        shl    bl,1
        or     al,bl
        out    dx,al         ;output top address
        ret
Position_Cursor_Top_Tseng_4000 endp
```

28.7.5   Controlling the Display Offset

As described in Section 10.4.22, no additional bits are provided for the offset address beyond the eight bits provided in the Offset Register. With word addressing, these bits can cover 2040 pixels in the 256-color mode and 4080 pixels in the 16-color mode on the ET4000.

28.8   THE CRTCB/SPRITE

The CRTCB/Sprite registers are a second CRTC generator. They can be used to control a sprite or to provide a second simultaneous window on the screen. The CRTCB addresses are relative to the active CRTC window and **not** relative to the display memory. These registers are listed in Table 28.15.

As per the standard, the width and height are loaded with one less than the desired number. The Start Address is a 20-bit address that describes where the Sprite pattern or image data resides within the display memory. This address is relative to the display memory and **not** the CRTC active region. The offset registers describe the number of quadwords between the start of one row and the start of the next row for the CRTCB or Sprite pattern. Note that this value must be a 2 when the Sprite is enabled since the Sprite offset is 64 * 2 bits/pixel = 128 pixels = 16 bytes.

The Sprite Color Depth Register is described in Table 28.16. The zoom factor determines the number of times that a line is repeated.

The Control Register is described in Table 28.17.

The Sprite Data format as stored in memory is stored in a contiguous 1024-byte area arranged in a linear "packed" format. A single row of the sprite occupies four contiguous double words. The second row occupies the next four contiguous double words and so on. Each byte contains four pixels. Thus, the first byte contains the left-most four pixels where each pixel is two bits. This is shown in Table 28.18.

TABLE 28.15 The CRTC/Sprite Registers

Index	Description
E0	CRTCB/Sprite Horizontal Pixel Position Low
E1	CRTCB/Sprite Horizontal Pixel Position High
E2	CRTCB/Sprite Width Low/Sprite Horizontal Preset
E3	CRTCB/Sprite Width High
E4	CRTCB/Sprite Vertical Pixel Position Low
E5	CRTCB/Sprite Vertical Pixel Position High
E6	CRTCB/Sprite Height Low/Sprite Vertical Preset
E7	CRTCB/Sprite Height High
E8	CRTCB/Sprite Start Address Low
E9	CRTCB/Sprite Start Address Mid
EA	CRTCB/Sprite Start Address High
EB	CRTCB/Sprite Row Offset Low
EC	CRTCB/Sprite Row Offset High
ED	CRTCB Pixel Panning
EE	CRTCB Color Depth
EF	CRTCB/Sprite Control

TABLE 28.16 Color Depth Register

Bits	Field	Description
7–6	Vertical Zoom	0=1, 1=2, 2=3 3=4 times zoom
3–0	Bits/Pixel	0=1, 1=2, 2=4, 3=8, 4=16 bits/pixel

TABLE 28.17 Control Register

Bits	Field	Description
2	Sprite Size	0=64x64, 1=128x128
1	B Pixel	1=CRTCB pixels overlay the CRTC 0=CRTCB Pixel data is output (2 bits/pixel sprite)
0	CRTC/Sprite	0=select Sprite, 1=select CRTCB

TABLE 28.18 Typical Word of Sprite Pattern

Bit Position	15	14	13	12	11	10	9	8	7	6	5	4	3	2	1	0
Pixel Number	7	7	6	6	5	5	4	4	3	3	2	2	1	1	0	0

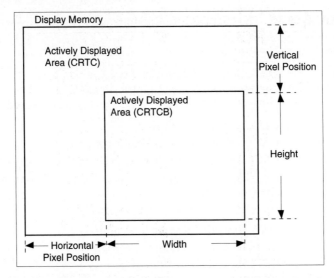

FIGURE 28.18 The CRTCB Simultaneous Display Window

The CRTCB window is shown in Figure 28.18 and the Sprite is shown in Figure 28.19.

The CRTCB Sprite Row Offset Register High also contains a 4-bit field in bits 7–4 that identify the chip.

When the sprite is enabled, the CRTC Width Low//Sprite Horizontal Preset Register contains the horizontal position relative to the beginning of the sprite

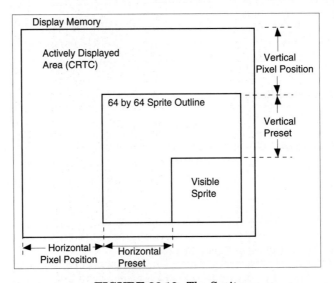

FIGURE 28.19 The Sprite

area at which the display of the sprite begins. The sprite does not wrap and always ends at position 63. Similarly, the CRTC Height Low//Sprite Vertical Preset Register specifies the vertical position relative to the beginning of the 64-by-64 pixel sprite area.

The CRTCB Pixel Panning Register controls the number of pixels that the display should be shifted to the left. Up to nine pixels are supported.

28.9 MEMORY APERTURE

Besides the normal bank swapping mechanism, there is a technique that uses a fixed size aperture through which the display memory may be accessed. The aperture varies in size depending on the system configuration. It is typically 8 Kbytes for VGA applications. The aperture may be relocated to begin on any byte boundary in the 4 Mbyte display memory space. This is shown in Figure 28.20.

The registers associated with this memory aperture technique are shown in Table 28.19. Each aperture has a Memory Base Pointer register that is 22 bits wide. This specifies the starting address of the aperture in the linear display

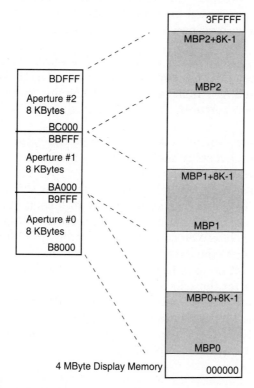

FIGURE 28.20 The Triple 8 Kbyte Memory Aperture

TABLE 28.19 Memory Aperture Registers

Offset	Description
0	MMU Memory Base Pointer Register 0
4	MMU Memory Base Pointer Register 1
8	MMU Memory Base Pointer Register 2; available on rev A only
13	MMU Control Register

TABLE 28.20 MMU Control Register

Bit	Description
6–4	Linear Address Control (LAC)
2–0	Aperture Type (APT)

memory. The MMU provides three independent apertures. The host selects which aperture to use based on the address. The offset of these memory mapped registers is with respect to the base address of the memory mapped registers.

The three memory base pointers are each double words where only the lower 22 bits are used. The MMU Control Register is described in Table 28.20. Note that both the LAC and APT fields are binary yet occupy three bits. This occurs since there are three apertures. Bit 6,2=Aperture 2, Bit 5,1=Aperture 1, Bit 4,0=Aperture 0.

The Linear Address Control (LAC) bit controls the organization of data in display memory. Thus, display memory can be accessed in a linear fashion, independent of the current display mode.

The Aperture Type (APT) bit indicates that accesses through this aperture should be directed to the accelerator and not to display memory. Thus, an APT=1 any memory write to the respective aperture will be directed to the graphics accelerator. Note: You cannot read from the graphics accelerator. An APT=0 will read or write the data to or from display memory.

The address translation uses the thirteen bits from the host address to the memory base pointer for the selected register. These thirteen host bits provide the 0–8191 address. If the APT=1 and the CPU Data Route is MixData, the host is supplying the MixMap data to the graphics accelerator, and the 13-bit host address is multiplied by 8 before being added to the memory base pointer. Thus the 8-to-1 color expansion is handled.

28.10 THE GRAPHICS COPROCESSOR

The graphics coprocessor includes an address sequencer and a data processor thereby reducing much of the overhead requreied by the CPU. The most common operation used by the graphics coprocessor is the BitBlt.

The accelerator operates on pixel maps. Each pixel map has a starting address into display memory and an offset that represents the number of bytes between consecutive scan lines. The accelerator operates on four pixel maps, these being Source, Pattern, Destination and Mix. The Mix pixel map is a binary map. Data from these maps is combined based on the current raster operation.

The Destination and Pattern Bit maps must reside in the display memory. The Source Bit map may reside in display memory or be supplied by the CPU during an accelerated graphics operation. The Mix map data may be supplied by the CPU or it may be fixed to a 1. In this case, it always uses the Foreground RasterOp. For a given graphics operation, the CPU can provide either source data or mix data but never both.

28.10.1 Starting an Accelerator Operation

A graphics operation is a two-dimensional operation. After loading the appropriate accelerator control registers, a graphics operation can be started by one of two ways. The host performs a write to the display memory using the MMU Buffer Space. If the APT bit is a 1, then an accelerator operation will begin. The address that is generated by the MMU translation is implicitly loaded into the Destination Address Register in the accelerator queue and the accelerator operation is begun.

The second technique involves loading the starting address of the Destination Map directly into the Destination Address Register followed by a write to the Accelerator Operation State Register. Both the Resume and Restore control bits must be set to 1. Once an operation is begun, the accelerator is responsible for generating all addresses. Thus, the MMU addresses can be changed while an operation is in progress. Only the first address is used.

28.10.2 The Graphics Queue

A one-level queue is provided for a set of coprocessor registers. In addition to the queue, there are registers internal to the accelerator that it uses as working registers. Thus, the host can modify registers in the queue while the accelerator is running. At the time an operation is initiated, the queue becomes full and all of the values in the queued registers are transferred to the accelerator internal registers. After the transfer, the queue becomes empty again and ready for loading by the host. The queued registers retain their values after a transfer takes place, and thus do not need to be reloaded each operation. Only the internal registers of the accelerator can be read back to the host.

28.10.3 The Graphics Coprocessor Registers

The Graphics Coprocessor maintains an internal copy of the Source Address, Pattern Address and the Destination Address Registers. At the end of an operation, these internal registers can be used as the starting addresses for the next operation. The accelerator also maintains an internal copy of the X Position and the Y Position as an acceleartor operation progresses. These can act as a reference as to how far the graphics coprocessor has proceeded on the current operation.

The Graphics Coprocessor Registers (ACL) are described in Table 28.21 and Table 28.22. Note that some of the registers are queued while others are not. These registers are memory mapped and the offset is relative to the base address.

28.10.4 Controlling the Coprocessor

An operation in the coprocessor can be suspended by setting SO=1 as shown in Table 28.23. Once a 1 is written to this register, the program should wait for the Read Status bit (RDST bit 0) of the ACL Status Register to be 0. At that time, the SO can be set to 0.

An operation can be terminated by setting TO=1 as shown in Table 28.24. Once a 1 is written to this register, the program should wait for the Read Status bit (RDST bit 0) of the ACL Status Register to be 0. At that time, the SO can be set to 0. Termination returns the graphics coprocessor to its power-on reset state.

TABLE 28.21 Non-queued Graphics Coprocessor Registers

Offset	Description
30	ACL Suspend/Terminate
31	ACL Operation State
32	ACL Sync Enable
33	ACL Write Interface Valid Bits Except Rev A
34	ACL Interrupt Mask
35	ACL Interrupt Status
36	ACL Accelerator Status
38	ACL X Position (all but W32)
39	ACL Y Position (all but W32)

TABLE 28.22   Queued Graphics Coprocessor Registers

Offset	Description
80	ACL Pattern Address
84	ACL Source Address
88	ACL Pattern Y Offset
8A	ACL Source Y Offset
8C	ACL Destination Y Offset
8E	ACL Virtual Bus Size
8F	ACL X/Y Direction
90	ACL Pattern Wrap
92	ACL Source Wrap
94	ACL X Position on W32
96	ACL Y Position on W32
98	ACL X Count
9A	ACL Y Count
9C	ACL Routine Control
9D	ACL Reload Control
9E	ACL Background Raster Op
9F	ACL Foreground Raster Op
A0	ACL Destination Address

TABLE 28.23   Suspend/Terminate Register

Bit	Name	Operation
4	TO	Terminate Accelerator Operation
0	SO	Suspend Accelerator Operation

TABLE 28.24   Operation State Register

Bit	Name	Operation
3	RMO	Resume Accelerator Operation
0	RSO	Resume Accelerator Operation State

A paused screen-to-screen accelerator operation is resumed by setting RMO=1. The state of the accelerator's queue is transferred to the internal registers of the accelerator if RSO=1. Setting either RMO or RSO to 0 has no effect.

Setting both bits at the same time transfers the queued state to the accelerator and resumes an accelerator operation.

If SE=0, a write to a full queue will be wait-stated until the queue becomes not full. If SE=1, a write to a full queue will be ignored.

Since the host processor and the accelerator are working together, it is essential that they remain in sync. There are two levels of synchronization, these being through hardware and software. At the software level, the host can poll the Write-Status bit before each write to determine if there is room in the queue for another data write. This adds overhead since each write requires a test.

At the hardware level, the host bus WAIT (Ready) line can be used for synchronization. Programming the Sync Enable bit to a 1 forces the W32 to insert wait-states into a host data transfer when the queue is full. This is shown in Table 28.25. The primary concern is to limit the amount of time that the host bus is held waiting, since long waits can crash some computers. It is wise to set the Virtual Bus Size to the largest value possible (usually 4 bytes) when passing Source Map data and to set to 1 byte when passing Mix Map Data.

The Accelerator Status Register provides status information, as shown in Table 28.26. If the ADST field is 1, the accelerator has data available for the host to read. It is used during accelerator operations that have the Accelerator Data Routing bit (bit 6 of the ACL Routing Control Register programmed so that the Destination Data is routed back to the host).

If the APNE bit is 1, the accelerator has new Destination Map data waiting in its pipeline to be written out to the frame buffer memory or to the host when

TABLE 28.25 Sync Enable Register

Bit	Name	Operation
0	SE	Sync Enable

TABLE 28.26 Accelerator Status

Bit	Name	Operation
7	ADST	Accelerator Data Ready Status; W32p above revA
6	APNE	Accelerator Pipeline Not Empty; W32p above revA
4	ASUS	Accelerator Suspended Status; W32p above revA
3	SS0	Screen-to-Screen Status
2	XYST	XY Status (Read/Write)
1	RDST	Read Status
0	WRST	Write Status

the Accelerator Data Routing bit (bit 6 of the ACL Routing Control Register programmed so that the Destination Data is routed back to the host).

If the ASUS bit is 1, the accelerator is suspended. It is suspended by setting the SO bit, bit 0 of the ACL Suspend/Terminate Register.

If SS0=1, the current accelerator operation is a screen-to-screen operation. This is valid only when the XYST bit is a 1. It is used by the State-Restore software to determine if a write to the RMO bit is necessary.

If XYST is 1, the Accelerator is processing an X/Y block. This means that the accelerator's internal XPOS,YPOS have not reached the terminal XCNT,YCNT for a given operation. This bit must be restored when the state is restored for a suspended operation.

If RDST=1, the accelerator is idle and the queue is empty, or the Accelerator is suspended. If RDST=0, the host is assured that valid data can be read.

If WRST=1, the accelerator's queue is full and cannot accept any more host writes. If WRST=0, the host can write to a queued register.

The Pattern Address, Source Address, and Destination Address Registers contains the 22-bit pattern and source and destination map addresses. If the host is providing the source data, the Source Address Register is not used.

The Pattern, Source, and Destination Y Offset Registers provide the 12-bit pattern and source and destination offsets. The offset is the number of bytes to be added at the end of each line to get to the next line. These values are one less than the actual offset.

The Virtual Bus size is a 2-bit field in bits 1–0 of the Virtual Bus Size Register as described in Table 28.27. It is used when the host is providing source map data or mix map data to the operation. The host interface waits for this many bytes and then releases the data to the accelerator. The Virtual Bus size also controls the amount addresses are to be incremented for each host data transfer. This increment value also depends on the ADR0 and DAR0 values of the ACL Routing Control Register. This is described in Table 28.28.

The Virtual Bus size is used to eliminate the effects of different physical system bus sizes such that the chip functions in the exact same manner whether it is connected to an 8-bit bus or to a 32-bit system. All CPU double-word writes to the accelerator must be double-word-aligned and all CPU word writes to the accelerator must be word-aligned when writing to the Source or Mix Map data.

TABLE 28.27 Virtual Bus Size

Value	Size
0	1-byte
1	2-byte
2	4-byte

Extra bytes at the end of lines that are not even multiples of the Virtual Bus size are ignored.

The ACL Write Interface Valid Bits Register is available in all but Rev A of the 32p chip. Bits 3–0 indicate the status of each byte in the write interface, where bit 0 represents byte 0 and so on. When a bit is a 1, it indicates that the host has written to that byte, and the accelerator has not yet consumed the byte. When 0, the host can write to that byte without concern for large number of wait states. It is used for state save/restore operations.

The address registers contain byte addresses, so when a Bitblt is moving in the decreasing X and Y directions, the initial address should point to the LAST BYTE of the map. This is independent of the Virtual Bus size. However, the Destination Address is DEPENDENT on the Virtual Bus size. If a write throught an MMU aperture is initiating the operation, the write should address the last "Virtual-Bus-Sized" element of the Destination map. For example, if VBS is four bytes, the initiating write operation should address the last double word of the Destination map. The accelerator internally takes care of pointing to the correct starting byte.

The ACL X/Y Direction Register determines the X and Y direction of BitBlts as shown in Table 28.29. If either the X or Y field is set to a 0, the accelerator operates from the lowest address to the highest address in an increasing direction. If it is set to 1, the accelerator operates from the highest to the lowest address in a decreasing direction. In the W32p processor, it is also used to control the direction of the line draw.

If 0, the Graphics OpCode field controls whether a BitBlt operation is to be performed. If 1, the line draw operation is to be performed. If a line draw is initiated, the LETQ field is set to 1. At the initiation of a line draw, the accelerator loads its internal error term from the Load Error Term Register as placed on the queue. If 0, the error term is automatically calculated from the value in the ACL Delta Major Register.

TABLE 28.28 Increment Amount Based on VBS, ADRO, and DARO

VBS	ADRO	DARO	Increment (bytes)
—	0	0	No CPU Data transfer
—	1	0	1
0	—	1	1
1	—	1	2
2	—	1	4
0	—	2	8
1	—	2	16
2	—	2	32

TABLE 28.29 X/Y Direction Register

Bit	Name	Chip
7	Graphics OpCode	W32p
5	LETQ Load Error Term	W32p
4	Line Draw Algorithm	W32p
2–0	Axial Direction	W32p
1	Y Direction 0=down 1=up	
0	X Direction 0=left 1=right	

The Line Draw Algorithm field, if set to the same as the Y-Direction bit, draws lines compatible with the IBM VGA hardware. If it is inverted from the Y-direction bit, the line is compatible with the XGA hardware.

The Axial Direction field occupies bits 2–0 of this register when a 32p is present. It controls the direction of the line, consistent with the eight quadrant directions.

When the host is supplying the Mix map for a graphics operation, the processing order of bits in the Mix map varies depending on the programmed X direction. If the X direction is increasing, the least-significant bit of the Mix data is processed first. In other words, the least-significant bit of the Mix map is anchored to the left-most edge of the Destination map. If the X direction is decreasing, the most significant bit of the Mix data is processed first. In other words, the most significant bit of the Mix map is anchored to the right-most edge of the Destination map.

The ACL Pattern Register and Source Register defines an x-by-y tile size for the Pattern map. Thus, a pattern can be replicated. After the accelerator operates on the wrap length number of bytes horizontally or the wrap length number of bytes vertically, the pattern pointer is set back this number of bytes or lines. This register is described in Table 28.30 and the X and Y wrap values are described in Table 28.31.

The X Position Register and the Y Position Register are 12-bit values used to determine the X and Y positions. These registers are used for saving and restoring the accelerator's current position when it is suspended. They should be initialized to 0 at the start of each operation. On read, they return the accel-

TABLE 28.30 Pattern and Source Wrap Register

Bit	Name	Description
6–4	PYWR	Pattern Y
2–0	PXWR	Pattern X

TABLE 28.31 Wrap Lengths

Value	Horizontal	Vertical lines
0	—	1 lines
1	—	2 lines
2	4 bytes	4 lines
3	8 bytes	8 lines
4	16 bytes	—
5	32 bytes	—
6	64 bytes	—
7	no-wrap	no-wrap

erator's internal positions, indicating how far it has progressed on the current graphics operation. As the accelerator is running, this register is constantly changing, starting from the value written to these registers and approaching the terminal value as programmed in the ACL X and ACL Y Count Registers. Writing to these registers will load the respective register in the queue, but will not affect the accelerator's internal copy of this register.

The X Count Register and Y Count Register are each 12-bit fields that contain the number of bytes or lines that the accelerator should operate. These should be programmed to one less than the desired number of bytes or lines. The formula for converting from number of pixels to X Count is as follows:

X Count = (number of pixels −1) * bytes_per_pixel;

For example, if the pixel depth of the ACL Pixel Depth Register is programmed to a 1, (two bytes per pixel), and the sixth pixel is the X dimension is to be operated on, then the X Count should be loaded with:

```
X Count = (6-1) *2 = 10   // Note: The accelerator will operate
                          // on twelve bytes.
```

The Routing Control Register provides routing information for CPU data. It is described in Table 28.32.

If bit 7 is set to 1, the multiport cache is not invalidated at the end of the accelerator operation. If 0, the multiport cache is invalidated at the end of the accelerator operation. It is recommended that this bit always be programmed to 0. If bit 6 is set to 1, the accelerator data is routed to the host CPU. If 0, it is routed to display memory.

If the ADRO field is 0, the CPU address is not used. If it is not used, the first write to an accelerated MMU aperture is used to determine the destination address. As the accelerated operation progresses, the destination pointer is updated automatically. If it is a 1, the CPU address is the destination address.

TABLE 28.32 Routing Control Register

Bit	Name	Function
7		Invalidate disable; W32p
6	ACRO	Routing of Accelerator data; W32p
5–4	ADRO	Routing of CPU Addresses
3	MXEN	MixMap Enable; W32p
2–0	DARO	Routing of CPU Data

The MXEN Field is used as the MixMap enable mask to control which bytes of the Destiantion map will be modified. The MixMap is used in this way only if the Background Raster operation is set to AA (no operation) and the Foreground Raster operation is not a function of the Destination map. This method of operation allows for faster drawing of transparent BitBlts since it avoids reading the Destination map data from the frame buffer. This bit is normally set to 1 at all times. The only reason to set this bit to a 0 is if the host wishes to read the destination directly.

The DAR0 Field determines the routing of CPU data and is described in Table 28.33.

If the CPU data is X Count or Y Count, the initial write to the accelerator operation stores the low-order eight bits of the corresponding internal X Count and Y Count Registers. The high-order bits come from the X Count or Y Count Registers in the queue. The Virtual Bus Size (VBS) field must be one byte in this case.

The Reload Control Register allows the next operation to begin at the end of the current operation. It enables reload of the Pattern Address (bit 1) or the

TABLE 28.33 CPU Data Routing DARO Field

MXEN	DAR0	Function	Mixed Data
0	0	CPU data not used.	Fixed to 1
1	0	CPU data not used.	From display memory
0	1	CPU data is Source.	Fixed to 1
1	1	CPU data is Source.	From display memory
0	2	CPU data is Mix.	From CPU
1	2	CPU data is Mix.	From CPU
0	4	CPU data is X Count.	
0	4	CPU data is X Count.	
0	5	CPU data is Y Count.	

Source Address (bit 0). When either field is set to 1, the accelerator's internal pattern or source address value will be the starting pattern or source address for the next accelerator operation. This internal value results from the previous accelerator operation. If it is a 0, the programmed pattern or source address value will be used as the pattern or source address. These bits should not be set to 1 on the first operation, since there is no known last state.

The Background and Foreground Raster Operation Registers provide the 8-bit raster op used between the Source, Pattern, and Destination maps. These are used when the CPU data routing is MIX data. If the data bit is 0, the Background raster op is used; if it is a 1, the Foreground raster op is used.

28.11 HARDWARE ASSISTED LINE DRAWING

The registers associated with line drawing are provided in Table 28.34.

The ACL Error Term Register contains the 16-bit error term used to initialize or restore the Bresenham Error Term for the accelerator's line draw engine. The LETQ bit of the ACL Direction Register controls whether the accelerator's Line Draw engine initializes its internal error term from this register or calculates it directly from the ACL Delta Major Register.

The ACL Mix Address Register contains the 25-bit Mix Address map. This is the absolute address in display memory for the Mix map. Since the Mix map has one bit for each byte processed in any other map, this register should be programmed to point to the first bit to be processed by a given accelerator graphics operation.

The ACL Mix Y Offset Register is a 12-bit register that indicates the amount to be added to the accelerator's internal Mix address pointer when going from one line to the next during accelerator operations. The actual value programmed is one less than the desired number of bits to be added. For example, if the Mix map is fourteen bits wide, a value of 13 should be programmed into this register.

The ACL Delta Major and Delta Minor Registers are loaded with the distance between endpoints of a line along the major or minor axis respectively. The axis of the line is defined as the dimension along which the endpoints are

TABLE 28.34 Hardware Line Draw Registers

Offset	Name
A4	ACL Mix Address
A8	ACL Mix Y Offset
AA	ACL Error Term
AC	ACL Delta Minor
AE	ACL Delta Major

the farthest apart. In other words, if delta-X has a higher magnitude than delta-Y, then X is the major axis and Y is the minor axis and the register is loaded with the absolute value of the difference.

The W32p has a built-in Bresenham Line Draw engine. The engine operates in units of pixels rather than bytes and the Pixel Depth Register is used to tell the accelerator how many bytes to process per pixel. An example of using the Line Draw engine is provided in Listing 28.12. Note: The accelerator computes the initial Bresenham Error Term based on the values of dx and dy.

LISTING 28.12 Line Draw Using the W32p

```
void     loadReg(int register,int value);
/* Input Parameters
      x1,y1   starting point
      x2,y2   ending point
      bytes_per_pixel   1,2,3,4
      bytes_per_row display offset
      algorithm  line algorithm MICROSOFT_VGA or MICROSOFT_XGA

DrawLineW32p( int x1, int y1, int x2, int y2, int
bytes_per_pixel, int bytes_per_row, int algorithm)
{ int dx,xdir,ydir,dy,ydir,adir,Xcount,Ycount,value,algrthm;
  long address;

// compute DeltaX
dx = x2 - x1;

// compute X Direction and take absolute value of DeltaX
if(dx<0) { xdir=1, dx = -dx; }     else   { xdir = 0;  }

// compute DeltaY
dy = y2 - y1;

// compute Y Direction and take absolute value of DeltaY
if(dy<0) { ydir=1, dy = -dy; }     else   { ydir = 0;  }

// compute and load Axial Direction, Count and Delta Major/Minor
// Registers
if (dx >= dy) {  // X is the major axis
  adir = 1;
   Xcount =  (dx-1) * bytes_per_pixel;
   loadReg(ACL_X_COUNT_REG, Xcount);
  // the Count Register along the minor axis is loaded with the
  // maximum possible value (0xFFF).
  // This ensures that the length of the line is limited by the
  // limit of the smaller of the two Count values, supporting
  // clipping of lines.
```

(continued)

```
   Ycount =  0xFFF;
    loadReg(ACL_Y_COUNT_REG, Ycount);
    loadReg(ACL_Y_DELTA_MINOR_REG, dy);
    loadReg(ACL_Y_DELTA_MAJOR_REG, dx);
   }
 else  { // Y is the major axis
   adir = 0;
   Xcount =  0xFFF;
   loadReg(ACL_X_COUNT_REG, Xcount);
   Ycount =  dy-1;
   loadReg(ACL_Y_COUNT_REG, Ycount);
   loadReg(ACL_Y_DELTA_MINOR_REG, dx);
   loadReg(ACL_Y_DELTA_MAJOR_REG, dy);
   }

// select Line Draw Algorithm
if(algorithm==MICROSOFT_VGA)    algrthm = ydir;
          else
algrthm = (!ydir) & 1; // XGA Line Draw Algorithm

// load Direction Register
   value =  0x80 | (algrthm<<4) | (adir<<2) | ydir <<1) | xdir);
   loadReg(ACL_DIRECTION_REG, value);

// load the Destination Address Register. The Destination Address
// Register is loaded with the address of the pixel at coordinate
// (x1,y1) to start the accelerator. If a pixel is more than
// one byte, the starting address depends on the X direction.

// If the X Direction is 0, the address must point to the
// lowest addressed byte in the pixel
address = (x1 * bytes__per_pixel) + (y1 * bytes_per_pixel *
bytes_per_row);

// If the X Direction is 1, the address must point to the
// highest addressed byte in the pixel
if(xdir==1) {
  switch(bytes_per_pixel) {
  case 1:  break;
  case 2:  address += 1;
  case 3:  address += 2;
  case 4:  address += 3;
   }
 }

 loadReg(ACL_DESTINATION_ADDRESS_REG,address);
}
```

28.12   CLIPPING

For the most part, rectangular clipping must be done by the software. Clipping with a data mask can be accomplished by using the Mix map and programming the Background raster op to DEST and the Foreground raster op as desired. This allows each bit in the Mix map to control whether the corresponding byte is processed or left alone.

28.12.1   Accelerator Clipping

The accelerator can support clipping through the loading of the Initial Error Term and through the length of the line being limited by either the X or Y count. Consider the case where a line starts at (x1,y1) and is outside the clipping region and the line passes through an edge of the clip region. The point where the line crosses the edge is called the intersection point (xi,yi). The unclipped remainder of the line can be drawn by the following: The Error Term must be determined for this intersection point and loaded into the Error Term Register. The intersection point is loaded into the Destination address.

Normally, the accelerator computes the initial Bresenham Error Term based on the values of dx and dy. This value is computed as (2 * DeltaMinor) − DeltaMajor. But with the LETQ bit of the ACL Direction Register set to 1, the programmed value of the error term is used as the initial error term for the line draw engine.

The equation to compute the Error Term at the point (xi,yi) is

X Major: ETi = ET1 + (abs(yi-y1) * (2 * dx)) - (abs(xi-x1) * (2*dy));

Y Major: ETi = ET1 + (abs(xi-x1) * (2 * dy)) - (abs(yi-y1) * (2*dz));

Note that a software algorithm must be employed to find the coordinates of the intersection point.

A second example is a line whose starting point is inside the clip region. In this case, there is no need for the CPU to compute if the line passes through the edge of the clip region. The software loads the X Count Register with the minimum value of DeltaX and the horizontal distance from the starting point to the left or right edge, depending on the X direction. The Y Count is loaded in a similar fashion. Table 38.35 summarizes how to program the X and Y Count Registers based on the line draw direction.

28.13   THE PCI INTERFACE

The ET4000W32P is the PCI brother of the ET4000W32. It is functionally identical with the exception of the PCI interface.

TABLE 28.35 Computing the X and Y Count

Direction Y	DirectionX	X COUNT	Y COUNT
0	0	min(DeltaX,xRight–x1)	min(DeltaY,yBottom–y1)
0	1	min(DeltaX,x1–xLeft)	min(DeltaY,yBottom–y1)
1	0	min(DeltaX,xRight–x1)	min(DeltaY,y1–yTop)
1	1	min(DeltaX,x1–xLeft)	min(DeltaY,y1–yTop)

28.13.1   Configuration Space Organization

The record structure for the PCI interface is restricted to 256 bytes. This is divided into pre-defined header and device-dependent regions. The configuration space for a device must be accessible at all times, including during the system boot up. Every device, including the W32p, must support the register layout of the 64-byte pre-defined header region as shown in Figure 28.21. The remaining 192 bytes are device-specific.

The system software must scan the PCI bus to determine what devices are present. To accomplish this, the vendor ID must be read in each PCI slot. The host bus to PCI bridge must unambiguously report attempts to read the vendor ID of non-existent devices. As 0ffffh is an invalid vendor ID, it is sufficient for the host bus-to-PCI bridge to return a value of all 1s on a read accesses to configuration space registers of non-existent devices. NOTE: These accesses will be terminated with a master abort.

PCI devices must treat configuration space write operations as no-ops. The access must be completed normally on the bus and the data discarded. Read access to reserved or unimplemented registers must also be completed normally and a data value of 0 returned.

Figure 28.21 illustrates the layout of the 64-byte pre-defined header portion of the 256-byte configuration space that must be supported by all PCI devices. Device-specific registers must be placed in locations 64 through 255. The lower address of multi-byte fields must contain the least significant parts of the field. Some fields contain bit-encoded reserved bits of no particular value. This requires that the software use appropriate masks to extract defined bits.

The pre-defined header portion of the configuration space is divided into two parts. The first consists of the sixteen bytes that are defined the same for all types of devices. The layout of the remaining 48 bytes can differ according to the base function of the supporting device.

PCI devices are required to carry Vendor ID, Device ID, Command, and Status fields in the header. Implementation of the other registers are optional, depending on device functionality. A device that supports the function that is defined by the register must implement it in the defined location and in the defined functionality.

28.13.2 Configuration Space Functions

PCI can potentially increase the ease of configuring systems as long as PCI devices provide certain functions that system configuration software can employ. Listed in the following sections are functions that require support by the PCI device registers as defined in the pre-defined header portion of the configuration space. The exact format of the registers is germane to the device. However, some rules are universal. Registers must be capable of being read back with the data returned indicating the value that the device is actually using.

Use of the configuration space should be restricted to initialization and error handling software, and it is intended for configuration, initialization, and catastrophic error handling functions. Device registers are manipulated by operational software's use of the I/O and/or the memory space accesses.

28.13.3 Device Identification

Following are the definitions for the fields presented in the pre-defined header of Figure 28.21. PCI devices are required to implement them. This standard allows software to determine what available devices are present on the PCI bus. These registers are read-only.

Vendor ID

Identifies the manufacturer of the device. Valid vendor identifiers are allocated by the PCI SIG to ensure uniqueness. The value 0FFFFh is not valid for vendor ID. The value assigned to Tseng Labs is 100Ch.

Bit in each Double Word

Byte	31 … 16	15 …	… 0
0	Device ID	Vendor ID	
4	Status	Command	
8	Class Code		Revision ID
C	Reserved		
10	Base Address Register		
14-2C	Reserved		
30	Expansion ROM Address		
34-38	Reserved		
3C	Reserved	Interrupt Pin	Interrupt Line

FIGURE 28.21 PCI Header

Device ID

Indicates the specific device. The ID is allocated by the vendor. Tseng Labs incorporates the Revision ID in the last four bits of this field. The Revision ID is 320x where x is the four ID bits read from the CRTC Indexed Register EC, bits 7–4. Revision ID is the same as found in the CRTCB/Sprite Row Offset High Registers at Index EC, bits 7–4.

Header Type

Identifies the layout of bytes 10h–3Fh in the configuration space and specifies if the device contains multiple functions. Bit 7 is equal to 0 indicating the W32p is a single function device. Bits 6–0 specify the layout of bytes 10h–3Fh.

Class Code

This register identifies the generic function of the PCI device and can indicate a specific register level programming interface. It is a 3-byte-sized field consisting of an upper byte at offset 0Bh, a middle byte at 0Ah, and a lower byte at 09h. The upper byte is a base class code indicating the type of function the device performs. Display controllers are given a base class number of 3. The middle byte identifies the function of the device. The lower byte is used to specify a particular register-level programming interface, if any, to facilitate interaction with device independent software.

Base Class = 03

The base class is used to define display controllers. No specific register level programming interfaces are defined by the W32p. The base classes for the PCI interface are listed in Table 28.36. Three subclasses of the 03 base class are shown in Table 28.37.

28.13.4   PCI Registers

The PCI registers conform to the basic PCI specifications as related to Display Controllers.

Command Register

The Command Register is configured at space address 04. It provides undefined control over a device's capability to generate and respond to PCI cycles. A zero written to the Command Register disconnects a device from the PCI bus except for configuration accesses. Bits that do not pertain to the device's functionality may not be used. For example, if a device does not implement an I/O space, it is not likely to implement a writable element at bit location 0. The Command Register is a read/write register as described in Table 28.38.

TABLE 28.36 Base Classes for the PCI Interface

Value	Description
0	Class code not finalized before device built
1	Mass storage controller
2	Network controller
3	Display controller
4	Multimedia device
5	Memory controller
6	Bridge device
7–FE	reserved
FF	Device does not fit any defined class

TABLE 28.37 Display Controller Subclasses

Subclass	Programming Interface	Definition
0	0	VGA compatible
1	0	XGA compatible
80h	0	Other Display Controller

Device Status Register

The Device Status Register is at configuration space address 06h. The status of the PCI bus-related events is recorded in the Device Status Register. Bits that do not pertain to the device's functionality may not be used. As an example, a device that acts as a target but will never signal target-abort would not implement bit 11. Reads to this register are handled normally; writes differ in that bits can be reset but not set. Bits are reset whenever the register is written with data in the corresponding bit location. For example, writing the value 4000 clears bit 14 without affecting other bits. The Device Status Register is shown in Table 28.39.

Interrupt Line Register

The Interrupt Line Register reflects the system controller interrupt connect pin. This register is at configuration space address 3Ch. It is a read/write register in bits 3–0. The value indicates the input of the system controllers to which the W32ps interrupt pin is connected. Revision A sets all bits to a 1. Revision B sets bits 7–4 to a 1; Revision C returns a 0 in bits 7–4 while returning the connect pins in 3–0.

TABLE 28.38 Command Register

Bit	Description	Access	Function
9	0	—	—
8	System error driver=0	R/W	1=error driver reporting address parity errors, 0=system error driver is disconnected.
7	Wait cycle control=1	R/W	1=address/data stepping is enabled, 0=disabled.
6	Parity error	R/W	1=device set to respond to parity errors, 0=device ignores parity errors. Must be reset to 0. Devices must generate parity even if parity errors are disabled.
5	VGA Palette snoop	R/W	1=special snooping behavior is enabled. The device must not respond to DAC write operations. 0=Palette accesses are not treated specially.
4	0	—	—
3	Special cycles	R/W	1=device is allowed to monitor special cycle operations.
2	0	—	—
1	Memory Space	R/W	1=device is allowed to respond to memory space accesses. 0=device response is disabled.
0	I/O space	R/W	1=device is allowed to respond to I/O space accesses. 0=device response is disabled.

NOTE: On parts other that Revision A and B, the W32p power up condition has bits 1 and 0 set to 0.

TABLE 28.39 Device Status Register

Bit	Description	Access	Function
11	Device Target-abort=0		1=set by target device whenever it terminates a transaction target-abort
10–9	Device Select Timing=0	RO	Timing of DEVSEL#; 0=fast, 1=medium, 2=slow
8	Bus Master=0		Implemented by bus masters only

Interrupt Pin Register

This register at configuration space address 10h tells which interrupt pin a device uses. This register bit 8 is permanently set to the value of 1 indicating the device is using INTA#.

Base Address Register

The bits 24–31 of this register are written to by the system BIOS to indicate where in the 32-bit address space to map a 16 Mbyte linear address space to be used when the W32p is put into system linear mode. Bits 31–30 will be compared with address lines 31–30 in PCI mode when the CRTC Indexed Register 36 bit 4 is set to 1. In Revision B, bits 31–30 are not physically compared with address lines 31–30.

Expansion ROM Base Address Register

This register is at configuration space address 30h. This register handles the base address and size information for expansion ROM. In Revisions prior to C, Bits 31–1 are hardwired to the VGA compatible C0000h. Bit 0 is a read/write bit and is used to control whether or not the device accepts access to its expansion ROM.

In Revisions C and greater, bits 21–28 are read/write with a power up condition of 0. If the DISB PORI bit is set, then writes to these bits will have no effect. All zeros in this register locate the address C0000h. When any other value is written to these registers, the ROM is remapped to a 256-Mbyte space that is designated by these bits 31–28. The actual ROM appears replicated at each 32-Kbyte boundary within this space.

Bits 27–1 are read-only and are hardwired to 0. Bit 0 is a read/write register used to control whether the device accepts accesses to its expansion ROM. When reset, the expansion ROM address space is disabled. When set, address decoding is enabled using the parameters in the other bits of this register. The Memory Space bit in the Command Register has precedence over this bit.

NOTE: Unlike the local bus implementation, moving the memory address range from A0000–BFFFF to any other location will not automatically disable the ROM. Disabling the ROM should be handled through bit 0 of this register.

28.14 THE IMAGE PORT (IMA)

The image port is an 8-bit asynchronous input port capable of accepting CPU or image data directly into the display memory. The ET4000W32p will keep track of the linear addresses being transferred as well as data transfer counts per line. The input data scan sequence can be interlaced or non-interlaced, and may be sent along with a bit mask so that only the differential motion data is transferred. Once in display memory, the IMA data may be displayed through either the primary display CRTC or the secondary display (CRTCB). The combination of the internal bandwidth of the W32p chip along with the IMA port make it possible to provide 640 by 480 at 24-bits-per-color full-motion (30 frames per second) video.

Sustained throughput of 40 Mbytes/second can be achieved using two-dimensional addressing via IMA Registers E0–E6h. The synchronization of address generation is by the way of frame/line and odd/even interface signals. The range of data transfer per line is specified in the Image Transfer Length Registers at IMA F3–F4. A byte mask input can be used to specify only the changing motion video data to be transferred to the ET4000W32p frame buffer. The masked data transferred can be used to reduce the bandwidth requirements.

Chapter 29

The Paradise Super VGA Chips

29.1 INTRODUCTION TO THE PARADISE/WESTERN DIGITAL VGA

The Paradise, trademark of Western Digital, Super VGA family of chips includes the PVGA1A, WD90C00, WD90C10, WD90C11, WD90C30, WD90C31, and WD90C33. The features of each are described in Table 29.1. Each chip is downwardly compatible to the newer generations. The first generation PVGA1A chip provides the framework for the second-generation WD90C00 chip. The WD90C00 builds upon the basic framework of the PVGA1A by adding additional extended registers and providing higher display resolutions. Similarly, the WD90C10 and WD90C11 are later versions of the WD90C00.

The WD90C10 is a stripped-down version of the WD90C00, not an enhancement. The WD90C10 exists mainly on motherboard implementations of the VGA. This chip supports only the basic VGA modes, no 256-color modes other than Mode 13 hex. It has a total of 256 Kbytes DRAM, providing the capability of 800-by-600 16-color, 1024-by-768 2- and 4-color graphics, and 132 column text modes. It will not do 640 by 400 or 640 by 480 in the 256-color modes as did the PVGA1A and WD90C00.

The WD90C11 is the enhanced version of the WD90C00. It provides improved data paths and memory addressing. Both of these provide improved performance. The WD90C11 supports 512 Kbytes of memory allowing it to support the 640 by 400, 640 by 480, and 800 by 600 in the 256-color mode, and 1024 by 768 in the 16-color mode. It will have twice the speed performance of the WD90C00.

The WD90C30 and WD90C31 are pin-for-pin compatible chips. The 90C30 supports 132-column text modes with up to 1024-by-768 4-bit and 8-bit-per-color modes. The 90C31 is a super-set of the 90C31. It also contains a hardware cursor and hardware BitBlt that assists display-to-display transfers and between display memory and a fixed I/O port. The WD90C33 is also a super-set

THE PARADISE SUPER VGA CHIPS

TABLE 29.1 Paradise/Western Digital Chips

Chip Name	16-color Max Resolution	256-color Max Resolution	Memory Capability
PVGA1A	800 by 600	640 by 480	512 Kbytes or 1 Mbyte
WD90C00	1024 by 768	800 by 600	512 Kbytes or 1 Mbyte
WD90C10	640 by 480	320 by 200	256 Kbytes
WD90C11	1024 by 768	800 by 600	512 Kbytes
WD90C30	1024 by 768	1024 by 768	1 Mbyte
WD90C31	1024 by 768	1024 by 768	1 Mbyte
WD90C33	1280 by 1024	1280 by 1024	1 Mbyte

of the 90C31 and also includes a high-performance 32-bit video bus and windows accelerator features.

29.1.1 The PVGA1A Super VGA Chip

The first-generation Super VGA chip, the PVGA1A, is straightforward and easy to program. This VGA implementation supports the high-resolution 800-by-600 16-color display modes but is limited to 640 by 480 in the 256-color mode. The VGA card is equipped with a maximum of 512 Kbytes of memory. Some vendors have implemented the PVGA1A with 1 Mbyte.

The PVGA1A has seven extended registers as indicated in Table 29.2. Access to these registers is typically locked, with the exception of the PR5 register. This register contains the enable key to the other extended registers. It is always unlocked.

TABLE 29.2 Paradise Extended Registers

Name	Usage	Designation	Port	Index
Address Offset A	Bank Switch A	PR0A	3CE	9
Address Offset B	Bank Switch B	PR0B	3CE	A
Memory Size	Memory Configuration	PR1	3CE	B
Video Select	Video Configuration	PR2	3CE	C
CRT Control	CRT Address Control	PR3	3CE	D
Video Control	Video Control	PR4	3CE	E
General Purpose	Enable Extended Registers	PR5	3CE	F

MDA and CGA emulation is available. EGA emulation is not handled separately from the VGA operation. Utilities are provided that change the display controller to emulate the 6845 CRT controller. This path was chosen over implementation of non-maskable interrupts (NMI) and autoswitching. This path was chosen to eliminate the problem that occurred when "smart" software checked to see what graphics cards were present. For example, the software would issue a CGA command, which would cause the hardware to switch state in an attempt to emulate the CGA card.

Both single- and dual-paging schemes are available to the programmer. The paging scheme is unique in that the banks are not fixed to 64-Kbyte intervals. Instead, they are controlled by the addition of the host address and the bank registers. This is very useful if a data transfer is known to be under 64 Kbytes. The bank register can be set up to point to the closest 4-Kbyte boundary and the 64-Kbyte transfer can proceed.

The 512 Kbytes of memory can be accessed through bank switching. A standard bank switching technique is available that utilizes either one- or two-bank registers. The memory can be configured into 64-Kbyte or 128-Kbyte segments.

The VGA BIOS contains extended function calls that allow extended mode setting, emulation, and access to the extended registers.

29.1.2 The WD90C00 Super VGA Chip

The second-generation Super VGA chip, the WD90C00, improves upon the performance of the PVGA1A chip by increasing display resolutions and providing support for interlaced and non-interlaced monitors. Like the PVGA1A, the chip can support up to 1 Mbyte of DRAM memory. Although a 16-bit host data path is provided, it operates only in the packed display modes. The planar display modes rely on the 8-bit data path.

In addition to the seven extended registers available in the PVGA1A, eight additional extended registers are provided in the WD90C00. These registers control interlaced timing and EGA hardware emulation. They also provide additional register locking, a software scratchpad, and additional addressing capabilities. These registers are located in the CRTC register group instead of residing within the same register group as the earlier extended registers.

Three new 16-color modes were added at the 1024-by-768 resolution. These provide a 4-color and 2-color graphics mode. Output timing can be constrained to be completely compatible with the 8514/A interlaced monitors.

29.1.3 The WD90C10 Super VGA Chip

The WD90C10 is a stripped-down version of the WD90C00. Functionally, these two chips are very similar. The WD90C10 has four additional extended registers, which provide additional control and status information. The WD90C00 provides enhanced system configuration ability to the hardware designer for inexpensive motherboard implementations. All features of the WD90C00 are directly applicable to the WD90C10 except some of the higher display modes.

29.1.4   The WD90C11 Super VGA Chip

The WD90C11 is the enhanced version of the WD90C00 and WD90C10. Due to improved memory accessing, the WD90C11 provides an 800-by-600 256-color display mode. One major WD90C11 enhancement is the ability to configure the PR0A and PR0B extended bank select registers. In the PVGA1A and WD90C00, these registers perform identically. Bank switching can be accomplished using the single PR0A Register or the dual PR0A/PR0B registers. In the 64-Kbyte memory dual mapping case, the PR0B Register is used when memory accesses occur to the 32-Kbyte host memory address space A0000–A7FFF. The PR0A Register is used when memory accesses occur to the 32-Kbyte host memory address space A8000–AFFFF. In the 128-Kbyte memory dual map case, the PR0B register is used when memory accesses occur to the 64-Kbyte host memory address space A0000–A7FFF. The PR0A register spans the 64-Kbyte space between A8000–AFFFF. Read or write operations can occur through either bank selection register.

In the WD90C11, the PR0A and PR0B registers can be configured so both are used when memory accesses occur to the 64-Kbyte host memory address space A0000–AFFFF. All read operations utilize the PR0A Register; all write operations utilize the PR0B Register.

29.1.5   The WD90C30 Super VGA Chip

The WD90C30 improved upon the early products by supporting both TTL or analog processors, adding high-resolution graphics with up to 1024-by-768 8-bit-per-color modes and supporting 132-column fonts. A zero wait CPU write operation was integrated along with the capability of supporting a 32-bit memory interface. In addition, it is capable of supporting 1 Mbyte of display memory.

29.1.6   The WD90C31 Super VGA Chip

The WD90C31 is pin-for-pin compatible with the WD90C30 and was capable of all of the 30's capabilities. In addition, a 64-by-64 pixel hardware cursor is capable of inversion, transparency, pattern fill, and two or three color modes. It also added a limited hardware BitBlt that supported raster operations, transparency, color expansion, rectangular and linear addressing, filled rectangles, and transfers to and from the host using an I/O port.

29.1.7 The WD90C33 Super VGA Chip

The WD90C33 increased the display resolutions up to 1280 by 1024 in both 4- and 8-bit-per-color modes, and added hi-color and true-color modes. The hi-color modes go up to 800 by 600; the true-color modes go up to 640 by 480. A true Windows-compatible accelerator was added. This accelerator has the hardware assisted features of the WD90C31 including the BitBlt operations using an I/O port and a hardware cursor. Additional graphics accelerator features include a Bresenham and strip-line line draw, hardware assisted trapezoid fill, and rectangular clipping.

29.2 CONTROLLING THE PARADISE SUPER VGA

The Paradise extended registers are typically locked and must be enabled through the PR field in the PR5 Register as shown in Figure 29.1. The programmer must write a value of 5 into the PR field to enable the extended registers. Any value other than 5 will lock out the extended registers The PR5 Register is always accessible. The extended registers are accessed through the indexed port pair at 3CE and 3CF. The Paradise Super VGAs can be controlled through the registers in Table 29.3. It is recommended that the programmer read the locking register contents, unlock the relevant registers, perform the desired function, and replace the locking register contents. This will provide compatability with future chips and BIOS versions.

29.2.1 WD90C00 Locking

The extended registers, PR10–17, reside in the CRTC register group. These are indexed through 3D4 and accessed through 3D5 in the color modes and through 3B4 and accessed through 3B5 in the monochrome modes. These registers are named PR10–PR18. Register PR10, shown in Figure 29.2, can lock these registers from read or write operations.

The WPR field controls the write protection of registers PR11–PR18 as listed in Table 29.4. PR10 cannot be write-protected. If it were, there would be no way to unlock it for use.

PR5 General Purpose Statuss and PR Register

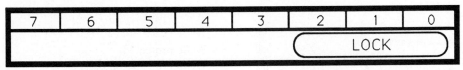

Index OF at Port 3CE   Port 3CF Read/Write

FIGURE 29.1 PR5 General Purpose Status and PR Register.
The LOCK field enables the extended registers.

TABLE 29.3 Resetting and Enabling the Paradise Super VGAs

Function	Register Name	Port	Index	Bits	Value
Index PR0A,B,0–5	Index Register	3CE	9–F		
PC Setup Mode PRO–5 Unlock	PR5	3CF	F	7–0	5
Index PR10–17	Index Register	3x4	29–30		
Read Unlock PR10–17	PR10	3x5	29	7,3	0–3
Write Unlock PR11–17	PR10	3x5	29	2–0	0–7
Scratch Pad (reserved)	PR12	3x5	2B	7–0	0–255
Enable Interrupts	PR14	3x5	2D	7	1
Disable Interrupts	PR14	3x5	2D	7	0
Enhance Host transfer Speed	System Interface Control	3C5	11	6–O	0–63
Don't Blink Cursor	Miscellaneous Control #4	3C5	12	6–O	1
Scratch Pad	Display Configuration	3C5	7	7–4	0–15

PR10 Unlock PR11–17 Register

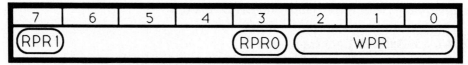

Index 29 at Port 3B4/3D4   Port 3B5/3D5 Read/Write

FIGURE 29.2 PR10 Unlock PR 11-17 Register. The RPRO and
RPR1 fields protect the PRlO-PR17 registers from being read. The
WPR field protects the PR11-PR17 registers from being written to.

TABLE 29.4 Write Protection of PR10–18

W 2	P 1	R 0	PR10–PR17
0	X	X	Write protected
X	1	X	Write protected
X	X	0	Write protected
1	0	1	Write protected

TABLE 29.5   Read Protection of PR10–18

RPR1	RPR0	PR10–PR17
0	X	Read protected
X	1	Read protected
1	0	Read enabled

The RPR0 and RPR1 fields form together to create the read-protection code as listed in Table 29.5. These registers protect registers PR10–PR18. It is recommended to write 85 hex into PR10 to enable read and write access.

The Paradise VGA extensions can be enabled or disabled through the macro code provided in Listings 29.1 and 29.2 respectively.

LISTING 29.1   Enable Paradise Extensions

```
Extensions_On_Paradise macro
;       extensions on
        mov   dx,3ceh      ;address PR5
        mov   al,0fh       ;index F = PR5
        mov   ah,05h       ; turn on extensions
        out   dx,ax

;       unlock PR10-PR17
        mono_or_color
        add   dx,4
        mov   al,29h       ;address PR10
        mov   ah,85h       ;unlock read and write
        out   dx,ax

;       unlock extended sequencer
        mov   dx,3c4h
        mov   al,06h       ;index Unlock Sequencer Register
        mov   ah,48h       ;unlock extended sequencer
        out   dx,ax

endm
```

LISTING 29.2   Disable Paradise Extensions

```
Extensions_Off_Paradise macro
        mov   dx,3ceh      ;address PR5
        mov   al,0fh       ;index F = PR5
        mov   ah,00h       ;turn on extensions
        out   dx,ax
```

```
;           lock PR10-PR17
            mono_or_color
            add     dx,4
            mov     al,29h         ;address PR10
            mov     ah,00h         ;lock read and write
            out     dx,ax

;           unlock extended sequencer
            mov     dx,3c4h
            mov     al,06h         ;index Unlock Sequencer Register
            mov     ah,00h         ;unlock extended sequencer
            out     dx,ax
    endm
```

29.2.2 Control of 46E8 Global Enable

The global enable registers control the enabling and disabling of the VGA chip. If the chip is on an adapter card, the location of this register is at 46E8. If it is on a microchannel card or on the motherboard, the location is at 3C3. Both of these registers are shown in Figures 29.3 and 29.4, respectively.

The 46E8 register can be enabled to be read at the E46 field of PR15. Typically, the 46E8 Register is a Write-only Register. The PR15 and PR16 registers

Global Enable Register

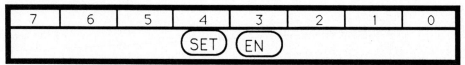

Port 46E8 Read/Write

FIGURE 29.3 Global Enable Register. Adapter Card Implementation at Port 46E8. Controls enabling and disabling of the VGA through the EN field. The SET field allows access to the 102 hex Wake Up Port.

Global Enable Register

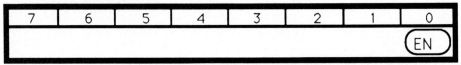

Port 3C3 Read/Write

FIGURE 29.4 Global Enable Register. Motherboard Implementation at Port 3C3. Controls enabling and disabling of VGA through the EN field.

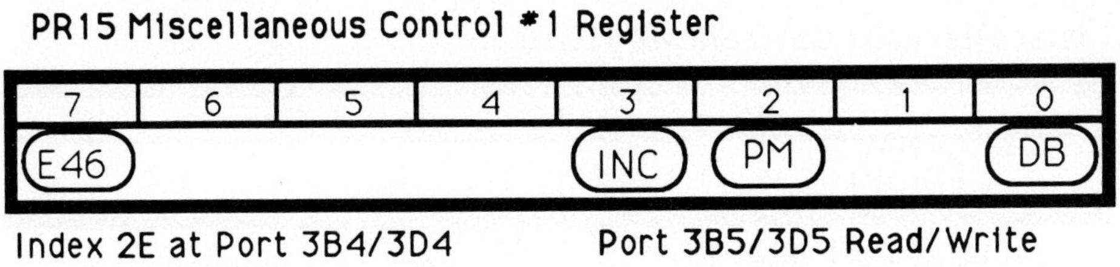

PR15 Miscellaneous Control #1 Register
7
6
5
4
3
2
1
0
E46
INC
PM
DB
Index 2E at Port 3B4/3D4
Port 3B5/3D5 Read/Write

FIGURE 29.5 PR15 Miscellaneous Control #1 Register.The E46 field enables port 46E8 to be read. The INC field provides interlaced compatibility to 8514/A timing. The PM field enables page mode addressing in alphanumeric modes. The DB field disables borders.

PR16 Miscellaneous Control #2 Register
7
6
5
4
3
2
1
0
MOD
TOP
MEM
Index 2F at Port 3B4/3D4
Port 3B5/3D5 Read/Write

FIGURE 29.6 PR16 Miscellaneous Control #2 Register. The MEM field selects standard VGA memory. The TOP field provides the top bits 16 and 17 for the display start address. The MOD field provides the limits to how high the CRTC address counter will count.

are shown in Figures 29.5 and 29.6 respectively. The PM field of the Miscellaneous #1 Register is discussed in Section 29.5.6. The DB field is discussed in Section 29.6.4.

29.2.3 WD90C10/11 Cursor Control

The WD90C10 and WD90C11 can enable or disable cursor blinking through the BLN field of the Miscellaneous Controls Register shown in Figure 29.7. If the BLN field is 1, cursor blinking is disabled in the text modes. If 0, cursor blinking is enabled.

29.3 INQUIRING ABOUT THE PARADISE SUPER VGA CONFIGURATION

The programmer can determine the memory size and memory map through the PR1 Extended Register. It can identify the VGA through data written into the ROM memory. Details for selecting the VGA status are presented in Table 29.6.

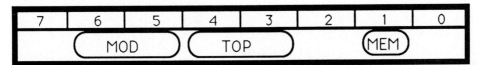

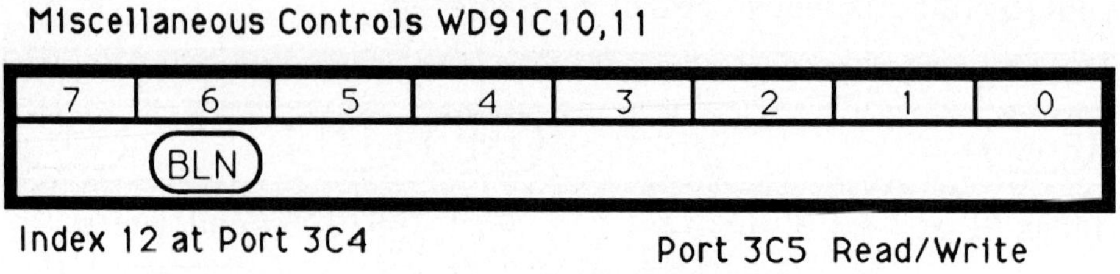

Miscellaneous Controls WD91C10,11

7	6	5	4	3	2	1	0
	(BLN)						

Index 12 at Port 3C4   Port 3C5 Read/Write

FIGURE 29.7 Miscellaneous Controls Register WD91C10 ,11.
The BLN field controls cursor blinking.

TABLE 29.6 Determining Paradise Display Status

Function	Register Name	Port	Index	Bits	Value
Memory Size	PR1	3CF	0B	7–6	0–3
Memory Map	PR1	3CF	0B	5–4	0–3
VGA Identification	Byte at C000:007D				"VGA="
BIOS Date	String at C000:0009				
BIOS Version	Byte at C000:0035				
Compatibility	Display Configuration	3C5	7	2–1	0,1
Mono/Color Mode	Display Configuration	3C5	7	3	0,1

29.3.1 Identifying the Paradise Card

The programmer can sense the Paradise card by looking at the VGA identification string at host memory address C000:007D. This string should be four characters long from 7D–80 and should contain VGA=. Code to identify the Paradise VGA is provided in Listing 29.3. This function calls upon the assembly language function in Listing 29.4. This code utilizes the assembly language function that actually acquires the string from memory.

LISTING 29.3 Determine if the Card Is a Western Digital (Paradise)

```
/* Output Parameters:
        1=card is a Paradise   0=card is NOT a Paradise
 Calling Protocol:
   Paradise= Is_It_Paradise()   */


int Is_It_Paradise(void)
{ char signature[9]; int result1,result2;

  Get_Paradise_Key(signature);   /* get signature */

  /* compare the two strings and return  the result */
```

```c
    result1 =  strncmp(signature,"VGA=",4);
    result2 =  strncmp(signature,"(c)",3);   // check for AST
    if((result1==0)||(result2==0)) return(CHIP_FOUND);
        else     return(CHIP_NOT_FOUND);
}
```

LISTING 29.4 Determine Which Western Digitial/Paradise Chip

```c
/* Output Parameters:
        identity     integer containing chip code
NOTE:   A subsequent consequence of this call is that the mode
        control registers are put into their new state.
Calling Protocol:
 identity = Which_Paradise()   */

int Which_Paradise(void)
{
    int base;
    unsigned char
old_value,new_value,wd90c10,old_index,new_index,value;
    unsigned int
old_value_w,new_value_w,value_w,BIT_ON_MASK,BIT_OFF_MASK;

Extended_On_Paradise();
if( (inp(0x3CC) & 0x01)==1) base = 0x3D0;  else base = 0x3B0;

// first find out if it is a PVGA1a
outp(base+4,0x2B); old_value = inp(base+5);   // get old value
outp(base+5,0xAA);  new_value = inp(base+5);    // try new value

outp(base+5,old_value); // restore old value
if(new_value!=0xAA) return(1);   // it is a PVGA1a

// distinguish between WD90C00 and WD90C10 by loading bit 6 of
// the Miscellaneous Control to a 0
outp(0x3C4,0x12); old_value = inp(0x3C5);

// set bit 6 to a 0
outp(0x3C5,old_value&0xbf); new_value=inp(0x3C5)&0x40;
if(new_value!=0) {
    outp(0x3c5,old_value);
    return(WD90C00); // its a wd90c00
  }

outp(0x3C5,old_value|0x40); new_value=inp(0x3C5)&0x40;
if(new_value==0) {
     outp(0x3c5,old_value);
```

```
        return(WD90C00); // its a wd90c00
    }

outp(0x3c5,old_value);
if(new_value==0) return(WD90C00);  // if it is a 0 then WD90C00

// distinguish between a WD90C10 and a WD90C11 by loading the
// extended register at 3C4/3C5 index 10 (The PR30 Memory
// interface write buffer and fifo control) hex bit 3 with a 0
// and then a 1

wd90c10=0;  // assume its a wd90c11

// get the current value for restore later
outp(0x3C4,0x10);  old_value = inp(0x3c5);

// attempt to set the bit 3 with a 0
outp(0x3C5,old_value&0xfb); new_value=inp(0x3C5)&0x04;
if(new_value!=0) wd90c10=1;  // if it returns other than a 0
                             // then 90c10

// attempt to set the bit 3 with a 1
outp(0x3C5,old_value|0x04); new_value=inp(0x3C5)&0x04;
if(new_value==0) wd90c10=1;  // if it returns a 0 then 90c10

outp(0x3C5,old_value);  // restore old value

if(wd90c10==1) return(WD90C10);  // if it is a 0 then WD90C10

// ++++++++++++++ now check to see if it is a 90C30 or 90c31
// first unlock this register by setting PR20 bits 6,4,3=101
outp(0x3C4,0x06);  outp(0x3c5,0x48);

// check to see if there is a PR33  index 13h.  If there isn't
// then it is a 90c11

// get old value
outp(0x3C4,0x12);  old_value = inp(0x3c5);

// output a 01 to bit positions 01
  value = (old_value&0xfc)+0x01;
  outp(0x3C5,value);

// check to see if 01
  new_value = inp(0x3c5)&0x03;

//  restore the original state
        // restore old value
```

```
            outp(0x3C4,0x12);  outp(0x3c5,old_value);
            // relock extended regs
            outp(0x3C4,0x06);  outp(0x3c5,0x00);

// if not then exit since 90c11
if (new_value != 0x01) return(WD90C11); // return since it is a
                                         // WD90C11

// if it is then check to see if it is a 90c30 or 90c31. check
// for hardware cursor.  If there then it is a 90c31 else it is
// a 90c30.

// read back the current index
//  old_index = inp(0x23c0);

// first set the index at port 23C0h to a 2
  outpw(0x23c0,02);

// read back the changed index
//  new_index = inp(0x23c0);

BIT_ON_MASK = 0x0020; BIT_OFF_MASK = ~BIT_ON_MASK;

// get old value
  old_value_w = inpw(0x23c2); // read the hardware cursor
  read_hardware_cursor();

//  check if it can be set to 0
  value_w = old_value_w & BIT_OFF_MASK;
  outpw(0x23c2,value_w);

  new_value_w = inpw(0x23c2); // read the hardware cursor
  read_hardware_cursor();

  new_value_w &= BIT_ON_MASK; // read the hardware cursor

// if this bit 0 is not 0, then it is a 90c30
  if(new_value_w!=0) {
        outpw(0x23c2,old_value_w); // restore old value
        return(WD90C30);
        }

// check bit 8 which is 23c2 bit 0 to see if it can be set to 1
  value_w =  (old_value_w & BIT_OFF_MASK) | BIT_ON_MASK;
  outpw(0x23c2,value_w);
  new_value_w = inpw(0x23c2); // read the hardware cursor
  read_hardware_cursor();
```

```
    new_value_w &= BIT_ON_MASK; // read the hardware cursor

    outpw(0x23c2,old_value_w); // restore old value_w

    if(new_value_w!=BIT_ON_MASK) return(WD90C30); // it is a 90c30

// now distinguish between a 90c31 and a 90c33
    new_value_w = inpw(0x23CE);
    if(new_value_w==0xffff)  return(WD90C31);  // it is a 90c31
        else return(WD90C33);
}
```

29.3.2 Identifying the Paradise Chip

The Paradise Chip can be a PVGA1A, a WD90C00, WD90C10, WD90C11, WD90C30, WD90C31, or WD90C33. These are differentiated by the presence of specific registers. Each chip builds upon the register set of its predecessor. Each chip adds new registers. The presence of these registers determines which VGA chip is installed. Code to perform this function is provided in Listing 29.5 and a function that reads the hardware cursor registers is found in Listing 29.6.

LISTING 29.5 Get the Paradise ID Key

```
; Return the Paradise ID. The Paradise chips are identified
; by checking a string which is located at C000:007D.
; Output Parameters
;       signature         character string

; Calling Protocol:
;   Get_Paradise_Key(signature)

Get_Paradise_Key PROC FAR   USES DS SI ES DI, arg1:FAR PTR

;       set  up source pointer
        mov  ds,SegC000
        mov  si,007Dh   ;location of signature

        les  di,arg1    ;set up destination "c" buffer signature

;       Get  id
        mov  cx,4        ;move 4 bytes
        rep  movsb
        ret
Get_Paradise_Key        endp
```

LISTING 29.6 Reading the Hardware Cursor Registers

```
void read_hardware_cursor(void)
{ unsigned int i;

  for (i=0; i<15; i++)
          inpw(0x23c2); // read the hardware cursor
}
```

29.4 PARADISE DISPLAY MODES

The Paradise adapters support a wide variety of alphanumeric and graphic display modes.

29.4.1 Alphanumeric Modes

The Paradise adapter has four alphanumeric modes available to allow 25 and 43 lines of 132-column text in either the 4- or 16-color configuration. These modes are listed in Table 29.7. The PVGA1A-based character font bit patterns will be seven pixels wide when a fixed frequency monitor is present. These will be eight pixels wide when a multi-frequency monitor is detected. The monitor type is based upon the setting of a DIP switch. With the WD90C00, C10, and C11, the character font patterns will be nine dots wide. The resolution changes accordingly in both multi-frequency and fixed frequency monitors.

29.4.2 Paradise Graphics Modes

The Paradise family of Super VGA chips provides a wide variety of graphics display modes as indicated in Table 29.8. Included are 2-, 4-, 16-, and 256-color display modes ranging in resolutions up to 1024 by 768.

TABLE 29.7 Paradise Alphanumeric Modes

Mode	Rows	Columns	Font	Resolution	Colors	Monitor
54	43	132	8x9	924 by 387	16	fixed
54	43	132	8x9	1056 by 387	16	multi-sync
55	25	132	7x16	924 by 400	16	fixed
55	25	132	8x16	1056 by 400	16	multi-sync
56	43	132	7x9	924 by 387	4	fixed
56	43	132	8x9	1056 by 387	4	multi-sync
57	25	132	7x16	924 by 400	4	fixed
57	25	132	8x16	1056 by 400	4	multi-sync

TABLE 29.8 Paradise Graphics Modes

Mode	Resolution	Bits/Color	Chip	Char Size	Characters
58	800 by 600	4	pVGA1,WDC90Cxx	8 by 8	100 by 75
59	800 by 600	1	pVGA1,WDC90Cxx	8 by 8	100 by 75
5E	640 by 400	8	pVGA1,WDC90Cxx	8 by 16	80 by 25
5F	640 by 480	8	pVGA1,WD90Cxx	8 by 16	80 by 25
5A	1024 by 768	1	WD90Cxx	8 by 16	128 by 48
5B	1024 by 768	2	WD90Cxx	8 by 16	128 by 48
5D	1024 by 768	4	WD90Cxx, C11 (512K)	8 by 16	128 by 48
5C	800 by 600	8	WD90C11 (512K)	8 by 8	100 by 75
60	1024 by 768	8	30,31,33		
64	1280 by 1024	8	33		
	640 by 400	15	33		
62	460 by 480	15	33		
63	800 by 600	15	33		
	640 by 400	16	33		
	640 by 480	16	33		
	800 by 600	16	33		
	640 by 480	24	33		

29.4.3 PVGA1A Graphics Modes

The PVGA1A supports a limited number of graphics modes with a maximum resolution of 800 by 600 in the 16-color modes and 640 by 400 in the 256-color modes. A 640-by-480 256-color mode is available with 512 Kbyte DRAM. An 800-by-600 2-color mode is also provided.

29.4.4 WD90Cxx Graphics Modes

The WD90C00, WD90C10, and WD90C11 provide three high-resolution 1024-by-768 graphics modes. The 16-color mode 5D uses the VGA standard 16-color planar memory organization. The 2-color and 4-color modes 5A and 5B use a unique scheme of memory mapping.

29.4.5 Mode 5B 1024 by 768 Four-Color Display Mode

Mode 5B is a 1024-by-768 4-color graphics mode. It uses two bits per pixel. Thus, four pixels reside in the same display byte. This qualifies as a packed display mode. The display planes are chained together in a fashion similar to the 256-color modes. The basic difference is that there are four pixels per byte instead of one pixel per byte. This is illustrated in Figure 29.8.

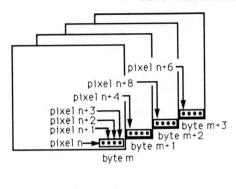

765 43 2 1 0 765 43 2 1 0

| • | ○ | ○ | ○ | ○ | • | • | ○ |

Byte m   Byte m+1

FIGURE 29.8 Memory Organization for Mode 5B hex.
Illustrates four-color packed organization.

The four colors reference palette registers 0–3. If the default palette registers for this mode are in place, these will reference color registers 0–3.

This chained mode has a 16-bit data path. Consequently, speed improvements can be realized if the 16-bit host data path is engaged.

29.4.6 Mode 5A 1024 by 768 Two-Color Display Mode

The display mode 5A is a 2-color packed mode that has eight pixels per byte. It utilizes an odd-even plane addressing scheme utilizing two display planes. Suppose that byte address m contains eight pixels, n,n+1,...,n+7, and this byte resides in plane 0. The neighboring (to the right) eight pixels would reside at byte address m+1, in plane 1.

A similar odd-even technique can be used in planes 2 and 3 to allow a second page to reside in display memory. This odd-even scheme is illustrated in Figure 29.9.

Accessing the display memory is accomplished by selecting the desired pair of display planes. If the image data resides in display plane 0 and 1, the Map Mask Register, discussed in Section 10.3.3, enables both planes 0 and 1. Similarly, the Read Map Register, discussed in Section 10.5.7, accesses either plane 0 or 1. If the image data resides in display plane 2 and 3, the Write Map Register enables both planes 2 and 3. Similarly, the Read Map Register accesses either plane 2 or 3. Enabling all planes 0,1,2 and 3 causes identical data to be written into both images simultaneously.

Displaying an image that resides in plane 0 is accomplished by enabling planes 0 and 1 through the Color Plane Enable Register. This register was discussed in Section 10.6.5. An image that resides in planes 2 and 3 is displayed

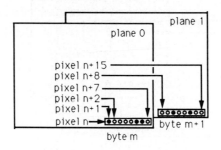

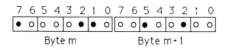

FIGURE 29.9 Memory Organization for Mode 5A hex.
Illustrates two-color-packed organization.

by enabling plane 2 through the Color Plane Enable Register. Enabling both planes 0 and 2 causes both images to be simultaneously displayed.

If planes 0 and 1 are used, the two colors reference palette registers 0 and 1. If planes 2 and 3 are used, the two colors reference palette registers 0 and 4. If the default palette registers for this mode are in place, these will reference color registers 0, 1 and 4. Note that color register 1 and 4 are selected since only plane 0 or 2 is selected to produce a color. By selecting both planes 0 and 2 through the Color Plane Enable Register, the images can both be overlayed producing a 3-color mode. Only three colors can be achieved since only color registers 0, 1, and 4 can be accessed.

This chained mode has a 16-bit data path. Consequently, speed improvements can be realized if the 16-bit host data path is engaged.

29.5 ACCESSING THE PARADISE DISPLAY MEMORY

The display memory can be accessed through single- or dual-bank registers. The memory size and mapping fields are configurable. In the WD90C00, the memory can be organized as the standard 256 Kbytes of VGA memory and a special feature allows paged alphanumeric modes. The register fields relevant to memory accessing are listed in Table 29.9.

In addition, the WD90C11 can configure the PR0A and PR0B registers to a dual-bank selection state where the PR0B Register is used exclusively for write operations and the PR0A Register is used exclusively for read operations by using 3C5 index 11 bit 7.

TABLE 29.9 Reading and Writing to Paradise Display Memory

Function	Register Name	Port	Index	Bits	Value
Bank Register A	PR0A	3cF	09	6–0	0–127
Bank Register B	PR0B	3cF	0A	6–0	0–127
Enable Dual Banks	PR1	3cF	0B	3	1
Enable PR0A Bank	PR1	3cF	0B	3	0
Memory Size	PR1	3cF	0B	7–6	0–3
Memory Map	PR1	3cF	0B	5–4	0–3
Enable Paged Alphanumerics	PR15	3x5	2E	2	1
Standard Alphanumerics	PR15	3x5	2E	2	0
Standard VGA Memory	PR16	3x5	2F	1	1
Extended Memory	PR16	3x5	2F	1	0
Read/Write Bank Select	System Interface Control	3c5	11	7	1
32k Bank Select	System Interface Control	3c5	11	7	0

29.5.1 Bank Addressing

The 512 Kbytes of display memory can be mapped into a 64-Kbyte or a 128-Kbyte host address space at A0000–AFFFF or A0000–BFFFF, respectively. The 512 Kbytes of memory are overlayed into this address space through the bank registers. There are three extended registers, PR0A, PR0B, PR1, and 3C5 index 11 bit 7, which control the bank switching. These registers are described in Table 29.10.

The programmer can elect to utilize either one or two bank registers based on the ENB field of PR1, index B of port 3CE bit 3. If the ENB field is set to 1, both the PR0A and PR0B registers are engaged. If 0, only the PR0A Register is engaged. Both the PR0A and PR0B registers contain a BANK field as shown in Figures 29.10 and 29.11.

The Bank field contains a bank value from 0–127 which is added to the system bus address bits 18–12. This provides a 4-Kbyte granularity, and the 128 * 4 Kbytes spans the entire 512-Kbyte display memory address range. The value in the BANK field is added to the host bus address as shown in Figure 29.12.

There are three distinct bank selection modes in the WD90C10 and WD90C11. The first uses just PR0A for the bank select. This applies to read or write operations. The second uses PR0A for the lower 32 Kbytes from host memory address space A0000–A7FFF and uses PR0B for the upper 32 Kbytes from A8000–AFFFF hex. The third mode is a read/write mode where PR0A is

TABLE 29.10 Memory Size Field MEM

MEM	Memory Size	Configuration
0	256 Kbytes	VGA standard
1	256 Kbytes	PVGA bank switching
2	512 Kbytes	PVGA bank switching
3	1 megabyte	PVGA bank switching

PR0A Address Offset A

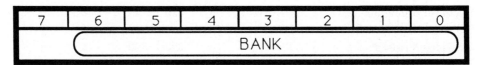

Index 09 at Port 3CE   Port 3CF Read/Write

FIGURE 29.10 PR0A Address Offset A Register. The BANK field controls the address bits 18-12 of the display memory providing a 4 Kbyte granularity.

PR0B Address Offset B

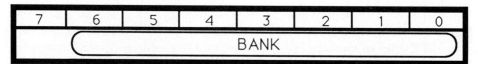

Index 0A at Port 3CE   Port 3CF Read/Write

FIGURE 29.11 PR0B Address Offset B Register. The BANK field controls the address bits 18-12 of the display memory address providing a 4 Kbyte granularity.

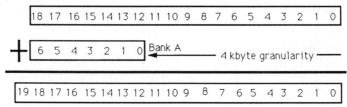

FIGURE 29.12 Creation of a display address using PR0A. A 20-bit address accesses 512 Kbytes of display memory.

used for all read operations that occur within the 64 Kbytes from A0000–AFFFF hex. In addition, PR0B is used for the write operations in the 64 Kbytes from A0000–AFFFF hex. Two macros are provided in Listings 29.7 and 29.8 that set up the VGA for the Single and Dual modes respectively.

The PVGA chip contains a single bank register used for reading and writing at PR0A. Functions that set the read and write bank for the PVGA chip are found in Listing 29.9. Chips beyond the PVGA including the WD90C10, 90C11, 90C30, 90C31, and 90C33 include dual bank switching based on reading versus writing. Functions that set the read and write bank for these chips are found in Listing 29.10.

LISTING 29.7 Set Up for Single Bank Mode

```
;   Calling Protocol:
;       Enable_Single_Banks_Paradise();

Enable_Single_Banks_Paradise    PROC FAR
        mov     dx,3c4h         ;access the System Interface Control
        mov     al,11h
        out     dx,al

        inc     dx
        in      al,dx

        and     al,07fh         ;zero bit 7
        out     dx,al
        ret
Enable_Single_Banks_Paradise endp
```

LISTING 29.8 Set Up for Dual Bank Mode

```
;   Calling Protocol:
;       Enable_Dual_Banks_Paradise();

Enable_Dual_Banks_Paradise      PROC FAR
        mov     dx,3c4h         ;access the System Interface Control
        mov     al,11h
        out     dx,al

        inc     dx
        in      al,dx

        or      al,080h         ;set bit 7
        out     dx,al
        ret
Enable_Dual_Banks_Paradise endp
```

LISTING 29.9 Load the Write Bank for the PVGA

```
;   Input with:
;        bank    Write Bank_Number   0-7 bank number indicating
;                desired 64-kbyte bank

;   Calling Protocol:
;        Load_Write_Bank_PVGA(bank)

Load_Write_Bank_PVGA    Proc far bank:BYTE
        mov     bl,bank
        mov     dx,3ceh         ;point to PR0A Register
        mov     al,09h
        mov     ah,bl
        shl     ah,1            ;adjust to 64 kbyte bank size
        shl     ah,1
        shl     ah,1
        shl     ah,1
        out     dx,ax           ;output bank
        ret
Load_Write_Bank_PVGA endp




;   Input with:
;        bank    Read Bank_Number   0-7 bank number indicating
;                desired 64-kbyte bank

;   Calling Protocol:
;        Load_Read_Bank_PVGA

Load_Read_Bank_PVGA    Proc far bank:BYTE
        mov     bl,bank
        mov     dx,3ceh         ;point to PR0A Register
        mov     al,09h
        mov     ah,bl
        shl     ah,1            ;adjust to 64 kbyte bank size
        shl     ah,1
        shl     ah,1
        shl     ah,1
        out     dx,ax           ;output bank
        ret
Load_Read_Bank_PVGA endp
```

LISTING 29.10 Functions to Load the Read and Write Banks Number for the 90C11, C30, C31, C33

```
; Function:  Load the Write Bank with a new start address for
; the 90C11, C30, C31, C3
;  Input with:
;       bank    Write Bank_Number  0-15 bank number indicating
;               desired 64-kbyte bank
;  Calling Protocol:
;       Load_Write_Bank_C11-30(bank)

Load_Write_Bank_C11-30    proc far bank:BYTE
        mov    bl,bank
        mov    dx,3ceh          ;point to PR0B Register
        mov    al,0ah
        mov    ah,bl
        shl    ah,1             ;adjust to 64 kbyte bank size
        shl    ah,1
        shl    ah,1
        shl    ah,1
        out    dx,ax            ;output bank
        ret
Load_Write_Bank_C11-30 endp


; Function:  Load the Read Bank with a new start address for
; the 90C11, C30, C31, C3
;  Input with:
;       bank    Read Bank_Number  0-15 bank number indicating
;               desired 64-kbyte bank
;  Calling Protocol:
;       Load_Read_Bank_C11-30(bank)

Load_Read_Bank_C11-30    Proc far bank:BYTE
        mov    bl,bank
        mov    dx,3ceh          ;point to PR0A Register
        mov    al,09h
        mov    ah,bl
        shl    ah,1             ;adjust to 64 kbyte bank size
        shl    ah,1
        shl    ah,1
        shl    ah,1
        out    dx,ax            ;output bank
        ret
Load_Read_Bank_C11-30 endp
```

29.5.2   Memory Size and Mapping

The memory size is controlled through the MEM field of the PR1 Register. Table 29.10 describes this field. It contains the amount of memory present and the configuration. Only the 256 Kbytes of memory can be configured as the VGA standard.

The memory map field of the PR1 Register is described in Table 29.11. The 20-bit address associated with the 1 Mbyte of display memory address space ranges from 0–FFFFF hex. If 256 Kbytes are present, the memory will be resident between 0–3FFFF hex. Similarly, 512 Kbytes will be resident between 0–7FFFF hex.

In addition, the WD90C00 allows the memory to be configured as the standard 256 Kbytes IBM VGA mapping through the MEM field of the Miscellaneous Control #2 Register displayed in Figure 29.6. If the MEM field is set to 1, the IBM standard memory configuration is selected regardless of the memory size bits described in the MEM field in Table 29.10. Typically, these bits will be set to 0 for VGA applications. Other values will cause memory conflicts in the PC environment.

29.5.3   Single Page Register Mode

If the PR0A Register is selected in a single-page mode, the 19-bit address necessary to access the 512 Kbytes of display memory or the 20-bit address necessary for the 1 Mbyte of display memory is obtained by using the PR0A Register as a bank address in conjunction with the host address. The host address is a 20-bit address in the form A0000–AFFFF for a 64-Kbyte segment and A0000–BFFFF for a 128-Kbyte segment. The 64-Kbyte segment pointed to by PR0A is mapped into the host memory space at A0000. This is illustrated in Figure 29.13.

29.5.4   32-Kbyte Dual Page Registers Mode

When the dual bank registers are engaged, the programmer can perform efficient memory transfers. The display memory space is configured into either 128- or 64-Kbyte segments. Figure 29.14 illustrates the 128-Kbyte configuration. Note that data transfers to A0000–AFFFF utilize the PR0B Bank Register; transfers to B0000–BFFFF utilize the PR0A Bank Register.

TABLE 29.11   Memory Configuration Field MAP

MEM	Memory Map	Configuration
0	A0000–BFFFF	VGA standard
1	0–3FFFF	1st 256 out of 1 megabyte Kbytes address space
2	0–7FFFF	1st 512 out of 1 megabyte Kbytes address space
3	0–FFFFF	1st 1 Mbyte address space

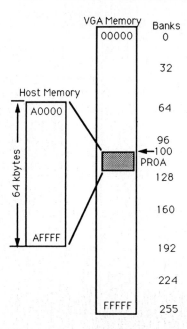

FIGURE 29.13 Using a Single Bank Register PR0A= 100 decimal to address 64 Kbyte segment from 64000 to 73FFF.

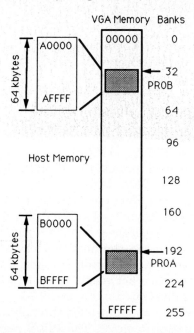

FIGURE 29.14 Using Dual Banks in a 128-Kbyte Configuration. PR0B=32 to address a 64-Kbyte segment from 20000–2FFFF and PR0A= 192 to address a 64-Kbyte segment from C0000–CFFFF.

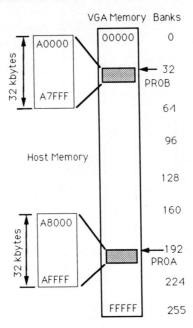

FIGURE 29.15 Using Dual Bank Registers in a 64-Kbyte Configuration.
PR0B=32 to address a 32-Kbyte segment from 20000–27FFF and
PR0A=192 to address 32-Kbyte segment from C0000–C7FFF.

Figure 29.15 illustrates the 64-Kbyte configuration. Note that data transfers to A0000–A7FFF utilize the PR0B Bank Register; transfers to A8000–AFFFF utilize the PR0A Bank Register.

29.5.5 Read/Write Dual Page Registers Mode

The WD90C10 and beyond allow an additional bank selection mode. This mode utilizes dual bank registers, PR0A and PR0B. The memory can be configured so all write operations are directed through the PR0B Register and all read operations are directed through the PR0A Register. The memory is mapped into the host address space through a 64-Kbyte segment at A0000–AFFFF. The display memory is segmented into 64-Kbyte banks. The PR0A and PR0B Registers can be used to access memory in any of these banks through the 64-Kbyte segment. When a read operation occurs to the host memory space between A0000–AFFFF, the PR0A Register is automatically invoked. Similarly, a write operation to the host memory space between A0000–AFFFF invokes the PR0B Register. This mapping is illustrated in Figure 29.16.

This bank selection technique is controlled through the R/W field in bit 7 of the System Interface Control Register. The PR0B register must be enabled through the ENB field in bit 3 of the PR1 Memory Size Register. If the R/W field is set to 1, the PR0A Register is used for reads and the PR0B Register is

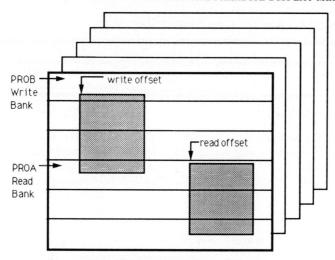

FIGURE 29.16 Read/Write Dual Bank Mapping. Display Memory
Addressing in the WD91COO. Read/write operations utilizing the PR0A
and PR0B Bank Registers. The R/W field of the System Interface Control
Register must be set to 1 for this bank addressing mode.

used for writes. If the R/W field is set to 0, either 64-Kbyte or 32-Kbyte dual-
bank or single-bank selection is in effect.

29.5.6 Page Mode Alphanumerics

It is possible in the WD90C00 and beyond to speed up alphanumeric transfers
by forcing screen refresh memory read cycles to use the page mode addressing
techniques. This page mode addressing is identical to the page mode addressing automatically used in graphics mode. Speed improvements of 30 to 40 percent can be achieved using this mode.

The PM field of the Miscellaneous Control #1 Register controls this function.
If the PM field is set to 1, the page mode addressing scheme is enabled. If the
PM field is 0, the page mode is disabled. Make sure that after setting this bit,
the font is reloaded into planes 2 and 3. That is, this bit should be set before the
font is loaded.

The 132-column character mode requires that the page mode addressing be
enabled. When enabled, the configuration and functioning of the Character
Map Select Register is modified. The normal configuration for this register is
described in Section 10.3.4. The new configuration is shown in Figure 29.17.

In this new configuration, the MEMSEG field selects one of eight memory
segments within planes 2 and 3. The host addresses for both planes are identical due to the plane overlapping. Each of these segments is 8 Kbytes long, filling the entire 64-kbyte segment.

Reconfigured Character Map Select Register

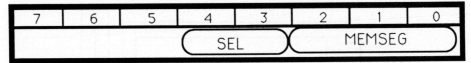

7	6	5	4	3	2	1	0
			SEL		MEMSEG		

Index 3 of Port 3C4   Port 3C5 Read/Write

FIGURE 29.17 Reconfigured Character Map Select Register. When the page mode alphanumeric addressing is engaged, the Character Map Select Register is reconfigured. Refer to Section 10.3.4 for original mapping. The MEMSEG field selects one of eight 8-Kbyte memory segments. The SEL field selects a character map.

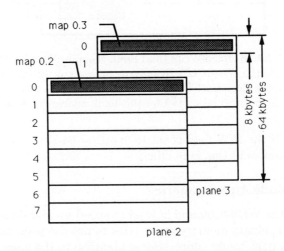

FIGURE 29.18 Page Mode Character Map. A pair of character maps exist in each of the eight segments in planes 2 and 3. In Segment 0, the banks are labeled bank 0.2 and 0.3.

A pair of character maps exist for each segment. One resides in plane 2 and the second in plane 3. This is illustrated in Figure 29.18.

There are a total of sixteen character maps. The character maps are labeled [0–7].[2-3]. Thus, the character map in segment 0 and in plane 2 has the name 0.2. The selection of the map from either plane 2 or plane 3 is accomplished redundantly through the SEL field and the bit 3 of the character attribute bit. The selection is detailed in Table 29.12.

29.6 CONTROLLING THE CRT ADDRESS GENERATION

The PRVGA1a and the WD90C00, WD90C10, and WD90C11 permit positioning the starting address and cursor address in any location in the extended display memory space. The relevant fields are listed in Table 29.13.

TABLE 29.12 Character Map Selection

SEL Field	Attribute Bit 3	Plane Selected
0	X	2
1	0	3
1	1	2
2	0	2
2	1	3
3	X	3

To position any portion of the image memory onto the display, it is necessary to provide an extended start address. Bits 16 and 17 are programmed through the STRT field in the PR3 CRT Control Register described in Figure 29.19.

The display starting address can be loaded through the code provided in Listing 29.11.

If the graphics card is equipped with 2 Mbytes of memory, a bit 10 of the start address is required. This is found in bit position 6 (CRTC Start Memory Address Upper Byte field) of the PR18 CRTC Vertical Timing Overflow Register. A function that accessess all eleven bits of the start address is provided in Listing 29.12.

TABLE 29.13 Paradise Display Address Control

Function	Register Name	Port	Index	Bits	Value
Start Address Bit 17–16	PR3	3CF	0D	4–3	0–3
Disable Border	PR15	3x5	2E	0	1
Enable Border	PR15	3x5	2E	0	0
Modulo of Address Counter	PR16	3x5	2F	6–5	0–3
Address Counter Offset	PR16	3x5	2F	4–3	0–3

PR3 CRT Control

Index 0D at Port 3CE   Port 3CF Read/Write

FIGURE 29.19 PR3 CRT Control Register. The STRT field contains bits 17–16 for the CRT address generation. CRT address can be multiplied by 2 through the MB2 field. The remaining fields are used to lock/unlock access to various registers.

LISTING 29.11 Load the Display Start Address for the Paradise

```
; Input Parameters:
;       top     top two bits of address
; Calling Protocol:
;       Load_Start_Top_Paradise(top)

Load_Start_Top_Paradise proc far top:BYTE
        mov     bl,top
        mov     dx,3c4h
        mov     al,0dh          ;index PR3 CRT Control
        out     dx,al

;       read current value
        inc     dx
        in      al,dx           ;get value
        and     al,0e7h         ;zero out start address 17-16 bits 4-3

;       or in new start address
        and     bl,03h          ;only want 2 bits
        mov     cx,3
        shl     bl,cl   ;shift left 3 to get bit in proper position
        or      al,bl
        out     dx,al           ;output top address
        ret
Load_Start_Top_Paradise endp
```

LISTING 29.12 Load the Display Start Address for the Paradise for the 2 Mbyte Systems

```
; Input Parameters:
;       top     top three bits of address
; Calling Protocol:
;       Load_Start_Top_Paradise_2M(top)

Load_Start_Top_Paradise_2M      proc far top:BYTE
        mov     bl,top
        mov     dx,3c4h
        mov     al,0dh                  ;index PR3 CRT Control
        out     dx,al

;       read current value
        inc     dx
        in      al,dx                   ;get value
        and     al,0e7h         ;zero out start address 17-16 bits 4-3
```

```
;        or in new start address
         and    bl,03h       ;only want 2 bits
         mov    cx,3
         shl    bl,cl   ;shift left 3 to get bit in proper position
         or     al,bl
         out    dx,al        ;output top address

;        process bit 10
         mov    bl,top       ;get top again
         and    bl,04        ;only want bit 10 (in bit position 2)
         mov    cx,4
         shl    bl,cl        ;shift left 4 to get into bit position 6

         mov    dx,3d4h
         mov    al,3eh       ;index PR18
         out    dx,al
         inc    dx
         in     al,dx        ;get PR18

         and    al,0bfh      ;zero bit 6
         or     al,bl        ;put in our start address
         out    dx,al        ;output
         ret
Load_Start_Top_Paradise_2M        endp
```

29.6.1 Controlling the Display Offset

The display offset determines the virtual image size. The 8-bit value is stored in the Offset Register in the CRTC Register Group, described in Section 10.4.22. In the word mode, which is typically the case, display offsets up to 1024 bytes can be defined.

29.6.2 Address Counter Modulus

The WD90C00, WD90C10, and WD90C11 allow the CRT address counter width to be controlled. The address counter can count to 64 Kbytes or 128 Kbytes of words or double-words. It may be desirable to utilize this modulus counter when virtual images exceed the resolution of the display mode. The MOD field of the Miscellaneous Control #2 Register in the WD90Cxx determines the modulus as indicated in Table 29.14.

29.6.3 The Display Offset

The upper address bits, bits 17 and 16, of the CRTC address counter can be offset to one of four 64-Kbyte boundaries spanning 256 Kbytes of display memory. The TOP field of the Miscellaneous Control #2 Register in the WD90Cxx

TABLE 29.14 CRTC Address Counter Width

MOD field	Counter Width
0	256 K
1	128 K
2	64 K

controls this offset as indicated in Table 29.15. These bits are summed with bits 4 and 3 of PR16.

29.6.4 Border Display

The border region of the screen is often problematic. The WD90C00, WD90C10 and WD90C11 have the ability to force the video outputs to 0 during the time that the border region is being displayed. The border, also called overscan region, can be forced to 0 by setting the DB field of the Miscellaneous Control #1 Register in the WD90Cxx to 1. If the DB field is 0, the border region is displayed as normal with the overscan color. The overscan color is located in the Overscan Color Register described in Section 10.6.4.

29.6.5 BIOS Extensions

Paradise provides a set of twelve BIOS Calls as shown in Table 29.16. These have to do with setting the display modes, emulation modes, reading the status of a mode set, and reading the extended PR registers.

29.6.6 Parametric Mode Set

The alphanumeric and graphic display modes, listed in Tables 29.8 and 29.9, can be invoked by using the Parametric Mode Set BIOS Call. The programmer provides the horizontal, vertical, and color resolution to the BIOS call. If a

TABLE 29.15 CRTC Address Counter Offset

TOP field	Counter Width
0	0 K
1	64 K
2	128 K
3	192 K

TABLE 29.16 Paradise Super BIOS

Function	AH	AL	BH	Feature
Parametric Mode Set	0	7E	0	Set a mode based on parameters
Set VGA Mode	0	7F	0	Old Set a VGA mode
Set Non-VGA Mode	0	7F	1	Old Set a non-VGA mode
Extended Mode Status	0	7F	2	Return status of last mode call
Lock VGA or Non-VGA mode	0	7F	3	Lock VGA into current
Set MDA Mode	0	7F	4	Set MDA emulation
Set CGA Mode	0	7F	5	Set CGA emulation
Set VGA Mono	0	7F	6	Set VGA into a mono mode
Set VGA Color	0	7F	7	Set VGA into a color mode
Write PR Register (1)	0	7F	09–0F	Write a PR Register
Read PR Register	0	7F	19–1F	Read a PR Register
Set Analog EGA Emulation (1)	0	7F	20	Sets analog EGA emulation

Notes: (1) WD90C00 or WD90C11

mode is supported that matches these resolutions, a mode set will be issued. It is not recommended to use this mode. The AH=00 Set Mode command described in Section 11.2 should be used to set the standard or extended display modes.

Inputs:

AH=00h	Mode Set BIOS Call
AL=7E hex	Parametric Mode Set Subfunction
BX=Horizontal Resolution	Horizontal Resolution
	pixels if a graphics mode
	columns if an alphanumeric mode
CX=Vertical Resolution	Vertical Resolution
	pixels if a graphics mode
	rows if an alphanumeric mode
DX=Color Resolution	Number of colors
	0=monochrome
	2,4,16,256 = number of colors

Outputs:
Selected matching mode is set

29.6.7   Set VGA Mode

This function is an old BIOS function designed to bring the VGA controller into a VGA emulation state after a soft boot operation. The technique involves setting up the desired mode using the standard Mode Set BIOS call. Next, this Set VGA Mode BIOS call is issued. This sets up the VGA so a soft boot will cause the chip to initialize in a VGA state.

Inputs:

AH=00 hex	Mode Set BIOS Call
AL=7F hex	Extended Mode Set Subfunction
BH=00 hex	Set Non-Extended VGA Mode

Outputs:

BH=return	Return parameter
	7F = valid call
	Not 7F = invalid call

29.6.8   Set Non-VGA Mode

This function is an old BIOS function designed to bring the VGA controller into a non-VGA emulation state after a soft boot operation. The technique involves setting up the desired mode using the standard Mode Set BIOS call. Next, this Set Non-VGA Mode BIOS call is issued. This sets up the VGA so a soft boot will cause the chip to initialize in a non-VGA state. If a monochrome mode is desired, set to MDA/Hercules emulation. If a color mode is desired, set to CGA emulation.

Inputs:

AH=00 hex	Mode Set BIOS Call
AL=7F hex	Extended Mode Set Subfunction
BH=01 hex	Set VGA Mode

Outputs:

BH=return	Return parameter
	7F = valid call
	Not 7F = invalid call

29.6.9   Extended Mode Status

The Extended Mode Status returns the status of the last mode call.

Inputs:

AH=00 hex	Mode Set BIOS Call
AL=7F hex	Extended Mode Set Subfunction
BH=02 hex	Query Mode Status

Outputs:

BH=return	Return parameter
	7F = valid call
	Not 7F = invalid call
BL=status	Status parameter
	0 if a VGA mode
	1 if a non-VGA mode
CH=memory present	Amount of memory present in 64-Kbyte chunks
CL=memory required	Amount of memory used for current mode

29.6.10   Lock VGA or Non-VGA Mode

The current mode can be locked so the VGA system will default to the locked mode after a soft reset. Some applications require the soft reset initialization to work properly.

Inputs:

AH=00 hex	Mode Set BIOS Call
AL=7F hex	Extended Mode Set Subfunction
BH=03 hex	Lock Current Mode

Outputs:

BH=return	Return parameter
	7F = valid call
	Not 7F = invalid call

29.6.11   Set Non-VGA MDA/Hercules Mode

This function brings the VGA system into a MDA/Hercules emulation mode. It emulates the 6845 graphics controller. It does not require soft booting and can be invoked at any time.

Inputs:

AH=00 hex	Mode Set BIOS Call
AL=7F hex	Extended Mode Set Subfunction
BH=04 hex	Set Non-VGA MDA/Hercules Mode

Outputs:

BH=return	Return parameter
	7F = valid call
	Not 7F = invalid call

29.6.12   Set Non-VGA CGA Mode

This function brings the VGA system into a CGA emulation mode. It emulates the 6845 graphics controller. It does not require soft booting and can be invoked at any time.

Inputs:

AH=00 hex	Mode Set BIOS Call
AL=7F hex	Extended Mode Set Subfunction
BH=05 hex	Set Non-VGA CGA Mode

Outputs:

BH=return	Return parameter
	7F = valid call
	Not 7F = invalid call

29.6.13   Set VGA Mono Mode

This function brings the VGA system into a VGA monochrome mode. It does not require soft booting and can be invoked at any time.

Inputs:

AH=00 hex	Mode Set BIOS Call
AL=7F hex	Extended Mode Set Subfunction
BH=06 hex	Set Non-Extended VGA Mode

Outputs:

BH=return	Return parameter
	7F = valid call
	Not 7F = invalid call

29.6.14   Set VGA Color Mode

This function brings the VGA system into a VGA color mode. It does not require soft booting and can be invoked at any time.

Inputs:

AH=00 hex	Mode Set BIOS Call
AL=7F hex	Extended Mode Set Subfunction
BH=07 hex	Set Non-Extended VGA Mode

Outputs:

BH=return	Return parameter
	7F = valid call
	Not 7F = invalid call

29.6.15   Write a PR Register

This function allows the programmer to write to one of the PR registers as shown in Table 29.17. This is available on the WD9xCxx generation of Paradise Super VGAs.

Inputs:

AH=00 hex	Mode Set BIOS Call
AL=7F hex	Extended Mode Set Subfunction
BH=desired register	Number of PR register to read. Refer to Table 29.18.
BL=register value	Value of PR register

Outputs:

BH=return	Return parameter
	7F = valid call
	Not 7F = invalid call

29.6.16   Read a PR Register

This function returns the contents of one of the PR registers as shown in Table 29.18.

Inputs:

AH=00 hex	Mode Set BIOS Call
AL=7F hex	Extended Mode Set Subfunction
BH=desired register	Number of PR register to read. Refer to Table 29.19.

TABLE 29.17   PR Register Codes for Write Operations

Code	Register	Chip
9	PR0A	PVGA1A or WD90Cxx
A	PR0B	PVGA1A or WD90Cxx
B	PR1	PVGA1A or WD90Cxx
C	PR2	PVGA1A or WD90Cxx
D	PR3	PVGA1A or WD90Cxx
E	PR4	PVGA1A or WD90Cxx
F	PR5	PVGA1A or WD90Cxx

TABLE 29.18 Read PR Register Codes

Code	Register	Chip
19	PR0A	PVGA1A or WD90Cxx
1A	PR0B	PVGA1A or WD90Cxx
1B	PR1	PVGA1A or WD90Cxx
1C	PR2	PVGA1A or WD90Cxx
1D	PR3	PVGA1A or WD90Cxx
1E	PR4	PVGA1A or WD90Cxx
1F	PR5	PVGA1A or WD90Cxx
29	PR10	WD90C00, WD90C10, WD90C11
2A	PR11	WD90C00, WD90C10, WD90C11
2B	PR12	WD90C00, WD90C10, WD90C11
2C	PR13	WD90C00, WD90C10, WD90C11
2D	PR14	WD90C00, WD90C10, WD90C11
2E	PR15	WD90C00, WD90C10, WD90C11
2F	PR16	WD90C00, WD90C10, WD90C11
30	PR17	WD90C00, WD90C10, WD90C11

Outputs:

BH=return	Return parameter
	7F = valid call
	Not 7F = invalid call
BL=register value	Value of PR register

29.6.17 Set Analog EGA Emulation

The EGA can be emulated when the VGA card is attached to an analog monitor. This is available on the WD9xC00 generation of Paradise Super VGAs.

Inputs:

AH=00 hex	Mode Set BIOS Call
AL=7F hex	Extended Mode Set Subfunction
BH=20 hex	Emulate EGA with Analog Monitor
BL=EGA switches	low nibble is EGA switches.

Outputs:

BH=return	Return parameter
	7F = valid call
	Not 7F = invalid call

29.7 EXTENDED REGISTERS

A complete list of the extended registers is provided in Table 29.19. All of these registers are read/write with the exception of the Unlock Sequencer Extended Registers at PR20, which are write-only.

TABLE 29.19 Western Digital Extended Registers

Index	No.	Name	Address
9	PR0A	Address Offset A	3CE/3CF
A	PR0B	Address Offset B	3CE/3CF
B	PR1	Memory Size	3CE/3CF
C	PR2	Video Select	3CE/3CF
D	PR3	CRT Control	3CE/3CF
E	PR4	Video Control	3CE/3CF
F	PR5	Unlock PO0–PR4	3CE/3CF
29	PR10	Unlock PR11–PR17	3D4/3D5
2A	PR11	Configuration Switches	3D4/3D5
2B	PR12	Scratch Pad	3D4/3D5
2C	PR13	Interlace H/2 Start	3D4/3D5
2D	PR14	Interlace H/2 End	3D4/3D5
2E	PR15	Miscellaneous Control 1	3D4/3D5
2F	PR16	Miscellaneous Control 2	3D4/3D5
30	PR17	Miscellaneous Control 3	3D4/3D5
3E	PR18	CRT Vertical Timing	3D4/3D5
3F	PR19	Signature Analyzer	3D4/3D5
31-3C	PR31-3C	Reserved	3D4/3D5
06	PR20	Unlock Sequencer Extended Registers	3D4/3D5
07	PR21	Display Configuration and Scratch Pad	3D4/3D5
08	PR22	Scratch Pad	3D4/3D5
09	PR23	Scratch Pad	3D4/3D5
10	PR30	Mem Interface Write Buf and FIFO Control	3D4/3D5
11	PR31	System Interface	3D4/3D5
12	PR32	Miscellaneous Control 4	3D4/3D5
13	PR33	DRAM Timing and Zero Wait State Control	3D4/3D5
14	PR34	Video Memory Mapping	3D4/3D5
15	PR35	Reserved	3D4/3D5

TABLE 29.20   PR18, CRT C Vertical Timing Overflow Register

Bit	Function
7	Enable 2 Mbyte Memory for 1280-by-1024 8-bit mode
6	CRTC Start Memory Address High bit 10

The PR18, CRTC Vertical Timing Overflow Register, provides additional bits for the CRTC Controller. The relevant bits are listed in Table 29.20.

29.8   HARDWARE CURSOR

The hardware cursor supports a user-defined pattern of up to 64 by 64 pixels. Each pixel is the standard two bits per pixel. The cursor pattern is stored in off-screen memory. The hardware cursor is accessed at Port 23C2h/23C3h when the register block pointer at port 23C0 has been set to 02h. The 12-bit hardware cursor registers are listed in Table 29.21.

TABLE 29.21   Hardware Cursor Registers

Index	Name
0	Cursor Control
1	Cursor Pattern Address Low
2	Cursor Pattern Address High
3	Cursor Primary Color Byte 0
4	Cursor Primary Color Byte 1
5	Cursor Primary Color Byte 2
6	Cursor Secondary Color Byte 0
7	Cursor Secondary Color Byte 1
8	Cursor Secondary Color Byte 2
9	Cursor Auxiliary Color Byte 0
A	Cursor Auxiliary Color Byte 1
B	Cursor Auxiliary Color Byte 2
C	Cursor Origin
D	Cursor Display Position X
E	Cursor Display Position Y
F	Cursor Register Block/Index

TABLE 29.22 Cursor Control Register

Bit	Function
11	Cursor Enable
10-9	Cursor Pattern Type
8	Cursor Plane Protection
7-5	Cursor Color Mode
4	Enhanced Hardware Cursor (24 bits per pixel)

29.8.1 Cursor Control Register

The Cursor Control Register is defined in Table 29.22. The cursor is enabled by setting the Cursor Enable bit to a 1. The pattern type is either 0 for 32 by 32 or 1 for 64-by-64 cursor pattern, each at two bits per pixel. For cursor plane protection, 1=enables, 0=disables cursor protection.

The cursor color mode defines the type of color codes used on the cursor. These may be a software compatible cursor if the field is 0, a two-color cursor with inversion if the field is 1, a two-color cursor with special inversion if the field is 2, or a three-color cursor if the field is 3.

The Enhanced Hardware Cursor bit=1 enables the enhanced 24 bit per pixel hardware cursor. The standard hardware cursor of 16 bits per pixel is enabled by Control Register 2 at index 1, bits 11–10–2.

29.8.2 Cursor Pattern Address Low and High Register

The cursor pattern address is a 21-bit address that specifies the location in the display memory where the first byte of the cursor pattern is stored. The value is independent of the cursor origin. The cursor pattern may be stored anywhere in the display memory but is usually in off-screen memory. NOTE: A write to either of the cursor pattern address registers or the cursor origin registers does not take effect until the beginning of a video frame following the next write to the Cursor Control Register.

Storing the cursor pattern in a planar mode is shown in Table 29.23. Storing the cursor pattern in a packed mode is shown in Table 29.24. In these cases, it assumes that A0000 is the starting address. This is, of course, a visible portion of the display memory and typically the cursor will be stored in an off-screen portion.

The cursor pattern is stored as shown in Table 29.25 when in a text mode. In mode 7, the CPU addresses are B0000h–B7FFEh.

TABLE 29.23 Cursor Pattern Storage in a Planar Mode

CPU Address	Map	Cursor Pattern Address
A0000	0	Byte 0
A0000	1	Byte 1
A0000	2	Byte 2
A0000	3	Byte 3
A0001	0	Byte 4
A0001	1	Byte 5
A0001	2	Byte 6
A0001	3	Byte 7

TABLE 29.24 Cursor Pattern Storage in a Packed Mode

CPU Address	Cursor Pattern Address
A0000	Byte 0
A0001	Byte 1
A0002	Byte 2
A0003	Byte 3
A0004	Byte 4
A0005	Byte 5
A0006	Byte 6
A0007	Byte 7

TABLE 29.25 Cursor Pattern Storage in a Text Mode

CPU Address	Pixel	Byte
B8000	0:1	Byte 0
B8001	0:1	Byte 1
B8000	2:3	Byte 2
B8001	2:3	Byte 3
B8002	0:1	Byte 4
B8003	0:1	Byte 5
B8002	2:3	Byte 6
B8003	2:3	Byte 7

TABLE 29.26 Cursor Color Modes

Pattern	Color Mode 0	Color Mode 1	Color Mode 2	Color Mode 3
0	All 0	Secondary	Secondary	Secondary
1	All 1	Primary	Primary	Primary
2	Transparent	Transparent	Transparent	Transparent
3	Inverted	Inverted	Special	Auxiliary

29.8.3 Cursor Primary, Secondary, and Auxiliary Color Registers

There are three sets of registers, each up to 24 bits long, that specify the primary, secondary, and auxiliary colors. The cursor color modes are selected by the Cursor Color Mode field and are shown in Table 29.26.

The special color generates the exclusive-NOR (XNOR) of the background and the Auxiliary Color Register. This retains the different from background color property of inversion while adding the ability to specify one preferred special inversion from a background color to any desired color. To use this feature, the Cursor Color Mode field must be set to special, and the cursor auxiliary color should be loaded with the exclusive NOR or the background color to be translated and the desired color to be displayed. When set in this manner, any screen pixel 0 of the former color covered by an inverting cursor pattern pixel will be inverted into the auxiliary color.

29.8.4 Cursor Origin Register

The Cursor Origin Register species the offset in pixels from the top-left corner of the pattern that is displayed at the cursor display position. This is referred to as the "hot-spot." Table 29.27 describes this register.

29.8.5 Cursor Display Position X and Y Registers

The Cursor Display Position X and Y Registers specify the location of the cursor in screen coordinates. These values represent pixel positions. NOTE: A write to either register does not take effect until the beginning of a video frame following the next write to the Cursor Control Register.

29.8.6 Register Block Index

All register blocks have an Index 0Fh that can be used to switch the block or index. Normally to change a register block or index requires the user to write to I/O port 23C0h with the values of the register block or index desired. To speed up block switching or to change the register index, index F can be used. This register is described in Table 29.28.

TABLE 29.27 Cursor Origin Register

Bit	Function
11–6	Cursor Y Hotspot
5–0	Cursor X Hotspot

TABLE 29.28 Register Block Index

Bit	Function
11–8	Register Index
7–0	Register Block Pointer

29.8.7 Cursor Plane Protection

The Cursor Plane Protection bit provides compatibility with the software cursor using a similar algorithm to the one used by the VGA attribute controller. In the 8-bit-per-color modes, a background pixel covered by the cursor is either replaced by a specified 8-bit color or it is inverted. For other modes, cursor plane protection is enabled.

When the Cursor Plane Protection bit of the Cursor Control Register is set, the two or four high-order bits of the background are replaced with the corresponding bits of the Cursor Auxiliary Color Register.

If bit 7 of the VGA attribute Mode Control Register is reset, cursor plane protection applies to the two high-order bits of the background. When this bit is set, protection applies to the four high-order bits.

29.8.8 Cursor Pattern

The 2-bit cursor pattern format is stored in 1024 or 256 consecutive memory byte locations. The cursor pattern is stored such that four pixels are packed into each byte. The most significant two bits of each byte represent the leftmost pixel in that group. The pattern is stored in a line-by-line fashion, with the top line first. A few lines of pattern are shown in Table 29.29. In this case, the offset is relative to the value in the Cursor Pattern Address Register. In packed mode, the BitMap (Map) is selected by the two low-order bits of the CPU address. The Cursor Pattern must start in map 0.

29.9 GRAPHICS COPROCESSOR

The graphics coprocessor is also called the drawing engine (DE) by Western Digital. It supports accelerated data transfers between regions of display memory. A full complement of raster operations are available, as is color expansion and transparency. The DE supports solid fill rectangles, pattern filled rectangles, line drawing, and trapezoid fill using trapezoid fill strip.

The DE supports text modes and monochrome, 4-, 8-, 15- and 16-bits-per-pixel display modes.

TABLE 29.29 Cursor Pattern

Offset	Map	Plane	Row	Column
0	0	AND	0	7–0
0	1	XOR	0	7–0
0	2	AND	0	15–8
0	3	XOR	0	15–8
1	0	AND	0	23–16
1	1	XOR	0	23–16
1	2	AND	0	31–24
1	3	XOR	0	31–24
2	0	AND	0	39–32
2	1	XOR	0	39–32
2	2	AND	0	47–40
2	3	XOR	0	47–40
3	0	AND	0	55–48
3	1	XOR	0	55–48
3	2	AND	0	63–56
3	3	XOR	0	63–56
4	0	AND	1	7–0
4	1	XOR	1	7–0
4	2	AND	1	15–8
4	3	XOR	1	15–8

29.9.1 DE Extended Registers

The drawing engine is controlled though a set of indexed registers, which are listed in Table 29.30 for block 1 and Table 29.31 for block 2. These registers are accessed by selecting this register group and writing the index into bits 15–11 of each word. The drawing engine registers are found at I/O port 23C2h.

29.9.2 DE Control Register #1

The DE Control Register #1 is shown in Table 29.32, and the drawing modes associated with bits 11–9 are shown in Table 29.33. The source formats associated with bits 4–3 are shown in Table 29.34.

TABLE 29.30 Block 1 of the Drawing Engine Registers

Index	Name
0	Control Register 1
1	Control Register 2
2	Source X
3	Source Y
4	Destination X
5	Destination Y
6	Dimension X
7	Dimension Y
8	Raster Operation
9	Left Clip X Position
A	Right Clip X Position
B	Top Clip Y Position
C	Bottom Clip Y Position
F	Drawing Block Index

TABLE 29.31 Block 2 of the Drawing Engine Registers

Index	Name
0	Map Base Address
1	Row Pitch
2	Foreground Color Low
3	Foreground Color High
4	Background Color Low
5	Background Color High
6	Transparency Color Low
7	Transparency Color High
8	Transparency Mask Low
9	Transparency Mask High
A	Mask Byte Low
B	Mask Byte High
F	Drawing Block Index

TABLE 29.32 DE Control Register

Bits	Function
11–9	Drawing Mode
8	X Direction; 0=positive, 1=negative
7	X Direction; 0=positive, 1=negative
6	Major Axis; 0=X, 1=Y
5	Source Select; 0=Screen, 1=Host I/O or Memory
4–3	Source Format
2	Pattern Enable; 0=No Pattern, 1=Pattern used as source
1	Destination Select; 0=Screen, 1=Host I/O or Memory
0	Last Pixel Off; 0=Last Pixel On, 1=Last Pixel Off

TABLE 29.33 Drawing Modes

Value	Mode
0	No Operation
1	BitBlt
2	Line Strip
3	Trapezoidal Fill Strip
4	Bresenham Line

TABLE 29.34 Source Formats

Value	Format
0	Color
1	Monochrome from Color Comparisons
2	Fixed Color
3	Monochrome from host

29.9.3 DE Control Register #2

The DE Control Register #2 is shown in Table 29.35, and the drawing modes associated with bits 11–9 are shown in Table 29.33.

The Host BLT Color Expand Data Bits/Host write values are shown in Table 29.36.

TABLE 29.35 DE Control Register #2

Bits	Function
11–10	Pixel Depth 0–4; 1=8, 2=16
9	Transparency Enable; 1=Enable, 0=Not enabled (Opaque)
8	Transparency Polarity; 0=Negative, 1=Positive
7	Monochrome Transparency; 0=Off, 1=On
3	Host BitBlt through Memory Port; 0=Data through I/O, 1=Data through Memory
2–0	Host BLT Color Expand Data Bits/Host write

TABLE 29.36 Color Expand Data Bits/Host Write

Bits	Value
0	Reserved
1	Reserved
2	2 Bits/CPU Write (16 bit/pixel only)
3	4 Bits/CPU Write (8 or 16 bit/pixel only)
4	8 Bits/CPU Write (4, 8, or 16 bit/pixel only)
5	8 or 16 Bits/CPU Write (4, 8 or16 bit/pixel only)

29.9.4 Source and Destination Registers

The Source X and Source Y Registers specify the source address for BitBlt operations. Similarly, the Destination X and Destination Y Registers specify the destination address for BitBlt operations. The X and Y locations of each refer to pixel positions in screen memory. The starting corner of source and destination can be any of the four corners as specified with the X direction and Y direction Bits of the DE Control Register 1. The starting corners are shown in Table 29.37 providing for overlapping BitBlts.

TABLE 29.37 Starting Corner Dependent on X and Y Direction

X Direction	Y Direction	Starting Corner
0	0	Top Left
0	1	Bottom Left
1	0	Top Right
1	1	Bottom Right

Pattern fill BitBlts are BitBlts with the Pattern Enable bit set. In this case, the Source X and Source Y are used to point to the staring location of the pattern.

29.9.5   Dimension and Row Pitch

The Dimension X and Dimension Y are both 12-bit addresses that specify the X and Y dimension of the BitBlt. Like most BitBlts, they represent 1 minus the actual value to be transferred. For BitBlt operations, the Dimension X Register specifies the width of the BitBlt, and the Dimension Y Register specifies the height of the BitBlt. For line strip and trapezoidal fill strip operations, the Dimension X Register specifies the length of the strip, and the Dimension Y Register specifies the number of line strips that have the same length. For Bresenham lines, the Dimension X Register specifies the length of the line. In graphics modes, the Dimension X and Dimension Y express number of pixels. In text modes, the Dimension X Register value is expressed in the number of characters multiplied by eight, and the Dimension Y Register value is expressed in the number of character rows.

The Row Pitch Register specifies the number of pixels offset from any location in a given row to the same location in the next row. The units are the same as the source and destination fields to which it applies.

29.9.6   Clipping

Four clipping registers are provided that define a rectangular area. Any pixel inside and on the boundary of the rectangular area can be updated during a drawing operation.

29.9.7   Address Mapping

The Source X and Source Y and the Destination X and Destination Y are converted internally to the linear address that point to pixel locations. The linear address is defined as the following:

$$= ((Y * ROWPITCH) + X) * S) + (MAP\_BASE\ ADRESS * 4\ K)$$

where: S is 1/2 for 4 bits/pixel = 1 for 8 bits/pixel and = 2 for 16 bits/pixel

The map base address provides a linear address offset from the start of display memory. Each increment of offset corresponds to a 4-Kbyte increment in display memory.

29.9.8   Foreground and Background Colors

The Foreground and Background Registers specify these two colors with depths from 4 bits per pixel to 16 bits per pixel. Each color can reside in one or two registers as shown in Figure 29.20.

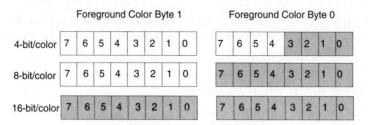

FIGURE 29.20 Color Registers

29.9.9 Map and Plane Masks

The Mask Register control both map and plane masks used in drawing operations. The Mask Byte 0 specifies a 4-bit mask that prevents data in the specified registers from being updated. This mask is needed for BitBlt operations in all text modes to prevent font data from being overwritten in a character-attribute mode.

The Mask Byte 0 and Byte 1 together specify an 8-bit or 16-bit mask that prevents data in the specified planes from being updated. This is useful during extended packed modes when plane masking is desired.

29.9.10 Raster Operations

The Raster Operations Register specifies a bitwise logical operation to be performed on the source and destination fields. This field is always active and must be loaded with the appropriate value even when a simple source copy is to be performed. A 4-bit raster operation is described in bits 11–8 of the Raster Operations Register. The raster operations supported are provided in Table 29.38.

29.9.11 Patterns

All 8-by-8 patterns can be rapidly and repetitively copied to large destinations. The host writes the 8-by-8 pattern to display memory in a linear fashion, usually to a non-visible location depending on the current addressing mode. The host then loads the source registers with the location of the pixel within the pattern corresponding to the top-left corner of the destination region. The Pattern Enable bit must be set to 1 to enable patterns to be used as the source.

The host must write a color pattern in the current mode and then use the control registers to specify a single plane when a monochrome pattern is to be used.

In a planar or packed configuration, the 8-by-8 source pattern must be stored in display memory in a 32-byte aligned area. It is stored as 64 consecutive pixels, not as a rectangular region. An anchor point is associated with the top-left corner of the destination region and the pattern wraps to the right and down from that point. The source address may point to any pixel within the pattern.

TABLE 29.38 Raster Operations

RasterOp	Function
0	Zero
1	AND
2	S * !D
3	Src
4	!S * D
5	Dest
6	XOR
7	OR
8	NOR
9	XNOR
A	Inv Dest
B	S + !D
C	Inv Src
D	!S + D
E	NAND
F	ONE

The anchored point is selected by Control Register 1, Bits 8–7 as shown in Table 29.39.

An example of an Anchor Point is shown in Figure 29.21. Note that the pattern is stored linearly and that the one-dimensional pattern wraps around through the two-dimensional output

29.9.12   Color Expansion

Color expansion is the conversion of a monochrome source to a color destination where each pixel whose value is 1 is replaced with a foreground color and each pixel whose value is 0 is replaced with a background color. When the source is

TABLE 29.39 Direction and Anchor Point

X (Bit 8)	Y (Bit 7)	Wrap	Anchor Point
0	0	Right and Down	Top Left
0	1	Right and Up	Bottom Left
1	0	Left and Down	Top Right
1	1	Left and Up	Bottom Right

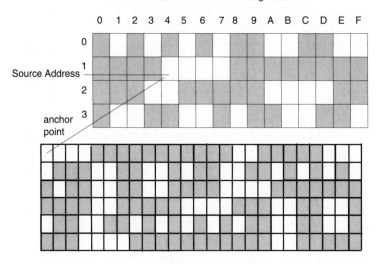

Destination Rectangle

FIGURE 29.21 Pattern Anchor Point

a fixed color, the entire destination will be filled with the foreground color subject to masks, raster ops, and destination transparency. This is the way that rectangles are filled.

29.9.13   Color Compression

Monochrome data can be extracted from color data when read from display memory by the color comparitors. Data extracted in this manner is replicated to each plane or map as if it had been read from memory.

Monochrome data can be extracted from color data when read from the host through an I/O Port during a BitBlt. Each 32-bit word written to the I/O port is treated in the same manner as if it had been read from display memory.

It is possible to extract a single plane from a color source field. The Transparency Color Register should be loaded with FFs and the Transparency Mask Registers should be loaded with a 0 in the map or plane positions to be extracted and a 1 in all other positions.

When the Monochrome Transparency bit is set to a 1, the monochrome source pixels that are 0 do not modify the destination regardless of the RasterOp.

29.9.14 Color Transparency

A certain color or range of colors in the source or destination field of a BitBlt operation can be specified as transparent. Transparent source data cannot overwrite the background. Similarly, opaque destination colors cannot be overwritten. Therefore, a transparent background color can be overwritten.

Color destination transparency is supported. The transparency color registers specify the 4-bit to 16-bit color to be used as the transparent color. The pixels of the destination are compared against the transparency color under the control of the transparency mask. Each bit of the mask that is a 1 makes the corresponding bit of the transparency color a don't care.

The Transparency Enable bit of the Control Register 2 specifies whether transparency is enabled. The Transparency Polarity bit specifies whether pixels matching the transparency color are considered transparent. In the case of a destination transparency, only destination pixels matching the transparent color can be overwritten.

29.9.15 Filled Rectangles

A BitBlt operation where the source is a fixed color produces a filled rectangle. The Source Format field in Control Register 1 must be set to Fixed Color, and the Foreground Color Registers should contain the desired color.

29.9.16 Host BitBlt Transfers

Host BitBlts transfer data from the host to the screen. The BitMap can contain from 8 to 16 bits per color. Either memory or I/O accesses are allowed. The Source X address refers to the offset into with respect to the source data. It is used to align byte and word transfers. For image transfer, every transfer must end on a 32-bit boundary. The Source X value determines whether the data starts at the beginning of the 32-bit boundary.

NOTE: Host BitBlts with Color Expansion are limited to 16-bits due to the memory bandwidth.

After starting a BitBlt, the host writes lines of the BitMap to the Read-Back-Latch. Memory access is faster than I/O Port access. The selection of memory or I/O access for HBLT data is controlled through the Control Register 2 BHLT Through Memory bit. If this bit is a 0, screen memory normal mode is used and I/O port 23C4 is used for the data transfers. If this bit is a 1, all screen memory is decoded for HBLT image data.

I/O access occurs differently for the different widths of I/O instructions as shown in Table 29.40.

During write operations, if the host is not ready to supply data, the drawing engine waits until the data becomes ready. If data comes from the host but the

TABLE 29.40 I/O Access for HBLT

I/O Bits	Access Port
8	23C4h, 23C5h, 23C6h, and 23C7h in sequence
16	23C4h, and 23C6h in sequence
32	23C4h

drawing engine is not ready, it is put into the write buffer. If the write buffer is full, the host is held off.

Example 29.1 Programming an HBLT

1. Wait for the command buffer locations to be available for all parameters.

2. Enter set-up parameters including destination, width, height, and foreground and background colors.

3. Use CLI to disable host interrupts that could cause conventional VGA access during an HBLT data transfer.

4. Write Control Register 1.

5. Wait for Command Buffer Locations Available=0, such that all eight locations are free. This allows the Control Register 1 write to reach the drawing engine. A previous operation may have the drawing engine busy and hold Control Register 1 in the command buffer until the previous operation is complete.

6. Transfer the image or bit map to the WD90C33. This transfer can be done through the 23C4 Register or memory.

7. Wait for Drawing Engine busy =0.

8. Use STI to enable interrupts.

During image transfers, every transfer of a line of host data must end on a 32-bit boundary. Pad bits can be added before and after the image to complete the 32-bit blocks. Any block contains data for one line and only one line. The least significant bit is displayed on the left for X-Direction=0 and on the right for X-Direction=1. The 32 bits of image data are accumulated in the Read-Back-Latch.

If Byte 3 is loaded and the X-Direction is positive, then the drawing engine is triggered. A second technique is to have the X-Direction be negative and write to Byte 0 of the Read-Back-Latch.

Example 29.2 Image Transfer

Assume:

1. Selected Mode is 8 bits per pixel.

2. X-direction is positive, Y-direction is positive.

3. Source X is set to 1.

4. Destination X is 1, Destination Y is 2

5. Dimension X is 4 (5 pixels).

A Source X set to 1 selects byte 1 of the Read-Back-Latch for the left-most pixel of the destination. NOTE: The Dimension X=4 results in five bytes being written. The source data is provided in Table 29.41. Note that the data 84 or 8C are not going to be written to the display. They would load into the Read-Back Latch Byte 0; since the Source X is set to 1, byte 0 of the Read-Back-Latch is ignored. The next three writes of 85, 86, 87 are written to the Read-Back-Latch in byte positions 1, 2, and 3. After the 87 is written, these 32 bits are transferred. The 88, 89, 8A, and 8B are then written to the display. Note that since

TABLE 29.41 Data Transfer

Address	Data	Pixel	Line	Notes
B800:0	84	—	—	32-bit boundary
B800:1	85	1	1	
B800:2	86	2	1	
B800:3	87	3	1	causes write
B800:4	88	4	1	32-bit boundary
B800:5	89	5	1	
B800:6	8A	pad	—	
B800:7	8B	pad	—	causes write
B800:8	8C	—	—	32-bit boundary
B800:9	8D	1	2	
B800:A	8E	2	2	
B800:B	8F	3	2	causes write
B800:C	90	4	2	32-bit boundary
B800:D	91	5	2	
B800:E	92	pad	—	
B800:F	93	pad	—	causes write

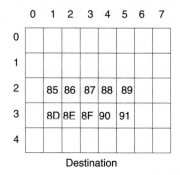

Destination

FIGURE 29.22 Image Transfer

the X-Dimension is 4 (5 bytes), the 8A and 8B are written to the Read-Back-Latch but not written to the display. The same sequence follows for the second line.

This results in data being written to the screen as shown in Figure 29.22.

29.9.17 Color Expanded HBLT

A color expanded HBLT requires pad bits for 8-bit boundaries. Any write contains data for only one line. The most significant bit is displayed on the left when X direction =0. For 8-bit writes, Control Register 22 bits 2–0 should be set to 5. Then, use a byte move instruction such as MOVSB.

For planar modes, Source X can be from 0 through 7 as shown in Figure 29.23a. For packed modes, all source X can be from 0 through 3. When Source X is greater than 3, it wraps around the 8-bit register as shown in Figure 29.23b.

In 16-bits-per-pixel mode, the color expansion works for Source X values of 0 and 1 only. When the source is greater than 1, it wraps around as shown in Figure 29.23c.

The procedure in Example 29.3 and its associated Figure 29.24 provide an example of a color-expanded host transfer.

Example 29.3 Color Expanded Image Transfer

Assume:

1. X-Direction is positive; Y-Direction is positive

2. Monochrome transparency is set to 0

3. Source X is set to 0

4. Destination X is 1; Destination Y is 2

5. Dimension X is 4 (5 pixels).

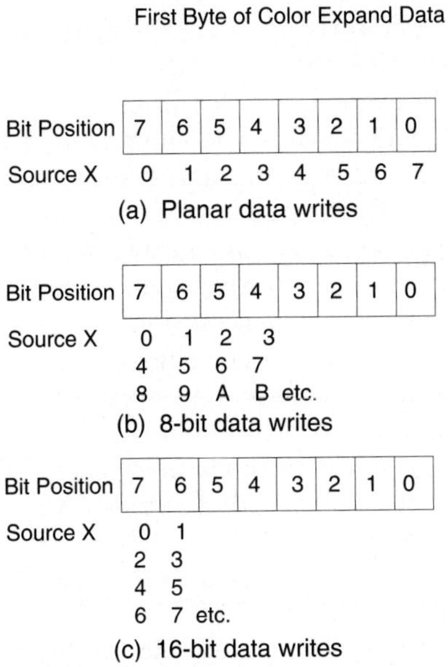

First Byte of Color Expand Data
Bit Position 7 6 5 4 3 2 1 0
Source X 0 1 2 3 4 5 6 7
(a) Planar data writes
Bit Position 7 6 5 4 3 2 1 0
Source X 0 1 2 3
4 5 6 7
8 9 A B etc.
(b) 8-bit data writes
Bit Position 7 6 5 4 3 2 1 0
Source X 0 1
2 3
4 5
6 7 etc.
(c) 16-bit data writes

FIGURE 29.23 Packed Mode Wrap Around (a) Planar (b) Packed 8-bit wrap around (c) Packed 16-bit-per-pixel wrap around.

29.9.18 Line Strip

Lines can be thought of as sequences of horizontal line segments. The length of each line determines the slope of the line. Drawing these horizontal lines in quick sequence can create lines of arbitrary slope, where each pixel of the line can be controlled. Bresenham lines, on the other hand, do not provide a pixel-by-pixel control. Often, filling closed shapes requires accurate control of which pixels are drawn on a line.

The hardware is designed to anticipate the needs of the line-strip drawing. For example, after a strip is drawn, the X and Y directions can be left alone,

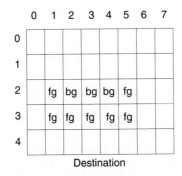

0 1 2 3 4 5 6 7
0
1
2 fg bg bg bg fg
3 fg fg fg fg fg
4
Destination

FIGURE 29.24 Color Expanded Host Transfer

incremented or decremented in anticipation of the next line segment. The hardware actually initiates the write operation when the Dimension X is written into, thereby eliminating the extra step of loading a control register. Therefore, all other registers must be loaded before the Dimension X Register.

Line strips provide flexibility in selecting the pixel to be drawn in a line. The hardware draws one strip with the length specified in Dimension X. At the end of the strip, if the X Direction Bit is set to 0, the hardware increments Destination X by 1. If the Direction bit is set to 1, the hardware decrements Destination 1.

The same operation can be done to Destination Y depending on the Y Direction Bit. The preceding operations are then repeated as specified in the Dimension Y. Following the last desired operation, Control Register 1, bits 11–9 must be set to 0 indicating no operation. This ensures that subsequent writes to Dimension X will not start a drawing mode operation. These steps are illustrated in an Example 29.4 and its associated Figure 29.25.

Example 29.4 Draw a line using the Line-Segment technique from (5,3) to (20,8)

Control Register 1 with 410h to force fixed color and Line Strip
Destination X = 5
Destination Y = 3
Dimension Y = 1 (2 pixels)
Dimension X = 2 (3 pixels)
Dimension Y = 0 (1 pixel)
Dimension X = 1 (2 pixels)
Dimension Y = 1 (2 pixels)
Dimension X = 2 (3 pixels)
Dimension Y = 0 (1 pixel)
Dimension X = 1 (2 pixels)
Control Register 1 with 010h to force fixed color and No Operation

29.9.19 Trapezoid Fill Strip

The trapezoid fill strip drawing mode is supported to quickly fill arbitrary shaped objects. This operation is similar to Line Strips except that the Trapezoid Fill Strip does not use Dimension Y as a count number and does horizontal strips only. Like the line strip, an NOP has to be loaded into the Control Register 1 so that the trapezoid fill operations are terminated.

The procedure in Example 29.5 will fill an area as seen in Figure 29.26.

Example 29.5 Using Trapezoid Fill Strips

Control Register 1 with 610h to force fixed color and Line Strip
Destination X = 12
Destination Y = 2

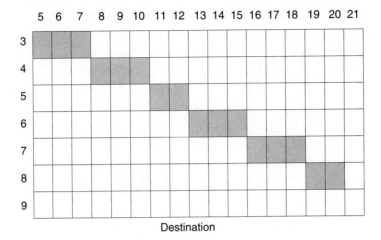

FIGURE 29.25 Line Strip Example

Dimension X = 4 (5 pixels)
Destination X = 14
Dimension X = 4 (5 pixels)
Destination X = 16
Dimension X = 3 (4 pixels)
Destination X = 16
Dimension X = 3 (4 pixels)
Destination X = 15
Dimension X = 3 (4 pixels)
Destination X = 13
Dimension X = 14 (15 pixels)
Destination X = 12
Dimension X = 11 (12 pixels)
Control Register 1 with 010h to force fixed color and No Operation

During trapezoid fill strip writes, if the command buffer is disabled, the writes to Destination X and Dimension X must wait until the drawing engine is not busy. If the command buffer is enabled, the buffer should be checked to ensure that enough locations are available.

The result of these operations is shown in Figure 29.26.

29.9.20 Bresenham Line

The Bresenham line draw requires the standard Bresenham constants and error terms as follows:

Destination X = xs
Destination Y = ys
Dimension X = xmax

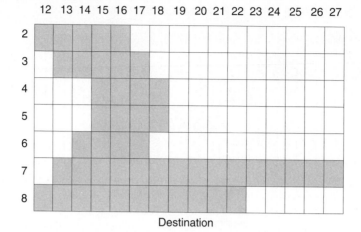

FIGURE 29.26 Trapezoid Fill Strip Example

K1 = 2 * min
K2 = 2 * (min – max)
ET = (2 * min) – max – 1 if (xs>xe)
ET = (2 * min) – max if (xs<=xe)
xs = X coordinate of the starting point
ys = Y coordinate of the starting point
xe = X coordinate of the ending point
ye = Y coordinate of the ending point
delta x = abs(xs–xe)
delta y = abs(ys–ye)
min = min (delta_x,delta_y)
max = max (delta_x,delta_y)

29.10   ACCESSING THE EXTENDED REGISTERS

All of the enhanced features of the 90C33 are controlled by the extended registers using indexed register block. Each indexed register block can contain up to sixteen 12-bit indexed registers. The 4-bit register index is written at the same time as the data in the upper four bits of the word.

29.10.1   Selecting a Register Block

To access one or more indexed registers within any register block, the desired register block must first be selected. A register block is selected by loading its address into the Register Block Pointer field (bits 7–0) of the Index Control Register at 23C0h.

29.10.2 Writing to a Register

To write to one or more indexed registers within any register block, the desired register block must first be selected. A register block is selected by loading its address into the Register Block Pointer field (bits 7–0) of the Index Control Register at 23C0h. A 16-bit word (4 bits of index and 12 bits of data) is then written to the register access port.

29.10.3 Reading from a Register

To read from one or more indexed registers within any register block, the desired register block must first be selected. A register block is selected by loading its address into the Register Block Pointer field (bits 7–0) of the Index Control Register at 23C0h . A 4-bit index is then written to the Register Index field (bits 11–8) of the Index Control Register. Thus, both the index of the desired register to read and the desired register block are written during the same write. This causes the selected register block to appear at the register access port located at 23C2. A 16-bit word is then read from the register access port. Remember, the index is still in the upper four bits of the selected word.

29.10.4 Auto-Increment

If the Auto-Increment Disable bit in the Index Control Register is reset (causing Auto-Increment), consecutive read or writes to or from the register access port will return consecutively indexed registers within the same register block in ascending order.

29.10.5 Direct I/O Ports

The relevant direct I/O port addressing registers are shown in Table 29.42. The Index Control Register is shown in Table 29.43.

TABLE 29.42 Direct I/O Port Addressing

I/O Port	Bits	Name
23C0	—	Index Control
23C2	15–0	Register Access Port
23C4	15–0	Host BitBlt Transfer Port 0
23C6	15–0	Host BitBlt Transfer Port 1
23C8	13–0	K1 Bresenham Constant 1
23CA	13–0	K2 Bresenham Constant 2
23CC	13–0	ET Line Draw Error Term
23CE	10–0	Command Buffer and Interrupt

TABLE 29.43 Index Control Register

Bits	Function
13	Invalid Register Block (READ ONLY)
12	Auto Increment Disable
11–8	Register Index
7–0	Register Block Pointer

The Invalid Register Block bit returns a 1 if the currently addressed register block does not exist. It returns a 0 if it does exist.

29.10.6 Register Blocks

The Register Block Numbers are provided in Table 29.44.

29.10.7 Command Buffer

The command buffer is located at I/O Port Register 23CEh. It is a FIFO buffer that can hold up to eight drawing engine (DE) register writes. When the DE is busy, the command buffer allows the host to continue sending commands instead of waiting until the drawing engine is finished. When the DE completes an operation, the contents of the command buffer are loaded into the drawing engine until the command buffer is empty or until another command begins. The hardware cursor and Standard VGA writes do **not** go through the command buffer.

29.10.8 Command Buffer Operation

The command buffer is enabled by setting I/O Port Register 23CEh bit 5 to a 1. The software should check the Command Buffer Locations Available bits before writing additional commands. The command buffer is described in Table 29.45.

TABLE 29.44 Register Block Numbers

Number	Register Block
0	System Control
1	Drawing Engine
2	Hardware Cursor
3	Drawing Engine

TABLE 29.45 Command Buffer and Interrupt Control Register

Bit	Function
10	Vertical Retrace Status (1=interupt pending)
9	DE Not Busy Interrupt Status (1=interupt pending)
8	DE Not Busy Interrupt Clear (1=arm for next DE not busy interrupt)
7	DE Busy (1=Operation in progress)
6	Command Buffer Overflow (1=overflow occurred since last enable)
5	Command Buffer Enable (1=Command Buffer Enabled)
3–0	Command Buffer Locations

If the command buffer is written to when it is full, the information usually is not stored and the Overflow bit, Bit 6 is set to 1. This bit can be read to determine the command buffer status. It is cleared by disabling the Command Buffer (bit 5=0).

The meaning of the Command Buffer Locations field is provided in Table 29.46.

When the command buffer is disabled, the Locations Available bits follow the drawing engine busy and can be polled to determine if a write operation can be performed. If the buffered registers are written to, the locations available status indicates empty=0 until the drawing engine operation starts. The status then changes to a full = 8. When the drawing engine finishes its operation, the command buffer locations available status returns to empty and another write operation can be performed. A program is provided in Listing 29.13.

TABLE 29.46 Command Buffer Locations

Value	Meaning
0	Empty 8 locations available
1	7 locations available
2	6 locations available
3	5 locations available
4	4 locations available
5	3 locations available
6	2 locations available
7	1 location available
8	Full NO locations available

LISTING 29.13 Command Buffer Initialization

```
;Input parameters
        count    ;number of FIFO locations required

CommandBufferReady proc far count:BYTE
        mov    cl,count
        and    cl,0fh        ; only can require 1-8
        xor    cl,0fh        ;invert it for value
        and    cl,07         ;save for later
        out    23CEh,0020h   ;enable command buffer

;       poll for command using three writes
try:    in     ax,23CEh      ;input the Register Access Port
        and    ax,000Fh      ;only want bits 3-0
        cmp    ax,5          ;check for 3 available locations
        jg     try           ;wait til three are ready

        ret
CommandBufferReady endp
```

Chapter 30

Weitek

30.1   THE WEITEK GRAPHICS CONTROLLERS

Weitek has introduced several graphics processors including the W5186, W5286, the Power 9000 (P9000), the P9001, and the P9100. The W5186 and W5286 are Super VGA controllers. The Power 9000 and Power 9001 are graphics accelerators and are typically configured with either the W5186 or the W5286. The P9100 is an enhanced graphics accelerator with an internal W5286 Super VGA controller.

30.1.1   The 5186

The 5186 is a VGA-compatible graphic controller capable of controlling DRAM or VRAM. It includes a "no-nonsense" graphics accelerator. It has resolutions up to 1024 by 768 in 4- and 8-bit-per-color mode, and 800 by 600 in hi-color modes. It includes a hardware BitBlt function and hardware line draws.

30.1.2   The 5286

The 5286 is a VGA-compatible graphic controller capable of controlling DRAM. It includes resolutions up to 1280 by 1024 in 4-bit-per-color mode, 1024 by 768 in 8-bit-per-color mode, 800 by 600 in hi-color mode, and 640 by 480 in true-color mode. Its graphics accelerator includes a hardware BitBlt function, hardware line draws, pattern fills, and color expansion. The 5286 hardware is found in the P9100 chip.

Due to the similarities between the 5186 and 5286, they are referred to as the 5186/5286 unless otherwise noted.

30.1.3 The Power 9000

Weitek's first generation high-powered graphics engine is the P9000. It includes powerful graphics primitives including line drawing, polygon drawing with pattern fill, BitBlts from screen-to-screen or host-to-screen, color expansion, plane masking, clipping, polylines, and a variety of raster operations. It is a single chip VRAM controller using a 32-bit host interface and supporting resolutions up to 1600 by 1200 in 8-bit-per-pixel mode, 1024 by 768 in high-bits-per-pixel mode, and 800 by 600 in true-color modes.

The P9000 is a register-based hard-wired graphics processor. It is memory-mapped into the host address space. The P9000 is not a VGA or Super VGA controller identical to the 5286. Boards that are based on the Weitek P9000 are based on two chips, one being the P9000 and the second being a VGA controller, such as the Weitek W5186 or W5286.

30.1.4 The Power 9001

The Power 9001 is a Power 9000 with a PCI interface.

30.1.5 The Power 9100

The successor to the P9000 is the P9100. It supports resolutions up to 1280 by 1024 in 24-bit true color modes while supporting up to 1600 by 1200 for hi-color modes. It fully accelerates all 8-, 15-, 16- and 32-bit-per-pixel operations. It draws lines and polygons with optional pattern fills and supports all of the features of the P9000. It also supports both the VL and the PCI bus. One important feature of the P9100 is that it contains an on-chip Super VGA controller. In addition, it supports a four-color pattern RAM that can be used to perform a four-color dither at full speed. The dither pattern is reduced to 8-by-8 from the 16-by-16 pattern in the P9000. In order to support the VGA portion, the aperture memory mapping can be mapped into a 64 Kbyte aperture in addition to its usual 4 Mbyte linear mapping. It supports the full 256 raster ops as described by Microsoft and performs text transparency.

The Power 9100 builds upon the P9000. The major differences are provided at the end of this chapter. Otherwise, the P9000 and P9100 are referred to as the 9000/9100.

30.2 DISPLAY MODES

The Weitek chips typically support the non-standard display modes shown in Table 30.1.The graphics accelerator does not support the 4-bit-per-color planar modes. Some implementations using the Weitek chips may support 4-bit-per-color planar modes.

TABLE 30.1   Display Modes

Mode	Resolution	Bits / Colors
101	640 by 480	8
111	640 by 480	16
103	800 by 600	8
114	800 by 600	16
105	1024 by 768	8
117	1024 by 768	16
107	1280 by 1024	8
112	640 by 480	24
115	800 by 600	24

30.3   THE 5186/5286 EXTENDED REGISTERS

The 5186/5286 extended registers are provided in Table 30.2

TABLE 30.2   The 5186/5286 Extended Registers

Port	Index	Lock	Name
3C5	5	W	Control Reg 0
3C5	6	W	Control Reg 1
3C5	7		Revision
3C5 R	10	R	User Bits
3C5 W	10	W	I/O Base
3C5	11	R/W	Miscellaneous
3C5	12	R/W	Output Control
3C5	13	R/W	Memory Base
3D5	19		Interlace
3D5	1A		Serial Start Address High
3D5	1B		Serial Start Address Low
3D5	1C		Serial Offset
3D5	1D		Total Characters per line
3CF	09		GHA Queue Base Address
3CF	A		GHA Queue Tail Pointer
3CF	B		QHA Execution Pointer
3CF	C	W	Extended Graphics
3C0/3C1	15		Overscan Color High
3CD	—		Bank Select

30.3.1 Unlocking Extended Registers

The technique used to unlock and lock protected registers is provided in Listing 30.1a and Listing 30.1b respectively. The process of unlocking is described in Table 30.3. Locking is described in Table 30.4.

LISTING 30.1a Unlocking the 5186/5286 Registers

```
Unlock5186/5286 macro
        mov    dx,3c5h
        mov    al,11    ;access the Misc. Reg
        out    dx,al
        in     al,dx    ;read the Misc Reg (Step 1)
        out    dx,al
        out    dx,al    ;write it out twice (Step 2)
        in     al,dx    ;read the Misc Reg again (Step 3)

        and    al,0dfh  ;zero bit 5 (Step 4)
        out    dx,al    ;write modified value back (Step 5)
endm
```

LISTING 30.1b Locking the 5186/5286 Registers

```
        mov    dx,3c5h
        mov    al,11    ;access the Misc Reg
        out    dx,al
        in     al,dx    ;read the Misc Reg (Step 1)
        or     al,20h   ;set bit 5 (Step 2)
        out    dx,al    ;write modified value back (Step 3)
endm
```

TABLE 30.3 Directions to Unlock all Locked Registers

1. Read the Miscellaneous Register.
2. Write this value back to the Miscellaneous Register twice.
3. Read the Miscellaneous Register.
4. Clear bit 5 to unlock the 5186/5286 extended registers.
5. Write this value back to the Miscellaneous Register.

TABLE 30.4 Directions to Lock all Lockable Registers

1. Read the Miscellaneous Register.
2. Set bit 5 to 1 to lock the 5186/5286 extended registers.
3. Write this value back to the Miscellaneous Register.

30.4 MEMORY CONTROL

The Memory Base Address Register defines the 1 Mbyte section of the address space where the display memory is located. This register is accessed through 3C5 index 13.

The Bank Select Register contains two fields as shown in Table 30.5 used for read and write banking.

30.4.1 Read Bank Selection

When the host address maps only the "A" segment to the display memory A0000–AFFFFh, and if bank switching is enabled, these four bits provide the most significant four bits of the 20-bit display memory address during read operations, bits 19–16. When 128 Kbyte banking is enabled, this register contains the segment for all access to the A0000–AFFFFh space. Note that 128 Kbyte organizations are not recommended.

30.4.2 Write Bank Selection

When the host address maps only the "A" segment to the display memory A0000–AFFFFh, and if bank switching is enabled, these four bits provide the most significant four bits of the 20-bit display memory address during write operations, bits 19–16. When 128 Kbyte banking is enabled, this register contains the segment for all access to the B0000–BFFFFh space. Note that 128 Kbyte organizations are not recommended.

Code that provides bank switching is provided in Listing 30.2.

LISTING 30.2a Setting the Write Bank of the 5186/5286

```
; Input Parameters
;       bl     bank number (0-15)

SetWriteBank5186/5286    macro    bank
          mov    dx,3CDh        ;Bank Select Register
          in     al,dx          ;get the value
          and    al,0f0h        ;zero bits (3-0)

          or     al,bl          ;add in the desired bank
          out    dx,al
endm
```

TABLE 30.5 Write Bank Select Register

Bit	Function
7–4	Read Bank/Bank 0 [0–3]
3–0	Write Bank/Bank 1 [0–3]

LISTING 30.2b Setting the Read Bank of the 5186/5286

```
; Input Parameters
;        bl     bank number (0-15)

SetReadBank5186/5286     macro     bank
        shl     bl,1
        shl     bl,1
        shl     bl,1
        shl     bl,1             ;put bank into bits 7-4
        and     bl,f0h           ;zero bits 3-0
        mov     dx,3CDh          ;Bank Select Register
        in      al,dx            ;get the value
        and     al,0fh           ;zero bits (7-4)

        or      al,bl            ;add in the desired bank
        out     dx,al
endm
```

30.5   THE EXTENDED SEQUENCER REGISTERS

30.5.1   The Sequencer Index Register

The Sequencer Index Register is important in that it contains some non-VGA standard bits as shown in Table 30.6. It is located at 3C4 and indexes registers into the 3C5 port as it is in the standard VGA.

The additional registers in the Sequencer group are listed in Table 30.7. Note that several are locked and can be unlocked through the code in Listing 30.1.

It is necessary to set bit 3 in order to reach the additional registers in the general register group, provided in Table 30.8. This provides 5086 downward compatibility. These registers can be accessed as indexed I/O registers by the 5186 only without unlocking this bit 3.

30.5.2   Control Reg 0 and 1

The relevant fields of the Control Register 0 Register are provided in Table 30.9. The Control Register 1 fields are provided in Table 30.10.

TABLE 30.6 Sequencer Index Register

Bits	Function
2–0	Standard index bits
3	Addition registers enable only on 5186
4	Index high bit

TABLE 30.7 Sequencer Additional Registers

Port	Bit 4	Bit 2–0	Lock	Name
3C5	0	5	W	Control Reg 0
3C5	0	6	W	Control Reg 1
3C5	0	7		Revision
3C5 R	1	0	R	User Bits
3C5 W	1	0	W	I/O Base
3C5	1	1	R/W	Miscellaneous
3C5	1	2	R/W	Output Control
3C5	1	3	R/W	Memory Base

TABLE 30.8 Additional Registers Unlocked by Bit 3 5186

Port	R/W	Name
300	R	BIOS ROM Status
300	W	I/O Base Address
301	R	User Bits
30A	R/W	Shadow ROM
320	R/W	Memory Base Address
32A	R/W	Output Control

TABLE 30.9 Control Reg 0

Bits	Name	Meaning
7	DVSAE	Dual Video Start Address/Offset Enable; see Section 30.6.1
6	BO	Bit Order 0=bit 7 displayed first (VGA)
2	SRS17	Bit 16 of the start address

TABLE 30.10 Control Reg 1

Bits	Name	Meaning
6	GHAE	Graphics Accelerator Enable; 1=enable, 0=halt
3	BSE	Special Text Attributes

The DVSAE field, if set to 1, enables the 17-bit serial start address registers as a second start address. The Serial Start Address is a 17-bit field located in bit 2 of this register and in the Serial Start Address Low and Serial Start Address High Registers.

The code in Listing 30.3 sets the serial start address.

LISTING 30.3 Set the Serial Start Address

```
; Input Parameters:
        top     bit 16 of the start address in bit position 0
        bottom  bits 15-0 of start address
        offset  offset of second display memory *4

setSerialStart  proc    far     top:BYTE,bottom,offset:BYTE
;    first lets enable the serial start address set of registers
        mov     dx,3c4h
        mov     al,5    ;access Control Register 0
        out     dx,al
        inc     dx

        in      al,dx   ;get the value
        or      al,80h  ;set bit 7 to enable dual start address
        and     al,0FBh ;zero bit 2 in the old word for bit 16

;       now lets set the serial start address bit 17
        mov     bl,top  ;get top in bit position 0
        shr     bl,1
        shr     bl,1    ;put top into bit position 2
        and     bl,40h  ;only want bit 2

        or      al,bl   ;put in bit 2
        out     dx,al   ;load Control Register 0
        dec     dx

;       now load the lower 16 bits
        mov     al,1bh  ;index start address low
        out     dx,al
        inc     dx

        mov     ax,bottom ;get bottom 16-bits
        out     dx,al     ;output lower

        dec     dx
        mov     al,1ah      ;index start address high
        out     dx,al
        inc     dx
```

```
        mov     ax,bottom   ;get bottom 16-bits
        mov     al,ah       ;put upper 8-bits of bottom
        out     dx,al       ;output upper
        dec     dx

;       now set up offset
        mov     al,1ch      ;index start address low
        out     dx,al
        inc     dx

        mov     al,offset   ;get offset
        out     dx,al       ;output offset
        ret
setSerialStart  endp
```

The GHAE field is the bit used to start or stop the Graphics Accelerator.

The BSE field is used to enable the special attributes. The attribute bytes is defined according to Table 30.11.

30.5.3 The Revision Register

The Revision Register is a read/write register that provides the device identification and revision level of the 5x86. It is described in Table 30.12. The 5186/5286 is identified by a 1 in the Device ID field. The 5286 is identified by a 2 in the Device ID field.

30.5.4 User Bits Register

The User Bits Register is a write-only register located at index 10h. It can be used identify the 5186/5286. Bits 7–4 always return a 9h. Bits 3–0 are defined by the board manufacturer and may contain useful information about the

TABLE 30.11 Special Attributes

Bit	Attribute
0	Color 0 (Half bright in monochrome)
1	Underline
2	Reverse Video
3	Blinking
4	Bold
5	Struck Through
6	Color 1
7	Color 2

TABLE 30.12 The Revision Register

Bits	Name	Function
7-5	DID	Device ID; 1=5186/5286, 2=5286
2-0	RL	Revision Level

monitor or memory. A function to identify if the chip is a Weitek is provided in Listing 30.4. A function that distinguishes between the Weitek products is shown in Listing 30.5.

LISTING 30.4 Is the Chip a Weitek

```
/* Output Parameters
        returns a 1 if the chip is a Weitek   0 otherwise
 Calling Protocol
        retval = isChipWeitek();   */

int isChipWeitek(void)
{  unsigned char value;

        outp(0x3c4,10h);
        value = inp(0x3c5) & 0xf0;    // get User Bits Register
                                      // bits (7-4)

        if(value != 0xA0) return(0);  // not a Weitek bits 7-4
                                      // should return a 1001

        return(1);
}
```

LISTING 30.5 Which Weitek Chip Is Present

```
/* Output Parameters:
        returns the value of the Weitek chip
                -1 = none  1=5186/5286  2=5286
  Calling Protocol:
retval =  WhichWeitek();  */

int WhichWeitek()
{  int retval=-1;  unsigned char retval;

 outp(0x3c4,7);  // index Revision Register
 value = inp(0x3c5) & 0xe0;  // get Revision Register bits (7-5)
```

```
switch(value) {
  case 0x20:  retval=1;   // 5186/5286
  case 0x40:  retval=2;   // 5286
  }
return(retval);
}
```

30.5.5 I/O Base Register

The I/O Base Address Register is a write-only register located at 3C5 index 10. It defines the most significant eight bits of the I/O register addresses. This register is accessed through location 3C5 index 10h. The default value of this register is 3 mapping the I/O register to 3xxh.

30.5.6 Miscellaneous Register

The Miscellaneous Register is shown in Table 30.13. It contains a Bank Switching Enable field and a Register Lock field. The Bank Switching enable field, if 1, allows the bank switching described in Section 30.4 to be enabled. It defaults to 1. The Register Lock field is described in Section 30.3.1.

30.5.7 Memory Base Address Register

The Memory Base Address Field, MBA, resides in bits 3–0 and provides the most significant four bits of the 24-bit AT bus address of the display. They define in which 1 Mbyte section of the address space the display memory is located. It defaults to 0.

30.6 EXTENDED CRT CONTROLLER REGISTERS

30.6.1 Serial Start Address

The Serial Start Address High Register, at 3D5 Index 1A, and the Serial Start Address Low Register, at 3D5 Index 1B provide the lower sixteen bits of the start address. These registers are engaged by setting bit 7, the DVSAE field of the Control Register 0 described in Section 30.5.2. It is used when there is

TABLE 30.13 Miscellaneous Register

Bit	Name	Function
6	BSE	Bank Switching Enable
5	CRL	Control Register Lock

sufficient VRAM to store two simultaneous frame buffers. One of the two frame buffers uses the standard start address registers. The second uses the serial start address and serial video offset registers. Thus, text and graphics can be overlapped in 8-bit planar graphics modes.

30.6.2 Serial Offset

The Serial Offset Register provides an 8-bit offset for the second frame buffer (see Section 30.6.1 and Section 30.5.2 for a description of the second frame buffer). The actual number of bytes per scan line is two or four times this amount depending on the clocking.

30.6.3 Total Characters Per Line

This register contains the total number of characters per line for the second frame buffer (see Section 30.6.1 and Section 30.5.2 for a description of the second frame buffer).

30.7 EXTENDED GRAPHICS CONTROLLER REGISTER

The graphics registers include the Queue Base, Tail, and Execution Pointer Registers. They are used to process GHA instructions.

30.7.1 Graphics Index Register

Hiding in the Graphics Index Register is a bit 7 used as a Graphics Engine Busy field. When read, if this bit is set to a 1, it indicates that the graphics engine is busy. If 0, the graphics engine is ready.

30.7.2 The Instruction Queue

A 4 Kbyte address space is reserved for the GHA queue. The queue must start on a 1 Kbyte address boundary. The host sends instructions to the GHA via a 4 Kbyte instruction queue that resides in off-screen frame buffer memory. Each instruction occupies sixteen bytes, so up to 256 instructions can be queued. Each instruction is a four-word instruction where each word is 32 bits wide.

30.7.3 Queue Base Address

This register specifies the 8-bit (0–255) pointer into the queue and points to the base of the 256 instructions.

30.7.4 Queue Tail Address

This register specifies the 8-bit (0–255) pointer into the queue and points to the tail of the 256 instructions.

30.7.5   Instruction Pointer

This register specifies the 8-bit (0–255) pointer into the queue and points to the current one of 256 instructions is being executed. When the GHA finishes an instruction, it increments the execution pointer and compares it to the queue tail pointer. If the two are equal, no more instructions are in the queue and the GHA halts and waits for a new instruction. Since the GHA executes synchronously from the host, it is possible that the GHA is updating the pointer simultaneously with the host reading it, giving the host an incorrect result. To ensure correct results, the host should read the pointer multiple times until two consecutive reads return the same value.

30.7.6   The GHA Bit Mask 5286 Only

The GHA Bit Mask Register inhibits writes to selected bits within each byte of memory in packed pixel modes. Each bit in this byte register represents one plane. A 1 in a bit position indicates that the respective plane is enabled for writes. It is located at index GRA 0D.

30.7.7   BCOLORL and BCOLORH Registers 5286 Only

These two registers, BCOLORL and BCOLORH, hold the 16-bit (low and high byte respectively), background color used for color expansions. These are found at index GRA 0Eh and GRA 0Fh respectively.

30.8   THE GRAPHICS ACCELERATOR INSTRUCTION SET

The instructions to the graphics accelerator are provided in Table 30.14.

30.8.1   BitBlts

The SBLT and LBLT instructions combine data from the source with the destination and place the result in the destination. The GHA performs raster operations as designated by the LOP bits. The BitBlt instructions require reading a byte from both the source and destination areas, and writing the resultant byte back to the destination. The LBLT instruction is used when two source bytes are required prior to writing one destination byte. A BitBlt is illustrated in Figure 30.1.

30.8.2   Screen Moves

Screen moves are variations of the BitBlt instructions. They are optimized for use when reading from destination memory can be avoided. The SMOV and LMOV instructions move data into a destination area. Raster ops that require data from the destination area are **not supported**. Screen move instructions can be used to fill, save, and restore video data. Only the first and last byte of

TABLE 30.14 GHA Instruction

Instruction	OpCode	Function	See Section
SBLT	0	Short BitBlt	30.8.1
LBLT	1	Long BitBlt	30.8.1
SMOV	2	Short Screen Move	30.8.2
LMOV	3	Long Screen Move	30.8.2
FLINE	4	Flat Line Draw	30.8.3
SLINE	5	Steep Line Draw	30.8.3
BLKMOV	6	Block Move	30.8.4

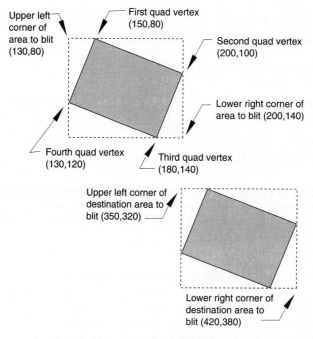

FIGURE 30.1 BitBlts

the destination memory are fetched for use with the START MASK and the
END MASK. The LMOV is necessary when the GHA has to read two source
bytes before being able to write the first destination bytes.

30.8.3 Line Draws

The SLINE and FLINE instructions draw a 1-pixel wide line in video memory.
The START MASK must have one and only one bit set to indicate the position
of the first pixel in the line. The END MASK must have all bits, up to and

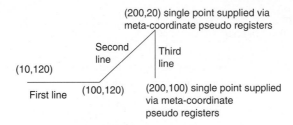

FIGURE 30.2 Polyline Draw

including the last pixel in the line, set. Set the ROTATE CNT to 1 for drawing lines left-to-right or to 7 for drawing lines right-to-left. Set the DIR bit to 0 for drawing lines top-to-bottom, or to a 1 for drawing lines bottom-to-top. Set the VERT TOTAL field to the number of bytes needed to draw the line. A flat line is defined as a line with a slope between −1 and 1. A steep line has a slope less than −1 or greater than 1. A polyline draw is illustrated in Figure 30.2.

30.8.4   Block Moves

Large contiguous blocks of data within the video memory can be moved using the BLKMOV instruction. The pitch values are normally set to the width of the VRAM registers.

30.9   A GRAPHICS ACCELERATOR INSTRUCTION FORMAT

Each GHA instruction specifies all parameters necessary for the instruction such as the source and destination addresses, inclusion masks for bordering pixels, and the color planes. Each instruction is sixteen bytes of data as shown in Figure 30.3.

30.9.1   Instruction Parameters

The instruction parameters, as shown in Figure 30.1 are listed in Table 30.15.

30.9.2   Instruction Handling

Once a GHA instruction is built, it must be placed in the instruction queue. This is done by writing four bytes to each of the four color planes at the position in the queue pointed to by the GHAPUT Register. The execution sequence of each GHA instruction is shown in Table 30.16.

30.10   THE P9000/9100

The three important aspects of the P9000/9100 to programmers are the parameter engine, drawing engine, and host interface. Graphics operations flow through the parameter engine and then through the stages of the drawing engine.

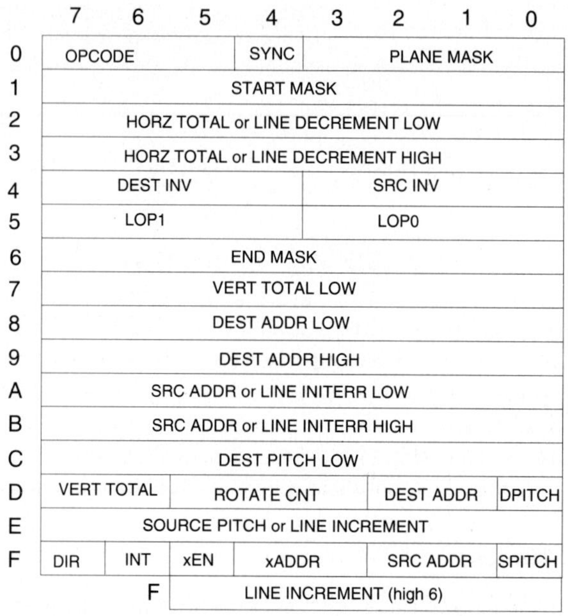

	7	6	5	4	3	2	1	0
0	OPCODE			SYNC	PLANE MASK			
1	START MASK							
2	HORZ TOTAL or LINE DECREMENT LOW							
3	HORZ TOTAL or LINE DECREMENT HIGH							
4	DEST INV				SRC INV			
5	LOP1				LOP0			
6	END MASK							
7	VERT TOTAL LOW							
8	DEST ADDR LOW							
9	DEST ADDR HIGH							
A	SRC ADDR or LINE INITERR LOW							
B	SRC ADDR or LINE INITERR HIGH							
C	DEST PITCH LOW							
D	VERT TOTAL		ROTATE CNT			DEST ADDR		DPITCH
E	SOURCE PITCH or LINE INCREMENT							
F	DIR	INT	xEN	xADDR		SRC ADDR		SPITCH
F		LINE INCREMENT (high 6)						

FIGURE 30.3 Graphics Accelerator Instruction Format

TABLE 30.15 Instruction Parameters

Parameter	Description
OPCODE	Instruction Opcode 0=SBLT 1=LBLT 2=SMOV 3=LMOV 4=SLINE 5=FLINE 6=BLKMOV 7=NOP
SYNC	Sync instruction with video raster. Setting this bit to a 1 causes the GHA to delay execution of the instruction until the next vertical retrace.
PLANE MASK	Color plane inclusion mask. Setting the mask bits enables writing to the corresponding color planes (0–3) for the current instruction. Data in planes that are 0 are write protected.
START MASK	Start byte inclusion mask. Setting the bits in this field enables writing to the corresponding bits of the first byte of each horizontal line processed. Bits for which the corresponding bits are 0 are write-protected.
HORZ TOTAL	Horizontal width of the operation area. This unsigned field defines the width (in bytes) of the area to be processed by this instruction. This does not include the last byte. To process five bytes, specify four in this field. One additional byte will be processed using the ENDMASK field. If only one byte is to be processed set this field to 1, the START MASK field to all 1's and the END MASK bits to 0.

TABLE 30.15 *(cont.)*

Parameter	Description
ROTATE MASK	Rotate inclusion Mask. Setting the bits in this field designates which bits will be retained from the previously processed bytes. When set, the corresponding bit form the source byte will be retained and used for merging with the next source byte. Use of this field may require a long instruction.
DEST INV	Destination inversion mask. Setting these bits causes the corresponding destination bits to be inverted prior to the operation specified by the LOP operator.
SOURCE INV	Source inversion mask. Setting these bits cause the corresponding source bits to be inverted prior to the operation specified by the LOP operator.
LOP1-,LOP0	Color plane logical operations. Setting the LOP bits specifies the logical operation to be performed between the source and destination data after possible inversion as specified by the DEST INV and SOURCE INV fields. Each bit in each LOP field corresponds to a plane. The lsb corresponds to plane 0. The combination of bit settings determines the logical operation for the corresponding plane. The logical operations are

	LOP1	*LOP0*	*Operation*
	0	0	Store
	0	1	AND
	1	0	OR
	1	1	XOR

Parameter	Description
END MASK	End byte inclusion mask. Setting the bits in this field enables writing to the corresponding bits of the last byte of each horizontal line processed. The remaining bits are write-protected and therefore unaffected by this instruction.
VERT TOTAL	Vertical height of the operation area. This field specifies the height of the operation area (in raster lines) or the length of the line being drawn (in bytes).
DEST ADDR	Destination address specifies the byte offset from the first byte of video memory to the first byte of the destination area for each plane.
SOURCE ADDR	Source address specifies the byte offset from the first byte of video memory to the first byte of the source area for each plane.
DPITCH	Destination pitch specifies the number of bytes from the beginning of one destination line to the beginning of the next destination line. This is a 9-bit two's complement value. The value is negative if the direction (DIR) is negative, or positive if the direction is positive.

(continued)

TABLE 30.15 *(cont.)*

Parameter	Description
SPITCH	Source pitch specifies the number of bytes from the beginning of one source line to the beginning of the next source line. This is a 9-bit two's complement value. The value is negative if the direction (DIR) is negative, or positive if the direction is positive.
ROTATE CNT	Rotate count specifies how many bits to right-shift the current byte before writing it to the destination. It is used with the rotate MASK for determining what bits are used from the preceding source byte.
DIR	Direction flag. Setting the bits in this field causes the GHA to process the operation address in reverse. If the DIR bit is set, the GHA processes the source and destination bytes from right-to-left and bottom-to-top.
INT	Interrupt disable. Setting this bit prevents the GHA from signaling an interrupt upon the completion of the current instruction.
xEN	Expand enable. Setting this bit enables the expand function to copy a single source plane to the other color planes.
xADDR	Expansion source. When expand is enabled, the source plane is written to the other color planes. This value in this field specifies the source plane (0–3).
LINE DECREMENT	Used for line draw instructions. Specifies the amount to subtract from the DDA error term when moving parallel to the minor axis.
LINE INITERR	Used for line draw instructions. The initial value for the DDA error term.
LINE INCREMENT	Used for line draw instructions. The amount to add from the DDA error term when moving parallel to the major axis.

30.10.1 Parameter Engine

The parameter engine prepares the drawing engine for its operation. Its basic function is to take the input coordinates from the host and convert them to a form usable by the drawing engine. The parameter engine performs its own tests regarding clipping and screen boundaries and scissoring. It prepares four kinds of polygons for drawing, quadrilaterals, triangles, lines, and points. It converts points, lines, and triangles into quadrilaterals by automatically replicating vertices. A point is a quadrilateral with all four vertices at the same X,Y location. The host passes one point coordinate pair to the parameter engine

TABLE 30.16 Execution Sequence for Each GHA Instruction

Step	Function
1	Read the next GHA instruction designated by the GHABASE and GHATAKE Registers.
2	Increment the GHATAKE Register.
3	Read the next source byte, beginning with SOURCE ADDR.
4	(For the first time on a new scan line and for long instructions only) Read a second source byte.
5	Read the next destination byte (if necessary), beginning with DEST ADDR.
6	Rotate the source data by ROTATE CNT.
7	Select the data using ROTATE MASK.
8	Combine the rotated source data with the destination data via the LOP function.
9	Write the result byte. Use START MASK or END MASK if the byte is first or last on the line.
10	Repeat steps 3 through 9 until the last byte of the line is processed.
11	Add SPITCH to the source and DPITCH to the destination.
12	Repeat the entire process VERT TOTAL times.

that then replicates this point four times and passes it to the graphics engine as a quadrilateral. The parameter engine also handles screen-to-screen and host-to-screen BitBlts.

If the drawing engine is busy or if the request contains illegal parameters, the parameter engine does not pass on the request. Operations such as setting color registers or video timing bypass the parameter engine.

The parameter engine performs clipping calculations on each X,Y vertex. It compares these points against all four edges of the screen and viewing window and against each other. It tests for trivial acceptance or trivial rejection. The parameter engine cannot correct an illegal request. For example, horizontally convex quadrilaterals must be rendered in software. The status register indicates such problems.

30.10.2 Drawing Engine

The drawing engine draws quadrilaterals (quad), performs screen-to-screen BitBlts (blit), and performs host-to-screen BitBlts (pixel1 and pixel8). The quad operation draws quadrilaterals in either the X11 mode that is X-Windows compatible or the Bresenham mode. Triangles, lines, and points can always be rendered correctly, but the drawing engine cannot draw horizontally convex quadrilaterals. This means that it cannot cross from the inside to the outside of an object more than once in a single scan line. A common example is that "bow-ties" cannot be drawn, but "hourglasses" can.

The blit operation copies a rectangular area of the display from one screen location to another. The pixel1 operation takes a monochrome, 1-bit pixel from the host, expands it, and writes it to the frame buffer. Up to 32 pixels can be transferred in a single word. The pixel8 operation takes color data 8-bit pixels and writes them to the frame buffer. Up to four pixels can be transferred per word. Hi-color and true-color modes use the pixel8 operation. The drawing engine accepts one drawing operation at a time from the parameter engine. When processing a drawing operation, it determines which pixels are touched by the drawing process (scan conversion) and then determines the color value of each touched pixel (rasterOp).

Scan Conversion

Two line-drawing engines follow the left and right edges of the quadrilateral on each scan line, and a pixel processing engine fills the region between these edges. The pixel1, pixel8, and BitBlt operations are limited to rectangular areas; the quad operation can have edges at any angles.

Raster Ops

The color of each pixel is determined by the raster op function. This is further conditioned by the contents of other registers.

The drawing engine can remain busy for long periods when drawing large quads or performing a large blit operation. The quad and blit operations are started by a read operation. The read requests that the operation take place and returns the contents of the status register. The Status register indicates whether the request was granted. The graphics engine does not accept a request if it is busy or if an exception has occurred. The software must check the status register that contains both exception and drawing engine status bits and resubmit any quad or blit request that is not accepted. While no new drawing operations can be started until the drawing engine is idle, the host can load the parameter engines coordinate registers with the vertices of the new operation.

30.10.3 Host Interface

The host interface uses the lower 22 bits of the host address bits. The P900 decodes a 4-Mbyte space and uses half of the decoded space, 2 Mbyte, for the direct frame-buffer access. The display looks to the host like a dumb frame buffer. 1 Mbyte of the space is used for non-Power 9000/9100 operations, and the remaining 1 Mbyte is used for P9000/9100 instructions. Both big-endian and little-endian addressing formats are supported. The P9000/9100 commands are specified by the address. This frees the data bus for data transfers, as opposed to instructions.

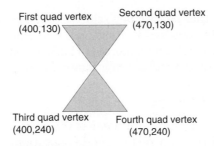

First quad vertex
(400,130)

Second quad vertex
(470,130)

Third quad vertex
(400,240)

Fourth quad vertex
(470,240)

FIGURE 30.4 Hourglass Quadrilateral

30.10.4 Drawing Quadrilaterals

The drawing engine assigns the two edges at either the top-most or bottom-most vertex to its two Bresenham line-drawing engines. These engines do not actually draw anything in the frame buffer. Rather, they transverse the boundaries of the quadrilateral on each scan line. The pixel processing engine then fills in the pixels between the boundaries found by the line-drawing engine. A simple quadrilateral is an hourglass as shown in Figure 30.4. This filling operation is also clipped against the clipping window and screen boundaries. This is shown in Figure 30.5.

The drawing engine draws in X11 mode or in oversized mode. Oversized mode is the common IBM mode; X11 mode is compatible with X-Windows standards. Oversized mode must be selected to draw points and lines since X11 drawing rules do not touch pixels in zero-width objects. In X11 mode, only those pixels that lie within the perimeter of the quad are drawn.

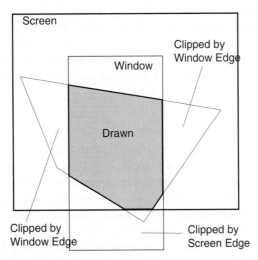

Screen

Window

Clipped by
Window Edge

Drawn

Clipped by
Window Edge

Clipped by
Screen Edge

FIGURE 30.5 Drawing a Quadrilateral Clipped Against the Window and Screen

Coordinates can either be specified relative to the clipping window (absolute) or relative to the previous vertex (relative). Polylines, meshed triangles, and meshed quadrilaterals are all supported. These are drawn by transferring the new vertices and issuing another draw command.

30.10.5 Drawing Bit Maps

The host first sets up the X,Y coordinates of the destination then transfers data to the P9000/9100 with the pixel1 or pixel8 operations. The P9000/9100 draws the pixels on the screen, auto-incrementing the current X,Y location after each pixel. Bit-map drawing proceeds from left-to-right. When it reaches the right-hand edge of the target bit map, the P9000/9100 automatically wraps to the next line.

The pixel8 operation draws multi-colored pixels. Up to four 8-bit pixels are transferred per 32-bit instruction. These are drawn through a single bus trans-fer. The pixel1 operation is used for color expansion. It expands monochrome bit maps into color bit maps. Instead of transferring four 8-bit pixels per opera-tion, it transfers up to 32 1-bit pixels that are expanded to the current color value. Pixel data must be padded out to multiples of four bytes per scan line for pixel8 transfers. Left-over pixels in the current word do **not** wrap to the next line; Pixel1 **does** allow the left-over pixels to wrap. This makes it especially well suited for sending narrow blocks of monochrome data such as character bit maps.

30.10.6 BitBlts

The blit operation moves a rectangular block of pixels from one part of the screen to another and handles overlapping source and destination blocks prop-erly. The source block arrives unchanged at the destination, as if it had been moved off-screen. It then copies back to the new destination.

Like the quad operation, the blit runs until completion. The host must test for busy before attempting another drawing operation when a blit could be in progress.

30.10.7 Color Selection

Once a pixel has been touched, the actual color is selected at five levels as shown in Table 30.17. Each of the five steps in Table 30.17 is executed in order.

The pattern RAM allows a 16-by-16 bit-repeated pattern to be applied on the data. The raster op function is a four-input Boolean function controlled by a 16-bit miniterm array. The four inputs are shown in Table 30.18. The raster op requires a 2-bit field to select from the four inputs. The 16-bit miniterm provides a raster op for each of the eight pixels. The plane mask is an 8-bit mask that write-enables

TABLE 30.17 Selecting a Color

Step	Source
1	The initial source color
2	The pattern color
3	The raster ops
4	The plane mask
5	The RAMDAC look-up table

TABLE 30.18 Sources into the RasterOP

Item	Source
1	Source color
2	Destination color
3	Foreground color
4	Background color

individual bits in the 8-bit pixel. The RAMDAC takes the pixel value from the frame buffer and uses it as an index into three parallel DACs.

30.11 INSTRUCTION AND REGISTER FORMATS

The host controls the P9000/9100 by setting registers, loading pseudo-registers, and issuing commands. P9000/9100 registers are all 32 bits wide and contain parameters and status information for the P9000/9100. Pseudo-registers minimize the number of parameters that must be specified per drawing operation. Commands initiate the drawing operations whose parameters are defined by register and pseudo-register settings.

The P9000/9100 is memory mapped. Its address is divided into control fields that determine the actual operation to be performed. Each register or command is addressed as a memory location. There are many more addresses than there are registers and commands. Taking advantage of this, bit locations in the addresses are used to transfer information as well as addresses. Only the least significant 22 bits are used or the P9000, but all 32 bits are used for the P9100. NOTE: The sections of memory reserved for the P9000/9100 addresses must be marked as non-cacheable.

All tasks are performed sequentially. The host ensures that requests before drawing operations are accepted, by checking P9000/9100 status to verify that the previous drawing operation has completed before issuing a new request. For operations that return status, the status must be checked.

30.11.1 General Address Formats

The registers and commands in the P9000/9100 are organized into groups consisting of video and system control registers, user registers, pixel addresses, RAMDAC registers, and non-P9000/9100 registers co-resident with the chip. Registers are accessed through the direct or indirect address scheme on the P9100. The P9000 supports only the direct addressing scheme.

30.11.2 Indirect Addressing on the P91000

The indirect addressing scheme is shown in Figure 30.6. It uses a prefix field in bits 31–15 of the address. Bits 14–0 represent the coprocessor address. Bit 15 is a don't care such that the prefix is set to 000Ah, thereby mapping the indirect addressing into the A0000h address range. Note that in the Configuration Register 65, both the NA_ENABLE and the NA_SELECT fields must be set to 1 for this indirect addressing to work. The coprocessor address works the same for both the indirect and direct addressing schemes.

30.11.3 Direct Addressing

The direct addressing mode is the only addressing mode available on the P9000. The P9100 also uses this direct mode, but has an indirect addressing mode as well. It is called direct addressing because the data is directly accessed by the address. Not all of the address bits are used to address; some are used for data. A sample address format is shown in Figure 30.7. Note that the P9000 shown in Figure 30.7a uses the lower 22 bits, but the P9100 uses all 32 bits, as seen in Figure 30.7b. Note the b, H, and H fields in bit locations 18–16 in both cases. They are actually data fields indicating the format of the associated data.

In the P9100, bits 31–24 refer to the value in the WBASE field of the CONFIG register number 19. This is the base for the P9100 native (non-VGA) mode.

```
31                              16 15 14                    0
┌──────────────────────────────┬──┬──────────────────────┐
│          000A hex            │ - │  Coprocessor Address  │
└──────────────────────────────┴──┴──────────────────────┘
```

Note: In this case, the H, B and b swapping are specified indirectly from the CONFIG[65].H, CONFIG[65].B, and CONFIG[65].b fields. This indirect addressing is availalbe if CONFIG[65].NA_ENABLE = 1.

FIGURE 30.6 Indirect Addressing on the P9100

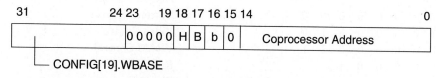

(a) P9000 22-bit Direct Addressing

(b) P9100 32-bit Direct Addressing

FIGURE 30.7 Direct Addressing Address Format (a) P9000 (b) P9100

It represents the memory space address relocatable every 16 Mbytes. If the P9100 is configured in a PCI bus, then this field is set through the configuration process. If the P9100 is in a VL bus, this field is set through an I/O operation, typically through BIOS.

In the P9000, the GROUP field located in bits 20-19 specifies the register group as shown in Table 30.19. A 0 in bit position 21 selects the registers and commands while a 1 in bit position 21 indicates a direct frame buffer address.

Except for the configuration registers in the P9100, the frame buffer memory, and the ROM BIOS, access to all remaining native mode items are controlled through the coprocessor access protocol.

TABLE 30.19 Register Groups in the P9000

GROUP Field	Register Group
0	Non-P9000 Registers (Note bits 19–0 are used as address)
2	Video Control and VRAM Registers
3	Command Registers

30.11.4 Direct Address Register Mapping on the P9000

In the direct addressing mode, the registers are address mapped. The decoding of the address bits for the P9000 write operations is shown in Table 30.20. The address bits for read operations are shown in Table 30.21.

TABLE 30.20 P9000 Write Address Decoding

21	20	19	12	11	10	9	8	7	6	5	4	3	2	1	Specific Address
															Register
0	0														Non-P9000/9100
0	1	0	0	0	0	0	0	0							System Control
0	1	0	0	0	0	0	1	0							Video Control
0	1	0	0	0	0	0	1	1							VRAM Control
0	1	0	0	0	0	1									RAMDAC Control
0	1	1	0	0	0	0	0	0	0	0	0	0	1	1	Pixel8 Command
0	1	1	0	0	0	0	0	0	0	0	0	1	0	1	Next_pixels Command
0	1	1	0	0	0	0	0	1							Pixel1 Command
0	1	1	0	0	0	0	1	1							Parameter Engine Control
0	1	1	0	0	0	1									Drawing Engine Control
0	1	1	1		0										Parameter Engine Coordinate
0	1	1	1		1										Meta-coordinate Pseudo-registers
0	1														Direct frame buffer

TABLE 30.21 P9000 Read Address Decoding

21	20	19	12	11	10	9	8	7	6	5	4	3	2	1	Specific Address
															Register
0	0														Non-P9000/9100
0	1	0	0	0	0	0	0	0							System Control
0	1	0	0	0	0	0	1	0							Video Control
0	1	0	0	0	0	0	1	1							VRAM Control
0	1	0	0	0	0	1									RAMDAC Control
0	1	1	0	0	0	0	0	0	0	0	0	0	0	0	Status
0	1	1	0	0	0	0	0	0	0	0	0	0	0	1	Blt Command
0	1	1	0	0	0	0	0	0	0	0	0	0	1	0	Quad Command
0	1	1	0	0	0	0	1	1							Parameter Engine Control
0	1	1	0	0	0	1									Drawing Engine Control
0	1	1	1	0	0										Parameter Engine Coordinate
0	1	1	1	0	1										Meta-coordinate Pseudo-registers
0	1														Direct frame buffer

30.11.5 Direct Address Register Mapping on the P9100

The decoding of the address bits for the P9100 write operations are shown in Table 30.22 while the address bits for read operations are shown in Table 30.23.

TABLE 30.22 P9100 Write Address Decoding

Address Bits													*Specific Address*
14	13	12	11	10	9	8	7	6	5	4	3	2	Register
0	0	0	0	0	0	0	0						System Control
0	0	0	0	0	0	1	0						Video Control
0	0	0	0	0	0	1	1						VRAM Control
0	0	0	0	0	1								RAMDAC Control
0	0	0	0	1									Video Coprocessor Interface
0	1	0	0	0	0	0	0	0	0	0	1	1	Pixel8 Command
0	1	0	0	0	0	0	0	0	0	0	0	0	Next Pixels Command
0	1	0	0	0	0	0	1	0	0	1	0	1	Pixel1 Command
0	1	0	0	0	0	1	1						Parameter Engine Control
0	1	0	0	0	1								Drawing Engine Control
0	1	1	0	0	0	0							Parameter Engine Coordinate
0	1	1	0	0	1								Meta-coordinate Pseudo-registers
1													Pixel8 Command

TABLE 30.23 P9100 Read Address Decoding

Address Bits													*Specific Address*
14	13	12	11	10	9	8	7	6	5	4	3	2	Register
0	0	0	0	0	0	0	0						System Control
0	0	0	0	0	0	1	0						Video Control
0	0	0	0	0	0	1	1						VRAM Control
0	0	0	0	0	1								RAMDAC Control
0	0	0	0	1									Video Coprocessor Interface
0	1	0	0	0	0	0	0	0	0	0	0	0	Status
0	1	0	0	0	0	0	0	0	0	0	0	1	Blt Command
0	1	0	0	0	0	0	0	0	0	0	1	0	Quad Command
0	1	0	0	0	0	1	1						Parameter Engine Control
0	1	0	0	0	1								Drawing Engine Control
0	1	1	0	0	0	0							Parameter Engine Coordinate
0	1	1	0	0	1								Meta-coordinate Pseudo-registers

30.12   THE P9000/P9100 CONTROL AND COMMAND REGISTERS

30.12.1   Video and System Control Register Formats

The formats for the video and system control registers are shown in Table 30.24 and in Table 30.25. The register field selects the register for data transfer. (See specific register accesses descriptions). The Index value in this field is shown in the index field of Table 30.25. This is used to select the appropriate register. Indexes and register names for the video and VRAM control registers are not described since they control hardware issues typically not relevant to the programmer. Note that the ALT_READ_BANK and ALT_WRITE_BANK Registers are available on the P9100 only. The Index refers to the specific register being accessed in the Register field address bits 6–2.

TABLE 30.24   Format for Video and System Control Registers

Bits	Definition
21	Always 0
20	Always 1
19	Always 0
18	Half-word swapping; 0=do not swap half words, 1=swap half words
17	Byte swapping; 0=do not swap bytes, 1=swap bytes
16	Bit swapping; 0=do not swap bits, 1=swap bits
8–2	Register field used for index to related registers (see Table 30.20)

TABLE 30.25   Video and System Control Registers

Index	Register	Function	Group
1	SYSCONFIG	System Configuration	System Control
2	INTERRUPT	Interrupt status	System Control
3	INTERRUPT_EN	Interrupt Enable	System Control
4	ALT_READ_BANK	Alternate Read Bank	System Control
5	ALT_WRITE_BANK	Alternate Write Bank	System Control
—	Not relevant to this book	—	Video Control
—	Not relevant to this book	—	VRAM Control

30.12.2 User Register Address Formats

The address formats for the user registers are shown in Table 30.26 and in Table 30.27. The Register field selects the register for data transfer (see specific register accesses descriptions).

The user control registers consist of the registers and commands shown in Table 30.27.

30.12.3 Pixel Address

The pixel address format is shown in Table 30.21. It allows direct access to the pixel map. Unlike other address formats, the pixel address format does not specify half-word byte and bit swapping. Instead, the System Configuration Register (SYSCONFIG) provides this information. Data in the frame buffer is

TABLE 30.26 Format for User Registers

Bits	Definition
21	Always 0
20	Always 1
19	Always 1
18	Half-word swapping; 0=do not swap half words, 1=swap half words
17	Byte swapping; 0=do not swap bytes, 1=swap bytes
16	Bit swapping; 0=do not swap bits, 1=swap bits
15	Always 0
14–0	Register field used for index to related registers

TABLE 30.27 User Control Registers and Commands

Registers and Commands	Section
Parameter Engine	30.14, 30.15
Status	30.14.2
Drawing Engine	30.16
Meta-coordinate Pseudo-registers	30.18
Quad Command	30.19.1
Blit Command	30.19.2
Pixel8 Command	30.19.3
Pixel1 Command	30.19.4
Next_Pixels Command	30.19.5

TABLE 30.28 Format for RAMDAC Registers

Bits	Definition
21	Always 0
20	Always 1
19	Always 0
18	Half-word swapping; 0=do not swap half words, 1=swap half words
17	Byte swapping; 0=do not swap bytes, 1=swap bytes
16	Bit swapping; 0=do not swap bits, 1=swap bits
3–2	Controls transfer as defined by the RAMDAC specifications

always stored as big-endian. When the host issues a pixel address, the P9000 accesses the display memory as if it were normal memory.

30.12.4   RAMDAC Address Format

The RAMDAC addresses are shown in Table 30.28.

30.12.5   Non-P9000/9100 Address Format

The P9000/9100 ignores the address format when both bits 21 and bits 20 are set to 0. Some boards that utilize the P9000/9100 will use this format to communicate with non-P9000/9100 registers.

30.13   SYSTEM CONTROL REGISTERS

The system control registers control all but the video portions of the P9000/9100. They can be read or written at any time and are accessed via the general video and system control register address format described in Table 30.19.

30.13.1   System Configuration Register

The System Configuration Register (SYSCONFIG) provides various system configuration controls as shown in Table 30.29. NOTE: Bits 13–11 determine the swapping control for pixel accesses only. This is unlike other address formats. For pixel accesses, the address format does not provide this information. The Pixel_size field is also relevant to the P9100 only.

30.13.2   Interrupt Register

The Interrupt Register, shown in Table 30.30, is a read/write register that provides status information. These bits are set when an occurrence of a specific

TABLE 30.29 System Configuration Register

Bit	Field	Contents
30–29	Shift 3 (P9100 only)	Shift Control 3 of horizontal resolution
28–26	Pixel_size (P9100 only)	Size of pixel; 0=8 bits, 1=16 bits, 2=24 bits, 3=32 bits/pixel
22–20	Shift 0	Shift Control 0 of horizontal resolution
19–16	Shift 1	Shift Control 1 of horizontal resolution
15–12	Shift 2	Shift Control 2 of horizontal resolution
13	pixel_swap_half	Half-word swapping; 0=No swap half words, 1=swap half words
12	pixel_swap_byte	Byte swapping; 0=No swap bytes, 1=swap bytes
11	pixel_swap_bits	Bit swapping; 0=No swap bits, 1=swap bits
10	pixel_buf_read	Select buffer for reads; 0=buffer 0, 1=buffer 1
9	pixel_buf_write	Select buffer for writes; 0=buffer 0, 1=buffer 1
2–0	version (P9000 only)	P9000 version number

TABLE 30.30 Interrupt Register

Bit	Field	Contents
5	Mask	Write mask for vertical blanking done
4	Vertical blanking done	0 = no vertical blank done 1=vertical blank done
3	Mask	Write mask for Pick
2	Pick	0=no pick done 1=pick done
1	Mask	Write mask for Drawing engine idle
0	Drawing engine idle	0=drawing engine busy 1=drawing engine idle

interrupt occurs. They remain set "sticky" after the condition occurs and must be cleared by a host register transfer. Each condition bit is preceded by a field write control bit that must be set to 1 to write into the field. If this field write control bit is 0, the respective field is left alone during the next write. Thus, it acts as a write-protect mask.

30.13.3 Interrupt Enable Register

The Interrupt Enable Register shown in Table 30.31 specifies the conditions under which the P9000/9100 asserts the interrupt signals. Each condition bit is preceded by a field write control bit that must be set to 1 to write into the field. If this field write control bit is 0, the respective field is left alone during the next write. Thus, it acts as a write-protect mask.

TABLE 30.31 Interrupt Enable Register

Bit	Field	Contents
7	Mask	Write mask for vertical blanking done
6	Master Enable	0=disable all interrupts, 1=enable all interrupts based on enables
5	Mask	Write mask for vertical blanking done
4	Vertical Blanking Done	0 = no vertical blank done interrupt, 1= interrupt on vblank
3	Mask	Write mask for Pick
2	Pick	0=no pick done interrupt, 1=interrupt on pick
1	Mask	Write mask for drawing engine idle
0	Drawing Engine Idle	0=no idle interrupt, 1=interrupt on idle

30.14 PARAMETER ENGINE REGISTERS

The parameter engine registers supply the coordinates for a drawing operation, provide control for the drawing operation, and maintain status information. These are accessed via the general user register address format described in Table 30.26.

30.14.1 Device Coordinate Registers

The Device Coordinate Registers supply the screen coordinates for a drawing operation. These supply the four screen coordinates required for each drawing operation. There are four X and four Y registers, one for each X and Y value required. The X and Y values can be supplied as a 32-bit or a 16-bit value. This is indicated by the YX field in the address format. When a 16-bit value is supplied, the X and Y values are packed and transferred in a single 32-bit read or write. The device coordinate register format is shown in Table 30.32. The YX format specifies the data format as specified in Table 30.33.

30.14.2 Status Register

The Status Register is a read-only register shown in Table 30.34. Its contents reflect the current status of the drawing engine and coordinate register clip checks. Access to the Status Register is obtained via the General User Register Format described in Table 30.26.

The status information can also be accessed by issuing a quad, blit, or pixel8 command. The specific address format bits 15 through 2 are zero; all other bits are identical to those shown in the general user register address format.

TABLE 30.32 Device Coordinate Register Format

Bits	Field	Function
7–6	Reg	Coordinate pair i.e., 0= X[0],Y[0], 1= X[1],Y[1]
5	REL	0=perform absolute screen addressing, 1=relative
4–3	YX	Data Format

TABLE 30.33 YX Format Field

Value	Format
0	Not used
1	R/W 32-bit X
2	R/W 32-bit Y
3	R/W 16-bit X (high 16-bits) and 16-bit Y (low 16-bits)

TABLE 30.34 Status Register Format

Bits	Field	Function
31	issue_qbN	0= may start quad or blit operation, 1=can't start either
30	busy	1=drawing engine is busy
7	picked	1=pick detected (same as field in Interrupt Register)
6	pixel_software	1=Exception encountered for pixel command
5	blit_software	1=Exception encountered for blit command
4	quad_software	1=Exception encountered for quad command
3	quad_concave	1=concave quad requested
2	quad_hidden	1=source coordinates for quad draw are trivially rejected
1	quad_visible	1=source coordinates for quad draw are trivially accepted
0	quad_intersects	1=source coordinates for quad draw straddle window

30.15 CONTROL AND CONDITION REGISTERS

The Parameter Engine Control and Condition Registers control and monitor the P9000/9100 operations. The address format for each of these registers is shown in Table 30.35.

TABLE 30.35 Control and Condition
Registers Access Address Format

Register Entry	Register
Bits (6–2)	Selected
0	not used
1	oor
2	not used
3	cindex
4	w_off.xy
5	pe_w_min
6	pe_w_max
7	not used
8	ylip
9	xclip
10	xedge_lt
11	xedge_gt
12	yedge_lt
13	yedge_gt

30.15.1   Out of Range Register (oor)

The read-only register is illustrated in Table 30.36. It identifies the X and Y values that are out of range of the drawing engine for the current drawing operation. The P9000/9100 updates this register every time the X and Y Coordinate Registers are modified. There are four coordinate pairs, 0–3, and each has a bit in this register.

30.15.2   Index Register (cindex)

This read/write register supplies the current index into the X and Y coordinates as a 2-bit binary integer. The value is used for meta-coordinate computation as described in Section 30.18.

TABLE 30.36 Out of Range Register (oor) Format

Bits	Field	Function
7–4	x_oor	0= X value is in range 1= X value is out of range
3–0	y_oor	0= Y value is in range 1= Y value is out of range

30.15.3   Window Offset Register (w_off.xy)

This read/write register supplies the offset of the current window on the display as two packed 16-bit two's compliment binary integers representing the X and Y coordinates. This is required by coordinated computation operations to calculate addressing relative to the window. It has no effect on clipping.

30.15.4   Parameter Engine Window Minimum (pe_w_min) and Maximum (pe_w_max) Registers

These read-only registers provide the minimum and maximum values. They are copies of the drawing engine window minimum and maximum registers (w_min and w_max) as described in Section 30.16.10.

30.15.5   Clip Registers (xclip and yclip)

These read-only registers define the results of clip checks, as summarized in Table 30.37. They are updated for every new set of X and Y values loaded into the coordinate registers. Each of the four bits in each field represents that one coordinate of the four coordinate pairs.

30.15.6   Vertex Relationship Checking Registers (xedge_lt, xedge_gt, yedge_it and yedge_gt)

These read-only registers define the results of checks on vertices to verify that the requested drawing operation is acceptable as shown in Table 30.38. through Table 30.41.

TABLE 30.37   Clip Register (xclip and yclip) Format

Bits	Field	Register	Function
7–4	x_It_min	xclip	0=x value not less than w_min.x, 1=x value is less
3–0	x_gt_max	xclip	0=x value not greater than w_min.x, 1=x value is greater
7–4	y_It_min	yclip	0=y value not less than w_min.y, 1=y value is less
3–0	y_gt_max	yclip	0=y value not greater than w_min.y, 1=y value is greater

TABLE 30.38 Vertex Relationship Register (xedge_lt) Format

Bits	Comparison result
5	x[0] > x[2]
4	x[1] > x[3]
3	x[3] > x[0]
2	x[2] > x[3]
1	x[1] > x[2]
0	x[0] > x[1]

TABLE 30.39 Vertex Relationship Register (xedge_gt) Format

Bits	Comparison result
5	x[0] < x[2]
4	x[1] < x[3]
3	x[3] < x[0]
2	x[2] < x[3]
1	x[1] < x[2]
0	x[0] < x[1]

TABLE 30.40 Vertex Relationship Register (yedge_lt) Format

Bits	Comparison result
5	y[0] > y[2]
4	y[1] > y[3]
3	y[3] > y[0]
2	y[2] > y[3]
1	y[1] > y[2]
0	y[0] > y[1]

TABLE 30.41 Vertex Relationship Register (yedge_gt) Format

Bits	Comparison result
5	y[0] < y[2]
4	y[1] < y[3]
3	y[3] < y[0]
2	y[2] < y[3]
1	y[1] < y[2]
0	y[0] < y[1]

30.16 DRAWING ENGINE REGISTERS

The drawing engine registers are pixel processing registers that provide storage and define the foreground and background colors, plane mask, pattern and pattern origins, pixel drawing window limits, and raster operation parameters as shown in Table 30.42. Access to the status register is obtained via the General User Register Format described in Table 30.26.

30.16.1 The Foreground and Background Registers

These registers contain the 8-bit number that specifies the foreground and background color for use in subsequent raster operations. Note that there are two registers available on the P9000; these are the foreground and background registers. There are four such registers on the P9100.

TABLE 30.42 Drawing Engine Registers

Bits 8–2	Name	Chip	Register
0	fground	P9000	Foreground Color
1	bground	P9000	Background Color
0	color 0	P9100	Color 0
1	color 1	P9100	Color 1
2	pmask	both	Plane Mask
3	draw_mode	both	Draw Mode
4	pat_originx	both	Pattern Origin X
5	pat_originy	both	Pattern Origin Y
6	raster	both	Raster Op
7	pixel8_reg	both	Pixel8
8	w_min	both	Window Minimum
9	w_max	both	Window Maximum
E	color 2	P9100	Color 2
F	color 2	P9100	Color 3
40	Pattern 0	P9100	Pattern 0
41	Pattern 1	P9100	Pattern 1
42	Pattern 2	P9100	Pattern 2
43	Pattern 3	P9100	Pattern 3
44	Software 0	P9100	Software 0
45	Software 1	P9100	Software 1
46	Software 2	P9100	Software 2
47	Software 3	P9100	Software 3
40		P9000	Pattern [0..1]
41		P9000	Pattern [2..3]
42		P9000	Pattern [4..5]
43		P9000	Pattern [6..7]
44		P9000	Pattern [8..9]
45		P9000	Pattern [A..B]
46		P9000	Pattern [C..D]
47		P9000	Pattern [E..F]
50	b_w_min	P9100	Byte Window Min
51	b_w_max	P9100	Byte Window Max

30.16.2 The Plane Mask Register

This register supplies the 8-bit plane mask. Bit 0 corresponds to bit 0 of the pixel data in the frame buffer. Setting a bit to a 1 enables the plane. Resetting the bit to a 0 masks the plane.

30.16.3 Draw Mode Register

This register controls writing within a picked window and selects the destination buffer for drawing operations. This is described in Table 30.43.

TABLE 30.43 Draw Mode Register

Bit	Name	Function
3–2	Pick	Pick write enable. 0=suppress any write operation outside the window. Allow any write inside the window. 1=suppress any write operation inside the window. Allow any write outside the window.
1–0	Dest_buf	Destination buffer. 0=select buffer 0 as the destination buffer 1=select buffer 1.

TABLE 30.44 Raster Register

Bit	Name	Chip	Function
17	Use_pattern	both	Pattern enable. 0 = disable pattern for quad draw operation. Force pattern to all ones. 1=enable pattern.
16	Quad_draw_mode	both	Quad draw mode 0=X11 mode 1=Oversized mode (VGA).
15	Pixel1_transparent	P9100	0=disable pixel 1 transparent mode, 1=enable.
14	Pattern depth	P9100	Pattern depth 0=2-color 1=4-color.
13	Solid_color_disable	P9100	0=solid color enabled, pattern disabled. 1=solid color disabled, pattern enabled.
16–0	Miniterms	P9000	Miniterms for Boolean raster operation (see Section 30.10.7).
7–0	Miniterms	P9100	Miniterms for Boolean raster operation (see Section 30.10.7).

30.16.4 Raster Register

The raster register specifies the raster op as shown in Table 30.44 and described in Section 30.10.7. Note the new fields in bits 15–13 on the P9100 and the different size of the miniterms field.

30.16.5 Pattern Origin Registers

The two Pattern Origin Registers, Pat_originx and Pat_originy, supply the 4-bit origin of the pattern to be used by the quad command to fill polygons on the display screen. Only the lower four bits of each register are used because the pattern is a 16-by-16 pattern.

30.16.6 Pixel8 Register

This register provides a temporary storage for excess bit data from a pixel8 operation. The data is stored in the lower end of the register. It may be useful when a pixel8 operation is aborted in the middle of a scan line.

30.16.7 Window Minimum/Window Maximum Registers

These registers supply the window limits that the pixel processing engine uses to determine if a pixel should be drawn. This register is described in Table 30.45.

30.16.8 Pattern Registers

These read/write registers contain the pattern for quad fill operations. Note that there are eight registers available on the P9000; these are the foreground and background registers. On the P9100 there are four such registers.

30.16.9 Software Registers

On the P9100, there are four registers available for the software application. These can be used for any purpose by the software application.

TABLE 30.45 Window Minimum/Window Maximum Register

Bit	Name	Function
28–16	xvalue	Minimum x value in the w_min register; maximum x value in the w_max register
12–0	yvalue	Minimum y value in the w_min register; maximum y value in the w_max register

30.16.10 Clipping

Two sets of window registers called the p_w_min and b_w_min hold the minimum values; p_w_max and b_w_max hold the maximum values. The b_w_min and b_w_max registers are available only on the P9100. Each of these registers contains the x value (either minimum or maximum) in bits 28–16 and the y value (either minimum or maximum) in bits 12–0. Clipping is always enabled and imposes no performance penalty. The units for the b_w_min and b_w_max registers are in bytes for both the x and y coordinates. The units for the of the p_w_min and p_w_max registers x value is in pixels and the y value is in scan lines. The p_w_min and p_w_max registers are write-only.

30.17 VIDEO CONTROL REGISTERS

The video control registers control the horizontal and vertical timing. The registers are accessed through the register field in bits 6–2 as shown in Table 30.46. The Screen Repaint Control Register has some fields that are relevant to this book, which are shown in Table 30.47.

TABLE 30.46 Video Control Registers

Bits 8–2	Name	Register
1	hrzc	Horizontal Counter
2	hrzt	Horizontal Length
3	hrzsr	Horizontal Sync Rising Edge
4	hrzbr	Horizontal Blank Rising Edge
5	hrzbf	Horizontal Blank Falling Edge
6	prehrzc	Horizontal Counter Preload Value
7	vrtc	Vertical Counter
8	vrtt	Vertical Length
9	vrtsr	Horizontal Sync Rising Edge
A	vrtbr	Vertical Blank Rising Edge
B	vrtbf	Vertical Blank Falling Edge
C	prevrtc	Vertical Counter Preload Value
D	sraddr	Screen Repaint Address
E	srtctl	Screen Refresh Timing Control
F	sraddr_inc	Address Inc

TABLE 30.47   Relevant Fields in the Video Control Registers

Bits	Register	Function
5	srtctl	Enable video. 0=blank, 1=normal operation
3	display_buf	Display buffer. 0=buffer 0, 1=buffer 1

30.18   META-COORDINATE PSEUDO-REGISTERS

These write-only registers allow you to issue the minimal number of coordinates required for a drawing operation. The registers will format the data for the quadrilateral format required by the graphics engine and facilitate the drawing of quadrilaterals, degenerate quadrilaterals, polylines, and meshed quads. Access to these registers is obtained via the general user register format described in Table 30.26.

The address format for a meta-coordinate pseudo-register is shown in Table 30.48 and the type of graphics operation field is further described in Table 30.49. If the REL bit is a 1, screen addressing is relative to the previous vertex. If the REL bit is a 0, screen addressing is relative to the window offset. The YX field controls the type of coordinates that will follow. A 0 indicates that a 32-bit X value is present. A 1 indicates that a 32-bit Y value is present. A 2 indicates that a 16-bit X address is located in bits 31–16; the 16-bit Y address is located in bits 15–0.

TABLE 30.48   Meta-coordinate Pseudo-Registers

Bits	Field	Function
8-6	Vtype	Type of graphics operation
5	REL	Relative or absolute addressing
4-3	YX	Type of access

TABLE 30.49   Vtype Field of Meta-coordinate Registers

Value	Function
0	Point
1	Line
2	Triangle
3	Quadralateral
4	Rectangle

30.19   COMMANDS

The commands initiate functions on the P9000/9100 as shown in Table 30.50. Access to these registers is obtained via the general user register format described in Table 30.26.

30.19.1   Quad Command

The Quad command draws and fills the quadrilateral defined by the vertices specified in the coordinate registers. This command sets the busy flag, performs the operation scan line by scan line, applying the current pattern with the left and right Bresenham engines and establishing the outlines of the left and right boundaries as the fill engine fills the quadrilateral. Four vertices are required for this command. The command will fail if the quad is concave or at least one coordinate is out of range of the drawing engine. If it fails, the quad_sw bit is set in the Status Register.

30.19.2   Blit Command

The Blit command copies a rectangular area of the display from one screen location to another (source to destination). When these two regions overlap, the P9000 ensures accuracy by automatically setting the correct direction of transfer.

   The Blit command requires the vertices of the upper-left $(x[0],y[0])$ and lower-right $(x[1],y[1])$ corners of the source plus the upper-left $(x[2],y[2])$ and lower-right $(x[3],y[3])$ corners of the destination. Both areas must be the same size; specifying different sized areas produces undefined results. If the destination is out of range, blit sets the blit_software bit in the Status Register. Otherwise, it determines the direction and performs the transfer.

30.19.3   Pixel8 Command

The Pixel8 command transfers one word of pixel data from a linear host memory array to a rectangular display memory array in the frame buffer. The source (in host memory) must contain lies that are multiples of four pixels wide.

TABLE 30.50   Commands

Command	Function
Quad	Draw a quadrilateral
Blit	Copy a rectangular area of the display from screen-to-screen
Pixel8	Transfer one word of pixel data from linear host to rectangular display
Pixel1	Transfer up to 32 pixels from linear host to rectangular display
Next_pixels	Advance the drawing area for a pixel8 or pixel1 operation

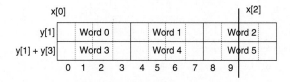

(a) Host Memory Source Area

(b) Display Memory Destination Area

FIGURE 30.8 Pixel8 Operation

The Pixel8 Command requires the vertices of the left edge of the block to be transferred (x[0]), the point at which to begin the transfer (x[1],y[1]) and the right edge of the block to be transferred (x[2]) . In addition, it requires the increment by which to increase the y coordinate at the end of the scan line (y[3]). This command is initiated with a write command.

Each Pixel8 command writes one word into the frame buffer unless the word being written overlaps the end of the current scan line. When this happens, the scan line is filled and the excess data is saved in the pixel8_reg register. This is illustrated in Figure 30.8.

30.19.4 Pixel1 Command

The Pixel 1 command is a color expansion form of the Pixel8 command. It can transfer up to 32 pixels from a linear host memory array to a rectangular display memory array in the frame buffer.The Pixel1 command requires the vertices of the left edge of the block to be transferred (x[0]), the point at which to begin the transfer (x[1],y[1]) and the right edge of the block to be transferred (x[2]) . In addition, it requires the increment by which to increase the y coordinate at the end of the scan line (y[3]). It also requires the total number of pixels to write (loaded into the register as the number − 1) and the pixel data. Each bit from the host data bus represents the data to write to one pixel with the color value of 0 to 255. This command is initiated with a write command.

Each bit from each data word in the source is expanded to a color value (0 to 255). When the last pixel on the scan line is reached for the defined area, it continues writing pixel data in the buffer for the next scan line. For example,

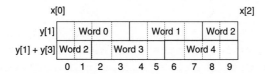

Bit
Word 31 30 29 28
0 (0,0) (1,0) (2,0) (3,0)
1 (4,0) (5,0) (6,0) (7,0)
2 (8,0) (9,0) (0,1) (1,1)
3 (2,1) (3,1) (4,1) (5,1)
4 (6,1) (7,1) (8,1) (9,1)
5 (0,2) (1,2) (2,2) (3,3)
(a) Host Memory Source Area
x[0]
x[2]
y[1]
y[1] + y[3]
Word 0
Word 1
Word 2
Word 2
Word 3
Word 4
0 1 2 3 4 5 6 7 8 9
(b) Display Memory Destination Area

FIGURE 30.9 Color Expansion Using the Pixel1 Command

suppose that the screen area is ten pixels wide and that the pxiel1 command requests an expansion of four bits from each data word from the host. This is illustrated in Figure 30.9 and described in Table 30.51.

Data formatted starting at 0 and working towards 31 can be achieved by setting the little-endian format in the address format.

TABLE 30.51 Color Expansion Using the Pixel1 Command

Step	*Function*
1	Expand the data from the host data word 0, bit 31, and write it to the frame buffer for pixel 0,0.
2	Expand the data from the host data word 0, bit 30, and write it to the frame buffer for pixel 1,0.
3	Expand the data from the host data word 0, bit 29, and write it to the frame buffer for pixel 2,0.
4	Expand the data from the host data word 0, bit 28, and write it to the frame buffer for pixel 3,0.
5	Advance to host data word 1, ignoring the remaining bits in data word 0 and repeat 1–4.
6	Advance to host data word 2, ignoring the remaining bits in data word 1 and repeat 1–4.
7	Continue the process until done with the specified number of pixels.

TABLE 30.52 Next_pixel Modifications
to Coordinate Registers

Coordinate	Becomes
x[0]	x[2]
x[1]	x[2]
y[1]	y[2]
x[2]	x[2] + width

30.19.5 Next_Pixels Command

The Next_Pixel command specifies the next area of the frame buffer to load for consecutive pixel8 or pixel1 drawing operations. It advances these to the next step in a sequence of operations. It requires the right edge of the previous block transferred (x[2]), the top edge of the previous block transferred (y[2]) and the width of the next transfer. The coordinate registers are modified as shown in Table 30.52.

30.20 DRAWING OPERATIONS

30.20.1 X11 Drawing Modes

The P9000/9100 supports two drawing modes. The X11 drawing mode strictly conforms to the rules of X-Windows as shown in Table 30.53.

30.20.2 Oversized Drawing Mode

Besides touching the pixels in the X11 format, the oversized drawing mode also touches the pixels along the boundary of the quadrilateral following the Bresenham algorithm. A line or a point is drawn as an infinitely thin quadrilateral.

30.20.3 Quadrilateral Drawing Method

All four points of each quadrilateral must be supplied in the device coordinate registers. To specify a degenerate quadrilateral, repeat one or more coordinates or use the meta-coordinate pseudo-registers.

30.20.4 Miniterms

The raster operation replaces the destination with some combination of the foreground, background, source and old destination. The function is performed on a plane-by-plane (bit-by-bit) basis. There are sixteen miniterms for each of

TABLE 30.53 Rules Regarding the X11-Drawing Format

1.	The boundaries of the quadrilateral are considered to be infinitely thin.
2.	Only those pixels whose centers are completely within the boundaries of the quadrilateral are touched.
3.	If the center of a pixel is exactly on the boundary, it is touched if and only if the interior is immediately to its right (in the increasing x direction).
4.	A pixel with its center on a horizontal boundary is handled as a special case. It is touched if and only if the interior is immediately below (in the increasing y direction) and the boundary is immediately to its right, in the increasing x direction).

the four arguments, thus the Boolean operation can be expressed as a 16-bit number. Note that this produces 64 Kbyte possible raster ops. Most, of course, are not relevant in most cases. Four useful defines are provided in Table 30.54.

The technique used to determine the miniterm relies on the data in Table 30.55. Note that each logical combination of the four arguments is assigned a value from 0 to Fh and any logical operation can be represented as a sum of products. Each desired logical operation is broken down into a sum of products term. Each one of the products is converted to a value from 0 to Fh using Table 30.55. The sum of products then represents a collection of 0 to Fh values. No product terms can be the same since A OR A = A. The 16-bit value is then determined by setting the bit position corresponding to the 0 to Fh value to a 1. All other bit positions are a zero. Four examples are shown in Table 30.56.

In a normal BitBlt, the source is copied to the destination. The miniterms are set to FF00h to copy the source to the destination. In a non-transparent text display, the source is 1 bit per pixel. If the bit is 0, the destination is set to the background. If 1, it is set to the foreground. The miniterms are as follows:

(IGM_S_MASK AND IGM_F_MASK) OR (! IGM_S_MASK AND IGM_B_MASK)

To display text in a transparent mode, the source bit is 0, and the destination is left unchanged.

(IGM_S_MASK AND IGM_F_MASK) OR (! IGM_S_MASK AND IGM_D_MASK)

In a draw quad operation, every pixel touched is set to the foreground color. Therefore, the IGM_F_MASK is used.

TABLE 30.54 Useful Definitions

Value	Function	Definition
FF00	Replace destination with foreground	IGM_F_MASK
F0F0	Replace destination with background	IGM_B_MASK
CCCC	Replace destination with source	IGM_S_MASK
AAAA	Replace destination with destination (NO OP)	IGM_D_MASK

TABLE 30.55 Miniterm Definitions

Hex Value	Binary	Miniterm
0	0000	!f !b !s !d
1	0001	!f !b !s d
2	0010	!f !b s !d
3	0011	!f !b s d
4	0100	!f b !s !d
5	0101	!f b !s d
6	0110	!f b s !d
7	0111	!f b s d
8	1000	f !b !s !d
9	1001	f !b !s d
A	1010	f !b s !d
B	1011	f !b s d
C	1100	f b !s !d
D	1101	f b !s d
E	1110	f b s !d
F	1111	f b s d

TABLE 30.56 Examples of Miniterms

f !s d	= f !b !s d + f b !s d	bits 9 and D are on = 2200h
sd	= !f !b s d + !f b s d + f !b s d + f b s d	bits 3, 7, B and F are on = 8888h
s + d	= s !d + s d + !s d = !f !b s !d + ... + f b !s d	bits 1,2,3,5,6,7,9,A,B,D,E,F on = EEEEh
s XOR d	= s !d + !s d = !f !b s !d + ... + f b !s d	bits 1,2,5,6,A,B,E,F on = 6666h

TABLE 30.57 Rules Regarding Program Flow

Step	Rule
1	Access to non-drawing engine registers can be assumed to be instantaneous.
2	Access to drawing engine registers are valid only when the drawing engine is idle. (Status Register Busy Bit = 0.)
3	The quad and blit drawing operations are invoked by a read on the host bus. This read always completes immediately and returns the Status Register. If the drawing engine is ready (Status Register issue_qbN=0), the operation is initiated. If the drawing engine is busy, the request is ignored. The software is responsible for reissuing the request if busy.
4	The pixel1 and pixel8 operations wait for the drawing engine to become idle. Sequences of these operations can be executed without checking the status of the drawing engine. It is assumed that any preceding operation is short. When this is not certain, the software should wait for the drawing engine to become idle (Status Register Busy Bit = 0) before issuing the command.
5	Before drawing a horizontal line just after performing a blit, check the drawing engine for idle (Status Register Busy Bit = 0).

30.20.5 Program Flow

The host processor issues read and write operations that must not hang up the bus. The rules provided in Table 30.57 must be followed.

30.20.6 Exception Handling

It is up to the software to check the Status Register to detect an exception.

30.21 THE DIAMOND VIPER

The Diamond Viper is the most popular card utilizing the Weitek P9000/9100 and is therefore described in some detail.

30.21.1 Viper BIOS String

The Diamond Viper has an identification string in BIOS as shown in Listing 30.6. The Viper may contain a Weitek 5186/5286, a Weitek 5286 or an Oak OTI-087 VGA. This is indicated in the version number in the BIOS string.

LISTING 30.6 Viper BIOS Identification

```
1.  Location - C000:37
2.    'VIPER VLB Vers. 1.00 (c) Diamond Computer Systems, Inc.'
3.    VIPER VLB w/Weitek 5186/5286/5286 VGA
              1.XX
              2.XX
```

```
4.   VIPER VLB/PCI w/OAK OTI-087 VGA
             3.XX
```

30.21.2   Viper BIOS Call

An additional Int10 BIOS call is provided to get information regarding the Viper as shown in Listing 30.7.

LISTING 30.7   Viper VLB/PCI Get Info Function

```
1. Use INT 10h function.
2.   Save registers AX,BX,SI,DI.
3.   Input   AX=01DAAh        get Diamond VIPER info
             BX=0FDECh
4.   Return  AH       VIPER dac/hardware info
       bits 3-0, dac type (always BT485 or compatible)
          =00h Normal 8-bit dac
          =01h Sierra hi-color dac
          =02h Diamond music dac
          =03h BrookTree 485 or compatible dac
       bit 4, VGA type
          =0 Weitek 5186/5286/5286 VGA
          =1 Oak OTI-087
       bit 5, BUSTYPE
          =0 VIPER VLB
          =1 VIPER PCI
     AL               VIPER VRAM amount/type
       =01h, 1 MB, 8 128x8's
       =02h, 2 MB, 8 246x8's or 16 256x4's
       =10h, 1 MB, 8 256x4's
     SI:DI            Segment:Offset VIPER BIOS String
location
```

30.21.3   Viper Sequencer Register

The Viper VLB Sequencer Register is located at 3C4/3C5h index 12h. Its bit definitions are shown in Table 30.58 for the VL Bus and in Table 30.59 for the PCI Bus.

NOTE: Reserved bits in Sequencer Indexed Register 12h should be masked during updating of the register and should not be modified.

30.21.4   VL Local Bus or PCI

Use _setup_addr_parms module to determine if BusType is VESA LOCAL BUS or PCI. If VLB, read from VIPER.INI to setup P9000/9100 MemAddr and BT485 Command Registers. If PCI, use INT 1Ah to determine P9000/9100 MemAddr from P9000/9100 Base Register1 and BT485 Command Registers from P9000/9100 Base Register2.

TABLE 30.58 Viper Sequencer Register for the VL Bus

VIPER VLB Sequencer(3C4h) Indexed register 12h bit definition:

Bits	Description
1,0	P9000/9100 Base Memory Address
0,0	No Address decoding
0,1	A0000000 or B0000000
1,0	20000000 or 30000000
1,1	80000000 or 9000/91000000
2	Reserved (=0)
3	Reserved (=1)
4	P9000/9100 video signal enable
	0 VGA provides video signals to ramdac
	1 P9000/9100 provides video signal to ramdac
5	P9000/9100 horizontal sync polarity
	0 positive
	1 negative
6	P9000/9100 vertical sync polarity
	0 positive
	1 negative
7	5186/5286 video signal enable
	0 if bit 4 is 1
	1 if bit 4 is 0

TABLE 30.59 Viper PCI Sequencer Register (3C4h) Index 12h for the PCI Bus

Bits	Description
1,0	Reserved (always 1,1)
2	Reserved (=0)
3	Reserved (=1)
4	P9001 video signal enable
	0 VGA provides video signals to ramdac
	1 P9000/9100 provides video signal to ramdac
5	Reserved
6	Reserved
7	Reserved

30.21.5   Viper PCI P9001 Base Register

The Viper PCI P9001 Base Register is located in PCI Configuration Space offset 12h. This register contains P9001 Base Memory Address.

30.21.6   Viper PCI P9001 Extended Base Registers

The Viper PCI P9001 Base Register1 is located in PCI Configuration Space offset 14h. These extended registers are I/O mapped as described in Table 30.60.

30.22   MAJOR DIFFERENCES BETWEEN THE P9000 AND THE P9100

The major differences between the P9000 and the P9100 are shown in Tables 30.61 and Table 30.62. The new registers present in the P9100 are described in Table 30.61 and more fully in Section 30.23. Registers that have changed are decribed in Table 30.62. The minor differences are provided in the respective sections where they are described for the P9000/P9100.

TABLE 30.60   Memory-Mapped Viper PCI P9001 Base Register 1

Offset	*Description*
x000h	SVGA Windows A Bank Register. This is a 7-bit read/write register to access Windows A in SVGA space(A0000h–AFFFFh). Bank size is 64 Kbyte.
x100h	SVGA Windows B Bank Register. This is a 7-bit read/write register to access Windows B in SVGA space(B0000h–BFFFFh). Bank size is 64 Kbyte. It is **not recommended** to use Window B.

x200h	SVGA Enable Register (Read/Write)
	    bit 0=0 Disable all memory accesses to A0000h–AFFFFh.
	    1 Enable all memory accesses to A0000h–AFFFFh.
	    bit 1=0 Disable all memory accesses to B0000h–BFFFFh.
	    1 Enable all memory accesses to B0000h–BFFFFh.

x300h	Monitor Power Down (Read/Write)
	    bit 0=0 (PW0) Horizontal Sync enabled.
	    1 Horizontal Sync disabled.
	    bit 1=0 (PW1) Vertical Sync enabled.
	    1 Vertical Sync disabled.
	    bit 2=0 VGA VCLK enabled.
	    1 VGA VCLK disabled.

TABLE 30.61 New Registers in the P9100

New Registers	Notes
Configuration	Registers specify PCI or VL bus including device and vendor identifiers, enable the RAMDAC Palette, memory-space access and I/O-space access, specify base addresses, enable VGA, and select the P9100 or the SVGA modes.
Color 0 – Color 3	Color 0 replaces P9000 foreground register. Color 1 replaces P9000 background register. Both are used in two-color patterns. Color 2 and Color 3 are used in the new four-color patterns. Each is 32 bits wide.
Pattern 0 – Pattern 3	Replaces the P9000 pattern registers. Each is 32 bits wide.
alt_read_bank	Specify the high-order address bits in register its 22–14 when alternate aperture frame buffer banking logic is used to read directly from the frame buffer.
alt_write_bank	Specify the high-order address bits in register its 22–14 when alternate aperture frame buffer banking logic is used to write directly to the frame buffer.
Software 0–3	Reserved for system software use.
SVGA	The P9100 contains all of the registers found on the 5286. They are identical to the 5286.

TABLE 30.62 Changed Registers in the P9100

Changed Registers	Notes
System Configuration	A new field is present in bits 28–26 specifying whether 8, 16, or 32 bits per pixel should be used for the drawing engine. The version field in bits 2–0 of the P9000 are now contained in a configuration register (see Table 30.53). Bits 2–0 are always 0.
Memory Configuration	Several new fields in this register are used to control the memory hardware.
Raster	New fields include bit 15 that enables the pixel1 transparent mode and bit 14 that specifies the pattern depth. If 0, a 2-color pattern is used. If 1, a 4-color pattern is used.

30.23 NEW REGISTERS IN THE P9100 NOT FOUND IN THE P9000

The most notable of the new registers in the P9100 are the 5286 Super VGA registers. They are described in Sections 30.2 through 30.9. The new registers are described in Table 30.52.

30.23.1 Configuration Registers and the Local Bus

The PCI bus specification requires a group of configuration registers. These same registers are supported in the VL bus implementations by mapping the configuration registers into the I/O address space.

30.23.2 Configuration Registers on the VL Bus

These registers are accessed by two double words in the I/O address space. The first is used as an index into the configuration address space. The second is used as the data transfer register. These registers are present regardless of whether the P9100 is in the native or SVGA (5286) mode. The index registers can be placed at several locations in the I/O address space depending on the adapter card or motherboard implementation. The location is called the CFGBA field. It can be read in the Power-up Configuration Bits Register (PU_CONFIG) as shown in Table 30.63.

The CGFBA field specifies the value that goes into bits 14–3 of the Configuration Index and Data Registers. This field is described in Table 30.64.

The Configuration Index and Data Registers are described in Table 30.65.

30.23.3 Configuration Register Descriptions

The Configuration Registers are described in Table 30.66.

The Config Register is described in Table 30.67. Note that these fields are copies of the similar fields in the Power Up Configuration Register of Table 30.62. The CFGBA field was described in Table 30.64.

The Mode Configuration Register is shown in Table 30.68 and a general purpose control register is shown in Table 30.69.

TABLE 30.63 Power-up Configuration Bits Register PU_CONFIG

Bits	Name	Function
31–30	Bus	2=VESA VL bus, 1=PCI Bus.
29–27	CGFBA	Configuration address for Index and Data Registers.
26	INIT_MODESELECT	Initial value for the CONFIG[65].MODESELECT field.
25	INIT_VGA_PRESENT	Initial value for the CONFIG[10].VGA_PRESENT field.
4	MEM_DEPTH	Depth of memory chips. 0=256K, 1=128K.
0	MBOARD	Implementation. 0=Motherboard, 1=Adapter Card.

TABLE 30.64 CFGBA Field for I/O Address Determination

Value	Index	Data
0	9100	9104
1	9110	9114
2	9120	9124
3	9130	9134
4	9108	910C
5	9118	911C
6	9128	912C
7	9138	913C

TABLE 30.65 Configuration Index Registers when on the VL Bus

Register	Bits 31–16	Bits 15–3	Bits 2–0
Index	0	PU_CONFIG.CGFBA	0
Data	0	PU_CONFIG.CGFBA	4

TABLE 30.66 Configuration Registers

Index	Name	Bits	Function
0	Vendor ID Low	0–7	0Eh
1	Vendor ID High	0–7	10h
2	Device ID Low	0–7	0h
3	Device ID High	0–7	91h
4	Configuration	0–7	Shadow DAC, Memory and I/O enable
7	Status	0–7	Status Reg
8	Revision ID	0–7	Current Revision
10	VGA Present	7–5	0=VGA Present, 1=VGA Absent (see Table 30.55).
11	Type of Controller	1–0	Set to 3 for Display Controller.
19	Base for Native Mode	7–0	Memory space address for VL or PCI.
48	BIOS ROM decoding	0	0=ROM Decoding disabled (PCI), 1=enabled (VL).
49	ROM Base Address	7	Bit 0 of the ROM Base Address (default is 0).
50	ROM Base Address	7–0	Bits 8–1 of the ROM Base Address (default is 0Ch).

TABLE 30.66 *(cont.)*

Index	Name	Bits	Function
51	ROM Base Address	7–0	Bits 16–9 of the ROM Base Address (default is 00h).
64	Config Reg	7–0	Copy of Power Up Configuration (see Table 30.59).
65	Mode	7–0	Mode select (see Table 30.60).
66	Clock Sel	7–0	Clock Hardware Related.

TABLE 30.67 Config[64] Register

Bits	Name	Function
7–6	Bus	2=VESA VL bus, 1=PCI Bus
5–3	CFGBA	Configuration address for Index and Data Registers
0	EEDAIN	Current state of clock select pin

TABLE 30.68 Mode Configuration Register at [65]

Bits	Name	Function
7	Half-word swap	1=halfword swap for commands A0000–AFFFF
6	Byte-word swap	1=byte swap for commands A0000–AFFFF
5	Bit-swap	1=bit swap for commands A0000–AFFFF
3	NA_SELECT	Select 0=Frame Buffer, 1=Coprocessor
2	NA_ENABLE	0=don't respond to A0000–AFFFF, 1=respond (0=default)
1	MODESELECT	0=P9100 native mode, 1=P9100 VGA emulation (5286)

TABLE 30.69 Configuration Register Index 4

Bit	Field Name	Function
5	SHADOW_DAC	Shadow access to RAMDAC. 0=no shadow, 1=shadow (default).
1	MEM_ENABLE	0=no access to memory space, (default) 1=access memory.
0	IO_ENABLE	0=no access to I/O (PCI), 1=access I/O (VL).

30.23.4   Color Registers

The four color registers are located at register addresses as shown in Table 30.70. These registers are used by the pattern and pixel1 logic to expand colors. When in an 8-bit-per-color mode, the byte color must be replicated four times, once in each register. Similarly, when in a 16-bit-per-color mode, the byte color must be replicated two times, once in each register pair.

30.23.5   Pattern Registers

The four pattern registers are located at register addresses as shown in Table 30.71. These registers are used during quad fill operations to specify the pattern. The four color pattern uses all four registers only in the 8-bit-per-color mode.

The pattern registers are described in Table 30.72. Note that the patterns are Intel-ordered such that bit 31 contains pattern bit 0 and bit 24 contains pattern bit 7.

30.23.6   Alternate Read and Alternate Write

The Alternate Read Bank Register specifies the high-order address bits when the alternate aperture frame buffer banking logic is used to read directly from the frame buffer. Similarly, the Alternate Write Bank Register specifies the high-order address bits when the alternate aperture frame buffer banking logic

TABLE 30.70   Color Registers

Register Index	Register
00	Color 0
01	Color 1
0E	Color 2
0F	Color 3

TABLE 30.71   Pattern Registers

Register Index	Register
40h	Pattern 0
41h	Pattern 1
42h	Pattern 2
43h	Pattern 3

TABLE 30.72   Pattern Register Descriptions

Register	Pattern Bit 31–24	Pattern Bits 23–16	Pattern Bits 15–8	Pattern Bits 7–0
Pattern 0	[1][0][0–7]	[1][0][0–7]	[1][0][0–7]	[1][0][0–7]
Pattern 1	[0][2][0–7]	[0][2][0–7]	[0][3][0–7]	[0][3][0–7]
Pattern 2	[1][4][0–7]	[1][4][0–7]	[1][5][0–7]	[1][5][0–7]
Pattern 3	[0][6][0–7]	[0][6][0–7]	[0][6][0–7]	[0][7][0–7]

is used to write directly from the frame buffer. The bank address, either read or write, is contained in bit positions 22–16 of these double words. These registers reside in the system control registers at register locations 4 for the Alternate Write Register and 5 for the Alternate Read Register.

30.23.7 Software Registers

The four software registers are located at register addresses as shown in Table 30.73. These registers aren't used by the software for anything.

TABLE 30.73 Software Registers

Register Index	Register
44h	Software 0
45h	Software 1
46h	Software 2
47h	Software 3

Index

Note: page numbers followed by an asterisk (*) denote C or assembly language code.

Special Offer for Software

Programmer's Companion Disk Super VGA Toolbox
Graphics Accelerator Toolbox

Programmer's Guide Companion Disk includes all software listings contained in this book.

Super VGA Toolbox contains over 300 source code and demonstration functions that identify the SuperVGA, perform intelligent mode setting, and VESA support. Text in both alphanumerics and graphics modes, line, circle and polygon drawing, raster graphics, and indexed, Hi-Color or True-Color support. Both real or protected mode versions are provided. A 100-page manual is included.

Each *Graphics Accelerators Toolbox* supports one of the many Graphics Accelerators. These include support for host-display, display-host and display-display BitBlts, solid and patterned line drawing, transparency text and hardware cursor. Each toolbox is specific to a single chip and not all chips are supported. Please inquire before ordering.

Note: The *Super VGA Toolbox* and *Graphics Accelerators Toolboxes* are constantly updated to support new chips and cards as they become available.

Methods of payment: Check, Money Order, Bank Wire Transfer or Domestic COD. All payment in US funds only. Payment should be made to:

Richard F. Ferraro
2568 NE 188th St., Seattle, WA 98155
(206) 362-2520

Programmer's Guide Companion Disk	$ 30.00
Super VGA Toolbox	$200.00
Specific Graphics Accelerator Toolbox per chip	$150.00 (please inquire)

Shipping: *(rates are subject to change).*

UPS Ground	$10.00
UPS Domestic 2nd Day	$15.00
Domestic Next Day	$20.00
Foreign Express Mail	$30.00
COD	add $7.00
Washington State residents	add 8.1% sales tax

Richard F. Ferraro is available for consulting services. He provides direct quotes and rapid turn-around as per your special requirements.

For additional ordering information call or fax Richard Ferraro at **(206) 362-2520.**